Contemporary Literary Criticism

Guide to Gale Literary Criticism Series

When you need to review criticism of literary works, these are the Gale series to use:

If the author's death date is:	You should turn to:
After Dec. 31, 1959 (or author is still living)	***CONTEMPORARY LITERARY CRITICISM*** for example: Jorge Luis Borges, Anthony Burgess, William Faulkner, Mary Gordon, Ernest Hemingway, Iris Murdoch
1900 through 1959	***TWENTIETH-CENTURY LITERARY CRITICISM*** for example: Willa Cather, F. Scott Fitzgerald, Henry James, Mark Twain, Virginia Woolf
1800 through 1899	***NINETEENTH-CENTURY LITERATURE CRITICISM*** for example: Fedor Dostoevski, Nathaniel Hawthorne, George Sand, William Wordsworth
1400 through 1799	***LITERATURE CRITICISM FROM 1400 TO 1800 (excluding Shakespeare)*** for example: Anne Bradstreet, Daniel Defoe, Alexander Pope, François Rabelais, Jonathan Swift, Phillis Wheatley
	SHAKESPEAREAN CRITICISM Shakespeare's plays and poetry
Antiquity through 1399	***CLASSICAL AND MEDIEVAL LITERATURE CRITICISM*** for example: Dante, Homer, Plato, Sophocles, Vergil, the Beowulf Poet

---

Gale also publishes related criticism series:

CHILDREN'S LITERATURE REVIEW

This ongoing series presents criticism on authors of all eras who write for the preschool through high school audience.

SHORT STORY CRITICISM

This series covers the major short fiction writers of all nationalities and periods of literary history.

ISSN 0091-3421

Volume 47

Contemporary Literary Criticism

Excerpts from Criticism of the
Works of Today's Novelists, Poets,
Playwrights, Short Story Writers, Scriptwriters,
and Other Creative Writers

Daniel G. Marowski
Roger Matuz
EDITORS

Sean R. Pollock
Robyn V. Young
ASSOCIATE EDITORS

Gale Research Company
Book Tower
Detroit, Michigan 48226

STAFF

Daniel G. Marowski, Roger Matuz, *Editors*

Sean R. Pollock, Robyn V. Young, *Associate Editors*

Jane C. Thacker, Thomas J. Votteler, Bruce Walker, *Senior Assistant Editors*

Kent Graham, Michele R. O'Connell, David Segal, *Assistant Editors*

Jean C. Stine, *Contributing Editor*

Carolyn Bancroft, Mary Nelson-Pulice, Debra A. Wells, *Contributing Assistant Editors*

Jeanne A. Gough, *Production & Permissions Manager*
Lizbeth A. Purdy, *Production Supervisor*
Kathleen M. Cook, *Assistant Production Coordinator*
Cathy Beranek, Suzanne Powers, Kristine E. Tipton, Lee Ann Welsh, *Editorial Assistants*
Linda M. Pugliese, *Manuscript Coordinator*
Donna Craft, *Assistant Manuscript Coordinator*
Jennifer E. Gale, Maureen A. Puhl, Rosetta Irene Simms, *Manuscript Assistants*

Victoria B. Cariappa, *Research Supervisor*
Maureen R. Richards, *Research Coordinator*
Mary D. Wise, *Senior Research Assistant*
Joyce E. Doyle, Kevin B. Hillstrom, Karen D. Kaus, Eric Priehs,
Filomena Sgambati, Laura B. Standley, *Research Assistants*

Janice M. Mach, *Text Permissions Supervisor*
Kathy Grell, *Text Permissions Coordinator*
Mabel E. Gurney, Josephine M. Keene, *Senior Permissions Assistants*
Eileen H. Baehr, H. Diane Cooper, Anita L. Ransom,
Kimberly F. Smilay, *Permissions Assistants*
Melissa A. Kamuyu, Martha A. Mulder, Lisa M. Wimmer, *Permissions Clerks*

Patricia A. Seefelt, *Picture Permissions Supervisor*
Margaret A. Chamberlain, *Picture Permissions Coordinator*
Pamela A. Hayes, Lillian Tyus, *Permissions Clerks*

Library of Congress Catalog Card Number 76-38938
ISBN 0-8103-4421-1
ISSN 0091-3421

Computerized photocomposition by
Typographics, Incorporated
Kansas City, Missouri

Printed in the United States

Contents

Preface

Literary criticism is, by definition, "the art of evaluating or analyzing with knowledge and propriety works of literature." The complexity and variety of the themes and forms of contemporary literature make the function of the critic especially important to today's reader. It is the critic who assists the reader in identifying significant new writers, recognizing trends in critical methods, mastering new terminology, and monitoring scholarly and popular sources of critical opinion.

Until the publication of the first volume of *Contemporary Literary Criticism (CLC)* in 1973, there existed no ongoing digest of current literary opinion. *CLC,* therefore, has fulfilled an essential need.

Scope of the Work

CLC presents significant passages from published criticism of works by today's creative writers. Each volume of *CLC* includes excerpted criticism on about forty authors who are now living or who died after December 31, 1959. Nearly 1,900 authors have been included since the series began publication. The majority of authors covered by *CLC* are living writers who continue to publish; therefore, an author frequently appears in more than one volume. There is, of course, no duplication of reprinted criticism.

Authors are selected for inclusion for a variety of reasons, among them the publication of a critically acclaimed new work, the reception of a major literary award, or the dramatization of a literary work as a film or television screenplay. For example, the present volume includes Philip Roth, whose novel *The Counterlife* won the National Book Critics Circle Award; John Masefield, Poet Laureate of England from 1930 to 1967; and Walker Percy, whose recent novel, *The Thanatos Syndrome,* received significant critical attention. Perhaps most importantly, authors who appear frequently on the syllabuses of high school and college literature classes are heavily represented in *CLC;* Arthur Miller and Marianne Moore are examples of writers of this stature in the present volume. Attention is also given to several other groups of writers—authors of considerable public interest—about whose work criticism is often difficult to locate. These are the contributors to the well-loved but nonscholarly genres of mystery and science fiction, as well as literary and social critics whose insights are considered valuable and informative. Foreign writers and authors who represent particular ethnic groups in the United States are also featured in each volume.

Format of the Book

Altogether there are about 600 individual excerpts in each volume—with approximately fifteen excerpts per author—taken from hundreds of literary reviews, general magazines, scholarly journals, and monographs. Contemporary criticism is loosely defined as that which is relevant to the evaluation of the author under discussion; this includes criticism written at the beginning of an author's career as well as current commentary. Emphasis has been placed on expanding the sources for criticism by including an increasing number of scholarly and specialized periodicals. Students, teachers, librarians, and researchers frequently find that the generous excerpts and supplementary material provided by the editors supply them with vital information needed to write a term paper, analyze a poem, or lead a book discussion group. However, complete bibliographical citations facilitate the location of the original source and provide all of the information necessary for a term paper footnote or bibliography.

A *CLC* author entry consists of the following elements:

- The **author heading** cites the author's full name, followed by birth date, and death date when applicable. The portion of the name outside parentheses denotes the form under which the author has most commonly published. If an author has written consistently under a pseudonym, the pseudonym will be listed in the author heading and the real name given on the first line of the biographical and critical introduction. Also located at the beginning of the introduction to the author entry are any important name variations under which an author has written. Uncertainty as to a birth or death date is indicated by question marks.

- A **portrait** of the author is included when available.

- A brief **biographical and critical introduction** to the author and his or her work precedes the excerpted criticism. However, *CLC* is not intended to be a definitive biographical source. Therefore, *cross-references* have been included to direct the reader to these useful sources published by the Gale Research Company: *Contemporary Authors,* which includes detailed biographical and bibliographical sketches on more than 89,000 authors; *Children's Literature Review,* which presents excerpted criticism on the works of authors of children's books; *Something about the Author,* which contains heavily illustrated biographical sketches of writers and illustrators who create books for children and young adults; *Dictionary of Literary Biography,* which provides original evaluations and detailed biographies of authors important to literary history; *Contemporary Authors Autobiography Series,* which offers autobiographical essays by prominent writers; and *Something about the Author Autobiography Series,* which presents autobiographical essays by authors of interest to young readers. Previous volumes of *CLC* in which the author has been featured are also listed in the introduction.

- The **excerpted criticism** represents various kinds of critical writing—a particular essay may be normative, descriptive, interpretive, textual, appreciative, comparative, or generic. It may range in form from the brief review to the scholarly monograph. Essays are selected by the editors to reflect the spectrum of opinion about a specific work or about an author's literary career in general. The excerpts are presented chronologically, adding a useful perspective to the entry. All titles by the author featured in the entry are printed in boldface type, which enables the reader to easily identify the works being discussed. Publication information (such as publisher names and book prices) and parenthetical numerical references (such as footnotes or page and line references to specific editions of a work) have been deleted at the editor's discretion to provide smoother reading of the text.

- A complete **bibliographical citation** designed to help the user find the original essay or book follows each excerpt.

Other Features

- A list of **Authors Forthcoming in** ***CLC*** previews the authors to be researched for future volumes.

- An **Appendix** lists the sources from which material in the volume has been reprinted. It does not, however, list every book or periodical consulted during the preparation of the volume.

- A **Cumulative Author Index** lists all the authors who have appeared in *CLC, Twentieth-Century Literary Criticism, Nineteenth-Century Literature Criticism, Literature Criticism from 1400 to 1800,* and *Classical and Medieval Literature Criticism,* with cross-references to these Gale series: *Short Story Criticism, Children's Literature Review, Authors in the News, Contemporary Authors, Contemporary Authors Autobiography Series, Contemporary Authors Bibliographical Series, Dictionary of Literary Biography, Something about the Author, Something about the Author Autobiography Series,* and *Yesterday's Authors of Books for Children.* Readers will welcome this cumulated author index as a useful tool for locating an author within the various series. The index, which lists birth and death dates when available, will be particularly valuable for those authors who are identified with a certain period but whose death date causes them to be placed in another, or for those authors whose careers span two periods. For example, Ernest Hemingway is found in *CLC,* yet a writer often associated with him, F. Scott Fitzgerald, is found in *Twentieth-Century Literary Criticism.*

- A **Cumulative Nationality Index** alphabetically lists all authors featured in *CLC* by nationality, followed by the volume numbers in which they appear.

- A **Title Index** alphabetically lists all titles reviewed in the current volume of *CLC*. Titles are followed by the corresponding page numbers where they may be located. In cases where the same title is used by different authors, the author's surname is given in parentheses after the title, e.g., *Collected Poems* (Berryman), *Collected Poems* (Eliot). For foreign titles, a cross-reference is given to the translated English title. Titles of novels, novellas, dramas, films, record albums, and poetry, short story, and essay collections are printed in italics, while all individual poems, short stories, essays, and songs are printed in roman type within quotation marks; when published separately (e.g., T.S. Eliot's poem *The Waste Land*), the title will also be printed in italics.

• In response to numerous suggestions from librarians, Gale has also produced a **special paperbound edition** of the *CLC* title index. This annual cumulation, which alphabetically lists all titles reviewed in the series, is available to all customers and will be published with the first volume of *CLC* issued in each calendar year. Additional copies of the index are available upon request. Librarians and patrons will welcome this separate index: it saves shelf space, is easily disposable upon receipt of the following year's cumulation, and is more portable and thus easier to use than was previously possible.

Acknowledgments

No work of this scope can be accomplished without the cooperation of many people. The editors especially wish to thank the copyright holders of the excerpted essays included in this volume, the permissions managers of many book and magazine publishing companies for assisting us in securing reprint rights, and the photographers and other individuals who provided portraits of the authors. We are grateful to the staffs of the Detroit Public Library, the Library of Congress, the University of Detroit Library, the University of Michigan Library, and the Wayne State University Library for making their resources available to us. We also wish to thank Anthony Bogucki for his assistance with copyright research.

Suggestions Are Welcome

The editors welcome the comments and suggestions of readers to expand the coverage and enhance the usefulness of the series.

Authors Forthcoming in *CLC*

To Be Included in Volume 48

Jorge Luis Borges (Argentinian short story writer, poet, essayist, critic, and scriptwriter)—Among the most eminent and distinctive contemporary Latin American authors, Borges is particularly noted for his innovative short stories, in which he blended imaginative fiction with historical detail and philosophical speculation.

Buchi Emecheta (Nigerian-born novelist, autobiographer, scriptwriter, and author of children's books)—In such novels as *In the Ditch* and *Second-Class Citizen,* Emecheta addresses difficulties faced by oppressed African women who are forced to live under a patriarchal social system. She exposes such traditional African customs as polygamy, servitude, and arranged marriages as practices which render women powerless to assert their individuality.

Loren D. Estleman (American novelist and short story writer)—Writing in the "hard-boiled" detective tradition established by Dashiell Hammett and Raymond Chandler, Estleman employs a terse yet vividly descriptive prose style to examine the sordid world of urban crime. Among the novels to be covered in his entry are *Sugartown, Kill Zone,* and *Roses Are Dead.*

Sheila Fugard (English-born South African novelist and poet)—A respected author who examines life under apartheid in South Africa, Fugard combines feminism and the Gandhian concept of nonviolent resistance to address her country's social problems in her recent novel, *A Revolutionary Woman.*

Ellen Gilchrist (American short story writer, novelist, and poet)—Gilchrist is best known as the author of the short story collection *Victory over Japan,* for which she received the American Book Award in fiction. Her recent volume of stories, *Drunk with Love,* has elicited significant critical attention.

Julien Gracq (French novelist, critic, short story writer, dramatist, and poet)—Influenced by Surrealism and the work of André Breton, Gracq creates phantasmagoric novels characterized by elegant prose and evocative imagery. Gracq's third novel, *The Opposing Shore,* won the Prix Goncourt in 1951.

Tina Howe (American dramatist)—Best known for her humorous plays about human interaction, Howe often sets her dramas in such unlikely locations as art museums, restaurants, and fitting rooms. Among her recent works are *Appearances, Painting Churches,* and *Coastal Disturbances.*

Medbh McGuckian (Irish poet)—McGuckian is praised for her innovative and descriptive verse imbued with a feminist sensibility. In such volumes as *The Flower Master* and *Venus and the Rain,* she experiments with language and conveys personal themes.

James Tiptree, Jr. (American short story writer, novelist, and critic)—Among the most acclaimed authors of science fiction to emerge during the 1970s, Tiptree combined the tight narrative style and aura of amazement attributed to literature of the "Golden Age" of science fiction with the moral and psychological emphasis often associated with the genre's "New Wave" movement of the 1960s.

Richard Wright (American novelist, autobiographer, short story writer, and nonfiction writer)—Best known as the author of the novel *Native Son* and the autobiography *Black Boy: A Record of Childhood and Youth,* Wright was one of the first modern American writers to confront the dehumanizing effects of racism by revealing the physical and psychological torment produced by segregation and discrimination.

To Be Included in Volume 49

Richard Aldington (English poet, novelist, short story writer, critic, and autobiographer)—Regarded as one of the most significant poets of the Imagist movement, Aldington is also recognized for his later verse, in which he explored romantic love, modern warfare, and historical themes.

Gwendolyn Brooks (American poet, novelist, autobiographer, and author of children's books)—The first black author to win a Pulitzer Prize, Brooks is distinguished for blending elevated speech and colloquial dialect in lyrical, inventive verse that objectively addresses the injustices confronted by contemporary urban black Americans.

Humberto Costantini (Argentinian novelist, dramatist, poet, and short story writer)—In his novels *The Gods, The Little Guys, and the Police* and *The Long Night of Francisco Sanctis,* Costantini employs black humor and satire to depict political oppression in Argentina during the 1970s.

H. L. Davis (American novelist, short story writer, poet, essayist, and critic)—Davis's works, set primarily in the American West during the nineteenth and early twentieth centuries, explore such universal concerns as initiation, alienation, the nature of love, and the relationship between past and present. The recent reissue of *Honey in the Horn,* his 1936 Pulitzer Prize-winning novel, has generated renewed interest in Davis's career.

Nadine Gordimer (South African novelist, short story writer, critic, and editor)—Gordimer is respected for examining the effects of the South African apartheid system on both ruling whites and oppressed blacks. Criticism in Gordimer's entry will focus upon her recent novel, *A Sport of Nature.*

Spalding Gray (American performance artist, dramatist, and actor)—Gray has won acclaim for his humorous dramatic monologues in which he transforms personal stories and anecdotes into larger reflections on contemporary society. His entry will cover *Sex and Death to the Age 14,* a collection of monologues, and *Swimming to Cambodia,* which relates Gray's experiences in Thailand during the filming of *The Killing Fields.*

Tommaso Landolfi (Italian novelist, short story writer, critic, poet, dramatist, essayist, and translator)—Among the most innovative stylists in modern Italian fiction, Landolfi demonstrated a surreal vision and a preoccupation with language similar to those of Franz Kafka and Italo Calvino. His most respected books include *The Moon Stone* and *The Two Spinsters.*

Elmer Rice (American dramatist, novelist, scriptwriter, editor, and autobiographer)—A prolific and diverse dramatist whose career spanned more than fifty years, Rice is best remembered for such plays as *The Adding Machine* and the Pulitzer Prize-winning *Street Scene,* which contributed to the development of a socially conscious American theater.

Vladimir Voinovich (Russian-born novelist, short story writer, essayist, and nonfiction writer)—A Russian exile since 1980, Voinovich is well known for his satires about life in the Soviet Union. Recent works to be covered in his entry include *The Anti-Soviet Soviet Union,* a collection of prose pieces, and *Moscow 2042,* a futuristic novel.

W. S. Wilson (American short story writer and novelist)—Best known for his short story collection *Why I Don't Write like Franz Kafka,* Wilson imbues his fiction with scientific and philosophical language and methodology to explore such topics as human relationships, epistemology, and the nature of fiction.

Aharon Appelfeld

1932-

© Jerry Bauer

Rumanian-born Israeli short story writer, novelist, essayist, and poet.

A survivor of the Holocaust, Appelfeld uses muted symbolism and understated, parabolic prose to examine the effects of anti-Semitism upon assimilated European Jews. Although Appelfeld avoids commenting directly on the politics and horrors associated with the Third Reich, his fiction, often set in Nazi-occupied locales immediately prior to World War II, poignantly foreshadows the Holocaust to come. Appelfeld's protagonists usually reject or minimize their commitment to Judaism in order to assimilate with European society; confronted with anti-Semitic attitudes, they experience feelings of worthlessness, inferiority, and self-hatred. According to Ruth R. Wisse, "Appelfeld knew anti-Semitism from the inside, from the anti-Jewishness of his own home, before he encountered it in society, and it is this initial discovery that has remained the more decisive. The hostility of outsiders seemed almost proper retribution for the spiritual meanness of his assimilating family."

Appelfeld was interned in a concentration camp in Transnistria, Rumania, in 1940. He escaped in 1943 and survived the remainder of World War II hiding and scavenging in the forests of the Nazi-occupied Ukraine. Upon immigrating to Israel in 1947, Appelfeld wrote poetry in several languages before deciding to write fiction exclusively in Hebrew.

Appelfeld's early literary output includes hundreds of short stories addressing the effect of the Holocaust on Jews; several of these pieces appeared in the English translation collection *In the Wilderness* (1965). *Badenheim, 1939* (1980), Appelfeld's first novel translated into English, received high praise from British and American critics and elicited frequent comparison to the works of Franz Kafka for its hallucinatory prose style and detached characters. Set in an Austrian spa in the summer of 1939, the novel portrays a group of vacationers, many of nominal Jewish faith, who are forced to register with uniformed agents of the "Sanitation Department." After the entire community is revealed to be Jewish, the visitors blandly accept their removal to Poland. Robert Fyne called *Badenheim, 1939* "a work of extraordinary merit, a novel carefully constructed in simplicity, an allegory lyrical in style and content, a story expressing pathos and happiness, humor and mirth, surrealism and impending doom." In Appelfeld's second translated novel, *The Age of Wonders* (1981), a young boy watches as his father, an assimilated, anti-Semitic Austrian of Jewish descent, is destroyed by his inability to conceal his background. Although the boy survives the Holocaust and is invited to resurrect his father's writings, he chooses to embrace Judaism rather than accept his father's hatred for his own race.

Critics compared the story line and the fable-like simplicity of Appelfeld's next novel, *Tzili: The Story of a Life* (1983), to Jerzy Kosinski's novel *The Painted Bird*. In Appelfeld's work, Tzili, a retarded peasant girl who is an embarrassment to her Russian-Jewish family, is abandoned at the onset of the Holocaust but survives by foraging in forests and learning to mimic uneducated peasants. Tzili's perseverance and endurance through instinct are contrasted with the respect of other Jewish characters for refinement and intellect. In Appelfeld's next novel, *The Retreat* (1984), Jewish senior citizens gather at a remote camp in Austria to purge themselves of their cultural traits in order to assimilate more completely with European society. Confronted with the hostility of neighbors and the impossibility of being accepted, the characters revert to their old habits. Although several critics faulted Appelfeld for relying on stock characters and dialogue, Jakov Lind deemed *The Retreat* "a small masterpiece, the vision of a remarkable poet on a passage of our contemporary history, given in an unassuming little volume of elegant prose."

In Appelfeld's recent novel, *To the Land of the Cattails* (1986), a woman who had rejected her Jewish heritage to marry a gentile returns home with her son, Rudi, many years later to reconcile her doubts regarding Judaism. After encountering increasing anti-Semitism on their journey, the pair become separated. As the novel ends, Rudi joins a group of Jews by the railroad tracks to await an unknown destination. Patrick Parrinder noted: "By stopping short of its terminal horrors, Appelfeld renders a journey which ends in the gas chambers in the form of an austere and resigned pilgrim's progress."

(See also *CLC*, Vol. 23 and *Contemporary Authors*, Vol. 112.)

JOYCE CAROL OATES

[***Tzili: The Story of a Life*** is a] slender, elegiac and resolutely unemotional account of a dull-witted Jewish girl who almost inadvertently survives the Holocaust. . . . Like its highly acclaimed predecessors—***Badenheim 1939*** and ***The Age of Wonders***—***Tzili*** focuses sharply on an individual whose experience is too profound to be intellectualized or even adequately absorbed. Far less complex in design than ***The Age of Wonders*** (whose Jewish protagonist returns to Austria long after the war has ended to suffer the past superimposed on the present), ***Tzili*** unfolds with a parablelike authority in which landscapes, weather and the passage of the seasons are frequently presented with as much dramatic emphasis as Tzili's progress into maturity. Anti-Semitism, so painfully described in ***The Age of Wonders,*** is made to seem in ***Tzili*** as remorseless and inevitable as any event in nature, in which human wishes count for very little.

The war itself, remote from Tzili's experience, is never anything more than abstract to her and to us. A grief too horrific to be borne washes through her to become "empty and pointless." . . . Emotion too is remote and abstract. That Tzili becomes pregnant at the age of 15, only to lose her baby in a refugee camp, is as inevitable in this fictional world as the change of seasons. That with a boatload of other Jewish survivors she is bound at the novel's end for Palestine (where "everything will be different") is fated as well and not the consequence of anything she chooses or directs. Her destiny lies outside her, apart from her. Like Aharon Appelfeld himself, who managed to escape from a labor camp at the age of 8 and wandered the forests of Central Europe in the early 1940's, Tzili triumphs simply by enduring.

Though ***Tzili*** bears resemblance to Isaac Bashevis Singer's *Shosha* (in which a retarded Jewish girl is a redemptive figure) and Jerzy Kosinski's *Painted Bird* (in which a mute child suffers unspeakable brutalities at the hands of Polish peasants), it is a highly original work, as much for the purity and austerity of its language as for the character of Tzili. The novel begins: "Perhaps it would be better to leave the story of Tzili Kraus's life untold. Her fate was a cruel and inglorious one, and but for the fact that it actually happened we would never have been able to tell her story. We will tell it in all simplicity."

This distant, impersonal, achromatic tone is never violated throughout the novel's brief chapters; the author retains his omniscient point of view, so that Tzili's experience day by day and season by season is rendered with the uninflected authority of history as fairy tale. The author has elsewhere extolled Kafka art, and it is not difficult to sense his brooding presence in these pages, though Mr. Appelfeld, trusting the miraculous in the "merely" natural, creates no surrealist metaphors or landscapes. What need of art to invent images like that of the torture machine of Kafka's "In the Penal Colony" when the Holocaust itself has outdistanced all such images?

Our heroine is "devoid of charm and almost mute." She is the lastborn child in a large, poor Jewish family in which academic performance has become an obsession. Because her failure at school is considered an insult to the family, she is routinely punished and ridiculed; it is significant that in an agnostic Jewish household, Tzili, the feebleminded, is alone given religious instruction. When war breaks out, the family simply abandons her as if she is of no worth, but Tzili feels no anger or resentment toward them. Indeed, regardless of how cruelly and sadistically she is treated by the various people who shelter her during the next several years, she never flares up in rage, never plots revenge. Though the reader becomes numbed by the recurring acts of senseless violence she endures—she is often beaten "religiously"—it seems that in her passivity Tzili is possessed of a wisdom that allows her to transcend her physical suffering. . . .

Because, early on, she is mistaken for one of the daughters of a gentile prostitute named Maria, Tzili's life is spared and she is even given shelter with various people, among them a diseased prostitute who drifts into madness and abuses her. By degrees, without calculation, she learns to mimic the peasants with whom she lives, so that when she meets a fellow Jew in the novel's most extended and hallucinatory sequence, he is amazed at her "change." . . . This refugee, a mentally unstable man in his 40's named Mark, becomes Tzili's lover and the father of her ill-fated child. . . .

Tzili contains a number of eccentric characters in addition to Mark—among them a former engineering student, a survivor of a death camp, who is distressed at having his studies "broken off in the middle" and hopes to return for the second semester—but Tzili passes no judgment upon them. She develops a considerable attachment for Mark, though he later abandons her; but even he is eventually forgotten in the physical agony Tzili endures when her baby is born dead. Though this spare, muted allegory certainly does not move to a conventionally happy ending, the fact that Tzili's European experience is now behind her and another life waits in Palestine allows the novel to end on a relatively benign note. . . .

It is a measure of Aharon Appelfeld's uncanny skill that a narrative so deliberately shorn of familiar human relations and emotions should bear so much power. This is fiction in the service of a stern and highly moral vision, in which details yield to a larger design and individuals participate in a historical tapestry they cannot comprehend. The riskiest of Mr. Appelfeld's three novels, ***Tzili*** completes a triptych of sorts, of which ***Badenheim 1939*** and ***The Age of Wonders*** are more readily accessible but not more memorable.

Joyce Carol Oates, "A Fable of Innocence and Survival," in The New York Times Book Review, *February 27, 1983, p. 9.*

THOMAS LeCLAIR

If the Grimm brothers had described modern German terror . . . if Faulkner's Benjy Compson had lived through the sound and the fury of the Holocaust: these are the comparisons one needs to suggest the strange subject and estranged style of ***Tzili.*** Tzili Kraus is a feeble-minded Jewish girl abandoned by her family when "the soldiers" (presumably German) invade her "remote district" (perhaps Poland) in a year unspecified. . . . It is through [her] mind, both lucid and severely restricted, that we gather the fear, suffering, achievement, and even comedy of survival, Tzili's three years of eluding private and mass death. If, as editors say, less is more, in ***Tzili*** least is most, for Appelfeld's self-imposed limitations of character and perspective give his tale an unusual emotional purchase and, surprisingly, a subtle cultural commentary. (p. 3)

Appelfeld's subtitle is "The Story of a Life," but perhaps "Story of Life" would suggest more precisely Tzili's progress through eons of evolutionary time in the book's three years. An instinctual loner, she learns to care for and love another escaping Jew, a middle-aged man whose child she bears. Tzili learns to think, to use language, to distinguish among the values of the other refugees she joins in the trudge to war's and novel's end. Her transformation from thing to member of the wandering tribe is Appelfeld's counterexample for those survivors, inside and outside his book, who let themselves be reduced to less than nothing. Nothing to begin with, Tzili climbs to humanity in the worst of times and places.

Sentimentality is an enormous danger for such a story. Adults, especially writers, sentimentalize children. Appelfeld seems to record rather than create Tzili. Because she does not indulge herself with the adult melodrama of nostalgia or lost expectations, her responses to matters large and small are direct, appropriate, not exaggerated. Emotionally sound, intellectually innocent, Tzili has authority. She sees both the brutality and heartiness of peasants, the lechery as well as courage of partisans, suicidal Jews with survivor guilt and celebrating Jews without it, good merchants and bad messiahs. Eighteen years ago Jerzy Kosinski's supposedly autobiographical story of an adolescent wandering through the Holocaust—*The Painted Bird*—made him famous. Now, and next to ***Tzili***, that book seems forced, innocence controlled not so much by history as by authorial manipulation. Appelfeld's story has instead the naive elegance of eyewitness accounts, unspoiled by ideology or literary exigency.

Hemingway once said that easy writing makes hard reading. The simplicity of ***Tzili***—its folk-tale language, one-thing-after-another structure, and avoidance of complex thought—makes it a Holocaust primer, a novel that adolescents can and probably should read as an introduction, for it treats the before and after of the death camps without describing that central horror. But ***Tzili*** is also "hard" enough—subtle enough in its cultural materials—for readers more familiar with Holocaust facts and fiction. Appelfeld likes to rub against the grain of stereotypes or trace their ironies. Anti-Semitism is directed against the stereotyped city male—educated, rootless, immoral—yet it is Tzili's impregnation by such a man that gives her reason to survive. Lusty, fun-loving women, both Gentiles and Jews, are Tzili's helpers along the way. Tzili finds that the rush for advantage can turn the folk against the Jews, the Jews against themselves. Zionism is a pompous voice on a loudspeaker as well as a delivering ideal.

Appelfeld's shaping irony is that Tzili survives because she isn't smart. Ignorant of German, she has the protective coloring of peasant dialect. In Appelfeld's other two novels, ***Badenheim 1939*** and ***The Age of Wonders,*** the Jewish characters' obsession with German, the repository of high culture, deludes them and helps identify them for destruction. In ***Tzili*** a character says "There's no culture without language," but his loyalty to the grand phrases of civilization destroys him. Tzili's sensory vocabulary and earned wisdom are the saving alternative to abstraction and cultural pretense.

In both the highly praised ***Badenheim 1939*** and in ***The Age of Wonders,*** Appelfeld examined pre-war Jewry with an almost anti-literary irony, yet in the holiday-notes style of the first and the dual narration of the second the artist's hand is always evident. In ***Tzili*** the sophisticated novelist absents himself, and in so doing presents the fundamental values only implicit in the other novels' satire. There are risks of telling a story "in all simplicity"—dehistoricizing the Holocaust, muting its horror, losing experiential and novelistic texture—but ***Tzili*** is consistent in its economies, authoritative, and, most importantly, original in its effects. When ***Tzili*** is read with Appelfeld's more explicitly literary novels, the reader sees and admires an author continually pressing his imagination to defamiliarize—make newly strange and affecting—a subject that must be retold again and again. (p. 6)

Thomas LeClair, "Passage through the Inferno," in Book World—The Washington Post, *April 3, 1983, pp. 3, 6.*

ROBERT M. ADAMS

Aharon Appelfeld's ***Tzili*** takes on a technical problem familiar to realists of as much as a century ago, including Maupassant, George Moore, and Arnold Bennett. The problem is to present a major social event by way of a very limited, in fact a dull, reflector. The difficulty is simply not to interfere—not to explain, not visibly to arrange, not to underline or remotely to imply extraneous judgment—while at the same time avoiding the merely dreary. For all Mr. Appelfeld's exquisite self-effacement, a game is going on around his brief and cogent novel; it is the completion by the reader in his own mind of the huge and grisly pattern within which a single life must take its place. What we build that pattern from is very largely what the character does not see and the author does not say.

Tzili Kraus is a Jewish girl living in a Russian village and barely in her teens when the war breaks out. To the anger and frustration of her family, she has been a backward student in school; . . . they leave her behind and run away. After waiting a while for their return, she too drifts off. Only half-aware of what she is running from, and having no notion that there is anything to run to, she wanders out into the woods. (pp. 35-6)

Tzili is cold, hungry, ragged, disease-ridden; but by an instinct she never articulates, she stays away from towns, and by a good fortune of which she is never conscious, she encounters no soldiers and no authorities. Deep in the woods, she does meet an older fellow Jew named Mark. . . . With Mark, Tzili survives a grim winter, living in a kind of burrow hut. . . . In the spring, she is pregnant. Mark goes off to trade for food, but never comes back. . . . [Tzili's] child is born dead. Without knowing exactly where she is going, or why, she finds herself on a boat for Palestine.

[***Tzili***] is a narrative of the utmost simplicity, told with a complete absence of self-consciousness on the narrator's part. Tzili hardly seems to recognize how miserable she is—not altogether because she is stupid, but because she has never known any time when she was not abused, reviled, battered. Nothing good can conceivably happen to her, and indeed nothing good does. She has been given the very simplest rudiments of religious training, but . . . embodies no allegorical principle. Her story is told in short declarative sentences. It seems utterly empty. Yet the things not said, the anguish not voiced, make it strangely full. And though it certainly cannot be described as agreeable reading, ***Tzili*** by no means leaves its reader feeling crushed. Its steadiness of vision and quiet acceptance of life reduced to an absolute minimum give it, in the end, a sense of buoyancy the more moving for being apparently effortless. (p. 36)

Robert M. Adams, "Double Exposure," in The New York Review of Books, *Vol. XXX, No. 10, June 16, 1983, pp. 34-6.*

RUTH R. WISSE

Appelfeld's short stories and novels are concerned with the effect of the war on the assimilated Jews of his boyhood milieu. His work is classified as Holocaust literature because of its subject matter and because of the sense of doom that presses down on most of his characters even when they temporarily manage to elude their earthly predators, yet Appelfeld's writings are actually more engaged with the world into which he was born than with the forces that determined its extinction. Like Kafka, the writer with whom he is often compared and to whom he acknowledges a major debt, Appelfeld knew anti-Semitism from the inside, from the anti-Jewishness of his own home, before he encountered it in society, and it is this initial discovery that has remained the more decisive. The hostility of outsiders appeared to be almost proper retribution for the spiritual meanness of his assimilating family. (p. 73)

The dreamlike quality of Appelfeld's fiction is immediately palpable in ***Badenheim 1939,*** the book that introduced the author to English readers. The novel opens as spring returns to the Austrian resort town of Badenheim, bringing with it the vacationers who form the basis of its economy. Townspeople and visitors have established over the years a routine of mutual accommodation. But this year, even as the guests begin to arrive, ominous changes are noted. . . . [The] "Sanitation Department" extends its jurisdiction into many areas of once unassailable privacy, requiring that all Jews, permanent residents as well as visitors, be registered.

The Badenheimers, however, have reached such a remote stage of acculturation that some of them have never even been recognized as Jews; the drama of their progressive unmasking is like the prolonged climax of a successful masquerade. Throughout the summer, as the town adjusts to every new discriminatory measure, the Jews, one by one, reluctantly or persuaded by an inner logic, accept the condition that has been forced upon them, and which culminates in their "return to Poland." By the time the trains come to gather everyone up, some of the reconstructed Jews are even looking forward to the New Jerusalem they hope to find on Polish soil.

The book's English title signals its prevailing mood of predestination. . . . As if to underscore the element of frivolous self-deception in the whole process of Jewish assimilation, the characters are enclosed in their hotel as in a great amusement center. . . . For so long the Jews had expressed their appreciation of European culture through dedicated participation in its high artistic forms. Now their German-Austrian hosts have rewarded them by casting them in the leading roles of this year's drama, to be performed (like the passion play at Oberammergau) with the whole town's cooperation. (p. 74)

One reviewer of [***Badenheim 1939*** (see Gabriele Annan, *CLC*, Vol. 23)], in pointing to the Jews' creative embrace of their function and to the spiritual verve with which they bring the drama to its conclusion, has praised Appelfeld for imbuing grim historical events with a real sense of artistic decorum, a *commedia dell'arte* charm. It is certainly true that the reader, if he does not derive actual pleasure, is spared undue pain from this stylized work of fiction whose plot is known in advance and whose characters all seem to accept its ineluctable denouement. The final image, of Jews sucked into trains "as easily as grains of wheat poured into a funnel," leaves a lulling sadness, but no sharper emotion—no moral outrage, no disquieting hatred of the murderers, no panic about the human condition. The novel, like its characters, succumbs to the Germans and Austrians as if they were fate itself. It suggests that the return to Poland in cattle cars was implicit in the initial attempts of Westernizing Jews to transcend their identity, and that the best of them *accepted* the ironic reversal that restored them to their origins. In this way ***Badenheim 1939*** spares its readers any confrontation with history, a process determined by the choices of living persons.

Though one can see why Appelfeld's narrative scheme of fatal entrapment has been compared to Kafka, there is none of Kafka's mystery here, nor any of his metaphysical doubt. Kakfa's view of incomprehensible authority arose from within himself, and was then projected outward; Appelfeld comes at writing from quite the opposite direction, taking the real terror imposed from without by real human forces and internalizing it, thereby further obscuring its origins and meaning.

The Age of Wonders is a less controlled and more complex novel. The narrative is divided into two sections: the first deals with the period immediately preceding the war, as remembered by the young son of an assimilated Jewish family in Austria, whom one cannot help associating with the author; the second recounts a visit by this son, the sole surviving member of his family and now a resident of Jerusalem, to his native town "many years later when everything was over." In between has occurred the metamorphosis that accounts for the "wonders" of the title.

The novel traces the remorseless pressure of anti-Semitism in the late 1930's upon a family that is ill-equipped to understand or to escape it. Under Nazism, the boy and his mother—expelled from an idyllic summer retreat—become aware of the meaning of their identity. The boy's father, who had just begun to attain some recognition as a writer, is set upon in print by anonymous critics, and is gradually cut off from all his cultural outlets. This is the more unbearable to him since he shares in the general hostility to Jews, of whose evil and unpleasant ways he considers himself free. (pp. 74-5)

The son's return to his native Knospen many years after the war is inspired by an unwelcome invitation to help in the republication of his father's works. The unchanged physical nature of the town, filled with so many familiar landmarks, leaves him unprepared for the difference he finds. . . . [At] the very end of his stay, he makes real contact with one of the few local residents he still remembers from his childhood. This bitter old cripple allows the returning son to confront the past and warns him to get out of town, and to stop stirring up the old demons. "My hatred for the Jews knows no bounds," he says with proud malice. Although the old man has fallen to the ground and is lying there helpless, the Jew hits him in the face at this provocation and replies, "Now it will be easier for you." Having performed this act of purgation, he returns at peace to Jerusalem.

The ontological condition of this book is anti-Semitism, and one can think of few such thorough descriptions of its spread among Jews themselves. . . . The boy, grown to a man, avenges his father by a peculiar act of definition: if six million corpses were not enough to satisfy the anti-Semite's hatred, the Jew can at least refuse to play the complementary role of the self-hater. So he slaps his enemy, returning the aggression where it belongs. But he cannot slap his father for the inglorious and ugly legacy he has been given, nor can he free himself from its oppressiveness. . . .

Unfortunately, Appelfeld himself cannot seem to get beyond this point, which may be summed up, in this reading, as the disgraceful Jewish desire to shed an unwanted Judaism in favor of all that once appeared so much grander: liberal, post-Romantic idealism; the mystical intensity of Christianity; the unexceptional bliss of a European bourgeois existence free of anti-Semitic persecution and history. Yet was it, finally, the desire that was venal, or the forces that first encouraged hope and then brutally denied it? ***The Age of Wonders*** ends with a view of the Jews filtered through a corner of the same anti-Semitic lens that first distorted their own view of themselves. (p. 75)

In ***Tzili,*** the latest of Appelfeld's novels, the author seems to want to take a somewhat more affirmative view of his subject: rather than the sorry disintegration of the European Jewish collectivity, he treats the survival of a single worthy individual. The main character, Tzili, is a slow-witted girl, resilient and good-tempered but without the verbal facility and intelligence that are considered characteristic of the Jews and that are indeed characteristic of her highly assimilated and ambitious parents and of her studious brothers and sisters. . . . When the war breaks out, the family flees, leaving Tzili to her fate.

The book takes its revenge on this family. All but Tzili disappear, presumably forever, while she alone adapts successfully to the ensuing animal hunt. Her plain instinct for survival teaches her to endure the brutality of those who take her in as a servant in the winter rains, and to forage independently during the summer when she has no need for human shelter. One day she meets a stray Jew. . . . She instructs him in the mountain life, but as soon as he is sufficiently strong he is drawn back down to the people in the plain, and disappears. Tzili is left pregnant with his child and with a few remembered sentences that she holds precious.

As the war ends, Tzili joins the flow of refugees westward, survives the loss of her baby, and prepares to board a ship for Palestine. In the final pages of the book the company of callous, isolated refugees is addressed thunderously by Zionist organizers, whose words are as incomprehensible and inappropriate as were the injunctions of Tzili's parents in the beginning. Nonetheless, though the words remain beyond her understanding, Tzili has rejoined the Jewish people. She has come through the war alone, intact.

This story of a life is told in a spare manner, as if adjusted to the limited mentality of its heroine. In its partisan sympathy for the simpleton over the worldly wise, it corresponds in form to many well-known folk tales. In Jewish folklore, Tzili may be considered a female version of the *tam,* the character of limited intelligence who is at a particular disadvantage in a community that places such value on learning and brilliance but who nevertheless triumphs in the end over those older and smarter. As the narrative structure suggests, Tzili wins a victory not so much over her would-be Nazi destroyers (unnamed and remote) as over those who in their hubris belittled her ability and were themselves destroyed.

Tzili is also reminiscent of one of Appelfeld's earliest fictional heroines, a slightly retarded girl named Kitty who in the story **[''Kitty'']** is granted asylum in a convent during the war as long as she seems a suitable prospect for conversion to Christianity. But once Kitty begins to develop into a young woman, and to take some interest in her physical life, she is suspected by her would-be ''saviors'' of being a damnable Jew. As the end of the war draws near, and ''a final ceremony was still needed,'' Kitty serves as a sacrifice. The Germans overrun the convent, and the young Jewish girl is betrayed and executed.

If preoccupation with her body is responsible for Kitty's downfall, in ***Tzili*** the same preoccupation becomes a saving grace. Tzili stands in opposition not to the religious values of the convent, however, but to Jewish hyper-intellection and guilt. While all around her Jews are drawn to their death (several, having survived mass murder, commit suicide), she concentrates instead on the stark requirements of animal existence. Her survival, based as it is on growing strength and accumulated experience, is made to seem less a felicitous accident than the consequence of her difference from all the other Jews whose subtlety is here exposed as obtuseness.

Some critics have claimed that Tzili's endurance is emblematic of Jewish survival. So Appelfeld may possibly have intended it; but it is in fact rather the opposite. The Cinderella of her own Jewish family and community, she exposes their self-absorption, the failure of all their protective strategies, their weakness, baseness, folly. ***Tzili*** is thus an emblematic tale of how and why the European Jews, in their vast majority, did not survive. (pp. 75-6)

In his writing, Aharon Appelfeld struggles with a very difficult personal inheritance—the culture of self-rejection in which he was raised and to which, despite everything, he remains attached by strong filial bonds. His desire to confront his past is inhibited by the terrible fate inflicted on the world of his childhood—as well charge your father with parsimony when he has been murdered for his wealth. In trying to achieve the necessary detachment, Appelfeld has cultivated an uninflected style, emotionally neutral, distant, impersonal. But the stifled anger of the son has been transferred onto the parents. Fate sits in judgment on all the ugly, assimilated Jews—fate in the form of the Holocaust. The result is a series of pitiless moral fables, more damning of the victims than of the crime committed against them. (p. 76)

Ruth R. Wisse, ''Aharon Appelfeld, Survivor,'' in Commentary, *Vol. 76, No. 2, August, 1983, pp. 73-6.*

WALTER GOODMAN

The retreat imagined by the Israeli writer Aharon Appelfeld [in ***The Retreat***] is a sort of camp for Jewish senior citizens in the magic mountains of Austria. The period is not specified, but the events seem to be taking place shortly before World War II.

The camp is run by Balaban, who was raised in the country, where he grew strong and adept at un-Jewish skills like training horses. Through exercise and clean living, Balaban hopes to help those Jews who find their way to his camp to shake off all the distasteful traits that he believes are responsible for the world's antipathy to them. . . .

[***The Retreat***] is a parable that aims to teach, among other things, that the Jew who cuts himself off from his fellows in a non-Jewish world is truly adrift. Try though he may to imitate the majority, he has no hope of being accepted or, when persecution strikes, of being spared.

The ailments that these Jews are seeking to escape have of course been diagnosed for them by the non-Jewish world. One of them, Lauffer, for example, described by Balaban as ''an incorrigible Jew,'' is ''frivolous, nimble, shifty as they come and capable of exerting a spellbinding charm on Gentile women.'' One resident reports that he has counted 200 defects among Jews, from inflamed nerves to shortness of stature. . . .

Alas, none of these campers seem capable of redemption. They keep reverting to their bad habits, like playing poker every night. . . .

But even those who attempt to change and go jogging around the mountains to build up their bodies cannot escape either their own natures or the hatred of the outside world. These

Jews in retreat from their Jewishness finally have no one left to count on but each other.

As he demonstrated in his earlier works, Mr. Appelfeld, who was born in Eastern Europe and spent time in a Nazi concentration camp as a child, has a powerful vision to impart. Unfortunately, it only flickers [in ***The Retreat***]. The characters seem to be concealed by the mountain mists. Even Lotte, with whom we spend the most time, remains vague.

And then, there is the language. Mr. Appelfeld's style at its best is unadorned and direct, but in this translation, it becomes a shop of second-hand phrases. In a space of 50 pages, there is a silence that "you could cut with a knife," somebody who "lived to a ripe old age," somebody else who takes "a new lease on life" and also feels "cold shivers down her spine." Things prey on someone's mind; wool is pulled over one's eyes; someone can't curb her tongue; things go "from bad to worse." Can it be that Hebrew makes use of the same stock phrases as English? A generous interpretation might be that this is a device of Mr. Appelfeld or his translator to demonstrate that having lost their identity as Jews, these people are unable even to express their feelings in an individual way.

(The translator, Dalya Bilu, incidentally, has an affection for the word "transpire," but seems a bit shaky about its usage. "She was a farmer's daughter, it transpired, born in the mountains." . . . "It transpired that Isadora's last requests were to be buried without Jewish rites.")

The result, it transpires, is disappointing from the writer who, in ***Tzili*** . . . , molded such a strong character and so forceful a tale with his economical prose.

Only as it reaches its conclusion does ***The Retreat*** build up comparable force. The enemy is growing more relentless and, for purposes of persecution, no distinction is made among Jews, short or tall, observant or emancipated, poker players or no.

Walter Goodman, in a review of "The Retreat," in The New York Times, *April 3, 1984, p. C17.*

JAKOV LIND

In one of Aharon Appelfeld's earlier novels, ***Badenheim 1939,*** the regular summer guests of a resort live through the summer before the outbreak of war still clinging to a last vestige of hope. . . . About to be deprived of their Austrian citizenship, lacking the means and connections to emigrate, they are a pathetic, confused and forlorn lot. . . . The tragic self-delusion of the emancipated and assimilated Jew culminated in passive resignation to the inevitable.

In ***The Retreat,*** Appelfeld returns to the same prewar period and to a similar though slightly more desperate cast of characters. The setting, "not far from Vienna," is a small place, yet remote and inaccessible as Kafka's Castle. . . . [Balaban] bought it and announced his intention of converting the place into a sanatorium, offering mountain air, medical supervision and a kosher kitchen. This last turns out to have been a mistake, giving rise to the suspicion he is advertising a Jewish old age home. He brings out a different prospectus, omitting the kosher kitchen and offering horse riding, swimming, seasonal hunting, organized hikes. . . .

We are evidently witnessing the last fortress against the incoming tide. The Jews in ***Badenheim 1939*** still hoped against all hope. In ***The Retreat*** all hope has vanished. Lotte Schloss, an aging actress, . . . is delivered here by her daughter, who is married to an Austrian farmer. Like the rest of its inmates, Lotte hates other Jews; the idea of having to live with so many of them in this ramshackle house standing alone on top of a hill depresses her. In this isolation of the house itself, Mr. Appelfeld found his perfect literary metaphor. The battle has been lost, and those who lack the finances and papers to leave prepare themselves for a dignified end. Nothing can save them—neither better accents nor less pronounced Jewish gestures. . . .

[***The Retreat***] is a small masterpiece, the vision of a remarkable poet on a passage of our contemporary history, given in an unassuming little volume of elegant prose.

Jakov Lind, "Despair on a Lonely Hill," in The New York Times Book Review, *May 20, 1984, p. 38.*

VIVIAN GORNICK

Uniformly pervaded by a dreamlike impressionism, each of [Appelfeld's] four [novels] is placed in Europe on the eve or in the middle of the Second World War, and is absorbed with the folly and deception of Jewish assimilation. [***The Retreat***] is set in and around a provincial town in Austria in the spring of 1927. An aging bit-part actress, Jewish and long out of work, suddenly realizes she is permanently unemployed. . . . [She] hears of a place not far from the town, on a hillside above the plain, a kind of spiritual retreat for Jews. . . . As it turns out, the retreat, Jewish-owned and operated, is designed for people like her—Jews who had considered themselves Austrians. Its purpose is teaching these self-deceived Jews how to purge themselves of their lingering Jewishness and return to the town more genuinely Austrian.

A year passes. The actress is enthusiastically learning how to pronounce her lines "properly." Another resident has become a great jogger. Yet all in all, not much progress has been made. The Jews keep putting on weight, and they cannot be stopped from playing cards. Sooner or later, most residents revert to this degenerate practice. . . .

In time there are suicides, breakdowns, runaways. . . . We are moving toward the autumn of 1938. The novel stops abruptly, with the residents simply waiting for the doom we all know is at hand.

The Retreat fashions a self-consciously mythic circumstance, characters without human particularity, a great many portentous sentences. It provides neither textured description nor interesting ideas nor even a serious working-out of the allegorical implication. The author imagines that merely to construct this prose skeleton is to make literary meaning out of the situation of the European Jews. He thinks that the skeleton is a fully formed creature, alive and in motion.

For Aharon Appelfeld, the history of the Jews in the 20th century has achieved mythic status. This myth is his territory; here he travels comfortably. But it is in the nature of an achieved myth that its boundaries are fixed and its terrain is well-mapped. Live writing occurs when the writer moves through a country of the heart where boundaries are fluid, territory is uncharted, the landscape not yet penetrated. Surely, the timid journeying of mythic repetition cannot be good for the Jews, who have a penchant for asking: what is the point and where are we going?

Like any writer working with historical figures or events, the Holocaust writer must transcend the historical source. The Holocaust in literature can no longer be about itself; it must be put to metaphoric use. Holocaust writers must have something they are burning to say and find that only the charged imagery of the Holocaust allows them to say it. (But that would make them more than "Holocaust writers," would it not?)

Jewish identity as such—Jewish outsidedness, Jewish crucifixion—can no longer command the existential attention it commanded after the Second World War. If Jewishness is to be a contemporary writer's preoccupation, it must earn its way—emerge from the dictates of obsession or the live idiom of actual experience. It cannot claim attention as a museum piece of remembered thought and feeling, now legendary in its character and nostalgic in its affect. . . .

Writers for whom Israel is the primary experience and Hebrew the first language are indeed absorbed by Jewishness, and out of this absorption comes literature. Jewishness provides the metaphor that communicates the taste of life being lived. Amos Oz, A. B. Yehoshua, Amalia Kahana-Carmon are writers of contemporary sensibility, with the power of language in them and the inward gaze necessary to achieve transcendence. . . . These writers know that being Jewish is not in itself a tale of interest; rather, Jewishness is a language through which one may still tell a story of consequence because somewhere in the world the idea and the actuality are one. Reading Aharon Appelfeld, we can feel neither the live terror of the destroyed European Jews nor the complex anxiety of Jews living as Jews today. The idea seems merely to pay ritual obeisance to the actuality.

Vivian Gornick, "End of the Holocaust Myth," in The Village Voice, *Vol. XXIX, No. 17, June 5, 1984, p. 51.*

MICHAEL F. HARPER

[***The Retreat***] is a cool, unsparing yet compassionate critique of "assimilation." Fired from their jobs, rejected by their friends, the assimilated Jews at the Retreat are oppressed by a racism that is truly insidious because it invades consciousness, structuring its victims' very identity.

Jewish Lotte has from her youth "felt an aversion for all things Jewish," and Isadora, a fellow-resident, complains loudly and bitterly about the "disgracefully Jewish arrangements." Assimilation is a precarious kind of schizophrenia just one step away from self-contempt and despair; Isadora kills herself, and her last request is to be buried without Jewish rites. . . .

Jewishness is a deficiency of nature—in fact its chief symptom is an estrangement from nature and an unhealthy affinity for culture, for books, music, theater. The prescribed therapy at the sanatorium, therefore, is massive doses of "nature"—peasant bread and yogurt for breakfast, "horseback riding, swimming, seasonal hunting, organized hikes and . . . assimilation into the countryside."

The therapy, needless to say, is not effective—how can it be with a "disease" rooted not in biology but in ideology? The ideology of anti-Semitism has brainwashed the assimilated Jews into accepting a particular culture—the culture of peasant Austria—as "natural" and therefore healthy and desirable. . . .

The Retreat is a story of persistence—the heroic persistence of sanatorium inmates in the face of increasing deprivation and hostility, and the tragic persistence of their delusions as their lives move toward an end written not by Appelfeld but by history. The novel's power lies in Appelfeld's incisive depiction of the effects of discrimination on the consciousness of its victims, and in his dissection of an ideology riddled with paradox and contradiction but nonetheless devastatingly effective.

The prewar Austrian concept of "nature" may not stand up to critical examination, but it did not have to: Power over language—the power to stipulate and limit the meanings of words such as *nature* and *health*—is power to determine the self-concepts of those who must think themselves in that language, and power like that translates easily into a more familiar kind of power, its operations more open, its brutal effects more obvious.

Michael F. Harper, "Assimilation, Humiliation, Human Being, Being Human," in Los Angeles Times Book Review, *July 8, 1984, p. 2.*

JOHN GROSS

[***To the Land of the Cattails,*** published in Great Britain as ***To the Land of the Reeds,*** takes place in] the summer of 1938. A mother and her son have made their way eastward from Austria to Bukovina, traveling first by train, then by horse and carriage. The mother, Toni, is a woman of 34. Seventeen years ago she ran away from a traditional Jewish home in the region together with a non-Jew; once they reached Vienna, they married and had a child, Rudi, but by the time she was 20 she was divorced. Now, after coming into a legacy from one of her many lovers, she has been seized by an urge to revisit her native village and see the parents with whom she has lost touch, taking Rudi with her. . . .

Like several of Aharon Appelfeld's earlier novels, most memorably ***Badenheim 1939, To the Land of the Cattails*** is a story about Jews on the brink of the Holocaust. Destruction and its attendant horrors wait in the wings, and our foreknowledge of them conditions everything we feel about the immediate situation that Mr. Appelfeld describes. But the politics of the period—the names, the slogans, the headlines—are never directly referred to; Toni and Rudi move forward on their pilgrimage as though through a dream.

Nowhere is this dreamlike quality more apparent in the book than in the way the passage of time gets mysteriously stretched out. Almost every stage of the journey takes far longer than it would in reality, even horsedrawn reality. Summer gives way to autumn, and by the time Rudi finally reaches his destination (his mother, at the last minute, has gone on ahead) another autumn has come round.

Along the road, mother and son stop at lodging houses and inns. . . . [Toni] and Rudi arrive at an inn and find that the landlady has just been murdered—not as a result of anything she did (she was by all accounts unusually open-hearted) but simply because she was Jewish.

From this point on, the atmosphere grows far more ominous. Peddlers they meet warn them that anti-Semitic disorders have broken out in the surrounding countryside. . . . Nostalgia has made Toni romanticize her native land—the land of the cattails growing by the river, fondly remembered from childhood. Now she is gripped by fear; and it is fear—"the feeling of closeness, with nowhere else to turn"—that makes her realize she is truly drawing near home.

To the Land of the Cattails is not only an account of a journey toward doom, however. It is equally concerned with the relationship between mother and son; and though the two stories are entwined, they are by no means identical. If Rudi's feelings about Toni fluctuate, if the scorn that has long overlaid his earlier devotion to her has begun to drop away, it is as a result of a more general emotional awakening. There are strong sexual undercurrents in the story, and complicated adolescent tremors.

Still, the Jewish theme keeps recurring, inescapably. One of Toni's purposes in setting out to see her parents is the hope that Rudi will absorb some of the Jewishness that his upbringing has lacked; as the journey proceeds, however, she becomes increasingly preoccupied with what she thinks of as Jewish failings. At first, by contrast, the half-Jewish Rudi seems much more at ease with his Jewish loyalties. But then his rage at the prejudice in the air turns in on itself; he starts drinking, his appearance coarsens, he mutters anti-Semitic catch phrases that he picked up at school.

At the last inn where they stay, a few miles from the journey's end, he relents, and he and Toni are reconciled. It is then that she decides to slip ahead by herself, to minimize the shock caused by her homecoming. A couple of days later Rudi follows her, only to find that she and her parents have disappeared.

There can be no half-measures with a story like this; either the spell works, or it fails. And, speaking for myself, I have no doubt that it works, that Mr. Appelfeld has succeeded in creating an effect of utter inevitability. The strong spare narrative impels the reader forward, as though in a folktale or a ballad; how could any of it be otherwise—alas?

At the same time, I can imagine some readers who have followed the story unquestioningly up to the final section parting company with it at that point. In the closing pages, after learning that the Jews in the region are being rounded up for deportation, Rudi wanders over the countryside . . . [and joins] a group of Jews waiting quietly at a small railroad station for the train that is coming to take them away.

It is all very subdued, with none of the dreadful scenes that accompanied such departures in actuality. Yet once again, it seems to me to work, though in a rather different way from what has gone before. Certainly there is nothing innocent, still less evasive, about the apparent naiveté of the conclusion. What it reflects are the feelings of a child abandoned by its mother that come to the surface once Rudi has been separated from Toni, even though we know that in reality she herself is a helpless victim. Or so I would tentatively suggest—tentatively, because a fable as compact as ***To the Land of the Cattails*** doesn't necessarily yield up all its secrets the first or second time around.

John Gross, in a review of "To the Land of the Cattails," in The New York Times, *October 24, 1986, p. C31.*

MERLE RUBIN

[Appelfeld] uses the medium of fiction, not to portray life and death within the [Nazi concentration] camps, but to evoke the strange and treacherous calm before the deluge. The foreboding, dreamlike atmosphere of his earlier novels also permeates ***To the Land of the Cattails***. . . .

The novel begins in the summer of 1938, a year fraught with danger and alarms of war. But these perils seem very far off as we follow Toni, a 34-year-old Jewish woman, and her adolescent son Rudi on a journey from Vienna to the land of her birth.

Absorbed by her private dream of homecoming, Toni travels eastward through Ruthenia like a somnambulist. We see her through the eyes of her son, who loves her, fears for her, is by turns touched and exasperated by her behavior, cares for her, mysteriously loses her, and desperately seeks her. Rudi is the son of Toni's brief marriage to a Viennese gentile. He "looks" non-Jewish, like his father, but is Jewish by virtue of her maternity. His demeanor strikes people as "non-Jewish," but he feels a strong allegiance to his mother. She belatedly and confusedly, upon leaving cosmopolitan Vienna for the rural world of her parents, attempts to explain "Jewishness" to her son. In view of what is to happen, attempts at self-definition will make very little difference.

The dreamlike ambience of Appelfeld's fiction is a means of re-creating the stillness before the storm. But this quality of stillness has further significance. The life that was lived at an ordinary pace before the catastrophe takes on the appearance of stillness when viewed retrospectively, through the fire and smoke of the Holocaust. And so, the characters seem to move as if in a dream: the novelist's dream and our dream. Their words and actions take on a deceptive simplicity. There seems a lack of connection between action and consequence. Ordinary solid objects—an inn, a tablecloth, a cup of coffee—are portrayed as if strangely insubstantial, yet filled with an ineffable value. The lives of these people are a dream not only because they do not realize what is about to happen to them, but also because their reality seems dreamlike to us, we readers who see their helplessness as they cannot and who recognize in it the helplessness dreamers feel in nightmares.

Merle Rubin, "Novel Evokes Dreamlike Stillness before Holocaust Nightmare," in The Christian Science Monitor, *November 12, 1986, p. 38.*

GABRIEL JOSIPOVICI

Novels are written for many reasons; only a very few convey the impression that they are written because they have to be. But Aharon Appelfeld's are of this kind. Like the poems of Wallace Stevens they may sometimes be puzzling, sometimes obsessive, but they carry the authority of something which had to be done, which could not be avoided.

They are also difficult to write about because they catch the many flickering changes that occur between people and within people every minute of the day, but which, for obvious reasons, most novelists find it easier to ignore. . . .

[In ***To the Land of the Reeds,*** mother] and son set out, first by train and then in a cart drawn by two horses which they buy on the way, for the Bukovinian town she had left so long before. One moment Toni is full of happiness, sure she has made the right decision, but the next she is full of doubts, sure that her parents will reject her, fearful that her son will leave her as she left her own mother, fearful too that he will turn out to be more goy than Jew. For his part the boy veers between love for his beautiful mother, annoyance at her childishness and stupidity, and pity for her weakness and confusion of mind. . . .

The journey sometimes seems to be taking decades, then to be rushing by in a second. As with the early scene between mother and son, so with the book as a whole: nothing happens and everything happens—which is how we experience our own lives but not how novelists usually depict life. Eventually, and with a kind of terrible lack of awareness of what is happening, mother and son are separated. There are a great many people wandering about these large open spaces, we suddenly realize. Before we fully understand, we are, as in so many of Appelfeld's novels, at the end, and the end is a quiet country railway station. . . .

With another writer we might have thought a point was being made about Jews colluding in their own destruction, or how man prefers to have the void for a purpose than be devoid of purpose. But that is not Appelfeld's way. His dreamlike (or nightmarish) books do not make points. They leave that sort of thing to other writers, and to readers, if they wish. He is content merely to pay his respects to reality.

Gabriel Josipovici, "Time on the Palms of Their Hands," in The Times Literary Supplement, *No. 4378, February 27, 1987, p. 207.*

PATRICK PARRINDER

[***To the Land of the Reeds***] transmutes the destruction of the Jewish populations of Eastern Europe into the material of legend and folk-tale. A mother and her son set out eastwards from Vienna in 1938, driven by a compulsion to revisit their ancestral home in the farthest recesses of the old Hapsburg Empire. Soon they have embarked on an immemorial journey by horse and cart across an apparently endless pastoral landscape. . . . With eloquent simplicity Appelfeld evokes the experiences of these archetypal travellers, whose high hopes gradually deteriorate into nightmare. The Jewish villagers and innkeepers who once welcomed them turn out to be living in fear for their lives, while the pastoral landscape degenerates into a no man's land of starving fugitives and abandoned ruins. . . .

To the extent that it is a Holocaust novel, Appelfeld's haunting and stylised fable does not purport to say anything new. It is a story that has been told before, and that surely cannot be told too often. But ***To the Land of the Reeds*** filters the persecution and deportation of the Jews through two quite ordinary and more universal forms of narrative, the journey homeward and the growth of alienation between a mother and her son. Toni, the mother, is obsessed with the need to atone for her immoral life and for her desertion of her parents and her native community. Rudi, the half-Jewish son rapidly approaching adulthood, is confusedly trying to discover both his own identity and the secret of escaping from his mother's influence. It is, of course, too late to go home, and too late for either the mother or the son to identify with anything but the impending catastrophe.

Does the estranged form of a novel like this succeed in giving it a significance independent of the precise historical events to which it alludes? This is hard to say. If it does, the metaphor of a reckless and doomed return home to the 'motherland' ought to be applicable to modern Zionism as well as to the prewar condition of Eastern Europe. But, like so much in this terse and sometimes lyrical story, Rudi's self-destructive frustration and anger and Toni's restless determination seem as enigmatic as they are inevitable. The singlemindedness of the narrative discourages speculation as to its possible meanings. Like Toni's familiar grumbling refrain, 'A person is not an insect,' everything in ***To the Land of the Reeds*** points to one end, which is extermination. The beauty and pathos of the final sequence, in which Rudi gives in to his destiny and voluntarily joins the other deportees quietly waiting at the railway station, invokes one of the appalling paradoxes of Holocaust literature. Here the persecution and defeat of the body are seen as stages in the renunciation of self and the purification of the spirit. By stopping short of its terminal horrors, Appelfeld renders a journey which ends at the gas chambers in the form of an austere and resigned pilgrim's progress. (p. 16)

Patrick Parrinder, "Charmed Lives," in London Review of Books, *Vol. 9, No. 8, April 23, 1987, pp. 16-17.*

Paul Auster

1947-

American novelist, poet, translator, critic, nonfiction writer, and editor.

Auster is best known for his novels *City of Glass* (1985), *Ghosts* (1986), and *The Locked Room* (1986), which comprise *The New York Trilogy*. In these works, he employs elements from hard-boiled detective fiction and *film noir* as well as literary references and epistemological concepts to create a style that Dennis Drabbelle termed "post-existentialist private eye." While experimenting with standard elements of the mystery genre, the novels address the relationship between past and present and the elusive nature of language and identity. Quinn, the protagonist of *City of Glass,* is a writer of mystery novels who sometimes uses the pseudonym William Wilson. Mistaken for a detective named Paul Auster, Quinn assumes Auster's identity in order to investigate one of his cases; meanwhile, Quinn increasingly confuses himself with his own fictional detective, Max Work. Quinn's assignment is to shadow a linguistics professor who is so obsessed with rediscovering humanity's primordial language that he has isolated his son in a closet for nine years. In the more abstract *Ghosts,* Auster identifies characters only by such designations as Black, White, and Blue. The unnamed detective of *The Locked Room* is often mistaken for his close friend Fanshawe, the missing man whom he has been hired to find. The similarities between Fanshawe and the detective go beyond physical appearance, however, as the detective begins to appropriate facets of Fanshawe's personality and eventually marries his wife. The innovative quality of this complex series prompted Geoffrey O'Brien to note: "[*The New York Trilogy*] suggests that in the apparent dead ends of genre conventions, infinite fresh possibilities can still be found. By turning the mystery novel inside out, Auster may have initiated a whole new round of storytelling."

Auster's other works evidence his knowledge of international literature and further display his attention to experimental prose styles and linguistics. *The Invention of Solitude* (1982), a nonfiction work written after his father's death, details Auster's relationship with and impressions of his father. Through a discursive and fragmented presentation, this book also contains discussions of such authors as Stéphane Mallarmé and Carlos Collodi. Auster's recent work, *In the Country of Last Things* (1987), is an epistolary novel depicting a dystopian American city of the future. Like his other prose works, *In the Country of Last Things* integrates realism with Auster's interest in language. Auster has also written several books of poetry, including *Unearth: Poems, 1970-1972* (1974) and *Wall Writing: Poems, 1971-1975* (1976), and he has translated works by Jean-Paul Sartre, Jacques Dupin, and Stéphane Mallarmé.

(See also *Contemporary Authors,* Vols. 69-72 and *Contemporary Authors New Revision Series,* Vol. 23.)

W. S. MERWIN

Paul Auster's [***The Invention of Solitude***] starts with an event at once ordinary and unique, commonplace and incommunicable. His father, after a divorce and 15 years of living alone in a big house in New Jersey, "in the best of health, not even old, with no history of illness," suddenly died. Their relationship had been composed in great part of remoteness and absence. Most of the feelings it had engendered and fostered had been unarticulated and unnoticed. Indeed, his father's inability to notice him had seemed to Mr. Auster one of the principal and abiding elements of their knowing each other. . . .

© Jerry Bauer

It is not surprising that his father's sudden death—the abrupt ending of a bond so frustrated, unexplored, undeveloped, so seldom, apparently, present—should have stunned Mr. Auster. It overwhelmed him not only with shock but also with a desperate need to examine at last his memory of the man who had been his father, his own feelings about both their lives, and to put it all into words. . . .

The Invention of Solitude starts with Paul Auster's urge to save his father's life from vanishing along with his father. It leads initially to an evocation of his father's conduct and oddities, a reconstruction made of remembered scraps and impressions. The groping account takes the form of a series of relatively brief paragraphs and essays that examine his father's behavior toward his family and business acquaintances, as well as his social life after his divorce. (p. 10)

The consideration of what has survived in Mr. Auster's memory, his "Portrait of an Invisible Man," occupies the first half of the book. The approach to the subject is clearly as direct as he could make it: an effort to get the "material," as he suddenly conceived of it, into language. The notion that there is in fact a relatively solid body of material that exists on its own and can really be put into words is one of the abiding and essential delusions of writers—a delusion that may assert itself with particular vigor at moments when the subject is pressing. Partly because of it, I think, the first section of ***The Invention of Solitude*** has some of the virtues and rawness of letters written under stress. The clearest and most telling passages—including those that convey glimpses of remoteness, absence and speechlessness—are direct and immediate and seem to have emerged more or less as they are out of the guiding impulse.

But the telling itself was a surprise for Mr. Auster. . . . The subject, approached directly, eludes the pursuer. Evanescent to begin with, it dissolves. Mr. Auster therefore turns from his subject to an examination of the attempt to write about it, self-consciously tracing a self-consciousness that occasionally affects the style and form of his account without benefiting them.

For years Paul Auster has been a gifted, sensitive, learned translator of contemporary French literature, especially poetry, and the practice of responsible translation may have served to nourish the illusion of a discrete body of material waiting only to be written down. His book was conceived and begun with honesty, earnestness and intelligence. When his subject proved invisible, he moved in the second half of the book to an extended examination of analogous situations bearing on his relationship with his father and to the themes of isolation and speech, memory, and the present.

This part of ***The Invention of Solitude*** is called "The Book of Memory"; while it contains some ambitious and illuminating passages, it is marred, more than the first part, by recurrent pointless mannerisms apparently suggested by contemporary French "experimental" writing—among them a tendency toward ponderous and sententious notation. He decides to refer to himself in the third person and informs us of this grave decision. . . . The value of the book and above all of the second half emerges in spite of some of the means and flourishes employed to set it forth; even the most original and penetrating sections are sometimes impaired by the author's urge to supply a final weighty generalization.

But there are in the second part of the book moving, delicately perceived portraits of lives and relationships. And there are a number of glosses that reflect on Mr. Auster's own story—commentaries on Collodi and Pinocchio, in particular, on Jonah and on Vermeer. Mr. Auster has also written criticism for years, and perhaps it is not surprising that some of these pages of critical comment, ostensibly the most distant from his original subject, are among the most skillful, sure and realized in the book. And having found both his father and his father's father to be invisible in the first section, the account of his maternal grandfather's life and death in the second part is a clear and unhesitating evocation of a touching, likable man. The mode that Paul Auster affects at moments throughout ***The Invention of Solitude***—that of the notation intended or half-intended or as though intended for later writings—is often obtrusive in this book, but it suggests that much of the story has yet to be told. (pp. 11, 29)

W. S. Merwin, "Invisible Father," in The New York Times Book Review, *February 27, 1983, pp. 10-11, 29.*

JACQUELINE AUSTIN

Titles, pictures, quotations, clippings. Coincidences which are, at first, only significant to the person who initially notices them, but which then are drawn out, riffed on, exegized, until they become larger. Fragments. Literary bits of thought. Old self, new self, self as parent as self. These are items which form a journal. They also form Paul Auster's ***The Invention of Solitude,*** which turns out not to be a journal, but a literary evocation of one.

This book happens in two parts. In the first, the unexpected death of Auster's father precipitates a complex examination of his effects—and also of related literary effects. In this section, "Portrait of an Invisible Man," the literary effects are kept subordinate to the material they evoke. Grief, remorse, and shock make strong glue. In the second part, literature takes over. The resulting series of critical meditations, recollections, and fragments presents itself as the self-conscious creation of a self-conscious tradition; it is by *auteurs* as much as by an immediate author, and it is as much about reading, and being read, as writing.

From its beginning to its end, ***The Invention of Solitude*** is intelligently constructed, especially on the larger structural levels. One idea leads to the next not by the rules of causality or chronology—though these rules are employed within sections of strong narration—but by those of emotional proximity. . . .

Coincidences run strong in this book. They have their problems, even when linked, to use Barthes' phrase, in a "psychological image-system." Auster tends to link coincidences aphoristically, relying on exterior chance and precedent to an almost frustrating degree. The particular coincidences of location and event which Auster uses sometimes seem overdone and forced; they can short-circuit an otherwise delicately wired narration. In an early section of his book, Auster writes that "The house became the metaphor of my father's life," an overexplanation which is not very expressive, and which jars not only because it pushes the skeleton unpleasantly out from beneath the skin, but because Bachelard, in *The Poetics of Space,* said the same thing, so well, at such great length. To Auster's credit, this does not happen very often in ***The Invention of Solitude.*** His most basic sources, French culture bibles such as Proust, Blanchot, and Barthes, are not those about which he talks. Mallarme is, but he is presented later in a delightful discussion about his and Auster's sons, who happen to look very much alike, upon whom Auster projects similar concerns, and who thus permit their fathers to play together. But when such overexplanation does occur, it makes Auster seem less deserving of respect, less successful, than he actually might be.

This problem is sometimes joined by another, which is often inherent in the journal (or pseudo-journal) form: that of staying on the surface, of skimming, of being too brief and easy about particulars. The journal form forces the writer to accrete meanings, often contradictory ones, after having written down events and images. When meanings are uncovered too soon, forced through coincidence, or edited before they have reached their ripest stage, they dull, rather than enhance, the reader's process of discovery. Are certain aspects of Auster's subject too painful, too delicate, for lengthy consideration—or are they just too private? A strained coincidence, or a gloss such as "It sufficed him to remember. And this, in itself, was a startling discovery . . ." just does not tell the reader enough. We want and expect something wiser, more idiosyncratic, and more lengthy, especially when the writer has constructed paragraphs in other sections, with exactly the right blend of terseness, evocation, and image.

The book becomes more problematic, and more "modern," in its second half. The focus changes from the immediate to the general, from the son's father to the son's son, from the richness of the house to the spareness of the writer's empty room. Though the fragments are coherently placed, they unfortunately become shorter and more provisional. The writer begins to refer to himself, in the third person, as "A." Under the stress of changing from past to future, the stable doors spring open and all the horses of this season's technique come galloping out: Reflexiveness. Defamiliarization. "Nostalgia for the present." Translation. The techniques of "post-modern" description. Stress on rhymes, word transformations, coincidences: ". . . the grammar of existence [which] includes all the figures of language itself . . .".

Again, this is a time when Auster's brevity does him a disservice. Just because techniques are fashionable does not mean they are not legitimate, and here the techniques are both assimilated and sincerely used. Bachelard's "valorization of a center of concentrated solitude," his house which "furnishes us dispersed images and a body of images at the same time," has had an opportunity to become something related, but different, but it has failed because Auster has not been sufficiently kind to his readers. Some of the postmodern technical horses are more rideable than others. . . .

There are relatively few writerly lapses; Auster is extremely sensitive both to language and ideas. For a short book, ***The Invention of Solitude*** contains quite a bit to read. Lovely things are done with high-quality, eclectically-chosen sources that fit together in quirky, personal, yet coherent ways. . . .

Any book which can include such diverse *auteurs* as Marina Tsevetayeva, Holderlin, Thurman Munson, and Collodi, and fit them all together in unquestionable coherence, deserves cheers. I do wish, though, that the connections had been pursued further; I felt that huge amounts of material had been denied for over-fashionable reasons, perhaps despair at encompassing the subject, perhaps something more rarefied. . . . The second half of the book, a meditative search for the meaning of the past and its effect on the present, is truly catalyzed by the initial search for the invisible father. "Like everyone else, his life is so fragmented that each time he sees a connection . . . he is tempted to look for a meaning in that connection. . . The connection exists. But to give it a meaning, to look beyond the bare fact of its existence, would be to build an imaginary world inside the real world, and he knows it would not stand . . .". Yet elsewhere Auster has affirmed Jonah's internal process: "Death has frightened him into opening his mouth . . . And even if there is no answer, the man has begun to speak . . .". In "The Book of Memory," we should be given more uninterrupted time to hear that speech, more time in which the speech is allowed to say something to us, whether we, or the author, will believe it or not.

Proust has described the self as a being who stands at the apex of an imaginary pyramid, watching the rest of the world fall away beneath him in descending tiers. The writer who wants to describe self, or that extension of self, the family, has to at once build the pyramid, climb it, be it, and vanish. It is a complex and absolute task. The self, as Holderlin, Barthes, Proust, and countless others have described, must be experienced alone, reinvented, placed. It's no wonder that a simple autobiography might be both boring and successful, or that a complex one, in its self-confessed, even overasserted, failure, might be both interesting and ambitious. I respect ***The Invention of Solitude***. It does falter, I feel, when examined as a whole in the shadow of the other monuments which surround it. But then, Auster has chosen to construct his pyramid, without smirking, blushing, or smashing his thumbs, in the same crowded patch of desert which supports some of the best tombs of France.

Jacqueline Austin, in a review of "The Invention of Solitude," in The American Book Review, *Vol. 6, No. 1, November-December, 1983, p. 23.*

TOBY OLSON

In Paul Auster's remarkable ***City of Glass,*** the ostensible mystery derives from the book's odd and often strangely humorous working of the detective novel genre. The real mystery, however, is one of confused character identity, the descent of a writer into a labyrinth in which fact and fiction become increasingly difficult to separate.

The city of the title is New York, the only truly constant character in the book, and it is the fate of this city to be walked through and interpreted by the writer Quinn and the philosopher and former convict Stillman. . . . Always it reflects Quinn's and Stillman's search for arcane truth or psychological peace.

Quinn writes mystery novels under a pseudonym, and as ***City of Glass*** begins, with a wrong number, "the voice on the other end asking for someone he was not," Quinn is drawn into an actual world of mystery where he begins to take on the characteristics of his fictional detective, Max Work. Early on, we learn what Quinn likes about writing mystery novels and reading them:

> In the good mystery there is nothing wasted, no sentence, no word that is not significant. . . . Since everything seen or said, even the slightest, most trivial thing, can bear a connection to the outcome of the story, nothing must be overlooked. . . . The center of the book shifts with each event that propels it forward.

As the story of Quinn's case develops, taking up issues as diverse as language acquisition and biblical history, both he and the reader find themselves in a world in which the possibilities of chance seem to be dissolving. "Nothing must be overlooked" here either. Each detail, each small revelation must be attended to as significant. And such attention brings ambiguity, confusion and paranoia. . . .

One way in which "the center of the book shifts" involves the reader's discovery that the anonymous phone call Quinn receives is a call for the detective Paul Auster, the identity Quinn takes on as he enters the confusion of the case. When Mr. Auster himself enters the novel, we cannot even be sure who the author of this mystery might be.

In ***City of Glass,*** Mr. Auster's prose shifts its essence in the same ways that the accumulation of significant events shifts the reader's focus. At times the prose is transparent, at others it humorously calls attention to the mystery novel genre with light parody. . . . Always the prose moves with grace and sureness, and the reader is moved along briskly. Even in its difficult and complex discussions, the book is a pleasure to read, full of suspense and action.

City of Glass is the first volume of ***The New York Trilogy***. . . . [One] can only wait with much anticipation for the second installment of this strange and powerful new adventure in his art.

Toby Olson, "Metaphysical Mystery Tour," in The New York Times Book Review, *November 3, 1985, p. 31.*

DENNIS DRABELLE

If I had to supply a label for [***City of Glass*** and ***Ghosts***] . . . it would be something like *post-existentialist private eye*. Though they are steeped in the stuff of the hard-boiled detective story, ***City of Glass*** and ***Ghosts*** evolve into studies in obsession and withhold the last-chapter solution obligatory in the unadulterated genre. It's as if Kafka had gotten hooked on the gumshoe game and penned his own ever-spiraling version.

Other comparisons might be drawn—to Nabokov, to Dino Buzatti, to Witold Gombrowicz—and presumably Auster would welcome them. . . .

Auster is more successful, I think, in ***Ghosts.*** From the outset it is clear that we are in Abstractland. A client named White hires a detective named Blue to follow a man named Black. Gradually Blue realizes he's been ruined. All he can do is stare at Black, eternally writing a book in the rented room across the street, and draw a weekly paycheck. Black and White are probably the same person, and Blue is "trapped . . . into doing nothing, into being so inactive as to reduce his life to almost no life at all."

Auster fleshes out this, well, austere tale with vignettes of old New York. Blue's and White's apartments are located on a street in Brooklyn Heights where "Walt Whitman handset the first edition of *Leaves of Grass* . . . , and it was here that Henry Ward Beecher railed against slavery from the pulpit of his red-brick church." He tells the story of the invalid Washington Roebling, who presided over the construction of the Brooklyn Bridge from his house in the Heights, with forceful economy. But then Auster's prose is always economical—clipped, precise, the last word in gnomic control.

The syndrome of being obsessed with and paralyzed by an idea you've talked yourself into seems a particularly European one, not viable on a continent where you can easily pick up and desert your past. That is, until now. Auster, who has spent several years in France and edited *The Random House Book of Twentieth-Century French Poetry,* has brought the idée fixe mentality home. In his detectives who degenerate beyond the standard seediness into self-jailing voyeurs and bagpersons in the cramped streets of New York City, he has provided a striking vision of contemporary American stasis.

Dennis Drabelle, "Mystery Goes Post-Modern," in Book World—The Washington Post, *June 15, 1986, p. 9.*

REBECCA GOLDSTEIN

Ghosts is the second volume of ***The New York Trilogy,*** and like the first, it is a mystery novel—of sorts. The mystery does not take place so much within the story as on some higher level; how much higher the level is is, in fact, very much a part of the mystery. It is a very slim little tale, the pared-down elements of the detective story. One man, Blue, is hired by another man, White, to watch a third man, Black. But from the beginning one knows that this story goes beyond itself. With the very first sentence, one is given the conviction (but, then, mystery writers are so coy, and this one is coyer than most) that this is all going to mean something: "First of all there is Blue. Later there is White, and then there is Black, and before the beginning there is Brown." A slightly oracular tone, no? The author seems to be informing us that he need not bother with those details of realism that encourage the reader to sink himself deep into the story. Hence the names: Blue, White, Black and Brown, and later Green, Grey, Gold, Red (a bartender) and violet (a blowsy tart).

This ironic detachment from the reality of the story is sustained throughout. So too is that oracular tone.

> Little does Blue know, of course, that the case will go on for years. But the present is no less dark than the past, and its mystery is equal to anything the future might hold. Such is the way of the world: one step at a time, one word and then the next. There are certain things that Blue cannot possibly know at this point. For knowledge comes slowly, and when it comes, it is often at great personal expense.

Is the conclusion to be avoided that all this stands for something, something that smacks of the philosophical—perhaps, given all this talk of knowledge, the epistemological? We are not being asked to submerge ourselves in this story, to believe in its reality. We are to stay above it, to read it as, well, metaphor; and our fanatical attention to details and frenetic attempts at deduction (both necessary for reading a mystery novel correctly) are to be directed upward toward the question, what does it all mean?

The detective in this story, like the mystery writer turned detective in ***City of Glass,*** is brought to the edge of destruction in his obsession to get at the answer. About to go undercover, he informs his fiancée that he will be unavailable for the duration of the case. The case continues for years; he never gets in touch with her; and when he happens to pass her in the street, her arm linked through another man's, she attacks him, pounding him on the chest, "screaming insanely at him, accusing him of one foul crime after another." Pursuing his case, Blue has become inhuman, a ghost. Is Mr. Auster using the mystery novel to present a tale meant to point a finger at the destructive underside of the dispassionate intellect, the very faculty exercised in our reading of mysteries? But there is more; things happen between Blue and Black. And then there is White, who truly is not the man he seems.

As this is a mystery that clearly goes beyond both itself and its genre, we cannot complain that it lacks the absolute sine qua non of the mystery—the solution that leaves no questions. We get the answer to the questions within the story; we find out who White and Black are and what they have been up to. But we don't get the answer to the metamystery. What, in fact, did it all mean? Perhaps nothing at all. That would be coy indeed. The ghosts of the title, then, would be meanings, conjured up in the fever of our shared intellectual delirium. If this is what the book is all about, it has betrayed itself into inconsistency. If the meaning is that there is no meaning, then there is a meaning. Or perhaps Mr. Auster is writing of the violence (for there is violence in the end) with which we demand that our own lives be made meaningful. In any case, what does one call a seamless little detective story that forces one to ask questions such as these? I call it nearly perfect.

Rebecca Goldstein, "The Man Shadowing Black Is Blue," in The New York Times Book Review, *June 29, 1986, p. 13.*

GEOFFREY O'BRIEN

The simple pleasures of narrative were expelled from paradise by modernism's archangels, but for some time they've been creeping in again through the back door of structuralist and semiotic analysis. In the process, of course, they turn out not to be simple at all. When a writer ventures into the realm of pure storytelling, he enters a paradoxical space where freedom and restriction mirror each other, and every getaway becomes an oblique imprisonment. The reader of genre fiction thinks he escapes, but where? Does he ever get there, or is he simply lured on by the continual promise of something about to happen? Out of such questions Paul Auster has fashioned the skeletal thrillers of his ***New York Trilogy,*** an enterprise which may signal a tidal shift, as theory finally gives way to practice. Auster is not content to disassemble genre; he wants to put it back together as well.

These are novels of desire: the desire to write a detective novel, to read one, to inhabit one. But a price must be paid for indulging in such shadowy pleasures. To write a detective novel, for instance, one must become someone else, a writer-as-author capable of deceiving the writer-as-reader. Mind hides from itself, spinning a labyrinth of detours and false leads. Thus in the trilogy's first volume, ***City of Glass,*** a detective novelist named Quinn sometimes mistakes himself for his fictional creation, Max Work, who in turn is mistaken for a real-life detective named Paul Auster. . . . Toward the end we encounter yet another figure, the unnamed author of the novel we have been reading. ***City of Glass*** is a dance of doppelgängers that culminates in the only resolution its structural logic permits: an empty room, a disappearance, an unbroken silence.

Ghosts, the trilogy's second installment, is—in accordance with the iron laws of genre—the same as its predecessor, only different. More detectives, more doubles, more disguises, more cabalistic excavations of a literary text (this time it's *Walden*), more investigations that coil in on themselves and threaten to shatter the frame of the narrative. . . .

In this stripped-down generic story, the only thing colorful about the characters is their names. Yet every move they make connects them to real locations and real historical moments. The narrative mechanism tries to establish a hermetic space, but the world keeps intruding. It's 1947; down the street they're showing *Out of the Past,* and its intricate plot becomes part of the texture of Auster's tale, along with the Dodgers, *True Detective,* and a phantasmal Fuller Brush man. Auster skillfully wards off the double demons of nostalgia and pastiche, managing to appropriate the signifiers of *film noir* and the bric-a-brac of local history without being appropriated by them.

Ghosts is neither homage nor parody; instead it uses genre clichés as a personal language. Auster has watched the same movie so many times that it's become an extension of his psyche. But since we've all seen that movie, since the stories of our lives are patched together from pieces of that movie, the private world of ***Ghosts*** is a public domain, a fill-in-the-blanks landscape where there is no privacy even in solitude. . . . Each individual represents a link in a chain of solitudes. Real freedom, real relationship can exist only outside the text.

For all their obsession with negativity and absence, ***City of Glass*** and ***Ghosts*** convey a mood of controlled exhilaration. Their subject is their construction, the sleight-of-hand by which Auster creates stories out of nothing at all. That he lays his cards so openly on the table makes his feat all the more remarkable. We see every move, watch him build the mystery sentence by sentence. The process is so overt that it can give us the uncanny impression of writing the book ourselves—an impression that provides the final twist in Auster's game of hide-and-seek. The ***New York Trilogy*** . . . suggests that in the apparent dead ends of genre conventions, infinite fresh possibilities can still be found. By turning the mystery novel inside out, Auster may have initiated a whole new round of storytelling.

Geoffrey O'Brien, "And Then What Happened?" in The Village Voice, *Vol. XXXI, No. 29, July 22, 1986, p. 46.*

GARY G. GACH

The plot [of ***Ghosts***] is the routine assignment of most private investigators: the stakeout, the tail. "White wants Blue to follow a man named Black and keep an eye on him for as long as necessary." The attraction of this genre is seldom the plot, rather it is the chance to look at the darker side of American life. However, by reducing the characters to colors, and the language to the plainest—in jettisoning the whodunnit's chief attractions of character and language—in its resulting austerity the book focuses in upon itself. As a made thing, art is reflexive, implying an audience. Here its reflexivity doubles back upon itself.

The "obstinate individualism" of the detective merges with that of the author. As the detective's code becomes the artist's job description, it becomes evident that its self-reflexive treatment of *genre* is not a subtext so much as a pretext, in the same fashion as was Thoreau's going to Walden.

On its own merits, ***Ghosts*** is nearly perfect. And perfection, obedient to life's imperatives of transformation, always carries its own subversion. Thus far, the ***New York Trilogy*** has managed to maintain its sense of the perfection of sheer being while simultaneously remaining vigilant to the nightmare inevitable to its elaboration. Paul Auster displays a unique gift for storytelling and has moved from the nonpaying profession of poetry into a wider arena with a skill at hardball prose that commands great respect.

He has not exactly broken out of our century's preoccupation with itself, its hall of mirrors—at least not yet. Yet ***Ghosts*** records the struggle of doing so. As a "read," its author's struggle becomes ours, through the depth of his commitment and the power of his craft. Writing and reading are both enacted in solitude.

"Every age has the renaissance of antiquity it deserves," as Aby Warburg has pointed out, and Paul Auster has found ours in that wellspring of mainline American literature, the mystery. That the frame of ***Ghosts*** purports to be both 1948 and the present leaves the residual problem of continuity to be dealt with in the concluding book, ***The Locked Room.*** It promises to tie up and explain the mysteries of its two predecessors, but, naturally, not Mystery itself. (pp. 6-7)

Gary G. Gach, in a review of "Ghosts," in San Francisco Review of Books, *Vol. XI, No. 3, Fall, 1986, pp. 6-7.*

GARY GACH

[*City of Glass*] is a mystery novel. Modern, certainly, but somewhat short on the realism expected of most detective fiction. Hard-core mystery addicts are habituated to material description, evidence, things—all details being possible clues until the illuminating show-down, the wrap-up. Instead, and a very pleasant surprise it is, this story and its attendant architecture, characters, and props consist only of the writing and the reading of the book itself.

It is a mystery more of ripples forming in a still pond, or of footprints leaving their tracks in a virgin snowfield. Which is not to say that this book isn't replete with its share of stunning twists of plot, nor that it doesn't capture the pulse of contemporary urban life. Rare feat, Paul Auster has written a "page-turner" without building the plot on scandalous sex and violence.

Rather, drawing deeply upon the solitude of the act of writing, he has communicated the great solitude of great cities. In sharing so generously with us his daily act of placing a blank rectangle of paper on the cleared rectangle of his desk, he elicits from us the most intimate experiences of our daily urban aloneness.

City of Glass opens with a seemingly random occurrence narrated by an author who writes detective stories under another name, and now gets pulled into the maze of a "real" mystery. Readers who like deep complications ought to know that the author, Paul Auster, writes mass-market detective books under a pseudonym.

Discussion of the plot of ***City of Glass*** might easily topple the delightfully intricate house of cards Auster constructs. . . . I noted a structural peculiarity which appeared throughout the book. Its thirteen chapters each seem to be a variation on the opening premise, or setup. That initial form is replayed each time within a discrete, different mirroring device, in one case entries from the protagonist's notebook, the speech of a seemingly insane man in another, and in yet another chapter the protagonist's notes on a book one of the characters has written reexamining the myths of the Fall and of the Tower of Babel.

As suspense mounts within the overall "meta-mystery" framework of the book, through its successive variations, the theme that finally emerges concerns identity and individual communication. To be sure, there've been other such mystery novels before—Christie's *The Murder of Roger Ackroyd,* Perutz' *The Master of the Day of Judgment,* and more recently, Hjortsberg's *Naked Angels*—with which ***City of Glass*** can join company on any discriminating Mystery shelf.

As this is the first volume of a trilogy in progress, we'll have to wait and see whether and how Paul Auster can continue to pour new wine into the old bottles of fiction, not to mention of popular fiction. My hunch is that we may be witnessing something auspicious enough to compare to Samuel Beckett's fictional trilogy, both in its establishment of a new quality of writing in a postwar era as well as in its use of the semi-detective story of the Seeker and the Sought.

One last comparison: when the revolutionary Russian film-maker Sergei Eisenstein was in America, he contemplated making a film based on a proposed Frank Lloyd Wright tower of glass. In the tower in which Eisenstein wanted to shoot, everything—walls, ceilings, floors—would be glass; only, nobody would look at each other. . . . A similar *imagination* of America is at work here, only within a world of real walls, and of people speaking, from time to time, across them.

Gary Gach, "Magna Civitas, Magna Solitudo," in The American Book Review, *Vol. 8, No. 5, September-October, 1986, p. 16.*

STEPHEN SCHIFF

The quirky richness of Paul Auster's ***Locked Room*** took me by surprise. This is the final volume in his ***New York Trilogy,*** and the first two, ***City of Glass*** and ***Ghosts,*** left a sour, medicinal taste, as if I had swallowed something terribly good for me but not very toothsome. Widely lauded as postmodern and postexistentialist and post a few other things, these two slender novels turn the detective genre into something tonier: the gumshoes in their chilly pages keep meeting doppelgängers and spitting out references to *Don Quixote* and Hawthorne and Thoreau. And the more they stalk their eccentric quarry, the more they seem actually to be stalking the Big Questions—the implications of authorship, the enigmas of epistemology, the veils and masks of language.

For mystery fans whose pleasure in the genre consists in putting together puzzle pieces, Mr. Auster's glassy little jigsaws can be seductive. His plots—decorated with death threats and "dark-eyed" women and all the other private-eye flotsam—draw one in like those of any other page-turner. But once the door bangs shut, the clue-sniffing reader finds himself on a swift elevator to a loftier plane. Soon he is deposited, still sniffing, on the heady heights of meta-fiction, where "Who done it?" has been transformed into "Who's asking?" and "What does who done it mean, anyway?" Mr. Auster has hit upon something. By changing the nature of the clues from the physical to the metaphysical, he harnesses the inquiring spirit any reader brings to a mystery, redirecting it from the grubby search for a wrong-doer to the more rarefied search for self. . . .

The trouble with ***City of Glass*** and ***Ghosts*** is the absence of a flatfoot worth hoofing around decrepit New York with; in addition, one longs for characters more robust and more resourceful, less wan, less cipherlike. Mr. Auster is boyishly smitten with solitude. . . . [Auster] has filled the trilogy's first two volumes with the depictions of lost-soul wanderings and stir-crazy journal-keeping and the disintegration of identity—stuff that makes us think our putative detective may presently strip off his disguise to reveal a neurasthenic grad student cooped up with his final thesis too long.

But ***The Locked Room,*** which works best if you have read the other two books first, is a brilliant leap forward, a beguiling entertainment that accomplishes nearly everything the first two books set out to do and provides a diverting main character as well. It is the only first-person narrative in the series, and this helps enormously. Mr. Auster's philosophical asides now sound heartfelt instead of stentorian and his descents into semiological *Angst* feel genuinely anguished and near. The nameless narrator, whom we are meant to identify with Mr. Auster himself, is not a detective but a biographer; which is much the same thing: a chaser of facts, details, clues. The man he is researching is his recently vanished friend, Fanshawe, a golden boy who calls to mind the golden Fanshawe of Hawthorne's first novel. Hawthorne plainly viewed his solitary hero as some noble and untarnished aspect of himself, and so does our narrator, who is frequently mistaken for his old pal. But this Fanshawe's early life has been borrowed wholesale from Mr. Auster's own, so the narrator and the object of his pursuit both represent the author. In short, we are watching the writer hunt down his own identity. . . .

To compose a fiction is very much to be a private eye, gazing inward, investigating characters who may or may not be oneself. The closer one comes to one's hidden identity, the more harrowing the chase, and the novel's most vivid passages conjure up a true dark night of the soul.

> Something monstrous was happening, and I had no control over it anymore. The sky was growing dark inside—that much was certain; the ground was trembling. . . . I could no longer make the right distinctions. This can never be that. Apples are not oranges, peaches are not plums. . . . But everything was beginning to have the same taste to me.

In that eloquent passage, and others like it, Mr. Auster puts his finger on the pulsing locus of language and identity. He understands that the detective of the self is trapped, forced to use that clumsiest of tools, language, to ferret out what mere language can never discover. Putting a name on something makes it at once available and all the more elusive, at once fixes it in front of us and obscures it forever. In ***The Locked Room,*** Mr. Auster proclaims the urgency of that dilemma, not just for writers but for all those who seek the truth behind the fictions they read and the fictions they live.

Stephen Schiff, "Inward Gaze of a Private Eye," in The New York Times, *January 4, 1987, p. 14.*

DANIEL MAX

Paul Auster is a tricky writer. In ***In the Country of Last Things,*** as in the earlier ***New York Trilogy,*** he appears motivated by the straight-forward desire to tell a story. Yet beneath the polished words, the question of language and its relation to itself and to society is elegantly struggling to get out.

The ***New York Trilogy*** was one of the literary surprises of 1986. The three brief volumes, ostensibly detective novels—***City of Glass, Ghosts,*** and ***The Locked Room***—borrowed their tone from the hard-boiled school of Raymond Chandler and the *film noir*. But for their subject they ranged much further afield. . . .

In the Country of Last Things belongs to a different genre. A young girl, Anna Blume, goes on a wilderness journey in search of her brother, a missing journalist. The twist is that the wilderness Anna sails for is an East Coast American city of the near future, a New York, Boston, or Washington that has fulfilled the worst predictions of every prophet of doom. Anna relates her experiences in this nightmare land through a journal or never-sent letter. . . .

The city is crumbling, its buildings and streets near collapse. The military government no longer even tries to keep the civil peace. It is erecting a great wall along the harbor to keep out attackers (and keep in citizens). Garbage—everything from heirlooms to feces and dead bodies—is the city's most precious industry. The government officially licenses scavengers to comb the streets with big shopping carts and collect anything at all—orange rinds, pieces of cloth—to sell to the wealthy Resurrection Agents to be made into new products or burned for fuel. The authorities collect bodies in great hoppers and burn them at Transformation Centers. . . .

As in ***The New York Trilogy,*** Auster's special literary concern is how words control and shape our thoughts. The crazed Columbia professor in ***City of Glass*** believes the creation of an Eden in America can come only with the discovery of man's natural language. In ***Country of Last Things,*** language is dying with its people. . . . Here is the true power of Auster's dark age vision—not only has horror replaced all the good of our society but the good can no longer even be remembered because the words are gone with which to think of it.

Daniel Max, in a review of "In the Country of Last Things," in Boston Review, *Vol. XII, No. 2, April, 1987, p. 26.*

PADGETT POWELL

One prepares, when picking up a novel that promises to be postapocalyptic, to change his critical kit bag. One prepares to find moral guidance and instructions for living in novels of the next world, in a way we've learned it is sophisticated not to find them in novels of this world. The assumption is that whatever horror is contained in the next world may, if we buy the prophecy and the route from here to there, serve to change our current imprudent behavior and steer this unhappy world away from the unhappier one the novelist warns us is ahead.

The opening pages of Paul Auster's ***In the Country of Last Things*** confirm that "last things" denotes an end-of-the-world-as-we-know-it, and one gets ready for those warnings and prophetic detour signs, and then stops. There is entirely too much in these pages about the world *as* we know it. (p. 11)

The setting, though unnamed, may without dislocation be thought of as New York, and the economy depicted may be termed *late* service. An industrialist's true nightmare: there are no current manufacturers, and most folk are involved in one form of rude salvage of the broken remnants of "last things." The services are primarily the reclamation of the things and the government collection, for fuel, of corpses and feces. The landscape is a rubble-intense evocation of what could already be parts of the Bronx if buildings there were actually allowed to fall down and remain. The monetary unit is a "glot," and the government—what there is of it—changes hands rapidly. Along with body and waste collection, its main goal is distributing misinformation.

In all, the world is reminiscent of the Great Depression, carried to about, say, the third power, and it is inhabited, mostly, by a race of bag people. One Anna Blume comes into this "grim" (one of her favorite words) scenes looking for her brother, William, who, on journalistic assignment from an uncollapsed world to the east (we may assume it is the Old World—and the fallen one the New), has disappeared. The novel is Anna's letter home to an old friend from childhood.

Into this letter, this chronicle of unrelenting travail for Anna Blume, Mr. Auster, author of the highbrow mysteries of ***The New York Trilogy,*** proceeds at a trilogist's pace and with a series of high-novel dares. During an introductory anatomy of the bag world, a summary of how Anna comes to be looking for William and of the horrors confronting her—the very building William was said to be in is gone—we get no real, live characters on stage other than the narrator herself. When we do get some, on page 40 or so, they are doozies: the quintessence of bag people, precisely the denizens we might lazily expect following Anna's anatomy of her bag world. Moreover, they are Isabel and Ferdinand—Ferdinand carves tiny ships that go into bottles, a "lilliputian fleet of sailing ships and schooners," and certain historic and mythic contours are set up. Anna Blume is become a latter-day Columbus in a world anything but New.

Ferdinand just happens to be reminiscent of Louis-Ferdinand Céline as well. "'The smaller the better,'" he says to Anna one night, "bragging about his accomplishments as an artist. 'Some day I'll make a ship so small that no one can see it. . . . They'll write a book about me, I'll be so famous. Then you'll see what's what, my vicious little slut.'" Anna concludes, "One non sequitur after another, rushing out of him like some poison that had accumulated in his blood." That he inhabits the very kind of world Céline seemed to prophesy is not lost on us.

These are daring touches, and they let us drop all notion of having to suffer a didactic, finger-wagging account of how we ruined ourselves. Not Mr. Auster's game at all. What *did* happen? "Collapse" is the entire explanation offered—late in the book—again, the worst word conceivable for the free-enterprise believer, yet nowhere is there a suggestion that a socialist order has prevailed. As if to further not let us worry on this score, Mr. Auster keeps on offering novelistic dares.

He will try to surprise with the obvious, and he will advance the story with the madly (but somehow not maddeningly) coincidental. The boldness of these maneuvers—rather like the big lie—allows them to work. (pp. 11-12)

The main music, the game perhaps, is linguistic, even though Anna Blume is a most regular, most unexperimental, most conventionally "elegant" writer. . . . Anna confronts a grimmer and grimmer degeneration each day and yet tries to generate more words from it. From nothing, something: she is the last manufacturer in the New World; she is, again, a Columbus, sending back not what she wanted but *something* to show for it all.

Mr. Auster seems most interested in this problem of confronting a limited *thing* with talk that shall not be, or cannot be, limited. . . .

It is an asymptotic approach of expression to the nothing it finally defines, an infinite series of effables toward the ineffable. It is not simply objects that are disappearing. Human things are on the wane too. Mr. Auster offers Anna nothing in the way of hope and wants her to make a generous, human account of it anyway. In light of this aim, if indeed it is Mr. Auster's, it is telling that (Louis-) Ferdinand is bumped off early, and that Anna, facing a world ever bleaker than Céline's, remains resilient, plucky, apologetic for uncivilized behavior necessary to survive, and hopeful yet. She promises to write more of her continuing search for William. If in the beginning there was only the Word, she wants to say that in the end It will still be. (p. 12)

Padgett Powell, "'The End is Only Imaginary'," in The New York Times Book Review, *May 17, 1987, pp. 11-12.*

George Bowering

1935-

Canadian poet, novelist, short story writer, critic, editor, and nonfiction writer.

A leading Canadian experimental writer, Bowering devises inventive literary forms and techniques to explore themes related to art, language, and identity. Underscoring his commitment to playfully examine the creative process of art, Bowering has stated: "I'm not interested in the results of thinking, I'm interested in the process of thinking itself." His preoccupation with art and language is tempered by irreverent humor, sensuality, and an abiding concern with Canadian society and culture. Although Bowering's prolific output is considered uneven by many critics, he is generally regarded as an important contributor to contemporary Canadian literature. Brian L. Flack asserted that "there are a *number* of reasons for [Bowering's] success: constant innovation, clarity of thought, dedication to the imaginative, and structural sophistication."

Deakin University, Victoria, Australia. Courtesy of George Bowering.

While a student at the University of British Columbia in Vancouver during the late 1950s and early 1960s, Bowering was inspired by the verse of William Carlos Williams. He found especially fascinating Williams's poetic experiments intended to intensify ordinary language and subject matter. Along with Fred Wah, Frank Davey, and other poets, Bowering founded *Tish,* a poetry newsletter that served as a forum for unconventional literature. Stimulated by a series of lectures featuring such Black Mountain poets as Robert Duncan and Robert Creeley, the *Tish* group developed a poetics based on the tenets of Williams and the Black Mountain group, patterning the syntax and line structures of their poems on the inflections and rhythms of everyday speech. Another Black Mountain principle central to Bowering's verse involves self-reflexive writing, a mode through which the poet's thoughts and the act of creation itself are reflected in the form and content of the composition. These concerns are evident in the lyric poems of *Points on the Grid* (1964), in which he examines such topics as art and love. In *Baseball: A Poem in the Magic Number 9* (1967), Bowering strays from the lyric form to create a long poem in which he muses about life and poetry while discussing the intricacies of the sport of baseball. In his most acclaimed early volumes of poetry, *Rocky Mountain Foot* (1968) and *The Gangs of Kosmos* (1969), both of which won Governor General's Literary Awards, Bowering contrasts the natural beauties of the wilderness with the problems of civilization while recreating the Western Canadian idiom. Many of Bowering's early pieces are collected in *Touch: Selected Poems, 1960-1970* (1971).

Between 1970 and 1982, Bowering published more than a dozen volumes of verse, several of which were later collected in omnibus form. *The Catch* (1976) contains *George, Vancouver: A Discovery Poem* (1970), *Autobiology* (1972), and a section of new poems. In *George, Vancouver,* Bowering focuses on various discoveries made by three men named George: George Vancouver, an eighteenth-century navigator and surveyor who mapped the shoreline of Western Canada; King George III of England, who dispatched several explorers to claim uncharted lands; and Bowering himself, an adventurous young poet. In *Autobiology,* Bowering blends poetry and prose in a surreal presentation replete with personal memories and associations to create an actively inquiring and introspective voice. *West Window: The Selected Poetry of George Bowering* (1982) includes several new poems in addition to four previously published volumes: *Curious* (1973), a series of prose poems about writers with whom Bowering was acquainted; *At War with the U.S.* (1974), in which Bowering declares his independence from American cultural influence; *Allophanes* (1976), in which Bowering employs a baseball game as a metaphor for life and presents divergent views on the conflict of art versus reality; and *Uncle Louis* (1980), a satire on Louis St. Laurent, Prime Minister of Canada from 1948 to 1957, that evidences Bowering's penchant for social criticism. *Particular Accidents: Selected Poems* (1980) contains representative poems composed during the 1960s and 1970s. Bowering's most acclaimed later volume, *Kerrisdale Elegies* (1984), is an extended poem loosely based on Rainer Maria Rilke's *Duino Elegies*. Evoking a somber tone to meditate upon death, Bowering writes from the perspective of a man who gradually realizes the importance of being aware of his surroundings and gains greater appreciation of life. The verse in Bowering's next collection, *Seventy-One Poems for People* (1986), deals with political and social issues.

Bowering is also respected for his experimental fiction. His first novel, *Mirror on the Floor* (1967), concerns an attractive young woman, her relationship with a college student, and her suffocating family life. Bowering was praised for recreating the middle-class and counterculture milieus of Vancouver. In *A Short Sad Book* (1977), Bowering satirizes postmodernist fiction and Canadian literary politics while exploring the creative process in a self-reflexive narrative that directly involves the reader. *Burning Water* (1980), which won a Governor General's Literary Award, juxtaposes the adventures of George Vancouver with Bowering's personal interpolations to simultaneously create and comment upon Vancouver's story. While critics found the blending of the two stories confusing, many agreed that Bowering had crafted an intriguing search for identity. In his recent novel, *Caprice* (1987), Bowering parodies Old West revenge tales by depicting a larger-than-life female protagonist who seeks to avenge the murder of her brother.

Bowering's short stories are collected in *Flycatcher and Other Stories* (1974), *Protective Footwear: Stories and Fables* (1978), and *A Place to Die* (1983). Several characters recur in these stories, including George Delsing, a sensitive man who approaches life with a sense of wonder, and Carter, an eccentric artist. *A Place to Die* contains pieces that deliberately work against the traditional short story form. Bowering's nonfiction books, among them *A Way with Words* (1982) and *Craft Slices* (1985), contain criticism, anecdotes, and literary theory.

(See also *CLC,* Vol. 15; *Contemporary Authors,* Vols. 21-24, rev. ed.; *Contemporary Authors New Revision Series,* Vol. 10; and *Dictionary of Literary Biography,* Vol. 53.)

MILTON WILSON

[***Points on the Grid***] is a cluttered, uneven, exciting collection, the work of a genuine poet who is very self-consciously, and sometimes very convincingly, finding himself. His mentors in the process have been Olson and Creeley. It was back in 1952, in *Cerberus,* that Raymond Souster suggested that Canadians might benefit from studying Olson, but it wasn't until the 1960's that any number of them took the hint. In ***Points on the Grid*** the student is sometimes in danger of outweighing the poet. Poetry is on the verge of turning into poetics, perception into epistemology. Bowering likes to watch himself in process, moving in and out, absorbing and projecting, relating the margin and the centre, filling the space between with a field of physical objects in which any distinction between word and thing is irrelevant, identifying his body and his poem. . . . The most inventive and exciting (if still a bit formula-ridden) of these "poetics about poetics about poetics" is a long (and structurally imaginative) poem called **"A Meta Physic in Things,"** which ends:

> the song sung where he is located in the middle of his
> poem
> that moves up & out thru the poem part that is his
> actual body /
> the whole physiological barrel of the poet of the poem!

Presumably, if the poet knows his business, the reader gets shot.

I take it that a reviewer's job with such a poet is to judge the accuracy of the aim, the quality of the ammunition, and the strength of the thrust. The job should be easier with his second book. This one is a very mixed bag, a clearing of the decks to signal the end of his apprenticeship. Some of the poems probably mean more in the education of the poet than they are likely to in the experience of the reader. **"Soliloquy on the Rocks,"** whose imagery and syntax get in the way of its sound just as Bowering says they shouldn't . . . is presumably included as a nostalgic gesture. (I first encountered it as long ago as 1959, in an early issue of *Prism,* and it hasn't changed a word since.) **"The Night Before Morning"** seems equally out of place. I can't imagine anyone being impressed by **"The Hockey Hero"** who has ever watched hockey, much less played it. Or take the Heathcliff and Jake Barnes poems. To use Olson's terminology, in some of these poems there isn't enough mind in the syllable or the right force in the field. . . . (pp. 362-63)

But enough carping. One of the most promising things about this book at its best is the variety of thrust, the range of rhythm, between one poem and another. Bowering likes to think that rhythm is his forte, and I'm sure he's right. . . . **"Benzedrine," "Hospital,"** and **"Locus Solus"** are all excellent Bowering, and their rhythmic skill is one of the chief reasons for their excellence, but they dance very differently indeed. Many of the best things in ***Points on the Grid*** are love poems. Bowering likes to write about girls-at-a-distance, outside "the margins of his mind," with the night between to be erased or a brief space filled (**"Dark around Light"** is the choice of these); but the wonderful **"For A"** has no such distance (how characteristic, by the way, that Bowering should measure love in syllables). Then there's the long, spasmodic, sectional poem that opens the book, **"Another Try at It,"** which manages to be about love and poetics simultaneously. I started off by calling this book "cluttered, uneven, exciting." The excitement looks as though it will last. I'm certainly anticipating his [next] book. (pp. 363-64)

Milton Wilson, in a review of "Points on the Grid," in University of Toronto Quarterly, *Vol. XXXIV, No. 4, July, 1965, pp. 362-64.*

W. D. GODFREY

Bowering has created in Andrea Henderson [the heroine of ***Mirror on the Floor***] a nubile triumph of the recent novel. At first you fear she is going to be nothing more than one of those lovely, horny harpies the Bowering-I is always meeting in dark college elevators and where not, but as she moves deeper down and farther out in Vancouver, like a black, spawn-spent steelhead, she becomes more than real, sadness hovers closer to her, she is that quirkily beautiful girl down the hall with the denim miniskirt and the eyes which predict her own doom. The one you regret not having talked to. You are glad Bob Small did.

But Bowering's hero, or perhaps more definitely the relationship between hero and author, is not quite so successful an accomplishment. And this stems, I am not certain precisely how, from the method Bowering uses to reveal Andrea. He shows her as Small sees her and loves her; he shows her as a voice on the confessional tape which she records and to which Small listens. But Bowering also drops all pretence of Small as total-narrator and shows Andrea's mind and memory directly. These are the finest portions of the novel: deftest, fullest, most carefully selective. We get a smaller amount of Small's insides and only as we see him respond to this interior misery of Andrea. With Andrea herself, the book moves towards a Yeats-Reaney richness of psychological myth. With Small, there is always the danger of phrases and ideas coming out as Penticton Kerouac. But definitely a novel to read. . . . (p. 46)

W. D. Godfrey, "Andrea or Andre," in The Canadian Forum, *Vol. XLVII, May, 1967, pp. 45-6.*

PHYLLIS GROSSKURTH

Mirror on the Floor is the story of a teen-age beatnik girl, Andrea, and her brief love affair with a college student. The desperation of her loveless home with its shrewish mother and sexually starved father is caught in one superb kitchen scene in which all three studiously ignore each other while the father exacerbates the girl's nerves as he slurps down an apple. Fleeing to a room of her own, she discovers that she is so emotionally damaged that love will be an experience forever closed to her.

George Bowering has accomplished a very difficult feat. He has captured the intonation, the mood, and even the pretentious self-consciousness of youth. His dialogue is extraordinarily believable. Indeed, the whole novel is so authentic that it moves to the ultimate violence of its catastrophe with bleak inevitability. (p. 39)

I have never read a novel which evoked the flavour of a Canadian city so successfully. Vancouver, the smell and feel of its fog, the beaches, the bridges, Stanley Park, the sleazy bars of the dock area are all absolutely there in a way that has been curiously difficult for other novelists to capture. (p. 41)

Phyllis Grosskurth, in a review of "Mirror on the Floor," in Saturday Night, *Vol. 82, No. 5, May, 1967, pp. 39, 41.*

RALPH GUSTAFSON

Look at the last page of George Bowering's ***Rocky Mountain Foot:***

> nobody
> belongs anywhere,
>
> even the
> Rocky Mountains
>
> are still
> moving

Even the comma in there doesn't hold us up. Yea, verily. We all are moving gravely. Our "small durance," as Hopkins says, naught availeth much. . . . [An] epigraph / epitaph says "all / Life death does end and each day dies with sleep." Are you out of breath? Dead sure? Yup, I'm dead sure, as George Bowering might say—and does. And because he does, his book is full of life. Paradox? Figure it out for yourself. Many people can't. I too am always being accused of seeing the skull beneath the skin, and answer to know you are dead is a sure way to keep yourself quick. As Kierkegaard says, "Man must live his contradiction." And this present book is one that does. Look, now, if you aren't completely out of breath, at the bottoms of the pages (all of them). Here you will find some pretty nasty counterpoint (usually in prose; counterpoint to Bowering's poetry which sometimes is, alas, prose). (pp. 74-5)

Bowering has a serious mind. Take that frivolous bit of counterpoint . . . about the Reverend John McDougall who ran up and down a valley in the Rocky Mountains faster than any man alive; "not because I was a good runner, but because a big buffalo was after me." That bit of fugue punctures pretension. Fugues generally do. . . .

Now, go right back to the last page of the book (got your second wind?) where he says nobody belongs anywhere. Apart from this slippery foothold on today, Bowering certainly does; smack in Alberta (too bad it has to be a smack involving Queen Victoria; why couldn't the province be named Minnewissawatagan or some such?). The book celebrates Alberta as it seldom has been celebrated—and in a way that provincial Albertans won't much care for.

It's an elegy, in essence; an elegy with wit. Bowering mourns the blight of civilization, "this present enormity"; shows us how humanity pollutes mountains. (p. 75)

His elegiac stance is mighty precarious, however. With nostalgia and neuralgia, the poet would wipe out everything, everything but irradiating wild flowers; his realistic grasp of the horrible present yearns itself into the impossibility of a longing for the "untouchable blue mountain." The attitude is inverse romanticism. Bowering's saving grace is that he knows that in dreams begins responsibility.

His verse is an easy-going, projective verse, with an occasional wit-clinching rhyme. There are several descents into self-conscious rhetoric (that poem partly quoted above); and the stenographic syntax and blunt line eventually make one long for the grand style. But (as you have gathered) this is an accomplished, jolting, entertaining book of Canadian poetry. (pp. 75-6)

Ralph Gustafson, "Virtue Is Not Enough," in Canadian Literature, *No. 4, Autumn, 1969, pp. 72-7.*

WILLIAM HEYEN

Reading George Bowering's ***Rocky Mountain Foot,*** a sequence of lyrics and poems interspersed with prose passages, I feel what Thor Heyerdahl must have felt on his last voyage when he discovered floating swamps of sludge in mid-ocean. The sensibility here loves the solitude and grandeur of the land, but is invaded by the civilization that despoils the Canadian Dream. Bowering's details of, on the one hand, primitive nature and, on the other, "progress", deepen into symbol: "the mountains to the left / blurred by a passing / Cadillac." His "car radio tuned to music / of distant Mozart", his "eyes indulgent on old women", he is bombarded by crooked politicians, chiropractors in the pulpits, tourists dropping candy wrappers and butts. The speaker moves to acceptance—not a carefully reasoned acceptance, but one emotionally necessary.

Rocky Mountain Foot demonstrates a remarkable range of voices, from the quiet lyricism of **"The Grass"** to the pyrotechnics of **"Above Calgary."** Bowering sometimes descends into a version of Hollywood Indianese ("I sit on stump") that is disconcerting, but the voyager's vision here is powerful. We in America have lived through what certain Canadian poets are making their theme: the death of the land's promise. As Bowering puts it, "property / . . . is / another name for / history." But it is a happy thought that the frontier still holds its dream, that the poet still finds words. For better or worse, the journey is not over, the end is not yet in sight: "nobody / belongs anywhere, / even the / Rocky Mountains / are still / moving. . . ." (p. 429)

William Heyen, "Sensibilities," in Poetry, *Vol. CXV, No. 6, March, 1970, pp. 426-29.*

ELDON GARNET

To Bowering, the past is very important. In true romantic fashion he likes to reach back into his past and pull it forward into the present. ***Touch: Selected Poems, 1960-1970,*** as a selection of poems from the most productive decade of his writing, brings the high moments of Bowering's poetic past into the present. He prefers not to call these poems a representative collection, or a personal selection, but rather poems grouped without any plan or any set guideline. In the introduction he describes his method of selection: I "fell to typing out my strophes & let's see, what will happen on the way to a book full."

Besides being mementoes of his past work, the poems themselves deal with aspects of Bowering's personal past. Some poems deal with the settings of the past. Others concern themselves with the men of his past: his grandfather, Jabez Harry Bowering, who "strode across the Canadian prairie / hacking down trees / and building churches." There is a four-part poem to William Carlos Williams, one of the major influences on Bowering's poetic form, in which he describes part of his literary past: "Words / coming together / moving at one another / traction for the tongue."

By the act of memory and by the writing of it in a poem the figures of Bowering's past live again, ascend to "a new life, reborn, from him, from time, out / into the air, shaking off the dust like a / dust-rolling dog."

The book is not made up merely of souvenirs of the personal past spilling onto the page. Combined with the poet's personal recollections of the past are the tellings of past legends, legends for which Bowering is merely the modern spokesman of a collective memory.

Touch as a whole represents Bowering's re-ordering of the past; it stands as a subjective selection of what has been in his writing, with a re-ordering for the present. (pp. 46, 49)

For Bowering, the identity of a person may be contained within an object. In the baseball is the man who throws it. In the furnishings of a house are hints of the man who lives there. A man may be discovered, revealed through the objects which surround him. . . . This method of working with objects, which Bowering learned from William Carlos Williams, and re-learned from those who had learned it from Williams, has always formed a major part of his poetry. In ***Genève,*** . . . his latest attempt at the longer poem, the method has been carried to new heights.

Each part of this serial poem relates to a specific Tarot card from a Swiss deck. A card is dealt and Bowering reacts to the card. He works his way through the deck, writing one poem for each card. From the object emerges the poem. The object becomes the window, and the poet looks out through the opening.

He gives each card the richness of his observation. To each card he adds the poet Bowering interpreting how he personally fits into the card and its story, and describing how he is affected by the card. He allows his imagination to roam freely over the tangible object of the card until the poem moves from object to dream. The card becomes an extension of his dreams. . . .

The poems and the Tarot cards are intricately related, but either may stand alone. The reader may look at a card, and then read its related poem. By relating the card to the poem both are opened. A reader may see where the card leaves off and the poet's imagination begins, or he may see how a poet comes to poetry from the inspiration of an object.

Genève may be considered an elaborate process of looking: of the poet looking at the cards, or the reader looking to the poems and to the cards. It is a process of looking closer for subtleties, for what is hinted at, and for what has been enriched. In the complex processes of looking, the divisions between the card, the poet, the poem, and the reader seem to break down, until all are one. The poems become more than Bowering's interpretations, they become extensions of the reader's own dreams. (p. 49)

For the author there is an emotional involvement with the Tarot cards. Bowering is possessed with a certain fear of the cards, with their mysterious life and order. In the presence of his imagination they are more than an opportunity for description, they are a lesson in life. As the cards are being dealt specifically for Bowering each card which falls reveals something about him; something can be read from the order in which they fall. It is the self, Bowering's self, that the cards reveal; their power is to discover what is known and unknown, what has been and what will be. The cards by their nature deal with the dark recesses of the man. As each card falls the poet is the figure of the card and cannot help but identify with his fate. He is the card; it is his life. . . . It is not strange that Bowering, who believes in the power of the cards, cannot help at times but fear and hate what he sees being revealed.

Add up the poems in ***Touch*** and ***Genève,*** and the poet as a person emerges with his past, his present, and possibly his future reflected; all three with a mystery and accuracy which parallels that of the Tarot cards. Like the Tarot cards these two books deal with the past and the future of the poet; the one content with resting in the past, and the other unable to remain at rest, but compelled to move on. (pp. 49-50)

Eldon Garnet, "Two Bowerings Embrace Past, Present, Future," in Saturday Night, *Vol. 86, No. 11, November, 1971, pp. 46, 49-50.*

JOHN L. NUGENT

Touch is a collection of George Bowering's "short and middle distance" poems, most of which were originally published in the early sixties. It includes none of his more recent, longer works which he thinks of as "poetry books" rather than books of poetry. The single exception is **"Baseball"** a clever metaphor of life in nine innings. "In the beginning was the word, & the word was 'Play Ball'".

The first thing that strikes a reader not previously familiar with Bowering's poems is the arrangement of the words on the page. Bowering's adventuresome stanza configurations are often helpful but sometimes distracting.

In the introduction to the volume Bowering asks that the poems be read aloud, a request which if granted, permits a more sensitive appreciation of the effect of his typography. . . .

Bowering's subject matter runs the gamut from Veracruz to Mars, Indian folk-lore to grain elevators and his approach never becomes ostentatious—after all how could the author of the lines "I say to you, / marriage is a boat" swamp his readers in affected erudition or contrived profundity. That is not to say his poetry lacks substance, on the contrary, but his treatment of themes is very down-to-earth.

The poems of this collection successfully couple emotional and intellectual appeal and considering his sensitivity to diction and syntax one gathers the impression that Bowering wishes to play the role of gadfly rather than pedagogue. (p. 109)

The selected poems of ***Touch*** make up a very readable presentation and serve as a compelling introduction to George Bowering's poetry. (p. 110)

John L. Nugent, in a review of "Touch: Selected Poems, 1960-1970," in The Fiddlehead, *No. 92, Winter, 1972, pp. 109-10.*

DONALD STEPHENS

[***Flycatcher and Other Stories***] is Bowering at his prose best. The stories are bright and clean, and Bowering does not attempt in any way to confuse the reader with references to a private world that are not clear. He uses a kind of autobiographical persona to tell the stories, so that the reader is not only aware of what is being told but also by whom; with this device a proper distance is acquired by the reader so that he, too, can "half listen and half compose" as he reads the stories. Bowering moves from British Columbia to Calgary to Mexico, recording random experiences as the narrator, George Delsing, looks for his friend, Ebbe Coutts. But Bowering never tries to make the ordinary extraordinary; instead, he attempts to record the awe in being ordinary and having average relationships within normal landscapes. In his poetry Bowering senses the wonder at being alive, and this sense infuses his latest book of short stories with a strength that is missing in his other attempts at fiction. (p. 102)

Donald Stephens, "Insistent Fluidity," in Canadian Literature, *No. 64, Spring, 1975, pp. 101-04.*

LOUIS K. MACKENDRICK

George Bowering's chief persona, George Delsing, is a self-indulgent creation who wars with coherence and reader attention in [***Flycatcher and Other Stories***]. As a manuscript reader complains in one story, "Jesus, this isn't a *story,* I mean, Christ, you have to have some discipline over your craft", and narrators in others often cheerfully deny the necessity of meaning or continuity. Bowering's style is sometimes poetically clotted and efflorescent, and suggests the sponsorship of Jack Kerouac—as does the matter. Delsing's obsession, though hardly the reader's, is Ebbe, a post-beatnik grotesque whom he desperately attempts to see as a model of knowing—somewhat like "Flycatcher", an alleged pervert who *knows* through constant victimization. The best stories here are straightforward and objective: **"Apples"**, a symbol-burdened sexual mechanism; **"The Elevator"**, where a chance liaison reinforces the isolation in a world not captivated by television; **"Time and Again"**, a would-be writer's discovery of how superficially he knows his roots; and **"Ricardo and the Flower"**, a Lawrencian pastiche set in Mexico which pits feminine intuition and blood-conscious boy against the camera-toting, tourist-minded male. (pp. 107-08)

Louis K. MacKendrick, in a review of "Flycatcher & Other Stories," in The University of Windsor Review, *Vol. XI, No. 2, Spring-Summer, 1976, pp. 107-09.*

MICHAEL BRIAN OLIVER

No one, not even Irving Layton, has published as many bad poems as George Bowering. All through the 1960s and early '70s his books came out regularly, and all this time readers had to suffer through his embarrassingly juvenile, self-important, even silly poems. Worse, they had to tell themselves it was for their own good: George Bowering was, after all, one of Canada's best young poets. . . . How George Bowering got to be one of Canada's most reputable poets is perhaps the greatest mystery in Canadian literature, but there he was and there he is. Mr. Bowering is remarkably persistent; he simply would not nor will not go away. Still, persistence pays off. In the last few years he has finally published some poems worth reading. ***In The Flesh*** . . . demonstrated that he really could write lyrics after all, something he had long been claiming without much proof, and ***Curious,*** a book of his personal impressions of other poets . . . , turned out to be the right subject and mode for his abiding literary narcissism. Now we have three new books at hand: one inane, one interesting, and one important.

The Concrete Island is a monstrous resurrection from the wastebasket. These poor verses should have been left to rest in peace. . . . Their excuse for existing in the first place was Bowering's stay in Montreal in the late 1960s. . . . Obviously these were important times lived in an important place, but after reading this little book, we see that they were wasted on G. B. I do not mean that he, or anyone else, should write political or journalistic poetry, however active his society. Bowering's personal theme, stated with clarity, and typical cleverness, is a valid one: "My sojourn in the east took me out of place & took place out of my poetry." But this statement of the barrenness of the east for him is all that we get from this book. Like a freshman writing a bad essay, he tells but he doesn't show. We have to take his word for it that Montreal is a concrete island, and I for one am not willing to put that much faith in flat statement, whereas I would be willing to believe in poetry.

Bowering calls these writings the last of his lyrics (promises, promises), but really they are more like frustrated scribblings. Not that this is surprising. There are plenty of his notoriously gasping line breaks, his half-witticisms, plenty of solipsism, and more than enough slightness to swamp the most devoted dilettante. . . . So what, George, you don't like Montreal—who cares! *You should make us care*. . . . There lies the problem. These verses are almost totally transparent, not windows on the soul but windows to nothing more interesting than boyish daydreams. The only possible defence for this book is to say that its very nothingness proves the barrenness of Montreal for Bowering, and therefore he has fulfilled his intention.

Anyway, this brings up an important fact that we should always bear in mind while reading Bowering—namely, that he is by his own claim an experimental poet. He defines an experimental poet as one who asks, what would happen if. . . ? ***Allophanes*** is an experimental book, a product of the author's "symphonic period" as he likes to call these last few years. Before writing this long poem, Bowering obviously asked himself, what would happen if a poet tried to find God, or any of His synonyms, in modern literature? He then sets out to play the old game, 26 innings of Art versus Life (History versus Nature, Literature versus Composition, whatever). The outcome doesn't matter; it's how you play the game. If you noticed that echo, you know how Bowering plays it. ***Allophanes*** is a half-recalled, half-created assembly of quotations, allusions, and puns which taken together attempt to prove that appearance is sometimes different from reality. Yes, everything about this sounds familiar, but it is all juggled just enough to make it sound almost profound, sort of a hipster's *Waste Land*.

Only it isn't hip. The central metaphor of this poem, and of many of Bowering's poems, is that everything is a baseball game. Well, as Holden Caulfield said so long ago, "Game, my ass." Sorry, George, but games are simply not hip: their predetermined, moral structures are antithetical to the hip life which is open, free, and flowing. ***Allophanes*** is performed by Bowering not improvised, in spite of its loose appearance. In fact the main motif of the poem, the snowball in hell, which becomes of course a baseball, the planet Earth, and so on, illustrates the unoriginal playfulness of Bowering's style. No poet was ever happier in hell! He's having a ball, tossing around twisted quotations and adolescent puns—a regular Huckleberry Finnegan as he calls his hero. No worry about Bowering committing suicide. (pp. 159-60)

The roots of ***Allophanes*** are surreal, and its message is orthodox existentialism: we exist as part of nature and any attempt to understand ourselves takes us out of nature. Thus both poetry and history are suspect and inadequate for salvation. Meaning too breaks down. . . . Still he does suggest that poetry and the reflective life can be authentic, though his formulation of this vision may not yield to the most imaginative cogitation: "Pure poetry," he says, "has no presence / but only its own being." This is what the whole book tries to prove; it is a portrait of the poem as a poem. Of course we can argue forever over the definition of 'pure' poetry or the distinction between 'presence' and 'being.' This vision, like all intuitions, demands faith. Personally I would be much more willing to believe if the poem were not so cluttered with grandstand word plays. Nevertheless, ***Allophanes*** deserves close and repeated readings. It is a genuine experiment in philosophical poetry and poetics. (p. 161)

The Catch presents Bowering the poet composing and Bowering the man composed. It is by far his best book to date, and it is a landmark in Canadian poetry.

The Catch consists of two previously published long poems, ***George, Vancouver*** and ***Autobiology,*** together with a new series called **"Cereals For Roughage."** ***George, Vancouver*** provides the reader of Canadian poetry with an alternative to Atwood's *Journals of Susanna Moodie* and her Survival Theory. The main difference is implicit in the sub-title: ***George, Vancouver*** is "a discovery poem," and Bowering makes the most of his subjective, existentialist bias to allow us to discover the Inland Sea for ourselves, to join Captain Vancouver in finding what was really there two hundred years ago. In other words, by fusing imagination and historical record, Bowering composes the discovery in his poem: he places us in the act without ever presuming to tell us its meaning. It's no accident that he focuses much attention on Vancouver's botanist—or biologist—Archibald Menzies. Throughout the poem Bowering emphasizes the experimental quality of the voyage and the fact that although Vancouver failed to find the North West Passage, his exploration was still authentic. Northrop Frye has called Franklin's attempt to find the North West Passage Canada's unwritten epic, but Bowering makes Vancouver's search equally significant, especially when he suggests Vancouver's sense of being on a fool's errand and his turning back with nothing more than his charts and Menzies' weed-book, which were ironically important finds in their own right. Frye calls Canada a journey without an ending; perhaps he has not recognized what Bowering seems to. The ending is not truth but reality. By the end of the poem the explorer and the poet become one and the same. . . . Ultimately the difference between Bowering's treatment of the origins of white Canada and Atwood's (or Purdy's or even MacEwen's) is more one of method than message: Bowering writes us into discovery whereas the others stand back from it and explain it neatly and formally. ***George, Vancouver,*** apart from its western perspective, the other difference, tells us nothing different from, say, MacEwen's "Dark Pines under Water" as far as meaning is concerned: "This land like a mirror turns you inward." The difference is distance and feeling; Bowering is more primary a poet than the others: he moves through the experience and moves us with him; he is not removed. For this reason alone ***George, Vancouver*** should be required reading in every class of Canadian Literature.

Autobiology is Bowering's most original symphonic work. It is a composition that breaks the barriers between poetry, poetics, fiction, autobiography, psychology, philosophy, and a few other things. It is not about consciousness; it is consciousness on the page, and "Consciousness is how it is composed." More than any of Bowering's other poems the forty-eight page long chapters of ***Autobiology*** take us inside a consciousness—George's own of course: he has always been more curious about himself than about anything else. But then aren't we all self-absorbed, really? What is especially interesting and important about this work is that it includes a considered and deeply felt poetics for all the surrealists since Kafka and all the existentialists since Kierkegaard. Bowering's practice is not new, but it does help illuminate the main direction in which twentieth-century literature has consistently tried to flow: away from the sequence into the whirlwind, away from cause and effect into association, away from objective social realism into private natural consciousness. . . . Bowering moves through his life in this poem, through his childhood, through his thoughts and feelings, through his obsession with baseball, even through his phsyical breaks and scars. Mind you, Bowering's life is not all that interesting, but his method is, and that is enough to make this work significant. More important, his idea of poetry is one to be reckoned with by critics and poets alike. As I have already pointed out, Bowering sees poetry as a natural action, and he combines art and nature in the word "composition." Furthermore, "Consciousness is how it is composed." What the poet must do according to Bowering is take the reader from "here, on this side of the page" into the composition, the consciousness, the art *and* nature of the experience: "Composition / is not there it is going to be there & you are / here . . ." His metaphor for reading is cracking the Captain Marvel code without paying to join the club; in other words, getting into the world on the page by an imaginative co-operation—in an act of "prophecy" as he calls it later in the book—with the poet who is already "there." Thus, though few have realized this, Bowering is a surrealist to the point of being a visionary, and, more surprising, he offers the only readable alternative in Canada to the poets with Myths and Messages.

The Catch concludes with three middle-length poems, two of which are hardly even noteworthy (one is dull as catatonia). **"Desert Elm"** though is excellent, one of the best poems I have ever read about a son's feeling for his father. This poem takes us into the relationship, the intangible web of heritage itself: the orchards where Bowering's father "spent thousands of hours in those trees / picking pennies," his father's heart attack on a golf course, the poet's dream of a tree growing down into the earth, and so on. . . . If only Bowering were this good all the time! But perhaps his theory of composition precludes self-editing, which is after all a removed effort antithetical to the action of poetry. Anyway, the fact that he can be this good makes him mandatory, maybe even major in years to come. (pp. 161-64)

Michael Brian Oliver, "Clever, Curious, Sometimes Composed George," in The Fiddlehead, *No. 116, Winter, 1978, pp. 158-64.*

MATT COHEN

In ***Protective Footwear,*** a collection of Bowering's stories . . . and his first major prose work in ten years, one has stories dating from the early 1960's, some of them recently rewritten, and one has recent stories, some of them based on events in the earlier ones. As Bowering himself is only about forty years old, this collection cannot help but be seen, among other things, as an astonishing act of faith in his own juvenilia; this impression is reinforced by the fact that after each story there appears the date when it was written, and the date, or sometimes dates, of subsequent revision.

This concern to see oneself in the present from the point of view of the past would seem to be crippling to most writers, especially those who have publicly stated that their writing is autobiographical, but in Bowering's case the theme is at the centre of his most successful stories.

The first, and my favourite, story is called **"ReUnion"** and is about the poet-narrator's high school reunion. With his wife, whom he has carefully instructed in the rituals and details of his past, he has returned to the small town in the B.C. interior where he went to high school. Although, at the beginning of the weekend, it appears that his main interest is in seeing his old girlfriend, it turns out he is also curious to compare himself to his former classmates, secretly hoping that they are fatter and balder than him, wondering if he should tell them that although he was not, in high school, much of an athlete, he now bats .375 on the Coast.

Although some of his classmates know he has become a successful writer, have even read some of his work and are impressed, the reunion is anticlimactic. The old girlfriend disappears from the story, no one is either overwhelmed by or scornful of his achievements. In the end nothing happens and, almost apologetic about this, he says: "Right now I'm writing like a halfback, gliding off tacklers and hoping to make a few yards with each carry." This statement is remarkably like one that appears later in the book: "You do a painting a day, one sitting, and you don't come back to it. If you don't make it that day, you try again the next. There is no limitation on the chances you get."

What's so attractive about **"ReUnion"** is the slow realization that in this story it's the poet, the supposedly eccentric one, who has stayed the same: the poet has married a girl from the same high school, fulfilled his childhood ambition to become a poet, has even in middle age fulfilled the athletic and sexual fantasies that eluded him in high school. Not only has the narrator fulfilled these youthful goals, but they have remained consistently in the centre of his life; and it has been affirmed that the most desirable values a man may attain are those desperately wished for at fifteen.

Like **"ReUnion,"** many of the stories in ***Protective Footwear*** have George Delsing and / or his friends at the centre, and of these friends the most dwelled-upon is Ebbe Coutts. In **"The House On Tenth"** there is a moment when Ebbe is winding his way through the dense party: "I had seen Ebbe pass from the kitchen into one of the bedrooms, his hands up high so he could squeeze through the crowd, a quarter-full bottle in one hand, pack of cigarettes in the other . . ."; and that detailed sight of Ebbe Coutts, where suddenly the narrator's absolute fascination with his *pose* is somehow conveyed, typifies for me what is Bowering's most interesting quality as a prose writer—the stringing together of a series of successively irrelevant details so complex that finally you become lost in them and for a moment actually see just what Delsing / Bowering wants you to see.

Because of this lovingly irrelevant and modest approach I have always been interested in Bowering's stories, especially the Delsing stories. Yet ***Protective Footwear*** was a bit of a disappointment to me because it not only omitted some of my favourite Delsing stories, but seemed, in many of the old stories, to be divided between Delsing stories that are simply trivial and non-Delsing stories that have mostly an archaeological interest.

Reading some of these old stories we see abandoned techniques, masks the writer might have assumed had he not assumed his own. **"The Lawnmower"** is a Ray Bradbury type sci-fi story, very well done, with a suitably venal attitude towards TV and advertising. **"The Big Leagues"** is a more arcane direction, the kind of instant pop history that Bill Hutton brought to unequalled and obscure perfection. In **"The White Coffin"** we get perhaps the most ambitious story in the book, and yet, because it is set in Mexico, and is somehow indignant in a way which seems forced in the context of the rest of the stories, it doesn't quite work out.

In these and other non-Delsing stories, which range from science fiction to a story which might be a satire on *Beautiful Losers,* I felt I was reading competent stories which might stand on their own in a magazine, but in a book, surrounded by the greater warmth and confidence of the Delsing stories, seemed like they shouldn't be there.

An exception was the story **"The Hayfield."** It tells of an amateur painter who is painting a hayfield. A mysterious symbolic stranger turns up and furnishes a few learned remarks about art. Then a third person enters, the young man who owns the field. After a long discussion about the painting, which is only modestly valued by its creator, the farmer offers to buy it from him for the price of a bale of hay. A perfect transaction has been witnessed.

The last piece in the book, **"Protective Footwear,"** is a very short and very effective story about a father taking his young daughter for her first walk in the woods. Desperately wanting her to like the woods, he practically turns himself inside out trying to control the situation. Finally the afternoon is rescued: they get lost. And by the end of the story one feels that despite the manipulated situation and the absolute need the father has to impress his daughter, the love he has for both her and the woods has actually worked something: in some way this new place has been opened for her. It is a good story to have picked for both the title story and the concluding story, because it is a story which is only ambiguously one of the Delsing series. It is the only story in the book in which the present is the measure of the past, rather than vice versa. And while the tone is not yet the accomplished Delsing tone, it is convincing enough to seem as if this may be more than another directional experiment—perhaps Bowering's fictional voice will now take a jump in an unexpected direction. (pp. 53-5)

Matt Cohen, "Bowering's Act of Faith," in Essays on Canadian Writing, *No. 12, Fall, 1978, pp. 51-5.*

GWENDOLYN DAVIES

In an interview with Donald Cameron in 1971, George Bowering speaks of the evasiveness of the novel form as he conceives of it. For Bowering, the novel follows none of the conventions of linear structure or characterization commonly associated with it, but instead represents a free flow of associated ideas. "I sit down," says Bowering, "and I don't really know what the subject is. I get ready to start moving, and if a useful line comes along, one that I haven't made up, then I can keep going. If I make up the line it's usually a case of writing it down on an index card and throwing it in my desk drawer, and then later either throwing it out or selling it to the university library."

These remarks illuminate a reading of three of Bowering's fictional works, for in ***Concentric Circles*** (1977), ***A Short Sad Book*** (1977), and ***Protective Footwear*** (1978), the reader finds the illusion of Bowering's theory carried into practice. It is only an illusion, however, for, in spite of Bowering's assertions to the contrary, the three books under discussion are patterned and unified by recurring symbols, characters, images, and points of view. They are equally unified by their preoccupation with the act and process of creation. ***Concentric Circles,*** the earliest of the three fictions, explores this process by depicting a confrontation between the artist and the state. The result is the destruction of the artist, but not before Mel has terrorized the state with his mysterious black box and Brown has painted the state's representative into parody. The drama is sparely and understatedly told, and the reader feels as if he is in the midst of a Beckett play. Events just seem to happen, and when Mel and Brown die in the end, it is the culmination of a series of seemingly unconnected events, each one of which reveals the artist as gadfly and sacrificial lamb in the state's highly organized scheme of things.

In ***A Short Sad Book,*** the process of creating is again explored, but this time through the persona of an indulgent, intruding author-narrator. Whereas the reader of ***Concentric Circles*** is in limbo, the reader of ***A Short Sad Book*** finds himself involved in the process and act of writing the novel. . . . The narrator's self-consciousness is one of the most prominent features of ***A Short Sad Book.*** The narrator-author provokes, teases, and poses. He objectifies himself and describes "George Bowering . . . still sitting at his desk and now . . . scratching out line after line." What emerges from this creative activity is not a novel to satisfy conventional expectations, but a novel which is itself a character in the story. One almost feels oneself plunged into the technical world of *Tristram Shandy,* but Bowering's emphasis is different from Sterne's. It is not the author, the narrator, or even the process of novel-writing which ultimately dominates, but the politics of Canadian Literature. And this contributes to the failure of ***A Short Sad Book*** as much as it contributes to its uniqueness. While it may be fun to explode the shibboleths of "Can-Lit" by sending Evangeline up the mountain with Sir John A. or Margaret Atwood to a tryst with the drowned Tom Thomson, it is also ingrown and limiting to write a book out of in-jokes and privileged information. This is too rarified a world about which Bowering writes, with nicknames, coined names, and puns on names only thinly disguising a cast of "Can-Lit" luminaries: Al (Purdy), Frank (Davey), Peggy (Atwood), Stan (Bevington), and Sparrow (Robin Mathews). The politics of literature is a fascinating area to explore, but to create literature out of it is to produce a work removed from the realm of everyday experience. Does it mean anything to the average reader of ***A Short Sad Book*** to know that David McFadden (both as character and poet in the book) wants the author-narrator to call the novel *The Black Mountain Influence?* Or that Milton Acorn "has tasted his cigar"? To those initiated into Canadian Literature and its literary circles, the jokes and the plays may mean something, but the mockery and fun in the novel are those of an in-group and must surely elude the majority of readers.

The obscurity of ***A Short Sad Book*** emanates not only from its subject matter but also from its form and idiom. The book is part novel, part essay, part autobiography, and part poem. One can argue that it not only mocks the Canadian Literature hierarchy in central Canada but also "sends up" the traditional novel form. Yet this does not explain why Bowering resorts to the particular patterns of language and idiom that he employs. An author deeply concerned with creating a "personal language" in his works, he uses signs instead of words ("&"), media-spelling ("pumpt"), run-on sentences, and small case letters. While these devices reinforce the colloquial quality of his work, they do little else. When one alters the established spelling of the language ("pumpt," "thru," "finisht"), it is usually to enhance the tone or statement of the work. But here the linguistic and stylistic texture of the novel seems over-done for the level of feeling and satire that one finds in ***A Short Sad Book.*** The book may be a lovely "Can-Lit" lark, but it is a lark limited in range and depth.

With ***Protective Footwear,*** Bowering seems to have broadened his scope to explore not only form and language but also character and its response to a world of change and ambiguity. The stories are mere "mind pictures" in which moments and fragments of people's lives are shown to be interlocking. A recurring figure is George Delsing, a poet who constantly tries to describe his friend, Ebbe Coutts. But Ebbe is an elusive figure who defies the power of the author-narrator to contain him in words. Nor will language order the existence of Eduardo Williams, a character whose life is made up of bizarre and unrelated fragments which the self-conscious Delsing tries to connect. . . . As in the earlier books, there is a concern here for the act of creating and for the role of the narrative voice that Bowering describes as the "I, someone, that voice speaking to you at last, the intrusion you will probably call it, though I have been here all along, of the first person." But although the narrative voice can joke about his role in describing the chaos, he cannot explain the absurdity of the situations and people he witnesses. When the narrator-poet, George Delsing, is found murdered by Eduardo Williams in **"Owning Up,"** the outcome seems a fitting end for a relationship forged in the general aimlessness and inexplicability of the world depicted in these stories. Only love seems to mitigate the violence and impotency found in this environment; and in the narrator's feeling for his friend, Ebbe, or in the family warmth of **"ReUnion"** and **"Protective Footwear,"** there are encouraging glimpses of a world saner than that in which the Ebbe Coutts, Eduardo Williams, and George Delsing relationships have developed and unfolded. (pp. 134-36)

Concentric Circles, A Short Sad Book and ***Protective Footwear*** are clearly vehicles for Bowering as he works out his theories on language and its versatility. For many readers, the results will be disappointing and abstract, or, as is the case with ***A Short Sad Book,*** elusive. However, in spite of the failure of some of these works to elucidate the relationship between language and response, they do act as a revealing gloss on Bowering's theories and his development as a prose writer. The "kind of a tune in my head" which he follows may not be universal in the audience it attracts, but it is nonetheless reassuring to have on the Canadian scene a writer and theorist of such on-going vitality and experimentation. (p. 136)

Gwendolyn Davies, in a review of "Concentric Circles," "A Short Sad Book," and "Protective Footwear," in The Fiddlehead, *No. 121, Spring, 1979, pp. 134-36.*

JANET GILTROW

In this book about George Vancouver in the Pacific Northwest [***Burning Water***], George Bowering asks his readers to take an interest not only in the travels of the great eighteenth-century navigator and surveyor, but also in how the twentieth-century novelist and poet came up with the story. Casting himself in the third person, Bowering tells about his own creative venture: imagination, he says, implies "a travelling, or a trip," and Vancouver's itinerary is punctuated with reports of the author's physical and imaginative comings and goings. Bowering uses this auxiliary narrative to explain the relations between subject and author, or "art and life. . . . Or at least life and literature."

The explanation hinges on certain coincidences connecting these Georges and their journeys. Some of the connections precede the text, and become in effect pretexts for the novel: Bowering shares a first name with the navigator; and he lives in Vancouver, the other George's name-place. Another class of connection is more complicated. To begin his work on this man who travelled west, the author goes east, to Europe. During later parts of the book, when Vancouver presses north, Bowering goes south, in an inverse mimicry of his hero. With these European and southern journeys, Bowering makes more connections. (p. 118)

Conveying some very ordinary details of the writer's life, the interpolated narrative embarrasses the text, lingering like an unnecessary excuse. The interpolations are formally unmarked, and this, combined with the author's presence in the third person, creates pronominal confusion. Chapters beginning "He . . ." are no doubt deliberately ambiguous in reference; but when the antecedent George turns out to be Bowering rather than Vancouver, the reader is disappointed, for this version of the life of Vancouver is interesting, and the delays in advancing the story are exasperating. Happily, the interpolations diminish in conspicuousness if not in frequency even as the story gets under way. This fancy part of a plain narrative withers and falls like a superfluous ornament.

Much more convincing is Bowering's fundamental sympathy with his hero, and his pride in Vancouver's accomplishment and even in his high-minded devotion to Empire. Nothing shows this pride more than Bowering's contemptuous view of the Americans who pass in and out of the scene. With their obtuse mercantile attitude, the Yankee traders offend and brutalize the natives, and show their own meagre spirit: "They crawled all over the trading post like flies on pastry, trading in liquor and arms, gathering in furs and gold coin, and looking for an opportunity to scoop up some real estate."

Bowering respects Vancouver's office as surveyor of the coast, and in describing the navigator's honourable work he sticks closest to plain truth—the kind of hard facts his sceptical hero revered. For three seasons, Vancouver sailed methodically up and down the intricate shore, measuring and plotting its devious design. So complex was the coast that it seemed to promise *somewhere* a concealed, fog-cloaked corridor to a Northwest Passage. But Vancouver penetrated every sound and inlet, discovering the finitude of each. In doing so, he repudiated the longstanding notion of easy passage through a marvellous strait.

When he comes to reconstructing his protagonist's character, Bowering must depart from this plain truth. The more obvious tasks in exploring Vancouver's uncharted personality—accounting for his strict attitude of command and for his devotion to accuracy and exactitude—are accomplished rather superficially. Vancouver, Bowering tells us, felt himself "special," even as a boy. Fanatically devoted to Cook, loyal to his sovereign, he embraced his duty wherever it fell. More daring, and more interesting, are Bowering's speculations on Vancouver's love-life, here unexpectedly explained in terms of Vancouver's relations with Quadra, the Spanish commander who relinquished Nootka to the British in 1792. Bowering postulates that, with Quadra, the nearly virginal Vancouver found love at last. (pp. 118-19)

There are weaknesses in this book. The interpolated narrative is a nuisance. Some of the anachronisms in the main narrative are too trivial: a local chief answers Vancouver's inquiries about the climate by remarking that, in winter, "it rains all the time, but we always say that at least you don't have to shovel it." But these weaknesses are attributable to the ambitiousness of Bowering's intentions. He wants to write in his own, modern way about something that has all along commanded its own prose form: voyage narrative is conventionally linear and forthright. It sets one thing after another, locating events consecutively in time and space. Bowering overthrows this linear orientation to make room for his record of the imaginative origins of the text, and to make plausible characters out of the eighteenth-century travellers who came all this way. Certainly, Vancouver, Quadra, and Menzies are substantial creations, and worth the trouble. Yet an old subject can get the better of a new form, and some of the best parts of the book are the accounts of where the *Discovery* goes and why. The structural commotion of flashbacks and fast-forward leaps pesters this plain-speaking with stops and starts and recursiveness, making the narrative spasmodic just where the logic of travel demands that the story be advanced. Bowering may see this as a contest between traditional and modern fiction (he envies the simpler task of the old-fashioned "realist novelist"), but this is not really the issue. Voyage narrative is neither realistic nor novelistic: it is documentary and compellingly linear. Against this serious straightforwardness Bowering works, interrupting itinerary with his interpolations and fictional inferences. Some of these interruptions are unwelcome, but others are worthwhile. (pp. 119-20)

Janet Giltrow, "Fast-Forward Man," in Canadian Literature, *No. 89, Summer, 1981, pp. 118-20.*

ANTHONY S. BRENNAN

In [***Burning Water***], Bowering undertakes the difficult feat of trying to reconstruct the life and circumstances of the indefatigable explorer of the north-west Pacific, George Vancouver. On his tiny ship, the *Discovery*, this stubborn perfectionist of the late eighteenth century devoted four years of his life to the charting, with extraordinary accuracy, of the world's most complicated coastline. Here was an age in which adventurists were legion and dedicated explorers few. Captains lied to their monarchs about fabled wealth, talked for decades of the will-o-the-wisp North-West passage—only a few inlets away. The Admiralty longed for tall-tales, and any explorer who did not adjust his disposition to that need was liable to be forgotten. It was a rare man who was able to focus on and appreciate the riches before him as much as the imaginary wealth that haunted his mind. This European itch, the overvaluing of what we do not have to the neglect of the treasures all around us, was a part of the Canadian experience from the outset. . . . It is obvious to Bowering from the outset that "the fancy cannot cheat so well / As she is fam'd to do, deceiving elf." Vancouver, in his precise naval manner, endeavours to resolve the conflict.

> "The imagination," he said. "You speak of it as if it were the opposite of facts, as if it were perhaps the enemy of facts. That is not true in the least . . . The imagination depends upon facts; it feeds on them in order to produce beauty or invention, or discovery . . . The true enemy of imagination is the idleness that provides fancy."

Thus we have a proposition of a balance of forces that Bowering's book cannot follow through on. The characters catch fragmentary intimations of immortality, shadowy glimpses of poetry. They are never dull, but they are limited. The book is true, perhaps, to a certain aspect of Canadian experience—the eternal puzzlement with or search for identity, the frustration that because we were not born in turmoil we are not a mixture of deep and volatile contradictions, the rooted conviction that there is something missing and that it is probably to be found outside the country. Bowering produces flesh and blood creatures who are varied and convincing in their interactions, but who seem undramatic and incapable of change or growth.

The story seems to be in low-gear or merely ticking over for long periods. It is written as a mosaic in fifty-nine chapters. It has the loose quality of being tacked together as if from several diaries. We have notes from Bowering, the novelist, on how he is progressing in Trieste and Guatemala, on his work on Vancouver's life. These passages are often written in a way that makes us unsure for a few sentences which George we are with, Bowering or Vancouver. For all the insight generated about the continuity of conflicting ideas despite the revolutions in modes of transportation, they could have been dispensed with. Collected together they might provide a self-justifying letter to the Canada Council on why it was necessary to go to areas very remote from British Columbia in order to understand George Vancouver's charting of it. It is a wry joke that Bowering obviously enjoys, but it is flogged to death.

The novel does not, however, mire itself in pretentiousness. It does not announce heavy themes and then proceed with dull solemnity. Such a book could easily have become a Conradian symphony played on a penny flute. Bowering adopts a light, offhanded tone, a jokey raciness that is of the locker room and as near as he can guess of the masculine bluntness of the navy. History here is neither marmorealized nor trivialized. Bowering is not after an authentic, precise reconstruction. Archaic syntactical forms and modern slang are jumbled in together so that we may feel that the tensions Vancouver wrestled with have yet to be resolved. The time frame of events is at times deliberately yet maddeningly imprecise, and in line with other modernist affectations Bowering tries the occasional sleight of hand with point of view. . . . Unfortunately the subject matter too often lacks substance to justify the cumbersome machinery, and we are left in many of the lightweight fragments with too much foppery. We are invited in imagination to be the contemporaries of long-dead sailors, and they are press-ganged into being ours. We can nod in agreement that those who do not learn from history are condemned to repeat it, but we do not have to submit so easily to the flippancy of homogenizing human experience.

The central focus of the book is on Vancouver's essential loneliness and on his ambiguous relationship with two men. The battle between naval commanders and the scientists they were obliged to take with them has a long history in British annals. An early battle with Sir Joseph Banks and his extensive equipment is merely a foreshadowing of the four year simmering feud that Vancouver conducted with his Scottish naturalist, Menzies. Though there ought to have been a natural alliance between them, their relationship was fraught with tension. The relationship, in all its delicate shading, is meant to have central weight in the novel, and yet it takes too long to come into focus. Bowering takes far too long to assemble the idiosyncracies of his characters, but he does eventually draw us in to a fascination with the willfull stiff-necked stubbornness of these proud men stuck together for four years on a ninety foot ship.

Vancouver travelled half way round the world to settle a treaty, the Nootka Agreement, with the Spanish admiral Juan Quadra. Vancouver, the Puritan of Dutch extraction, would seem to be poles apart from the luxuriously sensual, Catholic Quadra, and yet they developed a deep love for each other. Bowering is not over-eager to strip away the mystery that shrouds the relationship, nor does he try to simplify the tenacious pride and the drive for perfection that animates them. We are given very little of the background and upbringing of any of the characters. One cannot fault Bowering for resisting the urge to plaster research detail all over his work. The characters do have a degree of authenticity, but ultimately the absence of a richly varied texture condemns us to episodic repetitions. There is something missing from the book, and one could spend a good deal of time puzzling out what it is. Is this the Canadian habit of ignoring what is there and carping about what is not? I hope not.

Bowering makes the strategic error of devoting two episodes to extracts from Vancouver's diary. These passages are swift-moving and vivid in a manner that is so rare elsewhere. No doubt narrative has its limitations and pace isn't everything. The novelist cannot passively lean on a rail; he must turn over rocks and be as tenacious as Vancouver in taking soundings or Menzies in collecting horticultural exotica. He must eschew the idea that there is a North-West passage that leads straight to the truth. Perhaps Bowering is accommodating himself to an irony that is central to his book—what we achieve is never quite what we want or aim at. Vancouver produced magnificently accurate charts, and yet he would much have preferred to be embroiled in naval combat with the French; Menzies collected a huge variety of rare specimens for four years and lost them all in a tempest one week from home; Bowering aimed to write a novel about George Vancouver and ended up with notes for a novel. The book itself becomes an image of the attempt to understand the characters within it and of the cruel paradox that Hamlet notes:

> Our wills and fates do so contrary run
> That our devices still are overthrown;
> Our thoughts are ours, the ends none of our own.

(pp. 85-7)

Anthony S. Brennan, in a review of "Burning Water," in The Fiddlehead, *No. 131, January, 1982, pp. 85-7.*

JON PEIRCE

[***West Window: The Selected Poetry of George Bowering*** is] redundant, tasteless, and as carelessly crafted as any book of Canadian poetry I've read in the past 10 years. (p. 28)

About a third of the book's 130 pages are devoted to a reprinting of Bowering's ***Curious,*** a series of prose-poem-portraits of his literary colleagues. First published in 1973, ***Curious*** was excerpted as recently as 1980, and it isn't the kind of writing that improves with further acquaintance. As the following selection from **"George Oppen"** illustrates, the voice we hear is immature, self-indulgent, and above all derivative:

> He stood & said his poems & I sat & cried in front of him. I sat on the chair & it was solid there. He stood on his feet & said it plain & it was so plain & it was not pain it was weeping. I was weeping. That has never happened before.

It is difficult to see how any intelligent person could begin to take such talk seriously. And even the reader willing to engage in the necessary suspension of disbelief will quickly lose interest upon discovering that this sort of thing has already been done 10 times better by Gertrude Stein.

The rest of the collection is no stronger. In ***At War with the US,*** Bowering drivels away a good opportunity for significant political satire by indulging in obsessive self-parody, baby talk, and assorted other mind games not worth dwelling on here. Thanks to Bowering's efforts, a real villain like Richard Nixon emerges as a kind of comic-strip heavy. His talent for self-trivialization is deployed even more tellingly in ***Uncle Louis,*** a satire on the longtime Liberal prime minister. Potentially the strongest piece in the collection, the poem would have worked had it not been for Bowering's insistence on conducting a running commentary upon himself by means of footnotes, which vitiate most of the intended satiric effect.

From here, things go downhill even more rapidly. ***Allophanes,*** another twice-recycled piece, supposedly on the poetic process, is virtually incoherent, with the exception of a single moderately lucid section on history. As for **"Between the Sheets,"** the only thing that can be said in its favour is that unlike the rest of ***West Window,*** it has not previously appeared in book form. While all the poems in this section are vapid and derivative, the title piece, consisting simply of a list of titles of well-known Canadian poems interspersed between repetitions of the single line "between the sheets," seems to me to indicate a new low, even for Bowering.

I wouldn't be reacting so strongly to this collection, pitiful though it is, if I thought it were the best Bowering could do. Such enjoyable and well-crafted earlier poems as ***George, Vancouver,*** **"Inside the Tulip,"** and **"Esta Muy Caliente"** show that he can write poetry when he wants to. But if he expects to be taken seriously by his readers, Bowering will have to show them a good deal more respect than he has recently. It is high time he quit playing with himself and us and started in on some serious work. (pp. 28-9)

Jon Peirce, "The Poet as Traveller," in The Canadian Forum, *Vol. LXII, No. 722, October, 1982, pp. 27-9.*

JOHN ORANGE

The almost simultaneous publication of two books by George Bowering—one a selection of his critical articles [***A Way With Words***] and the other a selection of his poems [***West Window: The Selected Poetry of George Bowering***]—affords an opportunity to test his theories against his practice. His essays are indicators of his taste, what alerts his interests, and indirectly, his theory of poetry; so one book can serve as a gloss on the other. His allusions to Keats and Shelley in the first few essays, for example, attest to his roots in Romanticism, and his dabbling references to Barthes, semiotics, and post-structuralism in the final essays demonstrate his alignment with some of the various theoretical positions which come under the heading of post-modernism. . . . There are, in fact, a number of points of intersection between the two books. His comments on the "self" as process, his rejection of notions of centricity, his puzzling assessments of versification and music, to cite only a few examples, all help to locate the context within which to appreciate (even understand) the poems. It is handy, then, to have the poems and essays collected together as they are in these two volumes.

What of the books examined singly? In ***A Way With Words*** Bowering resembles a tour guide taking us through a greenhouse of his favourite exotic, albeit indigenous plants. He points out a particularly colourful marking on a leaf here, a cluster of blossoms there, the shape of a flower over there. He mentions root systems in passing, lingers over an unusual hybrid for a minute and then hurries us on, filling in the time between observations and impressions with anecdotes about how one plant nearly died or how he cross-fertilized another. His commentary is associative, selective, benevolent and, when necessary, sprinkled with enough jargon to remind us that he is an expert. All in all, the tour is informative and we nod our assent at how agreeable our guide is. Even the odd petulant remark only piques our interest; these kinds of tour guides are supposed to be a little eccentric anyway.

The specialist in the field might be less enchanted with the tour these essays provide for a number of reasons. . . . Does Bowering still believe that Davey's "*Weeds* is as good a book as any that has ever been composed by a Vancouver poet [and] one of the most brave and beautiful and important books of our time," or does that judgment come out of a specific historical context? The essays are also badly documented so that when Bowering writes, "All images are symbols—Frye says that," there is no reference given that would enable the reader to verify the accuracy of that statement. . . . Too often Bowering seems to be an *apologist* for the *Tish* poets in both the positive and negative senses of that term. His criticism is often far more elaborate than the poems seem to warrant, and at times one senses that he is reshaping the poetry to suit his own predilections.

Having said all of that (mostly out of duty), it should be emphasized that Bowering's impressionistic approach to these poets is very helpful, because he has a special talent for picking up nuances, cadences and subtleties of form that are often difficult to articulate. His essays on Avison, Jones, Kearns, and Davey are the kind that teach us how to read these poets and nothing could be better than that. His anecdotes give readers something of the flavour of a poet's personality as it relates to his writing, so they are a bonus: "[Fred Wah] does not write fiction because his aesthetic is not geared to construction. (Once, trying to build a cabin, he put the hammer through his front teeth.)"

West Window is a collection of previously published books. ***Curious*** (1973) is a collection of poems which record Bowering's responses to his meetings with forty-eight poets. The poems are prosaic in rhythm, often polemical and mannered, but never flat or dull. ***At War With The U.S.*** (1974) does not seem to stand up very well and parts of it are boring, while ***Allophanes*** (1976) is beginning to look better and better. ***Uncle Louis*** (1980) is a lighter series of poems about the Louis St. Laurent era and it carries a running commentary which is even funnier than the poem; the mischievous interplay of the two is the real poem which turns out to be about Canadian poetry. The final section entitled **"Between the Sheets"** is a collection of five shorter pieces . . . which seem to be left over and dangling at the end of this book. (pp. 104-05)

[The] poems are samples of Bowering's post-lyrical phase. They are often experimental and they hold all the promise of success, and danger of failure, that any experiment holds. There are sudden flashes of insight and wit when the language works for him and long flat areas when he plays around to see if he can do it again. . . . The line lengths, rhythms, spaces and notation also seem to be struggling for form most of the time and these things, too, can try a reader's patience, but the rewards can be considerable for the reader who "takes his time." If to display "mind in process," "language in action," "poetry creating itself" is the purpose of writing, as Bowering indicates it is, then the collaborating reader will find many delightful passages in this volume. The energy and playfulness in many sections are in themselves enough to recommend the poems. If, on the other hand, you sympathize with that little poem about process versus product which McLuhan used to quote (it ends: "So that is reckoned wisdom which / Describes the scratch but not the itch"), then you turn these pages at your own risk. (pp. 105-06)

John Orange, "The Scratch, Not the Itch," in Canadian Literature, *No. 98, Autumn, 1983, pp. 104-06.*

JEANETTE SEIM

All of Bowering's short stories are on one level satires of the traditional short story form and the tenets of realist fiction. ***A Place to Die*** carries this impulse even farther. Exhibiting the typical Bowering archness and wit, these stories represent an apocalyptic kind of writing in which the "real" death is the death of traditional fictional realism.

In his essay **"The Painted Window: Notes on Post-Realist Fiction,"** Bowering remarks that "whereas the realist had seen his writing as a window, the post-realist presents something opaque." Perhaps the most striking feature of the stories in ***A Place to Die*** is their opacity. Most of them are about *not* finding something out. The stories work away from a sense of resolution. Anti-climactic, ambiguous and deliberately banal endings undermine the achievement of dénouement, the traditional vehicle of resolution in short fiction. **"Match Boxes"** ends with someone having a drink. **"Carter Fell"** concludes with a musical score.

The characters in these stories are similarly opaque. **"Carter Fell,"** the first story in the collection, involves the first person narrator's attempt to reconstruct a personality—that of Carter. A recurrent figure in Bowering's short fiction, Carter is the friend-artist-eccentric-mentor who is ultimately unknowable. The narrator's quest for Carter, or knowledge / understanding of him, is fragmented into webs of nostalgia and convoluted remembrances. We receive only pieces of a personality.

Like other post-realist writers, Bowering is more interested in time as a *repetitive* phenomenon than in time as sequential and linear. **"The Clam Digger"** is a pseudo-fable about repetition, transformations that are the same and different. **"Arbre de Décision,"** perhaps the most opaque and antilinear story in the collection, deals with an event—an obscene telephone call—that happens over and over. There is no real plot; the story is more like a series of "takes" on one incident. Reading this story is like watching a Jean-Luc Godard film. The voice on the phone repeatedly interrupts the protagonist engaged in the sex act with a myriad of real or imagined lovers. The story explores the limits of narrative: how much recursion and interruption does it take until no narrative remains? Ironically, the final conversation between Arthur, the protagonist, and the caller (in this particular take the voice is a genteel spokesman of culture) is about language. . . . (p. 33)

Each story in this collection engages some aspect of traditional fiction. In **"A Short Story,"** for example, Bowering parodies the formulae of the short story by dividing his story into sections entitled "Setting," "Point of View," "Protagonist," "Symbolism," "Plot," "Theme," etc. In "plot," something is supposed to happen. It does: "Donna turned a smooth quick arc, & shot her mother's face off." The narrator of **"A Short Story"** makes fun of the over-zealous narrator who tells instead of shows: "She thought of the universality speaking through her condition." Narrators parodying narrators are not uncommon in Bowering. Similarly, **"Four California Deaths"** is a story about reading a story.

A Place to Die is a strong collection, a decided contribution to Canadian post-realism. These stories constitute a critique of the short story form, just as Bowering's novel ***Burning Water*** exploits the conventions of the historical fiction genre. In spite of its characteristically playful tone, Bowering's writing is a serious exploration of language and literary form. As Matei Calinescu remarks, "fiction is a matter of life and death. But it also enables us to play." (p. 34)

Jeanette Seim, "Not Finding Out," in The Canadian Forum, *Vol. LXIII, No. 736, February, 1984, pp. 33-4.*

BRIAN L. FLACK

George Bowering has a reputation for stories and poems that delicately straddle the fine line between the bizarre and the absurd. This is not a criticism of his intentions or the degree of success he achieves; it is simply a statement of fact. Because he has consistently flirted with (even courted) excellence, Bowering has been rewarded with a mittful of Governor General's Awards—each deserved for a variety of reasons. The interesting element is that there are a *number* of reasons for his success: constant innovation, clarity of thought, dedication to the imaginative, and structural sophistication.

There is, however, a great problem inherent in the process of continual trail-breaking that must be carefully addressed and requires total authorial vigilance. Once set astray from the intended and narrowly defined goal, there is every possibility that the adventurer will fall into a pattern of aimless circling, perhaps even crossing and recrossing already travelled paths. Bowering has victimized himself in this manner in his collection of short stories, ***A Place to Die.*** This is not to say the stories are uninteresting or even failed. Most are not. In fact, one or two of them are almost superb. (p. 26)

[Aside from **"A Short Story"** and **"Old Bottles"**], most seem repetitive of intent, structurally cloying, and absurd. **"Arbre de Décision,"** a multi-narrative exercise in reader confusion that uses the telephone as an image for imprecise and gratuitous communication, begins and ends nowhere. Hard to follow and punctuated by transitions between the real and the imaginary, it makes one wonder whether some integral detail was overlooked on the way through. **"The Clam Digger"** begins like a fairy tale (a young man is carried on the back of an enchanted turtle to a deep-sea kingdom where he is installed as a prince with no limits on his self-indulgence), but degenerates into a trite moral tale that reaffirms Thomas Wolfe's souring dictum: you can't go home again.

Readers may also be annoyed by Bowering's stylized use of structural devices: "and" is replaced by ampersands; "through" becomes "thru"; the apostrophe is dismissed from contractions. These, as always, remain minimally effective tools. Tired is a charitable way to describe them.

At his best Bowering exhibits a skill for penetrating and manipulating the stylistic nuances that make literature enriching, but in ***A Place to Die*** there is little evidence of this rare quality. On the one hand, the prose seems hurried and often poorly thought out, creating both sense and interpretation difficulties. On the other, Bowering seems to be making a valiant attempt to lure us into linguistic and structural mazes that promise uniqueness but do not deliver. In the few stories that are free of these weaknesses, one is aware of the authorial control and intricate levels of meaning that characterize Bowering's usual virtuosity. It is unfortunate there is such a dearth of that expertise. (p. 27)

Brian L. Flack, "Lost in the Maze," in Books in Canada, *Vol. 13, No. 5, May, 1984, pp. 26-7.*

GEORGE GALT

Young poets can be excessive, brash, self-admiring, arrogant and ridiculous—and get away with it. They can fly off in all directions, rockets full of energy, burning up received wisdom in a wild bet on radical insight. Often we read them just to watch the risk-taking, the cutting loose, the lofting into their personal unknown. Occasionally they reveal something we can keep, but many beginning writers burn up so much fuel along the way that the trip seems more memorable for the noise and smoke than for its durable revelations.

George Bowering, I used to think, was such a young poet. Though he more than occasionally recorded moments worth keeping, his early cosmic rockets generally described parabolas of heat, not light. Still wandering the universe in this his most far-reaching book, no longer young but still taking large risks, Bowering now can mix old wisdom and fresh insight without wasting an ounce of fuel. The scope of ***Kerrisdale Elegies***, essentially one long poem broken into 10 parts, is breathtaking, and its accomplishment matches its ambition.

These meditations are offered in immediate, tactile language, which is not to say they are devoted to the immediate, tactile world, though that too. Mortality, but more interesting, the challenge of being fully conscious of mortality while being wholly alive, are the book's preoccupations. . . .

For this poet the vanishing present is born earthbound and heaven-connected, a dialectical mix of mud and metaphor in which the lawns of Kerrisdale (described on the back of this book as "one of Vancouver's most gracious residential areas") are descended from the farthest star. Immersed in the immediate, his nose in the roses, he is also face to face with the transcendent beyond. . . .

About consciousness, these meditations are also about poetry. Writing about writing can be tedious to read, but here it is handled unself-consciously as a natural appendage of awareness. Like the houses and gardens of Kerrisdale, the writer is a neighbourhood artifact. His books, his papers, his bones are disintegrating as quickly as the trees in the yard. Only the permanence of words can leapfrog us backwards and forwards out of the dot of time our bodies inhabit.

There is lively wit in this book as in the echoes from Eliot when Bowering's robin is

> skidding across his own wakened air,
> like a pen across a modern poem.
>
> Let us go then,
> heart and eye,
> to look as
> always,
> attend as always,
> look at the world and never
> out of it.
>
> It begins to fall down a little.
> We renovate and proudly show our friends.

It begins to fall down, begins to die. But this poet has the renovating gift, the ability (and felt responsibility) to snatch death out of slack-jawed everyday life. . . . (p. 19)

George Galt, "Mud and Metaphor," in Books in Canada, *Vol. 13, No. 6, June-July, 1984, pp. 19, 21.*

KARL JIRGENS

This zingy collection of literary slices [***Craft Slices***] finds its historical antecedent in the satiric essays of Addison, Steele, and Johnson, and has less in common with Pope's *Dunciad* than the cover note would suggest. Bowering serves views on literary theory and tradition with observations on writers sandwiched between views on geographic locations and their possible influences on artists and writers.

He mixes these musings with spicy pot-shots at the educational system, and tops them off with personal experiences, insights into his own creative recipes, and self-critiques of his earlier spreads. To the literary gourmet, some of this will smack of older fare, though it's not without zest. . . .

At this point I could enter into post-structural analysis and say that Bowering shifts the centre of his essays, deconstructing them by showing their preconstructions, by revealing his thought roots, by having himself interviewed by an invented "Canadian Tradition" only to demystify its self-referentiality through the narrator's pose of *faux naif*. I could say that Bowering blurs genres here, is self-reflexive, uses inter- and intra-textual references, appropriates and dis-appropriates methodologies, redefines the roles of author, artwork, audience. I could also say this is a significant book for theorists, perhaps an essential book for scholars. But that would be taking half the fun out of it; that would be eating the sausage without mopping up the *jouissance*.

Karl Jirgens, in a review of "Craft Slices," in Books in Canada, *Vol. 14, No. 8, November, 1985, p. 23.*

DAVID LEAHY

Craft Slices is structured as alphabetical entries "about the world of writing," but as Bowering muses in "slice" **"ABC"** he "wanted order but not development . . . I wanted any entry to be a place of entrance." The ensuing naming and criticism happens in no "significant sequence" and many of the entries read as if they are thinly recycled book reviews, but they are also often witty, thought-provoking touchstones for the theory and practice of post-modern literature in Canada.

Not surprisingly, Frank Davey is lauded as the "post-modern letters" don who "has put thematic criticism to rout" and shown Canadians the necessity of writing literary theory (though Bowering's vanguardism does not prevent him from perpetuating the myth that the "Confederation Poets" are "imitations of Wordsworth"). In **"Posthumous Fiction"** and other entries, in keeping with his long-established critical pronouncements, realist authors are just too "serious in the sense of solemn" for Bowering's post-modernist sensibility. On the lighter side, a section such as **"Brown Tish"** is a delightful send-up of eastern Canadian poets' paranoia about the *Tish*-rooted (and American "Black Mountain Poetry"-inspired) literary mafia.

As in ***Seventy-One Poems for People,*** which is dedicated to Dorothy Livesay and Milton Acorn, politics keeps coming to the fore. For instance, the two sections on Eliot dissect his fascist tendencies as a bourgeois "spokesman for the modern Anglo-American mercantile middle class" (and are remarkably reminiscent of Livesay's Marxist critique of Eliot in the 1930s). By contrast, Bowering praises Gerry Gilbert's "horizontal" political aesthetic and Milton—the "Romantic Carpenter"—Acorn for not "glamourizing the poor in the way the bored bourgeoisie do," and contends that "Wayman is proof that you can combine economics and love in one poem, that the political poem can be well made, and not only in Latin America." ***Craft Slices'*** political cutting edge is contradicted, however, by Bowering's insistence that criticism should not be sociological. Likewise, he fails to acknowledge how Livesay's *The Unquiet Bed* was as political—in sexual and feminist terms—as anything else she has ever written.

Contrary to predictable conservative naysaying the political verse of ***Seventy-One Poems*** is not "less subtle" nor "more programmatic." The collection's thematic divisions have barbed titles like "Cops" or "Our Other America" but many of the apparently more recent poems suggest Bowering is ready "to leave off wit and do / the important work, now" as his moving elegy to Red Lane records the latter once advised him to do. A poem questioning the *Tish* movement's philosophy of poetry as the "highest calling" may not strike one as political until we read **"The Canada Council Poet"** in which Bowering chastises established poets, as Thoreau did Emerson, for shirking their duty of the "line up . . . in the police station."

Commensurately, **"Survival Course"** attacks the merchants' control over artistic production and marketing, while **"London, Ontario"** envisions an interstice of rebellion "125 miles from Detroit, / 125 years from revolt"; the ambiguities leave us wondering if Bowering regrets the antiquity of the 1837 rebellion or is anticipating one which will surpass it. (pp. 412-13)

Frequently the more refined and equally more "committed" poems are adaptations from Latin American poets such as Manuel Pacheo or Robert Sosa. There is probably no better political poetic *oeuvre* for contemporary poets to apprentice themselves to, but it is too early to tell if Bowering will be able to make it his own the way Livesay absorbed Auden's, Spender's and C. Day-Lewis' work during the Depression and made it anew for the Canadian context. In the meantime, poetry's "poor powers" may be "weak and useless" in the face of exploitation but this does not prevent Bowering from translating works of hope and beauty out of the South American inferno. . . .

Formally speaking, ***Seventy-One Poems*** is too varied and reflects too large a time span to isolate representative characteristics and devices. And in the dot-matrix conservative '80s many of the poems in this collection demand and deserve a wider audience than they will likely receive. Perhaps then Bowering should take a cue from the American visual artist Jenny Holzer and install an electronic screen of these or similar poems in a mall in Vancouver or Toronto's "Harbourfront." As they are, the primacy of language is not lost in the protest and exultation and it is work worthy of Livesay and Acorn, which only time will tell whether or not Bowering will continue to produce. (p. 413)

David Leahy, in a review of "Craft Slices," "Seventy-One Poems for People," and "Feeling the Worlds: New Poems," in Queen's Quarterly, *Vol. 93, No. 2, Summer, 1986, pp. 412-14.*

STAN DRAGLAND

A friend of mine opened ***Kerrisdale Elegies*** in a bookstore, read a few pages, replaced it. Maybe he noticed the reference to Rilke in Robert Kroetsch's blurb on the back of the book; anyway, he detected Bowering poaching on *Duino Elegies* and it put him off. Like any good browser he was looking for the book he could fall in love with at first sight. Which is how ***Kerrisdale Elegies*** took me. What I liked first was the voice, which is curiously un-Rilkean, unless we were to imagine how a Rilke reborn and settled in present-day Vancouver might sound. That voice has its modulations, but one very important thing it does is swallow all influences. Therefore ***Kerrisdale Elegies*** is not like, say, ***Burning Water,*** into which Bowering introduces undigested chunks of other books. In the novel, shifts of style are the only signals that the ground has changed. Of course that's for fun. Nobody whoops it up in an elegy. *Duino Elegies* and ***Kerrisdale Elegies*** are really like night and day—caught at the same hour on the same globe. Despite the powerful presence of another powerful poem in it, I still read ***Kerrisdale Elegies*** every time with admiration for its originality.

We are not talking about *Duino Elegies* as a general model, as for Dennis Lee's *Civil Elegies* or Jack Spicer's unfinished group of elegies. ***Kerrisdale Elegies*** is actually, in part, a free translation of *Duino Elegies*. At times the two poems go along together almost line for line, though Bowering makes changes no translator would be permitted. A translator doesn't substitute a baseball team for a family of acrobats, as Bowering does in "Elegy 5." A translator doesn't all but throw out Rilke's angels, dispersing their function among humans, as Bowering does. It is amazing but true that the spirit of *Duino Elegies* doesn't evaporate as Bowering writes his own time and place, his own life across it. (p. 14)

Duino Elegies is a sort of core text which Bowering courts in a rhythm of departure and return. Sometimes he is quite near; sometimes he goes off where there is no Rilke to follow. Since there is always something more than translation going on, Bowering is always in dialogue with Rilke. Sometimes he explicitly interrogates his source. But always there is this sense of vindication of the essential vision of Rilke, always the feeling of homage being paid, and ultimately of two powerful voices contrapuntally celebrating life lived in the shadow of death.

Bowering's poem is full of his own versions of Rilke's "Things" to be valued and praised for themselves, and also as part of the rich ensemble of life so loved that the prospect of leaving it is agonizing—until pain is recognized as a principle of that life. . . . Bowering endorses Rilke's conviction that the world is recreated and sustained in the eyes of the committed beholder. That is their answer to mutability. It takes hold . . . when we stop trying to leave our home in suffering.

Bowering's type of this committed individual, more explicitly than Rilke's, is the poet, and the poet at the centre of the poem is quite like Bowering himself. ***Kerrisdale Elegies*** is an unchronological portrait of the artist in formation, but Bowering manages to handle the autobiographical element impersonally and with self-irony. He doesn't grandstand. If he did, the reader would not feel welcome to share the immensely difficult task of sustaining the spirit of the things that are.

So who is Bowering in ***Kerrisdale Elegies***—an audacious pirate or a self-effacing participant in tradition? He is surely both, and if I stress the latter mask it's to argue for the seriousness of his wonderful poem. The fact that it *matters* could easily be lost as critics move in on the question of influence. A reader needs to be relaxed about what Bowering is doing, and that means first simply responding to his words. Then one can safely enter the labyrinth of influences. Holding on to what the words actually do, wherever they came from, one never gets lost.

I wonder if I'm the only reader who almost prefers to get his Rilke in Bowering's words. I love *Duino Elegies,* but I can't read German and it's unsettling to go from translation to translation. Something of poetry comes through and the something is probably Rilke's, but there is no definitive Rilke in English, whatever various publishers and reviewers claim. This is Bowering's opportunity. Released from the impossible demands of exact fidelity to the German he can make real poetry in English.

I like seeing double myself, and I think anyone who studies the intertextuality (presence of one text in another, by quotation, paraphrase, allusion, echo and so on) of ***Kerrisdale Elegies*** will need to like it too. Such a person will also want to remember the context of Bowering's other writing—like ***Allophanes,*** whose playful intertextuality throws out this manifesto-like unattributed line from Yeats: "Talk to me of originality / and I will turn on you with rage." Why not take Bowering at Yeats' words?—which might mean reading ***Kerrisdale Elegies*** alongside *Duino Elegies* the way scholars read Malory's *Morte Darthur* as both an original text and an edited translation of French originals, an origin Malory doesn't hide. Even the idea of offering under one's own name a text borrowed from a writer in another language is far from new, and there are modern precedents like Pound's "Chinese" poems.

Kerrisdale Elegies sounds nothing like *Duino Elegies*. The two poems look completely different too, and at one level the arrangement of the poem on the page controls how it sounds, but this is not so much in the way Bowering effortlessly catches the idiom of his time and place. He never speaks "poetically," in fact he never raises his voice, and yet he comes across with authority, speaking levelly and conversationally to his peers, with confidence that people will listen. His language is bare of artificial ornament, there is no straining at figures of speech; quiet conversational rhythms carry much of the effect, while avoiding the banal or monotonous. In everything from the short burst to drawn-out periodic sentence (see the last page of "Elegy 5") in tones from jaunty to hushed, diction from correct to slangy, ***Kerrisdale Elegies*** strikes the ear in an authentic North American accent. The lines are as natural as speech, if you imagine speech that is everywhere active, like a chord augmented with a fifth or a seventh note—on its way somewhere else. . . . Bowering's voice could not be colloquial in the same way as Rilke's, given the gap between their time and place and language, but there is an even greater disparity in the deeper principles of sound and sense caused by Bowering's distinctive notation, with alternation between full lines and stepped half lines and shorter units. Bowering makes the page a unit of composition and his page might show a number of opened-up couplets or tercets or longer staves. Visually there is a lot more open space than there is in *Duino Elegies*. The amount and disposition of space is not constant; it depends on the words it surrounds. These are all arranged along the traditional horizontal axis, though the stepping introduces a degree of verticality into the wordscape, but they do sometimes seem to rise and float on a white ground. There is almost the feeling that if the page weren't opaque you could see past the words to something else. Writing or typing out the lines makes you feel their physicality, their almost sculptural interaction with white space. That is also an interaction between sound and silence. Variations in these, together with subtleties in the use of traditional schemes of sound arrangement like repetition and refrain, give an improvisational feel to the music of the poem. It never settles into a predictable pattern.

Rilke is the most important literary presence in ***Kerrisdale Elegies,*** but by no means the only one. In all of Bowering's elegies but the third, adding up to the "magic number" of nine, there suddenly appear a few untranslated and unattributed lines of French poetry. None of the passages sounds like Bowering (and none of them reads like any other) but the French lines do not seem out of place in terms of content. Sometimes the lines follow the sense of what Bowering had just been doing, so that a bilingual reader will feel only an enharmonic change of language; sometimes the lines are not locally related but pick up or point ahead to something elsewhere in the poem. Occasionally freely translated phrases from the French poems appear in Bowering's text proper (though the more we look into this matter, the fewer words we find that seem to be merely Bowering *propre*). (pp. 14-17)

Whatever one makes of the French poets, adding their presence to that of Rilke, both sorts of source make sense as part of an intricate web of conscious intertextuality that includes the epigraph stanza from Emily Dickinson, reference to H. D., quotation of Margaret Avison, dedication of "Elegy 8" to Michael Ondaatje, general references to famous dead poets in "that great anthology," allusions to and echoes of all sorts of specific poets, vestiges of Bowering's other work, even the poem's doubling back on itself as it reconfigures certain clusters of thought and feeling in refrain and self-quotation. The self-reference works us back towards the central figure of "Bowering" and his poem as the container of all that tradition. A highly self-conscious poem, at times about itself. So the reader is entertained with a view of the writer writing—discovering the poem—and is shown certain pressures of the passage of time on the very lines being read. In the postmodern way, then, the reader is shown the process of poem-making. In the case of ***Kerrisdale Elegies*** that means watching the tip of a living tradition unfold. (pp. 17-18)

Stan Dragland, "The Bees of the Invisible," in Brick: A Journal of Reviews, *No. 28, Fall, 1986, pp. 14-25.*

NOAH ZACHARIN

In ***Seventy-One Poems for People,*** George Bowering has gathered two decades of "lyrics about public struggle," and in so doing carries on a line of committed poetry begun in 1947 by Dorothy Livesay and *Poems for People,* and continued by Milton Acorn with his 1972 publication, *More Poems for People*. Appropriately, Bowering dedicates his addition to the forebears from which the torch is passed.

The book is divided thematically into six sections: "Some People," "Cops," "Canadian Scenes," "Vietnam & Other Wars," "Our Other America," and "The Poems of Ed Prato" who, it is rumoured, is one of the author's personae with much to say about Canadian poets and the scene with which they surround and swaddle themselves. The poems in each section are as straightforward as the titles of their sections.

However, the task Bowering sets for himself is not as simple. To write a consistently successful book of poems is hard enough; to write one composed of convincing topical work is even harder still. Much of ***Seventy-One Poems for People*** is an attempt to restore the immediacy and importance of some of the distant concerns of the sixties, and thereby recreate a political sensibility that was, to a large degree, created by the ethos of the times. Much of what was hip then is hackneyed now, and an attempt to revive it is almost certain to fail.

Yet there is much that is wonderful in this book. Fifteen adaptations of work by relatively obscure Spanish-language poets are exquisitely crafted into English poems that boil with image and emotion. Bowering as veteran craftsman and satirist also writes his own: "Ah, violence, ah violence, ah viet cong / infiltrating the faculty club," he begins one section of a poem about the 1969 Sir George Williams University computer centre incident. **"The Deathmaker at San Quentin"** speculates on the psyche of that institution's executioner. Without possible recourse to fact, Bowering creates the poetry of the subject's possibilities, and shows that a poem grown in imagination's fertile soil need not betray the emotional seed that started it. (pp. 145-46)

Not surprisingly, some of the best of Bowering's work is personal in nature. **"The Dead Poets of Vancouver"** is one of the most moving pieces in this book, and a serial poem that is a lovely elegy for the poet Red Lane ends with a mysterious and moving ambiguity: ". . . I am reduced // to these simple words, / to say I love you, sleep, // I love you, sleep."

There is no denying that ***Seventy-One Poems for People*** has its failures: throw-away poems, in-poems, ephemeral poems. But it also has its bright moments, and this, one could say, is an accurate mirror of the world the poet is dealing with. Perhaps this is an apology for Bowering, but he has earned our respect, both as the young writer whose early lyrics everted reality as they quick-stepped over the page with quirky yet careful dance-steps, and as the writer of longer works, most recently, and perhaps most notably, ***Kerrisdale Elegies,*** a book that displays sustained thought and a calm, mature wisdom. Perhaps then, this same writer can be permitted partial failure of a move in another direction.

But there is enough of both art and commitment here to satisfy all who would place themselves between the aesthete and his arid inanimate world, and the "doctrinaire believers who state that all artiness must be expunged from people's poetry, because it serves the taste & cause of the bourgeoisie." In ***Seventy-One Poems for People*** there is a sufficiently energetic meeting of poetry and politics to convince the reader that these are the words of a poet, who happens also to be a human being struggling with the rest of us to remain human in a beastly world, by responding as eloquently, and as honestly as he can. (p. 146)

Noah Zacharin, "For People," in Canadian Literature, *No. 112, Spring, 1987, pp. 145-46.*

PAUL ROBERTS

If Clint Eastwood were a woman, he would have no trouble playing Caprice, the Amazonian heroine of Bowering's [new novel ***Caprice***]. She's six feet tall; she can ride a horse and handle a bullwhip and gun as well as any trail hand; she's the object of every man's lust and every woman's bitchy envy. And, what's more, she's a poet.

Bowering attempts to turn the whole hack-western revenge genre on its head by fleshing out stereotyped characters to a point approaching credibility, and then setting them free in a story that is so straightforward that, paradoxically, there is something not at all straightforward about it.

Caprice—as much the object of the author's passion as anyone else's—has spent much of her early life in Europe, where wealth and poetry filled her days. Of this former life, we learn little. What is central to the story is that her brother—from Quebec, as she originally was—has been gunned down by a squalid outlaw named Frank Spencer, and she must henceforth devote her days not to poetry but revenge. And so she rides her magnificent black stallion down to New Mexico and back to B. C. on Spencer's trail. As the pages turn, however, it becomes less and less clear who is tracking whom.

A traditional cowboy villain, Spencer has little going for him. He's dirty, mean, and a bad drunk, besides being a psychopathic killer. But he is tight-lipped enough to be enigmatic. Like Iago, he's a baddie because that's his nature, and Canada's no place for baddies. You can't even get into a decent gunfight, because nobody has a gun. Why, he even has to tolerate being called "Sir" when he goes into a bar.

His sidekick doesn't help matters either. "Strange Loop Groulx" is hardly a name to put the fear of God into honest folks, let alone the stuff of which legends are made. In fact, Groulx, who is also from Quebec and who still considers himself an "apprentice outlaw", is considering changing his name to the "Savona Kid". Does the following sound like the kind of dialogue the James Gang exchanged?

> "I been studyin' on a name. I mean if I am going to be an outlaw I should ought to have an outlaw name."
>
> "How about the Fuckface Kid?" suggested Spencer.
>
> "Why do you have to talk like that?"
>
> "You ain't no kid, Groulx. You ain't been a kid for twenty years. Likely you never were a kid. You were probably a goat from the time you were dropped."

If this kind of low verbal play were peculiar only to this duo of dangerous duds, it would be an acceptable indulgence. Unfortunately, it runs rampant throughout the novel: almost everyone in the book has a shameless weakness for groaning puns or etymological parlour games. This author-behind-his-scenes stuff threatens to ruin the book on countless occasions. Yet, curiously, it becomes the very thing that takes ***Caprice*** to where no hack-western has been before. If it's possible, this is the classic Western as post-modernist chic. The components of the novel could be shuffled almost endlessly to create any novel you want. Bowering presents a deck of cameos and a plot so conventional, its flexibility is endless.

For example, framing the story's events—tracking the trackers, if you like—is another dubious duo. Known simply as "First Indian" and "Second Indian", they function much like a Greek chorus or Shakespearian clowns, shedding light on the white man's folly while plodding through a folly of their own. . . .

Similarly adrift are all the other evocative and irreducibly precise cameo appearances Bowering conjures up as essential elements in his photo-album of a novel. And, beyond all reason, they work—often with heart-breaking poignancy: the poor, lonely Italian immigrant, Everyday Luigi, makes a dash to possess the vision that Caprice's beauty represents; his resulting misery is oddly tempered and transformed by the reader's compassion. Set against his romantic yearning is the image of his boss, Soo Woo, the original Chinese entrepreneur, whose instinct for profit would have other minorities complaining of racism. Roy Smith, the teacher and Caprice's lover, is torn by a Canadian choice—passion or duty; the "photograph maker" out to make a record of what is already gone; the pompous journalist sent from Austria-Hungary to write wild yarns about a West that has outgrown its wild; and the whores, the hoteliers, the bankers, the kids—all of them living out their reality in a land that too many others still view as fantasy.

So intent on arguing this point is Bowering—as if intoxicated by the notion of one age slipping imperceptibly into another—that he at times forgets the needs of a story, even digressing, albeit exuberantly, into fascinating irrelevance. Fortunately, he has at all times the assistance of a tough, insistent plot. One simply has to find out what happens when Caprice meets up with Frank. And with this ploy, Bowering is unforgivably sly.

Between the alpha and the omega are too many letters, all connected and all threatening their own tale. All men want a taste of Caprice's Wonderwoman mystique, yet I cannot help but feel that it's only George Bowering who gets it.

Paul Roberts, "Bowering's Western: Woolly Post-Modernist Chic," in Quill and Quire, *Vol. 53, No. 5, May, 1987, p. 19.*

KENNETH McGOOGAN

Set in the Canadian West in the 1890s, ***Caprice*** is replete with good guys and bad guys, cowboys and Indians, and a central figure who is obsessed with tracking down a killer and bringing him to justice. It's an old-fashioned western, then—except that the hombres have ethnic identities, the Indians debate metaphysical questions, and the eponymous, would-be avenger is a gorgeous, red-headed, French-Canadian woman who is six feet tall, carries a European bullwhip, makes poetry when she isn't suffering from writer's block, and has a schoolteacher boy-friend who plays baseball, can't understand her quest, and wants her to settle down. What we have here is an entertainment with a polemical subtext—not an old-fashioned western but a post-modern one. In drawing attention to the conventions of genre, George Bowering is reasserting the aesthetic that informed his controversial 1980 novel, ***Burning Water:*** "You're reading a story, amigo, and don't you ever forget it."

The plot of ***Caprice*** is simple enough. A ruthless American gunslinger named Frank Spencer kills a French-Canadian wrangler who calls himself Pete Foster—shoots him in the back over a couple of bottles of whisky. Foster, otherwise known as Pierre, dies with his sister's name on his lips: Caprice. This we learn in an early flashback, the narrative having opened with Caprice's arrival in the West to embark on her quest. She rides a beautiful Arabian horse named Cabayo, and pursues Spencer from Canada to the Mexican border and back again. (p. 15)

In ***Caprice,*** Bowering distinguishes fancy from imagination, rejects motivated characters in the name of fate, and invites his readers to collusion: "We can look back to what they (the characters) looked forward to." Old familiar ploys. Yet the novel differs from ***Burning Water*** in another significant particular. Though Caprice the woman is larger than life—a mythical figure—she never does anything magical. Bowering has resisted the temptation (one can only imagine the agonized writhings) to thumb his nose at realism by introducing, say, horses that suddenly soar into the air. Some readers will miss the hyperbole, the unruly excessiveness of the earlier approach, but the strategy is wise. ***Caprice*** insists on its own reality, but more subtly than ***Burning Water.*** It will alarm and alienate fewer readers.

Once in a while Bowering indulges in corny jokes ("The two riders approached fast, their horses wild-eyed. One of the horses was brown-and-white. The other was white-and-brown"), and his oft-repeated insistence on "now, or rather then," together with its variations, is an annoying affectation ("He hoped that he could forget [his anger] for two hours on the field this afternoon, or rather that one"). But these are peccadilloes. If the world of Canadian letters were a classroom, Bowering would be the kid who sits at the back of the room with his feet up on the desk, making wisecracks. That's his chosen pose. Behind the banter and bravado is one of Canada's most interesting novelists. (pp. 15-16)

Kenneth McGoogan, "As for Me and My Horse," in Books in Canada, *Vol. 16, No. 5, June-July, 1987, pp. 15-16.*

Dee (Alexander) Brown

1908-

American nonfiction writer, novelist, and editor.

Best known as the author of *Bury My Heart at Wounded Knee: An Indian History of the American West* (1970), Brown is noted for his informative and enlightening historical accounts of nineteenth-century America. Intending his works for a popular readership, Brown writes in a simple prose style and highlights his narratives with entertaining vignettes and colorful portraits of historical figures. Much of Brown's work involves the American West and comments upon the exploitation of natural resources and the injustices suffered by American Indians. For example, *Bury My Heart at Wounded Knee* chronicles from a native American perspective the ruthless mistreatment and eventual displacement of Indians during the westward settling of the United States. N. Scott Momaday observed: "Having read Mr. Brown, one has a better understanding of what it is that nags at the American conscience at times . . . and of that morality which informs and fuses events so far apart in time and space as the massacres at Wounded Knee and My Lai."

Brown's other historical works are informed by his career as a librarian for various departments in the United States government. He often incorporates diaries, letters, journals, government records, and oral tribal histories to authenticate his studies. *Grierson's Raid* (1954) recounts the military adventures of Benjamin Harrison Grierson, a music teacher who led an unruly band of Union cavalrymen into Confederate territory during the Civil War. In *The Gentle Tamers: Women of the Old Wild West* (1958), Brown reveals the important role women played in settling the western United States, and in *The Year of the Century: 1876* (1966), he offers a sketch of America at the time of its centennial celebration. *Hear That Lonesome Whistle Blow: Railroads of the West* (1977) exposes through its study of the early development of the Union Pacific-Central Pacific Railroad the rampant corruption and destruction spawned by the Industrial Revolution.

Brown is also the author of several historical novels in which he recreates episodes from the American frontier and the Civil War. In *Wave High the Banner* (1942), he recounts the adventures of Davy Crockett, the legendary pioneer and politician. *Creek Mary's Blood* (1980) chronicles the hardships of an American Indian woman and her descendants and examines how exploitation of native Americans and their land contributed to the destruction of Indian culture. Brown's next novel, *Killdeer Mountain* (1983), traces a newspaper reporter's attempts to uncover the truth behind the mysterious life of Major Charles Rawley, a revered military figure. The conflicting stories of those who knew the man complicate the reporter's efforts. Brown based his recent work, *Conspiracy of Knaves* (1986), on a group known as the Copperheads, who attempted to create a second Confederacy during the Civil War. While the Copperheads never realized their intentions, Jack Hurst contended: "Such considerations might loom larger if this book evinced high-flown historical or literary pretensions. It doesn't. It appears intended solely to entertain and does so." In addition to his historical fiction, Brown has written several conventional western novels and *They Went Thataway* (1960), a parody of spy and thriller fiction.

Photograph by Linda Brown. Courtesy of Dee Brown.

(See also *CLC*, Vol. 18; *Contemporary Authors,* Vols. 13-16, rev. ed.; *Contemporary Authors New Revision Series,* Vol. 11; *Contemporary Authors Autobiography Series,* Vol. 6; *Something about the Author,* Vol. 5; and *Dictionary of Literary Biography Yearbook: 1980*.)

JOHN K. BETTERSWORTH

The fine art of raiding, wherein Americans have always excelled, was never so well practiced as in the Civil War. Achieving little except as psychological warfare, raids perhaps diverted war-bored civilians more than enemy forces. But Americans loved the daring, the suddenness, the "touch and go" of it all. . . .

[Benjamin Henry Grierson, featured in D. Alexander Brown's ***Grierson's Raid***], was an Illinois music teacher who despised horses and "would have much preferred leading an orchestra instead of a brigade of wild-riding cavalrymen." Yet this paradox of a soldier led 1,700 western cavaliers over the 600 miles from La Grange, Tenn. to Baton Rouge, La., his only guides a Colston map and a handful of "butternut" scouts in captured uniforms.

Grierson set out on April 17, 1863, feinting at the well-guarded Mobile and Ohio Railroad but heading for the poorly protected Southern Railway, the only supply line from the east to Vicksburg. Grierson disrupted rail and telegraphic communications before the "Rebs" realized what was happening. Then, while Pemberton neglected Vicksburg to run Grierson down, the foolhardy raider set out to join Grant, who was preparing a landing south of Vicksburg. Never being able to contact Grant and beset by aroused Confederate pursuers, Grierson finally had to race southward to Baton Rouge, arriving on May 2 with his forces almost intact. . . .

Mr. Brown exhibits a proper respect for the epic and dramatic qualities of the Grierson story. Indeed, Civil War fact has hardly been so imaginatively handled since the days of Stephen Vincent Benét. Here is an exception to the trite ritual of military history, which tends often to be as deadly as its subject. The author never fails to see the men for the battles. One relives the adventure with all its sights, sounds and smells, as Grierson's men swear, sweat and swagger their way the whole length of Mississippi. Even enemy civilians cheered the foolhardy Yanks, if somewhat patronizingly.

John K. Bettersworth, "A Daring Dash through Dixie," in The New York Times Book Review, *December 5, 1954, p. 26.*

STEWART HOLBROOK

The promise implicit in the title of [***The Gentle Tamers: Women of the Old Wild West***] is not broken. Mr. Brown has assembled a notable collection of women who took part in the migrations westward, mostly in the period 1850-1880, and presents them, often with enthusiasm and always with sympathy, as they proceeded, each in her own manner, to put rings in the noses of men who liked to believe they were operating in a world of complete masculinity. . . .

Mr. Brown seeks to dissipate "The Sunbonnet Myth," a stereotype invented by he-men types including such articulate romancers as Emerson Hough, who saw the westering woman as a gaunt and sadfaced figure "sitting on the front seat of the covered wagon, following her lord where he might lead, her face hidden in the same ragged sunbonnet which had crossed the Appalachians and the Missouri long before."

The Western woman, says Mr. Brown, was far more than a face hidden by a ragged sunbonnet. Often the bonnet was gay with color and plumes; sometimes she wore French millinery. And no matter what her dress "she had endurance, she had courage, and sometimes she was wilder than the land she tamed." Having said so much, the author selects as wide a variety as possible, ranging from gentle missionaries like Narcissa Whitman and Eliza Hart Spalding to ungentle Amazons who were as notorious as Belle Starr and Lola Montez.

Although less reflective collectors of women might have loaded the scales heavily in favor of types like Cattle Annie, Cattle Kate, Pearl Hart and others of unquestioned immorality, Mr. Brown is content to mention them in passing rather than to stress their efforts. But Julia Bulette, a noted madam of the Comstock, gets several pages and one picture, while Mrs. Martha Cannary Hunt Blake Burke White Dorsett Dalton, called Calamity Jane, gets two pictures and generous biographical notice. . . .

Almost any Western reader of this excellent book will naturally think of omissions from Mr. Brown's charming gallery. There is only one I deeply regret. She is Abigail Scott Duniway, who devoted the enormous energies of her long life to the end that the women of the Pacific Northwest should not only vote in any and all elections, but that they should cease being dolls and drudges and take their rightful places in business and professions as the equal to the lords of creation, many of whom came in time to blanch at the very mention of Mrs. Duniway's name. . . .

I thoroughly enjoyed Mr. Brown's book, which has sixteen pages of photographs and prints, many of which will likely be new to most readers.

Stewart Holbrook, "A Gallery of Western Women, Very Few with Sunbonnets," in New York Herald Tribune Book Review, *April 13, 1958, p. 3.*

MARSHALL SPRAGUE

There is, to be sure, nothing like a dame, and [in ***The Gentle Tamers: Women of the Old Wild West***] Dee Brown proves the point once more in a wise and witty report on those indomitable females who came, saw and conquered the West. . . .

Though careful to preserve an illusion of soft helplessness, these Western dames were mostly hard as nails. Wives of the Donner party survived [an] awful winter of snowbound death far better than the males. While passing through Montana in September, 1849, the men of the Riker family parked the wagon with Janette Riker in it and went hunting. They never returned. Janette kept herself alive alone in the wagon until Indians found her the following April.

Mr. Brown has turned up endless samples of feminine ingenuity. A woman in Washington Territory was planting precious seed corn, which was eaten by a rooster. When she caught on, the woman pounced on the bird, cut it open on the spot, removed the kernels and planted them again. An officer's wife carried her baby across the Arizona desert in a champagne basket. Sarah Royce rode horseback with her baby in her lap, canteen and diapers in one saddlebag, a pail in the other and necessities hanging from the pommel. (p. 6)

Underlying the book's fascinating comedy and pathos and terror, there is a sociological overtone. Mr. Brown shows that the reactions of these women to their frontier experience were as important as male reactions in the development of American mores and American democracy. Brigham Young's curious kingdom collapsed in part because pioneer Mormon wives rebelled against plural marriage and yearned for finery beyond the means of the average harem-burdened husband. . . .

Dee Brown, a librarian at the University of Illinois, has produced an entertaining as well as an instructive work to add to his ***Trail Driving Days*** and other Western studies. (p. 37)

Marshall Sprague, "On the Western Trail There Was Nothing Like a Dame," in The New York Times Book Review, *April 20, 1958, pp. 6, 37.*

RICHARD B. HARWELL

They Went Thataway is a light hearted and delightful spoof, a finely drawn caricature of a spy novel. Such parody requires more skill than the real thing on the part of its author, and Dee Brown shows that he has served his apprenticeship as a serious historical writer well. But let him never turn back from this kind of fun book, fun for the reader, that is.

Philip Faraday, a doctoral candidate at a midwestern university, is doing research in Washington on a mythical Gen. Comstock. . . .

The fun begins when the sexy daughter of his boarding house landlady describes his work to a friend in Intelligence. And it shines bright thru a hilarious interlude in the Kentucky archives, continues thru a slapstick Fourth of July celebration at Sanderson university, and reaches a wildly funny climax in the wastelands of Wyoming.

Brown sets a fast pace for his story, but he never lets it flag. He pokes fun at some of America's most sacred cows: intelligence agencies, the doctoral degree, movies, the spy story, the western novel, and sex. But neither does his humor flag. It is light and breezy, sometimes even subtle.

Richard B. Harwell, "Spy Novel Caricature," in Chicago Tribune, *April 24, 1960, p. 3.*

BELL I. WILEY

President Lincoln in September, 1864, lent his support to a previously initiated move to recruit Union troops from among Confederate prisoners. The move received considerable impetus from adoption of General Grant's suggestion that units formed from prisoners be not employed against their erstwhile comrades but against Western Indians. . . .

It is fortunate for Civil War history that D. Alexander Brown [in ***Galvanized Yankees***] elected to tell the little-known but fascinating story of the turncoats of the 1860's. Since these men served on the Western plains in 1865-1866, the knowledge of that area and period that he acquired in writing such books as ***The Fighting Indians of the West*** and ***Trail Driving Days,*** stood him in good stead; and because they functioned largely as mounted troops, he benefited much from acquaintance with Civil War cavalry derived from ***Grierson's Raid*** and ***The Bold Cavaliers.*** From long service as a librarian at the University of Illinois came a familiarity with sources and reference tools that enabled him to locate obscure and scattered materials. . . .

Galvanized Yankees is an accurate, interesting and sometimes thrilling account of an unusual group of men who rendered a valuable service to the nation in a time of great need. It is also a fresh and informative study of the Old West in transition from frontier to stable society.

Bell I. Wiley, "The Untamed West Was a Way Out," in The New York Times Book Review, *May 31, 1964, p. 6.*

WALLACE D. FARNHAM

The historian who can shut his ears to the din of battle finds in the Civil War a cluster of enduring human issues, of which the nature of loyalty is surely one of the most fascinating. The war troubled men's allegiances in varying ways, but a unique kind of distress must have assailed those who took up arms against a country they had repudiated and then found themselves its captives. It was only to be expected that some would forsake their rebellion, and even wish to switch uniforms. A penetrating study of those prisoners who exchanged gray for blue, setting their whole experience against that of more stable Confederates, might considerably extend our understanding of the great conflict. In ***The Galvanized Yankees*** Brown has written about these men. By toiling faithfully in appropriate sources he has learned much about them, and his book is not without merit. Unhappily, it does not measure up to its subject.

The book's value lies in its parts rather than in the whole, for the great difficulty with it is that there is no whole. Six thousand captured Confederate soldiers become six regiments of Union volunteers and march west to fight Indians, and with that fact the unity in Brown's story fades. Thereafter he simply follows one outfit after another on its travels, until each has been mustered out at Fort Leavenworth. . . . In handling each group separately, the author turns out sketches of frontier soldiering that are sometimes full and instructive, if also uninspired. Yet the virtues come as by-products of the pervasive fault of incoherence. There is little in these adventures to hold the story together, Confederate origins seeming not to give the men much in common or to set them apart from the true Yankees with whom they often marched. The truth is that as Brown handles things he does not have a genuine subject, or at least one worth a full book. . . . In short, there is much sand and little cement. He leaves mostly unused the cement he might have found in an exploration of the nature of loyalty, of civil strife, or perhaps of the mind of Johnny Reb. But these are profound themes, and Brown has not tried to be profound. He has set down reliable, if not very important, information in a fair narrative style, but he has not applied the qualities of intellect and imagination needed to do justice to the galvanized Yankees or to satisfy the minds of thoughtful readers. (pp. 502-03)

Wallace D. Farnham, in a review of "The Galvanized Yankees," in The Journal of American History, *Vol. LI, No. 3, December, 1964, pp. 502-03.*

A. L. TODD

In his research for [***The Year of the Century: 1876***] Dee Brown must have spent many hours feasting on succulent meats that many of us have had only limited time to taste—those colorful, exaggerated, highly inaccurate newspapers of the golden age of yellow journalism. The year 1876 was a great one for unrestrained newspapering, and Mr. Brown's extensive reading in the files of those spicy old issues is clearly evident in his account.

Any book on the events of the 100th year of American independence is based on a purely mechanical device. Centennials and other anniversaries have their place, but they are best used as today's vantage point from which to measure our progress in a given period. Waxing rhapsodic, as the author sometimes does here, over the alleged deep significance of a centennial celebrated 90 years ago is stretching the anniversary idea a bit thin. It is highly doubtful that a "sense of climacteric or watershed" was felt anywhere but in a few pompous orations. . . .

[Brown] would have done better by discarding his restraining centennial formula and giving us instead a "Bedside Reader of the Yeasty Seventies." In many places his book is just that. It is a highly amusing, episodic slice off the frothy top of life in the Gilded Age. The stories come in short spurts. You can put the book down, but you are impelled to pick it up again to read the next episode.

A. L. Todd, "When We Were 100," in The New York Times Book Review, *September 11, 1966, p. 61.*

EDWIN H. CADY

For Dee Brown [in ***The Year of the Century: 1876***] the Centennial Year surges with color, vitality, and fate. It was a year of events. In Washington the Grant regime ended in sensational scandals, perhaps ringing down the curtain on the Gilded Age; and nationally the Hayes-Tilden campaign and its aftermath brought to its close a year fraught with tragic implications North and South. In the West, Jesse James and his band held up trains and banks; the Youngers were shot down in Northfield and Wild Bill Hickock in Deadwood; Buffalo Bill Cody had the immortal luck to kill Yellow Hand in view of a posse of newspapermen only days after the news of Custer's defeat. . . .

Centering on the national jamboree of the Centennial Exposition in Philadelphia, Brown contrives to suggest that his chosen events were symbolic as well as colorful. But the difficulties attendant on his methods are those endemic to "popular history." Temptations to facile irony and other razzmatazz rob his style of precision. His perspective is largely interior and intimate; therefore his canvas is very broad, he resorts to poster strokes and colors, and one is comfortable with his history in a ratio inverse to one's independent knowledge of the materials.

Edwin H. Cady, in a review of "The Year of the Century: 1876," in The Journal of American History, *Vol. LIII, No. 4, March, 1967, p. 833.*

HELEN McNEIL

Now that Vietnam has brought the United States to the point of accepting national guilt for the first time, this scholarly and passionate chronicle [***Bury My Heart at Wounded Knee***] has attained US bestsellerdom by fixing the image of the nation's greatest collective wrong: the extermination of the American Indian. A deliberately revisionist history, ***Bury My Heart at Wounded Knee*** tells the story of the Plains Indians from an amalgamated Indian viewpoint, so that the westward march of the civilised white men, 'like maggots', according to a Sioux commentator, appears as a barbaric rout of established Indian culture. Conversely, when General Custer (known to the Indians as Hard Backsides, Long Hair and chief of all the thieves) made his last stand at the Little Bighorn, it is shown to be the Cheyennes and Oglala Sioux making a last stand against invaders of sacred land traditionally theirs and specifically promised them by the Treaty of 1868. The new perspective is startling, even if the success of Dee Brown's empathy depends on a shared assumption that Indians can still be spoken for safely; a history of slavery written by a white 'from the Negro viewpoint' would hardly be so well received.

For a study whose proximity to national illusions would seem to make stereotypes inevitable, ***Bury My Heart*** is amazingly myth-free. The central scenes of each chapter show famous chiefs and warriors like Red Cloud, Crazy Horse and Geronimo acting as parts of a larger tribal whole, thus avoiding the more convenient image of the individual Indian, who is unsurprisingly usually depicted in literature as the Last (or the only visible) Mohican. The contemporary incarnation of Indians as The First Ecologists is accepted by the author, which is fair enough, though uncritical, since by anthropological definition a primitive society does not exhaust its environment. If it did, it would destroy itself, unless compensatory technology came along.

A great revelation of Brown's Indian historical viewpoint lies in its contrast to the vulgarity of the 'Turner thesis', which dominated American historiography for over 40 years and has been surfacing again in Nixon's White House. In 1893, Frederick Jackson Turner proposed simply that the 'empty land' of the frontier had removed America from European historical precedent, and the continuous re-creation of civilised society out of conflict in the West kept breathing idealism into a languishing democracy back East. Thus Turner's mystic spring has fed both US isolationism abroad and imperialism at home. For the Indians, unacquainted with the ideals of Manifest Destiny, each new incursion into their homeland meant suffering from the brutality, greed, hypocrisy and sanctimoniousness which many soon recognised as hallmarks of white civilisation. The Indians, one realises, knew exactly what was being done to them. ***Bury My Heart*** reproduces their words, transcribed at tribal councils or treaty conferences, or dictated in memoirs, indicting the invaders more eloquently than any third-person account could. (pp. 444-45)

When white settlers arrived in the early 19th century, the Plains Indians were at a cultural peak dazzling enough to inspire the clumsy tribute of a recent title: Peter Farb's *Man's Rise to Civilisation as Shown by the Indians of North America from Primeval Times to the Coming of the Industrial State*. ***Bury My Heart*** awakens a more authentic sense of that grandeur with the moving speeches of the great chiefs. The catalogues of tribes and warriors, the accounts of when, where and how battles were fought, even the precise descriptions of the heroes' wounds, all give a strangely Homeric quality to this epic. Like the Trojans, the beautiful Sioux and Cheyennes were rich in robes and horses, but their end had come. Gods to protect the Indians are missing from the scene. Brown's panorama is almost too broad and uniformly tragic. As each tribe is seen in its moment of agony, his distinctions between tribes, never made emphatic, begin to blur. One isn't reminded that the Navahoes were settled, the Apaches predatory, the Poncas gentle or the Utes lazy, since in any case the same fate awaited them all. (p. 445)

Helen McNeil, "Savages," in New Statesman, *Vol. 82, No. 2115, October 1, 1971, pp. 444-45.*

PETER J. OGNIBENE

At first people regarded the railroad as a force for good. "When I hear the Iron Horse make the hills echo with his snort like thunder, shaking the earth with his feet, and breathing fire and smoke from his nostrils," wrote Thoreau, "it seems as if the earth had sent a race now worthy to inhabit it."

In a matter of years, as the impact of the railroads and the financial manipulations of their "robber barons" became known, people began to see things differently. Thoreau, too, changed his mind. "We do not ride on the railroad," he now said. "It rides upon us."

Hear That Lonesome Whistle Blow takes the reader through a transition similar to Thoreau's. We begin with the noble men who pioneered the Iron Horse and see how they were inexorably forced out by financiers who did not want to build railroads so much as exploit them.

Brown makes an implicit distinction between free enterprise and private enterprise. The former died when the industrial revolution overturned America's village economy. An illicit marriage of private interest and government subsidies replaced it. This was called "private enterprise."

Entrepreneurs bribed members of Congress with cash or stock certificates. In return, they were awarded exclusive construction rights and western land grants totaling 155 million acres. Construction estimates were grossly inflated so the railroads could pocket the difference between the congressionally subsidized price and the actual cost of building the rail line. Additional profits were made by stock manipulators who bankrupted their opponents or, in some instances, their partners. Whenever Indians blocked the path of the Iron Horse, Congress quickly extinguished their tribal rights to disputed lands, and the Army was sent in to enforce the national will. Usurious interest on farmland drained immigrants of their meager savings while exorbitant freight rates devoured their agricultural earnings. . . .

Brown has written a short book about a tall subject, and some individual stories have gotten short shrift. For example, Jay Gould, the worst of the "robber barons," thunders onto the stage but soon becomes lost among the other players. Also I think too many pages were given to 19th-century travelogues and too few to the hardships of the men who laid the rails. These are, I hasten to add, minor flaws.

Brown has an impressive grasp of the political and economic dynamics which turned the building of the western railroads from an initially noble enterprise into a national disgrace. It is a fascinating story, but at another level it is a cautionary tale.

Peter J. Ognibene, "How the West Was Overrun," in Book World—The Washington Post, *May 15, 1977, p. H7.*

PHILIP FRENCH

[Brown's publishers call ***Hear That Lonesome Whistle Blow***] 'the story of the great American railroads'; it is in fact the case *against* the great American railroads. The outlines of this story are familiar enough and Brown tells it passably well within the limits of the muckraking tradition.

Put pretty crudely, and that's more or less the way Brown puts it, groups of unscrupulous robber barons got together in the east and west to make fortunes out of railways that nobody needed. . . . As a consequence the Indians were dispossessed, the buffalo destroyed, the ecology ruined, millions of immigrants lured from Europe to cultivate unsuitable land, and the nation presented with miles of poorly built railroads and a hopeless communications system that had to be bailed out time and again by the government. The mobile communities of brothels, saloons and gambling dens that accompanied the construction gangs across the west were dubbed 'hells on wheels'; Brown's remorseless indictment almost proposes such a city as an image of American history. Though he takes time out for a few bland chapters on foreign travellers' experiences crossing the Continent and names a few token 'good railwaymen' . . . , he moves inexorably towards his final pages, where he extols the anti-railroad National Grange organisation which sprang up among western farmers in the 1880s and the Populist movement that followed it.

It is characteristic of Brown's approach that Lincoln and Brigham Young figure in his saga principally through close-ups of their hands trapped in the till, and that he should elevate to emblematic significance the fact that the unscrupulous financier Thomas Durant (boss of the Union Pacific) through inexperience or excess of champagne twice failed to hit the final golden spike at Promontory Point, Utah, on 9 May 1869. Such things should not be overlooked, yet the constant emphasis on shoddy deeds serves not merely to qualify almost out of existence the epic nature of the undertaking, but to deny a true complexity to the events and a full humanity to the participants. This reductive process also takes away from the abiding heroism of the men who physically laid the tracks and ran the trains, leaving them as hapless victims. Above all, despite the contemporary quotations, Brown fails to create the atmosphere of the post-Civil War 'Gilded Age', or to capture the magic of the railways—not that romantic side which has such nostalgic appeal for us now, but rather the way in which the steam train frightened and excited the world, and transformed the way we think about space and time.

Perhaps, as a corrective to pre-war Westerns like *Union Pacific* or old-fashioned school histories, Brown's book has its uses. An understanding of American 19th-century history is impossible without appreciating the pervasive corruption and the railroad companies' contribution to it. Some quite reputable historians tend too easily to excuse these evils. To make them the central issue, on the other hand, is to abuse history and forge a false link to the past. (p. 452)

Philip French, "Hell on Wheels," in New Statesman, *Vol. 94, No. 2428, September 20, 1977, pp. 451-52.*

GENE LYONS

Any reader of modern fiction will find the preamble to Dee Brown's [***Killdeer Mountain***] familiar. "In a way," says the narrator, St. Louis newspaper reporter Sam Morrison, "the story is a puzzle . . . because each of us sees or feels or uses the senses in differing degrees from all other human beings, and inevitably there are conflicts in the tellings. The world we view is a complex mirror that tricks us with false images. . . ."

If the point of view here seems contemporary to a fault, the subject matter of ***Killdeer Mountain*** is not. Like all of his books, including the best-selling history ***Bury My Heart at Wounded Knee,*** Brown's latest novel takes place in the nineteenth-century American West. It's an almost Conradian tale of high ideals, dishonor, betrayal, redemption and "the deadliness of righteous men." After covering General Sherman's march through Georgia, narrator Morrison has been posted by his editor, in the spring of 1866, "up the wretched Missouri River," where a sporadic Indian rebellion in the Dakotas promises "more stories of conflict and gore." . . .

Brown has a compelling tale and a powerful theme in ***Killdeer Mountain.*** But he seems a bit uncomfortable in the narrative mode he has chosen. Sometimes his characters say too much, as when one describes a firing squad observed from a distance: "Tiny puffs of pearly smoke lifted and vanished in a sky filled with frightened birds." Then, when the reader needs unfamiliar history or Indian lore explained, verisimilitude gets in the way. Even so, fans of Western novels will find themselves well entertained.

Gene Lyons, "Varnished Truth," in Newsweek, *Vol. CI, No. 13, March 28, 1983, p. 71.*

JOHN RECHY

Once we ignore the expectations aroused by Brown's earlier ***Bury My Heart at Wounded Knee,*** a moving, resonant book; once we forget the jacket's fatuous promise that with "uncompromising brilliance'' the author will explore ''the mysterious ways of the human soul''; and once we forget the jacket itself, one of the ugliest ever foisted on a book, we will most likely enjoy this good novel [***Killdeer Mountain***].

La Rochefoucauld noted that ''well-placed flaws'' in certain works may gleam more brightly than ''virtue itself.'' In this yarn, flaws occur with full knowledge of the author that they enhance the primary pleasure of his engaging book.

To get away with this, Brown elicits trust by immediately creating adventure and suspense as his narrator travels by boat on the Missouri River in 1866 to ceremonies honoring the dead Indian-fighter and war hero, Capt. Rawley. . . .

Brown creates an exciting battle, a journey in a blizzard, a spectacular fire, and surprises till the very end.

Now what are the flaws that, together, make this tale ''shine''? Brown uses a cliche or two or three. Women do ''whatever it is that females do when they are together.'' Liquor unleashes confessions. His heroine is ''the soul of feminine beauty and vivacity.'' And ''winter arrived early.''

Pages of information monologue are disguised as dialogue by allowing a hapless listener (as opposed to the intrigued reader) only convenient questions: ''How can that be?'' ''How was it that he failed?'' ''You were here?'' In a flimsy shelter during bitter cold, a character announces: ''Talk passes time, tell us about. . . .'' And we read long, required, spoken narrative.

Brown withholds information awkwardly to enhance suspense. . . . Coincidences abound.

Questions logically asked when certain information is first delivered go unanswered for only one reason—the author's. He nudges his readers into attention. . . . (p. 2)

Yet these flaws give the narrator's adventure a plausibility by arousing an accepting, old-fashioned naivete, which suspends disbelief. On the level of entertainment, Brown's book succeeds wonderfully. (p. 9)

John Rechy, ''The Flaws to Make a Fiction Shine,'' in Los Angeles Times Book Review, *April 3, 1983, pp. 2, 9.*

JONATHAN COLEMAN

Reading Dee Brown's engrossing, though not totally successful, new novel [***Killdeer Mountain***] reminds me of the many times I used to sit spellbound on my grandparents' porch, late on summer evenings, listening to them tell me wonderful stories about events that had shaped their lives: the two world wars and the Great Depression that came between. But what I remember most is that whenever they recalled these events, or a particular person they both had known, their accounts were strikingly different.

Different versions of what is essentially the story of a Major Charles Rawley and his exploits during the Civil War form the basis of this solid, old-fashioned mystery-and-adventure yarn. . . .

Filled with, and sometimes made top-heavy by, such timeless themes as honor and dishonor, loyalty and betrayal, cowardice and redemption, decency and ruthlessness, the novel opens just after the Civil War. Sam Morrison, the narrator, is a young reporter for The Saint Louis Herald, traveling aboard the steamboat Roanoke ''up the wretched Missouri River in search of more stories of conflict and gore.'' What he finds instead is a fascinating array of people on their way to the dedication of Fort Rawley in the Dakota Territory. The fort is being renamed in honor of Major Rawley, the son of a famous Ohio senator, and is a replacement for Fort Standish, where the major reportedly died in an explosion a few years before. I say reportedly because that, like so much else in the novel, is intentionally unclear and mysterious. The men and women Morrison meets all knew Charles Rawley or *thought* they did. And, just to make things even more interesting, there is the possibility that Rawley, or someone who might be impersonating him, is alive and on board the Roanoke. (p. 15)

Mr. Brown's gift for strong narrative far outweighs his skill at writing dialogue, which, at times, hurts his novel by trivializing it. When he can describe a person's eyes as having ''an ashen sadness, a resignation that comes only to those who have struggled against great odds and lost,'' he can also produce such banal lines of dialogue as ''Humans are no more than snowflakes. . . . Blown about. No more control over our lives than a snowflake.''

As far as his characters are concerned, some are more successfully drawn than others. While one is absolutely entranced by one woman who ''had a way of making her eyes lock into the eyes of whatever male happened to be exchanging looks with her,'' we never really learn why another is ''a woman of some passion.''

Finally, though Mr. Brown does a fairly good job in using the complex mystery of Charles Rawley as the main vehicle for moving his novel along, this intriguing story does not reach a terribly satisfying conclusion. It's too open-ended, as though the author partially forgot his responsibility to the rather puzzled and somewhat exasperated reader. Still, much of Mr. Brown's considerable audience will not be disappointed. (pp. 15, 21)

Jonathan Coleman, ''Atoning for an Act of Mercy,'' in The New York Times Book Review, *June 5, 1983, pp. 15, 21.*

THOMAS FLEMING

In two of his previous historical novels, ***Creek Mary's Blood*** and ***Killdeer Mountain,*** Dee Brown explored the anguish of white-Indian relations. ***Conspiracy of Knaves*** is another ambitious excursion into the American past. It examines an almost forgotten drama of the Civil War—the Copperheads' Northern Conspiracy.

The Copperheads were in a sense the war resisters of the 1860's. Their critics saw them as poisonous snakes, sinking their fangs into the Union. They turned the tables on this reproach by wearing the Liberty Head on the copper penny as a badge of honor.

The Copperheads, who were mostly Democrats, saw Abraham Lincoln as a dictator out to destroy the United States of America. . . .

To undo ''King Lincoln,'' the Copperheads planned a massive revolt in the summer of 1864 that would rip Indiana, Ohio and Illinois out of the war to form a second Confederacy. The scheme was eagerly supported by the South with guns and money.

Here, it would seem, is material for a story seething with conflict. Especially when added to the plot were Gen. John Hunt Morgan and his cavalry, ready to surge up from Kentucky to storm through Indiana and Illinois on the promise of Copperhead support. (p. 12)

Mr. Brown tells this panoramic tale through the eyes of Belle Rutledge, a pretty actress who signs aboard as a Union spy and goes to Richmond, where she is promptly hired as a Confederate spy. She is assigned to a team of Rebel agents, led by a handsome Kentuckian, Maj. Charles Heywood. I fear that making Kentucky-born Belle a double agent was an artistic mistake. It drains almost all the emotion and much of the suspense from her narrative. There is not a shred of idealism in her support of the Union; she was just a woman who needed work.

There are richer characters in the real story, such as beautiful, willful Lucy Williams, who was accused by her husband of infanticide and adultery and who many think betrayed Gen. Morgan to the enemy. Beside her, Mr. Brown's fictional Belle is tame and dismayingly prim. He seemed to sense his story would go awry and suddenly let Belle tell some of it through the eyes of a Morgan cavalryman, Johnny Truscott. Here we get closer to the passion and frustration in the drama. But Truscott is soon captured and he spends most of the book in jail yearning for Charles's cousin, Marianna Heywood. (pp. 12-13)

Mr. Brown's historical research is sound. But I wonder if it was wise to make the pusillanimity of most Copperheads the main point of the novel. These were people caught in one of the riptides of history and not all of them were knaves. Some were honest men, appalled by the list of dead and wounded in the newspapers each day, who were desperately trying to rescue their country from a seeming holocaust. There is no hint of this anguish in Mr. Brown's story.

Above all, ***Conspiracy of Knaves*** lacks a sense of the real reason why the Copperheads failed. Frank Klement, their best historian, put it succinctly: "Copperheads would not admit . . . Lincoln's qualities of leadership." There were knaves aplenty swirling around the South and the North during the Civil War. But there were also men and women who responded to Lincoln's sympathy and sincerity, who came to share his tormented idealism. I wish Mr. Brown had tried to deal with that side of the story. It would have made the knaves more poignant, his novel more compelling. (p. 13)

Thomas Fleming, "Rebel Belle, Double Agent," in The New York Times Book Review, *January 11, 1987, pp. 12-13.*

JOHN BYRNE COOKE

It is obvious from the outset [of ***Conspiracy of Knaves***] that Brown (a Southerner by birth) knows the Civil War period as well as he knows the Indian War and the taming of the West. Details of dress, speech, customs, incidents in the war, politics, horsemanship, military tactics and equipment, all are woven into the narrative by a consummate storyteller. The rivers flow, the winds blow, the nights are full of secrets and the days pulse with real life.

The characters are an interesting lot, each with quirks and peculiarities. Brown's first-person narrator is Belle Rutledge, an actress who quickly becomes involved in spying for both sides, sometimes dressing herself in men's clothing. . . .

Many readers may find Belle and the story's other virtues sufficient to carry them through to the end without a second thought. Some, like myself, may feel that the tale never fully catches fire, although all the ingredients are present.

Brown carries off the 19th-century women's writing style well, but in the end his perhaps too-conscientious fidelity to the style hinders rather than helps the story. Belle is a wonderful character, well-suited to appeal to 1980s readers. She is a double agent, an actress who has appeared in "racy" skits and danced in tights, a headstrong young woman unconcerned with conventional morality, yet she writes like Jane Austen. She proclaims at the outset that she is setting down her own version of the story because she is "the only one who moved through the three sets of knaves and knows the whole truth." If, in pursuit of that truth, she were to say also, "Convention be damned, I'll tell this my own way," no modern reader would blink. But she never shakes off her self-imposed Victorian restraints, and one result is that it is difficult to feel much passion in her affair with Charley Heywood—the central personal drama in the novel. . . .

Then there is the Northwest Conspiracy itself, which ended with a whimper, not a bang. I don't want to give away the ending, but if history fails to provide the novelist with a dramatic climax, he can still invent one for his fictional characters. Whether or not Brown has done that in ***Conspiracy of Knaves,*** each reader will have to decide for himself.

If there are failings here, they are minor. Dee Brown knows American history well. He takes delight in dusting off neglected incidents and using them as elements in his stories. As a member of the same company, I wish him well in all his efforts. But I would have liked to hear Belle Rutledge's story told with a bit more of, say, Anais Nin in her voice, and a bit less of Jane Austen.

John Byrne Cooke, "Dee Brown's Tale of Convicts and Confederates," in Book World—The Washington Post, *January 18, 1987, p. 7.*

JACK HURST

During the last, desperate months of the Civil War . . . wild plots ran rampant.

One of the wildest was a Southern one in which a handful of Kentucky Confederates were to spearhead a move by Southern-sympathizing Midwesterners to [1] liberate thousands of Confederate soldiers imprisoned at Camp Douglas in Chicago, [2] set fire to Chicago itself, [3] launch an uprising to lead the "Northwestern" (now Midwestern) states out of the Union into a Confederacy of their own and [4] thus force President Lincoln to abandon his war to keep the South in the federation.

Dee Brown's [***Conspiracy of Knaves***]—an energetic, engaging narrative—fictionalizes the weird machinations of this convoluted conspiracy. . . .

Much of the charm of the book lies in its antique tone. It purports to be a memoir of the conspiracy by its most knowledgable participant, and the picturesque detail—quickly sketched in wartime Richmond, Cincinnati, Toronto and especially Chicago—is offhandedly well-done. Many of the characters also are drawn with a Dickensian eye for variety.

If there is a problem, it lies mostly with Charley Heywood, the man with whom Jennie/Belle becomes so smitten that she is unable to perform her duties to the boss to whom she has sworn primary allegiance: Lincoln. Perhaps because of Brown's method, which is to tell the story in the style of a book of the

1860s, Jennie/Belle primly discloses so little of what goes on behind closed doors that the reader may end up wondering why she fell so hard for Heywood in the first place.

The reader may also fleetingly wonder, if he pauses to consider, whether this is all much ado about not much, since the central conspiracy the story is based on is a non-event: it never came about. When the conspirators tried to bring it off the week of the Democratic Convention in Chicago, history tells us, it haplessly fizzled.

Such considerations might loom larger if this book evinced high-flown historical or literary pretensions. It doesn't. It appears intended solely to entertain and does so, thanks considerably to the unsinkable and, for the 1860s, outrageous character of Jennie/Belle, a woman 120 years ahead of her time.

Best of all, ***Conspiracy of Knaves*** ends well. The denouement is unanticipated and powerfully lifelike.

Jack Hurst, "Spies in Chicago," in Chicago Tribune, *January 25, 1987, p. 5.*

Basil Bunting

1900-1985

English poet, editor, and critic.

An innovative poet of the Modernist movement, Bunting is perhaps best remembered for *Briggflatts* (1966) and other long poems in which he attempted to duplicate musical forms. These highly allusive works, termed sonatas by Bunting, evidence Modernist and Objectivist contentions that poetry convey emotion through sound, be structured according to the words it contains, and treat clarity of meaning as secondary to rhythm. Bunting repeatedly relied on monosyllabic words derived from Anglo-Saxon roots and his own Northumberland vernacular, and he often employed alliteration, compressed lines, and onomotopoeia to further imbue his verse with musical qualities. While his *Collected Poems* (1968; expanded, 1978) preserves a relatively small body of work, most critics concur with Tom Scott's assessment: "Bunting stands apart, one of very few dedicated poets of incorruptible integrity of purpose and talent, a subtle and original craftsman of consummate technical skill."

© Thomas Victor 1987

Educated in English Quaker schools, Bunting was briefly imprisoned as a conscientious objector during World War I. Following his release, he contributed in an editorial capacity to Ford Madox Ford's *transatlantic review* in Paris and, later, became a music critic for *The Outlook*. Critics note that Bunting's early poems display the influence of T. S. Eliot, Louis Zukofsky, and Ezra Pound, all of whom experimented with musical forms in literature. Bunting's first collection, *Redimiculum Matellarum* (1930), was privately printed in Italy, where both he and Pound resided and collaborated on various projects. *Redimiculum Matellarum* contains "Villon," the first of Bunting's sonatas, which, like Eliot's *Waste Land,* was severely edited by Pound. "Villon" alternates between the point of view of fifteenth-century poet François Villon and a contemporary narrator who, like Villon and Bunting, had spent time in prison. Subsequent poems by Bunting from this period appear in the *Active Anthology,* which he edited with Pound, and in Louis Zukofsky's *Objectivist Anthology*.

Following the publication of *Redimiculum Matellarum,* Bunting began to travel extensively and held several government and military positions. Although he published little new poetry during this time, Bunting's experiences provided the subject matter that informs much of his later verse. A prolonged stay in the Middle East during and immediately following World War II furnished him with extensive knowledge of Persian languages and culture. Bunting evidences these concerns in the lyrical "Odes" from *Poems, 1950* (1950) and in *The Spoils* (1965). Originally published in 1951 in *Poetry* magazine, *The Spoils* is the least musical of Bunting's sonatas and reflects his belief that Western civilization would benefit greatly from an understanding of Eastern culture. *Loquitur* (1965), a revision of *Poems, 1950,* and *The First Book of Odes* (1965) increased critical and public recognition of Bunting's work.

Bunting's last sonata, *Briggflatts,* secured his reputation as an important modern poet and is considered by many critics a landmark of twentieth-century poetry. Described by August Kleinzahler as "the finest long poem of the century," *Briggflatts* displays a pastoral sensibility within a framework that is characteristically erudite and musical. Although subtitled "An Autobiography," this work focuses on Bunting's impressions of his experiences and his lifetime of studying literature rather than rendering actual occurrences in his life. The greatest achievement of *Briggflatts,* according to many critics, is the myriad of emotions, knowledge, and lyricism Bunting instills in lines that consistently display his control and mastery of technique.

(See also *CLC,* Vols. 10, 39; *Contemporary Authors,* Vols. 53-56, Vol. 115 [obituary]; *Contemporary Authors New Revision Series,* Vol. 7; and *Dictionary of Literary Biography,* Vol. 20.)

LOUIS ZUKOFSKY

[In ***Redimiculum Matellarum***], Mr. Bunting's poetic care is measure. He is aware that quantity has naturally to do with the tones of words. His diction, as a result, tends to a classical selection, even when his themes are modern, as in his epigram to Narciss and in his sonnet beginning "An arles, an arles for my hiring.'' At the same time, reversing this relation, the past meets the present as in **''Against Memory''**:

> Ten or ten thousand, does it much signify, Helen, how
> we
> date fantasmal events, London or Troy? Let Polyhymnia
> strong with cadence multiply song, voices enmeshed by
> music
> respond bringing the savors of our sadness or delight
> again.

The diction often seems to collect no more than the experience of classical poetry: ''The distant gods . . . abstracts of our spirit,'' at the end of **''While Shepherds Watched,''** themselves ''rabbits sucked by a ferret''; the preoccupied but outwardly integrated mythology of the **''Chorus of Furies—Overheard—guarda, mi disse, le feroce Erine.''** . . . (p. 160)

But Mr. Bunting would not be among the isolate instances of Englishmen concerned with poetry in this time, were his content only the product of a classical ear directing a polished manner. All his poems, and especially the **''Villon,''** are grounded in an experience, though the accompanying tones of the words are their own experience. . . . (p. 161)

His indictment of Bertillon in [**''Villon''**] is violence that an intelligent man confronted with historical fact has had to express, even if the name has joined the decorative scheme of his poem. The coda of the **''Villon''**—

> How can I sing with my love in my bosom?
> Unclean, immature and unseasonable salmon—

is the logical humility consequent on Mr. Bunting's bitterness. The rhetorical wrench of the last line is self-mitigated because the writer's metaphor has become the objective equivalent of his personal irony.

Mr. Bunting's adaptation of Lucretius' invocation to Venus even indicates a safer art and a more certain direction. . . . So much so that the French epigrams opening and closing his volumes and laying restraint on the extent of his expression (*Bornons ici cette carrière*) are unnecessary. (pp. 161-62)

Louis Zukofsky, '' 'London or Troy?' 'Adest','' in Poetry, *Vol. XXXVIII, No. 111, June, 1931, pp. 160-62.*

HUGH KENNER

Mr. Bunting's verse has been inaccessible since the *Active Anthology* (1933) went out of print; after eighteen years there should be a few hundred people to be interested in [***Poems, 1950***]. What he has to offer that is not in the work of his elders doesn't depend on his having read different books, gone to a different school, and formed a preference for different women, adjectives, and cheeses. Neither Mr. Bunting's interest nor his readers' is focused on Mr. Bunting's insides. The reflection has preceded the poems, has preceded, as it were, the very mapping of the interests they articulate; the poem isn't a transcription of the poet's trying to think, nor a noise attending spiritual indigestion.

Let the reader not be put off by talk about thought; we are not in the presence of versified dogmatics. . . . [It] isn't on sonority that Mr. Bunting habitually depends. The solidity of image, the absence of fuzz and duplication, the weighing of epithet, the continual interest of the rhythms (none of them conspicuously borrowed), underlie single lines arresting and rich . . . and a range of tone that can extend in a single poem all the way from

> Crack, rush, ye mountains, bury your rills!
> Spread your green glass, ocean, over the meadows!
> Scream, avalanche, boulders amok, strangle the dale!
> O ships in the sea's power, O horses
> on shifting roads, in the earth's power, without hoofhold!
> This is the earthquake, this was
> the great earthquake of Genryaku!

to

> Summer? Cuckoo's *Follow, follow*—to
> harvest Purgatory hill!
> Fall? The nightgrasshopper will
> shrill *Fickle life!*
> Snow will thicken on the doorstep,
> melt like a drift of sins.

And the thematic range of the collection extends with equal sureness from

> We built no temples. Our cities' woven hair
> mildewed and frayed. Records of Islam and Chin,
> battles, swift riders, the ambush, tale of the slain,
> and the name Jengiz

to wry contemporary observation. . . . (pp. 361-62)

It is probably the novelty of encountering verse not held together solely by a sense of the writer's personality that makes Bunting seem, at first, fragmentary. The reader brought up on the presently popular tradition of more or less dramatic introspection may need to be persuaded at some length that a thing is what it is, that anything honestly recorded has the incalculable value of honesty. . . . [Close reading of **''Chomei at Toyama''**] may persuade us of the pleasure to be derived from writing that confines itself to discovering what are the essentials of the job in hand and setting them down.

> Lofty city Kyoto
> wealthy, without antiquities

precisely defines a quality; but six words are apt to be overlooked if one assumes a point to be unimportant unless dilated into witty rhetoric. Mr. Auden would have fashioned this distich into a whole chorus.

Bunting's extreme concentration is not unconnected with an air of contrivance. Not that his verse is the null product of a will to turn out so many lines on a theme; it is the contrivance of a man who knows what it is he means to contrive. Word never suggests word, mood is never prolonged because a groove held it. On the other hand, one has only seldom the sense that—as with Pound or Yeats—the right words are miraculously presenting themselves instant by instant. This is only to say that Mr. Bunting isn't (and doesn't claim to be) a major poet. He has done a few things right; his superiors (whom at his best he isn't inferior to) did more things well, and weren't betrayed into publishing their attempts on subjects a little beyond their skill. Bunting's virtue is that he always knows what he wants to do; he does it so deliberately that one occasionally notices the hand reaching for the next tool. The beginning of the **''Villon''** monologue . . . is unnecessarily strained into patness: an attempt to crush the daisy-pickers who a page later are evaporated by the full heat of the poem. When the heat comes, however, the over-laboured irony of the opening not only suffers, it vanishes from the mind. . . . (pp. 363-64)

Mr. Bunting has learned from Pound, but gotten far beyond the early "*Personae*" at which most Poundlings stick. (His debt is rather to "*Cathay*" and "*Propertius*".) He has learned from W. C. Williams, and been sufficiently original to dissociate the assimilable techniques from the highly personal (and hence, to the imitator, far more tempting) astringencies. He has learned techniques where others have borrowed voices. His defects (occasional strain after a contrast; rhythm bogging while attention pauses on lexicographic concision) depend on virtues. He is alive to much more than the things he has read about, or the commonplaces which assume a spurious uniqueness when they happen at length to *me*.

Of these 54 pages some 5 may or should enter the *corpus poeticum;* a way of saying that Bunting's subjects and treatment have an interest outlasting the area in which they were conceived. (p. 365)

Hugh Kenner, "A Resurrected Poet: The Chisel," in Poetry, *Vol. LXXVIII, No. 6, September, 1951, pp. 361-65.*

THOMAS COLE

One coming on [***Poems, 1950***] for the first time may think it shows a disregard for form. But on reading closely one discovers that Mr. Bunting is more concerned with overall structure (i.e., as we use the word in music) than with stanzaic forms. The short poems do, as in the delicate odes, often have a stanzaic regularity. I suppose most of the poetry in this first collected edition was written during the Twenties when free verse was popular. Yet, this is a strong verse, never loose, never flat, never really free. The meter for an opening line is not necessarily the ground beat for a thorough reading, but always a marked rhythm is developed which is rich in a way that metrical regularity seldom is. As might be expected, it is only after a second reading that most of these poems open themselves to the reader and show an easy, fluent line, a bare beauty. This "bare" quality is the outcome of Bunting's concern with the concrete image, his clarity of thought, and his simplicity of language. These are qualities not unlike those of Pound's and Williams'.

There are at times abrupt modulations of subject matter in the longer poems, modulations akin perhaps to Joyce's latter work, or better, Eliot's *The Waste Land*. These occur notably in **"Villon," "Attis,"** and **"Aus Dem Zweiten Reich."** But overcoming such difficulties in Bunting's poetry one comes on the real merits. The . . . little poem (**"Ode 32"**) **"To Violet, with prewar poems,"** is an excellent example of Bunting's lyric quality. . . . Here rime is used to fine advantage, making one wish that Bunting had used it more often.

The detachment of the real critic and the concern with human values are evidenced in just about every poem, and especially in the long poem **"The Well of Lycopolis"** which concerns the latter day ruminations of

> Mother Venus, ageing, bedraggled, a
> half-quartern of gin under her shawl, . . .

This is a brilliant tour de force on age and memory. And there is Bunting's concern with the simple life as presented to us in **"Chomei at Toyama"** (another long poem). Here we have a 12th Century Japanese nobleman migrating to Toyama to live out his life amid the simplicities and beauties of nature. The poem contains much of Bunting's railing against the ultimate decadence which follows bad government and the over-crowded conditions in great capitals. It is surprising with what ease Bunting operates amid social ideas (which ideas I suspect have helped keep him out of the picture in English poetry these past thirty years). Bunting ironically parallels, with a double image, the decay and destruction of the ancient Japanese capital Kyoto with, prophetically, present-day New York City. Along with the **"Chomei"** poem there are such shorter "companion" poems as **"They Say Etna," "Gin the Goodwife Stint," "The Complaint of the Morpethshire Farmer"** and several of the Odes. Mr. Bunting in these poems presents the plight of the poor, the exploited farmer, the city worker of England as the result of the pitiful workings of politics. (pp. 366-67)

Bunting often reminds me of Pound. Both these poets have a deliberate, easy usage of the language. In particular, one can put Bunting's long narrative poem **"How Duke Valentine Contrived"** beside the early "Italian" Cantos, say VIII to XI. Each presents fragments from the 15th and 16th Centuries of Italian history and in similar styles and manners. I was very much taken with the beginning of part 4 of **"Villon."** Immediately I set it against the second stanza of part II of Eliot's *Ash Wednesday,* which opens: "Lady of silences / Calm and distressed / Torn and most whole . . ." Eliot, in his poem, speaks of a Christian "Lady" while Bunting develops the theme of another lady—Helen. There is a wonderful control of the lines in both these poems, and a great similarity in rhythms. . . .

Bunting's **"Ode 34"** is a poem which I might have expected from Yeats in his latter years. Bunting's poem might stand close scrutiny with "Lapis Lazuli" for temperament and language. (p. 368)

It is difficult to believe that the poetry of Basil Bunting has gone uncollected until this excellent edition appeared. Heretofore no one has had the opportunity to read him. I hope the situation will now be rectified, for Bunting's poetry can hold its own against any England has produced these past fifty years. (p. 369)

Thomas Cole, "Bunting: Formal Aspects," in Poetry, *Vol. LXXVIII, No. 6, September, 1951, pp. 366-69.*

CHARLES TOMLINSON

For too many years the work of Basil Bunting was unobtainable and now we have it in bulk, made available by the courage and perspicacity of two small publishers. . . . Mr. Bunting has made a few minor additions to [***Loquitur,*** a reprint of ***Poems, 1950***] and he has deleted what might be called the only downright bad piece from it, namely **"They Say Etna".** On the subject of ***Poems,*** Hugh Kenner once wrote: "Of these 54 pages some five may or should enter the corpus poeticum; a way of saying that Bunting's subjects and treatment have an interest outlasting the area in which they were conceived" [see excerpt above]. Certainly the best works and the best parts of them stand out a long way in ***Loquitur*** from those elegantly written pieces on tickling young ladies in the back of taxis. **"The Well of Lycopolis", "Chomei at Toyama", "Vestiges", "Let them remember Samangan", "The Orotava Road",** these are a few of the contexts where Bunting shows as a distinctly individual poet, where he makes good Kenner's claim that from Pound and Williams "he has learned techniques where others have borrowed voices". Pound's voice, however, certainly dogs him—even in **"Samangan"** usurers head the list of villainies and elsewhere Pound's presence overwhelms poet and reader. . . . (p. 11)

Bunting's art, like Zukofsky's, "aspires to a condition of music"—"accompanying tones of the words" that "are their own experience"—and in coming to **"The Spoils"** (1951) one sees time and again how the music achieved there was of the greatest possible transitional importance for the all-over musical structure of ***Briggflatts,*** published fourteen years later. In **"The Spoils"**, experience prepares the ground and music plays over against that ground. First there is the experience of semitic culture, the sons of Shem, Arab and Jew; in the second section, Persia, and finally a home-coming after the war to "Cold northern clear sea-gardens" . . . Experience confronts all with the fact of mortality—the spoils are God's. Music edges experience, a counterpoint with nature:

A fowler spreading his net
over the barley, calls,
calls on a rubber reed.
Grain nods in reply.

Such replies densen the musical structure of the later ***Briggflatts*** without hazing it, and we get a foretaste of the music of that poem when, at the climax of the second section of **"The Spoils"** Bunting puts before us a falcon, figuring his theme "Man's life so little worth / do we fear to take or lose it?". "The accompanying tones of the words", in Zukofsky's phrase, take on a new power of interlacing sounds. . . . (p. 13)

The music of ***Briggflatts*** lies not only in tones, rhyme, the articulations of syntax, but in the use throughout of recurrent motifs. A number of these—spring, bull, slowworm, a mason chiselling letters on a gravestone—are introduced at the opening in a landscape of space and time, and analogous with the entry of the various voices in a madrigal. . . . (p. 14)

The music Bunting refers to for his imagery (Byrd, Monteverdi, "Schoenberg's maze") suggests voice against voice, line against line—madrigal and canon, not impressionistic sound-painting. The achievement of the poem—and here one is reducing to abstraction all that is art and art's particulars—derives from the attempt to bring Then into as close a relation with Now as possible. The aligning of the two comes about by the central device of imitating "the condition of music". Then and Now are brought to bear upon each other as are the different voices in a madrigal. In the poem this cannot be done simultaneously; but, by juxtaposition, Now can be played over against Then as Then—summoned up by motif and left echoing in the mind—stands forth, counterpoised rather than counterpointed, against the ensuing motif of Now. And yet, in the beautiful image of the slowworm, simultaneity can be and is achieved, by a radical innocence that has persisted as a possibility in the poet's own mind:

light from the zenith
spun where the slowworm lay in her lap
fifty years ago

Then and Now: that incident of fifty years since and other incidents in Northumbrian history of a greater starkness, Eric Bloodaxe and Aneurin numbering over the dead, all now the spoils of time, are held over against the present moment and landscape, the quality of that wet spring night informing this present moment and demanding all the intricacy of musical form that Bunting brings to the confrontation. A prose example can perhaps best illustrate what the musical form of ***Briggflatts*** renders possible: "Music," writes J. Hillis Miller in *The Disappearance of God,*

> is the very model of a use of time to transcend time. It proceeds by repetition, with variation, echo, reverberation . . . Music constantly circles back on itself. Its aim is not to go in a straight line from place to place, but to achieve the most complete exploitation of its primitive germ. . . . The listener is diffused throughout the musical space and copresent to all parts of it at once and all these parts interpenetrate one another in the closest intimacy . . .

For "listener" read "reader" and for "primitive germ", "spring, slowworm and mason"—all elements of that musical "preparation" of which De Quincey speaks, "pregnant with the future". Words are not notes and the music of poetry, traceable in tones, rhyming, syntax, repeated motifs, implies analogy not identity with musical experience. To my own mind, Bunting is most successful in confronting Then and Now, when he uses incidents and motifs *as if* they were musical elements. He goes wrong—the fault is marginal but significant—when he brings to his aid an orchestra which one *cannot hear* and which cannot work as an analogy for comparable emotions in the poem because the sounds which he asks us to imagine in such a passage are extra-verbal and hence unachievable within the poem's acoustics:

Young flutes, harps touched by a breeze,
drums and horns escort
Aldebaran . . .

or

Great strings next the post of the harp
clang, the horn has majesty,
flutes flicker in the draft and flare . . .

The sentimentality of "young flutes" and the lameness of "the horn has majesty" are a poor substitute for a real horn and real flute tone: music must inhere for the poet in his verbal meshings not in "sounds off". And indeed, it is precisely in those verbal meshings, rhyme disposed in its time sequence counter-poising a Then and Now, that Bunting's "musical" successes come. (pp. 15-16)

From the measured quantities of ***Loquitur*** through the more intricate rhyme and line of ***The Spoils,*** Bunting has come, in his late poetry, to a music that combines strength and delicacy in patternings that to the reader are a constant delight and that to the young poet should prove of intense and liberating technical interest. Not least among the poem's achievements is the way an erotic incident that could have been sentimental or, in the manner of some of the ***Loquitur*** poems, trivial has been made as real for the reader as for the poet, realised, as it is, with a novelistic specificness. We can completely accept, for the purpose of the poem, his valuation of it, which is a measure of how far Bunting has come since "the teashop girls" of his earlier verses. (p. 17)

Charles Tomlinson, "Experience into Music: The Poetry of Basil Bunting," in Agenda, *Vol. 4, Nos. 5 & 6, Autumn, 1966, pp. 11-17.*

KENNETH COX

The most obvious characteristic of Mr Basil Bunting's verse is its compression of language. This characteristic is so consistent and at times so extreme that, whatever the intention or the instinct at its origin, it is likely to strike the reader as a practice fortified by long use and possibly buttressed by some theory. Given a knowledge of Mr Bunting's famous pun *dichten = condensare* he may then suppose the objective to be a simple quantitative brevity, such as is recommended in those manuals which tell you to prefer short words to long and never to use two if one will do. But Mr Bunting's condensation covers a number of different techniques as well as processes which can hardly be described as technical at all. There are, it is true, times when what is written appears to be the result of a mere saving of unnecessary words, such as we aim at in composing a telegram, or to have a curt and offhand manner. Traces of these idiosyncrasies persist throughout Mr Bunting's work but the method which gives his style its individual mark is not at all scrimping or casual. His aesthetic, his sense of the beautiful, does not depend on mechanical measurement, although the criterion of brevity may be used as others might use metre or consonance, to prompt revision and suggest improvements.

The foundation of the method is a close involution of the idea consisting in the use of phrases which are, as it were, knotted as tight as they can be yet are easily unloosed. It disdains any gradual leading up to the meaning or the fumbling which makes it necessary to qualify or supplement what has just been said. It is not concerned with progression, development or illustration: the meaning is given in full and at one go, in a quick and as far as possible inclusive shot. With this onceness there goes a paring away of inessential elements. In turning itself for the quickest presentation the idea drops the encumbrances of cliché and avoids the adventitious meanings which cling to it. The result, if successful, is clean, bare, limpid and perhaps a little awkward.

It may be desirable to add that the technique described does not require the meaning itself to be without nuance. There would be less merit in giving sharp expression to a crudity. It is the art of Mr Bunting to give succinct and accurate expression to firm, delicate and uncontaminated observations.

Sometimes the meaning is turned in such a way as to let it out in the gnomic forms typical of the most ancient poetry. . . . (p. 20)

The concept of the turn (tropos. trope) lies at the basis of syntax. It is not merely a matter of deciding the order of words or, as in the political rhetoric of antiquity, the figure of speech which will best ingratiate the speaker with his audience. Presentation, in the obstetric sense of the term, is nevertheless its object. On which way up or which end first the writer presents his idea will depend the immediacy and the accuracy of its impact and the amount of delay in any delayed action he may have deliberately intended. The possibilities are numerous and the choice may be difficult. (p. 21)

[It is apparent] from many instances in the history of literature, that the introduction of new tropes or the restoration of old ones is not a mere social or linguistic trick but the result of a reliving of ideas, sometimes agitated and prolonged, whose effect is to make the tropes already established look rhetorical and ridiculous. In presenting himself to the world through the medium of a language renewed in this way a writer compels himself to examine himself and cannot, it seems (the mechanism is obscure), perform the operation of stripping and reassembly without some moral discipline. There emerges in the end not only a spareness but also a purity of line.

Another method of attaining concentration of meaning, supplementing work on the fabric of the phrase, is the narrative or dramatic method, consisting in the clever selection and arrangement of what comes before. So prepared, a few words possibly unremarkable by themselves accumulate a charge which can shock. The principle will be familiar from Ibsen and the sagas.

If there is, as W. P. Ker thought he could discern at the origins of Old Norse and Old English verse, a basic difference between their movements and systems, then it is from what he called the Norse that Mr Bunting's verse derives. Its continuous single-stroke movement promotes pointed observation and epigrammatic vehemence, in contrast to the longer line or couplet of the so-called English tradition which, by favouring the introduction of a second element, promotes balance, modification and antithesis. Unless singularly adapted to the matter, for instance in drama or argumentation, the second element is liable to duplicate or weaken whatever is in the first. So Pasternak found the power of expressing reality heightened by shortening the lines, not so much to develop any specific quality they contained as to escape the tyranny of a humdrum metre.

Whether or not this is a typically northern process, there is to be seen in the spareness and purity of Mr Bunting's line, especially manifest in his earlier work, the tempered and taciturn spirit of the border ballads. His compression of language can be regarded as a compression of emotion, as of speech through compressed lips. Such speech not only rejects fripperies, it keeps as close as it can to the feeling which generated it and to the object it describes. (pp. 21-2)

For all its artistry the poetry of Mr Bunting stays, in the stark tradition he adorns, close to the state of inarticulateness. Such a state may arise from concentration, passion, madness, sleep or even stupidity: any of these can turn into a matrix of poetry, because free of sophistry. The resulting speech utters what has only just escaped being unspoken, almost as if speech were painful or inappropriate to the circumstances, and it bursts under strong pressure but strict control into the nearest expression capable of speedy termination. (pp. 22-3)

The re-emergence of this tradition may be of interest to those critics who stress Mr Bunting's acknowledged obligations to Ezra Pound and who ask to what extent and in what manner the example of the American master can be assimilated to a native heritage. A poetry which remains close to the state it describes gives rise to certain difficulties. How far can the close expression of reality be freed from the feeling of disgust? And what elements of colloquial speech is it possible to reproduce? It is also a disadvantage of the method that, with a rendering so close to the subject, firsthand knowledge of the object may be needed to appreciate the fidelity of the rendering. Who, who does not remember Churchill or see old newsreels, will get the picture of him *clowning with a cigar*?

One of the paradoxes of the situation is that a direct transcription of the vernacular easily looks false. Mr Bunting's Cockney imitation of Villon rings untrue. It is hard to say why: it seems that the feel of living speech comes through only when some of the subtlest elements of movement and intonation join in a meeting governed by rare and unpredictable conditions, similar to those which govern the evanescent existence of the elementary particles, and that these conditions commonly escape the meshes of the grammarian's net, fine as these are now. The prestige of Wordsworth's theory [expounded in the preface to the second edition of *Lyrical Ballads*], the political movement of which it is part and our modern interest in radio and the tape-recorder may temporarily have obscured the truth that even the colloquial style is acquired *by sedentary toil / and by the imitation of great masters*. The real, it seems, is not to be won by direct assault but is to be wooed with humility and display. It is demonstrable that the most authentic achievements of colloquial utterance usually crown a lifelong exercise in revision, imitation and translation. (pp. 23-4)

Few of Mr Bunting's rhythms depart from the limits ordinarily set by the internal movements of the human body—systole and diastole of the heart, expansion and contraction of the lungs—which set the norms for expression of the emotions. But there is also to be found in his verse a slower movement keeping time not with the movements or gait of the body but with the longer stronger motion of the sea. When drained of feeling or evoking a reality outside human life it is to this movement, as to a prenatal source, that his verse returns, for example in the coda to ***Briggflatts.***

It may be doubted whether anyone can really (without losing his personality) step outside his own personal rhythms, whatever the nationality of the vocabulary he may temporarily employ. Mr Bunting's rhythms offer great variety within a small compass: the delights of perfect freedom of movement are difficult to combine with the satisfactions of remaining close to earth. His verbal concentration also precludes certain auditory effects. Although it may be lightened by playfulness, his verse is occasionally also clogged by the ornament the Arabs call *jinas,* correspondence of consonants without correspondence of meaning. (It differs from the *cynghanedd* of Welsh poetry in that it does not constitute an organic part of the structure of the verse but only knits it closer together.) In an example like

Fear of being imputed
naive impeded thought

the idea is not only in-turned but in-grown and a surgical operation is needed to release it.

After economy the next most notable characteristic of Mr Bunting's verse is risk. The omission of intervening or supporting structures exhibits both characteristics, while his choice of words tends towards the slightly unexpected. Part of this tendency is due to the continuous process of expelling poetic diction. The direction of his choice is towards the more familiar and the more sensuous word: ramparts no longer *hug* a town, they *cuddle* it. The constant undercutting of his expectations may excite in the reader a pleasure continually reactivated and mingled with a suppressed apprehension. When he sees that an exercise of skill and daring has been successfully performed his pleasure is complicated by relief that the danger has been avoided and by amusement that it could ever have been overestimated. Out of a number of such slight deviations the style achieves at its best a new coherence regulated by an appropriate movement. . . . The phrases succeed one another easily, without hurry or slip, with *never a boast or a see-here,* but with extraordinary marksmanship. Though bare of ornament the diction is rich by virtue of economy and enterprise; what may be called its specific gravity must be one of the highest in English. This is the accomplishment of *Mauberley,* poetry of the second order but the finest quality.

The felicity of the descriptions shows that the focus of interest is an observation half created, half acutely perceived and exactly recorded. The fascination exercised by some incidental aspect of the physical world constitutes the tenuous but unexpectedly solid foundation of the art. We know how such perceptions obsess the attention and govern the appetites, without understanding how they operate. Those of ***The Spoils*** are principally visual, those of ***Briggflatts*** aural, but both convey a perception of total grace not easily communicable by means other than verbal, unless the essential force of these percepts may be reduced to the equation of a curve.

Mr Bunting's verse is not only concerned with *the angle a slut's blouse / draws on her chest*. . . . [It] also honours those who themselves acknowledge and manage these perceptions. From the girl with *delicate ignorant face (preoccupied rather / by the set of her stockings)* it goes on to celebrate a Persian miniature painter, Italian fiddler, Cumbrian dog-trainer. This cultivation of the senses has two extraneous consequences of some importance. First, by progressively increasing the definition of the verbal record, the expression of observation drives the language to its primal resources, till it draws upon the qualities which bind words to things. Secondly, by monopolising the mind these observations act as a preservative against propaganda of all persuasions and so make possible the commemoration of innocence achieved in the first section of ***Briggflatts.***

The problem is to fit the bits together. Some of Mr Bunting's longer poems look like tesserae or catenae of particulars. ***Briggflatts*** arranges them in patterns copying musical forms. To both matter and pattern the world, both animate and inanimate, created and manufactured, is made to contribute. From its opening line (*Brag, sweet tenor bull*) the poem plays on the whole realm of sound, inarticulate but not inexpressive, and on the gesture related to it by rhythm, harmonising the units into a chorus of selfpraise. . . . In one sequence the movements of nature are expressly related to the work of certain musicians. This is the Orphic interpretation of the earth which René Ghil attempted.

The underlying themes of Mr Bunting's poetry are not easily brought to the surface because the volume of his preserved work is small and sudden perfections discourage thematic analysis. Certain deductions may be permitted. In its description of the external world much of his writing is concerned with appearances of desolation: the deserts of the Middle East, the borderlands of northern England, the Paris of Villon, the thirties, the sea. In these settings man comes close to facing the conditions beyond which life is not possible. . . . If he survives he can say with the quiet arrogance of the bedouin: *What's to dismay us?* The impoverishment of the actual world stems the flow of the verses, reducing them to a pure trickle of which every drop is to be valued. Economy, the free use of few resources, is seen to be another aspect of the same concern, thematic as well as technical.

By another of the correspondences one comes to expect the idea of risk also appears thematically, most clearly in ***The Spoils.*** The dominant theme of this poem is that of opposition between the calculating and the reckless. The calculator (moneylender, administrator, policeman) imposes arbitrary rule and measure; the reckless (singer, soldier, seaman) gives without counting. The difference between them is determined by the presence of death. The calculator works to an end beyond the scope of an individual lifespan, but it is the risk of death that gives zest to life: without death life is not worth living. This bourgeois-romantic dichotomy is counterpointed by a secondary opposition running in the contrary direction. In spite of the care and precision of their operations the art of the calculating is rhetorical and false: *Roman exaggeration and the leaden mind of Egypt*. But the art of the gay in the shadow of death is cool and fine: it is by taking risks that we preserve proportion. The thesis is illustrated by reference to Persia and the second world war.

Briggflatts, somewhat unfairly, makes Mr Bunting's earlier poetry look like preparatory work. Its subject is repossession after long absence: *Heureux qui comme Ulysse* . . . It returns to the north country with English both purified and enriched, the past and its studies absorbed. Here and there is a southern warmth, an eastern courtesy, the skill of a Latin poet in placing a long word, the audacious finality of Dante:

One
plucked fruit warm from the arse
of his companion, who
seeking to beat him, he screamed

But in general the debts are present only as harmonics. Yet it is the long practice of the translator, the persistent testing of every word, which has probably made possible the unfailing discretion with which the life and appearance of the country is represented without trace of provincialism or lapse into the banal. In addition to romantic theory and symbolist technique it infuses into the native tradition the sensuality of oriental poetry and attains, not by imitation but by a revival of its primitive elements, the standard of the King James version of the Old Testament. . . . (pp. 24-8)

Skills and accidents by which we make contact with poets distant and past, or by which we seem to establish a relation with the non-human world, convince us that in cultivating the art we are not just playing with words, toys of our own invention, but that we do indeed perform, in ways we cannot understand but know for sure, parts in a rite able to dignify and perpetuate our common life. It may also be allowed that in obeying its laws we do a little to appease the dead. The achievement of Mr Bunting is to have demonstrated yet again and by concrete example the classic conclusion of his early poem:

"The Emperor with the Golden Hands"

is still a word, a tint, a tone,
insubstantial-glorious,
when we ourselves are dead and gone
and the green grass growing over us.

(p. 28)

Kenneth Cox, "The Aesthetic of Basil Bunting," in Agenda, *Vol. 4, Nos. 5 & 6, Autumn, 1966, pp. 20-8.*

THOMAS CLARK

With one or two minor changes [***Loquitur***] consists of a republication of Bunting's ***Poems 1950,*** which has been out of print for some time and is very hard to get hold of: I left a borrowed copy of the earlier book on a London bus in 1963 and later learned the copy had been sold in a used-books shop for $75! (p. 110)

[In] Bunting's poetry generally the real accuracy of the senses that brings about (for me) such a sharp and immediate sense of reality isn't visual but rather the "picturings" of auditory and tactile experience. . . . But what turns this skill into *poems* is a true and articulate discourse or "voice"—the spoken elaboration of syntactical ideas.

A great and (at its best—as in **"Villon"**) simple dignity in the placement of words provides an equal light and clarity in Bunting's poems—the consummation and creation of experience as language is so complete that the central personality is reduced to a transparency through which the action of the words can be seen. I think it's for this reason that the narrative passages (especially in Bunting's adaptation of Machiavelli in **"How Duke Valentine Contrived"**) have an amazing directness, the events allowed to stand clear and describe themselves. A similar ability to withdraw before the *self*-disclosure of a given subject matter occurs in Bunting's Northumbrian dialect poems like **"Gin the Goodwife Stint."** Here there's a real "transference" of emotion in disposing the words so as to let a content of feeling implied in the situation appear. Like Pound's Bunting's expertise as a translator comes not from an acquired style but from a natural insight into the emotional structures of other men.

And so it's not only influence (there's that too) that makes Pound's voice audible in ***Loquitur.*** These great, sad poems aren't ever cranky or self-pitying—there's too great an equivalence of tone for that—and the pessimism of many of Bunting's works is really what used to be called realism. . . . The similarity to Pound in Bunting's works is less a matter of technique than of attitude, a toughness of regard that makes possible the expression of bitterness as a description of realities and not simply as a complaint. And in the end the two poets differ very much—beauty is perceived in Pound's work both as immediate ecstasy and as regret, in Bunting's only as the latter. That he hasn't this vision of majesty doesn't *only* make his work more "modest"—there's a great concentration, yielding actual wisdom, but always as product of attention:

The sea has no renewal, no forgetting,
no variety of death,
is silent with the silence of a single note.

(**"Villon"**)

This goes right to the core, the seriousness that is Bunting's distinction of feeling and intelligence. The first time I read this book I was shaken, without knowing anything more about Bunting than a few biographical facts concerning his relation with Pound. Today, copying out some words to include them in this review I was as struck by their integrity as I was on first reading. The poetry here is permanent—it's a really important publication. (pp. 110-12)

Thomas Clark, "New Lines," in Poetry, *Vol. CIX, No. 2, November, 1966, pp. 110-12.*

RICHARD HOWARD

[***The Spoils***] offers precisely the discriminating welter of whining sensuality ("Condole me with abundance of secret pleasure") we like to associate with those Moslem epicureans so attractive to English poets since Fitzgerald. . . . [***The Spoils***] is like the best of the *Cantos,* or anyway the prettiest: Turkish delight, and indigestible without something more fibrous along the way. In 1951 fiber evidently still meant the anti-Roosevelt line Pound had been following since the thirties (Bunting appears in the *Active Anthology,* 1933), and some of ***The Spoils*** is spoiled by the shrill "bastard-Roosevelt" invective that waters down to paranoia: "counsellors of patience / lie in wait for blood, / every man with a net." Zukofsky quotes in his *Test of Poetry* eighteen perfect hexameters of Bunting's, an imitation of Lucretius which closes:

. . . Alma Venus! Trim my poetry
With your grace; and give peace to write and read and
think.

The peace was given, apparently, in the Middle East, where Bunting translated Firdusi and dropped out of sight. Early last year, of course, *Poetry* published his masterpiece, ***Briggflatts,*** in which Pound's music has been fused with the kind of understanding which surpasses peace, giving us the Northumbrian fantasia on themes of king-killing and masonry-as-meaning which enclose their own magisterial poetic:

Flexible, unrepetitive line
to sing, not paint; sing, sing,
laying the tune on the air . . .

Briggflatts suggests an alternative convention of prosody, one afforded by "modernists" as centrifugal as Perse and David Jones and, taken with the best parts of ***The Spoils*** (over 400 lines), proves Pound to have been quite right, again, about the man to whom he wrote in 1936: "The poet's job is to *define* and yet again define till the detail of surface is in accord with the root in justice." Thirty years later, we can see what he meant. (pp. 196-97)

Richard Howard, in a review of "The Spoils," in Poetry, *Vol. CX, No. 3, June, 1967, pp. 196-97.*

HUGH KENNER

Basil Bunting's ***Briggflatts*** [is] a celebration by a Northumbrian poet in his sixties of a Northumbrian village with just four houses: which village denotes origins, all that roots mean, all that can be returned to, all that can neither be returned to nor forgotten.

The short harsh words (have thirty pages ever exhibited so many monosyllables?) are a stark speech reaching back to Eric Bloodaxe; lovingly heard, lovingly set into lines ("laying the tune frankly on the air"), they make a wiry texture of sound, utterly new, that comes with the authority of some lost tradition. . . .

We are meant . . . to pay attention to the aural identities of simple words, of many such words at once. The patterning of sound is a homage to the words, an affection for the words, an eliciting of their sound on a northern tongue. . . . (p. 1217)

Mr. Bunting has spoken of ***Briggflatts*** as the culmination of a long effort to shape something fit to exist in the same universe with Scarlatti's sonatas, and just past its mid-point the poem incorporates an explicit homage. . . . It's a consonantal music, as Scarlatti's is a music of plucked strings. A word's identity is in its pattern of consonants, as the telephone book demonstrates by abbreviating plmbr, bookpr. A Tennysonian fulsomeness with vowels, on the other hand, affronts, blurs, swamps, melts, conceals the words; submerges them in modulated sound; deplores consonants and cannot abide sibilants; wishes English were a dialect of Italian.

Bunting's celebrations of identity, each word audibly, lexicographically, the word it is, are continuous with his theme, the identity of a village in time, of a language persisting in time; the identity of the man who returns, despite all he has undergone, with the man who left. With years in France and in Italy and at sea and in Persia marking his mind and his body, it is still to the English monosyllable as to a tonic that his speech returns. . . .

If there's a hope just now for English poetry—poetry written in England—it's here, in this return to actual plain speech (not "simplicity": Bunting isn't an easy poet). . . .

It is Bunting's unique distinction that he has opened, in his seventh decade, a new career, after being in his forties the most accomplished school-of-Pound poet alive. It's ultimately Pound's lesson he is now rethinking in local conditions, the speech of the places of his boyhood, the here-and-now he spent a lifetime leaving behind him: the lesson of the exact, the local, the word that names, the thing that is what it is. There is more to be learned about poetry from ***Briggflatts*** than from most anthologies. (p. 1218)

Hugh Kenner, "Never a Boast or a See-Here," in National Review, *New York, Vol. XIX, No. 43, October 31, 1967, pp. 1217-18.*

THOMAS LASK

If the English poet Basil Bunting is better known to poets than to the public, there are reasons. For one, there hasn't been much of his verse around. [***Collected Poems***] numbers only 160 pages, but it represents work going back more than 40 years. The earliest poems are marked 1924. Nor has he appeared frequently in book form. Though he has seven titles to his credit, the last three, ***Loquitur, Briggflatts,*** and ***Collected Poems,*** were published in the last four years.

The situation is not because of a faltering muse. The poetry suggests that as much was thrown away as was kept. **"Ode II,"** uncharacteristically fierce with anger, berates a compliant colleague, saying, "my numerous cancellations prefer / slow limpness in the damp dustbins amongst the peel / tobacco-ash and ends" to "one review-rid month's printed ignominy / the public detection of your decay that reeks." And of a lady who has his prewar poems, he asks that she "count the sharp study and the long toil" for "this unread memento be / the only lasting part of me."

But scarcity is not the only reason for Mr. Bunting's limited public. His work is compact and tight, with frequent cryptic allusions not easily grasped the first time round, and with a mind-jumping imagination that makes unusual associations between ages, people and events. These are more obvious to him than to the reader at least on first meeting. In a long and dense poem, they are qualities that act as a brake on the understanding. But they can also be explosively illuminating. One poem tells of an ordinary girl, with a "delicate, ignorant face," whose life is slipping away:

Men are timid,
hotels expensive,
the police keep
a sharp eye on landladies.

In the final stanza the poet reminds his friend, Postumus, that in the same situation years ago, they used the cinema. But with the repetition of his friend's name, the reader is carried back to Horace's ode on the fleeing years. The reference not only underlines the poet's own aging, but the girl's anguish as she feels the years slipping away fruitlessly before her.

This ability of encompassing past and present is seen also in the wonderfully shaped and worked out poem, ***Briggflatts.*** It is a kind of autobiography that identifies with Northumberland legends, names, language, usage and myths. Another major poem, a version or an "imitation" of the work of a 12th-century Japanese poet, Kamo-no-Chomei, is not an exercise in Orientalia but a modern poem throughout. In the foreword, Mr. Bunting acknowledges a strong debt to Ezra Pound. He could scarcely hide it. . . . But he has moved away from this earlier manner. Now the lines are hard, spare and weighted. The beat is almost reminiscent of Anglo-Saxon verse. Alliteration, inner rhyme, controlled vowel effects, carefully manipulated musical values combine to make a poetry that is always technically fresh and challenging. . . . Mr. Bunting will be a pleasure to all who cherish the craft of verse. His is not the kind of poetry that wears away with a single reading.

Thomas Lask, "Each in His Own Voice," in The New York Times, *March 8, 1969, p. 27.*

ROGER GUEDALLA

Basil Bunting is primarily known as the author of the long poem ***Briggflatts,*** and as one of the two poets whom Ezra Pound celebrated as "strugglers in the wilderness" in the dedication of *Guide to Kulchur* in 1938. . . . For most of us [***Collected Poems***] provides our first comprehensive image of his work. It places ***Briggflatts*** in its true context as one of six long poems entitled "sonatas" and modeled on the musical form. The book also confirms Bunting as a poet who has worked all his life in two areas absolutely central to the development of 20th-century poetry. Pound's admonition, succinctly stated in the phrase "make it new," describes the concern of many modern poets, including Bunting, to refashion the past in terms of the present and to reaffirm the immediacy of past poetry in a contemporary context. Also, Bunting's use of the baroque sonata form as a structural model is comparable to Pound's and Zukofsky's use of the fugue, Yeats's use of the song cycle, and Eliot's "Preludes" and *Four Quartets*. Those poets were attempting to confirm what Renaissance poets knew: that there must be a close link between music and poetry. (p. 216)

In keeping with Bunting's varied life, his study of literature is eclectic—and highly idiosyncratic. The ear can detect in his poem the presence of Spenser, Villon, Dante, Whitman, Wordsworth and Mallarmé, as well as Pound. Yet Bunting, insofar as he is read and talked about, is almost always referred to simply as a Poundian. Pound's influence is clear, especially in the early poems, and Bunting received Pound's kindness and support in his youth, as did so many other poets. One does not so much need to play down Pound's influence as to put it in perspective and note, for example, that Bunting's use of alliteration and hard, compressed consonants derives as much from his independent reading of Anglo-Saxon as it does from his reading of Pound. The ***Collected Poems*** contains translations from Horace, Lucretius, Catullus, Firdosi, Rudaki, Sa'di, Manuchehri and Machiavelli. Other poems contain borrowings from earlier poets indicated by quotation marks and sometimes by footnotes as tantalizing as "parodies of Cino da Pistoia and Lucretius can do no damage and intend no disrespect," or, "the long quotations from Villon and Dante will of course be recognized." Still other poems incorporate material from other authors with only the most oblique indication. It is enough, for Bunting's purposes, that the reader be aware that he is "making it new." One recalls the stricture in ***Briggflatts,*** "follow the clue patiently and you will discover nothing." Bunting not only enjoys teasing scholars but also wishes to emphasize that the poem is a made object that stands on its own, uncluttered by notions of meaning that depend on an accumulation of dubiously relevant facts. His idea of poetry, deriving from his knowledge of music, has at its base a concept of multiplicity that specifically differentiates poetry from prose.

The musical model which was to provide him with a structural basis was the baroque sonata. The form is essentially simple, and it is capable of sustaining seemingly endless complexities in the hands of a skillful practitioner. Its inherent requirement of at least two voices, themes, or keys, which are stated, contrasted, developed, mixed, and eventually reconciled, provides an appropriate vehicle for the kind of literature Bunting believes poetry to be. (pp. 216-17)

Another element which depends as much on musical as on literary principles is Bunting's love of the sound of words, especially brief words in thick tongue-twisting groups that almost defy articulation and demand close attention to every syllable. . . . His admiration for Scarlatti, Corelli, Monteverdi, Vivaldi and other baroque composers lent impetus to his quest for tense precision. This expresses itself in his poetry in a variety of ways including his use of compressed epigrammatical, almost gnomic phrases:

> It is easier to die than to remember . . .

often containing marvelous puns:

> Every birth a crime,
> Every sentence life.

But, whatever his experiences and readings may incorporate, they come together in the fashioning of what is really important: the poem.

Above all, the poem is conceived as a made thing, an object created with the care of a craftsman doing an essential job of work. Bunting denies the commonplace distinction made between artists and craftsmen. For him a poem is a finely wrought object; the better the poet's technical equipment the better the poem will be. Bunting has kept sixty-four of his poems for inclusion in the ***Collected Poems.*** He has discarded about six early poems and published two or three since the book appeared. Not a large output for a lifetime devoted to poetry that began fifty years ago and includes publication in Zukofsky's *Objectivist Anthology* and Pound's *Active Anthology* and *Profiles*. Bunting pares his work down, discarding and cutting poems for the sake not only of brevity but also of concision and precision. ***Briggflatts*** was originally 15,000 lines long, but there are only 700 lines in the published version. As he says in that poem,

> Brief words are hard to find
> shapes to carve and discard.

Bunting traveled too much and stayed away from universities for too long to be limited by a single school or group of poets. He defies classification, and his contribution to English poetry is unique. But his very independence seems to limit his reputation, much to the frustration of his admirers. Certainly many contemporary poets and critics have written well of him. . . . If the function of poetry is, in Bunting's words, to "stretch the limits language sets to thought, to make other thoughts available, to make what was vague precise, what was unknowable knowable," then the sixty-four poems in this book demonstrate the full realization of that function. (pp. 217-18)

Roger Guedalla, "Struggler in the Wilderness," in The Nation, *New York, Vol. 212, No. 7, February 15, 1971, pp. 216-18.*

KARL MULLER

Precise images, closeness to spoken language, musical rhythm and free verse became essential to Bunting's theory and practice through the influence of Pound. With these aims in mind, Bunting developed a linguistic concept of his own in order to achieve clarity and concreteness in the presentation of experience. These notions arose from an investigation of language as a system and of constituents which go unnoticed and are thus responsible for imprecise and abstract words and sentences. (p. 16)

Pound's most obvious advice to Bunting was to acquire a style and message of his own by means of translation and imitation. Thus **"Villon," "Attis: or, Something Missing," "The Well of Lycopolis,"** and **"Chomei at Toyama"** emerged in substance and in language from underlying texts. These long poems can be regarded as constructions of translations, adaptations and quotations from authors such as Catullus, Villon, Dante or Milton, mingled with genuine passages from Bunting. As in Pound's poems, the thematic coherence of images and ideas is not ensured by linear formation and conventional consistency, but by contrast, variation and repetition, justifying the structural label "sonata" for six of his long poems.

Bunting's adaptation of Villon's poetry had its roots in Pound's imagistic claim that poetry should render particulars exactly and not deal in vague generalities, and T. E. Hulme's dictum that the great aim is accurate, precise and definite description. Villon served Pound and Bunting as a model from literary history to achieve these goals because, "Villon has the stubborn persistency of one whose gaze cannot be deflected from the actual fact before him: what he sees, he writes." (pp. 16-17)

The blending of several impressions which form a visual chord as in Hulme's "Above the Dock" or in Pound's famous "In a Station of the Metro" have little relevance for Bunting. One reason for the minor importance of this use of imagery to Bunting was the fact that it was in practice mostly connected with the short poem, which he was not willing to write, as his derogatory remark of 1932 reveals: "Everybody looks for polished versification on the first imagistic model." Bunting wanted to present whole situations which were too complex to be framed in interrelated images. To achieve this aim without sacrificing the imagistic principle of clear presentation, he also emphasized Pound's comparison of poetry with good prose as a second principle of Imagism which had been neglected by Hulme. While the latter feared the danger of abstraction in prose, Pound held that concreteness and directness could be learnt by shortening and condensing long narrative texts. (p. 17)

Concern about economy of language and brevity of treatment led Bunting to a closer inspection of the relation between words and objects. He expressed his ideas about an efficient language which realizes the principles of exactness and clarity of presentation in the article **"Some Limitations of English"** in 1932. Such linguistic questioning was again initiated and influenced by Pound and his coined "logopoeia," poetry that emphasizes nothing but language, and by Ernest Fenollosa's "Essay on the Chinese Written Character," to which Bunting refers. Pound himself valued Fenollosa highly, because the latter "seems to have convinced [him] that if he will recognize the true verbal basis of language, we can write a poetry that will attain the desired closeness to nature".

But Bunting's observations gain actuality because he refers to Ludwig Wittgenstein's *Tractatus* and adopts the principal ideas that the restrictions of thinking reflect those of language, which in turn determine the immediacy of things rendered. Under this premise the imagistic goal of precision and directness presents itself as a problem about the linguistic restrictions and requirements which structure the reproduction of actions and things in language. (p. 19)

[Bunting's] condensation by means of a strict linguistic economy was derived from imagistic precepts. The importance of Bunting's own contribution lies in the fact that he has explored the imagistic goal of immediate presentation at the level of syntax. His awareness of the complexity of language has led to an attempt at strengthening the referential force by deletion of primarily functional words and the avoidance of oblique constructions. Thus Bunting has identified himself in theory and practice with the aim of a regeneration of language from the weak and abstract constructions into which the poetry of the 19th century had fallen. By shifting from images to language as a system, he has overcome imagistic weakness in structure and thematic scope. Although this development was not independent of Pound's influence, Bunting has gained a voice of his own. His later long poems ***The Spoils*** and ***Briggflatts*** have a stronger coherence than Pound's *Cantos* and treat a subject matter which is free from the influence of his master. (pp. 23-4)

Karl Muller, "Basil Bunting's Linguistic Poetics," in Forum for Modern Language Studies, *Vol. XIII, No. 1, January, 1977, pp. 16-24.*

ROLAND JOHN

[Basil Bunting] is a hard man to place, as it would be possible to discuss him in the company of others and this is a mistake, as Bunting has made a unique contribution to English poetry. The vogue for poetry readings brought his poetry to a wider audience and it would be easy to include him in that strange crowd, who made 'reputations' as platform performers. He has said, "Poetry, like music, is to be heard" and "Poetry lies dead on the page, until some voice brings it to life, just as music on the stave is no more than instructions to the player." In Bunting's case the musical voice and Northumberland accent added to his reading. It would be unfair not to include him with the modern movement, his name is not out of place with Pound and Eliot, or again it would be reasonable to list him as a regional poet—doing a MacDiarmid for the North of England, his gruff remarks about the South are reminiscent of MacDiarmid's grumblings. Then there is the obvious American connection, Zukofsky, Duncan and Olson. Although it would be possible to add him to any of the above groups, somehow he doesn't quite fit. He is far more than a regional poet and far too English to be lost amongst Objectivists and their followers and his control keeps him away from the loose verse makers of the diluted Pound sort.

That he has benefited from many sources is true; but it has never been a simple imitation, he has assimilated the lessons from the bulk of English poetry, learned from Pound and Zukofsky and added an edge, a tone and sensibility of his own. A tone peculiarly English, traditional, yet augmented with a *foreignness,* that gives a sharpness—learned no doubt, as in Pound, by careful study of the best models in other languages and by translation.

Like Pound, Bunting can use the technique of the *persona* and the past to produce poems like **"Chomei at Toyama,"** a poem in which Bunting thinking as Kamo-no-Chomei turns Chomei's prose Ho-Jo-Ki into a kind of elegiac poem, suggesting that this was Chomei's true intention. It is interesting to note that Bunting did not work from the original; but used an Italian version as his source, a typical modern distancing technique. . . . This is more than a translation, or reworking; in this poem Bunting has actually attempted to be Chomei and finish a work, that the writer never had time to turn into a poem. (pp. 101-02)

Unlike many of the moderns, Bunting has a full humour, often expressed in short, witty poems; one of the best examples is **"The Passport Officer."** . . . The poem has a hardness and is straight to the point; but unlike so many others, Bunting does not moralise, nor overwork his theme.

In all his poems, and translations there is this exactness. Perhaps it is this quiet mastery of forms, that makes critics ignore him. He is not part of a school, nor can he be used as a measuring rod for other writers and this makes him of little use to comparison makers. It is time that we accepted Bunting as unique, someone who has taken the best materials, invented some of his own and worked them into a poetry of high standard. There is not a published poem that fails to interest; his output is small, but consistently excellent, again hard for critics to compare one period of work with another. It is this consistency that allows his critical neglect. He is certainly part of the modern movement; but his suppression kept him from most of us and we had to wait until 1968 to read any great quantity and so some of the surprise of his forms was removed, we had become used to them: but the dates of the poems should not be overlooked and they put Bunting amongst the inventors of the new.

Thus we have a highly individual poet, writing with clarity an erudite verse; but a verse that does not demand a specialised knowledge from the reader—unlike some of his contemporaries—his references, when unknown are traceable, or explained in notes. He is successful in getting us to understand immediately, his special knowledge of history and place does not stand in the way of the poem's meaning, nor is it there just for effect. He does not browbeat us with philosophical, religious or economic dogma, his poems tell—and above all entertain. Bunting's plea is for and to the civilised; but there are no barriers and anyone can enter into his poetry. There is something of the renaissance man in him, wide learning, knowledge of languages, particular historical periods, geography, optics, even astronomy. (pp. 103-04)

A traveller who has brought back spoils and given us some of this knowledge, in a direct, clear way. For the erudite, parodies, quotes, translations, references to other poets and poems can be discerned giving another level to his work. Always a disciplined metric, but never merely mechanical, nor brutish, there are personal statements and a concern for civilisation, even though this concern is often covered by an arrogance. Bunting expects more from civilization and our shortcomings and frailties annoy.

We have then an expert, a master craftsman, a witty translator and explainer, a poet whose rhythms move towards music and with all these talents it is hard to see why Bunting is not a major poet. Admittedly the output is small; but there are splendid long poems like ***The Spoils*** and ***Briggflatts,*** so often the mark of a major poet. I believe that he fails due to his lack of didacticism, he does not preach nor demand disciples, he has founded no school. (pp. 104-05)

For too long we have avoided Bunting's poems, they are some of the best that this century has produced; but because of their lack of a philosophy they keep the role of major poet from him. However he is more than just a minor poet, once again this difficult man refuses to be assigned a stereotyped position.

We must be content to acknowledge him as an unique talent, who has constantly produced, and still is producing poetry of an extraordinarily high standard and who has brought back to poetry the pleasure of reading. The sadness is that that this excellence was kept from us for so long and that it was left to magazines and smaller publishers to print him. I do not know the reasons for his suppression, but I am aware that it was a serious disservice to English poetry. It is time that we had a serious critical assessment of this unique and very English poet. (p. 105)

Roland John, "Basil Bunting: A Note," in Agenda, *Vol. 16, No. 1, Spring, 1978, pp. 101-05.*

BEN HOWARD

After decades of neglect, the poetry of Basil Bunting is now enjoying extraordinary acclaim. . . . Bunting, a disciple of Pound and a survivor of the modernist period, brings to contemporary poetry qualities that have now become rare, such as polyglot allusiveness, wide geographical reference, and a deep awareness of European history and culture. But for this reader, at least, Bunting's appeal lies less in his modernist complexities than in his moral weight, his timeless felicities of style, and his gift for combining elements usually found apart. Bunting has the power to integrate such disparate materials as Northumbrian history and Greek myth, local dialect and Latin mottoes, colloquial speech and allusions to ancient Persian tales. And of all these fusions, none is more striking or more central than Bunting's peculiar blend of realism and lyric intensity. At their extremes Bunting's bitter realism turns to satire and his lyricism to pure song, as though his voice were the issue of Swift and Keats, or Juvenal and Wordsworth. To his subjects, as to the sea, he has come "with teeming sweetness to the bitter shore." (p. 169)

The severity and directness of Bunting's view of life are reflected in his art. His slim, superb ***Collected Poems*** gathers the work of a lifetime, beginning with the celebrated **"Villon,"** an ambitious monologue written when the poet was twenty-five, and ending with a short meditative lyric entitled **"At Briggflatts meeting house,"** which returns Bunting, after residence on four continents, to the Quaker hamlet in Northumberland where he spent his earliest years. Between these two points lie the residues of nearly five decades: fifty-odd poems, grouped as "Sonatas" and numbered "Odes." For the most part, the odes are pithy free-verse lyrics, by turns satirical and elegiac, whimsical and harsh, abrasive and tender. By contrast, the sonatas are ambitious compositions in several movements, employing personae as diverse as Villon, Venus, and a Twelfth Century Japanese poet named Chomei. Through all the changes of tone, scope, and form, however, one hears a voice of uncommon authority, a "chiseled voice" brooding on loss, poverty, corruption, natural beauty, the harmony of art and nature, and the sad impermanence of things. Not infrequently, Bunting's attention turns to the making of poems, a process he compares to that of the stonemason, or, alternately, the composer. Here, as elsewhere, a classical sense of human limitation prevails over a native romanticism, as Bunting says of his work:

> It looks well on the page, but never
> well enough. Something is lost
> when wind, sun, sea upbraid
> justly an unconvinced deserter.

Those lines catch Bunting's pessimism and hint at his sense of resignation. (pp. 170-71)

Bunting's satire attacks a broad range of targets. His invectives against the literary world vary from sneers at Bloomsbury aesthetes, critics, and poetasters ("All the cants they peddle / bellow entangled, / teeth for knots and / each other's ankles . . .") to a vicious lampoon of T. S. Eliot, whom Bunting likens to Attis, the eunuch who sacrificed his manhood for the goddess Cybele. His attacks on the bourgeoisie focus on philistinism and complacency, and his targets range from the "chairman" who regards poetry as a "hobby" to the teashop girl, who is "untroubled by / earth's spinning / preoccupied rather / by the set of her stocking." His denunciations of Filthy Lucre, reminiscent of Pound's broadsides at usury, range from caustic remarks on social inequity to an intricate meditation entitled ***The Spoils,*** in which the disruptive influence of Babylonian moneylenders, who have "planted ink and reaped figures," contrasts with the natural rhythms of an agrarian economy, where "the ewes go out / along the towpath striped with palm-trunk shadows" and "there is no clamour . . . no eagerness for gain." But eagerness for gain, at the expense of social harmony, is only one aspect of general human blundering, which Bunting impales on sharp, intemperate statements:

> But their determination to banish fools foundered
> ultimately in the installation of absolute idiots.

Bunting's satire is seldom blunted by good will. . . . Bunting might well remind one of [Samuel] Johnson in his awareness of human limitation and his unflinching confrontation with fact. . . . (pp. 172-73)

[**"Search under every veil"**] is memorable for stylistic reasons. Its enjambed trimeter couplets, its elaborate but supple syntax, its deft placement of caesurae, and its subtle but forceful rhymes create a miniature enchanting *fado*. To be sure, such music, mishandled, might become an affront to its subject, a pretty lament in the presence of someone else's plight. And the one flawed line in the poem, "come nightly more amiss," is disappointing not only because its rhyme seems forced but because, all too mellifluous, it reminds us that we are reading poetry. Here and at other points in Bunting's work, one feels that if the view of life were less stern, the diction less austere, the lines might dissolve in the sweetness of their sounds.

But music and sober realism strike a balance in Bunting's art. And as we turn to the longer poems, we find the one element playing contrapuntally against the other. Where Bunting's realism attacks and penetrates, his melodies enlarge and celebrate. And where his realistic imagery is coarse, his lyric moments are melodious and pure. (p. 174)

The image of a relaxed informal conversation, interlaced with medieval Persian poetry and the song of the nightingale, epitomizes Bunting's lyric mode, in which the threads of art, nature, and the common life form a single delicate weave. At the center lies the art of music, which in Bunting's work becomes a way of perceiving the natural world, a poetic motif, and, most centrally, a model for poetic composition. "Brag, sweet tenor bull," ***Briggflatts*** beings, "Descant on Rawthey's madrigal." . . . Not everyone will be convinced by this Wordsworthian idyll, in which the river Rawthey becomes a polyphonic composition and, reciprocally, the "mason times his mallet / to a lark's twitter." For my own part, I find such visions easier to like than to believe in, since they take little account of the random violence of the natural world. Nature, as flood victims know, has a way of dropping her cymbals.

Even more problematical are Bunting's analogies between poetry and music. (From 1925 to 1928 Bunting wrote music criticism for *Outlook,* the London newspaper.) These analogies might be seen as deriving largely from Pound, but it would be fairer to say that Pound nurtured Bunting's lifelong interest in poetry's sister art. When Bunting was a child, his aunt, a concert pianist, played Scarlatti sonatas at his request. Fifty years later, the impression lingers:

> It is time to consider how Domenico Scarlatti
> condensed so much music into so few bars
> with never a crabbed turn or congested cadence,
> never a boast or a see-here; and stars and lakes
> echo him and the copse drums out his measure,
> snow peaks are lifted up in moonlight and twilight
> and the sun rises on an acknowledged land.

As a stylistic ideal this seems unassailable. It proposes a compromise between clarity and condensation, naturalness and intensity—a standard to which any poet might reasonably aspire. For the most part, Bunting's example is equal to his precept. His cadences, to be sure, are sometimes congested. . . . But more often they are fluent and lucid. . . . (pp. 176-78)

Beyond a concept of style, Bunting's musical analogies embrace a concept of structure. In four long poems written early in his career—**"Villon," "Attis: Or, Something Missing," "Aus dem Zweiten Reich,"** and **"The Well of Lycopolis"**—Bunting made a conscious effort to imitate the classical sonata. As he tells it, he began with Beethoven's sonatas but turned eventually to Eighteenth Century composers like Scarlatti and Johann Christian Bach, whose sonatas demonstrated "a simpler way of dealing with the two themes." Bunting's poems, like Scarlatti's sonatas, introduce themes and counterthemes (e.g., imprisonment and poetic creation in **"Villon"**), develop these themes in contrasting contexts, and recapitulate them in a final movement, sometimes concluding with a coda. While allowing for freedom of invention, the form remains strict.

However useful Bunting's analogy might have been as an aid to composition, it is less than helpful as a basis of evaluation. Poems written with sonatas in mind must still be judged as poems. And these early experiments, for all their formal rigor, are very uneven. To begin with, they are glutted with recondite allusion; and Bunting's coy footnotes are not very instructive. (Of **"The Well of Lycopolis,"** for instance, we are told that "Gibbon mentions its effect in a footnote." Happy hunting!) Obscurity, it's true, is partly in the eye of the beholder. Moreover, the allusions don't always matter. **"Villon,"** for example, is an exquisite monologue in which the voices of Francois Villon and Basil Bunting, who was imprisoned as a conscientious objector, become one. . . . (pp. 178-79)

[Beyond] their opacity, the ill-tempered tone of these poems and their ungenerous treatment of contemporaries detract from the high quality of the verse. In **"Aus dem Zweiten Reich,"** for example, Bunting caricatures Gerhart Hauptmann as one "Who talked about poetry, / and he said nothing at all; / plays, / and he said nothing at all; / politics, / and he stirred as if a flea / bit him. . . ." In **"Attis,"** Eliot is even more savagely attacked. . . . Bunting calls **"Attis"** a "sonatina," but it contains little that is musical or pleasing. Its tone is that of witty malicious gossip.

Bunting's longer "sonatas" are far more impressive. In this trio of poems—***Briggflatts*** (1965), ***The Spoils*** (1951), and

"Chomei at Toyama" (1932)—Bunting exploits the compositional techniques of the earlier poems: development of theme and countertheme, tonal contrast, and so on. As a result, these poems are more coherent than most postwar poetic sequences and far more unified than Pound's *Cantos,* which they superficially resemble. At the same time, they have a fluidity and freedom greater than that of the earlier "sonatas." Their structure might be described figuratively as that of "impressionistic polyphony"—Ralph Kirkpatrick's term for the harmonic structures of Domenico Scarlatti. (pp. 179-80)

Bunting's structures do show affinities with Scarlatti. But to acknowledge such affinities is to raise a further question. What does the analogy of poet as rococo composer have in common with Bunting's other analogy: the poet as stonemason? Are the two figures compatible? Throughout his work Bunting has favored both analogies without, to my knowledge, exploring possible conflicts between them. . . . [It] may well be that two aesthetic ideals are in tension in Bunting's poetry. One is that of chiseled verse and stony austerity. . . . The other is one of opulent sound, enriched by inversions, complex syntax, and archaic diction. . . . (pp. 181-82)

The remarkable thing is that Bunting has managed to balance these contrasting styles and to create from disparate idioms a unified whole. But balance, as we have seen, is Bunting's forte. He is a living, thriving example of Coleridge's primary imagination, which effects a "balance and reconciliation of discordant qualities," whether those qualities be satire and song, or assaults and exaltation. The unifying force is Bunting's aggressive personality; and the unifying perspective is that of tragic irony—a perspective Bunting has made his own in over five decades of writing. Such is the viewpoint of **"Chomei at Toyama,"** where Bunting's persona observes that "This is the unstable world and / we in it unstable and our houses." (p. 183)

Ben Howard, "Teeming Sweetness," in Parnassus: Poetry in Review, *Vol. 8, No. 1, Fall-Winter, 1979, pp. 169-83.*

GEOFFREY O'BRIEN

[Basil Bunting] insisted that his poetry could be fully experienced only if sounded out loud. For him a poem's published text was little more than a musical score, lifeless unless performed: "A poem is a series of sounds in the air, just as music. Other things can be included or loaded onto it, but the essential thing is just the *noise.*" Fortunately a recording exists of Bunting reading his masterpiece ***Briggflatts,*** so we can hear its parallel assonances and craggily knocked-together consonants precisely as intended. But Bunting is just as much a poet for the eye. The mere sight of phrases like "rut thud the rim" and "pricked rag mat" and "fellside bleat," stacked up in a firm rough-hewn structure, creates a kind of orthographic landscape. In Bunting the words seem to have just been unearthed: here and there his vocabulary has been scratched by glaciers, dented by axes, buried under generations of rotted leaves. The words are no one's personal property.

The ***Collected Poems*** is at once remarkably slim and remarkably dense. It was Bunting who, in a German-Italian dictionary, came across the definition which Ezra Pound promptly adopted as a maxim: "*Dichten* equals *condensare,*" i.e., to write poetry is to condense. Bunting compresses immensities of experience into clipped, tightly stitched lines. The miniature epic ***Briggflatts*** is only 22 pages long, but in the mind it expands to infinitely greater length, as if a lifetime's duration were somehow secreted within and between its syllables. . . . When words are given their true weight of inherited connotation, they become heavy indeed: "Pens are too light. / Take a chisel to write."

Although Bunting described ***Briggflatts*** as "an autobiography," the reader will find in it no chronicle of his evidently adventurous life. . . . The poem's a memoir without a memoirist, in which the word "I" is used sparingly and with shifting signification. The poet makes himself an instrument of the world, constructs a summing-up of earthy elements, a catalogue of smells and colors, the distillation of a life into essential—and often microscopic—perceptions.

Bunting's method had been established as early as 1925 in **"Villon"** . . . and honed in the abrasive satires of the early '30s. After nearly two decades of silence came ***The Spoils*** (1951), with its panoramic scope and soaring music, a homage to the classical Persian culture from which Bunting had drawn so many of his aesthetic imperatives. . . . Whatever else a poem might be, it had to be an artisan's work. The focus was form, not revealed truth: "I don't give a damn whether I falsify experience or not. I'm out to make a good poem. I'm not there to provide raw material for psychologists. . . . I have never supposed a poem to be organic at all. I don't think the thing grows, it's built and put together by a craftsman." The poem is to be approached as a free-standing artifact, without regard to its essentially irrelevant maker. Bunting would have felt quite comfortable as one of the poets known to us as Anonymous.

He had little interest in intellectual originality, and suggested that "poets are wise to do as they usually do and stick to commonplaces." Insofar as the content of his poetry can be summarized, it has to do with the most ancient of perceptions: the body's frailty, the futility of desire, the ramshackle unsteadiness of human works. He was a great nature poet obsessed by the heartlessness of nature; his "gay thrush" sings of "familiar things, / fear, hunger, lust." **"Chomei at Toyama,"** his wonderful adaptation of the 12th century Japanese *Hojoki,* starts in a vein of Orientalist prettiness (no one was prettier than Bunting when he wanted to be), only to crash abruptly through the exotic spell:

> Empty markets, swarms of beggars. Jewels
> sold for a handful of rice. Dead stank
> on the curb, lay so thick on
> Riverside Drive a car couldn't pass.
> The pest bred.

His reverence for the beauty of song did not disguise the sordid context of that beauty: quite the contrary. His lyricism had nothing remotely ethereal about it.

The progress of Bunting's poetry resembles a homing in on his own roots. In the early work he writes as a voyager, a foreign resident; the settings are France, Germany, Japan, Iran. The music still echoes Pound and, beyond him, Dante and Catullus. Had he stopped writing after ***The Spoils,*** we might remember him as a distinctive minor modernist. Instead—after another 14-year gap—he published ***Briggflatts*** at 65, and thereby decisively changed the ear of the poets who came after him. It seemed nothing less than a resurrection of English poetry, with a fullness of body that had been so long lost as to become unimaginable. . . . The sensual delights of sound were themselves reborn, and through them, by implication, all the other senses. . . . It was a poem without high points, a continuously metamorphosing flow of sense impressions. Each of its elements, considered separately, shone keenly and icily clear, yet at the same time blended into the malleable current of the whole: a triumphant vindication of Bunting's formal concerns. He never again published anything on that scale, but in a series of brief odes continued year after year to perpetuate the lingering harmonics of ***Briggflatts***. (pp. 43-4)

Geoffrey O'Brien, "Solid as a Rock: Country Poems, Made to Last," in The Village Voice, *Vol. XXXI, No. 3, January 21, 1986, pp. 43-4.*

Frederick Busch

1941-

© Jim Kalett

American novelist, short story writer, critic, and editor.

Busch is admired for his realistic fiction in which he experiments with different narrative voices to examine the private lives of his protagonists. In many of his novels and short stories, Busch explores the strength of familial relationships and depicts the quiet heroism of characters who confront domestic catastrophes. While his writings often examine such subjects as death and alienation, they also affirm Busch's faith in the nobility of human life. Busch's ability to render incidents in a lucid prose style prompted John Romano to comment: "[Busch] is one of a small party who are resuscitating an ancient use of words, to connect us to our feeling, to refresh our vulnerabilities, to waken in the mind the prospect of an edifying pain."

Busch's first novel, *I Wanted a Year without Fall* (1971), a humorous contemporary adaptation of the *Beowulf* legend, was followed by his celebrated novels *Manual Labor* (1974), *Domestic Particulars: A Family Chronicle* (1976), *The Mutual Friend* (1978), and *Rounds* (1979). These works garnered Busch recognition as an author of novels that poignantly convey human emotions through diverse points of view. *Manual Labor* evokes the grief experienced by a couple endeavoring to save their marriage after the wife suffers a miscarriage. The novel is related through the husband's journal entries, the wife's thoughts presented in the form of an unmailed letter to her mother, and the voice of the dead child. Similarly, in *Domestic Particulars,* several members of an American family recount their ancestry and history from 1919 to 1976. The strained relationships within the family and their encounters with real and imagined crises are tempered by their enduring love for one another. *The Mutual Friend* relates the story of Charles Dickens's final years from the perspective of George Dolby, Dickens's secretary. Praised for its narrative structure and depictions of nineteenth-century America and England, *The Mutual Friend* is often cited as a brilliant departure from Busch's examination of contemporary concerns. *Rounds* returns to familial concerns in its examination of pediatrician Eli Silver. Estranged from his wife following the death of their son, Silver suffers guilt and loneliness while trying to order his life through the discipline of his profession.

Busch's novels of the 1980s continue to depict domestic situations. *Take This Man* (1981) follows isolated events in the lives of Tony Prioleau, Ellen Larue Spencer, Tony's occasional lover, and Gus, their illegitimate son. Alternately comic and sad, this novel generates interest by contrasting the insecurities and hopes of its protagonists. *Invisible Mending* (1984) recalled to some critics the works of Bernard Malamud, Saul Bellow, and Philip Roth in its depiction of a Jewish protagonist who struggles to come to terms with the Holocaust and its relationship to his heritage. In *Sometimes I Live in the Country* (1986), Busch explores marital discord and racial prejudice from the viewpoint of a suicidal urban adolescent who is removed to a rural community.

Busch has also published several volumes of short stories, including *Breathing Trouble and Other Stories* (1973), *Hardwater Country* (1979), and *Too Late American Boyhood Blues* (1984), in which he examines themes similar to those of his novels. In *Too Late American Boyhood Blues,* Busch ironically adapts Ernest Hemingway's prose style in stories about sentimental and emotionally insecure males.

(See also *CLC,* Vols. 7, 10, 18; *Contemporary Authors,* Vols. 33-36, rev. ed.; *Contemporary Authors Autobiography Series,* Vol. 1; and *Dictionary of Literary Biography,* Vol. 6.)

STEPHEN GOODWIN

The trouble with American novelists is that they wish to be great, not good; and consequently they are neither. That, anyway, is Gore Vidal's opinion, one of those clever half-truths which a novelist like Frederick Busch turns upside down. Busch has always aimed at being good, not great, and if he keeps on being so good, he will surely be recognized as great.

Take This Man is Busch's eighth work of fiction in 10 years. His previous books have been published to virtually unanimous acclaim—and then, somehow, ignored. There is nothing flashy or even fashionable about his fiction. His themes are mostly domestic, his techniques realistic, his characters ordinary men and women who try to lead just, intelligent, loving lives. Ho-hum, says the Average Reader, and slides down the rack to the books which promise an experience Larger Than Life.

Busch's fiction is very much like life; he always gets the scale right. He deals in drama, not melodrama; sentiment, not sentimentality; love, not romance; passion, not panting. This is not to say that his characters are paragons of virtue and wisdom. They are subject to the same delusions and vanities as the rest of us—and, in time, they have to pay for them. (p. 3)

Take This Man is the story of a small family, man, woman, and child, that lives beyond the law. The man is Anthony Prioleau, a southerner whose uncertain origins—he is suspected of having Negro blood—prove to be a destiny. He never quite fits anywhere. He's the sort of man who manages to foul up everything he touches—and who, therefore, touches very little. In his love affair with Ellen LaRue Spencer, it is she who must take the initiative, who must, literally, *take* this man.

She takes him first in 1944; when Prioleau is working as a television technician—he's been let out of prison, where he was serving time for conscientious objection—at a desolate and insignificant Army post in Illinois. She arrives there by accident, though Prioleau works up the nerve to declare that he's been waiting for her since puberty. "Pewberty," she corrects him. "Not pooberty; that sounds ugly and it's incorrect." Ellen is a schoolteacher, small, spirited and resolute. She is on her way to California in a gasping car to meet and eventually to marry another man; Prioleau feels seduced and abandoned when she continues her journey.

In 1956 he sees someone else he has been waiting for—his son, the issue of that first seduction. The boy, Gus, steps off a bus in the same Illinois town where Prioleau is now working as a TV repairman. "I heard you were my father," he says simply, not at all surprised to find Prioleau meeting him. Nor, a bit later, is Ellen surprised to arrive in town and find that Prioleau is still in love with her. She takes him again—Gus will always think that the three of them *slunk* eastward to Maine—and they live together as man and wife. "I liked the idea of being married to someone who couldn't find me," Ellen tells Gus when he's grown, "and of not being married to someone who could."

The invisible lines that bind these lives together work again in 1963, when Gus runs away to an island with a pair of activists who intend to bring the military to its knees by blocking radio transmissions. This section of the novel, while a little pat and pointed—Prioleau was a conscientious objector, remember, and Gus' attitude toward one of the activists, a strong-willed woman like his mother, is surely a kind of replay of Prioleau's first feelings toward Ellen—is nevertheless uncanny. Both Prioleau and Ellen, pursuing Gus independently, arrive on the right island, where they discover each other in the darkness. (pp. 3, 13)

What else happens? They bring Gus home, time runs on, and the last section of the novel is set in 1980. Gus has grown up, but the essential configurations of this triangle of man, woman, and child haven't changed. All I will say about the ending of ***Take This Man*** is that it seems at once inevitable and mysterious, as life itself gives way to death itself.

This story encompasses 40 years, and the durable image that emerges is that of a profound, lifelong union between a man and woman. It's a love story, though the word *love* is hardly mentioned. When Prioleau does say it, Ellen is as short with him as she was when he mispronounced puberty. Yet love is the only thing Prioleau doesn't foul up, the one thing that lasts.

The minor characters in ***Take This Man*** are brought on without a fuss; they're just there, like the landscape or the weather or thought or desire or the TV. It's all there, all without a fuss. The details are so right that they're unobtrusive; Busch creates a large and recognizable world with effortless grace.

He has a reputation as a writer's writer, but I don't think it can be very long before he's better known as a reader's writer. (p. 13)

Stephen Goodwin, "Frederick Busch and the Mysterious Lines of Love," in Book World—The Washington Post, *September 13, 1981, pp. 3, 13.*

DAVID QUAMMEN

The man in question is Tony Prioleau, a part-Choctaw Cajun of gentle heart and hopelessly clumsy hands who floats like a chicory chip through Fredrick Busch's eighth work of fiction [***Take This Man***]. He is a *schlemiel* in the Thurberesque vein—so fully in that vein as to perilously approach stereotype—but with the critical distinctions that Prioleau is capable of deep and abiding love, and that although resoundingly unvalued by the world, he is passionately valued by the two people who know him and matter to him, his common-law wife and his bastard son. ***Take This Man*** is the portrait of that valuation.

In the earliest of the novel's four main sections (designated "1944," "1956," "1963," "1980"), Prioleau is a conscientious objector working on a secret but risible war-research project on the prairie outside Patoka Plains, Ill. . . .

Prioleau manages to get himself seduced and abandoned by a strong-willed, impulsive redhead named Ellen LaRue Spencer. . . . [In] "1956" a natural son named Gus appears in Patoka Plains on Prioleau's doorstep, and Ellen shows up soon afterward. With these more slapdash and cartoonish parts of the novel out of the way, the potent emotional transactions begin. The lives of Ellen and Prioleau are not merely, as it had seemed, random flying molecules that collide and then carom away. They are random flying molecules that collide and stick.

Mr. Busch's technique is to present the story of Ellen and Prioleau and Gus not in continuous pageant but by the set of four dated samplings, looking in on them at key moments and giving us enough flashback (more than enough) to fill the gaps. Generally that technique seems quite apt. These are not, after all, especially eventful lives; by some standards they would be judged rather empty. Their interest lies chiefly in the unusual power of their unusual bonds with one another, and in the rare heights of bizarre ordinariness that each of the three—through an excess of some ordinary virtue like steadfastness, forthrightness, ingenuousness—at times attains. Nevertheless one of the more curious things about ***Take This Man,*** such a small quiet book and seemingly so carefully written by a man with a small quiet reputation for fine craftsmanship, is that it is so uneven.

Its indisputable emotional force is of a cumulative sort that is rather a long time coming. This is due largely to a diffuseness of focus, a number of ill-considered digressions and other defects of invention and selection in the first half of the book, whole portions of which read like scrupulous, workmanlike padding. It seems almost as if, with Prioleau maundering through both "1944" and "1956" before Ellen and Gus have taken a firm grip on him, the narrator can figure nothing better than to maunder a bit himself.

He straggles off on extended forays into the lives of secondary characters, forces himself to try on their points of view with middling success, and further dissipates our attention with chattering set pieces from tertiary figures who are neither relevant to plot, nor freshly conceived or amusing. In fact his fast-talking radio promoter who aims to build a television empire, and his famous broadcasting shyster evangelist, to cite the worst, are both quite hackneyed. The entire first half of the book is redeemed only by a few poignant moments, and many fine dabs of dialogue.

But the second half of the book (in particular the depiction of the final arrangements for a deathbed wedding in which Ellen will at last take this man Tony Prioleau as her legally wedded husband) easily earns Frederick Busch indulgence for earlier lapses. ***Take This Man*** is not a novel you *must* read; but if you happen to, you'll find delights scattered along the way, and some very genuine emotional power at the end.

David Quammen, "Quiet Virtues," in The New York Times Book Review, *September 20, 1981, p. 15.*

SUSAN LYDON

Take This Man is a generational novel, and I suspect one of the reasons I enjoyed it so much is that it's about my generation. The protagonists, a male and female, meet during World War II. Tony Prioleau is a part-Indian with a gentle heart and clumsy motions. Ellen LaRue is a willful, determined woman, on her way to see her intended off to combat. Tony and Ellen meet, and it is the woman who seduces and then abandons the man. The novel seems rather aimless in the first half. . . . But it picks up steam in later episodes. . . .

Although there are many comings and goings, secondary characters, and eternal details meant to dramatize contrasts between the various decades of the episodes, in the end it is the bonds between the members of this unlikely, unintended, and sometimes hilarious family that make the book interesting. Busch has a gift for the exploration of gentle feelings. I found this same quality in ***Rounds,*** one of his eight previous novels. . . .

In the broadest sense, ***Rounds*** and ***Take This Man*** seem to tell the same story—love lost and love redeemed. Busch's insights into the hearts of these men touched me, almost despite myself. His characters, groping toward reunion with the women they love, are also groping for a way to carry on relationships with some integrity in an age when all the rules have changed.

Susan Lydon, in a review of "Take This Man" and "Rounds," in The Village Voice, *Vol. XXVI, No. 45, November 4-10, 1981, p. 44.*

EDITH MILTON

Frederick Busch's new novel, ***Take This Man,*** is . . . about the peculiar life of one odd family. . . . A simple story of love and loss, to all appearances: Ellen LaRue meets Tony Prioleau in 1944 when her car breaks down in the middle of Patoka Plains, Illinois. . . . They fall in love, then part. Twelve years later, a boy steps from the bus in Patoka Plains, where Tony has settled down, and announces that he is Gus and that Tony is his father.

If this sounds like a movie, it should. Busch traces the modes of his family's experience through the times' changing fashions in theatrical entertainment. Echoes of *It Happened One Night* sound through Tony and Ellen's love affair, the army bits are straight from a 1940s farce, and Gus's arrival in Patoka Plains flirts with TV melodrama and situation comedy. But over the somber final section, which takes place in 1980, isolation, guilt, and silence preside with contemporary appropriateness. Busch loses his way somewhat in the penultimate section when Gus, now an adolescent, takes flight from his parents into the *Easy Rider* chaos of 1960s revolutionary poses and the fringes of the drug culture. But he more than makes up for that with the resonance of the last section and the splendid insanity of moments early in the novel: the school play, for instance, in which the Nazi persecution of the Jews miraculously becomes high comedy about American naïveté and arrogance.

In this comedy of changing manners, Busch suggests it is the form only which alters while the content remains the same. A growing sadness pervades that sameness. For the novel suggests that what remains unaltered is the fact that to love people is to lose them and leave them. In every section, in every part of the novel, children are looking for their fathers, parents are looking for their lost children, lovers search for the beloved, husbands follow wives, as the pursuers become the pursued and the searchers in time flee from what they were looking for. Gus comes for Tony across half a continent, only in turn to run away from him later.

But the novel begins and ends with Tony's dying, and the sense that all loss, all flight from love is, in the end, permanent, while all pursuit of it is, in the end, frustrated. And in a marvelously modulated reference to a jazz song, "The Boy in the Boat," which both opens the book and, in image at least, closes it, Busch celebrates a universal sorrow and the various means we have invented to distract ourselves from it. (pp. 262-63)

Edith Milton, "Fables for Our Times: Six Novels," in The Yale Review, *Vol. 71, No. 2, Winter, 1982, pp. 254-66.*

ANATOLE BROYARD

When Zimmer, the hero of ***Invisible Mending,*** was a small boy, his mother took him to a chiropodist who advised him to walk less heavily on his heels. A few years later, while explaining "the facts of life" to him, Zimmer's father strummed discordantly on the family piano.

In these two images, Frederick Busch notifies us that, in his adult life, Zimmer will always come down too hard on the delicate surfaces of things and his sexual experiences will usually be accompanied by the nervous, discordant music of self-consciousness and guilt. . . .

[Zimmer] seduces Rhona, his first love, with "stories of ineptitude and bookishness and fear." In certain quarters, Mr. Busch gives us to understand, these qualities are felt to be lovable and aphrodisiac. The helpless antihero appeals to the new, competent woman as the innocent girl used to appeal to the capable man. As the author of several unconventional novels and a collection of short stories, Mr. Busch is a connoisseur of contemporary inversions.

Rhona's father survived a concentration camp at Birkenau, and now she sees anti-Semitic fascism everywhere in New York City in 1980. During her affair with Zimmer, she tracks down a man she identifies as a Nazi war criminal, pursuing him through the streets to his apartment, punishing him with her presence, her silent reproach.

If he wants to share her bed, Zimmer is obliged to share Rhona's conception of Jewishness as a state of perpetual vigilance and inquiry. For her, love is an offshoot of vengeance, a sort of indemnity from life. Though Zimmer feels absurd following the elderly alleged Nazi into Macy's men's room, he accepts Rhona's conditions because, like her, he can't conceive of unconditional love.

When his affair with Rhona ends, Zimmer meets Lillian, his future wife, at the Baseball Hall of Fame in Cooperstown. She is weeping over a film clip of the life of Babe Ruth, and for Zimmer this is a revelation. Lillian is, as Flaubert put it, "in the real." Zimmer marries her in an attempt to make a legal claim on the real. Why she marries him is not so clear. . . .

While Zimmer is happy after a fashion with Lillian and their son, Sam, he can't locate the literature of happiness. He doesn't know how to categorize it, and he puts more energy into the explication of the text than he does into the joy of sex. Love, for Zimmer, is a nonprofitable poem of anguish, a function of the tragic sense of life. He sees it mainly as something you can *lose*. Sex is a series of rebellious uprisings against that loss.

Zimmer dosn't understand that love is a transaction, not a passive tribute. When he says "I love you," it is as if he were offering himself as a sacrifice. He feels jilted because his wife is "more comfortable in the world" than he is. While Rhona lives in history and Lillian lives in the real, Zimmer lives only in the slum of his consciousness. In "making a secular mystery out of the holiest simplicity," he ruins his marriage.

Invisible Mending has some interesting things to say about the lunatic fringes of love, a field in which Mr. Busch is an acknowledged explorer. While he offers us a hero who would try the patience of the American Civil Liberties Union, his book manages at the same time to be funny, sad, possibly true and pretty well written.

Now and then a strong image rises up in Mr. Busch's pages. There is an elderly blind man, for example, who sits, idly, all day in a public library. When someone questions him about this, he explains that he is an author and he is hoping to hear someone ask for his book. Perhaps Mr. Busch is making a melancholy joke about authors, suggesting that they can only sit by blindly, hoping to be called. With ***Invisible Mending,*** a considerable improvement over his earlier books, he may not have to wait much longer.

Anatole Broyard, in a review of "Invisible Mending," in The New York Times, *March 15, 1984, p. 19.*

NORMA ROSEN

Frederick Busch's earlier fictions, which were widely praised for their clarity and dignity, celebrated rural life in New England and the Midwest. In ***Invisible Mending,*** Mr. Busch gives us something else—Zimmer, New York Jew and first-person narrator, whose voice is nervous, sentimental, wisecracking, garrulous. "Can I come home?" is the plea Zimmer recalls from his panicked childhood; the phrase applies as well to the 40-year-old Zimmer's present plight. He has a wife, a son, an editor's job in a publishing house, but he still feels lost. . . .

"Inauthentic Jews," Jean-Paul Sartre wrote in "Anti-Semite and Jew," "are men whom other men take for Jews and who have decided to run away from this insupportable situation." This seems a fair description of Zimmer. When Zimmer was a boy, his assimilated, liberal parents bad-mouthed Jews and gave him Christmas, but Zimmer has to reject them anyway when he marries the gentile Lillian and adopts her family, "with their gold hair and delicate cheekbones," in place of "those squat and un-Americanized" people from whom he sprang.

Zimmer's marriage to Lillian and his subsequent fathering of their son, to whom he now in turn gives Christmas, are acts with which no champion of free choice would wish to quarrel. Zimmer's relationship to the Holocaust, however, is another matter. Before Lillian, there had been Rhona, a Jewish lover who introduced him to the Holocaust to win back his "Jewish soul." Though years later Zimmer still can't decide whether it was "sex or history that drove me on," he embarked on a tormented reading of Holocaust books and let Rhona drag him into a humiliating Nazi hunt. The outcome (it's all right to reveal it because the reader knows long before Rhona, who refuses to see copious clues) is that the "Nazi" turns out to be a Jewish refugee. . . .

Because Zimmer is so dedicated a narrator-rememberer and Mr. Busch so skillful a novel constructor, the story can slip from past to present and back again (sometimes dizzyingly), cantilevering its way across decades. The technique creates a simultaneity of mood and event that keeps Zimmer's ambiguities always before us. It also keeps authorial stance obscured. At what ironic distance from himself does Mr. Busch want us to read about his character Zimmer, who must make farce of the Holocaust in order to rid himself of it? Whatever signposts the author provides are ambiguous.

When, after 12 years of marriage, Zimmer leaves Lillian and their beloved 8-year-old son, his reasons are fuzzy. And the tone is uncertain: The poor little overdetermined boy cries out in what sounds like parody, "Do we still get to have Christmas, Daddy?" The breakup mainly seems to occur so Zimmer can re-encounter Rhona and reconfirm his choice of Lillian. . . .

In place of obsession, Zimmer looks for the single idea that will be a shortcut to meaning and exclaims about this or that event that it would make "a dandy metaphor." He finds what he seeks on a tailor shop window. "Invisible mending" becomes his metaphor for what love can do when applied to the world's sorrows. Even Lillian feels moved to remind him that "invisible mending" won't work if the Ku Klux Klan takes over America. "The only place where you can run to . . . is Israel. . . . Home for the Jews? Remember?"

Zimmer is not without his charm, not the least of which is that he is the first to tell us the bad news about himself. What he seems not to know is that he suffers from the emotional thinness of someone who can believe in nothing but language. When he looks at *I Never Saw Another Butterfly,* a book of poems and drawings done by children in the Terezin concentration camp, he thinks, "They were children of language," before emotion seizes him and he hurls the book away. . . .

For all his rushing about, Zimmer is as isolated from true encounter as a man locked in a room.

Having learned about Nazis, Zimmer feels free to quip about Abraham's binding of Isaac, "He was only obeying orders." Yet Zimmer also tries to get his firm to publish the poems of the Holocaust poet Paul Celan. Where lines from Celan's "Deathfugue" appear, they flood the pages with a tragic grandeur that all but drowns Zimmer's voice. It is as if Zimmer—or his author—had remembered that biblical Jews sometimes wrestled with angels and came away wth new identities and names.

Mr. Busch lavishes language on Zimmer but never gives him a first name or a completed identity. The book, in fact, sends out confusing cross-messages. A clear relationship between author and character is lacking, and this reader had the impression that narrative technique was used to avoid coming to grips with the moral implications of the story. The novel's cozy ending is contrived at the cost of engaged authenticity for either Zimmer or the book. The reader's mind (fatally for the novel) wanders outside this fiction to recall that there are real Nazis and real Nazi-hunters whose "paranoia" is justified. The novel shrinks to a nursery fictional world shielded from the terrors of the real world, where the mountain of Holocaust documentation yearly looms higher and where Jew and Christian alike struggle with agonized questions at the heart of their post-Holocaust relationship. Neither Zimmer nor Frederick Busch ever faces up to that.

Norma Rosen, "Hunting Metaphors and Nazis," in The New York Times Book Review, *April 1, 1984, p. 12.*

KARL KELLER

The Holocaust has been the central fact of the arts of our half-century, as a subject and as the prime measure of whether art is ever adequate to the larger facts of life. But, I believe, it is quickly being replaced by the Second Holocaust, the bomb. A Jew living, a Jew dying, a Jew knowing how to live and die a Jew hangs on—still significant but weaker now. For better or worse, one cannot let go.

Nathan Zimmer, in Frederick Busch's [***Invisible Mending***], has tried to let go. He calls himself "a Jew-manque, a conscious one." . . .

Everyone around Nathan Zimmer is in a panic over the issue of being a Jew. He just wants to let go. . . .

Guilt is how people around him try to get Zimmer. He can't enjoy Christmas because it means he has "betrayed the many dead whose sacrifice had somehow gotten me from Europe, in various bloodstreams, to the U.S.A. I betrayed the living and the dead." . . .

But Zimmer escapes. "Such failures to feel guilty," he reflects, "were one of maturity's rewards. This is what I have been growing up for." . . .

By the end of his story, Zimmer will no longer speak of "gee-dash-dee" but only of "a God one of whose names, if there had to be one, ought to have something to do with comfort or love." His alternative to the Jewish self-consciousness, then, is simple sex. "Maybe good love," he muses, "leaves some of the self in place." For the Law of Return (to one's blood, to oneself, or to one's Zion) Zimmer substitutes a longing for love—someone warm and living beside him in bed. . . .

And it is in this fact I think that Busch's novel breaks in half inexplicably and sadly fails its theme. One half confronts, in both profound and hilarious prose, such issues as racial identity, belief, suffering and death. The other half is all orgasms as an answer, an escape, an alternative. "Sex," Zimmer insists, "is that behavior which coexists with death and flight." But that trivializes everything else in the novel.

"What have we learned?" is the large Jewish question of the novel. Instead of "worshiping history," Zimmer just wants to "come home" and love someone. But is this, even to Frederick Busch, really sufficient "invisible mending" when all the stuffing may have come out of life, out of *lives*?

Karl Keller, "Freedom from Guilt: Escaping the Demands of Jewish History," in Los Angeles Times Book Review, *May 27, 1984, p. 4.*

ANATOLE BROYARD

In Frederick Busch's new collection of stories [***Too Late American Boyhood Blues***], love is a night-school course or second career. Many of his characters have already made their initial mistakes, gone through their undergraduate enthusiasms. They're winded, still panting from their exertions, feeling a stitch of desperation in their sides.

The men and women in ***Too Late American Boyhood Blues*** are no longer young. They're thinking not so much about attacking life as defending themselves against it. They've moved beyond what they want to what they need. In the back of their minds is an ominous question: Not can I live with this person, but can I die with him or her?

It is not the women, but the men who are sentimental here. After childbirth and mothering, women are too much aware of the mechanics of love to be sentimental about it. Only men, in their vagueness and self-absorption, can still afford to fling themselves about, can drive through the night to distant loves, or make large promises. . . .

Some of these stories in ***Too Late American Boyhood Blues*** are about children. We watch them practicing for adulthood, studying their mothers' and fathers' mistakes and wondering whether they're worth repeating. Because they feel themselves to be the most interesting mistakes their parents have made, they have a natural prejudice in favor of continuing the tradition. When they grow up, they say to themselves, they'll make bigger and better mistakes, bolder ones.

Mr. Busch's stories often take place in forlorn or desolate small towns. He seems intent on proving to big-city dwellers that life in small towns is just as intricately disheveled as theirs, that you can go crazy with panache even among a population of 20,000. One of his characters has a job looking for locations for a movie company, and there's no question that Mr. Busch's stories could furnish forth a dozen depressing movies.

The author himself also seems to be looking for a location in his stories, some formal scheme in which human irrationality makes sense and might even flower. He has written quite a few books, and he's still searching for new risks to take. This collection in particular might be regarded as a comprehensive example of the technical vicissitudes of short-story writing in our time. **"Stand, and Be Recognized,"** the last piece in the book, is an orgy of failed experimentation.

Is it condescending to say of a fiction writer that he makes you think? Maybe we might like to feel a little more, along with our thinking. Some of Mr. Busch's readers would be willing to concede that, yes, life is difficult, but not precisely in the terms he describes. He seems to be displacing some of the main issues, they might argue, with digressions that he finds too appealing.

At his worst, Mr. Busch is pretty bad. At his best, he's pretty good. Most of his stories, though, are in the middle range. One of them, **"The New Honesty,"** offers a clue as to what's the matter. A middle-aged couple in this story are shocked when they are told by an antiques dealer that all the furniture in their house, all the things they cherish, are worth only $800 on the market.

Mr. Busch's characters are a bit like that too. Though they've seen hard times, their experiences are not always as valuable, authentic, original, cherishable or representative as he'd like to believe.

Anatole Broyard, "Looking at Life," in The New York Times, *September 1, 1984, p. 12.*

JANE BEIRN

Too Late American Boyhood Blues is a collection of short stories, focusing on what Hemingway called "the great American boy-man." Frederick Busch looks at this phenomenon within the context of the fragmented American nuclear family—single parents, stepparents, dual-career couples—exploring the domestic conflicts that erupt.

The young boy, still in touch with his emotions, tries to sort out the behavior of his elders or struggles for expression beneath the facade of the mature man who has learned to "talk easily without intimacy," who has found communication and camaraderie in the silences between words.

Busch, however, does not use the short story format to best advantage for this provocative theme. Too often, the kernel of his story is lost in a network of plots, or obscured by the introduction of secondary characters who detract from the salient point of his story. In **"Time Is Money,"** Busch sets out to explore the reunion between first-time lovers who meet by chance 20 years later. The opportunity to compare notes with one's first love, the temptation to explain how one has grown into a sexual being, is an intriguing premise. Had Busch fleshed out the encounter more completely, and cut back on the tangential material which he used to set the tone, his story would have delved more satisfactorily into the boy/man theme and made for more absorbing reading.

The more successful stories in this collection are about writers who use their craft as a substitute or refuge for their own emotional lives. **"Critics"** is narrated by the 9-year-old son of two fairly successful writers who possess an ability to shift back and forth between reality and fantasy with utmost facility. This habit, meant to smooth out the wrinkles in reality, instead accentuates the competition in the marriage ("everybody is a critic") and confuses their son, who still needs both the enchantment of fantasy and a way of coping with a reality that is separate and distinct. . . .

Some of the more poignant moments in Busch's stories occur in explosive confrontations between men who have known each other in a "silent companionship" for many years. In **"Rise and Fall,"** two brothers are compelled to discuss the nature of love for the first time: Jonas is about to desert his family; Jay is toying with the idea of commitment. At this juncture, Jay reaches back into what he thought was their shared past to discuss the time their parents almost separated. Jonas, the younger brother, stares in amazement—he had never known of the possible demise of their parents' marriage, "No way, not them. That's a couple," Jonas says of his parents. Jonas openly weeps. His brother moves to touch him in a gesture of compassion.

There are glimpses here of the wit, the perception about human nature, and the well-crafted prose style that earned Busch critical acclaim for his novels. The flaw in this collection is lack of proportion. Busch, perhaps more accustomed to the ample structure of a novel, fails to pare away extraneous material; as a result, the impact of many stories is diminished.

Jane Beirn, "Hurdles on a Path to Manhood," in Los Angeles Times Book Review, *September 23, 1984, p. 13.*

JOSEPHINE JACOBSEN

It is cheering, in view of many instances to the contrary, to find an experienced novelist as alert as is Frederick Busch to the deep differences between the needs of the novel and those of the short story. In [***Too Late American Boyhood Blues***], his second collection of stories, Busch knows just what he is about. Without the slightest sense of constriction, the stories have both beautiful form and that pace, whether disguised or overt, so vital to the short story. . . .

Need and control—attained, or slipping, or lost—are the focal points. Love, always needed, always desirable, always ambiguous in promise and failure, is so beset by circumstances and vulnerabilities, by the ludicrousness of mistakes, that it is never a constant. Need is always there; and the greatest need is for control over one's own future which so dizzyingly becomes one's present. Sex has, in general, become a medication, essential but with drastic side effects. Love cannot carry a marriage or an affair over the shoals of personality and circumstance; it can only make the foundering more painful. And the most pitiful and sinister aspect of the collapse in confidence is that the misery or failure of another becomes a sort of self-justification: I'm a mess; I didn't make it. But neither did he, or she. . . .

Almost every story ends in a departure, from a belief, a person, a place—a departure without a destination in any real sense. In a very short, practically flawless story, **"Critics,"** a boy learns that tales told him by his father, not as truths but as friendship offerings, are not even that—they can be trashed in a minute as counters in an adult game of hostility. In the very first story, **"The Settlement of Mars,"** a young son, sensing in the words "separate vacations" all that is ahead of him undefined, scary, and immense, is almost literally blinded by the fact that no one will define what he senses, and that words are used as hiding places. Fidelity—to the young, the dead, those present and absent, to the concept—is a need; one rarely filled, and then in damaged ways.

One might assume that these stories, filled with universal dissatisfaction, with scarred yet clinging relationships, with lethal intimacies, with derailed, ferocious and pathetic adolescents, would be both depressing and monotonous. The fact is that this is simply not so. Busch's great gift is that he can make the reader care, not just about what happens to these people, but about the people themselves. Because his characters are neither smug nor artificial, nor without some mangled hope, the total effect of the book is not a sort of viscous depression, but an experience of value and insight. The examination of the results of these particular American boyhoods is nót a sententious all-purpose diagnosis. In spite of the stories' unity, Busch is not telling us This Is How It Is. He is telling us that this is how it is with these human beings, and we can judge for ourselves how universal or endemic is their plight. He has taken a very solid risk in a collection avowedly on a common theme, and that risk has inevitable results. These stories should be read with time between each, and while this is in general true of all collected short stories, it is peculiarly true in this case. The obverse of the risk is the advantage of weight, the cumulative effect the stories bring to bear.

Busch depends on our sensibility; what we get are our cues, and our satisfaction is in our response. Description—that albatross for the neck of the short story—is detailed, but flexible and full of motion, whether it is of driving by night in a snowstorm, or the revelation by a brief look in a house, of the identity of its inhabitant. The ability to compress a trait, an emotion, a crisis in tension, into a sentence is one of his special gifts; and perhaps the book's least successful story, **"The News,"** is the only case in which he is conscious of length. But actually it is difficult to imagine Busch writing an uninteresting story.

He is subtle without pretentiousness, and often very funny. ***Too Late American Boyhood Blues*** has the feel of life, and if it says little of cheer about our predicaments, it never settles for them. And that at least is a good preliminary.

Josephine Jacobsen, "Writings of Passage," in Book World—The Washington Post, *November 11, 1984, p. 6.*

DAVID LEHMAN

The 10 stories collected in Frederick Busch's ***Too Late American Boyhood Blues*** concern, for the most part, men who tend to stand in the kitchen with a dish towel on the shoulder, "feeling needful." These are men whose wives have left them—and who are spurned or kept guessing by the women they pursue, sometimes with masochistic glee. Harry, the tabloid journalist in **"The News,"** is an extreme instance of this tendency. He chucks his job, drives in a treacherous ice storm from New York City to a remote upstate village, and descends unannounced on his reluctant former flame—all on the strength of a tersely noncommittal postcard she has sent him after four years of silence.

The trouble with Harry is that he's feeling "like a spinster" now that he's approaching 40. In Mr. Busch's universe, only the men are likely to get called by that somewhat anachronistic term; Kathy, who sent Harry packing four years back, is quite self-sufficient with her two sons and her job at the local historical association. "The kind of love you're talking about, the kind of relationship you're talking about, I think it isn't in the picture for me now," Kathy solemnly declares. "I feel like I'm Lady Brett and you're Jake," Harry replies, adding a literary dimension to their chatter.

The reference to *The Sun Also Rises* is a pointed one. These stories represent, indeed, an effort at Hemingway revisionism, at cutting Papa down to size. For his epigraph, Mr. Busch takes Hemingway's line about American men remaining boys all their lives—but his view of this phenomenon differs rather strikingly from Hemingway's. It's as though it were too late in our culture for the masculine bravado of Hemingway's *Men Without Women*.

In **"Making Change,"** one of the stronger stories here, a middle-aged novelist labels himself "the Ernest Hemingway of the teapot set." "I don't go in for enough absinthe and heroin and racing cars and killing myself," he confides. "My agent thinks that's my big problem. I diminish my marketability by not killing myself enough." The theme is echoed in **"Stand, and Be Recognized,"** where a Vietnam-era draft escapee recalls living the cafe life in the south of France: "I used to sit there and drink pastis until I admitted that I wasn't Hemingway and anise gave me the runs." In short, heroic adventure just isn't in the cards for these characters. They're determined, rather, to begin—or begin again—"the crawl toward adulthood."

There's something terribly disheartening about Mr. Busch's vision of the "great American boy-men" (Hemingway's phrase) and the way they live now. And no doubt Mr. Busch intends it that way. Though his stories are set in a variety of venues, he is particularly effective at evoking rural bleakness in upstate New York: houses with imitation brick siding and interiors furnished by Montgomery Ward, motels where "portly traveling salesmen" sit on barstools and watch "on the television set above the bar precisely what their preadolescents at home are watching." Mr. Busch has a caustic wit that serves him well. He also works hard at structuring his stories. Characteristically, he modulates from a salient boyhood memory to the grown-up predicament it foreshadows—though, alas, sometime the symmetries seem forced and the clunk of artifice can be heard.

In **"The New Honesty,"** Mr. Busch cites Ambrose Bierce's definition of destiny as "a tyrant's authority for crime and a fool's excuse for failure." That's a no-win situation any way you look at it, since there isn't an awful lot of room for free will in these stories. Mr. Busch speaks of "the new honesty" with requisite layers of irony, but one suspects that he wouldn't mind if the phrase were applied to his work.

David Lehman, "American Male Throws in the Towel," in The New York Times Book Review, *November 18, 1984, p. 20.*

MARK HARRIS

I don't always know what to say about a book—"It gave me a certain feeling . . . I liked it because it haunted me . . . took me somewhere strange I've never been." I might eventually say, as I think I must say with [***Sometimes I Live in the Country***], that I admire it, it is a worthwhile work, the author is a serious man, but I wonder whether I can honestly tell anybody he or she ought to spend $16 for a book that seems to me so much to be admired for its craft, but so stingy with its emotion. It achieves a triumph of technique, the mastery of a certain task it set for itself, but there's not the excitement of responding to someone living life very hard through crisis.

There's this boy. His name is Petey. Petey's father, until recently a New York City policeman, has broken with Petey's mother and spirited Petey into cold country in northern New York. Petey's father's desire to remain concealed, and thus to thwart Petey's mother's search for them, presents one of their major problems. They are being—for complicated reasons—harassed by the Ku Klux Klan, but they cannot report their harassment to the local or federal authorities since such an action will reveal their past.

Petey, as a matter of fact, misses his mother a great deal, though he loves and enjoys his father, who reciprocates Petey's love as well as he can under difficult circumstances. Father also loves the company of women, which Petey cannot entirely understand. A great deal of father's private business becomes uneasily available to Petey, who eavesdrops through the ventilation system upon father's conversations with visitors.

Petey, for those reasons, and for other reasons perhaps less obvious, is suicidal. In the opening lines of the book, he puts the barrel of his father's revolver into his mouth and pulls the trigger. "He didn't want to pull the trigger, but he did. He closed his eyes, and that made it easier. He tightened on the trigger and the sight came up onto the roof of his mouth and he heard the click inside his head. Then he took the revolver out of his mouth and wiped it on his shirt. He put the safety back on and went down the hill across from their house." This is a gripping way to begin, no less effective for its being in the tradition of the time-worn "narrative hook," nor is this the last time Petey plays Russian roulette with himself. I wait each time for the terrible report of his losing.

My problem is that I don't really see things as Petey presumably sees them, and I think the reason is that the author has achieved such technical virtuosity that his story is clouded by the limitations of Petey's viewpoint. Petey has been compared by boosters of this book to masterpieces of viewpoint—to Huckleberry Finn and to Holden Caulfield—and I do not want to condemn a book because of the enthusiasm of its supporters. But the creators of Holden and Huck supplied their creations with the art or techniques of translation, a filter, a process whereby the very nature of the boys' diction makes me see not only what they see in their limited range but what I, as an adult observer, would see if I were there. They offer double vision, double hearing, as this book by Frederick Busch somehow does not.

Busch has not struck the balance between Petey's comprehension and mine well enough for me to understand what Petey sees and hears in his terms as well as in mine. This is a difficulty facing an author who is ambitious to achieve a style that shall be interesting, not merely workaday. In the end, the style of the book attracts notice at the expense of the clarity or the liberation of emotions of the characters. For it is Huck's and Holden's emotional liberation that endears them to us, not the clever styles of their tales: Those are phenomena we study afterward, once having absorbed the emotional power of the work. In this book by Busch I feel myself invited to study clever technique without first being captured by the power of its narrative.

Mark Harris, in a review of "Sometimes I Live in the Country," in Los Angeles Times Book Review, *April 27, 1986, p. 2.*

CHARLES BAXTER

When first seen, Petey, the 13-year-old protagonist of Frederick Busch's vivid, moving novel [***Sometimes I Live in the Country***], is playing Russian roulette. Having stuffed the cold barrel of his father's handgun into his mouth, he is about to pull the trigger when he remembers to open his eyes. "He didn't want to miss anything." This is suicide-as-sideshow, and Petey is a true American adolescent—entertained by his own despair.

The entertainment of despair has two primary tones, sorrow and comedy, and in ***Sometimes I Live in the Country*** Mr. Busch mixes them with generally effective results. He has transplanted that perennial character, the American boy, from this particular boy's original home in Brooklyn to the rural wilds of upstate New York, and given him an affectionate, alcoholic ex-cop father, known throughout the novel only as Pop. . . .

The American boy—insufferable, insightful, ubiquitous, pathetic—has been much on Mr. Busch's mind lately, and lost, stolen or strayed children have appeared with increasing frequency in his recent work, from the 1980 novel ***Rounds*** to the 1984 collection of stories, ***Too Late American Boyhood Blues.*** In that book, the American obsession with innocence, and with process rather than product, is underscored by Mr. Busch's knowing use of a quotation from Hemingway concerning the "great American boy-men," who "stay little boys so long . . . sometimes all their lives."

If anyone should know about the effort to retain one's innocence, it's Hemingway, who also stuck a gun in his mouth, and who codified the styles of virile innocence for the whole modern period. And what is immediately noticeable about Mr. Busch's new novel is that it is written in full-frontal, blatant Hemingwayese, as both *hommage* and critique. "His father used to run the back of his hand along Petey's cheek when he was smaller. He used to do that and look at him. Once in a while he still did it. Peter would stand there and let him. What the hell."

It's hard, reading this passage and many others like it, not to think of Hemingway instead of Petey, and not to think that there are two books struggling with each other to get themselves down on the page: one book is about the implacable power of a pre-existing literary style to define the self (Mr. Busch's novel ***The Mutual Friend*** addressed this subject directly), and the second book is about a lonely kid in upstate New York, exiled among what he calls "cornheads." The occasional result of this struggle is that Petey's private story is displaced by the public-address voice of Papa.

When Petey's voice and spirit take control of the page, as they often do, the results are funny and moving in a homespun surrealist way. Mr. Busch knows exactly how adolescent agony phrases itself in exaggeration and metaphysical muckraking. In a restaurant, feeling accused, Petey "thought his head would fall off and bounce down the aisle and the waitress would trip over it." Insights with the intensity of poetry leap at him: "He got out the flashlight he'd taken from his bureau. He turned it on. Nothing happened. He wasn't surprised. He was the guy whose flashlight made things darker." He notices every anomalous adolescent sensory shock, including a high school that "smelled like hot water and creamed corn," a creepy adult whose "shirt was ironed so hard with starch that it didn't move when the guy did" and the fraudulence of the night sky: "Some of the stars were supposed to make the shape of a scorpion. He looked. The stars were a ripoff. They looked like stars."

Petey's phobias and epigrammatic innocence are set up against the much more sinister innocence and fearfulness of the upstate New York Klan members he and his father encounter. Mr. Busch presents the Klan members as shifty American boy-men in sheets, obsessed (as Petey is) with libraries and strangers, and crazed with the conviction that things should always be the same, always pure, always white.

The Klan members, and in fact nearly all the inhabitants of the community, are painted with a very broad writerly brush. All those blessed with real intelligence are from the city. As pictured, the lifetime country dwellers are 100 percent grotesques, with crooked teeth, bad breath and prosthetic hooks for hands. . . . In ***Sometimes I Live in the Country*** the villains look like villains.

Though the Klan members are dramatically presented as the products of rural poverty and social injustice, the flattening of their characterizations has the effect of making Petey's climactic moral choices seem easy. Petey thinks that people who live in the country are cornheads, and as it turns out, the book makes it appear that he's right. What he understands about his own family and what he sees he must do to help save it come as no immediate surprise.

Mr. Busch is an immensely gifted and mindful writer with an old-fashioned love for exuberant plotting and big finishes. As curious as it is stylistically, the novel has great resources of humor and—who even uses the word anymore?—tenderness.

Charles Baxter, "Petey among the Cornheads," in The New York Times Book Review, *June 1, 1986, p. 35.*

HOWARD FRANK MOSHER

Frederick Busch is a shrewd and sympathetic chronicler of modern American family life. "Is visiting old parents like visiting old friends?" he speculates at the beginning of a characteristic recent short story called **"Obits."** With a clear-eyed affection for his characters reminiscent of John Cheever's, he proceeds to examine the mutual concerns between a middle-aged couple and their elderly parents, their own children, and one another. Yet like Cheever, Busch is never content merely to tell and retell his own stories. In [***Sometimes I Live in the Country***], he has ventured deep into the heart of a strange backwater of the Northeast to explore the themes of family tension and racial prejudice in the unlikeliest of places. The result is a powerful account of coming of age in an isolated and forbidding pocket of contemporary rural America. . . .

Sometimes I Live in the Country isn't going to delight everyone with an RFD mailing address. As much as I admire the book myself, for that matter, I can't help wishing that Busch had shown us more of that substantial majority of rural citizens anywhere who do not retail hate, ban classics, shoot fawns, burn crosses, or string up newcomers. . . .

Yet, as Petey suddenly realizes one day in social studies class, prejudice has always been an inescapable part of American history, in the provinces and in the greatest cities, just as it has been an inescapable and tragic part of human history everywhere. Frederick Busch is far too skillful a storyteller to resolve all of his characters' problems at the end of his novel. But with this sobering insight, Petey has made a giant stride toward understanding one of the hardest and saddest truths of living not just in the country, but anywhere at any time.

Howard Frank Mosher, "New York State Gothic," in Book World—The Washington Post, *June 8, 1986, p. 4.*

Orson Scott Card

1951-

American novelist, short story writer, dramatist, critic, and editor.

Best known for his Hugo and Nebula Award-winning novels *Ender's Game* (1985) and *Speaker for the Dead* (1986), Card is a prolific and popular author of science fiction and fantasy literature whose predominant concern involves the development and moral growth of his inexperienced characters. Card's young protagonists are usually thrust into chaotic situations; their ability to quickly gain maturity and self-awareness often determines the fate of a community. Although some reviewers fault Card for gratuitous violence and implausible plots, he is praised for the accessibility of his narratives and his sympathetic characterizations.

Card received the John W. Campbell Award for best new science fiction writer in 1978. His first book, *Capitol: The Worthing Chronicle* (1979), is a collection of interrelated short stories set on a planet consisting of one immense city. The stories detail a revolt by the masses for control of a drug that prolongs life over several centuries. In his first novel, *Hot Sleep: The Worthing Chronicle* (1979), Card further explores the theme of what Fred Niederman termed ''skipping-stone immortality.'' *Songmaster* (1980) features a young man who achieves maturity through singing, an activity which has acquired religious significance in his society. Card blends elements of myth, satire, fairy tale, and fantasy in *Hart's Hope* (1983), a cautionary tale about extended life and immortality written in an archaic, obfuscated dialect. Don Strachan called the novel ''a full-blown epic, a lusty, bawdy pastiche evoking Rabelais, Shakespeare, Joyce.''

Card's next novel, *Ender's Game,* features a six-year-old genius who is manipulated into killing insect-like extraterrestrials through training in space battle games. Some critics faulted Card for employing the familiar science fiction premise of a superbeing who saves Earth from alien invaders. Others, however, praised Card's ability to maintain reader sympathy for Ender, despite his brutality in battle, by asserting his essential innocence and his empathy for the beings he has destroyed. *Speaker for the Dead,* a sequel to *Ender's Game,* focuses on Ender as an adult. In this book, Ender encounters an intelligent species who pose a viral threat to the human race. In addition to his science fiction works, Card has also written a historical novel, *A Woman of Destiny* (1984).

(See also *CLC,* Vol. 44 and *Contemporary Authors,* Vol. 102.)

Photograph by Jay Kay Klein

PUBLISHERS WEEKLY

[***Capitol***], concerned with the struggle between a humanistic sensibility and a mechanistic one, traces the rise and fall of Capitol, a planet that is one vast city. Here, a drug enables the privileged few to spend years in a state of suspended animation, stretching their lives to centuries or millennia, while the masses only dream of it. Eventually, a popular revolt led by a genius named Abner Doon, who has infiltrated himself into the highest levels of government, reduces Capitol to a dead steel shell, and mankind is reborn on the planet Answer. This collection of eleven interrelated but self-contained stories demonstrates a fine talent for storytelling and characterization, if a rather dour outlook.

A review of ''Capitol,'' in Publishers Weekly, *Vol. 214, No. 23, December 4, 1978, p. 62.*

BRADLEY SINOR

[In ***Capitol***], Card has produced a cycle of stories that describe the rise and fall of an interstellar empire. The keystone of the series is the drug somec, which gives man virtual immortality. The center of government in man's galactic empire is located on a planet its inhabitants call Capitol.

The individual stories range from Russian-dominated America to a far future universe ruled by a handful of immortals. There are no continuing characters except for Abner Doon, who moves behind the scenes manipulating key events for his own private reasons; and on the whole, the cycle, while entertaining, does not hang together very well. Card is a skilled craftsman, a writer to watch—perhaps his promise will be better realized in his next book.

Bradley Sinor, in a review of "Capitol," in Science Fiction & Fantasy Book Review, *Vol. I, No. 3, April, 1979, p. 27.*

FRED NIEDERMAN

Returning to the setting of his first novel, ***Capitol,*** Card explores a new set of variations on the theme of skipping-stone immortality, where citizens alternate periods of waking and suspended animation, living their 80 years spread across the centuries. [***Hot Sleep: The Worthing Chronicle***] suffers to a lesser degree from the same major problem afflicting ***Capitol***—a tendency to jump from one scene of action to another, creating a sense of short stories cobbled together rather than a novel. This new book is somewhat smoother, being unified by the personality of Jas Worthing, who evolves from hunted prodigy to politically-enmeshed space pilot to the god-like founder of a new world. What saves this book is the fact that each section is fresh, intelligent, and interesting.

Fred Niederman, in a review of "Hot Sleep: The Worthing Chronicle," in Science Fiction & Fantasy Book Review, *Vol. I, No. 11, December, 1979, p. 155.*

MICHAEL BISHOP

Hot Sleep is a weird, as well as a bad, book. The title comes from a physiological side-effect of the drug "somec," which all of Card's characters inexplicably crave as an open sesame to immortality—even though, rather than extending life, somec merely permits one to parcel out a normal life span over a period of centuries. A second unattractive attribute of the drug is that it deprives its users of their memories, a potentially ruinous inconvenience recently countered by, perhaps you've guessed it, "new brain-taping techniques." Although the phrase "hot sleep" neatly subverts the old sf bromide "cold sleep," Card seems to relish nearly every other hoary convention of the field.

Like a brutally halved watermelon, ***Hot Sleep*** splits right down the middle. Both halves are pulpy and overripe. The first is a paranoiac van Vogtian melodrama—with alarming echoes of *Slan,* in particular—set primarily against a city-planet so reminiscent of Asimov's Trantor that, like Steve Brown in a recent issue of *Thrust,* I wonder if Card is "reinventing the wheel" in blithe and total ignorance of its preexistence. The second half of ***Hot Sleep,*** meanwhile, is a post-Edenic saga devoted to the struggle of a group of colonists, all beginning with tabula-rasa minds, to formulate new identities and establish a viable civilization on another world. A good old-fashioned space battle with an unnamed enemy has destroyed the somec-soused colonists' braintapes in transit, you see; as a consequence, under the hands-off tutelage of Jazz Worthing, telepath and starship captain, the world must begin anew.

Neither half works very well, but the second is the better. Here Card jettisons some of the cheap science-fictional baggage with which he has encumbered his story, stops writing egregious lines like "two blond, blue-eyed gorillas with cheerful smiles on the front of their microcephali," and concentrates on developing a few believable and occasionally poignant human interactions. Nevertheless, ***Hot Sleep*** suffers from muzzy religio-political parallels, ill-conceived character motivations, an almost willful refusal to evoke place or mood for the reader, and some shamefully awkward prose.

Michael Bishop, in a review of "Hot Sleep," in The Magazine of Fantasy and Science Fiction, *Vol. 58, No. 1, January, 1980, p. 35.*

RICHARD A. LUPOFF

Songmaster, by Orson Scott Card is the story of one Ansset, a "Songbird" in a galactic empire of the fairly remote future. Like many such empires, the one created by Card is a strange mixture of the super-advanced (namely, interstellar travel) and the regressive (emperors, courts, armies, peasants, castles).

It's a too-familiar picture, but Card adds a most striking feature, the Songhouse of Tew. Here singing is raised to the level of a philosophy, virtually of a religion. And the finest of the singers, the Songbirds, are sent to the most deserving throughout the galaxy. The Songbirds are apparently all sopranos, sent out in childhood, their sexual maturation delayed a few years by drugs. Even so, by their mid or late teens, Songbirds return to the Songhouse to serve the rest of their lives as teachers, administrators or the like.

Ansset is the galactic emperor's own Songbird, and provides a unique point of view for a novel of personal growth and exploration melded into a tale of interplanetary politics and court intrigue. Card strives for emotional intensity and often achieves it. On occasion he deals from a stacked deck, as when he withholds information regarding a side effect of the Songbird's drug—from Ansset and the reader alike—for the sake of a melodramatic moment. But most often he plays fairly and he plays well.

If the book has a major—or even semi-major—flaw, it is a certain sense of coldness and austerity. Card is too controlled a writer for this to be inadvertent; perhaps the calculated starkness of the background is intended to make the story's physical drama and emotional intensity stand out. If so, Card sells himself short—he would have succeeded anyway. ***Songmaster*** is a first-class job, far superior to Card's previous novel, ***A Planet Called Treason,*** which was miles better than the still earlier ***Hot Sleep.***

Richard A. Lupoff, "Beasts, Songbirds and Wizards," in Book World—The Washington Post, *August 24, 1980, p. 6.*

KIRKUS REVIEWS

[***Unaccompanied Sonata and Other Stories*** is an] amiable but mostly toothless first story collection . . . from the whimsical, rather mushy and juvenile author of ***A Planet Called Treason*** and ***Songmaster.*** Best of the bunch: the gleeful and pointed **"I Put My Blue Genes On"** (colonists returning to Earth find a world devastated by an 800-year-long biological war, but devolved jingoists still keep the banners waving); **"Ender's Game"** (a well-reasoned yarn about child soldiers training in war games); and **"The Porcelain Salamander"**—a controlled and comely fable about the lifting of a misapplied curse. Other, less original tales strain for effect: [**"Unaccompanied Sonata"**]—about a genius who creates haunting music despite heavily contrived ostracism and mutilation—slips into mawkishness; **"Kingsmeat"** (people-eating bug-eyed monsters) and **"Closing the Time-lid"** (death as the ultimate orgasm) disgust rather than horrify. And, weakest of all, there are some awfully preachy items involving repentance and lessons from alien races. Again, as in the novels, the impression is one of promising ideas and good intentions undermined by lack of discipline and puerile tendencies. . . .

A review of "Unaccompanied Sonata and Other Stories," in Kirkus Reviews, *Vol. XLVII, No. 23, December 1, 1980, p. 1542.*

PUBLISHERS WEEKLY

Ideas are at the crux of SF's excitement, and Card certainly has them. You need them if you're going to build a reputation on short stories, and that's what Card, whose best work so far has been in the short form, has done. So it's not surprising he won the 1978 Campbell award as best new SF writer, and it's no surprise that [***Unaccompanied Sonata and Other Stories***] is a fizzing sparkler of a collection, with 11 stories that span the spectrum from fantasy to hard science. . . . Card's writing still leaves a lot to be desired in literary terms (beneath their surface flash his stories can be shallow and synoptic; too often he settles for easy emotion or cheats on background, as in [**"Unaccompanied Sonata"**], for the sake of an interesting idea). But this collection has exactly what [science fiction] buyers are looking for—the excitement that first hooked them on SF—and they'll overlook the author's shortcomings.

A review of "Unaccompanied Sonata and Other Stories," in Publishers Weekly, *Vol. 219, No. 1, January 2, 1981, p. 49.*

GEORGE R. R. MARTIN

Card has been the victim of a curious critical whiplash; vastly overblown praise for his first efforts, followed within the blink of an eye by savage critical "reassessments." Neither verdict was justified. The truth is that Card is a young, talented, and ambitious writer who is still in the process of growth and you can see him growing visibly in [***Unaccompanied Sonata and Other Stories***]. The title story [**"Unaccompanied Sonata"**], one of his most evocative works, demonstrates how far he has come since the early pieces that open the book, though it restates some of the same themes.

One cautionary note: ***Unaccompanied Sonata*** is often grim reading. In a brief afterword, Card says all these stories have happy endings. If so, I pray I am spared Card's sort of happiness. Story after story deals with death, pain, mutilation, dismemberment, all described in graphic detail—Card is not one to look away. One story features a detailed account of a woman's breasts being cut off and eaten. A later tale has for a horror a thing that looks like a thalidomide baby, flippers and all. The protagonist drowns it in a toilet and cuts up the body with a knife. The hero of [**"Unaccompanied Sonata"**] suffers one mutilation after another. Each of these tales might be powerful, read in isolation. Read one after the other, they are rather much. I am pleased to add that Card seems to be changing in this regard, too. In his more recent work, he seems less obsessed with graphic violence, and what remains of it is handled in much less heavy-handed fashion. (p. 11)

George R. R. Martin, "Scanning the Stars of the Short Story," in Book World—The Washington Post, *January 25, 1981, pp. 9, 11.*

ROLAND GREEN

[In ***The Worthing Chronicle***], Jason Worthing returns to take a hand in the development of the colony of refugees from the collapsing society of Capitol he founded thousands of years before. Portions of this exceedingly odd volume appeared previously as parts of Card's ***Capitol*** and ***Hot Sleep*** and his disjointed narrative technique will be troubling to those who have not read the earlier books. However, Card's fertile imagination and the sheer power of some of his characterizations—notably Worthing himself and Lared, the blacksmith's son he befriends—carry the book.

Roland Green, in a review of "The Worthing Chronicle," in Booklist, *Vol. 80, No. 2, September 15, 1982, p. 134.*

DON STRACHAN

The best science fiction creates not just a fictional world but a fictional pattern of thought, internally consistent and intersecting our own. This is just a minor achievement of ***Hart's Hope*** . . . : the tangled tragedy of Orem, who seeks to break an all-pervasive spell; his merciful, bloodstained father, King Palicrovol; a vengeful queen less forgivable than Card argues; and a Flower Princess who speaks only truth. These archetypal characters live out a full-blown epic, a lusty, bawdy pastiche evoking Rabelais, Shakespeare, Joyce. Feasts of rude wordplay, myth-twisting relationships, Homeric passions and images from the dungeons of the collective unconscious spill across these blood-soaked pages, reciting a hair-raising, psyche-scalding, tragi-comic quest straight from the ancient mind.

Don Strachan, in a review of "Hart's Hope," in Los Angeles Times Book Review, *March 6, 1983, p. 8.*

MICHAEL R. COLLINGS

In ***Hart's Hope,*** Card weaves a tapestry of myth and fantasy, fairy tale and religion, language and emotion, at times attaining to—and exceeding—the lyricism and power of ***Songmaster.*** The tale of Palicrovol and Orem (the Little King) seems at first austere and distanced. The formal "Proem," the direct addressing of Palicrovol by an unnamed narrator, and the simplified, at times almost biblically repetitive and formulaic prose structures (*not* diction) suggest at once high seriousness, epic density, and a sense of immediacy that deepens as we gradually discover who the narrator is. Interwoven with these elements are others that transport the reader further and further into the world of Burland and Hart's Hope. Card's poetic style blends with constant emphasis on Truth and (more to the point perhaps) the Naming of Names as a source of reality as characters are re-named to give them increasing depth. . . . In true epic fashion, Card virtually allows names to become the *thing* themselves—Beauty's son, through whom she will be restored to power, is Youth.

In addition, ***Hart's Hope*** incorporates a number of traditional literary devices, simultaneously altering each to make it fresh and new.

Traditional Christianity contributes the motif of the sacrifice of the Son (on many levels and in many manifestations). Card deftly handles Christian imagery, with echoes of Poe, H. Rider Haggard and T. S. Eliot, uniting them and other mythic elements almost flawlessly to generate a stirring narrative that moves to an irrevocable climax.

Several of Card's earlier themes recur here, suitably altered. He touches on longevity and immortality, as he did in ***Capitol***—and to much the same result: such powers are ultimately destructive. He again displays hesitant kingship, coupled with self-sacrifice, as he did in ***Songmaster***. Yet ***Hart's Hope*** is fresh and original, well-written and deeply moving, showing off Card's considerable skills to their fullest. (pp. 21-2)

Michael R. Collings, in a review of "Hart's Hope," in Science Fiction and Fantasy Book Review, *No. 15, June, 1983, pp. 21-2.*

TOM EASTON

[***Hart's Hope***] offers us a calling of a different sort in the realm of fantasy. In a world whose gods are the Hart, the two Sweet Sisters, and God, once lived a wicked king and his daughter, Asineth. Palicroval, one of the king's lords, rebels, kills his master, weds Asineth by rape, and exiles her in his mercy. She bears his child, learns magic, and uses the child's blood to gain awesome power. This power she uses to oust the rebel husband from his capital and enslave his new bride, his general, his prime wizard, and the gods. Her husband and his allies she afflicts with sundry boils and cramps. The people of her regained city she rules lightly. The people of the land beyond she leaves to Palicroval.

And so it goes, for three centuries, until the gods manage to engineer for Palicroval a son, Orem Scanthips, Hart's Hope. . . .

Card tells the story in a novel, effective way. The narrator, unidentified until the last page, is addressing a finally victorious Palicroval, trying to dissuade the man from killing Orem, who had occupied his throne for a time. The narrator's approach is through a series of tales, reminders to Palicroval of past history, supplies of new information, bids for sympathy and understanding. Many of the tales stand more or less alone, in form rather like myths or legends. The book thus feels ancient—not antique, nor archaic, but more like a volume of fairy tales. It seems a far more effective vehicle for fantasy than the more usual style that tries to present the fantastic as if real.

Tom Easton, in a review of "Hart's Hope," in Analog Science Fiction/Science Fact, *Vol. CIII, No. 7, July, 1983, p. 103.*

PUBLISHERS WEEKLY

Written with painstaking attention to historical detail, but not with a great deal of life, [***A Woman of Destiny***] is a novel based on the true story of Dinah Kirkham. Her father John leaves their Manchester, England, home in 1829, abandoning his wife and three children. . . . Their lives change with the appearance of an American Mormon preacher, who immediately converts Dinah, one of her brothers and their mother. The three (along with father John, who reappears) leave for America. . . . The family settles in the Mormon town of Nauvoo, Ill., and the Prophet Joseph Smith takes Dinah as his "secret" second wife (the practice of polygamy is not yet out in the open). When Smith dies, Brigham Young takes over as Prophet, and Dinah becomes *his* wife. This rambling, 700-page saga sags under the weight of Mormon dogma, which seems to take precedence over the development of characters and their relationships.

A review of "A Woman of Destiny," in Publishers Weekly, *Vol. 224, No. 22, November 25, 1983, p. 59.*

KRISTIANA GREGORY

[***A Woman of Destiny***] has a cover hinting cheap romance, but from its first vivid scenes of slums in industrial England, there's more depth than dirt. Orson Scott Card, author and direct descendant of heroine Dina Kirkham, is a powerful storyteller with the gift of making mundane details sparkle. In his engrossing epic, he brings to life this courageous pioneer who migrates to the Mormon settlement of Nauvoo, Ill., and marries Joseph Smith, the church's polygamous prophet. After his murder in 1844, she and hundreds of others flee to Utah where she becomes a stalwart leader—and one of Brigham Young's many wives. Historical events are meticulously researched; the religious doctrine is weighty but fascinating.

Kristiana Gregory, in a review of "A Woman of Destiny," in Los Angeles Times Book Review, *July 22, 1984, p. 8.*

JANRAE FRANK

When science fiction writers tell stories of military conflict set in the far future, they are saying that, in their world view, the elements in our characters that create war are so deeply rooted that we will still have been unable to eliminate them thousands of years from now. The first two volumes of Orson Scott Card's ***Ender*** trilogy, ***Ender's Game*** and ***Speaker for the Dead,*** are rife with this dyspeptic view of the human race, but Card is a writer of compassion and his heart breaks for the individual men and women of good will who find themselves caught up and forced to participate in the race's homicidal crossfire.

Ender's Game is the story of a 6-year-old computer genius whose childhood is ripped violently from him when the military, seeking to exploit his talents in a war against an alien race, drafts him into a savage "battle school" where children make war on children. Here Card focuses on the question: What happens to the heart and soul of those, unremittingly trained for war but essentially innocents, who for the (possibly delusional) safety of their people commit what amounts to genocide? Can a person redeem himself, especially in his own eyes, after helping to wipe out every man, woman and child of another people? ***Speaker for the Dead,*** set 20 years later, offers Ender—who had been tricked into xenocide in the first book by being told the battle he waged was a computer simulated practice run—a chance to redeem himself.

Once again humanity is on the verge of committing xenocide, this time against a highly intelligent but socially primitive culture whose genetic structure threatens Homo Sapiens with a devastating viral plague and, although biologists have already learned to contain it, frightened humanity as usual would rather shoot first and ask questions later. The climaxes of both volumes invoke quasi-religious images and themes . . . which suggest either some unresolved inner conflict on the author's part or else the subject matter to be dealt with in the concluding book of the trilogy.

Janrae Frank, "Wars of the Worlds," in Book World—The Washington Post, *February 23, 1986, p. 10.*

Louis-Ferdinand Céline

1894-1961

(Born Louis-Ferdinand-Auguste Destouches) French novelist, essayist, and dramatist.

The Granger Collection

A major stylistic innovator in twentieth-century literature, Céline is credited with freeing French letters from the rigid, formalized language of much nineteenth-century fiction and with introducing an immensely influential, hallucinatory prose style that posits the primacy of emotion over reason. Céline's reputation rests primarily upon his first two novels, *Voyage au bout de la nuit* (1932; *Journey to the End of the Night*) and *Mort à crédit* (1936; *Death on the Installment Plan*), which, like his later works, condemn depravity and violence through extensive use of Parisian slum vernacular, neologisms, vulgarities, ellipses, and ruptured syntax. In his fiction, Céline often drew upon personal experience to render a pessimistic and horrific vision of twentieth-century existence. Erika Ostrovsky commented: ''Céline's entire work—both in theme and style—is an illustration of the view that existence is an endgame played out on a cannibal isle or in a cosmic jungle, in an irrational and vicious setting with a multiple décor of slaughterhouse, asylum, and dunghill.''

Céline grew up in a Parisian suburb among France's lower and middle classes. He enlisted in the French armed forces in 1912 and received a medal for heroism after being severely wounded at Ypres in 1914. Following World War I, Céline studied medicine, receiving his degree in 1924, and began to travel on medical missions to Africa, Cuba, and the United States for the League of Nations. In 1928, he established a private medical practice in the ghettos of Clichy.

Many critics attribute Céline's misanthropic world view to his unhappy childhood environment, his wartime traumas, his negative experiences abroad, and his medical practice among the poor. In *Journey to the End of the Night,* generally regarded as among the twentieth century's most innovative works of fiction, Céline uses frenetic rhythms and ellipses to vitalize speech patterns and to create a nightmarish picture of a mad, disordered world beyond redemption. The novel depicts the picaresque adventures of Ferdinand Bardamu, a World War I deserter who flees life's insanity but ultimately realizes that only self-delusion can protect him from the truth at the heart of the human condition—death. The theme of human mortality is again explored in *Death on the Installment Plan,* a novel often cited by critics as Céline's most mature stylistic accomplishment. This work embodies Céline's conviction that adulthood represents the gradual death of faith and ethics. Although *Death on the Installment Plan* is essentially a *bildungsroman,* employing expressionism, grim humor, and fluctuating time frames to depict a rebellious youth's struggle to reject petit bourgeois values and familial pressures, the novel also condemns colonialism, industrialism, patriotism, Christianity, immorality, and war. Irving Howe called *Death on the Installment Plan* ''a prolonged recital of cheating, venality and betrayal: the child as victim of the world.''

Between 1937 and 1941, Céline published four controversial political pamphlets that substantially damaged his reputation. Céline's belief that Jews were conspiring with England and the United States to drive France into war with Germany fueled the anti-Semitism expressed in these essays, and following their publication Céline never fully recovered his former prominence. In the pamphlet *Mea culpa* (1937), inspired by a visit to the Soviet Union in 1936, Céline indicts the Soviet communist system for its inbred arrogance, materialism, and hypocrisy. *Bagatelles pour un massacre* (1937), *L'école des cadavres* (1938), and *Les beaux draps* (1941) contain strident anti-Semitic sentiments as well as denunciations of communism, Zionism, freemasonry, and war. Following the liberation of France by Allied forces during World War II, the French government accused Céline of wartime collaboration with Nazi Germany. Céline fled France and traveled through Germany as the war was ending; although he found sanctuary in Denmark in 1945, he was arrested and imprisoned by the Danish government on various charges for eighteen months before being granted a conditional release. When the French government finally exonerated Céline in 1951, he returned to France to resume his medical practice.

Guignol's band (1944) and the posthumously published, unfinished sequel *Le pont de Londres: Guignol's band II* (1964) explore Céline's motif of death and disintegration in savage comic terms. Like his previous works, these novels follow an alienated protagonist through strange incidents that test his perseverance. Allen Thiher described *Guignol's band* as ''a work of the comic imagination. It is a *guignol* where Céline sets forth a macabre yet hilarious puppet show animated by a lyric verve and a sense of the comic that is unique in his work." *Féerie pour une autre fois* (1952) and *Féerie pour une autre fois II: Normance* (1954), regarded by many critics as transitional works, are less passionate than Céline's earlier novels and emphasize his revolt against politics. In *Entretiens avec le Professeur Y* (1955; *Conversations with Professor Y*), an imaginary interview between an insane writer and a brilliant professor serves as a pretext for Céline's attacks on publishers, consumerism, education, and television. This book also takes the form of an artistic manifesto in which Céline likens his stylistic innovations to those of the Impressionist painters.

D'un château l'autre (1957; *Castle to Castle*), *Nord* (1960; *North*), and the posthumously published *Rigadon* (1969; *Rigadoon*) form a trilogy of novels in which Céline chronicles his escape from possible execution in France and his attempt to reach Denmark through Germany in 1944 and 1945. Written, according to John Weightman, as an "impressionistic, paranoiac monologue," the trilogy provides a poignant account of the destruction of Berlin and of Céline's quest to save himself, his wife, and his manuscripts. George Grant called the trilogy "one of the great masterpieces of western art and the greatest literary masterpiece of this era."

(See also *CLC,* Vols. 1, 3, 4, 7, 9, 15 and *Contemporary Authors,* Vols. 85-88.)

ALLEN THIHER

Céline is known primarily as the author of two novels, ***Voyage au bout de la nuit*** (1932) and ***Mort à crédit*** (1936). . . . Céline wrote, however, one more major novel, ***Guignol's Band,*** before his flight from France and his post-war exile in Denmark destroyed his health and nearly ruined his creative powers. The first part of ***Guignol's Band*** appeared in 1944, during the chaotic moments of the last months of the Occupation, and immediately before Céline's compromising exodus to Germany. Upon returning to France in 1951, Céline discovered that the manuscript for the second and concluding part of ***Guignol's Band*** had disappeared, perhaps stolen in the looting of his apartment. (p. 67)

Shortly after Céline's death in 1961, however, his secretary found by chance the missing manuscript lying in a closet. After some editing by Robert Poulet, it was published as a separate work in 1964 under the title ***Le Pont de Londres.*** This title, however, is not Céline's, nor should it lead one to suppose that the 1964 publication is a new and separate work. . . . But with the publication of ***Le Pont de Londres*** is it now evident that ***Guignol's Band*** is of the same stature and importance as ***Voyage au bout de la nuit*** and ***Mort à crédit.*** Reflecting little of the hysteria to which Céline gave vent in the polemical pamphlets that appeared between 1936 and 1941, and none of their anti-Semitism, ***Guignol's Band*** deserves the same critical attention that has recently been given to Céline's earlier novels.

In his first two novels [***Voyage au bout de la nuit*** and ***Mort à crédit***], Céline had written sordidly powerful masterpieces that were unique in their capacity to convey an immediate sense of physical disgust and delirium as a reaction to life's demented hostility. ***Guignol's Band*** is, in one respect, a continuation of the earlier works. Céline's language, fragmented and twisted, a savage blend of argot and obscenities, mimics hallucination in ***Guignol's Band*** much as in ***Mort à crédit.*** Death and destruction are again the central leitmotifs in Céline's third novel; and it is again Ferdinand, Céline's quasi-autobiographical but quite fictional hero, who must seek to survive in a world given over to pointless self-annihilation. Yet, ***Guignol's Band,*** for all that it has in common with the earlier novels, is plainly of a different stamp. As its Anglo-French title suggests, the novel is a work of the comic imagination. It is a *guignol* where Céline sets forth a macabre yet hilarious puppet show animated by a lyric verve and a sense of the comic that is unique in his work.

Another mark of difference between ***Guignol's Band*** and the earlier novels is the plot's harmonious movement. It would appear that Céline, for the first time using relatively few autobiographical sources for a novel, found himself free in ***Guignol's Band*** to write a work in which he could structure the pattern of narrated events with greater precision than he had in ***Mort à crédit*** or ***Voyage au bout de la nuit.*** In typical Célinian fashion, ***Guignol's Band*** begins with a prelude in which Céline calls forth the experience to be narrated and situates the story's narrator, though it appears at first that the narrator is to be Céline himself. For ***Guignol's Band*** opens with a horrible and sometimes incoherent vision of disaster in which French refugees are roasted by German fire during the exodus of the 1940 defeat. Céline cannot tolerate this vision and turns the narration over to his fictional narrator, who, in turn, leads the reader away from the detestable present and back in time to the London of World War I. The prelude acts through its graphic repulsiveness to compel the reader to escape and seek refuge in the wonderland of the *guignol* that Céline will present him in ***Guignol's Band.***

Céline's hero and narrator, Ferdinand, recuperating from wounds received on the Flanders front, has found shelter in London with a "band" of French pimps and prostitutes who may be likened to the puppets in the *guignol*. While under the influence of some strange cigarettes, Ferdinand participates in the accidental murder of a grotesque pawnbroker. He must spend the rest of the novel attempting to avoid the band and Scotland Yard. Failing in an effort to re-enlist, Ferdinand meets a strange Frenchman, a self-proclaimed mage who dresses as a Chinaman, and joins him in his catastrophic efforts to aid a beserk English colonel win a gas mask contest. The novel's events move circularly to come to an end when the band can find and dispose of the pawnbroker's corpse and thus free Ferdinand from his past. Ferdinand finds himself again in the same situation as at the beginning of the novel. After going through a ritualistic series of trials, he has vanquished all foes, though his principal enemy, as is always the case in Céline's universe, is death. After disposing of the damning cadaver, which incarnated death in its most material form, Ferdinand is liberated only to find himself again "down and out" in London. He crosses London Bridge, an act which reintegrates him into the *guignol* from which he had been dispossessed but which also seems to indicate that he must face anew the burlesque challenges that death forever presents. As in every *guignol* show, there is no true ending, only interludes.

Within this framework of bizarre events, which seems to be modeled on the structure of the *roman populaire* or the mystery story, Céline has displayed a lyricism quite unlike anything found in ***Voyage au bout de la nuit*** or ***Mort à crédit.*** Anger and revolt, two constants in Céline's earlier writing, have been transmuted into a *délire* of wonderment and poetic enchantment, which is the proper setting for a *guignol*. London, for example, is a fairyland in which the youthful hero is overwhelmed by its fabulous riches. . . . [Céline] has endowed his first person narrator with a scope of vision that goes far beyond the narrow limits that Céline forced on his earlier narrators. The universe is set dancing as the *guignol* players go through their ritual art.

Céline's lyricism is allied to his interest in the dance. For this Parisian doctor, the summit of esthetic perfection was incarnated in physical motion as stylized by the dance, in the perfect co-ordination of body, music, and poetry. In ***Guignol's Band*** Céline seems to attempt to imitate the vibrancy of the dance through linguistic mimesis; his broken syntax and language fragments capture rhythms that convey the emotional resonances suggested by the frenzy of the dance. Moreover, in ***Guignol's Band*** Céline has united his lyricism and passion for the dance with his obsessive concern with death. For death can be incarnated in the puppet-like characters and, on the occasion of a delirious orgy, forced to go through an extraordinary dance. Ferdinand believes he has murdered a member of the band, Mille-Pattes; yet, to Ferdinand's surprise, they later meet on a London street. Wishing to be amenable to his stinking host, Ferdinand accompanies "Lord Mille-Pattes" to a club where the cadaverous puppet throws himself into a boisterous *danse macabre*. . . . This comic dance of Thanatos presents Céline's equivalent of a "dancing god" who, through the power of farce, can negate death's power. The dance is seen through the eyes of a quite possibly hallucinated observer, for Ferdinand's battered physical state seems to be the "cause" of his fantastic visions. But it is obvious that Céline is taking advantage of his narrator to portray a vision of death in which the dance, death's own dance, is a form of exorcism. By comic reduction, Céline attempts to reduce the obsessive dimensions of death to those of a puppet dancer. (pp. 68-71)

Guignol's Band offers the most complete illustration of Céline's dance with death, though all of his novels are, in one way or another, a kind of thanatopsis. The journey to the end of the night is a journey that ends in a cry of revolt. Death on the installment plan is only one miserable way of getting to the grave, though Céline's hyperbolic black humour in [***Mort à crédit***] suggests that he was already trying to exorcise his own vision. Only in ***Guignol's Band,*** however, has Céline "tuned" his work so completely with death, has he found the animated lyricism that vibrates throughout the *guignol* play and sets death in motion as a dancing puppet. ***Guignol's Band*** ends, for example, with a dancing orgy that is the only suitable conclusion for this novelistic act of ritual. The band throws itself into an orgiastic celebration that parallels the rowdy orgies that take place at the beginning of the novel, while the bewildered hero is left alone with his own hallucinations. . . . Dance and delirium are interrelated in Céline. To be continually aware of life's absurdity, death, is a scandal that leads to *délire,* yet the freeing of the self through the emotional release of the dance is also a form of *délire*. Dance and death, the dance of death, are at the heart of Céline's vision. (pp. 71-2)

[In ***Guignol's Band***], Céline seems to have distrusted his lyrical impulse, perhaps from fear of falling into some form of mere sentimentalism, such as is in fact found in ***Voyage au bout de la nuit.*** In his ballet scenarios, published collectively as ***Ballets sans musique, sans personne, sans rien*** (1959), Céline amused himself by treating traditionally sentimental subjects in a whimsical or a satirical vein, such as in ***Voyou Paul. Brave Virginie.*** In ***Guignol's Band*** he refuses to allow his exuberance to go beyond the boundaries of his *guignol* and its comic framework, even though the boisterous poetry of London does tempt him frequently to unleash his verbal power in an exercise of poetic *élan*. Céline prefers to parody the raptures of youth that he might have exploited in a different manner. For Ferdinand, his young protagonist, is a romantic lover, which is unique in all Céline's writing. He is, in fact, a delirious version of Bernardin de Saint-Pierre's Paul, who, if he is not quite a *voyou,* is considerably more lascivious than the original model. (p. 73)

The grotesque is an element of Céline's work that has never been satisfactorily studied. Ferdinand's raptures, through comic reversal, possess a hilarious dimension, but they also are part of Céline's repertoire of grotesqueries. Ferdinand quickly becomes the lascivious dog or the slobbering pig, and his antics, though comic, are repugnant. In ***Voyage au bout de la nuit*** the initial picaresque satire gives way to a series of sluggish scenes where Céline seemed to feel the necessity of accumulating all the misery, in its most grotesque forms, that he could drag in from the Parisian *banlieue*. In ***Mort à crédit*** the grotesque abounds, often in comic forms, but often in scenes where physical delirium explodes in such a hyperbolic fashion that it is hardly tolerable. The mass vomiting by a crowd crossing the English channel, or the sexual grotesqueries that Ferdinand undergoes with Madame Gorloge seem to incarnate the world's insanity at its most feverish intensity. Yet, Céline's presentation of a demented world, of its disgustingly grotesque physical nature, is only a counterpart to his lyricism; it is a reversal of the lyricism that vibrates in much of ***Guignol's Band.***

Guignol's Band is thus quite necessary for a full assessment of Céline's work, for it is here that we can fully see how Céline's fear of his lyricism, a lyricism which must ultimately derive from his impossible thirst for transcendence, led him in his earlier novels to subvert all positive values and to decry the world with all the vehemence in his command. In Céline's case, this vehemence had one of the most extraordinary verbal talents in the history of French literature at its disposition. Céline's lyricism, then, is a chant of anger and disappointment. . . . Trapped between his indignation at the world's refusal to answer to his need for lyrical perfection and his own distrust of his sentimentality, Céline turned to his work to force an exorcism on the physical reality he detested—and yet looked to for salvation. Thus the dance, the imposing of lyrical form on physical existence, is the essence of perfection and, at the same time, participation in existence's madness. Thus the romance of youth is both a moment of grace and a moment of comic but hyperbolic madness; indeed, it is comic precisely because it so fully participates in the extravaganzas of the *délire* that holds Céline's world in its grasp.

Guignol's Band was the final work in what now appears to be Céline's trilogy. In ***Voyage au bout de la nuit*** Céline gave a portrayal of the picaro's education and then a forceful statement of his mature resignation and revolt, for Ferdinand and Robinson, Ferdinand's double, present complementing attitudes in their common refusal to accept existence. ***Mort à crédit*** is the tale of childhood's ghastly misery set against a mock epic depiction of destruction. And ***Guignol's Band*** is a delirious romance where youth acts out a parody of its obsessions. Céline has set forth a saga that encompasses childhood, youth, and maturity, a saga that is unparalleled in its depiction of destructive misery and savage humor. (pp. 74-5)

Allen Thiher, "The Yet to Be Salvaged Céline: 'Guignol's Band'," in Modern Fiction Studies, *Vol. XVI, No. 1, Spring, 1970, pp. 67-75.*

ULRICH WICKS

In both ***Journey to the End of the Night*** (1932) and ***Death on the Installment Plan*** (1936) Céline renders the night-side of life: "Shut your eyes, that's all that is necessary. There you have life seen from the other side." To see life from the other side is perhaps to see it (imaginatively) from death's point of view; and it is a life that provides the cash that pays the installments on death: life is seen not as a segmented growing-old but as a segmented death or dying. The world of order, norms, and continuum is slowly chopped up by inevitable darkness itself. (p. 25)

The withdrawal into the night-side of life is, paradoxically, also an immensely *assertive* act. In the old picaresque sense, it is the picaro's way of fighting back at mad life with a madness that itself has tremendous force. Céline's dark world begins with his prose, which seems discontinuous, full of shifts and changes of direction, full of strange verbal gestures, the posing of questions which seem to be made in the present and yet apply to the past his narrator is telling about—all this has nothing to do with flowing prose. It is a verbal energy that heightens the distorted world it renders. Yet the effect is flowing, is continuous; the three dots bridge the shift from thought to thought and from gesture to gesture much better than a final period, which has the effect of pause. ***Death on the Installment Plan*** as a whole is one continuous flow. The lack of chapter divisions gives the effect of one tremendously energetic outburst, one stutter-like yet continuous burst of language rendering the installments on death, mirroring in its unrelieved pounding the very onslaught of the chaos-world itself. ***Death*** begins as though chopped off from some previous thing:

> Here we are, alone again. It's all so slow, so heavy, so sad . . . I'll be old soon. Then at least it will be over. So many people have come into my room. They've talked. They haven't said much. They've gone away. They've grown old, wretched, sluggish, each in some corner of the world.

And it ends, or rather stops, the same way. This burst of narrative comes from the element that seems basic to Céline's art: immense verbal energy. Céline's version of the picaro is first of all thoroughly energetic—a picaro whose tactic in asserting himself against the world, in order to survive outside of it, is to use his picaresque energy verbally.

Where the more traditional picaro exists in a world full of bits of chaos, Céline's Ferdinand exists in a chaos full of bits of world. He hopes, in moments of despair, to turn it into some sort of stable thing:

> . . . All these assholes, these pests . . . you'll never see them again . . . soon they'll be gone . . . all these harmless people parading along the shop fronts . . . I wanted to jump out on them . . . to plant myself in front of them . . . and make them stop where they were . . . Grab them by their coats . . . a dumb idea . . . and make them stop . . . and not move anymore . . . stay where they were, once and for all . . . and not see them going away anymore.

But the very force and energy of his own narrative act negate any stability. Whatever the world out there may be like, Céline's narrator converts it into a constantly moving, constantly shifting and constantly pulsating thing. He compresses onto every page (indeed, into every verbal gesture, every phrase) the panoramic sense of movement and teeming life which the traditional picaresque conveys only in much larger narrative segments. He exhausts the reader, not by tedious length, but by compression, a delirium inherent in the world and in the act of perception itself. The result, as David Hayman points out, "is a vehicle capable of carrying everything, a tidal wave—or, to use Céline's own tongue-in-cheek expression, a 'métro émotif' (emotive subway) sucking the outer world into its dark maw and spewing it out again reconstituted."

Ferdinand, as narrator of his life, has stepped out of the normal, ordered world—if there even is such a thing in his world-view—and from a perspective outside the continuum of things he dares to give us an absurd portrait of the world as though his vantage point were also the *atalaya* or "watchtower" of human life of the picaresque. But his vision is a distortion, a grotesque image projected on life from a fantastic vantage point that is more like a projector than a watchtower. The more traditional picaro, the receptacle of experience, might say that this is how things are in the world, but Céline's picaro would have to add *for me*. Though we may find crazy truths and absurd meanings in Ferdinand's nightmare of waking life, he has set himself so far apart—from his world, from us—that we as readers hover precariously between being victims of his verbal onslaught (and wanting to be) and feeling superior to him because he sees himself as the victim of his world. He is the bitter clown, with a squirt gun that shoots fouler stuff than water. Only the individual, who like some wild-funny-sad-mad clown, dares to act as though he were the only man, really exists outside the continuum of things. Ferdinand is an *onlyman* who dares to do what we perhaps would like to do but cannot: step totally out of daylight and into night and chaos. Perhaps he satisfies our desire to be corrupted, "safely" through art. He may be a victim, corrupt and corrupting, but he is also his own judge. We can identify with Ferdinand and his grotesque landscape, but we would never go out and do what he does. He is our surrogate victim, and thus he becomes a purger for us. In becoming a kind of radical onlyman, Céline's Ferdinand does the dirty work for us in the circus of life. (pp. 26-7)

Ulrich Wicks, "Onlyman," in Mosaic, *Special Issue: The Literature of Exile, Vol. VIII, No. 3, Spring, 1975, pp. 21-47.*

PETER PETRO

That eminent connoisseur of eccentricity and eccentrics, Dame Edith Sitwell, has defined eccentricity as 'some rigid, and even splendid, attitude of Death, some exaggeration of the attitudes common to Life.' In the modern novel, eccentric literary characters exhibit the contrast implied in this seemingly vague definition: between the serious and the comic; the tragic and the parodic; and, finally, the transcendent and the satirical. Such eccentric characters often prepare the reader for a highly original, sometimes even shockingly unusual world view embodied in some innovative modern novels. That the reader accepts these worlds is often due to the device of the eccentric character who, through his idiosyncratic attitude, thinking, perception, or behaviour, provides the key to the no less idiosyncratic point of view proffered by the author. (p. 48)

In the comic, parodic, and satiric branch of this eccentric taxonomy belongs the genial pseudoscientist of Céline's ***Mort à crédit***: the magnificent Roger-Marin Courtial des Pereires, balloonist, publisher, inventor, exhibitionist and author of countless pamphlets. . . . Courtial's aeronautic ascents and escapes into charlatanry which, for him at least, are just another mode of perceiving or ordering the world, complement the delirious universe in which the narrator and Courtial's unwitting disciple, Ferdinand, participate. (pp. 48-9)

Courtial finds the world of theories, controversies, and pioneering inventions to his liking, though perhaps in a manner that suggests that it—like the ascents in his balloon or his hiding in the cellar—represents yet another means of escape from reality that bewilders him as much as it does the young Ferdinand. Nor is this an escape from a chaotic reality into a world of reason. . . . The best evidence of this is his apparently serious preoccupation with 'tellurism.' Here, his instinct betrays him when he provokes a riot with a series of talks on 'L'orientation tellurique et la mémoire des hirondelles,' and even more so when he gambles everything on one card, his radio-telluric growing of vegetables. For both Ferdinand the narrator (who is a Sancho-like disciple) and his quixotic master Courtial, the world is full of unexpected traps that spring up from nowhere in the guise of creditors, police, and mobs of disgruntled inventors and subscribers to Courtial's periodical *Génitron*. The relationship between the young disciple and his master, and their quest for survival, evoke a similar one found in H. G. Wells's *Tono-Bungay* (1908). Survival in Céline's world is highly problematic. The harassment, the constant badgering, and the many subterfuges periodically coalesce in scandals, in bestially erotic pursuits, and stupendous explosions, that—in the manner of fireworks—lend Céline's work the delirious quality which his disjointed style breathlessly apes. This is far from the elegant, systematic, and hagiographic portrayal of the eccentric des Esseintes by Huysmans, a creation which, Mario Praz tells us, 'resembles Poe's Usher—an Usher who follows in the footsteps of Bouvard and Pécuchet,' but who, at the same time, yearns for a cataclysm that would annihilate the modern world with raining fire on the cities of the plain!

At first it seems that Courtial des Pereires is not against modernity; he *is* modern science, running amok, puncturing the boundaries of science, and entering the domain of pataphysics. Courtial growing telluric potatoes is like Bouvard and Pécuchet converted to pataphysics by Doctor Faustroll of Alfred Jarry, for pataphysics is 'la science des solutions imaginaires,' and while Bouvard's and Pécuchet's attempts to make a killing at growing fruit end in disaster, without, however, damping their urge to learn, Courtial's disastrous radio-telluric potatoes teeming with maggots lead to his solitary death on a country road when he kills himself with a shotgun.

What can the young and cynical Ferdinand learn from Courtial? That science, like its practitioner-*manqué*, is a fraud? Or that, at best, it supplies one with knowledge which, fascinating as it often is, still remains absolutely irrelevant to the misery in the *Passage* from which emerges daily the martyred mother of Ferdinand, almost blind, hawking her wares? It seems that Ferdinand is a good listener and observer. He learns Courtial's 'science.' But, we suspect, he outgrows his master when he realizes that, far from engineering or controlling the delirious events, Courtial is as much their victim as is Ferdinand. The flight into radio-tellurism, as well as pataphysics, suggests the rejection of modernity. In this, Coutial's significance corresponds to that of des Esseintes. And, at the same time, it provides a key to Céline's hate-filled rejection of modernity that he expressed with an originality that few are willing to acknowledge.

In his next work, ***Guignol's Band*** (1944), Céline creates a grotesque reincarnation of Courtial in Hervé Sosthène de Rodiencourt. A certified mining prospector, explorer of occult hearths, and initiated engineer with a rich but soured career as a magician and illusionist, Sosthène is accompanied by a masochistic American nymphomaniac. Sosthène, sensitive enough to feel the emanations and exhalations from Tibet, is sadistic toward his companion, and, as such, is a decadent variant of the eccentric character. But he too rejects the present, prefiguring the late Céline with his prophecies of the Yellow Peril. What is more important is that Sosthène, like Courtial, helps the reader to orient himself in the phantasmagoric environment of the novel that goes far beyond the delirium of the previous one. (pp. 49-51)

Peter Petro, "Four Eccentrics: The Eccentric Character in the Novels of Céline, O'Brien, Gombrowicz and Solženicyn," in Canadian Review of Comparative Literature, *Winter, 1981, pp. 48-60.*

GEORGE GRANT

English-speaking people may find it difficult to recognize that Martin Heidegger, the leading philosopher of this western era, and Louis Ferdinand Céline (1894-1961), its greatest literary artist, were both acquiescent (at the least) towards the Nationalist Socialist regime in Germany. I do not make this claim for Céline because of his two famous novels of the 1930s, ***Journey to the End of the Night*** and ***Death on the Installment Plan,*** but because of his three books about his wanderings around Germany during its collapse in 1944-45, ***Castle to Castle, North*** and ***Rigadoon.*** The first purpose of this article is to state that this trilogy is one of the great masterpieces of western art and the greatest literary masterpiece of this era. It would be more prudent to flatter this age which worships "individuality" and confine the claim to my "personal" opinion. Aesthetics would be a "subjectivist" way of looking at the matter. But let's leave these clever difficulties aside for the moment.

Such homage to Céline appears necessary because in the present literary scene in the English-speaking world his works have been shunted aside, because of his anti-Jewish pamphlets of the 1930s and his passive acceptance of the German occupation of Paris in the 1940s. The contemporary way of writing about him is generally the following: here is a writer whose two main novels in the 1930s were stylistically immensely influential, and for these he will be remembered; but in the later 1930s he degenerated into mad and vicious polemical writing and collaborated with the Nazis. He will remain in the history of literature for those two remarkable early novels, but his later writings are not worth our attention. . . . To all the contempt that has surrounded Céline the central answer is just to say, "Read."

To say this, however, is not to deny that questions arise if one reads Céline with any knowledge of his life. In the light of all the nonsense that has been written about him and in the light of his greatness, it is necessary to proceed carefully in the formulation of the question. At its most simple, the question might be: How can one be enraptured by the art of somebody who wrote anti-Jewish pamphlets in the thirties? But this is not the best formulation. Dostoevski's dislike of the Jews does not stand in the way of being enraptured by his novels. (pp. 801-02)

The question can be best formulated in a slightly different way. Céline's judgments of the thirties make suspect for us the actuality we seem to be given in the trilogy about the fall of Germany. We are forced to ask as we drink from the chalice of his art whether its ingredients are not poisoned and therefore not to be commended to our own lips. If in the 1930s he can write as if the crisis of imperial technological Europe can be explained primarily in terms of the responsibility of the Jews, then is his art not marred at its core by simple failure of vision? To put the matter in the limited terms of my own experience: I am given in the trilogy the wonderful sense that this is the way things are; this is a monumental chronicle telling the truth about a great event in terms worthy of Homer. Then that apperception falls away as made suspect by the remembrance of the particularity and violence of his political judgments of the 1930s. I prefer this formulation of the question to those that are based on some supposed understanding of the worthlessness and odiousness of his character. I prefer it to those who say that he ought to have had better political judgments. It is best to say that the extremity of some of his earlier writing makes suspect the very substance of his later art.

In terms of that formulation, it is necessary to discuss (*a*) Céline's "madness" and (*b*) his politics. These two questions are, of course, closely related. But I will discuss the first one simply in terms of the evidence for it in the trilogy. The second will be discussed in terms of a knowledge of the details of his life. It may seem tiresome antiquarianism to raise in detail the political questions of half a century ago. However it seems important to do so, because of the claims I am making about Céline's genius. First it is necessary to say something about what the trilogy consists in as a story. (pp. 802-03)

[***Castle to Castle, North,*** and ***Rigadoon***] describe how Céline and his wife Lili and his cat Bébert struggle through collapsing Germany in their effort to escape to Denmark. He had reason to want to escape. The French Left were baying for his blood. To put it violently but accurately: the plagiarizer of Heidegger was calling for his execution. The journey takes place while the Russian armies get closer and closer, and while the American and British bombers flatten and reflatten the cities. Roosevelt's unconditional surrender is in full swing. Europe is being demolished by the two great continental empires with the help of the British. Céline's chronicle is of the collapse of that Europe and is laid before us with prodigality.

From that last sentence three points must be expanded. First, it is a chronicle—a chronicle "of wasted time." . . . Second, it is a chronicle of great events. A great subject is necessary but not sufficient for a serious work of art, as the novels of Hemingway and Mailer tell us negatively. I do not know whether Aristotle is correct in saying that war is coeval with humanity. But up to this point it has been. Therefore it has been a central subject of art. In our era war has been particularly prevalent because of technology, and has taken new forms because of technology. . . . Céline chose for his last masterpiece technological war. (He died the day that ***Rigadoon*** was completed.) Third, it is a chronicle told with prodigality.

I must pause to say carefully what I mean by "prodigality," because its presence in Céline is central to this tribute. For us it must be a pregnant word, for it is used in the English translation of a parable in divine revelation. The shorter Oxford English Dictionary says that it means lavishness to the point of waste. Therefore the word may not seem appropriate to great art. Who would dare say that there is waste in Shakespeare, Mozart or Raphael? But what other word will do for this essential quality which seems common to the great artists? "Profligacy" is the word for the vice, and the distinction therefore implies that prodigality is not of necessity vicious. "Profuseness" means the ability to pour forth. But it sounds ridiculous to say that Shakespeare or Mozart was profuse. Indeed the use of the word in the translation of Christ's parable points to its meaning in the present connection. The prodigality of the son is related to the particular joy in the father's welcome. An analogy may also be taken from nature. In nature there seems to be an extravagant waste that would not have been the case if a sensible human being had made it. It seems that all the very great artists share in this mysterious lavishness. . . . It is this prodigality which above all raises Céline's art to a different level from that of Proust or Joyce, James or Lawrence. The chronicle is spread out before us—ruined soldiers, refugees, collaborationists, SS leaders, dying women, the animals, etc., etc., talking and running, cheating and dying, loving and fearing, defecating everywhere from Pétain on down. About the magic of the art in which the dance of this prodigality is achieved—well, it is magic, and I cannot speak of it here and perhaps not at all.

What about Céline's "madness"? I do not mean by madness here that divine frenzy which Plato tells us is necessary to the greatest poets. I am the last person to say that Céline did not possess that "mania." But those who write of Céline's madness do not mean that. They mean paranoia as the OED defines it: "chronic mental unsoundness characterised by delusions and hallucinations." When people speak of his madness they mean some unsoundness which makes him distort reality in his art. Is his art corrupted by such distortion, as indeed much art has been? In such art reality is not laid before us so that we can take it to heart; what is laid before us are the compulsive fantasies of the writer as if they were the truth.

Two preliminary remarks are necessary before I proceed to the question. First, the old cliché: "Just because you're paranoid doesn't mean you aren't being persecuted." To repeat, throughout the 1940s and 50s the Left in France called for [Céline's] blood. . . . Secondly, hatred is present in all his books. He had grown up in the lower reaches of the small bourgeoisie; in that class which was always trying not to be proletarianized, never having enough to eat and always having to toady in order to stay out of destitution. He describes it in the account of his youth in ***Death on the Installment Plan.*** "If you haven't been through that you'll never know that obsessive hatred smells like . . . the hatred that goes all through your guts all the way to your heart." But are hatreds a mark of madness? Aren't all of us, other than the saints, full of hates of one kind or another? To deny that most human beings hate is to confuse the immediate facts with the highest end, and to deny that that end is supernatural.

To return to the centre of the question: Is reality distorted in the trilogy by Céline's madness? Those who think so fail to grasp what the book is. Céline is telling the story of himself and his wife and his cat wandering around a bomb-wrecked Germany. He is there as storyteller, and he is there acting in the story. It is not some novel where the writer lives "standpointless" outside the book. Céline's art may give the impression of madness because he is able to hold inwardness and outwardness together in a marvellous way. Céline is always present in the 1950s as well as in the 1940s. . . . When at the height of the highest of the three books, ***Rigadoon,*** he is in the midst of the destruction of Hanover by the flying fortresses, we are present in his hallucinations when he is hit by a brick. But is this madness? How can one better tell what it is like to be in the midst of saturation bombing? When one says this, it is well to remember that English-speaking people have done most of the bombing of this era, not so much suffered it.

Céline's inwardness is not madness, but the art whereby he is present in the books both as storyteller and participant. Old men like to tell stories about the events of our lives. In comparison with the unity of the inward and outward in Céline's writing, Proust seems a Trollope of the Faubourgs and Joyce's Mollie Bloom a literary device. This is not somebody who would qualify as the ideal of what psychiatric social workers want us to become. But it is worth remembering that the society which lives under this ideal is not one which seems to produce great works of art.

If I were to use a colloquial title for this writing, it would be "Up Yours, Matthew Arnold." To see life steadily and see it whole is an admonition that is likely to be self-defeating for poets. Yet those who call Céline mad would have liked to have lived by it. To repeat: it is reported that the saints in prayer can at moments touch that love wherein "the tears, the agony, the bloody sweat" can be loved. But for the rest of us all too often the attempt to see it steadily is a method for not seeing it whole. . . . Céline was a dedicated doctor who at the height of his poetic art wrote of technological war with incredible tenderness. A steady story of what he had lived through would have been a distortion and corruption.

The definition of poetry as "emotion recollected in tranquility" must be given greater respect than the "steadiness" business, because it comes from a greater poet than Arnold. After Céline had been cleared by the court, he had enough immediate tranquility to write his epic poem. Recollection certainly required tranquility at that basic level. But why should the storyteller in the suburbs pretend in his recollecting that he is some jolly old reconciled gent who has put on a mantle deemed appropriate by those who feed our academic fodder machines in cosy universities? Indeed it appears to me that those who write of Céline's madness and how it vitiates his art are in fact trying to put aside the truth he is telling us. They often seem to go further and wish for him to be mad so that what is told herein can be emasculated. This is of course closely related to the opinion that he must be mad, for how else could he have held such political opinions?

What then of Céline's politics? I must first state that it seems to me unimportant to take seriously the political judgments of most of us. They are caused mainly by necessity and chance—occasionally a little by good. They are better understood in terms of comedy than by behavioral science. And this still remains the case despite our extreme politicization in the technological age. It certainly applies to Céline's politics. They are only to be described because they have stood in the way of the proper recognition of his art—particularly in the English-speaking world. It is useful therefore to look at his politics—albeit they have no contemporary significance and are an historical curiosity.

Céline's first political principle was that war between France and Germany should be avoided at all costs. As a youngster he had been thrown into the carnage of the 1914 War, and had been badly wounded. He wanted the Europeans to stop killing each other before they were swallowed up by the alien empires which surrounded them. . . . Céline wanted to save Europe (for him above all France) from tearing itself up, and from invasion by the two continental empires which waited in the east and west [the Soviet Union and the United States]. . . . As war approached, Céline thought that the Jews and the English were trying to push the French into war with the Germans, and that this should be avoided at all costs. (pp. 802-08)

Céline's intensity of desire that there should be no repeat of war between Germany and France led to his politicized writing, based on an inadequate premise—namely, that the overriding cause of the European crisis in the 1930s was the Jews. He certainly must be credited with a major mistake in political judgment and a great lack of moderation in writing about it. Beyond this, he must certainly also be seen as somebody whose life and art is packed full of the modern ideas that had come to flower in the last centuries and which swept over Europe at the time of its collapse as a civilization. But this last has been a state common to all western art and thought in this terrible era. Its consequences have, of course, been worse for philosophy than for art. Céline at the best of times was, both for good and for ill, a singularly unphilosophical being. He had all the contempt of the deprived for theories. This was good in that the immediacy of his art is not thinned by general ideas; it was for ill in that the absence of philosophy left him open to the "spirits" of the age.

Céline often spoke of his "disaster"—the period of his life from 1930 to 1950. He seems to have meant that period when he wrote of the public world, and the consequences he paid for it in persecution. Indubitably that long disaster is something to be regretted in the life of a great artist. In that disaster what is marred for us in Céline is his judgment, albeit at a time when such failure was widespread. By the time Céline is writing this trilogy in the 1950s he is all political passion spent. His hopes have been burnt out of him by prison and persecution, by poverty and by age. The splendor of his art lays before us Europe's collapse. Indeed, the very high splendor of his art is somehow related to the fact that his hopes have been burnt out. In this sense the question about this writing can be answered negatively. The greatness of his art is not corrupted by the follies of his "disaster." His trilogy is not a poisoned chalice. We drink from it the truth of the human condition. (p. 812)

George Grant, "Céline: Art and Politics," in Queen's Quarterly, *Vol. 90, No. 3, Autumn, 1983, pp. 801-13.*

PATRICK McCARTHY

Maudits soupirs pour une autre fois is an early version of ***Féerie pour une autre fois*** and of ***Normance*** or ***Féerie II***. Toiling through a thousand pages of Céline's often illegible handwriting, Henri Godard has assembled a text that begins with Clémence Arlon's visit, depicts the Royal Air Force bombing of Montmartre and concludes with the narrator's quest to find a safe place for his manuscripts before he flees to Denmark. . . . ***Maudits soupirs*** is so interesting that it deserves a wide and not merely a specialist audience. Moreover the frequent blanks and the notes indicating that the manuscript contains two or three words instead of one, or that names are being changed, remind us of Céline's finished novels, where the text often corrects itself in order to warn the reader that the seeming perfection of the traditional literary work is a mystification.

In one respect ***Maudits soupirs*** is better than ***Féerie***. There Clémence Arlon visits the narrator, Ferdinand, because he is about to be murdered by the Resistance; curiosity about other people's demise is a familiar but banal theme in Céline's work. Here she comes because she has copies of his books and she wants him to sign them, which he will not do. The notion that the written language is alienating is widespread in modern thought, but few have gone as far as Céline in identifying writing with a criminal act of violence. So Ferdinand refuses to sign his name or to take responsibility for his books and, when eventually he does so, the RAF arrive and the bombing begins.

This episode is less good than ***Normance*** although the villain-hero is the same: Ferdinand's other self, Jules, the painter who has "a forelock like Hitler's" and who orchestrates the bombing, turning Paris into one of his canvases. But Jules's seduction of Lili, who as a ballet dancer incarnates the liberating power of art, is missing and the dance-like structure of ***Normance,*** where different artists gain control in turn, has still to be worked out (it is surprising that no choreographer has turned ***Normance*** into a ballet). In particular the superb scene where the actor Le Vigan takes over and transforms Paris into a silent film was invented later.

Féerie contains a long monologue delivered by Céline from his Danish prison and there are echoes of it in the last segment of ***Maudits soupirs,*** but the principal narrator is the Ferdinand who prowls the Montmartre streets in 1944. Interwoven with depictions of Céline's friends like Marcel Aymé, who appeared to Céline the model of the clever writer, is a lament for the past Montmartre. As so often in Céline's books this nostalgia is not very convincing because there seems to be so little in the past that is worth conserving. Céline may or may not have been a Fascist but he was no Tory. The ***Féerie*** monologue where the demonic writer gains revenge on his persecutors by imposing his language on theirs is better, but there is a hint of this motif in ***Maudits soupirs*** where the manuscripts are to be saved so that Céline's vision of history—or rather his legend, for one of the manuscripts is the Krogold saga—may oust the Resistance version.

Patrick McCarthy, "The Villain-Hero Unmasks," in The Times Literary Supplement, *No. 4340, June 6, 1986, p. 625.*

NANCY RAMSEY

In ***Conversations with Professor Y*** [Céline] set out to restore his reputation as an innovative literary stylist. . . . Professor Y is a fictional foil for the author's digs at formal literature, and much of ***Conversations*** is hilarious. Céline is self-mocking as he tries to get his name back into circulation. He compares an eager genius to the new Big Bubbly soap product, is adamant in his revulsion at the ascendancy of ideas over emotion and is passionate in his desire to capture the immediacy of conversation on the page. "*The emotion of spoken language through the written form!* Just reflect on that a bit, dear Professor Y! get your noodle in gear!" Poor Professor Y! This dull academician (whose most intelligent comment is "Why, holy moly! you're afloat in dialectics!") is led on a dizzying tour of Paris, overwhelmed by a crazed author who claims he's on the brink of a revelation just when the professor expresses a need to find a bathroom. ***Conversations*** is essential for Céline fans, and a good, if tame, introduction for the uninitiated.

Nancy Ramsey, in a review of "Conversations with Professor Y," in The New York Times Book Review, *August 31, 1986, p. 13.*

ALLEN THIHER

In publishing [***Maudits soupirs pour une autre fois***], the tireless *célinien* Henri Godard is not offering us something of the same importance as ***Le pont de Londres.*** He has, however, given us some materials about Céline's attempt to save his manuscripts, and in publishing them he has rendered a good service to students of modern French literature.

As Godard makes clear, what he offers are essentially early drafts of texts that preceded Céline's completing ***Féerie pour une autre fois I*** and ***Normance*** (or ***Féerie pour une autre fois II***), a single work that Céline began during his stay in prison in Denmark and finished during the fifties in Paris. ***Normance*** ends with a cascade of papers showering down on Céline as he wanders in occupied Paris after an Allied bombardment. These papers are the manuscripts that he wanted to save. ***Maudits soupirs*** shows how central that preoccupation with his manuscripts was to Céline, for the most original part . . . is essentially a tale of Céline's trying to find a safe place for them, before, as he would have it, he was eviscerated by one of the victorious powers.

Maudits soupirs actually offers three manuscripts: a hundred or so pages of text that would appear to be a first version of ***Féerie I,*** presenting Céline in his apartment in Montmartre; a second manuscript of another hundred pages that might have been a third *féerie* coming as a narrative after ***Normance;*** and finally, a briefer third section, apparently part of a version of ***Normance,*** that also presents Céline's attempts to escape from his savage neighbors while protecting his manuscripts. Godard fills in with some résumé from another manuscript, though in no sense do the materials fit together as a unified narrative. For the reader who has made his way through Céline's snarling at him at the beginning of ***Féerie I*** and through the fantastic bombardment orchestrated by the diabolic artist Jules in ***Normance,*** the new texts do provide insight into the way Céline reworked his material. They also provide some choice moments of Céline's caustic verve as well as show, once more, how little contrite he was for his insane polemic against the Jews. In any case, *céliniens* the world over will be grateful to Godard for the work involved in deciphering what are often very comic texts.

Allen Thiher, in a review of "Maudits soupirs pour une autre fois: Une version primitive de Féerie pour une autre fois," in World Literature Today, *Vol. 60, No. 4, Autumn, 1986, p. 594.*

ANATOLE BROYARD

There's no doubt that Céline was a great novelist in ***Journey to the End of the Night, Death on the Installment Plan*** and ***Castle to Castle.*** Leon Trotsky, of all people, described him as well as anyone. Writing in *The Atlantic Monthly* in 1934 when ***Journey*** was translated into English, Trotsky said that Céline "walked into great literature as other men walk into their own homes."

Yet it is also true that during World War II Céline published several virulent anti-Semitic pamphlets, and the relation between his genius as a novelist and his anti-Semitism has never been satisfactorily explained. It is my theory that in his paranoia Céline saw the Jew as an "influencing machine," just as schizophrenics often report themselves persecuted or dominated by mysterious agencies or forces. Paraphrasing Trotsky, we might say that Céline wrote those pamphlets as some men walk *out* of their homes.

A degree of madness in literature is nothing new. For the past 100 years novelists and poets, especially in France, have been looking covetously at the irrational as a kind of reservoir of the absolute. Baudelaire put it best when he said, "I cultivate my hysteria with joy and terror.'' Going farther, the Surrealists saw the irrational as a panacea, confusing it with art. In 1932, in the Surrealist issue of *This Quarter,* Salvador Dali wrote an essay on the ''paranoiac-critical'' theory of literature, and in our time paranoia has become a popular mode for trope in fiction, one that comes with a ready-made structure and intensity.

The difference between Céline and the Surrealists is that his insanity is *serious*. More than any other major novelist, he provides us with a full-blown case history. He demonstrates what he himself called ''the novel's revenge.'' Like a mad dog turning on its master, the novel sometimes repays our liberties and our experiments by getting ugly. In our own fiction, we can see this in books like *Gerald's Party* by Robert Coover or Norman Mailer's *American Dream*. (The American dream is our most popular version of the influencing machine.)

In Céline's work, as in Mr. Mailer's and Mr. Coover's, the irrational is a profounder form of profanity or obscenity, a gesture almost as striking as suicide or murder. There's a hint of uncanniness in craziness: we see, or at least we think we see, to the bottom of personality. Céline's insanity is so startling because, more than anyone else, he found the inevitable voice for it. . . .

Voice is the most insidious appeal in literature: it reminds me of those heartbreaking tenors in Bach cantatas who represent the soul pleading with God. Sanity is, in a sense, a skepticism about one's voice—not believing in it too much. Céline's voice can be spare, as in ''Almost every desire a poor man has is a punishable offence,'' or baroque, as in ''A well-cared-for body always suggests the possibility of theft, of a lovely, direct, intimate intrusion into the reality of wealth and luxury, without the fear of punishment.''

As Parisian slum doctors, both Céline and his protagonist Bardamu did postgraduate work in misery. Céline's doctoral dissertation was on Ignaz Semmelweis, a Hungarian obstetrician who slit his fingertips and plunged them into the corpses of women who had died in childbirth in order to prove, by infecting himself, that puerperal fever could be transmitted by the physician. When his colleagues ignored him, Semmelweis stood on street corners hawking his pamphlets and crying ''Wash your hands! Wash your hands!'' Céline's whole career as a novelist might be seen as an unsuccessful attempt to wash his hands of humanity—when this failed, he turned to attack in the pamphlets.

Céline naïvely saw himself as ''inventing'' the sound of spoken language in literature. He raved about his ''three dots,'' his ''emotive subway,'' with which he broke his sentences into fragments. The truth of the matter is that ***Journey*** reads better, not in the ''faithful'' translation of Ralph Manheim, but in the earlier rendering by John H. P. Marks, in which the punctuation is conventionalized. It's difficult to achieve a good complex sentence or any kind of rhythmical variety when every clause is isolated by three dots.

''Don't give it [emotion] a chance to dress up in sentences,'' Céline said—but that's what literature is: emotion dressed up in sentences. Falling for the old imitative fallacy, he splutters like a street corner evangelist, his three dots flying like spittle. While modern fiction relies increasingly on voice, it is necessary to remember that the final, most intimate voice is the one that only the author can hear. Insanity talks primarily to itself. All too often, Céline's voice turns Pentecostal and speaks in tongues. His was a journey to the end of the voice, the last stop on his emotive subway.

The trouble with voice in literature is that it can so easily grow garrulous. We hear this already in Dostoyevsky's *Notes From Underground,* which paved the way for Céline, just as he in turn made *Tropic of Cancer* and *Portnoy's Complaint* possible. Reading the long paranoid harangue about publishers at the opening of ***Castle to Castle,*** we remember the Underground Man talking our ear off in Dostoyevsky's first section. People don't deserve our restraint, Céline said—but he forgot that art does.

The irrational voice slides too easily toward harangue. It discourages qualification and contact, and the reader is reduced to the role of voyeur rather than sympathizer. Literature, by definition, is a mitigation of our madness, a conspiring with it—not a surrender to it. We can only bear edited versions of one another. Even lovers don't mean it when they cry ''Tell me everything!'' A literature that tells us everything talks itself out of art.

Anatole Broyard, ''Writing Off the Deep End,'' in The New York Times Book Review, *February 1, 1987, p. 11.*

STEPHEN DAY

Observed as a whole, Céline's work is a journey through the events of the twentieth century with its wars, chaos and apprehension. And a great part of Céline's urge to write is the desire to achieve a mode of expression capable of relating them. In attempting to do so, Céline must constantly put himself in jeopardy in order to feel intensely, and ultimately to be part of the quest. Frequently, he says about himself: ''j'ai risqué ma peau—I stuck my neck out'' (understood: unlike other writers), in order to justify his life, his vision and his style. Except for a few short ballet scenarios, none of Céline's books is removed from the present, from the moment of its composition. One might assume that his novels, pamphlets and ''chronicles'' constitute three distinct literary modes. Nevertheless, they are intertwined and produce a constant flow of the same voice whether it is narrative, reflective or prophetic.

Céline was officially punished for his pamphlets, and only for them. But in a later preface to ***Journey,*** he asserts that the most ''wicked'' of his books is his first novel [***Journey to the End of the Night***]. And indeed, there is a growing awareness that very early Céline willed his fate, even engineered his own damnation, in order to write. (p. 82)

Céline encountered his first enemies with the publication of ***Journey.*** He had fashioned a style of writing hitherto unknown in French letters and expressed that which few authors before him dared to say. Céline was renovating the French novel, giving it a pace and tone unheard of since perhaps Rabelais. In 1932 this produced conflicts, the most famous of which was the splitting of the Goncourt prize committee. Céline lost the Goncourt, but in the long run was delighted with his status as a famous loser (the winner has been almost completely forgotten). Although it departs from the traditional novel, ***Journey,*** because of its structure, does remain a novel. Its fiction rests mainly upon the distance which separates Bardamu, the protagonist-narrator, from Céline, the author. Despite some character-resemblance and the similarities of their war experiences and travels, Bardamu is still a fictional hero invented by Céline. Yet the book outlines some characteristics of the future chronicler: the manner in which Bardamu connects seemingly disparate events in order to draw moral conclusions or to project his vision of an endless night. In ***Death on the Installment Plan,*** the narrator is more sharply in focus. Ferdinand, Céline's own second name, is a doctor who tells about his childhood until the moment he decides to join the army. ***Journey*** and ***Death*** are then written in reverse sequence. Their sequel, ***Casse-Pipe*** (***Break-Neck***), in which Ferdinand has become a soldier, exists only as a fragment. The manuscript was almost entirely destroyed when Céline's apartment was pillaged in 1944.

Céline wrote his pamphlets between 1936 and 1941. The shorter ***Mea Culpa*** is a blueprint for the three major ones, ***Bagatelles pour un massacre*** (***Trifles for a Massacre***), ***L'École des cadavres*** and ***Beaux Draps*** (***Fine Mess***). The first was the result of Céline's visit to the Soviet Union where he wished to spend the royalties that the Russian translation of ***Journey*** had brought him. In ***Mea Culpa,*** he denounces the Communist myth, provoking a backlash against himself by those who thought him to be a friend of the proletariat. With the subsequent anti-Semitic, pacifist pamphlets, Céline was to put his life in danger. It should be noted that during the Occupation, Céline regularly insulted Hitler and the Nazis verbally and in print. Germany remembered this during his precarious exile there. But once again this was to be a boon, giving rise to the powerful account of his odyssey in ***D'un château l'autre*** (***Castle to Castle***), ***Nord*** and ***Rigodon,*** in which the narrator, chronicler and author meld into one character: Céline, the pariah, the hunted animal, the target. (p. 83)

[***Conversations with Professor Y***] presents several of Céline's preoccupations and techniques. At the time, Céline was attempting to re-enter the literary world and regain the interest of the reading public. He creates an imaginary interview with Professor Y—who is also a retired colonel in disguise, with a prostate problem. The "interviouwe," as Céline writes it in the original text, rapidly becomes an opportunity for him to rail against publishers, readers who borrow books rather than buy them, the mentality and practices of a consumer-oriented society, institutions, education, the arts, television, other writers, and much more. But progressively, these jibes give way to a more formal discourse on the nature and purpose of Céline's literary style. In many ways, we are reminded of Diderot's allegorical *Jacques le Fataliste*. Here, as in other works, Céline creates a grotesque double who becomes a foil. In this way, Céline is able to dialogue with himself, or with another self, playing all the parts simultaneously, mocking himself while deriding others, whom he makes to speak like him. The more Professor Y tries to argue or object, the better Céline is able to devastate him.

A great part of ***Conversations*** is devoted to the definition, justification and illustration of Céline's style. "I have no ideas, myself! not a one! there's nothing more vulgar, more common, more disgusting than ideas! libraries are loaded with them! and every sidewalk café! . . . the impotent are bloated with ideas! . . . and philosophers!" But, ever so modestly, he does claim that he is "just a little inventor" of a special "technique," a "gimmick" in the area of stylistic expression. And he compares himself to the Impressionists, who after the invention of photography developed a new emotional approach in order to transpose reality on canvas. Céline's innovation is "to pin emotion down on the printed page."

> Emotion is only found, and that with great difficulty, in the spoken word . . . emotional can be tapped only in the spoken language . . . and reproduced through the written form only by hard labor, endless patience such as an asshole of your sort could not even suspect!

Inevitably, Céline is drawn to his long-standing image of writing and reading experienced as a journey. Another component of his invention is "le métro émotif":

> I take everybody, willy-nilly, with me! . . . charge along! . . . the emotive subway, mine in a dream! no draw-backs, nor congestion . . . never stop, nowhere! . . . straight through! destination! in emotion! . . . powered with emotion! only the goal in sight: full emotion . . . start to finish! . . . Thanks to my streamlined rails! my streamlined style!

Throughout ***Conversations,*** Céline claims for himself the same status given to creators in painting, architecture and music. It seems paradoxical that he disowns the stolid, plodding, fossilized forms of traditional literature, while at the same time he formalizes the result of his reflections and practice over many years in this manifesto, as if it were a quest for classicism. But in his lucid and succinct introduction to the volume, Céline's translator invites the reader to enjoy the work without misgivings:

> ***Conversations with Professor Y*** is no scholarly treatise on the art of writing, no codification of precepts to be followed. . . . The ***Conversations*** are not simply a genteel exchange of views on the subject of literature. Far from it. They become a brawling, incontinent stampede across Parisian streets and parks, a maniacal buying binge, an alcoholic guzzle, an insane nude frolic through public fountains and finally the calm of exhaustion. Now that is a statement backed up by example. A poetic art to be remembered.

Translating Céline is an enormous challenge, as Stanford Luce is well aware: "Since no French writer has yet equalled Céline's style, it is obvious that in another language such a feat is all the more improbable." One is confronted with far more than conventional problems of lexical and grammatical subtitles. Céline's style is poetic, so that rhythm and tone must be considered; it breaks away from formal French grammar and syntax, but then sometimes reverts to them to achieve parody; Céline uses all the resources of *argot,* slum slang, shop talk, the language of pimps, prostitutes, bums, criminals in addition to the discourses of professionals. But "equally important as part of the Céline impress, is the invention and deformation of words. Many specific examples can be found where meaning and emotion (fear, derision, exaggeration or violence) are combined in one term." In such a situation, many readers will all the more enjoy and be grateful for Luce's facing-page bilingual edition (not a practical possibility for most other Céline's works owing to their bulk). It will be seen that for the most part Luce has been able to maintain a close parallel to Céline's phrasing and rhythm. But the transposition of standard idioms as well as Céline's own appear to present the translator with a disproportionate amount of difficulty; and it must be admitted that occasionally, if the French text were not *vis-à-vis,* the English one would be incomprehensible. (pp. 87-9)

[This problem] should not deter readers interested in Céline and in the adventure of an extremely difficult translation. ***Conversations*** is an eminently satisfying reading experience made possible by a dedicated Céline researcher. . . . [Although] many comparisons may be made, as a writer and as a man Céline is remarkable in that he reminds us of no one else. (p. 90)

Stephen Day, "Louis-Ferdinand Céline Observed and Translated," in Queen's Quarterly, *Vol. 94, No. 1, Spring, 1987, pp. 81-90.*

Andrée Chedid

1920-

Egyptian-born French novelist, poet, dramatist, and essayist.

Chedid's works reflect a blending of European and Middle Eastern cultures. Noted for her poetic language rich in symbolism and metaphor, Chedid depicts archetypal characters and situations to explore such concerns as love, communication, oppression, and identity. She frequently blurs distinctions between memory and fantasy and between past, present, and future to focus upon the intense emotional states of characters involved in personal crises and social conflicts.

Of Egyptian and Lebanese descent, Chedid moved to France while she was in her early twenties and began her literary career writing poetry. While her first volume of verse, *On the Trails of My Fancy* (1943), was written in English, her succeeding volumes have been composed in French. As in her novels and plays, Chedid's poetry evokes the settings and cultures of Egypt, Lebanon, and France and explores themes related to youth, death, war, love, and time. She employs lyrical language, and playfully juxtaposes such devices as metonymy, synecdoche, apostrophe, personification, and tropes to create shocking and jarring effects. Bettina Knapp commented: "In Chedid's inner world, words and letters are activated, expand, dilate, influencing her earthborn verbal pictures as attested to in so many poems appearing in *Textes pour une figure* [1949], *Textes pour un poème* [1950], *Textes pour le vivant* [1953], *Textes pour la terre aimée* [1955], *Terre et poésie* [1956], *Double-pays* [1965], and other volumes." The verse collected in *Fraternité de la parole* (1975) is representative of Chedid's primary poetical concerns. This volume encompasses such topics as rebirth, her strong feelings against violence and destruction, pleas for recognition of the positive qualities of life, meditations on humanity, and such common lyric topics as nature, love, and art.

In Chedid's novels, murder, war, disease, and death underscore her exploration of personal, social, cultural, and religious themes. *Le sommeil délivré* (1952; *From Sleep Unbound*) focuses on the repression of women in the Middle East. In *Jonathan* (1955), a confused young protagonist must choose between religion and revolution. *Le sixième jour* (1960) suggests that introspection can serve as a means for spiritual rebirth. *Le survivant* (1963) examines the effects of separation and loss on personal identity. Chedid uses archetypal characters to investigate the quest for identity in *L'autre* (1969), motherhood in *La cité fertile* (1972), the actualization and demise of a utopian dream in *Nefertiti et le rêve d'Akhnaton* (1974), and inner awakening in *Les marches de sable* (1981).

Chedid's plays are characterized by austerity, technical experimentation, and suspense. *Bérénice d'Egypte* (1968) is set in ancient Alexandria and relates the story of Egyptian ruler Ptolemy XI and his virtuous daughter, Bérénice. Fragmented dialogue, portrayal of dreams, and use of puppets and symbolic masks are among the innovative techniques Chedid employs in this work. *Les nombres* (1968) is based on the spiritual struggles of Deborah, the biblical judge and prophetess. *Le montreur* (1969) is perhaps the most inventive of Chedid's plays. Alternately lighthearted and tragic, this work centers on the attempts of two puppets to kill a puppeteer. Although the protagonists begin as paper and string, they eventually become flesh and blood. *Echec à la reine* (1984) is set in a palace and centers on the interaction between a lonely queen and her constant companion, a clown. The play culminates in a tense confrontation between the queen, the clown, and the queen's runaway son, who returns home near the end of the play.

Courtesy of Andrée Chedid

EVELYNE ACCAD

More than any of Andrée Chedid's other volumes of poems, [***Fraternité de la parole***] reflects an agony to communicate through words universal and brotherly themes, words becoming symbols of understanding, words becoming a link connecting differences and loneliness. . . .

This volume of poems has won her the Prix de l'Académie Mallarmé.

The poems are divided under five headings: "the movement," "ceremony of violence," "always—briefly . . . ," "the fire from inside," "multiple voices." The first and longest expresses the movement of rebirth, with poems on the condition of women, life, men, words, rivers, flesh, love. The second is an outcry against violence, wars, death and destruction. The third is a prayer of request for the fulfillment of life in spite of all its miseries. The fourth is a long meditation on how to get to the core of things, the universe, man, and includes a hymn to humanity. And the last is a collection of short poems—two to five lines of suggestive words put together, with silences in between. . . .

There is maturity, depth, growth and variety in these poems, the agony of a person who has tried to touch life through diverse paths and who is able to transcend barriers and limitations through words.

Evelyne Accad, in a review of "Fraternité de la parole," in World Literature Today, *Vol. 51, No. 1, Winter, 1977, p. 57.*

BETTINA L. KNAPP

Andrée Chedid's latest book of poetry, ***Cérémonial de la violence,*** touches very deeply. It is an outcry against slaughter and torture from one who knows the meaning of such pain. Of Lebanese extraction, Andrée Chedid has made her home in Paris since her departure from Egypt. She has become the spokesman for the oppressed and pain-ridden, for those facing the harrowing experience of civil war. When she writes

Comment te nommer, Liban?
Comment ne pas te nommer!

Comment crier du fond de tes abîmes
hors des camps et des clans
loin des catéchismes de la discorde

she speaks of humanity's seemingly uncontrollable bent for self-destruction and demands a reassessment of values and ideations. Her language is that of the soul, deeply moving and passionate. Her cry is for justice and love.

Bettina L. Knapp, in a review of "Cérémonial de la violence," in World Literature Today, *Vol. 52, No. 1, Winter, 1978, p. 77.*

BETTINA L. KNAPP

Classic in its starkness, penetrating in its vision, musical in its color tones, rhythmic in its having yet restrained emotions, Chedid's [***Les marches de sable***] depicts the world of the ascetic—women in search of an *absolu*. The time: the third and fourth centuries after Christ; the place: Egypt. A period when paganism was experiencing its death rattle—but not completely, since it infiltrated (transmuted) into the nascent Christian religion. Gnosticism was also making inroads into mystical climes, threatening the concept of the All-Good God. It was a period when asceticism and sacrifice (or masochism, as some may allude to such ways today) lived side by side with unspeakable cruelties perpetrated by all philosophical and religious schools. It is the eternal aspect of human nature, with its impulse toward Good and its immersion in Evil, that the author emphasizes.

The three protagonists, though emerging from different backgrounds and varying in age and purpose, are really one person. . . . [They] have withdrawn from their earthly existence into the desert, to a closed, monastic life, that of the anchorite—each having discovered a "zone" within herself that no mortal could inhabit, only that transcendental entity called Divinity. Athanasia, the wife of a magistrate, the mother of two sons, has withdrawn from pain into the desert world. Husband and son, martyred and dying, have left her once-fulfilled existence vacant. Emptiness and sorrow fill the days of her life.

That the desert should be the locus for inner awakening is not surprising. . . . The three women, each of an age bearing the number three or a multiple of it—a number so meaningful to mystics of all faiths, really One—all know a life bathed in the terror of existence. The withdrawal of each from life may be considered an initiation, her night sea journey, her period of indwelling, of subliminal peregrinations from which she emerges at the end, healed, awakening into daylight and life.

Les marches de sable is a quest, a personal probing, a subjective questioning, leading to the beauty of fulfillment as woman—artist and mother—in all its plenitude. Highly recommended for its depth of feeling and its poetry. (pp. 297-98)

Bettina L. Knapp, in a review of "Les marches de sable," in World Literature Today, *Vol. 56, No. 2, Spring, 1982, pp. 297-98.*

MARY ANN CAWS

Between proofs and trials, *preuves* and *épreuves,* between looking and reassembling, to each of which are devoted several poems, [***Épreuves du vivant***] stretches its narrow though serious path. The poems are concerned with the true and its appearance, with language and the cry, with the capitalized nouns of our existence: The Earth, The Nation, The Word.

The texts render homage to the act of writing and to the work of seeing. The dust and the dispersion of the wanderer are salvaged by the seeing eye of the child and the speaking mouth of the poet: the duty of both is to reinvent the earth. Brief, the poems are of the descriptive sort, of which perhaps the critic had best say little.

Mary Ann Caws, in a review of "Épreuves du vivant," in World Literature Today, *Vol. 57, No. 4, Autumn, 1983, p. 607.*

BETTINA L. KNAPP

Andrée Chedid, one of France's outstanding novelists and poets . . . , is also known for her innovative plays: ***Bérénice d'Egypte, Les nombres, le montreur*** and more. Her latest theatrical endeavor, ***Echec à la reine,*** is a highly charged work—mythical in dimension. Not only does it incarnate a personal vision, but it dramatizes a collective experience: not a one-time event, but cumulative and eternal situations and relationships. (p. 564)

The curtains part on a palace hall, an empty throne, a large convex mirror which distorts, a queen with long blond hair who stands immobile, back to the audience, facing an invisible crowd. Jok, her clown and constant companion, is dressed to the hilt: grotesquely, with pointed slippers, a colorful costume upon which are attached all kinds of bells, a donkey's headdress, plumes, a false nose and more. Jok is crouched at the foot of the steps leading to the throne; he caresses the Queen's train. Since her husband's death and her son Slif's departure from court, she reigns in all her radiant loneliness. Jok is there to entertain; their relationship is ambiguous: love and power are motivating factors. He orders the queen to obey, to turn around. She does, and in so doing tears off her crown and wig, emerging from her disguise as a frail old woman. Like her jester, she too is a collective figure divested of identity. . . . (pp. 564-65)

As the drama progresses, the queen and Jok grow younger and younger. They spend their time at play for the most part. . . . Only on the surface is this jovial attitude maintained; beneath, we are made privy to incantations and poetic interludes replete with pathos, yearnings and cruelties. A second couple intrude upon the scene: Slif and Zina. Conflict and tension increase between mother and son—and Jok. . . . Suffice it to say that ***Echec à la reine*** is captivating and fascinating for its drama, poetry, style and psychological insights. (p. 565)

Bettina L. Knapp, in a review of "Echec à la reine," in World Literature Today, *Vol. 58, No. 4, Autumn, 1984, pp. 564-65.*

BETTINA KNAPP

Andrée Chedid is one of France's outstanding literary figures. Her work is profound and sensitive; her vision innovative in its archetypal delineations; her aesthetic, lyrical, dense, symbolistic, a blend of the real and the unreal, the Occident and the Middle East. Chedid's protagonists emerge from a universal mold; they are eternal in their philosophical and psychological configurations, for they have stepped into life full-blown from the dream. . . .

Chedid has repeatedly said that she is the product of two civilizations, two ways of life, two psyches. These dichotomies are fused, however, in the works of art that are her writings, distilled in giant frescoes, visualizations and dramatizations replete with mysterious and arcane forces, spheres bathed in subliminal darkness, insalubrious realms, as well as crisp, stark luminosities that crystallize sensation, revealing the most subtle shades of feeling. (p. 7)

Chedid's writings for the most part are situated in Egypt, the land of her birth; yet all of them bear the veneer of the Middle East and Europe. Ancient and modern civilizations fascinate Chedid—the known and the unknown. The past is ushered into being; creatures are enticed to spin their webs, to evolve, to act; and as they do, each in his or her own way reveals a tarnished or unblemished inner world. Chedid's characters are endowed with a sense of proximity and distance, rootedness and rootlessness. They are paradigms of a personal quest and a collective search: the need to communicate not only with one's own multileveled self but also with those organic and inorganic forces that surround each being. (p. 8)

Her works, then, are stamped with universal feelings as well as with personal yearnings, each set apart or opposed to the other. The tension that results from this dynamic is sometimes evoked in muffled and muted tones, sometimes in blazing cacophonies that feed on and then dilate the imagery that abounds in her writings.

Language for Chedid is an instrument that allows her to decant her feelings, to concretize her thoughts, her philosophical and aesthetic views. Set in single and multiple sequences of energetic patterns, rhythmic groupings, and lyrical sonorities, her writings resound with subtle blendings that capture and hold the reader in their flow. A voice always presides in each of her works; disconcertingly at times, assuagingly at others, it expresses the pain, anguish, joy, and sensuality that exists inchoate in the mysterious subclimate of a human soul. Emanating from the very depths of being, this voice links past, present, and future together in ductile essences and sensations. It is attached to the land; it speaks out strongly yet softly of Egypt, Lebanon, France—indefinite and also limited in an endless poetic vision. The voice inhabiting Chedid's novels, poems, and dramas transcends geographic boundaries; it bears the stamp of universality. (pp. 8-9)

Chedid's characters are archetypal in dimension. They are energy centers that exist in ingrained and firm realms once they have been incarnated, their joys and agonies becoming real and palpable to the reader. At the same time, however, they are amorphous and indeterminate in their substance, divested of overly specific or limiting personalities. As such, these created beings into which Chedid infuses the breath of life are connected, linked, nurtured by their spiritual, psychological, and visceral configurations as well as by environmental and national considerations. Solitary, they frequently must tread their own dismal lonely path, a prey to fantasies and terrors, not always of their own making, but imposed upon them—at least in part—by centuries of social conventions. Such beings yearn to be understood, to share their anguish, to bridge over personal distances, pierce through matter, and luxuriate in a wall-less world by a sensate sun, rather than be confined to icy climes or a sphere engulfed in blackness.

Le Sommeil délivré, Chedid's first novel, introduces the reader to a world of ambivalent and complex emotions, to text and subtext, conversations and subconversations all flowing into an audiovisual matrix. Chedid sniffs out her details, as if lying in wait for the slightest nuance to emerge: a wavering smile, a quiver around the mouth, a muted glance, so as the better to seize and apprehend those repressed feelings that precede an action, those sensations that prod the maneuverer. Repetitions, underscoring recurrent perceptions and impressions, are interspersed throughout the peripeteia, increasing the multiple and intricate conduits that interlock and depersonalize the characters. Like a sculpture by Giacometti, each of Chedid's characters is stripped of all unnecessary accessories, both visual and verbal. As the protagonists move about, weaving in space their intricate patterns, they also bear a resemblance to figures in some ancient fresco dimmed by the patina of time. The pace of the dialogue likewise injects a sense of timelessness and atemporality into events and beings, capturing the stillness and terror of eternity.

Le Sommeil délivré is the story of a woman bound fast by the tentacles of a decaying society, imprisoned by ancient conventions, primitive, rigid, and immutable customs that have not evolved since the darkest of dark ages. It is a novel that generates narrative excitement, not by exaggerated twists of the plot or rhythmic effects, but by the juxtaposition of restrained tempi, constrained feelings and yearnings. An urgency, extreme and traumatic, emerges powerfully at the very outset of the novel. Indeed, the book opens with a crisis. Compressed feelings explode as in classical Racinean tragedy—with a stabbing.

Le Sommeil délivré takes the reader directly into the heart of a woman's world. Samya is the product of a contemporary Middle Eastern upbringing, with its harsh and brutal customs, particularly in regard to women, whose earthly existence is wholly devoted to serving certain specific purposes—to service man and to procreate. (pp. 12-13)

Le Sommeil délivré captures not only one woman's world but that of all women, whether living cloistered and closeted in a Middle Eastern land or liberated to all intents and purposes in a modern metropolis yet still imprisoned within their own psychological worlds. (p. 15)

• • • • •

Written before the more recent conflicts and tensions broke out in the Middle East, ***Jonathan*** deals with the choice that many young Christians make between religion and revolution; choices that may often occur today in the third-world (in South America, for example) where the church is still very traditional and conservative. Envisaged symbolically, however, ***Jonathan*** may be considered a rite of passage, disclosing the triturating conflicts that are engendered as youth is transformed into man.

Jonathan, the young protagonist of the novel, has been brought up in a Catholic orphanage. Of unknown parentage, he is represented as a virtually anonymous force, an archetypal figure. . . . Who is Jonathan, this man without antecedents, with supposedly no past and an uncertain future? Jonathan just seems to be there—a symbol, an essence, a semiotic device. Unable to enter into complicity with him, as one may say in the case of Gide's and Malraux's heroes and of many others peppering the novels of the nineteenth and twentieth centuries, Chedid encourages the enigma to prevail. (p. 16)

Jonathan delineates an aborted rite of passage. It reveals the difficulties that arise when a young person attempts to take on the world and is unprepared to do so, to broach dangers when still living in an unconscious, childish state. That the protagonist dies indicates his inability to assume the active role of revolutionary: his inner vision is still too undeveloped, unarmed, not strong enough to carry out his ideations. Jonathan is only a shadow figure who dreams of wrestling with reality but who is still living under the aegis of . . . [others]. Only his soul longs for something different, but it is airy and atomized, not cohesive and substantive. His one heroic stance fails him at the end. Unlike Samya in ***Le Sommeil délivré*** who shoots her husband in an anguished attempt to free herself from his dominion and her own spiritual and psychological paralysis, Jonathan is the recipient of a brutal deed: vulnerable, he has succumbed to forces more powerful than his own with which he is unable to cope. In both cases, however, murder brings to an end an impossible situation which has been trenchantly built up during the course of the novel.

To die, however, is only to end a certain phase in the life experience; to pass to another, which may or may not yield its fruits.

• • • • •

Like a classically constructed tragedy, all three closeknit parts of ***Le Sixième jour*** are weighted with import. Each bears its own melody and pace. Past sequences infiltrate into present realities, echoing and re-echoing the silent and ineluctable march of events. Repetitions, like so many waves, reverberate throughout the course of the novel, and in so doing, take on visual and oral configurations, mirroring feelings and events in a variety of blendings and amalgams, thereby adding to the novel's density and impact.

Le Sixième jour can be seen as a death and resurrection myth, like that of Osiris, Dionysus, Christ. Every force, being and object in the novel gravitates around the mother principle, a collective image representing good, and not evil, an image restorative and not destructive in its power. A cholera epidemic raged in Egypt in 1948, Chedid tells us, and this simple fact inspired the novel. Like Camus' *La Peste* (1947), cholera may be looked upon here not only as a disease but also as a stigma, a blight, that battens on society, entering the human domain cyclically to attack its prey—the vulnerable, innocent, and defenceless.

Om Hassan, whose only daughter has died some years before the incidents related in the novel, is devoting her life to bringing up her grandson, Hassan. ***Le Sixième jour*** is the struggle waged by Om Hassan—driven by some inner power, some energetic force—to save her grandson's life. It is the tale of one whose faith in nature, in existence, is immeasurable. (pp. 21-2)

Le Sixième jour is Chedid's most moving novel. The intensity of the emotions expressed and their authenticity invest it with the power of classical Greek drama, in which archetypal forces vie with one another and with the natural world. Those unassailable powers with which Om Hassan must deal dictate their own laws, subduing, even annihilating, those obstacles that would alter their course. In certain respects, ***Le Sixième jour*** is reminiscent of Paul Claudel's *L'Annonce faite à Marie* (1911), but divested of Claudel's religious frenzy and ferocity, his violence, sensuality, and rage. The rituals in both Chedid's novel and Claudel's play take place in a grotto or in a symbolic one; in both, a child is brought back to life. Both children were the cause of extreme suffering and both thereby empowered the mother figure to connect with cosmic forces, linking their separate being with the whole.

Om Hassan is not to be thought of as merely one grandmother, anymore than Samya is to be considered only an individual woman. Both are archetypal in nature. As we have seen, they represent the feminine principle, which aids in the process of birth and gestation and which nurtures what would otherwise expire or be barren. The room and the cubbyhole on the boat, where darkness and pain were felt at their most excruciating levels, may psychologically be looked upon as a paradigm of the Self (the entire psyche) nourishing the ailing ego (the consciousness), which sees only to its own needs and frequently does not take vaster implications into consideration. Only with the help of the Self can the subliminal sphere begin functioning in the workaday world, expanding consciousness and bringing forth fresh attitudes. With Hassan's rebirth, a new life, a fresh being becomes incarnate: the world is rediscovered. The child, born during the six days of recreation—that symbolic realm of time—will, unlike Jonathan, know his course in life.

• • • • •

In ***Le Survivant,*** the reader is plunged into a world where notions of death and separation are fleshed out, objectified, and analyzed in an attempt to discover whether or not an individual is capable of living independently and realizing life alone. Although realistic and identifiable, the characters do not live out their lives a prey to various external forces and situations as they do in Chedid's previous novels. In ***Le Survivant,*** they exist solely as phantasms and are conditioned by the personal world of a single individual. Experiencing life only through that person's eyes, they may be viewed as intrusions from the subjective realm of shadows, as unconscious forces seeking to find an acceptable environment, as memory images yearning to reenter a world of contingencies.

Le Survivant begins as Lana emerges from sleep. It is morning. So deep has been her slumber that, upon awakening, she is still out of touch with objective reality; she has forgotten that her husband, Pierre, left yesterday on a business trip, that she herself saw him off at the airport. From the very outset, the reader knows that a dual time scheme will be experienced: linear time as Lana deals with the unfolding empirical situation, the developing crisis, and cyclical time as it is experienced by her unconscious. Such layering allows Lana to come into contact with past, present, and future events, all of which are integral to the text. All sorts of people, real and imagined, emerge full-blown, helping her to breach spatial distance and formal time schemes—and thus to open wide the gates for the visionary experience that is so powerful an element in ***Le Survivant.***

As Lana stretches, enjoying the warmth of the day being born under a summer sun in Paris, the phone rings, jarring the peaceful calm that inhabits the atmosphere—between sleep and waking. A woman's voice is heard. It is an official at the airport calling. Lana refuses to listen. A plane has crashed, the voice is insistent. Lana's mind turns back to Pierre's departure. The voice is adamant. The dialogue is now lived out in two modalities, yesterday's and today's; each tone and the emotional equivalents it arouses are superimposed upon one another, interrupting Lana's previously smooth-flowing mood and mounting disquietude. Listen! the voice demands. All were killed but one. There is one survivor. Call back at noon. (pp. 26-7)

Lana calls the airline agency at noon. There is only one survivor, the voice repeats. The other eight bodies found near the wreckage are so mutilated that they are unidentifiable. Lana is now determined to go to the airport and take the next plane to the site of the accident. (p. 28)

In due course, Lana leaves for the desert to confront the loss in which she still does not believe. In her fantasies she continues to see Pierre. . . . Intense togetherness is experienced in the lyrical intrusions marked by Pierre's verbal presence; also by the dichotomies involved as she separates the world of contingencies from the cyclical sphere, and in so doing, enforces a contrapuntal rhythmic effect that transforms the disparate into the single. The fusion of two beings—the *nous*—which resounds throughout the novel like a protracted threnody, allows barriers at times to vanish, encouraging Lana to pursue her psychic trajectory. A virtual telepathic experience is enacted in ***Le Survivant,*** fascinating as an innovative literary technique, but also deeply moving because of the beauty and depth involved in the emotional happenings.

The fact that ***Le Survivant*** begins with an awakening—as does Marcel Proust's *A la recherche du temps perdu*—causes intuitions and perceptions to emerge into consciousness and previously forgotten memories to take on breadth and scope and function in a seemingly routine manner for Lana. Conversations between her and Pierre pursue their course, both temporally and atemporally. Lana feels free to continue her search: unbound, liberated from the constricting world of contingencies, with its divisiveness, its rigid opposition between life and death. . . . Pierre lives so vitally in Lana's unconscious that when he asks her to allow him to continue to dwell there—in that no-man's-land, that in-between zone—she joyfully agrees. . . . Then Lana wonders, doubts intrude. Pierre's voice, she questions, is it really hers? (pp. 29-30)

The delicate use of shifting time sequences, of waking and dreaming states, of vivid verbal description, forcing participation in the events and raising feelings and emotions to a heightened pitch of awareness—all this encourages the reader to consider this novel as the most personal of Chedid's endeavors, providing a catharsis for her, as well as being a distinct literary achievement for our time.

• • • • •

All Chedid's writings are marked by their intermingling of tragedy and hope, and ***L'Autre*** is no exception. (p. 31)

Unlike ***Le Survivant,*** which concentrates on death, ***L'Autre*** is a canticle, a hymn, to life. It is also an exploration into the meaning and impress of self-identity and into the framework of human relationships in general. An earthquake has leveled a hotel and surrounding buildings; a young man, a stranger to the town, is buried alive. Just moments earlier, he has been talking to an old peasant named Simm. The novel centers around the efforts expended by Simm to save 'the other'—the unknown lad, and in so doing, to halt the powers that destroy and hurl the living into oblivion.

Stylistic innovations are again effectively used in ***L'Autre.*** Instead of the narrative style implicit in ***Le Sommeil délivré, Jonathan, Le Sixième jour,*** various literary devices and techniques are introduced into the novel's very structure. Dialogue, for example, which is particularly inherent to the theatre; poetry, which Chedid felt would encourage the reader to reflect, pause, and look inward; scenarios, like those used in films, with the words printed on the right and the image descriptions on the left of the page, endowing each step of the process with visual, rhythmic, and aural equivalents. Other typographical novelties are prevalent in ***L'Autre:*** italics are used during certain monologues so as to underscore their import and importance. When a voice is heard from within the earth, it uses the familiar *tu;* capitals indicate moments of heightened tension; and during such sequences, letters may be reversed or even be simply printed in a disorderly fashion in keeping with the emotional tension of the moment. (p. 32)

Unlike Marguerite Duras' *Les Petits cheveux de Tarquinia* (1953) which deals also with a man's gratuitous death and thereby instills a negative atmosphere over the entire work, the seeming death of Chedid's text spells life. Both novels delineate gratuitous deaths; the former bathing in the negative sphere, the latter emerging into the positive one. Death would have worked its way into ***L'Autre,*** had not Simm's perseverance, tenacity, and belief in the adventuresome nature of life not prevailed. In this respect, ***L'Autre*** is comparable to Jean Giono's *Le Chant du monde* (1934) and *Que ma joie demeure* (1935)—two novels that bear the stamp of the ordeal and of the conqueror's jubilation.

A life reborn, the life created for Chedid in ***L'Autre*** requires, as does the resurrection ritual, an exile from the outside objective world, a withdrawal to where the seed and the word can gestate, and inspiration come to term—only then can the book, the work of art, sprout into being. (pp. 35-6)

• • • • •

[***La Cité fertile***] is the work of a consummate artist. The images now imprinted on Chedid's verbal canvases are alchemical in quality, primary colors merge there in sequences of stark blendings. A city, for example, is depicted in terms of multiple molten metals, as though exposed to intense heat. Flowing outward through a maze of intricate verbal patterns, the elements of earth, water, and air are transformed by the wizardry of Chedid's creative powers into rows of concrete houses, vast landscapes, clumps of bushy trees, flowers of pastel shadings. As for the protagonists, they appropriate to themselves whatever admixtures and blendings suit their personalities—from blues to ochers, from greens to mauves. (p. 36)

The most important image in ***La Cité fertile,*** as it is in ***Le Sixième jour,*** is the figure of the archetypal mother. In ***La Cité*** *fertile,* this figure is universalized in the person of Aléfa the dancer. . . . Ageless, Aléfa could be a hundred thousand years old, as Chedid writes; she practises one of the most ancient of the arts, dancing, an elemental form of expressing human emotion. Aléfa, however, is no ordinary entertainer. When she walks, she 'oscillates,' when she moves her limbs, she concretizes them in a series of hieratic gestures, transforming them at times into natural forces: a tree, a stone, silence, air, a city, tears. (pp. 36-7)

Aléfa nurtures, encourages, yields to the embrace of those in need of her. . . . She is earthborn, collective. She is the one that animals, children, and adults approach for counsel, for warmth, for an infusion of creative energy. She is clairvoyant, a seer, a medium. Some feel that she belongs in the desert or in a grotto or in one of those sacred places where oracles made their pronouncements in ancient times; but her life is centered around human beings. (p. 37)

What remains with the reader are Chedid's extraordinary visualizations and the dynamism of the dancing figure, Aléfa, who sweeps into the story, arrests the reader's attention, then vanishes only to return moments later, energizing feeling, act and word. It is she who stands above and beyond the others, eternal as an earth force, consummate as an artist, revered for her spiritual and visceral power!

• • • • •

Nefertiti et le rêve d'Akhnaton differs from Chedid's previous novels in that it combines history and fiction. It plunges the reader back into a remote period, 1388-1344 B.C.—the eighteenth dynasty in Egypt—when the pharaoh, Akhnaton rebelled against polytheism in favor of monotheism, of the concept of one God as manifested in the visible Sun. (p. 39)

In order to prepare the reader for the unfolding events, Chedid returns to an even more distant past: to 3400 B.C. and Menes, Egypt's first historic ruler, who unified the upper and lower kingdoms and established a new capital, known later as Memphis. She recounts the incidents associated with Menes' reign and also those of other well-known Egyptian rulers. By fusing the real with the imaginary, Chedid gives credence to her narrative, solidity to the unfolding tale, broadening in this way the novel's structure and adding to its dynamic.

As is implicit in Chedid's previous novels, so ***Nefertiti et le rêve d'Akhnaton*** may also be considered a prose poem; its dissonances, prolonged silences, reverberating cadences, create a very specific emotional response in the reader. As for the characters, their joys and sorrows are woven into palpable living patterns that capture and hold the reader's attention. Psychologically, the voices that are heard, which emerge from some spectral realm like so many disembodied tonalities, haunt, provoke, and traumatize the audience because their concerns are so contemporary, their ideals so vital, to present-day society. Colors, so significant to the ancient Egyptian, are important factors in Chedid's writings always, since they set up a rapport between the individual's affective state and the mood of the scene as a whole. Here, however, the colorations are more varied. When, for example, Nefertiti and Akhnaton don their regal costumes, these are daubed with gold, lapis lazuli, white, and coral—acting as a spur to the senses and the imagination. Their very beings, when bathing in these striking hues—depicted in powerful verbal lines—take on the physical configurations of those ancient, perspectiveless hieratic paintings, visible today on ancient Egyptian stellas, which capture the immobility and elegance of those powerful rulers of old—those Gods in human guise.

Nefertiti—mother, wife, woman of insight and strength—is the focal figure around whom Chedid centers her positive feminine principle. As attested to in ***Le Sixième jour, La Cité fertile,*** and other novels, Chedid excels in her portrayal of woman; she understands her many faces. In Nefertiti's case, she shows her as gentle yet forceful, sensitive yet wise, profound yet persevering. The novel indeed centers on Nefertiti, who recounts her life in all its pain, anguish, and joy to her old scribe; his insights are added, rounding out the narrative, exploring further the rise and fall of a Utopian dream. (pp. 39-40)

• • • • •

Egypt, Lebanon and France are focused upon in her verse, as they are in her novels. Chedid endows them with soul and psyche, form and flesh. Their different mores and topographies are underscored by tracing out their lifelines, their currents, crosscurrents, and undercurrents, in accumulations of charged imagery. Distinct in their own ways, under her aegis these disparate lands form a cohesive whole. Frontiers, for Chedid, whether spiritual, political, philosophical or literary, are artificial obstructions, barriers that prevent human beings from communicating freely with one another; impediments erected by those whose vision is stunted, short-sighted, whose cares are mundane, even retrograde, whose desires are petty and conventional. Such forms and formalities do not exist for Chedid. Humanity, as far as she is concerned, possesses a common meeting ground, an area that exists within each person and which she continually probes in her writings—the collective unconscious, the deepest layer of the psyche. In this, despite their profound differences, she may be said to join poets such as Claudel and Perse. The world of particulars bathes its component parts in this limitless oceanic sphere, allowing the poet to immerse herself in the entire history and evolution of the human psyche—in all of its cultural and spiritual manifestations. (p. 50)

Chedid's poetic themes are multiple and plurivalent. Childhood and youth, for example, those precious periods of awakening and discovery that Jean Giraudoux, before Chedid, presented in such misty and dreamlike sequences and that Jean Cocteau mythified in oblique glances and yearnings. Chedid's delineations of these very special years, when wishes are vigorous and disappointments lacerating, are perhaps more subtly hewn and their tones more harmonious than those of her predecessors. Leaner certainly than those of the 'precious' Giraudoux, Chedid builds her secret relationships—those existing between word, image, and rhythm—with sparser equipment reminiscent more of Guillevic. Ambiguity rules in her world; and so does mystery. Like Cocteau, Chedid also shocks and jars by her juxtaposition of strange metaphors, unusual images, that reverberate throughout the poems as a whole, triggering dormant memories, transforming barely recognizable subliminal forms into terrifying configurations. At other moments, as in **"Jeunesse,"** they take on the shade of aerated essences, phantasmagorias. (p. 51)

Death, too, makes its inroads into Chedid's poetic vision, as it does, though in dissimilar fashion and intention, in that of her contemporaries Yves Bonnefoy and Philippe Jaccottet. Having witnessed brutalities and cruelties on all levels during wars, uprisings, persecutions, Chedid not only knows the meaning of loss and separation, but expresses it viscerally in her verse by cutting and cleaving images. . . .

"Le Compagnon de la dernière heure" swells with aching torment as the agonizing destinies of those killed in action, in ambushes, in mine accidents, or simply because of different political and religious views, are invoked. (p. 52)

When Lebanon's civil war detonated, Chedid wrote ***Cérémonial de la violence.*** Her rage, though contained, screams out her pain at the massacre in spasmodic, hoarse, yet blatant tones. . . .

Chedid does not live in an ivory tower. She is part of the earth, attached to the soil, to its people. She takes and bestows life from every aspect and part of the universe. She deals with problems at hand, never turning aside from them, never diffusing her energies in order to avoid hurt. Her images in ***Cérémonial de la violence*** lancinate for this reason, stab and spear as she disgorges the slaughter and torture perpetrated by fanatics whose uncontrollable lust for blood has compelled them to sniff about and lap it all up. . . .

But love poems are also part of Chedid's repertoire. In **"Notre hublot"** feelings are disclosed in mitigated and ephemeral verbal portrayals, in evanescent transparencies, but with ever more powerfully echoing reverberations. (p. 53)

Time, always an important factor for Chedid, is also poeticized. Past, present, and future are mirrored in both cyclical permutations and fugacious eschatological enumerations. In **"Prendre corps,"** hours, minutes, seconds, are eternalized in a temporal present. . . . Figurations infiltrate in **"L'instant II,"** saturating the atmosphere with time become concretion: an object that strikes, hammers its way out of an anonymous void onto a spaceless sphere where it takes on dimension and weight. . . . Time is both attacked and shunned, welcomed and enjoyed, and explored because of its immanence and transcendence. (pp. 53-4)

If one were to generalize, one could say that Chedid's poems are for the most part plainchants in honor of life; hymns to the earth and the heavens, to the vastness of the cosmic experience. (p. 55)

• • • • •

Chedid came to playwriting late in life. While still in Egypt, she worked closely with a number of amateur groups, but only as actress and not as dramatist. She has always been aware of the difficulties involved in this perilous art, however, understanding that great maturity is needed to wrestle with stage language, that each word must be ground out, carved from the flesh and re-injected with life. Distancing and objectivization need to coexist with sensitivity and understanding, not only in the creation of the drama itself but in the unification of the disparate elements required to bring forth a true theatrical spectacle. (p. 57)

Chedid's theatre is not absurdist nor does it profess to have a thesis, whether this be existentialist, political, or one advocated by any other school or group. Unlike the plays of Alfred Jarry and his successors, hers are not spontaneously irrational, nor are they grotesque in quality, satirizing humanity's greed, hypocrisy, and eccentricities. Neither are they farcical like Arrabal's, derisive like Pinget's, biting in their macabre humor like the outpourings of Ionesco and Genet or cerebral like the parlor games of Sarraute. Rather they are deeply felt poetic visualizations, which although firmly anchored to the world of reality, give primacy to fantasy, suggestion, evocation. Violence, shock, and hurt are, however, implicit in some of Chedid's hallucinatory lines; her concerted rebellion against injustice, partiality, and inhumanity never falls silent. When this raw emotional response emerges full-blown from the mouths of the players, it serves to dislocate the stage happenings, to dissociate the images, and to reveal a willfully chaotic disorder—and malaise.

Although classical in their simplicity, Chedid's dramas are modern in their direct force and inner power, their effulgence of spirit, their blending of singular terms, images, sensations and perceptions; yet they are also strikingly different from the brews offered by her contemporaries.

Chedid's plays are simple, poignant. There is no extraneous action, nothing superfluous. Everything onstage emerges directly from the body of the written text. Her protagonists are flesh-and-blood beings, but they also are atemporal, archetypal, arising from the deepest layers of the unconscious. Chedid's characters do not develop psychologically as in conventional theatre. When they move about on stage weaving intricate patterns in space, each becomes an energy center, diffusing its own aura which either attracts or repels the others. Her frequently statically paced dialogue injects her plays with a sense of timelessness, capturing thereby the stillness and terror of eternity. Suspense is accentuated not by exaggerated rhythmic effects nor by plot, but rather by the juxtaposition of images and oral emanations. Actions and gestures are studied, restrained, rarely flamboyant. Silences, breathing, both spasmodic and in long protracted intervals, heighten the feelings of apprehension implicit in . . . [***Bérénice d'Egypte, Les Nombres,*** and ***Le Montreur***]. (pp. 57-8)

A classicist in the density of her prose, its concision and imagistic vitality, Chedid creates plays that deal with significant events and problems; they are food for the mind as well as for the senses. They are to be studied, probed, examined not only after the spell of the theatrical happening has faded into oblivion, but long afterward—deep into the night. She is, also, a modernist in her use of technical innovations: lighting and sound effects which jar as well as heal and subdue; the breaking up of scenic continuity which makes her theatre real, actual; the characters, not of flesh and blood, but reminiscent of ambulatory hieroglyphics whose silences and articulated sonorities are equally evocative. Hers is compelling theatre; it speaks to the individual and to the multitude! (p. 78)

Bettina Knapp, in her Andrée Chedid, *Rodopi, 1984, 81 p.*

BETTINA L. KNAPP

Poetic, sensitive, and imagistic, Andrée Chedid's latest novel, ***La maison sans racines,*** strikes at the heart of the matter: Lebanon as battleground between Christian and Muslim. Few if any are in a better position than the Egypto-Lebanese Chedid . . . to write about the tragic saga dominating that land. Never maudlin or self-pitying, ***La maison sans racines*** dramatizes the deepest of traumas—the cutting down of a budding life, the destruction of future hope—in a stylistically innovative manner. Three time schemes emerge: the family's and narrator's past, and the visitor's present. Their intersections and diffusions, in keeping with the pace of the events, heighten or slacken the pulsations and innervations of the protagonists, while also expanding their consciousness and dilating their sense perceptions. In so doing, they involve the reader in a continuously deepening visualization of the happenings; enfolding him (or her) in a complex of emotional, religious, and political situations.

The plot is stark: Kalya, in her fifties and living in Paris, has never seen her granddaughter Sybil, whose home is in the

United States. She has begun corresponding with the twelve-year-old girl, whose ethnologist parents decide to send her to Lebanon during the summer months while they go to the Amazon on a research trip. As in classical theatre, Chedid begins her work with a crisis: Kalya, at home, observes the goings on in the distant square from her window. Two friends, whom Kalya loves dearly, Ammal and Myriam, Muslim and Christian respectively, are walking toward each other. A burst of volley fire is heard; screams, groans, blood. Has one of them been killed? Both? Wounded? Kalya cannot see clearly from her perch, nor can she go out for fear Sybil might follow her. She waits patiently, then makes the child promise not to budge from the doorstep, where she can observe the happenings. Though the child obeys, she worries, having already grown to love her grandmother, now an indispensable force in her life. Kalya leaves on what proves to be an interminable journey to the square: it is not merely a walk taken to reach a particular spot, but one which takes her and the reader back into time. . . . (pp. 357-58)

Kalya's venture into this space-time continuum lasts throughout the entire novel. Like a tonic chord sounding at regular intervals, her walk brings the reader back to a present reality that fades out of the picture at specific junctures, only to invite another reality to occupy the reader's attention. We learn about Kalya's past, not in Paris or in Egypt alone, so dry and parched during the summer months, but also in Lebanon, where the cool breezes cleanse the body and nature's exquisite colorations. Chedid excels in her depictions of nature; one has the feeling of being there, of experiencing tactilely, orally, olfactorily, the very *livingness* of this ancient land. Particularly important are Chedid's discussions centering on the variety of religions and sects in Lebanon, each anchored to its own limitations, its materialism, its power drives, its egocentric view of what should be considered a Universal Power—God. . . .

La maison sans racines is a work of art which must be read not for its plot alone, but rather experientially. Like a giant wave, it is not only endowed with energy and momentum; as it crests, force and gusto empower whiteness to emerge. A brilliant sun, shining powerfully upon the happenings, cleanses what had grown putrescent, encouraging those once deeply glimmering crystals to transform blood and gore into the most precious of elements—the life principle! (p. 358)

Bettina L. Knapp, in a review of "La maison sans racines," in World Literature Today, *Vol. 60, No. 2, Spring, 1986, pp. 357-58.*

JENNY DISKI

Andrée Chedid's ***From Sleep Unbound*** is a passionate study of life imprisonment. The prison is the social world that Samya, the main character, inhabits; the jailers, the men who maintain and reinforce the system.

It is not a new proposition perhaps, but this translation from the French reaches us over a decade after its original publication. And the difference between this feminist *cri* and many others we have read is the efficiency of the system it describes. The novel takes place in Egypt, where patriarchy reigns supreme and where even the modicum of awareness and discomfort that has seeped into western patriarchal attitudes is entirely missing. The system is intact and unreflecting.

We follow Samya from prison to prison. Already, at convent school, caged by uniform and rigid discipline, she is drained of life. Then to her home, motherless and populated by a father and brothers who have no interest in her beyond their concern to find her a husband as soon as possible to take on the burden of keeping her fed. Finally, at 15, to marriage where she is no more than a vessel for producing a male heir. There is not a glimmer of warmth from anyone in her life, and yet, as she moves from one incarceration to the next, each holds some hope before it is entered, merely because it is different. An illusion, since each stage is no more than another aspect of the same patriarchal structure. Boredom and oppression combine to drive all energy away. Chedid depicts a social world that denies psychic life to half the population. It is a narration of despair.

Even Samya's fantasies of happiness are circumscribed by the totality of the system. How a prisoner perceives release depends on what kind of prison they are in. Samya's prison is cold and devoid of love, even affection. Lovelessness is the central torment. Her dreams are of a happier kind of prison. . . .

When she is confronted by the women of the village and wants to make contact she offers them a version of her life warmed with a fantasy of how it should have been: her father's pain at her loss; the flowers and love letters sent by her suitor. Freedom or independence from those who hand her around for economic motives is not an available dream. Even fantasies must have some basis in reality.

The reader must be content with the single act of rebellion that begins and ends the book. Samya, finally physically as well as psychically paralysed, shoots her husband and waits passively for society to take revenge. The single gleam of hope is a young girl she has befriended who runs away, we are to suppose, towards independence and creative freedom. The trouble is that the writer has done her job too well. You can't imagine where this girl could run to in such a world where the men are cold, unloving oppressors, the women obedient and furtive. We are given no hint of other possibilities. On the contrary, Chedid offers us Samya's husband as the archetype, the source of all oppression. 'I hated Boutros . . . I saw him and all the Boutroses in the world in their rigid authoritarianism. They ruled over destinies; they crushed plants, songs, colours, they crushed life itself. And they reduced everything to the shrivelled proportions of their own hearts. All these Boutroses advancing! But a day would come . . .'

Chedid is sometimes over-explanatory, tipping uncomfortably into the polemic. We are told too often of the universality of Samya's condition in a tone that approaches rhetoric. . . . The strength of the novel lies in the way it communicates despair. We, as readers, are required to live through the hopelessness, share in it. It should be possible, of course, both to participate in the experience of despair and to analyse its causes, but the flights into rhetoric weaken the power of the narrative and begin to seem over-simplified. The unswerving cruelty of all the men and the insensitivity of the women who uphold the status quo is presented, but never examined in any depth. We get only heartless cyphers. I found myself wanting more than this. What kind of victims are the men, and the women who reinforce the male view? If love is the answer, as Chedid suggests, then, in this loveless world, everyone must be losers and the oppressors as much victims of the system as the oppressed.

Jenny Diski, "World without Love," in New Statesman, *Vol. 113, No. 2930, May 22, 1987, p. 28.*

James (Lafayette) Dickey

1923-

© Thomas Victor 1987

American poet, novelist, critic, essayist, scriptwriter, and author of children's books.

A prominent figure in contemporary American literature, Dickey is best known for his intense exploration of the primal, irrational, creative, and ordering forces in life. Often classified as a visionary Romantic in the tradition of Walt Whitman, Dylan Thomas, and Theodore Roethke, Dickey emphasizes the primacy of imagination and examines the relationship between humanity and nature. He frequently describes confrontations in war, sports, and nature as means for probing violence, mortality, creativity, and social values. In his poetry, Dickey rejects formalism, artifice, and confession, favoring instead a narrative mode that features energetic rhythms and charged emotions. Dickey has stated that in his poetry he attempts to achieve "a kind of plain-speaking line in which astonishing things can be said without rhetorical emphasis." In addition to his verse, Dickey has authored the acclaimed novels *Deliverance* (1970) and *Alnilam* (1987), symbolic works that explore extremes of human behavior.

Dickey commonly draws on crucial events in his life for his subject matter. His early poetry, for example, is infused with guilt over his role as a fighter pilot in World War II and the Korean War, ruminations on his older brother's death, and reflections upon his Southern heritage. In his first three volumes of verse—*Into the Stone* (1960), *Drowning with Others* (1962), and *Helmets* (1964)—Dickey explores such topics as war, family, love, death, spiritual rebirth, nature, and survival. These poems are generally arranged in traditional stanzaic units and are marked by an expansive and affirmatory tone. James Schevill observed such characteristics of Dickey's early verse as "a unique unmistakable tone, an awareness of the physical forces of the world that flow beyond time, beyond history." These volumes also contain several poems about the wilderness in which Dickey stresses the importance of maintaining the primal physical and imaginative powers that he believes are suppressed by civilization. *Buckdancer's Choice* (1965), which won the National Book Award, signaled a shift in Dickey's verse to freer, more complex forms. Employing internal monologues, varied spacing between words and phrases in place of punctuation, and subtler rhythms, *Buckdancer's Choice* investigates human suffering in its myriad forms. Dickey expresses ambivalance toward violence, most notably in "The Firebombing," a long poem that juxtaposes the thoughts of a fighter pilot as he flies over Japan and his memories twenty years later. *Poems, 1957-1967* (1967) encapsulates what most critics consider Dickey's strongest phase as a poet.

During the 1970s, Dickey devoted more time to fiction, television and film scripts, literary criticism, journals, and children's books. His verse composed during this period evidences a more self-reflexive voice and an increasingly restrained, meditative style. Dickey also began to employ what he termed "country surrealism," a technique by which he obscures distinctions between dreams and reality to accommodate the irrational. Throughout his later poetry, Dickey laments the loss of youth, expresses a profound fear of mortality, and explores visionary qualities and creative energies. For example, "The Eye-Beaters," published in *The Eye-Beaters, Blood, Victory, Madness, Buckhead, and Mercy* (1970), examines blindness, artistic vision, and the pursuit of truth. *The Zodiac* (1976) is a long, self-referential poem about an intensely visionary alcoholic artist who has difficulty distinguishing between illusion and reality. The title poem of *The Strength of Fields* (1979), which Dickey read at Jimmy Carter's presidential inauguration, affirms faith in humanity while addressing various human dilemmas. In *Puella* (1982), Dickey blends myth and reality to portray his young wife's maturation from adolescence to adulthood. Peter Balakian praised *Puella* for "tautness of rhythm, a clustered density of imagery, and a voice that speaks with conviction."

In the novel *Deliverance,* which was adapted into an acclaimed film, Dickey reiterates several themes prevalent in his verse, primarily the rejuvenation of human life through interaction with nature. This work concerns four suburban men who seek diversion from their unfulfilling lives by canoeing down a remote and dangerous river. The characters encounter human violence and natural threats, forcing them to rely on primordial instincts in order to survive. Many initial reviews assessed *Deliverance* as a sensational adventure story that exalts violence and machismo. Subsequent evaluations, however, noted Dickey's skillful use of myth, biblical references, and Jungian archetypes, and several critics have compared *Deliverance* to

Mark Twain's *The Adventures of Huckleberry Finn* and Joseph Conrad's *Heart of Darkness*. Dickey's second novel, *Alnilam,* is an ambitious experimental work centering on a blind man's attempts to uncover the mysterious circumstances of his son's death. The man's son had been a charismatic leader of an elite corps of army pilots who held vaguely sinister revolutionary aspirations. While Dickey celebrates the pleasures of flying with vivid imagery, he denounces the misuse of power, creating what Robert Towers described as "a vast, intricate work distinguished not by its forward momentum but by its symbolic suggestiveness and its bravura passages, some of which rise to visionary heights."

Dickey is also an esteemed poetry critic. In such volumes of essays and journals as *The Suspect in Poetry* (1964), *Babel to Byzantium: Poets and Poetry Now* (1968), *Self-Interviews* (1970), *Sorties* (1971), and *Night Hurdling: Poems, Essays, Conversations, Commencements, and Afterwords* (1983), he offers subjective viewpoints of poetry and asserts his preference for artistic intensity and intuition.

(See also *CLC,* Vols. 1, 2, 4, 7, 10, 15; *Contemporary Authors,* Vols. 9-12, rev. ed.; *Contemporary Authors New Revision Series,* Vol. 2; *Contemporary Authors Bibliographical Series,* Vol. 2; *Dictionary of Literary Biography,* Vol. 5; and *Dictionary of Literary Biography Yearbook: 1982*.)

SEYMOUR KRIM

I have rarely read a poem by James Dickey which did not give me an experience. It may well prove out that Dickey will have to pay the price for his accessibility by being denied a berth in all future *Oxford Book(s) of Verse* but it is a price well worth paying. He writes for us now with every jot of passion, pain, imagination, and genuine independence that he can summon up, and gets through most of the time. He actually cuts across the infinite static to which we're all subjected to commemorate important things and moments in everyone's mutual experience.

This is no empty claim. Pick up ***The Strength of Fields,*** and see the number of poems that get under your skin—perhaps only seven or eight out of 30-odd, but how they reverberate! Surely the effectiveness of these poems is the centrality of their themes. An eight-year-old girl previewing the erotic power of a grown American woman; the sad hopes of a small Sherwood Anderson town at night; basic-training war games in Louisiana during World War II ("prepared for death and unprepared / For war . . ."); a mature man recalling his mother in the bathtub; a U.S. war vet (Dickey) playing his guitar for an English war vet who had a leg shot off in Burma; nightflying (Dickey was a pilot) over the South Pacific in WWII; the poet braving the sneers of the barbershop boys in Columbia, S.C., by wearing a jacket on which his daughter-in-law has stitched the word "poet."

Even though some of this subject matter is undeniably male—and I've heard Dickey patronizingly referred to as a Hemingway-type—let no woman think for a moment that he writes in a locker-room code that prevents identification. Dickey merely writes out of personal experience; he happens to be a man, he is not gay, he likes but is not a snob about sports, and he was involved in the crucial war of his and my generation. Beyond that, he writes for everyone who can appreciate the honest, kinetic excitement of being alive and often bewildered in the big swirling washing machine of today's America. . . .

Nabokov once told us that "the great writer is first of all an enchanter," and great or not, nothing this poet sets down is devoid of those conjurer's threads that bind the reader to him. . . .

It may well be lowbrow to enjoy James Dickey on a New York scene that is forever doubting and changing its taste, but we are speaking here of a national poet who speaks beyond the box-seats to the bleachers. The word "universal" has been so hyped in our time that one blushes to use it; besides, Dickey is not without his hickeys, he indeed comes up with lines that are bummers, he is surely as fallibly human as these poems never fail to demonstrate one way or another. He even owes a debt to Dylan Thomas and Theodore Roethke, if an amateur poetry detective can claim competence in this area. But he is writing for us even more than for himself and it is an honor for me to recommend his book and his words to you.

Seymour Krim, "A Poet for the Bleachers," in The Village Voice, *Vol. XXV, No. 5, February 4, 1980, p. 40.*

ROBERT PETERS

Most of these new poems [in ***The Strength of Fields***], with a pair of exceptions, instead of soaring off easily into the empyrean, skim the tops of trees and occasionally crash. They generate weakly, and . . . they are like tortoises plodding along, testing their way, being maddeningly self-indulgent, as they rest after every 3 or 4 words. Also, Dickey now reflects what I call *Momentosity,* an easy metaphysics, a yanking of the poem into *Significance,* which doesn't always work. It's as if Dickey feels that a poet as famous as he is is obligated to say Big Things—the poet as a Shelleyan universal Sky-Pilot for Mankind. Further, he frequently has trouble moving his poems, in their casual dispositions across the page, past the middle; by grabbing onto some vague concept, he tries to propel the poem on to its landing (hand-thrown rather than jet-flown projectiles). Finally, there's a sentimentality based in part on his affection for the male world of *men's* feelings (the only women in the book are either dead or are memories), recollections of military service, guitar-strummings, jogging, and football. The fact that he still manages some good poems containing the old high-octane revved magic makes us regret there aren't more such poems. As a poet who himself owes a good deal to Dickey, I sincerely hope that this book is merely a hiatus in his career; obviously, there is evidence in ***The Strength of Fields*** that there are good things still to come, possibly. (p. 160)

Robert Peters, "The Phenomenon of James Dickey, Currently," in Western Humanities Review, *Vol. XXXIV, No. 2, Spring, 1980, pp. 159-66.*

TURNER CASSITY

If you write in lines so long that your book has to be printed sideways, it seems to me you might well reconsider your methods. However, James Dickey has always been the least succinct of poets, and here, in a grand horizontal sprawl, is ***The Strength of Fields,*** a collection of lyrics and of adaptations from other languages. Dickey writes with undiminished vigor, but I am not sure I can say this as praise. Intellectually, he is so seldom on secure ground that he ought perhaps to proceed with caution. (p. 177)

Within his limits—one cannot really call them self-imposed; that would imply a sense of focus he does not have—he can be effective. **"Root-light, or The Lawyer's Daughter"** is a very amusing put-down of the idea of the Platonic Idea. Or would be if one could rescue it from its surrounding welter of verbiage. It is the dread Southern urge to use eight words wherever one will do. (pp. 177-78)

I do not understand why he sets up the poem typographically as he does. If there is any rhythmic measure, or any non-random relationship of sentence to line, I cannot discern it. I have heard him read the poem—most engagingly—and still cannot. As a lyric it is marred by a leering resemblance to a *Playboy* cartoon, but it does represent the poet at his least pretentious.

"False Youth: Autumn: Clothes of the Age" (even his titles are long) shows him at his most pretentious, but may nevertheless be the most successful poem in the book. . . . [Unlike] root-light, its details are relevant to its subject, and do not paralyze the narrative. (p. 179)

"The Rain Guitar" suffers from being a sequel to or trial run for the dueling banjos scene in ***Deliverance***—that abyss—and from our suspicion that what a man of Dickey's age should really be playing is a ukulele. The guitar reappears in **"Exchanges,"** a notably bad performance. The poet, with no hint of irony, is apparently going down a checklist of cocktail party chic: smog, offshore drilling, freeways, the quality of life, and the death of whales. All too appropriate, unfortunately, for a Phi Beta Kappa poem, "being in the form of a dead-living dialogue with Joseph Trumbull Stickney (1874-1904)—(Stickney's words are in italics)." Italicizing was not necessary. It is perfectly obvious which words are Stickney's: his are the ones that make sense. In the Dickey text nothing has anything to do with anything else. You cannot call it free association because there is no association. The narrator is sitting on a bluff above the Pacific Ocean outside Los Angeles (where else?) and playing Appalachian music to a companion while worrying about environmental pollution. "We sang and prayed for purity." A reader who will believe that will believe anything, although I should say in its defense that it is the most straightforward utterance in the poem. (pp. 180-81)

It would be just as easy to hatchet **"For the Death of Lombardi,"** a maudlin threnody for the iconic coach. It would be easy but counter-productive. We should regret instead that someone who is uniquely qualified to give us a good poem on the world of the locker room has failed to do so. Very few writers play football, and we should have our understanding enlarged if a poet could convey to us what it is actually like. (pp. 181-82)

The writing in **"Lombardi,"** as writing, confronts us with what three generations of modern poets have been unwilling to face: no amount of talent is going to help if the rest of your mind is a mess. Common sense is as useful in poetry as it is elsewhere.

I do not want anyone to think I underrate Dickey's talent. The best phrase in the poem is very good indeed.

> the weekly, inescapable dance
> Of speed, deception, and pain

It is no accident that it consists of abstractions (you can be sure in any modern poem that dance does not actually refer to dancing). (p. 183)

I am not familiar with the originals of the translations in ***Strength of Fields,*** but I conclude either that the translator likes long-winded poets or that he can make anyone seem long-winded, even an oriental. (pp. 183-84)

It would be agreeable to say that in the translations we are at least freed of Dickey as a persona, but the voice of most of them is relentlessly first person. . . . Dickey's egoism has generated a thousand self-perpetuating anecdotes, yet the truth is, he is less imprisoned in his psyche than most poets. Whatever his poems are, they are not claustrophobic. Extroversion is an attractive thing about them, and may well account for their popularity. The poets he translates are, compared to him, closeted.

Speaking in his own voice he is a lyricist whose gift for the dramatic moment, for the accurate, vivid observation quickly rendered, is dissipated in non-structures enormously inflated. I seem to be describing Meyerbeer, and one could say that, like Meyerbeer, he will be immortal in his lifetime and for a few months after. The identification is not capricious: Meyerbeer may be said to have invented publicity—advertising—as we know it, and publicity has made Dickey one of the better poets who has ever been really popular. (pp. 184-85)

Turner Cassity, "Double Dutch," in Parnassus: Poetry in Review, *Vol. 8, No. 2, 1980, pp. 177-93.*

DAVE SMITH

The Zodiac is a poem about fear and estrangement and what poetry can do to make felt "The star-beasts of intellect and madness." Dickey's preface tells us this is:

> . . . the story of a drunken and perhaps dying Dutch poet who returns to his home in Amsterdam after years of travel and tries desperately to relate himself, by means of stars, to the universe.

Organized in twelve zodiacal and seasonal panels, occurring within twenty-four hours, and being an approximation of the dying poet's mind-flow mediated through Dickey, with intrusive commentary by Dickey, ***The Zodiac*** is not a narrative progression except as the poet-hero's madness implies the eternal story of "connecting and joining things that lay their meanings / Over billions of light years," or the madness of failure and fear. Nature, in ***The Zodiac,*** is either the meaning of stars or their deadness. Dickey's oscillating journey, in the poet's "story," is now between the failure of everything on earth (history, time, love, home—all betrayals) and whatever, if anything, stars are saying. In this sense, ***The Zodiac*** is entirely self-referential and everything to which the poet responds leaves him aware he is only a prisoner of illusion. Darkness reigns.

The Zodiac seems to me important as an impressive failure and as a transitional poem for Dickey. Its failure is caused partly by the absence of narrative and hence by an absence of event which might generate the storm of emotional rhetoric, and partly by the artificial organization of zodiacal panels which remain static and shed little if any of the Pythagorean aura of divine immanence. Drunk not only on *aquavit* but on cosmological abstractions, Dickey's poet is harassed by images of Time in both the world-city and in the "Peaceful-sea-beast-blue" of universal space, but his life in time is a failure and an imprisonment. He has no life in or out of the world and his homecoming is the occasion to ruminate, while attempting to write, on all the great unknowns. But why this apparently diseased and world-bruised symbolic man should particularly constitute a window into some universal reality, or how, is never quite clear. For all the poem's tortured anguish and virtually hacked-out-alive language, it has the feel of ideas sketched hugely but not dramatically. There is no sense the emotional progression comes to rest except that the poet sits writing a prayer for "the music / That poetry has never really found." Lacking necessity and motion, failing to coalesce around the secret it wanted, ***The Zodiac*** turns Dickey's spatial organization into spatial occupation. On the other hand, there is so much plainly good and true writing in the poem I am tempted to feel it is impertinent to cavil. (pp. 351-52)

If ***The Zodiac*** suffers from Faustian explosion, Dickey's newest collection [***The Strength of Fields***] on the whole does not. This is perhaps because ten of the poems in **"The Strength of Fields"** section were published by 1973 and are, in character, continuous with the style appearing late in ***Poems 1957-1967*** and in ***The Eye-Beaters, Blood, Victory, Madness, Buckhead and Mercy*** (1970). The poems in this section are not walls of words but they avoid such conventions as a continuous left-hand margin, stanzas, repetitive line-lengths, and consistent punctuation. Ordinarily such matters have little to do with what poetry is, but Dickey calls our attention to them to insist he is working less with narrative than with spatial suspensions of states of being. In fact, there is little new in these fourteen poems, nor does that compromise their general excellence. In all of them we find Dickey's obsessive and linking image patterns of water, flight, evasion, ascent, descent, the ghosts of the dead, and mythopoeic animals, though Dickey's metaphoric transformation with the beast-world is remarkably absent. Dickey seems, since ***The Eyebeaters,*** to locate his poems more firmly in the social and public house of human society and the genesis of the energized man finds its most dramatic moments in sexual epiphanies and the dangers of war. At age 58, Dickey's vision of heroic glory remains intact, but the Melville-like dark abysm against which the powerless man contends has come, like the military drums of Fort Jackson, closer to the living place. Still, Dickey's problem in ***The Strength of Fields*** (1977) is:

> how
> To withdraw how to penetrate and find the source
> Of the power you always had

especially when all one's best strengths and efforts have revealed that icily indifferent universe of ***The Zodiac***. It is possible now, I think, to argue that that pattern of oscillation in Dickey's poetry was also between a tragic anguish and a comedic joy. Where earlier Dickey's vision of connection and resolution seemed dominant, perhaps the product of a war survivor's faith in the future, his poems now stand in the present of "death-mud shaking" and look backward in tragic despair.

Dickey's title poem, **"The Strength of Fields,"** believes however that "We can all be saved / By a secret blooming." In it Dickey, as before, skates the thin ice of fear and trembling, courageously and believably assuming the role of the Chosen Man doomed to bring back from the psychic underworld the secret of life's fertility and renewal. There is no dramatic occasion or plot save the presiding ghost of the monomyth's rite of passage but the poem has the force of the private man's public declaration of faith in the earth and the dead who speak to us through "the renewing green" and "the homes of men." Straight through Dickey speaks with the power of a man who has seen beyond the surfaces of things and, as hard as it is to say it, he redeems us.

Each of the thirteen other poems in Dickey's first section aspire in one way or another to acts of redemption. **"Root-Light, or the Lawyer's Daughter,"** the tightest of them all, is an epiphany of passion's beginning, a kind of folk religion's "Image / Of Woman to last / All your life" as she was once seen diving into and rising up from the St. Mary's River. Its reverent excitement matches the sexual aura and jittery magic of **"The Voyage of the Needle,"** in which a man taking a bath remembers himself as a child who learned from his mother the "scientific trickery" that lets a sewing needle float. **"Remnant Water"** alone returns Dickey to the animal world and, here, to the death of a pond. As if an extension of the last, dying carp, Dickey is the shamanistic genius of the place whose words alone can redeem "my people gone my fish rolling" and whose mission is "Suffering its consequences, dying, / Living up to it." There are five poems of war experience (Dickey had once called this collection *War Embrace*) and each is a kind of latter-day redemption of those lost not to war deaths but to war's betrayals of ordinary human responsibility. None of the poems glorify combat but in the context of "O why / In Hell are we doing this?" each seeks to celebrate those who passed through the valley of death with human distinction, which is to say, committed acts of fearful evasion and bright courage. **"Camden Town,"** which may be the best of all of Dickey's war poems, shows a cadet pilot's training flight, the fear which causes him to hide under his instruments so that his ship becomes a Flying Dutchman until he gathers himself and swings the ship "East, and the deaths and nightmares / And training of many." It is not too much to say that with these poems Dickey reminds us that all war survivors may be psychological and emotional flying dutchmen. We live in a time once again of rattling sabers and one has only to read these poems to comprehend the huge psychic wound of war, a debt really and one whose amortization is endless.

The best of these poems, however, are **"False Youth: Autumn: Clothes of The Age"** and **"Exchanges."** The latter takes the form of an interlineated dialogue with the dead poet Joseph Trumbull Stickney. Here exchanges are not the transformations Dickey used to make but a juxtaposition of what we give and are given of value in our lives. (pp. 353-54)

In spite of the general and significant accomplishment of ***The Strength of Fields,*** the book has some pronounced disasters. **"For the Running of the New York Marathon"** reminds me of Dickey's early and uncollected poem **"The Sprinter's Mother."** It is a bathetic and sentimental grabbing of the cosmic hand-mike to proclaim they also win who only show up and trot. A similar failure, with better moments, is **"For the Death of Lombardi,"** a poem which demonstrates by implication Dickey's formidable power and a singular weakness. Ostensibly Dickey hovers near the legendary football coach, as he lies dying of cancer, one hero paying homage to another's manly courage, pride, passion, and sacrifice. Lombardi, we remember, said "Fatigue makes cowards of us all." But he also said "Winning isn't everything. It's the only thing." Was Lombardi a tragic hero? There is every opportunity for a great elegy of interrogation, drama, and grand resolution and Dickey seems to have had this in mind but there is no dramatic occasion out of which oracular moralizing *must* arise, so that Dickey is just gratuitous when he says "Did you make of us, indeed, / Figments over-specialized ghosts / Who could have been real / Men in a better sense?" Such writing smacks of superior post-season banquet bouquets. (p. 355)

Fourteen poems comprise the second half of Dickey's book, "Head-Deep In Strange Sounds: Free-Flight Improvisations

From the Un-English,'' and are, apparently, what he called in ***Sorties*** ''misreadings.'' Each carries an acknowledger such as *from, after, near* and most hail poets like Montale, Aleixandre, Paz. **''Three Poems With Yevtushenko''** are near-translations, though what precisely the others are I do not know, and therefore treat them as new poems. All continue Dickey's theme of the heroic Energized Man, but all are, in style, radically discontinuous with Dickey's characteristic work. They are short, terse, and intensely imagistic of body though written mostly in long, gap-punctuated and spatially dispersed lines. There was always a surreal quality to Dickey's poetry and it is strong here. If there is a precursor in his poems, it is ***The Zodiac*** and its heightened dream of vitality surrounded by disease, death, and doom. Each poem feels like a parable but is not, being essentially a kind of nakedly psychic speech, studded with image clusters, that blurs both dramatic occasion and public clarity. . . . [Several] seem to me virtually impenetrable. The best of them all is perhaps **''Purgation,''** which is addressed to the ninth-century Chinese master-poet Po Chu-yi and which describes the emotional ''season for wildfire'' and renewal. It is a stunning and wonderfully gentle piece. . . . (p. 356)

I cannot help feeling that these poems from the UnEnglish and ***The Strength of Fields*** ''[carry] the day despite everything,'' as Dickey said of Jeffers, but not merely because of his embodiment of *his* Truth. No, it is because he returns us to our most deeply longed for lives, and shows us those lives, as few are gifted to do. There are changes in James Dickey's poetry, a deepened sense of mortality and fragility, a less frenetic impatience with the constraints of form, and a joy less the result of making literature than of setting the large visionary personality against fear and trembling. No one was ever a greater lover of poetry, of the sheerness of sound and the honesty of feel that poetry makes our first and last way of knowing the labor that life is. No one has demanded more of art as the ungulled and absolute measure of the individual existence. Dickey's strength, the strength of this book, is that he is not a poet of argument but one who turns the world ''tall / In the April wind.'' (p. 357)

Dave Smith, ''The Strength of James Dickey,'' in Poetry, *Vol. CXXXVII, No. 6, March, 1981, pp. 349-57.*

RICHARD TILLINGHAST

The publication of any new work by James Dickey is cause for readers of poetry to sit up and take notice; the publication of his new book, ***The Strength of Fields,*** is cause for celebration. In the current ''poetry boom'' (the term itself a negation of poetry), a reader searches to the point of exhaustion without finding poems as powerful, exhilarating, and radically original as those in ***The Strength of Fields.*** Dickey is back with a vengeance, and it is fascinating to see the ways in which he has grown.

Alone among his contemporaries, Dickey has a quality of exuberance that one must go back to Whitman to see equaled. By contrast Allen Ginsberg's enthusiasm sounds hollow, manic, trumped-up, as though he is trying to reproduce something he admires in Whitman. This exuberance has hurt Dickey among critics, just as it has hurt Whitman; with Randall Jarrell in his praising mood a notable exception, a critic almost by nature dislikes exuberance and rejects it when he sees it.

Trying to view Dickey's work ''from inside,'' it would seem that his main technical problem is getting the language to bear the live currents of expression without blowing a fuse. Sometimes he does blow a fuse. But in this book he partially solves the problem through his use of syntactic dislocations and rearrangements. . . . Dickey could be accused of incoherence; but I believe he succeeds in creating a ''hot'' language that bears in one moment the charge of sense-experience, memory, judgment—no mean achievement. He has the uncommon ability to see, and to transmit a verbal experience of, the unity of life, which is the real meaning of metaphor. A few lines from **''The Rain Guitar,''** about the poet's encounter in the rain, on an English stream, with a fly fisherman, give a glimpse of this vision of unity:

> I picked, the guitar showered, and he cast to the mountain
> Music. His wood leg tapped
> On the cobbles. Memories of many men
> Hung, rain-faced, improving, sealed-off
> In the weir.

A new note—thoughtful, tragic—enters Dickey's music in this book. Whether, as Yeats said, ''We begin to live when we have conceived life as tragedy'' (I doubt very much that James Dickey would agree), this darkening of his poetry gives it a dimension it has not always had. His great early poems are ecstatic trances; **''Exchanges,''** the major poem of [***The Strength of Fields***], is ecstatic too, yet at the same time it entertains a powerful, complex awareness of tragedy and death. Part elegy for a dead lover, part meditation on Southern California as the ecological and spiritual death of the American continent and the American Dream, the poem is an exchange between Dickey and Trumbull Stickney, who died of brain cancer in 1904 at age 30 and whose lines appear in italics. . . . This poem ranks with James Dickey's finest achievements, with poems like **''The Firebombing,'' ''The Owl King,''** and the many others. Yet with its darkness, its compassion, its unforced complexity, it excels them. The verve and the brilliance of Dickey's language place him above most living poets; in human terms, his willingness and his ability to grapple with the things that matter to all of us, his ''participation in large common actions'' (to use R. W. Flint's term), give his poetry major importance and make his novel ***Deliverance*** a popular classic. Yet this new book, and in particular the poem **''Exchanges,''** make me believe that his best work still lies ahead of him. (pp. 455-57)

Richard Tillinghast, ''The Growth of James Dickey,'' in The Southern Review *(Louisiana State University), Vol. 17, No. 2, Spring, 1981, pp. 455-57.*

WILLIAM HARMON

Vicissitudes of reputation notwithstanding, James Dickey remains an extraordinary talented poet. . . . [In] a sense, Dickey's personal and professional fortunes soared and sank along with those of another toothy James (well, all right: *Jimmy*) from Georgia. The 1977 Inauguration may be likened to a sort of solstice for Dickey, and since then he seems to have become a less public celebrity.

Which brings us to Yeats's forced zero-sum choice between perfection of the life or perfection of the work. For a while, Dickey seemed to have chosen a gaudy perfection of the life, whereupon the work drifted ever further from perfection, reaching one nadir in ***The Strength of Fields*** then bouncing along to another in ***The Zodiac.*** But now—and I am delighted to say so—Dickey's new book, ***Puella,*** impresses me as his best work since ***Buckdancer's Choice.***

The poet has kept some of his now-familiar idiosyncrasies. With the exception of the final poem, **"Summons,"** ***Puella*** consists of rather modest poems in which every line begins with a capital letter and is centered on the page, with some portentous liberties taken with the spacing and line-feed. Apart from that typographical continuity, ***Puella*** differs substantially from most of Dickey's earlier work. The book presents, in eighteen poems, a complex persona named Deborah whom the dust-jacket identifies as the poet's "young wife." The dedication of the book reads, "To Deborah— / *her girlhood, male-imagined*." (p. 91)

Dickey's ***Puella*** works as both a rare encomiastic tribute and a courageous dispatching of the imagination. A notoriously macho poet, for whom 1982 will be his sixtieth year to heaven, fancies himself privy to the sensibility of a character nearly the opposite of himself: a woman who seems to be quite young, no more than twenty-five. The title suggests outright girlhood, but no one has exactly surveyed the boundary between *puella* and *mulier*, "girl" and "woman." The heroine of Cummings' *Puella Mea* is certainly an adult. (p. 92)

One gets no sense of Deborah as a housewife or a citizen outfitted with a local habitation, a family name, a Social Security number. (She does sound pregnant at the end.) With only a first name, and with a book called something as abstract and general as ***Puella,*** the character undergoes a metamorphic elevation into pure Girl, her lineaments mostly symbolic, heraldic, totemic, mythic, atavistic, primal. . . . Deborah's voice, powerful and occasionally obscure, comes through as poetry from a Delphic doorstep, echoically poised between Girl and Woman, *farouche* and much-hyphenated. Over the language of such poems, a number of familiar spirits brood. Hopkins and Rilke, sophisticated poets of naive "betweenpie" states of becoming, are honored by epigraphs. Hart Crane's hyperactive syntax is here, as is the metamorphic spondaic rhythm of Pound's Canto II. Everything is exaggerated, but most of the time Dickey's invention is rugged enough to take the strain.

Now and again, the vocabulary of these poems seems to belong outside the persona's native precinct. Some expressions are writerly conceits ("End-stopping a creek," "off-prints / of lightning"); others suggest the warfare and aviation of Dickey's earlier verse ("flame-outs," "search-and-destroy"); still others come out of current popular science ("black-hole," "anti-matter," "steady-state," "light-sensitive" twice, and "flash point" twice). None of this diction is necessarily alien to Dickey's *puella*-persona, and the book provides many moments of intense somatic realization for which Germanically compounded adjectives and nouns seem entirely appropriate. . . . I, for one, am happy that Dickey exploits an increasingly common feature of the American language and his own distinctive idiom to create a sympathetic character with an answerable style. Usually, he manages not to run hyperbole into the ground. (pp. 92-3)

Poems whose torque comes from sex and myth are easy to begin; prosecuting a series of such poems seems to be an enterprise that comes to Dickey easily, naturally, leaves to a tree; but satisfactorily ending the series, or even one of its units, must be impossible. How should such poetry stop, end, terminate? This has been one of the difficulties besetting Dickey for a long time now. He has a good eye, his heart is somewhere near the right place, his ideas are original, he gives his poems those helpful titles (against the grain of the age, which seems to favor such nothing-title poets as Creeley and Ammons), he follows through both tenderly and robustly, he has a sense of humor. But he seems not to place enough trust in his reader, and he definitely cannot end a poem or a sequence without recourse to tacky platitude. The worst poem in ***Puella***—and the only bad one, I judge—is the last, **"Summons,"** and the very worst part of it comes at the end, where the four portentously spaced, portentously italicized lines are arranged in portentous echelon:

unending
invention
go for it
unending

I had just seen "Rocky III" when I read this part of ***Puella,*** but that experience may not explain all of my recoiling from the reverberating wrongness of that "go for it." Restraining the impulse to bad-mouth the sadomasochistic-birdbrained-Vince-Lombardi-jock-ethic of Dickey at his worst, I'll just say that here the poet took quite a chance, ransacking the threadbare thesaurus of sport, and it didn't pay off. But the feeble dud of an ending is no total loss. This pathetic moment, even at the end, cannot ruin what is after all a very good book. (p. 94)

William Harmon, "Herself as the Environment," in Carolina Quarterly, *Vol. XXXV, No. 1, Fall, 1982, pp. 91-4.*

J. D. McCLATCHY

In [***Puella***], James Dickey has taken his young wife, Deborah, as his labyrinth and clue. A note (presumably written by the poet himself) explains that Dickey "embarked on his own male voyage into the realm of womanhood" and that ***Puella*** offers eighteen glimpses into, or versions of, her "crucial and exalting passage" from girl to woman. . . . Because the book is a sustained and unified sequence—a rhapsody, really—it is better than Dickey's previous two collections. Still, it makes me wince, as if watching a silk scarf pulled backward through a mangle.

It has been fifteen years now since Dickey wrote a good poem, a poem with the flexed narrative skill and outsized gestures of his first work. Even then he walked—so he once boasted—"the razor's edge between sublimity and absurdity." Since then, the sublime has been shoved aside by a vulgarity of tone and a banality of attention to make room for an absurdity that has embarrassed his first champions. ***Puella,*** too, for all its new efforts to elide and control, is a bloated affair. (p. 148)

Instead of the left-hand margin's point of departure and return, Dickey chooses a kind of firehouse pole down the middle of a poem around which the phrases spiral down into action. Rather than "center" a poem, the device loosens it; the episodes float in a solution of adjectives and images. Perhaps it should be read as a field of force. Certainly—whether or not apt to a young girl's sensibility—energy is all. Art historians use the term *Knollenstils* to describe a style of exaggerated, grotesque musculature, and that has become Dickey's trademark. Worse, it is accompanied here by the jargon of hype: "high-concentrate," "super-nerved," "time-releasing," and "no-win" (as in "the sea's holy no-win roar"). It is never pleasant to chart the further decline of a poet one used to admire. (pp. 148-49)

J. D. McClatchy, "Labyrinth and Clue," in The Nation, *New York, Vol. 236, No. 5, February 5, 1983, pp. 148-51.*

DANIEL MARK EPSTEIN

By now James Dickey's position in the constellation of American letters is secure. He is rightfully considered the most significant poet the South has produced since Robert Penn Warren, to whom one poem in this collection is dedicated. Lovers of poetry will be reading **"Buckdancer's Choice," "The Celebration,"** and many other of Dickey's poems for generations.

So it is with great curiosity and some apprehension that we confront a retrospective such as Dickey has arranged for us in ***The Central Motion.*** This book brings together under a single cover the volumes ***The Eye Beaters*** (1970), ***The Zodiac*** (1976), and ***The Strength of Fields*** (1979), with a preface by Dickey explaining how this work demonstrates the "central motion" in his life as a poet. . . .

Regarding the poet's method, anyone familiar with Dickey's career knows the most dramatic change occurred during the writing of the poems in ***Buckdancer's Choice*** (1965). It was the sort of spectacular mid-career style change that many poets attempt but few accomplish. In that book Dickey breaks with the formal prosody of his highly successful lyrics, developing what he calls the "block format" in order to accommodate rangy narratives and internal monologues. Visually, the poems fill the page, rather like prose poems, their rhythms indicated by spaces between syntactic units rather than by versification. This method dominates the succeeding volume, ***Falling,*** the title poem of which records the impressions of an airline hostess plummeting several miles to her death. (p. 47)

Dickey is an American romantic, by D. H. Lawrence out of Walt Whitman, and when the beast in him is aroused, the poem resulting is a mystical, primal force.

This is not to suggest that Dickey's poems lack delicacy or thoughtfulness. . . .

It is difficult to understand why Mr. Dickey chooses to argue that these books represent a central motion with regard to his subjects. The poems of 1979 draw as heavily upon experiences of the military, sports, illness, and astronomy as do the poems of 1968. Perhaps the key is in the middle book, ***The Zodiac*** (1976). It is a single long poem, an internal monologue based upon a poem by Hendrik Marsman, "the story of a drunken and perhaps dying Dutch poet who returns to his home in Amsterdam after years of travel and tries desperately to relate himself, by means of stars, to the universe." The subject of ***The Zodiac*** is the process of making a poem, this particular poem. It is an exercise in postmodernism, as is practiced with precision and wit by John Barth, John Ashberry, and John Cage, all calculating ironists. This is no medium for a naturalist romantic. The alcoholism of Dickey's protagonist blurs his perceptions. The language is sometimes hysterical, at other times vague, and nowhere do we get the ironic distance that such a poem requires. In choosing his artistic processes as his subject in ***The Zodiac,*** Dickey is showing us his back. Perhaps he means to suggest, in his preface, that the central motion of his work begins and ends with the external world as subject, with an intervening turn inward, to self-study. Certainly this is the movement within his poems.

If deconstructionism, in contemporary criticism, has arrogated to the critic certain powers formerly reserved by the creators of literature, it seems that Mr. Dickey is trying to even the score by interpreting as well as editing his own poetry. I wish he wouldn't, because I am sure he has more important things to do. The poems speak for themselves. When they are as good as **"Victory"** or **"Exchanges,"** they are blindingly good and need no cheering section. When they are not so good, it is better for them to sink of their own weight, like the lesser works of Wordsworth and E. A. Robinson. Let them go, for the artist survives entire in his best work. (p. 48)

Daniel Mark Epstein, "Surviving Entire," in National Review, *New York, Vol. XXXVI, No. 9, May 18, 1984, pp. 47-8.*

LOUIS D. RUBIN, JR.

The Central Motion consists of poems that have hitherto appeared in several collections; it is dated 1968-1979, which means that these are the poems of Mr. Dickey's middle years, written after he became a full-fledged public personality. The poems here reprinted, he says in his preface, represent for him "a change of subject matter and method," and in the future he intends to move toward "further, perhaps more extreme, changes." . . .

To know the wellsprings of Mr. Dickey's poetry, consult the lyric entitled **"False Youth: Autumn: Clothes of the Age,"** from ***The Strength of Fields*** in the present collection. The poet goes into a barbershop in Columbia, S.C.; he is clad in a hat made of fox skins, from Brooks Brothers. As he finishes getting his hair cut, another barber remarks, "Jesus, if there's anything I hate / It's a middle-age hippie."

> Well, so do I, I swallow
> Back: so do I so do I
> And to hell . . . I get up, and somebody else says
> When're you going to put on that hat,
> Buddy? Right now. Another says softly,
> Goodbye, Fox.

As the poet leaves he puts on his denim jacket, the back of which features an embroidered eagle in threadbare condition and clutching a banner. Defiantly Mr. Dickey pauses by the door to allow everyone to get a good look at the one-word legend on the banner,

> . . . . soaring loose
> In red threads burning up white until I am shot in
> the back
> Through my wings or ripped apart
> For rags:
>
> Poetry.

In other words, do your worst, boys, but that, by God, is what I am. It is out of precisely this clash, potentially violent, between his middle-class Georgia origins—the redneck barbers—and the intensity of his artistic impulse that all of Mr. Dickey's best work comes. On the one hand there is the esthetic sensibility, the lover of words and images, the private imagination, and on the other the wish to be one of the Buckhead Boys, as he calls them, the athlete, the hunter, the lover boy if you will, together with the fear of being thought incapable of properly fulfilling that role.

Each of Mr. Dickey's characteristically recurring themes—football, war, bow-hunting, snakes, country music and guitar playing, flying, death by drowning, fear of and fascination with suicide—can be linked to this issue. His best work confronts it bravely and quite often magnificently. As in the poem cited above, he must wear the fox skins, flaunt them, be not merely different but flagrantly and gorgeously so, even though he knows and fears what the rednecks are thinking and the possible violent consequences. The poem is the statement of the schism, and, by dint of being written, its ritualistic flouting. It is a characteristic American literary stance. I think, most of all, of Ernest Hemingway; and like the prose of Hemingway, this man's best poems will be read and admired for a long time to come.

Louis D. Rubin, Jr., "Rituals of Risk," in The New York Times Book Review, *June 3, 1984, p. 23.*

PAUL CHRISTENSEN

The problem besetting Dickey's ***The Central Motion: Poems, 1968-1979*** is that he has tried to deal with middle age, his own, and fails to perceive in it value or meaning. It is only negative—a loss against which he loudly and dramatically declaims. The collection reprints three books of the 1970s: ***The Eye-Beaters*** (1970), ***The Zodiac*** (1976), and ***The Strength of Fields*** (1979). The poems span his middle years from his mid-forties to the age of fifty-six. Hence the title, the central motion, with its insinuation of a central *e*-motion. There is a centering drive in much of the work: the lines of most poems are balanced on an axis, "hung," Dickey remarked to me some years ago, "as if on a string, like a mobile." Sometimes the enjambments are awkward, with lines broken at random to make them fit his expanding and contracting shapes, his balances. The poems spread out like Rorschach blotches, or balloon up and down like a breathing bulb. In their conscious shapings, they express the craftsmanship, if not the vision Dickey struggles to impose here. To center anything thus is a nerve-racking act of precision, and there is a good deal of trembling and frustration in the tone of these poems. The lyrics are often shrill, at times agonized to find a dramatic finale to essentially uneventful experience.

The exaggerated tension in the book suggests Dickey's dread of his subject, as if growing older were a terrible curse with grim consequences. The opening poem, **"Diabetes,"** is nearly frantic with fear of debility and death. The persona lugs his ailing body around at night full of "self- / Made night water." His doctor has made him swear off booze and all his other vices, or else he can look forward / To gangrene and kidney / / Failure boils blindness infection skin trouble falling / Teeth coma and death." It is not a promising start for a book about the wisdom years. Instead, it begins with a dark threat against one's desire to remain recklessly young under one's soft chin and sagging belly. This pitch of rhetoric is sustained throughout all three books, into the final poems, which are Dickey's loose renderings of fourteen foreign-language poems, also about old age, dying, illness, and a serene final resignation to it all.

Dickey cannot find a justification for his own mortality; the loss of youthful powers is irreplaceable by wisdom or any nourishing vision of the remainder of life. There are no rituals or rites of passage for the mid-life adult to undertake to redeem himself. He can only dread the further loss of his powers, or remember with poignance the range of his youthful passions. The figure stumbling around in **"Diabetes"** has lost his bearings: everything he believed in had to do with strength and courage. This is where the Southern dream of manhood aborts—when older age becomes the waking nightmare. Now it is upon him, and a terrible throe ensues in operatic, shrilly pitched lyric thrashings. The language is anguished, distorted, the syntax skewered into Lear-like raging soliloquies. Dickey means to play out to the end his own final curtain as a Southern male; but the passions running through the poems are very toxic, the potent confusions that drove Hemingway to suicide. Missing here are the resourceful and cunning self-rescues in Saul Bellow's mid-life novels, *Henderson the Rain King* (1959) and *Herzog* (1964).

But for Dickey there is no going forward; to dwindle in strength and courage is unthinkable. He plies his theme with melodramatic hyperbole, but keeps an eye on the effect he is having on his audience. Dickey knows when he is hamming his emotions and when they cause him genuine *angst;* but the poems merge candor and bombast into one lyric keen. He can change his act on a nod; some of the poems take an abrupt turn from self-pity to show us his fatherly affections, as in two poems on his sons, **"Messages,"** with their tender words from an otherwise hard-boiled parent. Soon after, he is off once more, raging in his ambulance on the way to the emergency room, having collapsed in the street, shouting his fustian and gesturing like an old tragedian in the poem **"Mercy,"** arms outstretched as he delivers this close:

My lips   hold them down don't let them cry
With the cry   close   closer   eyeball to eyeball
In my arms, O queen of death
Alive, and with me at the end.

This peroration is intended for his favorite nurse, who has rushed down to find her old warrior dying again. The tone of this poem is murky—a mixture of pathetic sincerity and self-mocking irony. It turns over its own psychological ruse by minimizing and clowning in a serious crisis. (pp. 207-09)

Death is nothing; life is everything, but exactly what life is remains unspoken. It is merely a continuation of the struggle. But this undimensional imperative counters all thoughts of death but the fear of it. Dickey is at an impasse in this book—he has gone from youth to age, only to dread the progress. The poems do not penetrate experience; instead, they build up a wall of extravagant evasions to it. The forays back to youth and wartime memories are brief escapes from torment; the illness poems are full of self-mocking humor. The obsession with death fears is everywhere; he transforms all his experience into it, but this momentary fiat of imagination is then blocked by an unwillingness to argue for relief or consolation. That is why the sudden appearance of **"The Eye-Beaters"** is so extraordinary in the stagnant relation of the other poems. It suddenly leaps off in a new direction, alien to the other poems.

The eye-beaters of the poem are blind children in an asylum who beat on their eyes to experience visions; they beat them till they bleed and turn black. An older man narrates his visit to them and sympathizes with, almost approves of their tortuous behavior—he, too, is blind and has no vision of his own. The poem seems to acknowledge the intellectual catch of all the preceding poems—the aging persona who cannot drink, smoke, or womanize must now preserve what health remains, even as he dreams of youth and escape from his ailing body. The children are in a similar intellectual paralysis, prisoners of their own malfunctioning organisms who also need to be consoled and delivered. As they beat on their eyes, visions form, he imagines, that are nothing more than hemorrhages, but to the inner eye are like the scrawls of cave walls—the figures etched in feces and vegetable dyes by primordial man, who was also "blind" and desperate to create a consoling vision for his life. The children re-create for themselves the same archetypal images that were first seen thirty thousand years ago in the corridors of the Dordogne caves. In a way, history is static in this poem—a suspended state of desire in which the same archetypes appear across the whole human era, from beginning to now. There is considerable merit to the thesis, and other poets have recently been exploring the notion of such archetypal patterning in the deep imagination—in the work of Robert Bly and even more recently in Clayton Eshleman. (pp. 210-11)

It is a good poem, and its roots go far back into earlier work—into other poems touching on the human relation to the animal world, as in **"The Sheep-Child"** and **"The Shark's Parlor."** In its dread of life and loneliness, it bears relation to other classic poems in the vein, among them Yeats's "Among School Children" and Dylan Thomas's "I See the Boys of Summer." But personal solace is not forthcoming in Dickey's poem; it ends on a note of indeterminacy. The goal of the poem was the agony, not the relief. It is a grotesque poem in the original sense of the word, from grotto, the cave, the dark soul. It bears pointing out that Dickey, like few others in American poetry, is a grotesque writer—from the tradition of Bosch, Goya, Céline, Burroughs—whose energies have always been directed at the hidden depths of pain and distortion in life. Its negative tradition is a running commentary through the centuries on different notions of the Sublime, the Beautiful—but in reverse. Solace for Dickey is not in escape from the pain but in finding commiseration through others also in pain, the exploration of pain itself, its myriad volatile images and fused emotions.

The line of reasoning in **"The Eye-Beaters"** prompted the ambitious, failed effort called ***The Zodiac,*** which appeared six years later, in 1976. The poem is about another eye-beater, a Dutch poet whose "triangular eyes" look into the cold Christian heaven and alter all its abstractions with animal totems of his own invention. Reordering the zodiac and paganizing the lifeless divinity of the Christian view somehow consoles his besotted mind, though how is never clear or persuasive. The book-length piece is a dark, sweaty, booze-laden sequence, monotonous in pace, raspy-voiced in its slangy lyric climaxes and repeated epithets. It is disheveled in every way—with a laundry-line typographic scheme that drapes the onrush of phrases over the whole page space. Dickey is at sea trying to make up a new mythology through the guise of his deranged persona.

Both **"The Eye-Beaters"** and ***The Zodiac*** bear much in common—they constitute Dickey's forays into the speculative realms of Charles Olson. By 1970, Dickey was played out on the themes of youth and heroism. Olson died the same year and left behind a contentious canon and a bevy of admiring young intellectuals to spread its heady gospels. Dickey was not amused by Olson's brief spate of publications, but he paid attention to them through the years, as did other major figures who frequently took aim at Olson in the journals. . . . Dickey tries out the notion of a valid primordial "sight" in **"The Eye-Beaters,"** but in ***The Zodiac*** he seems to be writing a *Maximus Poems* in miniature, under flamboyant disguises and with disclaimers posted at the outset. This may seem an awkward thesis to put forward in the light of the harsh words Dickey wrote in ***Babel to Byzantium*** (1968, 1981), but he could turn around even there and say, "Yet I have a weakness for long poems of this kind." "His mind," he wrote, "seems to me a capable one," and his *Maximus* poems, though "unsuccessful," contain a "few moderately interesting sections . . . worth reading."

By 1966, in **"The Poet Turns on Himself,"** he wrote: "I began to conceive of something I called—doubtless misleadingly—the 'open' poem: a poem which would have none of the neatness of most of the poems we call 'works of art' but would have the capacity to involve the reader in it, in all its imperfections and impurities, rather than offering him a (supposedly) perfected and perfect work for contemplation, judgment, and evaluation." But this is precisely what Dickey complained of in 1961 in Olson's "structure of fortuitous association," which five years later is grafted onto Dickey's poetic, since he is now "interested most of all in getting an optimum 'presentational immediacy,' a compulsiveness in the presentation of the matter of the poem that would cause the reader to forget literary judgments entirely and simply experience." (pp. 211-13)

The turn to Olson, however veiled or half-conscious, is curious and problematic: the Southern poet regarded himself as a force of conservation of certain Western values, which in Olson are under attack. Olson had specified a disorder that released creative energies; the Southern legacy put a value on controlling one's materials as a siphoning off of essences in the poetic act. Even Poe retained the graces of lyric and its sturdiest conventions of the European tradition. With few exceptions, Southern writers, though of perplexed emotion, held out for order over materials as an imperative of art. One must wonder if it is the *Zeitgeist* of the mid-century or the disarming arrogance of Olson that made Dickey question his own rules and conventions and throw them out.

But one affinity between Olson and Dickey is always just under the surface of Dickey's poetry: his "permanent interest . . . in the forfeited animal grace of human beings, occasionally redeemed by athletes . . . and the hunter's sense of understanding with the hunted animal." Both Americans expressed attitudes toward the natural world previously articulated by D. H. Lawrence, which sets them apart in the distinctive, rebellious direction of recent poetry. Whereas poets like Theodore Roethke and James Wright admired the grace and peace of certain animals, Dickey, Olson, and Lawrence longed for the violent, untamable animal realm that would overpower the frailties of human awareness. They wanted reunion with a primal world of violence and instinct, which they glimpsed in certain primordial images. All three writers expressed an intense masculinity and dreaded the loss of their animal powers through the refinements of human evolution.

The drama of these uneven poems of middle life is of a Southern poet moving out of the boundaries of his literary heritage into a great uncertainty of composition and idea, which he deals with by incorporating principles of his most suspect contemporary. Olson at least asked big questions and wondered aloud in his messy compositions, and sought no firm conclusions to his arguments. It was more important to be lost in one's creative confusion, which Dickey now wanted for himself—the "conclusionless poem," with its language at once "open" and "ungeneralizing," the poem "un-well-made." If Faulkner exploded the sentence to lay bare the paradoxical content of his own feelings, it is not until Dickey that the line of Southern poetry is finally broken open to allow a disorderly subjectivity to tumble out of it. The "tradition" of Southern writing, rich as it is, eccentric and volatile as it may seem, was bridled by its inherited European aesthetic. The line from Faulkner to Wolfe to Barthelme is a dissent and an opening out of the prose structure of fiction; it cannot be traced in poetry much before the wild, disordering tendencies of Dickey's poems in the mid-1960s.

For all that, ***The Zodiac*** is not very good. As a long poem, it lacks the mosaic infrastructure required for suspense and rapid, jagged movement forward; it rarely achieves the fortuitousness desired; and it labors to show a mind liberated from old assumptions, which comes and goes in a boozy haze of imprecision and feigned madness. The long poem is essentially a ritual, a "dark game" which, when carried out well, shows a Western poet seated among the fragments of his own culture and of others, which he sorts through and reassembles in order to bring off his own eccentric perspective on life. Dickey's persona can't do that; the poet behind him is not speculative by nature but sure-handed and too exacting. The kind of mind Dickey wants to invent—the Olsonian speculator of lofty, difficult notions—is simply too foreign to him. Instead, he falls back on his old maunderings and bellyachings through his speaker—whose alcoholism threatens his life and whose desire to bring "God's crazy beasts" back into metaphysics simply fades out. . . . Dickey can only record the sweating melodrama of the effort, not its steps of mental progress. Sadly, his poem becomes a Hollywood treatment of the long poem—scenes and dialogue, little of the essential substance of its subject. (pp. 213-15)

The Strength of Fields (1979), the third and last book of ***The Central Motion,*** is a slight but fluid collection of original poems, with an appendix of fourteen translations. Dickey has made some adjustments to style in it—an emphasis on sound and the musically enriched phrase, and away from a crisp narrative focus. The poems seem reluctant to tell anything—an image will do, as in **"Root-Light, or the Lawyer's Daughter,"** with its rush of baroque imagery, its subject withheld until the final lines, when a naked girl dives from a bridge into a river as a lasting memory of youth and beauty. **"The Strength of Fields"** was commissioned for Carter's inauguration, and it is an elegant tribute to a new President. It explores the delicate sense of fealty between one isolated self and the lives that fill the surrounding cosmos as a low, baleful train whistle is heard in the distance to remind one of change and mortality. The poem's elegant sophistications of language are tempered a bit by the form they construct—an open-ended variation on the blues ballad of freight trains and lonely travel. **"The Rain Guitar"** is a silly bit of mythmaking, with Dickey as magic minstrel again, playing his regional music as an English fisherman helplessly dances in excitement. It is a throwback to the magical realism Dickey produced earlier, but its self-glorifications hardly seem naïve any longer.

Especially interesting is the poem **"For the Death of Lombardi,"** which is Dickey at his vintage best. In Lombardi Dickey finds a mystical Southern father—someone who drove the boys to manhood, who died and is lamented self-consciously in mythical terms as a source of Dickey's own manhood. His death by cancer is metaphorical of a terrible inexorability, which Dickey fears now that he is "middle-aged and gray." (p. 216)

Mortality, old age, and death are the terms of this poetry, but Dickey seems to have found peace with himself. The poems are less shrill and frenzied; they balance once more on their plumb lines, the lines tapering and expanding as he packs all the music he can into their lumpy, jarring phrases. Some of the language reads like tongue-twisting elocution drills, but there are also somber themes that buoy up the dizzying lyric spells. In the closing poem of Part One, **"Exchanges,"** Dickey merges his words with lines from Joseph Trumbull Stickney, as both describe the California coast. The Stickney lines are romantic and reverent, while Dickey's are sober and realistic: together they merge the two halves of history—the beautiful wilderness, the gloomy sea of oil rigs and pollution. It ends on Dickey's most persistent theme: the human curse upon nature. . . . (p. 217)

The Central Motion is the waffling poetry of a major writer of the 1970s. It's a slim volume with a few very good poems in it; the rest is confusion and ramblings, awkward experiments and grim failures. It comes after a decade of remarkable successes and awards and was perhaps an inevitable falling off. The seventies were themselves unheroic and inward-looking, and their atmosphere wears off in this work. The view is almost always within, at failing health and waning convictions; it is a book about struggle and grief, arguments with the self, a desire to go on as the feet grow leaden. It is partly about being caught in one's own confected image, the duties that it imposes, which are false and wearying. Americans took to Dickey, even non-readers, who flocked to his readings. Sporting-goods manufacturers plied him with canoes and power bows, hoping for his endorsements. The book seems to sigh under the load of that publicity and vanity, as real things ensue—mortality, death of loved ones, illnesses, qualms, and fears. It is a book of thrashings and throes by a man who cannot easily face his aging. Unlike Lear, who reached an epiphany of sorts—that man is a bare, forked animal gripped by change—Dickey's voice keeps arguing alone in the dark, in thickets of confusion and ill humor, trying to find the drama and the lyric ebullience to somehow get through it. But all Dickey can argue here is that youth is everything—and to lose it is the only tragedy. (pp. 218-19)

Paul Christensen, "Toward the Abyss: James Dickey at Middle Age," in Parnassus: Poetry in Review, *Vol. 13, No. 2, Spring-Summer, 1986, pp. 202-19.*

JOHN CALVIN BATCHELOR

Alnilam is the mythical and sinister second novel of an internationally prominent poet, appearing 17 years after his folkloric ***Deliverance.*** It combines James Dickey's curious opinion of the relationship between blindness and truth with his gift for evoking the tall-tale Southland, where language stalks with the ferocity of a hunter. The novel is also possessed by the mystical notion of flying like a predatory bird. . . .

There is a spooky strangeness to ***Alnilam,*** however, that may discomfit readers accustomed to Dickey's rough-hewn, regional voice. Set on a world-scale canvas during World War II, the novel pursues the ambitious art of myth-making. And what Dickey has to say, slowly and angrily, amounts to a vertiginous decrying of the 20th century's military cults, from imperialism to communism to fascism to, just perhaps, American jingoism.

The novel's title is the initial oddity; it derives from the central star in the belt of the constellation Orion, the warrior-hunter. Alnilam is Arabic for "a belt of pearls." . . . (p. 1)

The title is not just poetry, though; it is also the name of a secret boy's club among the cadets at an inconsequential Air Corps training base. The time is the middle of World War II; the place is the make-believe Peckover, N.C., somewhere between the Cape Fear River and Piedmont plateau.

In the manner of a Greek yarn, Dickey's story begins simply. Frank Cahill, a 54-year-old Atlanta amusement park owner, receives a telegram informing him that his only child, Joel, has perished in a training accident at Peckover. Cahill is a brawny, unapologetic, vain, self-confident man whose pregnant wife left him 19 years earlier.

Therefore he has never seen his now dead son, and his fate is doubly dark, for Frank Cahill has recently been blinded by diabetes. For the simplest of reasons then, idle whim, he sets out by bus to bury his son's remains, taking along with him the sentinel Zack, a murderous black wolflike dog who provides eyes and security.

The mystery spirals when Frank Cahill learns from the camp commandant that they have not been able to find Joel's body. Joel is said to have been a gifted cadet-pilot, yet inexplicably he swooped over a brush fire, was pulled down by a downdraft, was rescued in bad shape by a farmer, then escaped the farmer to flee first back into the fire and then into the nearby river, where he finally disappeared after what one notes was an ancient progression: air, earth, fire and water.

Cahill hears the explanation and is neither aggrieved nor repelled; he is merely curious. Why is everyone being so solicitous, from the colonel to the fellow cadets and flight instructors? He is invited to stay on until graduation Sunday, when Joel would have gained his wings. He is offered the run of the camp, out of pity but also out of respect. Frank Cahill shrugs. It does not come to him, as it does to a suspicious reader, that he is caught up in the Oedipal drama, except topsy-turvy: Laius is blind and alive, Oedipus is missing-in-action. Ineluctably, Frank Cahill begins an exploration of the quintessential truth: Who was this boy Joel Cahill to die like that?

It is important to note that Frank Cahill is a truth teller as well as seeker. And Dickey emphasizes his insights with a stylistic innovation. Now and again, the text page is divided into two columns. The left hand in bold face is what the blind Frank Cahill senses and thinks even as the right-hand column is what the narrator describes, the actions of everyone else. The effect is difficult on the eye and often disorienting. One soon learns to read the right side the way one uses a fast forward button, and then to review Cahill's brooding thought for more clues.

Frank Cahill enlists several apparently reliable confederates in his quest, two of them combat veterans, one Joe's former flight instructor, another the flight surgeon, and, most elusively of all, a "wild mountain girl of the cotton mills." Each of them describes something not only of Joel but also of the nature of flying. Accordingly, in what must be a hard-won memory of his own ordeals, Dickey lavishes some excellent prose on combat-flying. . . . (pp. 1-2)

Episodically, Frank Cahill assembles a recon photograph of his son: flush-faced, psoriatic, adolescently defiant, mathematically adept, sexually sadistic, what one man calls someone "who doesn't question himself," another calls unmilitary, and another calls a "demon from the pit." Frank recovers a broken front tooth from the crash and confronts Joel's comrades, the Alnilam echelon. What he learns in the end is pathetic for so brief a life; it is also creepy.

It would be bad manners to reveal more of the puzzle except to say that the narrative explodes with a climax revealing the depravity of a world of boys at war, European, Asian or American. As far-fetched as it sounds, Frank Cahill unearths a conspiracy that resembles, in its wacky brutality, the same sort of totemic cabal that originally launched Lenin, Mussolini and Hitler, and that may have collected around more up-to-date militants.

Yet questions worry a measure of ***Alnilam.*** How far does Dickey want us to interpret all of this? He writes splendidly of flying yet opines that "the airplane is a mutilation machine." He speaks convincingly for the magic of the sky yet warns against windy cranks creating starry-eyed cults, even back-handing Christianity. And he offers the strangest assurance that those who plot for ultimate power will ultimately fail because of the inevitable Judas and because they always go too far. Betrayal and mass murder? If that is our common defense against military cults, then justice is not simply blind; it is tardy. (p. 2)

John Calvin Batchelor, "James Dickey's Odyssey of Death and Deception," in Book World—The Washington Post, *May 24, 1987, pp. 1-2.*

CHRISTOPHER LEHMANN-HAUPT

There are wonderful things in ***Alnilam.*** There are also things about it that justify one's initial suspicions that Mr. Dickey has failed to write a novel as taut and exciting as ***Deliverance*** was.

The story of ***Alnilam,*** for all its length, is surprisingly simple and absorbing, at least on the surface. In the year 1943, Frank Cahill, a 54-year-old carpenter from Atlanta who has recently gone blind from "early onset diabetes," receives a telegram informing him that his son, Joel Wesley Cahill, has been killed in a flight training accident. Though Cahill has never met his son, his wife having left him before Joel's birth, he decides to cooperate with the telegram's request to "please contact" the training field's commanding officer in Peckover, N.C.

With his seeing eye dog, Zack, he takes a bus to Peckover, meets the colonel in command, and begins to investigate his son's death. It soon turns out that Joel was an extraordinary young man whom the other cadets idolized, indeed, a cult had formed around him involving prophecy and revelation. Moreover, his "accident" occurred under mysterious circumstances that possibly may have left him alive. Whatever is going on, Frank Cahill soon discovers that he is at the center of it.

As for Mr. Dickey's typographical experiment: the boldface (or dark) columns describe what Cahill in his blindness is experiencing, while the colunms opposite show us what the other characters see. Although it's often hard to tell which version one is meant to read first, the device is often effective, particularly when Cahill is taken for a night flight by one of the flight instructors.

Yet balanced against the originality of the story and its divided narrative is Mr. Dickey's insistence on spelling out to the point of tedium every detail and nuance of what Cahill goes through. Moreover, the novel's main characters talk in a rural vernacular that sometimes reminds one of Eugene O'Neill at his most heavy-handed. . . .

Still, one reads on, intrigued with the developing mystery and the meaning of the code word "Alnilam." Whether the payoff is worth all the effort is a matter of interpretation. At the center of the cult involving Joel Cahill is an estatic vision of flight that is partly religious and partly ideological—as if the Italian futurist F. T. Marinetti had seen in Mussolini the second coming of Christ. . . .

Anyone who's bothered by this sort of mystical fanaticism, will find plenty of support in Mr. Dickey's pages. The cadets' commanding officer dismisses the Alnilam group as nothing more than "boys" who "don't like authority." The head doctor of the base compares them to Nazis and the Ku Klux Klan. A literal-minded reader is inclined to agree.

But Mr. Dickey seems ambivalent toward his Ubermensch, just as he was toward Lewis, the fanatical leader in ***Deliverance*** who overreaches himself but sets a standard for his less ambitious companions to match. Though the rational characters in ***Alnilam*** dismiss Joel's group for its fanaticism, it is his followers who get the last word. . . .

The guiding intelligence of ***Alnilam*** remains fascinated with power—the power of flight, the power of machines, the power of the human body, the power of the imagination, the power of youth. For readers captivated by Mr. Dickey's vision, there is an intricate network of symbols to explore: fire, air, water, the Phoenix, the maze, the snake, the constellation of Orion, Sirius the Dog Star and on and on, down a slope as dizzying as a fall from the sky. But skeptical readers will find such symbols labored. For them, ***Alnilam*** may never get off the ground.

Christopher Lehmann-Haupt, in a review of "Alnilam," in The New York Times, *June 1, 1987, p. 17.*

HENRY TAYLOR

One of Dickey's great strengths as a poet has been his extraordinary ability to give plausibility to nearly incredible situations and events. This is harder to do in fiction, of course, but ***Deliverance*** demonstrated that Dickey is aware of the different ways in which the two genres present this problem. A bare summary of the events in ***Alnilam*** would stretch credulity, but the detailed and absorbing narrative provides the necessary background and motivation for even so outrageous a scene as that in which a blind man [Frank Cahill] goes up in an airplane and wrestles the controls away from the pilot for a few minutes. . . .

The strength of the novel lies in the thoroughness with which Cahill enters the life of the camp for a few days, and in the gradually emerging picture we get of Joel, who has been a charismatic figure, the leader in a secret society of cadets who have named themselves after the middle star in Orion's belt—Alnilam.

This group is an extreme example of the rebelliousness that develops among schoolboys or convicts or soldiers in training. Joel Cahill came among them with a few strange ideas gleaned from the 19th-Century poet James Thomson and from science fiction; the force of his personality has been enough to involve several cadets in rituals and secret messages, the aim of which is to mold an elite corps of pilots who will be beyond the Army's control. The final purpose of their activity is obscure, because they are committed to such notions as "flying without the airplane." But they manage to create considerable havoc after Joel's death, acting on the belief that Frank's coming to the base has been foretold to them, and that Joel is not really dead, but is still out there somewhere, directing their actions.

Cahill's arrival at the base, and the willingness with which the commanding officer, Col. Vernon Hocclave, permits him to wander around, are made convincing partly by the circumstances themselves—Joel's crash is the first accident to have occurred at Peckover—and partly by the sheer force of Cahill's character. (p. 1)

But it is the existence of the small group of young fanatics that makes possible Cahill's freedom to wander around the base, asking questions and making discoveries—about his son, about flight, and about himself and the resources he can call on to negotiate this strange environment. He has not been blind long enough to stop marveling at his rapidly developing aptitude for sensing his surroundings, and this lends a pace-quickening intensity that makes the book feel shorter than it is.

In several passages, Dickey uses parallel columns, the left in boldface representing Cahill's sightless perceptions, and the right representing a sighted view of the same action. Most of the time this technique works surprisingly well. The contrast is sometimes almost humorous, as when Cahill works up mental descriptions of the people he is talking to, and the right column reveals how wrong he is. At other times, these passages handle the more ambitious business of presenting a deeper impression of things than either viewpoint alone could give. Unfortunately, there are places where both columns go on unbroken for several pages, and it becomes annoying to have to decide when to switch back and forth.

There are a few brief passages in which the style becomes self-conscious, or where the intensity seems too laboriously worked up. But Dickey's ear for Southern talk, his understanding of the sensations involved in flying, and his interest in a wide array of minor characters, make the novel rich and rewarding reading. ***Alnilam*** is a solid achievement. (pp. 1, 6)

Henry Taylor, in a review of "Alnilam," in Los Angeles Times Book Review, *June 17, 1987, pp. 1, 6.*

ROBERT TOWERS

Alnilam (hard to pronounce: the stress falls on the last syllable) is a vast, intricate work distinguished not by its forward momentum but by its symbolic suggestiveness and its bravura passages, some of which rise to visionary heights. It is, for better and worse, very much a poet's novel, Mr. Dickey's extended hymn to air, light, wind and the ecstasies of flight.

Alnilam opens with the detailed account of the sensations of a recently blinded man trying to find his way downstairs on a wintry night in an unfamiliar boardinghouse—and then outdoors to relieve himself; he is accompanied by a large dog. . . .

The man is Frank Cahill, the rough-spoken, middle-aged owner of a small amusement park in Atlanta. A sudden onslaught of adult diabetes has destroyed his vision, leaving him with the constant impression of exploding lights against the darkness. The dog, Zack, is not a trained and harnessed guide dog, but a huge, wolf-like creature who sticks close to his master, guiding and defending him when necessary. After the almost hallucinatory opening, many pages of flashback pass before we learn Cahill's mission: he is on his way, summoned by telegram, to an Army Air Corps training camp in rural North Carolina where his son, Joel, whom he has never known, has just crashed while flying over a brush fire and is presumed dead. The time is January 1943, in the middle of the Second World War.

For most of its nearly 700 pages, ***Alnilam*** shuttles back and forth between the little town of Peckover and the adjoining base, with periodic returns to rhapsodic moments—evoked with a wealth of sensory detail—in Cahill's earlier life. The present action spans less than a week. At the base Cahill meets everyone—officers, trainers and cadets—who knew, or knew of, Joel. Gradually a rather contradictory account emerges of this strange and charismatic young man, whose body has never been found and about whom a cult has formed. Joel, it turns out, was the founder of a secret society of cadets called Alnilam (Arabic for "string of pearls") after the bright star in the center of Orion's belt.

A daring and gifted pilot, Joel inculcated in his followers a mystical reverence for the special properties of air, together with a Zenlike belief in the coextension of subject and object, of self and machines—particularly planes. His doctrines are bolstered by his gnomic sayings, which he apparently wrote into the margins of an anthology of 19th-century poetry; his followers recite these, along with incantations based on the ''Prometheus Unbound'' of Shelley (that most light-struck and aerial of poets) and ''The City of Dreadful Night'' by the Victorian poet James Thompson. The members of Alnilam, who refuse to believe that Joel is dead, see themselves as the forefront of a revolutionary movement that has already been spread, in coded messages, to other air bases and that will eventually alter human consciousness. For the present, they are plotting a maneuver that will introduce panic and chaos into the graduation execises a few days hence.

Cahill has trouble (as the reader might well have) making sense of the esoteric message of Alnilam, but he feels drawn to its followers and is in turn seen by them as a kind of totem figure, whose arrival was prophesied by his lost son. Through his initiation, we are introduced not only to the mysteries of the cult but to the mystique of flight. In one remarkable set piece, into which Mr. Dickey pours a lavish measure of his verbal resources, the blind Cahill is taken up in a plane by a flight instructor, McCaig, who is in sympathy with the movement. . . .

Readers will react variously to writing of this sort. Powerful? Overblown? Such set pieces occur at intervals throughout the book. Some—such as a fight in which Zack dispatches a whole pack of local dogs—are sadistically ferocious. Others, such as Cahill's sleepover with a young woman who is given to self-punishing fantasies and torrential nosebleeds, are more quietly written and absorbing. There are numerous digressions as well as Cahill's extended flashbacks; nearly everybody has a story to tell and some are told at considerable length. From this medley a richly detailed picture of a region and an era emerges. At his best, Mr. Dickey captures the sounds, the textures, the smell and, above all, the *feel* of the town and the base with the most loving exactitude; he can make the technology of flight more interesting (and convincing) than its exaltations.

These achivements counteract, with considerable success, the tendency toward overwriting and windiness that periodically afflicts ***Alnilam***. Another of the novel's strengths is to be found in the characterization of Cahill. Proud, touchy, truculent and earthy, Cahill is a stalwart and often moving figure as he struggles to gain independence *through*—rather than in spite of—his affliction. The minor characters, too—especially the Southerners—spring vividly to life as they befriend or thwart the blind man and regale him with their tales; Mr. Dickey's ear for their dialect and eye for their mannerisms seem to me impeccable. Only Joel, the centerpiece of the cult, remains (purposefully, I assume) an enigma and a confection. He is partly a Shelleyan skyborne figure with intense blue eyes and bright curly hair, partly a dangerous monster of ego, partly a seer mouthing oracular nothings. And his character never coheres, nor are his power and influence made credible.

This ambitious, overreaching, alternately impressive and pretentious novel is, I think, handicapped by its inordinately slow pacing. On many of its pages, the symbolic contrasts between blindness and sight, between darkness and light, are typographically rendered. The page is split down the middle into two columns. The left, which represents Cahill's internal sensations and thoughts, is printed in dark type; the right, which contains the objective narration of speech and events, is printed in ordinary type. Such a device has, of course, the effect not only of dividing one's attention, but also of modifying the degree of one's involvement in what is taking place. Cahill's interior monologue is thick with imagery and often requires close scrutiny—or skipping—before one can get on with the story. Often such scrutiny is rewarded by some arresting or original play of language, but in a book that moves like lava oozing from a fissure, the further slowing down can be maddening. Melvillean in its aspirations and scope, the novel lacks a propelling action energetic enough to sustain its digressive and centrifugal aspects. The mystery of Alnilam is too vague to engage us, and the planned demonstration of its power is too weakly anticipated and too mechanically carried out to have the impact one longs for. ***Alnilam*** needs a white whale to pursue.

Robert Towers, ''Prometheus Blind,'' in The New York Times Book Review, *June 21, 1987, p. 7.*

Janice Elliott

1931-

Photograph by Tara Heinemann

English novelist, critic, short story writer, journalist, editor, and author of children's books.

A prolific author, Elliott is particularly noted for her novels examining the aftereffects of World War II on English domestic life. Her characters are usually upper middle-class liberals whose need for love and acceptance leads variously to manipulation, benevolence, or despair. Critics have compared Elliott's oblique prose style to those of Virginia Woolf and Iris Murdoch, and she is particularly noted for her characterizations, her ability to recreate period settings, and her elegant dialogue and imagery.

Elliott's first novel, *Cave with Echoes* (1962), portrays a young social outcast whose search for love and companionship leads to rejection and, eventually, to mental breakdown. In *The Godmother* (1966), Elliott's first book to achieve wide critical acclaim, family and friends react with varying degrees of antipathy to an eccentric and domineering matriarch who is nearing death. In *Angels Falling* (1969), Elliott employs elements of realism, the fairy tale, and melodrama to explore contemporary family relationships. Rebelling against grandiose parental expectations, the children in this novel create destructive mythic roles for themselves as means of attaining self-definition. Jonathan Raban maintained that ''[on the] level of documentary myth, *Angels Falling* works very well; it has the compulsiveness of a family scrapbook, stuffed with press cuttings and yellowing photos.'' In *The Kindling* (1970), one of Elliott's few novels to feature a working-class protagonist, a coal miner attempts to escape his dull provincial origins by fulfilling his literary aspirations but finds happiness by compromising his ideals with reality.

In the early 1970s, Elliott began a trilogy of novels delineating the social and economic effects of World War II on the life of upper-class English liberal Olive Armitage. According to David Haworth, the theme of the first novel, *A State of Peace* (1971), is ''the lost peace of those years and the uncertainties in trying to come to terms with the pedestrian problems of readjustment by people robbed of the heroic opportunities of war.'' In this book, Olive flees her restrictive family to work with underprivileged people and becomes romantically involved with communist Bob Wilson. *Private Life* (1972), in which the couple is married, addresses Bob's disillusionment with England's Communist Party and Olive's adjustment to domestic life. In the final book of the trilogy, *Heaven on Earth* (1975), Olive realizes that her marriage has become meaningless and that her children have rejected her values to pursue their own ideals. Olive attempts to revive her failing marriage, however, and she and Bob discover a tenuous peace in the country.

Elliott's later novels make use of fantasy, realism, and satire to explore contemporary relationships. In *The Country of Her Dreams* (1982), Mary and Nicholas Lamb, troubled by the violence of the modern world, travel to a foreign country which Mary recognizes from her dreams. Her sense of foreboding is realized when Nicholas is abducted by terrorists and she becomes involved in an extramarital affair. Ironically, when the danger passes, the Lambs return to their everyday lives, seemingly enriched for having witnessed and accepted humanity's violence. In *Magic* (1983), the most overtly mystical of Elliott's novels, an old man attempts to save an ancient magical stone from destruction by England's Ministry of Defence. Reviewing this novel, Miranda Seymour commended Elliott's talent ''for making the improbable likely, for tinting the mundane with the greys of mystery, and for briefly drawing the reader into a charmed world where anything but the predictable may happen.'' Elliott's recent novel, *Dr. Gruber's Daughter* (1986), centers on a woman confined to a wheelchair who dominates a houseful of stateless immigrants following World War II. Among these characters is a reclusive, elderly German, referred to as Dr. Gruber, who is terrorized by his daughter. Several critics contended that the question of the man's historical identity imbues the novel with intrigue and suspense, and Sylvia Clayton deemed *Dr. Gruber's Daughter* essentially ''a fable, a legend about the nature of evil.''

Prior to writing novels, Elliott served as a journalist and critic for numerous publications. Her short stories, book reviews, and essays have appeared in such magazines as *Harper's Bazaar, Twentieth Century,* the *New York Times,* and *New Statesman.* Elliott has also written two books for children, *The Birthday Unicorn* (1970) and *Alexander in the Land of Mog* (1973).

(See also *Contemporary Authors,* Vols. 13-16, rev. ed.; *Contemporary Authors New Revision Series,* Vol. 8; and *Dictionary of Literary Biography,* Vol. 14.)

RICHARD PENN

[***Cave with Echoes*** is a first novel] of great promise. Jonah, its hero, is a misfit and from the hospital bed where he ends up he recounts his strange and lonely life; at school, at Oxford and in London. The reader is drawn irresistably into a fantasy world, sinister and eccentric, which is skilfully managed and imaginatively described.

Richard Penn, in a review of "Cave with Echoes," in Time & Tide, *Vol. 43, No. 35, September 13-20, 1962, p. 25.*

THE TIMES LITERARY SUPPLEMENT

Janice Elliott's first novel [***Cave with Echoes***] tells the story of Jonah, a misfit who feels himself miserably distinguished from the rest of the world. Hunting always for affection yet unable to assume a proper place in society, he passes from an asthmatic childhood through an unusual education and unsuccessful marriage to attempted suicide. . . . But unfortunately he is too fluid and passive a personality to emerge into prominence as the central figure of the book. He remains a sensitive pad absorbing pain and suffering, and dangerous to touch, while his story, told in the first person with a carefully balanced and coherent style, weakens the impression of a man bordering upon insanity.

A review of "Cave with Echoes," in The Times Literary Supplement, *No. 3160, September 21, 1962, p. 746.*

BRIGID BROPHY

[*The essay from which this excerpt was taken originally appeared in* The Sunday Times *in April, 1964.*]

Janice Elliott's new novel [***The Somnambulists***] is beautifully strange. When the red-headed Purdy children are orphaned, Jessie, the eldest, is already forceful enough to hold at a distance the adults whose 'moon faces' loom above, offering succour. She accepts a minimum of material care for herself and Andy, her fat brother: but emotionally she creates round the two of them a world the adults cannot enter. When she and Andy become adults themselves, it proves a world they cannot get out of.

Even their brother, the youngest Purdy, does not impinge on his siblings. He lives in his own fastness: by one of the strokes of bizarre poetry with which Miss Elliott's book effloresces, he is a deaf baby. He wins the notice of Jessie and Andy only once in childhood, when he is likely to die, and once in adulthood, when he does. . . .

Jessie and Andy begin to arrange their childish impressions according to the logic of the real world. At twelve, Andy wonders if orphanhood is, 'against all his inclinations, his specialty'. He explores Jessie's as well as his own character through their separate relationships with the violet-scented 'Mummy Schultz'—who is in fact not a mummy and to whom the orphans are therefore emotional prey. But the brother and sister, though they learn to make sense of, never make contact with, reality. (p. 171)

[***The Somnambulists***] is marvelously wrapped in the somnambulistic sensation of the title. In their submerged world, Jessie and Andy move 'like dancers beneath the sea'—but a tropical sea, in which everything is visible with sharpest clarity. Miss Elliott's fabric is sprigged with knots of condensed observation (the river at night *smells* cold) and shimmers with lyrical metaphors: girls lying in the sunny park are so impressionistically equated with flowers that a tulip can button her cardigan. Miss Elliott remarks that 'in a sense, nothing happened' to her hero and heroine. Yet the narrative is deeply exciting—through the sheer, unforced *bizarrerie* of her vision, which has the utter, almost alarming truthfulness only pure imagination can achieve. (p. 172)

Brigid Brophy, "Some Writers and Books: Janice Elliott," in her Don't Never Forget: Collected Views and Reviews, *Holt, Rinehart and Winston, 1967, pp. 171-72.*

ELIZABETH JENNINGS

The Somnambulists—a little pretentious, more than a little sophisticated—declares, rather unconvincingly, that the feelings of the story's chief characters, the orphans Andrew and Jessica (drawn together by a semi-incestuous relationship), reflect a common human condition—the longing and yet the failure to live in the world, the final acceptance of any comfort which can be found.

This could have been a grim and moving story; as it is, it remains bizarre and often merely clever. One never feels that Miss Elliott is really very deeply involved with her characters or, for that matter, with 'a common human condition'. Jessica and Andrew, with their cruelty to their young deaf brother and their own casual relationships with other men and women, seldom convince the reader that they are really capable either of understanding the often bleak melancholy of the human condition or, indeed, any tragedy beyond their own. Their final return to each other seems glib and altogether unreal. Perhaps what is the real fault of this novel is that Miss Elliott was not sure what she really wanted to do. Briefly, she never seems to have decided whether to elevate the book's theme to a tragic level, or simply to make the most of its curious, but also undoubtedly comic, aspects. These are faults in design and treatment. That Janice Elliott can write, and write often with skill and perspicacity, there is no doubt at all.

Elizabeth Jennings, in a review of "The Somnambulists," in The Listener, *Vol. LXXI, No. 1830, April 23, 1964, p. 693.*

THE TIMES LITERARY SUPPLEMENT

If ***The Buttercup Chain*** were a profounder book, it might be highly disconcerting to all kinds of people, but as it is it slips down like junket and no one is much the wiser—or sadder, or more disconcerted. It is about the kind of life made possible only if two things till recently thought indispensable are dispensed with: privacy and guilt. Making love to her husband's best friend, more or less in the children's presence, Manny forgets to keep a close enough eye on the youngest, who crawls into the sea and is drowned. When telephoned with the news, husband Fred fails to answer because he, too, is in bed with someone else (Manny's best friend this time), but the child conceived by Manny in these circumstances is rapturously received by everyone concerned (including Fred, in spite of Manny's having spent her pregnancy with yet another lover, an elderly gun-runner), and named after Fred's sister, who has killed herself for love of Manny's lover who was the child's father. And so it goes on.

Losses and betrayals that in another age or atmosphere would warrant fury, hair-tearing or at least outrage and self condemnation are taken so much for granted that they scarcely cast a shadow over the sunny relationships of those involved. No one has shame or secrets, no one feels guilt or regret, and, in the mini-morality of this pigmy paradise where adults are not childlike but dwarfish, so long as one is young and beautiful one's actions are beautiful to match. . . .

Miss Elliott writes very readably, in breathless little sentences you can almost read a lisp into. She shifts scenes as fast as her characters swap beds and takes us briskly round the Mediterranean and Scandinavia as well as Soho; in a whimsical car called Madame Bovary we go for picnics galore, eat photogenic sounding meals, watch photogenic sounding clothes and scenes and expressions. The talk is monosyllabic, which tires no one. In spite of some thick symbolism towards the end, it is all as bland and meaningless as the adman's posed landscapes with figures.

"Bed and Bored," in The Times Literary Supplement, *No. 3404, May 25, 1967, p. 471.*

NORA SAYRE

[As] the anthropologist Geoffrey Gorer has explained, most modern Anglo-Saxons treat death with the prudery which the Victorians reserved for sex—an embarrassing and disgusting phenomenon that few want to acknowledge. But Janice Elliott's ***The Godmother*** is a magnificent acknowledgment: here, an old woman's gradual dying appears almost as an achievement. True, her eccentric detachment from the present vexes her relatives and friends; with alternating admiration and resentment, they recall all of the roles which she has played: godmother, aunt, sister, daughter, "virgin spinster," never (but nearly) a wife or mother.

As the emotional scenery shifts, she appears as a comforter, a destroyer, a "love goddess," an invalid, a clairvoyant, a potential murderee, a benign magician, a malignant witch, and finally—in senility—as a child to be protected. Miss Elliott's characters are muted, respectable people who long for violence. They want to shout at and strike one another. . . . (p. 219)

Miss Elliott's primary concern is the passive and almost arbitrary interaction of people who are far from fond of one another. They're seduced by the belief that others are responsible for their horrors or delights, or that "things just happen," or even that an absent-minded old woman can predestine and guide their experiences. None of them wants to be an engine of control; hence their irritable insistence on making "the godmother" a mythic figure from whom miracles are expected. Thus, she lives and dies personifying other characters' imaginations—as, indeed, some solitaries do. Since she once seemed "immemorial," she is not forgiven for being mortal.

There are several plots sufficient for separate novels here: a drifter murders one old woman because another took too long to die; a chill but resilient divorcée experiments with nonlove; a woman, crimped with jealousy of her sister's lover, tells his wife that she's a cuckold—the wife promptly kills herself, and the complacent informer inherits the suicide's husband and child. But none of these quietly savage themes is really developed. Miss Elliott concentrates on reverberations rather than events, self-deceptions instead of confrontations. All of her characters wear the stripe of madness: the kinds of psychosis that need not prevent prosaic functioning, or even an orderly life. (For these, violence is tempting because it suggests the virtue of self-assertion, of which they're usually incapable.) The novel gives meticulous testimony that almost everyone feels—or is—insane at certain moments. The book's only flaw is an overdependence on E. M. Forster's Marabar caves: although the spelling has been altered from "boum" to "Boom," those infinity-echoes really do belong to him, and are disturbing in a novel that's otherwise unique. Washed throughout by recurring undersea imagery, Miss Elliott's prose also distills a series of frighteningly lucid observations: "there was something almost mad about their dedicated sanity as if balance taken too far breeds its own imbalance." As a study in delusions, ***The Godmother*** makes the word "sensitive" a compliment—which it hasn't been for decades. (pp. 219-20)

Nora Sayre, "Certain Aspects of Death," in The Nation, *New York, Vol. 205, No. 7, September 11, 1967, pp. 219-20.*

MARY SULLIVAN

Janice Elliott's fifth novel [***The Singing Head***] is a disappointing surprise. She seems to have been tempted away from the shrewd moderation of her earlier work, into a land of dispiriting daftness. Only people with shiny names (Bella, Ariane) inhabit the small college where Marcus Wilson is professor of English. Only two actual students manage to impinge on the busy lives of their teachers, whose intrigue and scandalmongering find a victim in their friend Marcus. He meanwhile is brooding on his wife's death, for which he may have been responsible. The plot is disastrously lashed to the myth of Orpheus, and beats you over the head with quotations from Ovid and Graves at the opening of every chapter, in case you didn't get it the first time. These trappings wouldn't matter if they were decorating something of substance, but they're offered *as* the substance, stating relationships instead of showing them at work. Yet every now and then, in a sentence of reflection, there is a glimpse of the hard sense of the previous novels.

Mary Sullivan, "Visible Men," in The Listener, *Vol. 79, No. 2031, February 29, 1968, p. 279.*

THE TIMES LITERARY SUPPLEMENT

A sigh of disenchantment, even in the most earnest student of fiction, would be understandable at the dust-cover disclosures on Miss Elliott's new novel [***The Singing Head***]. The myth of Orpheus, retold in the setting of a college campus on the Sussex Downs? Surely lady novelists ought to be wary, not only of how often this myth has been squeezed for sentiment but also of the symbolism which somehow didn't hold up in that Murdochian exploration of the severed head? Miss Elliott makes no bones about her intention to recreate poor widowed Orpheus, the eternal figure of the persecuted artist. Indeed, she breaks her narrative constantly with short quotes from Ovid and Robert Graves—clues to the forgetful or unacademic of how her "spiritual detective thriller" will be unravelled in subsequent chapters. But this very boldness, in sticking for her main characters to such as can be obviously identified with the Gods and Goddesses, soon pays off. One does, in fact, become intrigued how she will adapt the savage Maenad execution, the rivalry of Aphrodite and Athene, the legend of the singing Dionysiac head outdoing Apollo's oracles in popularity, to make them significant or convincing in rural Sussex. And, as in all her novels, Miss Elliott is never so absorbed by the intricacies of what her characters are feeling or thinking—usually with a query at every stage—that she ignores the necessity for a fast, taut plot.

Marcus Wilson, who often sees himself wryly as the caricature of the middle-aged academic, has begun to recover from the sudden death of his crazy and beautiful wife Ruth. Crowfield, the "experimental educational foundation" soon to be granted university status, has already proved an illusory haven of solitude for him—the Principal, a satyr-like snow-man called Donner, keen on computers and gracious living, is a dangerously smooth enemy. Marcus cannot understand why the other members of the Senior Common Room—notably the seductive, irrepressible Bella, married to a lame and longsuffering metal craftsman—insist on waging an embarrassing campaign on his behalf. . . . He values most the taciturn friendship of a rustic student, Brogan, but is not at once aware of the danger when he stumbles on Brogan's girl in the Principal's arms. Rumours of Marcus's homosexual corruption of the young are carefully circulated; too absorbed in the guilty questions that sing in his head about Ruth, his true desires, his fitness for the job, and the origin of all this furore to act decisively, he discovers with almost grateful self-pity that it is not only the "baby Bacchantes in mini-skirts" who are out to destroy him, but that Bella, her old enemy Donner's wife, even the fairest-minded of their sex, resent his silent acceptance of implied guilt.

Crowfield becomes a national scandal, and the final dismemberment of Orpheus is enacted against microphones and the hounds of the press. How Marcus manages to turn his martyrdom to our version of sanctity provides Miss Elliott with an ingenious ironic conclusion.

There are, as always in Miss Elliott's novels, some excellent moments of baroque fantasy. . . . One could fault the almost obsessional self-absorption of Marcus—here is an Orpheus not altogether credible as the founder of poetry, endlessly perplexed about his abnormalities rather than concerned with creation. And occasionally some of the mythical characters, particularly Bella and Donner, overact their properties and become caricatures. One mistake—a pity in any detective story—is the inconsistency about those anonymous notes, cut from newsprint, yet identified by typewriter. But Miss Elliott has become too good a novelist to carp at—her control of events and her use of dialogue and image are outstanding in her generation, and this book will certainly whet appetites for her next.

"Orpheus on Campus," in The Times Literary Supplement, *No. 3444, February 29, 1968, p. 197.*

THE TIMES LITERARY SUPPLEMENT

One member of the Garland family, whose fortunes are chronicled in this weighty novel [***Angels Falling***], is Frances the "lady novelist", who wonders about the possibility of writing truthfully about one's own time. "When you look back", she says, "you mythologize. You can't help it. Even historians, they're artists in a way. They give shape to something that probably had no form at all." To see events in symbolic patterns, or to describe them in a way which makes them seem more like myth or fairy-tale, has in the past been characteristic of Miss Elliott's own novels, but this time she has, it seems, consciously ventured into a genre which places fictional characters, as solidly and "historically" as detail can, against a background of outside, "real" events. Has she reconciled the artist's desire to give form to a family saga covering the past half-century with "writing truthfully"?

Lily Garland is dying in her gracious Oxford house, and her four children are summoned to attend her deathbed. At once it is made clear that we are to consider the Garland family as pretty remarkable. . . . It is the family as a myth, self-imposed by each member, where each is acting and reacting against some melodramatic role for the benefit of the others, that concerns Miss Elliott—and flummoxes the various outsiders who marry or become involved with any Garland. Not that the flashback to Lily's youth as an upper-class beauty of independent mind who goes off slumming and campaigning for votes suggests any particularly theatrical behaviour; she has a nasty shock in Brighton when Maud, her much admired Amazonian mentor, kisses Connie behind the potted palms, and she turns gratefully to Andrew, Connie's brother, who has made himself notorious by walking from the trenches with the severed head of his friend, and is now by way of becoming the prototype pacifist poet-hero. Their romantic marriage stales fast. Andrew's high ideals, from which his children and the public had hoped so much, are put away "fine and useless", his life comforted by a series of drab, comforting little affairs with younger and younger girls. . . .

[From] their children's point of view, both Lily and Andrew are failures as parents—even dangerous enemies. Frances, the eldest, runs away from school and stumbles on her father in bed with some tart; Melvyn, the beautiful, stony boy, his mother's favourite, steels himself against all hurts by becoming, at Oxford, as sinful a Catholic as he can—he is frequently described as Lucifer, goes in for passionately cruel remarks, and feels compelled by the Furies to search for pure evil. . . . Barbara settles for domestic stagnation, the only one who can bear to look after their increasingly silent and absent father. Adrian—again, described frequently in picturesque religious language—is seen by them all as a good angel, or an odiously virtuous villain, or a "genetic accident", able alone of all the Garlands to pursue a real and uncorrupted ideal of helping others.

The scene shifts cleverly both in time and place—Bloomsbury, Battersea, boarding-school on the Downs, Oxford, Rome, East Africa . . . and it is well peopled, often with Powell-style coincidental encounters, by minor characters such as the sinister Father Ferdy van Groot, Lady Maud and her Bronsky, or the newspaper proprietor of turncoat political iniquity, Landenberry. Much of the zooming and fading, with elegantly blurred descriptions of the Blitz, snow over Oxford at Christmas gaiety in the Home Guard canteen or literary interviews at the Television Centre, succeeds in creating an authentic period mood, and the various questing conversations about each other between the Garlands and their lovers or confessors appear as unbelievable glimpses into a few civilized unhappy private lives.

And yet, when—not for the first time—someone remarks that the Garlands are "rather fascinating", it is tempting to ask just what the reader is expected to be fascinated by. Except for Frances, who observes (for her novels) and copes forcefully with her solitary life, none of the Garlands emerges as more "real" than Adrian's refugee wife suggests—"You all behave like characters in a play . . . it's no way to live.'' Perhaps the agonizing is an intentional protest against Miss Elliott's own attempt to present the past ''truthfully''; yet, if this is what she has tried to do, it seems wilfully melodramatic to make quite such liberal use of the symbol of gilded angels—sought for, unappreciated, and ultimately destroyed.

''Family Feeling,'' in The Times Literary Supplement, *No. 3523, September 4, 1969, p. 969.*

JONATHAN RABAN

The decline of the Bloomsbury family, from the heights of imaginative prosperity in a distant England of fervent causes, Edwardian summers, blossoming little magazines and elegant *thé dansants,* down to the pop underworld of the Sixties, full of drunken TV demagogues, *démodé* cranks and sour, ironic lady novelists, is a theme which seems to have become an obsession in contemporary fiction. First there was Angus Wilson's *No Laughing Matter,* then, earlier this year, Doris Lessing's *The Four-Gated City,* and now Janice Elliott's ***Angels Falling.*** The characters and structure of all three novels are extraordinarily similar; a generation of contemporary Londoners working on the fringes of the arts, the mass media and the social services, imprisoned by the grandiose family dreams of their parents. Miss Elliott's Garland family were born to adorn the cultural life of England; they end up by poking tired, self-mocking fun at that edifice of failed aspirations and decayed talents. The declining fortunes of the family act as a mirror for the fate of England at large, sliding from the grand idealism of the League of Nations and the cause of Universal Suffrage towards the playpen culture of the King's Road—a nation of victorious democrats and men of vision transformed in one easy stage (1939-1956) into a nation of camp interior decorators.

Miss Elliott's novel, like those of Wilson and Lessing, has the large and absorbing structure of a myth; it attempts to create an imaginative whole out of the paradoxes and inadequacies of recent history. It's largely built with heightened and instantly recognisable set-pieces from the patchwork panorama of English social life from the death of Queen Victoria to the present. . . .

On this level of documentary myth, ***Angels Falling*** works very well; it has the compulsiveness of a family scrapbook, stuffed with press cuttings and yellowing photos. I'm not so sure about the symbolic engine which is wheeled in at intervals from the wings: there is war in the heavens (with Satan and Michael played by Andrew and Lily Garland) and the entire family are called upon to perform the roles of good and bad angels. Furies attend. At the death of Lily the family waits for Adrian, the saintly son, who is flying in from Africa for the funeral; but unlike Christ in his Miltonic flying machine, Adrian dies in a plane crash from which there are no survivors. A pity, because the historical substance of the novel is firm enough to stand on its own, without being hauled along on this symbolical Emett railway.

Jonathan Raban, ''Family Scrapbook,'' in New Statesman, *Vol. 78, No. 2008, September 5, 1969, p. 315.*

THE TIMES LITERARY SUPPLEMENT

Miss Elliott is becoming—one might almost say risks becoming—as prolific a novelist as Miss Iris Murdoch; ***The Kindling*** is her seventh to be published within about as many years. The comparison is not made simply because both are highly intelligent women writers who wear their learning lightly; although no professional philosopher, Miss Elliott is very good at introducing general concepts and giving the discussion of meaning a convincingly natural place in the conversations her frequently academic characters enjoy. More than this, the imaginative experience from which the material for her novels comes is not only as various and apparently inexhaustible as Miss Murdoch's, but it is, in the same way, backed by a professional attention to factual detail which, as Mary McCarthy has wisely said, is too often lacking in modern novels; you feel not merely that some discriminating homework on background has been done, but that the author has enthusiastically absorbed it into the world she is creating, so that all manner of different settings and people can appear genuinely convincing—and the dull Midland town in which ***The Kindling*** takes place is as much a part of Miss Elliott's imaginative experience as Edwardian London. . . .

But whereas Miss Murdoch's preoccupation with changing relationships so often—and deliberately—appears like a formal dance, with partners swapping and various permutations of kith, kin, and sex engineered in a mysterious game, Miss Elliott prefers to let chance appear the *deus ex machina,* often haphazardly causing friends and couples to exchange love and loyalties. She is particularly fond of following the fortunes of a small group of young contemporaries, any of whom might, but for some ironic chance, have paired off with any other. The latest group is a tiny pocket of talented and intelligent youngsters, friends partly because they despise the dreary respectability and dead-end provincialism of their home town, but chiefly because, as sixth-formers, they have come under the influence of a local teacher, Herbert Wolf, whose slim volume, now out of print, on Lawrence whom he had briefly known, has established him as a minor literary figure of somewhat shocking liberal views. It has also, as his acolytes know in their jollier moments away from him, been the ruin of Herbert Wolf as a man likely to achieve either happiness or success; his bohemian household—not least the beautiful and bright daughter, Laura—and his wonderful gift for encouraging pupils and stimulating ideas, are really the façade for a sad failure of a life.

But the central character is not Herbert Wolf, although the repercussions of his ideas and his suicide, after a dubiously revealing incident with a small boy, effectively destroy his image and change the lives of his young friends. The central character is Jack Wolstenholme, miner's son and spare-time poet, the only one of his friends whose escape from stifling Burleigh seems, at first, both vital and most hopeful, yet hardest to come by. To persuade Jack to escape is a good thing, because his ambivalent feelings about poverty, lack of education, social success and, above all, Laura Wolf, keep him in restless intellectual hibernation at his bicycle factory and in the loft with his late father's carrier pigeons. . . . Events decide. Jack, resigned to marrying a local girl Pat whom he has got pregnant, discovers slowly and painfully that their son, who almost dies and helps reduce Pat to a breakdown, matters enough to re-orientate his ambitions. His own innocence has gone—perhaps with Herbert's image—and the urge for change has been equally shaken by the disastrous involvement of his friend Ted with a revolutionary group of arsonists finally charged with murder. But the child's innocence, and the possibility of retrieving a love more lasting than Laura's inside his marriage, are something to stabilize and give him hope.

This could have been a sentimental little tale of local boy growing up, of trite conclusions concerning the loss of illusions and the awareness of moral values. Miss Elliott does sometimes overdramatize the significance of a crucial moment, overplay the admiration we are all intended to feel for Jack's sterling character, and may seem to some readers somewhat over-indulgent in those meaningful, vague, elliptical discussions of love, life and purpose of which she is very fond. But whereas in her early success, ***The Buttercup Chain,*** the idealistic soul-mates were often ineffectual and tiresomely self-centred, pretentious hedonists or high-minded bores, these people in Burleigh are seen with a mature, even very occasionally comic, eye to the Midland clay on their feet: the empty hopes of many young people during the 1950s, and their gradual adjustment to sober facts no less depressing but better faced than escaped from, are extremely well caught—Jack and his friends, with their "messy yearnings", already offer a sad and dated comment on the years when freedom was still at the end of the rainbow and conventions still powerful enough to blight its pursuit.

"Young Contemporaries," in The Times Literary Supplement, *No. 3563, June 11, 1970, p. 631.*

MARY BORG

Those of us who grew up in the provinces in the Fifties know very well that feeling of stifling in a climate still deeply Victorian, but encroached upon by our adolescent apprehension of Lawrentian freedoms. For some, London and Oxford glittered as the ultimate release. Janice Elliott accurately places ***The Kindling,*** her subtle novel of ambition and yearning, action and compromise, in this particular milieu, displaying a sure intuition for fitting them together.

Jack Wolstenholme is a working-class poet, working in a cycle factory, deeply influenced by Herbert Wolf, his ex-English master. . . . Jack fences with ideas of total freedom and irresponsibility, but is enmeshed in the lives of his wife, Pat, his mistress, Laura—Herbert's seemingly strange and elusive, but ultimately disappointing daughter—and his friend, sensible Ted, who commits himself totally and disastrously in his relationship with a tough, unpleasant fire-raising revolutionary girl. Jack ends up giving himself to compromise, returning to his wife, beginning to write again and perjuring himself for Ted in court in the name of friendship.

Miss Elliott writes with intense intelligence, glancingly drawing together fine strands of intention and significance. She builds up meaning from snatches of dialogue, exact portrayals of scenes and moods, elliptical fragments. Jack's growth is at once delicately and remotely recounted, but one is deeply impressed with the reverberations of the story. The effect is of gradual osmosis. (p. 845)

Mary Borg, "Escapes," in New Statesman, *Vol. 79, No. 2048, June 12, 1970, pp. 845-46.*

DAVID HAWORTH

To write of very recent history, inviting all the risks of readers' comparisons with their own memories, is a more formidable job than it might seem. Janice Elliott is not in the least daunted in [***A State of Peace***]. She evokes the immediate post-war period with accuracy and panache. Her theme is the lost peace of those years and the uncertainties in trying to come to terms with the pedestrian problems of readjustment by people robbed of the heroic opportunities of war.

Mrs Armitage, getting on in years, cannot adapt to the new circumstances. She was happier dealing on the black market and being an archetypal mother-protector than coping with what she sees as the dangerous aspirations of her children, who seek out their own solutions. Her only protection is to hide behind a shabby façade of gentility and prejudice, which events, both personal and national, threaten to sweep away.

The core of this strongly felt re-creation of the political and social dilemmas during those years is the relationship between the mother and her daughter, Olive, who breaks out of the straitjacket of her upbringing and joins the communists with touchingly naïve intentions. The ferocity of the encounters between these two is dramatic and real. Indeed, it's easy to give yourself up to the sweep of this novel's ambitions. They are wholly sympathetic—and successful.

David Haworth, "Gland Manner," in New Statesman, *Vol. 82, No. 2104, July 16, 1971, p. 89.*

THE TIMES LITERARY SUPPLEMENT

A reader new to Janice Elliott might easily assume from [***A State of Peace***] . . . that she was reliving adult experience of those grey and confused years after the war, when English domestic and political life underwent such painful reappraisal. But Miss Elliott, who was still a child in 1945, is now firmly establishing herself as a novelist with notable talent for recreating times past; [***The Kindling***] was set in the north during the early 1930s, [***Angels Falling***] during the Suffragette struggles, and all three capture a remarkably authentic, solid and evocative background. Yet it would not be wholly complimentary to describe ***A State of Peace*** as belonging to the somewhat ponderous Snow tradition; here, as in her two other fictional slices of history, Miss Elliott is really more concerned with private, individual adjustment to social change than with documenting newsreel events. What is more, she has a merciful, although not always unembarrassing, penchant for the flight of fancy, the poetic and literary image intended to crystallize a timeless moment; her narrative, like her style, is consciously elliptical.

Thus the scene opens not with the crowds celebrating outside Buckingham Palace, but behind quiet streets of Kensington, where gracious Mrs Armitage toasts peace with a glass of water, succeeding, at least in her own view, in creating for "the young people" round her candlelit dinner table something of a feast. . . . But already the family scene forebodes anything but peace. Olive, tense in her grubby ATS uniform, is shaking with outrage over Hiroshima, determined her mother's world must be discarded. Christopher, charming and lazy, prefers to go and build boats with his army pal—anything to avoid "Madam" and her ambitious schemes for her adored only son; Catherine, her stepsister, a silent and lumpy 16, prays for their happiness—her own, at home with a mother who's ashamed of her, shows no prospect of ever materializing.

Although the generation conflict is one strand in the narrative, and Mrs Armitage just survives the realization that she no longer belongs, is nothing but an irrelevant burden on her children's lives, Miss Elliott rightly focuses attention on Olive—the idealism and independence she proclaims so aggressively will clearly involve a readjustment just as crucial as her mother's, and she alone, by the end, has faced up to a chaos outside her own life. Olive drifts into marriage with Dennis, the immature leader of a left-wing cell. The failure of this marriage only hits her when, pregnant and torn by "victims crying to her from so many rooms" in her fragmented life, she falls in love with a tough, wise, protective working-class widower, lifelong Party loyalist yet also dismayed by what is happening to the society he hoped to change. . . .

Survival becomes all that any of the characters cling to. Politics and good works emerge as sham creeds—even love, Olive learns to suspect, may be less unselfish than masochistic.

Yet this is not a depressing novel, perhaps because, in the midst of a good many portentous pages of soul-searching and discussion, Miss Elliott sometimes lets us glimpse the comic detail. It is her ironic little observations, rather than the worthy themes and doubts she is anxious to raise, that make Miss Elliott's novel memorable, even if somewhat too down-to-earth to arouse great enthusiasm.

"Postwar Pangs," in The Times Literary Supplement, *No. 3621, July 23, 1971, p. 849.*

J. G. FARRELL

Janice Elliott's ***Private Life,*** the sequel to ***A State of Peace,*** covers that period after the war to whose lack of style and charm the Festival Hall stands as a monument: indeed, one of her characters is reported to be working on the Festival site for a while. The novel is built on a foundation of throwaway touches like this, not all of them so remote. They serve to re-establish the reader very much in his own recollections of that time, though few people can have suffered such a claustrophobia as settles on Olive and her friends, most of whom are preoccupied with social and political matters. I wonder whether the author deliberately chose a form which resembles *Mrs Dale's Diary* to convey the spirit of the Fifties. People drop in for coffee, get pregnant, have meetings, dig in the garden, don't feel well, have more coffee, more meetings, get pregnant again, have drinks, feed children, see psychiatrists, have coffee, see other people's children, discuss their relationships. Closest to Olive, at the centre of this whirlpool of domestic information, is Bob, her second husband, losing his faith in both Communism and politics—which he duly does, but not quickly enough for me. The book is written with honesty, intelligence and sympathy, but makes dispiriting reading.

J. G. Farrell, "Aristocrat," in The Listener, *Vol. 88, No. 2275, November 2, 1972, p. 611.*

THE TIMES LITERARY SUPPLEMENT

In times of war, so medical statistics show, there are remarkably few cases of mental breakdown—as the psychiatrist who briefly appears in ***Private Life*** puts it, "I nearly went out of business". But what of the aftermath? In ***A State of Peace,*** to which this is a sequel, Janice Elliott gave us a chunk of immediately postwar experience: Mrs Armitage, resolutely Kensington, dismayed by the new social (and socialist) order, seeing the "values" she cherished in the 1930s rejected by her children, crumpled into an unloved old age, taking in lodgers. One daughter, . . . Olive, who resisted her conditioning and chose poverty with a working-class group of "amateur do-gooders" and "pie-in-the-sky socialism", seemed by the end of the book to have tackled the problems of peace.

Yet by 1951, when this volume opens, it is in these disparaging phrases that Olive herself thinks of those brave aftermath years. The group's crusading spirit has foundered on political dogma, her first marriage of true idealistic minds come to grief, and finally been replaced by a vision of private domesticity, with baby and apple tree and shabby house, shared with safe, loving, rocklike Bob. The happiness has come true. But neither his past nor her social conscience is so simply appeased. . . . Korea is a haunting if distant mushroom cloud, and the homecoming of Bob's angular son Alan, full of rage at their reluctance to enthuse over unilateral disarmament, precipitates a return to commitment. For Bob, formerly an active member of the CP, and at fifty suffering a private crisis of disillusionment, idealism has been inseparable from politics and the new committee is clearly doomed to failure; yet, as a bridgehead to repair the relationship with Alan, it may offer freedom from guilt.

Olive drifts into her old role of coping, though with growing despair and panic; not merely with a new baby, but with . . . her mother's emotional blackmail, with her stepson and his girl . . . and, overriding all else, with Bob's tortured withdrawal beyond her help or comprehension. His break with the Party, dominating the book, crystallizes a much wider reorientation of the early 1950s; to be told "Comrade, you no longer exist" is to divorce his belief in freedom from all his life has meant, yet still to be haunted—in reality as well as nightmare—by spies from the past. . . .

In focusing what is clearly intended as a symbolic gesture of painful awakening, perhaps of acceptance that survival is an inescapable compromise, Miss Elliott inevitably gives both Olive and Bob a weighty burden of self-consciousness that is sometimes overdone. Their realization of crisis, of cosmic doubt and disorientation, is repeatedly analysed, the sense of impending doom a spectre, in Olive's weary and somewhat elderly ponderings, at every feast. Yet to have conjured up this tangibly authentic image of what is now history, without obtrusive recourse to journalistic documentation, is a remarkable achievement. It may be that the solipsistic form we accept as axiomatic in fiction can do no more than gloss the past; what is gained by private detail sometimes . . . outweighs the loss in objective or symbolic vision. Miss Elliott's study of Olive and her time is perhaps comparable with the Olivia Manning trilogy, in which background texture rather than protagonists satisfies the imagination; and there is certainly room for Miss Elliott to pursue her study into a third volume.

"Withdrawal Symptoms," in The Times Literary Supplement, *No. 3687, November 3, 1972, p. 1305.*

SARA MAITLAND

Janice Elliott's new book [***Heaven on Earth***], completing the trilogy that also contains ***A State of Peace*** and ***Private Life,*** is a dense, intense novel about growing older gradually and noticing it suddenly. Olive Wilson, the protagonist, seeing a friend from her past on the Underground, is jolted from a comfortable complacency into an agonising appraisal of her present and potential future. She can no longer bear the facts that her marriage has been effectively dead for 15 years, her children are strangers, her job is fatuous and her friends have fallen gently short of the ideals and aspirations of their youth. And it is too late to do much about it. In the end, she reaffirms the necessity of her marriage—less than a passion, but more than a habit—loses her children with a slightly chilling detachment, and retreats from London into rural Sussex: not a victory, but a meaningful and moving endurance. The theme is not startlingly original, but Janice Elliott brings to it a specificity, an accuracy of eye and ear, which gives her characterisation remarkable power. Moreover, by pinning her creations to a very particular background—London, 1968, middle-class, middle-aged left-wingers (Hungary, not Czechoslovakia, their disillusionment), the external details precise and definite—she offers us an objective reality against which to judge her perceptions, and which gives them conviction. In fact, the conflicts of political stances not only give intellectual substance to the characters, they also entitle the book to lay claim to a significance beyond the private domestic situation in which the plot appears to function.

With such richness here, it is a pity that Janice Elliott should, at times, be so heavy-handed. She appears to have no faith at all in her readers' intelligence. From the plot (and the title) we are able to grasp that she does not believe in Eden, in Heaven on Earth; but she has to bang this home. The words 'heaven', 'Eden', 'paradise', 'fiery swords', 'no heaven on earth' are seldom off her characters' lips and they are repeated in every image. . . . This becomes not a leitmotif, but the rolling drums and crashing cymbals of pantomime entrances, annoying and insulting. However, although Janice Elliott is not a subtle writer, she is considerably more than a bright-eyed observer-recorder. She recognises the patterns of what she sees, and she illuminates areas of emotional and intellectual truth.

Sara Maitland, "Out of Eden," in The Listener, *Vol. 93, No. 2396, March 6, 1975, p. 318.*

GAY CLIFFORD

Heaven on Earth, like many recently published novels, derives its plot from the activities of the far Left. This does not mean, however, that it is a political novel. Janice Elliott's interest is in showing the effect of various (real) international events and (imaginary) sectarian incidents on the domestic life of her heroine, Olive Wilson, a nice, middle-aged, middle-class woman whose family is connected with both the old Left and the new.

In the first scene of the novel Olive sees a woman suffering from hunger and exhaustion nearly trampled to death during the evening rush-hour on the Tube: she is an acquaintance from the old days on the left, the wife of the anarchist Tim Connor. A year later, near the end of the book, Olive's son, attempting to blow up the college where her husband works, is almost killed when a bomb provided by Connor explodes prematurely. Two accidents, both involving individuals caught up in forces they cannot control, both associated with "the ghost of Tim Connor ranging like a mad cat round the town". . . . Although the novel is not wholly free of portentousness—events loom large for Olive if not in themselves—these incidents are mercifully not presented as symbolic comments on modern society or the fragility and self-destructiveness of the Left: their significance is largely seen in a family perspective.

Jan Palach's suicide, the American moonshots, rebellion and counter-coup in Africa, a new generation demonstrating in Grosvenor Square: these feature simply as an allusive backdrop to Olive's separation from her husband, a former member of the Communist Party, and their children's various attempts at creating heavens on earth. . . . Olive reacts, but though supposedly intelligent, rarely analyses. Her passivity is reflected in the acquiescent ending: back with her husband, going to live in their cottage, opting into the cocoon of the personal. If one compares ***Heaven on Earth*** with, say, Doris Lessing's *Four-Gated City,* which gave such a strong sense of the Cold War period, one can only regret that the extraordinary world of the late 1960s should be muffled in such conventional wrappings.

Gay Clifford, "Life on the Left," in The Times Literary Supplement, *No. 3809, March 7, 1975, p. 241.*

VALENTINE CUNNINGHAM

Novels about growing up in the provincial proletariat can be—as ***A Loving Eye*** is—wonderfully receptive grab-alls. The novel as dustbin-lorry, in fact. Into the eagerly mashing jaws they all go: anything and everything the novelist has known, debris and gobbets, fag-ends and cabbage-stumps in loving eye-fulls, memories of bread and scrape and pikelets, of chapel picnics and the scholarship exam. . . . And so irresistibly on, in this case, through the Thirties to the Left Book Club and Spain, Oxford and war. An over-rich mix, perhaps, a contingency too messy by far, a particularity too utterly particular; but then, happily, dustbin-lorries don't suffer indigestion, and they're always filled with what Janice Elliott's hero David recognises as the 'stink of life'.

The strain of making all this telling vividness coherent does, unsurprisingly, begin to tell a bit towards the end, and the narration resorts to some old tricks for getting across rocky passages. But generally Janice Elliott manages her people, grotesques and all, with delightful skill, commanding the necessary rhetorical shifts and switchbacks with amazing ease. In short, she *knows*—and without becoming coyly knowing. Knows for instance about young politics in the Thirties, so that her account of the Jarrow Crusade being welcomed in David's Derbyshire town stands up well against the moving enthusiasms of actual records of such arrivals. The hostile outburst from a drunken prole friend against David's other, slummingly leftist, bourgeois pals aptly locates, for him and us, one of the period's big tensions. David endures 'a dream of violence'; precisely Spender's phrase for Auden's *Orators*. It's as informed, all this, as the novel's inside story of the 'holy tricoteuses' of the chapel, and of David's mum's man, the un-frocked Methodist drinker, once an inveigher against Lucifer's bottle, convinced now his God has left him. 'I wonder', David muses to his journal, 'if writing things down doesn't make them seem true—even make them happen, like magic . . .' Indeed it does; at least Janice Elliott's writing does.

Valentine Cunningham, "White Trash," in New Statesman, *Vol. 94, No. 2419, July 29, 1977, p. 156.*

PETER ACKROYD

If you're going to write family 'sagas', or turn somebody's life into a mixture of sex and anguish, then it's as well to make no bones about it, just sit down and write a best-seller. The only reason for writing conventional novels is to make money; and the popular demand for novelistic reassurance is so great that a conventional writer stands at least an even chance of doing so. But not, I'm afraid, Janice Elliott. She has got all the ingredients, in ***A Loving Eye,*** for something big and brassy and televisable; but they never quite cohere.

A novelists 'eye' and 'ear' are not enough; you've got to have style as well. There are so many warm feelings and loving memories and painful anxieties rattling around in the traditional novel that, if you are going to make any sense of them at all, you have to severely restrict their range, send them up outrageously, or at least throw them against a hard edge of incredulity. Janice Elliott doesn't do this; she takes the worth of 'the novel' at face value, and so treats its conventional devices too seriously. And because she is soft about her own writing, she becomes soft about her characters, too. Davy Middleton is a young boy growing up on the fringes of a mining community, with his genteel mother now down on her luck, and with rougher and tougher friends who stand no nonsense from him. He is, in other words, a typical character in a typical novel—and when he turns out to be intelligent, sensitive and also modest, there is no way he can avoid his novelistic fate. The book takes him through the Depression and into the War, through marriage and separation, through childhood fears and adult anxieties.

Setting the novel in the 'thirties and 'forties, when presumably its readers would also have been children, gives Janice Elliott the opportunity for arousing all kinds of infantile comforts and reassurance. And novels really ought to be the best medium for nostalgia of this kind: themselves part memory and part fantasy, part rhetorical and part genuine, they should be able to handle the special pressures which nostalgia can bring. But in the 'seventies our sense of time has slipped beyond repair, as decades are reconstructed and then destroyed on the small screen, and the conventional novel's usual evocation of the past merely seems dumb. The hesitant and broken quality of the narrative suggests that Janice Elliott knows this, too, but she only has the strength to express the problem in the mouth of one of her 'characters': '. . . the difference between the life she secretly and steadfastly imagined, and the way people did live'. The difference, implicit but never stated, is one that ruins the book.

And because her writing is flawed, Janice Elliott can't actually handle the problems and the complexities of Davy Middleton and the book gradually retreats into a threnody on sadness and decay. You can always tell a novel is about to lose its direction when 'Nature' is suddenly introduced: 'Though he did not formulate the concept in so many words, what he sensed was that if there were a power here, it was not God but Nature, a force indifferent to human affairs . . .'. And when you start invoking a power 'indifferent to human affairs', at the same time you're actually supposed to be writing about them, something has got to give. In this case it is not Nature; it is Janice Elliott.

Once she starts trying to evoke all of the mysterious natural processes of inheritance, life, love and sex she loses the battle with her own writing. ***A Loving Eye*** becomes more shallow the harder it tries to probe the 'depths'. Novelists are not philosophers, nor are they particularly wise or well-informed, and the references to 'God' and 'Nature' ring false.

Even her characters eventually turn against her and defeat her purposes by becoming insipid or incredible. . . .

[A novelist called H.N.] is Janice Elliott's greatest mistake because he clearly represents what, for her, a 'novelist' ought to be: 'H.N.'s self-absorption was equalled only by his passionate interest in others.' He is rumbustious, down-to-earth, wise, and full of good advice. To most people he would simply be a pain in the neck, but for Janice Elliott he is obviously some kind of seer expounding the mysteries of life. It's all rather reminiscent of John Braine's claims that because he is 'a novelist' he is somehow wiser and more perceptive about human affairs. It's ridiculous nonsense since, as Janice Elliott proves in this book, you must never confuse realistic art with life.

And so when it's revealed at the end of the novel that the liveliest and most puzzling character is actually impotent—and that his colourful personality was simply a camouflage—then the secret fear of the novel is unconsciously revealed. The novel, too, is really impotent—trying to disguise the fact, of course, with emotional scenes, 'acting out' feelings as though they were real, using 'life' and 'nature' as a form of therapy. But the book is sterile; all realistic fiction is sterile; but no one will admit to it.

Peter Ackroyd, "Acting Out," in The Spectator, *Vol. 239, No. 7779, August 13, 1977, pp. 21-2.*

ANNE DUCHÊNE

The great drought in England in 1976 caused even the most rational men to admit—with a touch of anthropocentric complacency—to sneaking thoughts about nature going awry through man's fault; and one may well imagine that a group of middle-aged, middle-class liberals setting up a commune just then in a borrowed stately home might have found the conditions particularly challenging. With so much unwonted stripping off, something odd might well happen down by the lake. Such a group being the subject of Janice Elliott's new novel [***The Honey Tree***], one embarks on it hopefully.

Liberal scruples, and the confusions they cause, have always been one of this writer's happiest grounds. Her trilogy—***A State of Peace, Private Life*** and ***Heaven on Earth***—was a valuable witness to left-wing experience in contemporary England, and there have always been readers to contend that she writes as "brilliant" a novel as, say, Iris Murdoch, but more wittily and less wilfully, and for unjustly less acclaim.

So it is sad to find that this new novel sinks under the weight of its multiple signals, and that the author's taste for elegant, allusive incisiveness—which makes her rather heady stuff scampi to the general, prized not only for its worldly comedy and insight, but for the kind of agreeable intellectual giddiness it induces—has taken a further, and regrettable, turn into a rather clogged, portentous short hand. . . .

A great deal is still very enjoyable. The commune is initiated by Minette, a celebrated gynaecologist whose caesareans and hysterectomies are "famous in the trade", and who talks about nature "familiarly, as of a wild sister to whom she is perforce attached but whose behavior she deplores". She is defeated chiefly, one is led to feel, because, like some mother Maenad figure, she tries to boss nature a bit too much. The other principal protagonist, Francis, has an engaging stammer and works with a firm of international futurists who say things like "Now, let's dialogue some specifics". Francis escapes from the smothering fecundity and insatiably inventive sexuality of his wife, Naomi, into the kindlier embraces of Gemma, a gentle Jewish woman assailed by thoughts of death. Naomi goes mad, briefly. Francis himself goes blind, temporarily. Their elder, nubile daughter sets fire to herself; their youngest cherubic infant begins to want to see pigs killed. Gemma, after a pregnancy of exalted calm, gives birth to a still-born monster. But everything, after some rain and snow, reverts to the recognizable, and Francis and Gemma go off to what the book's last words affirm is a "HAPPY ENDING".

It is not really a comedy about what happened to a group of aging liberals in that hot summer, so much as a parable about what happens when such people are scorched by stepping outside their normally brain-conditioned (as others are air-conditioned) lives. And as such, of course, it might have worked out well; only, alas, it is so loaded with numinous allusions, and the anthropological undercurrents run so strongly and surface in such bewildering eddies, that one begins to flinch at the very mention of a corn-dolly.

Anne Duchêne, "A Bad Case of Sunstroke," in The Times Literary Supplement, *No. 3993, October 13, 1978, p. 1142.*

PETER KEMP

Janice Elliott's ***The Honey Tree*** takes place in 1976: water-rationing, power-cuts and petrol economies all come in for mention. It seems, too, that when she wrote her book the author had the motto, 'Conserve Energy', hanging well in view. Listlessly, the novel pelts a middle-class commune with limp epigrams—'the only Englishmen who do not wear Harvard T-shirts are those who have actually been to Harvard.' Sentences are often short on verbs and pronouns—don't seem quite all there. And the would-be brittle dialogue sometimes sounds slightly cracked. Evidently despairing of giving her characters any human credibility—they are like 'golden Martians', she explains—Miss Elliott falls back on suggesting they are mythic archetypes.

'You've been reading too much Frazer,' a character is told. What the author seems to have been reading too much of is Iris Murdoch.

As in that writer's *The Nice and the Good,* the sun here beams down on twins, a difficult girl, a Jew troubled by thoughts of the concentration camps, and a goddess-like figure who holds everyone in thrall. More general similarities can be seen as well—in tone, technique and incident. This is no way to write books. (p. 591)

Peter Kemp, "The Nice and the Nasty," in The Listener, *Vol. 100, No. 2584, November 2, 1978, pp. 590-91.*

PAUL ABLEMAN

[***Summer People***] belongs to that relatively new genre, the female subjective novel. Since contemporary fiction is as securely, or perhaps precariously, in the hands of women as Afghanistan is in the hands of Russians, it is clearly a hazardous admission to make but I consider the form a self-indulgent aberration. Admittedly, it already includes some considerable works. *Fear of Flying,* to give one outstanding example, was both funny and moving. But, by presenting a hypertrophied portion of reality as the whole of, or at least the dominant part of, reality, these works seem to me inimical to the health of fiction. . . .

Having laid my head on the block, I might as well utter a few more heresies before the axe falls. The female subjective novel is actually a less effective instrument for the exploration of specifically female experience than the classical novel in the hands of a competent novelist of either sex. . . . The female subjective novel is actually based on the concept of objective differences [between sexes], but, over-compensating for the real or imagined historical neglect of women by novelists, relegates male experience to the margins of life.

This results in considerable distortion rather than rectification. When the world beyond the womb is thinned to a shadow-play the womb itself is drained of meaning. What is the point of having babies at all if they are merely destined to vanish over the frontier into a kind of 'dreamtime'? This is not only *Hamlet* without the Prince of Denmark but *Hamlet* without Denmark at all.

As if uneasily aware of such considerations, Janice Elliott strives to give [***Summer People***] some general significance. She sets it, for example, in the future 'a few short years since 1984 came and went without cosmic disaster'. This device allows her a rather perfunctory SF content. We learn that, presumably a decade or so hence, there are '. . . whole continents coming up to the boil, the polar cap melting, the economy of the West collapsing, civil war in Ireland, the American President assassinated (again), civil war in Africa . . .' and so on. But these simple linear predictions (almost certain to be discredited by the inexorable law of paradox) are almost wholly irrelevant to her main theme since what really concerns Ms Elliott is the consciousness of women.

In order to examine this, she invents a summer beach community of middle-class people. Her heroine is Bea Tyler and the second lead is Erin Willings. Also beached are a beautiful potential suicide called Francine and a hard-swearing, hard-screwing American called Jeannie whose breasts have been amputated. In orbit around these planets are a variety of husbands and children. The action ostensibly concerns family relationships but its true subject is the micro-structure of the womens' psychologies and emotional states. . . .

The children, some of them young adults, are endowed with a certain degree of autonomy but remain essentially expressions of the fecund women. The men, although credited with physical features and careers, and who service the women as husbands and lovers, remain ciphers. Bea's husband, tagged 'corporation executive', is 'permanently air-borne'. It is only when he flies home that he starts, like *Star Trek*'s Captain Kirk 'beaming down to the planet's surface', to solidify and he only achieves even ancillary substance in the immediate neighbourhood of his wife. So in spite of that melting polar cap and the motorcycle gangs alleged to be roaring past on the coast road, reality essentially extends no further than the 'women talking about babies'.

The result is like a Picasso beach scene where monstrous figures of women are planted in reverie. Fragments of their interior monologues evoke old lovers and aspirations but these, like concrete events in the outside world, are mere glints in the long brooding of the women. . . . Truth, in the female subjective novel, is narcissism, women musing on femininity.

So, although the genre can reveal details of feminine consciousness too fine for the classical novel, it only achieves this by a focus that excludes any broader vision. It would be a pity if women writers, while seeking to win a new province for the novel, actually subverted the kingdom.

Paul Ableman, "See the Joke," in The Spectator, *Vol. 244, No. 7917, April 5, 1980, p. 20.*

JOHN MELLORS

Janice Elliott's families migrate annually to their summer homes by the sea. The time is the near future, when 'there are dreadful things going on in the world . . . genocide here, genocide there, crazy prices, fall-out in milk, radioactive leaks, terrorists absolutely everywhere'. Bea and Herman are envied by their friends for what looks like a perfectly happy marriage and for having a teenage son who causes them no problems. No one else in the cast of ***Summer People*** seems as lucky or as normal. . . .

Everybody wants things to go on being as they used to be, but the signs are not good this year. Wild dogs roam the sands. Beach-bums occupy the caves. Motor-cycle gangs rule the coast road by night. A wrecked tanker spills its oil: 'like a detached retina, it casts a shadow over a corner of their vision.' It begins to look as if Bea's and Herman's perfect marriage might be on the rocks, too; their son is horrified to hear them quarrelling in bed.

Summer People is a perceptive, witty and disturbing book. The use of the present tense and the way places are described like paintings—the mackerel boat 'will always be making no progress through the milky water towards the lighthouse and the ocean'—produce a sultry, threatening atmosphere, like the lull before a cosmic storm. (p. 483)

John Mellors, "Dreadful Things," in The Listener, *Vol. 103, No. 2657, April 10, 1980, pp. 482-83.*

WILLIAM BOYD

"Holidays are long now—so much has changed in the few short years since 1984 came and went without cosmic disaster". The scene [in ***Summer People***], some ten years hence, is an unspecified stretch of English coastline where an assorted mix of middle class families are gathering for their summer holidays. Our attention focuses on the Tylers—Herman, Bea and their moody adolescent son Timbo—whose preternaturally secure and envied marriage hesitantly edges towards some dim crisis. . . .

Summer People bowls along at a fair pace in short segments rarely longer than two pages, often only a few lines. It is told in an intimate short-sentenced style in the present tense. Point of view changes sporadically and from time to time the author intrudes in a half-hearted metafictional way, exploring possible directions the story could take or chattily notifying readers of their privileged status:

> actually, Erin doesn't know it but Merlyn is a secret novelist. He has been writing a novel for ten years . . . Poor Merlyn. Still, as long as he never finishes, who may cast him down?

If this were an orthodox analysis of a segment of society in the traditional comedy of manners mode it could be counted a modest success. Janice Elliott has a sure, deft touch and assuming you've no ideological objection to her silly characters with their inconsequential worries and grumbles they are convincingly and economically drawn and tolerably engaging. But, plainly, ***Summer People*** has larger ambitions than this and it's here that certain dissatisfactions arise. Most puzzling is its slight sci-fi element which is in the end so tentative that it proves only an annoying affectation. The post-1984 world consists of a few layabout hippies on the beach, wandering stray dogs, hints that essential services are not all they could be, and dark talk of violence in the cities. The apocalyptic doom-laden atmosphere that's so patently striven for just doesn't emerge and odd references to the oil running out and planes called Super-Jumbos strike one merely as afterthoughts.

Our attention is explicitly drawn to two other novels that lurk behind this one like shadowy fictional parents: John Updike's *Couples* and Virginia Woolf's *To the Lighthouse*. Both authors are alluded to in the text and we are clearly invited to make connections. The interactions of the various couples are closer to Updike but certain symbols and echoes of *To the Lighthouse* make that link more prominent. There's a visit to a lighthouse for a start, Erin—who paints—takes over the Lily Briscoe role and Bea is a Mrs Ramsay figure, whose central consciousness in the book somehow unites the less than satisfactory characters around her. In one sense there's the possibility that Janice Elliott is offering us a debased late twentieth century version of the earlier book (for example Lily's final line in her painting becomes in Erin's the grey line of the wrecked tanker) but it can only be an educated guess: overall the similarities—though inescapable—are too diffuse to cohere in any satisfying formal manner.

William Boyd, "The Longest Days," in The Times Literary Supplement, *No. 4021, April 18, 1980, p. 430.*

JUDY COOKE

[Like Caroline Blackwood's *The Fate of Mary Rose,* Janice Elliott's ***Secret Places*** is] concerned with the death of innocence but it is a much sadder, deeper book, reflective rather than moralistic. It is a story of adolescence, set in a girls' school during the last war. The pupils go home 'swinging their satchels and gas-masks' to an absence of fathers, brothers and boyfriends—that is, until the Yanks arrive. The teachers encourage favourites, punish independence and watch factions develop, sometimes conscious of their own involvement, sometimes responding blindly to politics or passion. The claustrophobia of the all-female community is beautifully realised and against this backdrop we see the main protagonists: Nina, the authority on Life and Fashion; Barbara, the bully, good at games; Patience, clever, plain and bound to be rewarded; dreamy Rose, always remembering other people's birthdays; the newcomer, Laura, exotic and vulnerable, a refugee, a focus of sexual and social rivalries.

It is difficult to do justice to this quiet, authoritative text within the compass of a short review. The friendship between Patience and Laura carries the seeds of its own destruction; we know that from the first and read on with a sense of dread which is at every turn defeated. The book is full of surprises. It examines the human tendency to distrust the outsider; the lust for a scapegoat; the poignant truth that unacknowledged love can cause more suffering, even, than outright hatred. Pace and style are faultless, characterisation is subtle and the overall design has been triumphantly achieved. (pp. 22-3)

Judy Cooke, "Losing Innocence," in New Statesman, *Vol. 101, No. 2607, March 6, 1981, pp. 22-3.*

LINDSAY DUGUID

[In ***Secret Places***], Laura and Patience are pupils at Albert Lodge School for Girls in the north of England in the early days of the Second World War. The members of Form IV T, including gentle Rose, sexy Nina and insignificant Posy, are totally taken up with school. They spend their free time sitting in the boiler room where they dream, talk about having babies or examine Posy's chilblains (Janice Elliott has caught perfectly the mixture of cosiness and boredom).

Laura introduces a dangerous note of the exotic into this tight and wholesome English community. It is not just a matter of her foreign ways (she has an "air") or of her strange home-life (she lives with her dramatic mother in a dark and glittering flat), but that she introduces notions of freedom. Patience learns that the teacher may not simply be "Them" as opposed to "Us"; that war is not simple; that you can be imprisoned for your ideas and that rules are "a flimsy tissue . . . a conspiracy between those who obey and those who are obeyed". Patience, who is characterized by her peers as sensible and a good listener, and who thinks of herself as someone who will never marry but be "a famous author or help people instead", also learns about love: not only her own passionate friendship for Laura, but also the love between her parents, Nina's sordid seduction by an American airman, and the undercurrents of emotion that exist between the teachers. ***Secret Places*** is not simply the story of Patience's awakening, however; the personalities surrounding her unfold and become more complex, a saga of treachery and blood begins to unravel.

For this is also a novel about women without men . . . and about women who are trapped: "Women together. Time of year, time of war." The war progresses and the seasons change. A German PoW camp is built in the Arboretum in the school grounds. Laura's father Dr Meister is interned. The girls become infected with anti-Jewish and anti-German hysteria, and Laura is persecuted both for being a German and a Jew: she is sacrificed "for the good of the school" by Miss Swinnerton and Miss Trott, who are themselves disturbed by warring forces. Shut away in an attic at the top of the school, Laura tries to cut her wrists on a piece of broken mirror. After the final examinations and as the war draws to a close Albert Lodge is destroyed by bombs and Dr Meister and his fellow internees are revealed to have been testing the H-bomb. It says much for the power and subtlety of ***Secret Places*** that such an ending does not seem portentous.

Much of the book is funny somewhat in the style of *The Prime of Miss Jean Brodie*. . . . But we are never far from a substratum of violence: "Schoolgirls", Janice Elliott tells us, "are cruel as everyone knows but they also draw blood." This may come as no surprise to convent-educated readers, but Janice Elliott introduces a strong and distinctive note of menace. There are many references to blood: the suicide of the Victorian industrialist who built Albert Lodge; Laura's own attempted suicide; menstruation; Nina shaving her legs with her brother's razor; the junior girl who impales herself on the railings in an "English against Jerries" fight. Other disturbing elements are provided by Laura's mother Sophy, who is a morphine addict, and by a mad young shaven-headed German in the Arboretum camp. All these details are woven to form a seamless and convincing whole.

Lindsay Duguid, "Lessons of War," in The Times Literary Supplement, *No. 4067, March 13, 1981, p. 279.*

PETER ACKROYD

Janice Elliott's ***The Country of Her Dreams*** opens in a deceptively comic vein: a party of writers and artists has arrived at an Adriatic resort to participate in a Congress, which will decide where and how to protect Western works of art in the event of a nuclear war.

Despite the ostensible seriousness of the theme, Janice Elliott conveys the absurdity of such a cultural enterprise with a few passages of deft satire: one cannot, after all, anticipate the path of violence. When it comes, it will be with the suddenness of an hallucination. And in fact her style, in this and in previous novels, has a curiously soft and unfocused quality: so that the most important things seem to be going on at the penumbra of her characters' consciousness, just beyond the range of clear vision. The central character, Mary Lamb, has been to this Adriatic city before, in her dreams, but "I always woke up before the end". . . . [An] air of menace is combined with a strange, wraith-like atmosphere in which ordinary human reality is suspended.

And, of course, Mary Lamb witnesses "the end" of her dream. Her husband and a number of other delegates are kidnapped by a gang of terrorists: death and destruction follow on swift feet. On one level, ***The Country of Her Dreams*** is a fable about the peculiar softness and blindness of the West. But if this is the thematic centre of the novel, its imaginative centre lies elsewhere: in the depiction of violence, the kind of violence which is customarily beyond our experience and even our imagining, the violence which destroys the ordinary face of the world. "Every journey," Janice Elliott writes, "matters, even those we would not choose to take." One gets the impression that she believes such violence to be in some sense cathartic, perhaps even necessary, because only within it do her characters come to terms with the darkness within themselves. It is not a particularly appealing message but she outlines it here with a formidable clarity.

Peter Ackroyd, "The Paths of Violence," in The Sunday Times, *London, March 14, 1982, p. 42.*

SAVKAR ALTINEL

[In ***The Country of Her Dreams***], Mary Lamb and her husband Nicholas arrive in a communist country by the Adriatic for a conference whose aim is to select those works of art which should be moved to a lead-lined shelter in the event of nuclear war. . . . [Mary and Nicholas] are successful in their careers; they are very much in love with each other; and they have two nice grown-up children. They are, as one of their friends puts it, "obscenely" happy people.

Almost at once, however, things begin to go wrong. Mary is convinced that, although she has never been in this corner of Europe before, it is familiar to her from several disturbing dreams. This upsets her; she is right to be worried, for the country is in fact in a tense condition. The previous President, who had kept it non-aligned, and who is still referred to by everybody as the "Old Man", is dead, and both East and West are itching to move in.

Unknown to everybody, there are also terrorists about, and these soon manage to take the conference delegates hostage. The usual demands (freeing of political prisoners in West Germany, a plane to Algiers) and threats (shooting of prisoners, blowing up of the conference building) are made, but before any action can be taken there is an attempted coup by a pro-Moscow faction in the country, and the confusion gets even worse. . . . Meanwhile, the Lambs' marriage falls apart. She is unfaithful to him, he is almost unfaithful to her, and by the time they are finally rescued they both know that they can no longer take anything about their relationship for granted.

None of this is particularly original. There is no shortage of novels about happy couples who break up as soon as they step outside the confines of domesticity, or intellectuals who find themselves unable to cope with "real" life, or smug Northerners who come to grief in Mediterranean lands. But this derivativeness is openly admitted, and, indeed, emphasized. References to Forster abound; an allusion is made to Lawrence;

there are frequent appearances by a Panama-hatted figure reminiscent of the straw-hatted man who follows von Aschenbach about in *Death in Venice*. All this is merely Janice Elliott's way of indicating where her sympathies lie. The knowledge of literature she both displays herself and demands from her readers is a part of her defence of culture.

We are left in no doubt that being happy, leading a civilized existence and worrying about what might happen to art treasures in a nuclear war are all irrelevant in a world which is actually violent and chaotic, and there are plenty of jokes at the expense of unworldly intellectuals. . . .

Yet the author does not fall into the trap, common in this kind of novel, of using intelligence and wit to denigrate intelligence and wit and to uphold the "natural" life. She knows that, however artificial happiness, order and rationality may be, the alternative, which is chaos, is only painful and unproductive. The final sentence of [***The Country of Her Dreams***], which describes the Lambs' flight home—"The higher they flew, the simpler and more beautiful the earth appeared"—is both ironic and sincere, and neatly sums up this humorous, tender and provocative book.

Savkar Altinel, "Coming to Grief in the Real," in The Times Literary Supplement, *No. 4120, March 19, 1982, p. 306.*

PENELOPE LIVELY

I kept thinking, reading ***The Country Of Her Dreams,*** that narrative skill is extraordinarily underrated. We expect the novelist to tell a story (well, most novelists) and sit back to enjoy the ride; if it is a bumpy one we do not always question the basic framework. And by that I do not mean the structure of the plot, which can creak a little without foundering the whole venture, but the more subtle business of the unobtrusive organisation that is going to keep the reader turning the pages over in the first place. Those who are in the trade know only too well that creative despair is seldom induced by the intransigence of one's characters or deficiencies of inspiration about where to put them and when: the problem is what they are to do next, and how to tell it. Some writers never master the skill; others seem to achieve it by instinct. Janice Elliott, in [***The Country of Her Dreams***], tells the story with that high professionalism that makes it all look easy, and it is a measure of her success that the reader happily ignores the odd creak of the plot because, quite simply, it is necessary to find out what happens: you have to keep on turning the pages.

A happily married couple, Nicholas and Mary Lamb, attend with cronies and acquaintances a congress devoted to discussing ways of preserving crucial items of European culture in the event of a nuclear war. The congress takes place in a country that sounds like Jugoslavia and which is in a state of internal unrest; there is rioting, suggestions of a military coup. And in the middle of all this a group of the congress members including Nicholas is seized and held hostage by terrorists. . . . Mary Lamb, awaiting her husband's release, takes up with a slightly shadowy figure, Hugo Cross, ex-British Council (he turns out to be some kind of spy), and, quite uncharacteristically, holes up with him for several days and vaguely suggests that she might stay with him even if Nicholas gets out. But Nicholas is released, the eruption of violence into hitherto tranquil lives ends, the Lambs return to England. And it is all so persuasively related that any objections to areas of improbability—the inherent dottiness of the congress, Mary's extraordinary behaviour—are silenced, at least for the duration of the novel. The orchestration of characters and story is masterly. . . . (pp. 88-9)

Mary herself has a curious sense of *déja vu* about the country, upon arrival: she has dreamed about it, she realises. And this prescience or hallucination is discreetly offered as the key to Mary's strange response to her husband's possible death, which is a mixture of what you might expect and an almost dream-like irresponsibility: "Nice Mary, good child, loving wife and mother . . . had been shouldered aside by some woman not at all nice, the woman who had awaited her in this country of her dreams." Excessive circumstances, it is suggested, can unleash "the serpents in oneself." The story, for all its surface dash and verve, is setting out also to be a parable about violence and loss of personal innocence. Nevertheless, I had my doubts about Mary, I'm afraid, and was much happier with the scenes in which the hostages and terrorists sit it out in the besieged tea-room: a convincing sequence in which fear and prosaic irritability are nicely combined, in which strengths and weaknesses are unnervingly revealed. Along with that deft narrative ease goes much nicety of observation and agreeably understated authorial presence. . . . In the last analysis, here is a novel that is an extraordinarily good read, in which the reader's churlish objections are met half way by the competence of the pretence: and what more can you ask for, as a demonstration of fictional skill? (pp. 89-90)

Penelope Lively, "Backwards and Forwards," in Encounter, *Vol. LVIII & LIX, Nos. 6 & 1, June & July, 1982, pp. 88-90.*

MIRANDA SEYMOUR

Janice Elliott is as stylish as she is inventive and ***Magic*** is the most original of her books. The last two novels [***Secret Places*** and ***The Country of Her Dreams***] showed her moving steadily away from pleasantly anodyne autobiographical novels set in the fifties into worlds fringed by menace and the unknown. Here, she treats directly of the inexplicable, but with a humour and a firm grip on character and plot which allow her to make the zaniest of propositions seem convincing and engaging. She shares the talent of Alice Thomas Ellis . . . for making the improbable likely, for tinting the mundane with the greys of mystery, and for briefly drawing the reader into a charmed world where anything but the predictable may happen. . . . (p. 30)

[Oliver Hartley is] a retired diplomat and amateur historian with a keen and matter-of-fact sense of his existence in previous incarnations. . . . It seems wholly appropriate that this eccentric old man should be living on an island of magical properties, the last spot of England to be converted to Christianity, and that an attempt by the Ministry of Defence to buy the ancient site of Cerdic's Throne should provoke sinister happenings. A strange humming emanates from the throne; Alcestis, the Hartleys' cat, takes on super-feline qualities; their cleaning lady, Susan Humble, has visitations from a homely Virgin Mary who drops in on the pub or the vegetable patch with delightful insouciance.

Affairs take on a Murdochian twist of inter-familial passions with the arrival of grandson Sandy and his curious girlfriend. Dora Phenicule, like Oliver Hartley, lives very comfortably on two planes. In her other life, as Modigliani's model-mistress, she walked out of a fifth-floor window in response to his invitation to join him in Paradise. One meeting with Oliver Hartley is enough to convince her that he is Modigliani reincarnated and that she has a duty to transfer her affections. The rejected Sandy retreats to London to take revenge, and to suffer a Dostoevskeyan plague of guilts when the media invade the island's privacy. Normality, or whatever passes for normality in magic places, returns only when Oliver, the island's self-appointed Prospero, ceremoniously jumps off a cliff and Cerdic's Throne is repossessed by Sandy and his pregnant Dora. Sentiment threatens, but is held at bay. "As he plunged into his proper home, above the shush of the sea, there was a sound: a crack of laughter from the universe."

The story intrigues. The style is incisive and elegant. My only quibble is with a gratuitous dating of events. In a novel which has a great deal to do with the timelessness of things, it is a pity that we should be conscious that Anna Ford has just left the evening news and that Sue Lawley is ubiquitous. Such conscientious placing does carry the danger of dating a book. (pp. 30, 32)

Miranda Seymour, in a review of "Magic," in Books and Bookmen, *No. 336, September, 1983, pp. 30, 32.*

ANGELA HUTH

I admit being somewhat fainthearted when it comes to novels about magic. But when so fine a writer as Janice Elliott takes it for her subject, there is nothing for it but to brace up and feel willing to be captivated.

The setting of ***Magic*** is an unnamed British island wherein lives one Oliver Hartley, possibly dying. A self-indulgent old fellow befriended by one of those precocious fictional cats, Alcestis, he clings to his dreary routine fearing otherwise 'chaos might enter, birds peck his marrow, leaves dance in his skull.' At his beckoning various members of his rather unappealing family assemble in his house. They include his unemployed son, Sandy, whose girlfriend Dora is observed with accurate humour: bones in her hair, joss-sticks and brown rice in her shopping bag.

While within, the Hartley family reflect on the past and squabble a bit; without is a local problem. A granite stone planted on 'the last place in England to be converted to Christianity', is put up for sale. In protest, it begins to hum. . . .

But there are no fears about reading this book alone on a stormy night. The supernatural, after all, is not its *forte*. Its real magic lies in fragments of description. . . .

There is a bizarre note at the end when we are conjured into the mind of the Virgin Mary who had 'lately become interested in the Feminist movement.' But perhaps this is a joke, part of a whole which is not meant to be taken too seriously. Evocative in small parts, it is to be hoped that Miss Elliott's magical revels are now ended, and with her next book she will return to her more memorable territories. (p. 23)

Angela Huth, "Love and Magic," in The Spectator, *Vol. 251, No. 8097, September 17, 1983, pp. 22-3.*

RICHARD DEVESON

The Italian Lesson is a Tuscan-holiday story, jetting in where E. M. Forster has already trodden. But Janice Elliott is no fool—far from it. Her novel is highly intelligent, rather knowing, a very skilfully made web of Forsterian motifs ironically elaborated for the 1980s. Two English couples are staying in the hills above Florence and, as happens even to self-conscious, well-read English people on holiday in novels, their ideas about abroad are shaken up and the troubles they transport from home reassert themselves, to be resolved or not as the case may be. Numinous woods, Pan and panic, a baby and what to do about it, symbolic accidents and coincidences, 'trouble and muddle'—to these are now added sanitised modern tourism and terrorist bombs. The book is perhaps just too self-conscious for its own good, but it is conscious of being self-conscious and it *is* good. (p. 32)

Richard Deveson, "Nor Iron Bars," in New Statesman, *Vol. 109, No. 2824, May 3, 1985, pp. 31-2.*

MIRANDA SEYMOUR

The Italian Lesson aims at significance and peters away in arch and mildly entertaining inconsequence. Portentous references to bomb scares and terrorism, bacchic rites and E. M. Forster don't succeed in elevating from the ordinary a pleasant account of Florence as seen through middle-aged English eyes. Miss Elliott is prepared to trip with unwearyingly playful humour where angels might fear to tread. 'Language is funny,' her heroine Fanny says, but I found it an effort to derive much amusement from the endless jokes about the inappropriateness of phrase-book Italian in real situations. The irony lacks bite, although it is snappish enough. The tragedy (Fanny Farmer's loss of her own child and then someone else's) left me tearless. After the subtle pleasures of ***Magic***, Janice Elliott's last novel, this is a disappointment. (p. 35)

Miranda Seymour, "Perfect Happiness," in Books and Bookmen, *No. 357, July, 1985, pp. 34-5.*

SYLVIA CLAYTON

Janice Elliott blurs slightly the edges of her Oxford novel [***Dr Gruber's Daughter***]; her dingy lodging-house to the north of the city is set in the Radpole not the Radstock Road; the Martyrs' Memorial becomes the Martyrs' Cross, but Oxford is emphatically there, accommodating a weird crew of refugees in the Coronation summer of 1953. One of these, a fierce old woman in a wheelchair, who feeds on hatred and raw liver and calls herself Ilse Lamprey, dominates a household consisting largely of illegal immigrants, European survivors of the shipwreck of war.

All these lonely passengers Ms Elliott describes with a sharp, elegant wit, the formidable Ilse herself and her obedient henchman Babokov, the hospitable Hungarian countess, the handsome Polish boy who speaks no English and the one legitimate tenant, Elenora Flitch, an outwardly cool, inwardly neurotic English don. Their relationships twist and unravel, drawing in Professor Mowle and his feather-brained wife, who carries on a perpetual conversation in her mind with Lilibet about the corgis. The lodgers form a frieze rather than a group, for in spite of the documentary references to climbing Everest, Workers' Playtime and Algerian wine the core of this novel is not fact but fable, a legend about the nature of evil.

In the attic lies a sickly old man who never goes out, and whom his mysterious, waif-like daughter terrorises with ease. It is a flaw in this well-written book that his identity comes as no surprise, and that once it has been disclosed the cast of lovers and grotesques simply melts away. (pp. 35-6)

Sylvia Clayton, "Oddities," in Books and Bookmen, *No. 371, September, 1986, pp. 35-6.*

ANITA BROOKNER

This slim novel [***Dr Gruber's Daughter***] contains a plot so voluminous that it would have furnished a good 400 pages had a more dogged writer had the wit to invest it in something intentionally serious. As it is, it sits uneasily at the heart of a confection that prefers to think of itself as a fable and adopts a lighthearted, even superficial, tone to suit its resolute decision to skim the surface. It has to be said that this tone is remarkably unified, although it manages to incorporate hints of Muriel Spark and Fay Weldon without in any way reflecting the stoicism of the one or the fury of the other.

If you can imagine the aged Adolf Hitler holed up in an attic in North Oxford . . . you will have no difficulty in accepting his ultimate demise in Coronation year, just as Gloriana's barge sinks with all hands in what must be the Cherwell and midsummer madness parts and reunites all the characters in a final masque which is allowed equal time with Hitler's long delayed disappearance.

If, further, you can accept that Hitler and his daughter (yes, he has a daughter) exist less in the body, as material forms, than in the mind, that they in fact exist as incarnations or emanations of evil, as Satan once did, then their presence in North Oxford and their eventual mutation will seem less worrying and less anomalous than they might otherwise appear to readers of a more sensitive historical disposition. . . .

The strong woman of the novel, however, is not Dr Gruber's daughter, for all her demonic powers, but Ilse Lamprey, who acquired her house in North Oxford with mysteriously obtained money. She presides over a collection of refugees, all of them stateless. . . . The household contains one English woman, Elenora Flitch, a Chaucer specialist of virginal appearance and disposition, and a variety of more colourful, or at least more resourceful characters disposed around Elenora's ground floor and Gruber's attic: Babakov in the basement, Countess Rakosfalvi and Janusz Grzyb on the first floor, and Ilse Lamprey above all, chairbound, bewigged, focussing her opera glasses on the nearby convent, and theoretically writing a novel on her portable typewriter.

Across the road is the household of Professor Gustavus Mowle (these funny names could have been avoided), his wife Valerie, their dog Cuffy, Valerie's phantom pregnancy, and her empathetic acquaintance with Queen Elizabeth II, always ready to drop in and confide her weariness with the prospect of the Coronation, always ready for another of Valerie's fairy cakes, although she knows that Mr Hartnell will scold her if she adds another millimetre to what the author cruelly describes as her overweight figure. It has to be said that Janice Elliott frequently does duty for the rude child buried somewhere in all of us, particularly when detailing Miss Flitch's attacks of the vapours, during which coarse and lewd thoughts rise to the surface. These thoughts are eventually transformed into action when a student named Derrick Sproke comes to read her his essay on the Wife of Bath and is not allowed to leave until the early hours of the following morning. This subplot is negligible and more than a little tasteless, particularly when collated with the story of Gruber's of Hitler's residence in the attic of 161 Radpole Road and the events that bring his continued existence to light.

He has been seen, of course, notably by Countess Rakosfalvi. . . . He has also been seen by Detective Sergeant Rainbird, who has to be removed by Special Branch and sent to a rehabilitation centre in case his sensational declarations should clash with the Coronation. He has been found, moreover, by his witch-like daughter, Vera, who has inherited all his evil propensities and turned them to more feminine ends: she combines a gift for creative housework with a desire to kill cats, and she is after Dr Gruber's gold, the gold that he brought out of the bunker and was forced to share with Ilse Lamprey and Babakov as they hurried him through the subway tracks below the Wilhelmsplatz, through the Russian lines, to a hazardous form of survival. . . . It is only when he interrupts one of the Countess's little parties to complain of the noise and inform them that his patience is exhausted that his existence is revealed to the full cast of characters. What they do with the information is perhaps the cleverest part of the book.

Those who take their knowledge seriously have to be punished, for seriousness is out of order in Coronation year, when the university is mounting its own river pageant with Miss Flitch as Gloriana. There is a good deal of fairly grotesque pairing off, of a floundering and perfunctory nature. That disposes of the English characters, always regarded with a sceptical, albeit partial, eye by the author. The Detective Sergeant has been rendered free of all memory through the agency of the State's psychiatric services. The Hungarian Countess continues to cultivate her garden, the Pole, who in any event understands no English, finds happiness with one of Miss Flitch's students, and it is left to the survivor, Ilse Lamprey, to tap out on her portable typewriter the history of her meeting with Gruber and Babakov.

This is very well done. The irritations of the action subside to reveal the original plot which has been too easily overlaid with farce, much of it conveyed in short paragraphs of Weldonian length and substance. And the reader is at last allowed access to a grown-up world which might have seemed to be in danger of more or less total eclipse. Whether the grown-up world is more palatable than the world of surreal university junketings is something that same reader will have to decide. It is above all the sheer embarrassment of certain historical events and their irruption into normal peacetime concerns with which Janice Elliott seeks to tease us. I finished the book with considerable admiration for her insight, an admiration that contrived almost to dismiss my earlier impatience with her levity.

Anita Brookner, "Surreal Oxford Junketings," in The Spectator, *Vol. 257, No. 8252, September 6, 1986, p. 28.*

MANSEL STIMPSON

Janice Elliott's splendid new novel [***Dr Gruber's Daughter***] falls into two parts. In the first, a thin, shadowy girl calling herself Vera gradually makes her way to the house known as 161 Radpole Road. A home for illegal immigrants and for one English woman (the middle-aged don Elenora Flitch, who is living in exile from a world which makes her uneasy), it is ruled by a foreigner, Ilse Lamprey. Bewigged and confined to a wheelchair, Ilse is an absurd figure but also a formidable one. The darker tone is confirmed by her premonition of a girl arriving to confront her. So, while the reader enjoys being introduced to those living in the house (the Countess, the servant-like Babakov, the young Pole Janusz, Gruber in the attic), expectation is increased by our realization that the threatening figure imagined by Ilse, who wishes to dismiss her as pure fancy, is real and is getting nearer.

The success of ***Dr Gruber's Daughter*** lies in its strikingly individual and daring combination of comedy and drama. The involvement of the snooping Sergeant Rainbird leads to scenes of farce, with his own men regarding him as a suspicious figure, and a narrow escape from arrest as a rapist. Humour surfaces elsewhere too, not always with equal aplomb. A neighbouring couple, the Mowles, also feature in the story—Mrs Mowle's fantasy friendship with the Queen . . . seems a bit forced. But Elenora Flitch's late discovery of her own sensual feelings leads to a finely calamitous attempt to lose her virginity with a student who is less experienced than she supposes. . . .

Yet the book's themes are serious ones. Mother Martin in the local convent remarks to herself that there is no certainty of ease within or without these walls. The experience of life portrayed in the book reflects that, on all levels, including its mismatched relationships. Elliott grasps the nettle early on, inserting in a fantasy of Babakov's a reference to the ovens of Auschwitz. Even the farce turns black; only the youngsters, Janusz and his English girlfriend Posy, are innocent enough—being romantically self-absorbed—to be largely oblivious to the conflict between good and evil. . . .

When it is revealed, the secret of 161 Radpole Road proves almost too clever—it threatens to turn the book into a certain kind of thriller. Yet the novel goes deeper than that would suggest. Remembering the Nazi past, the book confidently asserts that people will be caught up by history in the same way in the future: there will be other monsters, other victims, other passengers.

Meanwhile the day-to-day struggle between good and evil goes on. In ***Dr Gruber's Daughter*** the latter seems to produce the more striking representatives, even though religious figures are there in the background. These are not immune from the writer's mockery, as when the convent hires a television set to watch the Coronation and it is revealed that Mother Martin's preference is for "I Love Lucy." Yet, just as the book's comedy is not a denial of its seriousness, such humour does not prevent the good being represented by the forces of faith: Janice Elliott's finest stroke comes in the last paragraph, when she unexpectedly evokes a distant echo of another serious comedy, T. S. Eliot's *The Cocktail Party*.

Mansel Stimpson, "No Certainty of Ease," in The Times Literary Supplement, *No. 4355, September 19, 1986, p. 1029.*

Raymond Federman

1928-

French-born American novelist, critic, editor, poet, short story writer, and translator.

Photograph by Zoe Leonard. Courtesy of Raymond Federman.

An important figure in American experimental fiction, Federman is a practitioner and theoretician of "surfiction," a term he uses to describe "writing that does not imitate reality, but that exposes the fictionality of reality, writing that proceeds . . . to produce meaning." Federman began his career as a literary critic; his interest in Samuel Beckett's fiction, which he interpreted as "a reflection on fiction by its own language," resulted in his first book, *Journey to Chaos: Samuel Beckett's Early Fiction* (1965). Beckett's influence is reflected in Federman's fiction through his stylistic innovation, syntactical experimentation, and eschewing of conventional plot, character, and chronological development. Featuring wordplay, typographical oddities, multiple narrators, self-reflexiveness, and frequent digressions, Federman's work often explores the nature of fiction and reality as well as the implications of his traumatic childhood.

The critical event in Federman's life occurred in 1942, when Nazi soldiers captured his Jewish family in Paris and sent them to their deaths in concentration camps. Federman survived because his mother hid him in a closet before the Nazis arrived at the family's apartment. In his fiction, Federman attempts to comprehend the meaning of this experience but concludes that language cannot sufficiently reveal the horror and truth of the tragedy. His first novel, *Double or Nothing* (1971), features many unconventional typographical elements to underscore the difficulties faced by a young Jewish survivor of the Holocaust as he attempts to write about his experiences. Ronald Sukenick commented: "It is as if to say that the experience of the Holocaust is more than language can comprehend or communicate." Sukenick continued: "The typographical game-playing in this book is a kind of dialogue with the blank space of the page—what can you say?" The eccentricities of form, multiplicity of voices, dark humor, and digressions characteristic of this work also surface in *Take It or Leave It* (1976). Ostensibly about a young immigrant's adventures while on leave from the United States Army, this novel includes ruminations on politics, philosophy, aesthetics, language, literary theory, and American values.

The Voice in the Closet/La voix dans le cabinet de débarras (1979) is a bilingual book that includes "Echos à Raymond Federman," a critique by Maurice Roche, positioned between the English and French versions of the novel. More stylistically and structurally concise than Federman's previous fiction, this work centers upon a young boy hiding in a closet who ponders the meaning of his family's extermination by Nazis. Peter Quartermain observed that *The Voice in the Closet* "reads as the chronicle of a mind struggling with questions of its identity and origins, of the accuracy of its memory and the authenticity of its feelings." In *The Twofold Vibration* (1982), Federman employs three narrators to relate the tale of an old man about to be exiled to a space colony on New Year's Eve, 1999. Moving backward and forward in time, the narrators attempt to discover the reason for the man's deportation and to rescue him. As in all of Federman's work, this novel focuses upon the relation between fiction and reality. He again explores this concern in the American Book Award-winning *Smiles on Washington Square* (1985) by obscuring the details of a love story. In this work, according to Allen Boyer, "Federman treats all events as possibilities rather than facts." Federman has also published two volumes of poetry, *Among the Beasts* (1967) and *Me Too* (1976), and has edited several books of critical essays, including *Surfiction: Fiction Now and Tomorrow* (1975).

(See also *CLC*, Vol. 6; *Contemporary Authors*, Vols. 17-20, rev. ed.; *Contemporary Authors New Revision Series*, Vol. 10; and *Dictionary of Literary Biography Yearbook: 1980*.)

THE TIMES LITERARY SUPPLEMENT

By the nature of his work, Samuel Beckett is less exposed than Joyce to the refinements of scholarship, but he is fast becoming an equal sufferer from far-fetched and piecemeal interpretation. Since the early essays on Proust and Joyce have proved so relevant to the later fiction, Mr. Federman's plan [in ***Journey to Chaos: Samuel Beckett's Early Fiction***]—to investigate the fictions prior to *Molloy* in their relation to the trilogy and *Comment c'est* in order "to gain a deeper understanding of these complex and abstract works"—seems both sensible and promising. But complexity and abstraction do not always (or even often) go together, and it may be argued that, as Mr. Beckett has progressively pared away the "illusions" of the external world in his search for an adequate metaphor for what living is like, his writings have become more abstract and less complex. *Comment c'est* is easier to apprehend than *Watt,* and, like his critical predecessors, Mr. Federman more frequently uses notions derived from the later novels to interpret the earlier ones than *vice versa*. In the chapter on *Watt* this procedure is serviceable, and although no convincing, overall account of the novel is achieved, much of the discussion is helpful. But the backward look at *Murphy* produces serious distortions, such as the conclusion that the disposal of Murphy's ashes

> represents a flippant indictment of all those who, like Murphy, seek freedom in the mind, but refuse to accept the consequences of such a condition and allow worldly concerns to interfere with intellectual or artistic aspirations.

This sentence is the culmination of an account of the novel which presents the hero as one who fails through defect of character or loss of nerve, instead of one who fails because life is a tragic farce in which aspiration and failure are two sides of the same coin. There are similar distortions in the discussion of the short stories, *More Pricks than Kicks,* and, in general, Mr. Federman seems more at home in the works immediately preceding *Molloy*. . . .

"Joyce Exagminated," in The Times Literary Supplement, *No. 3349, May 5, 1966, p. 388.*

WALTER A. STRAUSS

My first inclination, when I opened Professor Federman's [***Journey to Chaos***] was to cavil at the title. Journey *to* chaos? after all, Beckett's fiction is really a journey *in* chaos. But Professor Federman is right, after all, since this study begins with the earliest Beckett, that of the *Dream of Fair to Middling Women* and *More Pricks than Kicks,* and stops short of the great trilogy *Molloy-Malone meurt-L'innommable*. And the author has done a splendid job in serving as a guide through the progressively disintegrating landscape of Beckett's fiction from 1932 through 1945. . . .

Professor Federman keeps his attention strictly focused on Beckett's own fictional journey: the perception of chaos, the survey of chaos, the immersion into chaos. The difficulties of such an enterprise should be evident to any admirer of Beckett: the problem of analyzing Beckett's fiction runs up against the problem of Beckett's intellectual framework (for Beckett *is* a thinker, and a very acute one) constantly; and the major obstacle in writing about Beckett is the avoidance of monotony in discussing a series of works that—as Professor Federman demonstrates—become increasingly monochromatic in their execution. This second problem has not been solved altogether satisfactorily in this book: there are too many repetitions. . . .

Professor Federman had the excellent idea of initiating his study with . . . *Comment c'est;* it is altogether appropriate, in this particular instance, to allow the tail to chase the dog, and Professor Federman's observations on this puzzling and difficult work are highly perceptive. The same is true for his handling of *Watt*. I am less impressed by his treatment of *Murphy;* it seems to me that Murphy's reliance on astrology represents a good deal more than an alibi for physical indolence: it is also a retreat into a "closed system", a more successful attempt than Watt's to close the circle of intellection. Treated under this rubric, Murphy's horoscope-obsession might easily have strengthened Professor Federman's general argument. Also, I feel that Beckett's debt to Joyce, particularly in *Murphy,* needs to be emphasized, even if this means treating Beckett as a Joyce *à rebours*. (p. 505)

But the most gratifying aspect of Professor Federman's book—as well as of a great deal of recent Beckett criticism—is the fact that a real *prise de contact* with Beckett as a writer and thinker has begun to take place; there is still a great deal to be said about Beckett, from both points of view, and the Beckett enigma will tantalize many commentators to come. But a substantial beginning has been made, at least since the appearance of Professor Kenner's book, which remains the most seminal study of Beckett so far. I believe, however, that Professor Kenner's book, to which Professor Federman is greatly indebted, has tended to emphasize too strongly Beckett's critique of Descartes and of the Occasionalist philosophers. Beckett also reveals in his work a close acquaintance with Scholastic thought, with the philosophy of the entire seventeenth century, with Berkeley, possibly with logical positivism, and equally possibly with phenomenology and existentialism. Professor Federman seems to be aware of some of these aspects but does not take the next step, which would be to interpret Beckett's thought as an elaborate *reductio ad absurdum* of Western philosophy, particularly in its attempts to find a solution to the mind-body problem. (pp. 505-06)

Walter A. Strauss, in a review of "Journey to Chaos: Samuel Beckett's Early Fiction," in The Modern Language Journal, *Vol. L, No. 7, November, 1966, pp. 505-06.*

RONALD SUKENICK

Suppose that, in order to fully exploit the visual aspect of their writing, novelists operated within a convention that allowed them to use the placement of print on the page as an expressive component of style—like metaphor—rather than just laying it on margin to margin, with the occasional exception of a paragraph indentation?

Double or Nothing is a novel that operates on that premise. A young man comes to America after World War II. His parents and two sisters have been slaughtered in the concentration camps from which he escaped only by jumping off a train and surviving as a child laborer on a farm. He is met on the pier by a distant relative with whom he cannot communicate because he speaks no English. They take the subway to the Bronx and during the ride he is sexually aroused by a flirtatious black woman. They arrive at the home of an obnoxious Jewish family who seem to express a sly vicarious interest in his experience of the Holocaust, and they have a meal of noodles. This is the story of the novel.

It is a story that never gets told except as fragments in the mind of the narrator, who is preoccupied with his preparations for telling it. These consist mainly of renting a room and stocking it with survival supplies for a year of concentrated writing. It is the trivia of this preparation that constitutes the bulk of the book—which then becomes a long evasion, a refusal to talk about the young man's arrival in America or the Holocaust that led him there. Instead, we get printmaking designs on the page, typography defeating the language it symbolizes, the reduction of meaning to visual patterns. Each page is a separate frame, an empty canvas to be filled with a design more prominent than the information it communicates.

If what we have here is an evasion, it is an evasion so urgent and obsessive that it becomes a symptom, a symbol and finally, in a negative way, a statement: "(*you can't avoid the facts*). But we must forget about that about the Jews the Camps." The narrator's murdered mother, father and sisters are referred to only as "XXXX." It is as if to say that the experience of the Holocaust is more than language can comprehend or communicate—except, perhaps, by a denial of language, an admission, finally, that some experiences are so terrible as to be beyond the formulations of language.

The determined omission of such formulations, an omission made so glaringly, is what saves ***Double or Nothing*** from its own trivia and from the sterility of mere literary doodling. The typographical game-playing in this book is a kind of dialogue with the blank space of the page—what can you say? There's nothing to say, one might as well make patterns to fill up the emptiness. But the patterns, like a frame around a blank canvas, make the emptiness visible.

After having said all this it must be admitted that in the experience of reading the book the trivia is often not that interesting—here and there you just look at the designs, you skim. It's fun but raises the question of whether this kind of thing can't be done with a sequence of detail that is more compelling.

Double or Nothing breaks up that solid page of print we are all too ready to expect in fiction, and suggests a new convention more persuasively than any novel I know of, including those of Michel Butor, who has worked in a similar style.

It is a considerable achievement—a deliberate and complicated doodle, a perversely trivial book that forces you to take it seriously. And that also opens interesting possibilities for contemporary fiction. (pp. 40-1)

Ronald Sukenick, "Refugee from the Holocaust," in The New York Times Book Review, *October 1, 1972, pp. 40-1.*

HARRIS DIENSTFREY

Is there any reason why novelists should not continue to use the regular text format of over two hundred years, with lines of equal length ranked in standarized columns page after page? Is there any reason why they should? If they don't, what's their point? What's the point of the traditional format?

These questions are prompted by Raymond Federman's ***Double or Nothing,*** a comic, dazzlingly inventive, elegantly written, moving book that seems to me a small masterpiece. (I say "small" because I do not think the book strikes deeply into human experience. But I know that there are others who might consider such a characteristic a quintessential virtue.) It is a book that follows none of the usual conventions. Its page size is nearly as large as an 8½ by 11 sheet of typing paper, the text has been photographed off of a typewritten manuscript, and most bizarre of all, the arrangement of the words on the pages, far from just deviating in a regular way from the standard arrangement, changes radically almost from page to page throughout the book. Is this just wilfulness, the concoction of an imagination absorbed with nothing other than itself? Is there a point?

Let's begin with description. The narrative of ***Double or Nothing*** has three tracks. On the first is a narrator who worries a good deal about the nature of fiction and who is attempting to tell the story of a writer/gambler who somehow (the possibilities are various) has won enough money, if he budgets it carefully, to secure himself in a hotel room for a year to write the story of someone else. The second track is the story of the writer/gambler, steeling himself to sit down and write, and diverting himself with obsessive calculations of just what he will need to fulfill his plan. The third track is the story he wants to tell—the entrance into America, several years after the Second World War, of a young Frenchman, orphaned by the death camps. The book is a story within a story within a discourse about fiction, and the novel dips and weaves from one to the other, developing all three parallel to each other. Among other things, the page-by-page design is a neat device for moving from track to track.

A sizable part of the novel's pleasure comes from the comic inventiveness with which it tells the story of the writer/gambler and the story of the young Frenchman. The humor of ***Double or Nothing*** might be called the humor of persistency. Like a good screwball comedy, the novel is always read to give the screw another turn.

The writer/gambler, in trying to nail down every contingency that might arise for a man planning to live for a solid year in a hotel room, pursues his calculations relentlessly. . . . The outlandishness of his calculations are a lovely metaphor for the situation of any artist who must balance off the needs of his or her work against the other needs of life.

The problems of the young Frenchman are of a different order. While the writer/gambler wants to leave no possibility unaccounted for, the young man is entering a world where not a single possibility is known to him. The result is pratfalls and windfalls, pies-in-the-face and pie-in-the-sky. The circumstances of the young Frenchman make ***Double or Nothing*** kin to the legion of immigrant-come-to-America tales. But it is an odd America he comes to. Like the fabled country of Kafka's *Amerika,* the most fantastic of all immigrant stories, it is as much a country of the imagination as of reality. (pp. 147-48)

In the balancing of its narratives and in its page-by-page format, ***Double or Nothing*** is a kind of game, a game of art and, in another way, a game of anxiety. Its format is a statement about fiction. To ***Double or Nothing,*** fiction is concoction, invention. Fiction is whatever the imagination (and the determination) of the conceiver decides it will be. Rules guide the creation of fiction, but these rules are conventions, and they can be chosen and changed at will. So the words on one page can be arranged in a solid block, on another from bottom to top, on a third in three columns to be read across the columns. These conventions are part of the game of invention—which is another name for the fancier phrase "the art of fiction." The choice of inventions is what rules fiction, and the exercise of choice is one generating source of ***Double or Nothing.***

The choice of inventions is also freedom. The "fictioneer" behind a book like ***Double or Nothing*** does what he or she wants, goes from page to page, which means decision to decision, in a surge of self-determined movement. The choice of inventions is the expression of a continuing series of free acts. The page-by-page format of ***Double or Nothing*** is a tightrope performance that has the effect of being a celebration of the imagination and the will. Watching this performance is like watching any other virtuoso demonstration of skill: it causes wonder and it gives delight.

Yet one other critical element shapes ***Double or Nothing***—a central element of anxiety. On each page, the story begins again. The book's structure, of narrative within narrative, is in this case an expression of nervousness: a narrator who invents a writer/gambler who is determined finally to tell the story of a young Frenchman—why all the preparation? why the intervention of the writer/gambler? Telling is invention and choice, but invention and choice is a demand, and the questions of the person behind ***Double or Nothing*** are: Can it be done? Can I get my story told? Self-doubt, fear that the game may be too difficult, hovers over the narrative. The self-doubt of the writer/gambler is an expression of the book's self-doubt. The book tells its story in pieces and in shifting layers almost as if the psychological tension in it could not sustain any larger continuity. The game, in effect, is not just a device, a definition, and a celebration, it is also by way of being a necessity—the means to inch the story forward, page by page, to get the story told despite the fierce self-doubt that plagues the teller.

In the end, the story does get told, and this telling is in fact the book's triumph. The anxiety of the telling (and perhaps of the experience), for the sustained moment of the book, has been overcome. The beginning has succeeded in reaching an ending (though the very end of ***Double or Nothing*** suggests that the whole process might have to begin again: the writer/gambler has based his calculations on the assumption that a hotel room will cost him eight dollars, but "IF THE ROOM COSTS ONLY 7 BUCKS A WEEK," then all the possibilities are different). The book gets its wholeness, its integrity, its sense of completeness, from the completion of the telling, not from the completion of what is told. . . . For Federman, in ***Double or Nothing*** at least, the book is completed when the telling of the story is achieved. Federman has made the telling itself a challenge. Facing this challenge, by the doing of it, has become an essential part of his story. (pp. 149-50)

[The] adventure of ***Double or Nothing*** is complete—one of the rare successes among the rare novels whose story includes the pursuit of its own form and one of the most notable achievements of contemporary American fiction. (p. 150)

Harris Dienstfrey, "The Choice of Inventions," in fiction international, *Nos. 2-3, 1974, pp. 147-50.*

DORIS L. EDER

What is surfiction? Raymond Federman has chosen the word by analogy with surrealism; like surrealism, surfiction goes beyond realism. It is, says Federman, "the kind of fiction that constantly renews our faith in man's imagination and not in man's distorted vision of reality—that reveals man's irrationality rather than man's rationality". Unlike surrealism, surfiction does not necessarily mine below the surface; it may rise above it, but more frequently it remains on it. It is often called metafiction, fiction about fiction-making, which proclaims and rejoices in its own fictiveness. It no longer attempts to represent or to recreate reality, for reality itself is a fiction. Surfiction is thus anti-realist. It arrogates to itself a certain autonomy by abjuring mimesis; when fiction no longer attempts to represent life, it begins to exist for its own sake, not as mirror or allegory. In an age of mass journalism and of still and motion photography, the writer's aim cannot be to reproduce the world. In any case, writers with a truly contemporary sense of reality find their consciousness has passed beyond, has exhausted, and is betrayed by traditional realism. (pp. 153-54)

There is a definite need for the kind of book Raymond Federman has put together in ***Surfiction.*** Several of its best essays are reprinted, several are very awkwardly translated, and one can think of excellent articles on the subject of postmodern fiction that might have been included. Nevertheless, some of the pieces are exciting, most are thought-provoking, and the collection as a whole should inspire other writers, critics, and editors to similar, perhaps better ventures. Of the diverse essays in ***Surfiction,*** some are committed to spatial form, while others embrace the temporal-existential form. . . . (p. 154)

In Federman's introduction, **"Surfiction—Four Propositions in Form of an Introduction,"** two of his four propositions about postmodern fiction concern the abolition of plot and of character, as usually portrayed. (pp. 154-55)

Federman's first proposition calls for new freedom of format and typography in surfiction. Fiction should no longer be forced into the straitjacket of bound pages of solid type to be read from top left to bottom right of the page. Federman would also like to revolutionize syntax, again in the cause of enabling readers to find new, multiple, simultaneous ways of reading books. The medium is the message. Curiously, Federman says language is neither audible nor visible, but he believes the medium, the printed word, can be enhanced by making it more visual or more audible. ***Surfiction*** cites novels-in-boxes, printed on pages to be shuffled and rearranged in whatever order the reader pleases (Saporta); novels which may be read forwards or backwards (Cortázar's *Hopscotch*); fiction liberally interspersed with concrete or found poetry and graphics like comic strips (Handke); fiction based on mathematical formulae or spatial motifs (in Sukenick's *Out,* for instance, numbers of lines and lines of space vary inversely until language vanishes into space); and fiction based on or adorned with rebuses, puns, and metagrams (Baudry; Roussel). Such manifestations are a response to dissatisfaction with the linearity and temporality of fiction. In a multi-media age, the book strives to liberate itself from its old, constrictive format and incorporate features of other media. Fiction has become non- or cross-generic, if not multi-media. (pp. 158-59)

A reader wishing to examine a fiction employing visual techniques which dispose of words as though they were images might look at Federman's ***Double or Nothing.*** In this "real fictitious discourse," as the author calls it, a first person records how a second person holes up for a year to write the story of a third person. Later, a fourth person is postulated, a sort of camera eye who oversees the other three. All four persons or personae are fragments of the author. One notices that, in abolishing the distinction between life and art, surfiction overrides that between autobiography and fiction. Hence, much of this new fiction—Sukenick's is a good example—is autobiographical, but in a peculiar way. It is authorial stream-of-consciousness or stream-of-action, but deliberately kept flat and on the surface. And one cannot be sure when factual glides off into imaginary reportage. Life and fiction bleed together. In Federman's ***Double or Nothing,*** the third person, Boris, is himself when a young immigrant in the United States. The second person, the writer, is Federman some twenty-five years later, planning to write the story of his younger self. This second person has to be distinguished from the first, the recorder, because ***Double or Nothing*** is much more about the *writing* of Boris' story than it is about the story itself. Words are scattered in different visual arrangements over two hundred pages; scarcely two pages look alike. (The novel has been typed and then photo-offset.) In ***Surfiction,*** Federman says the old consecutive method of writing and reading is boring, but aside from the interesting notion on which ***Double or Nothing*** is based, it is hard to conceive of anything more boring than its cute typographical antics. Does this fiction convey "quick, vivid, simultaneous instants of experience?" No. Instead, we are given a sense of the tedium of writing—and of reading—which no amount of visual gymnastics can relieve.

While keeping an open mind on the subject, one should always ask if current visual or multi-media techniques in fiction are integral to the text or mere distraction and frippery. How often are graphics an excuse for the absence of any real talent with words? The essays in Federman's collection which insist on new formats for fiction are the least persuasive. Highfalutin theory may degenerate into a mask for mere whim or slobbery when authors really know neither the reasons for nor the effects of disrupting texts with mathematical formulae, visual objects, and typographical games. Examination of typographically limber fiction like Federman's and Sukenick's raises doubts. Who is going to bother to read a page of mirror-type printed backwards from lower right to upper left corner of the page? Should not prose which incorporates poetry be as choosy about its line-endings as free verse? What is the point of splitting up words as follows:

together they try to mak
e it work eventhough it is
a senseless hopeless situatio
n?

(This is taken from ***Double or Nothing***—a typical page, chosen at random.) The retort that there is no point only exacerbates a reader's irritation. (pp. 159-60)

The last and most troublesome of Federman's proposals for surfiction is that new fiction need mean nothing. It will be deliberately incoherent. "The new fiction will not create a semblance of order, it will offer itself for . . . ordering". Thus it will call for active reader participation. Writer and reader together may be able to invent, project, or extrapolate a meaning for or from a text, but not necessarily. Federman insists on spontaneous creation; meaning does not pre-exist the act of writing but emerges in that act, or in the act of reading, if at all. This is true to the existentialist creed that existence precedes essence. In "The Detective and the Boundary," [William] Spanos affirms that ends that are pre-existent, implicit from the beginning, should no longer be imposed on fiction. Since life knows no ends, in the sense of either goals or grand finales, the Aristotelian well-made plot is an act of bad faith. Despite their common attack on Aristotle, however, Federman's and Spanos' aims are different. Federman, for all his rebellion against traditional forms in fiction, seems to be an inverted formalist who delights in verbal playfulness for its own sake. Spanos believes literature should reflect and enhance life. He wants to see the modernist commitment to spatial form give way to contingent fictional forms which actively engage us in the chaos and absurdity of existence. (pp. 161-62)

Whether one is a devotee of temporal or of spatial form, however—and the two do not appear rigorously mutually exclusive—there is one question one cannot shirk. If fiction need no longer mean anything, why bother either to write or to read it? Even if one acknowledges existence to be absurd and chaotic, why should postmodern literature, which has abjured mimesis, insist on slavishly imitating life's meaninglessness? Reading has always afforded pleasures life could not: the pleasure of viewing people, events, and situations from all round, and of knowing characters *au fond,* as one cannot often in life. In other words, literature has been compensatory to life. It is probably true that it became too compensatory, too much a substitute for living, during the modern period. The postmodernist notion of fiction's role as being to teach people how to compose their own reality is an attractive and vital one. Still, what sustenance may be derived from fiction devoid of significance? "Meaning does not pre-exist creation, and afterward it may be superfluous," quips Sukenick. How true of life—but how untrue of any literature worth the name. For some purpose must precede the act of writing, and meaning may outlast the act of reading. Federman's emphasis on spontaneity seems mistaken, perhaps disingenuous. He insists fiction is based on experience that is not anterior to, but simultaneous with, the process of writing. Therefore, "writing fiction will be a process of inventing, on the spot, the material of fiction". Federman's fiction certainly stresses the process of writing—in itself rather a boring process (except to the practitioner), the more so as it lacks ardour, arduousness, or purpose. But shouldn't "the material of fiction" be the experience of a lifetime—vicariously, of many lives and times? (p. 163)

Doris L. Eder, "'Surfiction': Plunging into the Surface," in boundary 2, *Vol. V, No. 1, Fall, 1976, pp. 153-65.*

LARRY McCAFFERY

Take It or Leave It is Federman's third novel. Like his first two books, ***Double or Nothing*** (1971) and ***Amer Eldorado*** (1974, written in French), Federman's new book involves the adventures of a young ex-Frenchman, seemingly remarkably similar to Federman himself, who has arrived in the United States just after WW II. These strange and wonderfully funny adventures are, however, only one element of Federman's novels: they are also self-reflexive, metafictional tales which spend as much time discussing and analyzing the text before us as they do in presenting the "action" itself. At any rate, the "main plot" of ***Take It or Leave It*** is described by the dust jacket blurb as being "the hilarious and amorous adventures of a young Frenchman who has been drafted into the U.S. Army (the 82nd Airborne Division) and is being shipped Overseas to fight in Korea." Having received his shipping orders, the hero decides to see what he can of America in the thirty days left to him before his departure. . . . Thus summarized, the story would seem to be a self-conscious re-patterning of the classic American initiation story, in which the young initiate will discover America while he engages himself in a process of self-discovery. But this central narrative thread only serves as a sort of pretext which will allow the main portions of the novel to be told; these digressive sections include Beckettian ruminations, lengthy discussions about politics, sex, American values, current literary attitudes, Borgesian quotes and pseudo-quotes, a questionnaire ("Courtesy of *Snow White*"), and (the most frequent) specific commentaries about the text itself. Partly because of these digressions and partly because Federman creates a series of ironic reversals and cancellations in the plot, the "discovery novel" becomes no discovery at all; indeed, the trip in search of America is never even begun, and the entire premise on which traditional novels are built is undermined. . . .

The book ends with [the young man's] trip and all his hoped-for discoveries abruptly cancelled.

Cancelled, too, have been most of our own expectations about what to expect from an initiation novel—or any novel, for that matter; indeed, "cancellation" is one of the key elements in the inner-workings of the book. Early in the narrative Federman juxtaposes Ron Sukenick's novelistic strategy (in *Out*), "I want to write a book like a cloud that changes as it goes he said," with his own intentions in ***Take It or Leave It:*** "I want to tell a story that cancels itself as it goes I replied." The result of this strategy is a book which relies on "displacement and denial"—by impeding the action, altering the familiar novelistic formulas, introducing typographical disruptions, and by frequently pointing to its own fabricated, distorted nature, the book never allows us to believe in it and thus succeeds in "denying" itself. As one narrator proudly explains, what emerges is "the incredible astonishing magnificent result that the entire work cancels itself out not only as it progesses, but also in advance!"

Quite obviously, then, ***Take It or Leave It*** is created with the intention of defying the usual novelistic traditions of the well-made plot, character development, what materials are relevant enough to be included, and so forth. . . . Like so many other works of art in this century, Federman's books deliberately confound the real and the invented, and constantly remind us of their fraudulence even as they freely incorporate elements from the "real world" into their structure. Of course, to an extent, writers have always done this—which is precisely Federman's point: that writers must acknowledge the fictional elements which help them construct and relate to their own lives. In ***Surfiction,*** Federman noted that "reality as such does not exist, or rather exists only in its fictionalized versions." In ***Take It or Leave It,*** he summarizes this notion with a paraphrase from Celine which clearly outlines the key issue of all of his fiction: "after all let's be honest the biography of guy's past experience is always something one invents afterwards; in fact life is always a kind of fictional discourse." This view that fiction necessarily plays a part in our relationships with our past and that it is another structure to be used in helping us deal with the present is also the key to understanding Federman's peculiar digressive method in ***Take It.***

It doesn't take a reader of ***Take It or Leave It*** long to realize that, although he is going to encounter a variety of anecdotes and episodes, no "story-line" is going to develop in the usual sense (one is reminded of Tristram Shandy's inability to get his history under way). Indeed, the narrators multiply, the digressions continue to intrude, and the "background" information keeps pushing the main action off the page, the reader is likely to begin considering the possibility that Federman is deliberately conspiring to cover-up something, to deflect our attention from some mystery while he keeps us busy with an amusing game. And at least in one important sense, this "cover-up" is exactly what Federman is doing; like Beckett (and Beckett, along with Celine, seem to be the most signficant literary influences on Federman), Federman seems convinced that only by spewing forth words in the form of stories, anecdotes, and digressions can one confront what one is (or, perhaps more importantly, *avoid* this confrontation) and maintain an assurance that he continues to be. These various fictionalized versions of the past paradoxically aid in the process of ignoring the past; they are linguistic games which help cover-up, or even partially cancel the past—the frightening *was* of existence which for Federman and his autobiographical main characters involves being a Jew in German-occupied France, a family exterminated at Auschwitz, and a narrow escape from death himself.

What makes ***Take It or Leave It*** succeed, deliberately over-burdened at times with the self-consciousness so typical of contemporary fiction, is the enormous amount of energy with which nearly every page is conceived. Federman is probably the most exuberant writer around today, his prose filled with excitement and an almost childish awe at its own existence. Moving rapidly between different voices in tones which range from the scatological to the playful, ***Take It*** manages to sustain its almost manic sense of pace to the very end. Contributing to this tone is the book's typography, which changes for every page and often for each individual paragraph. These typographical effects are uneven—the book does not seem to possess ***Double or Nothing***'s consistent ingenuity in this respect—but they are occasionally startlingly successful (as with the reliance on the typographic symbol "X-X-X-X" to indicate his "cancelled" family). These typographical effects are created by Federman in the hopes of destroying the control which syntax, with the aid of traditional typography, has had over the power of words ("struggle of word-design, against word-syntax" is the way it is explained at one point in the book). Federman does not rely on traditional linear typography because as he notes, 'I don't give a damn about THE ORDER OF THINGS because me, I do not relate, I do not narrate, I do not recite in order to create order, rather not!" Hoping to produce the disintegration of *all* forms of language (another sort of cancellation), Federman also does not want to deny words any potential freedom—even if this means allowing the words themselves (along with the plot which they carry forward) to wander, establish new relationships, and even occasionally get lost. (pp. 145-49)

Federman's ***Take It or Leave It,*** as its title suggests, is a gamble for the reader, for it demands adjustments and provides the sorts of rewards which the reader has probably not encountered before. But if you're interested in new games, this is one of the most enjoyable, risky, and potentially profitable games to be found anywhere. (p. 149)

Larry McCaffery, "New Rules of the Game," in Chicago Review, *Vol. 29, No. 1, Summer, 1977, pp. 145-49.*

PETER QUARTERMAIN

The Voice in the Closet is a compelling book indeed, and it defies both description and label. It reads as the chronicle of a mind struggling with questions of its identity and origins, of the accuracy of its memory and the authenticity of its feelings, of the ways in which the act of voicing (and of writing) itself falsifies both the actuality of what once presumably happened and of one's attitudes towards it now. ***The Voice in the Closet*** is the voice on the page, obsessive and insistent, compelled by sheer need and battling the frustrations of defective language, memory, and thought as means. There are no sentences, as a result, in this book. Instead, writing weaves back and forth through layers of ambiguity and difficulty which manage—so carefully is this book crafted—to peel off layer after layer of falsehood and invention until desire itself is brought into sharp focus and the obsession, seen, recognized, can at last be (let me call it) satisfied, perhaps exorcised. The whole book is one sentence, without beginning, without end, though it starts (page one) and stops; it interweaves with itself largely through what the Greeks called *apu koinu,* where a word functions in a precedent and a subsequent clause or phrase simultaneously. Here, clauses and sentences, thoughts and feelings, simply merge one into another, feeding each other. Here is a simple bit, from page one: "it's winter now delays no more false starts yesterday a rock flew through the windowpane voices". The compression is fairly straightforward: no more delays, no more false starts (those were yesterday when a rock, and some voices, came through a window) and the thrust of the fragment pushes the possibilities in "delays now" into the back of our minds—until, as the book proceeds, we perceive it as the crux. This is a book of unusual power, written as carefully as a poem, demanding that the reader "re-scan" every step of the way. It is well worth it.

What is it "about"? If you flip the book over you find ***La voix dans le cabinet de debarras,*** the whole book in French. *Le cabinet de debarras* is French for what English people call a box-room, Americans a lumber-room, usually upstairs, a small room where you store unwanted or rarely used things, rubbish you can't quite bring yourself to get rid of. A closet, of course, can be the same thing, but that word carries with it connotations of secrecy, privacy, of things being put away, and so forth. The two languages cross-fertilize, in this book which the voice, at one point, labels *foutaise* (nonsense, rubbish) written *en fourire* (mad laughter, hysteria, foolishness) and they do so tellingly. One effect of them is to facilitate the act of concentration the reading demands, by focussing the attention on language, which becomes, in the "narrative", both the agent and object of experience. Yet the book does indeed (of course) refer to a pre-existent narrative: the Jewish child wearing a yellow star, hidden in the closet upstairs when the soldiers come and take his parents away, and his later emergence into the empty hostile house, his escape; the child in the closet needing to defecate, carefully wrapping it in a newspaper parcel and neatly disposing of it (on the roof? in the street?). The child, escaping, coming again into the world, alone, renamed. The child, federman/featherman; the adult, federman/featherman. A nightmare world of traps, fear, defenselessness, of exposure and nakedness; a world where everyone turns away. Father mother sisters down the stairs, yellow stars, to the furnace, he in the closet to be remade unmade to shade the light. At times the material the voice the book is painful to read, almost too much guilt anguish shame desire and confusion, distrust and sorrow. The voice in the closet becomes a voice in the typewriter, resisting the typist, resisting the reader, suspicious, resisting the naming perhaps maiming processes of words, figuring forth for us, readers as we are, the unreality of our world and of ourselves as we have invented them and allowed others to invent them for us, resisting with all the passion of its own *there*-ness. ***The Voice in the Closet*** astonishes partly because nothing in Federman's previous work, with its writerly and bookish determination somehow to demonstrate the world of writing as, say Derrida and Lacan envisage and describe it, nothing in his previous work prepares us for the obsessive immediacy of this. This book may be a one-shot, perhaps, but in it Federman has come to do what over a generation ago D. H. Lawrence enjoined readers as well as writers to do: trust the tale. (pp. 73-4)

Peter Quartermain, "Trusting the Reader," in Chicago Review, *Vol. 32, No. 2, Autumn, 1980, pp. 65-74.*

CHARLES CARAMELLO

Unfolding himself in the process, a narratorial "federman" [in ***The Voice in the Closet/La voix dans le cabinet de debarras***] spins an unpunctuated "disarticulation" across and through a block of twenty typographically blocked pages. It concerns these events: when "the soldiers" seize his parents and sisters to turn their "empty skins" into "lampshades," a twelve year old boy hides in a closet from which he later flees; the boy eventually becomes a man who closets himself in a room in order to tell this "real story." But the "real story" can only be, like Raymond Federman's first novel, ***Double or Nothing,*** "a real fictitious discourse"; it can only be, like some reprise of Federman's second novel, ***Take It or Leave It,*** "his exaggerated second-hand tale retold anew." Because the "real story" can only be about the voice articulating and "disarticulating" the primary event, Federman's text can only be about itself, ***The Voice in the Closet.***

That assertion involves a measure of disingenuousness. Federman agrees with Robbe-Grillet that to invent the novel is to invent man and the world; he agrees with Robbe-Grillet that in fiction it is "the style, the *ecriture,* and it alone which is 'responsible.'" Federman's polemics for a "surfiction"—a fiction of surfaces that represents its own reality rather than "reproduce a preexisting reality"—echoes Robbe-Grillet's *For a New Novel* and converts to practice in his own work. Composed in fragments that allow the reader to "leapfrog" at will in and out of an already disrupted narrative sequence, composed with typographical configurations that allow the reader to construct any given page in a number of orders, Federman's novels imply that people, places, and events are only a process of words, unattributable to an originary reality or an originary voice. . . . The slippages between Federman and "federman" and the pronominal ambiguity of "*his* exaggerated second-hand tale" signify the decentering slippages at the center of Federman's fiction, slippages between autobiography and invention, between invention and plagiarism. If Federman does not sustain myths of depth, these slippages suggest that his surfictional ***Voice*** still attends to their demise as a crucial problem. (pp. 10-11)

What Federman calls this novel's "second-hand teller" narrates to, and argues with, interlocutors who stand in for the reader. This voice, "Moinous," perpetually displacing "me" and "us," signifies both the slippages, or differences, through which multiple voices project and the absence that necessitates their doing so. Robbe-Grillet's warnings against metaphysical recuperation notwithstanding, this absence remains crucial to Federman's fiction. An insistent memory of the Holocaust suffuses his diffusion of voices. The narratorial "federman" of ***The Voice in the Closet***—the "divided I" of the boy and the man—proclaims himself only a plagiarized invention of writing. But he continually encounters a grim biographical past. It is Federman's. Federman needs to speak it, but he knows, like Proust and, more radically, Beckett, that he cannot speak it. Because he agonizes over that need and that knowledge, the problem that partakes of the "comic" in ***Take It or Leave It*** may partake more of the tragic in ***The Voice in the Closet.***

The problem is that the absence which must be mediated also ensues from the mediation. ***Take It or Leave It*** speaks of "the central primal loss (X-X-X-X): / HURTS to lose all the time / Hurts like hell near the heart / near the guts too." But Federman inscribes this central primal loss within an aesthetics that proscribes representation of external event and centrality of authorial subject. If the loss is that of Federman's family at Auschwitz, then Federman can no more write "about" the "event" of their extermination than he can cease striving to do so. His desire to recuperate his loss in writing militates against his commitment to the free play of ungrounded discourse, while his commitment to such discourse precludes recuperation of his loss. Federman can only indicate the event as "(X-X-X-X)" and weave elaborate digressions around this. "(X-X-X-X)" may *represent* the appalling anonymity imposed by technological genocide on its victims; and it may *represent* the unspeakability of that genocide to which writers from George Steiner to Edmond Jabes have testified. But "(X-X-X-X)" also *presents* the extermination of Federman's family as a scriptive event. As a result, the central event in Federman's fiction is not the extermination of his family; it is the erasure of that extermination as a central event. And since this, in effect, "cancels" the historical event—makes Federman an exterminator of his past—he continues to layer repetitions, interrogations, and interpretations in an attempt to discover and recover the event in the sedimentation. He creates "federman," whose guilt at having escaped becomes, in the dissociation through language from that escape, a doubled guilt at having effected the dissociation. The boy and the man are each caught in a dilemma wherein being entrapped implies an escape, but escape implies another entrapment. Hiding in the closet allows the boy to escape extermination, but entraps him in his becoming the man guilty for having escaped. The man can escape his room and perhaps the guilt imposed by memory if he can tell his story, but to do so would entrap him in the bad faith of representational closure. In fact, neither can escape, because the boy is the man is "federman," who can neither speak in a "single voice" nor attain the "voicelessness" sought in the final five pages of the text. Though "federman" is duplicitous, Federman is not morally obtuse: he knows that naming himself "federman" will not obviate confrontation with his past.

But Federman also knows that he can only name himself "federman," knows that the central loss is of the past and of himself as constituted totalities. His essential loss is that of recuperation of a perceived possibility. Federman's text asserts that it cannot tell "what really happened" in "federman's absence." This doubled absence—absence of the boy from the event of the extermination, absence of the man from the event of his own boyhood—necessitates Federman's speaking as "federman." Both bequeathed and willed, it is the name that the absent family gave Federman and the name Federman gives himself by writing. ***The Voice*** exhorts "federman" to "achieve the vocation of your name," to become "homme de plume hombre della pluma," to become the "featherman" who "sings his signs." It is the name by which Federman as Jew must recover his past; and it is the name by which, in doing so, Federman as writer will discover his future. . . .

To read the text of his past, Federman unfolds a name; to read Federman's text, we must do the same. For "federman" is also named "moinous," and the reader becomes one of this nexus of selves. The reader acts not only as an inquisitor, searching for the "real story" in the semantic and syntactic dislocations, but as a complicitor, helping Federman to avoid speaking the name of "(X-X-X-X)" and the name of Federman as subject. If folds and unfoldings occupy the absent center of the duplicitous ***Voice,*** they also occupy that of our complicitous reading. . . .

The fate of Federman and of "federman" is the fate of Jew and writer, perhaps an inextricably double fate as many on the contemporary French scene have suggested. . . . Federman must invent "federman" in order to excavate a past; but "federman" must bury that past in order for Federman to invent a future. This double invention, of course, also transcends the personal and the racial. . . . In ***The Voice,*** Federman applies Robbe-Grillet's dictum that the reader must assist in the fiction, must learn "to invent in his turn the work—and the world," to the specific question of the Holocaust. To be part of "moinous" is to be neither more nor less than a post-Holocaust human; as part of "moinous," the reader too must invent a future whose past contains the camps but is not contained by them. In this sense, Federman, knowing we are all implicated, seeks complicitors; in this sense, the folds and unfoldings of ***The Voice*** also constitute a serious meditation on the Holocaust.

Considered in this context, Federman's surfictional rhetoric and typographical play assume their more important aspect; they point us to relations of difference. . . . The divided "federman" may have to justify both his escape and his attempt to articulate it, but Federman apparently refuses to justify the resulting "disarticulated" discourse. He justifies the margins, rather than offer justifications in them. But these "boxes of words prisoner of their own form" equally imply something other than a commitment to formalism. Not only does each block of type suggest a closet, but the twenty pages together, justified in depth, form a closet. Federman has reconstituted himself as the voice of his text, and he has constituted his text as that voice's closet. The voice can no more find the door to its own end than we can find the door to its origin. Justifying the typography of his text, Federman does accede to an entrapment in form. But refusing to justify the existence of his text, he simultaneously asserts that the living form of collective writing may offer an escape.

Indeed, the plagiarisms and self-plagiarisms of Federman's text are only a part of an intertextualism that extends to its mode of publication. Initially, Federman published fragments of the text in four different places. . . . The slippages in ***The Voice,*** the slippages between its published fragments, the slippages between its English and French versions, continue in the complications of this particular book. It literally unfolds in two directions. We begin at one cover, read the English version, and encounter a drawing of a wall; we begin again, inversely and reversely at the other cover, read the French version, read Maurice Roche's "Echos"—a "deconstruction," to quote the promotional brochure, of Federman's text—and encounter the drawing of the wall again. I find the book too labored with its drawings of walls and doors, its drawings of Federman, its pagination effected by the progressive construction of linear boxes within boxes, its printing of Roche's text on the recto of each page mirrored on the verso. But it does unmake itself as a "book," puts into question Federman's "responsibility" as writer, his "authority," and hence his identity as "subject." (p. 11)

Perhaps because it is not pure form, ***The Voice in the Closet*** is the best stuff Federman has written. It is the text by which he continues to fold and unfold his past, the text by which he seeks to escape entrapment in *its* form, the text by which, through "federman," he invents his future. But this may be too optimistic. Given "federman's" dilemmas, ***The Voice*** may also be the text by which Federman entraps himself in duplicities. Federman knows this. But then, Federman is only the name according to which his complicitors keep folding and unfolding his fiction . . . and, in some measure, our own. (p. 12)

Charles Caramello, "Duplicities/Complicities," in The American Book Review, *Vol. 3, No. 3, March-April, 1981, pp. 10-12.*

RICHARD MARTIN

Within the last decade theory and speculation entered the tunnel of post-modernism, slowly worked its way through the shades, and has now emerged, slightly sobered, on the other side. In the process we have witnessed the death of the author (Barthes and Foucault), of the novel (Barth and Sukenick), of literature itself (Ehrmann), and even of reality (Federman), and yet in some metamorphosed way, all have risen from the grave to experience the fascination of resurrection. In a sense, this collection of essays [***Surfiction: Fiction Now and Tomorrow***] is a record of that process.

After some of the less disciplined, more esoteric and thus quicker to perish pronouncements of the followers of the founding voices of postmodern criticism, it seems to make good sense when, in his opening statement **"Surfiction—Four Propositions in Form of an Introduction,"** Raymond Federman writes, "The sort of fiction I am interested in is that fiction which the leaders of the literary establishment . . . brush aside because it does not comform to *their* notions of what fiction should be." . . . It is salutary to remember that theorists of innovative literature are concentrating on a literature that is defiantly non-consumer-oriented, non-profit-making, and thus non-commercial. Such a definition often seems to fit much better than most of the programmatic statements and theoretical jargon one has gotten used to hearing. One of the few acceptable theoretical positions has been to concentrate, as Federman does, on "that kind of fiction that tries to explore the possibilities of fiction; the kind of fiction that challenges the tradition that governs it; the kind of fiction that constantly renews our faith in man's imagination and not in man's distorted view of reality." This becomes for Federman the definition of what he has labelled "Surfiction."

The essays collected in this volume (originally published in 1975) cover a wide span representing heterogeneous theoretical positions of the decade 1965-1975. It is perhaps a measure of the tempo of the times that ***Surfiction*** may today be approached almost as a historical document, a collection of New Fiction classics. I am thinking here particularly of the essay already quoted by Federman, and the essays by John Barth ("The Literature of Exhaustion," 1967), Ronald Sukenick ("The New Tradition in Fiction," 1972), Italo Calvino ("Myth in the Narrative," 1971), and Philippe Sollers ("The Novel and the Experience of Limits," 1968).

Framed between Federman's 1973 **"Surfiction"** essay and his 1978 paper, **"Fiction Today or the Pursuit of Non-Knowledge"** (the only addition to this enlarged second edition), we find essays which range greatly in quality and interest. (p. 2)

The essays in the closing section are the most theoretical and have, according to the prefatory note, "been gathered in an effort to determine, define, analyze what is the present state of fiction . . . and, to some extent, in an effort to suggest . . . what will be the fiction of the future." It is only, however, the essays by Jacques Ehrmann and Jonathan Culler which really put forward ideas of some significance. Ehrmann . . . in his 1972 essay, "The Death of Literature," suggests that

> Poetry (or fiction) is . . . not to be found *within* texts of a given (conventional) type but, virtual and diffuse, within language itself, that is, in the relationship between writer and writing, reading and reader, and, even more generally, in the play of all communication.

There is a sense in which this is the key statement of this collection. There is a fruitful novelty in the idea that not only should we seek creativity in the process of communication, but that *fiction* itself is to be found, not merely in the moment when writer sets pen (or IBM machine) to paper, not only in the moment when the reader reads the page, but in the totality of the creative / receptive process. That this process itself may be fiction, that there is a fiction of the author and of the reader, as well as a fiction of the text, could well be one of the major discoveries of the Seventies which will take fiction on into new realms in the 1980s.

This idea is underlined by Jonathan Culler in his brief and fascinating essay, "Towards a Theory of Non-Genre Literature," where he points to the "astonishing human capacity to recuperate the deviant, to invent new conventions and functions so as to overcome that which resists our efforts. These texts which fall at the interstices of genres enable us to read ourselves in the limits of our understanding." This last phrase combined with Ehrmann's idea of fiction existing in the process of communication, hints at the extent of the revision in the critical standpoint: the author loses his significance, the text as an autonomous entity loses its significance, the reader gains in stature and above all, fiction becomes the process whereby and in which we learn to read ourselves.

It might, therefore, appear that when Raymond Federman adds as an afterword his essay on fiction as "the pursuit of non-knowledge," he is out of tune with these ideas. He states openly, "the new novel seeks to avoid knowledge deliberately." But this is not so far from the positions already outlined; Federman's point is once again to focus on the foregrounding of language, the invention and discovery of a new reality in fiction, and, outwardly, fiction's greatest task and greatest value: a remobilization of human imagination. . . . Federman demands that fiction should reclaim for literature the value and function that it once had—perhaps a postmodern demand for premodern status. This essay goes far in the attempt to provide a unifying theme—some rallying point—for the diffuse contributions to this volume, when Federman attempts to place Surfiction in the framework of the following observation:

> basically, there seems to be today a kind of unified effort to regain one's balance towards the world and the condition of man in that world, and it seems to me that the new fiction writers are working in that direction, are trying to make sense again out of the world.

Sense is conveyed through fiction, through a fiction that sees the world as non-sense, that sees the purpose of fiction as the pinpointing of non-knowledge.

The value of this collection, with all its weaknesses, is to provide us with a compendium of the way in which both writers and critics have surveyed the field of fiction over the last fifteen years and have attempted to suggest ways in which fiction is moving. It will be an invaluable document for all students and readers, writers and critics of contemporary fiction, and though it often drives one to exasperation, it will never fail to stimulate. (pp. 2-3)

Richard Martin, "Focus: American Fiction 'The Preserve of Idiots'?," in the American Book Review, *Vol. 4, No. 2, January-February, 1982, pp. 2-3.*

MARK ROSE

Raymond Federman has long been associated with the literary avant-garde both as an editor and expounder of Samuel Beckett and as a coterie novelist. Idiosyncratic typography has been one of the trademarks of his fiction. Each page of his first novel, ***Double or Nothing*** (1971), for instance, was designed as an independent visual image, and his later ***Take It or Leave It*** (1976) not only employed various emblematic devices such as swooping or sagging lines but also omitted page numbers in order to emphasize that the sequence is arbitrary. As a result of Mr. Federman's studied refusal to succumb to the lures of sustained narrative, these earlier novels soon became tedious going. ***The Twofold Vibration*** is more conventional and more successful. Here Mr. Federman's wit and intelligence, his humor and sense of verbal play combine with his acute awareness of the problems of fiction to produce a mildly avant-garde cream puff with a science-fiction flavor.

It is New Year's Eve, 1999, the night of the turn of the millennium. A nameless old man sits alone in a sterile "antechamber of departure" awaiting deportation to the space colonies where undesirables of all sorts, the aged and infirm as well as criminals and perverts, are sent. Exactly why is he being deported? Has he somehow offended the "authorities"? Can anything be done to save him? These Kafka-like questions provide some continuity for the narrative's investigation of the old man's life. Gradually pieces of his picaresque history emerge. . . .

We learn that he is a Jew born in Paris, like Mr. Federman himself, and also like the author a survivor of the Holocaust, a writer and an admirer of Beckett. In fragments we learn about the concentration-camp deaths of his parents and sisters and his own experiences in Nazi Europe. The anonymous old man in some ways conspicuously resembles the author, and yet as a larger-than-life figure of vitality, protest and suffering, he is also meant to represent essential humanity. We are all in a sense displaced persons awaiting deportation for reasons that are not apparent. But the book's narrative appeal derives less from its insistence on the old man's representative status than from the effectiveness of some episodes. In particular I was impressed by the fine and complex story—by turns farcical and pathetic, sardonic and affectionate—of the old man's visit to Dachau in the company of a Hollywood show-biz couple and a sentimental widow from Teaneck, N.J. Here and elsewhere Mr. Federman reveals considerable ability as a storyteller.

Nevertheless, he does not wholly yield to the illusionism of conventional narration. . . . Indeed, so pervasive is the book's self-reflexiveness that it might be said to have a two-tier plot. On one level is the ostensible subject, the story of the old man. On another are the comic squabbles and debates between the narrator and his two doubles, Namredef and Moinous, about how the old man's story should be told. At this level of metafictional farce the book's interest depends less on storytelling than on Mr. Federman's ability to generate a continuous stream of rhetorical energy in the manner of Beckett. (p. 12)

The ambiguous relation between fiction and reality is, I take it, the central concern of Mr. Federman's novel, as it was also of the very first novel, *Don Quixote*. What is surprising, then, about ***The Twofold Vibration*** is less the old theme than the way this still potentially radical idea comes trippingly off the tongue. Mr. Federman does not so much renew the theme as rehearse it, running through it once more with skill. Although his novel is not profoundly innovative, it is a slick piece of work and good fun to read. (p. 26)

Mark Rose, "The Time Is New Year's Eve, 1999," in The New York Times Book Review, *November 7, 1982, pp. 12, 26.*

BRIAN MORTON

[***The Twofold Vibration***] is in every way superior to ***Double or Nothing*** and its other recent predecessors, ***Amer Eldorado, The Voice in the Closet,*** and ***Take It or Leave It.***

The Twofold Vibration describes the involuntary exile of an unnamed "old man" to one of earth's space colonies—distant worlds set aside for criminals, perverts, the old and sick, Jews, and the artistic avant-garde. Federman resists the urge to write another parable of the Holocaust but, nevertheless, it influences his theme. The intrusive narrator (Federman himself) and two friends, Moinous and Namredef, reconstruct the old man's life in a complex, three-handed, free-flowing narrative.

A wider historical canvas is new to Federman and, perhaps surprisingly, Céline and Garcia Marquez join Beckett as the tutelary deities of the novel. For the first time with any success, Federman (like Walter Abish, though with a more acute historical perspective) combines a sense of time and consequence with the spatial concerns of radical postmodernist fiction. . . .

The Twofold Vibration is a disturbing book; thin on "plot", heavy on circumstantial development. At its most vicious and sexual it is reminiscent of bad Charles Bukowski; at its best it really does rival Beckett.

The irritating tics and tricks of the early books, however, are still there: the tags from Beckett—"two-fold vibration", "imagination dead, imagine, bah"; tricksy names like "Namredef" (Federman reversed); "*moi-nous*"; too much "nature of fiction" stage business. But the book evinces a new humour, compassion and self-awareness; after a casual reference to *déboires,* the author, mindful of past criticism, warns himself; "watch that French stuff Federman".

If this is not what John Gardner called "metaphiction for the millions", it is at very least an entertaining and salutary journey through the darker and more troubled outlands of contemporary history and fiction.

Brian Morton, "Room for a View," in The Times Literary Supplement, *No. 4157, December 3, 1982, p. 1344.*

DAVID LEHMAN

The Twofold Vibration fails to deliver the goods it promises. Hiding behind its relentlessly self-regarding prose, garrulous and coy by turns, is far too much perspiration and far too little inspiration. The writing does have a humorous edge that can charm, and the author's critical intelligence surfaces now and again in the form of "naive profundities" and interesting asides. In the end, however, the one-sided proportion of talk to action leaves the reader feeling decidedly grouchy, rather like the character in the book who exclaims, in understandable exasperation, "Why don't you tell the story straight and stop playing games?"

The trouble is, there isn't very much of a "straight" story to tell. ***The Twofold Vibration*** aims, in its author's words, to "explore the future retrospectively," surveying what is past, or passing, or to come, from its vantage point on the eve of the twenty-first century. Federman is disappointingly reticent on the immediate future, though we do learn about the Dismarital Law of 1990 which, for the sake of population control, has abolished marriage in favor of "triangular sexual accommodation." Sounds ominous, but there's good news too. With the elimination of national boundaries, the United States of

Peaceful Earth has come into existence in 1993 and brought about a number of Utopian changes: we have the author's word for it, if few details.

There's trouble in Tahiti nevertheless. Federman's plot, skeletal as it is, consists of essentially unrelated episodes—"pre-reminiscences"—centering on the life and times of a nameless old man awaiting deportation to "the space colonies," from whose bourn no traveler returns. Why have the authorities singled him out? Is he, like Kafka's Josef K., guilty despite having done nothing wrong? As he sits in "the ante-chamber of departure," no fewer than three puppet "narrators" review the old man's career, trying to make sense of his ambiguous destiny. "One must have the courage of one's narcissism," Federman pithily remarks, and this the writer certainly has. His three narrators are versions of me, myself, and I. There's Namredef, the author's mirror image; Moinous, whose name splices together the French words for "me" and "us"; and Federman himself, presiding over the trio as, in the Freudian model, ego presides over superego and id. Add to this that the old man's pre-1980 history tallies in many (undisguised) particulars with that of the author, and it seems only fair that Moinous is sometimes also called Moimoi. Nothing if not elaborate, these contrivances seem gratuitous and scarcely worth the bother; they amount to so much excess baggage, weighing us down.

The Twofold Vibration comes closest to success when, futuristic fantasies forgotten, it honors an autobiographical intention. At the cost of a lifetime supply of guilt and psychic damage, the French-born Federman narrowly escaped the Nazi nightmare that claimed the lives of six million of his co-religionists. It was by nothing short of a miracle that he survived. With the Gestapo knocking on their Paris door in 1942, Raymond's parents saved their young son by hiding him in a closet; there he crouched, in terror and confusion, while sisters and parents were dispatched to the death camps, "moaning yellow stars on their way to their final solution, to be made, remade to shade the light." To this central event in the "old man's" past, ***The Twofold Vibration*** returns again and again, and when it does the writing comes to life. Dramatizing the gulf between language and the impenetrable heart of the Holocaust, Federman's disjunctive style of narration, borrowed from Samuel Beckett's *How It Is,* serves him well in these passages. By contrast, the old man's adult (and adulterous) adventures—his experiences as a tourist in Dachau, for instance—lack vitality in the fragmented telling.

Notwithstanding his disparaging references to "literary junk," Federman gives us a good strong dose of it, charting out the parallels between his old man and Dostoyevski, who faced a firing squad and lived to tell the tale. Having cheated death, the old man becomes a compulsive gambler, as Dostoyevski was and as winners at Russian roulette are apt to be. He loses a small fortune in the casino at Baden-Baden, which Dostoyevski called "Roulettenberg" in *The Gambler;* using that novella's last sentence as a suicide note, he tries to hang himself in his hotel room, but history, repetitive as ever, has other plans for him—he is doomed to be saved again. (pp. xii-xiii)

The example of ***The Twofold Vibration*** reminds us that those who talk up a good case for vanguard writing aren't always its ablest practitioners. (p. xiii)

David Lehman, in a review of "The Twofold Vibration," in The Yale Review, *Vol. 72, No. 3, Spring, 1983, pp. xii-xiii.*

DOUG BOLLING

The Twofold Vibration develops a number of the ideas and directions of the earlier ***Double or Nothing*** but does so in a far more readable and challenging way. Even with the many echoes and reverberations from the past writings, there is a somewhat new and valid quality in the latest book. The ironies, the reflexivity, the lucid dimension and the digressions are all in place—but now they engage the reader within a context of horror, a challenge to our very humanity and our perceptions of worthiness—the Holocaust itself. The boldness (and the value for contemporary experimental fiction) lies in the confrontation of the postmodern aesthetic of disavowal and an event in recent history which demands a passionate response. A dialectic emerges that will satisfy and stimulate some readers and dismay others: the free-floating, disengaged, ironizing narrative voice (voices in this case) on the one hand and the unspeakable Final Solution on the other—the two "synthesized" by Federman's tough-minded determination to salvage something human and vital from the maw of the savage and inhumane. As both the author and Beckett remind us, we swim in both past and future, not one but both. The danger, of course, is that the former will overwhelm the latter—specifically our capacity to define ourselves anew in the times ahead—and this the structure and conclusion of the novel endeavors to circumvent.

The plot of ***The Twofold Vibration*** centers on a character identified only as the "old man" (Beckett, perhaps, or Federman himself or the twentieth century Everyman or the past or . . .) as he recalls his earlier experiences and prepares to enter a spaceship for deportation to the space colonies (the year is 1999). . . . Obviously an autobiographical figment at one level—as in Federman's use of closet and escape symbolism . . . as taken from his earlier poem **"Escape"** found in ***Among the Beasts / Parmi les monstres*** and in ***The Voice in the Closet***—the old man is also a stereotype or abstraction of certain aspects of Americana and of American fiction.

The reader finds the old man on the tourist trail with movie star June Fanon (Jane Fonda) and later with aspiring starlet Miriam Millstein. With Miriam in tow he visits Dachau, and the novel deepens toward a level beyond the parodic and satirical. Aware that the horror of Dachau has been reduced to an "unreal" picture album inside the museum (reduced to status of a mere artifact and a commercialization), he nevertheless comes to know the nothingness waiting just outside the walls: "the whole Nazi machine has produced nothing, nothing but an absence, it was invented to fabricate death". The task awaiting the future—and the reader—is to find some way to fill the void with a viable humanness which will genuinely liberate without demanding surrender to yet another form of madness, emptiness. No explicit solution is offered at novel's end—to expect such would be to misunderstand Federman's stance. Rather, the narrator and the reader are left with "a barrage of unresolved events" and with the disappearance of the old man into the "long and empty" silence. . . . ***The Twofold Vibration,*** then, resolves nothing in conventional novelistic (modernist) terms—and that is exactly the point: it opens us out to the nothingness beyond symbol and theme and closure. It gives us back ourselves—in our bondage to an uninhabitable past and our need to create a future. It awakens us to the peculiar, crazed reality that is the twentieth century and in doing so does more than provide "answers": it raises the questions we need to engage.

Lest the above seem a bit too heavy, let me mention that, as always, Federman breaks up the "serious" textures of his work with the sanity-restoring posture of laughter. The philosophy of "laughterature" seen, for example, in ***Take It or Leave It*** surfaces in the new novel as a powerful source of vitality for the new novel's dialectic. The old man reminds his friends at Professor Marrant's funeral that

> If in the past, seriousness was looked upon as the dark backing that the mirror of life needed for us to understand anything, today it is clear, thanks to our departed friend's persistent optimism, that laughter is the translucent glass which allows us to perceive our survival.

This epistemology of *rire* runs throughout the novel and figures nicely at the end in the list of departees scheduled to join the old man on the space ride to oblivion. Having led the unsuspecting reader to believe that the old man is shortly to be dispatched to the space colonies, Federman suddenly injects a spoofing quality into the climactic moment by providing a list of his fellow victims. . . . The heavy stuff, the seriousness of life—and fiction—must be defused by a vital opposition. And not only the seriousness but the "facts" as well. As the old man earlier reminds, "There are no facts . . . no facts to be accurately described, only hypotheses to be set up, no choices of words will express the truth".

The last quote leads to a major point of Federman's philosophy in general and ***The Twofold Vibration*** in particular. To survive in a world such as ours, we must move beyond "observing and classifying" and "rationalizing and explaining" to "imagining and projecting" because "that's the only thing we can do, the only hope left". This last is what the new novel is all about: it is a novel set in 1999 so that its creator must necessarily use his imagination in "premembering the future rather than remembering the past".

The Twofold Vibration is the best work done by Federman to date. Better than the other books, this one manages to get together in one spatial/temporal continuum an absorbing story and its postmod accomplice—a probing anti-story. Where ***Double or Nothing*** probably remains valuable chiefly as a clever uncovering of possibilities latent in the ebbing of modernism, ***The Twofold Vibration*** builds solidly for both reader and theorist.

Doug Bolling, in a review of "The Twofold Vibration," in The American Book Review, *Vol. 6, No. 1, November-December, 1983, p. 7.*

RICHARD PEARCE

"Surfiction"—a term invented by Raymond Federman—exposes man as irrational and life as a fiction. Federman refers not only to the fictional nature of contemporary reality but, following Robbe-Grillet, to the fact that such a fiction has no preestablished meaning. Events gain meaning only in their "recounted form," their "verbalized version." Nor does language *reproduce* a preexisting meaning: it *produces* meaning, creates meaning as it goes along, as it does its tricks. It is just such a movement that Federman embodies in the striving of his narrative voices—which themselves arise from language doing its tricks on the printed page.

Take It or Leave It, as the subtitle proclaims, is "an exaggerated second-hand tale to be read aloud either standing or sitting." To be read aloud is the key, for Federman has composed a novel of voices for voices—declaimers, singers, bellowers, mumblers, addicts of sound and rhythm, suffering subvocalizers. A Frenchman who has lived in America for thirty-five years and preserved an "incredible accent" while cultivating a marvelous ear for American speech and jazz rhythms, he also owes a debt to Rabelais and Beckett, who in opposite ways extended the tradition of the oral narrative into print.

To Rabelais he owes a verbal torrent that seems to take on a life of its own, embracing both the demotic and the erudite, and accumulating—in description, narration, peroration, and characterization—a gigantic vitality. ***Take It or Leave It*** also follows Rabelais in being a comic quest for knowledge, an episodic journey into the known and the unknown. (p. 119)

But the journey is intellectual as well as physical and goes back as well as forward in time: it explores the hero's past as well as his politics, philosophy, and aesthetics. The journey also explores the many ways of telling about the past and the present—and this leads us to another French writer if not a Frenchman who also extended the tradition of oral narrative into print. Samuel Beckett is the subject of Federman's critical study ***Journey to Chaos,*** and the voices in Federman's novel often address Sam and unashamedly steal ("play-giarize") from Beckett's voices. In plays like *Krapp's Last Tape, Happy Days, Play,* and *Not I,* and in novels like *Molloy, Malone Dies,* and *The Unnamable,* Beckett reduces his characters to voices. He dramatizes the plight, the energy, the inventiveness, the minor victories and major defeats of characters who are compelled to tell their stories and say their say. But whereas Beckett's voices, trapped in a language that is not theirs, agonize over the need to speak, Federman revels in this situation. He takes joy in the fact that he cannot separate himself from his fictions, is flushed by the need to go on, to invent, improvise, extend himself into the unknown through language.

So many of Beckett's voices are alone, but Federman's main voice is always surrounded by noisy listeners. In fact, we never hear the principal voice directly. We hear it only through the mediating voice of a "secondhand teller" as he stands on a windy platform and tries to tell his tale to a group of listeners who continually interrupt, question, and harangue him. What we hear then (and we too are addressed among the listeners) is a tall tale told by a secondhand teller who often weaves the voice of his hero in with his own, as he argues with his interlocutors over the character of his hero, his motivation, his politics, as well as the mode of storytelling, the state of fiction, and the critics of fiction. The mediating voice of the secondhand storyteller magnifies the "told" or raises him toward an epic level by trying to tell about him over the voices of the listeners. And the mediating voice must go on, progress, create the "told" and the meaning of his story with words that are continually disputed or undermined. A major conflict, then, which competes with the conflicts in the storyline, is among the many voices in the novel. Or, to put it another way, the comic problem of mediation—of how the story gets to us and what keeps it from getting to us—is as engaging as the story itself.

What engages us, in fact, is not only the story and not only the voices but the story and the voices as they appear in the concrete language of the novel, or as they evolve from the blank page into the printed text. "All the characters and places in this book are real," we are told in the prefatory disclaimer, "they are made of words." The subject, as funny as it is, is always mediated by the voice of the secondhand teller; and his voice, as energetic and resourceful as it is, comes to us only through the medium of the printed words. Even the characters are made of words—are uniquely evoked by the novel's imaginative typography.

The typography, which I mention last though it engages us first, is the novel's medium and the novel's reality. Federman composes not by the sentence or even by the line but by the page—using a variety of typefaces and arranging the words in patterns that evoke a wide range of rhythms and conflicts as well as a visual experience that often engages us for its own sake. There is no way of representing the reality of ***Take It or Leave It*** because the reality is the entire novel continually evolving: concrete language, "doing its own tricks," creating voices, building momentum, going against the very obstacles it creates for itself, dallying with familiar forms but continually giving birth to itself, enlarging itself—and enlarging the consciousness of its reader. (pp. 120-21)

Richard Pearce, "Riding the Surf: Raymond Federman, Walter Abish, and Ronald Sukenick," in his The Novel in Motion: An Approach to Modern Fiction, *Ohio State University Press, 1983, pp. 118-30.*

ALAN CHEUSE

[In ***Smiles on Washington Square,*** Federman] appears intent on compressing and compacting his story, rather than allowing it to expand and puff up into words and sentences and paragraphs made completely of capitals that seem to bleed into the margins and squeeze out any hope of plausible narrative. The result is much more charming and readable than anything else of his in English. The symbolically named and shabbily attired hero, Moinous, is a Frenchman become American citizen who finds himself in New York City after the Korean War, out of work and loveless. At an anti-HUAC rally in Washington Square Park he meets Sucette, the left-liberal daughter of a wealthy New England family. She's living alone, taking writing classes at Columbia—and, as we learn about midway through the story, the entire novel may be something she's working on for her class, a tale in which "It may not be possible to describe Moinous & Sucette's love affair in detail . . . for it is difficult nowadays to speak of love." Mr. Federman, for the most part, turns this difficulty into a virtue, working in a pared-down style that at times seems reminiscent of Beckett, though the narrative occasionally loses its force and reads like a movie treatment. Basically, the novel succeeds because of its appealing voice. . . .

Alan Cheuse, in a review of "Smiles on Washington Square," in The New York Times Book Review, *November 24, 1985, p. 24.*

ALLEN BOYER

Smiles on Washington Square is the story of a couple who meet in Greenwich Village (although perhaps they do not meet) and pursue a love affair which ultimately ends (assuming, however, that it ever began). The book is more of a teasing exercise than a novel—long on intellect, but short on flesh and bone. Most of the story follows Moinous, a young French immigrant. Moinous served in the U.S. Army in order to gain citizenship. Discharged at the end of the Korean War, he finds himself alone, unemployed and homeless in New York City. The one thing that enlivens his gloom is a smile thrown his way by a woman at an anti-McCarthy rally in Washington Square. The woman is Sucette, a blond Bostonian who is studying creative writing at Columbia. Their meeting is only an exchange of glances across a crowd. . . .

Federman treats all events as possibilities rather than facts. . . . The book could be called subdued or spare, but precious would be a better term. Instead of sensation, passion, or plot, it offers a suggestion that life and art are necessarily related, competitive and tentative—and this idea is hardly new. ***Smiles on Washington Square,*** ultimately, is just another academic novel.

Allen Boyer, in a review of "Smiles on Washington Square," in Los Angeles Times Book Review, *February 9, 1986, p. 4.*

MARCEL CORNIŞ-POP

Federman's [***Smiles on Washington Square***] seems much more willing to break with the "primordial closet" (closure) of his characteristic discourse. In a form that is more fluid and relaxed, less typographically oriented and "engulfed by the tidal events of his narration" (***Take It or Leave It***), Federman promises a *story of possibilities,* not of impossibilities and self-cancellation, as before. But he lowers his stake from the beginning, to accommodate (part seriously, part in jest) our appetite for a story line: this time a passing exchange of smiles in Washington Square between Moinous and Sucette is "good enough to get things started, especially since they are both lonely that day and in need of human fellowship." As long as the two actants "are in a state of emotional availability within the confines of their loneliness, anything can happen"; even "a love story of sorts" (the novel's subtitle), moving with subtle alacrity among clichés and variants of the same possible narrative.

These premises (however ironic) are bound to hearten us readers. After all, in our unabashed craving for a type of "nutritional literature" (in Sartre's expression, quoted elsewhere by Federman) we are not going to worry over such "insignificant" details as the starting point of a story. Furthermore, the dust jacket of Federman's book promises a real love story, with all the right ingredients. . . . If these initial data still do not convince us of the possibility of a story, we can always fall back upon a venerable tradition (revisited and parodied by Federman) where "many great loves of the past were initiated by little more than a conniving smile."

What we will probably miss, especially through the early part of our reading, is the tenor and purpose of this revisitation. It may well be that, as Umberto Eco says in his own *Reflection on "The Name of the Rose"* "the postmodern reply to the modern consists of recognizing that the past, since it cannot really be destroyed, because its destruction leads to silence, must be revisited: but with irony, not innocently." Federman's recent book doubles this narrative irony with a serious philosophical perspective, emphasizing the conflict between narration and fictionality, authorial (or readerly) freedom to invent and textual determinism, or between the inner possibilities and the constraints of a narrative form (genre).

Consider the latter oppositions, as they unfold in ***Smiles on Washington Square.*** Federman (or his unidentified narrator) apparently wishes to establish his actors on a trajectory that would make a second (and a third, etc.) encounter between Moinous and Sucette possible. This would render the story not only possible, but also *necessary:* for, however hesitant in its premises, a story, "bears its complete organization in itself even before it is fully formed. For this reason despair over the beginning of a story is unwarranted.'' This principle of *inevitability,* presented to us as a quote from Kafka (!), may look like another metanarratorial hoax; yet Federman's novel seriously illustrates the subtle ways in which what starts as a project, a hypothetical scenario, may acquire justification and partial credibility. Thus, several narrative alternatives in this ''love story'' told in advance, before it actually happened (or could have happened), are later acknowledged as having come true; or they are ''verified'' through repetition, summarized again ''as previously established,'' and ascribed a position in the unfolding scenario.

Several times, while summing up the predicament of the characters before their ''blind date with love,'' Federman's book lapses into that ''direct form of narrative without any distractions/without any obstructions just plain/normal/regular/readable/realistic/leftoright,'' etc. that Federman ironically decomposed in ***Double or Nothing*** (1971). Most often, however, the ''biographical'' and narrative material is introduced by such oblique methods as *preterition* or *paralepsis:* a common enough procedure with the postmodernists who claim not to deal in story details, while implying them nonetheless in the very act of their negation. . . . One (initial) encounter prefigures another, in a kind of self-engendering process that emphasizes both chance and inevitability. Federman unfolds a ''love story of sorts'' in which the real theme is the probability/improbability of a second (mediated, meaningful) encounter with reality.

''Of course, all this happens several months after the exchange of smiles on Washington Square''; or may never happen ''unless Moinous and Sucette meet again, by chance.'' And Federman's book, as it moves forward or backwards from this initial ''encounter across a smile,'' implies, in true ''surfictionist'' fashion, a critique of the possibilities and limitations of a love story. Significantly, the most logical hypothesis in this book is that of the non-meeting, that is to say of the *non-story*. As a ''foreigner'' in a ''world that systematically disenchants'' and displaces him, ignorant of the American cultural framework and of the complexities of its erotic code, Moinous's chances of meaningfully relating to Sucette are very slim; he is too involved in self-analysis or adolescent fantasies, and Sucette is too busy in plotting ''a story/that/is not going anywhere,'' to be easily ''decoyed/by the narrator/into a gratuitous exchange of smiles which may not lead to anything, unless they talk to each other.'' Even if the love story has a real chance to get started, it will subsequently unfold towards a predictable ending already inscribed in it. And Federman's book ironically emphasizes the ambivalent regime of most of its narratorial situations and signs: the initial ''encounter'' is also a chance missed: ''that day they do not speak. No. They smile at each other, nothing more.'' . . . The background narrator often interferes to underline the hypothetical nature of their love story, its derivation from the conventions of the genre, its location in what Mas'ud Zavarzadeh would call a ''subjunctive field of narration'' (*The Mythopoeic Reality*). He anticipates several narrative possibilities, or summarizes them in retrospect; he also brackets the presumptive love story, projecting a time after the ''inevitable disappointment'' and separation, when Moinous and Sucette will have returned to their ''normal,'' floating reality.

Thematically and symbolically, Federman's book brackets a similarly uncertain space (see in this sense his two ironic, ubiquitous metaphors—of the incessant rain and the indifferent, useless umbrella). At the ''center'' he places an initial ''encounter'' (or pseudo-encounter, inasmuch as the protagonists do not acknowledge their presence beyond a hasty smile). His narrative of probabilities and ''inevitabilities'' unfolds circularly around this fragile encounter in/with ''reality,'' wanting to fill in the gaps, to squeeze a meaning out of it. . . . In Federman's book, not only Moinous's quasi-meeting with Sucette in the Washington Square Park, but also other similar ''encounters'' with (a partly autobiographical) reality, set the narrative mechanism in motion, proliferating tentative (and thwarted) versions of the same essential rapport.

From a certain point of view Federman seems indeed ''to move out of the aesthetically incestuous world of metafiction and directly engage the reality outside (rather than inside) the fictional discourse'' (Zavarzadeh). But from another point of view, this story (or project of a story) is just as enclosed in its fictional possibilities/impossibilities as other previous texts of Raymond Federman. It seems to fit well Moinous's mind, ''wallowing in the disorder of his obsessive imagination,'' with no distinct memory of past facts for future reference, and no capacity to discriminate between reality and fiction; it also fits his situation, stranded as he is between ''hope, the hole ahead that we try to fill or fulfill,'' and ''despair, the hole we leave behind.'' Moinous's ''love story of sorts'' is encased in several ways: in a predictable scenario, moving unavoidably from chance encounter through ''intensity of hope,'' consummation, and ''conditional disappointment'' (''for as soon as a love story begins it has already begun to end''). It is also limited by the stereotypes of the genre (with coffee interludes after ''moments of sensual pursuit,'' lofty conversations and confessions, procrastinations and conflicts—the narrator will often emphasize these consecrated moments of a love story and adapt his choices to them). It is also paralleled and reflected in a kind of ''internal mirror'' (to use Jean Ricardou's term) by Sucette's story of Susan meeting a young foreigner called Moinous, a story that itself breaks off with a ''miscarriage.'' Towards the end of the book this double and triple ''bind'' becomes inescapable: Federman's character, Moinous, will not be able to consummate his love with Sucette until she does not bring her own story of Moinous and Susan (a transparent alter ego) towards some kind of resolution. And everything is then further enclosed in a generic ''as if'' (reinforced in the last paragraph of the novel by a return to the subjunctive).

In many ways, the key philosophical (and surfictional) theme of this book is that of the relation between *chance* and *determination,* narrative ''accident'' (invention) and manipulation. From the outset, Federman's text uses alternatively both the authorial ''fiat'' . . . and the authorial hypothesizing/arbitrary selection. . . . As we pursue further this circular text, we move through a rhetoric of precision/imprecision (especially on a temporal and spatial level), and through the paradox of a ''destined'' meeting ''by chance.'' The grammatical constructions that announce this second encounter reinforce a similar ambivalence. . . . This is, finally, the ambivalence inherent in any *authorial stance:* on one hand the wished-for freedom of invention and choices; on the other the author's awareness of an unbeatable textual (and generic) determinism, engulfing love stories (or any other stories, for that matter), in the laws, stereotypes and constraints of the genre.

Through an ironic *mise en abîme,* most of Federman's narrational problems are ''mirrored,'' redoubled by Sucette's own story. She invents a character called ''Moinous'' that is already invented (in Federman's outer story), she ''writes'' a story that is ''coincidental'' with the enframing story, already projected in several variants. From this point of view her "story" can only unfold summaries, postscripts. But, viewed from the opposite direction, Sucette's exercise in story-writing is also a pre-text, a pre-story that feeds, in a perfectly circuitous way, Federman's outer text. In this paradoxical intersection of inner-outer, anterior-posterior, hypothetical-real, all narrative distinctions finally collapse; with them also the possibility of establishing a proper authorial center and direction for this book: the two "characters" perform even the important task of naming themselves, playing happily with their new names "as if they have just invented each other on the spot". They choose to enter a clever literary game which further displaces their "reality:" "we should imagine nothing beyond these two names. No past. No future." Their original encounter is thus transposed on a purely *textual plane:* it becomes the paradoxical confrontation, constantly deferred and revised, between a character (he) and an embracing text (she); between a (naive, empirical) reader and a deconstructive writer (see the imagined dialogue between Moinous and Sucette apropos of her story-in-progress); or between two characters locked in their respective texts (Jerome Klinkowitz, *The Self-Apparent Word. Fiction as Language/Language as Fiction*), with their parallel narratives meeting only on the imaginary horizon of intertextuality.

Smiles on Washington Square may lack something of the textual complexity (and emotional stake) of Federman's ***Voice in the Closet,*** for example. But it certainly projects an amusing and in many ways credible love affair between the disparate sides of the literary process. . . . More than on previous occasions, Moinous (Federman) seems reconciled to the "fraudulent" forms of imagination, more willing to sustain the flow of words that will "hold them together" in a love story of sorts. (pp. 67-9)

Marcel Corniş-Pop, "A Love Story of Sorts," in The North American Review, *Vol. 271, No. 1, March, 1986, pp. 67-9.*

MARIA VITTORIA D'AMICO

New York, "Washington Square and Its Arch": in the snapshot in front of us two persons, a man and a woman, are smiling at each other, apparently during a political rally. This is what confronts us at the beginning of Raymond Federman's latest novel, ***Smiles On Washington Square,*** and as the story progresses—and digresses—the man and the woman will replay that act over and over again.

According to what the author once told Larry McCaffery, his tales should allow us to "see all the words that went into the making." *Smiles, hope, desire, desperation*—are these the right ones? Apart from the too obvious *smiles,* the others seem to be the words most frequently used to connote the emotional state of Federman's protagonist. On these words the rhythm of this love story is drummed out, and through them we may trace the exact movements of its protagonists: Moinous, a French émigré and naturalized American (his only properties: an "abominable" and sexy French accent and the merit of having served in Korea); and Sucette, the true object of Moinous's quest, a Bostonian with a momentary penchant for dissidence, a well-off blonde who can add to money all the other waspish advantages, style and culture included.

During an outdoor rally against Senator Joseph McCarthy in Washington Square, Moinous and Sucette exchange fleeting smiles and from that moment on (it is even dated: March 15, 1954) the story grows, swells like a conspicuous aggregate of wordy bubbles, enchanting and fragile, perfect circumferences that seal and aggregate always at the same central point, Washington Square. They are always on the verge of bursting, as the fragile and impalpable American dream does: certainly this is the crucial metaphor of the story. (p. 22)

At a first—irreverent—consideration, ***Smiles*** might seem a sort of *Love Story,* with the familiar social roles reversed. The story appears rather sentimental, even bafflingly simple for those who remember (and probably miss) Federman's commitment to complex representational structures and typographic fantasies. But the author warns us by quoting Kafka, "the beginning of every story is ridiculous at first," and by saying, "love stories, real or imagined, are always full of clichés and ready-made fantasies." But we must confess rather timidly that, as readers, we do feel safer on this more conventional ground. We are far from the kaleidoscopic surfictional vertigoes of ***Double or Nothing,*** definitely removed from the verbal "boxes" of ***The Voice in the Closet,*** although ***Smiles*** deals with just another variation of Federman's favorite topic: his personal story.

On the other hand, any expectation of some formally predictable work would certainly be presumptuous. On second thought it seems obvious that such a whimsical and playful writer as Federman should consistently confound our expectations. Here, in fact, he does surprise us: not by an ebullient excess of artfulness, but on the contrary, by an oversimplified structure that is primarily founded on a process of expansion of what Federman defines as his "threshold sentence" (here, most probably, "They smile at each other"), the basic sentence on which the author makes his endless jazzy improvisations and variations. But, Federman readers, beware! On account of its apparent simplicity, the whole operation reveals an even subtler ruse than usual: the keynotes of the plot, with their deliberate repetitions, assume the ambiguous but relaxing charm of the *déjà vu,* and thus the reader's critical awareness may smoothly grasp that peculiar fictional quality of catastrophe/drama that Federman chooses to honor by fishing it out of the shipwreck of realism.

In either an elaborate fictional form or in a tale as compact as this one, Federman cannot avoid driving back to the original drama of his stories, to the true dramatic origin of some wandering characters, the source of their restlessness—to the holocaust. (pp. 22-3)

Kafka once hinted at the necessity of writing as an escape from the folly of life. In Federman's case ths necessity has been expressed through a delirious creativity in his previous works, or through a well-balanced alternation of elegiac and satiric tones. In ***Smiles*** elegy and satire reverberate directly from Moinous's suffering dreams for his absent sweetheart (but has it ever been real, even for just one instant?) and from his mocking reactions to the bourgeois platitudes of America.

After incredible linguistic and typographic orgies, Federman has decided to tell a story again, in a novel which not only reduces any experimental sharpness to circular devices (such as the converging units of Sucette's meetings with Moinous; or just the story within the story, the one composed by her) but also lets its readers feel the ancient strength of emotion, of sentiment—and Federman's declared admiration for a writer like George Chambers, to whom the book is dedicated, is no mere coincidence.

Given the sophisticated quality of Federman's irony, many readers may be struck by the satiric passages in the tale. Some sequences picturing Moinous's frictions with Sucette's family are small masterpieces of irony, such as the ones in which his vengeful reveries luxuriate in an imaginary chain of grotesque obscenities acted by the family members in their dining-room: true moments of sublime, pure, surrealistic fun, that might be compared to the sensuous pleasure radiated by the supreme creator of cinematographic surrealism, Luis Bunuel. But to more sensitive and demanding palates certain delicacies of the novel's elegy will be most flavored and valued: witnessing the shattered dreams of the protagonist, the reader sees one more case of offended innocence, as in the great tradition of American literature. Billy Budd, the stammering sailor, or Moinous, the outcast with an exotic accent, are both victims of the same chimeric dream. (p. 23)

Maria Vittoria D'Amico, "Smiles, Hope, Desire, Desperation," in The American Book Review, *Vol. 8, No. 5, September-October, 1986, pp. 22-3.*

Michael Frayn

1933-

English dramatist, novelist, journalist, scriptwriter, translator, and editor.

Photograph by Mark Gerson

In his newspaper columns, novels, and plays, Frayn employs satire and farce to explore the complexities and shortcomings of contemporary society. Among his targets are human foibles, middle-class values, the pitfalls of technology, and those aspects of popular culture that Frayn believes distort reality, including mass media, public relations, and advertising. Although he first established himself as a columnist and novelist, Frayn is probably best known for several acclaimed theatrical works he wrote during the 1970s and 1980s. In these plays, Frayn continues to explore topics found in his earlier writings while undertaking a more thorough examination of the relationship between language and reality. Frayn is widely praised for his wit, insight, and ability to unite comedy with serious, philosophical observation.

Frayn developed his comic talents writing satirical columns for the *Manchester Guardian* and *London Observer* newspapers. Featuring an array of amusing fictional characters, these pieces offer witty commentary on prevalent contemporary issues and trends. The columns garnered Frayn a devoted following and have been collected in *The Day of The Dog* (1962), *The Book of Fub* (1963), *On the Outskirts* (1964), *At Bay in Gear Street* (1967), and *The Original Michael Frayn: Satirical Essays* (1983). During the 1960s, Frayn began writing comic novels that expand on many of the social and political concerns of his journalistic pieces. His first novel, *The Tin Men* (1965), for example, is set in an automated future world where computers generate everything from organized sports to moral decisions. *A Very Private Life* (1968) humorously examines another future society in which the well-to-do isolate themselves in hermetically-sealed houses. *Sweet Dreams* (1973), generally considered his most accomplished novel, centers on a middle-class Londoner who enters heaven and eventually becomes a close colleague of God. Much of the humor in this work stems from Frayn's depiction of heaven as a competitive and fast-paced world similar in many ways to contemporary society. Margaret Drabble found *Sweet Dreams* "lucid, intelligent, delightful, stylish, extremely funny." Frayn's more conventional novels include *The Russian Interpreter* (1966), an espionage story set in Moscow, and *Towards the End of the Morning* (1967; published in the United States as *Against Entropy*), a satire set in a London newspaper office.

Frayn's dramas are usually fast-paced and are noted for their satirical barbs and outrageous situations. The influence of Ludwig Wittgenstein, a twentieth-century philosopher whose works Frayn has studied extensively, is strongly evident in many of his plays. Beneath their comic surfaces, these works often reveal a Wittgensteinian concern with the relationship between language, reality, and personal perception. In his first major theatrical success, *Alphabetical Order* (1975), Frayn analyzes the dichotomy between order and disorder by chronicling the efforts of a fastidious newcomer to organize a newspaper's archives and its slipshod staff. In *Donkeys' Years* (1976), several wealthy sophisticates attending their college reunion regress to the callow behavior of their undergraduate days. Blending farce with serious themes, Frayn presents an insightful and humorous comparison between the characters' youthful aspirations and their present positions in society. *Clouds* (1977) and *Liberty Hall* (1980) reflect Frayn's interest in political themes. *Clouds,* which centers on a pair of journalists touring Cuba, raises questions about the degree to which artifice and political belief influence individual perceptions of reality. *Liberty Hall* is based upon the premise that the Russian Revolution occurred in England and mocks the rigid atmosphere of cold-war politics. In *Make and Break* (1980), Frayn lampoons corporate mores and the adverse effects of free enterprise. Set in a German hotel that is sponsoring a sales conference, the play provides a darkly humorous portrait of a workaholic salesman whose actions and behavior have become as mechanical as the products he sells.

Noises Off (1982) centers on a production by an inept theater company and evidences Frayn's concern with illusion and reality. The offstage antics of the company contribute to the play's overall pandemonium and hilarity. Critics applauded *Noises Off* for its chaotic humor; Frank Rich commented that the play "is as cleverly conceived . . . a farce as Broadway has seen in an age." *Benefactors* (1984), which involves a young architect who is designing an inner-city housing development, is considerably more somber than Frayn's earlier dramatic works. When the architect's wife and best friend oppose the project,

Benefactors becomes a trenchant study of how love and friendship are affected by individual attitudes and perceptions. *Wild Honey* (1984), based on the posthumously discovered Anton Chekhov play generally known as *Platonov,* is a tragicomic farce about a young schoolmaster who becomes involved with several women. Frayn radically reduced and revised the original while maintaining Chekhov's esthetic and thematic intentions. John Simon remarked that Chekhov's work "is skillfully pared down and then ingeniously fleshed out by Michael Frayn. . . . Simply put, half a Chekhov and half a Frayn together spell a whole lot of not unalloyed but manifold pleasure."

(See also *CLC,* Vols. 3, 7, 31; *Contemporary Authors,* Vols. 5-8, rev. ed.; and *Dictionary of Literary Biography,* Vols. 13, 14.)

JAMES FENTON

As far as I can tell from hanging around in all the likely secondhand bookshops, those people who bought Michael Frayn's classic collections of humorous pieces are not inclined to part with them. They will chuck out the Longfellow, they will flog off Mrs Hemans, and vast numbers of them appear to have got rid of Clochemerle as soon as they read it. . . .

A further circumstance may have helped to render these books unobtainable—their value as a source of comic ideas for later, less original writers. The attentive reader will find [in ***The Original Michael Frayn***] many a promising trope on its first outing, and many a journalist may be obliged to blush and exclaim, "Oh I'd *completely forgotten* that one . . . I could have sworn *I* invented it." But I am afraid that, innocently or not, we have pilfered much from Michael Frayne, and it's time we returned what we snitched. (p. 9)

Fashions in humour may have changed since the 1960s, but I cannot believe that the humour itself of these pieces will appear dated. Michael Frayn's virtues as a comic writer were always based on an ability to evoke the instantly recognisable—the awful predicament, the common foible, the typical character. He is the funniest journalist of our time, and he is also *the* master of comic form. These are not merely sustained jokes. They are model essays.

After the form had lost its attraction, Michael Frayn turned to fiction and plays. It is, to the outsider, a very satisfyingly shaped career—precisely the same career (minus the TB) as Chekhov. I shan't push the comparison, I merely wish to point out that admirers of Frayn the playwright may be curious to see how the original Michael Frayn developed his craft. But for most people, of course, the sufficient reason for reading this collection is that, from now on, you are not going to be able to keep a straight face. (p. 11)

James Fenton, in an introduction to The Original Michael Frayn: Satirical Essays *by Michael Frayn, edited by James Fenton, The Salamander Press, 1983, pp. 9-11.*

SIMON HOGGART

Michael Frayn's essays appeared three times a week in the *Guardian's* old 'Miscellany' column and later weekly in *The Observer*. They were very funny indeed. . . . They weren't really satire . . . but simple social observation. For this reason the 20 intervening years haven't dated his characters, unlike those other fictional figures of the Sixties: the hairdressers, models, photographers, and long forgotten pop singers. Frayn's people are still around—it's just that Frayn isn't keeping us up to date with them any more. . . .

The only pieces in [***The Original Michael Frayn***] which seem locked into their period are those in which Frayn was parodying the journalism of the time, and particularly the tone of breathless upbeat silliness which marked the popular press. That seems to have been replaced by a more unpleasant, world-weary knowingness. . . .

As [James Fenton points out in his introduction (see excerpt above)], it is almost impossible to get hold of the four original collections in which most of these pieces appeared, and we owe him a lot for having dug out, or winkled from Frayn himself, 19 more unreprinted pieces. Some of these shade into that period before he quit and became more interested in Philosophy than Jokes.

Simon Hoggart, "Worth Stealing From," in The Observer, *November 13, 1983, p. 32.*

ERIC KORN

[In his introduction to ***The Original Michael Frayn*** (see excerpt above)] James Fenton asserts that Frayn's early books are so esteemed and sought after as to be unfindable "in all the likely second-hand bookshops". Piqued, I searched my own stock: there was ***The Day of the Dog*** (1962), there ***The Book of Fub*** (1963), here was ***On the Outskirts*** (1964); but since someone, doubtless myself, had written "not for sale" / "do not borrow or steal" / "Lay off" on the flyleaves, I suppose Fenton's point stands. There is an eager audience of 1960s survivors who have been waiting to rediscover that piece about carry-cots, that one about Old English Cocktail olives (I must avoid going on like this), that deathless one entitled **"I said 'My name is "Ozzy" Manders, Dean of Kings'".** Young persons who know Frayn only as playwright or novelist will likewise be doing themselves a bad turn if they assume this recollection is only of archaeolgical or geriatric interest, though I cannot speak for anyone else's sense of humour and there is doubtless the odd curmudgeon in yurt or igloo who will not get a shock of joyful recognition.

Despite its subtitle, ***The Original Michael Frayn: Satirical Essays by Michael Frayn*** is not all satire. Such targets as Horace and Doris Morris, the upcreeping Lavinia and Christopher Crumble, Rollo Swavely and Christopher Smoothe, MP (by now doubtless Lord Lanolin of Blandford) are only peppered in passing: the more durable victims are those big enough to hit back, such as the Class of all Classes that Contains Itself (the epistemological pratfall, or "how do you know that there is fog on the motorway if it is too foggy to see the sign that says 'FOG'?"), or God the Father. . . .

Frayn's future, or rather future perfect, dramatic development is foreshadowed (this may be Fenton's doing) in a number of strikingly theatrical pieces, most notably where he exchanges the scalpel for the custard pie (wouldn't it be pleasant if there were shops where you could do that), the method of precision for the method of cumulation, the timing of the epigrammatist for that of the *farceur*. I have been recalling with hilarity for fifteen years (off and on, admittedly) a sequence of Christmas cards which recounts the history of two families as names add to, drop from, or swap between the list of addressees and the list of signatories. . . . I've just realized that the technique here is exactly that of the immortal cabin sequence in *A Night at the Opera,* when a hundred assorted seafarers successively cram into a tiny stateroom. (If Frayn sometimes has difficulty with endings, this is because this side of heaven, even the best of farces cannot end with a terminally wonderful climax: it can only detumesce when the audience and cast can't take any more.) Through the literary tropes and verbal felicities of these early writings, one hears, like a distant music, the cupboards, French windows, and bedroom doors opening and closing, and opening and closing, and opening. . . .

Eric Korn, "Farcical Goings-On," in The Times Literary Supplement, *No. 4218, February 3, 1984, p. 118.*

FELIX BARKER

Ibsen, to whom Michael Frayn gives glancing acknowledgement early in [***Benefactors***], found a symbolic affinity between architecture and life. Man's ambition to build high is one way of expressing his personal aspirations.

There are more than echoes of this idea in a play which shows domestic behaviour and emotions affected by what was happening in the architectural world of the 1960s. Fortunately Mr Frayn never pushes symbolism further than a high-rise building can safely go.

David (doubtless an Architectural Association graduate and apostle of Mies van der Rohe) is a dedicated architect faced with converting an awkward suburban site into a modern housing complex. He starts just at the time when public opinion is veering away from post-war tower blocks.

Ibsen's Master Builder Solness was unable to climb as high as he built; Frayn's David is prevented from building as high as he would like to climb. Both are frustrated in their aims. Both unwittingly sacrifice family life to their professional ideals.

So preoccupied is David with his project and the bureaucratic battles he has to fight that he fails to see that a married neighbour Sheila, an inadequate insecure woman, has fallen in love with him. (pp. 24-5)

David's wife Jane, a sensible, very 'together' mother, takes Sheila's infatuation in her stride; she is far more worried about what her husband is trying to achieve with his buildings. When he has no alternative but to compromise and changes his 'Basuto Road Scheme' from low-level housing to high-rise blocks (and finally to an office tower) she sides against him and joins the conservationists.

Mr Frayn starts a good many hares, but dissertion is always subordinated to humanity. This is an evening less concerned with message, symbolism and dramatic structure than with the way people behave. The perception of his observation of the four main characters—the two husbands and wives—is acute. Their vulnerability, guilt-complexes, concealed antagonisms, flashes of malice and minor bickerings are conveyed with absolute fidelity. We are left sighing sadly at the way intelligent, educated, basically nice people mismanage their lives, injure their feelings and fail to communicate. . . .

Benefactors marks a decisive further step in Mr Frayn's development as a major playwright. (p. 25)

Felix Barker, in a review of "Benefactors," in Plays & Players, *No. 369, June, 1984, pp. 24-5.*

JOHN SIMON

[***Benefactors***] is surely the most provocative drama I have seen in years. . . . [It] can be described as a strangely unsettling, tragic vaudeville. (p. 62)

[***Benefactors*** is] about ideas and counterideas, theories and countertheories held, consciously or unconsciously, by its four characters. Consciously or unconsciously, they help or hinder one another, never quite knowing which is, or will turn out to be, which. Most plainly, ***Benefactors*** is about change, about how people, circumstances, and history change, or don't change, or both do and don't, with everyone evaluating this differently, contradictorily and even self-contradictorily, and being both right and wrong, though exactly how nobody knows—not the characters, not the audience, not the author. It is also a play about good and evil, about what people want or do not want, and about whether they have to be told what they want before they can start wanting it. It is about the way private and public issues intermesh and interact, about how there are at least two bedeviling sides to absolutely everything, about what (and whether) happiness is, and about the sadness or funniness of it all, of one only knew which. But mostly, and obsessively, it is about change—about whether everything or nothing changes, or whether, perhaps, change is the ultimate changelessness. The only thing about which it is *not* is adultery, and that in itself should clue you in on how original it is.

Benefactors, finally, is a play about everything, by a man who undertakes to be Heraclitus, Thomas Love Peacock, Shaw, Chekhov, and Anouilh; if he is a bit less good than any of them at his specialty, he is a match for all of them in this pentathlon. My companion disliked but respected the play, and got an understandable headache from it. I found it highly intelligent but unlikable after Act I, extremely ingenious and troubling by the end. Which was only the beginning. I had no peace until I had bought and read the text, only then to be properly haunted by its artless-seeming wit, harmless-looking subversion, lucid insolubility. Creepingly, imperceptibly, it overpowers you. (pp. 62-3)

"Whenever one hears of a play by Chekhov one cannot quite place, it is a sure sign that somebody else has tried to trim down his untitled 1881 play to manageable size." ***Wild Honey*** would be no exception to Simon Karlinsky's axiom, except that . . . it really works. Here the immature but by no means worthless Chekhov is skillfully pared down and then ingeniously fleshed out by Michael Frayn, whose affinity with the Russian master has already yielded winning versions of *The Three Sisters* and *The Cherry Orchard*. Simply put, half a Chekhov and half a Frayn together spell a whole lot of not unalloyed but manifold pleasure.

David Magarshack's complete translation of Chekhov's posthumously published piece of juvenilia runs to 177 pages; I would guess that Frayn's text is a little over one-third that length. Several characters and much of the social aspect of the story about a careless female landowner letting a splendid estate fall into *nouveau riche* hands (familiar?) have been cut, but most of the tragicomic imbroglio involving Platonov, a disillusioned, shoddily Byronic country schoolteacher, the four women (including his wife) who love him, and the various men (including the husband of one of them, Platonov's friend) who unsuccessfully love some of these women has been preserved. The result is a melancholy round dance, a ludicrous chase, a battle of wits and nitwits all centering on Platonov (the name of this un-Platonic lover is itself a wry pun), who—a clever, charming narcissist—toys with them all and so becomes irresistible to all of the women and most of the men.

The key line from the original, as translated by Magarshack, is Platonov's "It wouldn't have been so bad if I'd killed them some other way, under the pressure of some monstrous passion, Spanish fashion. But somehow I've killed them so—stupidly, Russian fashion." In sum, this is a play about sham and waste, passion without passion, amorality further debased by mediocrity. Indeed, Platonov does not kill any of these women (though he is the indirect cause of a peripheral murder); rather, it is the women, collectively, who drive *him* to his death. With some help from the 21-year-old Chekhov, Frayn has couched this in plentiful, fresh wit—stocks, rather than gallows, humor, what with everyone entrapped in the viscosity and boredom of imperial Russia's provinces. Frayn also gets in a healthy dose of contemporary relevance without noticeable gimmickry or strain. . . .

Chekhov or Frayn, [***Wild Honey***] becomes a sterling addition to our all too limited repertoire of black but comely comedy. (p. 63)

John Simon, "Frayn and Refrayn," in New York *Magazine, Vol. 17, No. 35, September 3, 1984, pp. 62-3.*

CLIVE BARNES

Not for the first time I find myself wondering what a Michael Frayn play is really about. The wondering this time is occasioned by [***Benefactors***]. . . .

Frayn has pinned down his even carefully named people with seeming accuracy.

David Kitzinger . . . is a rising architect. Jane, his wife . . . , is an anthropologist, who helps him secretarially and also on the city-planning, human-resources aspects of his work.

Their friends, Colin Molyneux . . . , a not very successful journalist, and his wife Sheila . . . , a former nurse now simply a mildly incompetent housekeeper, are almost entirely dependent upon the Kitzingers.

The Molyneuxs and their children have become virtually part of a Kitzinger extended family. Yet the relationship is more symbiotic than might seem on the surface.

While the Molyneuxs may be parasites, they repay their hosts, their benefactors, in emotional terms. After all, each couple gives the other something to talk about.

But there are hidden depths lurking beneath our four people, even as they carefully perform roles, specially selected and adopted, for the games they play.

The depths are charged and explode when David gets an assignment from the local housing authority to redevelop a slum site in South London, and decides that the only way he can achieve the desired zoning density of 200 persons per acre is to build up, skywards.

He conceives a plan involving two slab blocks 50 stories high, which would be the tallest housing development ever conceived in Europe.

Colin opposes the plan—largely because he enviously hates his old college chum, and can see that the scheme runs against current popular opinion.

More interestingly, Jane, for purely humanistic reasons, favoring the rehabilitation of old neighborhoods rather than their total rebuilding, finds herself, also, more and more in opposition to her husband.

At the end the characters—"middle-aged children," someone calls them—have learned more about themselves than we have. Yet they have scarcely changed, merely interreacted predictably with trite circumstances.

At one point Frayn mentions Ibsen's *The Master Builder,* and it may be that, like Ibsen, in, say, *An Enemy of the People,* he is trying to contrast private action with public morality. But he doesn't do that.

His customary flair for theatricality here creaks just a little. The Pirandellian asides to the audience, often with the rest of the cast caught in a cinematic freeze-frame, and his characters' *Rashomon*-like views of differing perceptions of reality, are altogether too contrived. (p. 91)

Well, it is certainly good to have some kind of social drama on Broadway—but one wonders whether the drama is all that relevant or its characters all that immediate.

But it should be—given a little critical luck—a snob success, or *succes d'estime,* as they prefer to say in the business. (p. 92)

Clive Barnes, "'Benefactors'—Noises On," in New York Post, *December 23, 1985. Reprinted in* New York Theatre Critics' Reviews, *Vol. XXXXVI, No. 19, 1985, pp. 91-2.*

FRANK RICH

When last heard from, in the uproarious ***Noises Off,*** the English playwright Michael Frayn was demonstrating how the clockwork machinery of farce falls crazily apart when careless actors lose their props, drink too much and tumble down stairs. ***Benefactors,*** Mr. Frayn's equally dazzling new play . . . , would seem a complete departure: It's a comedy only in the darkest sense.

Yet the two works are connected—and not only by the extraordinary talent of their author or by the superbly acted productions, both under the unerring direction of Michael Blakemore, that have brought them to New York. As ***Noises Off*** was set within the perfect order of theatrical farce, so ***Benefactors*** unfolds within the idealized order of modern liberal society: the setting is a late 1960's London community of happy families, good neighbors and utopian political credos. But in this world—the real world, not the theatre—it's a matter for heartbreak, not laughter, when people get careless. It is, as one character explains, "like one of those bad dreams when you suddenly realize something has gone wrong." What comes crashing down in ***Benefactors*** are marriages, principles and, most unsettling of all, man's plaintive and often sustaining faith in personal and social change.

"People—that's what wrecks all our plans," says Mr. Frayn's protagonist, David . . . , a well-meaning architect who dreams of "building the new world we're all going to be living in." ***Benefactors*** tells of how David designs a redevelopment project for a South London slum neighborhood known as Basuto Road—only to discover that practicalities breed compromise ("In the end, it's not art, it's mathematics'') and that the beneficiaries of his scheme don't even want the ''New York-style skyscrapers'' he envisions for them. . . .

Such is Mr. Frayn's prowess as a theatrical architect that ***Benefactors*** has as many levels as David's projected housing towers. This is not a problem play about urban planning, and neither is it a domestic drama about a would-be extramarital love triangle. Told in flashback 10 or 15 years after the events it describes—and narrated, in turn, by each of the four characters—this prismatic work circumscribes the disillusionment of an era, no less American than English, in which grandiose dreams of a universally benevolent democracy died. ''Basuto Road. There's the whole history of human ideas in that one name,'' says David. Basuto Road—which dates back to the 19th century, when England still had its African empire—eventually stands as a comic graveyard not merely for the vanished imperial West but also for the dashed hopes of the enlightened welfare state that replaced it.

Mr. Frayn dramatizes his dour view of civilization in both public and private configurations. As the title indicates, everyone in ***Benefactors*** wants to help other people. Although on opposite sides of the skyscraper debate, both David and Colin see themselves as helping the city and the poor. As nearly inseparable neighbors, each couple presumes to be helping to prop up the rocky marriage of the other. But Mr. Frayn upholds the principle, as Colin states it, ''that other people's lives are at least as complicated as your own.'' Is David really trying to build a better world in Basuto Road, or is he merely erecting (pun intended by the playwright) a monument to his own ego? In protesting David's plans, is Colin fighting for social good or venting his jealousy at a more successful friend? Which marriage, if either, is really unhappy? Which characters are really the do-gooders, which the destroyers?

The answers to these and other questions keep changing, never to be firmly resolved. The evening's final image—of David overhearing a poor Basuto Road woman laughing, but having no idea of ''what she was laughing about''—is emblematic of the entire work. Just as the schemes of social reformers can fail because the reformers don't understand the people they want to help, so Mr. Frayn's two couples constantly misjudge each other, naïvely mistaking evil for good, selfishness for charity. The characters kill with kindness as often as they help, and, for all their daily intimacies, remain strangers. . . .

In favor of benefaction but despairing of its attainment, Mr. Frayn aches for all four characters and for the unseen inhabitants of Basuto Road. The engineering term ''progressive collapse''—a potential calamity in high-rise structures—carries a sad double meaning throughout the evening. Mr. Frayn doesn't see society or his characters progressing. At the end we do hear much talk about rehabilitation and change—and, indeed, in the plot sense, all four lives (as well as ''public opinion'' about urban development) have been dramatically altered. But the people haven't so much changed as adjusted (with or without psychiatric help).

''Life goes around like a wheel,'' says Colin. ''People don't know what they want until they've got it,'' says Sheila. According to David, even ''new and amazing'' architecture leaves a site looking ''the same as before.'' Its allusions to *The Master Builder* notwithstanding, ***Benefactors*** is particularly reminiscent of Chekhov (of whom Mr. Frayne is a foremost translator). The evening's chipper ending, in which survival and wisdom prove to be life's pyrrhic victories, is about as happy as that of *The Sea Gull*.

The writing in ***Benefactors*** is as meticulously conceived in a witty, poetic vein as the farcical mechanics were in ***Noises Off***. The imagery of the opening monologue—with its delicate play of clouds and sunlight, present and past—establishes the kaleidoscopic method used throughout. . . . Although Act I still feels a bit attenuated, the recast New York ***Benefactors*** seems to exceed the London version in speed and warmth.

Frank Rich, ''Dreams Die Hard,'' in The New York Times, *December 23, 1985, p. C11.*

LEO SAUVAGE

Michael Frayn occupies a major place in today's British theater. His superb farce, ***Noises Off,*** was also enjoyed in New York and in Paris as much as in London. Other writings of his in different genres have resounded internationally, too. So it is not surprising that Broadway eagerly awaited the arrival this season of a new Frayn production [***Benefactors***]—praised in advance as deeply moving and a serious drama of ideas.

Far less clear to me is why ***Benefactors*** . . . is a solid hit. One indeed may wonder where the seriousness lies and what ideas are embodied here, or even whether Frayn's old-fashioned do-gooders do well enough on stage to justify a poorly put together work.

David . . . is an architect in charge of designing a public housing project for a low-income section of London. As in most Western European cities, repairing the devastation World War II caused has been followed in the British capital by a preoccupation with eliminating urban blight. Yet, again as on the Continent, private interests, political chicanery, bureaucratic bumbling, and/or architectural incompetence have turned many renewal undertakings into esthetic and social disasters. And according to a highfalutin monologue David begins in getting the evening under way, the playwright means to deal with this phenomenon.

Thrice restarted, the rather dreary monologue is about the Basuto Road development David envisions. Although the speech threads through practically the entire first act, it remains a pseudo-philosophical digression in a two-act play ultimately more concerned with the problems faced by a married couple unable to make a difficult decision than with urban scheming. (p. 21)

Actually, ***Benefactors*** itself is a combination of two plays, one based on socio-political, the other on domestic-psychological dilemmas. Neither is terribly original. Moreover, like his characters, the author appears unable to make up his mind about where he stands. Anthropologist Jane, for instance, works mostly in the kitchen serving her husband and their guests. She is a paragon of tolerance, devoid of any feminist awareness. That impression lasts until Jane suddenly decides to go out and agitate against her husband's project. Then, back in the kitchen, she tosses boiling stew into Colin's face. Perhaps she doesn't like the way he treats his wife. Perhaps her turning on him is an expression of loyalty to David. Or perhaps she has been aroused by her political ally's insinuation that David is sleeping with Sheila.

After Colin badly loses his election, receiving a pitiful 183 votes, we are asked by Frayn to sympathize, for loathsome as he is, Colin represents the opposition of the urban poor to crushing high-rise projects. Having punished him for meanness while ennobling his revolt against bureaucracy, the author next abandons well-intentioned Jane and David to their hopeless mediocrity and has Colin write an article attacking what he terms the arrogance of "foreign born" developers.

The cast of characters provides only first names for the couples. But from the action it is possible to grasp that David's patronymic is vaguely German-Jewish. Colin's surname is Molyneux. I do not know what Frayn intended, but the implication is a leading one, pointing to yet a third dramatic theme whose presence adds to the existing confusion. (pp. 21-2)

Leo Sauvage, "Mixed Manners," in The New Leader, *Vol. LXIX, No. 3, February 10, 1986, pp. 21-2.*

CLIVE BARNES

Imagine the craziest scene of amorous desperation—four screaming wronged women, one screaming self-pitying philanderer, a few half-empty bottles of vodka, a brother, a husband, a rejected suitor, a revolver, a law messenger, and an express train waiting in the wings. Of course it's Russian.

What a strange, wicked, funny play is Michael Frayn's ***Wild Honey.*** In a sense—more than a sense, a striking reality—it is properly speaking a play by Chekhov adapted by Frayn, but the strange thing about it is that Frayn has made it completely his own, without taking away anything from Chekhov. . . .

It's a terrific evening—but let's get some housekeeping historic facts behind us first before explaining just how terrific.

When he was in his early 20s, Chekhov left this play—or at least its basis—in manuscript. The title-page was lost, so we don't even know what he intended to call it.

The manuscript, written in Chekhov's own hand, was discovered in a Moscow bank vault in 1920, but it was not until 1954 that it was performed—and then in Sweden in Swedish.

French and Italian productions soon followed, and in 1960 it was given in Moscow, New York and London. I missed the New York Off-Broadway production, called *A Country Scandal,* but remember clearly the London version, going under the name of *Platonov*. . . .

I enjoyed . . . the play . . . a great deal at the time, but was unprepared for the swift certainty and authority of this new Frayn adaptation. . . .

The thing that has to strike everyone about this play is the uncanny manner in which it presages themes and characters in the later Chekhov canon.

The country estate threatened by Russia's new entrepreneurial developers, the aimless people dreaming of love, destiny and Russia, the shiftless hero, the flighty widow, the wife trying to poison herself, the drunken doctor—the play is like a trailer to Chekhov's dramatic future.

But Frayn has ensured that the play stands up here and now in its own right. He has avoided that specific tragi-comedy mood, where pathos blends with laughter, that we even call Chekhovian, in favor of a more directly farcical approach.

The humor was there in Chekhov to start with—it was evident enough in the Dmitri Makaroff adaptation used by George Devine and John Blatchley for Harrison—but Frayn has both broadened and sharpened it.

The play is now less like Chekhov's *Ivanov* and more like a Feydeau farce. And in the middle of it is this cosmically comic character, Platonov, one of nature's fools madly in love with love and himself, doomed like Anna Karenina to reap the steel harvest of an unhappy family.

This Platonov is a Frayn hero rather than a figure of Chekhov—simply he lacks what every properly bred Chekhov hero must have, an overdeveloped ability for introspection. The most introspective act of which Platonov is capable is to look in a mirror and weep.

Platonov apart, the characters are distinctly more Chekhovian—even if the merry widow is a little too red-blooded in her lusts for walks through the cherry orchard—but the speed of the action, the interleaving of the farce, is more like Frayn. . . .

This is one of the best evenings in the theater Broadway has given us over the past few years.

Clive Barnes, "'Honey' of a Farce," in New York Post, *December 19, 1986. Reprinted in* New York Theatre Critics' Reviews, *Vol. XXXXVII, No. 17, 1986, p. 105.*

JOHN BEAUFORT

[***Wild Honey***] is a triumph of bravura performance and inventive theatricalism. Michael Frayn, whose credits include ***Noises Off*** and ***Benefactors,*** has radically revised an early untitled play by Anton Chekhov, while remaining substantially faithful to the principal characters, relationships, and spirit of the original. (p. 107)

In his introduction to the published text of ***Wild Honey,*** Mr. Frayn estimates that the overwritten original would have run something like six hours, "with too many characters, too many disparate themes and aims, and too much action. It is trying to be simultaneously a sexual comedy, a moral tract, a melodrama, a state-of-Russia play, and a tragedy." Even in its present two-act form, the adaptation lasts for nearly three hours.

While Chekhov's fledgling effort contains hints of the great later plays (notably *The Cherry Orchard*), the central character of schoolmaster Platonov . . . remains what Frayn has called "overwhelmingly, wonderfully, appallingly" himself, an original.

Platonov's decline from brilliant university student to provincial schoolmaster and local eccentric conditions a character whose wit and arrogance coexist with his misgivings and disappointments. His life has been a promissory note which never paid off in the way his friends expected.

Sofya, the young newly married woman whom he later seduces, asks him, "Why haven't you . . . done better?" Platonov admits that there was nothing to prevent him from achieving something worthwhile but "the question is whether there was ever anything to be stopped. I wasn't put in the world to do things. I was put here to prevent others from doing them."

That is Platonov's intellectual malaise, for which irony provides no solace. But it is his moral instability that is more perilous to the women who are drawn to him. He resists having an affair with Anna Petrovna . . . , the handsome widow on whose provincial estate the action takes place. But he allows himself to philander with the aforementioned Sofya . . . , the pretty wife of his best friend, Sergey. . . . He treats his faithful wife, Sasha . . . , abominably and has a teasing relationship with Marya Grekova . . . , a bespectacled chemistry student.

Platonov's incorrigible behavior takes place amid the comic-melodramatic-atmospheric-tragic context indicated by Frayn in his introduction. The characters banter, argue, and philosophize; eat and overimbibe; take off into the birch forest that forms a permanent background for the changing scenes.

Wild Honey ranges in mood from the genuinely affecting to a farcicality with Gallic—or perhaps one should say Anglo-Gallic—flourishes. Not for the first time, the Russian soul reveals a funny bone. (pp. 107-08)

John Beaufort, "Slimming Down a Chekhov Play That Needed It," in The Christian Science Monitor, *December 22, 1986. Reprinted in* New York Theatre Critics' Reviews, *Vol. XXXXVII, No. 17, 1986, pp. 107-08.*

MEL GUSSOW

Writing about Chekhov's first extant full-length play, Henri Troyat (in his biography, *Chekhov*) says, "For all its melodrama, chaos and verbosity, this immature work contains all the great Chekhovian themes in embryo." Acting as Chekhov's collaborator and editor, Michael Frayn has reduced the melodrama, trimmed the verbosity and made the chaos seem more comic. The result, ***Wild Honey,*** is one of those rare adaptations that is faithful to the spirit, if not the letter, of the original. The play draws strength from the dual authorship—the young Chekhov's ebullience and incipient sensibility, combined with Mr. Frayn's knowledge of dramaturgy. If Chekhov had had the time and the inclination to revise and polish his early play, it might have become ***Wild Honey***—the comedy that Chekhov never wrote. . . .

In ***Wild Honey*** are the concerns that were to obsess Chekhov throughout his life's work. Women are starved for love and purpose (as in *The Three Sisters*). The hero, Mikhail Platonov, is trapped—trapping himself—in the role of seducer. Platonov is the dramatic progenitor of Ivanov and, later, of Trigorin in *The Sea Gull,* and Astrov in *Uncle Vanya,* men who become the obsessive object of female desire. Though the characters have different professions and different perspectives on their predicament, they all share a lassitude even as others extol them for their charisma. In contrast, there is Sergey in ***Wild Honey,*** whom Platonov casually cuckolds, the first in a line of self-dramatizing Chekhovian failures, flailing themselves with their own ineptitude while idly dreaming of a life of poetry and commitment. From Sergey, it is but a step to Uncle Vanya himself. . . .

As Chekhov matured, his characters refrained from histrionics. Farce was replaced by comedy emerging more from character, and people were less prone to philosophize at length, although they never stopped saying how bored they were. In his early plays, Chekhov was not yet fully aware that important things could be said without words, through indirection. In his adaptation, Mr. Frayn has the double obligation of keeping the youthful freshness of the work while removing the awkwardness of Chekhov's apprenticeship.

In order to understand the progression of the play from discarded manuscript in Chekhov's time to the Michael Frayn adaptation on Broadway, I looked at three published scripts: David Magarshack's unabridged translation, entitled *Platonov;* Alex Szogyi's abbreviated translation, produced Off Broadway in 1960 as *A Country Scandal;* and ***Wild Honey.*** The first is impossibly long and discursive, a full four acts and five scenes. Mr. Szogyi brings the play down to manageable performance length while following the structure of the original. In his ending, Platonov is not shot (as in the original), but dies of fright. The version is broad to the point of being farcical. With boldness, Mr. Frayn has served both as translator and adapter, excising minor characters, shifting scenes and locations and rewriting both the beginning and ending. Almost all of the second act now takes place in Platonov's schoolroom-home. The Frayn finale, neither homicide nor fright, is more dramatic as well as more symbolic. Platonov is less a manipulator than a victim of circumstance.

In contrast to previous translators, Mr. Frayn is himself an accomplished playwright as well as a Russian scholar. The language flows, as it does in Mr. Frayn's own plays—although the territory is far removed in style as well as content from that of ***Noises Off*** and ***Benefactors.*** Just as Tom Stoppard has demonstrated a kinship with the work of Arthur Schnitzler, Mr. Frayn has an affinity for the Russians—Tolstoy as well as Chekhov. The tone of ***Wild Honey*** is Chekhovian, with a Frayn comic twist. (p. 4)

Mel Gussow, "Distilling the Heady Flavor of Early Chekhov," in The New York Times, *December 28, 1986, pp. 4, 10.*

JOHN SIMON

Whichever way you slice it, ***Wild Honey*** is a play divided against itself. Written by Chekhov at, apparently, age 21, it was posthumously discovered in a manuscript without title page or title but with numerous corrections. . . . Huge and unwieldy, *Platonov* (as it is usually called) has been cut and adapted for production before, but never more boldly than by Michael Frayn (who, by the way, knows Russian), under its present, more erotic title. ***Wild Honey*** falls midway between not-quite-ripe *Cherry Orchard* and less joyously noisy ***Noises Off,*** and is, for all its faults, the best thing Fraykhov ever wrote: charming, funny, and deeply melancholy. . . .

The complete text of *Platonov,* as translated by David Magarshack, immerses one in 200 turgid pages, twenty confusing characters, and two different plays. . . .

But the two plays, and their variously satirical and wistful, outrageous and agonized tones, do not mesh into what was to become Chekhov's way, succinctly defined by Peter Szondi as a "resignation in which yearning and irony combine into a middle position." Nor could the adaptation, however ingenious, bridge the gap without wholly discarding the Chekhovian blueprint or forgetting all Frayn has digested—from Feydeau to the theater of the absurd—for the sake of a lost, by now inconceivable simplicity. (p. 49)

Chekhov has Platonov say, "Only those novels have happy endings in which I'm not the hero." Not bad, but how much better is Frayn's "The only stories that end happily are the ones that don't have me in them." Again, trying to ward off Anna's advances, Chekhov's Platonov concedes, "We may perhaps meet again many, many years hence, when both of us will be able to laugh and shed senile tears over these days." How much stronger is ". . . .when we're both old—old enough to laugh together and shed an ancient tear or two over the past. As the present will mercifully have become." Fraykhov is not nearly so good as the mature Chekhov, or even as Frayn without

Chekhov (though there is much funny stuff here that is pure Frayn and not in the original), but there is also a civilized, weary, heedless poetry that flashes forth from time to time with a brightness way beyond a Neil Simon's. (pp. 49-50)

John Simon, "Milking Honey," in New York *Magazine, Vol. 20, No. 1, January 5, 1987, pp. 49-50.*

ROBERT BRUSTEIN

Frayn is being praised again, this time for having taken an early and presumably useless piece of Chekhov juvenilia and transformed it into a usable theatrical vehicle called ***Wild Honey.*** I can speak with a little more authority about this production, since I actually *saw* it in Los Angeles before the New York opening, and I can say without hesitation that it's unbearable. The play already enjoys a number of perfectly decent adaptations under such titles as *Platonov* and *Don Juan in the Russian Manner,* the most effective being Alex Szogyi's *A Country Scandal*. This one . . . turns the play into an artificial sex comedy, a bubble-headed Feydeau farce.

I don't want to sound too custodial here; the play is hardly a neglected masterpiece. Chekhov destroyed the original manuscript when it was rejected by a Russian actress; what we have is a voluminous early draft, more valuable to scholars than to spectators. Still, one has to watch the damned thing on stage, with everyone circling each other like windup china figures. . . . Recognizing the power of old Pearl White thrillers, Frayn puts a choo-choo train on stage and makes Platonov commit suicide by throwing himself, smiling, onto the tracks. For all I cared about any of these artificial people, they could all have been run over by a train. (p. 29)

Robert Brustein, "Snarls from the Bedclothes," in The New Republic, *Vol. 196, No. 5, February 2, 1987, pp. 27-9.*

Gabriel (José) García Márquez

1928-

Colombian novelist, short story writer, journalist, critic, and scriptwriter.

Nobel laureate García Márquez is included among the group of South American writers who rose to prominence during the 1960s, a period of fruition often referred to as the ''boom'' of Latin American literature. Like Julio Cortázar and Ernesto Sabato, García Márquez wrote fiction for many years before gaining international recognition. The almost simultaneous publication of major works by these three authors, together with the appearance of skillful first novels by Carlos Fuentes and Mario Vargas Llosa and the acknowledged importance of such writers as Jorge Luis Borges and Pablo Neruda, led to recognition of Latin American letters as a potent force in contemporary literature. García Márquez's enthusiastic critical reception is usually attributed to the imaginative blend of history, politics, social realism, and fantasy displayed in his work. He often makes use of techniques of magic realism, embellishing his works with surreal events and fantastic imagery to obscure the distinctions between illusion and reality which, he implies, define human existence.

García Márquez was born in Aracataca, Colombia, where he lived for the first eight years of his life with his grandparents. The storytelling of his grandmother, the long decline of Aracataca, and the myths and superstitions of the townspeople all played major roles in shaping García Márquez's imagination. He became a journalist in the late 1940s, an occupation which led to travels in South America, Europe, and the United States. During these years, García Márquez wrote short stories in which he introduced Macondo, a fictional village based on Aracataca. Macondo's richly imagined locale and colorful characters have drawn frequent critical comparisons to William Faulkner's mythical Yoknapatawpha County, and García Márquez has acknowledged the influence of Faulkner's work on his fiction.

García Márquez's early short stories were written in the late 1940s and early 1950s and are collected in such retrospective volumes as *Leaf Storm and Other Stories* (1972), *Ojos de perro azul* (1972), and *La increíble y triste historia de la cándida Eréndira y de su abuela desalmada* (1972; *Innocent Eréndira and Other Stories*). These pieces have been compared to the works of Franz Kafka for García Márquez's dreamlike presentation. *El coronel no tiene quien le escriba* (1961), a novella included in the short story collection *No One Writes to the Colonel and Other Stories* (1968), was praised for García Márquez's insight into solitude, a recurring theme in his fiction. This condition is expressed through the character of a retired colonel, who waits with unflagging determination for news of his government pension. The title story of the short fiction collection *Los funerales de la Mamá Grande* (1962; *Big Mama's Funeral*) is one of García Márquez's first works to combine realism with myth and fantasy, thus lending a social and political dimension to fantastic events. Although critics disagreed as to the ultimate literary importance of García Márquez's *Collected Stories* (1985), Charles Champlin deemed the pieces contained in the volume ''precociously successful exercises in craft,'' and John Updike praised them as ''rich and startling in their matter and confident and elegant in their manner.''

© Lutfi Özkök

In his first novel, *La mala hora* (1961; *In Evil Hour*), García Márquez uses a montage-like narrative style to depict a backwater town torn by political oppression and moral corruption while also documenting *la violencia,* a state of violence which occurred in Colombia during the 1950s. García Márquez won immediate international acclaim and popularity with the publication of *Cien años de soledad* (1967; *One Hundred Years of Solitude*). This novel, which John Leonard called ''a recapitulation of our evolutionary and intellectual experience,'' chronicles the history of Macondo, from its harmonious beginnings under founder José Arcadio Buendía to its increasingly chaotic decline through six generations of descendants. The novel presents Macondo as a microcosm of Colombia and, by extension, of South America and the world. In addition to reflecting the political, social, and economic ills of South America, the novel is replete with fantastic events; for example, a baby is born with a pig's tail. Characterized by nonlinear narration and long, free-flowing sentences, *One Hundred Years of Solitude* is acknowledged as a comic masterpiece for its labyrinthine structure, epic scope, and stylistic complexity. Pablo Neruda called the book ''the greatest revelation in the Spanish language since the *Don Quixote* of Cervantes.''

García Márquez's next novel, *El otoño del patriarca* (1975; *The Autumn of the Patriarch*), depicts the evils of despotism as embodied in an unloved dictator, with solitude again emerging as a prominent theme. Described by García Márquez as "a perfect integration of journalism and literature," the novel represents a powerful political statement against totalitarianism and a poignant evocation of loneliness. This work is written as a phantasmagorical narrative in which shifting viewpoint and extensive use of hyperbole enhance comedic and horrific effects. Following the publication of *The Autumn of the Patriarch,* García Márquez vowed that he would issue no new fiction until Chile's Pinochet regime was either disbanded or overthrown. Following a six-year hiatus, he published *Crónica de una muerte anunciada* (1982; *Chronicle of a Death Foretold*), a fictionalized journalistic investigation embellished with stylistic devices common in his fiction. The story centers upon a murder that occurred twenty-seven years earlier and reportedly involved people with whom García Márquez was acquainted. Presenting eyewitness accounts that ultimately prove unreliable within shifting time sequences and a surreal atmosphere, *Chronicle of a Death Foretold* examines a tragedy that is fostered rather than averted by the inhabitants of a backwater community. Most critics interpreted the novella as a profile of a society trapped in its own myths, either unable to overcome the outmoded customs of its forebears or unable to triumph over fate.

Relato de un náufrago (1970; *The Story of a Shipwrecked Sailor*) was originally ghost-written by García Márquez in 1955 during a stint as a news reporter and film critic for the Bogotá daily newspaper *El espectador*. Recently translated, the book relates the survival of Luis Alejandro Velasco, a sailor who became a national hero after being washed overboard from the Colombian destroyer *Caldas* and surviving his ordeal at sea. After Velasco revealed to *El espectador* that the destroyer listed in heavy seas due to contraband appliances stacked on its decks, in opposition to official Colombian reports, Velasco was forced to leave the Colombian navy and *El espectador* ceased publication by decree of the government of General Gustavo Rojas Pinilla. According to Mario Vargas Llosa, *The Story of a Shipwrecked Sailor* "has a cleanness and sureness of touch which reveal that [García Márquez] has more gifts as a storyteller than a journalist."

(See also *CLC*, Vols. 2, 3, 8, 10, 15, 27; *Contemporary Authors,* Vols. 33-36, rev. ed.; and *Contemporary Authors New Revision Series,* Vol. 10.)

JULIO ORTEGA

[*The essay from which this excerpt is taken was originally published in Spanish in Ortega's study* La contemplación y la fiesta *in 1969.*]

In addition to its obvious quality, part of the great success of ***One Hundred Years of Solitude*** can be attributed to the fact that it is a lengthy tribute to the reader. This novel demands and obtains the best from each reader; it tests the reader's availability and then assaults and transforms it by transgressing verisimilitude, exciting the imagination, motivating the sensibilities, demanding a sense of humor, and evoking compassion. It also demands that a historical parallel be established with its scheme, with the century of Latin-American events whose vast possibilities of pain and happiness end in death and destruction. . . . The history of Macondo is another version of the Latin-American past, but it is in the novel itself—between the foundings and the apocalypse—that these births and destructions have their own scheme, motivation, and subtle dialectics.

These relationships between different worlds and times form the central structure of [***One Hundred Years of Solitude***]. This structure includes at least four sequences of worlds and times: (1) the mythical world and time of the founders; (2) the historical world and time ushered in by Aureliano Buendía and his wars; (3) the cyclical time of the old age and death of the initial characters and their world changed by the insertion of Macondo into a vaster reality; and (4) the deterioration of Macondo, *axis mundi,* by the depleting effect of the exchange of its reality of the external world and time, which is tantamount also to the extinction of the family line, the axis of Macondo. Let us examine these relationships in some detail.

The mythical world and time of Macondo's foundation implies a search for a lost paradise. Hoping to reach the sea, José Arcadio Buendía, patriarch and founder, has undertaken, together with various other families, an exodus through the jungle. (pp. 85-6)

This search, which can be seen as a search for a paradise, is not necessarily equivalent to a religious undertaking. It suggests above all the drive toward the rediscovery of the world, the need to conquer that world through a primordial identity, the dream of reestablishing an original reality. Thus, the journey and the founding are placed in the context of ritual. José Arcadio Buendía decides to leave his village after he kills Prudencio Aguilar to destroy the rumors of Buendía's unconsummated marriage. Already in the motivation of this journey, in this self-imposed expulsion, a ritual begins to form. This episode takes on even greater significance from the fact that Ursula, José Arcadio's wife, is his cousin; they are equivalent to the primordial couple. For this reason of kinship she tries to insist on not consummating the marriage, horrified by the curse of giving birth to a child with a pig's tail. The sin and punishment of an amorous relationship that is also a blood relationship thus appear at the beginning of this journey. The son is born without the feared pig's tail, but José Arcadio Buendía has killed a man in order to kill a rumor, and his guilty conscience drives him to undertake the journey, to expel himself from the village. The sense of humor with which Gabriel García Márquez relates these incidents and the way he expands them through hyperbole should not prevent our recognizing in them the roots and rituals of an archetypal fantasy: the guilt of love, the expulsion, the search for another world, the pursuit of another innocence. (p. 86)

In this primordial zone the world is organized archetypically: objects emerge for the first time; José Arcadio Buendía discovers through his own calculations that the world is round; death is still unknown ("The world was so recent that many things lacked names, and in order to indicate them it was necessary to point"); Macondo appears to be an island; and Colonel Aureliano Buendía reports that the region is surrounded by water. This isolated world is sustained by the fantasy of José Arcadio Buendía and by the presence of Melquíades, the magician, a sort of internal author of the work, a hyperbole of the author himself. An unrestrained desire for knowledge leads José Arcadio Buendía to experiment constantly with magnets, magnifying lenses, and maps. This quest is another mythical dream: the need for science, for knowledge. (p. 87)

José Arcadio Buendía announces the end of the mythical time when he states that "it's Monday" on a Tuesday and continues to affirm this even on Friday. . . . From the point of view of the other characters it is in fact not Monday, but in a mythical world time is not linear. Consequently, José Arcadio Buendía is taken for mad and tied to a chestnut tree, where he dies. But actually he does not die. Tied to the tree of life, the enormous patriarch is still the founder, the Father. Melquíades, a sort of serpent who invites his audience to eat of the fruits of science, also dies without dying. He is rejuvenated in the sacred zone of that world, the room of the successive alchemists in which Melquíades has written the history of Macondo and of the Buendías, his prophesies, which are the novel itself. Ursula, the mother, while being perhaps the most pragmatic character in this world, is also an archetypal character. With the exception of her initial march through the swamps, she is the only character who does not experience any transformation apart from that of aging. As the Mother, she is a mirror that reflects the events occurring around her.

After this mythical time, Colonel Aureliano Buendía's wars indicate that Macondo has become part of a more concrete, historical time. Time becomes historical as Macondo's second generation witnesses the expansion of its world. This historical time reveals its political dichotomies and its elements of social injustice in the banana company's transformation of the village through its methods of extortion. Macondo's world is infiltrated by a conflictive, outside world. In the mythical world time was a norm, and the narrator says, "time put everything in its place." In the world transformed by history, on the other hand, time is equivalent to chaos, and the narrator states, "time finally confused everything."

The ludicrous thirty-two armed uprisings instigated and lost by Colonel Aureliano Buendía, the contradictory fortunes of rebellion and politics, and the eventual destruction of Aureliano, who is bewildered by the hidden factors of power, suggest in the novel the madness threatening this history, as well as its deep confusion and its destructive thrust. The thirst for justice becomes in the end, a blind slaughter. (pp. 87-8)

As this historical time draws to a close, time becomes a spiral and cyclically recovers the world. In this world the notion of time is governed by the recollections of the characters: old age recalls a bygone time. When Aureliano Segundo asks Ursula if what he has read in the history left by Melquíades is true, "she answered him that it was, that many years ago the gypsies had brought magic lamps and flying mats to Macondo. 'What's happening,' she sighed, 'is that the world is slowly coming to an end and those things don't come here any more.'" (p. 88)

[Cyclical time as] suggested by the repetition of the family line is something akin to a game of mirrors. . . . When José Arcadio Segundo announces that he is setting out for the coast to search for a Spanish galleon that had gone aground many years earlier, Ursula shouts: "I know all of this by heart. It's as if time had turned around and we were back at the beginning." . . . Aureliano Triste plans to build a railroad and draws a sketch on the table: "Looking at the sketch that Aureliano Triste drew on the table and that was a direct descendent of the plans with which José Arcadio Buendía had illustrated his project for solar warfare, Ursula confirmed her impression that time was going in a circle."

At the vortex of this spinning time, Ursula can now judge the history of her family; she becomes aware of the full presence of her descendants and understands them for the first time. She realizes Aureliano had fought all his wars out of "pure and sinful pride" and because he was incapable of loving. . . . In this time she also realizes "that her clumsiness was not the first victory of decrepitude and darkness but a sentence passed by time. She thought previously, when God did not make the same traps out of the months and years that the Turks used when they measured a yard of percale, things were different." She wants then to allow herself "an instant of rebellion" as a protest for "over a century of conformity." . . . Thus, judging a depleted time, the Mother points to herself as the center of the enormous failure of a century destroyed by conformity.

This cyclical time, like the mythical time before it, brings out the recurring theme of the symbols, of the objects that become archetypes: the Colonel makes little gold fish that he then melts and pounds again into little fish, and Amaranta laboriously weaves her own shroud. This entire time, then, is filled with echoes, it is infiltrated by previous times and worlds. "It's as though the world was going in circles," Ursula says, because time repeats itself.

The death of the characters returns the mythical world to a reality complicated by experience. Death, like love, war, solitude, and the other factors affecting the life of the characters, is also transfigured in this novel through hyperbole. Thus the narrator always transfers us to another reference, to a new possibility of its thematization. In this zone in which the novel turns on itself, the possibilities of death also suggest the allegorical context that suddenly summarizes the life of a character. Raveling and unraveling time through the little gold fish he manufactures, before he dies Colonel Aureliano Buendía hears the shouting of the children and the music of the circus. . . . Aureliano sees in the circus the parable of his own life. As the fanfare ends he recognizes his solitude in the emptiness of the street. He derisively urinates on the tree of life, where the presence of his father can still be felt, and dies leaning against the tree. (pp. 89-90)

Caught in this spiral of time, the world begins to deteriorate when the family line, which is its axis, goes into a rapid decline. The expectant fullness of the mythical world and the fabulous confusion of the historical world are replaced by a decaying reality, by a decline leading to total destruction. (p. 91)

Macondo ages with the war and is rejuvenated by the banana boom, but its history demands destruction. The shifting realities and the comings and goings of its characters slowly bring about its decay. . . . The last descendants of the line of the Buendías love each other with the courage their ancestors failed to show, but they also bring about the end. They do not realize that they are aunt and nephew, and their child is born with a pig's tail. Amaranta Ursula dies in childbirth, and Aureliano sees his son transformed into "a dry and bloated bag of skin" dragged away by the ants. Then he recalls the epigraph on the parchments left by Melquíades: *"The first of the line is tied to a tree and the last is being eaten by the ants."* Studying the parchments again, he realizes that "Melquíades had not put events in the conventional time, but had concentrated a century of daily episodes in such a way that they coexisted in one instant." Reading the parchments, he discovers in them his own fate, his imminent death. A wind destroys Macondo, "the city of mirrors (or mirages)." In reading the parchments, in reading the novel itself, this character reads himself. The ancient metaphor of the "book of life" thus closes the world and time.

García Márquez has explained that ***One Hundred Years of Solitude*** is the story of a family trying to avoid the birth of a son with a pig's tail. He has stated that this is the unity of the novel, but aside from being an internal motivation, it would appear that this fear is just another thread in the plot. The unity of the novel, its coherence, is actually found in its structure, in its formulation. The stories of the various characters are interwoven by the author's skillful manipulation of a structure based on temporal discontinuity.

According to García Márquez, this novel was initially developed following a chronological sequence, but he soon realized that it was impossible to write a linear history of Macondo and the Buendías. The key to this structure is found in the sentence that attributes to Melquíades the arrangement of events to coexist in one instant (discontinuous time), rather than in the order of man's conventional, chronological time. The daily episodes of an entire century thus unfold at the same time, because the time of this novel is sustained by the time of reading: the reader constructs the temporality of the novel as he relinquishes his chronological notions of time. Hence the presence of the future in the present time of the narrative, a present time embedded in a weightless past, since the perspective of this writing requires the discourse of the chronicle. The temporal discontinuities, the leaps in time that juggle this century of episodes, are underscored by the profuse use of formulas such as "every year," "many years later," "long hours," "several years," "in a few years," "several centuries later," "for several weeks," and so on, formulas that never clearly state a temporal measurement but that insinuate it by broadening the reverberations of time, insuring a continuity that in fact is essentially temporal. In addition, these formulas evoke the narrative tone of legends and thus introduce a convention of verisimilitude at the very core of the fantasy. In this novel the play of reality and fantasy is never dual; the narrative presence of the temporal compels "fantasy" to be a part of "reality," to be a spontaneous possibility of it.

Fantasy and reality constantly shift back and forth within the only web they form, underscoring the various worlds of the characters. (pp. 91-2)

It is more frequent, however, to find the immediate reality being extended in fantasy, which is its echo, its own vision. The mechanism of this extension is hyperbole. Fantastic elements are routinely introduced directly into the narrative. . . . This method of evoking the realm of the fantastic, which is a primary clue to the reading of this novel, is based on humor and on a sense of amazement and of the dramatic, as illustrated by the rain of flowers at José Arcadio Buendía's burial, the ascension of Remedios the Beauty, and many similar episodes. But the fantastic element functions as a reverberation of the referent, especially when an anecdote is distorted by hyperbole. Humor and fantasy are thus provoked in the contrasts, in the intimate oppositions, in the spontaneous exaggerations, and in the use of accumulation and giantism, which García Márquez, a Rabelaisian in the end, prolongs. . . . [The fantastic element is] such a clear transparency of reality that García Márquez has not had to resort to objective and accumulate details to represent it. Instead, the hyperbolic mechanism freely sustains the sense of amazement in the chronicle itself. This accounts for the profuse use of adjectives; qualities here are always clearly superlative.

But even the zestfulness of the fantastic element as a prolonging reference eventually feels the drama of cyclical time and of the end time, because on the other side of the hyperbole, at the end of the exaggerated and fervent exercise of fantasy, lies the white circle of solitude and the terror of the curse. The solitude of these one hundred years of events lives in all the protagonists as a condition fixed in the spiral of their history. Solitude is one of the traits of the Buendías, and it is also a precarious form of union. . . . Solitude is also the mirror that recovers a life in the passing instant of a recurring time. . . . Ursula reviews the history of her family from the perspective of solitude as a clairvoyant awareness. The last characters are "secluded by solitude and love and by the solitude of love." In the end we are told that the "races condemned to one hundred years of solitude do not have a second opportunity on earth." Solitude is thus a many-sided condemnation pervading everything from the smallest habits (Ursula looks through the window following "a habit of her solitude") to the most significant moments and even to the summing up of an entire life. In a moment of lucidity in which she sees her life flash before her, Ursula senses her guilt in having lived "over a century of conformity." In the human condition, the novel seems to be saying, conformity condemns us to solitude, to the absence of communion. (pp. 93-4)

This conformity and its unchallenged bastion, solitude, are also bound together by an ancient taboo, by an absurd and fanatical curse: the son born with a pig's tail. This fear is spread, above all, by Ursula. It inhibits love and reveals feelings of guilt. Her children are born without the dreaded tail, but Ursula sees the curse in every potential evil. . . . However, the curse comes true only for the one couple that freely love each other. The end of the family line betrays the sin at the origin and the guilt in love, part also of the character of this century condemned by its own alienation. Man, who lost paradise and reconquers it by inventing an archetypal world, loses it again in the solitude that transpires in the proximity of punishment and death. The curse of the son born of sin points therefore to a region of explicit guilt and implied rebellion. It reveals the irreversible condemnation of an age, a family line, and a history. These one hundred years of solitude find in the dialectics of several worlds and time the exorcism by which this novel makes them beautiful and terrible and also claims a different time, a time of innocence. (p. 95)

Julio Ortega, "One Hundred Years of Solitude," in his Poetics of Change: The New Spanish-American Narrative, *translated by Galen D. Greaser, University of Texas Press, 1984, pp. 85-95.*

JONATHAN YARDLEY

What we have [in ***Collected Stories***] is a curious piece of publishing. . . . These are, as the title says, the Collected Stories of Gabriel García Márquez, but they are short by two notable omissions of being the complete stories. They are drawn from the three volumes of stories—***No One Writes to the Colonel, Leaf Storm*** and ***Innocent Eréndira***—. . . but they are incompletely drawn; the title stories of the first two collections [***No One Writes to the Colonel*** and ***Leaf Storm***] are not included in this volume because the author regards them as novellas—though they are of approximately the same length as ***The Incredible and Sad Tale of Innocent Eréndira and Her Heartless Grandmother,*** which *is* included. . . .

[These] omissions render the ***Collected Stories*** a largely useless, if most attractive, book. Inasmuch as the three original story collections are available in [paperback], . . . there hardly seems a legitimate reason for anyone except the collector of García Márquez's work to shell out $16.95 for a new book that does not include two of his most important works and thus falls considerably short of being the definitive volume one would expect such a collection to be.

The one justification for the ***Collected Stories*** is that the book reprints the stories in the order in which they were first published in Spanish—although, again, whatever benefits the reader derives from this are significantly diminished by the omission of two pivotal tales, most notably ***No One Writes to the Colonel.*** Published chronologically, the stories make even clearer for American readers that García Márquez made an almost unimaginable leap from his apprenticework in the 1940s and '50s to the unblemished mastery of ***One Hundred Years of Solitude;*** it requires the skills of a literary archaeologist to locate the roots of that novel in the first 11 stories herein, assembled in a section called "Eyes of a Blue Dog."

The relationship of those stories to the great novel and the other work that has followed it is suggested only in an occasional glimmer, as when a woman's private demons are described as coming "from the heart of her father, who had fed them painfully during his nights of desperate solitude." For the most part, though, these stories contrast starkly with the author's mature work. There is in them little of the exuberant mixture of the fantastic and the literal that now characterizes García Márquez's work. Rather, they tend to be morose, interior stories—though there's precious little *story* to any of them—that muse gloomily about death. The one hint they give of work to come is their pervasive sense of twinning: mirrors, double images, actual twins are all employed to convey that sense of death in life, life in death, that pervades the novels and later stories.

It's at this point in García Márquez's career that ***No One Writes to the Colonel*** . . . assumes great importance. In it the author moves away from his preoccupation with death and toward a more energetic encounter with life; an early reference is made to Macondo, the town that subsequently became his equivalent of Faulkner's Yoknapatawpha County, and also to Colonel Aureliano Buendia, the larger-than-life figure who appears over and again in the major work [***One Hundred Years of Solitude***]. . . . But the reader of ***Collected Stories,*** of course, misses all of this.

Instead, in a second section of 10 stories called "Big Mama's Funeral," he finds himself quite suddenly in fictional territory that he knows well from the novels. Macondo is here, and Aureliano Buendia, and the astonishing magic that makes the mature work as distinctive as any in the world. . . .

Several of these stories are, as one would expect from García Márquez, quite splendid: ***Innocent Eréndira,*** **"One of These Days," "There Are No Thieves in This Town," "Balthazar's Marvellous Afternoon," "One Day After Saturday," "Death Constant Beyond Love."** Inescapably, though, by contrast with the two great novels [***One Hundred Years of Solitude*** and ***The Autumn of the Patriarch***] and even with the more slender one, ***Chronicle of a Death Foretold,*** they seem minor and tentative. Whether fairly or not, one tends to read them less for their own intrinsic virtues than for what they show us about the roots of the masterpieces; the delight we feel upon a chance and unexpected encounter with the name of Aureliano Buendia, or upon hearing a man speak of "the sign of solitude," is the delight of finding ourselves suddenly back in a landscape we love. They are very good stories, and the hint of greatness is in them, but only in the novels is it fully realized.

Jonathan Yardley, "The Magical Realism of García Márquez," in Book World—The Washington Post, *November 18, 1984, p. 3.*

CHARLES CHAMPLIN

[In a recent interview] Gabriel Garcia Marquez said:

> It always amuses me that the biggest praise for my work comes for the imagination, while the truth is that there's not a single line in all my work that does not have a basis in reality. The problem is that Caribbean reality resembles the wildest imagination . . . actually I'm a very realistic person and write what I believe is the true socialist realism.

In his ***Collected Stories,*** written between 1947 and 1972, an old male angel with filthy and lice-infested wings [in **"A Very Old Man with Enormous Wings: A Tale for Children"**] is kept on display in a crude backyard pen until he is at last able to fly away "with the risky flapping of a senile vulture." . . .

The beguiling aspect of the Garcia Marquez stories is that he is not, by his own lights, being coy, or twice fanciful, when he insists he is writing out of reality. His stories are indubitably the work of a fabulist's imagination, but the wellsprings are in the legends, folk tales, superstitions and indeed in the prevalence of miracles in the orthodox faith, of Latin America.

The socialist realism is everywhere present as well; it is the arid, unyielding rock on which the tales are built, and from which the tales are an escape. The observed world is of poverty, hopelessness, exploitation, despotic and demonic rulers—tyrants in government or in ownership. (p. 3)

Some of the stories have special interest because they offer glimpses of Macondo and the dynasty of Col. Aureliano Buendia, celebrated in full in ***One Hundred Years of Solitude;*** this novel . . . helped win Garcia Marquez the Nobel Prize for Literature in 1982.

Never, it may be, was a Nobel winner so *enjoyable* to read.

Garcia Marquez sometimes seems a litanist at heart, creating lists, at once absurd and surprising and exotic, that in the childhood observances of ancestral faith, might have been saints' names or catalogues of Marian virtues.

"Big Mama's Funeral" is a blackly funny recitation of the last days of a mammoth and tyrannical old woman, so powerful the Pope himself came to her last rites. Big Mama on her deathbed begins to dictate the list of her invisible estate. It commences with "the wealth of the subsoil" and reaches to "the underprivileged classes and statements of political support," also including "liberal ladies, the meat problem and the purity of the language." Alas, before she could finish, "Big Mama emitted a large belch and expired." The earliest stories are fascinations with death, told through the consciousnesses of the dead, one of them a woman yearning for a taste of orange and realizing it's been 3,000 years between bites. These tales now read as precociously successful exercises in craft.

The subsequent stories grow steadily more interesting for their ingenious interminglings of fantasy and reality, for their lyricism (ironic and blackly comedic as it sometimes is) and now and again for their simple narrative power.

In **"Sunday Siesta,"** a poor woman and her young daughter travel to another village to claim the body of her son, shot as a thief. In its economy and its emotional impact, the story suggests the technique of early Hemingway, but with an implicit compassion particular to Garcia Marquez.

Like dreams that redeem the sordid day, Garcia Marquez makes preposterous enchantments that confound the cruel and give the oppressed and the deluded a last, fantastical laugh. At the end of ***The Incredible and Sad Tale of Innocent Erendira,*** the beautiful Erendira, after a lifetime of enforced debauchery, is allowed to escape.

She runs

> past the saltpeter pits, the talcum craters, the torpor of the shacks, until the natural science of the sea ended and the desert began, but she still kept on running with the gold vest beyond the arid winds and the never-ending sunsets and she was never heard of again nor was the slightest trace of her misfortune ever found.

Like all the best stories anytime, these dark lyrics of Garcia Marquez demand to be read aloud. (pp. 3, 12)

Charles Champlin, in a review of "Collected Stories," in Los Angeles Times Book Review, *December 16, 1984, pp. 3, 12.*

JOHN SIMON

Frequently the history of literature (or the history of human gullibility) spews up a novel that becomes an "intellectual best-seller"—a book that all persons with literary or intellectual pretensions feel obliged to acquire, and some even to read. It may be the worst work by an established artist whose "best-seller time" has come. . . . Or it may simply be the book of a mediocre but newly emerged writer of strange origin or bent that strikes even some usually judicious people as unusual, original, unique (never mind that it is factitious, trivial, and, to be honest about it, boring). Such a book is—was—Gabriel García Márquez's ***One Hundred Years of Solitude,*** which earned its author the Nobel Prize, won by such other prodigious Latin American writers as Miguel Angel Asturias (at least unpretentious) and the unspeakable Gabriela Mistral, but never by Jorge Luis Borges, the one who most deserves it.

To read ***One Hundred Years of Solitude*** is to dive into a mountain of cotton candy head first and brain last, and endlessly, suffocatingly, sickeningly try to eat one's way out of it. This book that, without false modesty, could call itself *One Thousand Years of Solitude* is repetitious beyond anything but an old-time movie serial, with characters that even a genealogical chart cannot individuate (why should it? since when is the writer's job done by a chart?); the same sticky-sweet mixture of fantasy and social satire stretches on and on. Its mischievousness loses whatever edge it might have through iteration, lip-smacking enjoyment of its own cleverness, and flights into a fancy that seems to me the evasion rather than the extension of truth.

I had no better luck with two short novels by this writer, ***The Autumn of the Patriarch*** and ***Chronicle of a Death Foretold.*** Still, it seemed possible that he could achieve more with less—in the short story, which might curb his passion for prolixity. And indeed there are in the ***Collected Stories*** a few relatively unassuming, predominantly realistic tales that qualify García Márquez as a potential Hispanic Somerset Maugham. There is even one concluding novella in the author's dubious surrealist manner that works well enough, aside from some straining for effect and misfired jokes. For the rest, despite the odd powerful image and some passages of acerb mockery, these stories are mostly exercises in epigonous surrealism, with fantasy squeezed as desperately and self-destructively as when a novice milkmaid mistakes a bull's scrotum for a cow's udder.

The earliest stories, from the collection ***Eyes of a Blue Dog,*** are the poorest, though here the author has the excuse of his early twenties. In several of them, the protagonist is either a corpse somehow still alive or a living person relentlessly verbose in death. Death-in-life, life-in-death—these parvenu archetypes are pounded in with elaborately contrived, carefully self-contradictory detail. "Madam," says the doctor in **"The Third Resignation,"** the opening story,

> your child has a grave illness: he is dead. Nevertheless . . . we will succeed in making his organic functions continue through a complex system of autonutrition. Only the motor functions will be different. . . . We shall watch his life through growth, which, too, shall continue on [sic] in a normal fashion. It is simply 'a living death.' A real and true death. . . .

Here the preposterous conceit—it has no satirical thrust—has at least a kind of fairy-tale diaphaneity. Presently, pseudo-psychological obfuscation sets in. The living corpse hears terrible noises inside his head: "The noise had slippery fur, almost untouchable," yet our cadaver-hero will "catch it" and "not permit it to enter through his ear again, to come out through his mouth, through each of his pores. . ." etc. But forthwith this "furry" noise "[breaks] its cutglass crystals, its ice stars, against the interior walls of his cranium." Nevertheless, our hero proposes to "Grab it. Squeeze it. . . . Throw it onto the pavement and step on it [until it is] stretched out on the ground like any ordinary thing, transformed into an integral death." Notice that the noise goes from soft and furry to hard and crystalline and back again to something squeezable, thence to something animate that can be stomped on and stamped out with an "integral death." A pious hope, that; in García Márquez no death is integral enough.

Surrealism is all very well if it has some fidelity to its own bizarre self. A Max Ernst must remain an Ernst; it cannot, must not, transform itself into a Tanguy, a Matta, a Wilfredo Lam, at the whim of its undisciplined creator. Let the image be as crazy and hellish as it wants to be, but let it stay in focus. Out of focus, hell itself is not hell any more. It is only an amorphous blur. Yet from García Márquez's paragraphs of chaos a fine image, at times, surfaces—such as that "silence, as if all the lungs of the earth had ceased breathing so as not to break the soft silence of the air."

In the second story, **"The Other Side of Death,"** a similarly living corpse is haunted by a smell instead of a sound. If, in the previous story, the author played around with tenses, here he fools with pronouns:

> They were traveling in a train—I remember it now [this 'I' comes out of nowhere]—through a country-side—I've had this dream frequently—like a still life, sown with false, artificial trees bearing fruit of razors, scissors, and other diverse items. . . . He'd had that dream a lot of times but it had never produced this scare in him. There behind a tree was his brother, the other one, his twin, signaling—this happened to me somewhere in real life—for him to stop the train.

Note the confusion of they, I, and he in what is mostly a third-person-singular story. Note also the sloppiness of "other diverse items." And note the theme of the brother, the twin, the alter ego, that crops up with tiresome frequency in these stories—once it is even a mirror image that bleeds when the shaver does not—and later in the same paragraph another García Márquez favorite, the tumor. (pp. 32-3)

"Bitterness for Three Sleepwalkers" is even less scrutable. It may—just may—be about the death of a mother as perceived by her three sons. In any case, "she," whoever she is, seems to "become dissolved in her solitude" and to have "lost her natural faculty of being present."... In the title story, **"Eyes of a Blue Dog,"** a man and a woman inhabit each other's dreams but cannot find each other when awake, because the sleeper, upon waking, forgets the watchword "Eyes of a blue dog" with which to recognize the other. Kipling did this sort of thing better in "The Brushwood Boy."

There follows a straightforward story about a whore who has killed one of her johns and elicits a fake alibi from an ugly restaurateur who adores her and feeds her free of charge. Entitled **"The Woman Who Came at Six O'Clock,"** it is a neatly managed mood piece, situated in the bar-eatery before the evening's clients arrive, and containing such nice turns of phrase as "the man looked at her with a thick, sad tenderness, like a maternal ox." But in **"Nabo: The Black Man Who Made the Angels Wait,"** we are back in the thick of the old farrago with yet another figure hovering in a state that is neither life nor death, and a plot, if that is the word for it, obscurer than any. We get several more such stories, some with ghosts in them, and one, **"The Night of the Curlews,"** that is totally impenetrable. But it is the first to offer a favorite García Márquezian theme: the curious behavior of certain animals. In this instance it is curlews, who blind three men for no apparent reason.

In the stories from the next collection, ***Big Mama's Funeral,*** Macondo, the mythical locale of most of García Márquez's fiction, becomes more important yet. This Macondo can be anything from a pathetic hamlet to a good-sized town running to seed, and is peopled with the author's stock company of characters who pop up throughout his fiction, short or long. Here the writing is more assured, and some of the besetting mannerisms are kept relatively at bay. They are replaced, however, by new tricks no less annoying. Thus **"Tuesday Siesta,"** is a potentially interesting story about a poor woman who travels wretchedly, with her small daughter, to a distant town where her son, caught in the act of robbery, was killed and buried. She carries a cheap bouquet to lay on his grave, and rouses the indolent priest, during the hot hour of the siesta, for the key to the cemetery. But the townsfolk, aroused by her presence, gather ominously around the priest's house as the story abruptly ends.... We know something about the mother, very little about the daughter, and nothing at all about the townspeople except that they love their siesta. There is not enough to make up for missing confrontation. There is not even a denouement, only an anticlimax of the thudding rather than the teasing variety. García Márquez has said that he considers revelations "a bad literary device" and consequently avoids them. The avoidance, I think, is mutual.

Finally, the stories from the ***Eréndira*** volume, written between 1968 and 1972, are in the author's maturest style and perfectly display its generous flaws and niggardly virtues. Here the surrealism has become formulaic: in **"A Very Old Man With Enormous Wings,"** a senile, moth-eaten angel falls out of the sky and confounds Macondo, which, however, loses interest when the side-shows of an itinerant carnival become more popular. Eventually, the angel just flies away. Conversely, in **"The Handsomest Drowned Man in the World,"** the sea washes up a gorgeous, oversized male corpse, impeccably preserved; as the townswomen all fall in love with him while dressing him in whatever large enough finery they can muster, he has to be tossed back into the waves.

The long and fairly controlled title novella, ***The Incredible and Sad Tale of Innocent Eréndira and Her Heartless Grandmother,*** is probably all the García Márquez one needs to read for a full sampling of his ideas, strategies, and techniques. A mélange of the surreal, scurrilous, and occasionally poetic, it tells of a monstrous, larger-than-life grandmother who, having always exploited her lovely granddaughter Eréndira, now travels all over with her and prostitutes her to all comers until her alleged debt for supposedly causing their house to burn down is paid back.... Along its way, the novella takes satirical potshots at government, religion, capitalism, family relations, passion, and whatnot, and generally maintains its narrative propulsion despite its curlicues and discontinuities. Though there is wit, horror, and even wistfulness aplenty, the supernatural elements contribute little beyond a superficial exoticism, and one must finally wonder whether the story's eccentricities do not cancel one another out. (pp. 33-4)

[The pieces in ***Collected Stories***] sorely lack a philosophical or emotional center. "In García Márquez's world, love is the primordial power that reigns as an obscure, impersonal, and all-powerful presence," wrote Octavio Paz in *Alternating Current*. Obscurity and impersonality, to be sure, abound in these ***Collected Stories,*** but they contain more obfuscatory deliquescence than concentrated power. And they seem to have precious little to do with love, unless you can love a minor writer's obsession with telling tall tales such as his beloved grandmother told him, a boy of eight, to make him sleep. "Nothing interesting has happened to me since," García Márquez has said, and we are compelled to believe him. But he has certainly learned his grandmother's lessons well: with his fabulating, he can put even grown-ups to sleep. (p. 34)

John Simon, "Incontinent Imagination," in The New Republic, *Vol. 192, No. 5, February 4, 1985, pp. 32-5.*

MARLISE SIMONS [INTERVIEW WITH **GABRIEL GARCÍA MÁRQUEZ**]

Gabriel García Márquez is in the midst of a new novel, and a predictable order is imposed on his life. The 1982 Nobel Prize in Literature is behind him and so is the publication of his most recent novel, ***Chronicle of a Death Foretold.*** Still, his fans seek out the 57-year-old author of ***One Hundred Years of Solitude***—the book that made him a celebrity. (p. 1)

[Simons]: *You're writing a happy love story, as you've called it, a love affair between two very old people.*

[García Márquez]: It's the story of a love that begins when the boy and girl are very young. But it is suspended. It stays in a cocoon. It's renewed when they are in their 80's.

It began with an idea, an image I had. The point of departure for a book for me is always an image, never a concept or a plot. The first image I had for this book is that of an old couple fleeing by boat. An old couple, happy on a boat, dancing on the deck. But I don't want to talk about the book yet. That will bring me bad luck.

You've always said that a writer spends the rest of his life writing about his youth. Now you're inventing a period of your life that you haven't lived yet.

Yes, I'm anticipating. But in a way I've always done that since I was young. My two first books (both published in the United States as the title stories of collections) were about old people. In ***Leaf Storm,*** an old man no longer knows what to do and hangs himself. And ***No One Writes to the Colonel*** is about an old man waiting for a letter that never arrives. If I think about it, about all those characters in ***One Hundred Years of Solitude,*** I always seem to have observed my elders. I've never written about children.

Perhaps because as a child you lived for some time with your grandparents?

Yes, that was very important. Basically my grandparents were the models for many of the people in my books because I knew how they talked, how they behaved. To make sure the characters were real, I would always use my grandparents as a reference point. But I was trying to reflect the behavior of my elders without really penetrating what was happening inside them.

I am beginning to become conscious of old age now. This book I'm writing obliges me to think six hours a day about things I had never seriously explored: old age, love and death. It is having an effect on me. You leave a lot of yourself in a book, but a book leaves you with a lot of reflections. I never thought so seriously about death until I began to try and see how it affects people in their old age. I was used to my characters never dying. They were living endlessly.

Except the ones that were hanged, shot or otherwise assassinated.

Yes, through violence. But they didn't die of old age, there was no aging process. Now that I'm getting older, I'm concerned with how age affects the sentiments, which after all is the most important. (pp. 1, 18)

Did you study old age or read how other writers have treated it?

No, I don't work that way. I only read Simone de Beauvoir's book *The Coming of Age*. I try to let the writing, the imagination and invention tell me the secrets of old age. I imagine that afterward, specialists and old people themselves may say that it's not like this. So it may have to be the old age of my book and not that of life. . . .

What I don't do is prepare myself to deal with an overall theme. I may consult on small points. For ***One Hundred Years of Solitude*** I didn't study the economic or social conditions of Colombia. I could have made a serious investigation about the drama of the foreign banana companies. But I asked a few questions and look what happened. I went to check how many dead there were in the banana workers' strike of 1928. It was a tremendous national scandal. It's not exactly known, but I was told about 17. For my book, 17 dead would have been a joke. I needed enough bodies to fill a train. I wanted the train instead of being loaded with bananas to be loaded with corpses. History was against me, with 17 dead. That would not even fill a wagon. So I put 3,000. And so not long ago, during a commemoration of the event, someone in a speech talked about the massacre of the 3,000 compatriots.

So what I'm trying to say is that I don't make a study. I am not inclined to theorizing. I do not want to turn any of my experiences into theory and I also read very little literary theory. But of course I may look up some episodes someone has written or check some statistics. . . .

Do you work very differently now than when you were young?

The writing process is very different. When you are young, you write almost—well, every writer is different, I'm talking about myself—almost like writing a poem. You write on impulses and inspiration. You have so much inspiration that you are not concerned with technique. You just see what comes out, without worrying much about what you are going to say and how. On the other hand, later, you know exactly what you are going to say and what you want to say. And you have a lot to tell. Even if all of your life you continue to tell about your childhood, later you are better able to interpret it, or at least interpret it in a different way.

When you are older, when the inspiration diminishes, you depend more on technique. If you don't have that, everything collapses. There is no question that you write much more slowly, with much more care, and perhaps with less inspiration. This is the great problem of the professional author. . . .

There is a story called **"The Night of the Curlews,"** one of my first. It was the time when we put out a weekly literary magazine in Barranquilla, called *La Crónica*. At one point the editor suddenly found he was left with two empty pages. So in the evening I sat down and wrote that story.

I couldn't do that today. If I had it completely worked out, I would still need at least two or three weeks to write it. Worse, not many years ago, I wrote a story of 15 pages and bought a package of 500 sheets of paper. When I finished the story, I had used up all 500 to write the 15. . . .

Another great difference between one age and another to me is memory. I never used to write down all the ideas that occur to me while writing. I believed that if I forgot them they were not important, and the ones that really mattered were those I remembered. Now I write them all down. It makes me very anxious to know that I thought of something but I forgot, something I was going to say, that I read, where I read it, a melody I cannot recall. (p. 18)

After the Nobel Prize you said that success, the prize, are a burden that makes it more difficult to write. Do you still feel that way?

It's a private joke of mine that I have been famous for a long time but nobody knew about it. No, recognition is not a burden for me. I've always had my projects and I haven't changed them. . . .

Perhaps it's an excess of vanity, but I've always felt all this was going to happen. My commitment to my writing is no different, it's always been very deep. Even in journalism.

Now all my newspaper stories have been dug up in Colombia, whatever I wrote since I was 18. Six volumes have already been published and there are two or three to go.

Imagine the shock I got when I heard people wanted to do this. Then I realized it was going to happen anyway, sooner or later. Or they wait till I'm dead and do it then. So I figured the best thing was to have control over it. I read almost all of them and I don't have to regret anything. There are no great gaffes and no important contradictions. But I've always known that whatever you write down, it will pursue you, even after you're dead. There it is. You cannot say, I didn't write that.

But fame has not created greater pressures?

You could ask me if today I'm more frightened than before when I sit down to write. All my life I've been frightened at the moment I sit down to write.

Every day?

Every day. Terribly frightened. (p. 21)

Marlise Simons, "Love and Age: A Talk with García Márquez," in The New York Times Book Review, *April 7, 1985, pp. 1, 18, 21.*

ROBERT PHILLIPS

[García Márquez] would have been better served by rigidly chosen selected stories than by a big collection [***Collected Stories***]. In this chronologically arranged collection, more than the first 100 pages of early stories are negligible—imitations of Kafka and perhaps Aichinger (**"Eva Is Inside Her Cat"**), Hemingway (**"The Woman Who Came at Six O'Clock"** and **"Tuesday Siesta"**), and Faulkner (**"Nabo: The Black Man Who Made the Angel Wait"**). Another obvious influence is Virginia Woolf and her technique of the interior monologue. Part of the problem with this apprentice work was García Márquez's extreme youth at the time of composition; he began publishing stories at the age of 19.

The ***Collected Stories*** begins to acquire an individual voice and vision with a story he published in 1962, when 34. Called **"There Are No Thieves in This Town,"** it describes the events that occur after a village youth impulsively steals three billiard balls from the local pool hall. The balls cannot be sold, and they cannot be replaced. The social life of the town is interrupted, and the thief's life is ruined, not so much for being dishonest as for being a fool. With this tale, García Márquez abandoned the totally intellectual material of his literary experience, and began linking literature to life as he saw it around him. It is the beginning of his leftist social fictions for which he is now honored. . . .

[Later] stories are full of eerie, magical images, comic exaggerations and exotic dreams. There is a marvelous bird cage, more beautiful than anyone has ever imagined; a spectacle of dead birds that plagues a town; "the greatest funeral in the world," attended by the Pope; a wily snake healer; an ancient angel who falls to earth; a sea that gives off the fragrance of roses; and "the handsomest drowned man in the world." Perhaps the most fantastical fiction of all is ***The Incredible and Sad Tale of Innocent Eréndira and Her Heartless Grandmother,*** a 46-page novella of exploitation and evil whose characters and processions would be at home in the wildest Fellini film.

That story is the last in the book. In the 12 years since, García Márquez has devoted himself exclusively to writing novels. As the last two-thirds of this collection testify, he became a masterly teller of tales. One hopes he will return from time to time to the shorter form.

Robert Phillips, in a review of "Collected Stories," in America, *Vol. 152, No. 17, May 4, 1985, p. 379.*

JOHN UPDIKE

[The pieces in ***Collected Stories***] are rich and startling in their matter and confident and elegant in their manner. For the reader who has exhausted the wonders of García Márquez's masterpiece, ***One Hundred Years of Solitude,*** they probably constitute (along with its fine precursor, ***Leaf Storm***) the next-best place to turn. They are—the word cannot be avoided—magical, though for this reader the magic sparkled unevenly through the spread of tricks and was blacker than he had expected. García Márquez did not begin, as some of his interviews have suggested, as a realist who then broke through to a new, matter-of-fact method of fantasy. . . . [The] first story collected here, composed when García Márquez was a mere nineteen, with quite characteristic aplomb details the thoughts of a young man's corpse as it lies in the coffin. . . . The mature García Márquez's gift of linkage, his way of letting implausible threads intertwine and thicken into a substantial braid, already flourishes in these stories composed when he was a student and youthful journalist in Colombia. The next in order of composition takes up the thoughts of the dead boy's twin: "The idea of his twin brother's corpse had been firmly stuck in the whole center of his life." There is so much spiralling Faulknerian indirection that it is hard to know who is dead and who is merely imagining it; pronouns float in and out of embodiments, and a host of creepy sensations flicker by—"Death began to flow through his bones like a river of ashes . . . The cold of his hands intensified, making him feel the presence of the formaldehyde in his arteries." . . . The ideas of living death, of consciousness travelling within an immobilized body, of piecemeal dying within the garish trappings of Latin-American burial . . . dominate these stories, with their disagreeable sweetish stench of precocity, of adolescent terror turned outward. Though this spectral field will be extended into a sociological realm of closed houses and frozen lives, a geographical limbo where only the bitter past animates thought, García Márquez's great theme of suspended motion is announced here at the outset, along with a smooth and dandified indifference to the conventions of realism. (pp. 118, 121)

One story in this first collection moves out of the surreal into the orbit of Hemingway. **"The Woman Who Came at Six O'Clock"** gives us a nearly empty restaurant, a lot of unadorned dialogue, a woman of shady habits, a courteous barman, a whiff of criminal violence. But even here the sluggish tide of semi-death sweeps in, drowning reality. . . . Nonsense, of a sombre sort, nibbles at the edge of many a sentence, the rereading of which threatens to plunge us into a hopeless world of glutinous, twisted time. . . . Spatial disorientation also occurs within the unpredictable prose. . . . [For example, a] woman's consciousness wanders for no clear reason into that of a cat and hangs for no less than three thousand years over the desire to eat an orange. . . . **"Nabo: The Black Man Who Made the Angels Wait,"** ends with a monstrous run-on sentence in which García Márquez, at the age of twenty-three, in bravura fashion lays claim to his authorial power. A method of centrifugal revelation, wherein a set of images at first glance absurd or frivolous gradually coheres into a frozen, hovering world that we can recognize as the site of an emotion, of dread and pity: this is to become the method of ***One Hundred Years of Solitude.***

The second, middle set of stories, all dated 1962, are more naturalistic, and but for the title story and **"One Day After Saturday"** are located not in Macondo but in El Pueblo—"the town," and a town differing from Macondo mostly in the relatively straightforward, staccato style with which it is described. Evidently García Márquez's lush early style had been chastised by his fellow-leftists. . . . He lived, in the late fifties and early sixties, abroad, in Europe, Mexico, and Venezuela; for a time he worked for Castro's news agency, Prensa Latina, in its New York bureau. Yet the stories of ***Big Mama's Funeral*** seem scarcely political, but for their convincing rendition of stagnation and poverty, and the rather farcical condemnation of Big Mama's empire. They are brighter-humored, with more comic touches than the earlier stories. . . . There is a new epigrammatic loftiness: "She bore the conscientious serenity of someone accustomed to poverty." . . . García Márquez, a well-travelled man of the world, is contemplating his remembered Caribbean backwater with a certain urbanity, preparing to make a totally enclosed microcosm, a metaphor, of it. The young author's eerie muddling of the concrete and the abstract, his will to catch hold of a terrible vagueness at the back of things, now works within single polished sentences. . . . (pp. 121-22)

Several of these tales are García Márquez's best. **"There Are No Thieves in This Town,"** the longest of the lot, with magisterial empathy describes the confused, self-destructive behavior of a handsome young idler, Damaso, the love borne him by his considerably older wife, Ana, and the small-town boredom that stretches stupefyingly to the horizon. The town is so low on entertainment resources that Damaso's theft of three battered billiard balls creates an enormous vacuum; with no overt touches of the fabulous, an enchanted environment, shabby and stagnant yet highly charged, is conjured up. **"Artificial Roses,"** showing how a young girl's love secrets are detected by her blind grandmother, and **"Tuesday Siesta,"** sketching the arrival in town of the mother of a slain thief, are smaller but not inferior in their purity and dignity of treatment. **"Balthazar's Marvelous Afternoon,"** a parable of artistry in which the town rich man, José Montiel, defaults on paying for "the most beautiful cage in the world," sidles toward fantasy, and the prize-winning **"One Day After Saturday"** enters broadly into it, as the town suffers a plague of dying birds. **"Big Mama's Funeral"** (attended by the President of Colombia and the Pope) is firmly fantastical and celebrates Macondo, the territory of imagination where the author was to strike it rich. (p. 122)

The third and last group of stories were mostly composed after the completion and triumph of ***One Hundred Years of Solitude,*** and they have the strengths and debilities of an assured virtuosity. One of them, **"The Last Voyage of the Ghost Ship,"** is a single six-page sentence, and two of them, **"A Very Old Man with Enormous Wings"** and **"The Handsomest Drowned Man in the World,"** are subtitled "A Tale for Children." For the first time, we feel a danger of cuteness: "They wanted to tie the anchor from a cargo ship to him so that he would sink easily into the deepest waves, where fish are blind and divers die of nostalgia." . . . Such imagery has become a mere vocabulary, used a bit glibly, though with flashes of the old murky power. García Márquez's conception of an angel as a dirty, muttering, helpless old man with bedraggled wings is ominous and affecting, and scarcely less so the drowned corpse so tall and beautiful and virile that "even though they were looking at him there was no room for him in their imagination." But the sea he keeps evoking has the unreality not only of sleep and dreams but of, in the words of the old song, a cardboard sea, a sea that indeed could be packed up and sold like the sea in his novel ***The Autumn of the Patriarch.***

The longest and latest of these later stories, ***The Incredible and Sad Tale of Innocent Eréndira and Her Heartless Grandmother,*** has been made into a movie, with a script by the author and under his control, so the two forms of illusion can be fairly contrasted. Having seen the film before I read the prose, I was struck by how much that had seemed obscure was easily clarified—the photographer, for instance, who in the film appeared wholly gratuitous and of unrealized significance, is explained in the story as a natural adjunct of the carnival that grows up wherever the prostituted heroine is encamped. The comings and goings of Eréndira's young lover Ulises, baffling on the screen, make simple sense in print. . . . The scene of Eréndira's defloration, which in its written paragraph is swathed in subaqueous imagery, in the movie flays the eyes with its real girl, its real man with his three-day beard, its real shack, its real torrents of rain, its real brutality. The film, in short, had a power to stir and scare us quite unrelated to any cumulative sense it was making; its script was logically so loose that García Márquez could insert into it another story, **"Death Constant Beyond Love,"** for the sake of its photogenic episodes of a painted-paper ocean liner and of peso notes that become butterflies. The one image in **"Death Constant Beyond Love"** that penetrates into our own experience and lends it a negotiable significance—the frightened yet captivating odor of the heroine (not Eréndira), like "the dark fragrance of an animal of the woods . . . woods-animal armpit"—could not, of course, be captured on film. Thrown into real landscapes, with flesh-and-blood actors, the careless cruelty of "the incredible and sad tale" glared at the moviegoer confusingly, not quite action and not quite poetry. Seeing real human beings go through his motions, we realized how much stylized dehumanization García Márquez offers his readers.

There is a surplus of sadism in these later stories. Eréndira is made to submit to masses of men and her grandmother is prolongedly slain by a lover who is then spurned; the fallen angel is relentlessly abused and teased; and in **"Blacamán the Good, Vendor of Miracles"** a child is transformed into a miracle worker by a diet of pain. . . . The child has his revenge: when he becomes a miracle worker, and his master is dead, he revives him in his tomb and leaves him inside, "rolling about in horror." . . . Not a pretty tale, but then, we might be told, neither is life in Latin America. Nor were García Márquez's two post-***Solitude*** novels, ***The Autumn of the Patriarch*** and ***Chronicle of a Death Foretold,*** pretty tales. The former seemed, to this reader eager for more tropical dazzlement, tortuous and repetitive, and the latter astringent and thin. Both left a sour taste. (pp. 123-25)

[García Márquez's ***Collected Stories*** suggests] that his inspirations are extremely private and subtle. And, it may be, fragile. . . . To write with magical ludicity along the thin edge where objective fact and subjective myth merge is a precarious feat. Though he emphasizes technique—"Ultimately, literature is nothing but carpentry," he said to *The Paris Review*—there is much in the process beyond conscious control, however artfully monitored the promptings of the subconscious are. ***One Hundred Years of Solitude*** was a work of consummate ripeness. The author's sparse production in the eighteen years since its writing betrays the effort of fending off rot. (p. 125)

John Updike, "Living Death," in The New Yorker, *Vol. LXI, No. 13, May 20, 1985, pp. 118, 121-25.*

MICHIKO KAKUTANI

The year was 1955, and Gabriel García Márquez—who decades later would win the Nobel Prize for such works as ***One Hundred Years of Solitude, The Autumn of the Patriarch*** and ***In Evil Hour***—was working as a newspaper reporter in Bogotá, Colombia. One of his assignments that spring was to interview a sailor named Luis Alejandro Velasco—the sole survivor of a terrible accident at sea—and to ghostwrite an account of his ordeal as a 14-part series for the paper. The story, based on 120 hours of interviews, was first published in book form under Mr. Márquez's name in Spanish in 1970.

Mr. Velasco was instantly declared a national hero when news of his survival became public, and the immediate effect of Mr. García Márquez's series for *El Espectador* was to double the paper's circulation. Other, more sobering repercussions, however, were waiting in the wings. Mr. Velasco had revealed in the story that his ship—the Colombian destroyer *Caldas*—had been carrying contraband at the time of the accident. The Colombian Government responded, writes Mr. García Márquez, "with a series of drastic reprisals that would result, months later, in the shutdown of the newspaper." Mr. Velasco would be forced to leave the navy, disappearing "into the oblivion of everyday life," and Mr. García Márquez would leave for exile abroad.

In themselves, such dramatic circumstances do not add appreciably to our interest in the apprentice work of a celebrated author, but in this case, the text of ***The Story of a Shipwrecked Sailor,*** itself provides Mr. García Márquez's followers with certain insights into his preoccupations and the development of his craft. Though the narrative is completely written from Mr. Velasco's point of view, though it suffers from the multiple cliffhanger structure of serial writing, though its flat, reportorial language bears little resemblance to Mr. García Márquez's famous Faulknerian prose, the story does embody—or has been made to embody—many of his mature concerns. Not only do Mr. Velasco's adventures touch upon complicated questions about man's relationship with Nature and Fate—capsulizing, in a very undeveloped form, themes addressed more fully in later novels and short stories—but they also take on a familiar hallucinatory quality in which time and memory are distorted, reality and fantasy blur.

What's more, Mr. García Márquez has managed to turn Mr. Velasco's story into a kind of fable, in which the sailor's specific experiences come to symbolize something rather more general. Conscious or unconscious allusions are made to such sea literature as *Robinson Crusoe* and "The Rime of the Ancient Mariner," and the book's subtitle, too, has the effect of making us see the protagonist not as Luis Alejandro Velasco, but as the quintessential shipwrecked sailor "who drifted on a life raft for ten days without food or water, was proclaimed a national hero . . . , and then spurned by the government and forgotten for all time."

Yet if that little précis of the book has the unfortunate effect of sentimentalizing Mr. Velasco's story, of trivializing his actual experiences in favor of turning him into a larger-than-life hero, the actual narrative of this book remains surprisingly direct. Mr Velasco has a remarkably good memory—or imagination—for details, both physical and emotional, and Mr. García Márquez duly sets them down in a straightforward, documentary fashion. . . .

What would seem monotonous in its horror—spending 10 days on a raft, alone at sea, dying of hunger, thirst and exposure—becomes, in this account, a minutely textured experience. In noting the survival stratagems he concocts minute to minute, day by day—trying to fish with his hands, eating three business cards he's found in his pocket—Mr. Velasco also retraces the wildly fluctuating graph of his emotions: the initial calm he feels, confident that he will be rescued; the increasing sense of loneliness, followed by despair and resignation; the hope he feels on seeing a seagull or a plane pass over ahead, and the desolation experienced in watching the plane fly on. . . .

Though the descriptions of Mr. Velasco's ordeal hold our interest throughout ***Shipwrecked Sailor,*** they prove neither distinctive enough nor fierce enough to resonate long afterward in our minds. In that sense, this book remains a fairly ephemeral piece of journalism and only a very provisional blueprint for what Mr. García Márquez would accomplish in the years ahead.

Michiko Kakutani, "Early García Márquez," in The New York Times, *April 26, 1986, p. 10.*

PIERS PAUL READ

[***The Story of a Shipwrecked Sailor***] was ghostwritten in 1955 by Gabriel García Márquez for a young Colombian sailor named Luis Alejandro Velasco, who was swept off his destroyer into rough seas on a voyage from Mobile, Ala., to Cartagena, Colombia. He found himself next to a life raft and scrambled aboard. His four shipmates who fell into the sea at the same time were drowned as they struggled to join him. For 10 days Mr. Velasco drifted in the Caribbean Sea without food or fresh water. His spirits rose and fell like the waves around him—sinking as he heard the cries of his drowning friends, rising as he realized that he would soon be rescued, sinking again as airplanes flew overhead and their pilots failed to see him. . . .

After 10 days at sea Mr. Velasco's raft reached the coast of Colombia. With his last remaining reserves of will and strength he swam to the shore and, after a final struggle against the strong undertow of the waves, found himself on dry land. He was picked up by a peasant on a donkey and escorted by 600 men to the small town of San Juan. The Government of Gen. Gustavo Rojas Pinilla took charge of him and proclaimed him a national hero. . . . He was hired to advertise his watch, which had never stopped, and the shoes he had been unable to tear apart. He became rich as well as famous, and only when all the established forms of exploitation were exhausted did he come to the opposition newspaper, *El Espectador*.

Here starts a story of a different kind; for the young staff reporter assigned to ghostwrite his story was the 27-year-old Gabriel García Márquez. Mr. García Márquez saw in Mr. Velasco not only a chance to strike a political blow at the regime, but also a perfect front for his own narrative skill. In 20 daily sessions, each lasting six hours, he pieced together the true story of Mr. Velasco's ordeal, discovering as he did so that this sailor "who looked more like a trumpet player than a national hero, had an exceptional instinct for the art of narrative . . . and enough uncultivated dignity to be able to laugh at his own heroism."

It was this latter quality that had political significance, for it enabled Mr. García Márquez to say through Mr. Velasco that his survival proved nothing about the nobility of Colombia or the valor of its armed forces. . . .

What his narrative implicitly revealed, however, was the corruption and inefficiency of the Colombian Navy. No lifesaving equipment was stored on the life raft, and the destroyer had only listed in the heavy seas because contraband refrigerators and washing machines had been stacked on its decks.

The Government of Rojas Pinilla was incensed at this smear against the navy and took its revenge. *El Espectador* was closed, Mr. Velasco was forced to leave the navy. . . . Mr. García Márquez fled to France and began his "nomadic and somewhat nostalgic exile that in certain ways also resembles a drifting raft." . . .

[The value of ***The Story of a Shipwrecked Sailor***] to Mr. García Márquez's admirers will be largely as a literary curiosity. Certainly Mr. Velasco's story is well told, with a kind of clipped realism that in itself must have been a form of protest against the inflated rhetoric of Rojas Pinilla's authoritarian regime. The emphasis is on the nasty banality of survival—the oozing intestines of [a] sea gull, the impenetrable scales of a captured fish. Mr. Velasco says little of himself, his family or his friends. He prays to the Virgin of Carmen, but we are given no glimpse into his soul.

The structure of the book is that of a serialization: We are left in suspense at the end of each section as if we had to wait until the next day rather than the next page for the subsequent episode. We are also more familiar with stories of survival than we were 30 years ago, and so are less astonished at Mr. Velasco's ordeal. Indeed it is only fair to Mr. García Márquez's talents to say that if this translation had appeared, as did the original, under the name of Luis Alejandro Velasco, no one would rush out to buy it; and that those who now do so because it bears the name of Gabriel García Márquez are likely to be disappointed if they expect from this slim volume the same dramatic intensity and poetic brilliance they found in ***Chronicle of a Death Foretold.***

Piers Paul Read, "The Hero Who Lived to Regret It," in The New York Times Book Review, *April 27, 1986, p. 11.*

JOHN ARCHER

[In his preface to ***The Story of a Shipwrecked Sailor,*** García Márquez states]:

> I have not reread this story in 15 years. It seems worthy of publication, but I have never quite understood the usefulness of publishing it. I find it depressing that the publishers are not so much interested in the merit of the story as in the name of the author, which, much to my sorrow, is also that of a fashionable writer.

Gabriel García Márquez's comments in his introduction to ***The Story of a Shipwrecked Sailor*** for the Spanish edition of 1970 hold true for this English translation.

This is not a new work of fiction from Colombia's winner of the Nobel Prize for Literature. It is a piece of journalism, presented as originally published in 14 daily instalments in a Bogota newspaper in 1955. It tells, in the first person, the story of the Colombian sailor Luis Alejandro Velasco who spent ten days adrift on a raft in the Caribbean without food or water. . . .

The Story of a Shipwrecked Sailor was published as a book in Barcelona in 1970, the year that ***One Hundred Years of Solitude*** was first charming readers and puzzling critics in its British edition. Now, 31 years after its newspaper publication, readers care more for the writer than the sailor. Márquez regards his journalism as some of his finest work. It is a brilliant piece of 'new journalism', that old idea the Americans have now rechristened 'literary journalism'. It gives the story to its subject, a stirring reminder of what journalism can be. In Britain today, where discussion of journalism tends to be only of economy and technology, Alejandro Velasco would be flogging his tale as a drama-doc for television—no newspaper would give it the space.

The story has curiosity value, but there's no doubt that if it had not been written by Márquez then it would have not been translated. Historically it is significant in that it sent Márquez into the exile that eventually led him to tell his own tale in ***One Hundred Years of Solitude.*** But the publishers would be serving us better if they translated and published Mario Vargas Llosa's critical and biographical study of that masterpiece. And it would be reassuring to know that Alejandro Velasco, last heard of sitting behind a desk for a provincial bus company, was getting a cut from the royalties.

John Archer, "Man Overboard," in The Listener, *Vol. 116, No. 2986, November 13, 1986, p. 24.*

JUSTIN WINTLE

[***The Story of a Shipwrecked Sailor***] certainly is more than a curiosity. Enjoyment of it is by no means restricted to the discovery of pointers toward the later fiction. . . .

[***The Story of a Shipwrecked Sailor***] is an example of Marquez's emerging art. Day by day we are taken through Velasco's ordeal. He eats nothing except three name cards, a slither of seagull's thigh and two mouthfuls of raw fish. The sharks gather and soon he is hallucinating. Sometimes he talks to his drowned comrades, sometimes he imagines himself back in Mobile, dancing with his girlfriend, Mary Address. The land, he thinks, should there be any, is teeming with cannibals.

There is nothing particularly new in all this, especially if you have already read *Pincher Martin.* Unlike Golding's book, however, Marquez's is written with the utmost simplicity, the utmost clarity, and it is this that indicates the better storyteller. 'Some people tell me this story is a fantasy,' Velasco signs off. 'And I ask them: If it is, then what did I do during my ten days at sea?' His is not the government version, but governments, Marquez suggests, are also capable of fantasising. Reality is frozen out, that is the condition of combat.

Justin Wintle, "There Was a Ship," in New Statesman, *Vol. 112, No. 2903, November 14, 1986, p. 31.*

JOHN BUTT

[***The Story of a Shipwrecked Sailor***] is non-fiction, we hope. It is a translation of a 1970 reprint of a story originally ghost-written by Gabriel García Márquez in 1955 and told by a sailor who was washed overboard from a Colombian destroyer, survived ten days of thirst, starvation and sharks, was cast ashore and briefly became the darling of the Colombian media at a time when all but politically anodyne news was banned under the dictatorship of Rojas Pinilla. . . .

As far as I know, nothing that García Márquez published under his own name before ***100 Years of Solitude*** aroused much interest, including ***Leaf Storm, In Evil Hour*** and ***No One Writes to the Colonel.*** The enormous success of ***100 Years*** predictably encouraged the publishing houses to overturn this verdict of silence not only on those novels, but even on his most forgettable newspaper pieces, with the result that their author is being saddled, in Spanish and now in English, with a swelling *oeuvre* of reprints of, to put it mildly, middling value. Consequently he is starting to look like one of the most overrated modern Hispanic authors. ***Story of a Shipwrecked Sailor*** is a shocking example: García Márquez was obviously embarrassed to see the dust blown off these cuttings which had appeared fifteen years earlier under the name of an obscure seaman. . . . And there one might let the matter rest, were it not that this mildly exciting but run-of-the-mill tale of endurance on the high seas throws light on García Márquez's development as a writer. It exemplifies his training in a certain tradition of reporting. The hagiographers may try to build a legend of fearless investigative journalism on this book, but the pursuit of hard fact at any price was not García Márquez's style in those days and has not always been since. He makes it quite clear in the preface that at the time he had no inkling of the controversial nature of the seaman's story and was earning his bread turning in "politically germ-free" copy "to entertain the readers". Although there is no reason to question the basic facts in the sailor's account, it is in places luridly over-written and for all one knows generously embroidered, since, by his own cheerful admission, his reporting standards were not exactly rigorous. He said in an interview in *El Tiempo* that when news was short on *El Espectador* "we invented all sorts of things" and went on to admit to having faked a story about a demonstration in Quibdó and another about a helicopter landing at the Tequendama falls. Nor will readers of his more recent Wednesday articles in the respected Spanish daily *El País* have forgotten that, in his weekly catalogue of exaggerations and superficialities, he claimed that during the Falklands War British soldiers had to subdue by gunfire the sodomitical fury of the Gurkhas against Argentine prisoners.

But his inadequacies as a journalist—for instance a certain impatience with prosaic fact—are part of the secret of García Márquez's success as a writer of fiction. The techniques of popular journalism, a taste for hyperbole, melodrama and sensation, and for imaginative worlds that are ten times larger than life, are so deeply ingrained in his writing that sentences like these are the hallmarks of the prose: "his pistol went off as it hit the floor, and the bullet wrecked the cupboard, passed through the wall, roared across next door's dining room, and reduced to dust a lifesize plaster statue of a saint on the high altar in the church at the other end of the square" (***Chronicle of a Death Foretold***). . . .

This love of whimsical overstatement is the basis of the humour of ***100 Years of Solitude,*** which, as the author regretfully complains, is not "serious", ie. it is a comic masterpiece ambiguous in its implications and not, like most of his other work, a volley of more or less earnest social criticism aimed point-blank at huge and predictable targets like Latin-American violence and injustice. ***The Story of a Shipwrecked Sailor*** is among the earliest of García Márquez's attributed works, and it already shows an imagination straining to be let off the leash. Vargas Llosa remarks delicately of it that "it has a cleanness and sureness of touch which reveal that its author has more gifts as a story teller than as a journalist", and one can see his point. . . . It is pretty clear that García Márquez had to disentangle his literary powers from [his] less fortunate gift for writing hack copy if he was ever to write anything as good as ***100 Years of Solitude,*** and his subsequent career has been a hard and not always victorious campaign against the baleful legacy of that early newspaper training. His best work depends on uninhibited fantasy, on reviving what is essentially a child's vision of the world—on forgoing reportage, journalism and "comment" in every sense. The trouble is that the commentator, and with him the views, tends to creep in whenever the imaginative impetus of his novels falters and the realist comes to the fore. He once said that his "great regret" was that he was no longer a reporter, but readers of ***The Story of a Shipwrecked Sailor*** and his other journalism will surely agree that this nostalgia reflects a puzzling misjudgment of the nature of his own talent. But it may explain why ***100 Years of Solitude*** is something of an isolated phenomenon in his work. If there is a marked difference between it and his other books, it may be because he does not find it easy to live too far from current affairs in the apolitical, or at least only obliquely and ambiguously political, world of the former novel, and feels that he ought to stiffen his writing with a fair amount of obvious social comment and clumsy political satire. He often seems to hanker after the strident clarity of the reporter, all too evident in ***The Story of a Shipwrecked Sailor,*** despite the fact that the points he needs to make come through much more effectively in the ironic, indirect style of his masterpiece.

John Butt, "Resurrection of a Ghost," in The Times Literary Supplement, *No. 4365, November 28, 1986, p. 1333.*

JOHN STURROCK

In *Mayta* Mario Vargas Llosa bends his very high skills as a maker of fiction to the serious political purpose of showing how only a modest truthfulness can save. That is an irony that would be altogether lost, to be sure, on the Colombian Gabriel Garcia Marquez, a hothead impatient with the political moderation and decent meliorism that are what Vargas Llosa would ask for. He likes to call not for changes but for Change, the big one, some vague but redemptive coup and escape into a harmonious future from the demeaningly violent, narrow cycle of Colombian history. . . . (p. 15)

The Story of a Shipwrecked Sailor is not a new Garcia Marquez novella, but a piece of journalism dating back thirty years, so styleless and so topical it is a mystery why anyone thought it worth putting at this late date into English. . . . In 1955, when he was a young journalist in Bogota, Garcia Marquez ghosted this story of a Colombian sailor who had been washed overboard with a number of others from a destroyer in the Caribbean, had lasted ten days on a raft without food or water, and had then swum a mile or more ashore in Colombia, to be lionised as the one survivor of the disaster, and then forgotten. Ten days adrift became 14 in print: the story is spun out through that many instalments, with whatever suspense—will the plane see him? will the sharks get him?—and graphic particularities—nibbling visiting-cards when extra-hungry, carving into a seagull with his keys—can be found to animate it. But all these years on, it is a pretty dead affair. (pp. 15-16)

John Sturrock, "Darkest Peru," in London Review of Books, *Vol. 9, No. 4, February 19, 1987, pp. 15-16.*

(Samuel) Dashiell Hammett

1894-1961

(Also wrote under pseudonym of Peter Collinson) American novelist, short story writer, scriptwriter, editor, and critic.

A celebrated author of American crime fiction, Hammett is widely considered the originator of the ''hard-boiled'' detective story. Writing in a terse prose style frequently compared to that of Ernest Hemingway, Hammett focused on the investigations of callous, cynical private detectives who became the archetype for scores of protagonists in American television, popular literature, and film. Although Hammett retained elements of the traditional English mystery, he abandoned the genre's genteel, idealized characters and exotic settings, favoring instead an ambiguous approach to the seedy world of urban crime. In Hammett's fiction, gangland criminals, corrupt officials, police, and even detectives share a degree of guilt. Critics have praised Hammett's colorful characterizations, his accurate reproduction of vernacular, and his use of realistic detail. Julian Symons characterized Hammett as ''an original in style and approach, and there are few of whom one can truly use the word. The least of his work is interesting, the best has a permanent place in literature.''

The Granger Collection

Hammett began his literary career writing short detective stories in the 1920s, many under the pseudonym Peter Collinson for the pulp magazine *Black Mask*. Although these stories are considered inferior to Hammett's novels, they exhibit his spare prose style and were among the magazine's most distinguished and popular pieces. The stories feature an unnamed detective known as the Continental Op, whose adventures are based on Hammett's experiences as a private investigator with the Pinkerton Detective Agency. Through the Op's first-person narration, the reader is offered a harsh, realistic view of detective work during the Prohibition era. Hammett's early short stories were first collected in *The Continental Op* (1945) and *The Return of the Continental Op* (1945). Later collections include *The Big Knockover: Selected Stories and Short Novels* (1966) and *The Continental Op: More Stories from the Big Knockover* (1967).

Hammett began writing longer fiction at the insistence of *Black Mask* editor Joseph T. Shaw. After publishing two of Hammett's novellas, *Black Mask* serialized what later became his first novel, *Red Harvest* (1929). An extremely violent book which includes more than twenty murders, *Red Harvest* details the brusque, ruthless means by which the Op divides and conquers a city overrun with gangsters and crooked politicians. Adhering to a work ethic common to all of Hammett's protagonists, the Op views his task merely as a job that must be completed, and the question of his personal guilt for the series of deaths he initiated by his crusade is assuaged by a wider portrait of civic corruption. Although *Red Harvest* did not achieve best-seller status, the novel received substantial critical acclaim. John G. Cawelti called it ''a bitter and ironic parable of universal corruption and irrational violence.'' *The Dain Curse* (1929), often considered Hammett's least successful work, was faulted for its complicated and melodramatic story line. By the end of this ominous Gothic novel, the Op cures a young woman of drug addiction, disproves a family curse, exposes a bogus religious cult, and solves a dozen murders. *The Dain Curse* was Hammett's last work featuring the Continental Op.

Hammett's third novel, *The Maltese Falcon* (1930), earned him wide popular and critical acclaim. This work, in which Hammett adopts an objective, third-person narrative to obscure his characters' motivations, remains among the most discussed works of detective fiction. Although the book ostensibly concerns detective Sam Spade's efforts to bring his partner's murderer to justice, Spade quickly becomes involved in an illicit scheme to locate a reputedly priceless statuette known as the Maltese Falcon. Much critical debate surrounds the intentions of Spade; while some critics contend that he is as heartless and corrupt as the novel's villains, others argue that his amoral behavior is a guise which best allows him to efficiently perform his duties. *The Maltese Falcon* has been adapted for film on three occasions; the most famous version, written and directed by John Huston, is a classic of American cinema.

The Glass Key (1931), regarded by many critics as Hammett's finest novel, provides a vivid portrait of an American city mired in political graft. The book's protagonist, Ned Beaumont, is a gambler and confidant of Paul Madvig, a corrupt political racketeer involved in securing a state senator's reelection. When the senator's son is murdered and Madvig is accused of the crime, Beaumont saves his friend by exposing the senator as the murderer. Reviewers noted such traditional themes in this novel as the relationships between power and corruption and personal and professional loyalty. Annica Leenhouts observed: "*The Glass Key,* though technically a murder mystery, is not a 'whodunit.' Instead, the killing . . . is used as a catalyst in an examination of human relations, more particularly those between Ned Beaumont and Paul Madvig, within the framework of a corrupt society's endangered status quo." *The Thin Man* (1934), although a highly popular novel, departs from the style of Hammett's previous works and is generally considered a lesser literary achievement. Written in a light, jocular tone, this book focuses on a wealthy, eccentric couple who unintentionally become involved in a murder mystery. *The Thin Man* was adapted for film.

Hammett wrote intermittently for Hollywood studios from 1930 to 1944. His screenplays include *After the Thin Man, Another Thin Man,* and *Watch on the Rhine;* the latter script is an acclaimed collaborative effort with dramatist Lillian Hellman. Although Hammett virtually abandoned fiction writing after 1944, substantial critical commentary and republication of his work attest to his enduring popularity and literary prominence. According to Ross Macdonald, "Hammett was the first American writer to use the detective-story for the purpose of a major novelist, to present a vision, blazing if disenchanted, of our lives."

(See also *CLC,* Vols. 3, 5, 10, 19 and *Contemporary Authors,* Vols. 81-84.)

JULIAN SYMONS

[*The essay from which this excerpt was taken was originally published in the book* The Crime Writers *in 1978.*]

It is difficult today to imagine the effect of reading Hammett short stories in the early or mid-1920s. Their plots were like others of the time, cramming as much violence as possible into a few pages, but the harsh tautness of the writing was new, and so was the hatred of corruption implicit in several stories. It was implicit, because Hammett never explained things. In these stories, as later in his books, he described events as they happened, without any comment by the author. Yet in spite of this deliberate detachment, an attitude is being conveyed in the opening sentence of the very early (1923) story **"House Dick":** 'The Montgomery Hotel's regular detective had taken his last week's rake-off from the hotel bootlegger in merchandise instead of cash, had drunk it down, had fallen asleep in the lobby, and had been fired.'

The suggestion, without a word being positively said to that effect, is that if you are a detective you should be honest, you shouldn't get drunk, and if you are dishonest and drunk on the job, it is right that you should be fired. This code of honesty is extended to include all sorts of loyalties, loyalties which are always personal and not corporate. 'When a man's partner is killed he's supposed to do something about it,' Sam Spade says, and this is so even though the partner is fairly worthless. A similar code of loyalty between men is invoked in ***The Glass Key,*** although there all sorts of subtleties and contradictions are involved. There is also an ethic of the job. The princess in **"The Gutting of Couffignal"** (1925) is certain that the Op won't shoot her if she tries to escape, and is astounded when he puts a bullet through her calf. This deliberate shooting of a woman must have outraged many readers at the time. . . . Several of the early stories anticipate scenes in the novels, and the Op's treatment of the princess prefigures Spade's sending up of Brigid O'Shaughnessy.

The obvious likeness of style in early Hammett stories to those of Hemingway's first work has prompted arguments about possible influences. Hemingway could not have influenced Hammett because before 1925 he had published nothing in America, and it is not likely that early Hammett influenced Hemingway. Times of social change are often accompanied by changes in literary style, and the United States after World War I was a society in turmoil. The new world created by Prohibition, gangsterism and the loosening of sexual and social restrictions could not be adequately expressed in the prose of Edith Wharton or even by the flat realism of Sinclair Lewis. Hammett and Hemingway used a prose which seemed to them at the time the only possible way of showing the world they were writing about: in Hemingway's case a world often of warfare and almost always of action, in Hammett's a violent, brutal and corrupt section of society. It was their intention to eliminate as far as possible the author's voice, in the hope that what emerged would be genuine and not synthetic. (pp. 169-70)

One must not claim too much for [Hammett's early] short stories. Hammett himself thought little of them, and allowed them to be reprinted only after constant pressure by publishers. Their merits are those of sharpness, hardness, bareness, but the determination to cut out unnecessary adjectives and to avoid purple passages means that the author is sometimes not much more than a photographic recorder. The style is interesting, particularly in comparison with what was being published elsewhere, but it is deliberately drained of colour, so that even scenes of action tend to be played down rather than up. . . .

[The turning-point in Hammett's career occurred] in the middle twenties, when he became discontented with what he was doing, and realized that it would be possible for him to write a full-length book in which he could criticize the society in which he lived through the medium of a violent story about crime. (p. 171)

The result is [***Red Harvest***], a novel remarkable in its attitude towards violence and towards the police, and in the way it conveys through the acid prose the stench of society in Personville, which is called Poisonville. This is a town in which all of the police are crooked, not just one or two. . . . The Op cleans up Poisonville by playing one gangster against another, so that they are wiped out. The end of the story offers little cheer to believers in good government. Personville, with all the gangsters dead (there are twenty-eight violent deaths in the book by my count, but it is not easy to be exact) is 'developing into a sweet-smelling and thornless bed of roses', but it is under martial law. (pp. 171-72)

After ***Red Harvest,*** it would seem that Hammett felt there was a limit to what could be achieved by direct accounts of violence, that the same points could and should be made more subtly. His first attempt to do this was the confused and disappointing ***The Dain Curse,*** with a distinctly softened Op telling the story. ***The Maltese Falcon*** . . . replaced the Op by Sam Spade, and also took most of the violence off-stage. We are told about people being killed, but don't see it happening.

Hammett's books can be seen from one point of view as a series of dialogues and confrontations through which the plot is revealed and tension built up. In ***The Maltese Falcon*** we begin with Spade and Brigid O'Shaughnessy, and move on to Spade-Dundy, Spade-O'Shaughnessy, Spade-Cairo and so on. Much the same applies to ***The Glass Key.*** These are stories in which conversation is made to do the work of description, and also of characterization. We are never in doubt that Gutman and Joel Cairo are villains, but what about Spade himself? 'Don't be too sure I'm as crooked as I'm supposed to be', he says to Brigid, but he never directly answers her question, when she asks whether he would have gone along with the villains if the falcon had been real. And in ***The Glass Key*** we are left in doubt about the relationship between Ned Beaumont and Paul Madvig. We can see that Madvig is a crooked politician in the American style, bluff and shrewd but really not too quick in the uptake. Beaumont works for him, protects him by staging a fake quarrel which Madvig believes to be real, later gets beaten up for him, but what is Beaumont's own attitude? Are we to regard him as less corrupt than Madvig, and if so why does he work in Madvig's organization? To such questions Hammett deliberately returns no answer. These ambiguities are essential to the art with which, in these two books, he approaches the complexities of guilt and innocence.

They helped him to create a new type of hero-villain, a character now common enough, but never rendered with the depth that is brought to the depiction of Spade and Beaumont. Such a hero-villain was characteristically an American of the Prohibition era and the Depression. He reflected the contradictory feelings of respectable people towards bootleggers and gangsters. (pp. 173-74)

In [such works as ***Red Harvest*** and ***The Glass Key***], Hammett pushed outwards the boundaries of the American crime story. Homosexuality was not unknown in such fiction, but it was not a common theme, and Hammett's depiction of the homosexual gunman Wilmer and his relationship with Gutman was very bold. So, of course, was the fact that Spade slept with Brigid. Within the context of the time, Hammett's treatment of sex was extremely frank. The beating-up of Beaumont by the apish Jeff in ***The Glass Key,*** Jeff's insistence that Beaumont likes it . . . , and the use of Jeff's instinctive sadism by Beaumont in killing Shad O'Rory, remain perhaps the most horrific scenes of their kind in any crime story. In ***Red Harvest*** the Op speaks of getting a rear out of violence, and this is made specific in ***The Thin Man,*** where Nora asks Nick, after he has tangled with Mimi Jorgensen, 'Tell me the truth: when you were wrestling with Mimi, didn't you have an erection?' (p. 175)

The Glass Key is a masterpiece of plotting, but one hopes and believes that Hammett ranked it in a different class from the rest of his books because in it, for the first time, his mastery of technique was truly used for artistic ends. The relationships between the characters, and not just the chief characters but those concerning such a minor figure as Opal Madvig, are conveyed with wonderful restraint. In addition the main theme of corruption, social and personal, is handled in a way beyond the reach of any other American novelist of the time. The book can bear comparison with any American novel of the thirties: it does not look out of place when put beside what Hemingway, Faulkner, Fitzgerald were writing at the time.

After ***The Glass Key***—or so one sees with hindsight—Hammett could go no further with fiction in the form of the crime story. It had become hampering to him, as once it had been a liberation. If he stuck to it now, there was no way he could go but down. And down, sure enough, Hammett went in his last, and immensely popular, book ***The Thin Man.*** (pp. 175-76)

[***The Thin Man*** is] a sparkling comedy done in terms of a murder mystery, in many places a very funny story. For Hammett, however, it was taking an easy option. He returned to first person narration, which had been given up in the two previous books. . . . This provided for him, as for Chandler later on, a comfortable ration of wisecracks and side-of-the-mouth comments. Everything is sacrificed to easy, flip reactions and to the relationship of Nick and Nora, which is done very well but necessarily remains superficial because, after all, this is just a comedy. No doubt Hammet deceived himself into thinking that this was an interim book, written between better ones, but if there had ever been a chance of this, the novel's tremendous success made it impossible. ***The Thin Man*** was the end of a career.

In his twelve years as a writer. Dashiell Hammett did a great deal, apart from being the Onlie Begetter of the true American crime story. ***The Glass Key*** is a magnificent novel, ***The Maltese Falcon*** remains a model of the detective thriller, no other book of the time gives violence and corruption the raw reality of ***Red Harvest.*** Almost everything he wrote, after the earliest pieces, was stamped with a personal mark. He was an original writer in style and approach, and there are few of whom one can truly use the word. The least of his work is interesting, the best has a permanent place in literature. (pp. 176-77)

Julian Symons, "Dashiell Hammett: A Writer and His Time," in his Critical Observations, *Ticknor & Fields, 1981, pp. 166-77.*

JOHN S. WHITLEY

Following the example of Steven Marcus [see *CLC,* Vol. 10], we may point to a number of features or incidents in Dashiell Hammett's novels which seem to break sharply with previous conventions of the detective story. I do not refer to the important changes of direction brought about by the "hard-boiled" school and instanced by such matters as the professional detective, organized crime, dark urban streets and a spare, colloquial, "tough" style. Rather, I wish to concentrate on features which are unexpected even *in* the context of "tough-guy" writing and which occur unexpectedly in order deliberately and provocatively to remind the reader, in the midst of an easily-identifiable style, of other styles and methods of enquiry into human behaviour and ultimately, of another and very different world-view which must be placed against the world-view of the rest of the novel. By adopting this technique, Hammett succeeds in drawing attention not only to the limitations of his particular kind of popular fiction but also to ways in which these very limitations can be used. The aspects of Hammett's novel to which I began by referring are not separated stylistically from the rest of the novel. But they nonetheless suggest to the reader that the first-person narrator might have to be viewed in a context other than that in which he normally presents himself for the reader's judgement (and, frequently, approval). (p. 443)

In the classic detective novel a murder is committed and the remainder of the story shows how the detective uncovers the culprit and his motives. Sometimes, during the subsequent investigation, a second or even a third murder may occur, but their place will clearly be subsidiary and they will arise directly from the initial crime and its investigation. One of Hammett's earliest contraventions of the classic formula was precisely not to render it more realistic, as implied by Raymond Chandler's famous statement that: "Hammett gave murder back to the kind of people that commit it for reasons, not just to provide a corpse. . . . He put these people down on paper as they are, and he made them talk and think in the language they customarily used for these purposes.'' Hammett raised death to a level of almost Jacobean melodrama which rendered it at once common and absurd. In the classic detective novel murder is seen as a monstrous aberration from the true path of society and this is strengthened by the use of very isolated locales, the country house, the monastery, the snowbound train, so that the crime can be solved without ''society'' being involved and the small group of people involved are cleansed by the detective's solution and sent back to society by the striking of a comic chord, usually the successful conclusion of an emerging romance between suitable juvenile leads. ***Red Harvest,*** on the other hand, is set *in* society, a society so poisoned, like the world of Jacobean melodrama, that one death is neither here nor there. The poison lies deep in the system and only a succession of furious blood-lettings will go any way towards purification. (p. 444)

[In ***Red Harvest***], the death-count must be well over thirty. Yet the first killing, of Donald Willson, the man who first brings the Continental Op to Personville, is solved before the novel is a third of the way through and the culprit turns out to be a lovesick bank clerk who has no direct connection with the gangsterism rampant in the city. From then on there are different small mysteries as various low-life characters slaughter each other and the task of solving these mysteries is, for the detective, far less significant than that of cleaning up the city, a 1920s equivalent of Western ''town-taming.'' Yet his method of ''purifying'' the city is markedly different from the manner in which the detective in the classic tradition solves his cases, from a detached, ratiocinative standpoint; and from the stance taken by the town-tamer, who is often an isolated man of steely integrity, a reluctant hero forced to take on the job only when the corruption becomes unbearable. Hammett's Op immerses himself in the destructive element. In a city where everyone says one thing with his mouth and another with his eyes; where language has become such a debased currency that the Chief of Police, Noonan, finds everything that happens ''fine''; and where a father can, without compunction, set his son up as a patsy, the Op finds himself at home and ''stirs things up.'' He becomes a master shape-changer, a liar, a treacherous manipulator until his identification with the diseased society . . . has taken him as far as possible from the stance of the classic detective. Like the Malcontent of Jacobean drama he exposes a society of which he is a mirror image. . . . Dinah Brand is one character who does sense how dangerous the Op is. The narrator has previously responded in a minor way towards her humanity by noting the slovenliness of her dress, hardly the mark of a femme fatale. Yet Dinah, like the Op, is branded by the nature of her world. She uses in order not to be used and is appalled to find that the detective plays the game more adroitly. . . . (pp. 445-46)

She is right to be appalled, for shortly afterwards the Op gives evidence of the extent of his ruthlessness when he betrays Red at the peace meeting, a betrayal which leaves even such a hard-bitten thug as Red astounded at such treachery: ''He stared at me with dumbfounded eyes. He gaped. He couldn't understand what I had done to him.'' Shortly after this incident the detective goes to see Dinah Brand again. She asks him if he has been up to more of his ''cute tricks'' and instead of answering her: ''I went back into the kitchen, opened the top of the refrigerator, and attacked the ice with an ice pick that had a six-inch awl-sharp blade set in a round blue and white handle.'' He makes the drinks and then, apparently, lets his guard slip for the first time in the novel. He tells Dinah Brand that all the killing is making him ''blood-simple'' and that it is the place's fault: ''It's this damned burg. . . . It's what this place has done to me.'' . . . The chapter (XX) ends with Dinah giving the Op a good deal of gin liberally laced with laudanum. (p. 446)

[Chapter XXI of ***Red Harvest***] opens with the Continental Op having two dreams. In the first he walks most of the main streets in America searching for a woman wearing a black veil whose name he cannot remember. In the end she meets him in the lobby of a railroad hotel and embarrasses him by kissing him in front of a number of people. In the second he searches with an open knife through the streets of a strange city for a small brown man in a large sombrero whom he intends to kill. He runs at the man over the heads and shoulders of a large crowd and chases him to the top of a high building. As he closes his fingers on the man's egg-sized head they both plunge off the roof and the Op awakens to find himself clutching the handle of the ice-pick which is embedded in Dinah Brand's left breast. As soon as he has examined the situation he carefully wipes everything clear of fingerprints, leaves, and arranges an alibi by working out a deal with one of Personville's toughest gangsters, Reno Starkey. The first dream makes clear at least the minimal lure of Dinah Brand and suggests that the Op is both attracted and repelled by it. The second dream suggests both that he does tread dangerously on many people in his efforts to effect a ''solution'' to the problem of Personville and that there may be a strong affinity between the hunter and the hunted, an affinity underlined by their dual plunge from the high roof.

The classic detective story has little time for dreams. Even a detective as enamoured of intuition and imagination as Poe's Dupin would give only half the credit to the poet and couldn't avoid giving the other half to the mathematician. The relatively logical, ratiocinative processes by which most classic detectives sift the clues, weigh the personalities and build up the chains of causation do not allow for the murky half-truths, the promptings of the subconscious, the illogical premonitions flashed forth by dreams. As this point in ***Red Harvest,*** Hammett lines up less with Chandler and Ross Macdonald than with Patricia Highsmith who repeatedly uses the *doppelganger* motif to blur the roles of pursuer and pursued, manipulator and victim, and to suggest that the classic detective story, concerned with justice rather than compassion, assigns guilt far too easily and narrowly. (p. 447)

Certainly Chapters XX and XXI of ***Red Harvest*** overwhelmingly suggest that the Op's dream has a powerful rightness. He *was* responsible for Dinah's death because he ''stirred things up.'' He did have a reason to get rid of her because she offered a human life-line he couldn't afford to grasp if he was to do his job. She represented, that is, a tarnished but real humanity that his vision of Personville could not allow for. It cannot be an accident that the gangster Reno who gives the Op his alibi turns out to be Dinah's real killer. . . . The dream has told the reader a kind of truth which the Op could never admit in the daylight world and which the formula of the hard-boiled detective thriller would otherwise have little opportunity to express. In a brief but illuminating treatment of ***Red Harvest*** in his book *Adventure, Mystery and Romance,* John G. Cawelti argues that Hammett, in order to maintain the hard-boiled formula, pulls away from the implications of the dream sequence and legitimizes all the Op's activities by refocusing on the violence and corruption of Personville, which the Op finally clears up, leaving it under martial law [see *CLC,* Vol. 19]. According to Cawelti, ". . . Hammett must somehow pull his hero out of the moral dilemma created by his immersion in violence, thus freeing him from the devasting awareness of personal guilt."

Obviously there is a good deal of truth in this view. What would happen if the Op did realize and accept such overwhelming personal guilt? A dark night of the soul? Abandonment of the case? Suicide? At all events the formula would have to be broken asunder by such a revelation, and the problem with breaking the formula is that the novelist asks too much of the reader in jumping from one kind of novel to another and risks creating too many frustrations by his failure to follow the formula to a satisfactory conclusion. . . . Hammett, it seems, would rather work within the formula and render it as flexible and inclusive as possible. However, the problem with Cawelti's view is that it is the Op who insists that it is the place's fault and not necessarily Hammett.

The Op himself makes no editorializing comment on the dreams and on waking and finding himself in such a compromising position he reverts swiftly both to his detective expertise and his unerring sense of self-preservation. . . . In other words Hammett sets up, throughout the novel, patterns of association between the Op and the world he is supposed to be cleansing which act, for the reader, as reinforcements of the guilt and self-loathing suggested by the sub-conscious through the medium of the Op's dream. There is no evidence that the Op realizes the meaning of his dreams and certainly no indication that he would be prepared to act in any different manner as a result of realizing them. The dream, nonetheless, may act as a clear wedge between the narrator and the reader; a point where the narrator has moved further away from the reader's moral norms, making narrator/reader collusion in the "truth" of the formula more difficult to sustain. The only way in which the Op can solve the "problem" of Personville is by pretending to be as evil as its denizens; but is he only pretending? Little in his behaviour suggests loyalty to ideals, human relations or even abstract conceptions of the law. He believes only in himself in the narrowest possible sense. It is therefore easy to see why a number of contemporary critics of Hammett would join with Cawelti in calling him "a bleak and stoical pessimist"; yet I would suggest that the episodes of the dream and its related components in the novel, especially Dinah Brand and the minimally warm relationship she offers, bring the reader a brief glimpse of another moral and social order which the Op denies but which the reader must retain to balance against the "nada" of the detective's vision.

Another important feature of Hammett's writing is exemplified in his second novel, ***The Dain Curse*** (1930). In this novel the Op finds himself involved in a case of Byzantine complexity in which he is helped along by a writer friend, Owen Fitzstephan, who has a liking for Gothic mystery and "darkness." At the outset it may seem that Fitzstephan is no more than the hard-boiled detective story's equivalent of the detective's foil. . . . He is, however, separated from traditional figures by two factors. In the first place, his various meetings with the Op have the cumulative effect of a running debate on the nature of the detective work and ways of apprehending "truth." Fitzstephan is a Gothic Romantic. . . . He relates himself to Romantic fiction and compares himself with the Op in literary terms: "I've been thinking of Leggett in terms of Dumas, and you bring me a piece of gimcrackery out of O. Henry." The Op accuses him of "just being literary"; Fitzstephan counters with, "It's fellows like you that take all the colour out of life." The debate continues throughout the book until its dénouement, when the second factor comes into play: Fitzstephan stands revealed as the lunatic mind behind all the crimes relating to the alleged Dain "curse." His is a mind, like Iago's, which has decided to make the external world conform to its crazy theories about how it *should* work. This could, of course, be seen as the usual hard-boiled put-down of the romantic and the intellectual. Certainly an element of control in the Op's procedures involves countering any language which seems to be overloading its subject adjectively or by extensive cultural reference. . . . People who speak as though they had received even a modicum of education are often treated very brutally. (pp. 448-50)

Romanticism, too, takes severe punishment in hard-boiled fiction. In the short story **"Fly Paper"** (1929) Hammett makes the solution to the mystery hinge on the discovery of a romantic novel, *The Count of Monte Cristo,* amid whose pages he discovers several sheets of fly paper and realizes that they have been boiled to produce a lethal quantity of arsenic: the romantic novel as poison. A more sustained attack on romanticism occurs in the view Hammett's detectives take of women. In the story **"The Gutting of Couffignal"** (1925), a supposedly aristocratic woman is proved to be the villainess. The Op's description of her is significant: "The whiteness of her face was nothing to go by. . . . Her voice was smoothly cool. . . . Her strong slender body became the body of a lean crouching animal . . . out of it . . . rose the princess again, cool and straight." The problem with most of the women the Op meets is neither that they present a sexual threat nor that they offer the possibility of social compromise, so much as that they are shape-changers, indices of a world in flux, where nothing is what it seems and where order and control seem impossible. (p. 451)

Yet it seems there is more to the fingering of Fitzstephan than this clear aspect of hard-boiled fiction. In Chapter XI of ***The Dain Curse*** the Op, in a semi-drugged state, encounters a horrifying vision: "Its feet—it had feet, but I don't know what their shape was. They had no shape, no fixed form. . . . No feature or member ever stopped twisting, quivering, writhing long enough for its average outline, its proper shape, to be seen . . . [it] was as fluid and as unresting and as transparent as tidal water." The "God" apparition in this chapter is terrifying to the Op in the same terms as the woman in **"The Gutting of Couffignal"** and these terms are very much part of the Gothic machinery used to validate (possibly) the power of the irrational. It is particularly significant that the fluidity of the apparition is likened to the fluidity of water, the prime agent of the irrational in Brown's *Wieland* and in *Moby-Dick.* The Op, both in terms of his job and his personality, must water things down, by language and visual proof, to something well-defined and contextually understandable. Just as, after his discovery of Dinah Brand's body, he follows a usual methodical, self-protective routine, so as he escapes from the apparition he is relieved to be attacked again, when it is by a recognizably human assailant. (pp. 451-52)

Neither of the episodes I have treated are the usual material of detective fiction of any formula and both suggest other kinds of "truth" than those provided by the dénouements. In ***The Dain Curse*** this is made clear by the "truths" with which the Op opposes the "Gothic" developments. . . . As Steven Marcus pointed out, Hammett's detectives tend to substitute their own fictions for the fictions presented to them. These fictions may or may not be more coherent and feasible than those of the criminals but they cannot have the same pretensions to hold "truth" as the dénouements of, say, Ellery Queen. In ***Red Harvest*** the question of individual guilt becomes submerged in a wider view of social guilt, but this view is promulgated by the specific activities of the Op in "stirring things up": in a sense, he solves what he creates. (p. 452)

In the last chapter of ***The Dain Curse*** the Op draws the various threads of the affair together but his dénouement is based on Fitzstephan's courtroom testimony and the Op cannot be sure that everything Fitzstephan says is right. At one point in the novel the Op is using Fitzstephan as a sounding-board for his theories about the case, but the usual confidence in ratiocination is completely missing: "I hope you're not trying to keep this nonsense straight in your mind. You know damned well all this didn't happen. . . . If you want to believe that it did, all right, I don't. I'd rather believe I saw things that weren't there." Tongue-in-cheek as this may appear to be, it indicates, along with the other elements I have discussed, the way in which Hammett is subverting the generally accepted formula on behalf of a bleaker, much less reassuring view of the mysterious world. It is fair to say that we are left unclear about a number of aspects of the case, including the identity of Edgar Leggett's murderer and, indeed, the question of Fitzstephan's motives. Is he simply an insane plot-maker or is he a part of a genuine Dain curse, since he turns out (according to his own admission in the last chapter) to be a member of the Dain family? In this fog the Op's activity is not that of an Olympian jigsaw puzzle-solver but the creator of a puny, curiously solipsistic security. (pp. 452-53)

Hammett's detectives are often included, along with many of their successors, in the famous statement by Raymond Chandler: "But down these mean streets a man must go who is not himself mean, who is neither tarnished nor afraid." . . . I do not see Hammett contributing very much to this particular development in the figure of the private eye. His detectives (with the possible exception of Nick Charles—and no self-respecting private eye should be married) operate in no recognizable cultural or social traditions; their motives are bound to remain obscure since their rôles in the books are precisely that, an endless series of masks and masquerades in order to combat the chaos around them without becoming involved or revealing human weaknesses. Sam Spade's famous words have been used to demonstrate a viable identity located, like that of the most stable of Hemingway's characters, in doing one's job properly: "I'm a detective and expecting me to run criminals down and then let them go free is like asking a dog to catch a rabbit and let it go." Yet there is surely a terrible irony in vesting your identity in a job which cannot allow you to reveal a true identity but only a series of bogus identities; which cannot allow you any authentic relations with people or nature or ideas, but, indeed, forces you to destroy any possibility of such relationships. . . . [Hammett's detectives] rely on their own strength and invention to maintain their security, yet their strength resides not in a stable personality but in the ability to change like a chameleon to meet the needs of a fluctuating world, to hold to the security of the present moment, and their invention is always powerfully destructive in human terms. They operate not from the base of a recognizable interior self but from a deliberately created void. They cannot be seriously damaged because there is nothing there to damage. . . . Hammett's heroes persistently do harm without ever leaving themselves the chance to feel guilty. (pp. 453-54)

John S. Whitley, "Stirring Things Up: Dashiell Hammett's Continental Op," in Journal of American Studies, *Vol. 14, No. 3, December, 1980, pp. 443-55.*

JAMES NAREMORE

Dashiell Hammett is a profoundly romantic figure, and the most important writer of detective fiction in America after Edgar Allan Poe. During the years when he was doing his best work—chiefly the late 1920s—he managed to reconcile some of the deepest contradictions in his culture. He was a man of action and a man of sensibility, an ex-private-eye who looked like an aristocrat; he wrote five novels and a few dozen stories which provided material for scores of film, radio and television adaptations, but at the same time he evolved one of the most subtle and influential prose styles of his generation. (p. 49)

[All of Hammett's protagonists] speak with what might be called the Hammett voice. . . . Its diction is homely; its syntax mainly declarative statements strung together with conjunctions. It has a fine rhythm which depends on the rather calculated run-on syntax, the driving repetition of certain words and the variation between long and short periods; nevertheless, this rhythm is meant to seem more instinctive than eloquent. It is a transparent language, of the sort that wants to cut through the crap and get down to truths so basic to the culture that they seem like natural laws. (p. 50)

This less deceived language is always placed in the dialogue of the detective or in his first-person narration, rather than in the neutral, third-person descriptions, where Hammett's prose is much more ambiguous and stylised. It is a dramatised voice, taking the form of a virile man talking to women, children or mendacious crooks. It isn't quite the voice of Reason, as with Dupin or Holmes, because it has less to do with solving puzzles than with exposing various kinds of falsehood or naïveté. Nor is it quite the voice of Metaphysics or Morality, as with Father Brown (even though in a general sense any fictional detective becomes the story's omniscient narrator and hence a type of God), because Hammett is sceptical of absolutes and his heroes are not virtuous. It is more like the voice of Male Experience, and it usually speaks with brutal frankness after a period of reticence or silent knowingness. . . . Clearly it is a voice which cannot be taken in by abstract appeals to morality or even love, and while it situates itself on the right side of the law, it is too honest to give the usual reasons for being there. (pp. 50-1)

The sceptical, unpretentious honesty of Hammett's various spokesmen is one of the things that marks him as a writer with serious aspirations. But because he is a writer of detective stories, and because he is such a classic instance of the literary tough guy, he presents special problems for the critic who wants to take him seriously. His fiction is a rare combination of light entertainment and radical intelligence. He challenges the easy distinctions between popular and high art, and the critical language that normally sustains those divisions; any critical approach to him is likely to go awry if it becomes too serious, too sociological or too frivolous. A much greater problem is that the toughness of his characteristic voice is sexualised, linked to fantasies of male power, and nowadays especially it invites an easy clinical interpretation. . . . Hence the sexual case against Hammett needs to be acknowledged at the outset, in order to get at the complexities beyond it.

The pen may not always be a substitute penis, but with Hammett it often seems to be. His best prose has a Parnassian hardness, a lack of 'feminine' adornment, and many of his titles have a phallic quality. He writes about strong, silent men who have an acute sense of discipline, and about predatory women who have to be sent off to prison. His detectives are usually bachelors, but unlike their nineteenth-century predecessors they are loners, eating meals in various restaurants or hotel rooms, living as far from domesticity as a frontier scout. They are somewhat homophobic . . . and although they are attracted to the sexy females they encounter, the only women they trust are the ones who behave like boy scouts. (pp. 51-2)

Hammett was fond of blood sports and military camaraderie, and he wrote fiction in which women are always 'other' to a central male consciousness. It would be meaningless to call him a latent homosexual because everyone is always potentially another sex; nevertheless his work speaks a masculine ideology, generally portraying women as naïve students of male wisdom or as dangerously amoral creatures. What redeems Hammett is that his protagonists never become proto-fascist supermen of the James Bond variety. His novels are written in an impersonal, detached style that sometimes allows the male ethos to undermine itself, and his readers are not allowed to settle into a comfortable identification with characters like Sam Spade. . . . [A] properly useful analysis of Hammett's sexual politics should avoid glib ego-psychology; it should focus on Hammett's language rather than his 'personality', partly because he was always deeply concerned with problems of literary form, and partly because his style was an historical phenomenon.

American literature of the twenties was generally hard-boiled, and if Hammett had not become the 'father' of the tough detective, someone else probably would have. Actually his attraction to the detective story is as much a sign of his aestheticism as of his love of male action. Like Chandler, he began by writing verse, and like the other aesthetes of his period he found his true vocation by reacting against the genteel, prettified, vaguely homosexual tone of the nineties. . . . Hammett's distinction is that he applied the new literary sensibility to the pulps, attacking bourgeois values from below rather than from above. . . . Hammett was therefore very much a part of the literary atmosphere of his period, and it is no accident that he and Hemingway became popular at virtually the same moment. (pp. 52-3)

The reputation Hammett ultimately achieved is succinctly stated by his current paperback publishers, who describe him as the 'creator of the modern, realistic crime novel'. We should remember, however, that the origin of any literary form is impossible to establish. . . . Hammett's work seems real in the sense that it constructs a relevant model of his society, but also in the sense that it never departs truly from the realist conventions of the nineteenth century. He was a key practitioner of what was immediately named a 'modern' style, but much of his early work was geared to the demands of pulp fantasy. Before examining some of the more unusual aspects of his fiction, therefore, it may be useful to emphasise the typical fantasies he offers his readers. (p. 54)

[Hammett's] early fiction concerns [the Op], a short, fat, fortyish man with no name and no life beyond his job with the San Francisco branch of the Continental Detective Agency. He is an unglamorous and hence 'realistic' creation who, in terms of his general social status, probably resembles the majority of Hammett's first readers. There is in fact a potentially Walter-Mittyesque comedy (which Hammett takes care not to exploit) in the disparity between the Op's appearance and his physical powers. (p. 55)

[The Op resembles] other great detective heroes in being improbably heroic and a bit eccentric—outwardly the quintessential company man, he seems to love his rough life for its own sake. He is an effective instrument of fantasy precisely because he does not encourage readers to imagine that they are handsomer, younger or richer (W. H. Auden's test for 'escapist' literature); instead he encourages the notion that such things do not matter, given courage, stamina and a certain hard-edged view of life.

The Op needs these last qualities because he inhabits a world of almost cataclysmic violence; some of his longer adventures have as much action as a Keystone cops film and more corpses than an Elizabethan revenge tragedy. It is difficult to keep count of the dead in **"The Big Knockover," "$106,000 Blood Money," "Corkscrew,"** ***Red Harvest*** and ***The Dain Curse*** (1929), all of which have plots that leap from one killing to another and scenes of pitched battle that portray a society literally at war. (p. 56)

It is difficult to tell how much burlesque is intended in these over-heated visions—although Hammett seems to me to have a greater sense of humour in the Op stories than is usually recognised. The Op recounts everything in deadpan fashion, as if he were making raw reports under pressure. The style gives him a plausible character, and it suggests that Hammett himself has the same values as his protagonist, doing a quick professional job in a relatively disreputable but adventurous trade, with a minimum of fuss and single-minded determination to get the story told. In a sense, the plainness of the language contributes to the illusion of realism and honesty, especially when Hammett combines the spectacular events with documentary detail or accounts of the more quotidian aspects of the Op's job. He fills the stories with precise, almost city-map-style references to San Francisco street and place names, and he likes to include bits of information about the 'inside' of professional detective work. (p. 57)

[Hammett's later novels utilize] a third-person narration which presents everything from the detective's point of view without ever telling us what the detective is thinking. The narrator stands outside the character, like a camera watching an actor, describing only his movements. But it is typical of Hammett that this language of pure action sometimes calls attention to itself *as* language. Here, for example, is a scene from ***The Maltese Falcon,*** just after Spade has received a phone call telling him that his partner has been murdered:

> Spade's thick fingers made a cigarette with deliberate care, sifting a measured quantity of tan flakes down into curved paper, spreading the flakes so that they lay equal at the ends with a slight depression in the middle, thumbs rolling the paper's inner edge down and up under the outer edge as forefingers pressed it over, thumbs and fingers sliding to the paper cylinder's ends to hold it even while tongue licked the flap, left forefinger and thumb pinching their end while right forefinger and thumb smoothed the damp seam, right forefinger and thumb twisting their end and lifting the other to Spade's mouth. He picked up the pigskin and nickel lighter that had fallen to the floor, manipulated it, and with the cigarette burning in a corner of his mouth stood up.

(p. 60)

In part, this technique serves the interest of the mystery story, characterising Spade in terms of the objects around him, but keeping his chain of thought a secret until he solves the crime. By withholding information, Hammett gives the plot tension, investing the simplest movements with the importance that gunshots and fistfights had in the earlier fiction. As in the Op stories, the method suggests a world where actions are more important than thoughts; it portrays Spade as a sort of latter-day cowboy, rolling a cigarette while he ponders his next move. In other ways, however, the technique is less 'organic'. Except for the phrase, 'made a cigarette with deliberate care', the description of Spade rolling a cigarette is almost as defamiliarised as the pseudo-scientific account of Bloom returning home in the penultimate chapter of *Ulysses*. It makes Spade a technician, brooding on the fine points of a problem, but it also displaces the traditional ratiocinative values of detective fiction in favour of another quality that was always inherent in the form—a representative of the surfaces of things. Detective stories are the most fetishistic of literary genres because the trivial objects of the investigation—the 'clues'—function like the overdetermined symbols of dreams. But in Hammett's work this overdetermination extends to everything: the reader, confronted with impersonality and a cool, objective description, is invited to interpret the meaning of images. (p. 61)

Hammett was no avant-gardist, but the impersonal, ironic technique of his novels grows out of a deeply critical and sceptical attitude towards American society, a view of life that affects the form of his fiction in other important ways. The endings of his novels are always bleak, even in the early work where there is somewhat less emphasis on characterisation. . . . Always Hammett threatens to undermine the authority of the detective and the neat closure of the typical mystery plot; even the tough-guy ideology and the love of adventure which defines his heroes show signs of strain. The following brief review of his later work should indicate the delicate balance he sustained between popular forms and the deep questioning of those forms.

From the first Hammett was admired by critics who did not particularly like the detective-story formula, because in his novels the crimes were messy, the chase circuitous, the solution to the murder less important than the depiction of a *milieu*. To slightly revise Edmund Wilson's famous quotation, Who cares who killed Miles Archer? In one sense nobody, and that is the whole point of ***The Maltese Falcon.*** Archer's murder has a crucial function in the plot, and is part of a whole chain of enigmas; nevertheless, we and Spade soon become distracted by the search for the falcon, and one of Hammett's deepest ironies is that Spade himself has a possible motive and the right temperament to have committed the crime. Archer is an unpleasant fellow whom we meet only once, when he crudely looks Brigid up and down and pockets her money. He has been cheating on his wife, who in turn has been having an affair with Spade, and he is not particularly clever or trustworthy as a detective. Spade thinks he is a 'louse' and has been planning to sever the partnership anyway, by legal means. He tells Brigid that she has done him a kind of favour by killing Archer, and when he turns her over to the police the seven reasons he gives have nothing to do with revenge, justice or law and order. Commentators on his long speech usually claim that it shows a 'code' which sustains Hammett's heroes; looked at closely, however, the speech is about nothing more than self-preservation. Spade knows that somebody has to 'take the fall' for the murder, and that Brigid is likely to get a 'better break' from the police. 'When a man's partner is killed', he says, 'he's supposed to do something about it'; in other words he is *expected* to do something about it, and if he did not obey the conventional social ethic, his business would suffer. People would assume he is either incompetent or a killer himself. (pp. 62-3)

Spade's climactic speech indicates that Hammett isn't writing about guilt or innocence, or even about professional ethics, but about what he regards as a bewildering, predatory struggle beneath civilisation. Civilisation makes everyone, including the detective, an impostor. 'Don't be too sure I'm as crooked as I'm supposed to be', Spade tells Brigid. 'That kind of reputation might be good for business.' This remark may serve to reassure the reader about Spade's intentions, but it is a more ambiguous reassurance than we are usually given. It tends to mock the idea of a 'just solution' to murder, just as the Maltese Falcon itself mocks the idea of ownership or private property. Born out of a colossal hypocrisy—a 'Holy War' which, as Gutman says, 'was largely a matter of loot', the Falcon does not rightly belong to anyone. . . . The final irony, as Stephen Marcus has pointed out, is that the *rara avis* turns out to be as bogus as everyone else; a disguised (but rather phallic) signifier, it is supposed to have value beneath its skin, giving a meaning to the frantic, violent activity of the novel. But when the skin is peeled away, there is only a lead shape, an empty object of exchange.

Spade is the hero of this potentially anarchistic world, but he is a hero of an unusual kind. Morally he is hardly any better than his dead partner, and there is nothing particularly likeable about him. . . . He seems as potentially cruel as any of his adversaries. . . . (p. 64)

[Yet, ***The Maltese Falcon***] makes us respect Spade in a complex, qualified way, chiefly because of his intelligence and ability to master his own sometimes ugly instincts. His behaviour suggests that he has a heightened sense of the danger lying in wait for him should he try to join Brigid or Gutman. In the first chapter he is vividly contrasted with Archer, who serves as his foil. Spade has a suspicion of easy sex and money, a reserve that ultimately keeps him alive. He tells Brigid that life is not a 'clean orderly sane responsible affair', and what is especially interesting about this philosophy is that it means that he might as well be a crook as a cop. At some point he has become neither, operating a private practice in a legally indeterminate region between. Ultimately he serves the interests of official society, but not out of any faith in its justice. His job satisfies his taste for hunting and adventure, and he can survive best on the right side of the law.

It is almost a rule of Hammett's novels that at some point the detective's ambiguous position must be tested by a bribe. If he passes this test, his victory is mainly personal, a kind of survival of the fittest. There is no question of returning the society to some kind of order; if decent people exist in that society, they are always rather naïve, like Effie Perine and her family, or like the 'liberal' Donald Willsson, the first murder victim in ***Red Harvest.*** The only alternative to such innocence is the stoic, isolated intelligence of the detective, who is affected in various ways by the world he investigates. Thus another rule of Hammett's novels is that the detective is always personally involved in some basic betrayal of trust. In ***Red Harvest*** the Op complains that the violence of Personville (the most obviously symbolic of Hammett's names) is making him 'blood simple', and he feels vaguely responsible for the murder of Dinah Brand, the amoral lady who has been a sort of friend to him; in fact at one point he thinks he might have stabbed her while he was drunk or drugged. (p. 65)

The best example of this troubling, pessimistic quality of Hammett's work is ***The Glass Key,*** which gives such a detached, accurate picture of the politics of a moderately large American city that the detective story elements—a set of clues involving a hat and a fancy walking stick, a denouement in which an amateur detective forces a confession out of a killer—become somewhat obtrusive. To his credit, however, Hammett treats these elements ironically and makes them thematically functional. For example, the clue of the hat, emphasised throughout, is finally dismissed as 'unimportant'. The detective doesn't believe the confession, calling it a 'campaign speech' and leaving us in doubt as to what actually happened. As in ***Falcon,*** the victim deserved to die, and the detective says that the killer performed a 'favour'. Also as in ***Falcon,*** the only truly innocent characters are naïve females who live under the protection of corrupt men. Paul Madvig, the wrongly accused suspect, is a political boss who collects graft and intimidates the nominal leaders of the community into following his orders. He is a likeable enough fellow, with a sweet old mother and a certain working-class directness, and Ned Beaumont says he 'never had anybody killed'; nevertheless he is as crooked as anyone else. (p. 66)

The Glass Key has a good deal in common with modernist literature . . . , chiefly because it refuses to give the reader any comfortable position from which to judge the events it depicts. The crooked politicians, the sadistic gangsters, the criminally naïve females, the cruelly detached gambler-detective are all recognisable stereotypes from familiar cultural or literary 'texts', but they are presented without any narrative commentary and without any character (like Chandler's Marlowe) who could act as a moral norm. ***The Glass Key*** has all the adventure and heroics of a normal melodrama and much of the social detail of a muck-raking naturalist novel, but it presents this material neutrally. What, finally, are we to think of Beaumont and Madvig? How are we to judge the city without feeling like the 'respectable element' of comfortable bourgeois citizens whom Beaumont mocks? Pehaps the deepest reason why we feel Hammett is tough is that his commonplace, clear language is destructive of any liberal complacency.

After this impressive novel, however, Hammett seems to have become cautious. ***The Thin Man,*** written two years later when he was out of money, strongly resembles the classic detective story form. Nick Charles, the hero, is a retired detective who has married a rich young woman; she becomes his Watson, eager to go slumming in the New York underworld. The murder plot is elaborately complicated and more like a puzzle than Hammett's other work. The setting is a glamorous one, and the tone is largely comic—perfect and harmless escapism for the years of the Depression. (p. 68)

With only a slight turn of the screw ***The Thin Man*** could have been as unsettling as any of Hammett's other works. The chief metaphor of the novel is cannibalism, established in the long quotation from Duke's *Criminal Cases of America* in chapter 13. And like the previous books, it returns us at the end to a world where nothing has fundamentally changed—as the Continental Op says to his client in ***Red Harvest,*** the city is 'all nice and clean and ready to go to the dogs again'. Hammett again calls the solution to the crime into slight question: in the last chapter Nick explains everything to Nora, acting the role of the typical omniscient detective. Normally in such scenes the detective is a privileged narrator, but this novel is comic and Nora Charles is no passive Watson. Her questions continually upset our expectations by exposing the holes in Nick's story. 'But this is just a theory, isn't it?' she asks. Nick says he is only trying to describe what is most probable, and reaches for a drink. At the end Nora complains, 'it's all pretty unsatisfactory.'

Of course Nora's words actually function as Hammett's defence; by satirising his form he allows it to work. Nevertheless, it is interesting that these are his last words as a novelist, and it may be significant that he gave them to a woman. (p. 69)

James Naremore, "Dashiell Hammett and the Poetics of Hard-Boiled Detection," in Art in Crime Writing: Essays on Detective Fiction, *edited by Bernard Benstock, St. Martin's Press, 1983, pp. 49-72.*

JAMES F. MAXFIELD

The Glass Key is perhaps the most controversial and problematic of Dashiell Hammett's five novels. Julian Symons gives the novel his highest praise: "***The Glass Key*** is the peak of Hammett's achievement, which is to say the peak of the crime writer's art in the twentieth century" [see *CLC*, Vol. 3]; in Robert I. Edenbaum's judgment, "***The Glass Key*** is Hammett's least satisfactory novel" [see *CLC*, Vol. 3]. Edenbaum supplies clearer reasons for his negative assessment than does Symons for his laudation. Edenbaum sees the novel's central weakness as Hammett's failure (or perhaps refusal) to clarify the motives of his protagonist: ". . . it is impossible to tell what is under Ned Beaumont's mask." As a result, crucial actions of the novel's hero are left ambiguous. The effect of this ambiguity, Peter Wolfe suggests, is to deprive Hammett's characters of any depth: "The book's dark glimmering surface reveals characters who resemble silhouettes or sheet-tin cutouts."

The causes of the ambiguity are inherent in the stylistic method Hammett chose for his final three novels. He employs a completely objective approach, merely reporting the conversations and describing the surface actions of his characters, never directly presenting their thoughts and feelings. . . . This objective style enables Sam Spade in ***The Maltese Falcon*** for nearly the entire novel to conceal from both the other characters and the reader the fact that he has possessed the solution to his partner's murder from the moment he heard of the circumstances of the killing. Ned Beaumont similarly hides from the reader and Janet Henry his suspicions of her father. But more troublesome—since it is not unusual for the hero of a detective novel to hold back the solution to the mystery until the last possible moment—is the fact that the reader can only speculate on Ned Beaumont's motives for agreeing to take Janet Henry with him to New York at the end of the book. While Ned may be in love with Janet, he certainly never says that he is; and as we shall see later, the novel allows a very different interpretation of his motivation.

The result of the obscurity of Ned Beaumont's motivations, Robert Edenbaum says, "is not the richness of fruitful ambiguity but the fuzziness of inner contradictions." Yet for an unsophisticated reader imbued with the conventions of popular fiction such ambiguity or fuzziness probably does not exist. Ned Beaumont is the hero of the book (the detective who solves the murder); Janet Henry is the heroine (the beautiful girl who aided the detective in finding the solution). (pp. 107-08)

In making this undoubtedly naive assumption, the conventional-minded reader is likely correct because the preponderance of evidence in the novel supports it. The reason a sophisticated critic like Edenbaum finds it difficult to make the same assumption is that he is considering Ned Beaumont as merely a variation on the detective heroes of Hammett's earlier fiction, the Continental Op and Sam Spade, both of whom resolutely resisted emotional commitments or romantic entanglements. Although he shares a number of traits with Spade and Op, Ned Beaumont is ultimately a different person and a different kind of hero. The reasons why he is willing to make the kind of emotional commitment they are not willing to make can best be understood through an examination of both the ways in which Ned Beaumont resembles the Op and Spade and the crucial ways in which he deviates from their behavior patterns.

One thing Hammett's heroes have in common is that, according to Karen Horney's formulations, they are all neurotics of a certain type. Horney argues that one of the defining characteristics of neurosis is the individual's shifting of his energies "from developing the given potentials of the real self to developing the fictitious potentials of the idealized self." The heroes of detective fiction are virtually all neurotics of the type whose idealized self is that of the master or dominator. . . . Almost every fictional detective's concept of self-worth collapses when he appears unable to solve a crime or bring a criminal to justice—in short when he fails to assert his mastery.

The hard-boiled detective—for which Hammett's Op and Sam Spade established the archetype—is also a neurotic of the "arrogant-vindictive type." In real life the origins of this neurosis typically lie in an abused childhood. (Hammett never tells us anything about the childhoods of his heroes. . . . The Hammett hero refuses to be the victim of anyone or anything—including his past.) As a result of being treated harshly as a child, the arrogant-vindictive personality "has a need to retaliate for all injuries and to prove his superiority to all rivals. . . . He trusts no one, avoids emotional involvement, and seeks to exploit others in order to enhance his own feelings of mastery." What better profession for a person who distrusts others and needs to feel superior to them than that of the detective? . . . Hammett's heroes take their greatest pride "in being above hurts and suffering." As Edenbaum puts it, the Hammett hero aspires to (and within the limits of most of the stories achieves) "a godlike immunity and independence, beyond the power of his enemies."

One way in which the hero's immunity is displayed is in his ability to bear physical pain. Much in the same manner as Dostoyevsky's Stavrogin, Sam Spade is able to receive a blow in the face from a policeman and through sheer will power suppress his impulse to strike back. . . . Sapped and dumped into the middle of San Francisco Bay, the Op swims seemingly for hours until he is finally rescued by a passing boat just as he loses consciousness; upon reviving he refuses to be taken to the hospital, cures his chill by drinking "half a pint of whiskey" and rubbing himself "with a coarse towel," then goes off to confront the villains (**"The Tenth Clew"**). (pp. 108-10)

There are, however, more subtle threats to the Hammett hero's invulnerability than that posed by physical pain. Emotional vulnerability is a far greater menace than physical vulnerability. The Continental Op is on guard against feeling pity for any of the criminals he encounters, lest that feeling deflect him from the performance of his duty. (p. 111)

Sexual desire is possibly the greatest threat to the Hammett hero's invulnerability. In story after story the Op encounters a beautiful but thoroughly unscrupulous female who seeks to tempt him from the performance of his duty. Of Elvira (alias Jean Delano) in **"The House in Turk Street"** and **"The Girl With the Silver Eyes"** the Op says, "She was as beautiful as the devil, and twice as dangerous." He describes Ines Almed in **"The Whosis Kid"** as "appealing, and pathetic, and anything else you like—including dangerous." The Op recognizes his potential vulnerability to the temptation these women present. (pp. 111-12)

The Op's chief defense against the temptation posed by the attractive female criminal is his role as detective. With Ines he reminds himself, "when the last gong rings I'm going to be leading this baby . . . to the city prison. That is an excellent reason—among a dozen others I could think of—why I shouldn't get mushy with her." In **"The Gutting of Couffignal"** when the beautiful Russian Princess, who has masterminded the robbery of the wealthy residents of the island, attempts to bribe the Op not only with a share of the loot but also with her body, he tells her that his instincts as a detective make acceptance of her offer impossible: "'You think I'm a man and you're a woman. That's wrong. I'm a manhunter and you're something that has been running in front of me. . . . You might just as well expect a hound to play tiddly-winks with a fox he's caught!'" In effect the Op is saying that in committing himself to his role as detective he has significantly reduced the range of his humanity—and with it the extent of his human vulnerability. The single instinct, that of the manhunter, overrides all other instincts—like sexual desire—that might interfere with it. (p. 112)

Sam Spade, the most intense arrogant-vindictive neurotic of Hammett's heroes, is quite careful to select sexual partners who are unsuitable for long-term relationships because they fail to possess the kind of characteristics that would deserve respect or admiration from him. The only "decent" woman in ***The Maltese Falcon*** is Spade's secretary, Effie Perine, and his way of praising her positive qualities is also his way of declaring her off-limits for his sexual attentions: "'You're a damned good man, sister'." By sexually involving himself only with women he dislikes (Iva Archer, the wife of his partner) and/or distrusts (Iva and Brigid O'Shaughnessy), Spade feels totally justified in treating them in the classic manner of the arrogant-vindictive neurotic who, [in the words of Karen Horney], exploits "women for the satisfaction of his sexual needs with utter disregard for their feelings."

Spade's great fear, moreover, seems to be that someday he will meet a woman who will use him as callously as he has treated other women. Although he itemizes seven different reasons why he has to turn Brigid O'Shaughnessy over to the police for having killed his partner Miles Archer, it is clear from the way he obsessively repeats a certain phrase that one reason predominates over all the others. Seven times in less than four pages he repeats with only slight variation the statement: "'I won't play the sap for you'." (One additional time he substitutes "sucker" for "sap.") His true enemy is not even Brigid; it is his emotional susceptibility which makes him potentially vulnerable to her. . . . Perhaps Brigid's greatest sin in Spade's eyes is that she has considered him a mere mortal man—like all the "others"—and failed to realize that he, not she, was properly cast in the godlike role (unmoved mover) in their relationship.

Where the Op, in an almost monk-like way, withholds himself from intimate sexual relationships and Spade's involvements with women are purely exploitative (and neither character seems to have a close friend of the same sex), from the beginning of ***The Glass Key,*** it is clear that [gambler] Ned Beaumont is capable of human commitments. Paul Madvig is his friend and Ned is concerned enough about Paul's welfare to give him the sort of candid advice . . . that a mere hanger-on would never have the nerve to offer. (pp. 116-17)

Although political boss Paul Madvig possesses the money and the power in Beaumont's milieu, the younger man is clearly the superior in terms of knowledge and judgment. He freely advises Madvig on subjects ranging from gang warfare . . . to courtship etiquette. . . . While giving such advice clearly allows Beaumont to feel superior, it also seems intended to promote his friend's welfare. When Beaumont judges that Madvig is embarked on a self-destructive course of action, the gambler plans to leave town, completely abandoning the financial benefits of their connection. Although Hammett's objective style makes it impossible for the reader to know Beaumont's exact motive when he is preparing to leave for New York at the end of Chapter 3, the most likely possibilities seem to be a desire not to witness Madvig's downfall or through the threat of his leaving to shock the politician into reevaluating his course of action. That Beaumont's motivation is not a selfish desire to desert a sinking ship but a genuine concern for his friend is indicated by the gambler's decision to stay after he and Madvig have fought and made up.

A crucial difference between Beaumont and the two detective heroes who preceded him is that detection is not Beaumont's profession. Spade and the Op endeavor to bring criminals to justice because it is their job to do so. . . . But as a gambler and close associate of a corrupt politician, Beaumont has his true allegiance with the foxes rather than the hounds; his motives for involving himself in the investigation of Taylor Henry's murder are personal rather than professional. Although Spade and the Op try to rule out or suppress feelings in their investigations, Beaumont only solves the murder in ***The Glass Key*** because of his feelings first for Paul Madvig then for Janet Henry.

To be sure, Beaumont does sometimes share with the Op and Sam Spade a willingness to exploit others ruthlessly. He humiliates the newspaper publisher H. K. Mathews in his own home in front of his young wife and then, after the older man has gone upstairs to bed, drinks and necks with the girl. . . . When Mathews responds to his wife's betrayal by shooting himself, Beaumont wastes no time on remorse; he simply steals and destroys Mathews' last will so that the publisher will have died intestate, enabling a Madvig-controlled judge to appoint an administrator of the estate who will see that Mathews' newspaper *The Observer* ceases its attacks on Paul. Although Eloise Mathews is apparently at least half right when she accuses Beaumont of being responsible for her husband's death, he never shows the faintest sign of regret for what he has done to either husband or wife. (pp. 117-19)

In the last four chapters of the novel it may seem that Beaumont is using Janet Henry in much the same way he used Eloise Mathews. He allows her to think that he is gathering information that may prove Madvig to be the killer of her brother, but actually he is laying a trap for her father whom he suspects of the murder. Even after the quarrel that effectively ends their friendship—Ned has told Paul that Janet hates him, and Paul has responded by accusing Ned of coveting Janet for himself—Beaumont's feelings toward Madvig can be considered his primary motivation. Clearing Paul of Taylor Henry's murder becomes a way not only of saving Paul but of getting revenge on him—by showing him that the Henrys have used him ruthlessly all the time. By taking Janet Henry away with him at the end of the novel, Beaumont deprives his former friend of the thing Paul himself said he wanted. . . . Ned is simply using Janet at this point to hurt Paul—who remains, as he has throughout the novel, the only other important person in Ned's life.

But Hammett's objective style allows us to draw other conclusions. It is just as likely, for instance, that Ned tells Paul about Janet because it seems to him the honorable thing to do. In their final conversation Paul feels that he has wronged Ned, that he has turned his friend against him by lying to him. When Ned says he has to leave town, Paul replies, "'Well, it serves me right'." By asking Janet to come out of the bedroom so Paul may see her, Beaumont is revealing that his motive for leaving is not so simple or self-righteous. He and Paul can no longer be friends because Ned is taking the woman Paul loves. Nor is it illogical to conclude that the reason Ned is taking her is that he loves her too.

The preponderant evidence of the latter part of [***The Glass Key***] indicates that Janet Henry is much more to Beaumont than the mere instrument of his revenge on Madvig. Beaumont's relationship with Janet Henry is very different from the one with Eloise Mathews. Because Eloise was clearly using Beaumont to hurt her husband, the gambler felt no compunction about using her for his own motives. Although Janet and Ned use each other too, they do so much more openly and honestly. . . . [The] two characters are open with each other concerning their feelings—even feelings likely to be unacceptable to the other person. Janet admits her hatred of Madvig and her passionate desire for vengeance on him, and Ned frankly tells her, "'The part of you that's tricked Paul and is trying to trick him is my enemy'." Later he tells her of a dream of his which symbolizes his doubts about her (he caught an enormous rainbow trout and she "threw it back in the water") and admits "'I'm not sure of you'."

Janet responds to Ned's fish dream by telling him a dream of her own—although she suppresses its true ending until just before the end of the novel. The dream, which supplies the book with its title, sums up one of Hammett's major themes and, in its final form, shows that Beaumont and Henry ultimately share the same vision of life. In the dream Janet and Ned are lost in a forest; exhausted and hungry, they come to a small house, through the windows of which they see a "great big table piled high with all imaginable food." But when they find a key and open the door, they discover the floor of the house is covered with "hundreds and hundreds of snakes." In Janet's first version of the dream she and Ned slam the door on the snakes, then climb up on the roof of the house, open the door again to allow the snakes to slither away, and go inside to eat the food after locking the door behind them. Later she admits that in the true ending, "'the key was glass and shattered in our hands just as we got the door open. . . . We couldn't lock the snakes in and they came out all over us and I woke up screaming'."

The dream offers a wide range of interpretive possibilities, particularly psychosexual (with both the key and the snakes being standard phallic symbols), but its basic meaning is relatively simple: it shows what happens when we seek to obtain our desires. Throughout the novel intense desire leads to disaster. (pp. 119-21)

Janet in her first, altered version of the dream tries to deny the tragic perception her unconscious has revealed to her. She constructs a happy, wish-fulfillment ending in which it is possible to have and enjoy what you want and evade the dangers attendant on it. Ned, with his more consciously tragic perception of reality, doubts the truth of this version immediately upon hearing it ("'I think you made that up'"). By the end of the novel Janet accepts both his and her own realization of the truth of the message the dream conveys.

While it may be helpful for a man and a woman who link their lives together to share the same vision of life, it would seem something of a disadvantage for that vision to be one which holds all desire—including their desire for each other—to be ultimately destructive. As Robert Edenbaum puts it, the logical interpretation of Janet's dream is that "to get at the heart's need is to open a Pandora's box. . . . It would seem that the only safety is in not letting down your guard in the first place: do without the food and you escape the snakes." Yet in running off together Janet and Ned are in effect choosing to go after the food. How can they make such a decision which goes against both reason and the promptings of the unconscious?

Janet asks similar questions when she considers her feelings about Madvig and Beaumont after her father's exposure. Of Paul she says, "'I hated him . . . and I wronged him and I still hate him'." To Ned she says, "'And you . . . tricked me and made a fool of me and brought this on me and I don't hate you'." . . . Janet asks Beaumont to take her away with him not because she has any good reason to believe that pursuing her desire for him will turn out any better than her pursuit of vengeance, but simply because she nevertheless *does* want him.

Ned's response to her request indicates that his motivation is basically the same: "'Do you really want to go or are you just being hysterical? . . . . it doesn't make any difference. I'll take you if you want to go'." In essence he is saying that it doesn't matter to him whether she is motivated by love or hysteria—he still wants her. Neither the Op nor Sam Spade would have gone off with Janet, for as detectives they both strove to be ruled as much as possible by reason. But Beaumont is a gambler instead of a detective—a man used to taking risks. . . . Because he is willing to accept the risks that human commitments entail, Beaumont is, if not Hammett's ideal hero, his most completely human hero. (pp. 121-23)

James F. Maxfield, "Hard-Boiled Dicks and Dangerous Females: Sex and Love in the Detective Fiction of Dashiell Hammett," in Clues: A Journal of Detection, *Vol. 6, No. 1, Spring-Summer, 1985, pp. 107-23.*

Richard Howard

1929-

American poet, translator, and critic.

Howard is well regarded for creating intellectual poetry in which he explores historical and aesthetic topics. Strongly influenced by Robert Browning's experiments with various poetic voices, Howard often employs dramatic monologues to present intimate biographical details of historical figures. The poem "1915," for example, from Howard's Pulitzer Prize-winning collection, *Untitled Subjects* (1969), relates Jane Morris's deathbed reminiscences of her husband, William Morris, and includes references to such important pre-Raphaelite artists as Dante Gabriel Rossetti and Edward Burne-Jones. Howard's predominant concerns include themes related to human identity, mortality, and the permanence of art. In other poems, he explores homosexuality and groups himself with what he perceives to be an artistic and sexual tradition that includes Walt Whitman, Oscar Wilde, and Hart Crane. While Howard is praised for his technical expertise and knowledge of a wide range of esoteric subjects, his verse also contains puns, epigrams, and other forms of wordplay.

In his first two volumes, *Quantities* (1962) and *The Damages* (1967), Howard demonstrates a range of styles yet adheres to formal rhythms and structures which evidence the influence of W. H. Auden. In *Untitled Subjects* and *Findings* (1971), Howard refines his use of the monologue, enabling him to render nineteenth-century personae through such forms as the narrative, the epistle, and the journal. He expands this format to include a second speaker in *Two-Part Inventions* (1974), rejecting rhyme and meter in favor of more dramatic syllabic stresses. *Fellow Feelings* (1976) contains additional monologues as well as several poems alluding to Howard's homosexuality. Both *Misgivings* (1979) and *Lining Up* (1984) include portions of "Homage to Nadar," a sequence of poems that correspond to photographs of French authors taken by photographer Felix Tournachon, more commonly known as Nadar. In this sequence, Howard expresses affinities for nineteenth-century French literature and declares that art is a vital and timeless element of temporal human existence. Howard is also respected for his numerous translations of French literature and for his critical assessments collected in *Alone with America: Essays on the Art of Poetry in the United States since 1950* (1969).

(See also *CLC*, Vols. 7, 10; *Contemporary Authors*, Vols. 85-88; and *Dictionary of Literary Biography*, Vol. 5.)

CLAUDE J. SUMMERS AND TED-LARRY PEBWORTH

Among the most accomplished of contemporary American poets, Richard Howard may also be the most learned and the most literary. At a time when many poets self-consciously reject the past, Howard writes poems which evoke varied and rich traditions. In his six distinctive collections of poetry, he has developed from a follower in the Audenesque line of intellectual lyricism into a master of his own vision, worrying the subtleties of language and life in poems which are at once elegant and vigorous. Central to his poetry, in all six of his volumes, is an intense preoccupation with time; and the development of his artistry is paralleled by his progressive responses to time. As Henry Sloss has written, "Change is the subject of Richard Howard's poetry; to contain change is its project" [see *CLC*, Vol. 10]. Whereas the early Howard finds few satisfying resolutions to the problems raised by the fact of time's passage, the mature poet is able to see the continuity of human experience as a means of transcending the limits of time. By becoming a poet of "otherness," Howard affirms the shared values which bridge the narrow spaces of individual lifetimes.

Howard's first two books, ***Quantities*** (1962) and ***The Damages*** (1967), composed of original lyrics in several forms, translations, and imitations, are the work of a sophisticated and introspective young man, prematurely old and preoccupied with aging. In these poems, Howard is obsessed with personal loss and public malaise. He is a virtuoso of rhythmic and stanzaic form while at the same time a curiously vulnerable survivor. "At thirty-three," he asks in **"A Far Cry After a Close Call"** **(*The Damages*)**

> what else is there to do
> But wait for yet another great white moth

With eager, enlarging eyes
To land on my chest
Slowly, innocently choking me off?

Howard's consciousness of time contributes to this almost paralyzing ennui so prevalent in ***Quantities*** and ***The Damages***. . . . The reluctant acceptance of the inevitable, "it will be night," colors the poet's attitude throughout the early poems. Even traditional responses to the brevity of life are invoked with a distinctive twist, with a knowingness which renders ironic the strategies even as they are invoked.

Like the Renaissance poets of *carpe diem* whom he frequently echoes, the young Howard of ***Quantities*** and ***The Damages*** investigates the alleged capability of myth to arrest time or at least to join the particular moment to all time, the particular action to enduring human ceremony and ritual. In poem after poem in these early books he tests the viability of answers which others have found in the cycle of the seasons and in the atemporality of the pastoral. Several of the early poems which express the *carpe diem* impulse establish contexts within which the conventional call to action rings hollow. (pp. 13-14)

The brilliant and sophisticated poet of ***Quantities*** and ***The Damages*** wrestles time and again with issues of human transience. He offers few answers to the questions he raises, for he knows the traditional answers to be at best only half. And he often uses the dichotomy between the fact of life's brevity and the fiction of literary conventions to create poetry of surprising emotional power. It is only in his later work, however, that he approaches the question of time with positive attitudes and hopeful vision.

Howard's third volume, the Pulitzer Prize-winning ***Untitled Subjects*** (1969), marks an important turning point in his career and in his response to time within his poetry. A collection of fifteen dramatic monologues, letters, and journal entries whose subjects are nineteenth-century and early twentieth-century personages, actual and imaginary, famous and obscure, ***Untitled Subjects*** established Howard's reputation as an authentic successor to Browning in his understanding of character and in his evocation of the past to illuminate the present. Although manipulating the voices of historical "others," Howard's concerns in this volume are not merely "retrospective vignettes," as one reviewer complains. Instead, they are personal, as Howard reminds us in an allusion to Browning, "the great poet of otherness . . . who said, as I should like to say, 'I'll tell my state as though 'twere none of mine'" (Dedication, ***Untitled Subjects***). His fourth book, ***Findings*** (1971), consists of dramatic monologues and more obviously personal poems in which he continues to speak as a poet of "otherness." In his fifth collection, ***Two-Part Inventions*** (1974), he expands the dramatic monologue into dialogue and returns to the nineteenth and the early twentieth centuries for his subjects. Vital, witty, dramatic, the two-part inventions explore in a series of highly charged recognition scenes the shapes of completed lives. Howard's most recent volume, ***Fellow Feelings*** (1976), is a miscellaneous collection of lyrics, some cast in his own voice and some in the personae of fellow feelers, poets and painters. In this book Howard speaks with greater intimacy than ever before and with new insight into himself as a human being and as artist.

Howard's later work does not amount to a rejection of his earlier attitudes toward time, but it is informed by a larger vision, one which is able to incorporate questions of time and art into broader contexts. **"Presenting a Watch"** (***Findings***), for instance, confirms the implacable resignation to time which haunts ***Quantities*** and ***The Damages,*** but with a significant difference. In this later poem the poet recognizes the consolation of shared vulnerability as a positive consequence of dread time. This sharing cannot lessen the inevitability of death and age, but it may provide the basis of a bond which enriches the present. . . . In the later poems the poet is more capable of enjoying "the heavenly fellowship of men that perish" (Wallace Stevens, "Sunday Morning"), of seeing in personal mortality an opportunity for sharing fear and love. The poet comes to a new and fuller understanding of the *carpe diem* impulse, not as a means of arresting time, but as a means of binding together vulnerable individuals. In the later works Howard develops his concern with others, and in so doing he approaches the questions of time with new compassion and more equanimity.

By developing his concern with others Howard is able to see the continuity of human experience as a means of bridging past, present, and future. In the dramatic monologues and two-part inventions he manipulates past and present to inform each other. His understanding of the past enables him to invent fictions, often based on actual events tellingly altered, in order to probe questions of continuing significance. Conversely, his apprehension of contemporary issues, particularly those of sexuality and of art, directs his explorations of their historical roots. It is noteworthy that most of the dialogues and monologues involve aged individuals looking back on their personal pasts or younger speakers attempting to come to terms with the completed lives of others. Scott and Thackeray, at the end of their lives, take stock; Jane Morris, having outlived her era, repeats on her deathbed, "save it all"; a dying Ibsen returns to Capri and the scenes of his youth; an architect-designer learns on his deathbed that all his buildings have been destroyed; Edith Wharton and "Gerald Roseman" explore their relationships to the dead "Gerald Mackenzie," whose ashes they transport to Versailles and whom they both loved; Lady Trevelyan instructs her son as he undertakes to write her brother Lord Macaulay's biography, a work which turns out to be "a death-notice in three volumes," "the silver-chased fittings / of a coffin." . . . The reminiscences of these poems amount to more than nostalgia. . . . Howard's success in the historical poems attests to both the vitality of his art and the enduring power of essential lives. (pp. 17-21)

An important force in contemporary American poetry, Richard Howard has grappled again and again with issues which haunt the twentieth-century American psyche. Confronting the passage of time in poems of notable elegance and finish as well as vigor and vitality, he has grown from an urbane young sophisticate obsessed with age into a poet of vision. Central to his development has been his emergence as a poet of "otherness," one whose understanding of the lives of others has enabled him to transcend the limitations of a time-bound self. . . . Howard's movement from a narrow self-absorption toward an apprehension of the continuity of human experience may be a result of his mature understanding of the limits of our individual lives. . . . His identification of himself with fellow feelers . . . is not only a statement of human continuity, but also a recognition of shared values bridging the narrow spaces of individual lifespans. . . . It is precisely this ability to recognize his kind which Howard posits as a solution to the existential loneliness of an individual life limited by the exigencies of time. To transcend these limits by rejoining the fathers, by identifying with fellow feelers, by recognizing one's kind, is simultaneously to affirm and to escape the self. (pp. 32-3)

Claude J. Summers and Ted-Larry Pebworth, "'We Join the Fathers': Time and the Maturing of Richard Howard," in Contemporary Poetry, *Vol. III, No. 4, Winter, 1978, pp. 13-35.*

J. D. McCLATCHY

"A photograph," quipped Robert de Montesquiou, "is a mirror with a memory." Our memories of the flamboyant, voluptuary artists and lions of 19th-century France owe everything to the mirror—or, rather, the camera—held up to them by Félix Tournachon, called Nadar. [In ***Misgivings***] Richard Howard has chosen a dozen of them—from Baudelaire to Bernhardt, Gautier to the Goncourts—added a shot of the photographer himself, and set himself the task, in his sequence called **"Homage to Nadar,"** of turning each pose into poetry. So close are the two sets of portraits meant to be that the photographs are reproduced (not very sharply) beside the poems, which function, then, as extended captions or elaborate identifications of the images they accompany. By now, this is a familiar tack of Howard's; the characterizations that animate ***Untitled Subjects*** and ***Two-Part Inventions,*** and the moralized commentaries on paintings in his other books, have shown off the ability of his voice, not to project itself into others, but to absorb them into himself, to subsume both the sublime and the *mondain*. These new poems are more impatient and pithy, more spare than the earlier ones. (Perhaps spared the necessity of more local color by the black-and-white likenesses *en face*?) They are as sententious and aggressive as Susan Sontag, to whom Howard has dedicated the series, has asserted photography itself to be, and the lure of these verbal portraits by Howard is, similarly, that which Sontag proposes for photographs: "their hold on us is that they offer at one and the same time a connoisseur's relation *to* the world and a promiscuous acceptance *of* the world." Yet, despite his miscellany of subjects, Howard's intention is rather more single-minded than it's been before; and, last of all, he ascribes it to Nadar himself: "*All men are mad when they are alone, almost / all women:* that was your text and your testimony." Or so Howard claims, and then claims as *his* testimony, that counts up the high, indeed the fatal, cost of public success, the black secrets of private appetite, the stammer, blindness, folly, and failure underneath the works and days of these sacred monsters. (pp. 162-63)

In effect, each of these poems is a study in what he elsewhere calls "mortal will," the necessarily doomed prospect of being human while trafficking in eternity. The expected and unexpected absurdities set up some sniggering in Howard's hindsight, and some bitterness—but that keeps them from becoming the coffee-table poems they might have been—and a great deal of pathos. . . . (p. 163)

This smart and poignant **"Homage to Nadar"** is flanked by two groups of what can be called—at least in the case of a poet who can rise so well to them—occasional poems: specific responses to needs or losses. In the first group are an exercise in a foreign tongue, a commission for music to a theory about *Salome,* an excursus on an obscure landscape, a celebration of an abstract embroiderer, and, best of all, a meditation on the American Scene, called **"To the Painters: On the United States, Considered as a Landscape."** Howard surprises, as usual, by a fine excess. He has put together a pastiche of ideas and injunctions by three of our quintessential writers—Henry James, Walt Whitman, and Wallace Stevens—and devised a marvelous sketch, both literary and spiritual, of the body politic, "this beloved, / defiled and continuing body." Another poem in this introductory group, **"Thebais,"** ends with lines that anticipate the concluding group of poems in the book: any place / of trial is inconceivable without / a semblance of self-exposure." There is quite a bit more than a semblance of that in the several poems of trying and defeated love that give the book's title its true force. To judge by his present and previous successes, one might have supposed that Howard would second Remy de Gourmont's notion that one only writes well about things one hasn't experienced. Not so. The three last poems in the book are strong and strongly autobiographical, without being either inaccessible or cloying. **"Codes"** is a disconcerted musing on the range of languages and signs in which love repeats itself. Better yet is **"With the Remover to Remove,"** 45 tercets that recount a recuperative exile in the South Pacific, the poet his own Crusoe, finding what will suffice, encouraging and then enduring an uncommon self-recognition scene in the midst of a sea-change. A coral reef may seem a bizarre edge of doom, but Howard contrives to make it as familiar as a bar or dream, while he explores the alterations of love. And finally, from even further away, is **"With a Potpourri from Down Under,"** a sachet and conceit that release involuntary memories of times lost in and to love. It is a heavyhearted poem, braving one more immersion in "the intimate reek, the must of dark places." Indeed these are more intimate poems than Howard has given us before. His customary nervous poise—improvised, abandoned, re-improvised, like a dancer moving from point to point—is here. But also a new vulnerability, even a tenderness, that have an eloquence all their own. (pp. 164-65)

J. D. McClatchy, "Three Poets," in Canto: Review of the Arts, *Vol. 3, No. 1, 1979, pp. 154-65.*

ROBERT B. SHAW

To call a book of verse ***Misgivings*** is really asking for it. Richard Howard could get away with this audacity if all the poems in his latest volume were the equal of **"Thebais."** In this enchanting piece Mr. Howard describes in rapt, luminous detail a painting of saintly hermits in a landscape by Starnina, a 14th-century Italian master of whom virtually nothing is known. The near-anonymity of the painter is intuitively related at the end of the poem to the absoluteness of his art: "Look! a man may vanish as God vanished, / by filling all things with created life." One wishes that Mr. Howard would himself adopt such a strategy of self-effacement. In most of his poems, matter is subjected to a crushing weight of manner. His predilection for word play ("A stocky body in a body stocking"; "not to make the scene but to adore / the scenery") is hardly what one would call wit. It has more in common with a nervous tic.

I had hoped that the sequence **"Homage to Nadar,"** a set of commentaries on portraits by the great photographer, would illuminate 19th-century France as Mr. Howard's book ***Untitled Subjects*** did 19th-century England. I was disappointed: The Nadar poems have nothing like the richness of texture that made Mr. Howard's Pulitzer Prize-winning volume of 1970 so memorable. They approach their subjects—Victor Hugo, Sarah Bernhardt, Gustave Doré and others—by way of apostrophe; the effect is one of resolute artificiality. It is as though Mr. Howard had undertaken to recount to these heroes of culture all the unpleasant gossip about themselves that he could manage to assemble. The mild interest these pieces arouse is documentary, not esthetic. Like even the most artful photographs, they lack a convincing sense of their subjects' inner natures. Moreover, the commentator's gestures obscure the details he is bent on pointing out. Mr. Howard seems not so much to be writing poetry as producing rhetoric by rote. These poems cannot have been as hard to write as they are to read. The lonely excellence of **"Thebais"** suggests that he can do better. (pp. 9, 24)

Robert B. Shaw, "Mixed Report," in The New York Times Book Review, *February 3, 1980, pp. 9, 24.*

HAROLD BEAVER

The term "man of letters" may have become defunct; the species survives. Richard Howard, for one, embodies the term. It is more than an obsession. As Mr. Howard writes of Giuseppe Verdi in [the title poem of] ***Lining Up:***

we don't accuse
oysters of insincerity for making
their disease into a pearl.

"Disease" seems too strong. Yet the very epithet "man of letters" does suggest a personality unfitted to survive without constant literary and artistic dialysis.

Mr. Howard is eager to display such a personality. He pores over photographs by the 19th-century French portraitist Nadar of Berlioz, Delacroix, Michelet, Corot, lingers at the monument to Pierre Louÿs in the Jardin du Luxembourg in Paris or looks into R. W. Chapman's critical bibliography of Jane Austen. Again and again he pays homage or does a variety of "impersonations." . . .

His is donnish poetry, then—witty, discursive, learned, engaging—whose personal glimpses reveal little more than the making of the embryo man of letters.

Your name meant a row of red books, properly
  voluminous although not
Anatolian, as far as I could determine

begins a poem entitled **"Anatole France."** He cannot resist a pun (ogling the reader "with a wild surmise, silent on a pique") or imparting information (on etymology or the uses of photography). But when in this profusion of monologues can we leave the museum? Where can we meet real-life citizens and not another recount of Rodin's sculpture "The Burghers of Calais"?

Mr. Howard is good company as he moves with Alexandrian wit through the museums of the world. One is delighted to hear his annotations and be tugged along in the wake of his allusions. But what lies beyond the Palace of Art? How can we survive without Leda or Lewis Carroll to conciliate our desires? When contemporary life percolates through the encrustation, it is revealed partly in a bathhouse and partly in a backroom bar. At this point the fun is not nearly heady enough. When the emotions are fully engaged, the intellectual reflex becomes almost trite. . . .

[Howard's] poetry lingers precisely between "the craving to create" and mere contemplation. That is both its strength and weakness. Like the figures on his **"Attic Red-Figure Calyx,"** he circles around "an undisturbed absence at the center / of which we may never speak."

Harold Beaver, "Snapshots and Artworks," in The New York Times Book Review, *March 18, 1984, p. 30.*

JAMES FINN COTTER

Richard Howard presents his new book of poems [***Lining Up***] through a series of historical personages from the Belle Epoque, legendary characters of Greek myth, and people he knows. The title poem, **"Lining Up,"** establishes the gallery analogy for what follows; there is even a set of daguerreotypes of famous painters, musicians, and writers, accompanied by poetic commentaries. Delacroix, Corot, Berlioz, France and others are presented as sitters for the photographer Nadar; the poet converses with each person posing for his portrait. These dramatic monologues act as masks of Howard's own search for the relation between reality and art, between the passing moment and the object fixed in time, whether photograph, painting, musical composition, or poem. This self-consciousness is occasionally obtrusive, without that Keatsian negative capability to identify with the experience. One notes that there is scarcely any female presence in these poems. Jane Austen appears as a wise old maid and Penelope as a disappointed realist, but no *anima* animates the portraits. Howard is a master of the double take, the hesitation that gives way to quick recognition. He cleverly extracts his own attitudes from the vast classical and romantic information packed in his lines. They are chock-full of puns and allusions from Homer to Eliot; speeches of Shakespeare surface and fade. Baudelaire, Charles Dodgson, Proust, and Ford Madox Ford take part as listeners or partners in dialogue. The mask of irony is exquisitely carved, but the face behind it peers out with dark and empty eyes. The poet parodies Keats: "The Greek pot / and THE GREEK POTHOLE are one," identifying a red-figured calyx from Naxos with a bar in Texas. In both, figures move "with an undisturbed absence at the center." Art and the real race at last into the same void.

James Finn Cotter, in a review of "Lining Up," in The Hudson Review, *Vol. XXXVII, No. 3, Autumn, 1984, p. 502.*

J. D. McCLATCHY

In an essay about Richard Hugo, that attempts to define (and celebrate) his "regionalism," Richard Howard once wrote that "what a region finally suggests to a poet is not new content but new possibilities in the treatment of convention." And the best regional poet, he says, is never a stay-at-home; there is an "incessant movement binding outer weather to inner, connecting space with events, history with theory. . . . The conventions of a place have given him a vocabulary in which to accommodate his action in whatever place it occurs, have given him a means of dealing importantly with the privations and privileges of a life." Given this generous definition, it might be apt to describe Howard himself as a "regionalist." Certainly he has staked out a territory, which in turn has given him a vocabulary. His region is not a *place,* but that place in our lives High Culture occupies. It is the museum without walls and Borges's universal library combined. Howard's style, appropriately, is a highly literary one; it is adult, armchair, intellectual, wrought and ironic, the nimble language of a superior mind. It assumes everything can be articulated and therefore understood. With their Wildean multiplication of personalities, his poems seek to demystify "private" experience by seeing it in terms of other relational models—political, historical, cultural, artistic.

By now Howard has pretty thoroughly mapped his region, its subjects and tone. Those who know the territory will find little that is new in ***Lining Up,*** but much to delight. There is another of his ''two-part inventions,'' several more ''impersonations,'' arguments and homages, and a continuation of the series, begun in his previous book, of apostrophes to Parisian luminaries photographed by Nadar. This last is really a counterpart to a former sequence, scattered over several books and so perhaps as yet unrecognized: what might be called his Florentine sequence, intricate re-imaginings of paintings by Bellini, Simone Martini, Starnina, and others. (I want to call it more precisely his Uffizi sequence, but one of the best poems concerns Donatello's *David,* in the Bargello.) The Nadar sequence is fittingly more modern, more intimate and spare, tied to fact rather than released into speculation. Nine more are inducted here: Delacroix, Millet, Corot, Verdi, Meyerbeer, Berlioz, Michelet, Nerval, and Anatole France. They help clarify Howard's larger purpose in the whole sequence, which is to write a history of fame, that commerce between an artist and his society. (pp. 295-96)

In his seven books before this, Howard has known that art is no salvation, only a reprieve, but in this new book even that knowledge is temporized, and at times turned against himself. In the past, Howard has used paradox to explode pretense and hypocrisy, the bourgeois obverse of paradox. But now his eye is colder, blinking. He's read between the lines and found there (by implication, here too, in his own poems) an emptiness. . . . Howard's voice-overs, his way of speaking about or for others, may have become inadequate to the increasingly severe moral demands he makes on his material. It may, in fact, signal a crisis of subject matter—not his especial region necessarily, but subject matter itself: what a poem is ''about'' or up to—and mark a turn in his career. This sort of crisis is always a question of the poet's power over his material. When it is as strong as Howard's, there is a temptation to condescend. I do not want to leave off consideration of this book, though, with a question that may be impertinent and in any case is at present un-answerable. Instead, let me mention some sure strokes, some keen long views over gained ground. The title poem [**''Lining Up''**] is one, a plangent look at ourselves as we look at art. **''Narcissus Explains''** is another, shot through with dark wit. **''Move Still, Still So''** cuts between two voices, that of Charles Dodgson posing one of his undressed girls, and that of the girl herself, thirty years later a grown woman and on a different sofa—her analyst's, as she discusses her frigidity. It is an astonishing poem, at once macabre and moving. The poems in ***Two-Part Inventions*** were dialogues, and so the speech was pressured by the need to reply, to perform. In **''Move Still, Still So''** the two voices are juxtaposed across time, two monologues in antiphonal parts. Gone is the too self-conscious, topiary word play, what Howard himself has called his ''doodling . . . a way of hovering over utterance.'' More than in the earlier poems, Howard has here abjured his own voice and penetrated with telling effect both the dynamics of dramatic action and the mysteries of a haunted obsession. The most unusual poem in the book is **''Attic Red-figure Calyx, Revelling in Progress, circa 510 B.C.,''** a double view of the eponymous Greek pot and of **''The Greek Pothole,''** ''our favorite back-room bar'' in Texas. It is a dazzling blend of the ancient and contemporary, of hieratic primitivism and sleazy decadence, without the intervening civilization that is this poet's preferred vantage. (pp. 297-98)

J. D. McClatchy, ''Weaving and Unweaving,'' in Poetry, *Vol. CXLV, No. 3, February, 1985, pp. 291-306.*

Fanny Howe

1940-

American novelist, short story writer, poet, and author of children's books.

In her works, Howe focuses on alienation, the search for spiritual meaning, and the pressures of contemporary American society, particularly as these topics relate to women. Employing lyrical language and experimental forms, Howe evokes the psychological states of characters undergoing intense emotional experiences. For example, her first book, *Forty Whacks* (1969), contains six short stories about women driven to drastic actions because of their environment and their troubled relationships. In praising this work, Shaun O'Connell noted that "there is painful truth in Fanny Howe's artful apprehension of people caught in one another and the dilemmas of living."

Howe's first two novels, *First Marriage* (1974) and *Brontë Wilde* (1976), like the stories in *Forty Whacks,* depict the trials and adventures of alienated women. This pattern continues in *Holy Smoke* (1979), a fragmented experimental novel that features stream-of-consciousness passages, illustrations, and antithetical epigrams while portraying an eccentric young woman's attempts to locate her kidnapped daughter. *In the Middle of Nowhere* (1984) was Howe's first novel to draw significant critical attention. This work, which unfolds in a more naturalistic manner than *Holy Smoke,* details the struggles of four lonely individuals to find love and spiritual comfort in an oppressive New England town. Howe incorporates elements of Christian belief to underscore the spiritual quests of her characters.

In addition to her short stories and experimental novels, Howe has published a historical novel, *The White Slave* (1980), four young adult novels, and several volumes of poetry, including *Eggs* (1970) and *Robeson Street* (1985). In her verse, Howe examines such traditional lyric topics as love, friendship, and emotions.

(See also *Contemporary Authors,* Vol. 117.)

Photograph by Ben Watkins. Courtesy of Fanny Howe.

M. ANN PETRIE

Fanny Howe's ***Forty Whacks,*** a collection of six short stories, explores the condition of modern young women who have lost faith in traditional values and yet seem to have no resources of their own on which to rely. Living as they do in the 1960s, they are the true recipients of the old Chinese curse: "May you be born in interesting times."

The personalities of Miss Howe's women are of two rather limited kinds: assertive-destructive and passive. Whether by design or not, the first is usually rich or aristocratic, the second is always poor. Both feel helpless to change their condition; frustrated, they aim a terrible anger at themselves or others.

Although attractive and intelligent, these women do not know how to direct their potential in what they feel is a man's world. They are sophisticated without being mature, psychologically hip but neurotic. Hypersensitive to a fault, they cannot temper their emotions with compassion. In short, all are out of touch with themselves and the world—and they are lonely.

According to the jacket copy, the stories are about girls who are "more or less disastrously in love." Love is not the correct word, however, since it presupposes a giving of one's self in some way, and none of Miss Howe's characters has enough to spare.

Instead, they seem to attach themselves to men out of weakness and rage, with the inevitable result that for at least one of the lovers, the affair ends in tragedy. This all too familiar pattern, the basis for much bad writing, is kept from turning into melodrama by Miss Howe's wit and masterful technique. In fact, her skill is so fine that the stories often give the impression of dealing with deeper, more varied material.

Thus **"Forty Whacks,"** the title piece, touches upon a number of promising themes, but in the end hews close to the author's narrow line. (pp. 21-2)

On style alone, I much prefer the three pieces entitled **"Rosy Cheeks," "The Last Virgin"** and **"Plug Body,"** all written in the third person. The objective voice, I think, yields the most gratifying fiction, for it enables one to experience a story free from the narrator's interpretations. The reader derives much satisfaction from having to muster all his imaginative resources to absorb the full impact of the writing. This is especially true in the case of the short story—that most compact of forms—where emotional poignancy depends upon the artful selection of detail.

"Plug Body," the best of the trio, demonstrates Miss Howe's ability to control voice and plot to achieve dramatic effect. In this story, a successful builder burns down his childhood home, now a slum, when he discovers his daughter has spent the night there with its Negro tenant. Described simply, vividly and with complete credibility, his act is far more valuable an illumination of a complex father-daughter relationship than an "indepth" analysis.

Still, proper use of the first person remains the most effective way yet devised for an author to delineate a single character, even if it is to the detriment of the remaining dramatis personae. And Miss Howe, using this technique, portrays her women most strongly, albeit exclusively, in **"The Other Side of Lethe"** and **"Dump Gull."**

The first is narrated by a girl who has been found guilty of killing her lover, but acquitted on the grounds of insanity. Holed up in an isolated attic of a house that is about to be torn down, she sets down her account in a calm, detached manner. But the death of her lover, like a journey across the mythological river Lethe, has induced forgetfulness—the girl cannot remember the details of the killing. (pp. 22-3)

Because the story is told in retrospect, much of its dramatic potential is weakened. We are not allowed, for example, to witness the crime. Nor can we experience the full horror of the girl's cruelty, since through her memory lapse and detachment, she refuses responsibility for what she has done.

"Dump Gull," the longest and most ambitious piece in the collection, is more successful. The action is reported by the heroine at the moment it takes place, and an exhilarating effect is created by the swift movement through time and events. This excitement, accompanied by humor bordering on hilarity, is especially characteristic of the first half of the story, which depicts the early life of the narrator, Astrid, and her relationship with her husband, Patrick. But a bitter tone of near despair underlies all the gaiety and activity, so that reading this brilliantly written work becomes, paradoxically, a painful experience.

Astrid herself is a virtual composite of all the women in the collection: rejected daughter—hostile, helpless and cruel—destroyer and victim. And Patrick, although weak in many ways, is the strongest male character in the stories. There are moments when their marriage shows traces of warmth and love, but somehow Patrick's open nature seems to motivate Astrid to withdraw from him. . . .

Astrid, like all of the girls in ***Forty Whacks*** once the sophistication is stripped away, is heartless. Not one changes as a result of her experience, learns who she is or what she is doing, begins to relate to the world beyond her narrow, unhappy sphere. Angry child-women all, they hang suspended in their self-spun myth of helplessness.

A good collection of short stories, I believe, should create a new form from the combination of all its parts. Each piece should contribute some insight into an overall vision of life. In this sense Miss Howe's book is unsuccessful, excellent as the individual stories may be. (p. 23)

M. Ann Petrie, "Myth of Helplessness," in The New Leader, *Vol. LII, No. 22 November 24, 1969, pp. 21-3.*

SHAUN O'CONNELL

Things matter very much to her characters, her readers and herself in Fanny Howe's collection of stories, ***Forty Whacks.*** Girls are hung-up and strung-out in a variety of artfully apprehended ways. Though Fanny Howe unlike Coover makes so little of her technique, seems really just to be telling straight stories about anxious girls, that doesn't necessarily mean that her technique is neither apt nor original. Her technique, in fact, is more than sufficient to her ends; it is in the service of perceptions about the ways we create and destroy not only fictions but one another.

Two of her stories are related from the perspectives of half-mad, rationalizing narrators. They are as tightly told as Browning's dramatic monologues. The girl in **"Forty Whacks,"** though not fully clear to herself, is worming her way in between two of her friends, breaking up their marriage so she can have the husband (whom, of course, she no longer wants after she gets him). She keeps a careful journal, a record of her self-delusions, in which she sets down her mad rationalizations for doing things (like sleeping in her friends' bed when they are away)—(1), (2)—as though careful, numerical ordering of her motives justified her actions. In **"The Other Side of Lethe"** a woman explains to us—precisely and delicately, as though she were arranging flowers—how she murdered David, her lover, and was finally released from prison for insanity. Though she doesn't mind having killed, she is quite concerned with maintaining decorum in her discourse. ("David would die if he saw me now. But please excuse that vulgarity.")

Fanny Howe creates characters with angular collages of details which catch personality. ("Lizabeth controlling the car as if it were a motorcycle and required her shifting weight from side to side. She wore white-rimmed sunglasses, her nails were talons. The floor of the car was littered with beer cans.") She neatly interconnects her stories with motifs of symbols (sea gull), actions (whacks) and dialogue so that we have more than just a collection of stories, as in Joyce's *Dubliners,* fragments of a little world circumscribed in art.

"Dump Gull" is her longest and best story. A lovely, funny, not so comic epic of a girl of feeling, Astrid, who moves from her mother's shaping of her into the world of men. First Patrick, a shoe salesman who kisses her instep while selling her shoes, quits his job and goes off to marry her. Later, separated from Patrick, engaged to Julian, she frees herself from her mother at her rich fiancé's engagement party by placing a wax apple in her supinely drunken mother's mouth as the woman lies stretched out on the floor beside the dinner table. (In the context of the story, this wax apple is as real as an apple could be!)

Astrid promises to divorce Patrick and marry her fiancé, Julian. However, he, though decent enough, misuses language. So in a perfectly dramatic and alogically sound move, she turns away from him in the middle of her divorce proceedings, turns again to Patrick who, though crazy, used to comfort her by saying "Be loving, Puss." This may not be a rational or self-serving move for Astrid, but that's the way a sea gull over a dump survives, extracts "the sweet piece from the whole mess." (pp. 640-41)

[There] is painful truth in Fanny Howe's artful apprehension of people caught in one another and the dilemmas of living. (p. 641)

Shaun O'Connell, "Apples and Applesauce," in The Nation, *New York, Vol, 209, No. 20, December 8, 1969, pp. 640-41.*

ALAN HISLOP

[***Forty Whacks***] is a fascinating collection of stories about what used to be called the trials of womanhood. Fanny Howe creates both vivid and intractable characters, and situations that are humorous and moving. At times, she shies away from her characters, using her irony as a guard—but they usually come through. There is probably no ironic distance at which one could be safe from such a monstrous prig as the heroine of **"The Other Side of Lethe."** . . .

The best and longest story in the book, **"Dump Gull,"** is a love story—something one would have thought had vanished from the genre, along with antimacassars and patchwork quilts. There is more to this story than can be described here, but it has one special virtue that ought to be noted: it doesn't treat youth in hushed whispers, as if every one under 25 were a messenger from the Gods. Miss Howe is an exciting and promising writer. (p. 45)

Alan Hislop, "Life as a Series of Lost Directions," in The New York Times Book Review, *December 14, 1969, pp. 44-5.*

DAVID HAWORTH

[***Forty Whacks*** is a] a collection of adroit short stories, each illustrating the difficulties that place can cause the feminine psyche. All six of Miss Howe's heroines are poised *in extremis,* just risen from, or about to lie on, the psychiatrist's couch—providing a suicide or even a murder doesn't supervene. Whether or not Lizzie Borden did, as the old rhyme has it, take a chopper and 'hit her father forty whacks', she is the inspiration for refined agonies in New York, Boston and Reno which are the author's preoccupation.

If this sounds morbid, there is in each of them a sensibility which keeps mawkishness safely away. Nor does the occasionally improbable flourish spoil enjoyment. I wasn't so sure about the lady who had a fixation on her grandfather or the man who burnt down his own house where his daughter had been getting a bit on the side. **"Forty Whacks"** is a study of the way in which a desperately neurotic creature takes a termite's hold on another's marriage—with inevitable results. The amorality of her action and her cheerful determination in it are cleverly done. The last story, **"Dump Gull",** describes a young marriage's decline to the divorce court and the conspiracy of social pressures which bring this about. At the final minute the girl unexpectedly asserts her right to remain married. Miss Howe is working in a small compass and travels light. All the same, an interesting start.

David Haworth, "Resurrection," in New Statesman, *Vol. 81, No. 2081, February 5, 1971, p. 188.*

FRANK MacSHANE

Here are [Fanny Howe's] poems, ***Eggs,*** and she has laid them in an unabashed and forthright manner, for good or ill. The subjects are all human and personal, what it's like to be lonely and unloved, what sadness and grief, friendship, physical love are all about. These subjects are dealt with in a direct and uncomplicated way, which nevertheless produces the emotional complexity necessary to successful lyric poetry. . . . Miss Howe's lyric gift is like Lawrence's: she answers the question of how to deal with the disasters of life by simply dealing with them one by one. Her poems are drenched in human relations, and they are best when, as is the case with the work of William Stafford and Maxine Kumin, they are short. Stretched out, as in **"Time and Place,"** this effect becomes dissipated. Miss Howe's longer poems suggest she is interested in enlarging her range; as a writer of short stories as well, she might consider narrative verse, to give her impressions the grounding in felt experience longer works generally require. But even as it stands, ***Eggs*** is a fine and healthy book, full of human feeling and humor, and of poems as natural "as the leaves to a tree". (pp. 299-300)

Frank MacShane, "A Range of Six," in Poetry, *Vol. CXVIII, No. 5, August, 1971, pp. 295-301.*

PUBLISHERS WEEKLY

Such an unpromising title [***Brontë Wilde***] doesn't begin to suggest the pleasant surprise in store for the reader. And although the odyssey of Brontë Wilde, aka Mary Casement, takes her from Boston to Berkeley and into a radicalized existence, the author carefully avoids the clichéd pitfalls of the milieu. Her characterizations are truly handled; Mary is complex and eloquent, and if her best friend and alter ego Honey Figgis is less interesting, Honey's far-reaching influence on Mary is nonetheless altogether believable. . . . Howe is a serious writer, a caring craftswoman—a find.

A review "Brontë Wilde," in Publishers Weekly, *Vol. 209, No. 12, March 22, 1976, p. 48.*

MARTIN LEVIN

Fanny Howe's novel [***Brontë Wilde***] abounds in what James Joyce called "epiphanies"—brief moments that carry sudden perceptions. The collector of these impressions is a girl called Mary Casement, the adopted daughter of a pair of Boston psychiatrists who are full of good intentions but lacking in animal warmth. Mary's best friend is "Honey" Figgis, a near-psycho capable of cutting off her dog's ear while waiting for a phone call. Both of these relationships leave Mary on the outside of life, looking in. She shares neither in her parents' tidy routines nor in Honey's crazy compulsions. When the Casements are killed in a plane crash, Mary now 16 names herself "Brontë Wilde" and runs away, first to Greenwich Village and then to Berkeley, Calif. . . .

Some isolated moments in the book are appealing. . . . But there is no interaction of character to create fictional chemistry. So you are left at the end of the novel with no more than you had at the beginning—a sense of isolation, leading nowhere. It's a letdown.

Martin Levin, in a review of "Brontë Wilde," in The New York Times Book Review, *May 9, 1976, p. 42.*

PUBLISHERS WEEKLY

This short, labyrinthine novel [***Holy Smoke***] is written in an interior monologue that at times leaves the reader baffled and lost. One follows the ramblings and wanderings of the narrator, a woman who is a taxi driver in Manhattan. Her man, referred to as J. L., is found dead—again. When she won't hand over his notes, papers and belongings to Lucas, an abrasive man who appears at her house, he apparently kidnaps her adolescent daughter, Pepsi. The action then revolves around the woman's search for her elusive daughter, and for herself. . . . Howe has proven herself a skilled writer in previous stories, poems and novels, but ***Holy Smoke,*** a bit too thick and slow, is disappointing. (pp. 78-9)

A review of "Holy Smoke," in Publishers Weekly, *Vol. 215, No. 13, March 26, 1979, pp. 78-9.*

JAMES WOLCOTT

Howe—a poet and short story writer who's taught creative writing at Tufts, Columbia, and Yale—published her first novel in 1974, ***First Marriage.*** In that book, Howe indents her margins idiosyncratically, and heads her chapters with word-association piles, like this:

> GUILT: faux pas
> peccability
> pecker
> in flagrante delicto
> died without a name
> flaw
> blot

She also illustrates her narrative with humdrum drawings of gravestones, windows, wind-blown trees, lumpy clouds. These odd little touches aside, ***First Marriage*** is a brisk and bittersweetly conventional study of young women ricocheting through life only to arrive at a perplexed, rattled maturity. It's a slight and fluttery novel, but it's graced with a forlorn, everyday lyricism—icicles dripping in the spring light, cemetery flowers scenting the air with their fine musky rot.

In ***Holy Smoke,*** the lyricism has turned into a Wordsworthian riot of flowery raptures and the characters have become comic-book spies and deities. . . . [Howe] stuffs her book with miracles and surrealistic collisions. Oneida—heroine and narrator—is a taxi driver whose daughter, Pepsi, is kidnapped by a mysterious killer elite; she spends 100 pages or so in hallucinatory pursuit. The Virgin Mary gives her the finger and dispenses questionable wisdom. A character named Sgt. Pepper turns up, as do characters cutely named Poole, Brooke, and Water. Corpses are casually resurrected; Oneida inexplicably regains her virginity. Decorating the narrative are pictures of ashtrays, smiling cherubs, birds in flight, Yosemite Park postcards, palm trees, and Citgo signs; and tony quotes from Rilke, Byron, Emily Dickinson. The universe shrugs indifferently. Disorder. Madness. Doomsday debris shimmering in the doomsday sun.

All of which raises the question: Is there anything more tiresome than bastardized Barthelme? At least the Mandarin of Ironic Despair has mastered a cool, precise polyphonic style that suggests a gathering of bleak clarinets. ***Holy Smoke*** is all noise, flight, and nervous ejaculation. In a speech reprinted in a recent *Michigan Quarterly Review,* Tom Wolfe said that "the new fabulism" conjured up by Barth and Barthelme . . . is characterized by Lack of Realistic Dialogue, Inexplicable Visitors, Inexplicable Attitudes, Inexplicable Forces. ***Holy Smoke*** has all that, and something more, Inexplicable Violence:

> Hello, baby bitch, I said in greeting—then whopped her on the butt til my hand was aching and she was crying. She rushed to Sgt. Pepper for sympathy but was knocked away, as the woman was picking off the three men on the other side of the river with her rifle full of buckshot.

Howe isn't untalented—there are sentences that startle and please: "The kitchen table was rotten and cocoons bubbled between its legs." Or, "A tropical humidity languishes, like a nun, across my bed." But by whipping up a trendy chaos, Howe seems to be betraying her modest lyrical gifts. She doesn't "thrive" on impossibility, she chokes on it and ***Holy Smoke*** is a concatenation of cheap thrills. Even cameo appearances by Jesus's mother can't rescue a novel that ends like this: "Spiraling inwards, I know the end is near, a void more natural than nature itself. And between said nature is gravity, invisible, anonymous, and justice." Sounds like an arthritic translation of Goethe—or is it simple gas leaking out of Susan Sontag's tires? *Hsssssssssssssssssss.*

James Wolcott, "Unwanted Guests," in The Village Voice, *Vol. XXIV, No. 33, August 13, 1979, p. 75.*

FRANCIS BROWNE

In Fanny Howe's ***Holy Smoke,*** one is impressed by its aesthetic qualities. But whether or not we have a novel, as *novel,* or a combination of poetry-prose elements with a pastiche of other illustrative genres, is the question. Forms, instead of melding with a direct narrative line, tend to impede the work's movement. Maps, photographs, drawings, symbols, graphs, designs, impressions are scattered, however serendipitously, about its pages.

Essentially, the book concerns a young woman, Oneida, and her efforts to retrieve her kidnapped daughter, Pepsi. One is never quite certain as to why the child is kidnapped, although myriad hints prevail, some as arcane as cryptographic notes, loose philosophic ramblings, anarchistic activities, past associations, Cuban revolutionaries and other strange goings-on.

Throughout the book, Oneida hunts her abducted daughter, traveling down South, to Havana, Canada, in New York. During her peregrinations, she meets various shady persons—Lucas (a double agent?); Hart Christian, "a hippie freak"; a dog-faced sorceress; Selwyn, an effete lapdog, and other wispy characters. . . .

Pepsi is a child-sprite, both real and imagined, since Oneida is more involved with herself than anybody else. The child, once found, isn't too enthusiastic about rejoining her mother. After a series of protracted confessions by the kidnappers, whose deed was apparently done for political-social reasons to "test" Oneida's courage (in her post-revolutionary soul searching), and which, presumably, was engineered by her ephemeral phantom-like husband, once James-now Jacques, she whisks her child away to "live on a hypothetical continent with others of like mind." She however remains in a state of sterility:

> Daily we anonymous many lose more and more, including our children, our jobs, our lovers, our health and trust, until we are left only with our understanding of Thermodynamics.

Imposing a judgment of good or bad on a novel such as ***Holy Smoke*** has little meaning. Either a reader enjoys the work's playfulness with forms, antithetical epigrams, and its tongue-in-cheek satiric content—or he doesn't. For this work, if serious, must be seen as a parody of many kinds—of men and women, of religion, motherhood, sexual role-playing, art, literature, culture and philosophy. If not serious, then it is nothing at all, and no writer (even less so a reader) would waste the time.

Francis Browne, in a review of "Holy Smoke," in The American Book Review, *Vol. 3, No. 1, November-December, 1980, p. 15.*

THE SMALL PRESS REVIEW

[***In the Middle of Nowhere***] explores that uncertain territory at the edge of mystery and enigma, where men and women are forced to acknowledge the human and the divine. It opens at the onset of winter in a small New England town where the quartet of characters meet and become entangled in one another's lives. . . . The characters are quintessentially American: footloose, conscious that they are outside society, outlaws of sorts, who grapple with, but fail to achieve a sense of place.

The novel is structured in a series of screenplay-like sequences, sparse, dramatic scenes which build into blocks of emotionally charged narrative, interspersed with lyrical passages. A challenging, but satisfying book.

A review of "In the Middle of Nowhere," in The Small Press Review, *Vol. 16, No. 2, February, 1984, p. 8.*

JANET HAMILL

If a thriller can be defined as a work of fiction designed to hold the interest with a high degree of suspense, and if metaphysical is that which is or relates to the preternatural, then I think it's accurate to define Fanny Howe's new book [***In the Middle of Nowhere***] as a metaphysical thriller. What better way to describe this gripping tale of ordinary people set adrift in an abyss and heading for catastrophe under an umbrella of impending doom? It is as though a seasoned reporter and a theologian collaborated in Ms. Howe's person to present us with their combined account of the events which lead to a grisly newspaper headline. But the headline never appears, and the catastrophe, when it occurs, is not the grisly affair the reader's prurient imagination has been anticipating.

The setting for this preternatural suspense is Ashville, Rhode Island, a small, fictitious town "north of Providence, in the middle of nowhere." . . . [In] his bedroom, on a Friday afternoon in the late New England fall, the shy literate rector, Father Steele, blows his brains out, while the bell ringer is ominously ringing the church bell thirteen times.

Oddly, or not so oddly enough, all of ***In the Middle of Nowhere***'s central characters, including the deceased Father Steele, are outsiders, and as we're introduced to them, little by little we begin to glean a message from the title, which is more than geographical reference: Kathy, the unambitious high-school senior and virgin by choice, is the lead singer in the choir and the rector's greatest defender until his suicide utterly confuses her notions of God and turns her into a compulsive shoplifter; Elmer, Kathy's sometime date, is a drifter from the Southwest, an insomniac who sees "speed and cruelty everywhere," and whose sole comfort is studying maps to locate his next route of escape; Laclan St. George, the young minister sent to replace Father Steele, is a tall, outdoorsy product of old Boston who spends most of his weekends on a binge; and Caralisa, the object, in turn, of both Elmer and Laclan's sexual attention, is a welfare mother who nurses her chronic indecision with jugs of California burgundy in a remote cabin in the woods. What these people have in common, aside from their physical proximity, is a shared adolescence, an arrested development, that ironically, in the end, destroys the one person entitled to that state of being.

It is with clear, driving, minimal prose, occasionally interrupted by a page of mad, baroque rambling (from Father Steele's diary?), and serious metaphysical probing that Fanny Howe has drawn this very sympathetic portrait of four (five, if you count Father Steele) spiritually handicapped, aimless, drifting souls thrown together by circumstance—the kinds of souls who more and more come to populate a changing American landscape where traditions, like religions, have a very tenuous hold indeed, and momentum without direction spells disaster. . . . [The reader] will find ***In the Middle of Nowhere*** to be one of those books that just can't be put down.

Janet Hamill, "Arrested Development Thriller," in Exquisite Corpse, *Vol. 2, Nos. 5-7, May-July, 1984, p. 20.*

SARA LASCHEVER

Set in "Ashville," a small town between Providence and Boston, this ambitious, sad little novel [***In the Middle of Nowhere***] describes the temporary conjunction of four rootless lives. . . . In the unsettled world of America's middle class, as Fanny Howe portrays it, the unfulfilled promises of 1960's progressive politics, the "liberation" of women and the equivocal "I'm-O.K.-you're-O.K." position of the clergy have created a confusion of values and expectations. Her characters suffer acutely from the absence of new systems of guidance and reassurance to replace traditional social structures, and their uncertainty has fatal consequences. Unfortunately, Mrs. Howe stylizes her story with irregularities of format and punctuation that must be intended to evoke in her readers feelings of dislocation comparable to those suffered by her characters. As her narrative methods are fundamentally conventional, however, these fillips of typography distract more than they illuminate. She also uses some clinker phrasings ("her face a mask of angst"). Still, ***In the Middle of Nowhere*** is a harsh and original meditation on the lack of moral imperatives and the frustrated spiritual longings of our time.

Sara Laschever, in a review of "In the Middle of Nowhere," in The New York Times Book Review, *May 20, 1984, p. 30.*

LORI CHAMBERLAIN

For Fanny Howe . . . , "the middle of nowhere" is an existential condition. Kathy, one of [***In the Middle of Nowhere***'s] main characters, is undergoing a crisis of faith coincident with the turmoil of becoming an adult. She confronts these overlapping crises in a bathroom cubicle in the town library:

> Safe inside the green cubicle, she clasped herself tight, and experienced an emotional revelation so deep, she nearly fainted. Her body, in its pain, was nothing but a thing; and she,

> at root was no thing at all! *She was in the middle of nowhere*. She sat on the toilet, bent over, weeping for joy. That she was anonymous: nothing nobody, nowhere; that she was not lost, but free! And she thanked God for her suffering, and now she was reduced by it to naught.

What Kathy has come to understand is perhaps the main concern of the novel, signalled in its epigraph: "The nature of God is a circle of which the center is everywhere and the circumference is nowhere." But Howe also brackets Kathy's epiphany: the bathroom stall provides an ironic frame for her revelation. Thus, while Howe seems more concerned with the inner workings of her characters, she is also careful to point out the discrepancy between spirit and flesh and the superficiality of what is sometimes claimed to be the most deeply felt of experiences—religious faith.

The book focuses on the intersections among the lives of four characters, brought together from different directions by the opening action of the book: the suicide of Reverend Steele, Rector of the Episcopalian church. Kathy, a seventeen-year-old who sang in the church choir, is deeply affected, not simply because she admired Reverend Steele, but because his suicide calls into question her own belief. The new minister, Lachlan St. George—a person for whom *The Catcher in the Rye* "was the greatest influence in his life"—is, like his predecessor, torn by contradictions, though his seem more tawdry, less tragic—we are inclined to agree with Elmer's assessment of him: "A hypocrite without a collar, acting too chummy, eager to prove himself a regular guy."

Elmer works at the gas station, a quiet, handsome, but troubled character who tries to distract himself from the problem of "D—TH" by looking at maps and moving on from city to city. Elmer's and Kathy's lives cross at a blind date—a High School dance—and while theirs is the typical failure of blind dates, the two characters both suffer the loneliness of *being* in the middle of nowhere. In the course of his job at the station, Elmer meets and falls in love with Caralisa, an annoyingly passive and somewhat helpless divorced welfare mother with a small boy. She, however, falls in love with the new minister, who is struggling with the contradictions between his profession and the flesh.

The mortar of this novel is its language—the images, platitudes, metaphors that reside in two realms: the secular and the spiritual. The best example of this is Howe's play with the homily "seeing is believing," which already unites sight and insight. We see the novel as the characters often see things, through a window or their eyes, framed by their doubt, where looking out is like looking in. Thus, while characters look inward, they are also afraid of being seen through. . . . But Howe keeps an ironic eye on her character's self-reflections. . . . (pp. 114-15)

In the Middle of Nowhere seems to emerge from the American nineteenth century tradition of Poe, Hawthorne, and Melville. . . . At one point, for example, Kathy is visiting the town library "to uncover the history of the rectory, its GHOST," and discovers instead Poe's "The Purloined Letter." The word "purloin" provides a link between Howe's narrative concerns and her connection to this literary heritage:

> Pearl, loin, pearly loins, purloin like a neon fish, darting in green aquarium reeds—what a word! Then to discover it meant 'to steal, pilfer, take dishonestly' struck her as a form of revelation. She had been attracted to the word, consciously ignorant of its meaning, but maybe subconsciously aware of its special meaning for her. And it occurred to her that words were magic in some way, that fiction was true, not false, that she was the track of Truth!

The "special meaning" of the word for Kathy lies in its synonym "steal," the way that it thus conceals both the ghost of the Reverend Steele and Kathy's inclination for shop-lifting. But it also takes us to "pearl" and Hawthorne's *The Scarlet Letter,* whose structure is ironically repeated in the relationship between Caralisa and the *new* Reverend. Caralisa functions as a twentieth century version of Hester Prynne. . . . Thus, while Howe has inscribed her work within a tradition, she has also re-invented that tradition in contemporary terms.

Although ***In the Middle of Nowhere*** shares with most of Howe's work a concern with metaphysical themes, this novel is located more specifically—geographically and metaphysically—in the problems of twentieth century New England puritanism: the meaning of the work ethic, the conflict between the spirit and the flesh, the problem of individualism. It is a densely textual novel, quite different from her 1979 novel, ***Holy Smoke*** . . . , which has a more flamboyant narrative and an uneven, playful sense of allegory. (pp. 115-16)

Lori Chamberlain, "Lewis Warsh and Fanny Howe," in fiction international, *No. 16:1, 1985, pp. 112-16.*

ROCHELLE RATNER

The six long poems that make up Howe's new collection [***Robeson Street***] are difficult but extremely rewarding reading. Nonlinear for the most part, with images mounting to form their own rationale, they jolt the reader with unexpected rhymes. . . . Immigration, poverty, Catholicism, bearing and raising children, all the elements of Howe's autobiography come into play. There is an honesty and earnestness about this book that continually draws the reader back to it.

Rochelle Ratner, in a review of "Robeson Street," in Library Journal, *Vol. 110, No. 18, November 1, 1985, p. 100.*

Emyr (Owen) Humphreys

1919-

Welsh novelist, poet, short story writer, dramatist, librettist, and nonfiction writer.

Humphreys is respected as a novelist whose major themes center upon individual responsibility in contemporary society. Linking his prose with a nonconformist Welsh and Protestant heritage, Humphreys stresses the importance of personal example over ideology in furthering human integrity. In his works, idealism—either political or romantic—is depicted as fallible and corruptible, while pragmatism is shown to be more successful in initiating and maintaining positive change. Humphreys has written: "A soul cannot make progress *in vacuo:* many men are better for the existence of one good man, and one good man is the product of some kind of progress that was both individual and social." Humphreys's avoidance of omniscient narration underscores the austerity of his themes and ostensibly allows his characters to make their own choices.

In several of his early novels, including *The Little Kingdom* (1946), *The Voice of a Stranger* (1949), *A Man's Estate* (1955), and *A Toy Epic* (1958), Humphreys's characters seek or assume leadership roles but are rendered as opportunists with neither the intent nor the moral attributes necessary to enact desirable social growth. *The Voice of a Stranger,* for example, depicts individuals in positions of authority who are manipulated by carnal and political desires. In *A Change of Heart* (1951), *Hear and Forgive* (1952), and *Outside the House of Baal* (1965), Humphreys examines the inherited personality traits of protagonists whose moral strength is perpetuated through continuous contact with virtuous characters. In *Hear and Forgive,* for instance, a young, philandering teacher chooses to return to his wife and child because of the example set by his more responsible friend.

National Winner (1971), *Flesh and Blood* (1974), *The Best of Friends* (1978), *Salt of the Earth* (1985), and *An Absolute Hero* (1985) comprise a series of novels focusing on the life of Amy Parry. A Welsh orphan raised in poverty, Amy becomes a powerful and wealthy matriarch through a succession of unhappy marriages and personal sacrifices. These books detail early twentieth-century Welsh historical events and examine national politics as well as Humphreys's familiar themes.

(See also *Contemporary Authors,* Vols. 5-8, rev. ed.; *Contemporary Authors New Revision Series,* Vol. 3; and *Dictionary of Literary Biography,* Vol. 15.)

Photograph by Dewi Humphreys. Courtesy of Emyr Humphreys.

EDMUND FULLER

The particular quality of Mr. Humphreys's [***Hear and Forgive***] springs from its detailed self-portrait of a confessedly pusillanimous man. Most persons afflicted with the subtle brand of indecisiveness shading into moral cowardice that characterizes David Flint try desperately to pretend, both to themselves and others, that it isn't so. David lays it on the line, himself, in this quiet but interesting English novel.

He is a teacher by default; that is, for lack of any other appropriate wage-producing profession. His subject is Scripture, again by default. As he explains, "In order to get in a better type of school, and because I am religious enough by nature, I began to specialize in religious instruction. Teachers of Scripture were scarce." Here, as elsewhere, David's insight fails. The case might be stated that because he is *not* religious enough his whole teaching career is a passive opportunism.

Also, David is a novelist. But although Mr. Humphreys is a good enough novelist to make David just sufficiently interesting to carry his book on its quiet level, he cannot make us believe that David can be much of a novelist. A reviewer knows just the kind of novel David would write, for he reads a lot of them. . . .

The merits of Mr. Humphreys's novel, then, are in special departments and of rather limited interest. The personal, moral struggle is on such a subdued level that we can't become greatly exercised over it. The treatment of the problems of school life is on such a small, local scale that we are not absorbed by it. There remains only the psychology of David Flint, as he relates his story. The book has competence of execution, but lacks both scope and force.

Edmund Fuller, "A Peaceful Failure," in The Saturday Review, *New York, Vol. XXXVI, No. 22, May 30, 1953, p. 16.*

SYLVIA BERKMAN

Electra in the little retired seaside village of Pennant, North Wales—one might thus reduce the subject of Emyr Humphreys' many-faceted novel, ***A Man's Estate.*** Is the undertaking presumptuous, to present in terms of modern psychological dissection that ancient stark impassioned heroine? But Mr. Humphreys employs only general fable rather than strict parallel; and his wry twentieth-century intelligence will grant heroic stature to no character with whom he deals.

Only let the soul voice its hidden reverie, and we are all built of shifting, shaky stuff, he says. Therefore he has constructed his novel on the device of mirrors-reflecting-mirrors, so to speak: a given situation and set of characters as developed through the first-person narration of four of its principals.

Story, many critics have stated, though perhaps the least defining element of a good novel, is nevertheless the most imperative. Attenuation is desert, is death. Mr. Humphreys provides story in abundance. . . .

Mr. Humphreys does not answer in absolutes. We are all victims, and all victimized, he more than implies; all frail, misguided, weak; all capable of evil, all yearning toward good. Love elevates and transfigures; but is not the urgency of love merely the urgency in obverse of pitiable need? These thematic notes are not original perhaps; no broad human summation is, or can be. But transfused throughout a work taut with dramatic strength, buoyant with sensuous poetry, solid, exact, and sure in the world it creates, they seem to come afresh.

Sylvia Berkman, "With the Legacy, Disaster," in The New York Times, *August 12, 1956, p. 4.*

STANLEY COOPERMAN

For many years Irish writers were expected to sing sweetly regardless of the medium they chose. Yeats wandered in Celtic mist until the mist itself sickened him and he turned to more difficult and less musical verse; even realists like O'Casey and O'Connor have had to buck the verbal auto-intoxication that audiences demand from Irish writers. The problem, however, is no longer exclusively Irish; since Dylan Thomas made the literary world aware of Welsh rhetoric, the Welshman who writes fiction or poetry is all too often expected to be musical if nothing else. One can meet enthusiasts everywhere from the Bronx to Los Angeles who read Welsh writers aloud, with a great rolling emphasis, amid talk of "national genius."

Emyr Humphreys, author of ***A Man's Estate,*** is a novelist first and a Welshman second, for which his readers can be profoundly thankful. . . .

Mr. Humphreys' book, as a provincial novel, bears considerable resemblance to the work of William Faulkner. The children, for example, are either sensual and doomed, sensitive and impotent, or healthy and materialist. The older people are mummified eccentrics burdened by the corruption of past sin which finally results in madness. (p. 205)

Structurally, too, ***A Man's Estate*** has overtones of Faulkner. The novel develops through four separate narratives and four interlocking points of view, each spoken directly in the first person. While Mr. Humphreys does make some effort to vary the quality of the narrative according to the speaker involved, he fails to achieve the objectivity demanded by his method. The result, as in the earliest attempts to create interior monologue, is a distracting series of omniscient comments imbedded within subjective narrative, so that the book is without the freedom of one method and the spontaniety of the other. Mr. Humphreys' lapses in craft, however, are at worst minor irritations; his novel is an incisive and honest analysis of human pressures in a too frequently romanticized area. (pp. 205-06)

Stanley Cooperman, "Not Too Welsh to Write," in The Nation, *New York, Vol. 183, No. 10, September 8, 1956, pp. 205-06.*

AILEEN PIPPETT

At last we have a novel from England by a young man who does not appear in the least angry. True, [Emyr Humphreys] is Welsh, though not of the Celtic twilight variety, and that may account for some of the sprightliness with which he presents [***The Italian Wife***]. His characters are admittedly a mixed lot, liable to bounce to glory or blunder into tragedy at any moment, but he bears them no malice. . . .

The story moves at a great pace, with crisply revealing dialogue; the serio-comic aspects of the situations facing father and son are dexterously handled. Minor characters are clearly seen and firmly placed. There are compassion and poetry in these pages, interwoven with ironic strands of farce, a genial acceptance of human frailty which is both rare and refreshing.

Aileen Pippett, "Love's Counterfeits," in The New York Times, *May 25, 1958, p. 26.*

VIRGILIA PETERSON

[***The Italian Wife***] by the much-praised Welsh writer, Emyr Humphreys, differs not a little in setting and tone from its predecessor, ***A Man's Estate,*** though the author's deepest preoccupation with the damage we inflict on one another is unchanged. While ***A Man's Estate*** took place largely in an ingrown, exotic community of Wales, Mr. Humphreys' new tale of the wounding and the wounded reaches its climax in the more international atmosphere of an Austrian castle and a villa in Italy. The earlier novel was focused upon a young man in search of identity; in the new book, there is still an uncertain young man in quest of himself, and in the kind of confusion and unhappiness they suffer, these two young men are brothers under the skin.

Mr. Humphreys deliberately sets out, in this new family circle around ***The Italian Wife,*** to shift the emphasis from what parents can do to their children to what they can do to each other. It is upon Paula, the young, frail, talented Italian woman who became the second wife of a brilliantly successful English Jew, that he concentrates time and attention, as also upon the husband himself, Richard Roth, newspaper publisher, moving-picture magnate, self-styled Socialist, and arrant pig. When Paula acquired Richard as husband, she also acquired Chris, his adolescent son. But by the time we are introduced to the Roths, Chris, grown to a handsome, uneasy, self-engrossed, but tender twenty-one, has quite unsuspectingly imprinted himself upon his stepmother's heart. Built into this unhappy situation is its own fatality.

Determined as Emyr Humphreys has been, however, to center his interest upon the marriage of Richard and Paula and the study of Richard's power-hungry corruption and Paula's passionate potentialities, the fact is that it is not Richard and Paula, but Chris, the grown son, who steals the show.

"There was never any way," Chris finally realized, after various attempts to find someone upon whom to lean, "of making a pilgrimage except alone." If this can hardly be called an original idea, if it is the theme of inordinately many modern novels, it is still a universal and, therefore, richly legitimate experience to write and read about, and Mr. Humphreys brings to it a bitter little flavor of his own. As we read about Chris Roth, groping like a blindfolded player toward the freedom to love and hate, we experience with a new twinge of recognition that particular anguish that seems always to accompany coming of age. . . .

Although Mr. Humphreys has devoted less space to Chris than to his father and stepmother, deliberately subordinating him to the elders on the stage, Chris overshadows them. Perhaps, therefore, it is because ***The Italian Wife*** is out of focus that it lacks the power of the earlier book, ***A Man's Estate.*** But there can be no doubt that Emyr Humphreys has it in him to write telling novels and to make his writing sing.

Virgilia Peterson, "Of a Young Man in Search of Himself," in New York Herald Tribune Book Review, *June 1, 1958, p. 5.*

THE TIMES LITERARY SUPPLEMENT

Mr. Humphreys's career as a novelist has been full of ups and downs. ***The Gift,*** his eighth book, is about an actor at the precarious age of thirty-eight, whose career has also been full of ups and downs and is now very much in the balance.

The Gift is generally high-spirited and even gay. There is pointed light comedy of a kind that Mr. Humphreys has rarely attempted before. He has even taken pains to be less painstaking with his prose, adopting a jaunty slapdash manner and a smart modern idiom and frivolously dispensing with commas when he feels so inclined. He does, however, become somewhat diffuse. Too often he seems to be wide of the off stump, compelling no significant response from the reader. The section on a holiday in Italy, though agreeable in itself, is not at all relevant. One has the impression of waiting for the new ball to become available.

Mr. Humphreys is of course a remarkably gifted impersonator. The trouble is that once in a character he finds it difficult to get out. In ***A Toy Epic*** he had three first person narrators and in ***A Man's Estate*** he used four. This allowed him a measure of objectivity. ***The Gift*** is told entirely by the actor Sam Halkin, and although the blurb alleges that Mr. Humphreys is again creating "a subtle double image", by means of the "unwitting revelation of the different Sam Halkin that his friends and enemies see", this is not really the case. Indeed, if the blurb is right in supposing this to have been Mr. Humphreys's purpose, then he has hardly brought it off. . . .

Sam, however, is certainly a limited character. He is grossly self-centered and selfish, frequently trivial, and often presented as an empty vessel waiting for a new part to fill him. His frailties are human and sometimes endearing, but such a character in himself can hardly support a major work of fiction. Mr. Humphreys, unable or unwilling to escape from his persona, to act out of character, is too severely confined. Perhaps he wanted to say more, that Sam is not what he appears, that he is at bottom a poignant, self-deluding failure. But he has not managed it. Sam is no more a failure than Mr. Humphreys, whose books do not sell a million copies or challenge comparison with *War and Peace,* but who within the limits he sets himself accomplishes much.

"In Character," in The Times Literary Supplement, *No. 3177, January 18, 1963, p. 37.*

LAURENCE LERNER

The Gift is a story about the sophisticated world of television, cinema, boorish artists, nuclear disarmers, and pretty girls: entertaining, occasionally funny, and no doubt joyous reading for the Cinderellas whose drab lives never touch this polished world. Mr Humphreys seems to have shot this gay but trivial theme through with a darker purpose, but it is hard to say just what it is. Characters keep misunderstanding one another, then learning the truth; they speculate on the human condition, making fools of themselves yet leaving us wondering about what they say. In theme and tone it reminded me of Iris Murdoch's *Under the Net,* but it is neither so funny nor so boldly willing to indulge in metaphysical speculation. Mr Humphreys is a polished writer and a skilful novelist, but his confrontations and discoveries constantly seemed to me mechanical or evasive, and the book never worthy of the talent that is lurking in it.

Laurence Lerner, in a review of "The Gift," in The Listener, *Vol. LXIX, No. 1766, January 31, 1963, p. 215.*

CHRISTOPHER WORDSWORTH

I imagine that few novelists delight to be described as "professional," a left-handed dagger-word which can seem to imply both an eye to the main pecuniary chance and more competence than enterprise. As applied to Emyr Humphreys the term is tinged with admiration for a writer both versatile and deeply painstaking. But he has extended his range steadily from book to book, never content to re-exploit an area, and his nine novels amount to a solid corpus of achievement. Judging by ***Outside the House of Baal,*** he is still coming into his strength.

J. T. Miles, soldier of God in North Wales, poor blacksmith's apprentice who becomes a Calvinist Methodist minister, has based his life on the Sermon on the Mount, and is damned as "a soft old fool" by his wife, who leaves him, and Kate, his sister-in-law, who keeps house for him into old age, where we meet and leave him. It has been a harsh selfless life of literal Godfearing, doomed to an unsuccess that has imposed resentful poverty on his family. Miles's life unfolds in intricate flashbacks that are designed also to document an era, and I thought these documentary intentions the book's weakness.

It is nevertheless a work of some strength and pathos. The man's spiritual odyssey, and his relationship with Kate, is not memorable for any very subtle dissection. But there is absolute authenticity in the physical narrative—the human body, squalid, ageing, noble, is almost the hero-in-chief—and domestic interiors. This Wales of pulpits and refuse buckets and "the eighth deadly sin of sentimental vulgarity" is depicted with some of the passionate love-loathing of Caradoc Evans, and Miles's loyalty to it is a bitter lyric quite free of bardic flatulence. And, although it is a long book, it is bare of those standard scenic flights about the mountains and valleys. The author has deeper ways of conveying the texture of landscape.

Christopher Wordsworth, "Soldiering On for God," in Manchester Guardian Weekly, *May 20, 1965, p. 11.*

THE TIMES LITERARY SUPPLEMENT

Mr. Humphreys's method [in ***Outside the House of Baal***] is a departure from his usual practice. In his recent novels he has shown a preference for the first person and a tendency to identify very closely with his narrator. Here, by contrast, he renders himself invisible, not by putting on the cloak of his characters but by going away altogether and leaving a camera and microphone in his place. Objects and movements and human speech are recorded with great clarity of detail. Adjectives are chosen with the utmost care, anything incantatory or analogical being eschewed. Metaphors are out, similes starkly non-committal. He is debarred from the minds of his characters, and will venture no more than a deductive "he seemed satisfied that . . ." or "he appeared to be deep in thought . . .".

There are drawbacks to the method, the most obvious in this case relating to the characterization of the hero. For he is not a talkative or articulate man. He is apt, in response, to shake his head and smile. Some of the other characters, however, notably the spirited girl he marries and her doughty sister Kate, are much more vividly realized because they express themselves more freely and idiosyncratically, and act more positively. J. T. in comparison is only half revealed. He becomes familiar like a recurring figure in a family album, but there must always be more to him than meets the eye.

Though Mr. Humphreys has abandoned all claims to omniscience where his characters are concerned, he exercises it to the full in selecting the incidents of which the record is composed. Several years may elapse between these. With each incident the reader has to reassemble the pieces, fill in the gaps for himself, keeping a sharp eye open for the clues Mr. Humphreys has hidden. They are there, for it is a carefully constructed book. We know that if we are patient we will find out eventually how Kate lost her eye. We shall be able to guess with confidence what J. T. has been doing in the meantime. But by building the novel on a series of apparent discontinuities Mr. Humphreys obliges the reader constantly to start afresh.

Even so he has never written better. Sureness of vision and mastery of technique guarantee a genuine underlying coherence. He tells as no social historian could what it was like to grow up on a farm among the Welsh mountains, what stresses and challenges the twentieth century has imposed on the Welsh Presbyterian mind, of the binding and disruptive force of family, religion, and nationality. He makes no judgments, except occasionally through the mouth of an alien. There remains one awkward paradox. Mr. Humphreys has a fine command of English but his book ought to have been written in Welsh. All the important characters are Welsh speaking. If they are obliged to speak English Mr. Humphreys explains that they are doing so. There is thus the sense of remoteness from the source that even the best translations cannot avoid leaving.

"Wales Under Stress," in The Times Literary Supplement, *No. 3300, May 27, 1965, p. 409.*

SUSAN HILL

We are told that ***National Winner*** is the first of

> a sequence of novels to be called *The Land of the Living,* in which the subsequent relationships between the living members of this family will govern a pattern of story telling intended to reflect something of the complexity of the times in which we live.

I only hope Mr Humphreys didn't write that piece of pretentious blurb himself. But the intention behind the scheme must be his, and he has begun with a huge novel of incredible tediousness. I wanted to take a chopper to it. The characters are so dreary, their situations so mundane, their conversations so endless, I wonder the author could struggle to the end of the book, let alone plan to carry on with more. There are three brothers—one sensitive and withdrawn, one ambitious, one hip—whose father was a Welsh bard and who committed suicide. One brother is bent on finding out the truth about his death and getting a monument erected to his name. Their mother lives in a rambling mansion and plans to found a Community. The dialogue is full of profound thoughts or irrelevant chat. We know from his past books that Mr Humphreys has it in him to do much better than this. What has happened? Certainly he could learn a lot about the novel as iceberg. (p. 119)

Susan Hill, "Phi Principle," in New Statesman, *Vol. 82, No. 2105, July 23, 1971, pp. 118-19.*

ROGER BAKER

The family is a central concern of Emyr Humphreys' long, detailed novel [***National Winner***]. Peredur More is the youngest son of Amy, Lady Brangor, now widowed after three marriages. Peredur is a tutor at a red-brick university and becomes interested and finally obsessed with the mysterious circumstances of his father's death. His mother is very uptight about the affair, so he visits first his step-brother Bedwyr and his real brother Gwydion. In their different ways, both discourage Peredur in his plan to create a memorial to their common father.

The social function of the novel is to reveal change and development. The three brothers, their mother and father, all emerged from the same small, essentially Welsh, community. The father was poet and chaired bard at an Eisteddfod (a national winner) and the sense of these roots is very strong, even while the family has moved in different directions—Bedwyr is an architect, Gwydion on the maniac fringe of showbusiness. This novel is projected as the first of a sequence which will follow the subsequent relationships of this family. Humphreys has perfected a detailed, almost documentary style, in which scenes and conversations are given full revelation and weight. This has a tendency to make the pace slow until one becomes so involved that the minute recounting of events is seen as essential to the overall plan. (pp. 58-9)

Roger Baker, in a review of "National Winner," in Books and Bookmen, *Vol. 16, No. 12, September, 1971, pp. 58-9.*

PETER STRAUB

Any writer who embarks on a long sequence of novels must reckon despairingly with the certainty of being misunderstood at the outset, before the design can become clear, and reviewers, I suppose, should be charitable toward what appear to be lapses of pace, on the theory that later novels will bring out their relevance. I do want to be fair to Emyr Humphreys, and if his sequence begun by ***Flesh and Blood*** turns out to be a masterpiece I will rain flowers on his head in any public place he names. And yet. . . Although ***Flesh and Blood*** gradually picks up and, along about midpoint, becomes genuinely interesting, it is plagued by annoying structural tricks and long passages where even the author's interest seems to flag.

The narrative concerns the development from childhood to beautiful and hardheaded late adolescence of Amy Parry, a Welsh orphan who must escape the various traps and prisons set for her by others' affection, lust, weaknesses and enmity. Initially, the novel appears to be merely the presentation of a company of eccentrics—old women prostrating themselves before the rector, ego-bound cousins and uncles with their eyes on the next rung—but the pattern of Amy's self-liberation slowly emerges; the last sentence of the book has her jumping over a confining friend to get on her way to university. It is a good idea, but Humphreys does not fully trust his own narrative, and persistently falsifies it by creating meaningless enjambments of events. One anecdotal, would-be 'revelatory' scene mercilessly follows another; in every fourth or fifth of these, a number of offstage crises are packed into the scene in the hopes that this clumsy gimmick will be taken for ingenuity. The effect is like that of a film in which a weak director persistently shows important events reflected in mirrors or shop windows.

Peter Straub, "Whose Truth?" in New Statesman, *Vol. 88, No. 2264, August 9, 1974, p. 196.*

CHRISTOPHER WORDSWORTH

A "student of human nature,"—there's an old-fashioned term and one that the work of Emyr Humphreys dignifies more than most. He is a solid naturalistic writer who conveys the shape and feel of things and brings a careful eye to the manifestations and development of character. ***Flesh and Blood*** brings an orphaned girl, Amy Parry, to the threshold of maturity in Georgian Caernarvonshire through an album of episodes: bankrupt smallholding, Wesleyan in-fighting, a girls' hockey match, Nationalist pranks and fervours, attempted seduction in a ruin—"I was going to show you my mother's grave" says its dishevelled but still intact objective, having used her knee to some effect—scenes designed to plot the progress to identity. "Designed"—there's the rub, the novel is the first, chronologically, in a sequence and in spite of its solid physical grain the deaths and entrances read like the furniture of a mise en scene as the shutter clicks and clicks. . . .

Primarily this is an anatomy of Wales as it was in my and Mr Humphreys's childhood, and moreover of North Wales which, as anyone knows who has sampled the rail connections between Swansea and Penrhyndeudraeth on a Saturday, is another world from the South. . . . Mr Humphreys's scalpel cuts to the community bone, the unrewarding soil, the shibboleths, the beaten-down lay preacher stifling his adopted daughter's chances with windy texts—but still a man of glum wrong-headed courage, the answering ruthlessness of the secretive girl in the tricycle-and-First Investiture era. As it stands it seems more of a ground-plan than a self-contained novel. And although "mechanical" is too crude a word for a generally impressive book, events and emotions progress with a small but audible clank.

Christopher Wordsworth, "Land of My Fathers," in The Guardian, *August 24, 1974, p. 22.*

GORONWY REES

The Best of Friends is a sequel to Emyr Humphreys's previous novel, ***Flesh and Blood,*** and part of a sequence which, when completed, will have described the processes of growth, change and decay which have made Wales what it is today. For such a task Mr Humphreys is eminently well qualified. He knows Wales intimately, both from outside and from within, as it looks both to the native and to the foreigner, and it is not the least of his advantages that he is equally at home in both the languages in which it is natural for the Welsh people to express themselves. Best of all, Mr Humphreys is as interested in character as in environment, in nature as in nurture, and he writes in a style in which a gift of natural poetry is not incompatible with a sober realism.

Given such advantages, it is difficult to explain why one reads ***The Best of Friends*** with a certain disappointment. It is the story of two young girls, Amy and Enid, whom we have come to know from ***Flesh and Blood***. . . .

The time is 1928, a year in which Wales, after many and great tribulations, was looking for new roads, new ideas, new ways of life. For Amy these hopes and possibilities are symbolized by the charismatic figure of the Welsh Nationalist, Val Gwyn; for Enid, by the Welsh poet, John Cilydd, whose Eisteddfodic poem is rejected as "a heap of filth". After the two girls leave college the novel concentrates on the relationships between this quartet. . . .

Curiously enough, it is when Mr Humphreys concentrates on these relationships that his novel begins to lose its vivacity and momentum. It is as if his characters, initially so natural and spontaneous, have been allotted parts to play which are of less interest and importance than the background against which they play them, and though no one could be better than Mr Humphreys in bringing that background to life, his very success in doing so seems to have drained away the vitality from his characters and their personal experiences. Even the Welsh after all are human beings.

Goronwy Rees, "Class of '28," in The Times Literary Supplement, *No. 3989, September 15, 1978, p. 1010.*

JOHN MELLORS

The narrator in [Emyr Humphreys's] ***The Anchor Tree,*** Morgan Reece Dale, is a historian, a descendant of the 18th-century Welsh idealist, Robert Morgan Reece, who founded a city of Love and Peace in Pennsylvania. Dale goes to America and becomes obsessed with 'resurrecting' his ancestor's settlement, 'Cambria Nova'. Dale comes across as a somewhat wet romantic, and when he arouses the enthusiastic co-operation of a girl, Judith, half his own age, he falls in love with her. Mostly, he just adores her from afar, but when he sees her being attracted by the oafish Alva he tries, and fails, of course, to take her by force. At the end of the book Alva has made Judith pregnant and deserted her, and Dale has agreed to lend her money to go to Israel.

It is an unsatisfactory story, but Emyr Humphreys provides many incidental pleasures with the elegance and understated wit of his style. Dale talks to his pompous head of department at the nearby university: 'I was in fact repeating a form of words I had heard him use on more than one occasion. This facilitated his recognition of their basic wisdom.' Dale's sister, a capable, placid woman, walks through a graveyard, 'rotating with planetary calm among the tombstones'. An American says of Europeans: 'What they need is a strong dose of innocence.' Accurately though the remark may reflect the way many Americans see the perfidious people of the Old World, Humphreys's protagonist would have done better in America for a stiff dose of worldly wisdom.

John Mellors, "Norse Winds," in The Listener, *Vol. 104, No. 2672, July 31, 1980, p. 153.*

PATRICIA BEER

As a title, ***The Anchor Tree*** does not do justice to Emyr Humphreys's new novel. It belies the freshness of the book; there have been too many symbol-bearing trees among the titles of songs and stories throughout the ages. In any case, though the story is admirably clear, the title is opaque; it is introduced and explained on page 65 and there are recapitulatory allusions to it at various points in the plot, but it remains mysterious, in the wrong way.

Emyr Humphreys's sentence construction does not always do him justice either. He *can* write masterly sentences; the book is full of them. But all too frequently we get such sequences as: "I seemed to be listening only to the profound solidity of the house. Built from local materials. Rebuilt rather. Under their close supervision. Inspired by Frank Lloyd Wright." Apart from the architectural allusion it could be Mr Jingle speaking, and the narrator, Morgan Reece Dale, is no Mr Jingle, so it cannot be justified as a stroke of characterization.

Dislocation is clearly necessary to the recording of modern conversation, yet it still seems inappropriate to narration, even first-person narration. I can think of no reason why the following statement should be fragmented as it is: "Maybe I was a soft and pampered academic. Absorbed in his private puddle of misery. Like a pig in a spiritual factory farm. Nothing but wet slats to stand on and no room to move." If the pauses are intended to be pregnant, the pregnancy is hysterical.

But these are mere irritations. Emyr Humphreys is a persuasive storyteller, and he has cleverly solved the problem of how, when representing the banal realities of twentieth-century life, to be realistic without being banal.

In the first place, Idrisburg, the small town where the main events happen, is American not English, which makes a great difference. It is charming, clean and well-planned and the object of civic taste and pride, "with the blue hills in the distance and the tree-lined streets proclaiming the beauties of well-ordered existence". Significantly, one of the characters likens it to "an amalgam of a Tuscan town in the top right hand corner of a quattrocerto painting and an illustration from an old-fashioned children's book". It is out of this world in fact. In the second place, ***The Anchor Tree*** is by way of being a historical novel, set in the present. . . .

In its presentation of history ***The Anchor Tree*** goes back twice: firstly to the Second World War, which has formed or modified the fortunes and dispositions of most of the characters. . . .

The second and much longer leap takes us back to an earlier conflict, between Robert Morgan Reece (Dale's ancestor), and Oliver Lloyd, brothers in Christ who left Wales in the eighteenth century to found a community of love and peace in the forests of Pennsylvania. Reece being considerably more idealistic than Lloyd, they eventually disagreed. Reece founded Cambria Nova; Lloyd went on to establish the nearby settlement of Idrisburg. While Idrisburg, as we have seen, flourished, Cambria Nova collapsed into overgrown rubble.

Humphreys shows us enough of the two founders to capture our imagination, as they plod westward in Christian harmony, deep into Indian territory, pointing out to each other the turkeys, the creeks, the great Ohio river, the elk and buffalo and the marvellous fertility of the land. It is not surprising that Dale, reading the records they left, should decide to excavate the ruins of Cambria Nova and perhaps restore the community to life, and that so many citizens of Idrisburg should be inspired to join him.

The enterprise not only forms the framework of the plot but energizes the characters into something like total self-display. The notorious self-repetition of history takes the form of a latter-day struggle between idealism and pragmatism. It is all very convincingly done.

Patricia Beer, "The History Man," in The Times Literary Supplement, *No. 4036, August 1, 1980, p. 868.*

IOAN WILLIAMS

Like any other Welsh writer who uses the English language, Emyr Humphreys is often referred to as Anglo-Welsh. He dislikes this term himself, insisting that he is a Welsh writer, and although this creates some difficulties it helps us to bear in mind that his achievement must be considered against the whole background of Welsh literature. In rejecting the term Anglo-Welsh, Emyr Humphreys is reminding us that he, as a writer, is the product of the complex social and cultural reality of Wales which itself has shaped his mind and his art. The pattern of his development as a writer gives us a unique opportunity to study the nature of the world in which we all live, and at the same time a clear view of our society and culture is the best preparation for an appreciation of his literary achievement. As a Welsh novelist Emyr Humphreys has had to encounter special difficulties arising from the nature of contemporary Welsh society and from the conditions of the literary form he is employing. In struggling with these difficulties and in overcoming them, he has become one of the most important of contemporary Welsh writers and, as a novelist, has made a contribution of unique significance. (p. 1)

For a writer in his early twenties, Emyr Humphreys's earliest work was astonishingly mature and challenging and contained many of the elements most important in his later achievement. In his first two novels, especially, the typological view of character is strongly developed: character falls into certain patterns, according to the nature of the forces at work on it, and these forces are clearly seen in relation to ideas and institutions ultimately fuelled by human passion. But even here we may detect a fundamental tension between the typological view on the one hand and a theological tendency on the other. This tension becomes clearer in his next few novels, while his stance as a novelist changes. For an author who thinks that human character is formed by its environment, it is always difficult to come to terms with the existence of good and evil. In his later work Emyr Humphreys reconciles the two viewpoints by presenting moral choice as an essential condition of meaningful existence, an essential means of organising character and experience. In the early novels he was unable to do this, however, and, coming from a society pervaded by moral considerations, he gradually succumbed to a tendency to develop one at the expense of the other. His concern for moral assessment gradually overcame his tendency to take a typological view of character and began to influence, and indeed, to undermine, the structure of his work, giving rise to problems of focus and proportion which he was only able to overcome when the original tendency reasserted itself. (pp. 16-17)

The work of the years between 1951 and 1965 shows a loss of direction and loss of power. As he matured, instead of developing the vision implicit in his earlier novels, Emyr Humphreys set a new course for himself, which led him towards an increasingly intellectual approach to fiction and involved him in manipulation and uncertainty of focus. (p. 29)

With his ninth novel, ***Outside the House of Baal*** (1965), Emyr Humphreys created a new dimension for Welsh fiction and took up a standpoint from which he could effectively confront difficulties which had previously hindered his development. ***Outside the House of Baal*** presents the contemporary Welsh experience of disjunction and meaninglessness in an anglicised suburban estate in North East Wales. (p. 55)

Outside the House of Baal is so constructed that the past confronts the present, neither having precedence, but each reflecting on the other. They form part of a unified vision in which reductive comedy is a prominent element, in which individual human beings are seen in a constant struggle at varying levels of ideality, to realise themselves and relate to their surroundings. (p. 56)

In the novels which have followed ***Outside the House of Baal,*** Emyr Humphreys has maintained the technique he developed there. His stance remains fundamentally that of the traditional authoritative narrator, though he tends to exclude commentary and presents relatively little of what goes on in the conscious minds of his characters. His narrative technique resembles that of the film camera—highly visual and often moving very freely from one viewpoint to another. He is traditional in that he follows the lives and relationships of a group of characters over a period of time, the selection and proportioning of events depending on a clearly defined moral subject. On the other hand, his technique is original in so far as it suggests a larger perspective than is common among novelists. He does not present his characters primarily as actors in a drama. The action of his novels is derived from social history rather than the emotional involvements of individuals. Although their freedom of will is an important element, it is only one factor in their total significance, which derives from the fact that they are part of a whole greater than themselves. According to the vision of mankind implicit in his later technique, individuals are parts of a total social and cultural continuum which their actions and reactions define. This vision, which relates to all people in all places, has come to him as a result of the particular study of his own country. In Wales the problem is particularly acute—here persistent elements of altruism and idealism are at work in a world stubbornly resistant to any kind of coherent organisation, and we are continually brought up against the human dilemma which results. In this situation the novelist endures a particularly acute problem. His dilemma as an individual is compounded by his problem as a novelist, who seeks to create a coherent fiction which honestly reflects an incoherent world. In Emyr Humphreys's case the sharpness of this dilemma has effected a shift of emphasis, so that he is now looking for meaning not in individual experience but in the relationship between individual character and its environment. Depending more and more on history as a means of determining proportion and sequence, Emyr Humphreys presents a new vision of experience. (pp. 69-70)

The Best of Friends and its two predecessors [***National Winner*** and ***Flesh and Blood***] represent a major achievement, which goes a long way towards solving the dilemma of all Welsh literature in English. That is, it succeeds in transmuting the values of the past into the language of the present, without sentimentalism or affectation. We can go beyond this, too, and say that his consideration of specifically Welsh experience has brought Emyr Humphreys to a position from which he is able to realise aspects of human experience which are generally true in the modern world as a whole. The fundamental condition of his achievement has been his own moral integrity, even though it worked for years against his deepening his art to the fullest extent. When he brought this to bear on the elements in experience which had previously seemed to threaten it, he began to develop an original and convincing view of human character and the human condition. This could only happen when he had resolved his early confusion and fully translated his own demand for meaning into a desire for form. In this process his discovery of history was essential. The aesthetic unity of his later work derives from the interplay between subjective and objective aspects of experience—between man as part of a historical process and man as a feeling, willing being, complete in himself.

Since he has arrived in this position Emyr Humphreys has been working in the mainstream European tradition established by writers like Thomas Mann and André Malraux, but he faces a difficulty which may yet undermine the developing power of his art. The language of his work is in the main English, the language of his material largely Welsh. In a sense this is fitting, in so far as it reflects the historical process he is describing. We must accept the possibility of translation from one language at one time into another language at another. But the simple act of translation may be inadequate in a situation as complex as that which his work embodies. . . . Which of the languages concerned is the proper medium for the embodiment of such an experience? As far as I am aware no one has ever confronted the question before. It is a measure of Emyr Humphreys's status as a writer that he is the first; and in his response to it we will eventually find the full measure of his work. (pp. 83-5)

Ioan Williams, in his Emyr Humphreys, *University of Wales Press on behalf of the Welsh Arts Council, 1980, 97 p.*

ROLAND MATHIAS

Emyr Humphreys is not a novelist who happens by accident to be a Welshman but one whose qualities and intrinsic attitudes arise in the most direct fashion from his being one. His writing and its preoccupations are the result of Wales's heritage of the last three centuries: they begin in that Puritan seriousness about the purpose of living, about the need for tradition and the understanding of it, about the future of the community as well as the individual, that has almost no place in the writing of contemporary English novelists, however many wry soliloquies from the jazz of relationships they may from time to time throw out. Sadly, however, Emyr Humphreys stands alone as a writer, both in the context of his birth and in the choice he makes in celebrating the inheritance of his native land. (p. 64)

The Little Kingdom, his first novel, was published in 1946. Plainly he was part of the new generation displaced by the War, affected by the enforced mobility (which brought him Italy as well as Wales) and perhaps compelled it to accept experience faster than its predecessors. Equally plainly he was by birth and upbringing outside the coterie values and the rather precious aestheticism of pre-War practitioners of the novel.

Above all, he began with the impetus of a fresh start in the new peace.

But to leave him in the realist fold which, one cannot but be aware, he has never left, and to offer no further explanation is to suggest that this stance has become petrified. Nothing could be further from the truth. He is very certainly where he is as a matter of conviction. This point needs making because the realist novel has long since lost confidence. (pp. 64-5)

[To] Emyr Humphreys the concepts of art as forgery or as game are unacceptable, though he knows perfectly well what the limits of realism are and how far the picture can ever escape from the artist. The novel for him is essentially serious: "in our time", he wrote in 1953, "the novelist's attitude is more crucial than his manner of expression". Not for him, then, "the quiet sport of technical experimentation". Unfashionable as it may be, he has not abandoned the idea of *progress:* his insistence on plot, on narrative development, is not a sop to the conservative reader, it is his announcement that he is interested in other people rather than in the self shedding its skins as the ego perambulates: the subject of the novel is Life. Experiment he does, technically, in the use of time by intercutting the narrative (and, less significantly, in the matter of punctuation) but it will appear from what follows that such shifts do not contradict in any way a true chronology of the idea of progress. And the area of uncertainty he leaves for the reader is not a matter of technical manoeuvre or the deliberate omission of several pieces of the puzzle: the uncertainty he leaves begins at the point where our serious ideas about life fall off the edge of the world we know. Where has our society been and where is it going? What is *good?* How is a good man or woman created? How can our ideas of good best be applied to our society, to other people, to ourselves, so that more good may result? Are good standards passed on by the establishment of just organisation, by the example of an individual's absolute integrity, or by such integrity conjoined with political or social wisdom? Emyr Humphreys does not claim to know: he inclines only, and not infrequently with different emphases. But he is certain that the quest for goodness (and it will be left to the reader to determine whether goodness is a matter of a just and loving morality, conceived in human terms or whether it involves a mystery, a vision of the infinite, of God) is merely so remarkably difficult that it exhausts human energy and wisdom but that it is also exciting, life-giving, creative. Emyr Humphreys is a committed Christian and he has for long set himself to write what he once called "the Protestant novel".

One has only to read a page or two of any of his books to realise that what is in hand is no stuffy or censored tract. Nothing that I have written so far must be understood in that way. There is no relationship between, let us say, ***Hear and Forgive*** and Canon Farrar's *Eric* or *Little by Little*. Emyr Humphreys's purpose is neither hortatory nor deliberately evangelical. Where the *Catholic* novel exists in Britain, as for example in the works of Graham Greene and Evelyn Waugh, it confines itself to affirming the existence of evil (*Brighton Rock* and much of Waugh) or exemplifying (as in *The Power and the Glory*) or disputing (as in *The Heart of the Matter*) points of Catholic doctrine. In other words, though rarely as referential in this respect as Francois Mauriac, these Catholic novels have recourse to a centre of doctrinal certainty, even where, in secular terms, they have difficulty in arguing it. What Emyr Humphreys means by 'the Protestant novel' is something much less fixed than that. It draws attention to the principle of personal responsibility and the necessity of choice, not simply in the Existentialist sense that one makes one's own life by choosing (though that has its component of truth) but that choices have to be made with a responsibility both to the *status quo* (and everybody involved in it) and to the result hoped for, whether near at hand or distant. Where Existentialism is self-determining only, Protestantism is Christianly wedded to the City of God, to the ultimate community, to the salvation of all men. Choices therefore inevitably involve other people, and that is where the real responsibility comes in. The practice of *agape* or Christian love, at a time when, as Emyr Humphreys put it almost three decades ago, the human race was never harder to love, is infinitely difficult: such love often appears defeated, ineffectual, or successfully operative only over such periods of time or in such rarefied instances as scarcely to be worth bothering with. And yet there *is* progress—or our hearts think there is, however little we now believe in the claims of technology: our society, our world, moves on, perhaps immediately to violence and political extremism but also to honesty, compassion and continuing sacrifice. How does this happen? This is really Emyr Humphreys's terrain. (pp. 65-6)

[It] is implicit in Emyr Humphreys's work that love goes on despite sin and personal defeat and that its persistence and efficacy are not wholly examinable and testable against any law of probabilities that reason may evolve. This is neither to propose the visibly miraculous nor to assert the verity of the Apostolic Succession, as the end of *The Power and the Glory* does: it is to indicate the area of the unknown, to suggest some answers that do not work and one or two that on occasions do, and to approach God with the agnosticism of one who is well aware that all human answers fall short, even those of science. It is to look at life as a whole, murmuring repeatedly, "Lord, I believe: help Thou my unbelief".

Many readers of Emyr Humphreys may fail to recognise in this preamble any connection with their own recollection of his novels. There is in them such a wealth of incident, such a complexity of plot, such amusement and irony, so many characters and various, that the preoccupations I have outlined may seem restrictive and unreal. Any restriction that exists, however, is much more probably to be found in the reader's understanding of what Emyr Humphreys means by 'the Protestant novel', a restriction that I can best illustrate from my own mistakes in this context. When I first read Emyr Humphreys's article in *The Listener* in 1953 I had just finished ***Hear and Forgive.*** Taking the point about conscience and personal responsibility, I could see that David Flint, novelist and teacher of Scripture in a London secondary school for boys, who had been living, in a curiously blank and frustrated fashion with Lord Whiteway's comparatively wealthy niece, had, at the end of the book, come to the realisation that he *had* to return to his narrow-visioned, unintellectual wife in a provincial Shropshire town and to his spoiled and uncongenial son Stanley. Conscience required it, integrity required it, but there would be nothing pleasant or self-fulfilling about it. (pp. 67-8)

The idea of conscience in [the conclusion to ***Hear and Forgive***] persuaded me that what I was to look for in the Protestant novel was the character who was journeying through the wilderness of this world towards an ultimate and responsible choice and when I read ***A Man's Estate,*** Emyr Humphreys's next novel, I looked in vain for the same marking on the map and was entirely confused by the story's *dénouement*. . . . [A] closer observation would have made it plain that David Flint was not *journeying* at all: he was stuck, will-less, in his unsatisfactory predicament, and only the fact that his mistress Helen suddenly threw him over put him in the position to listen to his conscience. Even then he would not have listened to it but for his friendship with the headmaster, Edward Allenside, who nevertheless had addressed not one word to him on the subject. It was the fact of the emotional crisis and the existence in the mind's eye of an *example* that worked together to produce a new resolution in David Flint. Not even years of teaching Scripture and expounding the Bible had been able to create that moment for David on his own. The living, journeying character was in reality Allenside and the implications of that were still hidden from me.

But it is time now to put away errors and to indicate broadly what the various directions of Emyr Humphreys's novels are. . . . Let me begin with ***A Toy Epic*** (1958) which, in its original draft, was Emyr Humphreys's first novelistic writing. As one might expect, this takes the writer's experience to the limit of the then known and felt. It is the story of three boys, Albie, Iorwerth and Michael, schoolfellows who grow together and then separate again. Each of them has a social and a spiritual comment to make, but the heart of the book, in my view, lies in the relationship of Michael and Iorwerth. Michael was the rector's son, whose first lesson, impressed upon him by an ambitious mother, was that he was *different*. Privileged in school and in Sunday school, he chose to emphasise his difference by refusing to acknowledge that he could read Welsh. . . . For some years afterwards, during which Michael's academic prowess was no more than moderate, lack of confidence made him deliberately cultivate charm and choose popularity, especially when it meant bad company. Realising at length the emptiness of such acting, he worked harder, won an Open Scholarship to University and recovered confidence: with all the points of the *persona* clicking into place, he embraced the cause of Welsh Nationalism and became, in his own eyes, a man of destiny.

This sense of innate leadership is Emyr Humphreys's first target, then. What is its basis? Conscience? Belief? Or a psychological 'mix' which goes back to early environmental factors? The fact that the cause Michael chooses is very near to Emyr Humphreys's heart makes his author's disquiet the more poignant. A just cause must be led by conscience, not charisma. For observe Michael in the penultimate scene of the book. He dreams himself a dream of dedication to Wales, of which his friend Iorwerth, "in his naive innocence", is the soul, the potent symbol. But he has just been seen by Iorwerth in the wood beginning to make a not-very-interested love to Dilys Maurice, the minister's daughter, whose prospective partner Iorwerth has until then imagined himself to be. In other words, Michael betrays that soul, that symbol, before he starts. What is leadership when the leader despises the values of the led, however limited they may be?

Again, how does Michael come to see himself as leader? In the beginning by choosing his mother rather than his father, a Welshman of modesty and scholarship. How, from his initially anglicised position, does he come to embrace the cause of Wales? By arguing with Watkin at a Summer School, Watkin with the "sticky eyes behind thick lenses, a habit of sniffing, his lips always wet with excess saliva". Why is this? The novelist offers no answer. His experience suggests that that is how influence and example work: there is a time for them, and an occasion too, that often defy rationality. This is a problem with which Emyr Humphreys is engaged in all his books. (pp. 68-70)

A Toy Epic is a book of questions without answers, which its limitation to the days of school makes possible. Beyond them lies a great continuum of silence in which the answers may lie. (p. 71)

Emyr Humphreys's first-published book, ***The Little Kingdom,*** which appeared in 1946, takes the Michael figure further, into a new career as Owen. Owen is the son of a minister but he has been to public school. Michael, it may be recollected, was a public schoolboy manqué: it was the one respect in which his father was successful in blocking maternal ambition. There was a significant occasion at school when Owen was bullied, as indeed there was for Michael (in ***A Toy Epic***) when he and Iorwerth were at Llanrhos County School for the Scholarship exam (he regarded Iorwerth as having slipped out of the situation and deserted him). We should plainly add these ingredients to the already napoleonic confection.

Owen is older, post-university: he has also set himself a specific task, the prevention of the construction of an aerodrome on the land of his uncle Richard Bloyd and the damming of the anglicised tide that would certainly rise higher with the coming of new employment. There are echoes here, without a doubt, of the incident at Penyberth in Llŷn in 1936, but ***The Little Kingdom*** is set in true Emyr Humphreys country, in the precarious Welshness of Flintshire, and the plot develops by Owen murdering his uncle, taking over his money, land and the local newspaper and finally getting himself shot in an attempt to burn the hutments of the aerodrome. The case against false leadership is being taken further, obviously, but there is a strain on its dramatic credibility. What may be sensed in this novel and in the one that follows, ***The Voice of a Stranger*** (1949), successful as they are (the second more so), is that Emyr Humphreys is trying to kill two birds with the same stone: he is seeking to provide a well-plotted narrative with a wealth of dramatic incident of the kind attractive to readers whose attention is usually given to a more popular kind of fiction while working on one or two of the problems, in which he is himself interested. The effect of this dual intention, however, is that the writing is blurred in places. (pp. 71-2)

The Voice of a Stranger is that book of his (***The Gift*** only excepted) which can most easily be read without the smallest realisation that its author has particular preoccupations. Set in Italy, where the War took Emyr Humphreys as an official of the Red Cross, the novel is brilliantly plotted. It lacks nothing in the kind of growing tension and progressive readability that the general reader expects, and its backgrounds are authentic. What can be discerned in it is another illustration of the destruction of leadership—not, in this case, by the corruption of idealism but by the mistake of *eros,* by the apparently chance nature of romantic or physical love. The idealism here is unpoliticised Communism as felt by a wartime guerilla leader who has concentrated on the essentials of action. Guido Bordoni, the natural leader in the field, marries Marcella Vaspucci, the daughter of a liberal professor who is compelled to line up amongst his opponents in peacetime. Marriage 'across the line', so to speak, is a theme explored again in ***A Man's Estate.*** Whether or not Guido's idealism *could* have been applied to the trickier conditions of the post-war sort-out without fading or dirtying, in fact it gets no chance: his influence is increasingly nullified by the more experienced Communist hardliner Riccardo Forli, who not only knows how to manage the party but treacherously seeks to seduce his friend's bride. Failing in this, he has to eliminate Guido himself to cover his tracks. The genuineness of the love between Guido and Marcella proves to be no defence: and Professor Vaspucci, who might have straddled the gap between the two political factions, has betrayed his own position by his liaison with the Spanish refugee Rosaura, which gives the corrupt ex-Fascisti a hold over him. There are portraits of two do-gooders, Red Cross officials—Morell, with red hair and short, sharp burst of conscience, and the American Warner, whose Christian will to good is calmer and more persistent. But it is Warner who, like Guido, gets himself killed by Riccardo when he tries to help Marcella. *Eros* had begun to influence *agape* and the balance is lost. The issues are unmistakeable if the pressure of the plot leaves the reader time to think.

Love between man and woman, then, solves nothing outside itself, brings together no other persons or views that are sundered. And it may affect, deleteriously, the action of the kind of love which might work powerfully towards a wider unity. The direction of Emyr Humphreys's first two published novels is, behind the surface brilliance, *downward*, the cul-de-sac notice set firmly in the face of brash optimism. It is the presence of other and more forward-looking elements in ***A Toy Epic*** which suggests, despite its originally conceived limitations, that it was fairly substantially revised before it appeared in 1958.

A Change of Heart (1951), the third novel to be published, strikes one immediately, despite its sadnesses, as a warmer book. Emyr Humphreys begins in it to explore the positive. If there is truth, if there is honesty, if there is goodness, how is it transmitted? The background this time is that of a Welsh university and the chief characters are Howell Morris, Professor of English, who has made an ill-judged marriage with Lucy Davies, one of his students, and Frank Davies, her brother, himself a student and a poet but the product, like his sister, of a confined working-class home eastwards along the anglicised coast. The book opens with Lucy dead after many apparent unfaithfulnesses and Frank under the influence of Howell's enemy, Alcuin Phillips, who foments his conviction that Howell had given Lucy a terrible life. The burden of the book is essentially that of Frank's journey from darkness to light, through the tribulation of a love affair with the fickle and self-serving Gwen, through the rigours of work on a farm (to which his refusal of Howell's help and support has condemned him), to the final revelation, made by the Communist bus-driver Jimmy Hill, that Lucy died after the induced abortion of Alcuin's child. It is satisfactory enough, to be sure, to see the import of the narrative in the victory of one man's integrity over isolation and intrigue: but a survey of Emyr Humphreys's novels following must also make one aware that Howell Morris is the first of those who offer *example*. By whatever precise track influence passes, it must pass through a succession of such nodes of good.

> A soul cannot make progress *in vacuo:* many men are better for the existence of one good man, and one good man is the product of some kind of progress that was both individual and social.

Thus Emyr Humphreys, making his own exposition. But has this progress come about through politics? Not in the novels under survey. Carrog Ellis (in ***The Little Kingdom***) and Elis Felix Elis (in ***A Man's Estate***) both stand revealed as eloquent sellers of what truth and virtue they once had for the dubious mite of power. Does it come about through education? Not if Alcuin Phillips and Ronnie Miles (in ***Outside the House of Baal***) are the arbiters of moral health. And academic politicians, of course, are just politicians. How does it come about, then? By means of a succession of exemplars, whose connection with each other is not explicable rationally. Or not entirely explicable. The most obvious succession would be from parents to children, but in ***A Change of Heart*** there is the first demonstration that this does not work, at least not in any straightforward fashion. Lucy and Frank are brother and sister, children of conventional, limited and rather cowardly parents: what they have in common is academic ability, but Lucy plays faster and looser towards death and disaster (having a bravery of the wrong sort) while Frank is capable not merely of poetry but of recognising and choosing the good at the last (albeit to some personal advantage too). From this book onward Emyr Humphreys's novels become increasingly schematic and one plain reason for this is that he desires to examine the matter of inheritance (a term used here to cover the effects of birth *and* early environmental factors). Thus families appear, grandparents, parents, children: there are more and more generations of them. The move to the scale of ***Outside the House of Baal*** is significant, that to the quartet of books beginning with ***Flesh and Blood*** more significant still. Is the choice of the good predestined by the apparent accident of birth? Does the succession—the *real* succession—omit one or more generations? Or is the good man an existentialist from nowhere who chooses the good consistently because there is another kind of ordination which it is impossible to follow? Answers to such questions are hardly likely to emerge from the *schema* of the picaresque novel, where successive encounters and choices are likely to be meaningless except in terms of the passage of time. The unit of society under scrutiny must be tighter than that because Emyr Humphreys believes that inheritance is much the most likely as well as the most interesting bet, though his honesty compels him to show it working by such fits and starts, driving so often into cul-de-sacs, emerging again after an interval by roads that are not marked on the map. Free will and predestination, are they mutually exclusive? Perhaps not. The heart of the mystery for him lies somewhere there. And perhaps that is where God is. One does not know. (pp. 72-5)

I have already described the *dénouement* of ***Hear and Forgive*** and shall write the less about it now. But the character of Edward Allenside deserves a little examination. To begin with he is contrasted with his plausible rogue of a brother, Roger, and David Flint, in his capacity of novelist, works for some time on the sixteenth century brothers, Gay Tom and Protector Somerset, with Roger and Edward in the foreground as contemporary illustrations. Then we are shown the actual childhood of the two Allensides (at least from Edward's account of it): Roger in violent reaction against his pedantic, righteous but essentially well-meaning stepfather and Edward, the younger, accepting the *régime*. There are two points here, I believe: first, that revolt leads to no forward movement of the good (a view already noted): and second, that free will can nullify whatever benefits of inheritance there are as well as advance them. . . . We leave Edward Allenside . . . with none of his problems solved (as we leave Roger not quite in the hands of the police) and the good he stands for terminating with himself. But no, the spark crosses the void: his friend David Flint has at last learned from him and gone back to face his own responsibilities. That is perhaps, Emyr Humphreys is saying, one of the ways in which the good perpetuates itself.

I have already indicated that ***A Man's Estate*** (1955) puzzled me at first reading. That, it turns out, is because the inheritance theme is more complex and the real inheritor a much less forceful person than Edward Allenside. There is, too, a cross-theme of great, indeed fundamental, importance. Let me take the cross-theme first. Idris 'Flopper' Powell has come to Pennant as minister having renounced the love of his best friend's wife, believing that this has given him an impetus to love his not very lovable congregation. That impetus fades. This theme is devoted to demonstrating the folly of supposing that *eros* (even *eros* denied) leads into *agape*. (pp. 76-8)

The Italian Wife (1957) relates directly to ***A Man's Estate*** because it uses the latter's cross-theme in reverse. *Agape,* severely distressed, perceives its counterpart (or thinks it does) and is driven to express its yearning for communion in terms of *eros*. (p. 80)

The background of this book is international—England, Austria, Italy—and it may at first appear that this is why ***The Italian Wife*** falls somewhat from the standard of Emyr Humphreys's most demanding and successful novels. But this is not really so. Italy, it is true, might as well not be Italy but for a thumbnail sketch of Massimo, Paola's brother-in-law, known behind his back as Count Cheese. But in which of Emyr Humphreys's books has natural background—mountains, lakes, sea, air, sunset, morning, what you will—constituted an aesthetic factor, even a mood factor, in the argument? The world is people and Mr. Humphreys retains the old Puritan distrust of beauty as anything more than a pretended influence on conduct. No, the trouble with this book is that there are real people in it but no community, no natural framework for their moral perceptions and no connection which they can exercise one with another except their stated one of marriage and inheritance. It is a world like the broken language and the fragmented circles of the end of ***Outside the House of Baal***. . . . There is an impression from ***The Italian Wife*** that Emyr Humphreys is compelled, in the social medium he has chosen, to *state* rather than to illustrate and develop the significance of his theme. (p. 81)

The real difficulty facing Emyr Humphreys [in ***The Italian Wife***], I am confident, is that the rich, the playboys, the jet-set, do not constitute the natural medium for the Protestant novel. It is in closer societies that the concept of duty can be most intelligibly correlated with human conduct. Little dutiful Anton, the conscience of the next generation, seems just a shade unnatural here.

The Gift (1963) is the one book that might have been written by someone other than Emyr Humphreys. It followed ***The Italian Wife*** after an interval of six years, during most of which its author had been a drama producer with the B.B.C. This is not the place to begin any kind of discussion of the odds on self-destruction facing any creative artist who involves himself in day-by-day labour in television or radio. Suffice it to say that Emyr Humphreys wrote little or nothing during his five-year stint and when he realised, with the clarity necessary to the decision to depart, that he would write no more novels unless he freed himself, he decided that his first writing for some time must make use of his recent experience. Perhaps he was no longer entirely the man who had essayed the Protestant novel. And perhaps again he was, but temporarily submerged in a new and superficially attractive experience which must be made use of before the older preoccupations were resumed.

Intensely readable, the conversation always stimulating and often pointed, the narrative development no more than partly predictable, ***The Gift*** may well be the most popular and least Protestant of all Emyr Humphreys's novels (and although these adjectives belong to different categories their juxtaposition is not entirely meaningless). Sam Halkin (Flintshire is never forgotten, though rather titular in this book) is an actor approaching middle age, too often type-cast as a villain and still waiting for the fortunate 'lift' that will take him to the top of his profession. He is living, in the most casual way possible, with Polly Fleming and the main theme is concerned with Polly's increasing indispensibility, the undermining of the actor's sense of 'freedom' and the threat of marriage (still off-stage at the end). It could be argued, though not with much vehemence, that the book is about Sam Halkin and the approach of responsibility. Another marriage is looked at critically—that of the Danish producer Lars Steensen and his wife René—and the fact that Lars's diary falls into the hands of both Polly and Sam separately offers the opportunity for an appraisal of 'intelligence' and 'success as an actor' through at least three pairs of eyes. The background of plays, films and actors' talk reads authentically, even excitingly at times, and there is the by-now-ritual visit to Italy. Linsey Jones appears as the lead actor who is a successful business man as well and Da Parigi as the film producer, cultured and gentlemanly, who is nevertheless on the way out. As entertainment ***The Gift*** is little to be faulted and the implied happy ending adds to its attraction for many readers. Sam is perhaps 'over the hump' but Polly, whose beauty has brought her a film part, comes down from London to Cardiff to say that she prefers Sam and proposes not to take it.

But in the terms in which the other novels of Emyr Humphreys have been discussed here ***The Gift*** has little to say. Sam Halkin, despite his easy-going ways as a lover, is a decent sort of chap, unable to push himself as does Linsey Jones or to crush the weak in passing. But suspect as we may that he is to prove that Polly's Uncle Alfred's New Rules about asking for less and giving more (as a norm of conduct) are to produce his happiness if not the betterment of society, all that Sam really does is to lose his supreme chance in films because his 'friend' Linsey Jones won't let him have a part that is likely to steal the picture. He loses the shouting match that follows as well. Perhaps this, with his kindness to Lars, may suggest that he is the right match for Polly: but it has to be pointed out that he is a natural loser not a deliberate one.

Polly herself is, in any case, an even greater problem. The major architect of the happiness in the book, she is also every man's pre-liberation heroine, despite her odd beginnings as a teenage misfit. But how it comes about that she is an actress yet essentially untouched by the ideas of individual freedom widespread amongst her kind is not explained. Neither she nor Sam is shown *becoming,* so to speak: they have juvenile points of reference in Southport and Flintshire respectively, and Polly reveals herself as now appreciating and caring for Uncle Alfred, whom she once detested. But what does Uncle Alfred amount to? Why is he taken off to prison towards the end of the narrative (except to clear the flat)? Polly's supposedly enduring passion is love for Sam and 'the gift' is presumably hers to him (rather than his gift as an actor). This love crosses no social lines, however, as does that of Idris Powell in ***A Man's Estate***. In the free wheel of stage society what distinguishes Polly from other actresses is her closely domestic emphasis, something which safely ensures the romantic aura of the conclusion. The theme rests with an *eros* which is seen developing, optimistically, into the ground of an enduring partnership, but there appears to be no attempt on the author's part even to suggest an *agape*—which might, in any case, seem seriously unreal in the context of this novel. One might argue that the Protestant novel is as out of place here as with the jet-set, but it would be safer to regard ***The Gift*** as a popular and successful exploitation of particular and recent experience rather than any kind of development of the author's earlier philosophy of the novel.

With ***Outside the House of Baal*** (1965) Emyr Humphreys returns to his Protestant designs, which are enlarged schematically to cover four generations. It is the fullest and most elaborate of the drawings and inter-patternings to be considered in this essay and there will be space only to consider the themes that have been adduced thus far.

The intercutting time-scheme of the novel (which works painstakingly through a very short period in the present and brings the past more rapidly up to it) has many functions: but one simplifying thing it does—it tells the reader that J. T. and Kate are the people to watch. J. T. Miles, the Calvinistic Methodist minister, is the spiritual idealist in full-length portrait, the open, selfless spirit moving on through changing times, often impractical but never eloquently empty. A pacifist in the First World War, a man sympathising so strongly with the unemployed in South Wales during his ministry there that he foregoes part of his salary to be in communion with them, he is also the man who comes to be hated and betrayed by his wife for his neglect of his own and his family's interests, who comes to seem to her no more than a 'man of words' that are meaningless. He is the man, too, who, serving as a stretcher-bearer in that same First War, tries to rescue a wounded man against instructions and sees his comrade Cynwal killed in consequence. One of the developments of Emyr Humphreys's several themes here is plainly that Christian love, when practised, can bring its own share of sorrow and tragedy and can be seen as ineffectual, at least in the short term, against the heavy armour of power. Moreover, J. T. offers his wife Lydia *eros* within a life which is devoted to *agape* and still fails. *Eros* dies and *agape,* for many human beings in their unredeemed state, asks too great a sacrifice. (pp. 81-4)

In J. T. Miles Emyr Humphreys provides the kind of leader who cannot be faulted as Owen and Michael and the briefly-seen politicians are faulted. But he is human and *eros* separates him from the woman who would have stood by him. He moves forward by conscience, nevertheless, and seeks directly to influence the society of which he is part (as Howell Morris does not): but he sees, instead of a greater good, the godly community he loved broken into fragments and the worshippers flocking to the house of Baal. Behind it all lurks the enormous question of whether we know and understand what good is. . . . Is it meaningful to talk of *progress* within the span of a single life? Can we attempt to hasten *progress* by a positive leadership, even if it be of the most idealistic kind? May it not prove to be humanly mistaken and set *progress* back many years? Are there any actions we can take and views we can propound in society which are better and more effective for the advancement of the good than the simple reciprocities of love and kindness between members of the family, between neighbours and friends, between those to whom there comes a chance to show kindness and those who by chance receive it? In other words, is man stepping out of station in seeking to influence a society, a world, by means of politics, of education, even of what he sees as religious faith? May he not be usurping God's means?

Outside the House of Baal does not answer these questions. It leaves J. T. at a low point but still pursuing. We are not even certain whether he has been a carrier of good at all. He may be self-deluding. But he may also be Elijah whom God recognises even while he seems to desert him. There are no kings and priests whom he may appoint but a successor may have been provided nevertheless. (p. 87)

It is an ending for which the reader must call upon his own faith. Kate cannot quite keep track of J. T. in human terms, even in his seeming defeat. So he may be supra-rational, an agent who does indeed carry God's quickening spirit. And he may not be. Is there a succession other than that argued in *The Power and the Glory?* How are Protestant apostles chosen? *A oes gobaith?* Is there hope? Is there? (p. 88)

Roland Mathias, "Channels of Grace: A View of the Earlier Novels of Emyr Humphreys," in Anglo-Welsh Review, *1982, pp. 64-88.*

J.K.L. WALKER

In [***Jones,*** a] brief but compressed novel, Emyr Humphreys wryly explores, through the curriculum vitae of his hero Herbert Goronwy Jones, the rootlessness and rejection of responsibility that may underlie and vitiate metropolitan success. The success, in Jones's case, is more than usually relative. At the age of fifty-seven he remains a senior lecturer in Education at a London college, having, he imagines, remained politely standing so that his colleague Jolly may occupy the Chair; Jolly's contempt waxes on this evidence of slender ambition and still slenderer output of papers. Even Jones's Welsh smallholder parents see him as a failure because of his continued absorption in the London dream to the exclusion of such realities as taking over the farm, or a professorship at Bangor, or marriage to Glenys, the daughter of neighbouring Brynscawen. But having struck off the ball and chain of his Welshness, Jones to his surprise hears at the end an even more melancholy clanking at his heels, coming from the ghostly train of unfructified relationships. Early retirement beckons: sustained by the proceeds of his art collection and the unfailing services of the Royal Borough of Kensington, he will take up the role of a rich recluse.

Lying awake at four o'clock one morning, Jones thus puts together a major retrospective of his career. The exhibition is cunningly hung. . . . Interspersed are sketches of work in progress, as Jones prepares to abandon his dying career, and of the final stages of his involvement with his background: his father's funeral, his mother's widowhood, a visit to the farm, Brynllwyd, now a suburbanized retirement retreat for an ICI couple who, roses round the door notwithstanding, are doing their best by Welsh culture: the massive oak still stands among alien lawns, bringing tears to Jones's eyes. Back quickly to Ennismore Gardens.

Jones, of course, is a droll; and a Welsh droll at that. He knows all about himself, particularly his native disposition towards rhetoric which, given Humphreys's own Welshness, may not be seen as an unbalanced attack on a minority culture. He allows Jones a good deal of rope at times. . . .

Jones's treatment of Glenys is the moral fulcrum of the novel, occupying, as it does, much of its length: Glenys and Jones as children on the beach; Glenys as a brisk St George's probationer nurse, unhappy with Hyde Park Corner and its insincere surroundings; Glenys and Jones, engaged, driven by the Welsh proprieties to sexual intercourse against a tree in a parental valley; Glenys's final departure for America as the wife of Keith, a prospering neurosurgeon who bores practical holes in real skulls rather than dreamily stroking Benin heads, as does Jones. The memory of the final scene with Glenys similarly joins Jones's collection of precious artefacts: yieldingly offering her his unyieldable marriage block, he takes back the engagement ring with relief and puts another record on the gramophone.

Do you marry the girl from the valley or don't you? Upwardly mobile young men in the 1950s had trouble with this question; still more their fictional embodiments. Against it was the fear of entangling your newly fledged intellect and imagination in a net of prosaic affection; for it, acceptance and understanding. Nurses like Glenys were a particular danger. Jones's guilt over her is to some extent factitious, excluding as it does consideration of her gift for reducing Jones's flood of ideas to a warm shower of words—although, by the end, as he himself is aware, the two are not readily distinguishable. Jones is what those irreverent, introspective comic heroes of the 1950s have become—still, as old age and loneliness close in, compulsively fleeing dim provincial society and ending up jogging round in circles inside their own heads where, of course, you meet a better, or at least more entertaining class of person. That the London society presented here should emerge as perceptibly dimmer than the Principality is a weakness of the novel: shadowy characters and perfunctory backgrounds are no help when the reader is asked to believe in Jones's lifelong commitment to the metropolitan scene. That he should be more inclined to put his trust in Jones's valedictory "Truth was my religion. And still is in a circumspect sort of way" speaks for Humphreys's skill in creating a likeable and amusing protagonist, if at times an irritatingly prolix one.

J.K.L. Walker, "Pictures from an Exhibition," in The Times Literary Supplement, *No. 4245, August 10, 1984, p. 901.*

ANTHONY THWAITE

'Dogged provincialism' isn't the phrase for the spirit of Emyr Humphreys's third novel in his sequence about early twentieth-century rural Wales; but 'an irrelevant backwater' is the way one character in ***Salt of the Earth*** defines the place, and another calls it 'a fossilised zoo.' As in the earlier novels, Amy and Enid are at the centre, now in the 1930s. Amy (the 'free woman') is a teacher, Enid is married to a solicitor who will 'compose the new poetry that . . . would extend the frontiers of their native literature,' and an old arthritic clergyman declares 'What's good for Wales is good for the world!'

Chapel, communism and peace are the large forces and causes; but in their interstices personal matters often seem more pressing. Can Amy choose between her severely tubercular Val and the less admirable but seductive Pen, a fiery reformer? Will Enid's family become reconciled to her solicitor-poet husband, now that Enid is pregnant?

Humphreys is good at individual scenes and portraits, less good at knitting them together: the minutiae of personal relations don't come across against the backdrop of world, or even Welsh, events as sharply as he intends. I felt that a relatively minor character, clever young Eddie Meredith, who has a Lawrentian line in abuse, could have usefully been given more to say and do.

Anthony Thwaite, "Dogged Provincialism," in The Observer, *March 31, 1985, p. 26.*

GEOFFREY TREASE

[***Salt of the Earth***] is the third in a sequence of novels (following ***Flesh and Blood,*** 1974 and ***The Best of Friends,*** 1978) that seeks to trace the evolution of modern Wales, an ambitious project which Emyr Humphreys, a highly regarded award-winning novelist, poet and playwright writing in both English and Welsh (a language read by only a minority of that ancient people), is exceptionally well equipped to attempt. His scene is a small seaside town, his period the 1930s, his themes not so different from those that convulse society fifty years later—unemployment, memories and forebodings of wars, the fervent and desperate nationalism of a lonely few, the more widespread local agitation against a new bombing range. . . . But it is a claustrophobic little world to the outside observer and not all readers will find their sympathies deeply engaged. Only in the final pages does the leisurely narrative explode into unforeseen excitement.

Geoffrey Trease, in a review of "Salt of the Earth," in British Book News, *June, 1985, p. 362.*

MARGARET WALTERS

Emyr Humphreys's ***An Absolute Hero,*** set in a small Welsh town in the late Thirties, offers an intriguing study of a woman acting against her deeper feelings. Amy's closest friend has died in childbirth. She sets out to marry the widowed husband, who doesn't really attract her, to make a proper home for the motherless child. The roots of this decision are not fully explored; but there's a chilly sketch of how a young girl turns into a self-denying and self-righteous woman—a model housewife whose only outlet is her sentimentally possessive love for the child.

But it is little more than a sketch; and that's true as well of the 'absolute hero' of the title, the Communist who has a brief affair with Amy before he goes off to fight and die in Spain. The novel—the fourth in Humphreys's solidly crafted Welsh saga—doesn't quite stand alone. But the vigour and insight of some of the writing suggest that a leisurely re-reading of the whole sequence would be worthwhile.

Margaret Walters, "A Politician in Fairyland," in The Observer, *January 26, 1986, p. 51.*

VERNON BOGDANOR

'There's only one task that matters', says a character in ***An Absolute Hero,*** 'To create a public conscience.' It is the impact of that public conscience upon private relationships which forms the central theme of the [novel by Emyr Humphreys]. . . .

An Absolute Hero is the fourth novel in a sequence depicting the life of Amy Parry, a young Welsh schoolteacher, in the 1930s. Having witnessed the death of her best friend in childbirth, she determines to provide for the infant son, 'baptised on his mother's coffin', and marries the child's father. At the same time she remains attracted to her former lover, Pen Lewis. Resuming their relationship, she finds herself pregnant by him, while he, like Hardy's doomed trumpet-major, joins his companions-in-arms 'till silenced for ever upon one of the bloody battlefields of Spain' in the Civil War.

The theme could easily become the stuff of cliché, but Humphreys is a subtle and accomplished writer and moulds what might otherwise have been a sentimental and mawkish tale into something creative and fresh. ***An Absolute Hero*** is a novel of remarkable lyricism which one might call quintessentially Welsh if that did not imply confining a fine talent to a merely local setting.

Vernon Bogdanor, "Atoms Not Actors," in The Listener, *Vol. 115, No. 2948, February 20, 1986, p. 28.*

Fazil (Abdulovich) Iskander

1929-

Russian short story writer, novelist, and poet.

A popular author in the Soviet Union, Iskander gained international recognition with the publication of *Sandro iz Chegema* (1973; translated in two volumes as *Sandro from Chegem* [1983] and *The Gospel according to Chegem* [1984]). The tales collected in these volumes, many of which were first published in the Soviet journal *Novyi Mir,* help illuminate the people and customs of Iskander's homeland of Abkhazia, an autonomous republic of the U.S.S.R. located on the Black Sea. Largely autobiographical, Iskander's works are noted for their colorful descriptions of scenery and characters and their anecdotal narrative style. While not a dissident writer, Iskander manages with gentle satire and veiled sarcasm to ridicule Soviet policy. Critics praise the entertaining qualities of Iskander's works as well as his insightful observations.

Sandro from Chegem and *The Gospel according to Chegem* chronicle eighty years in the life of Uncle Sandro, a wily, strong-willed man who typically exaggerates his comical misadventures. Narrated by a newspaper reporter, these stories feature character sketches, anecdotes, reports, philosophical asides, and stories within stories relating to the townspeople of Chegem. Blending mythical and actual events, the volumes provide an informal history of Russia from the 1880s to the 1960s and examine such subjects as ethnic antagonism, Islam, the Stalin purges, and collective agriculture. Iskander also presents a broad picture of the mores and mythology of the Abkhazians and their reluctant adjustment to the intrusion of the modernizing Soviet government. According to Margot Frank: "The overall impression left by the epic is one of Abkhazian culture in gradual transition—notwithstanding the strong identification with tradition—modified as much by the influence of modern ways . . . as by Soviet intrusion." Although not overtly political, the *Chegem* books were heavily censored for publication in the Soviet Union. The English editions, however, collect unexpurgated translations of most of the tales.

Iskander's short stories are collected in *Zapretnyi plod* (1966; *Forbidden Fruit and Other Stories*) and *Zashchita Chika* (1983). Set in the late 1930s and early 1940s in the Black Sea resort city of Sukhumi, the capital of Abkhazia, the stories in *Zapretnyi plod* depict how the childhood adventures of the narrator contributed to his maturity. The pieces in *Zashchita Chika* center on the exploits of a precocious youth who is baffled by the hypocritical and contradictory behavior of adults. While most of the stories in these collections are lighthearted and humorous, some are poignant and tragic.

Iskander has also written several novels. *Sozvezdie kozlotura* (1970; *The Goatibex Constellation*) is a subtle political satire which recounts the crossbreeding of a goat and an ibex, leading to the "goatibexization" of a farming district. Set in the Krushchev era, this novel parodies the theories of a scientist who greatly harmed Soviet science by convincing both Joseph Stalin and Nikita Krushchev that he had disproved existing heredity laws. The book also ridicules propaganda and censorship through its portrayal of a local newspaper that capitalizes on the phenomenon. *Kroliki i udavy* (1982) is a satirical fable that metaphorically explores political manipulation and control. This novel depicts a power struggle between primitive reptiles and genetically advanced rabbits. Although the rabbits manage to break free of the snakes' domination, they fail to successfully alter their own society and fall prey once more to their savage masters.

Sovfoto/Eastfoto

(See also *Contemporary Authors,* Vol. 102.)

THE TIMES LITERARY SUPPLEMENT

Iskander is a gentle satirist who writes in the ironic, self-deprecating manner of, say, Vasily Aksyonov and Vladimir Tendryakov, but with even less respect for the pomposities of Soviet society than they have. Like many Russian writers of his generation . . . , he takes a look at Soviet (and Abkhaz) society through the candid eyes of children. All the stories in ***Zapretny Plod*** (***Forbidden Fruit***) are about a young, proud, often mischievous Abkhaz boy who takes an amused, baffled look at his eccentric Muslim uncles, and his officiously stern schoolteachers. He himself is not immune to the mean follies of his elders, for one day he decides that his uncle, who is known throughout the village to be a harmlessly benign lunatic, is really a spy, using madness as a cover. . . . So the boy, certain that he has found a meaningful clue in his uncle's odd habit of fishing without a fish-hook (he doesn't fish at all, but keeps microphones hidden in the rod), dreams of the article that will appear in the *Pionerskava Pravda* (the newspaper for young "pioneers") under the heading "Pioneer Unmasks Spy. Children, Be Watchful!".

Many of the stories in ***Zapretny Plod*** simply display the contented, abundant, vigorous life of Abkhazia, "our small, but charming autonomous republic"—the Muslim traditions, the Abkhazians' obsession with horsemanship, the rich agriculture interfered with by inexperienced town officials, the old men's hunting stories, the exotic food, details of which Iskander takes pains to explain to his Russian, therefore foreign, readers. And all this is done very naturally, without that wide-eyed extravagance with which Russian writers from Moscow and Leningrad have described the Caucasian mountains and the Black Sea for 150 years.

Iskander's most daringly humorous, satirical work to date is his novella, ***Sozvezdie Kozlotura*** (***The Kozlotur Constellation***). A *kozlotur* is a cross between a goat (*koza*) and an argali (*tur*). One day, "a person of importance, not in fact a minister, yet by no means inferior to a minister in rank", while on holiday taking the Abkhazian waters, is told of a *kozlotur* which has recently been bred (accidentally) in an Abkhazian collective farm, and he comments that the emergence of this new breed looks like "an interesting start". An interesting start? The editors of the local newspaper carefully analyse the phrase, and decide that the time has come for the "kozloturization" of the district. Frantic articles appear in the local newspaper praising the *kozlotur*'s wool yield, looking forward even to the day when Abkhazia will be a centre of Kozlo-tourism, attracting admiring onlookers from all over the world. Most of these articles are written by a single member of the staff, Platon Samsonovich, a man who becomes so obsessed with his subject (and at the same time objectionably self-important for having pioneered it) that he does not even have time to move into the new flat for which he has waited all his life. He prefers feverishly to type out essays on such topics as "The Kozlotur—a Weapon in the Anti-Religious Propaganda Drive". The trouble with the one *kozlotur* in existence is that it only eats cucumbers and refuses to be attracted by the nanny-goats placed at its disposal; in general the *kozlotur* is so impractical and time-consuming a beast that the collective farmers on whom it has been arbitrarily imposed by officials who know nothing about agriculture, long "to eat it at the funeral of the man who invented it".

At last, disaster occurs. An article unexpectedly appears in a "central newspaper" mocking the ridiculous "kozloturization" of the Abkhaz Autonomous Soviet Socialist Republic. There is panic in the local newspaper office. Platon Samsonovich is rudely demoted, and a long, careful process of "dekozloturization" begins, with hectic confessions of guilt from the local paper itself. In the end only a neon-light advertising a café called "The Kozlotur Spring" remains and here "a few local intellectuals would congregate in the evenings to look at the neon sign. They saw in it two things at once; on the one hand, some sort of liberal gesture of protest at something or other; yet on the other hand, the mean obstinacy of the dogmatists."

Iskander's work is more, however, than just a response to Soviet bureaucracy, although few of his sentences are not loaded with political allusions. (He cannot even make passing mention of a Cossack dancer without the deadpan comment that he was "famous in the thirties and recently rehabilitated".) His heroes have an endearing, not necessarily Soviet habit of losing their bus-tickets just as the inspector approaches, or of locking themselves out, or of getting drunk when they most need to be sober. Iskander is no anti-Soviet, and nowhere does he challenge the fundamental values of Soviet society. He asks only that it own up to its faults, and even laugh at them.

"Kids and Goats," in The Times Literary Supplement, *No. 3457, May 30, 1968, p. 546.*

CHOICE

[Fazil Iskander] is not the most "significant" or "controversial" writer of the U.S.S.R., nor are his works dramatic "exposures" of the Soviet system. A native of Abkhazia, an Autonomous Republic bordering on the Black Sea within the Soviet Republic of Georgia, Iskander writes delightful stories, in Russian, which have long enjoyed great popularity in the U.S.S.R. These stories about life and his childhood in Abkhazia are filled with gentle humor and irony which can charm readers anywhere. ***The goatibex constellation*** (first publication: ***Sozvezdie Kozlotura*** . . .) recounts the story of the crossing of a goat with an ibex in an Abkhazian collective farm. A young reporter is sent out to cover this significant innovation in animal husbandry. Along with his own reflections on life he delightfully describes the relations between the proponents and opponents of the "goatibex" experiment, Russians, Georgians, and Abkhazians, newspaper personnel, etc. All this is against the backdrop of the good life under the warm southern sun, mountains, and the famous Caucasian hospitality of good food and fine Georgian wines. . . . [The publisher pertinently notes], "neither dissident nor hack, Iskander belongs simply to the classification of good writers." Our picture of Soviet literature or indeed of the Soviet Union itself cannot be balanced let alone complete without reading the best Soviet writers published in the U.S.S.R.

A review of "The Goatibex Constellation," in Choice, *Vol. 12, No. 4, June, 1975, p. 542.*

MARGOT K. FRANK

The customs and life-styles of the colorful Abkhazian people have come to the attention of Western readers largely through the literary efforts of Abkhazia's illustrious son, Fazil Iskander. The tiny Caucasus republic, embedded in the Soviet Republic of Georgia, provides the background for most of Iskander's writing. His stories reflect the variegated heritage of a region which was once part of Colchis, later incorporated into feudal Georgia, exposed to Christianity but for many centuries subject to Turkey's Islamic rule. The clannish natives have preserved their ways and language despite incorporation into the Russian and subsequently the Soviet empire and now see their culture firmly chronicled and exported by Iskander. The area's literary heritage tends heavily toward poetry and folk-hero epics. Iskander continues both trends. His earliest works are verse collections, received with high regard by Russian readers and critics. (p. 360)

International recognition came to Iskander with his short stories, which are also being translated into other Soviet national languages and which continue the epic tradition of the area. These tales, including ***Sandro iz Čegema,*** are anecdotal in style, with a semi-picaresque flavor, loosely held together by a narrator who presents them as childhood remembrances. This narrator, clearly Iskander himself, supplements his plots generously with descriptions of Abkhazian culture, often depicting the incongruous situations resulting from grafting Soviet politics and technology onto an isolated, cunning, proud mountain people. The author's cheerful and humorous style avoids many a potential censorial objection, and he has managed to reach a wide and enthusiastic Russian reading public. There is much to attract the reader: The cloyingly sultry subtropical air of Abkhazia, so distant from Russia's harsher climate; the ingenious ways by which natives reshape Soviet directives to suit their own preferences; the reemergence of clan elders as collective-farm chairmen; the Abkhazian Party members who are psychologically unable to sovietize local tradition; the continuation of tribal marriage customs replete with female abduction rituals and threats of brothers' avenging a sister's violated honor. An appreciation of horsemanship, of ceremonial daggers, of absolute kinship loyalty looms larger in the Abkhazian mind and behavior than the imported Soviet organizational and ethical value system, despite the latter's better standard of living.

While [Iskander's] good-natured humor mitigates any political undertones, the occasional sarcasm of the narrator assures that the gentle stabs are perceived. . . . In ***Sandro iz Čegema*** (***Sandro from Chegema***) lazy and unqualified officials take bribes, spend their time mouthing slogans, are too eagerly looking for Abkhazian dissidents, praise Stalin (a gibe at neighboring Georgia, Stalin's home republic, which still reveres its notorious offspring). As long as Iskander's social anecdotes deal with postrevolutionary or other more distant conflicts, he seems to have few difficulties with censors. However, the new ***Sandro iz Čegema*** stories under review here contain contemporary taunts, including references to Vietnam, media inconsistencies, excessive Muscovite fears about Chinese invasion and semi-fantastic enemy neighbors. Also, these tales are harder to find on Soviet bookshelves. The current [American] printing thus ensures that these five tales, not included in the 1977 Soviet edition of ***Sandro iz Čegema,*** remain available in their Russian original. (pp. 360-61)

Iskander is well worth translating. The account of this small ethnic group's grappling with and adjusting to an alien, modernizing superpower provides a perspective seldom available in Soviet literature, which is dominated by Russian culture. Iskander himself has to draw on childhood recollections. Like many contemporaries, he was educated in Moscow, torn between ancient allegiance and the comforts of modern urban living; and though fluent in his native Abkhazian (part of the Ibero-Caucasian language group), he writes in Russian. However, Iskander transcends the limits of a provincial writer who pokes fun at Soviet rule. He qualifies in every respect as a creator of good literature. (p. 361)

Margot K. Frank, in a review of "Sandro iz Čegema" in World Literature Today, *Vol. 56, No. 2, Spring, 1982, pp. 360-61.*

SUSAN JACOBY

Fazil Iskander, an ethnic Abkhazian who writes in Russian and lives in Moscow, has written [***Sandro of Chegem***], a comic epic that, like Milan Kundera's novel *The Joke,* both depends upon and transcends the political context from which it arises. As it happens, Mr. Iskander belongs to the party of Swift and Gogol and Mark Twain.

Especially Mark Twain. I haven't laughed and groaned out loud so many times while reading a novel since I returned to Huck's adventures on the river at an age when I was finally old enough to comprehend *Huckleberry Finn*'s bitter elements of comic genius. Mr. Iskander's irreverent ruminations on Sandro's adventures, which span the period between 1880 and 1960, touch on just about every conceivable subject: erotica, Joseph Stalin (known as "Beloved Leader" and the "Big Mustache"), ethnic antagonisms in the Caucasus, Islam, local leaders who disappeared during Stalin's purges, collective agriculture and the comparative intelligence of dogs and mules.

Sandro of Chegem is not political in the same overt sense as, say, the works of Aleksandr Solzhenitsyn. Nor is the 54-year-old Mr. Iskander a dissident political *figure* in his native land—as Mr. Solzhenitsyn was. . . . Nevertheless, it is hardly surprising that when ***Sandro*** was officially published in the Soviet Union 10 years ago, only about 10 percent of the present manuscript appeared in print. The real surprise is that the censors managed to leave one-tenth of the text untouched in a novel that, among its many unorthodoxies, devotes long passages to an imaginative reconstruction of Stalin's thought processes—an endeavor that lends itself more naturally to tragedy but emerges here as comedy of the blackest hue. (p. 9)

Although Mr. Iskander may not be a dissident, the mule who narrates one of my favorite chapters in ***Sandro*** is downright subversive. He understands Abkhazian but not Russian, and his subversiveness is imperceptible to those around him because, while he can comprehend human speech, much to his frustration, he cannot talk.

Mr. Iskander's strong regional flavor travels every bit as well as Mark Twain's. The ancient land of Abkhazia, a part of the Soviet Republic of Georgia since 1921, has been known in the West chiefly as the home of those long-lived mountain dwellers who appear in yogurt commercials on television. . . . (pp. 9, 20)

Mr. Iskander has made certain that the mountain village of Chegem will join Chaucer's road to Canterbury, Sholem Aleichem's *shtetlach* and Twain's Mississippi in the universe of real places that have been granted a mythic, imperishable life. . . .

Mr. Iskander's humor, like Mark Twain's, has a tendency to sneak up on you instead of hitting you over the head. Nowhere is this quality more evident than in the long chapter entitled "Belshazzar's Feasts," in which Sandro, who is a prominent member of an Abkhazian dance troupe, meets Stalin at a banquet in Abkhazia in the 1930's. Some pages into the chapter, I remembered that Belshazzar was the Babylonian king who presided over the famous feast at which supernatural fingers produced the "handwriting on the wall" that predicted the destruction of his kingdom.

The cast of characters at Mr. Iskander's banquet is as ominous as any handwriting on the wall: Lavrenti Beria, who carried out Stalin's purges in the Caucasus and was his secret police chief from 1938 until he was shot after Stalin's death; Nestor Lakoba, head of the Abkhazian Central Committee of the Communist Party until he was executed on Beria's orders in 1936; Lakoba's wife, Sarya, who was tortured to death because she would not denounce her husband, and assorted party luminaries who travel from Moscow to enjoy Stalin's hospitality in his native region.

The most darkly comic passages in this chapter depict Stalin's sentimental ruminations at the sight and sound of folk dancing and music from his childhood home. . . .

Listening to a folk song, Stalin grows misty-eyed over the burden of power that has deprived him of the right to ordinary love:

> The minute you love a man you begin to trust him, but once you begin to trust, sooner or later you get a knife in the back. . . . Damn life, damn human nature! If only you could love and not trust at the same time. But that is impossible.
>
> But if you have to kill the ones you love, fairness demands that you make short work of the ones you don't love, the enemies of the cause.

The argument is perfectly logical: A leader who makes the supreme sacrifice of killing his friends must not discriminate against his enemies.

All of the episodes in ***Sandro*** can stand on their own, but they work beautifully as a unified whole. The sharp political passages provide a realistic counterpoint to Mr. Iskander's elegiac reflections on a cohesive tribal life that has largely disappeared. (p. 20)

Susan Jacoby, "An Abkhazian Mark Twain," in The New York Times Book Review, *May 15, 1983, pp. 9, 20.*

BONNIE CAREY

[***Kroliki i udavy*** is] Iskander's account of life in the kingdom of the Rabbits and in the underground world of the Boa Constrictors, of the mutual relationships and ecological balance between these two worlds and of the intricacies of political manipulation and control there. The mythmaking that provided Iskander with ample opportunity for political comment in his earlier works predominates in this one. Via the genre of the animal fable (*basnja*), the author exposes, criticizes and laughs at the weaknesses of the Rabbits and the injustices of the system that governs their lives, a system which is posited upon and unable to exist without the presence of evil.

The Boa Constrictors, less-than-noble descendants of the Dragon, are ruled by their stomach, the location of their soul, and they need an unlimited supply of Rabbits in order to survive. Equally fixated on feeding his stomach, the King of Rabbits panders to their greed by surreptitiously supplying unwitting sacrifices. He keeps his subjects passive and uncomplaining with the promise of a glorious future in which the Rabbits will feast on a marvelous (but fictitious) Cauliflower, constantly reported to be in various stages of development. May one assume that any parallels between the promised coming of the wonderful Cauliflower and the attainment of future perfection by modern states whose members suffer deprivation and lack of freedom in the present are purely coincidental?

The efficiency and stability of order is disrupted when The One Who Has Pondered exposes the false ideology that has made the Rabbits victims of the Boas. He discovers that the Rabbits succumb to hypnotism out of fear and that the Boas have no real power to put anyone into a trance. This discovery of freedom leads to a period of disorder and rebellion until the Boas adopt a new method of killing their prey by squeezing them to death. Then order returns, and once again evil reigns supreme. Iskander's gloomy message, punctuated with humor, is a Gogolian "laughter through tears."

Bonnie Carey, in a review of "Kroliki i udavy," in World Literature Today, *Vol. 57, No. 3, Summer, 1983, p. 478.*

DAVID TAYLOR

The absurdities of totalitarianism are conveyed . . . [obliquely] in Iskander's ***Sandro of Chegem,*** a discursive comic saga that ranges over 80 years of Russian history. Its focus is the legendary Sandro, village *tamarda,* ornament of Platon Pantsulaya's renowned Abkhaz Song and Dance Ensemble, its setting Abkhazia, the tiny republic on the edge of the Black Sea. I doubt whether this ought properly to be described as a novel. It is more a series of fragmentary incidents and tall tales (a talking tree which protests against collectivization) in which Uncle Sandro drinks, fornicates and dissembles his way into a legend that coincides hilariously with actual events in Russian history. As Uncle Sandro remarks: 'you couldn't poke your nose out of doors for fear of ending up smack in the middle of an historical event'. Chegem becomes the scene of a battle between the Bolsheviks and the Mensheviks. The dance ensemble performs in front of Stalin at a local banquet where all the guests are mentally torturing themselves over what level of sycophancy will be acceptable.

Much of this is irresistibly comic—Sandro sitting grazing his cow 'as if he had on tether was not an ordinary cow but a smallish wild aurochs, tamed by him personally'—and innocently so. It is not until about half-way through the book that one begins to realize why it was banned in the Soviet Union. Briefly, the mental attitude that emerges is one of fundamental irresponsibility, a sort of cheerful antinomianism that elevates local concerns at the expense of national ones. Stalin ('The Big Mustache') is merely a far-away fairy-tale ogre, taken into account only so far as his pronouncements affect the workings of Chegem. A discussion of the principles of Bolshevism and Menshevism degenerates into an argument about pig-farming. The revolution, so far as it affects Chegem, is merely an excuse for funny stories about the Bolshevik/Menshevik struggle in Abkhazia. All of this, of course, is nothing more than a terrific raspberry in the face of Soviet authorities, an indication that, whatever official notions of peasant solidarity, the feckless Chegemians will still contrive ways to look after their personal interests. Symbolically, Sandro gets himself elected to the Central Executive Committee out of a hankering to stand on its balcony and ogle the girls. Some of it is less subtle than this—there are some stinging remarks on the subject of collectivization, 'destroying the mystery of the peasant's love for his own field' and on one occasion the narrator ponders whimsically why it is that prisoners are always shot while standing against walls—but this in no way detracts from the book's achievement. ***Sandro of Chegem,*** combining droll humour with incisive satire, is the most powerful book to come out of the East since *The Yawning Heights,* proof that the most effective way of annoying a tyrant is not to take him seriously. (pp. 111-12)

David Taylor, "Calais and Beyond," in London Magazine, *n.s. Vol. 23, No. 8, November, 1983, pp. 109-12.*

MICHAEL SCAMMELL

Fazil Iskander is likened, on the jacket of his novel ***Sandro of Chegem*** . . . , to Gabriel Garcia Marquez, and the novel, by implication, to *One Hundred Years of Solitude*. The claim is far-fetched to say the least, and of course Iskander cannot be held responsible for it, but it is instructive to consider some of the reasons why the invocation of Marquez is so wide of the mark.

Iskander's tale of a tribal adventurer who rises from layabout to top dancer in a folk dancing troupe, then retires to escape arrest and becomes a celebrated toastmaster, is set, like *Solitude,* in a remote country at the outer edges of empire. Abkhazia, a tiny land at the eastern end of the Black Sea, once known to the Ancient Greeks as Colchis and later much buffeted by the competing ambitions of Georgia, Ottoman Turkey and Imperial Russia, is an excellent vantage point from which to contemplate the follies of empire building. And the events described in this Macondo of the eastern Mediterranean also span about a hundred years of turbulent history, starting with the period just after Russian annexation in the nineteenth century, continuing through the Revolution, four years as part of the independent republic of Transcaucasia, ten years as an independent republic within the Soviet Union, reduction to an autonomous region of Georgia, occupation by the Germans and "liberation" towards the end of the Second World War, not to speak of Abkhazia's involuntary ride on the roller-coaster of Soviet history: NEP, collectivization, purges, world war, more purges, de-Stalinization, de-Khrushchevization.

The subject-matter is rich in potential for irony and satire, especially when viewed from the village of Chegem, perched high in the mountains behind Abkhazia's capital city of Sukhum (best known as a holiday resort). Iskander, who has shown a gift for satire in the past (notably in his send-up of Khrushchev's agricultural policies in ***The Goatibex Constellation***), has peopled his novel with a cast of colourful characters. . . . And there are equally fascinating historical figures. . . .

Iskander has combined these elements in eleven chapters, each one a separate tale loosely woven around the character of Sandro, which take him from pre-Revolutionary times up to the era of Khrushchev. The progress is not strictly chronological, but it is useful to summarize it in that way. At the outset we find Sandro as the young lover of a Svanian princess and getting into a tight spot with the Mensheviks. In other early chapters he earns the praise and indulgence of Prince Oldenburgsky, gets involved in Kolya Zarhidis's epic gambling game and tries to play the Bolsheviks and the Mensheviks off against one another during a Civil War incident. The climax of the story comes when Sandro, as one of the stars of the Abkhazian Folk Dance Ensemble, dances for Stalin, and is later selected to accompany him on a fishing trip. Later still, as danger from the purges mounts, Sandro purposely injures his knee and retires to his native village of Chegem, where he becomes a celebrated *tamada,* or toastmaster, and betweenwhiles a watchman over the village orchard.

The trouble is that the book sounds more exciting even in this bald summary than it is in the reading. It suffers from two large faults. First, there is a failure of nerve. Iskander leaves us in no doubt as to his negative views on the impact of Soviet rule on Abkhazia, but, except in the very middle of the book, he prefers to keep these dangerous topics at arm's length, treating them to gentle ridicule instead of lashing them with the whip of satire. As a result, neither Sandro nor any of the other characters in the book ever comes truly alive. They remain figures in a comic opera, all lukewarm pleasures and pale regrets, in which the true-life monsters have walk-on parts. Eyes are averted from the bleak realities of modern Russia and the whole is lost in a haze of whimsical sentimentality. Only in two central chapters does Iskander break out of this haze. "The Story of the Prayer Tree", about the paradoxical fortunes of an ancient, hollow walnut tree that serves as the village oracle and the tricks it plays on the villagers, offers a wonderful parody of Soviet attitudes to religion. "Belshazzar's Feasts", where Sandro performs for Stalin's benefit and witnesses the effect the dictator's alternating bouts of seemingly spontaneous cheerfulness and sullen suspicion have on his sycophantic courtiers, is a memorable addition to the growing Russian literature on Stalin, given extra force, perhaps, by Iskander's intimate knowledge of Stalin's Georgian origins; this is one of the chapters that remain unpublished in the Soviet Union.

Two chapters, alas, are not enough to save a book (though they remind one of the strength of Iskander's talent when he is on form). The other (and related) major defect is the novel's slack and nerveless prose. Iskander writes not only as if in ignorance of the entire modern movement in fiction since James Joyce, but also, which is worse, as if Bely, Babel, Zamyatin, Bulgakov and Platonov had never existed. His leisurely, anecdotal narrative, with its clumsy asides to the reader, its plethora of "incidentally"s and "by-the-way"s, seems as if it had been written in Abkhazia rather than in Moscow.

There must be many and complicated reasons for this: cultural isolation, the difficulty for independent writers of obtaining any competent criticism once they abandon the sheep-pen of the Writers' Union, personal tensions. Iskander is a brave and admirable man, attempting the almost impossible: to remain in the Soviet Union and write truthfully. But it does him no favours to praise his prose indiscriminately or for the wrong reasons. Not the least of the evils of that political system that Marquez is said to admire is the assiduity with which it attempts to ensure that none of its subjects will write with the freedom of expression enjoyed by Marquez.

Michael Scammell, "Dancing for the Dictator," in The Times Literary Supplement, *No. 4205, November 4, 1983, p. 1215.*

JERI LABER

The Gospel According to Chegem is a collection of 11 interrelated stories, a continuation of Mr. Iskander's ***Sandro of Chegem*** (1983). Together these tales evoke the pastoral beauty of the Abkhazian landscape and the foibles and fantasies of the journalist/narrator's colorful clan—Uncle Sandro, a local patriarch whose adventure-filled life spans more than 80 years of pre-Revolutionary and Soviet history; his brother, Kyazym, illiterate and wise, distinguished by a spiritual dignity and grace; and a multitude of relatives, neighbors and friends who appear and reappear in a variety of intriguing situations as the stories unfold.

Mr. Iskander's unfettered imagination spins tales from the village of Chegem, where the establishment of a kolkhoz (a collective farm) hardly seems to have altered the traditional ways of the local peasants and goatherds. **"The Shepherd Makhaz"** is a timeless fable that portrays with stunning simplicity a classic drama of seduction, betrayal and retribution. **"The Foreman Kyazym,"** in a lighter vein, tells how Uncle Kyazym solved a series of robberies of the kolkhoz safe. **"Abduction of the Endursky Enigma"** is a hilarious account of Sandro's marriage some 50 years before to his friend's intended bride whom Sandro had helped abduct; it ends with a homily, as

Russian folk tales often do, this one a slightly disguised discourse on bureaucratic stupidity.

Mr. Iskander moves effortlessly back and forth between eras of history and between countryside and city. Some city stories, like **"Uncle Sandro and the End of the Goatibex,"** wickedly satirize the vagaries of the Soviet system. The beautifully written **"Uncle Sandro and the Slave Khazarat"** also begins in a city setting at a jovial restaurant celebration held by a former prince who, through connections, has just successfully quashed a drunken driving charge against one of his companions. Turkish coffee and Armenian cognac flow freely, as does the conversation, and we are soon listening to a haunting tale of clan warfare in a bygone era, of a 13-year-old boy seized in vengeance and kept as a slave on a chain in a barn for 20 years, until Uncle Sandro contrived to release him. We learn that "a slave doesn't want freedom, as people think. A slave wants one thing—to get revenge, to trample the man who has trampled him." There's no time to contemplate this bit of wisdom, for another tale has begun—this time a 1944 love story from the German front. And so it continues throughout the book—there are stories within stories, and more stories within *them,* each full of mystery and nostalgia, always touched with humor and often with sadness as well.

To the Abkhazian farmer, with his "peasant's knowledge of Russian," the Moscow leadership is as remote as some distant, primitive god. Lenin is known as "The One That Meant to Do Good but Didn't Have Time"; Stalin is disparaged as "The Big Mustache," against whom Lenin warned in his Final Testament. Two of the four points in Lenin's Final Testament, we are told, are of special interest to Abkhazians: "Don't round up the peasants into kolkhozes," and "If you absolutely can't do without kolkhozes, don't touch the Abkhazians, because when an Abkhazian looks at the kolkhoz he wants to lie down and quietly die."

Mr. Iskander's sharp eye and incisive satirical bent are tempered by the gentleness of his humor and the loving, never patronizing distance he sets between himself and his subject matter. His flights of fancy and seemingly inexhaustible ability to weave fantastic tales have led to frequent comparisons between his work and that of Gabriel García Márquez. But Mr. Iskander touches more lightly than Mr. García Márquez, while his interests are more deeply grounded in reality. . . .

Only a small portion of [***The Gospel According to Chegem***] has been published in the Soviet Union—for obvious reasons. For Mr. Iskander challenges all systems, especially those that justify present evils with promises of future good. His light-hearted mockery of bureaucracy is ultimately less threatening than his passionate love affair with the Abkhazian past. As he himself points out, "In idealizing a vanishing way of life we are presenting a bill to the future. We are saying: 'Here is what we are losing; what are you going to give us in exchange?'"

Jeri Laber, "Caucasian Collective Circus," in The New York Times Book Review, *June 10, 1984, p. 14.*

TIMOTHY SERGAY

"The nation that has Uncle Sandro," declares the Abkhazian Prince Emukhvari in Fazil Iskander's ***The Gospel According to Chegem,*** "will never perish." With the publication in English of this second and final volume of Iskander's wry epic, ***Sandro of Chegem,*** America gains not only Uncle Sandro but all the vitality and wisdom of Iskander's Caucasian homeland, Abkhazia. . . .

Iskander writes in Russian and lives in Moscow, where only about 20 percent of ***Sandro,*** his major work, has passed the censors. The entire novel has been published in Russian only in the West. . . . The novel relates the long and graced life of Uncle Sandro, which spans the history of his own peasant clan; of his mountain village, Chegem; of Abkhazia; Russia; "and all the rest of the world as it is seen from Chegemian heights," from the 1880s to the 1960s. Sandro is Chegem's premier *tamada*—"toastmaster," or elected head of table. He is thus a master storyteller, an "indefatigable drinker," "expert in human nature" and among the most responsible custodians of Abkhazia's elaborate system of customs. Through Sandro and his relatives, we learn about Chegem's mythology, its ebullient spirits and the severity of its moral life. . . .

[The] epic is an exuberant celebration of the integrity of national cultures, which Iskander observes in their twilight, passing irretrievably into the colorlessness of the modern state. (p. 363)

The subtle question of how much of Iskander's mythology reflects the true mythology of Abkhazia, and the simpler question of how much of his Chegemian history actually occurred, are, we soon sense, not to be asked. Several stories (especially those of war and blood vengeance) are perfectly sober and realistic; many others are obviously tall, lovingly embellished and generally unperturbed by the miraculous. In an episode from the early 1930s, Sandro's father, Khabug, ritually strikes the ancient walnut Prayer Tree with an ax, and the tree bellows a ghostly warning: "Kum-khozzz!" (the Abkhazian pronunciation of the Russian *kolkhoz,* "collective farm"). Khabug is perplexed not because the tree spoke but because "he had expected the deity to give a more complex, more mysterious reply, which he would have to interpret over and over. This was too clear, and therefore terrible." The cities and places Iskander names are for the most part real, and historical figures—Stalin, Beria, Nestor Lakoba—appear. But the truth Iskander expresses in belles-lettres is itself more art than history or "experience"; it is "the poetry in the life of the people. That is what matters."

In suppressing the publication of ***Sandro,*** the Soviet literary establishment has proved once again the shortsightedness of its censorship. As Carl Proffer has written, a fitting Soviet publication of Iskander's work might have made the West truly envious. It is, nevertheless, not surprising that the book has been suppressed in the author's own country. Iskander's critique of Soviet society can be as gentle as an ironic concession to official literary guidelines or as powerful as the portrayal of Stalin in the first volume as a Belshazzar, slogans for extermination campaigns crystallizing in his mind as lines of poetry might in the mind of a decent man.

Our first reaction to ***Sandro*** in the West might be to understand Iskander's epic as the story of the long struggle for survival of Abkhazia's peasant way of life against the expanding cruelties and folly of the Soviet system. But it would be a mistake to consider ***Sandro*** primarily political or dissident literature. There is a universally human lament in the background of Abkhazian life, even in the novel's most beatific passages. (pp. 363-64)

Iskander's protest is aimed at existential, not political, conditions. It is not Soviet history as such that overtakes Chegem; it is historical time itself. Like Milan Kundera in *The Un-*

bearable Lightness of Being, Iskander protests the irreversibility of linear time and the disappearance of the cyclical time that the anthropologist Mircea Eliade has identified with archaic cultures. The eternal, cyclical return of things gives moral solidity to human life, which is otherwise defective and terrifying, as well as weightless, empty, improvised and irresponsible. Kundera introduces *The Unbearable Lightness of Being* by proposing "the moral perversity of a world that rests essentially on the nonexistence of return, for in this world everything is pardoned in advance and therefore everything cynically permitted." He concludes with an elegy to the animal paradise of repetition: "Human time does not turn in a circle; it runs ahead in a straight line. That is why man cannot be happy: happiness is the longing for repetition."

In Iskander's Abkhazia, return takes the negative forms of the blood vendetta and the assurance of divine punishment for sins, and the positive form of national customs. The entire system guarantees that "a man doesn't end with himself" and that a nation's people can feel that "their country did not begin yesterday and will not end tomorrow. That way it's cozier for them to live in eternity, and easier to defend their soil." For Iskander, the vanishing of Abkhazia's peasant life is the story of countless cycles of familiar human experience spinning out their last melancholy turns, overcome by intolerable novelties. . . . (p. 364)

[Iskander's] concerns in ***Sandro*** are serious. Like Kundera's, they are broader and deeper than the anti-Soviet polemicism to which the West often confines its discussion of the Soviet world's émigré or censored writers. But for all its Abkhazian gravity, ***Sandro*** is a delight to read. Tragedy and pessimism alternate with bemused, Dickensian observations, and there are frequent thrills of transcendence occasioned by the ordinary: a faithful mule, Turkish coffee semisweet, the contemplation of another's happiness. The sentimentalism is never far from irony and subtlety. Iskander has been true to his idea of "real humor," which he described in his introduction to an earlier work, ***The Thirteenth Labor of Hercules***:

> I believe that to possess a good sense of humour one must reach a state of extreme pessimism, look down into those awful depths, convince oneself that there is nothing there either, and make one's way quietly back again. Real humour is the trail we leave on the way back from the abyss.

And so we begin in tears and end in laughter. The village life of Chegem, the "might and beauty" of its "moral sky": these may finally vanish from the Caucasus. But thanks to Iskander, they have been preserved in a fanciful and elegiac epic of real humor. Abkhazians have been famous since the first century B.C. for their extreme longevity. Perhaps it shouldn't surprise us to learn that Abkhazia itself will live forever. (p. 365)

Timothy Sergay, "Durable Tales," in The Nation, *New York, Vol. 239, No. 11, October 13, 1984, pp. 363-65.*

MARGARET ZIOLKOWSKI

An author of Abkhazian descent who writes in Russian, Iskander has succeeded in creating a self-contained fictional world, many of whose characters reappear in story after story. The most well-known of these is Uncle Sandro of Chegem, whose eighty-year life has provided subjects for numerous semi-independent tales . . . , some of which have been translated into English. (p. 116)

[***Zashchita Chika***] contains three stories concerned with Sandro or members of his family: **"Umykanie, ili Zagadka Endurtsev"** (**"The Abduction, or the Mystery of the Endurtsies"**), which describes the circumstances of Sandro's marriage; **"Bol'shoĭ den' Bol'shogo Doma"** (**"A Big Day at Big House"**), an account of a summer day in 1912 at Sandro's family home that focuses on his twelve-year-old sister Kama, the future mother of the narrator; and **"Brigadir Kiazym"** (**"Brigade-leader Kiazym"**), a tale of kolkhoz thievery which features Sandro's brother in the role of unofficial detective. The largest number of stories in ***Zashchita Chika*** (***The Defense of Chik***), however, is devoted to the adventures of the adolescent Chik, a resourceful and perceptive youth whose insights into adult behavior are as entertaining as his pranks and exploits. Of the other pieces in the collection, the most remarkable is the lengthy tale **"Dzhamkhukh—Syn' Olenia, ili Evangelie po-chegemski"** (**"Dzhamkhukh—Deer's Son, or the Gospel According to Chegem"**), Iskander's fanciful and idiosyncratic rendering of Abkhazian legend.

All these stories provide marvelous reading. The source of their appeal lies in the combination of humor and sensitivity with which Iskander's narrators and many of his characters apprehend their surroundings. While shedding fascinating light on both traditional and modern Abkhazian culture and mores, ***The Defense of Chik*** thus simultaneously enriches the fund of Russian satire. Anyone who has not yet experienced the delights of Iskander's unusual talent should find this collection a captivating introduction. (pp. 116-17)

Margaret Ziolkowski, in a review of "Zashchita Chika," in World Literature Today, *Vol. 59, No. 1, Winter, 1985, pp. 116-17.*

MARGOT FRANK

Iskander's success is in no small measure due to his narrative style and approach to subject matter. The reality of the Soviet presence, the intrusion of an alien, all-encompassing superpower, is kept at bay in many of the stories. Though the traditional economy of agriculture and animal husbandry, once the domain of the extended family, is now organized into collectives, the author depicts the activity still in terms of diligent labor over native soil, while local Soviet representatives continue to exhibit the mentality of their former clan-elder or tribal-leader status. Iskander's citizens manage by and large to graft Soviet directives onto indigenous custom to their advantage, and their cunning, as they craftily outwit neighboring groups and central authorities, is engagingly amusing but is also a reminder that Iskander's Abkhazian universe is not a true reflection of events under Soviet rule. In reality, Abkhazians so fiercely resisted agricultural collectivization that an enraged Joseph Stalin revoked their autonomous status and purged the local intelligentsia.

Iskander, following the conventions of epic genre, creates a slightly mythical world, where wishful thinking and self-glorifying mettle alter objective reality, though the canvas of native legendry, custom, behavior, and vague historical accuracy imparts an uncannily genuine flavor to the tales. The author can thus be thought of as a preserver as well as creator of local lore. His relaxed, sometimes even monotonously rambling presentation blunts the cleverly embedded controversial asides and in most cases leaves the impression of entertaining rather than tendentious portrayal. A generous dose of humor in his cheerful style contributes to the muting of politically sensitive passages, particularly since Iskander's barbs are also directed at home-grown follies and the incongruities of regional interethnic squabbles. Just the same, authorial sarcasm in various guises periodically punctuates the epic panorama. The very device, for example, of depicting Soviet rule from a seemingly guileless distant perspective results in ridicule, as barely literate and uncomprehending Abkhazian peasants endeavor to incorporate vacuous Soviet slogans into their simple speech.

The Caucasians' favorite literary expression is poetry, and Iskander too began his career in 1957 with a verse collection, followed by several others, before he turned to prose in the late 1960s. Whereas most of his efforts have been expended on his ongoing magnum opus, ***Sandro iz Chegema*** (1977; Eng. ***Sandro of Chegem,*** 1983, and ***The Gospel According to Chegem,*** 1984), . . . many of his earlier stories in one way or another reflect similar themes. His very first collection of tales, ***Dereva detstva*** (***The Tree of Childhood***; 1970), contains two of his most popular pieces, ***Sozvezdie Kozlotura*** (Eng. ***The Goatibex Constellation,*** 1975) and **"Kolcheruky"** (**"Old Crooked Arm"**; 1972). The former has a sharp satirical edge in that it parodies the theories of the pseudogeneticist Trofim Lysenko, who convinced both Stalin and Khrushchev that he had disproved existing heredity laws and who presided over the virtual destruction of Soviet science for many years. Iskander's parody echoes the inanity of that era by having a few enterprising Abkhazians breed an ibex with a goat in the hope of producing a meaty, wool-laden grazer sturdy enough to manage the steep local mountain slopes. The Abkhazian *Red Subtropics,* a publication that represents the press in many later stories, is depicted in its efforts to introduce "goatibexation" to all collective farms, and its methods add a humorously malicious dimension on production propaganda and censorship to the story. Counterarguments by genuine scientists are ignored or ridiculed by the paper, positive comments from workers are solicited or manufactured, skeptics become enemies of the people, and the hybrid goatibex appears in paintings, sculptures, emblems, and songs. Iskander then moves the narrative forward to post-Khrushchev times and the unmasking of the counterfeit experiments. The paper must now retreat and deny or rewrite what it has previously glorified, and so it initiates a prolonged countergoatibex campaign. Iskander's sarcastic edges are hidden in long stretches of innocuous material, making the work more the memoir of the young narrator-reporter's life than an exposé. An entire chapter is spent on the latter's boyhood reminiscences, not connected with the major event and poorly integrated into it. Many of the other chapters too have frequent diversions, which diffuse the focus of the satire. Iskander's technique resembles Nikolai Gogol's profuse meandering from one subplot to another with occasional touchdowns in the main plotlines. In Iskander's case, this approach facilitates both censorial approval and mosaic construction of the Abkhazian cultural landscape.

"Old Crooked Arm" continues the unhurried narrative mode but already introduces the type of folk hero later portrayed in the legendary Chegemian, Sandro. Old Crooked Arm's life consists of a series of picaresque adventures in which he proves his superiority and gains renown. The episodes tracing these exploits, however, illuminate important aspects of the society. Feuding and competition within the clan create animosities, yet there is instant bonding whenever outsiders threaten the community in some way. Old Crooked Arm's foremost local rival is the first to save him from government accusation of theft. Old Crooked Arm himself, a daredevil within his territory but unschooled in alien ways, freezes in confusion and fear when confronted by the workings and language of Soviet bureaucracy. The endurance of tradition over recently acquired Soviet status is reflected in the government representative investigating the theft. When he realizes that he is remotely related to Old Crooked Arm, he immediately ceases prosecution, instinctively responding to the customary prohibition against accusing a clansman. The final report that the village dispenses to the regional authorities is a hilarious example of local attempts to match official bureaucratese. Vaguely aware of the spy mania prevalent in the union, the missive argues in extended convoluted logic that Old Crooked Arm's theft was not part of a conspiracy, but rather was the isolated and irresponsible act of a prerevolutionary illiterate whom the czar failed to educate to minimum standards of behavior. The entire tale exudes the strength of ancient allegiances over superimposed Soviet ways.

Iskander's prose was widely published in the 1970s, and as his popularity grew, Moscow's Progress Publishers offered their own English translation of the collection ***Trinadtsaty podvig Gerakla*** under the title ***Forbidden Fruit and Other Stories*** (1972) and an expanded version under the English equivalent of the Russian title, ***The Thirteenth Labor of Hercules*** (1978). Most of the tales share similar literary devices. Usually a narrator frames the piece in the manner of the nineteenth-century *Rahmenerzählung* or frame story. Transitions between incidents tend to be simple or nonexistent, and the tales are largely autonomous, though a set of reappearing figures provides some continuity. In content, the tales relate facets of Abkhazian life.

Sandro of Chegem, which the journal *Novyĭ Mir* began to serialize in 1973, can justifiably be called an epic, for it charts the mores of an entire people, a still largely preliterate society living by ancient unwritten tribal custom rather than a set of codified laws. Sandro is the hero of the clan and, like all folk charmers, is depicted as larger than life, exaggerating his exploits and forever bent on surpassing those who would challenge his prowess. At the same time, his fame catapults him into the role of wise elder, whose advice takes on the force of legal judgment and who is expected to apply his wits for the benefit of the community. The author stresses that this is the story of a group rather than a single representative by making Sandro but one of the acknowledged sages and by excluding him altogether from a number of episodes so that others may display their craft. Iskander's Abkhazians, represented by the Chegemians, follow no rigidly prescribed religious rules, though their customs reflect Muslim heritage more closely than they do other major faiths. The region's one mullah who possesses and reads the Koran laces his prayers with ancient incantations and incorporates pre-Islamic rituals. A prayer tree substitutes for a religious edifice. The abundance of wine at Chegemian feasts attests to the lack of rigor in observing Islamic rites. Pork is excluded from the diet, but several enterprising peasants raise pigs for sale to "infidels." The Chegemians eschew institutionalized ethics and instead live by a guiding moral force embedded in their very behavior, handed down through generations and instilled in every native from infancy.

The twenty-one stories are not arranged in chronological sequence. Pre- and postrevolutionary incidents alternate in no discernible order of presentation, perhaps to underline the timeless quality of epic narrative. However, if the chapters are considered from a chronological perspective, one detects a change in characterization as the work moves into Soviet times.

Under czarist rule, the Chegemian elders still possess unchallenged moral authority; but after Soviet rule establishes itself, their power becomes more ritualistic and their previously bold exploits acquire a modicum of ridiculousness, of roguishness rather than valor, which imparts a picaresque flavor to sections of the novel. (pp. 261-63)

The bulk of the material sketches the generally deliberate pace of daily Chegemian routine. The author lovingly and at great length accumulates detail on how his people tend their land and flock, how they prepare food, what they eat and wear, and how hierarchical family relationships work themselves out. It is a lifestyle harmoniously close to nature and revolving around the agricultural seasons. Iskander often chooses the setting of the festive table to lead into an episode. A *tamada* or toastmaster ensures that everything transpires according to accepted practice, and the order of speeches, toasts, and dishes is starkly ritualized. As guests take turns recounting earlier heroic days and ancestral history, the region's traditions spring to life. A non-Abkhazian audience, reading the entire epic at one sitting, may lose patience with some of the long uneventful stretches, but this is Iskander's method of reaching deep into the culture. . . .

Outsiders are represented by both neighboring Caucasian groups and Russians. Although Iskander's evasively ironic approach tempers confrontation with the latter, the overall impression is one of reluctant accommodation to an ill-boding intruder. In a number of cases the negative references are overtly caustic, such as the description of the fluttering Soviet flag in **"Diadia Sandro i konets kozlotura"** (**"Uncle Sandro and the End of the Goatibex"**), which is compared to an ideological fan waving about a swarm of hostile ideas as if they were gnats. Iskander introduces a host of Soviet political figures into the novel, reserving most of his commentary for two Georgia natives, Stalin and Lavrenty Beria, chief of police from 1938 to 1953. It was particularly galling to Abkhazians to have the regional purges carried out by Beria, who came from the rival clan of Mingrelia. There are many allusions to Beria's terror, especially to his liquidation of the Abkhazian leader Nestor Lakoba, a prominent figure in the narrative as young Sandro's employer. (p. 263)

Other stories depict the political climate of post-Stalinist times. One recurring figure is the former president of the Abkhazian Council of Ministers, Abesalomon Nartovich, an erstwhile protégé of Stalin and later of Khrushchev who confides in **"Three Princes Carouse"** that no one in his family ever died a natural death. Iskander's narrator sets up parallels with Khrushchev's fate as he traces Nartovich's fall from power into well-pensioned retirement. In the end he fashions this man's death, after a long and comfortable old age, into an event of political and family history. (p. 264)

In creating the legend **"Dzhamkhukh—syn olenia ili evangelie po-chegemski"** (**"Dzhamkhukh, Son of the Deer, or The Gospel According to Chegem"**), Iskander provides the Chegemians with a genealogy. He uses the tale to fashion a semireligious, semifolkloristic ancestry for them by blending general Caucasian lore as well as elements of the major religions into all facets of their mythical forebear's biography: Dzhamkhukh, raised by a doe, acquires animal wisdom before becoming a renowned prophet in Abkhazia; he wins a beautiful maiden through superior mental and physical prowess; he gathers disciples to whom he relays, in parable and wise sayings, the commandments of the Great Weighmaster of Conscience; he loses the maiden to a scheming prince; he cleanses his spirit of impure attraction to her beauty by marrying a simple Chegemian girl, with whom he initiates the Abkhazian race before he is put to death by the treacherous prince. In true Iskanderian fashion, the legend spins on through many unexpected turns, eventually displaying Oedipal shading as the prince's son slays his father in order to marry the beautiful Gunda himself. The biographies of the disciples are also filled with ancient lore, including a St. George figure who frees the town of a maiden-devouring dragon. The variegated material reinforces the perception that Abkhazian heritage is a blend of many forces, that native custom shares a universal source. (pp. 264-65)

The overall impression left by the epic is one of Abkhazian culture in gradual transition—notwithstanding the strong identification with tradition—modified as much by the influence of modern ways (Iskander himself resides in Moscow) as by Soviet intrusion. This change is in no way presented as tragic or cataclysmic. Not only does the cheerful authorial tone temper a certain light ruefulness and distance the sorrows; the Chegemian panorama itself, especially as anchored in the Dzhamkhukh legend, suggests a people rich in and made strong by its multicultural heritage. It is a portrait of survivors. Unfortunately, Soviet citizens have thus far been unable to appreciate all of ***Sandro of Chegem,*** since censorship has limited publication to selected parts. The Russian original is available in its entirety only abroad. Soviet publishing, with the exception of ***The Goatibex Constellation,*** has favored those stories with subtle or no political allusions.

Iskander's more recent work, ***Kroliki i udavy*** (1982; Eng. ***Rabbits and Boa Constrictors***), too is available in an uncensored edition only outside the Soviet Union. The novel represents a stylistic departure for the author, but his capacity for irony is fully present as he unravels, via a fable setting, the political and social machinations of two opposed animal kingdoms in the African jungle. The surface level depicts a mythical revolutionary power struggle between primeval mammal-devouring reptiles and genetically more sophisticated rabbits. Though the latter manage to break free of the serpents, they fail to transform their society into an ethically superior one and in the end fall prey once more to their Draconian enemies.

In playing out this scenario, Iskander suggests a multitude of human-affairs parallels. One plot line implies not only that the hoped-for progress after the communist victory over czarism did not materialize but that the ills of the older order exist in direct and sublimated ways in the new one. There is little difference between the dictatorial methods of the reptile czar and the rabbit king; when internally threatened, they make common cause to ensure their survival. The political career of the rabbit king echoes that of Stalin, replete with purges, secret police, and party cadres. Iskander's parody falls heavily on writers. His rabbit court poet—a sarcastic portrait of Maxim Gorky—is forever looking upward in search of stormy petrels and consequently forever oblivious to the injustices of his society. Other members of the leporine intelligentsia, suspiciously similar in hierarchy and rank to the Soviet elite, are aware of their complicity in hypocrisy but loath to give up the privileges of special state carrot stores and other conveniences. Isolated dissident voices frequently challenge the king's authoritarianism yet fail to generate wide popular support. Iskander has given his major dissident, Zadumavshisia (The One Who Has Meditated), hues of Aleksandr Solzhenitsyn. This sage hare, through his great moral courage, cures his fellow creatures of dangerous psychological folly, but when he admonishes them to become spiritually pure by giving up thievery in human gardens, he encounters general indifference. In other aspects of the work Iskander appears to caricature irrational and ridiculous confrontations between superpowers, and toward the end he offers sad comments on the dichotomies of human nature in general. Incongruities in international dealings find humorous reflection when unlikely animal allies are driven to collaborate against third parties, perceived as enemies. At one point Iskander has humans hire pythons to guard gardens against rabbits, and their dependence on the reptiles becomes so great that they must overlook the occasional swallowing of a person. ***Rabbits and Boa Constrictors*** is a clever, stimulating fable and demonstrates that Iskander is by no means limited to the style and content favored in the Caucasian tales.

The author's uneasy relationship with censoring organs was exacerbated in 1979 by his collaboration on the banned *Metropol'* literary almanac. Actually, the two Iskander contributions are not unusually controversial. The first, **"Malenkiĭ gigant bol'shogo seksa"** (**"A Sexy Little Giant"**), is a rather uninspired history of a failed Don Juan figure, though it does include a mild homosexual scene, a generous lacing of expressive amorous phrases, and a mundane subplot involving Beria and his mistress. The second selection, **"Vozmezdie"** (**"Vengeance"**), is of much better quality. It depicts a contemporary Georgia in which petty and large-scale crime are everyday occurrences, and focuses on the confrontation between a local ruffian and a big-time extortionist, the latter in a Red Army uniform displaying the star of a Hero of the Soviet Union. The point of the story is nonpolitical. It concerns the simplistically black-and-white world view of a naïve young narrator who contributes to the violence when attempting to satisfy his sense of justice, but the background, always important in Iskander, maps an existence in which people have accepted crime as an integral part of their lives.

Despite Iskander's confrontations with Soviet publishing, he has managed to remain a published author whose work sells out immediately and is always in short supply. He encounters censorial delays but saw additional Chegemian tales brought out in 1983 and will no doubt continue as Abkhazia's major chronicler. (p. 265)

Margot Frank, "Fazil Iskander's View of Muslim Caucasia," in World Literature Today, *Vol. 60, No. 2, Spring, 1986, pp. 261-66.*

Pierre Jean Jouve

1887-1976

French poet, novelist, short story writer, critic, autobiographer, editor, essayist, translator, and dramatist.

A prolific writer often linked with several European literary movements of the early twentieth century, Jouve is particularly recognized for his later poetry, in which he integrates Christian and Freudian beliefs. Although Jouve's verse continued to evolve throughout his career, his work consistently displays a knowledge and appreciation of international music and literature. While his initial volumes were written in free verse, Jouve later developed a more fragmented and abstract technique through which he examined religious and psychological concerns. Following World War II, Jouve utilized the verset form to explore themes pertaining to language and memory. Although many critics consider Jouve among the most innovative modern French poets, little of his work has been translated due to its often difficult and obscure style.

The Granger Collection

Jouve's early writing displays his affinities with the French neo-Symbolists and Unanimiste groups. The neo-Symbolists adhered to the synaesthetic verse style employed by such nineteenth-century poets as Edgar Allan Poe, Charles Baudelaire, and Stéphane Mallarmé. The Unanimistes, led by Jules Romain, postulated that groups, cities, and societies may share a single, unified consciousness and believed that poetry could assist in integrating individuals into the collectivity. During this phase of his career, Jouve served as founder, editor, and critic for the Unanimiste journal, *Les bandeaux d'or,* and published his first works, *Les muses romaines et florentines* (1910), *Présences* (1912), and *Parler* (1913). During World War I, Jouve suffered from ill health and was forced to recuperate in neutral Switzerland, where he became acquainted with Romaine Rolland, whose humanitarian tracts inform Jouve's pacifistic writings of this period. These works include *Vous êtes des homme* (1915), *Poème contre le grande crime* (1916), and *Danse des morts* (1917).

Early in the 1920s, Jouve underwent a spiritual and intellectual crisis that he described as the beginning of his *vita nuova*. He eventually rejected all of his works written before 1925. Inspired by a revived religious orientation and the psychological teachings of Sigmund Freud, Jouve attempted to develop a terse poetic language capable of conveying what he perceived to be the unresolvable conflict between spiritual ecstasy and carnal impulse. While much of this poetry reflects Roman Catholic doctrine, Margaret Callander asserted: "Jouve's poetry is never the poetry of religious dogma: it is the purely personal record of fluctuations of hope, disgust and despair in a spiritual quest." *Les noces* (1928), *Le paradis perdu* (1929), *La symphonie à Dieu* (1930), and *Sueur de sang* (1933) are recognized by critics as efforts to document the tension between sexual passion and the worship of God while incorporating themes of guilt and death. In *Kyrie* (1938) and *La vierge de Paris* (1944), Jouve depicts World War II as the realization of the biblical "Revelation of Saint John the Divine" by portraying Adolf Hitler as the Antichrist. The apocalyptic tone and erotic content of these volumes blend into a highly original body of work that is often compared to the visionary writings of St. John of the Cross, St. Theresa of Avila, and William Blake. Jouve also wrote several novels, including *Paulina, 1880* (1925), *Le monde désert* (1927), *Hécate* (1928), and the diptych *La scène capitale* (1935), which reflect his concerns with God, guilt, sex, and death.

Jouve's work after World War II displays a more lyrical approach and relaxed response to the dichotomies of existence. Such collections as *Ode* (1950), *Langue* (1954), and *Lyrique* (1956) evidence his increasing concern with the capacity of language to express metaphysical concepts. Jouve's other works include an autobiography, *En miroir* (1954), and several volumes of music criticism. *An Idiom of Night* (1968) is a selection of Jouve's poems translated into English.

(See also *Contemporary Authors,* Vols. 65-68, rev. ed. [obituary].)

EZRA POUND

I take pleasure in welcoming, in Monsieur Jouve, a contemporary. He writes the new jargon and I have not the slightest doubt that he is a poet.

Whatever may be said against automobiles and aeroplanes and the modernist way of speaking of them, and however much one may argue that this new sort of work is mannered, and that its style will pass, still it is indisputable that the vitality of the time exists in such work. . . .

[*Présences*] is a book that you can read without being dead sure of what you will find on the next page, or at the end of the next couplet. There is no doubt that M. Jouve sees with his own eyes and feels with his own nerves. Nothing is more boresome than an author who pretends to know less about things than he really does know. It is this silly sort of false naïveté that rots the weaker productions of Maeterlinck. Thank heaven the advance guard is in process of escaping it. (p. 165)

I defy anyone to read [*Présences*] without being forced to think, immediately, about life and the nature of things. I have perused this volume twice, and I have enjoyed it. (p. 166)

Ezra Pound, in a review of "Présences," in Poetry, *Vol. I, No. 5, February, 1913, pp. 165-66.*

THE TIMES LITERARY SUPPLEMENT

To the English reader, and to most French readers as well, Pierre Jean Jouve is a poet, and there is a virtual conspiracy to confine him to that role. It is enough, we may feel, for any man. The consequence is that his novels have been greatly neglected.

It must be admitted that for many years a case of some sort could be made for this neglect. M. Jouve was recognized as a poet of great force and originality, but his novels were comparatively tentative and clumsy. Nor did it seem that they were saying anything which he was not saying far better in verse. One might have been justified in thinking them superfluous, in wondering rather irritably why he was bothering with prose at all. ***Paulina 1880*** (1925) was a neatly executed little book, treating a simple and unresolved conflict between good and evil, between salvation and damnation. It might have been written by a Mauriac lacking M. Mauriac's theological certitude. The Catherine Crachat series (***Hecate*** (1928) and ***Vagadu*** (1931)) are among the most *baffled* novels of our time. They are the work of a Samson Agonistes, blindly struggling with a medium which seems to become more intractable with every page. And it is not only the medium which proves stubborn; the idea itself is powerless to be born. In these books there is that passionate dignity of eroticism which M. Jouve has made his own; there is endless sin and there are innumerable deaths. The reader feels that something was desperately striven for, some great statement about the whole nature of our life on earth. But, try as he may, he cannot find the pattern which lies somewhere buried in this riot of poetic prose. There are indeed crudities of every sort, attempts on our emotion which embarrass by their simple-minded directness, gross clumsiness in construction, perpetual overstatement. It is typical that in ***Vagadu*** a psycho-analysis should be carried out before our eyes, the heroine's situation presented to us case-book fashion and complete with a whole series of her dreams. Other novelists have attempted this and it is always a disaster. No doubt it is a function of the novelist to incorporate the new discoveries of depth psychology in his work, but he can do this only by transmuting it, by seizing that essence of artistic truth which lies entangled among the jargon. In the consulting-room Catherine loses all our interest.

Any contemporary critic might have been justified in sourly ordering M. Jouve back to his verse. Yet with sympathy and imagination (and there were some critics who had enough of both) it might have been guessed that all this was leading somewhere, that a man of M. Jouve's stature would be unlikely to waste so much of his time and energy on so *obviously* abortive an enterprise. In 1935 he published ***La Scène Capitale*** and gloriously justified his previous labours in prose. His earlier novels became at once intelligible, not indeed as successful works of art—no retrospective judgment could make them that—but as necessary preliminaries, as directed and instructive enterprises, however unsuccessful. It is an unusual case: so many stutters before the statement is made, and then to find a statement of such astonishing confidence! (p. 225)

La Scène Capitale consists of two stories, intimately related in theme, though differing widely in environment and in key. They are more than variations on a theme; rather they are the two sides of a coin, the two antithetical outcomes of a similar situation. The first story, **"La Victime,"** is set in the German middle ages, and both its text and something of its atmosphere are taken from Luther. We are introduced to two students, Waldemar and Simonin, and we learn at once that Waldemar is in love with Dorothée, the patrician daughter of a civil dignitary. But we learn at the same time that the words "in love" are totally inadequate to describe his condition; he is possessed, diseased, half-destroyed by his passion for a girl whom he has seen only once. . . . Simonin is a magician, deriving his power directly from the devil, and he promises to bring about a meeting between Waldemar and Dorothée on the one condition that neither shall touch the other.

Meanwhile, we are translated to the house of Dorothée. The young girl wakes after a dream of great erotic significance, and feels herself compelled to leave the house for an assignation with someone as yet unknown to her. She prepares herself with an elaborate and newly acquired erotic skill, and the assignation takes place, Simonin playing on his magic flute somewhere in the dark streets behind the couple he has brought together. Waldemar and Dorothée walk beside each other in a sort of stupor of lust, and finally return together to her house. A moment's negligence from Simonin—the flute stops playing—and they have fallen together in a blind idiocy of passion. At the moment of achieving her satisfaction Dorothée dies; *la scène capitale* has been accomplished.

Now Simonin enters the house and upbraids Waldemar for his breach of the imposed condition, but promises to do his utmost to restore Dorothée to life. For this sin, he tells Waldemar, man can have no recourse to God. After an elaborate ritual, exalting all the symbols of the female, Dorothée opens her eyes, rises and rushes like a fury from the room. Meanwhile an organization called the Free Judges, long-established in the town to punish all sinners who escape the law, has learned of Waldemar's crime and Simonin's part in it. The two young men are seized and are to die by the sabre. Dorothée continues to move about her house, but always as if in a trance, without once speaking. Gradually a smell of over-ripe apples begins to be exuded wherever she goes. The physicians can discover nothing wrong with her and the theologians are summoned in their place. After a long argument between them, the most learned of these priests hurls an exorcism at the girl and her body tumbles to the floor with an appalling stench of corruption. It is agreed that she had been dead since her willing violation by Waldemar.

So much for the first panel of the diptych. The second is still needed before the pattern can reveal itself.

The atmosphere of **"Dans Les Années Profondes"** is as different as possible from the claustrophobic medieval urbanism of **"La Victime."** Here we are in the present time and high up in the sky-country of the Italian Alps. The hero and narrator is Léonide, a boy of sixteen who has been spending his holiday in the mountains. On the day before he had expected to leave he meets the beautiful Hélène de Sannis in the village street, and is enthralled by her. In this story the recurring symbol of feminine power is the glorious red-gold hair of Hélène. She accosts him with great directness and simplicity—"Voulez-vous être mon ami"—and within a few days he has made himself at home with Hélène and her husband in the Cas'alta de Sogno. Here there is also a sickly nephew of Léonide's own age, a sexual maniac whose function is to irritate and inflame the nervous lust for Hélène by which Léonide is possessed. The husband, by extreme contrast, is a strong man and hunter, dignified, courteous and aloof. By agonizing stages *la scène capitale* is approached, Léonide always pushing forward and Hélène holding back. Yet is is clear that she is not holding back in any hope or expectation of avoiding the climax; she is simply waiting for the ripe moment to come. For a period erotic symbols are exchanged between Hélène and Léonide, while the tension continually increases, the passionate crescendo swells to an almost intolerable pitch. Even the sexual act itself is accomplished after a preliminary fashion, without precipitating the final crisis. For on this occasion it was accomplished with only the maternal sympathy of Hélène. But on a second occasion passion is full and transporting on each side, and Hélène dies in the arms of her lover. By this *willing* sacrifice we understand that the soul and body of Léonide have been saved.

Perhaps no stories of our time lose more in the bare précis, for there is a mystery of poetic language in them both which is quite incommunicable. Recounted in this arid abbreviation ***La Scène Capitale*** may seem to be turgid, melodramatic and even unconsciously comic. At no moment is it any of these things, for each story is held together, integrated, by the controlling mind and purpose of the writer. Nothing in these stories is accidental or haphazard; nothing is added simply for extraneous effect. In spite of the richness of the language, the reader must feel that there is in this book none of the verbal over-exuberance which marred the Catherine Crachat series. Here is a writer who has suddenly become the complete master of his material, and, in this moment of triumph, is almost invulnerable. We know that such works of art do exist, rare expressions of some absolute possession, one might think, by muse or oracle. ***La Scène Capitale*** may be detested—in many ways it is a most detestable book—but it will be detested for the very power and completeness of its statement. (pp. 225-26)

The integration which M. Jouve achieves in ***La Scène Capitale*** makes any paraphrase more or less abortive. Indeed a reader's first reaction to this book may be something like the mere inarticulate reception of a blow. It is as if there had been an explosion in his mind, but he cannot find the cause of it. It may well be that this powerful impact is enough, and should be left to do its own subterranean work without any interference from the conscious mind. But the disease of critics is not to rest content with any simple impact; they must discover other terms for the writer's statement, although they know that their other terms will be, not more, but less clear than his own. And so we are embarked on the old pedestrian quest; what does it *mean*, this ***Scène Capitale*** of M. Jouve's? Why do the women die at the moment of sexual consummation? Why is Léonide saved but Waldemar lost? How, then, does M. Jouve really envisage our human condition?

It is clear that M. Jouve is preoccupied with sin. From the sins of Paulina to the final sin of Léonide, all the novels are suffused by their writer's obsession with the endless and recurring fall of man. But it is at least very doubtful whether M. Jouve's notion of sin can be equated, or more than barely related, to the doctrine either of man's first disobedience or of his subsequent sinful conception. We may choose to believe that it is rather the *sense* of sin which he finds implanted in us from our infancy, than any objective evil. Certainly it is very seldom in any of his novels, and never in his last one, that sin is presented simply as a falling away from God, or even as a passive and unconstructive submission to the devil. It might almost be said that the sense of sin is, in M. Jouve's conception, the one animating force in life, driving man to his only possible fulfilment in the commission of sin. Thus it would not be difficult to interpret M. Jouve as one of those "catholiques du côté du diable" whose paradoxes rather overburdened the later manifestations of the French romantic movement. At least it would not be difficult to do this if we examined either of these two last stories in isolation from the other. In **"La Victime"** we see a spectacle of an imperious and destructive lust against which it seems that no force can stand, whether human or divine. Waldemar and Dorothée are damned from the opening of the book, and it is nowhere suggested that salvation is open to them. In **"Dans les Années Profondes"** it seems to be the sin itself which leads to Léonide's salvation. Thus in one situation we have a world in which damnation takes an apparently *inevitable* course, and in the other salvation appears to be the paradoxical reward for mortal sin. From a strictly catholic point of view the situation is still further confused by the fact that the sin of Léonide, adultery, is far graver than the mere fornication of Waldemar. Why, then, do these two apparently similar situations lead in the one case to death and damnation, in the other to life and salvation?

Clearly no real distinction either of conduct or situation can be made between Waldemar and Léonide. Both are equally possessed, both are equally blind. Each pursues his end with the relentless and stupefied frenzy of an animal, and each, when the *scène capital* is accomplished, remains stricken with horror and incredulity. Yet Léonide is saved and Waldemar is damned. The explanation lies, of course, in the vast difference, both of attitude and action, between Dorothée and Hélène. Dorothée is as blind and possessed as either of the young men. Like them she is an automaton, unconscious of her destiny, impelled by forces quite outside herself. There is nothing in her which can ward off death or accomplish salvation. But Hélène *knows*. She knows all that is involved in her action and that the wages of sin is death. She is the willing scapegoat, consciously sacrificing herself for the salvation of her lover. By her knowledge and by her acceptance of her own necessary fate, she saves her lover.

This shows the impossibility of drawing, from M. Jouve's great book, any easy moral implication. It is in this that he departs furthest from the simplified latter-day ethics of Christendom, yet at the same time seems to revivify the ancient doctrine of the atonement. We are not saved by our own actions alone. Léonide has "deserved" salvation no more than Waldemar. But Hélène achieves salvation for him. Thus M. Jouve appears to embrace many of the floating and incoherent notions of our time and to carry them to a new level both of articulateness and of universality. Forster's cry ''Connect! connect!'' Martin Buber's passionate disbelief in the reality of the single man, the mysterious interdependence of the characters in Joyce—all these seem to find in M. Jouve a new simplicity of expression by reference to something very ancient (for the doctrine of atonement is older than Christianity by many thousands of years). There is something, too, of Luther in this attitude of M. Jouve's, for the salvation of Léonide is achieved by the workings of an irresistible grace, free—defiantly free—from the supplementary aid of works. But here the grace of God works indirectly. We are spared the unpalatable crudity of Lutheran theology by which God seems to sprinkle his gift quite haphazardly from on high. Here, on the contrary, there is a human agent of grace. By her conscious action it is Hélène who bestows grace on her lover, while jeopardizing it for herself.

This raises a question which it would be difficult, from the evidence of M. Jouve's work, to answer with any assurance. In both stories it seems that the possibility of salvation lies entirely in the woman. Is this a part of M. Jouve's theory, or merely an accident of the particular cases he has chosen to present to us? We can say at least that it is an accident which befalls both Paulina and Catherine Crachat. In all his novels the women are gigantic compared with the men. The spectacle reminds us of some genus of spiders in which the puny male plays only his little ignorant role before being consigned to death, or at least to oblivion. Indeed this is a matriarchal world, and it is always the women who are the vessels of fate both for themselves and for their lovers. This curious, and perhaps distorting, aspect of M. Jouve's world-picture springs from his passionate acceptance of Freudian theory. To him the woman must always be in some sense the mother, and in so far as she fails to play this part she brings death to herself and her lover. . . . [The] need for things to happen is at the bottom of M. Jouve's whole conception of life. The *conscious* doer is his ideal, and in this, though in nothing else, he approaches M. Sartre and the existentialists. Implicit throughout his novels is the horror of stagnation and refusal. And sin, accepted and recognized for itself, would seem to be the only active force in life.

Sin, love and death are the counters with which M. Jouve has always played. By his consciousness of sin man is destined for death, and only through love, properly understood, can he achieve life and the conquest of sin. . . . But this assuaging of sin through love is the greatest peril which man has to endure, for the sin itself lies embedded in the love. In the case of Waldemar everything is simple. He is obsessed by sin and he carries this obsession into his plan and act of love. Dorothée contributes no other element, and together they must perish. The sin and the love have not been disengaged, and the love is therefore abortive and powerless. But Hélène knows and accepts her destiny from the very first meeting with Léonide, and her destiny is to give life to her lover by her own death. It is the archetypal act of the loving mother, a division of herself into the son who shall live and the rest which must die.

It is at this point that the terms become recalcitrant, and that the critic begins to feel the impossibility of explaining this book in any words but its own. For M. Jouve's whole vocabulary is in some sense personal to himself. Sin, love and death are among the vaguest of our words, and as soon as we begin to use them we feel them slipping away, or we see their edges beginning to blur. Nor is it possible to extract these words from the context of M. Jouve's book and define them afresh. What, for example, are we really to understand by this ''death'' which is a cornerstone of M. Jouve's philosophy? In all his books it takes the simple form of a physical extinction, and it is perhaps only in **''La Victime''** that something both deeper and vaguer is suggested. The resurrection of Dorothée by Simonin is no mere *jeu d'esprit* (although it leads to the farcical fantasy of the theological disputation). In an extreme and symbolic form we are presented here with the spectacle of the Dead in Life, whose false appearance of life is only preserved by the devil's inhabitation of the lifeless body. The act of exorcism is no more than a device to show that spiritual death had followed immediately on the act of ignorant and therefore sinful lust. If we translate this symbolism to the second story it might seem that Hélène's death, too, is merely symbolic, and that she, too, had died in the spirit rather than in the body. Yet this interpretation destroys the whole story. By M. Jouve's quite explicit standards Hélène has acted ''rightly''; she has fulfilled the maternal role which her creator demands of her. So it is unthinkable that she should die in the spirit as Dorothée does. Indeed she, like her lover, is saved, though perhaps with no more expectation of salvation than had Faust. Consciously she accepted the possibility of her own damnation in order to avoid the damnation of her lover, but God, in the person of M. Jouve, the creator, will not allow her to suffer the full results of her sacrifice. Thus we must take the death of Hélène at its face value alone; she has lost only her physical life, although she believed herself to be risking her spiritual life as well. Is there, then, some confusion in M. Jouve's use of the word death? There may be, for it is quite certain that the death of Dorothée is a far more final and more dreadful thing than the death of Hélène.

What of the other two members of M. Jouve's trinity? Can we attach a single and definite meaning to his concepts of sin and love? It has been suggested above that the ''sin'' which he finds embedded in the soul of man from birth is rather an empirical discovery than a piece of theological anatomizing. At the risk of rationalizing his conception we can substitute ''sense of guilt'' for the more dramatic and authoritarian word ''sin.'' To bring it to its barest and most earthy terms, we can even talk here of the conflict between the *super-ego* and the *id,* the ''conscience'' imposed by heredity as well as by environment, at war with the purely non-human and instinctive drive to survival and aggrandisement. Man is born in torment; he is a battlefield from birth. Yet it must be admitted that there are many moments when M. Jouve seems to claim something more than this for his use of the word ''sin.'' The Freudian interpretation, which he certainly accepts, must be transcended, but his attempt at transcension seems to lead only to the old Augustinian dogma. Yet this confusion scarcely affects the two stories of ***La Scène Capitale.*** Reading them, we are not obliged to decide whether it is the *id* or the Fall which drives these creatures to their different destinies. That there is *something* which so drives them we can hardly fail to recognize, and we know this something in ourselves.

M. Jouve's concept of ''love'' is the simplest of his trinity. It is not the Christian love of neighbour; still less the Christian love of God (God plays very little part in M. Jouve's cosmogony). It is passionate love, but turned outwards away from the lover. It is the love of Hélène for Léonide, which demands, certainly, its own physical satisfaction but which can find its satisfaction only in the perfect harmony of giving and receiving. Hélène's act of love is a sacrament, altogether pagan but suffused with the highest pagan conception of passion. (pp. 226-27)

Guilt is the spur, love is the catharsis, death is the penalty for an inadequate love. Thus we might present the philosophy of Pierre Jean Jouve in bare and platitudinous form. It is a token, not of the occasional and almost inevitable ambiguity of his terms, but of his rich profundity that an exegesis of his great book could be made on many different levels. M. Jouve is a Freudian (Madame Jouve is a prominent psycho-analyst) and on one level Freudian terms can unravel nearly all the mysteries of his philosophy. Thus to have accepted the discoveries of Freud and to have transmuted them for his high creative purpose is by no means the least of his achievements. Many have attempted this transmutation, but perhaps only James Joyce has won an equivalent victory over the intractable material. M. Jouve is also a Christian, though inquisitors would find a rich crop of heresies in all his books. He is a paradoxical Christian, but one who is able to perceive the old enduring truths lying half-buried under the arbitrary curiosities of dogma. He is a moralist, too, though his morality is a curious and individual one. Finally he is a great artist, both in conception and in execution. ***La Scène Capitale*** is no *roman d'idées* in the ordinary sense of the phrase, and it may well be that a wrong and far too crude impression of the book has been given here by the attempt to disengage ideas which are in reality so closely linked to their context. The *integration* he achieves is an astounding literary feat. Atmosphere and vocabulary, personality and physical background are not the mere medium for purveying a theory of life. The theory is in them and they are in the theory. In this, his final work of imaginative prose, he writes with a supple fluidity and richness. (p. 227)

"The Prose of Pierre Jean Jouve," in The Times Literary Supplement, *No. 2412, April 24, 1948, pp. 225-27.*

THE TIMES LITERARY SUPPLEMENT

M. Jouve has always been, as he half-boasts, half-deprecates in [***En Miroir***], a figure apart, a solitary contractor-out from the literary schools and movements of his time. In England such solitude is near to being the rule, but in the Paris of proliferating schools and coteries it is genuinely remarkable. He is known best as a poet, and known, perhaps, to some of us for the beautiful translations of his verse made by his friend and admirer Mr. David Gascoyne. His prose, though he has written six novels and one of them a masterpiece, has been almost entirely neglected, in his own country no less than abroad.

The enigmatic impression which we had received from a long writing career—M. Jouve is approaching seventy—was of a passionate and original mind and of a writer who never feared to repeat himself in an obsessive spiral of intensity. A Christian heretic, a Freudian heretic, it was between these two poles of human thought and experience that he had been creatively extended. But the figure behind the work had always remained elusive, almost inhumanly unrevealed, until the appearance of this strange little skeleton of an autobiography. A disappointment? Of course it is, for no mystery has ever been uncovered without our regretting at least the vanished element of mystery. ***En Miroir*** turns out to be an apologia, suffering from all the conventional faults of self-justification. At its worst this particular note rises to a hysterical scream against imaginary accusers. . . .

When [M. Jouve] writes of Valéry's "opération poétique stérile, son classique à travers Mallarmé, et le jeu tout intellectuel de ses idées" we may feel that we require either more than this or less. Yet there are many pages where M. Jouve reviews his past life in a far more disinterested and far more poetical spirit than this. He is both touching and illuminating when he writes of his own operations and development as a writer. . . .

[This] little book is none the less a failure if it is considered in terms of the *genre* to which it belongs. M. Jouve seems to have assumed too lightly that self-revelation requires no practice, no hard experience, no bitter failures and fresh beginnings. Gide receives a casual side-kick in this book but M. Jouve would have done well to consider more carefully the laborious and heroic endeavours of that greatest of modern self-revealers. Journal, memoir, autobiography—these are art-forms no less legitimate than the poem or the novel, and in his brief attempt to combine them all a distinguished novelist and poet has shown himself to be a novice in fields which are unfamiliar to him.

It would be absurd if we allowed this comparative failure to influence our previous judgment of M. Jouve's poetry and novels. He has every right to resent the past neglect of his work, and may legitimately hope (he does so most explicitly) that posterity will judge him more kindly than the present has done.

"Self-Revelation of a Writer," in The Times Literary Supplement, *No. 2747, September 24, 1954, p. 607.*

DAVID GASCOYNE

Last spring, the *Mercure de France* published a new book of poetry by Pierre Jean Jouve: ***Langue,*** the fifth volume of his poetic work to have appeared since the end of the war. In the four previous volumes (***Hymne, Génie, Diadème,*** and ***Ode***), Jouve's poetic style has been seen to undergo a process of modification and renewal; the style of ***Ode*** was quite unlike that of anything that he had written earlier, while ***Langue,*** which is in a style that seems closely to resemble it, represents a still further phase of evolution, corresponding to the inner development of the poet in his struggle for spiritual significance.

It has been apparent for some time that the whole poetic work of Pierre Jean Jouve will eventually reveal itself to be constructed according to a consciously conceived plan. With the publication last year of the autobiographical commentary on his own writings called ***En Miroir*** . . . , the monumental outlines of the structure which his work as a whole represents may become more easily distinguishable. In its entirety this work will soon consist of at least a dozen volumes of poetry, four volumes of prose fiction (all pre-dating 1935), and five or six volumes of essays.

In ***En Miroir,*** Jouve has written: 'My passion becomes involved only when confronted with an idea, a scheme, that is at once the same, and different.' There are a number of themes that are fundamental and recurrent throughout his entire production, and one may be sure that, however unfamiliar the style and imagery of his most recent poetry, most of these themes will be found to recur, though possibly in transmuted or augmented form, in the poems of the sequence called ***Langue.*** It contains altogether forty-one poems, and is divided into three main sections. The dominant theme may be defined as the *a priori* non-existence of a language in which the unknown may be expressed, and the struggle to create, which is at the same time the prayer to be granted, such a language; and thus we may say that the work has a certain essential similarity to Eliot's

Four Quartets, although the latter is in most ways so very different in conception and style.

One of the most characteristic features of Pierre Jean Jouve both as a novelist and as a poet has always been his highly developed awareness of the Unconscious, of the guilt by which the Unconscious is dominated in all men, and of the struggle in the Unconscious of the instincts of life and death, which seem always to be locked inextricably together. Poetry, like the works of the great mystics, Jouve regards as proceeding from Eros, or rather, as representing the highest degree of sublimation of the erotic instinct (speaking, in the preface to ***Sueur de Sang,*** for instance, of *'l'élévation à des substances si profondes, ou si élévées, qui dérivent de la pauvre, de la belle puissance érotique humaine').* In ***Langue,*** it is clear that what the poet is attempting is above all the conjuration of a new transport of sublimation by means of which erotic energy may be transformed into the power to give reality through articulation in language to a hitherto unknown spiritual dimension. . . . At the same time, the poem is philosophical in the specifically Socratic sense of being a meditation directed towards 'preparation in view of death'. An experience of the approach of death, and of an Orphic reconciliation with death resulting in a restoration to life of the loved one, is embodied in the substance of the poem, and it is this which provides the subject of what are certainly the most beautiful and the most deeply moving pages of the whole text, in the passage which begins: *'Alors arriva d'un coup la face du Tonnerre.'*

In the concluding poems of the sequence, the poet's voice attains to a tranquility beyond desolation, and the principal theme of the whole is clarified in a last statement which is like the resolution at the end of a musical composition (the music-like structure of the work is another feature which it shares with the *Four Quartets).* (pp. 49-50)

At the present time it is reassuring to find that there can still exist in the world some poets entirely preoccupied, not with an art of agreeable diversion, but with an art that bears witness to the life of the spirit beyond and out of death. (p. 51)

David Gascoyne, "A New Poem by Pierre Jean Jouve: 'Language'," in London Magazine, *Vol. 2, No. 2, February, 1955, pp. 49-52.*

MARGARET CALLANDER

Pierre Jean Jouve is perhaps the greatest living French poet, and one of the more important writers of this century. Yet this author, with at least a dozen major collections of poetry behind him, is read by a very few among the cultivated public, and known to most in connection with only one work, ***La Vierge de Paris.*** (p. 1)

Certainly the re-orientation of Jouve's literary career in 1924 may have proved confusing and have lost him a following, but after forty years no reader can plead bewilderment. There has been plenty of time in which to come to terms with Jouve's new style. However, the poetry is in no respect easy to understand, and makes no direct appeal to the reader. Flashes of spiritual illumination run through the sombre matter which seems to represent the world given over to instinctive, inescapable sin, and the rhythms of hope and despair alternately quicken and solidify its curious heavy texture. Jouve demands that his poetry should become a spiritual instrument; all associations with pleasure and beauty are set aside in favour of this aim, and each poem becomes a wager with transcendental reality.

There was little in Jouve's earlier development to presage this release into mysticism. As an eager migrant from the provinces he had written first in a neo-Symbolist style, then as an admirer of Signoret, before apparently settling for a manner allied to that of the Abbaye group, which he accepted as the quintessence of modernity, and the only conscientious response to current needs. But the outbreak of war in 1914 shattered this exciting curiosity, so far mainly applied to his own sensibility, and also the vague humanism that had complemented it. The violence and suffering of war, which he experienced as a hospital orderly at Poitiers until illness took him to Switzerland, deepened a tentative social conscience into a distinct sense of mission. Jouve allied himself with Romain Rolland and launched into tireless propaganda work against national prejudice, capitalist self-interest and the unnecessary prolongation of the war. He poured out vituperative and abstractly symbolic denunciations of all those who profit from war and its horrors, and if he saw any hope for humanity it was in the Russian Revolution.

The close of hostilities threw Jouve back on his own resources. Embittered and exhausted, he analysed the despair that he found in himself, related it to his childhood emotions, offered it to God. This was the necessary prelude to what Jouve called his 'vita nuova', which comprised changes in his personal life, a renewal of religious faith, and a transformation of artistic outlook. This was one illustration of the 'tendance de rupture' which in his private life caused the abrupt shipwreck of various personal relationships, and in his literary life the formal disowning of all publications dating from before 1925. Many writers would look back on their most youthful essays into verse with emotions ranging from disgust to indulgence, but most would accept them as transitory yet indispensable phases in a process of natural development. However, for Jouve, who had tended to embrace each successive poetic apprenticeship as though it were a fresh religion, such phases took on the stigma of heresies and accordingly were totally suppressed.

After 1924 Jouve's poetry became the pursuit, through extremes of exaltation and abasement, of mystical union with an obscurely apprehended divine presence. This spiritual way is paved with voluntary suffering and renunciation, and the need for self-mortification finds its parallel in the broken, unrhetorical rhythms and undeveloped images of the new style. The ecstasy of renunciation outweighs, in ***Les Noces,*** the grim evidences of sin. But the sense of guilt that now pervaded all the poetry was sharpened and defined in ***Le Paradis Perdu.*** Jouve's is never the poetry of religious dogma: it is the purely personal record of fluctuations of hope, disgust and despair in a spiritual quest. This quest may inspire and generate his poetry, but its needs can finally be answered only by the poetry itself. However, Jouve has an intense and unrelenting intellectual curiosity, and this he felt obliged to turn on the problem of original sin. From his version of the Genesis story emerges an unorthodox and inherently pessimistic view of concupiscence as the primary sin, with an added element of predestination. All matter appears as fatally tainted, and the sexual relationship becomes a re-enactment, at once horrible and fascinating, of the original sin. The sense of helplessness induced by this realization is aggravated by Jouve's further conviction that body and soul are inextricably mingled and must be damned or saved together. Like Baudelaire, Jouve faces a being whose highest and lowest impulses are ambiguously inseparable.

This complexity was increased and rendered more serpentine by Jouve's appropriation for his art of some of the material discovered in his study of Freudian psychoanalytical methods and case-histories. Freud's polarities of the life and death instincts in man are translated, in ***Sueur de Sang,*** into the obscene writhings of a torrid, vegetable world. This poetry . . . reveals life as an endless, hopeless circle of lust and despair in a stifling sin-laden climate. But it is the instinctive energy of man, dissipated in the repetitious frustrations of lust, that Jouve aimed at diverting into a sublimation rather different from Freud's. Abstention is not enough, and any hint of compromise is abhorrent to Jouve. He envisages salvation as the conscious orientation of man's unconscious forces, and expressed this process in a series of images, mainly Biblical in inspiration. (pp. 2-5)

Jouve never renounced the desire to consolidate the brief flashes of Franciscan illumination that, in ***Les Noces,*** promise a purified universe. But the mechanism of redemption is elaborate and fiercely individual. It took Jouve away from the main currents of French poetry into a private and timeless world. He may have been one of the first writers in France to make direct use of Freudian material, but he did this with little show of avant-garde challenge, and his poems seem unconscious of their audience. 'Publiée, elle n'est pas un acte public' is how Yves Bonnefoy characterizes this quality of inner revelation that stamps all Jouve's poetry, however diverse. (p. 5)

When in 1938 the preliminaries of war found their echo in Jouve's poetry they appeared as part of a spiritual landscape that was merely widened to receive them. Jouve subjected a whole nation to the type of spiritual psychoanalysis that he had previously applied to the single soul, and, in the context of the Revolution and the Apocalypse, he prophesied disaster. After the manner of the Biblical prophets, his style became rhetorical, and all through ***La Vierge de Paris*** the two strains, private and public, alternate and sometimes mingle.

Jouve was never able to express the simple exultation of communal feeling and compassion that we find in Eluard's poetry at this time, but he succeeded, by his symbolic treatment of various aspects of the war, in endowing the suffering and bloodshed with dignity and significance. He saw the French people as jointly responsible for the catastrophes that overtook their country; they had failed to harness and understand the terrible forces unleashed at the Revolution. But conscious acceptance of guilt and readiness for self-sacrifice could transform death from the inevitable complement of sin into the instrument of salvation, part of a process of national regeneration. At the same time, the German forces were to Jouve literally Satanic, and he regarded the war as a crusade, the defence of a spiritual heritage. But he avoided abstraction and eccentricity in his treatment of these themes, so that the successive collections that were gathered into ***La Vierge de Paris*** were accepted freely and popularly as the voice of France, by the same right as the poems of Aragon, Eluard and Supervielle and the speeches of General de Gaulle. ***La Vierge de Paris*** is Jouve's most integrated and ambitious work, and it represents a point of balance between general and personal preoccupations. (p. 6)

Post-war France was bound to disappoint Jouve, who had seen in the Resistance and Liberation a potential national 'vita nuova'. After 1948 his poetry returned to its private meditation. However, his poetic universe was never again as narrow as before the war. The climate of the soul for Jouve had been associated with the very few places in Europe that offered to him 'un très puissant modèle de notre vie intérieure'—the Italian Alps, Salzburg, certain parts of a ravaged France. Now the scene became larger; seas, islands, deserts revolve in the wider and more flexible rhythms of a verset like that of Claudel, and a mysterious Oriental note recalls Segalen or Saint-John Perse. The poetry also appears less purely personal because it approaches the problem of the nature of language. Jouve is by no means the advocate of uncontrolled inspiration, but he is able to describe one of his war-time poems as being written 'apparemment sous la dictée'. He regards poetry as a mystery, and is impelled to penetrate it more deeply. Hence we find in ***Langue*** and other books the repercussions of a battle to create a language that will faithfully translate the unknown. Against 'le démoniaque contemporain' this quest appears to Jouve an urgent necessity. Art is the supreme witness to the spiritual world and its creation is a key to an otherwise elusive reality, 'Nous faisant plus vivants que vie avant toute mort'.

Jouve's excursions into novel and essay writing, his criticism and his occasional pieces, are all part of a remarkably consistent artistic vision, but it is as a poet that his stature must be measured. ***Matière Céleste, La Vierge de Paris, Langue***—with a special place for ***Les Noces***—these are the most unified and beautiful of his books, and, taken all together, his poetry represents a unique investigation of man's spiritual problems in the twentieth century. For a comparison one feels obliged to go outside France, as Jouve so often does in acknowledging his debt to Blake, St John of the Cross, St Theresa of Avila, or Shakespeare, whose *Romeo and Juliet, Macbeth* and sonnet cycle he has translated. At times Jouve appears to have something in common with Supervielle, Claudel, Milosz or Saint-John Perse; but it is poets like T. S. Eliot or Rilke that suggest themselves more readily, especially Rilke with his consistency and his free penetration of an invisible universe for which he struggled to find symbols. It would perhaps be more just, however, to link with Baudelaire Jouve's relentless wrestling with the presence of evil in men, in things, in Nature, and his attempts to release in them their tenuous and obscured potentialities for redemption. (pp. 7-8)

Margaret Callander, in her The Poetry of Pierre Jean Jouve, *Manchester University Press, 1965, 308 p.*

THE TIMES LITERARY SUPPLEMENT

The publication of [***Poésie IV***] is timely. It places in perspective the achievement of more than forty years of intensive poetic effort and it comes at a time when Jouve's poetry is beginning to be appreciated outside France. This is not to say that it has ever had a wide audience inside France. The difficulty and obscurity of much of his poetry and its apparent isolation from contemporary fashions have been serious obstacles to its popularity.

The reader is further disconcerted by an odd flatness, which probably derives, at least in part, from the fact that this deeply subjective poetry is rigidly controlled by an intellect determined to achieve and maintain its lucidity. One must be careful, however, not to exaggerate the intellectual quality of Jouve's poetry. The mind controls and guides Jouve's poetic exploration of the world within and around him, but recognizes that this world exists in its own right. Applying a similar method, Yves Bonnefoy, the French poet who has perhaps been most deeply influenced by Jouve, achieves a very different result. Bonnefoy's intellect not only controls his poetic world, it also creates it. Both poets are travellers engaged in an arduous quest for the absolute but, while Jouve's itinerary takes him across the vital, real terrain of the subconscious erotic self, Bonnefoy's, for all his efforts to the contrary, remains primarily intellectual. . . .

[***Poésie IV***] contains poetry published between 1956 and 1966, ending with a few previously unpublished poems. It is the poetry of an aging man, for Jouve was seventy-one in 1956, but this does not imply that it is the poetry of a declining talent. On the contrary, it reflects a poetic insight which is as vigorous as ever. What it does perhaps lack is the dramatic quality of his earlier mature poetry, from ***Les Noces*** to ***Matière Céleste,*** for those were the great years of Jouve's quest for a reconciliation between carnal love and love of God, a reconciliation finally achieved, as he indicates in ***Matière Céleste,*** through the notions of death and absence.

In the poetry of ***Mélodrame*** and ***Moires,*** Jouve continues to explore these basic themes, but it is, nevertheless, the poetry of a man preoccupied with the approach of his own death. This is to be the real confrontation with God and it is very different from the earlier metaphorical experience of death by a man in search of life. The poet wonders whether he really has ever come to terms with life, but above all he feels an overpowering weariness with life and a longing for death to end his quest and the suffering that goes with it—"Ah je suis fatigué".

He makes a final attempt to define the function of his art, and prays to be allowed to continue writing—"Que Dieu me donne encore le pouvoir d'écrire." He knows that what he has written will not only be ephemeral, but that it is also inadequate. "J'avais rêvé l'unité," he writes, but "Je ne verrai jamais mon ordre."

Jouve's poetry is by no means easy to translate into English, its obscurities often involve words which apparently make little sense in the French and even less in English. Jouve deliberately underpunctuates, so as to create ambiguities, and his very personal style of inversion requires an alert translator. In spite of these difficulties, [Mr. Keith Bosley, in ***An Idiom of Night***] has done remarkably well. One accepts most of his translations without hesitation as English poems, and, at times, he captures perfectly the delicate, almost timid lyrical quality of some of the originals. On the other hand, "god-body" (for "corps de dieu") and "bloodsweat" (for "sueur de sang") are not at all like Jouve, but these are quibbles.

"God and the Flesh," in The Times Literary Supplement, *No. 3494, February 13, 1969, p. 154.*

HENRY TAYLOR

Pierre Jean Jouve was born in 1887, and has long since established himself as one of the great figures in modern French poetry. ***An Idiom of Night*** is a selection from the whole course of his career, and so gives an adequate impression of the nature of his explorations and speculations. Keith Bosley's translations are for the most part very good, though there are occasional difficulties with the more formal poems. Jouve has been concerned for decades with the material made available by Freud, and his concern with form is therefore more complex than a simple struggle with the weight of poetic tradition. As he says in his ***Journal Sans Date,*** excerpts from which stand in place of an introduction to his volume, "We must start, then, with the problem of form. Deliberately setting aside accepted rational definitions (classical form, pure form, gratuitous form and the rest) we must pick out what seeks to limit and define itself by function. In the unconscious there is but one limit: it is represented by death. Thus what affects form through limitation is incontestably bound up with death." That kind of talk requires the authority of superb poetry to back it up; Jouve can do it, and even when he relies on more or less traditional consolations, such as God, he speaks with the authority of someone who has earned his vision. . . . (pp. 363-64)

Henry Taylor, "A Gathering of Poets," in Western Humanities Review, *Vol. XXIII, No. 4, Autumn, 1969, pp. 363-68.*

MARGARET CALLANDER

The aesthetic principles that have dominated Pierre Jean Jouve's mature artistic life have not varied greatly since the late 1920s when the first hints of their nature emerged. However, different aspects have been developed and emphasised, both in poems and in theoretical writings, according to differing stimuli. They have been used to test the work of others as well as to guide his own. They have been applied to painting and music almost as much as to poetry, and they form a remarkably comprehensive and stable group.

At the moment when in 1925 Jouve published ***Les Mystérieuses Noces*** he was in fact putting behind him the diverse, chequered literary affiliations of his earlier career, but the finality of this metamorphosis was only given overt expression in 1928, in a brief postface to ***Noces.*** Although Jouve has subsequently commented a little ironically on the tone of this declaration, it plunges directly into the central assertions of his whole aesthetic thinking in both their negative and their positive aspects. If it is to be at all authentic, poetry is seen as directly related to an imperious spiritual reality, and can be assessed only in this Christian context:

> . . . la plus grande poésie et la véritable est celle
> que le rayon de la Révélation est venu toucher.

This definition implies exclusivity, and indeed Jouve felt at this period a strong revulsion from what he saw as 'un ahurissant désordre des choses de l'art'. But if he judged the literary values of his contemporaries harshly, he was even more uncompromising in his condemnation of his own previous publications—'le poète renonce à son premier œuvre' is how his note ends.

The poems of Jouve's 'vita nuova' all exhibit the same rigorous self-scrutiny, the attrition, the difficulty-defined and beleaguered religious faith, spiritual illuminations, stifling sense of the omnipresence of original sin, and the conditions that apply to the man must apply also to the poet. It is difficult, at least in the earlier books, to discriminate between what Jouve is saying about his personal switch of direction and its attendant rejections, and what he is suggesting as a necessary experience for the artist in any case. But it becomes clear that he sees his own as in fact an exaggerated example of a common pattern in which the search for regeneration and for vocation must be related. Until the second World War Jouve made few pronouncements about his own work; his views have to be inferred from his poetry and from occasional pieces about the writing, music and painting of others. His most developed statements concerned the impact of Freudian concepts and material, and their potentialities for the artist. But the events of the war, particularly in France, convinced him that as a parallel to his poetic treatment of these events he could contribute most effectively by stating and defending artistic values. A profusion of texts attempted to define the relation of an artist to his country, to assess his role as 'témoin' of a national catastrophe, to reinterpret the work of artists of the past and present.

Subsequently Jouve has never ceased, although with less urgency and less expectation of touching an immediate chord, to develop and scrutinise his aesthetic ideas, and the often more expansive and speculative tones of this later poetry have allowed him to pursue a broader meditation on the identity and autonomy of language, on its power to consolidate, perhaps even to create, a spiritual reality.

Poetry, then, is 'une affaire de transcendance'. But for Jouve this means not so much defining the invisible as scrutinising the Pascalian 'misère de l'homme sans Dieu' and attempting a dialogue of which only one half can ever be spoken. For poetry partakes of the human condition, and language is not a neutral instrument but is composed of

ces mots universels menteurs
Et formés faux par le sang de naissance.

How then can it tell even a limited truth, how describe even the familiar reality of sin? From beginning to end of his work Jouve is haunted by the terrible sense that his words are not only inadequate but distinctly false, and it is in this form that he carries on and lives out Mallarmé's linguistic dilemma. The cry in ***Les Nouvelles Noces*** was 'J'ai peur de mentir', and some thirty years later he is still assessing failures in the same terms. . . . (pp. 192-93)

Jouve's poetry is not, however, permeated with defeatism and despair. His very strong belief in the artist as a 'dépositaire spirituel' leads him to a tenacious search for areas of validity, which will have to be meticulously tested and verified. One characteristic device is to suggest awareness of spiritual ambivalence by using words like 'vrai' and 'réel' with different meanings within the same phrase; and if familiar aesthetic criteria are applied to art these are rigorously redefined. It is inevitable that Jouve should be suspicious of the seduction and the implicit arrogance of formal aesthetic beauty, and he makes it clear that when he says of a painter 'il veut élever continuellement les images le plus obscures à un niveau de beauté et de lucidité', this beauty is to be an essentially spiritual quality—'je n'ai aucun goût pour la beauté formelle et d'harmonie, j'aime la beauté de forme, d'essence'. Once dissociated from trivial, static and limitedly sensuous identifications beauty can be released for a dynamic rôle in the 'coup de dés divin' that is the poem. It can hold together warring opposites and release their energies into a new harmony. . . . (pp. 193-94)

Jouve has elevated music to pride of place in his aesthetics. It was his earliest artistic preoccupation, as he has often stated, and is a continuing dominant influence. He has written studies of Mozart and Berg, and some of his strongest assertions of confidence in the power and validity of art have appeared in his comments on music and musicians. He continues the late nineteenth-century tradition of seeing music as the purest of the media, and adds a peculiarly Christian sense of revelation; music is for him 'avant tout autre art sur la voie d'accomplissement parfait dans la Promesse'. It is, however, through opera, which some people would see as a hybrid and therefore 'impure' art, that Jouve can most satisfactorily demonstrate the religious function of music. One of his own books of poems is entitled ***Mélodrame,*** and he sees as a privileged form of expression this particular mixture of drama and music, of orchestral and human sound. Whatever Mozart's conception or inspiration, his *Don Giovanni* is for Jouve 'essentiellement chrétien', demonstrating as it does the 'domination sur la Mort exercée par l'esprit de raison, qu'éclaire la Foi et selon la règle d'or de la beauté'. This last quotation contains in fact a precise formulation of all that Jouve hopes for from art, and a definition of the precarious but positive balancing of elements at a point of tension which he sees as necessary if art is to have a transcendental dimension.

But when Jouve speaks at this level of certainty he is commenting on a few works that he considers unique and exemplary. For his own poetry there is no short cut to spiritual transmutation, and the tainted words have to follow the same weary path as the poet. Jouve does not believe only in a single incontrovertible revelation, giving subsequent spiritual stability, but in an endless series of grim initiatives from an apparently desperate position. He subscribes to the paradox of 'He that loseth his life for my sake shall find it', but the process of abnegation, the extinction of pride and desire, the renunciation of all that can be achieved and possessed, even of art itself, all this is an exhausting and absorbing discipline. We see Jouve attempting various modes of detachment, propounding models of negation. A sacrifice of identity: the heroine of his novel ***Paulina 1880*** changes her name twice, and in his translations from Hölderlin attention is drawn to the poet's signature to his poems of madness, 'Avec humilité, Scardinelli', and to his cutting all but a few of the wires of his piano and then improvising on the remaining notes. A sacrifice of function: when Orpheus is evoked it is a torn and dying body whose severed hands still touch the lute. A sacrifice of formal beauty: many of Jouve's poems are abrupt truncated exclamations, and even in his more rhetorical constructions the syntax is wrenched away from its expected pattern; a similar reorientation of language is seen by him not only in Mallarmé but also in Baudelaire whose distinction is to 'briser en un certain sens l'instinct logistique de la langue française'. These manoeuvres have complex aesthetic implications, of course, but are also seen by Jouve, certainly in his own case, as part of a spiritual struggle. Finally there is the paradoxical sacrifice of all the accepted positive qualities of poetry, its material texture, its vision, its harmony, its autonomy. (pp. 194-95)

Jouve may very well seem to have appropriated poetry in a peculiarly personal quest for salvation, and indeed ultimately this is how his position may perhaps be interpreted, in spite of all that he has to say about the aesthetic validity of art. But at least it is clear that this quest is not exclusively self-centred. His view of the poet's rôle includes a preoccupation with contemporary problems and a sense of mission. His responsibility is to 'placer le trésor mystique bien près de l'humanité', and to engage with other men of good will in a stand against 'le démoniaque contemporain'. This 'démoniaque' takes many forms, from triviality to sadism; but its most public identification is with elements of German aggression in the second World War. In seeing the poet as 'le créateur des valeurs de la vie' Jouve is following the Romantic tradition, and for him this suggests a combination of Baudelaire's 'phares' and his 'intercesseurs'. He expects estrangement and solitude, though he may sometimes complain at what Pierre Emmanuel calls his 'fatalité salutaire'. This makes him particularly appreciative of the few artists whom he sees as sustaining kindred spirits. The names of these 'guérisseurs' appear often in his poetry as well as in his aesthetic comments, and, as with Eliot, quotations from their work are embedded in the texture of the poems. (pp. 196-97)

Jouve is exclusive in his artistic affinities; but, in addition to a group of mystical writers, these range from Dante and Shakespeare through Blake and Hölderlin to Segalen and Emmanuel; his musicians are Mozart, Beethoven, Mahler, Bartok, Berg; painters include Meryon, Delacroix, Courbet and Balthus. There is a special place for Nerval, Rimbaud and Mallarmé, but the most permanent presence in the poetry is perhaps what Jouve calls 'le réconfort Baudelaire', clarifying for him his own dualism, his sensuality, his spiritual sense, his aesthetics. Such affinities seem predestined to Jouve, and 'Quand on est très enfermé dans son monde, on n'accepte que les nourritures pour ce monde-là'; the rest is rejected, undifferentiated but disturbing. In the context of such a position, intransigent because intuitive, a late capitulation to Racine takes on an unexpected and moving quality. It might have been assumed that Jouve would have felt a special link with Racine, but in fact until the chance experience of a performance of *Phèdre* he had always considered seventeenth-century drama to be alien and artificial.

With this elective support to draw on Jouve found it easier to define the poet's function in a time of national disaster. He saw the second World War as specifically 'une guerre de la foi' and the French as recapturing the high moments of their Catholic and Revolutionary past. Such an apocalyptic view of history demands prophetic treatment, and here artists become the 'témoins' whose 'lucidité terrible' not only records the violence and suffering but reveals their inner significance of chastisement and purification. It is in this sense that Rimbaud appears as 'l'œil de la catastrophe', and that certain texts—Danton's speeches or Revolutionary popular songs—assume a special relevance. This was a period when Jouve could feel confidence in the immediate efficacy of art, since he saw its rôle as positive and unambiguous . . . and since, particularly during the Occupation, poetry did in fact become a much-prized mode of communication, the short-hand of fraternity, pity and resistance. He could broaden his canons to take in a number of his contemporaries—Claudel, Aragon, Saint-John Perse—since he felt that they shared his patriotic sense of mission or had contributed to defining the true spirit of France. For him there was no clash between the Christian and the Revolutionary elements in the national identity. . . . [The] sense that there is an inner coherence to a major artist's work, often imperceptible to contemporaries, is an important tenet of Jouve's aesthetics, and he has applied it when revising his own poems and novels for republication. (pp. 197-98)

Another area in which Jouve could feel certain of the ultimate justification and immediate benefit of his artistic activity was in his championship and adaptation of Freudian psychological findings. It was for him of the utmost importance that artists should identify and assimilate the potentially dangerous new material, should be the pioneers who would prevent its misappropriation, for they, just as much as the psychologists, are the 'spéléologues' the 'scaphandriers' of the human mind. The fact that Freudian ideas continued and confirmed at all points Jouve's existing religious conviction and image pattern made him all the more sure that artists are the only people aware enough to be able to fit the new concepts into a wider system of values. And they would immediately gain an aesthetic advantage. . . . Furthermore, the Freudian concept of sublimation is not just applied generally to the notion of artistic creation; there is a more precise parallel in that Jouve sees the necessity for art to be a charge of energy so powerfully directed that it can reverse the usual concentrations of man's psychological forces. In his poetry Jouve's imagery habitually suggests random explosions of energy and the mechanically repetitive play of erotic forces, all trapped within the static power of the death-wish. But just as the libido can transcend itself so art can suggest a quickening of the dead weight of evil. . . . (pp. 198-99)

There is an exuberance, a buoyancy in Jouve's welcoming of this challenge which is only matched by his excitement at finding in artists of the past anticipations of contemporary developments. One of his criteria of assessment is how far they are able to reveal to *modern* man something new about himself, and at the same time to offer a 'true' image of their own time. (p. 199)

But the discussion of some details of Jouve's literary activities, the definition of certain terms in his aesthetic vocabulary, may obscure what is perhaps the most crucial question that his poetry poses: the relationship between the mystic and the poet, whether their aims can be at all compatible, what difference there is between the mystic's account of his quest and the poet's. In a sense Jouve is asking that his poetry should give him spiritual certainty by breaking through the barriers of the finite and the material, and achieving the desired contact with a divine principle. If the mystic can feel that he has experienced this it will, however, have been a moment of essentially mute ecstasy and a denial of the material that a subsequent description can only hint at. Jouve is in fact well aware of this problem and its dangers, although the comment he makes on it may still seem ambiguous:

> la mystique commence par nier ce qui est le plus important pour l'art: l'orde suprêmement sensuel qui revêt la chose de la beauté. Et cependant tout 'grand' art doit *par paradoxe* contenir une fin mystique.

It is the maintaining of this paradox that produces much of the tension, the energy and the anguish in Jouve's own poetry. (pp. 199-200)

Statements about Jouve's view of poetry are the more confusing because critics bring to it preconceptions about what constitutes a mystical experience, what is its purpose and indeed value. It is really only possible to assess the effect of the poetry and to be guided by its emphases. There is no doubt that Jouve is committed to the idea of the supremacy of poetry and sees himself as first and foremost a poet. . . . [The] strength of his poetry is certainly its ability to suggest areas of matter being released from their own dark weight and transmuted into a glowing transparent buoyancy. This is the 'matière céleste', the sanctified flesh, the irradiated landscape, that is such a characteristic feature of Jouve's poetry, and by stressing its transmutation through art he is able to bring out all the pathos of the human associations but see them in a specific perspective. Again it is music that best conveys this poignant quality for him . . . but this quality is diffused throughout his own poetry and represents the point of balance between not so much the mystical and the aesthetic as the mystical and universally human. (pp. 202-03)

Margaret Callander, "Pierre Jean Jouve: The Idea of Poetry," in Order and Adventure in Post-Romantic French Poetry: Essays Presented to C. A. Hackett, *E. M. Beaumont, J. M. Cocking, J. Cruickshank, eds., Basil Blackwell, 1973, pp. 192-205.*

DANIEL E. RIVAS

Despite occasional efforts by critics to classify Jouve's poetry as religious or mystical, the poet's own pronouncements contain several *caveats* in this regard. Within the general movement of his poetry mysticism can be considered as an answer to the implicit poetics of ***Sueur de sang*** (1933), one of Jouve's earlier collections, that echoes, in its violent and anguished elaboration, the confrontation with erotic unconscious forces, a characteristic that belies the strong influence of Freudian psychoanalysis. Yet even in ***Sueur de sang*** this dimension of the poetry is coupled with a religious concern and imagery that appears subjugated and repressed by the onslaught of a most unrestrained sexuality.

The struggle between both facets of Eros is a consistent theme throughout Jouve's poetry, but its execution is not consistently even, as subsequent collections demonstrate. Thus ***La Vierge de Paris*** and ***Hymne*** constitute, in many respects and vis à vis ***Sueur de sang,*** a reversal, or more exactly the sublimation of an earlier instinctual eroticism as well as the inauguration of a mystical cycle. In this respect the *Nada* theme—already discernible in ***Les Noces*** and ***Sueur de sang***—achieves its full development, and the epigraph chosen by Jouve, "Para venir a serlo todo / No quieras ser algo en nada," clearly suggests the importance that nothingness is destined to play in the later poetry, and its manifest relationships with John of the Cross and the wider tradition of European devotional lyric, which in many instances constituted both a retreat from the religious and political upheavals of the age, as well as their reflection from another vantage point. Partially, at least, Jouve's modern devotional cycle is historically motivated, and its publication during the Second World War was enthusiastically received, for it voiced many of the concerns and hopes of the poet's compatriots at the time of France's occupation.

Apart from its particular historical import, Jouve's manipulation of the dark night of the soul theme provides an integral component in the overall design of his poetry. It expands on a dimension, religious in the broadest sense, and well suited to articulate a passage from the poet's negative view of the woman as a mediatrix between Christ and himself, as evidenced in the early poetry, and the later image of the "Vierge Noire," the highest expression of the Feminine. (pp. 325-26)

There is a persistent image that organizes many of the poems in ***La Vierge de Paris*** and ***Hymne,*** contributing to the unity of these two *recueils* and of Jouve's poetry in general. Alternately, it surfaces and submerges in individual poems, while other images, particularly darkness, furnish a backdrop against which the poet's mystical elaboration unfolds. The image in question is the dwelling place and its manifestations, the house or the room. . . . (p. 327)

Much of the effect achieved in this modern version of the dark night of the soul comes from a carefully selected, concentrated imagery that continually gravitates around nothingness, from an even more restricted vocabulary than is usual for Jouve, a skillful manipulation of syntax to highlight key themes, "oublier," "abandonner," "perdre," and a liberal recourse to homonyms and to anaphora. This reduction of language becomes a singular mirror metaphor of the mystical state, as the challenge becomes now, even more patently in Jouve's poetry, to diminish the raw elements of language while leaning upon certain techniques to safeguard a measure of variety. This poetic essay on negativity constitutes then a process of deconstruction, which the house exemplifies, becoming an icon, a sign of Jouve's own writing and of his poetry, particularly at this critical juncture. The linguistic overdetermination that functions here, and that by its very "reductiveness" engenders emptiness, leaves, at intervals, a space for internal and final rhyme that binds and closes the architecture of the poem, as the sounds that emanate from its reading become crucial elements of its fragile frame. . . . (pp. 328-29)

In Jouve's dark night of the soul many of the traditional elements of mystical baroque poetry are present, even direct borrowings from John of the Cross and his ascetical threefold path: purgative, illuminative, and unitive. All the props have been erected, all the accoutrements are there, save for one essential difference, that for John of the Cross Christ is a reality based on a distinct canon of religious beliefs, whereas for Jouve Christ is the "soleil des poètes," the "Christ de la poésic," statements that already deny extra-textual referential associations and beckon for an inter-textual self-referential reading, a dialogue on poetry with a revisionist attitude, in many ways showing signs of an "anxiety of influence," the weaker poet reacting against the strong one. (p. 331)

While Jouve may appear to be working within the structures of a literary religious tradition, his intentions cannot be considered "religious" or "didactic" (they are, in fact, but only in a literary context). (p. 332)

[Jouve's] dark night of the soul is one of the most remarkable and accomplished in French poetry of the twentieth century. (p. 333)

Daniel E. Rivas, "Pierre Jean Jouve's Dark Night of the Soul," in Comparative Literature Studies, *Vol. XVII, No. 3, September, 1980, pp. 325-33.*

MARY ANNE O'NEIL

In spite of the influence he has exercised on a generation of younger poets, notably Pierre Emmanuel and Yves Bonnefoy, Pierre-Jean Jouve remains in relative obscurity outside of France because of his hermeticism and the unusual turns taken by his career. During the first two decades of this century, he seemed little more than a clever imitator of several current intellectual trends: Neosymbolism, Jules Romains's Unanimistic philosophy, Romain Rolland's pacifistic idealism. His work did not acquire any true originality until 1925, when he experienced a conversion. . . . Thanks to his discovery of Christianity, he produced during the next ten years several novels and collections of poetry, all of which transcribe an attempt at autopsychoanalysis coupled with a quest for transcendence. As Hitler began his conquest of Europe, Jouve became convinced that the approaching struggle was the very holocaust foretold in the *Book of Revelation*. Armed with a new sense of prophetic mission, he composed shortly before and during the Second World War ***Kyrie*** and ***La Vierge de Paris,*** the two volumes that contain the bulk of his religious verse. After the war, he retreated from public life, devoting himself to the creation of an increasingly obscure poetic language until his death in 1976.

If, as [Terence] Cave maintains, the emergence of devotional verse requires a familiarity with the Ignatian meditative system, then it will be impossible to draw any meaningful comparisons between Jouve's poetry and that of a Sponde or of a La Ceppède. Although Jouve does hark back to sixteenth-century religious literature, he owes a debt not to the Jesuits, who stressed the development of the imagination, understanding and will, but rather to the Spanish mystics John of the Cross and Theresa of Avila, who counseled the abnegation of the powers of the soul in the pursuit of perfect union with God. Jouve's most important secular source, moreover, is not a religious thinker at all, but Freud. If, however, as I believe, devotional verse is not a genre tightly bound by historical circumstances, but instead a recurrent form of Christian poetry nourished by a variety of ecclesiastical writings as well as by related secular traditions, then Jouve's affinities with late Renaissance artists become more explicable. Obsessed with human depravity and divine vengeance, like poets of the Wars of Religion period, he immersed himself in the Bible and Catholic liturgy, where he discovered the themes, imagery and rhetorical patterns we commonly associate with the French Baroque lyric. Finally, the Freudian system of dream recreation and probing of the symbols of the unconscious in an effort to regenerate the will—a discipline that offers analogies to Loyola's threefold progression from composition to analysis to colloquy—may well have set Jouve on the path to meditation.

While both of Jouve's war volumes present a compendium of traditional devotional motifs, **"La Résurrection des morts"** of ***La Vierge de Paris,*** a sequence of fifteen short pieces ending with a six-stanza work, seems particularly germane to our discussion, since it explores Jouve's major preoccupation of the war years: the way in which catastrophe can become a means of purification aiding humanity's progress towards salvation. (pp. 259-60)

Although written over three hundred years after the Counter-Reformation, **"La Résurrection des morts"** exhibits most of the salient characteristics of French devotional verse of this period. Like the great religious poetry of the late sixteenth and early seventeenth centuries, Jouve's sequence finds its inspiration, as Cave has observed with regard to that earlier corpus of devotional verse, "in the Bible, the Father . . . the typological tradition and the liturgy." Based on the *Book of Revelation,* it contains quotations from the Gospels, allusions to the Epistles and Church doctrine. It presents the Last Judgment as a literal event, but also as an allegory that further explains the Old and New Testaments, while offering moral instruction. Like Sponde, La Ceppède and their contemporaries, Jouve exploits the central biblical antithesis of sin and salvation, which he expresses through contrasting images of light and dark, immobility and ascension, the grave and the blood of Christ. Finally, like earlier devotional artists, Jouve is a poet who recaptures both the thrust and the structure of Counter-Reformation spiritual exercises. He achieves a threefold appeal to the imagination, understanding and will, repeating the Ignatian progression from composition to analysis to colloquy.

Twentieth-century verse treatments of traditional religious topics like **"La Résurrection des morts"** suggest that our definition of the devotional genre, which in French literary criticism has been historically limited to the late sixteenth and early seventeenth centuries, requires revision. We must become aware of the continued influence of religious meditative tracts on contemporary Christian poetry, but also we must investigate the ways in which a poetry of meditation can develop independently of the handbooks, through the influences of earlier poets, the Bible and the liturgy, or even of secular sources. Unless we expand our notions of the devotional genre, we will find ourselves in the ironic position of discovering the forgotten religious artists of the Baroque age while losing the great Christian poets of our own day, writers like Pierre-Jean Jouve, who attempt to reconcile Christianity with the spiritual aspirations of their era and who succeed in creating exciting works of devotional verse designed for a modern audience. (pp. 271-72)

Mary Anne O'Neil, "Pierre-Jean Jouve's 'La resurrection des morts': A Contemporary Devotional Sequence," in French Forum, *Vol. 6, No. 3, September, 1981, pp. 259-73.*

Steve Katz

1935-

(Has also written under pseudonym of Stephanie Gatos) American novelist, short story writer, poet, and scriptwriter.

Courtesy of Steve Katz

Katz was part of a burgeoning group of American postmodern experimental fiction writers who gained prominence during the 1960s. Reflecting his conviction in the importance of spontaneous creativity and improvisation, Katz's fiction has a dreamlike quality in which the familiar is transmuted by bizarre, comic, and improbable events. Katz often depicts his characters and himself as being subjected to random and extraordinary circumstances, and his imaginative worlds mirror the chaos and irrationality of human existence. Much of Katz's fiction is concerned with the relationship between reality and art and with individuals searching for and inventing identities. Like most metafictionists, Katz's prose is extremely self-conscious and abundant with wordplay and absurd situations.

In his first work to draw substantial critical attention, *The Exagggerations of Peter Prince* (1968), Katz challenges the reader's expectations about books through visual, narrative, and spatial experimentation. He includes illustrations, supposedly deleted passages, parallel columns, and other typographical oddities. While these visual elements were regarded by some reviewers as gimmicks, Katz stated that he chose them "for their metaphorical and emotional resonances." In the book, Katz improvises on the name "Peter Prince," which represents at various times a character, a town, a ship, and a protagonist in another character's fiction. Throughout *The Exagggerations of Peter Prince,* Katz comments on the progress of writing the novel. The book's chaotic structure and nonlinear narrative baffled and angered some critics, while others admired Katz's whimsical and adventurous approach to fiction. Katz's next novel, *Saw* (1972), is a fantasy set in New York City in which characters interact with a humanlike sphere and a talking hawk. *Saw* metaphorically explores alienation, the importance of social intercourse, and New York's contradictory traits of beauty and ugliness.

Moving Parts (1977), Katz's most self-reflexive work, concentrates on how his imagination and personal aesthetics have shaped his perception of reality. For example, one section of this book details an actual trip to Tennessee which Katz had fictionalized in an earlier section to examine how closely his creation coincides with the real world. The experience proved to Katz that truth and reality are wholly subjective concepts. *Wier & Pouce* (1984) ostensibly focuses upon the lives of the two title characters and the changes they go through in childhood, college, and adulthood. Dusty Wier is an ersatz seer and an ingenuous Everyman who believes in the existence of an alternative "real" planet earth; E. Pouce is an illogical, undisciplined, and destructive man who serves as Wier's antithesis. The latter half of the novel encompasses dozens of interwoven tales which exhibit Katz's fertile imagination. The facts of Wier's and Pouce's lives fluctuate and become obscured until they come to respectively symbolize the preservative and nihilistic facets of human nature. Several critics noted that in this book Katz seems more intent on experimenting with narrative approaches and styles—including traditional realism, Joycean stream-of-consciousness, surrealism, and acronyms mixed with sestinas—than in writing a consistent and coherent story.

In addition to his novels, Katz has published two short story collections, *Creamy and Delicious: Eat My Words (In Other Words)* (1970) and *Stolen Stories* (1984). The pieces in *Creamy and Delicious* involve creative revisions of classical myths and mythic treatments of contemporary popular culture figures, whose lives Katz reconstructs in order to give them new identities. Larry McCaffery noted that Katz "seeks to disrupt any sense of myth's universality, fixated order, and immobilizing power by introducing new and actively disruptive elements into the system." *Stolen Stories* displays Katz's ability to meticulously create fantastic situations that have symbolic and moral meaning. Many of these works darkly satirize American social conventions and sexual mores. Brian McHale commented: "Some stories travesty the well-made story . . . leaving behind something just as satisfying, though a good deal harder to describe." Katz also has written *Posh* (1971), a parody of pornographic novels, and *Cheyenne River Wild Track* (1973), an epic poem about his experiences as a scriptwriter for a film set on a South Dakota Indian reservation.

(See also *Contemporary Authors,* Vols. 25-28, rev. ed.; *Contemporary Authors New Revision Series,* Vol. 12; and *Dictionary of Literary Biography Yearbook: 1983*.)

R. V. CASSILL

On its way to write [***The Exagggerations of Peter Prince***] Steve Katz's imagination was intercepted by the temptation to scramble the conventions that have prevailed—not only among novelists but among the typesetters and compositors who prepare the novel for publication—through all those dreary eras now being superseded by the revolutionary whimsy of the young. He found there were untried gimmicks and tried them. Consequently the chief interest of what he has produced can be pretty well illustrated by enumerating typical examples of distortion in typography and novelties of page composition. There are, indeed, shards, fragments, ligatures and lumps of more or less ordinary text incorporated in this montage. But the reader will encounter its real distinctions as readily by flipping from one typographical curiosity to another as by trying to read it in any traditional way.

Among the compositional novelties are: the device of overprinting a floor plan on a block of text—black on black to insure ultimate illegibility; . . . pages with two or sometimes three columns of boldface type, one column commenting on the text of those adjacent; and the neatly simulated lines of deletion that cross several pages to indicate that the author (once? why?) intended to eliminate them from the book. At the end of these included-deleted pages, the author directs a note to the reader: "Wahoo. I've done something for all of you, made it a little shorter through this book. . . ."

The cringing, yet importunate, diffidence of this direct address to the reader is recurrent. It is as if the author felt that to demonstrate and declaim that he is doing something uninteresting must, in itself, be interesting. . . .

By intent the putative title character is rarely more than a talking point, and sometimes only a typographic constellation of alphabetic symbols. The only constant character is the author, and he is not well realized. Instead of images we get his fingerprints—rather sticky ones, as if he had been eating [a] hot fudge sundae without a spoon while he fumbled the manuscript into its present sequence.

And, since the writer emerges as the chief agonist of his own *oeuvre,* I feel keenly frustrated in not learning why he was moved to produce it. It ought to have been, at least, fun for him. But in a poignant semi-acrostic he complains, "whilezIzamztypingzthiszeveryonezelsezhavingzfun."

On the basis of circumstantial evidence—the irrelevant inclusions, the deliberate admissions of circuitous false leads, the blatant lack of discrimination in selecting the stuff of parody, and the frequent, pointless fractures of sequence—one concludes that this novel must have been intended as a filibuster. But even so, it seems a filibuster without apparent object. For what could Mr. Katz be trying to delay?

R. V. Cassill, "Shards, Ligatures and Lumps," in The New York Times Book Review, *September 8, 1968, p. 4.*

THOMAS GORDON PLATE

Marshall McLuhan has argued that books are an outmoded form of communication and that TV, for example, the cool, non-linear medium, is more of our time. As if singlehandedly to prove the Great Communications Theorist a prophet in his own time, Steve Katz has delivered the kind of "novel" [***The Exagggerations of Peter Prince***] which tries its hardest to look like the anti-book that will spell the end of the book as we know it. He has produced the non-novel of non-novels, which amounts to minimum definition of the word "book": a bunch of well-bound pages of wood pulp on which a printer has impressed blotches of ink formally subdivided into letters, words, sentences, paragraphs, pages, and occasionally chapters.

Typographically speaking, Katz is quite clever. Parts of his text are crossed out with huge X's (though this device coyly leaves the "deleted" passages still legible). And he is engagingly self-conscious, archly revealing to the reader that the writing of his "thing" is not going too well. . . . At another point, he writes, "There are thirty pages of transition here which I have decided not to write . . . all of which could add up to sensitivity galore, but you'll have to take my word for it."

Then a bit of verbal striptease: "He caught her few tears on his lips and then sucked her mouth into his, and they began again that action that was mentioned above, but not described; action that deserves description and will be described later in this book, or in some other book." A plethora of "beeps" also papers over whole passages of possible prurient interest. Finally, Katz somehow persuaded the publisher, a very respectable and heretofore "solid" New York house, to smear stray words and letters all over selected pages to suggest, once again, that a book is in essence a bag of printer's tricks. (And for good-humored variety, Katz includes a few random illustrations, one, for example, of the male sex organ, another of a battleship steaming across the high seas.)

Katz's attack on the book as form is largely tongue-in-cheek of course, and, in a way, ***Peter Prince*** really disproves McLuhan, for Katz, perhaps in spite of himself, not infrequently comes off as an expert, and linear, craftsman. Some parts of ***Exagggerations*** are very entertaining. . . . (pp. 89, 92)

At points, the "story" breaks down into three separate stories printed side by side in three columns on the same page, and the reader gasps for air. But the real purple heart goes not to the reader, who may well be entertained by this unusual effort, nor to author Katz, who is in entire command of his maddening lunacy, but to his printer and publisher, who somehow managed to set the type and read the galley proofs of this idiot's delight that makes fun of their trades and threatens everyone's sanity. (p. 92)

Thomas Gordon Plate, "Tell Us a Story," in Newsweek, *Vol. LXXII, No. 11, September 9, 1968, pp. 89, 92.*

SARA BLACKBURN

Steve Katz may be a good writer, but it's hard to tell from this doggedly vacant novel [***The Exagggerations of Peter Prince***], in which intentionally comic-strip characters undergo an intentionally stupid series of (intentionally) wildly boring adventures, intent on attracting negative reviews. Every once in a while Mr. Katz drops his guard and lets in something that's *really* funny, but not often enough to make me believe that anyone but its proofreader has been able to read through every one of its beautifully designed pages.

Sara Blackburn, in a review of "The Exagggerations of Peter Prince," in The Nation, *New York, Vol. 207, No. 9, September 23, 1968, p. 286.*

MICHAEL ALEXANDER

Readers need not be put off by the hokey, pop-arty look of Steve Katz's first novel, ***The Exagggerations of Peter Prince.*** It appears to be terribly experimental, yet there beneath the layers of simultaneous action, interjections in the author's voice, and carefully crossed-out pages lies the conventional grand-tour novel that the author tried his darnedest not to write.

After a few false starts, including one promising adulterous interlude with the grass widow of a Vietnam soldier, Peter Prince skips out of the country to reappear in a number of exotic locales—Egypt, shipboard on the Mediterranean, Verona, even Ethiopia.

And along the way we meet such *interesting* people—some of them genuinely so, in spite of the author's obviously playful intent. . . .

The Exagggerations of Peter Prince (please note 3 g's) is a bit of a put-on. Among other things. Along the way, it is also the journal kept by the author during the writing of the Peter Prince episodes; a collection of appropriately mad though slightly disingenuous dialogs on the creative process; and a few embarrassing odds and ends tossed up from the author's kid past. Or Peter's. Who knows? There is no Peter Prince, really, just Steve Katz jumping around like mad behind the scenes doing tricks with his voice. Clever fellow.

But there is certainly no point in delivering a stern and resounding reproof to the author for failing to be *serious*. Seriousness is clearly—perhaps all too clearly—not his bag. Steve Katz stands for madness. Steve Katz supports whimsy. Steve Katz casts a big vote for *fun*! And there is plenty of fun to be had here—with a lot of pop-in-pop-out action, nutty illustrations, and what-will-happen-next asides from the author. And for that reason, ***The Exagggerations of Peter Prince*** is, shall we say, refreshing. Just how refreshing you consider it to be will depend on how turned-off you are on the old-fashioned, four-square, characters-and-plot sort of novel.

Michael Alexander, "A Bit of a Put-On, 'Peter Prince' Is . . . Uh . . . Refreshing," in The National Observer, *October 7, 1968, p. 23.*

PUBLISHERS WEEKLY

Much of [***Creamy and Delicious***] is devoted to what Mr. Katz calls "mythologies"—short, very short, half-humorous, half-horrifying, occasionally political tales about everyone from Homer and Faust to Sluggo, Mandrake, and, of course, Wonder Woman. There are, also, haiku, and a number of other stories. On the whole, the stories lack development. No matter how much you love the experimental, it's hard to get over the ill-conceived shift, false drama and abrupt endings of these tales. The three "Satisfying Stories" (the author's designation), which add up really to one medium long short story, is a captivating and rather lovely tale of a girl whose "voyage" ends in a "childbirth," in which the baby is a dolphin.

A review of "Creamy and Delicious," in Publishers Weekly, *Vol. 197, No. 18, May 4, 1970, p. 59.*

JONATHAN BAUMBACH

Creamy and Delicious, Steve Katz's far-out collection of abrasively funny short fictions, is deceptive. Playful, punny, self-mocking, it confronts us with a barely straight face. The tales are interspersed with mock chapters from a presumably larger work called "In Our Thyme" (the seasoning that makes the words edible?). There are pop illustrations by Richard Tum Suden. The jokes, some of them marvelous, flash by like a stand-up comedy routine: "I could look time in the face and tell him to brush his teeth." (**"Plastic Man."**) "As a pilot he was a real daredevil because he couldn't figure how to navigate." (**"Homer."**). Katz's dreamlike pop fables, zany and dislocating, are, at their best, mysteriously touching.

In their surreal preoccupation with everyday exoticism these stories share common ground with Borges, Burroughs, Barthelme, and Coover, though they have their own vision. Like many another cool writer, Katz, by means of distance and irony, resists sentiment and avoids the risk of feeling.

To describe the plot of a Katz fable is to give a minimal sense of its experience. In **"Nancy and Sluggo,"** for example, Nancy is a transvestite gunfighter, "hung up on the Code of the West," who has it out in a tragic finish with the wholesome bandit Sluggo, each killing the other. Thus Katz uncovers the disguises of our myths by creating correlative disguises.

His mythologies, as he calls them, resist explication. . . .

The world of ***Creamy and Delicious*** is mired with impedances, Katz's heroes take trips that go nowhere or lead back to where they began, as in the heavy weather of a bad dream. Within the nightmare there are moments of fulfilment, small victories, passing love, births inside deaths. The stories move in odd and surprising ways without seeming arbitrary or contrived, the necessity of obsession determining their form.

Whatever their other virtues, these eccentric fictions in ***Creamy and Delicious*** . . . are more tasty than most conventional fare. Small warning: at some point Katz's obsessions invariably touch home. The pleasures of this book are not without the pain of cognition and recognition. Don't come to it too lightly.

Jonathan Baumbach, in a review of "Creamy and Delicious: Eat My Words (In Other Words)," in Saturday Review, *Vol. LIII, No. 41, October 10, 1970, p. 34.*

PUBLISHERS WEEKLY

Once upon a time Steve Katz wrote ***The Exagggerations of Peter Prince*** and was saluted as innovative, fantastic, imaginative and whimsical. Now the fantasy has disintegrated to slovenliness, the whimsy to in-jokes and the innovations to grotesqueries. . . . The sphere episode [in ***Saw***] captures all the best of Katz: a ludicrous premise lovingly developed and concluded. Given the fact that he is a sphere, he is all one could desire, whether balancing delicately on a subway seat or making love as projectionless spheres must do. After that, laziness sets in, however. . . . The cylinder flattens everything, of course, . . .—it also flattens whatever Katz still had in mind for his fiction. Thereafter he is reduced to random anecdotes.

A review of "Saw," in Publishers Weekly, *Vol. 202, No. 3, July 17, 1972, p. 113.*

MARTIN LEVIN

I'm not certain about the sequence in ***Saw:*** when I was halfway through, my unbound review copy self-destructed, dribbling its pages all over the floor. Reassembling them as best I could, I concluded that Steve Katz . . . is a witty fantasist who can homogenize pop detritus, campy slang and hallucination to achieve inspired chaos.

Of the loose-jointed episodes, which began with Seventeen and ended with Seven, my favorite was Seventeen. This features a girl named Eileen, who feeds puppies to a hawk in Central Park, and is seduced by a sphere from *inner* space. . . . I wish I could be sure I had those pages in correct order. On second thought, it doesn't seem to make much difference.

Martin Levin, in a review of "Saw," in The New York Times Book Review, *October 1, 1972, p. 42.*

LARRY McCAFFERY

Steve Katz's trademark in his previous work has always been his ability to create bizarre situations which somehow produce mysterious resonances that illuminate events in our own lives. Katz's ability to convincingly create dreamlike situations is evident in the four loosely related fictions in ***Moving Parts:*** in one story, for example, a man receives a package containing 43 human wrists. Somewhat like Kafka, Katz develops even the most improbable scenes with careful precision. But the real center of interest in ***Moving Parts*** is Katz's exploration of the various ways our imaginative systems work their way into the world and affect our own personal sense of identity. In "Female Skin," for example, Katz first establishes the story's central premise (a man wearing a woman's skin) and then records the reactions of various real people to his story; with the assistance of journal entries, photographs, and assorted imaginatively recreated experiences, we observe the way that Katz's story began to have an effect on his own life and relationships with others. In the last of the stories, "43," Katz examines the use of the number "43" in his previous fiction and muses on the strange way this number seems to have begun intruding into his life. . . . This eruption of the arbitrary into reality is precisely the sort of event that demonstrates for Katz that "the potential for mystery is everywhere, it's infinite, but no predetermined order can circumscribe this world of events". . . . (pp. 114-15)

Larry McCaffery, "The Fiction Collective," in Contemporary Literature, *Vol. 19, No. 1, Winter, 1978, pp. 99-115.*

MICHAEL STEPHENS

Steve Katz gallops on to the page, galump, galump, a combination of Sancho Panza and Lawrence Sterne, waving his Poundian banner MAKE IT NEW! He is white knight astride his steed in dirty underwear, and the great beast champing beneath him is made, alas, of cardboard. So much for illusions. This is the Land of Illusion, and Katz is perversely apt at concocting spells. Katz writes of make-believe, only his fantasy world is laced with arsenic and phantasmagoria; it is unnerving, and probably alters consciousness. To have Katz waving Pound's banner is deserved, since the author has learned much of his craft from poets, especially the more wry and playful contemporary ones like Frank O'Hara and Kenneth Koch. Katz's intention appears to be to make imagination rampant, and his Marxian stratagem is mostly Groucho-like. What keeps his writing from becoming cute is a darker psyche lurking underneath the prose. His asides have the literary finesse of a Tristram Shandy and the cutting edge of a W. C. Fields.

Katz's first commercial novel was ***The Exagggerations of Peter Prince,*** perhaps the most circuitously baffling and beautiful literary work since *Tristram Shandy*. . . . To this day the novel remains one of the most daring and innovative books written out of the sixties experience. This was followed by further experiments, which comb through contemporary experience, culture, detritus, visual art, teaching, sex, childhood, stickball—you name it, Katz has probably written something about it. . . .

[***Moving Parts***] is less buoyant than the earlier books, and the sense of dread which undercut the humor in his earlier work has now come to surface in a story-section like "Female Skin" in which the writer describes peeling off Wendy Appel's skin and wearing it around town. The language still is inspired by poetry, but the vision has become formidable, sharing a kinship with another prose writer who learned his craft from poets—Hubert Selby, Jr. So often in these stories the placid surface leaves the realm of entertainment and erupts into abominable horror, and "Female Skin" is a study in this new genre. . . .

So often the writer makes the reader's skin crawl, as though to say, shouting breathlessly, We exist, we exist, it hurts, and it is painful. And if we needed proof of this statement, let this book suggest that. "Female Skin" is written in the diary form, although Katz chooses to make his style more prosaic to undercut the savage content. "Parcel of Wrists" continues the trembling when the aforementioned parcel in the title arrives at his doorstep. A picaresque journey to Tennessee follows, the counterpoint being like the gravediggers in *Hamlet,* while the content reads like Steve Martin rewriting the more macabre and morbid sections of John Webster's plays.

In his journey to Tennessee Katz becomes sublime in how he turns rural America into a Swiftian pilgrimage with the southern American landscape becoming as foreign and exotic as Lilliput. This section is written with such refined craftsmanship, with invention and imagination wedded together by a cutting and humane voice. Tennessee, for Katz, is a combination of real-time and fiction. Real-time seems to interfere with the imagination of the book, and this section does not bristle and bubble like the other moving parts, and yet it is an essential section for an overview of the book—obsession and imagination.

The obsession is most revealed in the section-story entitled "43," which delves into every arcane and apparent nuance and cavity of that number. It begins with an article the author read in *Scientific American* in 1964 and concludes with the journey down Route 43 in Tennessee, both real-time and author's Yoknapatawpha-time. . . . The obsession becomes terrifying: the need to find meaning where meaning does not exist. It is a drive for semblance when nothing is comparable or fits. Forty-three is God, religion, sex, meditation, dope, liquor, anything that narcotizes, relieves, and thereafter gives a hangover. As Steve Katz points out, forty-three nearly got him into a fight in the Tin Palace bar when he read the piece. Forty-three contains potential violence. ***Moving Parts*** ends on this obsessional note.

What the progression of this new fiction suggests is that Katz is less interested in entertaining or getting the laughs than he once was. It also shows a progression from imagination to invention, from joy to sorrow, from young man to older man, from lover to father. Steve Katz has become a surer craftsman and a maturer writer. His vision is fragmented and hallucinatory, but he is primarily a story teller-novelist and narrative remains one of his strong points, albeit he mainly chooses to lacerate this talent by cutting it off, turning it on, cutting it off again, quite consciously, quite willfully. While the information in ***Moving Parts*** is neither reassuring nor particularly hopeful, there is little sign of abnegation or despair. There seems to be a love of life in spite of life. And there is also the voice of a real artist operating, virtuoso-like at times, capable of pyrotechnics, blasphemes, and morphemes, a revved up epistemology of the heart, with signs and symbols, even photographs (nicely taken by author et al.), and those wonderful sidetracks and tangents.

Michael Stephens, in a review of "Moving Parts," in The American Book Review, *Vol. 1, No. 5, December-January, 1978-79, p. 5.*

LARRY McCAFFERY

Since "myths always lie in the most difficult places to ignore," [according to a character in Samuel Delany's *The Einstein Intersection,*] it is not surprising that one of the most common structural approaches employed by contemporary writers is to adopt directly a mythic framework as an organizing method. However, various factors mitigate against the use of myth except in an ironic, highly self-conscious manner. Thus in most recent works which employ overtly mythic materials—Barth's *Giles Goat Boy* and *Chimera,* Barthelme's *Snow White,* Pynchon's works, Zelazny's *Lord of Light,* Steve Katz's ***Creamy and Delicious***—there exists a central tension between the mythic framework's tendency to organize and rigidify its elements into teleological wholes and the ambiguous, fragmented nature of contemporary experience, which refuses to yield to formulas and patterns. The result is usually a sense that the textual elements are struggling against their roles, threatening to break out of the preset patterns in order to open us up to new constructive possibilities.

A good example of this tendency can be found in the "Mythologies" sections of Steve Katz's ***Creamy and Delicious,*** in which Katz, like Delany, aims at exploiting the transformational possibilities of myth. Katz, however, develops a more radical formal method of allowing prior mythic and literary materials to generate new fictional shapes. Roland Barthes has claimed that "the very end of myths is to immobilize the world; they must suggest and mimic a universal order which has fixated once and for all the hierarchy of possessions." Katz, on the other hand, seeks to disrupt any sense of myth's universality, fixated order, and immobilizing power by introducing new and actively disruptive elements into the system. In each of his "Mythologies," Katz begins by selecting a name which will be certain to evoke a rich series of associations from his audience. These names are "mythic" in the sense that they suggest specific story lines and clusters of other narrative elements. But in addition to the usual names (Faust, Achilles, Hermes, Goliath, Apollo), Katz devotes equal time to more recent mythological characters (Nancy and Sluggo, Wonder Woman, Plastic Man, Gandhi, and Nasser). Once the stories begin, however, Katz defiantly divorces the names from their traditional associations—as when Nancy and Sluggo are revealed to be a gay cowboy and a "terrible gulch-riding bandit," respectively—and goes about the business of creating pure narrative adventures. The "Faust" mythology, for example, begins:

> Don't believe any of those stories you had to
> read in college about Faust, the big scientist
> who wanted to know all the shit in the world,
> so he turned on with the devil. Don't believe
> all that. It's a big put-on, and maybe some of
> it is almost true, but none of it is really true,
> and if you fall for it you deserve to be pasted
> on the wall like a wall-paper pattern.

The remainder of the story has nothing to do with the Faust legend; rather, it tells of Faust, a farmer "who loved girls better than he loved his daily chores," his amorous adventures with one notorious Lulu, and a later encounter with a "befouled beauty" named Margaret. The Katzian Faust story, then, turns our expectations—which have been aroused by Katz's use of the coded signal "Faust"—upside down as he pursues a completely new story line. Since all received versions of the past have been fundamentally falsified in their transmission, Katz implies, the contemporary writer should feel free to invent whatever variations he chooses; indeed, Katz even suggests as the story concludes that "telling the truth" about Faust interferes with the storytelling impulse. . . . If Katz is intent on defying all the mythic patterns, we might ask ourselves, why use the name at all? The answer appears to be that Katz uses the name purely as an arbitrary formal departure point—it immediately establishes a context of meaning and story structure which Katz can disrupt (thus creating a sort of dialogue with the earlier text) while freely inventing a narrative line all his own. (pp. 31-2)

Larry McCaffery, "Form, Formula, and Fantasy: Generative Structures in Contemporary Fiction," in Bridges to Fantasy, *George E. Slusser, Eric S. Rabkin, Robert Scholes, eds., Southern Illinois University Press, 1982, pp. 21-37.*

J. KERRY GRANT

In "43," the final section of ***Moving Parts*** (1977), Steve Katz reveals and meditates upon his obsession with the prime number of the title, filling page after page with examples of its appearance in a wide variety of commonplace and esoteric sources. To the speculations raised by the first three sections of the novel, "43" seems something of an addendum, and yet its rambling and fragmentary meditations on the intrusion of reality into the minimal fiction of Katz's arbitrarily chosen number finally emerge as confirmation of the novel's concern with the relationship between art and reality and with the need to maintain a viable sense of connection between them. . . . Earlier in the novel [in the section titled "Trip"], Katz insists that "There's no intention here to make anything better, but just to lay open some possibilities of consciousness, explore the boundaries of identity." . . . ***Moving Parts,*** then, belongs with those other fictions of our time that attempt to grant our inventions a status equal to that enjoyed by our so-called facts in their capacity to shape and define our identities. (p. 206)

The novel falls into four more or less distinct sections (perhaps the moving parts of the title), "Female Skin," "Parcel of Wrists," "Trip," and "43." "Female Skin" consists of portions of an "ongoing fiction" interspersed with comments on its origins, entries from a journal, photographs, and one blank black page. "Parcel of Wrists" presents, without interruption, another fiction in which the narrator travels to Tennessee in search of the person who sent him a box of human wrists. On his return to New York City, the narrator discovers that the wrists he has planted before his departure have grown into huge plants which eventually bear fruit in the form of human body parts (again a suggestion of the title's provenance). The narrator feels obliged to devote himself to the plants and spends most of his time on the streets, trying to persuade passers-by to make use of his store of spare parts. In "Trip" Katz chronicles his own journey, three years after "Parcel of Wrists," to the Tennessee he had never visited, in search of the correlation between his fiction and the real geography of its imaginings. Both Katz himself and a Protagonist upon whom Katz attempts to impose the burdens and responsibilities of this undertaking are very much present in the narrative.

Some of the boundaries explored in the novel seem to be the familiar ones revealed in a good deal of contemporary fiction. "Parcel of Wrists," for example, can be read as an allegory of the plight of the artist, whose unique visions start him off on journeys that lead him inevitably beyond the community of which he is ostensibly a part, "doomed to make a pest of himself." Names in fiction can get one into trouble, but here one is certainly tempted to deduce from the name of the sender of the box of wrists—C. Routs—the elementary imperative that its recipient should make an effort to discover the roads that consciousness can travel. The parcel is postmarked Irondale, Tennessee, a place that, significantly enough, does not appear on any map, like all the true places of the American imagination. The narrator acknowledges the degree to which his own tendency to mistrust the conventional structures of society has caused his enslavement to his odd occupation. . . . There remains the mild paranoia of the artist who feels that his role has not been chosen but thrust upon him by some mysterious agent. "Who is it?" asks the narrator. "Who really exercises the control? That's an important question." . . . (pp. 209-10)

The question is not to be answered only within the confines of purely imagined constructs like "Parcel of Wrists." The portrait of the artist that is drawn there is not one that Katz would have us accept without question. The "Female Skin" section of the novel has already revealed to us a much more complex, fragmented, and therefore less authoritative portrait, this time of Katz himself, as artist, at work on one of the fictions that seems to be symbolically rendered in the spare parts peddled by the narrator of "Parcel of Wrists." The bulk of this section is made up of the bits and pieces of an experience that crystalizes finally in the story of the man stripping the skin from the girl. We have glimpses into Katz's own past, photographs (perhaps of his wife and of Wendy Appel, the prototype of the girl in the story), reactions of friends to the story in its various stages. . . . ***Moving Parts*** certainly tells the story of its stories, of its language, of its creator's anguish and exhilaration. (p. 210)

For reasons that Katz attempts to make clear, fiction is the inevitable mode of his exploration of himself. . . . There is scarcely any distance at all between "Fiction is inevitable" and "It's all fiction," an assertion made by Katz's "own lying proxy," the Protagonist in "Trip." Recognition of this fact allows for the kinds of discriminations within the category "fiction" that form the substance of Katz's exploration of "the boundaries of identity." If everything is invented, then legitimate and suggestive comparisons between kinds of invention become possible, collapsing the old dualities of fiction and reality into a single epistemology. Thus, for example, the fictional commune of "Parcel of Wrists" and the real commune in "Trip," though different, are both invented; one is "conceived in the mind," and the other is "blown from the mind of Adam." . . . One is the fiction of an individual consciousness, the other the fiction of a collective consciousness.

The potency of the latter kind of fiction is dramatized in the coming together of both inventions when Katz/Protagonist visits The Farm: "He went there on a story line, on an idea that was anticipated and nurtured for three years, and within a few minutes the reality of The Farm had scissored through and left him with no story at all." . . . When asked if it is possible to make art in the commune, Katz's guide appears nonplussed: "There are some writers here," he replies. "They work in the print shop." . . . In a collective situation, it seems, the writer is best confined to the reproduction of the codes by which the collective identity is sustained.

The resonances generated in ***Moving Parts*** by the art of telling, then, arise from such confrontations as these between the various fictions of which our lives are composed. By setting his stories—"Female Skin" and "Parcel of Wrists"—against the background fictions that constitute their origins, Katz reveals his need to escape as much from the confines of his own inventions as from the restrictions implicit in other people's. Private and collective fictions are both reductive, narrow versions of the possible; only the total fiction that results from the juxtaposition of these independent articulations can suggest an adequate means of knowing the boundaries of identity.

Towards the end of the "Female Skin" section of the novel, Katz records a journey to Woodstock:

> I go to Woodstock and drive up the mountain to Clarence Schmidt's acre. He was a folk artist of immense energy, an original explored consciousness, his place of enormous power. There in his crazed stonemasonry, and his disintegrating trash constructions I begin to appreciate my release. Clarence Schmidt's is like a sanctuary where I can feel what it means to be in one's own place, and devoted to the elaboration of one's own skin. I am released there into my own skin, to my own place. . . .

Similarly, at the end of "Trip," Katz finds himself liberated again into his own skin: "Now it's back in New York wholly sunk into myself again, in my own place." . . . (pp. 211-12)

Before he can achieve these moments of connection with himself, Katz has had to tell the story of his stories in exhaustive detail. Even deletions are left in as part of the experience. Photographs are used to connect the stories with the identities and geographies of the rest of reality. Separating "Parcel of Wrists" from "Trip," for example, is a photomontage of various pictures of Katz's own wrists, anticipating the transition from the individually imagined world of "Parcel of Wrists" to the societal structures encountered by the real Katz and the imagined Protagonist in "Trip." These fragments of himself seem to stand for those intrusions into the life of the Protagonist that ultimately lead Katz to a recognition of his own responsibility for the presence in his fictions. "Parcel of Wrists" is finally returned to sender when Katz is able to work through his desire to push that responsibility off on "envoys of personal pronouns and protagonists." In "Trip" the question of who really exercises the control is more or less answered. The Protagonist, records narrator Katz, "regrets my having shaved off my beard," not, as one would expect, "his having shaved off his beard." Katz shaves to assume the identity of the Protagonist, but the disguise is, like the skin assumed by the narrator in "Female Skin," scarcely sufficient to conceal the identity of the manipulator of the fiction. "Identity," you will recall, "is always one thing. Knowing it is all the others." Being in control of the separation between the two is what is important.

Katz's expression of the need to maintain flexibility in the relationship between art and reality places him well within the mainstream of contemporary fiction. (pp. 212-13)

J. Kerry Grant, "Fiction and the Facts of Life: Steve Katz's 'Moving Parts'," in Critique: Studies in Modern Fiction, *Vol. XXIV, No. 4, Summer, 1983, pp. 206-14.*

DAVID QUAMMEN

With a short story collection—especially one in which the author has ventured out beyond the conventions of style and technique—calling the work "uneven" should be taken, I think, as a compliment. The alternative extreme is repetitiveness, self-imitation and variations on a reliable and predictable approach. None of that for Steve Katz, who has previously published five novels and two books of poetry. He is neither predictable nor reliable. And this new assortment of his short fiction, ***Stolen Stories,*** is vigorously and intrepidly uneven.

Some of the pieces make no sense to me whatsoever. Into this category fall a number that Mr. Katz drily labels "essays"—bare, disembodied monologues with such ironically bland titles as "on THE PLAUSIBILITY OF FRIENDSHIP AMONG THE SEXES," "on LEADERSHIP" and "on PAID VACATIONS." Though the incorporeal voices that drone at us in these fragments are for the most part impenetrably Orphic, they do offer occasional flashes of relaxed wit. . . .

A few other stories are more accessible but still unsatisfying, like **"Mongolian Whiskey,"** the shaggy tale of a talking dog, a lonely salesman and a murderous married couple who lure the lonely man home from a bar. The story is bizarre, macabre and salacious, but it is also too neat, too coyly clever to be genuinely troubling. It is merely *Grand Guignol,* graced with a little deadpan humor. **"Mongolian Whiskey"** seems particularly disappointing because it remains just on the wrong side of a fine line—on the right side of which lies Mr. Katz's most potent work.

There is, for instance, **"Death of the Band,"** the story of a man who attends a performance of experimental music in which the composer participates by assassinating the band members one by one with a rifle, from his perch in a nearby tree. The composer, we are told, "leaned back against the tree trunk and cradled the weapon in his lap. This was the first piece he had written following strictly his ideas of irreversible subtraction." Of the man in the audience, who has gotten into the line of fire and received a chest wound, we hear: "If he took it to the hospital that would involve the police, and endless explanations, and put his favorite young composer through a lot of paralyzing legal rigamarole." The composer's successive creations progress toward a point of dramatic convergence with the wounded man's enthusiasm for the works. It is a wonderful story, full of insane, impeccable logic, suspense and faultlessly measured satire on the cant and rituals of Art. . . .

Then there is **"Friendship,"** a quiet but spectacular bit of work. . . . In this story Mr. Katz draws blood, with a very sharp and delicate razor. . . . But for that single story, which is absolutely worthy of Kafka, you might want to track down this small, interesting book.

David Quammen, "Of Cannibals, Paid Vacations and Talking Dogs," in The New York Times Book Review, *September 9, 1984, p. 9.*

MARY PJERROU

Steve Katz is full of so many tricks that you want to bash his head in, rather than turn another page of [***Wier & Pouce***]. But you do—and this is important—turn the page, if for no other reason than to see what fiendish, anything-goes-since-James Joyce, post-post-post modern, plot-twisting, weirdo device he's going to pull out next.

Starting with the title—an anagram for War and Peace (Wur & Piece)—Katz is up to no good. ***Wier & Pouce*** is about as far from *War and Peace* as war *is* from peace, although it's hard to know these days. Maybe they're the same. Maybe Katz belongs right up there next to Tolstoy, all things being equal. You can't blame Katz for reflecting what is obviously an ill American sensibility. How can you expect *War and Peace* in 1985 in the U.S. of A.? No. We get what we deserve. . . .

Katz hangs . . . precariously over a strange party that has been going on "Forever, darling. At least since the death of Bobby Kennedy. But I don't think of it as a party. It's an experiment."

Katz is talking about his novel here (although E. Pouce speaks the lines) and about life in general since 1968 when we all graduated into Sirhan Sirhan's world. His characters step out of graduation gowns into the soft ash of a civilization gone psycho. . . .

Katz has written *our War and Peace*—fractured, ignoble, farcical, bitter, incoherent.

Wier & Pouce is a rainbow of imitations of influences. Mark Harris. Hemingway. Fitzgerald. Fellini. Ken Kesey. Monty Python. Pynchon. Doctorow. Spielberg. It's like a Mensa game. How many influences can you spot? But Katz, whose writing is dense, self-referential and far too clever, still has a fire in his belly about something.

It flares up in the chapter entitled "Babebies," wherein a wonderful Italian ex-whore suffers and struggles hopelessly for dignity, and uses hero Dusty Wier as the bemused pawn in her revenge for World War II.

Elsewhere, Katz perversely defeats our interest in old-fashioned humanity and turns his novel so often at right angles to itself that he winds us into a maze of dissatisfaction and springs us from the maze with sudden grotesque evils. He does this with great glee.

Katz has one of his characters mention South American fantasists Borges and Garcia Marquez. But Katz doesn't have Borges' airy intellectual artistry, or Garcia Marquez's warm surrealism. Katz's dreams are peculiarly North American, neutron bombs. He smashes characters and feeds their children to a meat-eating lawn. His images are bludgeons. They are subreal. His novel twitches out of control. It's horrible, claustrophobic, unreadable, and quite, well, interesting, darling. Are we going to make it? Can we manage some sort of plot in this unasked for world of trashed dreams and endless battery?

Mary Pjerrou, "1985 Answer to 'War and Peace'," in Los Angeles Times Book Review, *January 6, 1985, p. 4.*

MONA SIMPSON

[The most obvious ambition of ***Wier & Pouce*** is] to deny and scramble ordinary narrative. This is a novel in which characters are named Dusty Wier, E. Pouce and Stormy, a novel that devotes a full chapter to cute permutations of the alphabet vaguely relating to the novel's characters. . . . It is very hard to distinguish Mr. Katz's motives, because his prose displays two seemingly contrary impulses—the tendency toward experimentalism, as well as absolutely stock, overblown scenes and descriptions of characters. A gang in the Bronx is, of course, "renowned for its rumbles," and the first chapter of the novel hinges on a baseball game between these bullies and the nicer team, of which Dusty is a member. If anything could save this book, it would be Mr. Katz's comic instinct, which sometimes serves him well, as when Dusty saves the day by bunting a baseball with his eye rather than the bat. However, too often the humor is sophomoric, and if the off-color jokes and scatological references had not already alienated this reader, Mr. Katz's almost amazing tolerance for triteness would.

Mona Simpson, in a review of "Wier & Pouce," in The New York Times Book Review, *March 24, 1985, p. 24.*

ALBERT MOBILIO

[In ***Weir & Pouce***] Katz chronicles the life of Dusty Wier, makeshift visionary, whose fascinations with the occult and belief in the existence of an alternative "real" planet Earth enrich this language-obsessed tale.

The novel unfolds episodically. Wier is seen in quick succession as an expatriate in Italy, unemployed denizen of the New York Public Library, and urban refugee on Cape Breton. The chronology, as you'd expect in a postmodernist saga, gets slippery—Wier's wife and kids vanish from one page to the next—but abrupt shifts in circumstance seem slight compared to changes in style and voice. Katz marshals a range of narrative techniques—traditional, surrealistic, Joycean—and deploys them in rotating chapters, making the book seem less a novel than a collection of stories. Plot is not catalytic here; Katz prefers to reveal his protagonist sentence by sentence, mirroring Wier's energetic imagination in a linguistic tour de force.

Wier & Pouce opens with a vivid evocation of New York street life in the '40s. A close baseball game between a Jewish boys club and some Upper Broadway Italian toughs is won by shy, overweight Wier. After the game, he's hiding in a storm drain that overlooks the Hudson, relishing his triumph, when he sees a beam of other-worldly light streaming between the bridge towers. Thrilled more by this than the day's heroics, he shouts, "I love you, Jimmy Piersall baseball mitt. . . . I love you bridge and I love you flying saucers. . . . I love you, rats." The sentiment—Whitman filtered through the Dead End Kids—clearly pegs Wier for a dreamer.

His college years come to us in a complex mixing of acronyms and sestina. Acronyms, drawn from the names Wier and Pouce, provide telegraphic distillations of these schoolmate adversaries: "*W*ad *I*mpatient *E*ating *R*affle & *P*anoramic *O*bverse *U*glification *C*acodyl *E*mbower." Fantasist Wier is well served by the conceit because it builds on the earlier portrait, whereas Pouce emerges unclear and insubstantial. Not only does the trickery muddle Pouce's introduction, but Katz's choice of increasingly difficult words makes the game seem forced. . . .

Ever versatile, Katz celebrates and satirizes the '60s in his surrealistic chapter, "The Death of Bobby Kennedy." Wier attends a bizarre Carib isle party thrown by Pouce—a spectacle inspired in equal parts by Lautréamont and psilocybin. Lawns devour children, caterpillars nesting in Wier's mouth emerge as butterflies when he speaks, Pouce cuts off his ear and force-feeds it to his ex-wife.

Shared billing notwithstanding, Pouce remains peripheral: a sideshow of exaggerated greed and cartoon violence. . . . Although Wier's dreams are staged in lush detail, he is an intellectually static figure in what passes for a coming-of-age novel. His rites of passage—sandlot baseball to rural commune—simply serve as points of departure for stylistic improvisation. Katz, while feigning the formal requirements of the genre, subverts its operative principle: he misses the causal link between experience and imaginative virtuosity. If Wier's stunted development deliberately short-circuits stock expectations, it also confines the character completely to the page as a bit of fictive handiwork. Nevertheless, the performance can dazzle. In the final scene, that vision above the Hudson is recalled: Wier stands at bat and watches a softball soar across the sky and assume the shape of the moon. Katz brings us full circle to assert his belief in the primacy of pure invention, a quality this novel displays in abundance.

Albert Mobilio, in a review of "Weir & Pouce," in VLS, *No. 34, April, 1985, p. 3.*

BOB HALLIDAY

No reader should be misled by the title of Steve Katz's new novel into dismissing it as a whimsical exercise in wordplay. ***Wier & Pouce*** is a work of power and imagination as arresting as anything which has appeared during the past several years. And although Katz has packed the book with acknowledging allusions to the novels and films that have influenced him, it is completely original. No other book comes to mind that resembles it at all.

The content of ***Wier & Pouce*** defies summarization, but the Tolstoyan pun of the title hints at the design which underlies the fantastic dovetailing of its many plots. The names belong to the two men around whom most of the action of the novel's seven sections centers. Both have strong personalities which Katz projects vigorously: Dusty Wier the decent guy and resourceful Everyman, the type who survives disasters and permits the species to keep on a peaceful footing most of the time; E. Pouce the embodiment of irrational, unmotivated evil who delights in destruction.

Wier and Pouce first meet in college, and Katz signals the importance of the episode by decking it out in a gaudy and deliberately artificial style based on permutations of the letters in their names. But this eruption subsides into an account of Wier's marriage to his college sweetheart Olivia and of his attempt to set up housekeeping for her in the small southern Italian town of Lecce, all told in an evocative style full of humor and compassion.

But not for long. Katz addresses the reader directly:

> Dear Reader: I never expected, nor did I ever desire, to say 'dear reader' again, but here I must beg your indulgence just one more time . . . The story of Dusty and his family broke up. The story of Dusty losing the woman he loved so bad . . . because fellas and girls, let me tell you this, some sweetest things is begun with a kiss; but when it's over, she's away and gone, it feels like your heart's shaved down to the bone. . . .

Dusty's agony of loneliness is then related in a relaxed version of Walter Abish's *Alphabetical Africa* style. . . .

This is the book's last fit of pure style, and also the end of its first, primarily realistic part. After the destruction of Dusty's home, Pouce-like irrationality gets the upper hand and straightforward narrative yields to a strange mix of fantasy and surrealism. The specific facts of the characters' lives shift and blur, until Wier and Pouce come to seem like characters in some huge, Bosch-grotesque folktale, embodying the sustaining and the destructive aspects of human nature.

When Dusty next appears, he seems never to have experienced either his marriage or the episode in southern Italy. Later, when a garrulous reader seated next to him in the New York Public Library bends his ear with tales of experiences in Lecce, it appears evident that Dusty has never been there, and the reader gets the strange sensation of this experience having been transferred to the talker like a forgotten garment. Pouce also undergoes a transformation. After losing most of his face in an accident, he becomes an elusive, phantasmal figure who conceives and realizes destructive projects on an apocalyptic scale, and there are intimations that he may actually be some projected dark aspect of Dusty's mind.

The latter half of ***Wier & Pouce*** incorporates dozens of interlocking tales, many of which are astonishingly imaginative and have the aura of dreams. One character discovers he can walk straight through a wall of his apartment because it is made up of millions of tiny blue-eyed bats, each holding captive the soul of one New Yorker. . . . Katz's writing matches the material in inventiveness—in one section he sustains three levels of narrative at once—but his phantasmagoria is carefully organized, and its many strands reunite at the novel's visionary conclusion.

With a book as striking as this, it is tempting to play the book reviewer's game of comparisons (''Reads like *Maldoror* rewritten by Ernie Kovacs''), but that won't do here, especially since Katz is so diligent about citing the predecents himself. At one particularly Garcia Márquez-like juncture, a woman has a realization: ''Now she understood the damn novel into which her life had been diverted; one of those trippy South American books, written from a position of privilege and political apathy . . .'' When all of the people who have figured in Dusty's life reassemble in Nova Scotia for a softball game at the novel's conclusion, a character points up the similarity to *8½* with the observation, ''Sometimes I feel like we live in a movie by Fellini.'' Nods are also given in the direction of Thomas Pynchon's *V* in ***Wier & Pouce***'s very last sentence, to Berg's *Wozzeck* in the unresolved catastrophe of its final pages.

Despite its complexity, ***Wier & Pouce*** is vastly readable. . . . Katz's sympathy for his characters gives it an emotional wallop of the type rarely found in fiction as determinedly anti-realistic as this, and once finished, it clings to the mind.

Bob Halliday, ''Meetings by Chance,'' in Book World—The Washington Post, *April 7, 1985, p. 9.*

BRIAN McHALE

[Katz] deliberately wastes the well-made short story, leaving behind him something just as satisfying, at its best, though a good deal harder to describe. Some of Katz's ***Stolen Stories*** in fact travesty the well-made story; they are *too* well made, fitting together with a derisively audible click. Of these, my favorite is **''Death of the Band,''** a parody of a detective story—the well-made genre *par excellence* . . . : the story opens with gunfire, as the composer Peter Glucks kills off his band in a gesture of musical innovation, and we wait expectantly for the reprise which, sure enough, arrives on the last page. Click. Other Katz stories stray farther from the beaten paths of story-writing, to the point where they seem no longer to bear any relation, not even a negative or parodic one, to familiar short-story economies. Deliberate *misfires,* these stories may please us, but without our being able to say *why* they do so. **''Mongolian Whiskey,''** for example, seems to be a parable of the sad fate of the sixties generation, its subsidence into consumerism, dog-eat-dog mutual exploitation, and kinky self-indulgence, all neatly symbolized here in the Gothic motif of cannibalism (literally dog-eat-dog). But if this is so, what accounts for the presence in **''Mongolian Whiskey''** of talking animals—a dog, a cockroach, even a stuffed owl—never explained, motivated, or even *used* in the course of the story, never, in other words, integrated in its internal economy. And what about the ending, a screwy vision of the Afterlife as a heaven populated by dogs—what is this, Walt Disney? You could, if you wanted to, show how the doggy heaven recycles the talking dog motif of the story's opening, thus giving it a form of closure; you *could,* but I don't see where that would get you, or how it would make any better sense of the mysterious coexistence of materials in this story. No, if **''Mongolian Whiskey''** is a ''satisfying story'' (the title that Katz gave to some of the texts in his earlier collection, ***Creamy & Delicious,*** 1970), its satisfactions are not those of tidiness and closure, not those of a well-made story.

Donald Barthelme, in an interview from 1980, speaks of his fondness for what he calls the ''backbroke sentence,'' one that is ''clearly clumsy but preparing itself for greatness of a kind.'' Now a sentence, as a number of people have surmised, is a sort of micro-narrative—or vice-versa, a narrative is a kind of macro-sentence—so the backbroke sentence can be seen as the equivalent, at the micro level, of backbroke stories like **''Mongolian Whiskey,''** an ill-made short story shrunk to sentence size. Barthelme himself, of course, is a master of this type of sentence, but so is Katz, and a number of the texts in ***Stolen Stories***—mostly the shorter ones, some of which Katz calls ''essays,'' but also **''The Perfect Life,''** one of the longer ones—are actually strings, or maybe just accumulations, of backbroke sentences. The effect is that of sliding around on a varnished dance-floor of language, skating from one small linguistic stupidity to another without ever being able to regain one's balance or arrest the forward skid. . . .

So these mostly *are* satisfying stories, one way or another—except the title-story, perhaps, which I confess escapes me. Something here refuses to be brought into focus. Maybe I could have focused it better if I had read it in a different context, that of Katz's novel ***Wier & Pouce***—a context spacious enough, and spacey enough, to have absorbed **''The Stolen Stories''** and almost anything else, for that matter. Like **''The Stolen Stories,''** ***Wier & Pouce*** is a kind of umbrella-story or meta-story, a story *of* stories. Stories pour down on Dusty Wier's head, or pour *out* of his head: real-life stories, fantastic stories, lying stories (''I don't believe in ruining a good story by telling the truth,'' says one good storyteller), stories about stories, stories within stories, stories that get in the way of other stories. Most of them are unfinished, pointless, or otherwise backbroke. Some of them Wier himself lives through; others belong to his life-story but are told to him as though they had happened to someone else—stolen stories, in short.

Sounds a little loose and untidy? maybe *too* untidy to qualify as a ''novel'' at all? The thing is, of course, that novels *are* untidy, by definition. ''Large loose baggy monsters,'' Henry James called the novels of his Victorian predecessors, and he thought he was putting them down. But *all* novels are more or less large, loose, baggy, and monstrous, not least of all the ones that Henry James himself wrote. . . . (p. 17)

As monsters go, ***Wier & Pouce*** is pretty baggy. Not only baggy, but a mixed bag. Some episodes give us all the familiar delights of capital-R Realism: the truth about an experience, told with all the honesty the author can muster, the sound of a language that people really use, the look and feel of a definite time and place—a provincial town in Italy, Cape Breton, New York City neighborhoods in the early fifties, the New York Public Library. Other episodes take off into implausibilities or the wild blue yonder of the fantastic: a cannibalistic lawn ingests a group of children, a manic plutocrat napalms his own house-party, a merchant sailor obsessed with bats spreads his wings and flies away, giants are sighted in offshore waters. . . . Katz even tries his hand at the sort of inorganic, function-follows-form fiction that Walter Abish and Kenneth Gangemi write, surrendering control of his story to the arbitrariness of language, letting it "be anonymous as the breeze of alphabets." These are not his most satisfying chapters; somehow they lack the tension, the edginess, that Abish manages to generate from his close encounters with the Signifier.

I don't want to give the impression that *nothing* holds ***Wier & Pouce*** together. For one thing, there are the title-characters themselves, threads on which to string the pearls of story: Dusty Wier, our Everyman of the late twentieth century, groping his way through the present, holding himself open to the future, and trying not to regret the past too much; and E. Pouce, Wier's college buddy and evil double, later on reduced to a "talking skull." Pouce obviously belongs to a different sort of fiction from Wier; he's Hyde to Wier's Jekyll, the Wicked Witch of the West to Wier's Dorothy—Svengali, Dracula, Goldfinger, every horror-movie bad-guy that Vincent Price ever played; larger than life, where Wier is as close to life-size as Katz can make him.

Apart from Wier and Pouce themselves, the other strands that tie this novel together read more like *parodies* of unity than the real thing. Take leitmotifs, for instance, that old favorite of academic unity-hounds everywhere. Katz gives us the motif of *bats*—bats as in baseball, bats as in winged rodents, bat as a three-letter word . . . and it's hard not to see this as a joke at the expense of the idea of leitmotifs. Similarly, Katz stages one of those Class or Family Reunions where all the characters gather one last time near the close of the book to tie up loose ends, like that big final *soirée* in Proust—except that this one is too transparently implausible, too obviously *staged,* to be anything but a parody of Tying Up Loose Ends.

So maybe ***Wier & Pouce*** is not a novel after all, but only a "novel"—that is, a novel only because that's what it advertises itself to be, and only to the degree that we accept its own self-description. If so, then all novels are really only "novels," in the final analysis. For the novel (unlike the short story) doesn't really exist at all; Katz, like Pynchon, and like Henry James and all the others before them, had to make it up as he went along. (pp. 17-18)

Brian McHale, "Unmaking the Well-Made Short Story/Making Up the Novel," in The American Book Review, *Vol. 8, No. 1, November-December, 1985, pp. 16-18.*

JESSICA AMANDA SALMONSON

Katz's stories [in ***Stolen Stories***] are populated by over-the-hill hippies but are by no means an homage to the wonderful '60s. These tales tease and deplore. They are extremely vulgar and intelligent. The themes, on the surface, concern adolescent men's obsessions, but the depth of awareness and the cruel whimsy renders such themes sparkling, imaginative, and psychologically complex. **"Friendship,"** about a cannibal girlfriend, could have been gynophobic and misogynist, but in Katz's hands is a fable of confusion in the sexual revolution. A friend of this bizarre pair of lovebirds tries to accept their relationship even while his happy, fulfilled chum vanishes piecemeal. It's as gross as Stephen King's "Survivor Type" but has, in addition, a genuine wisdom. A second cannibal story is **"Mongolian Whiskey,"** which includes one of the funniest unspoken puns (give the dog a bone) literature has ever implied. Again, it might well have been a grown adolescent's story revealing a castration complex. Instead, it's wickedly, almost intellectually, funny. The tale is also classically magic-realist, since only our doomed hero seems to notice the commentaries of a talking dog, cockroach, and stuffed owl. Is he hallucinating? His tendency to think of the past hints of a burnt-out druggy with LSD flashbacks. But no, this is real; the hysterical adventures immediately after his death say it all.

There are stories such as **"Two Seaside Yarns"** that would have been more appropriate to Katz's earlier collection, ***Moving Parts,*** where crazed surrealism borders on silliness. For the most part ***Stolen Stories*** [contains] sophisticated and well-developed modern fantasies with, perhaps, special appeal to anyone tired of fiction that waxes nostalgic over the 1960s, and is after something more jaded and true. (p. 24)

Jessica Amanda Salmonson, "Three Magic Realists," in Fantasy Review, *Vol. 9, No. 2, February, 1986, pp. 24-5.*

John (Edward) Masefield

1878-1967

English poet, novelist, short story writer, autobiographer, dramatist, nonfiction writer, critic, and author of children's books.

The Poet Laureate of England from 1930 until his death in 1967, Masefield is considered one of the leading transitional figures between the Victorian and Georgian periods of English literature. Masefield achieved notoriety early in the twentieth century with his first extended verse narrative, *The Everlasting Mercy* (1911), in which he employs violent action and vulgar language to depict the attitudes and manners of England's rural communities. This work proved enormously controversial, sparking heated debates between legions of critics who either perceived Masefield to be resuscitating poetry or debasing it, and established him as a popular writer gifted with humanitarian insight. In other poems, Masefield displayed his affinity for the work of Geoffrey Chaucer, adopting the narrative technique of *The Canterbury Tales* for *Reynard the Fox; or, The Ghost Heath Run* (1919) as well as composing *The Widow in the Bye Street* (1912) and *Dauber* (1913) in rhyme royal, a stanzaic pattern popularized by Chaucer. A prolific author in several genres, Masefield focused much of his writing on the sea and rural life to convey his sympathetic response to the working class and his reverence for all aspects of natural beauty. Contemporary appreciation of Masefield's work is varied; while conceding that his poetry is often uneven and careless, many critics praise the vitality of his language and his realistic depictions of commonplace characters and events.

Photograph by Mark Gerson

Orphaned as a youth, Masefield ended his formal education at the age of thirteen in order to pursue a career as a sailor. In 1895, he sailed to New York, where he held a succession of odd jobs and renewed his early interest in poetry. Upon returning to England shortly thereafter, Masefield worked as a journalist and a bank clerk before becoming acquainted with such prominent members of the Irish Renaissance as William Butler Yeats, John Millington Synge, and Lady Augusta Gregory. Masefield's first two volumes of poetry, *Salt-Water Ballads* (1902) and *Ballads* (1903), display a heavy Yeatsian influence tempered by use of realistic diction and subject matter and avoidance of symbolism. After several more collections which were moderate critical and popular successes, *The Everlasting Mercy* solidified Masefield's reputation as a significant poet and remains one of his most popular works. This long narrative poem centers on Saul Kane, a ruffian who is eventually reformed through his conversion to Christianity. The enthusiastic public response to *The Everlasting Mercy* helped save *The English Review*—the magazine in which the poem originally appeared—from financial ruin.

The Widow in the Bye Street, Masefield's next extended narrative poem, derives its story and form from Chaucer's "The Prioress's Tale." Composed in the rhyme royal scheme of seven iambic pentameter lines, *The Widow in the Bye Street* concerns an impoverished widow and her son, Jimmy, upon whom fate acts adversely. *Dauber,* first printed in *The English Review* and subsequently published in *The Story of a Round-House and Other Poems* (1912), is unique among Masefield's narrative poetry in its use of symbolism and allegory. Set aboard a sailing vessel, *Dauber* is noted for Masefield's accurate and vivid descriptions of life at sea as well as its themes of human alienation and artistic impulse. Perhaps the most critically successful of Masefield's longer verse was *Reynard the Fox,* a recounting of a fox hunt that is admired for its rich characterization of the hunters and its suspenseful story. Masefield's other extended pieces, including *The Daffodil Fields* (1913), *Enslaved* (1920), *Right Royal* (1920), and *King Cole* (1921), are generally considered of lesser quality than his earlier works. In 1930, Masefield was appointed Poet Laureate of England, and his subsequent poetry reflects in its topical nature his commitment to this position. During his tenure, Masefield was awarded several literary prizes and received many honorary degrees from Great Britain's most prestigious universities. While his reputation has declined since his death, Masefield is credited with having revived narrative verse in the twentieth century.

Masefield is also recognized for his accomplishments in other literary genres. Many of his verse dramas, including *Philip the King* (1914) and *Good Friday* (1916), center on religious and biblical themes. Masefield's prose plays, of which *The Tragedy of Nan* (1908) is the most popular, are characterized by his moral concerns and sentimentalism. In these and other theatrical works, among them *The Faithful* (1915) and *The Trial of Jesus* (1927), Masefield is credited with introducing elements of Japanese Noh and Kabuki drama to Western audiences.

Masefield also wrote more than a dozen prose works, including the short story collection *A Mainsail Haul* (1905) and the novel *Captain Margaret* (1908), both of which draw upon his experiences at sea.

(See also *CLC,* Vol. 11; *Contemporary Authors,* Vols. 19-20, Vols. 25-28, rev. ed. [obituary]; *Contemporary Authors Permanent Series,* Vol. 2; *Something about the Author,* Vol. 19; and *Dictionary of Literary Biography,* Vols. 10, 19.)

ROBERT SHAFER

Mr. Masefield must be set down as fundamentally pessimistic. There are bright spots in his work, of course, and many of them, but through it all there runs a dark thread, and at times the sinister aspects of life among the poor seem to have overpowered him. This is specially true of ***The Widow in the Bye Street*** and ***Dauber,*** his latest long narrative poem. This pessimistic outlook is evident not alone in Mr. Masefield's poetical work, but also in his plays, as any one will know who has read ***The Tragedy of Nan,*** which ends with a murder, a ptomaine poisoning, and a suicide.

Indeed, one cannot help but feel that Mr. Masefield, with his vivid sensitiveness to human suffering and misery, has let himself be carried away into, if not real untruthfulness, at least a certain misrepresentation. For we all know that the great mass of common working-folk do live; somehow or other they manage to get along, and even have the time and inclination for a considerable amount of loving, and hating, and marrying, and having children—especially having children, one sometimes thinks. And yet—and yet!—if their life really seemed to them the thing Mr. Masefield makes it out to be, I cannot help suspecting that they would all of them, long ere this, have rushed to the river and drowned themselves, even as did Mr. Max Beerbohm's odd thousands of Oxford undergraduates. Do not suppose that I am presuming exactly to condemn this pessimism, I wish merely to point the thing out with sufficient clearness. It seems, indeed, to possess certain fine and manly qualities—it has the elements of true impressiveness clinging darkly around it, and it has the supreme merit of being unmistakably sincere. Mr. Masefield's poetry is the work of a man who has known thoroughly that whereof he writes. We may not like it altogether, but we cannot fail of recognizing the noble truthfulness and deep seriousness of ***The Everlasting Mercy*** and of ***Dauber.*** That exaltation of the dime-novel *genre* which he gave us in ***The Widow in the Bye Street*** is a thing to forget rather than to censure.

Mr. Masefield's best work was done in ***The Everlasting Mercy*** and in a few short ballads of the sea which were published in London several years ago; these smaller poems have lately been reprinted with some additions in the American edition of ***Dauber,*** under the general title, ***The Story of a Round-House.*** In ***The Everlasting Mercy,*** Mr. Masefield gave us a representation of vital, red-blooded life that is palpitating with actual energy from start to finish, in its glories and in its debasement, in its spiritual exaltation as well as in its drunken frenzies. Saul Kane, reeling drunk, stripped naked, and ringing the fire-bell at dead of night as a herald of the coming of the devil to claim his own among the villagers, makes an image never to be forgotten, hardly to be surpassed in all its rude vigor and native strength. It is not quite enough to say that Mr. Masefield is the poet of Life: he is at the same time more, and less, than that—he is the poet of Common Life. (p. 493)

Mr. Masefield's song is rather a shout—the shout of one who has but just come from that of which he speaks, with the rudeness and exhilaration of actuality yet clinging about him. . . . There is much in the quality of Mr. Masefield's work that in certain minds compels immediate enthusiasm, but I suspect that, in the long run, . . . Mr. Masefield will be merely endured. (p. 495)

Robert Shafer, "Two of the Newest Poets," in The Atlantic Monthly, *Vol. 111, No. 4, April, 1913, pp. 489-95.*

GILBERT THOMAS

[When] Mr. Masefield's poem, ***The Everlasting Mercy,*** appeared in the pages of a contemporary, the water in the kettle of controversy began at once to bubble uneasily. A few critics rushed forth to place Mr. Masefield upon a pedestal the height of which must have made him dizzy; but many others came armed with sword and shield against him, denying him any claim whatever to the title of poet. The eternal question as to what does and does not constitute poetry was dragged forth again into the critical market-place, and for many weeks a none too dignified warfare was waged around it with somewhat blunt and rusty weapons. (p. 142)

Once more, however, the captains and the kings of controversy have departed into the oblivion of the newspaper files, and the poetry of Mr. Masefield remains. Now, therefore, that the air is a little cleared and cooled, it may not be uninteresting to attempt a reconsideration of the three long poems with which Mr. Masefield has entered into the public eye, especially in their relation to the new movement in poetry of which they are such admirable examples. And, to begin with, the main thing to be observed about this new movement as illustrated by Mr. Masefield's work is not the fact that poetry has succeeded in breaking away from such firmly-rooted traditions at all, but that it has completely, with one indomitable outburst of determination, so that it will never be possible again for that old bondage to reclaim it. Until recently poetry was content, as a general rule, to gather her grain where that grain was apparent and easily to be gathered. Now, however, she is wakening to the realization that it is no less her purpose to seek the grain in, and to winnow it from, the chaff. She has learnt that, the human soul being a more complicated affair than even she had suspected, the finest grain is often mingled with the coarsest chaff; and she is resolved that there is no aspect of human life or thought or emotion, there is no field, however forbidding in appearance (and how typically Victorian were the nineteenth-century poets in their attitude towards appearances!) that shall escape her threshing machine. In a word, she will not hesitate to trail her garments in the thickest dust, if so be that from that dust she may redeem some smallest gem.

The danger of the new movement will at once be apparent. The danger is that, while the true poet will delve in the dust for the sake of the gem, the false poet, who is always with us, will take the opportunities thus opened to him for plying his muck-rake in the dust for the sake of the dust itself. The danger is a real one, and it will have to be faced. But, after all, it is not so great as might at first sight be imagined. . . . Unfortunately, Mr. Masefield himself, in two at least of his three poems, falls a prey now and then to the obvious temptation. He is not always content with getting to the naked heart of things, as it is of the essence of his purpose to do; and occasionally he gives us, in consequence, touches of inexcusable coarseness, which will bring the blush to modest cheeks. Such infringements of reasonable restraint are, however, rare; and the fact remains that when everything has been said that can be said in demerit of Mr. Masefield—and in passing it must be added that he sometimes falls into an unmusical slough of despond—his poetry triumphs over it all, and triumphs conspicuously well. . . . Mr. Masefield shows us here and there the pitfalls which beset the new movement; but his work, taken as a whole, is sterling proof of what the new movement is capable of achieving.

Take, for instance, ***The Widow in the Bye-Street,*** which, though withheld for some time from publication, was the first of the three poems to be written. . . . Mr. Masefield has, let it be admitted, a slight tendency to caricature: but in its essence his story is true, and is one of no uncommon occurrence. It is one, however, which the Victorian poets would have regarded with dismay, and would have relegated to a place quite outside the pale of art. They might have been a little more generously disposed towards ***Dauber,*** which relates the history of a farmer's son, who, seized with a passionate ambition to paint the sea, embarks upon a vessel as ship's painter with a view to study the ocean "from the inside." (pp. 142-44)

[By Mr. Masefield's] daring in choosing a story outwardly repulsive, but nevertheless uncommonly rich in those elements of humanity and sympathy and dramatic irony—the grain which is the purpose of the true poetry to gather—but also by his equal daring in his method of treating the story, Mr. Masefield reaps a harvest infinitely greater than any that was ever capable of being reaped by the more exclusive and tenderly guarded Muse of the preceding generation. Both in ***The Widow in the Bye-Street*** and in ***Dauber,*** whole systems of nerves in the great and complicated organism of the soul which have hitherto lain unresponsive tingle into life; and surely the means is justified by the end.

But it is [in] ***The Everlasting Mercy*** that we see the supreme fruit thus far of the new movement. In ***The Widow in the Bye-Street*** and ***Dauber,*** Mr. Masefield has given us "remarkable" poems, which are destined to live as such; but in ***The Everlasting Mercy*** he has given us "a great" poem. . . . But not only does Mr. Masefield here show us how every ounce of gold may be extracted from the dust, but he shows us how the very dust itself may be transformed into gold. He takes the coarsest threads of realism and weaves them through some magician's loom into the finest fabric of spirituality. His story is only the story that may be heard at any street-corner where the Salvation Army musters. The man in the street, however, only sees the outward and cruder aspects of the change that often comes suddenly into a fellow-man's life, transforming it from evil into good. But Mr. Masefield, with true poetic genius, sees the inside; and what has been a matter for mild ridicule, sometimes upon the part even of the most cultured, he lifts upon the wings of interpretation into a thing of ethereal beauty. (p. 146)

[Where] in the whole of literature will you find more admirably captured than in the closing pages of ***The Everlasting Mercy*** the emotions of a man who had suddenly felt something "break inside his brain," and who knows that the past with all its shame and horror has for ever fallen from him, as he goes forth along the open road, while through the mist the sun comes up with the infinite promise of a new day, and the sound of an early plough upon the hillside, and the song of the first lark soaring into the silent heavens, and even the very noise of a railway engine shunting, are blended into one glorious symphony of regeneration?

And if it be another test of true poetry that sends the reader out along life's common road, refreshed and with new hope towards the dawn, then by this test also the author of ***The Everlasting Mercy*** is a great poet; and surely it is time that those critics who would deny to such vital literature its rightful honors should pull down their narrow barns of vision, and build greater.

In considering Mr. Masefield's work as it interprets the motives and methods of the new movement in poetry, it has been necessary to omit a consideration of certain of Mr. Masefield's more individualistic features. Much might be said, for instance, of the unrivalled passages of pastoral poetry which ***The Widow in the Bye-Street*** contains, or of the equally unrivalled manner in which in ***Dauber*** Mr. Masefield captures the spirit of the sea, which he knows and understands probably better than any man living. (pp. 147-48)

Mr. Masefield's success is due to the fact that there has been a large public eagerly hungry for poetry, but a public not willing to be beguiled by the drawing-room melodizings or the artificial extravagances which are all that recent years have had to offer. There has been a large public impatient for a poet who should prove his art to be not merely artifice, but something robust and something vital in its relation to life; and it is an encouraging sign that now that poet has arrived he has not come unregarded. (p. 148)

Gilbert Thomas, "Mr. Masefield's Poetry," in The Living Age, *Vol. CCLXXVIII, No. 3602, July 19, 1913, pp. 141-48.*

WILLIAM LYON PHELPS

In subject-matter and in language [John Masefield] is not in the least "traditional," not at all Victorian; he is wholly modern, new, contemporary. Yet while he draws his themes and his heroes from his own experience, his inspiration as a poet comes directly from Chaucer, who died in 1400. He is, indeed, the Chaucer of to-day; the most closely akin to Chaucer—not only in temperament, but in literary manner—of all the writers of the twentieth-century. The beautiful metrical form that Chaucer invented—rime royal—ideally adapted for narrative poetry, as shown in *Troilus and Criseyde,* is the metre chosen by John Masefield for ***The Widow in the Bye Street*** and for ***Dauber;*** the only divergence in ***The Daffodil Fields*** consisting in the lengthening of the seventh line of the stanza, for which he had plenty of precedents. Mr. Masefield owes more to Chaucer than to any other poet. (p. 428)

[***The Widow in the Bye Street***] is one of the best narrative poems in modern literature. It rises from calm to the fiercest and most tumultuous passions that usurp the throne of reason. Love, jealousy, hate, revenge, murder succeed in cumulative force. Then the calm of unmitigated and hopeless woe returns, and we leave the widow in a solitude peopled only with memories. It is melodrama elevated into poetry. The mastery of the artist is shown in the skill with which he avoids the quagmire of sentimentality. We can easily imagine what form this story would take under the treatment of many popular writers. But although constantly approaching the verge, Mr. Masefield never falls in. (p. 432)

No poet, with any claim to the name, can be accurately labelled by an adjective or a phrase. You may think you know his "manner," and he suddenly develops a different one; this you call his "later" manner, and he disconcerts you by harking back to the "earlier," or trying something, that if you must have labels, you are forced to call his "latest," knowing now that it is subject to change without notice. Mr. Masefield published ***The Everlasting Mercy*** in 1911; ***The Widow in the Bye Street*** in 1912; ***Dauber*** in 1912; ***The Daffodil Fields*** in 1913. We had him classified. He was a writer of sustained narrative, unscrupulous in the use of language, bursting with vitality, sacrificing anything and everything that stood in the way of his effect. This was "red blood" verse raised to poetry by sheer inspiration, backed by remarkable skill in the use of rime. We looked for more of the same thing from him, knowing that in this particular field he had no rival.

Then came the war. As every soldier drew his sword, every poet drew his pen. And of all the poems published in the early days of the struggle, none equalled in high excellence **"August 1914,"** by John Masefield. And its tone was precisely the opposite of what his most famous efforts had led us to expect. It was not a lurid picture of wholesale murder, nor a bottle of vitriol thrown in the face of the Kaiser. After the thunder and the lightning, came the still small voice. It is a poem in the metre and manner of Gray, with the same silver tones of twilit peace—heartrending by contrast with the Continental scene. It is the only poem thus far written about the war which I feel certain will survive. (p. 435)

What has Mr. Masefield done then for the advance of poetry? One of his notable services is to have made it so interesting that thousands look forward to a new poem from him as readers look for a new story by a great novelist. He has helped to take away poetry from its conventional "elevation" and bring it everywhere poignantly in contact with throbbing life. Thus he is emphatically apart from so-called traditional poets like Stephen Phillips, William Watson, and Alfred Noyes, who brilliantly follow the Tennysonian tradition, and give us another kind of enjoyment. But although Mr. Masefield is a twentieth century poet, it would be a mistake to suppose that he has *originated* the doctrine that the poet should speak in a natural voice about natural things, and not cultivate a "diction." . . . Mr. Masefield is a mighty force in the renewal of poetry; in the art of dramatic narrative he goes back to the sincerity and catholicity of Chaucer. For his language, he has carried Wordsworth's idea of "naturalness" to its extreme limits. For his material, he finds nothing common or unclean. But all his virility, candour, and sympathy, backed by all his astonishing range of experience, would not have made him a poet, had he not possessed imagination, and the power to express his vision of life, the power, as he puts it, of getting the apples back into the cart. (p. 437)

William Lyon Phelps, "The Advance of English Poetry in the Twentieth Century," in The Bookman, *New York, Vol. XLVI, No. 4, December, 1917, pp. 428-37.*

CONRAD AIKEN

The hasty critic who, when ***Good Friday*** was published, lamented that book as final proof of the decline of Mr. Masefield, meets something of a poser in ***Lollingdon Downs.*** Mr. Masefield is of that type of creative artist which is most distressing to the critic with a mania for classifying: he will not remain classified; he is for ever in a process of evolution. This is indeed the highest compliment that could be paid him. It is not every poet who is capable of growth and change of a creative sort. (p. 149)

If we look back on his career as poet, we see a perspective of ceaseless change. His first mood, in ***Ballads and Poems*** was unreflectingly, colourfully lyric: he was preoccupied with sensuous beauty, and with its transience, in the romantic tradition. In the group of novels which followed, we see a steady shifting of the attention away from the merely romantic, or decorative, and toward the real and human. The romantic attitude is not eliminated, to be sure; one feels here as later in the four long narrative poems which gave Mr. Masefield his greatest success, that though the material is often rudely naturalistic, it is still being used to an essentially romantic end. It is the romance of the realistic, of the crude and violent; it is romantic because it is always seen against a background of permanence and beauty. This use of the realistic element, the vigour of the commonplace, reached its height in ***The Everlasting Mercy, The Widow in the Bye Street,*** and ***Dauber.*** In ***The Daffodil Fields,*** which followed, one perceives the next change,—a distinct relenting of the naturalistic mood, a softening of both material and technique nearly to the point of sentimentalism. The hunger for hardness and virility having been satisfied in a brief and magnificant debauch, Mr. Masefield returned to his more natural taste for the sensuous and lyric. The poetic plays which followed were further developments of this. In spirit they are closely akin to the three later poetic narratives: the motive force, the emotional compulsion, is an almost obsessive feeling for the tragic futility of man's endeavour in the face of an outrageous and apparently unreasoning fate. At this everlasting door, Mr. Masefield says in effect, we beat in vain. One perceives in Mr. Masefield, as he says this, an almost pathetic bewilderment that it should be so,—but a bewilderment which has not yet reached the intensity of interrogation or rebellion. This point was finally reached in the sonnet series which composed the greater part of ***Good Friday.*** In these one gets a blind and troubled searching for spiritual comfort, a cry for some sort of assurance that beauty is more than a merely transient and relative thing. The tone at its best is tragic, at its worst querulous. The oracle is dumb, however, and Mr. Masefield implies, though he does not state (and in spite, too, of his passionate adherence to Beauty), that the silence is negative.

In short Mr. Masefield's evolution as a poet has been cyclic—it has revolved through many changes, but always about one centre. This centre, which has been at times obscured, and of which Mr. Masefield himself, like most poets, has been perhaps partially unconscious up to the present, is essentially romantic: it is clearly in the tradition of that romanticism which consists in a pagan love of beauty, on the one hand, and a profound despair at its impermanence and relativity, on the other. The sonnets in ***Good Friday*** showed us that Mr. Masefield had become partly aware that this particular emotional well was the feeding spring of his whole nature: it was his first attempt to dip directly from the source. Now, in ***Lollingdon Downs,*** he has completed this process. The echo of personal complaint which hung over the former work is practically eliminated. Mr. Masefield has seen himself in a detached way, as he might see a reflection; the tone has become one of calm and resignation; like Meredith he has managed a certain degree of objectivism and can accord without undue desolation when Meredith exclaims

Ah what a dusty answer gets the soul
When hot for certainties in this our life!

This volume has a singular and intriguing unity, a unity broken up by interludes and by a succession of changes in the angle of approach, and in time and place. The effect is that of a several-voiced music. It is panoramic, rich in perspective,—passing all the way from lyric and reflective sonnets to terse poetic dialogues and narrative lyric almost ugly in its bareness. It would be idle to pretend that Mr. Masefield is a philospher. He is not intellectual except in the sense that he is tortured by an intellectual issue; he is neither subtle nor profound. But he feels this issue intensely, and even more than usual he strikes music and beauty from it. On the technical side he has few superiors in power to write richly, richly not merely from the imaginative point of view, but also from the melodic. He modulates vowels with great skill; he knows how to temper sensuousness with vigour. Best of all, he is preeminently Anglo-Saxon in his speech. (pp. 150-54)

Conrad Aiken, "A Note on the Evolution of a Poet: John Masefield," in his Scepticisms: Notes on Contemporary Poetry, *Alfred A. Knopf, 1919, pp. 149-54.*

EDWARD DAVISON

Masefield's position in the gallery of contemporary English literature has been secure these ten years. The publication, before the war, of ***The Everlasting Mercy*** . . . marked a period in modern literary history. For this poem began the definite reaction against that thin and spiritless Parnassian type of verse which had survived Edwardian times from the naughty nineties. In it Masefield called a new tune which Rupert Brooke (particularly in his sonnet about Helen of Troy) and others, hastened in some respects to imitate. In short, he made verse masculine again after more than three decades of comparative effeminacy and decadence, unbroken save for the verses of a few minor poets like W. E. Henley. This is not merely to say that Masefield reintroduced violence, ugliness, and bad language into English poetry. There is no particular virtue is such passages as

"You closhy put."
"You bloody liar."
"This is my fence."
"This is my wire."

Taken as they stand, such things are only crude and sordid, as indeed much of the author's work actually is. But they were the immediately arresting signs of the real forcefulness and virility which John Masefield brought back to English verse. In their context such passages, with which his earlier work abounds, are very often (though by no means always) effective and inoffensive. Their ugliness sometimes paves the way toward his finest pages. The reader is dragged through some such stagnant pool of doggerel so that he may appreciate all the more that ensuing time when the poet carries him away on the rising wings of his verse to the sunlit, cleansing sea. But doggerel is, after all, doggerel. At its best this method of approaching the poetic climax can be very potent. Nevertheless it is always expensive and will not bear too much repetition. A time comes when the reader begins to see himself as the victim of what is, even at its best, a not very subtle mechanical trick. All poetry, of course, in one sense, is trickery; but poetry ceases to be poetry once the trickery becomes apparent. And, excepting ***Dauber,*** Masefield's earlier narrative poems are frequently marred by the overindulgence of this sleight. The key of the verse is switched too suddenly and too often from one extreme to the other. The resulting discord is not always resolved. Then the reader, shocked and arrested by an unexpected change, is forced to smile at the resulting incongruity. Thus Masefield, more than any other notable poet of today, has been the butt of all our best parodists. For good parody is always good criticism. And the parodists have been swift to discover and stab at this most vulnerable slit in his poetic armor, and it is impossible not to admit the fairness of their criticism. The reader of ***The Everlasting Mercy, The Widow in the Bye Street,*** and ***The Daffodil Fields*** might be likened to a man who is repeatedly thrust into a dark room: each new escape dazzles him momentarily. But when his eyes grow accustomed to the light he realized that it proceeds from a sun less bright than he suspected. (pp. 6-7)

Nevertheless those poems are vivid and powerful, in more ways than one. Quite certainly ***The Everlasting Mercy*** succeeds in translating a crude experience of religious salvation into terms of poetry, although some of Saul Kane's moralising cannot be reconciled with the general quality of his character as the poet draws it in the early parts of the poem. Between the extremes of beauty and sordidness Masefield has wrought some of his very best work. He makes no attempt to intellectualize the stories of any of his narrative poems. In these, as in all his work, we may observe a certain coarseness of the poetic texture, a coarseness extending beyond the surface limits of language and theme. This proceeds partly from his rough-and-ready imagination, and partly from his technical limitations, which, for so good a poet, are undeniably considerable. Despite his narrative power and the rather urgent themes of all his longer poems, themes requiring a fairly loose verse-structure, the lines recurrently incline to fall into doggerel, something less than the jingling kind of verse which may have been necessary in many places. A certain amount of looseness (though not so much as Masefield permits himself) may be expected in the style of any narrative poet who engages in the ancient battle with realism. It is impossible for his long poems not to sag sometimes. But if one complains of Masefield's failing in this respect it is not so much because his poems sag as because they frequently do so without actual necessity. The most prolific authors are, in general, the most careless craftsmen. Masefield, one of the most prolific poets of our time, is no exception to this rule. Haste and carelessness in workmanship leave their marks all over his collected works. He has never learned the whole lesson of poetic economy.

One other characteristic fault may be noted before passing on to Masefield's compensating virtues. It can best be described as a confusion regarding the true nature of simplicity. This, primarily, is an attitude of the mind, not a mere matter of subject-matter and language. Words and meter by themselves cannot translate simplicity out of life into poetry. The compromise between pure realism and ordinary speech is one of the most difficult problems of poetry. And however much we may theorize about it, the most successful poetic practice has shown that the language of everyday life (especially when it is the everyday life of people like Saul Kane and Jimmy Gurney) is not the language of poetry until it has been rearranged and rarefied. In short, unless poetry is to be sacrificed to prosaic realism, it is necessary to modify such language as would be employed by a real Saul Kane until its poetic equivalent has been found. To do this without passing to the opposite extreme of poetic diction is not easy. Wordsworth and Blake, the authors of some of the simplest poetry falling in this category, both poets of exceptional intellectual power and masters of poetic technique, struggled unceasingly with this same problem which Masefield so often has failed to solve. . . . His realism smothers the poetry, chiefly because he conceives simplicity as a mere matter of words. He gives us, as it were, a verbal photograph of an actual event, instead of translating a spiritual experience into poetry.

These defects, however, belong mainly to his earlier narrative poems. In the whole length of ***Reynard the Fox,*** his masterpiece, there is scarcely a false note. That this should be so suggests that he is a poet whose success is governed chiefly by his subject-matter. For in the later poem, ***King Cole,*** many of the former shortcomings reappear. Again, in ***Philip the King*** and ***Good Friday,*** dramatic poems written in dialogue, we recognize the same uncertainty of characterization that has already been noted in ***The Everlasting Mercy.*** Pilate, in one play, speaks in a voice indistinguishable from that of Philip in the other. Such technical devices as the particular form supplies are not sufficiently in the author's command. He cannot speak from inside his characters. They are nothing more than two names for his own voice.

But in ***Dauber*** and ***Reynard*** Masefield gives us the rarest of his presents, really long outbursts of beautiful, vivid poetry uninterrupted by the clamors and banalities of his more raucous Muse. There is little in the story of either of these poems to encourage new expeditions into sordidness. They contain no such gratuitous realism as may be found in the earlier works. . . . It appears that Masefield is always at his best when he sets out to describe men in the heat of action. All his love of reality (not realism) and movement are poured out in these two poems. In ***The Everlasting Mercy*** nothing surpassed the description of the fight at the beginning of the poem. Even this, however, is inferior to the magnificent account of the Dauber's voyage round Cape Horn. Here, happy in his mood as in his subject-matter, Masefield gives free rein to his genius and leaves criticism gasping for breath. (pp. 8-10)

[In ***Reynard the Fox***] Masefield, definitely modeling his poem on Chaucerian lines, surpassed the best of his former work. All the sounds and sights of the typical English meet, set in the loveliest countryside, are imbedded in his rapidly moving, sketchy verse. . . . The poem opens with a catalogue of characters comparing very favorably with the Chaucerian prologue from which it patently derives. But Masefield is no slavish imitator. If he takes the ready-made pattern it is not because he lacks matter and originality to weave it in his own way. The fox has even more character than the men and women who ride to the hunt. . . . There is no more exciting story in modern literature than the story of the Ghost Heath Run. Siegfried Sassoon, the poet, a great huntsman, once told the present writer that Masefield's account of the chase in this poem, through all its exhaustive particulars, is faultlessly accurate. Here at last the poet has achieved realism without sacrificing poetry by the way. He ensnares all our sympathies for Reynard without antagonizing us against the hunters. It was a great inspiration to introduce a second fox to cross the scent and divert the pack from its original quarry before the end of the chase. When the death cry begins the excitement rises to fever heat and the reader is too interested in the escape of Reynard to spare many of his sympathies for the less fortunate animal. At the close of this most thrilling poem we can pause to bask for a while in the full sun of poetic propriety (one might almost say ''poetic justice''). . . . Masefield has never done anything better. At the side of ***Reynard*** his lyrics and sonnets seem thin and pale. They have less of that grip and verve, that keen and nervous virility which makes every line in this poem contribute its full quota to the whole effect. There is no superfluity, no objectionable violence (in spite of the violence of the subject), no sentimental strain, such as we may see in his ***Salt Water Ballads*** and many of the short lyrics. His joy in the speed and pageant of the hunt and in the panorama of the landscape never fails him. Criticism recurs to a fact already noticed, the fact that Masefield, more than most of his peers, is easily victimized by his subject-matter. Unlike W. B. Yeats and Walter de la Mare, he cannot turn lead into gold. The imagination he brings to his service is something less philosophic than theirs. It is the product of a mind which remembers things loved without brooding over their metaphysical aspects. Action, movement, sound, color, light—all physical appearances move him chiefly, witness the catalogue in **''Biography,''** the best of his shorter poems. These, the qualities which have made him a popular poet, appeared in their cruder forms in his very earliest work, notably in ***The Salt Water Ballads,*** where the immediate influence of Kipling and W. B. Yeats were obstacles in the way of his own originality and power. The appeal of these poems is comparatively crude and superficial in the knowledge of his later work. The minor anthologists who inevitably choose to represent Masefield with such poems as **''Cargoes''** (that colorful hotch-potch lacking a finite verb) completely mistake Masefield's genius. It will be to the best of the sonnets in ***Lollingdon Downs,*** to such poems as **''Biography,'' ''The Wanderer,''** and the lovely stanzas to his mother that the anthologist of the future will look when he comes to take toll from the four volumes of the poet's collected works. (pp. 11-13)

Edward Davison, ''The Poetry of John Masefield,'' in English Journal, *Vol. XV, No. 1, January, 1926, pp. 5-13.*

STUART SHERMAN

[John Masefield] has given me more poetic pleasure than any other English poet living. Through his awakened personality I have felt mighty rhythms pulsing through forms of life that dissolve and decay; through waves that break, fields sown and harvested, foiled tragic lovers, hot races ending with blown steeds and fallen horsemen, and forlorn hopes ebbing out in blood-drenched, frost-bitten trenches by the Hellespont. His glorification of the invincible vanquished stirs me, I confess, profoundly. It is the inside story of human life. He tells it with swift, bright speed, and yet with a pathos which bites to the bone. (pp. 231-32)

Of course, I know that John Masefield has had his quarter century of productivity and his decade of fame, and that it is high time now for him to be slipping off the stage and leaving elbow room for the critics to haul the ascending stars into heaven. I know what the voguish critics are saying—that Masefield began with echoes of Kipling and Synge; that he spells Beauty with a capital letter; that the introduction of ''closhy puts'' and bar-room oaths into verse is no great feat once the trick has been suggested; that the tragedies are melodramatic through inadequate characterization; that the narratives are prolix; that the verse is padded with moral platitudes; that ''lasted'' is rhymed with ''bastard,'' as it is by many speakers; and that throughout the works there is a culpable indifference to the poetic uses of the file, just as there is in the works of the Master of all Makers.

Some of this critical pawing is captious. Masefield's apprentice debt to Kipling in ***Salt Water Ballads*** and to Synge in ***The Tragedy of Nan*** was soon stricken off the score. The mature Masefield is nobody's echo. He is a figure as independent and original as any man can be who works, as all the great English poets have done, for the vital continuation of an ancient and splendid tradition. Obviously, he learned his craft of the masters. For the forms and instruments of his music his debt is immense, to Burns, Byron, Shakespeare, Spenser, and Chaucer. ***The Everlasting Mercy*** is, if you please, an English "Tam o' Shanter"; ***The Widow in the Bye Street,*** a modern *Troilus and Cressida;* ***Reynard the Fox,*** a resuscitation of the Canterbury Pilgrims; ***Dauber*** is Childe Harold or Don Juan gone on a fresh pilgrimage; and the chief sonnet sequence carries on the Elizabethan quest for the soul and the divine idea behind the shadows of things. But that a poet suggests such comparisons, while writing with sharp realism of his own times and out of his own experience, marks him not a slave, but an heir.

Some of these exceptions, however, are well taken, and Mr. Masefield himself would probably sustain them. In the heat of the race, he has not always avoided knocking the top-rail off the fence. In his brief introduction to [the ***Collected Works of John Masefield***], glancing back over the performance of his generations, he says: "Often their work has been harsh, violent, and ill-considered." But their mission, he intimates, was not to gild the refined Tennysonian gold nor to paint the late Victorian lily white. Tennyson himself had kept an even balance between the native English tendency toward a robust rendering of life and the imported cult of artifice and technical finish. His imitators declined into a mere respectability, devoid of poetic courage or hope. The mission of Masefield's generation was to sally boldly into nature and restore vitality by reëmphasizing the native qualities: "character-drawing, humor, liveliness, and truth."

Certainly the apologist for Masefield should frankly concede his flaws and foibles to Mr. Squire and other parodists. He should take positive ground and defend him for the passionate expression of his tragic realism, his strength, and his sincerity. An English critic, Dixon Scott, moved to comment by ***The Daffodil Fields,*** began with a protest against the solemnity with which people take their poets. They, the poets, are just like other people, he would have us believe, not a race of "wilted priests," but "simple, jolly, frank, and friendly souls . . . engrossed in the grubby, glorious work of growing flowers." Well, a good many contemporary poets are like that. That is the trouble with their poetry. It is a kind of passionless floriculture. But John Masefield stands out as not in the least like that. Poetry has been in the place of religion to him; and he has served it like a priest—not with a linen ephod, but with Carlyle's "Baphometic fire-baptism." (pp. 233-35)

Masefield's long narrative poem, ***Dauber,*** is ordinarily praised as a superb picture of the sea. It is that, but it is more than that. It is a superb picture of artistic dedication. It illustrates the author's sense of the means by which a moribund art may live again. Here is a man who desires to paint the "windy, green, unquiet sea," ships scudding before the wind, and the destinies of men whose ways are on the great deep. Nautical pictures he might make from models in his studio. To know the might and mystery of the sea, he must give himself to it as the saint gives himself to God. Three years before the mast, he hopes, will teach his hand to paint the living truth when he shows the landlubber how billows break and a ship goes up the wave. From the fore-topgallant yard, the dedicated dauber tumbles too soon to his death. But such prices the gods exact of those who mimic the Creator's art.

The point is that with Masefield literature ceases to be hypnotic, a dreamily recreative "escape from life." It becomes a probe to the quick of the spirit, stabbing us "broad awake." It becomes an exultant hymning and glorification of life, even while it rushes on catastrophe. I do not know whether he became a sailor in order to learn to sing, or whether he sang because he had been a sailor. But that fine poem about his great joys, **"Biography,"** is proof enough that the prime sources of his passion were not "literary." He loves the taste of his own days, bitter and sweet, and his physical immersion in experience: swimming, racing, the first glimpse of strange mountains; but heavy labor, too, in quarry and mill, roads tramped in the rain, the rough talk of peasant and sailor, the long road westward through the springing wheat, [and] the comradeship of hard-palmed men following the sea. . . . (pp. 236-37)

One is tempted to say that the sensitive author of the sonnets and the lyrics, full of haunting cries and gushes of poignant sadness, has tossed his melancholy and the heartbreak of the *animula* into the west wind, and has voided the chamber of his personality in order to fill it with the ancient traditional emotions of the folk. It is one of many signs that John Masefield is a true poet of the taller sort, that he rises to a serene and joyous contemplation of the whole course of the "river of life" streaming down from Chaucer's time—with the eternal rhythm, and the fleeing waters that sparkle and pass. (p. 242)

Stuart Sherman, "In Behalf of John Masefield," in American Criticism, 1926, *edited by William A. Drake, Harcourt, Brace and Company, 1926, pp. 231-42.*

DAVID DAICHES

[John Masefield] was primarily a narrative poet, dealing both in the short narrative ballad and in the long tale. And . . . he preferred to write of humble folk, expressing his aim with a certain grandiose self-consciousness in his poem **"A Consecration":**

Not the ruler for me, but the ranker, the tramp of the road,
The slave with the sack on his shoulders pricked on with the goad,
The man with too weighty a burden, too weary a load.
The sailor, the stoker of steamers, the man with the clout,
The chantyman bent at the halliards, putting a tune to the shout,
The drowsy man at the wheel and the tired lookout.

His ballads have a thin vigor of their own, and his faculty for observation combined with his knowledge of sea life helped an undistinguished style to achieve conviction. His longer tales were written under Chaucerian inspiration—he himself tells us, in the Preface to his collected poems (1918), that the *Parliament of Fowls* converted him to poetry. In speed and slickness of narrative ***The Everlasting Mercy*** (1911) does show Chaucerian influence, but ***The Widow in the Bye Street*** (1912), ***Dauber*** (1912), and ***The Daffodil Fields*** (1913) have little suggestion of the early poet. The observation is close and clear, individual passages of description rise to considerable heights, but the stories as a whole mean much less than the author thought they did. Fundamentally a traditionalist and an idealist, Masefield uses realism as an incidental technique, a means to achieve a moral end whose function in the story is never very clear. A process of evaporation goes on, and though there are passages of strength and vigor that strike us as we read them, by the time we reach the end of the tale there seems to be nothing left. ***Reynard the Fox*** (1919), a more straightforward and highly colorful poem with distinct Chaucerian suggestions, is perhaps the most successful of all Masefield's narrative pieces.

Both [Wilford Wilson] Gibson and Masefield are in a sense lost poets. . . . At heart a sentimentalist and a moralist of the old school, a believer in Beauty in the Tennysonian sense, [Masefield] yet chose as his subject matter the "tough" aspects of contemporary life. The conflict however was less real in his case than in that of Gibson, for he was moved by no new social attitude. The ugly side of the social scene was for him picturesque because of its ugliness, and toughness was romantic. The meditative heartiness—strange combination!—that emerges from his work has a sort of dude-ranch quality. Later in his career Masefield gave up the struggle and cut the Gordian knot by reverting to a rather tedious traditionalism. Had he lived in an age when the cultural tradition was at once stable and vigorous, he might have done more justice to his talents. (pp. 48-51)

David Daiches, "Georgian Poetry," in his Poetry and the Modern World: A Study of Poetry in England between 1900 and 1939, *The University of Chicago Press, 1940, pp. 38-60.*

MURIEL SPARK

[There] are sides of Mr. Masefield's work which nothing the Georgians wrote, or that has been written before and after, can approximate to. It has the vitality to be remarked in such poets as Swinburne and Kipling; but with a range of human experience lacking in Swinburne, a broadminded sense of proportion lacking in Kipling; and naturalness of expression lacking in so vigorous a poet as Browning.

This vitality was overwhelmingly felt when ***The Everlasting Mercy*** appeared in 1911. The vitality was felt but its source never quite located, which I think caused some confusion in the ensuing controversy as to the merits and demerits of the work. (pp. 2-3)

The predominant conception of John Masefield formed at this time was, that with ***The Everlasting Mercy*** he had done something in poetry which liberated the feelings of the reader. He had brought about a wholesale catharsis. And this is a fact, as we have seen. Where the confusion arose, and where the error occurred in what I have called the Masefield 'idea' was over the more properly critical question of how he achieved this effect. Readers of English poetry at the time were not used to having their feelings exalted or, as some felt, outraged, by a poem so entirely impersonal as ***The Everlasting Mercy.*** In all the discussion there seems to have been very little assessment of what the poem really is: an objective account of sin and salvation as it existed in the life of an English rustic youth of the mid-nineteenth century. No one was prepared for such objective realism. It was assumed that the poem came straight from the heart of the author, which it did of course; but with this assumption went the further one that it was an exhilarating piece of propaganda for the evangelical cause which, as I see it, the poem is not. Intellectually, most people grasped that the poem represented 'realism', but emotionally the readers were not attuned to realism, especially in so emotional a poem. It was a new type of writing, and that always takes a long time to be properly understood. (p. 4)

[While] critics were exclaiming over the naughtiness of it all, while they were expressing the refinements of their own feelings, the real audacity of the poem, the all-over realism of it, was overlooked. The real audacity has nothing to do with oaths and curses and pub scenes, but in the rhythm, the arrangement, the verbal development, of lines. . . . (p. 6)

[***Reynard the Fox***] is not of the many-facetted order of poetry; it is depicted with intensity on a single level of experience. The fox is no symbol, but a very fox. In ***Reynard*** the poet's sympathy is with the fox equally with the many and miscellaneous human characters; the story is the thing. With the exception of ***Dauber,*** Mr. Masefield's narrative verse does not lend itself to a symbolist approach. It is not the sort of poetry which can be interpreted in several ways; it is the poetry of the surface; and I do not imply by this a distinction in merit, but in kind. For, Mr. Masefield's view of the surface of life is comprehensive. There is no limit or stipulation attached to the impressions he is prepared to receive. His subject-matter is everything on the face of the earth. We are not therefore to look in his work for a vision of Heaven-on-Earth, as we look in Blake; or for a vision of Hell-on-Earth, as we do in Baudelaire (to mention extreme examples). We must look for a vision of terrestrial life: a vision of its uniqueness and its unity.

It should be said that a great many critics paid lip-service to his 'objectivity'. But the degree of his objectivity was not thoroughly comprehended; even the wittiest parodists of ***The Everlasting Mercy*** assumed that the poet was secretly a benign patron to Saul Kane; the parodies failed, for they did not stab to the heart.

I would not be understood to be making out a general case for objectivity in poetry; only for a full understanding of the extent to which it is present in Mr. Masefield's writings. Browning defined the objective poet as 'one whose endeavour has been to produce things external (whether the phenomena of the scenic universe, or the manifested action of the human heart and brain) with an immediate reference, in every case, to the common eye and apprehension of his fellow-men, assumed capable of receiving and profiting by this reproduction'. There is in this definition that which Browning himself can be seen to have aimed at, though often failing to keep Browning out of the picture. The words can be applied accurately, though not as an inclusive statement, to John Masefield; and where Browning comes nearest to the definition he anticipates an aspect of Mr. Masefield. . . . Browning depicted human action in terms of poetic thought; John Masefield depicts poetic thought in terms of human action. And if this is true, as I think it is, then the property which has immediate reference to the 'common eye and apprehension of his fellow-men', as Browning has it, is in Mr. Masefield's case, action; in Browning's, poetic thought. It needs no elaboration of this to show that action has more immediate reference than has poetic thought; that is why Browning's attempts at objectivity, particularly in narrative form, show an obvious strain. Mr. Masefield's manner of conveying external things is comparatively effortless, and this, I think, causes the fallacy which prompted some of his contemporaries to think of him as a man of action who simply recorded things seen and done by him. Because he conveys human action with such immediate simplicity, it rather seems as if this is the case; indeed this impression signifies one of the essentials of his art; but it is not so. Whatever events of his life are reflected in his work are transformed by his imaginative grasp of them, they are changed by an intense vision of wholeness which does not attach to individual happenings in real life; and it is the vision, not the event, which is revealed to us finally in terms of action. That is the objectivity of Mr. Masefield, as I see it, and that is where he is unique. (pp. 8-11)

• • • • •

That [Masefield] is a born story-teller is apparent, not only from the fact that he is at his best when telling a story, but from his confident way—whether in the form of verse, novel or historical record—of attacking a tale and spinning it out, his way of bringing a story immediately before his audience. He takes for granted a larger and more receptive audience than most men of letters have the courage or justification to do. He addresses, not only the inquiring, the bookish or the purposive minds, but those with no particular purpose, and does so with effect. This alone makes for uniqueness. As one who adapts a story-telling capacity to several art-forms, he is distinctive in our time, when the art of narrative is almost entirely confined to the novel, which at its best has become confined to the narrative of ideas. His own novels I look upon as aspects of a poet; and as a narrator in prose and verse he can best be compared with other narrative poets. In this sense, he is unique not only in our own time, but in the period extending back to Chaucer, for though during that time the novel form has evolved and developed, though poetic narrative is by no means scarce in our literature following Chaucer, there is nowhere—not in Spenser, in Crabbe, Burns, Byron, Browning or William Morris (to name but a few narrative poets)—such purity of motive and in such abundance, as in Chaucer and in John Masefield. There are likewise refinements in the narrative verse of the six centuries which lie between these poets, which both lack; and there are differences between Chaucer and John Masefield which demand examination; but I am concerned here with Mr. Masefield's historical importance, so far as he possesses this purity of motive combined with abundance which had disappeared from English poetry for so long a time. (pp. 12-13)

The *motive* behind Mr. Masefield's narrative art is pure because it is apparently designed simply to convey a story in the most pleasurable and memorable form, without emphasis on moral, political or religious issues or issues personal to the poet. That is not to say that moral, political, religious or personal themes do not exist in his work; only that they are not emphasized by a didactic intention.

The *abundance* of Mr. Masefield's work is something that must be reckoned with, not in a spirit of quantitative judgment, but with the thought in mind that the abundance, in such variety as Mr. Masefield has given, is by itself a telling thing. In my own opinion he has produced a superfluity of writing; but there remains an abundance which is not superfluous and which betokens the uniqueness I speak of when allied to a sustained purity of narrative method. From well over a hundred publications which include poems, plays, historical episodes of the two world wars, verse and prose anthologies, essays, lectures; books on agriculture, on Shakespeare, on Rossetti, on ships and shipping, he emerges as a later type of epic writer; in which respect, of course, his resemblance to Chaucer ends. (p. 13)

[Mr. Masefield] is an objective, comprehensive and liberal observer of humanity and all the activities of man. He is not concerned with putting forward those individual impressions of society which have indeed enriched European literature; he is occupied with a vision of things—not a vision in the idealized sense, but a vision of things as they are as distinct from things as they sound in factual reportage. He concentrates therefore on those aspects of man and nature which signify, which look well in a ballad. Not that his work is stamped with the heroic spirit, as we take the phrase from the vocabulary of the critics; but that the poet evokes an heroic spirit nearer the life-size than the heroic spirit proper; and he does this through his reverence for man's powers of endurance, imagination and skill. (p. 14)

Mr. Masefield re-introduced flesh-and-blood into poetry. It will be said, what of Kipling? Kipling, it is true, dealt in flesh-and-blood but, with all respect to the recent and timely tendency inaugurated by Mr. T. S. Eliot, to do Kipling's verse justice, I do not mean, with regard to Mr. Masefield, the kind of flesh-and-blood Kipling dealt in. . . . [When] I say it was John Masefield who brought flesh-and-blood back into poetry, I mean also that he has a sense of the will of man, directing the flesh-and-blood for good or evil. . . . The purpose Kipling recognized was the purpose of the community, and it was not even a universal community: John Masefield is nothing like so abstract; he is aware of the will of man, and can be criticized so far as he does not sufficiently recognize the will of God. Still, it is the human species he is out to represent, and the human species is very seldom conscious of the will of God. It was an exclusive sense of the will of God operating outside of man, and almost no sense of man's freedom and purpose which makes Kipling's flesh-and-blood something of a caricature. (pp. 14-15)

Mr. Masefield has never been a cautious poet. Self-critical he must be to some degree, as his writings on the nature of poetry reveal. But he has never been self-critical enough. Therefore we find, as we do with all poets who give in plenty—with Browning, with Tennyson—we find, particularly among the poems, a great many that do not come off, along with the undoubted successes. But Mr. Masefield's lapses seem to differ in kind from those of Browning or Tennyson. If *dull* verse and plain *bad* verse can be distinct, then it is dull verse that bores us in Tennyson and Browning, and it is plain bad verse that shocks us in Mr. Masefield. For the great must always be dull at times—not only did Homer nod but St. Paul put a young man to sleep with one of his sermons. Dull work has its own sort of badness, but the quality of technical badness that comes sometimes from Mr. Masefield is truly incredible. And to confound us still more, this badness is often found no more than a few lines away from really fine verse. . . . Nor can it be said, in these cases where in the course of a single work, the very bad and the very good stand side by side, that the good compensates for the bad. They are both so alien to each other, so drawn as it were from different reserves of consciousness, that the relationship of compensation is inapplicable. And I would still hesitate to label this dichotomous element a lapse of taste, since the attribute of taste has so often attached itself in the past to the persistently mediocre, whereas genius frequently abounds with bad taste. If the phenomenon can be explained, the cause possibly has some bearing on the quantity of the poet's output. The degree of consciousness required even for the making of merely competent verse is one which operates outside the pressure of time, as do all forms of concentrated attentiveness. In fact, when the Muse has taken occasion to desert this poet, he seems to have rushed ahead without waiting humbly her return.

This intermittent falling-off can for the most part be located in careless rhyming, that is, rhyming which is accurate so far as it is a rhyme, but imprecise or incongruous where meaning is concerned. . . . John Masefield is not a reflective craftsman. No doubt he has revised his work, but without a reflective attitude. He relies on instinct which frequently leads him to do things of great skill in the way of poetic technique; but his instinct sometimes fails him badly.

Having made these observations, I feel it necessary to say that, granted the unevenness, one of the great delights of Mr. Masefield's poetry comes from the way he uses language. The vigorous sweep and naturalness strike a direct contrast to the stylization of Robert Bridges and to the 'poetic' poetry of the nineties; and makes small matter indeed of the Georgians, stylized as they too were, in their quasi-natural, Housmanesque manner. Such conversational ease in poetry had not appeared before Mr. Masefield, since Arthur Hugh Clough—that most neglected and rare of nineteenth-century poets. Anyone who can enjoy as poetry the language of *Amours de Voyage* and *The Bothie* will find the same satisfying effortless style (though not the sophisticated tone) in John Masefield. I do not mean the rhetorical parts of Mr. Masefield's poetry (nor of Clough's)—they are there for another purpose. But in the substantial functionary parts of any of the narrative poems; and in the shorter pieces too, the idiom has the same relation to common speech in Mr. Masefield's time as Clough's idiom had to the common speech of his day.

This naturalness was not easily acquired by John Masefield. It grew from experiments in prose, much influenced by Yeats and Synge; from the experiments in verse—the closest Mr. Masefield has come to Kipling—in ***Salt Water Ballads.*** It finds full expression in such narrative poems as ***The Everlasting Mercy, Dauber,*** and ***Reynard the Fox.*** His prose style has developed in quite a different way; not vigour, but patience, precision, grace inform the prose of his later novels and essays. The vigour of the poems and the 'sweetness and light' of the prose seem to me to meet in ***Reynard the Fox. Dauber*** is perhaps the most dramatically penetrating of the narrative poems; but ***Reynard*** is the most technically accomplished, the widest in range of characterization and action.

I have been speaking mainly of the narrative poems because I see him first as a narrative poet. But to speak of these is to represent only one of the numerous branches of Mr. Masefield's genius. (pp. 17-21)

Muriel Spark, in her John Masefield, *Peter Nevill, 1953, 186 p.*

NEIL CORCORAN

However lame and exasperating much of it seems now, [***The Everlasting Mercy***] is certainly a litmus paper for English literary taste and sensibility immediately before the First World War. It could well have replaced the disastrously lame and exasperating Greek and Arthurian poems in [John Masefield's ***Selected Poems***] (''Now she is trulling with her master, / That Lancelot of fame, / This spotless Queen of alabaster, / It is a shame'').

It is clear from the selection we do have that few poets have ever been so little introspective as Masefield. The book is a great bustle of activity and enterprise, a hubbub of human event. But faulty rhythms and dreadful strained rhymes (''comer'' / ''summer''; ''beheld'' / ''many-stelled'') contribute to the impression of a headlong, hectic rush, and they make it plain that Masefield sounds impressive only if you do not come too close: not as close, certainly, as Modernism and the New Criticism would. Admirers have respected his ''curiosity'', and it is true that his most interesting poems display a delighted fascination with the superficies of things. This can, however, become mere enumeration and itemization: of ships in **''Ships''**; of English place-names in ***Reynard the Fox;*** of shops in **''Shopping in Oxford''.** In the latter poem, indeed, Masefield's work disintegrates into the condition of a shopping list. If Eliot had such work in mind, he was displaying deadly accuracy when he remarked that ''the Georgians caress everything they touch''; and Masefield's touch went everywhere. It is tempting to import a phrase from a very different context in his letters and say that, even in a selection, there is far too much writing in which ''nothing is focused or kindling''.

This has something to do, probably, with sheer bulk and length. When he imposes the discipline of brevity on himself, it is usually—apart from his astoundingly incompetent sonnets—also a discipline of intensity, as it is in **''Cargoes''.** This much-anthologized poem does catch fire from its obvious delight in the exotic, which is also a delight in the commerce of Empire; but the poem—unlike much in Masefield—has clearly imposed a self-denying ordinance on itself: it has made a canny judgment about the point at which delight, if pursued, is likely to become indulgence. The critical judgment is apparent in the rapt entrancement with language itself. That ''Quinquereme of Nineveh from distant Ophir'' is rolled as lovingly on the tongue as Wallace Stevens's ''Chieftain Iffucan of Azcan in caftan / Of tan with henna hackles'' in ''Bantam in Pine-Woods''. But this is really not characteristic: much of Masefield's poetry is cripplingly disabled by unselfconsciousness about language.

What can actually be saved from the dross, then, is rather less than this selection offers. There is **''Cargoes''**, of course, and **''Sea Fever'',** that poem which will seem less like a poem and more like a Proustian *madeleine* to anyone forced, as I was, to learn it, at eleven or twelve, by a teacher over-respectful of Palgrave. There is the strange and uneasy **''C.L.M.''** which—reminding us that Masefield published, in 1910, a book called ***My Faith in Women's Suffrage***—draws together his mother's death when he was very young and his sympathy with turn-of-the-century feminism. There is the Roman Britain poem, **''Here the legions halted, here the ranks were broken'',** which, although it limps and collapses in its final stanza, has interesting affinities with Auden's ''Roman Wall Blues'' and David Jones's Roman poems. There are parts of **''Blown Hilcote Manor''** and **''Pawn to Bishop's Five'',** ghost poems caught halfway between Hardy and de la Mare. There is the long narrative poem ***Dauber*** . . . , which, despite some absurdities, has enough drive and zest, and an interestingly indirect autobiographical tension, to sustain it. Even so, it is unlikely that the new narrative poets with their finely poised obliquities and sleights of pen will find much of present use in Masefield's up-front obviousness. And there is, finally, his one wholly successful sonnet, **''The Lemmings''.** It is notable that, despite [the editor Donald Stanford's] advocacy, most of these poems are interesting precisely to the extent that they do not take any straightforwardly ''positive'' approach to life. In their moral complication, they avoid the monotonous, the reflex and the automatic which are crueller names for the ''positive'' in Masefield. They make us aware how narrow his conception of the poetic usually was.

It is a conception which could not make room for the First World War. Apart from the very early **''August 1914'',** written at a considerable level of abstraction, Masefield made virtually no poetic response to it whatever. In 1916 he published a volume of sonnets on "Beauty"; in 1917 ***Lollingdon Downs*** celebrated the Thames Valley; and in 1919 came ***Reynard the Fox,*** a huge poem about a fox-hunt which Stanford (and Muriel Spark [see excerpt above]) called Chaucerian, but which in my opinion is "Chaucerıan": a sentimental, overblown, rustic-rumbustious romp, in mind-numbing octosyllabics, dedicated to celebrating an enduring English social order against the grain of the available historical facts. (p. 469)

Neil Corcoran, "Too Much of Green," in The Times Literary Supplement, *No. 4282, April 26, 1985, pp. 469-70.*

Joseph (Prince) McElroy

1930-

Photograph by Nick Granito. Courtesy of Joseph McElroy.

American novelist, essayist, critic, short story writer, and dramatist.

Considered one of the leading practitioners of contemporary experimental fiction, McElroy constructs complex, encyclopedic novels characterized by an abundance of information, fragmented structure, a preoccupation with language and style, and extensive references to the social and physical sciences. In his work, McElroy is often concerned with such themes as the development of human consciousness and self-awareness, humanity's ability to structure and comprehend reality, the problems of art and the artist, familial relationships, and the continuities between past and present. An advocate of what he facetiously termed the "new maximalist novel," McElroy has frequently been compared to such authors as Thomas Pynchon, William Gaddis, John Barth, and Vladimir Nabokov. Although Thomas LeClair observed that McElroy "has unaccountably failed to receive the critical attention usually given to a writer of his ambition and achievement," Tony Tanner praised him as "a very important writer working with extraordinary energy and imagination right at the very boundaries of contemporary fiction; indeed he is redrawing some of those boundaries, and at times going beyond them."

McElroy's first book, *A Smuggler's Bible* (1966), concerns the narrator's attempts to organize a series of manuscripts consisting of memories from different periods in his life. Written in disparate styles and from various points of view through the narrator's intense projection into the lives of others, the manuscripts simultaneously attract and repel continuity. Described by McElroy as being "about disintegration and reintegration, . . . about the self putting itself back together again," *A Smuggler's Bible* also examines the structures of perception, the evolving relationship between the narrator and his father, and the dangers involved in imposing excessive order, as well as phenomenological, technological, and literary themes. McElroy's next book, *Hind's Kidnap: A Pastoral on Familiar Airs* (1969), is a labyrinthine psychological detective story centering on the experiences of a man obsessed with an unsolved kidnapping that occurred many years ago. When the clues lead to the protagonist's family and eventually to his own past, the kidnapping is transformed, in the words of J. G. Farrell, into "the vehicle for the hero's quest for his own identity and an examination of his way of relating to other people." Rich in wordplay, extended metaphor and analogy, and epistemological and ontological discussions, *Hind's Kidnap* also contains provocative considerations of such subjects as sports, education, architecture, logic, fatherhood, and love.

In *Ancient History: A Paraphase* (1971), McElroy continues to examine many of the central themes of his earlier novels. Having slipped into the apartment of a character who has apparently committed suicide, the narrator sits at the deceased's typewriter and proceeds to write, reflecting not only on the possible meanings of his friend's life and death, but also how they relate to his family and surviving friends. Characterized by linguistic abstraction, scientific terminology, verbal excess, blurred distinctions between present and past, and the narrator's attempts at discovering, in Stephen Donadio's words, "the deep coherence underlying all the disparate phenomena suspended in his consciousness," *Ancient History,* according to Tony Tanner, "is a remarkably interesting phenomenological novel about a very discernibly American spatial and temporal terrain."

The action in McElroy's fourth novel, *Lookout Cartridge* (1975), revolves around the destruction of a documentary film made by the narrator. His subsequent investigation into the cause of the deed combines elements of the conventional mystery novel with vivid evocations of differing natural landscapes, vast arrays of scientific theories, and cinematographic and computer terminology. *Lookout Cartridge* features simultaneous, inconsistent, and circular narrative progressions, fast-paced dialogue, discontinuities among characters, events, and settings, and themes related to love, marriage, fatherhood, power, and terror. Thomas LeClair observed that with this novel "McElroy creates a model that has less to do with the principles of the traditional novel than with the contributions of contemporary science, structuralism, and systems theory. Realistic in its details, *Lookout Cartridge* moves beyond the mechanistic realism of most contemporary fiction to a formal and conceptual correspondence with a reality the empiricist's eye cannot see."

McElroy's next novel, *Plus* (1976), is a radical experiment in linguistic density mediated by a plot structure derived from science fiction and a traditional mythical conceit: the departure, initiation, and return of the hero. In this book, the central figure is a disembodied human brain that has been carefully programmed, placed in a space capsule, and sent into orbit to transmit scientific information back to Earth. While in orbit, the brain slowly develops consciousness independent of its mission and begins to remember its past. The brain severs itself from ground control, develops physical appendages, gains extraordinary powers, and finally surrenders its physical form to become, in McElroy's words, "a circuit of conception" in the minds of human beings. While containing few disruptions in setting and time, minimal allusions to extraneous information, and a relatively small number of characters, *Plus* was described by Sheldon Frank as "a work approaching terminal unreadability," and it is commonly considered the most dense and difficult of McElroy's fiction.

McElroy's recent novel, *Women and Men* (1986), employs mathematic and scientific principles, historic and geographic information, intricate webs of characters and events, and conventional plot elements to explore the interconnected lives of two neighbors in a New York City apartment building who never meet. A comprehensive illustration of the multiplicity and density of human existence, *Women and Men,* according to Thomas LeClair, "is the single book—fiction or nonfiction—that best manifests what human beings can know and be and imagine now and, just as importantly, in the future."

(See also *CLC,* Vol. 5 and *Contemporary Authors,* Vols. 17-20, rev. ed.)

DANIEL STERN

In ***A Smuggler's Bible,*** his first novel, [McElroy] has undertaken precisely what a writer must do when he sits down to write today: the creation of the world. (Not *a* world. That's the conventional mystique of the artist. *The* world. From scratch.)

He starts, appropriately enough, with a character, David Brooke, who is utterly in the void himself. We encounter him in the process of a kind of breakdown, aboard a ship headed for England, with his English wife. But don't let the "breakdown" put you off. This is not merely a "psychological" novel. David Brooke is in the process of creating his own existence by projecting himself into the lives of eight people. Having done so, his task is then to smuggle himself out again. The theme sounds heavy, but the touch is light.

As we follow the eight manuscripts on David's desk, we encounter invented (and remembered) people full of enough juice for a half-dozen more characters. There is Peter St. John, an antiquarian bookseller who lives in Brooklyn Heights; James Judah Lafayette (formerly Lamentoff), bartender of Bunny's Bar on the upper West Side, and others too numerous (and, thankfully, humorous) to mention here. The title refers to a box bought to hold the final melding of the eight manuscripts into one, i.e., the final David. What turns out to be in it comes as a pleasurable shock rather than as a surprise.

McElroy employs the smuggler metaphor many times and in many ways, and though it never becomes mechanical or tired, it does at times seem overly ambitious. This is particularly true when David's inner voice says, "Do you see how people try to smuggle themselves out of life? To pretend to sneak across the mortal frontier—when in fact you stay right here after death . . . how Christ was in fact the most remarkable contraband of all time and simultaneously himself an arch smuggler?" Or again: "Sartre was wrong [in his comment, "Hell is other people"]; God is other people." Yet what McElroy proves in this virtuoso performance is that there is no need to retreat in the face of the void. By plunging into the unknown and dangerous territory of others we may be able to smuggle back the real prize: ourselves.

Daniel Stern, "Paper Worlds," in Book Week—New York Herald Tribune, *October 23, 1966, p. 16.*

JOHN COLEMAN

A Smuggler's Bible is nothing if not ambitious. Uncharitably, it might be described as an attempt to get the Great American Novel off the road and into bed with the *nouveau roman*. It has a modish and chastening epigraph, drawn from Pascal: 'Nature has made all her truths independent of one another. Our art makes one depend on another, but this is unnatural. Each has its own place.'

So Mr. McElroy, in search of a finer or more relative truth overall, adopts a bemusing stratagem. Roughly one-tenth of his eight-chapter book is devoted to a series of bridge-passages, or 'interchapters,' during which he archly chats up a fictional character, David Brooke, a thirtyish American struggling to put some writings in order in the course of a transatlantic voyage to London. The other nine-tenths, then, purport to be the book David wrote.

There is an arguable case for such a procedure. It certainly allows Mr. McElroy to mirror his doubts about the whole business of making fiction. . . .

But [these passages create their] own doubts in turn. Quite the worst writing in ***A Smuggler's Bible*** comes in the interchapters, as if a computer were trying to parody Nabokov ('dear dire dour *Dave,*' and so on). There are also all those hints about buried myths and biblical underpinnings: Midas, Theseus and Antiope, Gethsemane, the Garden of Eden. Only a devotedly misguided symbol-hound would be capable of finding these in the rest of the book. But perhaps that is part of Mr. McElroy's intention: to deflate such grand and Joycean aspirations. If so, his irony misfires. The only decent work done by his interventions is the transmission of two facts: David has written down his tormented memories of kin, friends and relations; David suffers from total recall.

No bad equipment for a certain kind of novelist, one would have thought, and indeed David/McElroy elsewhere proves to be a witty, frequently brilliant memorialist. The book moves easily around in time and stance, using all the conventional modes of creating character. Sometimes David's people tell their own stories, sometimes he narrates: occasionally a third-person or historical account is given. Gradually the outlines of an image of David himself emerge. The pieces begin to fit. Son of upper-middle-class parents, father Halsey a businessman, mother Julia a stylish music-lover, the boy is painfully intelligent and drifting. From his home in Brooklyn Heights he moves to a period at the sleazy Kodak Hotel, where he keeps charts of the inhabitants. On campus at one point he meets the gaudy pop-professor of history, Duke Amerchrome, a magnificent fake. There are later episodes on an Italian island and inside a fit of amnesia. The book winds remarkably down on a loving testimony to his father, a chapter that catches the peculiar hopelessness of some kinds of family affection to the life.

Mr. McElroy is a rare bird and, freed of apparatus, could probably write a very good novel—of the old 'unnatural' sort.

John Coleman, "Fiction within Fiction," in The Observer, *January 21, 1968, p. 31.*

JOHN HEMMINGS

Mr McElroy, it can be said, has [in ***A Smuggler's Bible***] written a novel—a very long and madly intelligent novel—about a writer who is himself writing a novel about a novelist's ambitions to be a good . . . mixer. David's PROject is to proJECT: self-projection into others is to deliver him from self-imprisonment. But the escape route, like the garden path in *Alice Through the Looking-Glass,* leads inexorably back to the point of departure. 'When I find out about a person I find all I've done is to come face to face with a thick mirror.' Self-projection should afford self-release, as it does in the sexual act. Right at the end of the book an analogy is suggested with the clamping together of the two hemispheres of plutonium which sets off the nuclear reaction. Any real union with another person is certain to be explosive; perhaps our sanity depends on our apartness.

The novelist projects himself as best he may by the intense, though seemingly absent-minded attention he pays to other people. He needs to be able to remember everything about them, he needs to have, like David, the power of total recall. 'The highest life demands the most ruthless and even amorous memory, yet everyone practises the art or, if you will, takes daily doses of the milk of amnesia.' Amnesia is what David finally opts for, succumbing to a pathological fugue which is the punning counterpart of the fugal design of the book, in which themes are constantly being stated, dropped, picked up and further developed. There are eight major narrative episodes linked by shorter passages apparently written by David's artistic super-ego, who expresses himself patronisingly in clever Joyceisms but grows crosser and crosser as the successive sections turn out to be less and less what he intended, and as he realises that he is being swept willy-nilly into the game, transformed from 'a scrier' into 'one of the descried'. These link passages also embody what hints the author deigns to let drop as to the real significance of the 'smuggler' motif. Here is a novel expressly designed, one imagines, for its own exegesis, and much better left to the aspirant PhD's who will, in due course, settle on it in swarms.

John Hemmings, "Only Project," in The Listener, *Vol. 79, No. 2029, February 15, 1968, p. 216.*

ROBERT M. ADAMS

Hind's Kidnap by Joseph McElroy is a long, mainly comic and fearfully successful novel about the difficulty of seeing the forest for the trees. Its setting is more or less Brooklyn Heights, its time the present and immediate past, its style the labyrinthine interiorities of the unvoiced monologue. (p. 5)

The book is written in a long series of tentative self-interrogations on the part of Hind (to which, before long, the reader finds himself responding with an automatic shrug of the shoulders and an offhand "Search me")—combined with looping, circumambulatory, long-drawn-out sentences, the syntax of which has to be paleontologized, vertebra by discrete vertebra, from under piles of paratactic lists and interpolated quasi-relevant details.

Past and present blur indistinguishably, scenes shift without warning, two-dimensional jokers and linguistic phantoms shoot past without pausing to identify themselves, crisis situations from high-school athletic events bob up amid whirls of indefinitely unrelated pronouns more or less from the kidnap case, a whole battery of etymological pinwheels sputters and sparkles in tangential discourses, and immense pseudological semi-structures flower and collapse like speedup movies under the vocalizing impulses of articulate cartoon-grotesques who recite and disappear, while it doubtless means something important that in Sylvia's long, beautifully entangled monologue, 39 of the 42 paragraphs begin with the letter "V." In short, the book doesn't make many concessions to a reader who's less than completely involved with it.

What rewards does the novel offer for the effort it obviously demands? Quite a few, as a matter of fact. Scenes of academic and industrial parody achieve a grotesque and wonderful absurdity—they're the open spaces of the book, and very welcome indeed. There is a lyric flow to Mr. McElroy's prose when he lets it go that overrides if it doesn't obliterate the verbal patter-work, and leaves the pronouns hanging where it doesn't *matter* about their antecedents. Even the puns and distortions and word-arabesques of the post-Joycean art-style (which can so easily look cute) and the cataractic involution of the underpowered overloaded sentence (which probably owes something to Faulkner) take on expressive qualities. When he wants to use them, Mr. McElroy has in his repertoire a vivid, evocative vein of language and a fine, throwaway wit; but Hind and his Sylvia, through the watery currents of their sleep-speech, will sometimes strike the reader as talking too directly to themselves. (pp. 5, 58)

Robert M. Adams, "Who Took Hershey Laurel? Did Anyone?" in The New York Times Book Review, *December 14, 1969, pp. 5, 58.*

J. G. FARRELL

[***Hind's Kidnap***] concerns a young man who has become obsessed with the unsolved kidnapping of a boy several years earlier. The case has long since been closed; the boy's parents are both dead, the boy himself and his kidnappers will by this time have grown older. The young man sets out to investigate it nevertheless on the strength of a number of highly ambiguous clues and chance encounters in his daily life. The manner of the book is strongly reminiscent of Thomas Pynchon's *The Crying of Lot 49*. Mr McElroy's intention is more serious than conspiracy-hunting, however: his kidnapping is used as the vehicle for the hero's quest for his own identity and an examination of his way of relating to other people. How far does the author succeed in his intention? It should be made clear that Mr McElroy is extremely difficult to read. He makes almost no concessions to the reader, frequently launches into discussions of characters as yet unfamiliar, loads his sentences with diversions and densely parenthetic offshoots, discusses abstruse and academic matters in an august manner worthy of Nabokov at his most impenetrable (this book also resembles *Ada* in many ways) and never for a moment calls off his pursuit of the theme to give the reader a chance to relax and get things sorted out. On the other hand, he writes with a control of his material which makes all these objections seem petty. He combines an acute intelligence with great learning (the discussion of language and meaning provides a powerful thematic undercurrent to the novel). He is often very funny, both in a Nabokovian sort of way playing with words (for example, he has a garage called 'Lubri-city') and also in a more normal descriptive way (he is particularly entertaining when describing his hero's landlord who is, no doubt symbolically, an undertaker, and the recipient of professional junk mail . . . 'San-O-Spray nips "post-mortem" odours' etc.). His observation of the physical details of life is sharp. He evokes characters with ease. The relaxed tone which he has selected for his book never falters. The result is a novel which is in many ways an unusual and distinguished work of imagination. At the same time, while reading it, one constantly has the feeling that the author is more interested in communicating with himself than with his reader, in solving, like Nabokov and Pynchon, his own elaborate and graceful puzzles.

J. G. Farrell, "Girls and Boys," in The Spectator, *Vol. 225, No. 7424, October 10, 1970, p. 407.*

STEPHEN DONADIO

Like his two earlier novels—***A Smuggler's Bible,*** which appeared in 1966, and ***Hind's Kidnap: A Pastoral on Familiar Airs,*** published in 1969—Joseph McElroy's ***Ancient History: A Paraphase*** is a strange, labyrinthine creation. Described by the narrator (named Cyrus, after the founder of the Persian Empire) as "my writing, my confession . . . my Memorial Span, my parallel lives," the work, which runs unbroken for over three hundred pages, undivided into chapters or clearly distinguishable parts, represents that middle-aged man's determined effort to follow out the thread of his past without losing his place in the present, to create a "charged field" in which experiences of past and present become "equi-valent." (p. 4)

Cyrus's record of his attempt to "plot" himself "among our shifting coordinates" is significantly addressed to an absent character named Dom or Don. Obviously conceived on the model of Norman Mailer ("talk about advertisements for yourself!" Cyrus exclaims at one point in mock reproach), Dom is depicted as "a radically active man who wrote key books *in* the selfsame field-situation he foretold and filled," a man possessed of a variety of "accents, Irish, Italian, southern," seeking finally to make himself "a complete image of our time, an actor never unroled."

For some time, Cyrus has followed the distinguished man's complex career with an interest bordering on religious devotion, and to those inclined to attack Dom for his contradictory ideas ("we don't have stars any more, we have community, and he wants to be the president of everyone. Left conservative he says he is, but it doesn't fool us. He wants the Nobel Prize for Personality") Cyrus feels called upon to explain that it is pointless to insist that the man be "consistent in that crazy old-fashioned way, think of his notions operating in a field-state . . . many forces acting in many directions through many distances."

Similarly, in contrast to those who find themselves decisively put off by the characteristically abrupt and occasionally violent alternations between Dom's disciplined expression of his genius and the wild excesses of his public behavior, Cyrus is convinced that the man's greatness is derived precisely from his manifest "will to interrupt [himself], to be a hero who would not de-oscillate the dialectic." Consequently, Cyrus comes to regard Dom as the "ideal listener" for his musings, since those musings are essentially concerned with the dynamic discontinuities of personality, with the divergent conceptions of the self which must be reconciled and balanced ceaselessly.

Indeed, until that long night which he spends setting down the intricate series of reflections and associations which constitutes the dense text of ***Ancient History,*** Cyrus has always imagined himself as the apex (C) of a triangle whose base is formed by (A) and (B), Al and Bob, a friend from the country and a friend from the city whom he has always deliberately kept from meeting one another in order to preserve his own tenuous sense of himself. But tonight the two friends will presumably meet, and Cyrus, his identity threatened, resolves to talk over the urgent matter with Dom, in whose apartment building he now lives.

When he arrives at Dom's apartment, however, he discovers that the great writer may well have committed suicide earlier that evening. Cyrus has not counted on this rather disheartening development, but making the best of a bad situation, he slips into the unlocked apartment, bolts the door behind him and, picking up a box of Sphinx paper, begins to fill the empty pages with the chronicle of his emerging identity.

Shuttling between past and present, linking repetitions, parallels, coincidences, contradictions, Cyrus becomes increasingly aware of the deep coherence underlying all the disparate phenomena suspended in his consciousness. "I think in interrupted scenes, Dom," he asserts, "but there is only one scene here. It is here." And referring to the book's governing analogy, that of the parabola, he concludes that the virtually inexhaustible scene which he has finally managed to reach "is an arc quite out of time and real not at all like those good and bad times and those bewildered distances that determine this arc."

Just as he used to connect the dots in newspaper puzzles when he was a child, Cyrus unravels the mystery of his experience by tracing out a whole constellation of isolated points in his past; but as it turns out, the picture that emerges, unexpectedly rich in detail, embodies far more than Cyrus's personal experience, far more than the bittersweet memory of a Brooklyn narrowly circumscribed by Brooklyn Heights and Poly Prep. For by revealing the contrasting textures and nuances of those items of experience recovered in the act of recollection—Weavers' concerts, unused Ramses, "the introduction to that 'Oh My Papa' trumpet solo"—***Ancient History*** succeeds in repossessing the lost world of the forties and fifties, and in locating that world in a continuum which embraces the present.

Unfailingly interesting, conceived with high intelligence, lucidity and wit, Mr. McElroy's third novel compels respect; but it is a difficult and disorienting book, and for a while the experience of reading it is like that of turning a familiar key in a familiar lock, only to discover that one has somehow entered a strange apartment. It is a proof of the author's mysterious power and perfect control that the reader, finding himself in that unfamiliar place, in time comes to believe that it could not look more like home. (pp. 4, 18)

Stephen Donadio, "Cyrus Connects the Dots of His Past," in The New York Times Book Review, *May 30, 1971, pp. 4, 18.*

MICHAEL HARRIS

[The protagonist] of Joseph McElroy's fourth novel [***Lookout Cartridge***] is Cartwright, an American living in England. He and a friend, Dagger DiGorro, have completed a film about "power being poached on when it had momentum but not focus.'' The film is destroyed by being exposed to the sunlight, and Cartwright wants to find out who did it and why. He inserts himself into a veritable switchboard of circuits that suggest—as far as he can tell from the energies pulsing through him as he sleuths his way from New York to London to Chartres to Corsica to the Outer Hebrides—an enormous conspiracy.

But a conspiracy of whom, and for what real object? The clues are, if anything, all too abundant. Each electrode Cartwright brushes against tickles an unexpected synapse, opens up new sources of power that he ''poaches'' on relentlessly. The conspiracy endangers both him and his family—yet at the same time there is no one who might not be involved in it. His wife, his ex-mistress, his son and his daughter, his business associates, his friends, utter strangers—all hold jagged pieces of the puzzle he must solve. The film, he suspects, must have threatened somebody, and he reconstructs it in detail from his notes and his memory.

The film shows an American deserter and a friend talking politics in an ''unplaced room,'' a softball game in Hyde Park, a bonfire in Wales, a Hawaiian hippie playing his guitar in the London Underground, ''hands laying out TNT like a xylophone and then standing each stick up carefully, and fingers dismantling a kitchen timer. The times we live in.''

But the film soon becomes only a metaphor for the world. Like many a serious novelist before him, McElroy is using the conventions of the whodunit to explore larger mysteries. What kind of a universe do we live in? Obviously, one full of hints and absurd dislocations and things falling apart—perhaps to hold in new centers. And Cartwright is curiously fitted to investigate it. He is a 20th-century Renaissance man, with an awesome command of all sorts of technologies—the calendar of the Maya, the properties of liquid crystals, how helicopters fly, peat is cut, wagon wheels were made. The answer to the fragmenting of our existence, he senses, may be to ride out the explosion, to assume all identities, to stretch like a film between the divergent particles until we see the correspondence of their internal structures—until the momentum of power is given a new focus.

We have seen variations on this theme before—for example, in Norman Mailer's *An American Dream*. But the differences are significant. The battleground in ***Lookout Cartridge*** is not the protagonist's psyche; Cartwright may surrender to the forces of chaos, he may kill in the Hebrides, but he is a ''morally stable'' man with few internal problems. The issue is how well he can mediate between his consciousness and the world, using the technological imagination slotted like a cartridge into both. The order he glimpses behind the multiplicity of systems—social, political, financial, sexual—is a utopian one where humans can possess godlike powers.

McElroy fills his 531 pages with a dense computerese that is, frankly, more than the average reader is likely to tolerate. McElroy, of course, does it all for a reason. He wants us to grope right along with friend Cartwright; he wants us to get a real sense of his world. Hence the flashbacks, flash-forwards, apparent digressions, unpunctuated dialogue and paragraphs so lacking in basic transition they might be stuck anywhere, like thick wordy cartridges. McElroy fans will find here a worthy successor to ***A Smuggler's Bible, Hind's Kidnap*** and ***Ancient History***. But the majority—while grateful for a novel of such energy, intelligence and conceptual richness—will not find its gratitude mixed with much pleasure.

Michael Harris, ''Metaphor Man,'' in Book World—The Washington Post, *March 9, 1975, p. 3.*

CYRA McFADDEN

A distant, distinctly American cousin to the French New Novel, ***Lookout Cartridge*** vividly illustrates the strengths and weaknesses, as well as the special demands, of the kind of fiction that subordinates plot and plausibility to small, closely observed details, subtleties of landscape and human relations, and degrees of light and shade.

Though it is described by the publisher as ''a gigantic mystery,'' ***Lookout Cartridge*** is many removes from conventional mystery or conventional narrative. . . .

Cartwright, the narrator and protagonist, is an American living in London, a successful entrepreneur whose latest venture is a film made in partnership with his friend Dagger DiGorro. Cartwright has a precarious marriage, a mistress who is his wife's best friend, a bright young son interested in computers, and a 17-year-old daughter he may or may not be able to trust. He also has a prolific, highly speculative mind, so that when DiGorro's house is broken into and their undeveloped film is exposed to sunlight, Cartwright becomes obsessed with finding out why. His account of that obsession is the novel.

A man with a strong bent toward mysticism, Cartwright sees the destruction of the film as secondary to the multitude of possible motives that may directly or indirectly explain what happened. His attempt to solve the riddle takes the form of abrupt transatlantic leaps, endless cryptic conversations, encounters accidental and deliberate, and experiences real and remembered. The plot as such rapidly becomes almost incidental to the greater goal of Cartwright's travels, his search for truth.

In a world of ambiguities and shifting perceptions, which events are real? Cartwright rephrases the question ceaselessly, using analogies ranging from the Mayan calendar to the properties of liquid crystals. Because his active life is less significant than his constant internalizing, he seems at times pure disembodied mind, and as the story progresses, his quest becomes increasingly hallucinatory.

Included in the book are glimpses of a vast, inscrutable conspiracy involving Druids, revolutionaries, a woman artist, and a film distributor, among others; extended descriptions of the film itself; and numerous passages . . . attempting to demonstrate in the language of film technology and computers Cartwright's belief that nothing happens at random. . . . (p. 21)

The constant distortion of the time sequence adds to the difficulty. Just as Cartwright keeps a film diary that is somehow another incarnation of the original movie, preserving and recreating its existence after it has been destroyed, McElroy is making his own experimental film on the printed page. His narrative moves with the freedom of the camera from past to present, present to future. Hence the rapid scene changes, suggesting jump cuts, from New York to London and back again, to Corsica, Stonehenge and the Hebrides—with long shots, closeups, flashbacks, flash forwards, and chapter titles such as ''Yellow Filter Insert.'' Hence, too, the lengthy stretches of ''cinematic prose,'' highly imagistic descriptions that are often stunning in themselves but are loosely connected to what precedes or what follows them.

These separate scenes are related only if one accepts the notion that all human phenomena are related. A murder at the beginning of the book, for example, is never really explained, despite the fact that the murderer is an old college classmate of Cartwright's and is later implicated in the vast, dim plot. The daughter, Jenny, plays a larger but equally confusing role. Is she somehow collaborating, albeit unwittingly, with her father's enemies? Cartwright thinks so, then changes his mind; neither position is particularly convincing because his personal mysticism and his enigmatic associational monologues obscure rather than clarify his thinking process. (pp. 21-2)

Lookout Cartridge raises the issue of what expectations one may legitimately bring to highly experimental fiction. Unless a person had somehow managed to hole up for the last two decades, reading nothing but Dickens, a novel like this one would remind him that the form of fiction is changing constantly and that someone who refuses to change with it might miss out on all the excitement. Certainly one can't read Robbe-Grillet the same way one reads *The Pickwick Papers*.

Nonetheless, I think even so gifted a writer as McElroy should be called to account for undue difficulty. For there are two bare-bones necessities of fiction, traditional as yesterday or newer than tomorrow, which, it seems to me, cannot be set aside.

The first is that the pieces of a narrative, whatever their separate shapes, eventually fit together into a coherent whole. The second, still more important, is the one ***Lookout Cartridge*** violates most damagingly: Joycean monologues, chic montages, unconventional punctuation, and other tricks of the novelistic trade work only when they point beyond themselves. Since McElroy makes the egotist's mistake of believing that everything interesting to him is equally interesting to us as well, Cartwright ultimately becomes a bore. (p. 22)

Cyra McFadden, "More Mystification than Mystery," in The New Leader, *Vol. LVIII, No. 10, May 12, 1975, pp. 21-2.*

IRVING MALIN

Plus is science-fiction about energies, "power in process," and consciousness. It begins with expected "awareness" of space: "He found it all around. It opened and was close. He felt it was himself, but felt it was more." But we soon recognize that Imp Plus, unlike McElroy's earlier narrators, is not a human designer. "He" (or it) does not know who (or what) he is. He shifts back and forth from "himself" to "more"; he feels in brief, primitive jumps.

Plus builds on repeated details. Impulses reign (rain); there is no pattern at first; we, along with Imp Plus, must establish contexts, connections, powers. There is thus a doubling effect because we learn only as Imp Plus does; we are enclosed in his pattern-making.

Gradually we do discover that Imp Plus is a disembodied human brain orbiting Earth in a capsule, an inhabitant of Interplanetary Monitoring Platform. The brain answers to Ground by means of transmitted impulses; it is, at the beginning, under control. But Imp Plus cannot exist in such regulated patterns. (Or so he thinks.) He slowly creates his own: he offers wrong information; he "camouflages"—a key word in the novel—reactions to sleep and glucose. (p. 102)

Although Imp Plus is the disembodied brain orbiting earth, he is also a language-maker. He remembers words from Earth; he eventually views them as charges (changes) of meaning. He puns. (Or does McElroy alone?) He thinks of "traveling light," "dim echo," "head for figures," "read me," and "me read." The words have multi-meanings, suggesting by their overall effect that language itself is a series of "never-ending" particles. (pp. 102-03)

Plus asserts, as do other science-fiction novels, that we live in a universe of forces, vectors, planes. But it maintains that if we are not somehow able to "transcend" (a physical word) the body, we can use it for our purposes. Imp Plus *becomes "more" through "camouflage."* Perhaps McElroy suggests that fiction affirms our flights of fancy, our potential for growth.

Plus ends, as it began, with the field. (Of course, the time suggested by these words, is suspended in the novel.) We are not certain of final solutions: "thought wondering then what chances now turned upon this fresh absence that would be as lasting as the glint of its arrival must have been brief for any who saw it in the sky: thought wondering, too, if at last the great lattice had let this happen or had been surprised." And as we "wonder" about the ultimate patterns—does Imp Plus let "this" (whatever) happen? do we have free will?—we are asking profound questions about Earth, Space and the Sun—*our positions in the universe*. Can we ask "more" from any novelist? (p. 103)

Irving Malin, "Ultimate Patterns," in The Ontario Review, *No. 5, Fall-Winter, 1976-77, pp. 101-03.*

SHELDON FRANK

Plus makes McElroy's earlier novels read like *My Weekly Reader*. It is a work of relentless virtuosity, but I suspect that the number of people who will actually read all of its mere 215 pages can be counted on the head of a pin. While it, too, like McElroy's earlier novels, provides a kind of intelligent pleasure not to be found in any other contemporary fiction, the price is far too high. It is a work approaching terminal unreadability.

The story itself is quite simple. (Although McElroy has written of his distaste for science fiction, ***Plus*** does resemble super-sophisticated sci-fi.) Imp Plus (Imp stands for Interplanetary Monitoring Platform) is a human brain that is orbiting the earth in a space capsule. It has been sent aloft, accompanied by some algae, in a solar energy project, and it has been carefully programed to simply transmit information about glucose readings, temperature, and the like back to its receiver on earth.

But slowly, inexorably, inevitably, Imp Plus begins to develop consciousness separate from its programing. It starts to withold information from its receiver; it begins to ignore commands from its earthly controls. As its consciousness expands, Imp Plus starts to grow weird, oddly named appendages (McElroy calls them wendings, faldoreams, shearows, and morphogens). Imp Plus wants to free itself from any dependence on ground control and, instead, commune directly with its real source of energy, the sun. Strange, almost indescribable transmutations occur until Imp Plus assumes its final form: It becomes a semiconductor—an array of molecules similar to a transistor. In short, Imp Plus has changed from brain to consciousness to hardware.

This brief synopsis may sound ludicrous, but to the degree that the reader can attend to the bewildering convolutions of McElroy's vocabulary and syntax, the saga of Imp Plus does have an eerie, compelling power. McElroy is off in totally uncharted territory, trying, in Beckett's words, "to eff the ineffable," to write a kind of natural history of the growth of human consciousness. An audacious undertaking. A novel of breath-taking daring. . . .

The achievements of Joseph McElroy remain a puzzle to me. He is gifted with rare, seemingly limitless powers of verbal and narrative invention; he is attempting to write novels unlike any other novels that have ever been written; he makes stupefying demands on his readers. But is it all worth it? I don't think so, but I'm not sure.

Sheldon Frank, "The Eerie Saga of Imp Plus," in The National Observer, *February 26, 1977, p. 21.*

THOMAS LeCLAIR

The most interesting and often the best American novels of the 1970s are excessive. The art of excess, as the word itself suggests, is relative and quantitative, different but not altogether new. The works of Joseph McElroy, Thomas Pynchon, William Gaddis, and others I mention below are often called experimental, but they do not claim a purity of invention or neutrality of intention as, say, the works of Stein and Robbe-Grillet do. The excessive novels of the seventies recognize and incorporate the norms of internal consistency, literary convention, and everyday empiricism in order to exceed these norms. Invited by initial familiarity, the reader has his expectations about proportion, propriety, and function transvalued by excess. That middle range in which the elements of fiction have traditionally been integrated is skewed to extremity by the exaggeration of one or more of these elements. In some works, excess provides a generous uselessness, a superfluity of art. In others, excess asserts the freedom of fiction from simple organic and mechanical models. And since most excessive fiction remains referential, the various means of excess defamiliarize the novels' subjects. (p. 15)

Joseph McElroy comes closest to equaling the achievement of Pynchon, for in McElroy's fiction, especially in ***Lookout Cartridge*** (1974), the art of excess works to create new imaginative models. For McElroy, more is less: the more information he gives the reader, the less the reader holds to old certainties and necessities encapsulated in conventional fictional forms. Quantitative differences near qualitative change; mass and energy produce originality. Both Pynchon and McElroy use informational overload as a basic strategy of excess, but because McElroy furnishes fewer links with popular culture and doesn't bother to amuse, his fiction has met a critical resistance that seems directly proportional to his remarkable intelligence and ambition. Although I cannot describe the massive complexity of his five novels in this space, I will comment on the informational excess that characterizes his work and discuss in some detail its effects in what I think is his best novel—***Lookout Cartridge***. (p. 16)

McElroy saturates his novels with extrinsic information from a remarkable variety of sources including familiar history and not-so-familiar sciences and technologies. The books are also intrinsically dense: bulky with detail, impacted by narrative techniques and linguistic improbability. I do not mean to suggest, however, that his five novels are inhuman stores of information that can be neither felt nor calculated. Except for ***Plus*** (1977), which is about a disembodied brain in space, the novels are set primarily and precisely in New York City and have characters who work and marry. They are Faulknerian in their attention to childhood memory, familial relations, and continuity, and Faulknerian as well in the complex treatment of these themes. The protagonists of McElroy's first three novels—***A Smuggler's Bible*** (1966), ***Hind's Kidnap*** (1969), and ***Ancient History*** (1971)—are extremely sensitized men obsessed with retrieving and understanding a past without translating their experience into some simplifying system. To express "an ultimate undecidability" of experience and to prevent the novels themselves from becoming simple, predictable systems, McElroy overloads them in various ways. In ***Lookout Cartridge*** he combines the methods of his first novels with an explicit interest in technology to produce his finest book.

The materials of ***A Smuggler's Bible*** are familiar from other first novels: the son's exile from and accommodation with the father. The narrator is an American in his thirties named David Brooke. As have most of McElroy's other protagonists, he has grown up in a Brooklyn Heights family of high intelligence and varied interests. Rather emotionally detached as a youth, Brooke decides to project himself into others' lives both literally and in the memoirs he writes. While sailing to England, David is revising the eight sections of his memoirs, which are written from various points of view. Because McElroy's presentation of his materials emphasizes their discontinuities, the relationships among the eight major blocks of the novel are improbable and the effect is a sense of overload. Materials collaborate or act together rather than lock into some chain of effects, and collaboration becomes a central theme in McElroy's fiction and a key word in his criticism. The way to this collaboration in ***A Smuggler's Bible*** is disorder: McElroy says the novel was "designed to break so that the reader would feel pieces reforming as if attracting and acting at distances from each other".

The novel is about, at least proximately, fathers and sons, their simultaneous search for and avoidance of one another; the uncertainties produced by chronological distortion and metamorphosing narration are analogues for David's psychological ambivalence. This conflict between father and son is also dramatized in short interchapters between the eight memoirs. There are two voices in these interchapters: Brooke's and some godlike or muselike or authorial voice that has fathered Brooke's voice yet is within it. Their argument over whether or not to unify the relatively discrete memoirs helps explain the rationale for McElroy's fracturing his material, but this conflict of "spirit-author" and author (or Holy Ghost and narrator) is more important as part of McElroy's exhaustive extension of the Biblical metaphor. Like the Bible, ***A Smuggler's Bible*** is concerned with the historical relation of father and son, split into separate "books" with different points of view and styles, and unified by theme and by a single agent of inspiration. Further, one motive of ***A Smuggler's Bible*** is the search for origins and ends, a continuity between genesis and revelation that would establish a configurative meaning. On the other hand, a smuggler's bible is only a means, an empty box used to transport valuables across frontiers. As the novel proceeds, various kinds of smuggling and allied dishonesties such as counterfeiting and forging are worked into the text, and by the end Brooke's manuscript is placed in a smuggler's bible on shipboard. Smuggling becomes an image for functional collecting and specious connecting, directly opposed to the more ambitious Biblical intentions of finding truth and meaning through separate acts. The metaphor of a smuggler's bible breaks when McElroy fully develops—overloads—each term's implications: the terms examine each other and cooperate for partial meanings but are finally separate as are the sections of the book. Just as David and his father move both toward and away from each other, the novel advances upon meaning and attacks its possibility, constructs and deconstructs itself as it expresses what McElroy identifies as its theme: "the powerful and mysterious coexistence of continuity and discontinuity".

Discontinuities other than the fracture of McElroy's title metaphor are also produced by excess. David Brooke breaks down because of his "total recall" of information; other characters fail in ambitious projects that exceed their powers. The memoirs and the interchapters include numerous items of extrinsic information—mechanical, mythical, geographical, and scholarly to name some categories—and various codes, including alphabetical, numerical, and linguistic, that the reader tries without success to sort into thematic continuities. There are connections, but they remain partial, short-circuited by mass. . . . The reader learns a great deal about the realistic materials of the novel, but the more data McElroy heaps upon him the less he is sure of its structure, meaning, and value. Overinformed, struggling with conventional codes for ordering the data, the reader learns to be satisfied with a collaboration among—rather than a configuration of—the elements of the novel and, presumably, of the world he can know. Because McElroy knows very well the ordinary life he here turns his attention to and because his characters are more than sums of information, the book has the emotional appeal of the best fiction about families. Ultimately, though, the achievement of ***A Smuggler's Bible*** is McElroy's creation of a sinusoidal epistemology, an alternating system that reduces the reader's expectations about continuity by giving exacting attention to both continuities and discontinuities.

The alternations of ***A Smuggler's Bible*** are essentially dialectical. In ***Hind's Kidnap,*** McElroy creates a field composition in which disparate elements have multiple, seemingly unlimited, and therefore excessive connections. His method is a Nabokovian overload of verbal networks and relations: the field of the novel is language itself, a semantically circular system of synonyms and associations. As in ***A Smuggler's Bible,*** McElroy embeds an equivocal paternal relationship in the difficulties and complications. The protagonist Jack Hind has spent years investigating the kidnap of a boy he has not known named Hershey Laurel; although Hind is married and has a child, he resumes the kidnap investigation as the novel opens. The more he tries to be a father to this unknown son, the more he discovers about his "guardian," his adoptive father who is actually his biological father. The first half of the book is detection: Hind follows elaborate verbal clues through a series of his friends. The second half is Hind's attempt to de-detect—to remove his friends and acquaintances from the plotted relationship he has put them into, to make them into ends rather than means. (pp. 18-22)

Language is both the cause of and analogue for Hind's confusion. His guardian has told him that "Language is the trap" and that "Language is what you build on"; it is both in the novel. For Hind, the city's "vertical message units" are the city. For McElroy, the words of the novel and their relations to other words, rather than to the words' referents, provide the information that he will exhaustively manipulate. . . . Puns, synonyms, connotations, allusions, quotations, alien perspectives, and noise create a multivalent system which can be used neither for the precise detection Hind first desires nor for the separation into discrete identities he later pursues. Hind's quest demands what he alludes to as a "mark-off series," but as the linguist Roman Jakobson has pointed out, "language is not a Markov-chain, whose every link is determined exclusively by the immediately preceding links, according to statistical laws of probability." Language in ***Hind's Kidnap*** and the novel itself are more akin to a synergistic system, a system of high unpredictability and therefore high information. Like Nabokov's *Pale Fire,* which McElroy admires, ***Hind's Kidnap*** makes unpredictability into intricacy or, as Nabokov's Shade says, an ornament of accidents. (pp. 22-3)

Poised between the discontinuities of ***A Smuggler's Bible*** and the overconnections of ***Hind's Kidnap, Ancient History*** deploys some familiar themes—retrieval of a past, influence of the father, the snooping self—but without the massiveness or authority of the first two books. The novel experiments with abstraction and nonliterary languages and displays a verbal excess that prepares McElroy for the achievement of ***Lookout Cartridge.*** The narrator Cy describes himself as a man with an "over-sensed" memory; he desires "the secret structures. . .which may make the continuing scene of my early life plain without doing violence" to the complexity of that scene. The "continuing scene," his memories of childhood and his later relations with country friend Al and city friend Bob, is presented in a very detailed, exact language. Cy tries to find "the secret structures" in several specialized and often abstract languages: the history and mathematics of his early schooling, which he calls "pure information"; the anthropology which is now his career; and the social systems talk of the writer Dom, his neighbor and a hybrid of Norman Mailer and Buckminster Fuller. Because these registers do not merge, because Cy does not finally want them to merge, the novel is a set of parallels, a paraphase (the novel's subtitle) rather than a paraphrase, which would be the translation of the concrete experience *into* abstractions. Cy thinks of himself as a parabola connecting the parallel systems, but at novel's end has to admit that the *ABCD* of Al, Bob, Cy, and Dom are points on many different curves. As in McElroy's first two novels, materials are distributed in a field, now explicitly defined, rather than integrated into some plot. (pp. 23-4)

In ***Hind's Kidnap*** the reader was overloaded with the concrete verbal connections of ordinary and literary languages. Here the overload is more a product of neologistic discourse and the fullness and opacity of abstractions. When McElroy mixes specific memories with Cy's interpretive languages, the range of implication and the possibilities for speculative connection are enormous. The interrupted way in which the reader receives information and the unfamiliarity of much of the extrinsic information also contribute to the novel's resistance to processing. The novel analyzes itself as a field system, but as in other works with a metafictional bent the self-analysis opens more questions than it closes. (p. 24)

McElroy speaks of his novels as "collaborative networks": these first three books are like graph paper contracted to an impossible density or expanded to show the empty spaces between the lines. In ***Lookout Cartridge,*** density, discontinuity, and a Möbius-like twisting of informations take place simultaneously to make this, more than any of McElroy's other fictions, a new, profound, and compelling imaginative model. It is a model in several senses of the word: a detailed imitation of surfaces and an experimental set of essential principles. Like the first three books, ***Lookout Cartridge*** is rooted in memory and moves by detection, but now the protagonist is more a father than he is a son, the novelist more an explorer of the future than the past, the novel itself an independent system: not referentially independent, for its materials are those of contemporary technological life, but independent of other novels because of the comprehensive range and original development of its materials. ***Lookout Cartridge*** is a macrosystem, an organon of subsystems, an encompassing construct of informations. In this novel, excess thoroughly displaces conventional expectations about selection and ordering by exhausting those expectations. Literary pragmatism—the text that "works" because it obeys a mechanistic model of proportion—is replaced by a planetary vision, the world seen through the microscope of massed details and the telescope of inclusive ideas. Because McElroy exceeds various literary norms, the reader is pressured toward, then released into the recognition that the computer-like circuitries and networks of information in the novel manifest and illuminate without explaining the countless, overlapping, collaborative systems he lives among without knowing. ***Lookout Cartridge*** is, as McElroy said of *Gravity's Rainbow,* a book that "tries to show forth the process of which human life is an instance". With *Gravity's Rainbow* and more than any other contemporary American novel I know, ***Lookout Cartridge*** dramatizes the interrelations of our plenitude and reaches toward some total realism of the open system. The results are, I think, the "wonder and awe" McElroy has reported the Apollo spacemen experiencing. In ***Lookout Cartridge,*** the reader's journey is through dense space, the novelist's substitute for awesome distances and lunar sight lines.

McElroy might well have written an encyclopedia of space; instead he exceeds the limits of the detective story—that old model of closed systems and unitary solution—to express his vision of mysteriously intersecting open systems, human and otherwise. ***Lookout Cartridge*** begins in traditional detective fashion. The protagonist Cartwright, a freelance merchant living in London in 1971, has made a documentary film with his friend Dagger DiGorro. When DiGorro's apartment is broken into and the film destroyed, Cartwright travels to New York City to investigate. When he arrives, someone tries to push him down a subway escalator. Cartwright asks the expected questions: Who has destroyed the film? Who has pushed him? And why? They are questions both Cartwright and the reader will pursue without ever fully answering through the 531 large pages of the novel. But these questions also begin to dissolve as the complex experience of the novel increasingly thrusts forward the question, what? What is this system the detective—protagonist and reader—finds himself in?

For the detective, who? suggests an agent or causal chain of agents following instructions. Identity is substantial even if identification is uncertain. The "who" of ***Lookout Cartridge*** is confusingly multiple; the novel has perhaps forty characters, many without surnames, some with identical given names. Although the book contains several conventional heavies—the inscrutable messenger Krish, the maniacal hit man Incremona, the bankroller Jack—and violence is done, responsibility is diffused over the multiple, partially interlocking groups. These groups have various motives for wanting the film destroyed and Cartwright's investigation stopped, so why? is also only partially answerable. . . . What the groups and Cartwright have in common is a need for information, that crucial element exchanged in transactions among open systems studied by systems theory. In the conventional detective story, the investigator ferrets, cajoles, or forces information from others. Here the process is reversible as well, with most of the characters drawn as information-providing and information-consuming beings. What the groups represent, in a concrete, rarely schematic way, are some of the primary power systems—political, social, economic, cultural, scientific, religious—of our time. Who? and why? are questions about character and causality. Although the consolation of character is reserved for few besides Cartwright in ***Lookout Cartridge,*** McElroy does not make the minor people into caricatures or functions of force as does, say, Heller in *Catch-22* or Gaddis in *JR*. The many groups do represent and do effect power, but the novel itself is more a system of informations than a system of actions. McElroy chooses to emphasize final rather than efficient causality, structural relations rather than functional mechanics, reversible circuits rather than one-way linkages, collaboration rather than independent action, analogues rather than sequences, probabilities rather than effects, simultaneity rather than linearity. These are the conceptual emphases that make ***Lookout Cartridge*** an original fictional system. By making his selection seem more inclusive, more open; by making order multiple; and by stressing the value of reciprocity and information, McElroy creates a model that has less to do with the principles of the traditional novel than with the contributions of contemporary science, structuralism, and systems theory. Realistic in its details, ***Lookout Cartridge*** moves beyond the mechanistic realism of most contemporary fiction to a formal and conceptual correspondence with a reality the empiricist's eye cannot see. (pp. 25-8)

Lookout Cartridge is long, wide, and dense. Its excesses ask the reader to see large and small sets, pipelines of plot and capillaries of style, in a simultaneous field: "the great multiple field of impinging informations". Cartwright speaks of the law of deformation, which rules the process of turning a sphere into a flat map. The excess of ***Lookout Cartridge*** is McElroy's novelistic deformation, his method for making a linear form dramatize simultaneous and circular systems. I think ***Lookout Cartridge*** is the most successful of McElroy's overloaded fictions because here overload serves the largest, most original vision; because the analogues and metaphors for that vision seem natural and necessary—true—rather than fabricated; and because the realistic materials—love, marriage, and fatherhood, multinational survival, power and terror—are most compelling. Furthermore, in ***Lookout Cartridge*** one understands the source of McElroy's excess. More than just an intellectual display, it grows from the attention McElroy gives to the world. Unlike the bitter knowledge one finds in other works of excess—Coover's *The Public Burning,* Gaddis' *JR,* even *Gravity's Rainbow*—McElroy's attention is passionately generous, welcoming while insisting on a reciprocal, a collaborative, attention from his reader.

McElroy's latest novel, ***Plus,*** is an extraordinary coda to his first four novels, an ontogeny that recapitulates the phylogeny of those earlier books, and an experiment in linguistic density that rivals those of Stein and Beckett. Like ***Lookout Cartridge, Plus*** uses as its base a popular genre, here the extraterrestrial journey of science fiction. To mediate the book's linguistic demands on the reader, McElroy gives it the mythical contour of Joseph Campbell's *The Hero with a Thousand Faces:* departure, initiation, return. A moribund engineer has his brain separated from his body and placed in an Interplanetary Monitoring Platform (IMP). While orbiting earth, the brain, now called Imp Plus, becomes conscious of itself as more than a monitor. It unfolds, remembers the past, unites with the algae beds in its capsule and braids with the sun, cuts itself off from ground control, and begins to create its body anew. The brain becomes other than itself—a lattice receiving and sending energy. It re-establishes contact with the ground, develops telepathic powers, surrenders vanity and desire, and finally sacrifices its physical existence in re-entry to become "a circuit of conception," a speculative idea in the minds of men.

This outline hardly does justice to the complex and emotionally affecting processes of growth and change that Imp Plus goes through, but it does suggest how ***Plus*** can be read as a coda to McElroy's fiction. The brain—intricate store of information, locus of collaborative processes—is the appropriate single metaphor for McElroy's work as a whole. The novel and the situation of Imp Plus (I am plus) within the novel indicate essential qualities and changing purposes in McElroy's fiction. The novel summarizes McElroy's increasing interest in scientific materials and the potential they bring to fiction; his concern with quantitative differences becoming qualitative change; his attention to "the relation between Outside and Inside"; his growing interest in growth itself: the need for and danger of expansion toward wholeness; his ever more complex themes of circling, collaborative systems; and his developing recognition that new language is new consciousness. Plus's situation within the novel reflects McElroy's self-imposed distance from "ground's" fictional conventions as a way toward some fuller communication with "ground's" attentive reader, and Plus's refusal of easy recovery points to McElroy's commitment to difficult conceptions. ***Plus*** explicitly affirms this novelist's methods and intentions: plus is more and plus is positive.

The overload of ***Plus*** is entirely linguistic. Few flashbacks interrupt the chronological line or the single setting of Plus's development. The reader encounters several characters (actually "Voices"), but there are almost no allusions to extrinsic information, and no grids of analogue to trace. The pace is slow, idyllic, a continuous present; repetition and subtle variation replace the quick-cutting of McElroy's other novels. Yet ***Plus*** is the most dense and perhaps the most difficult of McElroy's books. To portray a brain becoming aware of itself and becoming more than itself, McElroy had to create an original discourse that would express both the difficulties and the exhilaration of a coming into consciousness, that would in turn function as a model for any man's radical change in consciousness, for growth out of illness. At the beginning, McElroy reduces lexicon, simplifies grammar, and repeats; as in Stein's primer style, language is emptied of referential meaning. . . . As Hemingway remarked, easy writing makes hard reading: for a time the reader lacks specific information, and is overloaded with the opacity of abstractions and pronouns. As ***Plus*** develops, McElroy introduces concrete images from Plus's past and what Plus calls his "microsight"—the lexicon of neural physiology. Unfamiliar words with a very specialized referential meaning combine with simple abstractions to describe the complicated, even tortuous physical and conceptual growth of Imp Plus. This new language is played off against the chatty but purely pragmatic talk of ground control, which is capitalized throughout. As in ***Lookout Cartridge,*** but more radically here, excessive precision and excessive abstraction displace that middle range of expression that serves ordinary consciousness. Plus is overloaded by his experience—"It was far more than the words were equal to"—and the reader is overloaded by that squeezing and stretching of language that McElroy employs to express a mysterious presence of meaning and, almost more importantly, a significant absence of meaning. (pp. 34-7)

Although ***Plus,*** like Golding's *The Inheritors* and Burgess' *A Clockwork Orange,* is an imaginative tour de force, the radical linguistic experiment in ***Plus*** pushes toward what Cartwright in ***Lookout Cartridge*** calls "new modes of mind . . . a new privacy of collaborative process in which getting there or back here has become so minor as to be forgotten". Imp Plus changes from a channel of information to information itself. McElroy does not so much use scientific knowledge in ***Plus*** as he makes ***Plus*** its own science, not something we learn about or through but something we learn. ***Plus***—and McElroy's work as a whole—approaches the definition of information: an improbable quantity with maximum use. (p. 37)

Thomas LeClair, "Joseph McElroy and the Art of Excess," in Contemporary Literature, *Vol. 21, No. 1, Winter, 1980, pp. 15-37.*

TOM LeCLAIR

Women and Men is. . .the most important novel to appear in America since Thomas Pynchon's *Gravity's Rainbow* in 1973.

If you have been daunted by Pynchon's ravaging encyclopedia of entropy or by some of its massive successors in the 1970s—William Gaddis' *JR,* Robert Coover's *The Public Burning,* Don DeLillo's *Ratner's Star,* or John Barth's *Letters*—you will find McElroy's novel rather different, even longer than these masterworks of the decade but as earnest as the Victorian tripledeckers of Thackeray and Dickens, as attentive to the moving particulars of American family life as James or Faulkner. And unlike Pynchon and other contemporaries, McElroy is both fearful and hopeful about the survival of our species.

McElroy does make large demands on the reader, but they are the necessary consequences of his concern: to create a fiction that formally corresponds in some never-before attempted way to the concrete plenitude, intricate connections, and encompassing scale of the ecosystem. McElroy, in this novel, is our first planetary realist.

Set primarily in New York City in 1976-77, revolving around the lives of a feminist guru and a male science reporter, spreading outward into their large and sometimes overlapping circles of friends, taking in characters from Chile, New Mexico, and points between, ***Women and Men*** also ranges far beyond the merely human, backward into millennia of American landscape and forward to extra-planetary existence, downward into the ancient energies of earth's geology and upward to world-wide weather and the consciousness of spirits waiting to be reborn into human form.

Up and down, forward and back—these directions may recall the Great Chain of Being or suggest geometry's coordinate axes. But we know the ecosystem in which humans participate is as insistently and tightly looped as a baseball underneath its hide, and it is this criss-crossing, circling structure that ***Women and Men*** imitates, winding and rewinding itself to become a globe of life. If, as one of McElroy's characters says, "every little thing matters," then a minute change in a helix of DNA, a murder in Chile, the tilt of a lover's eyebrow, or a small shift along a fault line must be weighed into the relations of women and men. McElroy's ability to connect all that he collects and invents and to persuade us that this act of connection is crucial—this is the feat that humbles us, reminds us that our foursquare models of the world—novels we read, maps we consult, even dreams we have—are too often reductive, unworthy of our capacities.

Ten years in the writing, ***Women and Men*** is not an unexpected achievement. Since ***A Smuggler's Bible*** in 1966, McElroy has published four profoundly thoughtful and sophisticated novels—***Hind's Kidnap, Ancient History, Lookout Cartridge,*** and ***Plus.*** Though regularly praised by reviewers, and compared to Pynchon and Barth, McElroy has not had that "breakthrough" book that would bring him the readers his work deserves. ***Women and Men*** should be that novel, an accomplishment too large to avoid and a book that makes clear his intentions: to know enough about the sexes and the sciences of the present to write fiction for the future.

The two principal characters of ***Women and Men,*** while partly dividing this labor of knowledge, have all the everyday specificity we enjoy in more conventional domestic realism. Grace Kimball, a fiftyish feminist who runs nude Body-Self workshops in her Manhattan apartment, is a vulgar, charitable, witty and manipulative contemporary personality. As women of various ages and marital stages reveal their troubles to Kimball (and the reader), she reflects on her own marriage, friendships, and gender history, assuming the role of Great Goddess to help others activate their lives in the short-term future. As physical and frank as a longshoreman, Kimball reverses sexual stereotypes and plays off against her more detached neighbor, James Mayn, McElroy's other protagonist.

A much-traveled, middle-aged journalist who says he never dreams, Mayn is engaged by distant subjects such as solving the mysteries of his family past, including his grandmother's trip to the frontier and his mother's suicide when James was a boy. Mayn also attempts to understand his science-fiction daydream of a place where men and women will be joined as one being, and he investigates a multinational political plot that ultimately brings him closer to home when he discovers his daughter is involved. If Kimball is McElroy's voice of personal knowledge and myth, Mayn speaks for cultural traditions and science. Though they never quite meet, they do form, in the reader's mind, the unified woman/man that Mayn imagines.

Quite explicitly aware of the "awesome excess of data" his protagonists' lives generate, McElroy provides several conventionally suspenseful plots—finding secrets and love, preventing violence and disaster—to propel the reader on to what happens next. Webs of character, though, are McElroy's primary interest. Surrounding Kimball and Mayn are numerous people who would be protagonists in less expansive novels—a Chilean diva mixed up in sexual, artistic and political intrigue; a brilliantly observed teen-aged boy dealing with recently divorced parents; an 1890s feminist who returns to New Jersey from a trip to New Mexico with an Indian lover and a storehouse of myths; an idiot savant messenger, expert on the grid of New York City streets; a convict named Foley whose hundred-page monologue exposes prison life while proposing a new economics. These and many more minor characters braid together to fill out the seemingly pretentious abstractions of McElroy's title, making ***Women and Men*** the most comprehensive treatment I know of relations between the sexes.

To create what one of his characters calls a "simul-system," McElroy mixes together three kinds of chapters. One set presents brief *New Yorker*-style vignettes of contemporary city life. A second set is composed of streams and eddies of consciousness, most often Kimball's and Mayn's. The third set is McElroy's greatest risk. Called "Breathers," these chapters are the often long-winded meditations and gossip of souls waiting to be reincarnated on an earth they can observe. A new kind of omniscient and omniverous narration, the "Breathers" chapters are the minds of McElroy surveying personal, historical, and spiritual ecology. (pp. 1, 14)

That it frequently frustrates with its density and multiplicity, its microscopic observations and macroscopic abstraction, I will admit. I think, too, that McElroy favors his male Mayn at the expense of his female counterpart. And I realize readers will need stores of energy. But, finally, I believe that ***Women and Men*** is the single book—fiction or nonfiction—that best manifests what human beings can know and be and imagine now and, just as importantly, in the future. (p. 14)

Tom LeClair, "The Novel as Kaleidoscope," in Book World—The Washington Post, *March 22, 1987, pp. 1, 14.*

IVAN GOLD

Several of Mr. McElroy's earlier books (the others are ***Ancient History*** and ***Hind's Kidnap***) are in the 500-page range, and none, to risk a guess, was singled out for its accessibility. But ***Women and Men***—10 years in the writing, according to the publisher—is of a grander design. The Tolstoyan sweep of the title is the first clue to the scope of the enterprise. . . .

There does seem to be a svelte couple trapped inside ***Women and Men,*** a thin man and a thin woman trying to get out. They are James Mayn and Grace Kimball, two people who live in the same apartment building in New York and never meet, yet we will learn how their lives are connected. Mayn is a journalist or former journalist in his late 40's, divorced, with two grown children, with an alter ego named Spence who may or may not be stalking him, and he's plagued by the notion that he's come this way before, that is to say, has in some manner already lived his future life.

Grace Kimball is an attractive, sometimes brassy woman who presides over "Body-Self" workshops out on the cutting edge of feminism, or where some, in the 1970's, located that edge. It is not unusual for her students to get together in the nude and collectively masturbate, alone, and yet together. Grace is part American Indian, which provides a distant echo for Jim's constant brooding over tales his grandmother told him in his childhood about the comings and goings of a perhaps real, perhaps mythical Navajo Prince. These stories are of such eidetic urgency for Mayn that it becomes almost possible to understand, as he travels the world on mysterious para-journalistic errands, why he has difficulty distinguishing fact from fiction, or the present from the past. He is similarly obsessed by the possibility that his mother committed suicide (she disappeared, at any rate), and by his discovery later in life that his kid brother, Brad, is in fact his half-brother, the issue of his mother's brief affair. He loves his intellectual daughter, has little contact with his figure-skating son.

But his connection to Grace is more substantial than whatever is implied by her Indian blood and by the fact that the pair of them share a doorman—Jim becomes spiritual father to the distraught Larry, the son of a woman who attends Grace's workshop, a woman Grace is encouraging to seek a divorce. Larry, like Jim, may well be a "trace window," one of those channels through whom the past and future freely flow.

There is no shortage of data about the past and present lives of Jim and Grace, sometimes conveyed through the lively scenes Mr. McElroy is quite capable of inventing, but most often set forth in a viscous, arch, hectoring, information-crammed, unparagraphed series of the longest sentences since William Faulkner's.

Knowledge, not creation of character, is Mr. McElroy's long suit—the same sentences that describe the lives of Jim and Grace are made to give involved history lessons (more here than you might want to know about Coxey's Army, Ernie Pyle, American Indians, the U-2 incident, NASA, disarmament, America's involvement in Chile, etc.). And these same sentences are charged with keeping in the forefront of a reader's mind the author's seemingly private coordinates and metaphors for whatever might be going on—lengthy references to a "wide load," a "tapeworm," the aforementioned Navajo Prince, a Hermit-Inventor of New York and many more, equally arcane. A professional torturer makes interesting cameo appearances, but it is never clear, perhaps by design, whether he is torturing the characters in ***Women and Men*** or the reader, who is in any event, throughout the narrative, buttonholed and addressed as "you," pinned against a wall in a dark alley by a towering, nonstop voice. Mr. McElroy is said to speak to the preoccupations of our time, and he may well; there are simply too many preoccupations to house between the covers—however widely separated—of one novel.

Mayn, contemplating the dissolution of his marriage on page 1,004, observes: "Life's in parts, and some go together and some don't, and some incongruously don't, and the whole scheme is better left to itself." Had this insight come to him earlier, the shape of the book he inhabits might conceivably have altered. . . .

An academic critic could gear up for ***Women and Men*** (once past some jocular opening remarks on the "new maximalist novel"): its post-modernist reliance on blatant tricks of style, its canny melding and imploding of genres. For me, by the close, it was like having listened for several days to an all-news station in a foreign language: you have a rough idea of what's been going on, the news is worse than you imagine, and, while you feel more or less informed, you can't really say that you've enjoyed yourself. But one does not go to this novelist for the usual pleasures.

Ivan Gold, "Boy Doesn't Meet Girl," in The New York Times Book Review, *April 12, 1987, p. 18.*

ALBERT MOBILIO

Women and Men . . . constitutes an epic bid to isolate a small part of the limitless quality of experience. The paradox involved betrays the essentially poetic character of the job. Yet even by Pound's standards this is one very long poem. At work for 10 years, McElroy has produced a massive volume containing 1200 of the densest pages you're likely to read. Like other postmodern big books—*The Recognitions, Giles Goat-Boy, Gravity's Rainbow*—***Women and Men*** embodies the American notion of manifest destiny, a continent-sized ambition to speak largely in a large land. And with that title can one expect anything less than the vast embrace?

McElroy does not disappoint, but neither does he offer the tidal sweep of history or a single life examined from cradle to grave. The novel's "action" takes place in the time it takes to read it, much the way Molly Bloom's life takes place as she speaks it. ***Women and Men*** achieves its epic scale through the accumulation of details, a multitude of social and emotional gestures so dead-on specific they would delight Thackeray. Strangely enough, however, the abundance of the actual never displaces the narrator; ***Women and Men*** becomes, at its best, pure voice inside the head.

Obviously, such an enterprise doesn't yield easily to description, even less to summary. However, out of the dozen or more characters who mainly come and go, there are two, Jim Mayn and Grace Kimball, who occupy center stage. While these apartment house neighbors never meet, it is from their mysteriously connected worlds that McElroy spins an intensely nuanced web of other lives and other histories. (p. 51)

The flawed, unsettled state of current relations between the sexes is a topic some might say has been beat within an inch of its life. Universality and ease of affect assure its popularity with easy-read writers who believe some blues and a poignant freeze add up to a story. McElroy, however, ventures out on this well-worn turf with a novel that, whatever its ultimate merits, reads, feels, and sounds aggressively different.

What happens in ***Women and Men*** remains blurry, but what happened to this reader isn't. Aggravation and impatience mixed with cheers and real kicks. Overlong and too diffuse, the novel is exploding out of itself and you feel that. McElroy provides a personal introduction to the full-blown storm of immense sensibility, and the prose—propulsive, encyclopedic, and syntactically free-form—gives evidence of the encounter. . . . Page-long sentences that sound (some passages demand to be read aloud) like late James on alto are juxtaposed with elliptical clips of what could be Apollinaire: "Meanwhile, decades later in the near future two persons stand upon a metal plate waiting to be elsewhere." In the cadence of breathless conversation these sentences wrap close around the jolts and jags of real talk. Arriving in rapid, chantlike waves, what's being said sometimes gets lost in the vocal buzz: pure voice inside the head.

Amid this apparent free-for-all lies a subtly crafted strategy of connectedness. How things might possibly be made to fit together is a question McElroy has asked in each of his novels. ***Lookout Cartridge*** involves an effort to re-assemble fragments of a destroyed film. In ***Plus,*** a human brain orbiting the earth reconstructs its language, memory, and self from a few syllables. ***Women and Men*** uses cross-referencing and sheer accumulation, the techniques employed in those two novels, to connect its characters' atomized lives. McElroy orchestrates the appearance of a series of verbal and visual motifs—Ship Rock, the Chilean economist, Wide Load—that bind disparate texts and establish subconscious links for the reader between characters. It is a kind of poetry, building by increments.

The author's advice to readers of novels built to detonate when cause meets effect can be found in the preface to ***Lookout Cartridge*** but is no less pertinent here: "Trust your reactions to this book just as you have to begin trusting your own reactions to the powerful life in which you get your bearings every day. . . . Trust your sense of being in this book." McElroy rewards the effort. Brilliant and rigorously human, ***Women and Men*** offers a risky, brakeless drive at the far edge of what's possible in the novel. (p. 52)

Albert Mobilio, "More Is More: Joseph McElroy's New-Age Epic," in The Village Voice, *Vol. XXXII, No. 18, May 5, 1987, pp. 51-2.*

Arthur Miller

1915-

American dramatist, essayist, scriptwriter, short story writer, nonfiction writer, novelist, and autobiographer.

© Thomas Victor 1987

Miller's eminence as a dramatist derives primarily from four plays he wrote early in his career: *All My Sons* (1947), which earned him Tony and New York Drama Critics Circle Awards; *Death of a Salesman* (1949), for which he received the Pulitzer Prize in drama as well as Tony and New York Drama Critics Circle Awards; *The Crucible* (1953), which generated another Tony Award; and *A View from the Bridge* (1955), for which he was awarded a New York Drama Critics Circle Award. Insisting that "the individual is doomed to frustration when once he gains a consciousness of his own identity," Miller synthesizes elements from social and psychological realism to depict the individual's search for identity within a society that inhibits such endeavors. Although his later works are generally considered inferior to his early masterpieces, Miller remains among the most important and influential dramatists to emerge in the United States since World War II. Critics praise his effective use of vernacular, his moral insight, and his strong sense of social responsibility. June Schlueter commented: "When the twentieth century is history and American drama viewed in perspective, the plays of Arthur Miller will undoubtedly be preserved in the annals of dramatic literature."

Family conflicts are crucial to the plot development of Miller's early work and serve as a pretext for his examination of the relationship between the individual and society. In *All My Sons,* for example, Miller attacks American materialism, an ideal which he believes results in a conflict for most people between individual notions of well-being and social responsibility. In this play, set during World War II, Joe Keller sells defective aircraft parts to the United States Army Air Force to save his business. When this results in the deaths of American pilots, Keller allows his business partner to be imprisoned for the crime and takes over the company. At the play's conclusion, one of Keller's sons, a pilot, reveals that he plans to commit suicide because of his father's negligence, while Keller's other son demands that his father take responsibility for his act. Unable to cope with his guilt and with a world where social values contradict family loyalty, Keller commits suicide. Critics noted the resemblance of *All My Sons* to Henrik Ibsen's domestic tragedy *The Wild Duck,* and Miller has acknowledged Ibsen's influence on his work.

Death of a Salesman is widely considered Miller's masterpiece and is recognized as a classic of contemporary American theater. This play, which represents his most powerful dramatization of the clash between the individual and the materialistic American dream, chronicles the downfall of Willy Loman, a salesman whose misguided notions of success result in disillusionment. At the drama's end, Willy commits suicide, convinced that the wealth which eluded him will fall to his son Biff; however, Biff's ideals have already been tarnished by the same myths and illusions which destroyed his father. Critics often disagree with Miller's insistence that *Death of a Salesman* is a modern tragedy and that Willy emerges as a tragic hero; while some concede that Willy attains tragic dimensions by virtue of what Miller has termed an intense "human passion to surpass his given bounds," many reviewers maintained that the drama cannot be considered a tragedy in the traditional sense. Dan Vogel contended that Willy "is too commonplace and limited, [the play's] atmosphere is too dependent upon the delusions and weaknesses of an American materialistic society, and its problem is too ignoble."

Miller's most controversial play, *The Crucible,* is based upon the witch trials held in Salem, Massachusetts, in 1692. Featuring historical characters drawn from this period, *The Crucible* addresses the complex moral dilemmas of John Proctor, a man wrongly accused of practicing witchcraft. As the mass frenzy of the witch hunt mounts, Miller examines the social and psychological aspects of group pressure and its effect on individual ethics, dignity, and beliefs. Many critics interpreted *The Crucible* as a thinly-disguised critique of Joseph McCarthy's Senate investigations of communism in the United States. In Miller's next play, *A View from the Bridge,* Eddie Carbone precipitates his own downfall by harboring an incestuous love for his niece, Catherine. Jealous of Catherine's attraction to an illegal alien whom the Carbones are hiding, Eddie exposes the man to immigration authorities and becomes involved in a fatal confrontation with the man's brother. Some reviewers considered *A View from the Bridge* a contemporary drama written in the form of a Greek tragedy; like the tragic heroes of Greek drama, Eddie meets his fate with courage and dignity.

Following a nine-year hiatus from playwriting, Miller returned to the theater with *After the Fall* (1964), a drama that departs from his original style and thematic concerns. Whereas Miller's early plays center on problems of identity and societal pressures within realistic domestic settings, such later plays as *After the Fall* explore questions of social responsibility and personal guilt independent of family environments. *After the Fall* takes place, in Miller's words, "in the mind, thought, and memory of Quentin," a guilt-ridden man whose life resembles Miller's in many respects. By trying to come to terms with his past through conversations with an imaginary listener, Quentin realizes that human fallibility is universal rather than personal, and that every person must be held accountable for others. Although *After the Fall* received praise for its experimental structure, most reviewers faulted Miller for pretentious theorizing and artificial characterizations.

In *Incident at Vichy* (1965), Miller celebrates the strength of human dignity while continuing to examine the nature of deception and the limitations of personal guilt. This play, set in occupied France during World War II, features seven men who discuss their fate and the importance of social commitment to maintaining group freedom while awaiting interrogation by their Nazi captors. Their conclusions suggest that those who fail to resist oppression are as guilty as the Nazis of crimes against humanity. Miller's next play, *The Price* (1968), is a realistic family drama in which two brothers, Victor and Walter, are brought together after many years by the death of their father. When Victor accuses his brother of abandoning their father during the Depression, Walter refuses to accept the burden of guilt, and the brothers part in anger. *The Creation of the World and Other Business* (1972), later revised under the title *Up from Paradise*, is Miller's most radical deviation from his initial style. Written in a lightly humorous tone, this drama pits God against the devil in a debate concerning humanity's worth. This drama met with severe critical reprobation and closed after only twenty performances on Broadway.

The Archbishop's Ceiling (1977), set in a communist European country, is an intellectual drama in which Miller celebrates the power of the human will. This play chronicles the artistic struggles of a dissident novelist who reacts to government censure by shunning exile and fighting for his freedom. *The American Clock* (1980), structured as a series of vignettes that function as a social history of the United States, suggests that the hardship and suffering of the Depression served to unify and strengthen American society. Miller's recent drama, *Danger: Memory!* (1986), consists of two one-act plays which explore the relationship of the past to the present. In the first work, *I Can't Remember Anything*, an elderly man and woman meet to exchange views on a variety of subjects. Although the woman condemns contemporary society, the man concludes that there is still hope for the future. In *Clara*, the second one-act play in *Danger: Memory!*, a police detective ruthlessly interrogates the guilt-ridden father of a murdered social worker. They soon become involved in ideological debates over such topics as the Vietnam War, racism, and the Holocaust. Although some critics acknowledged the drama's occasionally compelling moments, most faulted *Clara* as ponderous and ostentatious. Frank Rich observed: "While Arthur Miller's admirable voice of conscience remains firm as always, *Danger: Memory!* is an evening in which the pontificator wins out over the playwright."

In addition to his dramas, Miller has published several works in other genres. His novel *Focus* (1945) offers an incisive critique of American anti-Semitism through the character of a gentile who is mistaken for a Jew because of his appearance. Iris Barry called *Focus* "a first-rate horror story, cleverly as well as passionately devised from the first premonitory touch." *The Misfits* (1961), a screenplay Miller created for his wife, Marilyn Monroe, is based on the short story of the same title collected in *I Don't Need You Anymore* (1967). *Situation Normal* (1944) is a nonfiction account of military training during World War II. *The Theater Essays of Arthur Miller* (1978) collects Miller's essays on theater craft, while *Salesman in Beijing* (1984) recounts his experience in China directing *Death of a Salesman*. Miller has also written an autobiography, *Timebends: A Life* (1987).

(See also *CLC*, Vols. 1, 2, 6, 10, 15, 26; *Contemporary Authors*, Vols. 1-4, rev. ed.; *Contemporary Authors New Revision Series*, Vol. 2; *Dictionary of Literary Biography*, Vol. 7; and *Concise Dictionary of American Literary Biography, 1941-1968*.)

IRIS BARRY

[***Focus***] is a courageous plea, on the part of a novelist with an urgent message, to "put yourself in his place" once again. His book is a fervent cry against intolerance and, specifically, against anti-Semitism. According to Mr. Miller (and he makes his contention dramatically real), a marked and growing ill-will toward the Jewish members of our community is already assuming Nazi-like proportions here. His fiction is rendered particularly effective because he asks his readers to put themselves in the place not of a Jew, but in the shoes of a humdrum gentile clerk, whose growing astigmatism compels him to get spectacles, and who is worried because he thinks the glasses make him "look Jewish."

The story, then, is that of this very ordinary citizen's misery and humiliation, of the persecutions to which he is subjected when it proves that he is indeed "taken for a Jew," and of the abominable temptation to which he is subject when fear half induces him to prove his Christian bona fides by joining a new local terrorist organization for running Jews out of his suburban neighborhood.

Admittedly, the picture presented is a lurid one. One's first impulse is to reject it as exaggerated and incredible. This is not likely to happen here; we do not persecute minorities in America or ostracize Jews, or banish them or any so-called alien groups from our own neighborhoods. Or hardly ever.

Yet some of the minor occurrences that come to harass and alarm the hero of this tale, as Mr. Miller so effectively relates them, do leave behind an uncomfortable and nagging sensation. . . .

This book is going to make a lot of people furiously angry. Nevertheless, it also sets out to ventilate what the author shows to be an extremely rotten state of affairs. Incidentally, it is a first-rate horror story, cleverly as well as passionately devised from the first premonitory nightmare touch, apt by its mere story-telling proficiency to enlist one's interest and thereby to plunge one inextricably in its sinister sequence of events, right through to the unexpected emergence of its hero from his intolerable dilemma. It is in a class with the propaganda novels of Charles Reade, or Harriet Beecher Stowe, which is a pretty good class to be in. The happiest fortune we can ask for it is that it may be read not by the completely tolerant members of our large populace but by those, so much more numerous, who either have not had occasion to face the problem it propounds or who chose simply to close their eyes to it.

Iris Barry, "Look through This Glass," in New York Herald Tribune Weekly Book Review, *November 18, 1945, p. 4.*

ALFRED BUTTERFIELD

[***Focus***] is a novel about anti-Semitism, a strong, sincere book bursting with indignation and holding the reader's attention despite its many faults. Its author handles his explosive materials skillfully, but not skillfully enough to keep his novel from sounding like a tract. And as a tract it depends too much on melodrama to be fully convincing. It would not be fair to Mr. Miller to examine his plot too closely. Its underlying device . . . is so fantastic as to look ridiculous considered apart from the clever superstructure. Perhaps Mr. Miller set himself too difficult a job in trying to lend conviction to a basically implausible situation. Perhaps he should have written his story straight. . . .

The transmogrification of Newman is a peculiarly unsubtle one, persecuted as he is by he roughnecks of the Christian Front. The most effective scenes of ***Focus*** are largely physical in nature, such as the picture of a Front rally, and of the great battle near the end where Newman takes up a baseball bat beside a Mr. Finkelstein. As the case history of a very strange human experience this novel has high merit. As a work of substantial meaning, it does not succeed.

Alfred Butterfield, in a review of "Focus," in The New York Times Book Review, *November 18, 1945, p. 15.*

JOHN WAKEMAN

Arthur Miller, for whom the theater is his serious business, his stern duty, writes short stories for his own pleasure and has now published a collection of them for ours. ***I Don't Need You Any More*** contains nine stories, eight of them written during the period of flux and transition which began for their author in 1956.

Plays and stories have certain affinities, as Mr. Miller points out in his foreword, and it is no surprise to find that he can sketch a scene or character with fine economy, or that he can do excellent impersonations. But these stories have other and less theatrical qualities. There is scant reliance on dialogue or dramatic action, and few signs of the sociological preoccupations that used to characterize the author's plays. Mr. Miller thinks the essential difference between a play and a story is a matter of the author's "distance" from his material; in a story he escapes from "the terrible heat at the center of the stage" to a position from which "the object, the place, weather, the look of a person's shift of posture . . . can all register and weigh."

Such things are made to register and weigh most effectively in **"The Misfits"** (1957), which in its original form is a story as stripped and significant as a bone, with none of the fleshing-out that partly disfigured the movie version. The two cowboys and the flyer are brought awake and to life, and the plane leaves to drive the handful of mustangs down from the mountains. The cowboys wait, their friendship warming and cooling in the "dead, sunlit silence" of the desert, until the horses come. There follows the controlled frenzy of pursuit and capture, during which the cowboys recognize the beauty and freedom of the horses. But "anything's better than wages," and their own freedom seems more important, though it is really the same freedom. Innocence is irrevocably lost. . . .

The earliest story here, relatively flat in its characterization, is **"Monte Sant' Angelo"** (1951), about an American Jew in Italy, a little envious of his ancestor-hunting friend, who discovers in his Jewishness a place and a history of his own. [**"I Don't Need You Any More"**], which examines a few critical hours in the life of a small boy, is the sort of presumably autobiographical exercise dear to the sad, subtle heart of *The New Yorker*. If the child's self-knowledge seems at times unacceptably precocious, the story is otherwise beautifully and lyrically observed, full of startling perceptions. It is also often funny (which will confound some of Mr. Miller's critics), as is **"Fitter's Night,"** a cautionary tale set in the Brooklyn Navy Yard during World War II. The most interesting (and least satisfying) piece here, the only one that seems to want to be a play, is a Chekhovian story called **"The Prophecy."** One reads it resenting the rather glibly ironic ending, and needing to know more.

Mr. Miller, who after all began as a novelist, sees life less simply than he did, and this is a handicap in the theater; he speaks rather wistfully of those playwrights who "at middle age so often turn to fiction and away from the unseemly masquerade." If he should ever join them it would, of course, be a loss to the theater—but, on this showing, a clear gain for fiction. This is exact, humane, knowledgeable writing, free of affectation and self-congratulation, its many successes honestly earned. (p. 4)

John Wakeman, "Story Time," in The New York Times Book Review, *April 2, 1967, pp. 4, 34.*

THE TIMES LITERARY SUPPLEMENT

As a short-story writer, Arthur Miller suggests, an author is less immodest than he is as a dramatist. Plays are aggressive, stories more personal and familiar so that the author is not so much a performer, an impersonator. . . . [One] persistent theme [in ***I Don't Need You Anymore***] is that of conflict between discipline and spontaneity. While most stories here require a smaller number of "impersonations" than plays demand (usually the author need imitate only one person, narrator or "hero"), one of them, **"The Prophecy"**, takes on a little too much, so that it is like a long and complicated novel which the writer has cleverly abridged. A young author called Joseph Kersh is criticized by a supposedly psychic old woman for writing works which are "a bit over-constructed"—an accusation which could be used against Miller himself, in this very story.

Another recurring element is Joseph's reaction to the old woman's strictures: "He did not like her. Women ought not to criticize. She was repulsively ugly." Upon Joseph's entry into this house of women, his immediate reaction was:

> Women discovered alone must have been talking about sex. He had believed this since his childhood, when his mother's bridge parties

> had always gone from screaming hilarity to matronly silence as soon as he appeared.

The same concern may be noted in his 1961 prizewinning story, **"I Don't Need You Any More."** This strong story sets down the author's demand for tradition, for family history, for Europe. Americans of Italian descent set the example—enviable to the Jewish character in **"Monte Sant' Angelo"**. A Navy fitter may boast a grandfather, "a throwback to some giants of old whose wit and ferocity had made them lords in Calabria, chiefs among the rocks". (This story, **"Fitter's Nights"**, is remarkable also for using tellingly the idioms of [Hubert Selby, Jr.'s] *Last Exit to Brooklyn,* for making descriptions of manual work interesting and for extending to Englishmen the infuriating patronage of racial tolerance.) The linking of maleness and tradition runs through a graceful vernacular monologue, **"Glimpse at a Jockey"**.

> The men are scared, did you see it where you been around? Nobody knows any more where he begins or ends, it's like they pied maps and put Chicago in Latvia. They don't allow nobody to die for loyalty any more, there's nothin' in it to steal.

This kind of feeling—that there is "a proper place" for everyone—is apparent in his concern for wild horses (**"The Misfits"**) and even for fish: "They'll live to a ripe old age and grow prosperous and dignified. . . . And see their children grown up!"

Some stories seem too "plotty" and play-like. Others are pure anecdote, like the funny Jewish story **"Fame"**, about an American playwright depressed by seeing his face (like a mask) on the cover of *Time*. The last story, **"A Search for a Future"**, eloquently combines the compelling themes in an account of an over-disciplined actor whose old, dying, spontaneous father escapes from the hospital.

"At Another Distance," in The Times Literary Supplement, *No. 3431, November 30, 1967, p. 1125.*

ENOCH BRATER

[***The Theater Essays of Arthur Miller***] comes at a most opportune time, for it serves to remind us that the realistic method Miller adopted has as its basis not merely a way of saying something, but something to say. . . .

Miller resolved to make his mark on the New York stage in the spirit of American pragmatism. "Wonder," he wrote in the introduction to the ***Collected Plays,*** "must have feet with which to walk the earth." Integrating new theatrical mechanics into the set for ***Death of a Salesman,*** he made the past literally simultaneous with the present in a practical dramatic solution above and beyond formalism. The staging of Willy Loman's psyche, his frustrated hopes and his unfulfilled dreams, could then strike his audience with astonishing immediacy and clarity. (p. 32)

John Gassner [see *CLC*, Vol. 26] and Joseph Wood Krutch pounced on poor Willy by stating unequivocally that his was a situation of pathos, not tragedy. One simply did not write tragedy about broken refrigerator fan belts. Miller's response was the spate of newspaper articles reprinted in this volume, defending the dignity of contemporary—albeit proletarian—man. Somewhere Aristotle gets mixed up in the turmoil and the affair develops into a *cause célèbre* between artist and critic, the latter coming off, as usual, to very great disadvantage. Audiences all over the world have paid tribute to the essential integrity of the Loman hero in countless productions. . . . Miller now admits that he has written far too much on the academic subject of tragedy, and readers of these essays will be quick to agree. Miller's most eloquent statement on this subject is the play itself, that "unsingable heartsong the ordinary man may feel but never utter." The controversy surrounding the academic reception of the play in 1949 pales into insignificance when we measure the brouhaha against the audience's continuing fascination with this work in performance.

Miller's accomplishment in the theater, his evocation of a drama which "ought to make sense to common-sense people," places him firmly in the tradition of Elmer Rice, Clifford Odets, and Lillian Hellman. All of them use the theater to examine the conflicts involved in being this new thing called a modern American, and all of them see the theater as a serious business, "one that makes or should make man more human, which is to say, less alone." It is this ability to specify a universal in very dramatic particulars that has given such maturity to the American theater these writers have helped to create. To them the European avant-garde had little appeal. Its methods were too oblique and its contingencies too dependent on the formally abstract. Americans needed a 20th century drama as forceful and practical as themselves. Miller plays a crucial role in this making of a new American drama, for his work takes root on native grounds. Handling issues rather than ideas, he dramatizes in play after play the societal implications of our own individual actions.

What makes Miller's essays important, then, is their mixture of praxis and esthetics. . . . [One is] impressed with Miller's stand on McCarthyism. Less strident and certainly less bitter than Hellman, Miller offers us sanity and hope. In his articles of that period he was consistent and courageous, saying in print those things that very much needed to be said. He emerges from a dark age with his humanism very much intact.

It is this same old-fashioned humanism, so desperately struggling to make a comeback at a time when so many of us are reluctant to take any stand at all, that distinguishes Miller's decisiveness in the theater from those works written by a younger generation of American playwrights. For Miller's plays confront us not only with observations, but with options. The human consequences of the choices we make in everyday life have always been at the center of his dramatic conflict. Miller's dramaturgy poses the question, "How does man make of the outside world a home?" It is a question that needs not only asking, but answering as well. (pp. 32-3)

Enoch Brater, in a review of "The Theater Essays of Arthur Miller," in The New Republic, *Vol. 178, No. 18, May 6, 1978, pp. 32-3.*

STEPHEN GRECCO

On the second page of his twenty-four-page introduction [to ***The Theater Essays of Arthur Miller***], Robert Martin declares that the theatre and drama essays of Arthur Miller "may well represent the single most important statement of critical principles to appear in England and America by a major playwright since the Prefaces of George Bernard Shaw." He need not have waited so long to make his declaration, for these twenty-three essays and three interviews immediately confirm what many have long suspected: that in addition to being one of our foremost contemporary playwrights, Arthur Miller is an eloquent and perceptive commentator on drama and culture—and has been ever since he wrote his now famous essay **"Tragedy and the Common Man"** almost thirty years ago, rightly the first piece to appear in this collection.

Because Miller grounds most of his plays in specific social situations, it has often been suggested that his concerns are too topical to encompass ideas of a more universal nature. **"On Social Plays,"** written in part to help correct this misunderstanding, demonstrates his affinity for the very same issues that obsessed the classical Greek tragedians. Of course, what a writer says about his work and what that work actually says to us can be two very different things. ***All My Sons,*** discussed in some detail in the **"Introduction to the *Collected Plays,*"** clearly lacks several of the larger dimensions he seems to assign to it. However, his remarks about ***The Crucible*** in the same essay deserve special attention. In effect, Miller invites us to have a closer look at what he considers to be his most important play, a work that goes well beyond seventeenth-century Salem and McCarthy's Washington in its relentless examination of the nature of evil. . . .

A thought-provoking and insightful volume. Shaw is in excellent company.

Stephen Grecco, in a review of "The Theater Essays of Arthur Miller," in World Literature Today, *Vol. 52, No. 4, Autumn, 1978, p. 631.*

CLIVE BARNES

[***The American Clock***] has been inspired by one of Studs Terkel's word-of-mouth documentaries, *Hard Times.* Terkel talked to people with his ever-ready tape recorder in attendance, and had people, in the Chicago area, tell what the Depression was really like.

Miller has used the Terkel material as a launching pad for his own memories and reminiscences of the Depression. He grew up at that time and paid his own dues. So did his family. Miller has taken Terkel's documentary vision of the past, and, I suspect, used that vision as a spotlight on his own family.

Whether this play is autobiographical or not is scarcely relevant. Miller is looking back, not really in anger, at historic circumstances that shadowed, perhaps even maimed his early life. (p. 81)

Miller gives us three central characters. A father, a mother and a son. The father is wiped out by the crash, the mother is fearful but indomitable and the son is the sort of boy Arthur Miller himself would have wanted to have been, and quite possibly was.

Can you have idealized vignettes of disaster? In ***The American Clock*** you can. Miller makes much of little, which is a good deal better than little of much. But these vignettes of crash, disaster and depression are pursued relentlessly by the hound-dogs of cliche and the wolves of overexposure.

Of course, and it is almost insulting to mention it, Miller knows his craft superbly. The scatter-shot image of the play, which probably derived from the first impulse of Terkel's book, is almost impossible to handle on stage. What Miller has here is almost a film script in search of a camera.

Yet so many things go so gracefully that while the play, in the ultimate terms of box office and the rest, will probably be a failure, and while it is never going to stand high on teachers' lists regarding style, method and grandeur of Arthur Miller, it does show the same kind of intimate, inner-voice writing that made ***The Death of a Salesman*** a masterpiece.

You find in [***The American Clock***] many wonderfully sensible instances of small people in the clutch of unfeeling disaster. . . . (pp. 81-2)

Clive Barnes, "This 'Clock' Is a Bit Off," in New York Post, *November 21, 1980. Reprinted in* New York Theatre Critics' Reviews, *Vol. XXXXI, No. 19, 1980, pp. 81-2.*

FRANK RICH

Sometimes it seems as if there's just no justice in the world—or at least in the world of the theater. Last spring . . . Miller's ***The American Clock*** was a flawed but powerful play about the great Depression of the 1930's. Mr. Miller was in touch with his best themes again; he seemed on the verge of creating an epic, tragic statement about a family caught in the midst of the collapse of the American dream. Last night, Mr. Miller's drama arrived . . . with an extensively rewritten script. . . . The result is a tragedy of another sort. Upsetting as it seems, the once beautiful pieces of ***The American Clock*** have been smashed almost beyond recognition.

What's gone wrong? It's almost too sad to talk about. Mr. Miller has tinkered with his play to the point of dismantling it. While he has reduced some of its unnecessary sprawl, he hasn't solved its structural problems; he also has injected too much sentimentality, thematic signposting and slapdash comedy. . . .

[The Baums are] a family that is not unrelated to those of Miller plays from ***All My Sons*** and ***Death of a Salesman*** through ***The Price.*** Moe . . . is a proud patriarch whose spirit has been all but broken by economic disaster. Rose . . . is a strong, complex woman who loves her husband but has a limited tolerance for human weakness. Their son, Lee . . . , is an aspiring writer who also serves as the evening's narrator. It is Mr. Miller's notion, potentially a great one, that the Baums' story can help tell the story of America itself during the traumatic era that gave birth to our own.

As it happens, neither tale is told well in ***The American Clock.*** Indeed, the Baums and history fight each other to a standoff. The play was loosely inspired by Studs Terkel's *Hard Times,* and Mr. Miller has struggled gamely but vainly to duplicate the book's oral-history technique. In his initial version, the evening's historical segments were thrown in like mini-documentaries: The story of the Baums would come to a halt and we'd suddenly see a scene showing the suffering of other, unrelated Depression victims. In the new version, such digressions are instead force-fed into the family's scenes. Where before there was an onstage confrontation between farmers and bankers, now a farmer turns up at the Baums' Brooklyn home and *tells* them of the confrontation. This is not an improvement.

Either way, the non-Baum characters—from patrician Wall Street titans to a redneck sheriff to poor blacks—are written as superficial archetypes. As before, they slow down and fractionalize Mr. Miller's domestic drama. The Baums' story, meanwhile, has now been expanded without being deepened. The familial relationships are often sketched in or announced rather than fully dramatized, and they are cluttered with additional deadwood characters. As acted by a shrill, hand-waving supporting cast, the assorted Baum relations and neighbors seem to have wandered in from a Norman Lear sit-com. . . .

An autobiographical stand-in for the author, the son [Lee] must set the tone for the evening. His confrontations with his parents, especially his mother, are ostensibly the most important in the play. His journey through the 30's, especially his brush with leftism, should give the evening its historical perspective. That's all gone here. . . .

Some of the play's more portentous historical transitions sound like "March of Time" newsreels: "All of a sudden, quick as death, the lights went dark in the casino." There's a running gag about Lee's college plans that cheapens the play's father-son relationship. The maudlin interludes are merciless. One minor character exists solely so he can commit suicide in Act II; a bit later, there's a sloshy and extraneous scene showing Moe and Rose in their golden years. . . .

The sadness, of course, is that Moe could have been as towering a character as Willy and that Rose could have been, as his son ultimately suggests, a woman who embodies the contradictions of an entire nation. . . . Mr. Miller has the inspiration for a potentially soaring play that could contain [these roles]. It's a bitter loss for the theater that ***The American Clock*** has arrived on Broadway unwound.

Frank Rich, "Miller's 'American Clock'," in The New York Times, *November 21, 1980, p. C3.*

HOWARD KISSEL

[In the first act of ***The American Clock,*** Lee Baum] speaks of "the crazy kind of expectation when there is no hope" that people felt during the Great Depression. [Baum], clearly a surrogate for the playwright as a young man, has just been deeply shaken by having to give his once-successful father 25 of the 35 cents in his pocket so his father can take the subway into town and also buy a hot dog.

The moment is one of many in the play—to my mind Miller's best since ***A View From the Bridge***—that drives home one of the traumas of the Depression, the task of absorbing the ever-deepening humiliations one has to share with those one loves. Out of this humiliation naturally grew unbearable tensions, absurd, grotesque sorts of pettiness, but ultimately a desperate sense of comedy so indomitable one still hears its echoes around us.

Much of the social and political history of the last 40 years has its roots in the emotional life of the Thirties, and Miller has recreated that life with profound resonance. He calls the play a "mural," an accurate description, since it is a collection of vignettes, simply, sharply etched, but with the impact of monumental figures frozen in time. One particularly telling sketch is a scathing comment on the intellectual life of the period, in which a woman well paid for writing a comic strip justifies her work and salary as a furtherance of Marxist enlightenment. Another beautiful scene is a public drama in which the young writer's father must disown him before a bureaucrat so his son can go on relief and then be eligible for WPA work.

The most powerful image of the Depression is the haunting portrait Miller has drawn of his mother, who manages to preserve a resilient exterior despite her emotional disintegration. In this heroic characterization, Miller has justified his conviction, voiced 25 years ago, that "it is not enough any more to know that one is at the mercy of social pressures; it is necessary to understand that such a sealed fate cannot be accepted." . . .

The American Clock is the sort of evening that revives one's faith in the American theater.

Howard Kissel, "The American Clock," in Women's Wear Daily, *November 21, 1980. Reprinted in* New York Theatre Critics Reviews, *Vol. XXXXI, No. 19, 1980, p. 82.*

JOHN BEAUFORT

Americans in crisis throng the landscape of Arthur Miller's spacious mingling of family portraiture and chronicle play [***The American Clock***]. . . . Mr. Miller has written "A Mural for Theater." Like the satellite map that forms a backdrop for the multiple episodes, it is sweepingly impressionistic, ranging widely in mood, time, and geography.

Central to these historic extracts is the Brooklyn home to which the Baum family retreats after Moe Baum . . . has lost his money and his business in the 1929 stock market crash. It is here that young Lee Baum . . . learns the hard facts of impoverishment as he takes his mother's jewels, piece by piece, to be pawned. . . .

Mr. Miller acknowledges Studs Terkel's *Hard Times* as the inspiration for ***The American Clock.*** But the playwright has stated that more and more of his own life went into the manuscript as he developed it. So this crowded, semi-autobiographical work becomes a selective group portrait of Americans in the depression years, with the Baums and their next-of-kin as central figures. The displaced and dispossessed of this sweeping retrospective include the rich and powerful, an evicted Iowa farmer who has somehow made it to Brooklyn, and a group of welfare applicants besieging a harried, irascible clerk.

Lee Baum, the play's narrator-participant, begins as a high-schooler in knee breeches and winds up realizing his ambition to become a bigtime sports writer after attending Ohio State University. On the way, he does menial labor, gets a job with the New Deal WPA, and works briefly on a Mississippi riverboat. (He hears a Roosevelt broadcast in the company of a red-neck Louisiana sheriff and a black cook in a diner.) Meanwhile, the depression is taking its toll of the elder Baums. Farther afield, Hitler is on the rise and Pearl Harbor is in the making.

The fleeting scenes—the narrative, personal drama, humorous observation, and folk color—all serve as fragments in the Miller mosaic of American social history. Indeed, ***The American Clock*** seems at times almost too fragmentary. Some of the scenes are played virtually like review sketches. . . .

Yet ***The American Clock*** never fails to hold the spectator's interest. Mr. Miller communicates his affection for and fascination with the people whose lives and times he is chronicling.

John Beaufort, in a review of "The American Clock," in The Christian Science Monitor, *November 24, 1980, p. 19.*

STANLEY KAUFFMANN

[*The essay from which this excerpt is taken originally appeared in* Saturday Review, *January, 1981.*]

Like every child of the Depression, Arthur Miller can't forget it, but all he has done in his new play is remember it. ***The American Clock*** (''inspired by Studs Terkel's *Hard Times*'') is not much more than a superficial ramble through the lives of a New York Jewish family in the Twenties and Thirties. Presumably it's somewhat autobiographical, with a narrator-reminiscer who makes us think of Miller himself. This narrator, called Lee, very soon pulls up his trousers to look like knickers and takes us back to his adolescence and flush times, with Mom and Dad in evening clothes worshipping the stock market; and after this depressingly platitudinous start, the play never improves.

The family's plight when the market collapses, the move to cheaper Brooklyn, the adjustments to grim changes, the strategies for survival, Lee's gropings toward jobs and education—these parade past in linear, shallow, unexplored scenes. The only consistent effect is the instant pathos that attaches to memory, especially when the rememberer is standing before us, stepping into and out of the past. . . . Miller used split time-planes well in ***Death of a Salesman,*** but here he merely leans on the form slothfully, meandering through material that must by now be substantively familiar even to those who didn't live through that era.

Occasionally there's a sharp line. (''Any girl with an apartment of her own was beautiful.'') Mostly it's the easy heart-tug of this easy form, sometimes varied with equally easy hindsight irony. (''This Hitler can't last six months.'') After a ramble down Memory Lane that could have been either shorter or longer because it has no intrinsic shape, the play ends with Lee talking to us about his mother, who is seated upstage at her piano, telling us that she is just like this country: full of contradictory views on a number of subjects. But this would have been just as true of her in Scene One. Why did we need to travel the length of the play to reach that end? And what did the Depression have to do with it? It would have been just as true if Wall Street had never crashed. (pp. 120-21)

In much of Miller's past work, one could at least discern what he was reaching for and fumbling. Here he seems only to be exploiting his position as a ''great'' playwright and the fact that he lived through the Depression. . . . ***The American Clock*** leaves Miller essentially where he was—a paradoxical figure, the ''great'' American playwright whose work is mostly mediocre. (p. 121)

Stanley Kauffmann, in a review of ''The American Clock,'' in his Theater Criticisms, *Performing Arts Journal Publications, 1983, pp. 120-21.*

ALAIN PIETTE

[Arthur Miller's latest one-acts ***Elegy for a Lady*** and ***Some Kind of Love Story***] lack credibility. In a note in the program, the playwright specifies that ''both works are passionate voyages through the masks of illusion to an ultimate reality.'' While the illusion contained in both plays is apparent, the ''passion'' and the ''ultimate reality'' are indiscernible. ***Elegy for a Lady*** centers around the personality of a well-to-do, middle-aged man who enters a fashionable boutique to buy a present for his dying mistress. We learn that she is much younger than he and no longer wants to see him. His preoccupation is to buy something that will not remind her of her condition. In an extraordinary display of tact, the owner of the boutique makes different suggestions. None of them is satisfactory, and the man starts speaking about his relationship with his mistress. Unfortunately, the central idea of the play is poorly developed. The man sees in the shopkeeper not only a confidante, but also a semblance of his mistress. . . . The atmosphere is almost intimate. The shopkeeper offers the man some coffee, comforts him from time to time, kisses him, and when he finally chooses to buy a jewel, she does not ask him to pay for it.

The thematic substance of the play is thin. We are presented with the crisis of an aging man, whose illusion of youth, his mistress, is on the verge of disappearing. But where is the ''ultimate reality'' the playwright alludes to in his program note? Why does the shopkeeper feel involved with the story of this strange man? Our questions remain unanswered. Passion is also absent from this short play. The characters' conversation is artificial and conceited: ''We have a passionate uncommitment,'' the man pompously declares. Many of the sentences are left unfinished, a hackneyed device suggesting a lack of communication. . . .

On the surface, ***Some Kind of Love Story*** sharply contrasts with ***Elegy for a Lady.*** The tempo is quick, the situation original, the language brilliant. Tom, once a police officer, now a private detective, is called in the middle of the night by Angela, a good-hearted prostitute. She has some information to give him concerning a case Tom has been trying to solve for five years. Though this is not the first time that Angela has called Tom, he does not seem to derive much information from these conversations. We are led to surmise that Angela has invented a complicated story of murder and corruption just to keep Tom near at hand. They have been lovers for some time, and Angela wishes they still were, but Tom no longer sleeps with her because he wants to remain ''objective'' in the conduct of his inquiry. The play is the story of Tom's desperate attempts to convince Angela to disclose to him whatever she knows. He threatens her, caresses her, talks to her, or pretends to go away. Each time he grows menacing, Angela breaks into a fit of schizophrenia, and Tom is obliged to call a psychiatrist to ask for advice. The psychiatrist tries to persuade Tom that there has never been a case at all, but Tom wants to keep on believing.

The swift succession of scenes and telephone calls, all remarkably interpreted, becomes increasingly funny as the play proceeds. Yet one cannot help feeling that Arthur Miller does not develop the argument of his play; as in the first work, the ''ultimate reality'' is missing and thematic substance is lacking. There is no justification for Tom and Angela's repeated confrontations, except perhaps the illusion of love they share.

Alain Piette, in a review of ''Elegy for a Lady'' and ''Some Kind of Love Story,'' in Theatre Journal, *Vol. 35, No. 4, December, 1983, p. 554.*

STEPHEN SPENDER

Arthur Miller, it seems, is rather sweetly and without the slightest reservation in love with every word of his 35-year-old masterpiece, ***Death of a Salesman.*** The fun of ***Salesman in Beijing*** is watching him, after intensive wooing, produce a Chinese performance of the play, which he falls equally in love with.

Until quite recently—and perhaps not even now—there have been no traveling salesmen in China. So Arthur Miller was considerably taken aback when Cao Yu, head of the Beijing People's Art Theatre, asked him, in 1981, to come to Beijing to direct a production of ***Death of a Salesman,*** and not, as had previously been suggested, ***All My Sons.***

After some hesitation, Miller, who does not know a word of Chinese, set out for Beijing with his wife Inge who does. She is also an excellent photographer, as the illustrations to this volume demonstrate. In the very earliest rehearsals Miller soon discovered that he could understand the Chinese dialogue spoken by his actors, so close was the excellent translation to his American speech rhythms. After this though he had a long struggle fighting Chinese mannerisms of acting, especially a tendency to melodrama and emphatic over-interpretation. He had to teach the players to act and speak their lines in his American style, while at the same time discouraging their enthusiasm for their own notions about Americans. . . . He had, on the contrary, to persuade them to present a Chinese interpretation of Willy Loman and his family, but this meant modifying considerably the rigid stylization of the contemporary Chinese theater.

The agony all ends in a great triumph, as the reader will have anticipated. He may perhaps find the blow-by-blow account of every fight with performers, theater, scenery, lighting, and, finally, international press and television a bit exhausting. But one is carried along by Arthur Miller's own character and style: his modesty combined with devastating self-confidence, his kindness and firmness, and above all his sense of having a mission to encourage these battered and still partly submerged outcasts, the Chinese intellectuals.

Stephen Spender, "Willy Loman Takes on New Territory," in Book World—The Washington Post, *May 13, 1984, p. 4.*

PAUL BERMAN

[***Salesman in Beijing***] shows more than a touch of arrogance. One wonders how much [Miller] actually knows about Chinese theater; he seems to have seen only one production on this most recent visit. There are plenty of passages showing his penchant for pompous, long-winded philosophical disquisitions. Arrogance and pomposity, however, aren't the worst of sins. He wasn't leading an army across China, he was leading a theater troupe, and he could hardly have done this if he didn't believe in the rightness and importance of his work. Whether his judgments of Chinese life can be trusted is another issue. He may well have fallen into the tourist fallacy of mistaking postage stamps for continents. His judgments don't strike me as silly or absurd, but then I wouldn't know. What I do know is how ***Salesman in Beijing*** compares to some of his other recent work. Critics have taken a dim view of Miller's recent plays. The plays almost make it seem that the man's intelligence has got up and gone. But the intelligence hasn't gone. His China diary is full of shrewd observations. The story Miller tells—there are glances back to McCarthyism, to the early productions with Lee J. Cobb, glances forward to Mao and sideways to Reagan, asides on stage lighting and international relations—could hardly offer a richer mix of history and theater. This casual diary is the best thing he's done in years.

Paul Berman, "Feudal Gesture or Capitalist Plot?: Arthur Miller Takes on China," in The Village Voice, *Vol. XXIX, No. 25, June 19, 1984, p. 43.*

SANTOSH K. BHATIA

All customary estimates of Miller—as a social realist, a clinical analyst, and a prudential moralist tend to ignore the tragic quality of his plays. (p. 115)

Conflict which is the soul of tragedy is there in each [of Miller's plays]. It invariably results from a struggle between the individual and the society. Sometimes this conflict is external and directly in the forefront in the manner of a traditional tragedy as in ***The Crucible,*** but more often it is reflected through the psychological tension in the hero's mind as in ***Death of a Salesman, A View from the Bridge,*** and ***After the Fall.*** The tragic feeling is aroused when the hero is called upon to face the challenge "which he cannot find it in himself to walk away from or turn his back on." The tragic status of the hero is usually determined by how well he meets this challenge.

In each play Miller tries to bring out that "moment of commitment" in the hero's character when he "differentiates himself from every other man, that moment when out of a sky full of stars he fixes on one star." His characters might lack the nobler or heroic qualities of the Greek and Elizabethan heroes and his themes might seem too banal or commonplace, but significant questions of choice and responsibility, love and survival, separateness and togetherness always emerge from the central conflict in each play. It turns the fate of the individual into an epitome of the fate of mankind, which in turn, raises his social plays into tragedies. . . . Miller combines some of the elements of traditional tragedy with those of the modern one so well that it gives him a unique place among the twentieth century tragic playwrights. For instance, his heroes, unlike the traditional tragic heroes, are not big or great people, but in matters of passions like love and jealousy, they are not too different from them. Be it Joe Keller or Willy Loman, John Proctor or Eddie Carbone, Quentin or Victor, they are all men of strong passions.

Suffering, the second important constant of tragedy, is also found in Miller's plays. As in all good traditional tragedies this suffering is mostly inward or psychological rather than physical. Willy, like Lear, suffers mentally and emotionally; John Proctor, confronting an evil world, reminds us of Prince Hamlet in his suffering; similarly, Eddie Carbone's anguish and suffering bring to mind the suffering of Phaedra. Where there is no open depiction of suffering, we have an over-whelming feeling of some terrible loss or a profound sense of waste as in ***After the Fall*** and ***The Price. All My Sons*** is an exception where the hero's suffering is not fully brought out. To that extent the play is comparatively weaker as a tragedy.

The third important common factor in all these tragedies is irony, which Miller employs with a masterly touch. The most potential source of tragic irony is the gap between the hero's aspirations and achievements. [In ***All My Sons***], Joe aspires to amass a lot of wealth and bequeath a rich business to his sons. He errs for his sons but the irony is that his sons prove instrumental in his punishment. The tragic irony in Willy's case is that he becomes a victim of his own success-dream. In trying to be a successful salesman like Dave Singleman, he even fails to be a successful father like Charley. The irony in ***The Crucible*** is so well executed that it is a predominant feature of the whole play. John Proctor has the reputation of being the wisest and maturest of all the people of Salem and fights heroically against evil, yet he becomes the cause of all the trouble since he has the taint upon him. Similarly, in ***A View from the Bridge,*** Eddie is seen committing the same error of informing, against which he warns Catherine in the beginning. In ***After the Fall*** and ***The Price,*** too, irony unveils the tragic situation and provides richness to the plays.

The awakening of the tragic hero is yet another vital element in tragedy. Normally experience leads to awakening; it comes as a culmination of suffering. That is the traditional mode of tragedy. But in Miller it is not always so. In some of his plays the awakening comes as a prelude to suffering. For instance, in the case of Quentin in ***After the Fall,*** the tragic awakening comes first and what follows is a whole process of intense mental torture and suffering. The same is true of ***The Price*** as well. In the case of ***Death of a Salesman*** the awakening is brought about in a highly dramatic manner in the form of a discovery by Willy Loman. Sometimes the awakening is simply suggested by an action of the hero as in the case of Eddie Carbone who dies in his wife's arms and indirectly accepts his error. (pp. 115-17)

Miller believes that the aim of drama is "something far wider than a purely private examination of individuality" for its own sake. He attempts to deal with more and more of the "whole Man," "not either his subjective or social life alone." The social matters in his plays are inseparable from the subjective psychological matters. In this he resembles the Greek playwrights who were unable to conceive of man or anything else except as a whole. The fate of Oedipus, for instance, is interlinked with that of the people of Thebes. His subjective existence cannot be isolated from his social existence. Similarly, Antigone's personal relationship with her dead brother brings her into one of the most violent conflicts with the State. Her subjective as well as social life is made the subject of treatment in Sophocle's masterpiece. The same is true of Keller and John Proctor and Eddie Carbone. Keller's crime has far wider repercussions in that society of which he is a member. Proctor's private guilt actually precipitates the whole Salem hysteria and his own fate is not sealed off from that of others. Similarly, Eddie's act of informing spawns forth a disharmony in the longshoremen community and leads to social fission. Despite some very important differences of subject and technique, the Greek tragedies and those of Miller are vitally similar; their chief character is social.

Besides, in the "family-social complex" of his plays the family is used as a prism to reflect the larger social world and its pressures. The blending of the social with the familial, helps in two ways. First, it helps him transcend the livingroom reality and his characters are seen confronting the non-familial or openly social challenges and forces. Secondly, since the forces which destroy the lives of his tragic protagonists are uncontrollable and lie outside the bounds of reason and justice, it helps raise his social plays into tragedies. The tragic heroes are made to reckon with social forces that can neither be fully understood nor overcome by rational prudence. This is important in view of the fact that where the causes of disaster are temporal or remediable we may have serious drama but no tragedy at all. No socio-economic reforms could have altered Willy's fate, no more pliant laws could have resolved John Proctor's dilemma, no psychiatric therapy could have saved Eddie Carbone; a third marriage with Holga would not exonerate Quentin from his past mistakes and responsibility; lastly, a reversal of choices between Victor and Walter would not let them escape tragedy. The ultimate tragic feeling in these plays is thus associated with two things: irrevocable deeds and irreparable loss. Rational explanation might sometimes look probable but it cannot be brought to bear effectively and, things being as they are, the fate of the tragic heroes could not have been otherwise. This precisely constitutes the metaphysical quality of these plays and makes them powerful tragedies.

Still another factor that provides tragic dignity to these plays is the use of archetypal mythical patterns and symbolic action. Myth is essential to tragedy and Miller has successfully exploited its usages in his plays. The success myth, for instance, is used effectively in ***All My Sons*** and ***Death of a Salesman*** and even in ***After the Fall*** and ***The Price.*** Similarly, a sustained use of symbols is also made in almost all his plays. It cuts across their narrow realism and lends them a poetic touch.

As a dramatist Miller is not simply realistic or naturalistic. His best theatrical devices belong to the expressionistic school although his interest in society and social problems makes him a realist-naturalist. His realism, too, is very complex. It is more of a technique that combines the free verse of Maxwell Anderson, the freedom of space and time of the Expressionists, the psychological insights of O'Neill and the intellectual devices used by Brecht and Thornton Wilder. He is a social dramatist but his plays are far from mere sociological plays. His chief interest always lies in persons rather than social problems or ideas. It helps lift his themes into larger universal themes; especially the theme of the individual's relationship with society which has been treated as an archetype. What he attempts to dramatize is the failure of man and society to maintain a fruitful relationship with each other but he does so in such an adroit manner that the intensity and effectiveness of his plays as tragedies do not suffer. The ultimate success of his plays as tragedies lies in that. (pp. 117-19)

Santosh K. Bhatia, in his Arthur Miller: Social Drama as Tragedy, *Arnold-Heinemann, 1985, 144 p.*

LEO SAUVAGE

A "new work" by Arthur Miller cannot be ignored—even when, like ***Danger: Memory!,*** it consists of two brief one-act plays, [***I Can't Remember Anything*** and ***Clara***]. . . . The works are united only by the author's penchant for treating splinters of big human problems in down-to-earth situations.

The first, called ***I Can't Remember Anything,*** gives us two characters for somewhat less than 50 minutes: 75-year-old Leonora . . . and her contemporary Leo. . . . Leonora has been a widow for 10 years. She loved her husband, but can't remember him quite as well as can Leo, who also liked him. Memory does not, however, seem to represent a danger for either Leo or Leonora. They used to be good friends, they still are, and although we suspect Leo once fancied Leonora, that is now ancient history. . . .

Leo is a retired scientist. He still likes to work out mathematical formulas, although they give him more trouble than they did a few years ago. He looks to the future and speaks of death dispassionately. Leonora, on the other hand, cannot get over her largely forgotten past and has lost interest in the present. . . .

There is certainly something symbolic in Leo's continuing profession of Communism. Is it supposed to mean that he can't remember what has gone on under Communist dictatorships during his lifetime? Or does Miller want to show us that the character, while suffering some loss of mathematical acuity, is nonetheless faithful to his "ideas"? Maybe what's dangerous here is the author's lack of memory.

Unexpectedly, the second one-acter, ***Clara,*** is a detective story. It opens with a man lying motionless on his belly in front of the first row of the audience, and a pool of blood spreading upstage from one of the wings. The man is not the victim—he has fainted because his daughter Clara is, and because he has suddenly become aware of a moral problem that overwhelms him, which police lieutenant Fine . . . makes it his business to elucidate.

Albert Kroll . . . cannot or will not remember anything about the friends his murdered daughter kept. She had been a social worker specializing in the rehabilitation of paroled criminals, and one of them, Fine discovers, visited her at Kroll's house and slept with her there. Bit by bit, Fine learns that the man is a Puerto Rican who had been in jail for murdering his girlfriend. . . .

Leaving aside the unsatisfactory ending, ***Clara*** might have been interesting for what it is—a demonstration of how a good detective extracts the facts from a reluctant witness. It is spoiled by Miller's lacing it with his irrelevant ethical-ethnical preoccupations. Lieutenant Fine, we are reminded several times, is Jewish. In the course of investigating the murder he is haunted by images of skeletal bodies in German death camps. Kroll, who as a white Army officer had commanded a segregated black battalion near Biloxi, is obsessed by the memory of a lynching mob that had menaced some of his men. The experience left him determined to do what he could from then on to protect minorities. His moving account of it, in fact, led Clara to a career in social work and, we are to suppose, to her death. That is one source of his guilt; the other is simple parental regret at having let his daughter sleep with a convict at home. But what—I ask because Miller doesn't—if the Puerto Rican is innocent? (p. 17)

Leo Sauvage, "Midseason Potpourri," in The New Leader, *Vol. LXX, No. 2, February 9-23, 1987, pp. 17-18.*

FRANK RICH

[The first one-act play in ***Danger: Memory!***] is titled ***I Can't Remember Anything,*** but it's Arthur Miller's nature that he can never forget. The horrors that haunt his characters today—the 20th century's police inquisitions, pogroms and wars—are the same specters that hung over ***After the Fall*** and ***Incident at Vichy,*** plays he wrote . . . more than two decades ago. What has changed with time is the writer's perspective. In ***I Can't Remember Anything*** and its companion piece, ***Clara,*** characters of Mr. Miller's American generation look back at history's cataclysms and their own liberal crusades to ask what, if any, good came of it all. The answers they find are at best ambiguous—a moral gray area where once the author of ***The Crucible*** and ***All My Sons*** would have found clear-cut blacks and whites.

As theater, ***Danger: Memory!*** is gray, too, resolutely resisting the efforts of a high-powered cast to inject drama. While the plays are meant to be casual . . . the writing is studied and ponderous. Mr. Miller seems to have begun with his themes and conceits, then worked backward to fashion (and diminish) his characters to fit the predetermined pattern. Despite the wide disparity of their settings and stories, the two plays share the same tone and even some specific metaphors (bridge building) and key props (phonograph records). While that parallelism may hammer in the author's message, it doesn't make for much spontaneity on stage.

The central character in each play suffers from a case of symbolic amnesia. In ***I Can't Remember Anything,*** the forgetful one is Leonora . . . , a wealthy New England widow who jousts over dinner with Leo . . . , her and her late husband's best friend. Disillusioned with a civilization still mired in brutality and lies after all these years, Leonora retreats into Scotch, reclusiveness and a questioning of the value of her own existence. Leo, an unregenerate Depression-spawned Communist, gently challenges his old neighbor by stubbornly refusing to relinquish entirely his hope for the world. . . .

Mr. Miller's sly sense of humor . . . surfaces in wisecracks about crossword puzzles and Nixon bumper stickers, as well as in Leo's amused, scientific view of the human race ("All we are is a lot of talking nitrogen"). But the play fails to deepen our knowledge of its characters or their differing, equally unremarkable credos. . . .

Clara is essentially a *Dragnet* episode, with middlebrow political ruminations substituted for suspense. . . . [Clara is] a murdered social worker whose killer may have been one of her "rehabilitated" former convicts. An inexplicably combative police lieutenant . . . grills [Clara's father] for clues, but the father keeps blocking out details of his daughter's life. Should [he] reveal the name of Clara's Puerto Rican suitor to the police? To do so would be to concede the bankruptcy of his lifelong political ideals—and to admit that those progressive beliefs may have helped precipitate his daughter's death.

Given that the detective, a lapsed liberal, proves to be the ideological opposite of the father, ***Clara*** soon severs all connections with its ostensible premise and becomes a bitter, unenlightening Sunday-morning talk-show debate about the continuing validity of Great Society social policy. In the process, the Vietnam War and the Holocaust are evoked, but, like the concentration-camp memories intermingled with the Marilyn Monroe episodes in ***After the Fall,*** the heavy-hitting historical references don't add tragic import to ***Clara*** so much as accentuate its pretensions. . . .

[Miller] can't leave anything unsaid, any ellipsis gaping: sooner or later someone will say what everything means, and maybe more than once. While Arthur Miller's admirable voice of conscience remains firm as always, ***Danger: Memory!*** is an evening in which the pontificator wins out over the playwright.

Frank Rich, "Arthur Miller's 'Danger: Memory!'," in The New York Times, *February 9, 1987, p. C15.*

JACK CURRY

Arthur Miller's ***Danger: Memory!***—two short plays about the pain of recollection—occasionally recalls the playwright's past brilliance. But in large part these pieces are far from unforgettable. . . .

Danger: Memory! seems small, unambitious and confused.

In Act 1, ***I Can't Remember Anything,*** an elderly woman . . . fumbles through a dinner meeting at an older man's . . . home. Their social intercourse is disrupted often by his crankiness and the memory lapses her senility causes. Tender, amusing but inconsequential, the play comes across as Miller's take on *On Golden Pond*.

Clara, the second-act play, challenges the audience more. The lights come up on a pool of blood upstage and a man face-down on the floor downstage.

Constructed vaguely like a mystery drama, the play asks, "Who is this man and how did this blood really get there?" The apparent answer—he's the father of Clara, the woman whose decapitation produced the puddle—may not be the right one.

Here memory is again blurred and imprecise, and unfortunately so is the play's message. The ambiguity of the piece will disappoint theatergoers.

Danger: Memory! poses no threat to the playwright's elevated position in the USA's pantheon. But it doesn't widen the niche he holds there, either.

Jack Curry, "Miller's 'Memory' Isn't Memorable," in USA Today, *February 9, 1987.*

JOHN BEAUFORT

[***Danger: Memory!***] is an evening of rituals and mystery. The rituals are small and the mystery is psychological rather than conventionally plotted. . . .

Arthur Miller dramatizes the role of memory in two vastly differing sets of circumstances with equally contrasting moods. Whether smooth or rugged, the path down memory lane achieves its destination within the limits the playwright has set himself.

Memories are clear as well as clouded in ***I Can't Remember Anything,*** the first of the two playlets. The dialogue begins with the entrance of Leonora . . . into the country kitchen occupied by Leo. . . . Widowed Leonora and her late husband have been longtime friends of Leo's. Nowadays, Leonora joins Leo of an evening to share a meal, drink his liquor, and compare notes on the state of the world and their own mortality.

Leo is an unreconstructed radical, a theoretical communist who keeps up with the world through the capitalist press. . . . Leonora is a disillusioned idealist who recoils from a world lost in "greed, mendacity, and narrow-minded ignorance." As they companionably bicker and reminisce and even briefly samba, Miller reveals the depth and constancy of the old friends' interdependence and mutual support. . . .

The genially comic tone of ***I Can't Remember Anything*** contrasts sharply with the dark probings of ***Clara.*** In the second half of the twin bill, Miller deals with the shattering aftermath of a gruesome murder. As the officer assigned to the case, shaven-headed Detective Lieutenant Fine . . . employs all the skills of a veteran interrogator to extract from Albert Kroll . . . , the victim's elderly father, the clues needed to advance the police investigation.

It develops that Clara, an idealistic young woman who worked with ex-prisoners, had been dating a man who had served time for killing a girlfriend. Kroll's state of shock combines with his deep-seated, unacknowledged sense of guilt that he had fostered in Clara the very openness that made her vulnerable.

In a highly charged flashback, Kroll recalls telling a young Clara of the World War II incident in which he rescued several of his black troops from a mob of Biloxi (Mississippi) whites.

The emotional outburst leads Fine to his first clue, but not before the hard-bitten cop has delivered his own assessment of a society dominated by "greed and race." In this case, the dangers of memory are inextricably linked to the unpredictability of human behavior.

John Beaufort, "Memories Infuse Two Miller One-Acters," in The Christian Science Monitor, *February 11, 1987, p. 26.*

GORDON ROGOFF

Failures of memory may lie at the heart of Arthur Miller's ***Danger: Memory!***—two short plays called ***I Can't Remember Anything*** and ***Clara***—but the real danger is Miller's carelessness. Am I alone in still wanting to know what Willy Loman sells? If I distrust Miller's Big Ideas, it's partly because the small, telling, relevant facts keep escaping me and him. "Rosebud" remained a mystery to Kane's survivors, but Welles didn't ignore the rest of us. Some facts may be more expendable than others (who cares how many children Lady Macbeth had or what Didi did for a living?), if playwrights make it clear that they are excluding one or another fact because they wish to focus on austere truths, rather than liberal rhetoric.

Miller's new plays are more modestly shaped than usual, less weighted with the need to Tell All. Even so, they are alike in their passing references to Issues and their refusal to get their stories right before doing anything else. In ***I Can't Remember Anything,*** Leo and Leonora meet in Leo's country kitchen, share a meal, and touch upon death, alcohol, the purpose of life, crossword puzzles, the old days (of course), the country's "greed and mendacity and narrow-minded ignorance," the war, women, and belief. Never clear is who they are to one another: Leonora was married to Frederick—dead 10 years—who was worshipped by Leo. Leonora is rich, Leo is still a Communist, and Frederick was famous for building bridges all over the world. . . .

At best, this is no more than it pretends to be: a glimpse into lives that are over but for the final blow. The characters can't remember much, but Miller can't find a way to tell what has been forgotten. Anecdotal, arbitrary in its transition—a sudden assault on incompetent dentists and doctors, a sentimental attempt at dancing a samba—the play is almost comfortably proud about its modesty, as if gentility might successfully pass for art.

More ambitious, ***Clara*** is also more elusive. Weirdly, bridge-building comes into this plot, too: Kroll, under questioning by Detective Lieutenant Fine about the murder of Kroll's daughter, Clara, reveals that he works for a New England construction company that does road building and bridges, though he only runs its central office in Poughkeepsie. If this is some sort of binding symbol—Miller's oblique homage to *The Master Builder*—there's no clear way of knowing. Fine is trying to trace Clara's past in order to uncover her killer, but to do so, he must dredge Kroll's memory for Clara's associations.

The play stands—and falls—on the premise that a New York detective has no resource other than Clara's father. "If you're not going to level with me," he says, "I'm out of business." Meaning you have to believe he wouldn't pursue Clara's friends, employers, or even her mother. Given such an opinionated detective, cynically persuaded that only "race and greed" matter, it's hardly likely that he's as helpless as Miller's convenient arrangement would have him. Yet without such a premise, there would be no time to pass over the memorable, unexamined Issues of Vietnam, Southern would-be lynchers, the effect of the holocaust, the horrors of battle, and guilt.

As it is, no time is given to them anyway. They're just there, footnotes to Clara's puzzling story. Her father brought her up to care about the poor, and she was murdered while living in the wrong neighborhood. Are we to believe that her idealism led to her death, that her Puerto Rican boyfriend—a man who had been convicted of killing his girlfriend—must be guilty because Kroll, an idealist-manqué, can't remember his name?

Kroll saw Clara kiss an older woman-friend goodbye, and Fine suggests that the boyfriend might have been a relief to Kroll. But does this mean that Clara's history includes lesbianism or that a good-bye kiss means anything at all? Who are these people? Unsophisticated and ignorant, perhaps, or just haphazard images from a story Miller has never wholly explored? . . .

Miller is continually presenting shadowy events that haven't quite happened within imagery that makes no sense.

Did Kroll himself kill Clara? Was she shot or decapitated? Should anybody care? Miller may be flirting with a Pinteresque departure in his playwriting, hoping that unanswered and unanswerable questions add up to profound mystery, but by the end it's clear that he doesn't entertain even Agatha Christie's respect for plot or the audience. In both plays, the most intriguing characters—Frederick and the grown-up Clara—never appear, which may mean that Miller's failures in diction are not far from his failures to find the play he wants to write. . . .

Danger: Memory! may be not much and nowhere, but Miller's earlier plays are everywhere these days. . . . At his best, he captures the bewildered in their semiarticulate squanderings of intelligence and will. His most effective scenes are confrontational duologues, challenging to act and often merciless in what they expose. While he deserves the twilight pleasures that eluded Tennessee Williams, he's not half as penetrating; the great, exhausting, splendid torments are not his to suffer or to give. He's famous again; that may be because theaters everywhere are settling for schematic arrangements and routine ideas.

Gordon Rogoff, "Treadmiller," in The Village Voice, *Vol. XXXII, No. 7, February 17, 1987, p. 99.*

JOHN SIMON

The two one-acters that make up Arthur Miller's ***Danger: Memory!*** seem to be about the reasons for which people forget things, although they are so flaccid, erratic, and lackluster that we cannot be quite sure they are about anything except wanting to maintain one's reputation as a dramatist even if one has nothing to say. The most charitable interpretation would be that they are meant as a demonstration of their ostensible theme on the audience itself, for, even as we watch them, we begin to forget them. They are the obverse of Proust's *petite madeleine:* As they come at you, you feel your mind going numb with indifference and blanking out from boredom. (p. 127)

I can't imagine a theater in the boondocks abject enough to produce this double bill, born of an amnesic rather than amniotic fluid, if it weren't signed "Arthur Miller." But if Mr. Miller wishes to trade in signatures, why not go directly to the autograph dealers and save us all the inconvenience of intermediate stages?

Miller has always been the sort of playwright who needs Big Issues on which to smuggle in his little melodramas. . . .

[Following ***After the Fall***], Miller ran out of Big Issues, and his plays became either recyclings of old Big Issues and family squabbles or attempts to go it without Big Issues, and, either way, fiascoes. In the present double bill, the first item is, according to Plan B, Big-Issueless, and as exciting and appetizing as an unfinished can of sardines left unrefrigerated for a few decades; the second reverts to Plan A, the Big Issues being generalized corruption, racism, and cowardice, with feeble echoes of World War II and the Holocaust—and this no longer plays, either. Having made himself one of the largest undeserved reputations in the theater, Miller should heed his own lesson—avoid the dangers of memory and forget about attempts to push his luck any further. (p. 128)

John Simon, "No Thanks for the Memory," in New York *Magazine, Vol. 20, No. 8, February 23, 1987, pp. 127-28.*

Marianne (Craig) Moore

1887-1972

American poet, essayist, translator, short story writer, editor, dramatist, and author of children's books.

Photograph by Arthur Steiner; reproduced by permission of The Rosenbach Museum Library.

One of the foremost literary figures in the United States during the twentieth century, Moore created poetry characterized by technical and linguistic precision, close attention to descriptive detail, and acute observation of human character. Her poems frequently employ loose rhythms and often reflect her preoccupation with the relationships between the common and the uncommon. In her verse, Moore espoused the virtues of restraint, modesty, and humor, advocating discipline in both art and life. Her frequent use of animals as a central image often serves to emphasize themes of independence, honesty, and the integration of art and nature. Although some critics consider much of her poetry overly precious and her subject matter inconsequential, Moore has been praised as an important poetic voice by such outstanding literary figures as T. S. Eliot, William Carlos Williams, Hilda Doolittle, and Ezra Pound.

Moore's first poems and short stories were published in the literary magazine of Bryn Mawr College, where she received a degree in biology and histology in 1909. During 1915 and 1916, Moore's poems began to appear in such literary periodicals as the *Egoist, Others,* and *Poetry;* her first volume, *Poems* (1921), gathers many of these pieces. Much of Moore's early verse is marked by originality and unconventional humor. Such poems as "Critics and Connoisseurs" and "Poetry" also indicate Moore's concerns with literature and art. While the works contained in *Poems* were collected and arranged by Hilda Doolittle and other editors without Moore's knowledge, the poems in *Observations* (1924) were chosen by Moore and represent the variety of her themes and forms. One of the more striking pieces in this volume, "Marriage," which had been published separately in 1923, is a long experimental work featuring collage-like assemblages of quotations and fragments in free verse. Moore employs wit and satire to comment on the tensions of marital coexistence. *Observations* also contains "An Octopus," a scrupulously described exploration of the flora and fauna of Mount Rainier. Deriving its name from the shape of the glacier that surrounds the mountain peak, "An Octopus" is often regarded as one of the twentieth century's great odes to nature.

In 1925, Moore became editor of the *Dial,* a position she retained until the magazine ceased publication in 1929. Her experiences with the *Dial* brought her into contact with many of the noted literati of the time and helped advance her international reputation. At the urging of friends, Moore published *Selected Poems* (1935), which features an introduction by T. S. Eliot and includes poems from *Observations* as well as pieces that had been published between 1932 and 1934. Among Moore's other volumes from this time are *The Pangolin and Other Verse* (1936), which attests to her interest in animals as subjects for art; *What Are Years* (1941), which combines poems from *The Pangolin* with several previously uncollected works; and *Nevertheless* (1944), which contains the frequently discussed poem "The Mind Is an Enchanting Thing." M. L. Rosenthal described this work as "true Marianne Moore in both its quiet abstractness and its detailed excitement." Many of the pieces in these books were also published in *Collected Poems* (1951), which was awarded both the Pulitzer Prize in poetry and a National Book Award.

Moore published several volumes of poetry subsequent to *Collected Poems,* including *Like a Bulwark* (1956), *O to Be a Dragon* (1959), *Tell Me, Tell Me: Granite, Steel, and Other Topics* (1966), and *The Complete Poems of Marianne Moore* (1967). Publication of the latter volume prompted John Ashbery to predict that Moore's work would "continue to be read as poetry when much of the major poetry of our time has become part of the history of literature." *The Complete Poems of Marianne Moore* contains all of *Selected Poems,* as well as several uncollected works and selections from her translations, *The Fables of La Fontaine* (1954). *The Complete Poems of Marianne Moore* (1981) is essentially a reissue of the 1967 edition but also includes revisions of Moore's earlier verse and five poems she composed late in life.

In addition to her poetry, Moore published several collections of prose. These works include *Predilections* (1955), which combines selections from Moore's numerous book reviews to form essays on poetry and language; *A Marianne Moore Reader* (1961), which contains previously published poetry, uncollected verse, and miscellaneous prose pieces from such diverse publications as *Vogue* and *Harper's Bazaar;* and *The Complete*

Prose of Marianne Moore (1986), which collects her essays, criticism, and short stories.

(See also *CLC*, Vols. 1, 2, 4, 8, 10, 13, 19; *Contemporary Authors*, Vols. 1-4, rev. ed., Vols. 33-36, rev. ed. [obituary]; *Contemporary Authors New Revision Series*, Vol. 3; *Something about the Author*, Vol. 20; and *Dictionary of Literary Biography*, Vol. 45.)

JOHN ASHBERY

I [once] wrote that ''Marianne Moore is, with the possible exception of Pound and Auden, the greatest living poet in English.'' After rereading her in this magnificent volume [***The Complete Poems of Marianne Moore***] (which reprints all her books of poetry starting with ***Selected Poems*** as well as a handful of uncollected poems and selections from the La Fontaine translations), I am tempted simply to call her our greatest modern poet. This despite the obvious grandeur of her chief competitors, including Wallace Stevens and William Carlos Williams. It seems we can never remind ourselves too often that universality and depth are not the same thing. Marianne Moore has no *Arma virumque cano* prefacing her work: she even avoids formal beginnings altogether by running the first line in as a continuation of the title. But her work will, I think, continue to be read as poetry when much of the major poetry of our time has become part of the history of literature.

Yet it seems to me that we underestimate Miss Moore. True, Eliot placed her work in ''that small body of durable poetry written in our time,'' and others have concurred; but there is a point at which her importance gets lost in the welter of minutiae that people her poems, and in the unassuming but also rather unglamorous wisdom that flashes out between descriptions of bizarre fauna and rare artifacts. Is she not a sort of Mary Poppins of poetry, or, to state the case against her as quickly as possible, an American La Fontaine, who, great poet that he is, always seems on the verge of becoming a tiresome moralist like Joubert or even Poor Richard? Prudence and good judgment are not virtues we associate with the highest poetry, and here is Miss Moore telling us that she distrusts ''merits'' (so do we); that ''A mirror-of-steel uninsistence should countenance / continence''; that ''Truth is no Apollo / Belvedere, no formal thing''; that ''the deepest feeling always shows itself in silence; / not in silence, but restraint.''

Caution, healthy disrespect, restraint: is this the way of poetry? She is the opposite of a mystic, and it is hard to believe that there can be poetry without a grain of mysticism, a dark corner somewhere. But Miss Moore is explicit:

> . . . complexity is not a crime,
> but carry it to the point of murkiness
> and nothing is plain. Com-
> plexity, moreover, that has been
> committed to darkness, instead of
>
> granting itself to be the pestilence
> that it is, moves all a-
> bout as if to bewilder us with the
> dismal
> fallacy that insistence
> is the measure of achievement
> and that all truth must be dark. . . .

(p. 1)

This is strong language, but strong not exactly in the way we expect from great poetry, which has never, including Milton, been overly concerned with setting the record straight and sending the reader about his business. Without, however, suggesting that there is in Miss Moore's work a strain counter to the sentiments she *seems* to be expressing here (and of course, we should not assume that they are hers merely because she uses the form of direct address), that the swarming details, each one crystal clear, often add up not merely to complexity but to a ''darkness'' which gives contours to her ''truth''—without going this far, one can still note that all here is not so modest, cheerful and brightly lit as the lines I have quoted seem to imply. She is not a moralist or an antiquarian, but a poet writing on many levels at once to produce work of an irreducible symphonic texture. If ''restraint'' is really an animating force in her poetry, then it is a strange kind of restraint indeed.

When we examine any of the poems that comprise the Moore canon—poems like **''The Steeple-Jack,'' ''The Fish,'' ''Novices,'' ''Marriage,'' ''The Monkeys,'' ''Bowls,'' ''In the Days of Prismatic Color''**—we are brought up against a mastery which defies attempts to analyze it, an intelligence which plays just beyond our reach. They start smoothly and calmly enough (''The monkeys winked too much and were afraid of snakes'') like a ride on a roller coaster, and in no time at all one is clutching the bar with both hands, excited and dismayed at the prospect of ''ending up in the decor,'' as the French say of a car that drives off the road. And, not infrequently, this happens. (pp. 1, 42)

And there are other cases in which I become aware before the end of a poem that Miss Moore and I have parted company somewhat further back. Sometimes, as in **''The Jerboa,''** the author has her say and retires, leaving you in the company of some curious little rodent. And her mode of direct address can be misleading: toward the end of **''To Statecraft Embalmed''** you become aware that she is no longer addressing an ibis, or even you, the reader; for the last minute she has been gazing absently at something terribly important just over your left ear.

These are not the manners of a governess, whether endowed with magic powers or not. ''There is something attractive about a mind that moves in a straight line,'' and though Marianne Moore's mind moves in a straight line, it does so over a terrain that is far from level. Only something like alchemy could account for the miracle of some of these poems, such as **''An Octopus''** which is for me perhaps the greatest of all of them. We start with an octopus, evoked with the customary precision (''dots of cyclamen-red and maroon on its clearly defined pseudopodia''), but the creature seems to be a glacier or else the two are superimposed, for now we are in a landscape of sierras and fir trees, while the author continues tacking imperturbably among excerpts from Ruskin, *The Illustrated London News, The London Graphic, The National Parks Portfolio* and a remark overheard at the circus, switching landscapes, language and levels with breathtaking abruptness, rising from botanical note-taking to pinpoint emblems of supernatural clarity that could be out of Shelley. . . .

Perhaps it is in her translations of La Fontaine, which I confess I prefer to the originals, that one sees most clearly her gift for language-making, for creating something where nothing was before. This sounds like a paradox since the poems are after all translations, but in trying to find an equivalent tone for La Fontaine's, she happened on a new language—new to poetry and new to her, since she had to abandon her glittering, allusive style to hoe the straight row of the original. And yet her speech, strict as it is, resounds with allusions and untapped possibilities. At the same time she has laid the hardheaded, bourgeois ghost that hovers over the ***Fables*** even at their happiest—Miss Moore's verses are snug but not smug. And the earlier poems tell us why: it is not La Fontaine who would have appended this moral to a poem: "The passion for setting people right is in itself an afflictive disease / Distaste which takes no credit to itself is best." Nor would he have written: "one is not rich but poor / when one can always seem so right."

In short one can never be sure precisely what she is up to; like the unidentified protagonist of **"In This Age of Hard Trying, Nonchalance Is Good And . . ."** whose "byplay was more terrible in its effectiveness / than the fiercest frontal attack," she has set about poetry with all the tools at her disposal. Common sense is just one; so are intelligence and integrity that dazzle, an eye and ear that are almost magical in their power to recreate reality for us, and a mastery of form that outpaces the most devoted reader. All of these are brought to bear, as through a prism, on the amorphous "world" that surrounds us. . . . (p. 42)

John Ashbery, "Straight Lines over Rough Terrain," in The New York Times Book Review, *November 26, 1967, pp. 1, 42.*

GILBERT SORRENTINO

From an elegant, restrained, restricted verse of enormous glitter and craft to the greeting-card doggerel of a dear old lady—such is the progress of Marianne Moore's ***Complete Poems.*** It is a volume that paralyzes the reader with sadness. A poet, presented as "major," who has worked for half a century, has avoided confronting, even once, in her entire body of work, the fact that the nation is brutalized, corrupted, and perhaps hopelessly psychopathic. But the clearly inept verse of the later books is strikingly prefigured in her early work. What happened to Miss Moore is that the costuming gave out; the language failed her. And the language failed her because it lost any touch with the reality that language bears. Miss Moore retreated from life; and her language retreated with her, until it finally died, it finally became good copy, bright and slick and incapable of carrying emotion to the page, to the reader. But since the poet had no emotion save that of the most bitterly conformist, no response but that which is the expected one in this time of the planned tear, the carefully bizarre, the language fits the poem to perfection.

What it is, really, is that the verse was always rooted in itself, i.e., was verse as artifact, as protection for the "refined" sensibilities of the poet. So the poem wore itself out upon itself as the poet grew older and further removed from the world. It is hideous to listen to the claptrap concerning Miss Moore's baseball fanaticism being an instance of her interest in the "regular things." It has nothing to do with what is true. It is a luxury for silly people. If Miss Moore could not, and would not, and most certainly did not engage the real when her juices were flowing, how much less could she do so in her old age: the poem, which sustained itself, sucked its own substance for nourishment, wore itself out over the years, grinding on itself, grinding itself to death. Miss Moore cast about for subject matter outside her own human terrors and desire and meanness—outside, that is, her own humanity, much like a classy Ogden Nash. The formal structuring of the poem, set in motion to poeticize the Brooklyn Dodgers, or Yul Brynner, or some footnoted speaker of some dull cliché, fell into cuteness, the scribbling of a harmless old eccentric. But this is the final product of what began as a harmless young eccentric. (Who knows how harmless?)

The formal composition of the early poems had a value to it: it made sense, that is, aesthetically. The prosy slabs with the careful internal rhyme, the subtle end rhymes, the enjambement used with such precision that the rhymes were muted and rang in the head alone, while devoid of the nervous energy of Williams' early work and the nobility of Pound's, had their verve, their poetic rationale. In the late poems, with the language drained of charge, the "look" of the poems is the same in many instances; but the sound, the formality of the made work is lacking. To compensate for her failed language, Miss Moore used the old suits in the closet. You can check, for example, **"The Steeple-Jack"** against **"Rescue with Yul Brynner"** for an exhibit of decadence.

But there are many other such exhibits. The wretched doggerel of **"Baseball and Writing"**; **"I May, I Might, I Must"** which hardly displaces the white of the page; . . . **"Hometown Piece for Messers Alston and Reese."** These are not simply the flagging energies of a tired poet displayed. The reason for the dreary failure of this work is that it is the perfect culmination of the Moore "machine" slowly coming to a halt—and it is indeed a machine that Miss Moore has been at work on all these years, one of glass. And although it still glitters with the look of beauty, and delicacy, and careful attention to detail, the machine is, after all, a toy. As it was from the start.

What is specifically salient about Miss Moore's poems? First, there is no sexuality. Which is incredible—i.e., that she should avoid such a basic human situation. So there are few men and women, those that exist are resplendent in their flat dimensions, clothed in the finery of the slow profundity. (Which takes the place of sex?) They are statues, or they are safely dead; they are ghostly words of wisdom, "Superior people never make long visits . . ." and "The deepest feeling always shows itself in silence; / not in silence, but restraint." Which, apart from the fact that both of these statements are patently untrue, except in Miss Moore's subworld, that is, the world where such dilettantish eccentricity passes for engagement and "trouble," are interesting in the use of "superior"—who are *they*? We know, though, who they are. They're the people who stand outside the world, annoyed at trifles, life a congeries of good manners. And "restraint" is, of course, like "continence." Thus, the whole crushing microcosm of Marianne Moore's universe, made clear in a very early poem.

What else? The animals are always pointed out as Miss Moore's private domain. Yet a look at the animal poems is enlightening because they come through, finally, as creatures out of Walt Disney. A bitterly ironic poem is the one, **"Peter,"** with the last lines

> To tell the hen: fly over the fence, go in the wrong way
> in your perturbation—this is life;
> to do less would be nothing but dishonesty.

—which agrees with the need for the cat to maim and destroy the hen, since that is his nature. Yet the "nature" of Miss Moore's poems is such use of it as to defend her very life, her heart, against all the incursions of a *human* nature as terribly compelling. She uses the exotic animal and the exotic habits of commonplace animals (with all their animalism removed) to draw pretty conclusions about a world which the animals, and myself, do not recognize—because it does not exist except within the shining machine of words.

In **"Critics and Connoisseurs,"** she sweetly scolds against "conscious fastidiousness" using a metaphorical swan who was guilty of this. Miss Moore deprecates the swan's actions, drawing the moral to extend to the human world. She brings an ant in, to the same effect. She does not like this kind of *person* and springs upon that attitude by using these picture postcard animals, these Walt Disney creations. (Who really did the same sort of dishonest thing in his anthropomorphic obsessions.) It is not, at this point, that one is complaining about anthropomorphism: it is that the animals are so *used*, lacking much of their juices. Miss Moore's cat, springing after the hen, will rend, slaughter, and tear the hen to bits when caught. This is also his nature, though this is the part of it that she will not see. The **"Critics and Connoisseurs"** works the same way. How can a poet *ask* of the humanized ant, what good the "experience of carrying a stick" is? She asks because the ant does not please her; he is metaphorically at fault in his "nature." The cat is not, so long as he doesn't engage in the ultimate rending.

A final note on this poem: She says, "Disbelief and conscious fastidiousness were / ingredients in its / disinclination to move." If Miss Moore's poems are not examples of "conscious fastidiousness," then what are they? Perhaps, at this time, she was struggling with herself, for it is in this book, published in 1935, that she includes **"The Fish,"** her best poem, with its absolutely awed, non-cute sense of the terror and evil inherent in the creation. There was never to be another poem like it.

The poems, as suggested, refuse to admit that living people live. One recalls William Carlos Williams defending his *Paterson IV* against Miss Moore's attack: "To me the world is something which to you must seem foreign. I won't defend my world. I live in it. Those I find there have all the qualities which inform those about them who are luckier," thinking, here, I'd guess, of himself as one of "those who are luckier." But Miss Moore does not, nor did she ever, want to be informed—to her, Lesbianism is evil and foul, so it does not exist. It is not for the poet to treat. I will be careful to state here that I do not take issue with Miss Moore's right as a poet to select her materials—but when the selection *grazes* that which lives, when it selects, then, from these living things, those qualities which render them nonliving, a mere projection of Miss Moore's hazy fantasy about what the world is, this selection is pernicious and ultimately destructive of the poem.

The fear of life, it seems obvious, is not really the same as being distrustful of life, or bitter about it. Nor is it the same as *being afraid*. One can be afraid, and *in life*—Miss Moore fears the entire slate, she withdraws herself and her poem, she scolds. **"In the Days of Prismatic Color,"** which I take to be her aesthetic, says:

> Principally throat, sophistication is as it always
> has been—at the antipodes from the initial great
> truths.

Which leads the reader to two points: What are these poems if not "sophistication"?—and, what does Miss Moore think the "initial great truths" are? The cat who stops short of killing? The "superior people" who don't stay too long? The ant with his stick, baldly anthropomorphized to use in a metaphorical or allegorical battering? Or is "the quadrille of Old Russia" as against "a documentary / of Cossacks" the truer image of reality? It is, of course, not an obeisance to "truths" at all that she cares for; it is an instance of Miss Moore's despair at the world which does not care about her Walt Disney creatures and her fantastic politics: people do not die; ideas die. (And a lot of them are such *nice* ideas.) Or people die so that ideas (Miss Moore's) may live and find their way into poems which are ideational set-pieces about people who are unconnected to reality. (pp. 158-61)

The poems truly take on, beginning with ***Like A Bulwark*** (1956), the cadence and shine of ad copy. They engage "subject" since there has been, for years, nothing left to engage, and the "subject" is the "Real Thing." Here is the beginning of Miss Moore's status as "beloved poet." Poetry, loved by everyone, loved by those who never read poetry, is produced. If one accepts the façade of America, as in 1956 Miss Moore had been doing for some thirty-five or forty years, one accepts the absolute language of that façade, and that language is the copywriter's. America, it must be obvious to even the most benighted by now, would literally cease to exist as the familiar entity it is without advertising copy: I would say that a great majority of the population would feel cheated, robbed, strangely empty and vague, without the advertisement. It is an integral part of the America Miss Moore loves and cherishes, i.e., the fake America. It is indeed an official language, violently opposed to the language of the poem, since its intent is to conceal. The concretists of today embrace the ad, and rightly so, since they have lost all pretension of caring about the use of clear language. It *is* the poem—the poem *is* the copy. (pp. 162-63)

"Spenser's Ireland / has not altered" is remarkable in that it works clearly on the two levels of decadence I have spoken of: The quick stab and glossiness of good ad copy and the blithe dismissal of certain facts that ad copy is better off ignoring, e.g., Swift, Parnell, the IRA, the Sinn Fein, Black and Tan butchery, Yeats, Joyce, Wolfe Tone, Robert Emmett, and so on. I am amazed that the Irish Tourist Board has not asked Miss Moore for permission to quote the first three or four lines of this poem, since it functions with great clarity on that plane they function on—dear old Ireland, ah, the peat, ah, the old priests, etc., etc. But how could Miss Moore write clearly of Ireland when she cannot write clearly of her own American experience? Of her own human experience?

It is impossible to lose all touch with the world without losing touch with the language; the language will betray you at every turn if you try to break and humble it to display an abstraction which you insist on believing is true. I am not sure if the converse is true, but I think it must be. So, as Miss Moore continually faced a world which frightened her, except in its more eccentric delights, mostly bookish, so she falsified her language. Emily Dickinson most certainly did not tell us of the "world" in her poems, probably knowing less about it than Miss Moore. Then why do we still, to our profit, read her?—it is, of course, because she went down into her own tortured heart and wrote of that specific. In Miss Moore's poems, we have neither the world nor herself; her anger is clearly removed from all emotion, save that which is safely to be vented. Who Miss Moore is, these poems will not tell, unless it is by default: what they do *not* say. Or, what they say charmingly, and offhandedly, as in the tensely hysterical assault on sex and sexuality in **"Marriage,"** surely one of the greatest attempts at sterilization in the language—all of it understanding, spinsterish language, skipping about "hearth and home"—never the bed. The language failed her as it lost its engagement with the real; and as time passed, Miss Moore added more and more supplementary material to her poems, in the form of scattered quotes from "public" sources mostly—newspapers, magazines, the writings of naturalists, etc. What is the effect of this cluttered poem, the strings of quote marks, the sounding of flat journalese in the body of the poem which builds itself around the quotes—not the opposite—the quotes used to heighten the effect of a particular line or stanza? The poem takes on the whole linguistic sense of the quotes; it creaks under the barrage of them; and, most importantly, the quotes elaborate on the idea of the poem, or elucidate it. We have the really juiceless phenomenon of the poem, rooted in sand, bolstered by secondhand quotes out of context, from sources whose sense of style is decidedly apoetic. The blind lead the blind.

I have mentioned the poem **"In the Days of Prismatic Color"** as striking me as Miss Moore's aesthetic, and her phrase therein, "great truths." Earlier on in the poem she says:

complexity is not a crime, but carry
it to the point of murkiness
and nothing is plain.

These "great truths," however, are strangely missing in Miss Moore's work. They are not found in the formal structuring of the poems and their engagement with the world; they are, indeed, these "great truths," a series of pegs upon which the poet hangs "ideas." She *says* it, but they are not to be found anywhere in the poems. We all know what she means by "great truths," don't we? Why, the "great truths" are . . . are . . . the, well, the "GREAT TRUTHS"! But the poem retreats at bewildering speed, and with a display of the most fantastic sleight-of-hand, from any sense of the real, at all. This, the shoring up of the poem with grand statements about Life, and Art, and Love, and Death, and so on, while the poem in its bones refuses to confront any of these things, is another instance of irony in Miss Moore's work. For what is this dazzling footwork but her proscribed "complexity"?—"carried to the point of murkiness" where "nothing is plain"?

"Style" reveals the poem destroyed as clearly as anything in this volume: The casting about for "subject" (there is nothing left, at this date, 1956), the "look" of the early poems, the bathos of the rhyme drawn out in great pain and carelessness, the great lack of sincerity, and the everpresent quotes. The rhyme is most instructive here, the fantastic wrenching of good straight syntax to get the rhyme to fall: "have an Iberian-American champion yet" to rhyme with "alphabet"—and that latter word used gratuitously, since it is followed by the phrase, "S soundholes in a 'cello"—this is bad enough, but the rhythmic sense of the poem falls from the merely incompetent and weary to the ludicrous with "fast fast fast and faster" to rhyme with "Etchebaster."

"In the Public Garden" is notable in that it mistakes Eisenhower for a "hardest-working citizen." This was in 1958, when he was President, and in a poem read at the Boston Arts Festival. It is on a level with Frost's inaugural poem in 1960—the public poem to delight the poetry-hating audience. (pp. 163-65)

For the poem **"Combat Cultural"** I refer the reader to Robert Duncan's remarks in his essay "Ideas on the Meaning of Form." Also, his general comments on the decline of Marianne Moore's work in the same essay.

James Dickey calls ***Tell Me, Tell Me*** Miss Moore's best book. In it we are presented with such poems as **"Baseball and Writing,"** which continues the bathetic note struck in **"Hometown Piece"**; **"In Lieu of the Lyre,"** which must be read to be believed; **"Granite and Steel,"** a poem about the Brooklyn Bridge, which, curiously, neglects to quote from the finest poem on that bridge, Hart Crane's "To Brooklyn Bridge"; and **"To Victor Hugo of My Crow Pluto,"** which must stand as the classic attempt at a conscious doggerel that doesn't succeed in its own intent.

"W. S. Landor" is a curious poem in its praise of Landor as someone Miss Moore would like. He throws a man through the window and worries about the plants beneath. It is not Landor's act which I hit at here, nor Miss Moore's approval of this gruff, "no-nonsense" English virility, all roast beef and Yorkshire pudding and baying hounds. It is the failure shown here to distinguish this kind of anecdote as being the propaganda of masculinity. There was a guard at Auschwitz who left his chores of murdering to return to his university and take his examinations in philosophy. A brilliant student, soft-spoken, well-educated, immaculately dressed. Perhaps he loved flowers. The man thrown through the window is a literary abstraction, like the swan, the ant, etc. The language in a vacuum.

"Rescue with Yul Brynner" carries on the spirit of **"Style."** It is Miss Moore crying in the movies.

In **"Hitherto Uncollected"** no further aberrations are revealed.

So, in reading through this body of work, these poems of an entire lifetime, one sees the clearest graph of decline imaginable in the work of a "major" contemporary poet. What I have tried to show in these notes, however, is that this decline did not come about through a sudden failure of power on the poet's part; but that the later, really bad verse, was absolutely prefigured in the earliest poems. The poet failed as her language failed, and her language failed because she shut out the real. (pp. 165-66)

Gilbert Sorrentino, "An Octopus / of Ice," in his Something Said, *North Point Press, 1984, pp. 157-66.*

LARRY P. VONALT

In practicing poetry Marianne Moore is in her own way practicing medicine. Her whole poetic career has been one long struggle with the diseases that most seriously afflict man: affectation, arrogance, timidity, materialism, selfishness—all the moral corruptions that fragment the self and isolate it in the terror of separateness. (p. 670)

Marianne Moore's medicines are those paradoxical and mysterious maxims men have known but seldom heeded; maxims which are encompassed by the idea that the spirit is stronger than the things of the world; what Robert Frost said every poem is about—"how the spirit is to surmount the pressure upon us of the material world". In her long career Miss Moore has concentrated on this one idea. For her, poetry provides "a spiritual happiness in which the intangible is more real than the visible . . . [and] belief is stronger even than the struggle to survive". . . . The conclusion of her poem **"The Staff of Aesculapius"** (1954) is emblematic of her concern with the way what was weak becomes strong, the way what "was inert becomes living". She asks rhetorically if this way is not "like the master-physician's Sumerian rod? . . . / staff and effigy of the animal / which by shedding its skin / is a sign of renewal— / the symbol of medicine".

Marianne Moore's medicines consist in observing precisely the various modes of existence. These observations may focus superficially on the ways of such creatures as the elephant, the jerboa, the pangolin, or the flora of nature; ultimately they expose these creatures as models for man's moral action. Like La Fontaine's or those of almost any other beast fabler, Miss Moore's depictions of animals or even of plants reveal the extent of man's failure to be all that he can. . . . The exclamatory delight and the iconographic moralizing [in **"Nevertheless,"** for example], are reminiscent of seventeenth-century writers—Sir Thomas Browne, Ben Jonson, Robert Herrick, Abraham Cowley—who found value in the esoteric and the common. In particular they could see significant relationships, bonds, among the varieties of existence. Their work was concerned with judgment, comparison and choice, and with wit. If T. S. Eliot found roots for his own poetry in the Elizabethan dramatists and the metaphysical poets, Miss Moore could have found a source for her poetry in that of Ben Johnson and his "tribe". She too conceives of poetry as a craft in which there is form, concentration, naturalness, honesty, steadfastness, and a freedom that is the result of self-discipline; most importantly, she too delights in relationships between the common and the uncommon.

Randall Jarrell, who has written more perceptively of Marianne Moore's poetry than anyone I know, pointed out that for her "the relations are the things; that the outside, looked at hard enough, is the inside; that the wrinkles are only the erosion of habitual emotion. She shows that everything is related to everything else, by comparing everything to everything else; no one has compared successfully more disparate objects." This ability to see likeness in apparent unlikeness is an attribute of all good poets. It is another way of saying simile or metaphor; it is the basis of wit and judgment. Such integration has a way of drawing the world together, of making the unknown known, of dissolving fear. (pp. 671-72)

The integrated vision is, as **"The Steeple-Jack"** makes clear, the artist's vision. The integration of art and nature is brilliantly established in the opening stanza when we are told that "Dürer would have seen a reason for living / in a town like this, . . . with the sweet sea air coming into your house / on a fine day, from water etched / with waves as formal as the scales / on a fish." The sea is the sea and it is also a picture, "etched / with waves", just as the waves are scales on a fish, and the scales, in turn, are waves. The artificial and natural sequence of time is suggested in the seagulls' flight "one by one in two's and three's, . . . back and forth over the town clock". In the third stanza both natural and artistic changes are depicted which imply the intimate relationship, the give and take, the balance, that is possible between the artist and nature—"a sea the purple of the peacock's neck is / paled to greenish azure as Dürer changed / the pine green of the Tyrol to peacock blue and guinea / gray." Even a storm in this town is a combination of and affects both art and nature: "The / whirlwind fife-and-drum of the storm bends the salt / marsh grass, disturbs stars in the sky and the star on the steeple. . . ." . . . To see the order amidst the confusion is to see . . . what is really there but is "disguised by what / might seem the opposite". Even in this obviously northern seacoast town, "the sea- / side flowers and / trees are favored by the fog so that you have / the tropics at first hand."

And Miss Moore treats the reader to a firsthand catalogue of these flowers. Interestingly, even this list of flowers suggests relationships between the artificial and the natural, the artificer and nature, for there are "moon-vines trained on fishing twine", and "crab-claw ragged sailors with green bracts". This catalogue (and Marianne Moore is one of the few modern poets who are really adept with catalogues) has been described as a digression and unnecessary to the poem. In fact, in the ***Collected Poems*** (1951) she cut this catalogue as well as the lines on "the college student named Ambrose". Certainly one reason for the restoration of these lines in the ***Complete Poems*** is their emphasis on the integrated vision, that ability to see the harmonies below the surface of opposites.

In this town where artifice and nature merge, where a northern sea-coast is tropical, and cats, not cobras, "keep down the rats", there is "nothing that / ambition can buy or take away". The town is the artist's vision—intact, whole, single. . . . It is like no town built by man, but like every town dreamed by man, "a fit haven", where danger is marked by signs and "the hero, the student, / the steeple-jack, each in his own way, / is at home," a town "of simple people". The town is not only the subject of the poem—it is itself a poem, and the steeple-jack, the artisan "gilding the solid-/pointed star, which on a steeple/stands for hope", is a poet. A poem provides a haven, a retreat from the confusion of everyday existence. It is a "still point of the turning world" where dangers can be marked out and signs of hope refurbished; it is a space and a time in which to reevaluate and re-create ourselves.

There is in "haven" and "retreat" the suggestion of withdrawing into some sort of protective shell, and Miss Moore has written much about protectiveness. Kenneth Burke, for example, has said that her "recondite menagerie is almost a thesaurus of protectiveness." But the armor she envisions for man is, like the whole armor of God, damned difficult to wear. Her conception of armor resembles her idea of medicine; it can make man whole again. Her armor is not, of course, steel, nor stone, nor anything to hide behind. It is patience, "the soldier's defense and hardest armor for / the fight". (pp. 673-75)

Almost all of [Miss Moore's] efforts have been toward restraint, not pulling away from what hurts, but rather a shaping of her judgments and a refining of her feelings, what she has called "the love of doing hard things". In **"Silence"** she writes, "The deepest feeling always shows itself in silence / not in silence, but restraint." Rather than "living self-indulgently until the moral sense is drowned", as Ulysses's companions do in **"Blessed Is the Man",** she tries to be always hard on herself. It is as if she realizes the power of compactness and compression, that to be "like a bulwark against fate" she must open herself to the adversities of life; she must be "nerved by what chills / the blood, and by hope rewarded—of toil". Life for her is only worth living when one has the "capacity to conquer one's detachment", to become involved, to be "made captive by / supreme belief".

Her belief, her armor, and, consequently, her medicines are old-fashioned. She is not interested in attacking and changing social institutions; what matters to her is the individual and the way he corrupts and loses himself in his obsession with ego. She is a leveler, who in leveling builds a stronger person; she is a surgeon who slices away the diseased tissue to restore the man. In her poems she has given the world emblems of determination, self-discipline, restraint, compactness, hope, and they are all, as she has titled one of her poems, **"Efforts of Affection"**. In that poem she suggests that "love's extraordinary-ordinary stubbornness" becomes "vermin-proof and pilfer-proof integration / In which unself-righteousness humbles inspection". Her poems are excellent antidotes in this age of self-righteousness when everyone else is guilty, when those "alive who are dead" are "proud not to see" that "trust begets power and faith is / an affectionate thing." Her trust and faith exemplify the virtues of simplicity—not simplemindedness, but simplicity that is the shearing away of excesses, of all those deceits and disillusionments that clutter and destroy life. In her affirmative—and no poem of hers is not affirmative—**"Love in America?"** she asks that love, "whatever it is, let it be without / affectation," for "feeling has departed from anything that has on it the touch of affectation." The effect of her work is best characterized by her description of the effect of T. S. Eliot's poetry. "The effect of Mr. Eliot's confidences, elucidations, and precepts," she wrote, "is to disgust us with affectation; to encourage respect for spiritual humility; and to encourage us to do our ardent undeviating best with the medium in which we work." (pp. 675-76)

Because she believes in the virtues of restraint and modesty, she knows the efficacy of humor, the relief in being able to laugh at one's own follies. "Among animals," she writes in **"The Pangolin,"** "*one* has a sense of humor. / Humor saves a few steps, it saves years." Ultimately, however, the source of her humor is also the source of her convictions: her integrated vision, her exceptional ability to see, as she said Sir Thomas Browne could, that "small things could be great things," and that in the universe man is, like the jerboa, the pangolin, the paper nautilus, or a snail, a small thing that can be a great thing. For her, as for Charles Ives, "the fabric of existence weaves itself whole."

I have not mentioned the failures of Miss Moore's work. Certainly not all of her poems succeed equally. Some are too abstract, too precious, or marred by rhythms almost impossible to speak. Sometimes her subjects seem almost too inconsequential for poetry, but, then, as I have tried to imply, what may seem trivial can, as so much of Miss Moore's work shows, be significant to our lives. There is much about her poetry that is difficult and much about it that is joyous. It provides medicines for the sinking spirit; it reveals the adversities and, particularly, the delights of living. . . . To judge whether her poetry is as great as that of her contemporaries is of little consequence, for, as she wrote of Anna Pavlova, "That which is able to change the heart proves itself." (pp. 677-78)

Larry P. Vonalt, "Marianne Moore's Medicines," in The Sewanee Review, *Vol. LXXVIII, No. 4, Autumn, 1970, pp. 669-78.*

MARY ALLEN

Queer creatures populate Moore's poetry—dikdik, echnidna, tuatera—drawn from scientific sources by the poet who was first a biology student and then a librarian. No stereotypes come to mind with these subjects. By handpicking them from afar, she takes a control not assumed with the surprise appearance of animals nearby. Moore's characters are kept at an emotional distance, just as most of them are geographically remote. They are strange but not frightening. As if viewed through a microscope, clear-edged shells or heavy hides, stripes or neatly arranged scales, and geometrical designs give a comforting sense of order. Moore's animals rarely attack; in fact, many of them barely move. Those who do are usually in flight, and motion is brought under control. The animal comes safely to rest.

Moore's stable, often hard-crusted animals more closely resemble *things* than any in American literature. Although she disclaimed herself as an imagist, Moore's emphases on the exact word, new and freer rhythms, clarity, and concentration are inevitably linked with imagism. And Ezra Pound's call for the direct treatment of a thing has a particularly literal bearing in terms of her animal subjects. Not only does Moore bring fresh vision to the object before her but she puts new objects into the light. The clear-edged brilliance of her images has been made the subject of a study by Kingsley Weatherhead [see *CLC*, Vol. 4], who finds in her clarity a kinship with Homer. She cites the Greeks for "distrusting what was back / of what could not be clearly seen." For Roy Harvey Pearce, she "more than any other American poet of her time respects (in a phrase dear to Stevens) 'things as they are.'" And no group of "things" is more prominent in Moore's poetry than her animals. A fourth of the ***Collected Poems*** (1951) are specifically devoted to animals, and they appear in almost all the others. The animal may serve as metaphor, but in most cases he walks away as himself, especially when the poem extends beyond two or three stanzas.

By Kenneth Burke's definition, Moore is an objectivist rather than an imagist, for by his analysis the symbolist makes the subject more important than the object; the imagist establishes equality between subject and object; but it is the objectivist who studies the object in its own right. Not only do Moore's animals have their own lives, but a persona is rarely present in the poetry to record a subjective response. To say that the objectivist *studies* a subject is also descriptive of Moore's technique, as facts are turned to poetry under her hand. Burke's linking of Moore with Henry James on the basis of a gratitude that invests their subjects with a "secular equivalent to the religious motive of a glorification" is also applicable to Moore's animals. In fact, Burke's analysis of Moore pertains to animals in American literature generally: they are secular subjects valued in their own right, yet sensed with a spiritual wonder. The intent of imagist and objectivist to eschew traditional symbolism is also pertinent, for even with the most prominent symbolic animals, at some point metaphor is stripped away to reveal the magnificently actual. As Moore puts it, "No anonymous / nightingale sings" from "palm-trees blurring at the / edge." (pp. 97-9)

The various roles of animals—art object, slave, hunter, plaything, by-product, guard, and free being—are all included in **"The Jerboa,"** all but the last under the heading **"Too Much."** Roman society is so lush with the accumulation of animals that one might be satisfied with its levels of artistry, were it not for the stunning appearance of a single desert rat, the subject of **"Abundance."** Art commissioned makes for the doubly contrived animal's form, "the peacock / statue in the garden of the Vatican." More appealing is the sight of baboons, not enslaved exactly but "put" on the necks of giraffes to pick fruit, and "dapple dog- / cats" engaged "to course antelopes." Without indignation, the poet quietly states the case: the Romans "looked on as theirs, / impallas and onigers, / the wild ostrich herd." While animals are considered possessions, without rights or sensations, a wealth of wild life is appreciated in a variety of ways. "Tame fish, and small frogs" ornament the garden, and the toy ichneumon (a weasel-like creature) and snake are given to the young boys. Animal by-products epitomize the life of luxury—goose-grease paint in bone boxes, honey, milk. And the king over all this, in his fear of snakes, must turn for protection to yet another creature, the mongoose.

The unique qualifications of animals are featured, not ignored, by the Romans—the height of the giraffe and the tensile ability of the baboons. They are not mistreated or even severely limited. But it is Moore's brilliance to draw a seductive picture of conditions that are nonetheless a graver danger than force—the affluence which calls increasingly for the domination of animals by man.

To remain free, the animal must protect himself. The most striking feature of Moore's animals is their armor—both an immediate physical defense and a long-range prevention against the more insidious penetration of the spirit. A philosophy of the shield is built on the principle of an inner discipline, manifest in the tough exterior that provides privacy and its accompanying freedom. In the exceptional case of armor as a weapon—the "battle-dressed" porcupine, for example, who wears a "pin-cushion thorn-fur" coat—the image is not aggressive. The quill is softened in its equation wih fur and with coat; the analogy with a pin cushion puts the sharp end of the quill to the inside, a blunt end pointing out. But make no mistake: the animal intends not to be disturbed.

If not a material covering, protective coloring, odor, or swiftness, then inner restraint alone serves as a shield. Donald Hall's theory that Moore's armor is used as a cage to check the wild spirit inside [see *CLC,* Vol. 4] simply does not describe Moore's genuinely peace-loving animals. Their solid surfaces *reveal* an inner security rather than contradict it. The "patina of circumstance can but enrich what was / there to begin / with." The concept of power in stasis is indeed the uncommon view in American literature—this vision of a poet who maintains that "a Chinese 'understands / the spirit of the wilderness.'"

Moore's fascination with animal coverings goes for the furnishings themselves, irrespective of the life of the animal. In a prose selection, **"My Crow, Pluto—A Fantasy"** (a crow who reverses gloom by answering only "Evermore"), Moore tells of her desire to own a crow that would accompany her on errands and then provide plumage for her hat (with no mention of the fate of a bird whose feathers are taken). New York is saluted as the center of the wholesale fur trade, not as a place of plunder but as the incarnation of " 'accessibility to experience' " (Henry James's phrase), which for Moore is called up in the splendor of fur: "tepees of ermine" and "picardels of beaver-skin; white ones alert with snow." As the "savage's romance," New York is "people with foxes," worn not in the spirit that " 'if the fur is not finer than such as one sees / others wear, / one would rather be without it'" but with unalloyed pleasure in the incomparable. The unusual case where Moore does meet the issue of the kill is coolly phrased in a poem based on an essay by a farmer of musk oxen: "To wear the arctic fox / you have to kill it. Wear / *qiviut*—the underwool of the arctic ox— / pulled off it like a sweater; / your coat is warm; your conscience, better." The easy transition from attainment of fur by the fatal method to one shown to be as harmless as undressing puts the graver issue at a distance, just as other threats are made remote.

Armor is frequently described in architectural terms. A vulnerable maternal care is displayed in the paper nautilus's rooms of thin glass shell where the eggs are kept. The lizard's shield is fireproof asbestos. Best known is the snail's quaint house, that charming model of compression, " 'the first grace of style,' " achieved through a contractility which is "a virtue / as modesty is a virtue." This house moves as a well-oiled machine run on the snail's own lubrication, a structure that like other armor *is* the animal himself, not an adornment. The only protrusion reaches out for perception, not locomotion—"the curious phenomenon" of the "occipital horn." The "absence of feet" is a benefit; feet are vulnerable, frequently superfluous. Besides, what's the hurry?

The hide that most graphically registers experience weathered is the wonderfully homely skin of the elephant. **"Melancthon"** shows age as a form of armor in itself, translated to the visible in the deeply rutted but carefully patterned hide "cut / into checkers." An analogy with a coconut shell accurately captures color and texture, while exaggerating solidity. More specifically than elsewhere, a definite threat is identified here: the soul shall not be "cut into / by a wooden spear"; the elephant (synonymous with his hide) is "that on which darts cannot strike," both images suggesting an abstract as well as a tangible encroachment. The more inclusive need for armor is, if not to resist, to absorb "unpreventable experience." The elephant is not merely earthbound; he is "black earth preceded by a tendril." But even the metaphor turns back on the literal, for the elephant's hide is incorporated with dirt. As atypically stated in the first person, "The sediment of the river which / encrusts my joints, makes me very grey but . . . do away / with it and I am myself done away with." Here is illustration not only of the exemplary hide but of the necessity for protection, as crucial for the massive as for the minute animal. (pp. 100-02)

The comfort Moore reflects through order does not stop at armor, formal arrangement, and factual data. Dead animals, properly arranged, make a thoroughly satisfying aesthetic image, as in the opening lines of **"The Steeple-Jack":** "Dürer would have seen a reason for living / in a town like this, with eight stranded whales / to look at." There is no melancholy in this image of whales, who do not even produce an odor: sweet air flows through the house nearby. Death is not Moore's subject; she is simply at peace with death. Evenly numbered, lined up, the impacted figures whose organs tend to the inside, bodies an extension of tail, provide a pleasure altogether apart from the life of whales. The apparent finality of their forms contrasts favorably with the dangerously tentative situation of the steeple-jack attempting to balance his star.

Animals work as a stabilizing pattern generally in this poem, from the aesthetic ideal embodied in the whales to the spider metaphor for the steeple-jack, with its reassurance of the spider's competence as the man works his way along a thread. At the pedestrian level "a twenty-five / pound lobster" provides fisherman and shopper with the pleasure of a prize whose value may be quantified. Animals are also central in the arrangement of the town's structures—"a schoolhouse, a post-office in a / store, fish-houses, hen-houses, a three-masted / schooner on / the stocks"—with food stores at the core. The church, being "a fit haven for / waifs, children, animals, prisoners, / and presidents," puts live animals at the center. An artistic distance from Moore's subject is never more evident than here where she who reveres the lives of her pangolin, her jerboa, is also capable of showing the various ways animals are integrated into human society, where the incongruity of affection for the living on the one hand and casual utility on the other is of no consequence.

Dead animals are, however, the exception. While the distinction between animals as matter and as living beings is often subtle, the revelation of life as motion is at last exquisite. The astonishing manifestation of the living is dramatized in the delicate unfolding of **"The Fish,"** where the mysterious combination of plant, mineral, and animal under water makes identification a compelling adventure. As animals are likened to objects or even to machines throughout Moore's poetry, here are "crabs like green / lilies." From one who inclines rather to adjective complexes than to metaphor, this simile does not represent the poet's ingenious linking of two unlike things: the analogy occurs in nature, where animal and plant (or mineral) are well disguised. Jellyfish, crab, and toadstools "slide each on the other." But "of the crow-blue mussel-shells," one opens and shuts itself—minimal movement, yet an indication of the self-willed life. That the inanimate shell moves is an enchanting puzzle (not unlike the miracle of machines). And the form of movement is characteristically gradual and directed by the urge for resolution: the mussel shell "keeps / adjusting the ash-heaps." Whatever the motive for action, the sign of life is exhilarating—the thrill of seeing a stone move. My God, the thing is alive!

Still, for Moore most movement is disturbing and must be controlled. After all, "a good brake is as important as a good motor." Speed indicates danger. Similarly, solid matter comforts, while the sea is **"A Grave"**: "you cannot stand in the middle of this." The quick gesture is brilliantly awkward, a mode of escape toward a home where the animal may stand or sit. (pp. 104-06)

Even the bird in flight moves with frantic necessity. Above the sinister wrinkling "progress" of the sea, "birds swim through the air at top speed," the verb accurately illustrating flight but transforming it from the classically free-spirited form to a desperate journey. The weightier frigate pelican *lies* on the air, his wings "uniting levity with strength," a brilliant occupation deactivated in the noun compound: this "hell-diver" prefers taking his fish from other birds to attacking for himself. The pelicans "move out to the top / of the circle and stop." Then this "most romantic bird flies / to a more mundane place, the mangrove / swamp to sleep." A bird may hide in the sky or escape back to earth, but he does not fly for fun.

The flightless bird is a more characteristic Moore subject, the kiwi, whose wings are used for an umbrella, and the ostrich, the world's largest bird, who **"Digesteth Harde Yron."** Moore finds in this bird as he swallows gravel for digestion the substantiality she seeks in all her animals—the size that works as a stabilizing, not a power, factor. With "leaden-skinned back," the big bird is solid enough to carry a man. That he is the symbol of justice interests the poet only as it ironically works to the detriment of the ostrich: his feathers are taken so man might appear just. Being valued by man is only a liability for an animal.

While the ostrich is a mighty runner, "swifter than a horse," Moore does not show him running. His speed as the potential for escape is enough. First noted as the "large sparrow . . . walking by a stream," he then stands guard over his chicks. That he "will wade / in lake or sea till only the head shows" makes even slow motion dangerous. Motion as an indication of vulnerability rather than might is expressed in the "compass-needle nervousness" of the neck, a delicately precise image built on the quivering of an instrument that points the way home. A strange mix of solidity and pregnability furthers the comic impression of this camel-sparrow with the "comic duckling head." (pp. 107-08)

As Pearce sees it, poets such as Williams, Aiken, and Cummings in their "chest pounding" conceal a "fear of the unknown" that is not to be found in Moore's poetry. Instead, in her assumption of the need for armor, the acknowledgment of threat as a first fact of life works to minimize fear or even to avoid it. As successful controls are imposed, a new sense of security becomes possible.

With scant physical armor, the jerboa, a tiny nocturnal rodent of Asia and North Africa, is the supreme case of inner discipline. Exemplar of abstinence, the jerboa is master of the enemy Moore has referred to as "fat living and self-pity." With no ivory bed, no palm trees, not even any water, the spare desert rat knows abundance—it knows *happiness*. Anything more than the stark self is "Too Much." Certainly being without companions is no detriment. As the wisely witty line from **"If I Were Sixteen Today"** maintains: "The cure for loneliness is solitude." The frontier of "boundless sand" armors the jerboa against civilization, serving as the bare stage upon which the individual stands. "Not famous" or of value to man, without material abundance, the jerboa is bared to a state requiring sheer self-reliance, a "sand-brown jumping-rat—free-born."

One of Moore's most notably adaptable animals, the jerboa is uniquely composed of what appear to be features of other animals: the "buff-brown" coat of the "bower-bird," "chipmunk contours," a "bird head," and a "fish-shaped" body. But "the fine hairs on the tail, / repeating the other pale / markings" bring disparate elements into a unique unity in the fragile exterior. (pp. 110-11)

This disproportionate creature leaps straight, as if inner spirit alone resolves exterior imbalance. And by setting irregular jumps to a musical measure, however unseemly the half-note effects, an underlying pattern leading to resolution is established. Likening the fragile bounce to the tune of flageolet catches an errant rhythm but also the pure tones of the flute-like instrument. Thus disturbing movement in the jerboa is brought under control, resolved in the final note, which Moore draws as a whole note. Delicate though they are, footprints show the beginnings of rootedness. Freed by obscurity, inner restraint, and stops between leaps, the sound little rodent makes it home.

Poetry has "a place for / the genuine," and Moore's favoring of animals as poetic subjects is a tribute to their genuineness. "Why an inordinate interest in animals and athletes? They are subjects for art and exemplars of it, are they not? minding their own business. Pangolins, horn-bills, pitchers, catchers, do not pry or prey—or prolong the conversation; do not make us self-conscious; look their best when caring least."

The obscurity of Moore's animals bestows the virtue of modesty, the gift of freedom. No less inclined to individual liberty than those who dramatize it more actively, she shows independence as the result of self-protection and discipline. In this, her animals incline to the stationary rather than to the expansive. Indeed, they would rather sleep than attack. And with the proper controls, they are free to do just that. (pp. 111-12)

Mary Allen, "Controlled Creatures: Marianne Moore," in her Animals in American Literature, *University of Illinois Press, 1983, pp. 97-112.*

DOUGLAS CRASE

In ***Predilections*** [Moore] linked reviews together to form essays, and mixed those with other pieces in such a way as to suggest that serene institution, a poet's essays—the detached, the Olympian reflection on matters aesthetical. In ***A Marianne Moore Reader*** she emphasized a more extroverted prose (a piece from *Vogue,* one from *Harper's Bazaar*) and, fitting her late image as the Mary Poppins poet in a tricorn hat who once threw out the first ball of the season at Yankee Stadium, she even included, over the objections of her editors, the correspondence with Ford Motor Company in which she proposed archly inappropriate names for the product Ford would later market as the Edsel. The new ***Complete Prose*** corrects both screwball caricatures by a method the poet herself applied to individual poems or essays, a method she calls—though she is quoting someone else of course—"an accuracy of abundance."

As Moore practiced it, this meant you might learn first what was *not* in abundance ("certain of Marsden Hartley's stark austerities not here, are preferred by us to some that are," she writes in a 1925 review). So the reader should know there are no interviews, no letters and no selections from her reading diaries in the ***Complete Prose.*** There's no fiction, either, unless you agree with the publisher that eight short stories by an undergraduate in the Bryn Mawr literary magazine add up to a showing in the form. And not much in the way of memoirs, though there is the sparkling, if decorous account of her tenure from 1925 to 1929 as editor of *The Dial,* present at the creation of Modernist American poetry. She "was our saint," said William Carlos Williams in retrospect. "She is one of the angels," said Wallace Stevens before he even met her. She's a "hysterical virgin," said Hart Crane at the time, when she was meddling with his manuscripts.

She was also the most engagingly original of the great Modernist poets born in the United States. Her first poems appeared in 1915 (the same year as "The Love Song of J. Alfred Prufrock" and "Sunday Morning") and one of them, **"To a Steam Roller,"** started out like this:

> The illustration
> is nothing to you without the application.

Thus began, as Eliot would point out a few years later, a brilliant use of "the curious jargon produced in America by universal university education." Today, this college vernacular has been so fully integrated into the American tradition that if you found those lines from **"To a Steam Roller"** lying around loose somewhere you might think they had been dropped by John Ashbery or one of his acolytes. But in 1915 nobody had written poetry this way before. "I want to know," wrote Ezra Pound in a letter, "whether you are working on Greek quantitative measures or on René Ghil or simply by ear (if so a very good ear)."

It was a good ear, one of the best; and Moore put it to work not just in her poetry but in a distinctive criticism that likewise answered to what the ear hears, as well as to what the eye sees. It is this criticism that dominates the ***Complete Prose,*** from a first, brief essay published in 1916 to an exiguous appreciation of Christopher Smart published two years after she died in 1972 at the age of 84. Moore once remarked that, whatever she wrote in prose, it would really be an essay. Apparently she was right, because the five kinds of criticism in this volume are distinguished not so much by form or quality as they are by length: essays of about five pages; reviews of two or three pages; comments, of a page or so, from *The Dial;* brief mentions, of a paragraph, also from *The Dial;* and blurbs. Yes, the "complete blurbs," and even these are little essays, as in the one for Hugh Kenner: "Entertaining and fearless, he can be too fearless, but we need him."

Since it is mostly criticism, the ***Complete Prose*** doesn't reveal what Pound was anxious to discover, the source of Moore's breakthrough poetics. But it does corroborate her poetics in ways that will make it easier and more fun to understand her. (p. 432)

Of course, if it's true that life consists in what you are thinking about all day (Emerson said it was), then the ***Complete Prose*** also represents a partial life of the mind of Marianne Moore. (In one month *The Dial* carried one review, one comment and three brief mentions all by Moore.) And because she was so deeply involved with the fortunes of Eliot, Stevens, Williams and the rest, it is also a life of Modernist poetry in North America, from its inception with Pound to its capitulation to Auden. (p. 433)

Still, to regard this book as primarily a concordance or a life would be to imply that a poet's prose is somehow ancillary to the poetry. That's a familiar attitude, predicated sometimes on the notion that poets should leave the "business" of criticism to those who are in it as a business, and sometimes on the notion that poets just can't think. One of these notions may even be true; but Moore, joyously quoting Eliot quoting Pound, actively believed that criticism and poetry are not exclusive ("They proceed as two feet of one biped"), perhaps not even separable. Criticism, she writes, "inspires creation." More than that, "a genuine achievement in criticism is an achievement in creation"—her own prose being the case that proves her point, if not exactly in the way she meant. Her reviews, and even her essays on poetics (with enchanted titles like **"Humility, Concentration, and Gusto"** or **"Idiosyncrasy and Technique"**), don't offer the kinds of intellectual recipes that explain poetry so much as they offer further examples of what goes on during poetry—Moore's poetry, to be exact. In the way that *Democratic Vistas* is more Whitman, or *The Necessary Angel* more Stevens, so the prose in these pages is *more* Marianne Moore.

No surprise then, if it can be as recalcitrant as the poetry. Moore is well known for saying that "one should be as clear as one's natural reticence allows one to be." It is easy to be amused by this, but it was not mere perversity on her part. . . . No, her reticence is designed to induce you to let her proceed until it is too late to do anything but catch up with her. Or as she puts it in one of the many collectibles waiting in this book:

> Poetry is an unintelligible unmistakable vernacular like the language of the animals—a system of communication whereby a fox with a turkey too heavy for it to carry, reappears shortly with another fox to share the booty.

No surprise, either, if the way Moore organizes an essay-review is also designed to share the booty (not to mention the burden) with the reader. "The objective is architecture, not demolition," she writes, indicating that she knew very well what we were likelier to think. Yet essays like **"Henry James as a Characteristic American," "Abraham Lincoln and the Art of the Word"** and the earlier **"Sir Francis Bacon"** do eventually reveal their architecture in paragraphs the way her poems reveal an architecture in stanzas. What appears at first to be an overturned file of quotations is really a stanzaic arrangement in which the quotations probably do more work by virtue of reassociation and antithesis than they did in the original. It is no coincidence that her first real review is built on the conceit of suggesting to Mr. Eliot how he might *rearrange* his book.

Readers, and I am one of them, who have been vexed by Moore's notorious revisions of her poems will recognize that she is following a similar impulse in this rearrangement of quotations into prose. In fact, given the examples and the dicta of the ***Complete Prose,*** we may have to consider that she knew exactly what she was doing to us.

> It may be true that the author's revisions make it harder, not easier, for hurried readers; but flame kindles to the eye that contemplates it.

There's a decidedly spiritual tone to that, and it recurs so frequently in the prose that I suspect Moore saw her rearrangements and revisions as a means to detain the mind—otherwise rapt with commerce—for decidedly spiritual ends. To rearrange a subject is truly to contemplate it. It is one thing in a review or an essay to express opinions, because opinions are easy to come by and much like everyone else's; most of the time they *are* everyone else's. It is another thing to rearrange, because choices are both morally and technically interesting, with the added chance of being original. This is the added chance Marianne Moore was always ready to take, and (in the rearranged words of another) she lets us know exactly why: "The 'ability to be drunk with a sudden realization of value in things others never notice' can metamorphose our detestable reasonableness and offset a whole planetary system of deadness."

If deadness was the evil, the salvation was idiosyncrasy, the "indigenous gusto" which, as she writes in praise of Auden, makes a good poet "unable to be dull." The problem is, salvation doesn't matter much if it's for poets only—a decent, realistic judgment that is implicit in this poet's statement to the readers of *Seventeen:* "Example is needed, not counsel." In fact, when you examine the "screwball" image of Moore's later life from this perspective, it doesn't look crazy after all, but exemplary. Like her poems, like her tenure at *The Dial,* her public prose and her public activities are examples of how Americans might contemplate the startling details of their own existence: the St. Louis Cardinals or the Camperdown Elm in Prospect Park; the "impassioned emancipator" M. Carey Thomas of Bryn Mawr or the middleweight champion Floyd Patterson; even the art of individual dress (just think of the effect on readers of *Women's Wear Daily* who learned under Moore's byline that "Whatever the cut, width, or foot, the wearer should be able to step with assurance—as Dante says, like a crane—'come una crana'").

So the woman who was among the first of poets to celebrate "plain American which cats and dogs can read" went on in her prose and life to demonstrate what a Dürer could do with the mix of fantasy and calculation to be seen in ourselves. As she said of one Modernist colleague: "In his modestly emphatic respect for America he corroborates Henry James' conviction that young people should 'stick fast and sink up to their necks in everything their own countries and climates can give,' and his feeling for the *place* lends poetic authority to an illusion of ours, that sustenance may be found here, which is adapted to artists." This was no jingoist or isolationist attitude, for already in her time she had seen how it was sublimely moral: a people who don't think themselves worth saving aren't going to care much about the rest of the world either. "The thing is to see the vision and not deny it," she writes; "to care and admit that we do." In a lifetime of seeing and admitting, Moore was so spirited and yet so careful to avoid hyperbole that she has earned the right to the last word, as she herself writes it (reviewing a very different stylist) in ***The Complete Prose of Marianne Moore:*** "But the book is a triumph, and all of us, that is to say a great many of us, would do well to read it." (pp. 434, 436-37)

Douglas Crase, "Quills from a Porcupine," in The Nation, *New York, Vol. 243, No. 14, November 1, 1986, pp. 432-34, 436-37.*

RICHARD EDER

By today's standards, Moore's poetry scarcely seems obscure, despite some difficult lines here and there. Although her verbal complexity is comparable to Wallace Stevens, whom she much admired despite his "bearishness"—"America's chief conjurer," she called him—she is much clearer than he is.

She would have been able to explain why. Difficult writing "should at least have the air of having meant something to the person who wrote it," she claimed, explaining why she felt that James Joyce and Gertrude Stein were fundamentally accessible. If you can sense the poet's attitude and commitment, the poetry will show through the complexity.

Stevens frequently vanished behind his words. It was always clear what Moore was doing. She was noticing and celebrating, whether it was the Verrazzano Bridge ("Enfranchising cable, silvered by the sea"), the universal resourcefulness of Yogi Berra ("He is no feather"), or the infrangible elusiveness of the jelly-fish ("visible, invisible / a fluctuating charm").

"More than any modern poet she gives us the feeling that life is softly exploding around us, within easy reach," wrote John Ashbery, one of our more difficult self-concealers.

It is not in her poetry but in some of the critical writing collected [in ***The Complete Prose of Marianne Moore***], in fact, that Moore can be hardest to fathom. Perhaps because in this kind of writing, it is clarity we particularly look for.

And we get it. But the clearer Moore is, the more difficult she can be, because what she is clear and exact about is a train of thought so individual that it lacks steps to climb aboard. . . .

There are more than a few such impasses in this collection of prose that goes from early stories in the Bryn Mawr college magazine through her time as critic and editor of *The Dial* and finally to essays and observations written for a wide variety of newspapers and magazines. From Moore's early *Dial* days, though, her eye and sensibility were acute; as the years went by, her style relaxed without ever losing its individuality. . . .

Had Moore been around to supervise the job, this "might have been a much slimmer volume," the editor writes. As it is, with certain themes recurring and with certain poets—Stevens, Ezra Pound, T. S. Eliot—written about repeatedly, we sometimes get a sense of undue reiteration. One of her favorite Stevens' couplets—"Chieftain Iffacan of Azcan in Caftan / of tan with henna hackles halt"—can be found six times. There are three citations of Dante's reference to Beatrice walking loftily, like a crane. But we forgive that one, because it so much suggests Moore's own high, delicate strides and her darting eye.

In short, there is a certain amount of sand in the raspberries. With a little rinsing, it is a feast, a slimming one. . . .

Her literary heroes were Eliot, Pound, Joyce, Stein, Stevens and William Carlos Williams. Perhaps it was the last two who meant the most to her, who especially reinforced her vocation as an American poet of high and concrete style. "Poetry in America has not died so long as these two 'young sycamores' are able to stand the winters that we have, and the inhabitants."

Her heart was nowhere on her sleeve, but it shows. Some of the pride as well as pain of her idiosyncrasy is reflected in these words of advice to young readers in a magazine column: "Fashion can make you ridiculous; style, which is yours to control individually, can make you attractive." And these: "The cure for loneliness is solitude."

"The most important influence in my poetry," she writes late in life, "has been ethical." Her poetry's lilt may make this puzzling; but it doesn't take much reading to make it evident. She is a poet of health, and her curlicues are of an astonishing straightness. "Any writer overwhelmingly honest about pleasing himself is sure to please others," she writes.

Richard Eder, in a review of "The Complete Prose of Marianne Moore," in Los Angeles Times Book Review, *November 23, 1986, p. 3.*

GRACE SCHULMAN

Of the major American poets born in the 1880's—including Moore, William Carlos Williams, Ezra Pound, Hilda Doolittle and T. S. Eliot—Pound and Eliot are regarded as eminent critics. Now ***The Complete Prose of Marianne Moore*** . . . demonstrates that Moore was another of the superlative critics. With inevitable exceptions but with resolute continuity, she tracks poetry from *The Wild Swans at Coole* by William Butler Yeats in 1918 to a posthumous collection of Randall Jarrell's poems in 1967, and she covers many novels, biographies and critical studies over five decades.

It is not, as she herself observes of Cervantes, that Moore needs to be rescued from oblivion. She has been celebrated for her achievement in poetry. Unfortunately, however, even the two volumes of her work that did include some essays have been out of print for some time. This new volume of prose is more or less complete, and it is dazzling. In it we find her attending to literature and also covering art, music and dance with an expertise born of tireless research.

She writes with an exuberance for real places and things; the neighborhood schools, the library and the cinema are elevated to excitement in a later essay, **"Brooklyn From Clinton Hill."** In her rapture for ordinary experience she resembles Williams and, especially, Pound, who felt he adhered to an American poetry of the commonplace inaugurated by Whitman. Her own enthusiasm was ignited by two prose craftsmen—Sir Thomas Browne, for whom, she points out, "small things could be great things," and Henry James, whom she describes in a major essay of 1934, **"Henry James as a Characteristic American."** . . .

New York is her territory. In *The Dial* from 1921 to 1929, she praises prints by Dürer and his contemporaries, notes Alfeo Faggi's masks of Noguchi and Dante and records "the bellows-warbled, now high, now low, hollow music of the circus" at Madison Square Garden. For *Dance Index* in 1944 she comments on the buoyancy, strength and "uncontaminated innocence" of Anna Pavlova. For *The New York Times* in 1967 and *Women's Wear Daily* in 1965 she examines fashion and manners with an elegance reminiscent of Castiglione's "Courtier." In *Dance Index* in 1946 she tells of *The Elephant Ballet,* an odd combination of George Balanchine's ballerinas and Ringling Brothers' elephants; her gaze fluctuates between the two, and she merges them finally when she sees "the spiral of the elephant's trunk repeating the spirals of the dancing. . . ."

Many similar perceptions appear in her poetry. Writing of a Dürer exhibit, she remarks that the artist traveled to the Dutch coast to see a stranded whale, and that image turns up, transformed, in her poem **"The Steeple-Jack."** Describing Faggi's sculpture, she develops the theme, recurrent in her poetry, of the writer's effort to join the visible world to invisible realities: "A reverence for mystery is not a vague, invertebrate thing. The realm of the spirit is the only realm in which experience is able to corroborate the fact that the real can be also the actual." Subsequently, in her poem **"The Hero,"** the figure so named is distinguished by "a reverence for mystery." In her poem **"Style,"** an image of the Spanish painter clearly has an antecedent in her prose observation that "Mr. Henry McBride finds in the painting by El Greco . . . a 'curiously lambent inner glow' that gives it 'an unearthly impressiveness.' "

The prose of Marianne Moore is not, however, simply a source for her poetry. For her it has its own integrity and importance. In 1925 she declares her indebtedness to—apart from Bacon, Browne and James—Defoe, Bunyan, Leigh Hunt, Edmund Burke and Joseph Conrad. She refers to many of them in her essays and learns from their methods. Writing of George Moore's prose, for example, she observes that he, like Defoe, has "preciseness without apparent effort to be precise, the effect of discursiveness unrehearsed." In her work she too labored hard to appear effortless. In 1965 she quotes George Grosz, the caricaturist, as calling for "endless curiosity, observation, research, and a great amount of joy in the thing." In an essential essay, **"Idiosyncrasy and Technique,"** she reveals: "One writes because one has a burning desire to objectify what it is indispensable to one's happiness to express."

It was as editor of *The Dial,* a position she obtained largely through the support of Pound, who was early to praise her poetry and her prose, that she came into her own as an essayist. In fact, her work at *The Dial* clarifies why she published no poetry (and claimed she wrote none) from 1926 to 1929, the years when she was editor. "A genuine achievement in criticism is an achievement in creation," she writes in a review of Eliot's book of essays *The Sacred Wood.* Just as she diminishes the importance of a division between prose and poetry, she writes criticism that is, like her poetry, an art of exactitude. She looks at her subject from all sides, and examines her own attitudes.

Her principles are stated in key essays such as **"Feeling and Precision," "Humility, Concentration, and Gusto," "Idiosyncrasy and Technique"** and the James piece. In the first she observes: "When writing with maximum impact, the writer seems under compulsion to set down an unbearable accuracy." Of clarity, which depends on precision, she writes: "We must be as clear as our natural reticence allows us to be," believing that the greater the emotional force is, the stronger the reserve and the drive to be exact will be. In **"Humility, Concentration, and Gusto"** she speaks of humility as acknowledging that, originality being impossible, the writer's unique mold is impressed on traditional material. "I have learned more about writing from Ezra Pound than from anyone else," she asserts, and she cites his call for directness, economy of words and "composition in the sequence of the musical phrase rather than that of the metronome." With her own emphasis on exactitude, intensity and idiosyncrasy (meaning individuality), she has a firm technical platform on which to base her comments. . . .

There is in her prose the democratic sense of mingling things, people and works of art. In 1951 she names in one breath Casals, Soledad, E. McKnight Kauffer, Hans Mardersteig, Alec Guinness and the Lippizaner horsemen as being among the artists of the time. While her most honored writers include Plato, Seneca and Plutarch, she is enchanted also by Christy Mathewson's *Pitching in a Pinch* and *My Garden* by the Duke of Windsor. This amassing of the ordinary and the unusual, the common and the great, creates an air of adventurous inquiry in her work like that she detects in Henry James's. With exclusive standards and an inclusive acceptance of anything that is exhilarating in its own way, she conveys fairness and the morality that is her mark. Her standards for prose are the same as her standards for life; she focuses on small objects to see beyond them to larger matters.

From 1929 on, especially during World War II, she writes of her wish for an end to violence and a peace built on affection. She commends Wallace Stevens for disparaging the lust for power and honors Conrad and Williams for their awareness of responsibility. In 1947 she applauds W. H. Auden for his emphasis on moral choice and his conviction that faith and purity are antidotes to fear and greed. She admires Confucius for his belief in sympathy: "What you don't want yourself, don't inflict on another" is, in her words, his command.

Finally, her humor, ranging from wit to hilarity, is understated, wry, epigrammatic. "Mr. Auden is not ashamed of seeming to have done some reading," she offers; or, "'Incredible,' 'fabulous,' 'rapturous,' used more than once in a lifetime, lose force." Her lightness indicates joy in the deeply serious, life-sustaining task that literature is for everyone.

Grace Schulman, "A Gusto for Dumbo and Balanchine," in The New York Times Book Review, *November 30, 1986, p. 13.*

BONNIE COSTELLO

Moore at her best (which by and large means before 1940) is a poet of wild decorum. She combines high civility with energy and inclusiveness, propriety with sincerity. This inevitably tense combination exemplifies a continuing American ambivalence about our European heritage and our native vitality. The Old World values of tradition and culture grow stale and superficial in excess; the new, frontier values of freedom and originality tend to become crude and rapacious. Moore's poetry situates itself at the center of this tension, presenting not compromise but a lively struggle toward an ideal fusion. In **"Poetry,"** Moore describes her ideal poets as "literalists of the imagination." They will write a poetry in which art and nature are one, in which refinement and gusto are not at odds. "In the meantime," she writes,

if you demand on the one hand,
the raw material of poetry in
all its rawness and
that which is on the other hand
genuine, you are interested in poetry.

Her animals (a jerboa, a pangolin, a paper nautilus) combine the virtues of freedom and restraint. Her poems join descriptive exuberance and epigrammatic tautness.

This same combination of qualities—bold feeling and formal precision—characterizes the style and stance of Moore's prose. Here, in [***The Complete Prose of Marianne Moore***], is a brave and ample commentary on an unprecedented range of subjects. There is nothing marginal about Moore's vision. She addresses the major concern of her time and her tradition: How should the imagination face the pressure of reality? But doctrine and dogma are antithetical to this mind enraptured by the particular. Her touchstone is always "strong enchantment"—in herself and in others—rather than any more impersonal concept of the modern.

Editorship of *The Dial* from 1925 to 1929 provided Moore with an ideal platform from which to review not only the contemporary literary scene, but whatever might evoke or instance this strong enchantment. Though Moore was always "picking and choosing" and was never attracted to a naive populism, she still resisted hierarchies. Just as her poems take up with equal vigor the topics of a desert rat and a painting by Dürer, so in the prose she is open to non-traditional and non-literary subjects. She celebrates the art of dressing well with as much passion as the art of writing well. Fine language catches her attention in the poems of T. S. Eliot, in the speeches of Abraham Lincoln, or in a guide to gardening. She can be "prepossessed by the impassioned explicitness" of a letter from the Federal Reserve Board and marvel at the lacework of a peacock's tail or the cursive ease of a Robert Andrew Parker drawing. Though she naturally comments most often on poetry, her reflections extend to the other arts, to living in Brooklyn, to visiting the zoo, to being 16. The world, for Moore, is a display of spiritual values; and those values are not "confined to one locality." Her models for prose (as for poetry) are less often the polemical writings of contemporaries than the reflective essays of 17th century writers such as Francis Bacon, Isaak Walton, Thomas Browne, and Robert Burton, for whom any natural or cultural phenomenon afforded an occasion for moral and aesthetic commentary.

Though her writing appeared in a variety of contexts (not only in *The Dial, Poetry,* and other literary magazines, but in *Harper's,* the *Nation, Mademoiselle),* Moore did not adjust that style significantly to suit the genre or the occasion. The writing is always inimitably hers, a patchwork of quotations backstitched with dexterous indirections and digressions to the fineness and patterning of brocade. Double negatives, circumlocutions, strings of dependent clauses give this writing a decidedly baroque look, despite Moore's espousal of the plain style. And her felicity with metaphor is as apparent in the prose as in the poetry: metaphors dropped casually on a meandering discursive path have a concentrating power. Her fondness for animal metaphors in describing her favorite poets recalls the aesthetic virtues she endorses in her famous poetic menagerie: Eliot "moves troutlike through a variety of foreign objects"; Cummings "settling like a man-o-war bird . . . shapes the progress of poems as if it were substance."

Moore's compendium of natural and technological fact, so apparent in the poems, provided her with ready analogies for the experience of art, with ways of coping with the difficulty and unfamiliarity of the new. On reading Gertrude Stein: "One is abashed not to have understood instantly; as water may not seem transparent to the observer but has a perspicuous opacity in which the fish swims with ease." Or on Williams's poetry: "The compressed fire in his work makes one think of the blaze in the blacksmith's forge, permeating dull iron until the metal gradually shows a clear red." Moore's metaphors function as part of her more profound talent for condensing the virtues of a subject into a sentence or two.

After all the deferential strategies, these essays depend finally on a concentrated voice that disarms the reader with its authority. (pp. 30-2)

The reader looking in these essays for clues to Moore's poems will not be rewarded with any lengthy discourse on poetics. The writing reveals by example, displaying the same predilections and employing many of the same strategies as the poems. Indeed, if poetry is prose with a higher consciousness, the level of consciousness in these essays is sufficiently subtle and intense to elude the careless reader with its "feigned inconsequence of manner." But as Kenneth Burke, one of Moore's best and earliest reviewers, argued, "when she quotes in her special way of quoting, we see her carving a text out of a text, much like carving a personal life out of life in general.'' Moore's essays, like her poems, use quotation beyond any familiar standard of evidence or exposition. But these quotations are part of her principle of economy, for while attending to some specific, often technical aspect of a quotation, Moore appropriates its statement.

The essay **"Humility, Concentration and Gusto"** is the most dramatic example of this concentrated indirection. Nowhere in the essay does Moore define explicitly the terms the title lists or invoke their traditions (in Herbert, for instance, and in Hazlitt). But the examples she chooses not only demonstrate, but often contain in their statements, clues to definition. As the essay develops, humility is redefined as sincerity, concentration as ambiguity, and gusto as impassioned explicitness. Although these qualities are identified, against standards of rhetoric and decorum, with apparent defects or oddities, they mark the presence of strong enchantment, and make a place for the genuine.

Thus William Cowper's ''The Snail,'' quoted in full, is prefaced only with the observation that it is ''a thing of gusto although the poem has been dismissed as mere description.'' Why Moore considers it a thing of gusto is left to inference. Undoubtedly she admired the precise rhyme and meter, broken by the isolated last line. Here the form echoes the sense, suggesting a personal interest in the subject of inhibition and solitude. But the real ''gusto'' of the poem, judging from the context of other quotations in which it is set, is the suggestion of self-reference that avoids self-display. . . . Moore's own poem **"To a Snail"** similarly speaks of itself. It begins: ''If 'compression is the first grace of style' / you have it.'' As in Cowper, the gusto of the poem depends upon a text that both hides and discloses the author's presence.

Though Moore was not a writer of critical manifestos, she became a tastemaker by the energy of her predilections. Her collected prose, not only during the years at *The Dial* but before and after them, offers one of the fullest assessments of the poetry of her time. It follows the careers of the major modernists through a period of 50 years. Stevens and Williams present two of the most complete cases of Moore's investment in the work of her contemporaries, and the most interesting cases of the poet defining her own sympathies and precepts through the evaluation of others.

Despite her ''capacity for fact,'' it is Wallace Stevens, the supreme fiction maker, who wins Moore's most unqualified praise. Moore was one of the first to recognize a prodigious talent at work in *Harmonium,* and her 1924 review **"Well Moused, Lion"** suggests that she found in Stevens a kindred attraction toward the exotic and an ideal of power and restraint. . . .Stevens also appealed to her as a poet of aural harmonies counteracting the visual riot of his imagery, as a poet responsible, for all his rage, to the higher orders of art. But Stevens compels her attention as much by his moral and philosophical as by his aesthetic power, especially since these are presented as aspects of each other in his later work (pp. 32-3)

Similarly, Moore's reviews of Williams, committed as they are to his courage and authenticity as a poet, contain many reservations about the presentation of uncensored, untransformed material in poetry, about the revolt against poetic tradition and decorum. . . . At the same time she recognized that Williams's uncompromising passion for the new, for the texture of the unaltered real, was an essential aspect of his poetic power. . . . Moore's comments on Stevens and Williams remind us how decidedly transformed Moore's ''real toads'' are in the imaginary gardens she arranges for them. Repeatedly the essays in this volume ask the question ''Is the real the actual?'' And they settle, without belying their acclaim of accuracy and particularity, on an Emersonian priority of spirit: ''A reverence for mystery is not a vague, invertebrate thing. The realm of the spirit is the only realm in which experience is able to corroborate the fact that the real can also be the actual.'' The fabulists, the conjurers, who transpose the textures of the real onto the imagined, most often delight her.

On all their topics Moore's essays pursue an integration of moral and aesthetic categories. ''Contractility is a virtue / as modesty is a virtue'' she writes in **"To a Snail,"** and she continues the theme in the essays. She sees the ethical in the technical, and vice versa. This identification of aesthetic and moral categories has a neoclassical flavor, and Moore's strong sense of decorum does sometimes hark back to a gentler age. One of Moore's master values was propriety, enlarged from our common usage to ''a tuned reticence with rigor / from strength at the source.'' She admired what she called Kenneth Burke's ''master-maxim'': ''Truth in art is not discovery of facts or addition to knowledge, it is the exercise of propriety.'' And she measured his and others' achievements by this maxim. A poet of tremendous aesthetic courage, she was a bold, but never indiscriminate, supporter of the new. Thus, reviewing the literary scene in 1936, she complains: ''Judged by our experimental writing, we are suffering today from unchastity, sadism, blasphemy, and rain-soaked foppishness.'' But she never calculated achievement by an impersonal standard of correctness. On the contrary, she repeatedly showed her sympathy for oddity or deviation driven by ''strong enchantment.'' In **"Feeling and Precision,"** she admits that ''feeling at its deepest—as we all have reason to know—tends to be inarticulate.''

Moore singles out for praise all those instances in which ''the inevitable warfare between imagination and medium'' has led to a final grace. Resisting polemics in herself, she was able to embrace a striking range of achievement. ''Hostile though specific theories may be and riotous as the artist may sometimes seem in his attitude toward the existing body of art,'' she says in one of her *Dial* comments, ''in so far as a thing is really a work of art it confirms other works of art.''

The breadth and the depth of this collection make it clear that the writing of essays was an integral part of Moore's career, not just an occasional supplement to the writing of poems. (The book includes Moore's several experiments in narrative as well, but these are more anecdotal than fictive, and often shape themselves around a discursive idea.) Her achievement in prose, as in poetry, is marked by an idiosyncrasy that is no barrier to profundity, by a personal predilection that carries the authority of measured judgment. Modernism was for Moore less a set of precepts or formal strategies than a responsibility to seek out and perpetuate the genuine. Her extraordinary essays meet that responsibility. (pp. 33-4)

Bonnie Costello, ''Strong Enchantments,'' in The New Republic, *Vol. 195, No. 26, December 29, 1986, pp. 30-4.*

Elsa Morante

1918-1985

Italian novelist, poet, short story writer, translator, and author of children's books.

Often considered one of Italy's leading postwar novelists, Morante frequently explored in her work conflicts between illusion and reality. Combining elements of fantasy with verisimilitude, Morante's prose style is indebted to surrealism and has been associated with Italian author Massimo Bontempelli's ''magic realism,'' which is characterized by lucid presentation of unreal events and stresses the value of imagination. Morante's central themes include the psychological implications of exclusion and separation, the common person's struggle against the institutions and ideologies of society, humanity's relationship to the external world, and the encroachment of reality upon dreams and memory. She often focuses on young protagonists, emphasizes the family as a fundamental human structure, and expresses sympathy for the socially disadvantaged. Although some critics have faulted Morante for expounding simplistic themes, most praise her vivid and fluent prose and regard her as an important writer of international stature.

© Jerry Bauer

Born and raised in Rome, Morante left her parents' home when she was eighteen years old; several years later, she married prominent Italian writer and antifascist Alberto Moravia. In 1943, due to the increased government pressure on antifascists that accompanied the Nazi occupation, Morante and Moravia fled Rome and lived for several months among peasants in rural Italy, an experience that occupies a central position in Morante's fiction.

Morante's first major work, *Menzogna e sortilegio* (1948; *House of Liars*), was perceived by Michael Caesar as ''the fullest exploration of the ambiguities of the imagination.'' Set in southern Italy at the end of the nineteenth century, this novel is narrated by an adolescent girl who has been left alone in a flat following the deaths of her parents and the prostitute who subsequently cared for her. By chronicling three generations in the history of her family, she hopes to exorcise the recurring hallucinations of her past and construct a tolerable world in which to live. The lies and illusions necessary to protect her fantasy become entangled, however, and her life is gradually destroyed. Michael Caesar commented that ''although the narrative is presented in the form of a sober chronicle, its assumptions are visionary: half-remembered, half-imagined, but more accurately evoked, like ghosts, the actors in the family drama move in a space occupied pre-eminently by insomnia, fantasy and day-dream.'' Morante's prose, which has been compared to nineteenth-century realism for its attention to detail and overriding concentration on character, contrasts with the novel's modern psychological concerns. Serge Hughes observed that ''in using a somewhat dated setting and technique, [Morante] has achieved a horror effect, like that sometimes provoked by a surrealist painting in which a familiar everyday object is placed in an utterly incongruous position.''

Morante's next novel, *L'isola di Arturo* (1957; *Arturo's Island*), is set on a fictional island near Naples and relates the experiences of Arturo, a young boy whose mother died during his birth and whose father shuttles between their island home and the nightclubs of Naples. Although the father devotes little attention to Arturo, his son worships him and often fantasizes about his heroic adventures at sea. When the father returns from Naples with a bride two years older than Arturo, the boy feels betrayed and abandoned, and the remainder of the novel focuses on his changing attitudes and emotions toward his father and stepmother. Essentially a psychological study of disillusionment, childhood trauma, and rejection, *Arturo's Island* is suffused with intimations of legend, myth, and Freudian obsessions and perversions. Employing intensely poetic imagery and lyrical, allusive language, Morante was praised for her psychological insights and her accurate rendering of the emotional fluctuations of youth.

La storia (1974; *History: A Novel*), a realistic depiction of personal suffering in Italy during World War II, is widely considered Morante's most ambitious work. The story of a lonely, half-Jewish peasant woman, her two sons, a small band of Resistance fighters, and their ghetto milieu, this novel portrays history's often violent and relentless effects on the lives of common people. Morante endeavors, in John Romano's words, to reveal ''that behind every human encounter, every turn in our lives, there is a pressure of historical reality, intimate psychic preparations, a universe of relevant detail.'' While acknowledging the tendency toward sentimentality that other critics had observed in this book, Romano questioned whether such a reaction is not an indication of the numbness of contemporary society to fiction: "We have forgotten how searing an experience the work of art made flesh can be." He concludes that *History* "bears the stamp of the best art: exalting life above itself."

The last of Morante's books to be published during her lifetime, *Aracoeli* (1982), returns to the theme of separation central to *Arturo's Island*. Distinguished from that book by its emphasis on the physical aspect of death and decay, *Aracoeli* has been viewed as Morante's bleakest work. Narrated by a guilt-ridden, neurotic, middle-aged homosexual, this novel is composed predominantly of dreams, bizarre fantasies, flashbacks, and childhood memories. Focusing his story on his mother's sudden mental and physical deterioration following the death of her second child, the narrator retreats into fantasy to escape his feelings of ugliness, hopelessness, and dissatisfaction with reality. In a final attempt to resurrect his mother's beauty and innocence, he journeys to the small Andalusian village where she was born; he encounters her spirit, but instead of comfort, it offers only ridicule and contempt. Raymond Rosenthal observed: "Not since Céline has there been so violent a protest against life's conditions, such outrage at the thought of death, so relentless an assault on the bare physical facts of human existence."

Morante's other titles include the short story collections *Il gioco segreto* (1941) and *Lo scialle andaluso* (1963); the poetry volumes *Alibi* (1958) and *Il mondo salvato dai ragazzini* (1968), in which Morante applies a variety of styles to explore many of the themes in her novels; and a children's book, *La bellisseme avventure di Cateri dalla tecciolina* (1942), which was revised and expanded as *La straordinarie avventure di Caterina* (1959).

(See also *CLC*, Vol. 8 and *Contemporary Authors*, Vols. 85-88, Vol. 117 [obituary].)

PAOLO MILANO

House of Liars (whose original, revealing title is "Of Lies and Charms") is Elsa Morante's first . . . novel, written during four years of seclusion. The girl who tells the long story (a recluse as well), looking for the source of her early sorrow and present estrangement, glances backward over the colorful obsessions which shaped the lives of her parents and their lovers and enemies.

At first, the characters look and sound like so many romantic heroes or villains: a young cousin, blond and dissolute; a wife who, in her deranged faithfulness to an adolescent idyl, will never forgive her husband for not being a rich aristocrat; a golden-hearted prostitute; two mothers who never tire of their sing-song competition in praise of their children. Gradually the reader, falling under the spell of Miss Morante's suggestive style, feels that her fable is not only rich in atmosphere but also meaningful and true. For many Sicilians of a provincial town do actually lead lives in which the years are filled by an old daydream or by a fossil resentment, while passions, grown out of the thinnest reality and more and more divorced from it, feed upon themselves and slowly burn people into ashes. Thus, the reader finds it natural that the straight narration should now and then give way to incidental poems—the best of these being the closing canto, in praise of a silent witness of many ruins, the cat Alvaro.

The felicity of such a novel rests, of course, chiefly on the writing. Miss Morante has chosen to clothe her perceptions, which are very modern, in a nineteenth-century dress; the effect of this contrast is as persuasive as it is delicate. There are dull pages and monotonous patterns; yet the impact of the novel grows continuously upon the reader and remains memorable.

Paolo Milano, "Slow Flames and Ashes," in The New York Times Book Review, *October 7, 1951, p. 5.*

SERGE HUGHES

Elsa Morante, wife of Alberto Moravia, the distinguished Italian novelist, reveals in . . . [***House of Liars***] a concern for that theme which has attracted and preoccupied almost every major European novelist of our times, the problem of personal disintegration and paralysis of action. The setting she has chosen for her moral disquisition is quite unusual: a warless Southern Italy of the late nineteenth or early twentieth century in which an amorphous lower middle class lives in constant dread of the poor and in the constant desire of gaining the favor of a few rich, decaying families. Unusual, too, are the rigorous exclusion of all ideological discussion, the embellishment with an introductory poem and a farewell epistle, and the richly melodramatic chapter descriptions. At first glance the novel would appear to be a belated realistic novel of the late nineteenth century. But it does not require much reading to become aware that the psychology which motivates the characters is completely, darkly modern, and that in using a somewhat dated setting and technique, the author has achieved a horror effect, like that sometimes provoked by a surrealist painting in which a familiar, everyday object is placed in an utterly incongruous position.

The story is told by Elisa, the young daughter of the heroine, who after the death of her parents and the prostitute friend who cared for her, is left alone in a Roman flat. There, trying to still constantly surging visions, dreams, and hallucinations, she undertakes to write down the history of her family. Aware that self-deceit destroyed her mother and father, she feels, nevertheless, that having had nothing else but those dreams, they could not be blamed. She, like the others of whom she writes, can only live alone in her room with her dreams of voices of the dead.

The characters she evokes are all very much alike. For all, self-deceit is the only adequate protection against outsiders: Elisa's mother, who goes out of her mind on learning of the death of her cousin, a wealthy, handsome nobleman she had wanted desperately to marry, and who collapses and dies soon after the accidental death of her husband, whom she does not love; Elisa's father, living with the illusion of being an intellectual, a person meant for a higher society; Rosaria, a prostitute, who is in love with the father, living only in the belief that he still loves her.

But lies are needed to protect the illusion, and sorcery to maintain these lies. And so the lives of all the characters become gradually indissolubly tangled, twisted, and slowly destroyed. Love, their only means of deliverance, is never possible for them; only sadism and Freudian complexes.

Regrettably, the tautness of the narrative is not matched by the plot, which becomes too involved, and one central character, the rich, aristocratic hero, who is oddly reminiscent of a Thomas Wolfe hero, remains hollow throughout. But if the reader will overlook these shortcomings, . . . he will have gained a sobering insight into a process of slow human disintegration. It makes Zola jovial by comparison.

Serge Hughes, "Human Disintegration," in The Saturday Review of Literature, *Vol. XXXIV, No. 42, October 20, 1951, p. 19.*

FRANCES KEENE

House of Liars is a vast work, and unlike our fat best-sellers of the "Woman of Property" type, it deals with a world which is to us exotic. Otherwise, I submit that it does not differ greatly from these overblown hunks of "literature." Miss Morante writes about what she knows, and she seeks fictional pegs simplified to suit her literary purpose. By projecting the Sicilian world against a screen she will at times silhouette and exaggerate certain details; at other times by putting a light behind a slide she will seem to diminish other views, making them appear as perfect and as unreal as detailed miniatures. Obviously, it is the family, the Cerentano of Palermo, who are silhouetted and exaggerated to heroic size, as indeed they saw themselves; and it is the rare and acutely etched Sicilian scenes, the religious fanaticism, the idiotic hierarchical social system, the life of the peasants as they grub to accumulate enough to educate a child, which are reduced to minute proportions. The author sometimes seems to query whether she is right in her dosage: so much emotional (not specifically sexual) perversions, so much world-weary pessimism, so much erotic adventure, so much local color, then let's do the turn over again. But she never settles on what that just percentage should be.

Morante's characters stand about as rather stunning effigies, while she admits her preference for the most perverse of them ("my incurable partiality for my character, Edoardo"). They are not rounded in their relationship to one another: hence her preferred character must be the *deus ex machina* who makes the others hop, for they have not enough visceral or cerebral validity to hop of their own accord. (pp. 357-58)

House of Liars is in the form of a flashback, a flashback which lasts 350 pages before we pick up the thread of the opening chapter. The author's narrator is, like herself, a young, brooding, and, we assume, solitary Sicilian who, by a trick of fate—that is, a bereavement—takes the reader into her confidence and retraces the story of her family, its inability to come to grips with either emotional or economic reality, its infinite capacity for illusion and for hate. (I do not wish to imply that the novel is autobiographical, which would be pure twaddle, but the narrator's eye is Miss Morante's and the reaction to the Sicilian world is hers, although the specific incidents may have little or no relation to personal, subjective experience.)

The thing for the foreign reader to decide is whether or not, when works of this kind come loudly heralded on to the international literary scene, there is such intrinsic merit in the book as will broadly communicate what is authentic in its background; that is, when the chips are down, is there enough of value in it to justify its introduction to that international public as the opening of a window on a hitherto partially or incorrectly known world. Certainly, the Morante book does effectively present aspects of the Sicilian genus which are largely ignored even in other parts of Italy. But it's a far cry from this admission to the heralding of the book as a piece of "fictional magic." Its structure is clumsy and verbose, its technique shows, and its characters move because they are moved, perversely and arbitrarily, by one of them. Now it is always easy to retort that these defects are not defects at all because they were consciously so planned by the author; and such counter-argument leaves the critic speechless, of course. But my admiration for Morante's obvious capacities is too great to hope that her errors were "plants": I believe she will do a better book next time. And since I am sure she is not a one-Gothic-tale author, I look forward to what she will offer us now that this great monster of a work is off her mind. (p. 358)

Frances Keene, "House of Nightmare," in The Nation, *New York, Vol. 173, No. 17, October 27, 1951, pp. 357-58.*

THE TIMES LITERARY SUPPLEMENT

Arturo's Island is a well-written, delicately constructed, richly coloured novel. It may also strike some of us as a bit of a bore. To call it too well written and composed . . . is not to demean skill but to say that this is one of those cases where skill defeats itself, where one remains conscious of the writing all the time, conscious of the effort and the calculations that lie behind it; just as one remains always aware of the precise degree of sensibility possessed by the authoress, of the dazzling literary values of the situation and ultimately, alas! of the exclusion from it of all factors except those which contribute to the literary effect.

The boy who is the centre of it is altogether the lonely, imaginative, passionately generous and fearful adolescent and nothing else. The stepmother, his father's child bride with whom he falls in love, is a sort of exquisitely composed archetype of dark-haired innocence, peasant simplicity and dormant fire, the sort of broad-hipped, long-lashed Neapolitan girl we have surely met before, seldom so expertly described, but often in the end with as much human truth. The father, who forms the third party in their little tragedy, is seen through the son's eyes to begin with as a handsome, fairy-tale hero, and then suddenly, also through the son's eyes, as the seedy, unloved traitor that he really is; and the very dexterity with which the image is composed and then destroyed is falsificatory, for adolescents, except in novels, do not have such clarity or single-mindedness of judgment at all. Finally, there is the island where it all, the boy's awakening to love of the bride and bitter knowledge of the father, takes place. Procida is a hot, close-fisted place, with a grim if sunlit reality of its own. Signorina Morante lavishes an undoubted talent on the description of it, but description it remains, with more than an element of the picturesque in it and little true inscape. Expertise is a bore if it is used factitiously, in an attempt to create literature rather than to contain life, and nearly everything in ***Arturo's Island,*** including the passions and the sorrows, are ultimately literary, no matter how richly done.

"Literary Art," in The Times Literary Supplement, *No. 2985, May 15, 1959, p. 285.*

THE TIMES LITERARY SUPPLEMENT

Elsa Morante's writing, especially in narrative and description, is extraordinarily attractive: fluent, delicate, "atmospheric", marvellously vivid and alive, with none of the rhetorical flourishes that often mar Italian prose (even today, when they are officially out of favour) and with what appears, at least, to be a strange lack of artifice, an air, very often, of thinking aloud rather than actually putting words down on paper. At the same time, its attractiveness has an underside of something very close to archness. Too many diminutives (sometimes several to a sentence), capital letters used for emphasis (whole phrases capitalized like banner headlines), a simplistic formulation of ideas, dialogue that is always childish and in [***La Storia***] actually includes page upon page of baby-talk: all this gives it, very often, a self-conscious, almost a simpering air that goes oddly with a story pointing the moral that history (the "storia" of the title) has beaten too many ordinary people into the ground.

La Storia has created a mostly admiring stir in Italy and has been hailed by some as the definitive war novel, saga, poem, politics and polemic all rolled into one. It covers the years 1941-47 (with flashbacks to earlier times), and includes a potted history of what is going on in the world in each grim period covered by the story. Its central character is a child known as Useppe (baby-talk for Giuseppe), fruit of the rape by a young German soldier of a prematurely aged schoolmistress, Ida (known as Iduzza), a totally friendless woman in Rome, half-Jewish, and terrified of the consequences of this for herself and her elder son, an enthusiastic fascist bully-boy called Nino (or Ninuzzo, Ninnarieddu or, by his small brother, *ino* or *aiè*). Useppe also calls the sun (*sole*) *tole,* the stars (*stelle*) *ttelle,* the dark (*buio*) *ubo,* voices (*voci*) *opi,* and Blitz his dog merely *i*. Over 656 closely printed pages, however pathetic, this and a great deal more of it becomes too much.

Useppe fills his mother's life for five or six years of loneliness, poverty, hunger, air-raids, sudden deaths, wholesale deportations, Nino's death and much else; and when he dies, Ida goes mad and is carried off to an asylum to linger on for another nine blank years. A large cast of characters, mostly old or very young, or animals ("Grrui grrruii hump hump hump", says Useppe's dog), suffers these disasters with toughness and ebullience; minor plots spill out in all directions; and everything is as boisterous, touching and monotonous as Useppe's cleverly recorded but whimsically envisaged prattle. Behind it all loom the lessons of history and politics.

The scope of these is limited, however, by the peculiarly undeveloped state of those learning them. Elsa Morante's limitation—in all her fiction, but in this, her longest and most ambitious novel, particularly—is that she seems incapable of dealing with adult characters or indeed of seeing anything from any point of view except that of a child or a painfully simple-minded adult. Her heroine Ida's real limitation is not her situation in life so much as her abysmal stupidity; she is a total victim—but less of circumstances than of her own IQ. Like the whole book, she is moving yet irritating, pathetic yet also absurd. Some novels can bear the full weight of horror; some, without creaking, cannot. ***La Storia*** is spirited and often attractive, and its heart beats (all too loudly) in the right place: but it is overwritten, long-winded and often gruesomely sentimental.

"Bambino Talk," in The Times Literary Supplement, *No. 3787, October 4, 1974, p. 1062.*

PETER S. PRESCOTT

Not all boring novels are bad, as I reminded myself when dozing over [***History: A Novel***]. To dismiss Elsa Morante's mammoth enterprise as an elegant soporific, or to say that her fellow Italians' appetite for it is as inexplicable as the Bedouins' zest for eating the eyes of their sheep, would be unfair. It seems to me that Morante has effectively achieved precisely what she wanted with her story; it's what she wanted that's so depressing. Furthermore, ***History*** has had in Italy a career remarkably similar to that of *Roots* in this country. By expressing a dangerously simplified view of history and posing as a kind of national epic that lends dignity to the oppressed, it became instantly a stupendous best seller, that rare book which not only unhinges the judgment of critics but is actually discussed on trains and in bars. For several reasons, I doubt it will do well here.

The central character, for instance, is an infant. The story begins in Rome in 1941, with the rape of a widowed Italian schoolteacher by a drunken German soldier. It ends in 1947 when Giuseppe, fruit of that rape, dies of epilepsy and his mother, Ida, is incarcerated in an asylum. Americans, generally, are quick to slobber over babies, but when a precocious kid like Giuseppe—early to walk, talk, love everybody, even to communicate with animals in their own languages—is introduced into a book or movie, the better sort of American reacts as W. C. Fields did to Baby Leroy: with a kick in the rump as soon as the opportunity arises.

To read this book at all, we must shelve such subversive thoughts. The war progresses. Ida, half-Jewish, is consumed with fear and guilt. Bombed out of her home, she fights starvation every day. Her legitimate son, Nino, is at first an enthusiastic Fascist, then a partisan; excited and insensitive, he is one of those who prosper only in wartime. Living with Ida in a corner of a room in a slum, Giuseppe sings with the birds, chats with his dogs, studies a cat's vocabulary ("To ask for something, she said: *myew* or *mayeu;* to call, she said *mau,* to threaten *mbrooooh,* etc., etc.").

During the war and after, the child Giuseppe hears grownups denouncing the social order. "Wherever there are Leaders," says Nino, "there's always the same stink!" And again, "History: that's their dumb joke, and it's got to end!" A friend of Nino's, a Jewish atheist and anarchist in search of Christ, says: "History, of course, is all an obscenity from the beginning." He goes on to suggest that all power is evil, that you can be either a part of the obscenity, or a healthy reaction to it—the kind of binary thinking that we heard a lot of here only a few years ago. For twenty pages or so this drug-ridden anarchist rages in what is clearly and unfortunately the author's own voice: "I realized that we, and all our fellow bourgeois, were the world's scum, and that man left in the street, and his fellows, were the aristocracy." It sounds, alas, like imitation Dostoevski.

Nevertheless, such oratorical tripe cannot quite bury what Morante does well: the delicacy with which she describes a soldier dying in Russia, a young girl giggling at reports of Nazi atrocities, or Ida's haste to put a paper bag over Giuseppe to protect him from the bombing. What *is* dismaying, for an American, is the novel's relentless naturalism. Obsessed with describing in detail rooms we will see but once, characters who have only a brief part to play, dreams, the thoughts of dogs and stained diapers hanging up to dry, Morante refuses her characters' claims to be anything but victims of heredity and history. (pp. 76-7)

Peter S. Prescott, "Italian Roots," in Newsweek, *Vol. LXXXIX, No. 18, May 2, 1977, pp. 76-7.*

JOHN ROMANO

History: A Novel is set in Rome during the war and just after. It is the story of Ida Mancuso, her two sons, and the people near to them in poor neighborhoods, refugee shelters, and the cadre of Resistance fighters to which the elder son belongs. To foreign observers, this is the world of neo-realist Italian cinema: Rossellini's *Open City*. To the Roman masses, it was the blasted, shabby, nearly hopeless actuality of long years. Though all the world, nearly, shared in the suffering of the war, it was perhaps in Italy that its chaos most abounded.

Miss Morante takes that chaos upon herself and declares that to grasp the immense public suffering one must look closely at the infinity of private circumstances in which it took place. . . . [We] learn that Ida's mother was a Jew from Venice; that her father, gentle and loving, was an anarchist from Calabria; and that as a child Ida suffered from mild epilepsy. We follow her to Rome with her husband, a poor, itinerant salesman who gives her a son, Nino, and then dies of cancer shortly afterward, leaving her in the near-poverty of her salary as a schoolteacher. It is the 1930's, when Mussolini has begun to imitate the racial policies of his German comrade, and Ida, half-Jewish, fears for herself and Nino. Gradually she, who has known no Jew except her mother, begins to frequent the Roman ghetto as if out of some protective herding instinct in the blood, like that of the animals to which characters in this book are constantly compared. And there she hears rumors, more terrifying daily, of what the Fascists have in store for the Jews of Rome. As these fears gather in her, Gunther [a German soldier] appears on her doorstep. "And on meeting, at the very door of her home, that uniform which seemed stationed there, waiting for her, she thought she had arrived at the terrible rendezvous preordained for her since the beginning of the world."

In the scene that follows, the mutual incomprehension of Ida and Gunther throbs like an open wound. Once inside he seeks lamely, pathetically, some basis for friendship. As he inquires with shy politeness about a photograph of Nino that hangs on the wall, Ida is frozen in the expectation that he will produce a "Wanted" photo of her son. He takes her in a confusion of rage and tenderness, she has a relapse of her *petit mal,* leaving her in a numbness which he mistakes for willingness, and he takes her again, lovingly. When she recovers he is asleep upon her. "Even the sleep of her aggressor, stretched out there before her, seemed to rest on the leprosy of all experiences—violence, fear—like a healing."

If the power of such a scene—and there are dozens of others like it in this long book—comes from the human fullness of its portraits, Miss Morante is also the master of the quick sketch, of which again there are countless vivid and memorable examples. But to account fully for her success one must go behind these qualities—qualities that have to do with her indefatigable interest in who people are and how they behave—to her broader involvement with historical forces moving outside the self and acting upon it. (pp. 60-1)

Among our many received notions about contemporary fiction is the idea that modern historical reality is too much for the old narrative forms, too destructive and overwhelming for storytelling in the traditional mode. Walter Benjamin observed that men came back from World War I as they had come back from no previous war—with no stories to tell. What they had seen could not be narrated, though perhaps it could be mimicked in the dire hallucinations of surrealism, or rendered brokenly in one of the other discontinuous modes of modernist art. But plot, sequence, the integrity of character and action, and causality itself were no longer appropriate.

It is, therefore, stubbornly old-fashioned of Elsa Morante to take on the most powerfully disorienting moment in modern times and to treat it by means of a plot-idea, and central figures, and a style out of Tolstoy, Dickens, or Flaubert. This applies not only to Ida—who does indeed recall the heroine of a 19th-century novel, the innocent, battered woman-child struggling at the base of dark, towering ruins, like Hardy's Tess of the D'Urbervilles—but also and especially to Giuseppe, the child conceived by Gunther and Ida in the first pages of the novel, who dies in its last. A frail, visionary child who has a precocious familiarity with loss and death, an instinctual closeness to animals, and a poetic enthusiasm for life, Giuseppe profoundly resembles the children of romantic poetry, or Dickens's Paul Dombey.

With Giuseppe's death scene some readers will inevitably feel that the novel has caved in under a load of anachronism and sentimentality. Yet this may be, rather, a sign of how jaded we have become in our responses to serious fiction. We have forgotten how searing an experience the work of art made flesh can be, how destructive of that distance between book and reader to which we have grown accustomed. *Gravity's Rainbow* is typical of what gets called a masterpiece today, because it is intellectually aggressive and demanding but emotionally blank. When a book tries to move us, and especially when it succeeds, we feel violated: Elsa Morante's novel is affecting enough to put vulnerabilities of this kind to the test. (pp. 61-2)

[***History: A Novel***] bears the stamp of the best art: exalting life above itself. (p. 62)

John Romano, "History into Art," in Commentary, *Vol. 64, No. 2, August, 1977, pp. 60-2.*

RUSSELL DAVIES

It is always dangerous to tax an author with what he "ought" to have done; but Elsa Morante's [***History***] is such a frankly mounted and honourable attempt on the title of Great Post-War Italian Novel that I feel she should have had more to say on the destination of the themes she sets in motion, if only for the sake of completeness. As it is, she has given us a story so defeated and issueless that it is hard to tell from it how Italy has staggered even the little way it has. Her admirably humanitarian aim has been to demonstrate the appalling distance set between shifts of power, changes in national performance etc, and the day-to-day, hand-to-mouth life of the barely surviving citizen; and there are times when this act of reverence at the tomb of the Unknown Civilian becomes profoundly moving. But, as one of the book's epigraphs (ascribed to a survivor of Hiroshima) warned, "There is no word in the human language capable of consoling the guinea pigs who do not know the reason for their death", and Elsa Morante has taken the long way round to an endorsement of this bleak observation.

Her central figure, Ida, is an unremarkable half-Jewish widow, a primary school teacher in Rome. By her late Italian husband she has had a son, Nino, a rash, brash, adolescent tearaway; during the war years, a delicate blue-eyed baby called (according to his own infantile mispronunciation) "Useppe" is born to her. Fathered, through rape, by a drunken and homesick young German soldier from "the rural village of Dachau"—killed, far away, only days after the conception—Useppe is both miraculous and doomed. Unaccountably bright, and with a gift for universal sympathy that makes him widely beloved among the bombed-out refugee folk who are the intimate witnesses to his childhood, he is also physically weak and small, with a predisposition, inherited from his mother, to epilepsy. So roundly does he personify the frailty of goodness that it is hard to resist seeing him as a second Christ-child, whom circumstance this time ritually prepares for submission to the cruelly indiscriminate laws of a god-forsaken world.

Little effort is made, before the event, to disguise the fact that "history" will speedily engulf and destroy all three of these bewildered souls. Nino, having survived the hazards of partisan guerrilla life and the smuggling trade, dies in a road accident following a police chase. Useppe succumbs to his hereditary disease; and Ida, from the moment of this second death, loses her faculties, and dies a lingering death in a home. Thus chance, predestination and the sheer grief of existence all get their opportunity to beat down human possibility.

What Elsa Morante would have us set against these overwhelming strokes of pessimism is the very considerable mass of behavioural detail in which they are encased. She is interested, certainly, in straightforwardly documentary material about How Things Were—and a lot of this is useful, particularly in reminding us how abjectly the Italian authorities eventually fell in with the Nazi Final Solution—but what keeps her going is the tiny twitching of life lived at the most basic and instinctive level: the spectacle of character liberating itself, if only momentarily, from the most sordidly reduced of circumstances. Here the character of Useppe acts as a kind of touchstone of goodwill—and also as a focus for the feeling of enveloping concern in which Elsa Morante manages to include all these creatures of hers. Perhaps the most remarkable feature of the book—and hardly a fashionable one in its heatedly feminist home country—is the mantle of maternal concern it casts over its entire world. Moments of violence, such as occur in Nino's partisan ambushes, have an air of horrible irruption upon a world in which watching and, if possible, cherishing are the natural modes of proceeding.

So no activity is more prized, by either the author or her characters, than the experiencing of sympathy with another being. For myself, I might have wished that Signora Morante had restricted herself to beings of the human sort; unfortunately she does not. Blitz, Nino and Useppe's first dog, ironically a victim of the phenomenon from which he takes his name, is a bearable presence; but in Bella, the white sheepdog who succeeds him as Useppe's guardian (and, for a couple of tacky pages, confidante), the narrator takes an interest that is simply too proprietorially loving. Here, one feels, is an invader not from the rubble of Rome but from somewhere much nearer the author's own fireside. Elsa Morante's willingness to plunge into the genealogy and social background of almost any and every animal that emerges from the woodwork shows her empathy running riot—and in fact is a symptom of a tendency to gush throughout the book.

A patch of verbosity which fails for a different reason—and more importantly—is the book's attempt to whip up its political and theoretical aspects into a belated climax of their own, through the dying ravings of an incidental character, Davide. This Jewish student, an anarchist turned partisan turned drug addict, is already a slightly unsatisfactory figure, his insubstantial form all too aptly complementing his abstract status as an embodiment of the pursuit of impossible ideals; so his last, black, nihilistic delirium is just too powerfully ambitious (and long) a statement to come from a voice we know only as a mouthpiece for ideas.

Punctuated at intervals by brutally simplified summaries of world-historical and military developments, the book closes with an especially distressing burst of these, emphasizing (as is only right) the fate of Vietnam, where civilian helplessness reached pitiful depths quite unknown to the most destitute of Europeans. As an expression of solidarity with such suffering populations, Elsa Morante's novel clearly claims and deserves international recognition: it is only at the domestic Italian level (and in the light of an ambitious title) that one must regret the chopping off at 1947 of the continuities which undoubtedly link the chaos of 1945 with the terrorized powerlessness of 1978.

Russell Davies, "The Unknown Civilian," in The Times Literary Supplement, *No. 3978, June 30, 1978, p. 729.*

MICHAEL CAESAR

Elsa Morante celebrates the miseries and splendours of the imagination with the passion of a devotee and the resolution of a proselyte. It is no exaggeration to say that the imaginary is the very stuff of which her characters live. . . . They and their author inhabit a world more amenable to mythical than to scientific explanation, where history is the surface rumbling of an obscurer cycle and human life in its essentials is not distinguishable from that of all other animals. To penetrate this world you must be prepared to draw on the metaphorical reserves of legend, dream and the imagination of children. Omniscience in Morante's narrators is not a question of positive knowledge, of being able to read off the facts of the case like an all-seeing eye, but rather of a kind of divination, the state of 'lucid insomnia' which is the main medium of the narrator's perception in her first novel. Rather than representing some abstract objectivity, the omniscient narrator in Morante is quite transparently the embodiment of her or his author's imagination. (p. 211)

Morante's cult of the imagination is nothing new in Western literature, even where imagination touches on magic and madness. Its roots lie deep in Romanticism, and it has continued to be fed by the author's wide reading in anthropology and epic and sacred writings, and by her travels and contacts with other, non-Western cultures. But the immediate sources of Morante's writing are to be found in the period between the wars, in Kafka and surrealism, and, more locally, in the 'magic realism' *(realismo magico)* which Massimo Bontempelli put forward in 1927-28 as the epitome of the avant-garde under Fascism: the combination of precise realistic detail and an atmosphere of 'lucid stupor', for which Bontempelli saw analogies in Quattrocento painting. The assimilation of art (or poetry) to magic is complete in Bontempelli: '. . . [Art] has all the characteristics of enchantment *(incantesimo)* and all its modes: it is the calling-up of dead things, the making visible of distant things, the prophecy of future things, the subversion of the laws of nature, brought about by the imagination alone'. Morante would not dissent from this view: the imagination, invested with this power, is the writer's only means of reaching the reality of things which it is his or her duty to represent. Where Morante parts company from Bontempelli is over the fact that he is in it for excitement: 'magic realism' on inspection turns out to be a kind of heightened awareness that restores a sense of adventure to dull suburban life, making the reader believe there is something else there, whether there is or not. In Morante, there is no trip, no journey into the unknown. It is the job of the writer to 'restore reality to others' through language. We should therefore think of a Morante novel not as an adventure of the imagination through time but as an enclosed and dark space—to use an image dear to the author—

empty at first, or flickering with insubstantial shadows, but receptive and filling, till at the end of the novel it is totally occupied by the intricate truths which the imagination has managed to recover. (pp. 212-13)

Morante does everything possible to make her vision communicable to the readers. The narrative form itself is a vehicle of 'exemplary' events; and the focus of the imaginative effort is on deep symbolic vocabulary of universal validity. But Morante's communication with her readers is assured not so much by these structural components, important though they are, as by her particular style of narrative prose. At first sight it is a difficult language, or at any rate a learned one, rich in adjectives, steeped in the archaic and Latinate forms of the literary tradition going back to Boccaccio, subtle, almost mannered in its discrimination of meanings. This lexical refinement, however, is supported by a syntax which, while it is not exactly simple (much depends on the artful placing of clauses in apposition), is for the most part linear, avoiding any too complex subordination, and readable. It is the language of a great realist: precise in every detail yet carrying the reader forward without hesitation.

This implicit criterion of communicability in its turn implies some limitation on the operations of the imagination, in the sense that, for the novelist (as distinct from the private person Elsa Morante), only what is in the last resort communicable can be imagined. This is the writer's defence against the obscure, the sentimental and the pathological, and also against the excesses and blind alleys of her characters. In some of her early stories—especially **"Il gioco segreto"("The Secret Game",** 1937)—Morante appears to be testing the forces of the imagination, marking out the limits in which she as a writer will perform. But it is her first novel, ***Menzogna e sortilegio*** of 1948 (translated as ***House of Liars***), that presents the fullest exploration of the ambiguities of the imagination and the equivocal stance of the sorcerer's apprentice who serves it.

The apprentice is Elisa, the twenty-five-year-old narrator who, alone in the world, begins to reconstruct the story of her family, painstakingly separating fact from fiction, truth from legend. It begins with her maternal grandmother, Cesira, ambitious and narrow-minded, a teacher up from the provinces in search of a good marriage, whose life with Teodoro Massia, a seductive but ageing and impoverished nobleman, will prove an inferno for both parties. The only consolation for Teodoro is the birth of their daughter Anna, a girl of fiery temperament who is as morbidly attached to the father who dotes on her as she is contemptuous of the mother who sees in her the symbols of her own humiliation. After Teodoro's death, Anna's love is concentrated on her cousin, the golden Edoardo, scion of the wealthier and socially more elevated Cerentano side of the family, who appears to her as a kind of sun-god, capricious, wilful and dangerous, and who, as far as his infinite selfishness will allow, loves her too, in a possessive and tyrannical fashion. What one owns one can also give away, and thus after an illness, Edoardo arranges for Anna to be married to his new-found friend, Francesco De Salvi, a young and eager law-student from the country who is both convinced of his own aristocratic origins, though he is in fact the illegitimate son of a peasant-woman and the Cerentanos' bailiff, and committed, at least verbally, to a radical socialism. The pieces are assembled from which will be produced Elisa, the only child of Anna and Francesco, and it is through her recollections of her childhood that we witness the final stages of her family's drama and decline. Ten years after her marriage, after a chance encounter with his demented mother, Anna learns that Edoardo has died, but she refuses to accept the idea, and joins with the old woman in an elaborate pretence that her lover is still alive by writing a series of letters purporting to come from Edoardo on his travels. Francesco, who in the meantime has taken up again with his old flame Rosaria, a vivacious working-class prostitute loved by both him and Edoardo, is gradually drawn into this game while unable to understand or accept that Anna's love for her cousin, dead or alive, is total and exclusive. The child Elisa witnesses her father, with whom she is sullen, become incapacitated through drink and her mother, whose indifference to her she repays with servile adoration, spin away into raving lunacy. The degrading death of both parents leaves Elisa to be brought up in another town by her 'second mother' Rosaria, with whose own death the story opens.

This rapid plot-summary comes only half-way to indicating on what a treacherous terrain the novel is set. The lies and deceits, the incantation and wizardry, alluded to in the Italian title, are not only those practised with varying degrees of success and varying degrees of malevolence by nearly all the principal characters, but also those of which the narrator herself is the protagonist and victim. For Elisa, the figures of her narrative are neither wholly fictional entities existing 'out there' in a realistic setting created by her, nor are they entirely 'remembered' from her own past and reconstructed on the page. . . . Although the narrative is presented in the form of a sober chronicle, its assumptions are visionary: half-remembered, half-imagined, but more accurately evoked, like ghosts, the actors in the family drama move in a space occupied pre-eminently by insomnia, fantasy and day-dream.

Thus the first thing that the reader notices about ***Menzogna e sortilegio*** is the degree of concentration with which each character is presented, as though spotlighted in centre-stage. In this way, even relatively minor characters are given all the space they need to act out their inner life, their fantasies, expectations, fears and frustrations. The external world becomes little more than a hazy background to a drama of pure consciousness, in which the real protagonists are not so much people as the images that they create of themselves, the ways in which they see themselves reflected in others, what others do effectively make of them. So the stage is also a prison, or a cloister, or a little room, or a hall of mirrors—all metaphors of enclosure that are repeated through the novel. (pp. 213-16)

The act of narration itself is posited as a liberation from the ghosts and traumas of childhood, a passage into adulthood, achieved by seeing the other adults' actions and fates in their true perspective (their 'legend' as a 'petty-bourgeois drama') and refusing the childish consolation of fantasies. The adult task is seen to consist in the shaping and ordering voice of reason, which exorcizes the ghosts of the past and chases away nightmares. A kind of bargain is struck in ***Menzogna e sortilegio:*** the disordered experience of the characters' imaginations (including Elisa's as a character), which is the subject of the narration, is balanced by the regular structure and relative calm of the narration itself. To achieve the necessary balance between imaginative freedom and communicability, Morante delegates these different functions to her characters on the one hand, and the narrator on the other. She keeps to this bargain throughout her subsequent writing, where the authority and lucidity of the narrative voice is never in doubt, even when it belongs to someone who speaks in the first person and is directly involved in the action, in short who is also a character. And at the same time the narration serves to distance the author and the reader from material which is frequently volatile: it is the crust of an emotional volcano.

The drama which Morante's players act out is that of exclusion, set primarily in the relation between child and parents, though the theme also has mythical (religious) and historical (political) dimensions for the author as we shall see. ***Menzogna e sortilegio*** introduced the theme, particularly in Elisa's story of her own childhood: it was expanded in **"Lo scialle andaluso" ("The Andalusian Shawl"),** a long short story written in 1951, which focussed on the possessive love-hate of a boy for his actress mother. Since then Morante has devoted two novels, separated by a gap of twenty-five years, to male protagonists whose lives are marked by a childhood trauma of rejection: ***L'isola di Arturo*** (***Arturo's Island,*** 1957) and ***Aracoeli*** (1982). Because of the thematic link between these two books, I propose to override the chronological sequence of Morante's production and consider them together. At the end of this chapter, however, I shall return briefly to ***Aracoeli*** in the light of the other two important works which immediately preceded it.

The rejected males desperately seek attention, approval and love, but are destined to a submissiveness which the Elisa of the first novel seemed at least capable of overcoming. The pain of this recurrent scene is made more acute precisely by the fact that it is narrated, that is, in Morante's terms, made conscious. Indeed, this is consciousness in a colder and crueller light than in Elisa's rationalist enterprise: here nothing is left to the mercy of the unexpressed.

Even so, ***L'isola di Arturo*** begins with the same strange silence as that with which ***Menzogna*** ended. Just as we do not finally know whether, by telling her story, Elisa has succeeded in breaking from her isolation, so in the second novel, which is a recollection of childhood and early adolescence, we do not know how old the first-person narrator is: in fact we know nothing at all about him as an adult. The present from which he looks back is blank and he himself without qualities. Childhood is evoked not as a preparation or as a stage in a progressive history, but as an experience entire in itself, separated from adulthood by a line which cannot be rubbed out. From the very first paragraph of the novel, the recollection of this special time is suffused in intimations of myth and legend. . . . (pp. 218-19)

Mythical references . . . colour the entire narrative and highlight the extraordinary situation of the protagonist. Arturo grows up on the island of Procida (near Naples) virtually an orphan. His young mother dies giving birth to him: he cultivates a respectful memory towards her. He is nursed in his earliest months on goats' milk by an adolescent boy, Silvestro, who then disappears from his life only to reappear at the end of the novel as the agent of Arturo's departure from the island. Arturo inhabits a rigorously masculine world. . . . His actual father, Wilhelm, is for the boy a marvellous and mysterious being. Frequently away on journeys, he is a stranger among the other islanders; fair-featured like Edoardo Cerentano, he is, like that character, arrogant, disdainful, cruel, and dominating. Arturo is his willing slave: . . . ('My childhood is like a happy country, of which he is absolute ruler').

This male paradise is broken when Wilhelm unexpectedly brings home a second wife, Nunziata, a girl from the slums of Naples. Arturo's maturation takes place through his evolving perception of Nunziata, as a rival for his father affections, as the usurper of his mother's place, but also as a companion of almost the same age, a playmate, a sister. He tries to establish his ascendancy over her by playing on her superstitions and mocking her ignorance. But even from the beginning his feelings towards the intruder are not unalloyed. Arturo needs affection, and Nunziata, human, warm and generous, seems ready to provide it. Her very presence on the island marks a kind of betrayal of Arturo by his father. The pages in which Arturo's confused emotions struggle to the surface as he spars on and off with Nunziata during her first afternoon and evening on the island are among the very best that Morante has written. Within a short time, Arturo also begins to see her as a lover. Three times he tries to possess his step mother sexually, three times she rebuffs him: on the third occasion he will leave the island. By this time, however, Arturo has learnt that his father's legendary journeys take him no further than Naples and that the band of faithful followers with whom he would one day take Arturo off to see the world is the homosexual circuit that he frequents in the city. Denounced as a 'parody' by a former lover who is now blackmailing him, Wilhelm can no more function as a model in Arturo's life than the mother who is dead or the stepmother who cannot replace her.

The departure from the island with which the novel ends can in a sense be seen as a liberation: Arturo, like Elisa before him, is freed of his fantasies. Certainly, the novel recounts a progressive disillusionment and a corresponding initiation into adult life as gradually Arturo's primal beatitude is disturbed and broken into. The hero crosses a series of threshholds and arrives on the brink of life in the grown-up world. But here we are faced with the problem of the blank after the narrated events which I mentioned at the beginning of this description. Progress into what? This is not a novel of 'sentimental education', in which the hero is gradually socialized and can therefore be left at the gate of life entirely prepared to enter. Arturo's experiences do not prepare him for the social world which he will encounter on leaving the island and which is as much a mystery to him at the end of his years there as it was at the beginning. . . . So the accumulation of Arturo's experiences cannot be seen as progressive in the sense of them leading anywhere. Rather they form a concentric pattern, each reproducing on a large scale Arturo's first and fundamental experience. The death of his dog Immacolatella, the intrusion of Nunziata, the birth of his half-brother Carmine Arturo, Nunziata's rejection of his sexual advances, the unmasking of Wilhelm and Arturo's final expulsion from the island are each a repetition and an expansion of Arturo's primal exclusion from the mother who died when he was born and denied herself to him.

If this interpretation is correct, Morante's most recent novel, ***Aracoeli,*** engages upon a striking return to the theme of separation from the mother twenty-five years after the publication of ***Isola.*** Only, in the new novel, the pattern of repeated exclusions is more directly and centrally organized around the relation of mother and son, which as in **"Lo scialle andaluso",** is the explicit theme of the book. ***Aracoeli,*** set in 1975, is organized around the memories of the protagonist-narrator, which are sparked off by his sudden decision, at the age of 43 (conspicuously the oldest of all Morante's heroes), to visit for the first time his mother's birthplace in Andalusia. Emanuele, the narrator, was six when his mother—who bears the liturgical name of Aracoeli (Altar of Heaven)—died. More than half the novel, in fragmentary episodes interspersed with more recent occurrences and the narrator's present journey as well as in longer narrative passages, is given over to the re-evocation of their life together, first in the 'exclusive intimacy' of a semi-clandestine life in the Monte Sacro district of Rome (she is a

Spanish peasant girl, Emanuele's father is a serving officer in the Royal Italian Navy: for a number of years they are unable to marry), then in the more public environment of a middle-class apartment block in the Quartieri Alti. In particular, it is the last year of Aracoeli's life which dominates the recollections of her son, the period during which, crazed by the loss of her second child, a girl, she rejects both the bourgeois decencies of the Quartieri Alti and the awkward attempts of Emanuele to restore the bliss of Monte Sacro. (pp. 220-23)

Emanuele's unsuccessful relation with his mother, who shortly turns to sexual promiscuity and prostitution, is taken in fact as the basis for the formation of a neurotic, unable to relate to other people whether as individuals or collectively except masochistically, barely capable of functioning in a physical and material sense, excluded on all sides and—what seems to be taken in the novel as a mark of particular deviance—homosexual. But his neurosis is only a question of degree: every living creature, animal as well as human, is condemned to search for love; all of us are . . . ('orphans and never weaned'), all of us like the stray dogs who keep crossing Emanuele's path. And universal exclusion leads to universal humiliation. Not by accident, Emanuele's search for his mother ends with him finding the memory of his last meeting with his father, in 1945. The ex-naval officer is reduced to an alcoholic wreck, but it is not *his* humiliation that we are concerned with. The twelve-year-old Emanuele is embarrassed and confused and simply wants to escape; only thirty years later does he realize that the obscure sensation he felt on leaving his father was the desire—impossible to realize—to make a declaration of love to him. Is the father here simply a substitute for the departed Aracoeli? Or is he in some sense the 'real' object of Emanuele's masochistic urge to submit to a loved one? It is an enigmatic presence at the end of the novel, but one which confirms the ideological lesson: we are all excluded.

Although, as I have suggested, ***Aracoeli*** returns to certain themes of the 1950s, the way in which the novel brings its ideological assumptions out into the open is much more in keeping with the trend of Morante's writing since ***L'isola di Arturo.*** This forthrightness has coincided with the writer's growing conviction that the fate of exclusion is common to us all, but is reinforced by society as it is at present organized for the oppression of the weak and particularly by modern industrialized and technological cultures: our collective condition is one of 'alienation' or 'unreality'. A few elect spirits escape this fate and attain, or rather retain, for most of them are children, the existential goal of wholeness *(integrità)*. The artist is entrusted with a social mission, to bear witness to the truth and alleviate the sufferings of the audience. . . . Morante sees herself as an anarchist, her declared political goal is Utopia; if she tries to 'speak for' others it is as a 'blessed propagandist' like Fra Angelico on behalf of beauty and unalienated reality, not as the accredited representative of a political party or ideology exercising or in pursuit of power. Her commitment is precisely that of the artist I described at the beginning of this essay, who risks all on the imagination.

Both of the books which follow ***Isola, Il mondo salvato dai ragazzini*** (***The World Saved by Little Children,*** 1968) and ***La Storia*** (***History,*** 1974), reflect these concerns and this commitment. ***Mondo*** is a collection of poems (most of them narrative or dramatic rather than strictly lyrical) in which, after a period of personal upheaval and wide travel, Morante draws on a new language, to some extent influenced by American models (Beat poetry, the blues) to specify issues that had previously been left vague, in terms that correspond exactly to the dominant themes of mid-to-late 1960s youth culture or counter-culture: the denunciation of military violence (especially in Vietnam) and of Fascism (the colonels' Greece being the topical case); the exaltation of certain values—love, happiness, carefreeness, youth itself—believed to be in dangerous conflict with the productivist mentality of neo-capitalism; the conviction (following R. D. Laing) that madness (neurosis, schizophrenia) is a social, not an individual, condition; an infinite suspicion of the mass-media and their power; the celebration of the imagination against the alienating effects of an imposed social order.

What immediately strikes the reader of the poems published in 1968 is a sense of urgency quite absent from the measured stateliness of Morante's earlier work. The poet howls a protest, desperately seeking to awaken her contemporaries to the violent and dangerous 'unreality' of their world. In this task, she can count at best on the understanding and support of the 'Felici Pochi', the Happy Few, who within themselves, whether the 'world' sees it or not, are beautiful and happy. The poems of ***Il mondo salvato dai ragazzini*** are like a gallery of these anarchistic free spirits: the young American painter Bill Morrow, loved and mourned by Morante (**"Addio, Farewell"**), a visionary Oedipus (**"La serata a Colono," "Evening at Colonus"**), and above all the Pazzariello, bastard, orphan, stateless, homeless, jobless, illiterate and resistant to all known forms of social discipline (**"La canzone clandestina della Grande Opera," "The Secret Song of the Great Opera"**). It is also a record of the constant attempts of Morante's Unhappy Many to suppress them—a conflict that will form the backbone of Morante's third novel. (pp. 223-25)

[***La Storia***] is centred on the brief existence of Useppe Ramundo, between January 1941 and the summer of 1947, in and around Rome. These are years of war and post-war deprivation. Useppe is conceived of a rape; with his widowed mother Ida he suffers bombing, homelessness, evacuation, hunger and illness; from his mother he inherits the propensity to epilepsy which will kill him. They are years of fear, and Ida's fear is such that she can barely function as an adult human being. They are years too of bitter civil strife, the slaughter of innocents, and genocide (not essentially different from the rest of history, in Morante's view), and Useppe will bear witness to these things and to the human wreckage that results. Yet Useppe is also a celebration in the novel, a 'festa', the focus of all those forces which exalt life over death, beauty over ugliness, reality (in Morante's terms) over the cruelty and repression of modern civilization.

What relation do these individual lives, Useppe, Ida, her other, teenage son Nino, the anarchist Davide Segre and all the rest, bear to the History (always with a capital letter) which gives the novel its title and to which the reader's attention is forcefully drawn before he even opens the book by the strong double qualification of the title (***La Storia*** is both 'A novel' and 'A scandal which has lasted ten thousand years')? The immediate answer is that from the point of view of the characters History is remote and foreign, something that conditions individual lives and at the same time is quite alien from them. But this withdrawal from History does not stop at mere ignorance or indifference, it goes beyond the mindlessness of the Unhappy Many so often denounced by Morante, in order to reach a reality, and an awareness of reality, that seems to be posited not only as different from History but as an alternative to it.

The process is clear in the opening pages of the novel. . . .

> (One January day in the year
> 1941
> a German soldier was walking
> in the San Lorenzo district of Rome.
> He knew altogether 4 words of Italian
> and of the world next to nothing.
> His Christian name was Gunther.
> His surname is unknown.)

These words are repeated and developed in the first couple of pages of the prose description that follows: the reader is now within the private world of the boy-soldier, and within that world an analogous distancing from History takes place. The youth comes from Dachau: the underlining of the *historical* significance of the place only serves to establish its *lack* of any significance for the characters in the story, starting with Gunther himself. And his other 'place', Rome, the city where he now finds himself on his way to the North African front, suffers a similar fate: the few bits of culture he's picked up at school are quickly forgotten under the pressure of more instinctual needs. . . . Wandering through the deserted working-class district on this warm afternoon, the wine he's drunk goes to his head, he wants to snuggle down and sleep like a child; homesick and just sick, he would be comforted by any female creature. . . . In a few lines Gunther has been transformed from soldier of the Reich to child, to small creature, an animal.

In a bizarre way, he meets his perfect match, for the female creature to whom it falls to mother Gunther (and the son Useppe that she bears him), Ida, is at once presented as a combination of all these features: terrified by History (its specific manifestation in her case is the race-laws: Ida is half-Jewish and living in the constant anxiety that the authorities will find out), she has been left by her fear of the world in a state of permanent childishness. . . . And when these two child-animals are finally brought together by the narrator in what it is difficult to remember is a violent rape, the violation itself is experienced by Ida in terms of something from her childhood (in fact a recurrence of her fainting fits), while it begins with another evocation of the name of Dachau and a strange transformation of Gunther's eyes; the eyes, like Ida's, are mentioned again at the end with their . . . ('tortured look, infinitely ignorant and totally aware').

This look, and the visionary state of consciousness to which it corresponds, crops up repeatedly in the novel, especially in Ida and, even more, in Useppe (his half-brother Nino, though he too is firmly on the side of life in the novel, does not have this insight: he is all movement and surface). It is in fact the privileged counterpoint to the historical discourse, the monotonous recounting of one outrage after another. It is the means by which History is seen through, and judged, but also suffered, by the most sensitive of its victims, those who are in some sense saved. It is used particularly to comment on the fate of the Jews of the Roman ghetto whose existence and destruction forms one of the leitmotifs of the novel. (pp. 226-29)

La Storia is the only one of Morante's full-length novels to date to use a third-person narrator. While this device reinforces the illusion that the narrator has a broad and superior knowledge of the events to be related and is, therefore, specially qualified to do so, it also leads to problems. The textbook historical summaries at the beginning of each chapter and the moments of intuitive prelogical insight I have just been describing are two extremes of a narration which for a great many of the novel's 700 pages does no more than register flatly the events of passing time: it is a kind of skindeep narration which refuses the explanatory potential of historicist writing and can only allude to the knowledge of the unconscious and the preconscious which was in a sense the touchstone of ***Menzogna e sortilegio.*** At this point we come back finally to Morante's next and most recent novel, for in ***Aracoeli*** she returns to the use of a first person and the dimension of memory. By doing so, she has given herself more space to do what she is really good at: to take what she calls . . . ('the seed of my tears') and explore its every component through the jungle of the imagination: the stifling heat of that jungle, if I may pursue the metaphor, suits her better than the airy plain she found herself on in ***La Storia.*** Not that this congeniality of technique makes her view of human destiny any less despairing. If anything, the internalization of the first-person narration reinvests her writing with an emotional force which tended to be dissipated in ***La Storia.*** But there is also in her new book an added note of what seems like renunciation. Whereas the 1974 novel recounts the slaughter of innocents, ***Aracoeli*** maps the self-destruction wrought by experience. Morante seems to take her distance equally from History, and from those who at one time seemed as though they might be the bearers of an alternative history. At any rate, she has chosen a middle-aged protagonist who admits: . . . ('I am by nature quite unsuited to history and politics: my attempts to deny it are foolish and vain'), who perceives demonstrating youngsters as mindless slogan-shouters and in whose experience the revolutionaries of 1968 have become exponents of what the novel satirizes as the 'Moderate Half-Right'. At the same time, however, Emanuele has lost the visionary confidence of his younger predecessors Elisa and Arturo: he is short-sighted and takes off his glasses when he does not want or cannot bear to see; he acknowledges repeatedly the fallibility of memory, he knows that his search is vain and that at the end of his journey he will find nothing: a private futility that is matched at the public level by General Franco's unconscionable time a-dying (we are at the beginning of November 1975). ***Aracoeli*** is not simply a throwback to the 1950s or a continuation of the ideological explicitness of ***Mondo*** and ***Storia,*** but introduces, it seems to me, a note of scepticism more pronounced than any we have heard in Morante before. (pp. 230-31)

Michael Caesar, "Elsa Morante," in Writers & Society in Contemporary Italy: A Collection of Essays, *edited by Michael Caesar and Peter Hainsworth, Berg Publishers, 1984, pp. 211-33.*

RAYMOND ROSENTHAL

Emanuele, a sad, guilt-ridden neurotic of 43 and the narrating voice of . . . [***Aracoeli***], remembers seeing himself in a mirror as his mother, the delicate Aracoeli, suckled him at her breast. It is all vivid, the darkly glowing, Byzantine-like beauty of his mother, her modesty, even hiding her breast from her baby, and his intense, overpowering emotion of love for her. He calls these flashes from the past his "apocryphal memories." Woven together with dreams, imaginary encounters, actual flashbacks, waking fantasies, and a river of whining and complaint—he feels old, ugly, unloved, miserable in his homosexuality, futile, it goes on and on—these memories form the book's chief subject matter and even its very texture. Most of the time one feels cornered, as one does when an importunate acquaintance tells a tale of woe that deserves pity but utterly fails to arouse either real interest or sympathy.

So Emanuele talks and talks, and in the interstices of this epic of sometimes brilliant nagging he also manages to tell the novel's story, which runs from just before the Spanish Civil War to 1975. We learn that his father, an ensign in the Italian Navy, met the young, illiterate peasant girl Aracoeli in Spain, fell in love with her, brought her back to Rome and set her up as his mistress in an apartment where she gave birth to Emanuele and then married her, over the objections of his strait-laced, bourgeois-patrician parents. Now Aracoeli, become a sort of proper middle-class matron who has learned such indispensable graces as how to mix cocktails and has read enough to read ladies' magazines and to distinguish a *chemisier* from a *tailleur,* suddenly undergoes a terrible change. Her next child, a girl named Carina, dies soon after birth. Aracoeli slides into a deep depression and emerges a wild nymphomaniac, forcing herself on every available man before the appalled eyes of her 7-year-old son. She runs away to work in a brothel and shortly afterward dies of a malignant brain tumor, which, it appears, was the cause of her demented, driven sexuality. The body, we are told, is a dark pit, "a sepulcher that we bear within us," the great demonic mystery. And whatever one may think of Miss Morante's rather Manichaean philosophy and her doubtful diagnostics, this entire sequence is frighteningly powerful and brilliantly told.

This is the main theme: the body betrays us into death, it ages and decays, mocks our unending desire for love; its iron law of determinism holds sway without the least alleviation on the part of the spirit. Emanuele hates his corpulent, awkward body, his bespectacled, befogged sight, his complete lack of grace. His few attempts at sex with women are grotesque and his homosexual affairs are far from gratifying. When as a grown man he envisions Aracoeli, he imagines her as a "loathsome old woman, sagging and painted," making gestures of "a frenetic indecency." Later on, Emanuele's father becomes a stumbling, pathetic alcoholic. Not since Céline has there been so violent a protest against life's conditions, such outrage at the thought of death, so relentless an assault on the bare physical facts of human existence; but without Céline's saving satiric humor and his lyrical poignancy. For instance, Emanuele only wants to "re-enter" his mother's womb, curl inside her like an animal in its den for all eternity. He thinks that it would have been better if she had eaten him at birth, as cats eat their malformed kittens. Finally, in despair, haunted by the pall of her ambiguous presence, he journeys to the small Andalusian village where she was born and lived, in the hope that he can somehow resurrect the wild, beautiful young girl that life had maimed and destroyed. Miraculously, on the trail up to the village he meets Aracoeli's ghost, "a minuscule sack of shadow"; when he tells her that he has sinned in his intellect, because he never used it to understand, she laughs and says that there is nothing to understand. And that is Miss Morante's farewell to Emanuele, the book she has written, and the whole problem she has raised.

But we can't leave it at that; we must try to understand why this strange, mocking book, despite a few fine moments, chiefly comic ones, proves in the end to be such a bleak failure. It would seem that Elsa Morante has turned against her innermost creative self and vision, her carefully nurtured private mythology, her special cult of the young and the innocent. This book reads as if she has surrendered to a blunt cynicism that doesn't work for her. Her earlier masterpieces, such as ***Arturo's Island*** and ***History: A Novel,*** were not achieved just by taking thought, they cannot be proved wrong because they misunderstand this problem or that, they live in their fabulistic world and have the truth of all fables, but above all they are what they are because of the immense charge of gaiety and joy that underlies even their most tragic moments.

Unfortunately, in this novel that playfulness appears only fitfully. What's more, the style has changed. The pure, singing, many-toned voice of her earlier books has given way to a heavy-handed imitation of the D'Annunzio of the middle period, the ornate prose of stories like his "Leda Without Swan," where almost every other sentence hinges on an elaborate comparison or simile, so densely embellished that it reminds one of the worst extravagances of baroque and rococo. One feels that this thick impasto of words is laid on to compensate for the author's uncertainty or disorientation. . . . But there is hope, for the light tap of frivolity and playfulness can be heard even in those portentous rhythms.

Raymond Rosenthal, "The Laughter of His Mother's Ghost," in The New York Times Book Review, *January 13, 1985, p. 24.*

REBECCA WEST

Elsa Morante's fictions are the fruit of intense sensitivity to inner experience, as well as of a deep love for storytelling. From her first novel, ***Menzogna e sortilegio (House of Liars)*** to ***L'Isola di Arturo (Arturo's Island)***, to the much-debated monumental war novel ***La Storia (History),*** Morante consistently plumbed the depths of what she once called, in an interview, "the first truth and most human reality of the human drama: psychological reality." She never deviated from her own, very personal, definition of realism: poetic invention that is, no matter how fabulistic in tone, event, and style, true to human psychology and to the portrayal of humankind's relationship to the external world. Her privileging of character over event is clear in her own discussions of her art. She once elaborated a typology of characters that represents the three basic psychological orientations, and the characters in her novels tend to adhere to this typology. There are the "Achilles" type (passionate and vital involvement in life); the "Don Quixote" type (solemn and epic evasion of real life through fantasy); and the "Hamlet" type (funereal contemplation of life that results in opting for real or figural non-being). Although Emanuele is most strongly identifiable as a "Hamlet," he partakes of some aspects of the other two types as well.

Other constants in Morante's novels reappear in ***Aracoeli:*** concentration on the family as the archetypal human configuration; emphasis on the interplay of memory and imagination as tools of knowledge; preference for child protagonists. Although Emanuele is an adult narrator, most of his memories center on childhood and the paradise of innocence that becomes the hell of mature disillusionment. In ***Il mondo salvato dai ragazzini (The World Saved by Children)***, a collection of poetry, prose, and drama never translated into English, Morante divides the world into the "Happy Few" and the "Unhappy Many." In the former category she places all those who retained a childlike exuberance into adulthood (Mozart, Rimbaud), and in the latter are all those who sold out to the "realities" of adult life. Children are, of course, marginal to the centralized institutions of power that organize and rule our adult world, and it is with the emarginated—youths, illiterates, the poor, the mad—that Morante's sympathies always lay. It is in this sense that she can be read as a political writer. In ***Aracoeli,*** both the naive peasant girl who becomes Emanuele's mother and her young partisan brother, an anarchist who dies in the Spanish Civil

War, are placed in sharp, if implicit, contrast to the bourgeois repressiveness of Aracoeli's husband's family, all of whom unthinkingly adhere to the values of fascism.

If we read ***Aracoeli*** as a political allegory, we might understand Emanuele's preference for fantasy, as well as Aracoeli's extreme sexual rebellion (she becomes insatiable and eventually leaves the family home to live as a whore), as desperate attempts to escape the "mature," stifling environment of Italian society under the fascist regime. But the novel is too complex to be read in a monotonal key. Aracoeli's decline from a beautiful girlish mother to a crazed whore is also the result of bodily decay. She is ruined by disease (we can assume cancer) that diminishes her corporeally and spiritually as brutally as does the more abstract force of repressive politics. The same is true of her husband, who descends into the hell of alcoholism after her death and dies a ruined man. Emanuele becomes physically repulsive as he ages; many passages recount his intense self-hatred as an overweight, sagging, middle-aged man. This emphasis on the horror of the body—a stark *memento mori*—distinguishes this novel from Morante's earlier books.

In vivid contrast to the negative details of "real life" are those passages in which Emanuele reveals his native temperament that, in his own words, is "more inclined to visions than to inquiries." Like his creator, he is not interested in documentable fact and readily admits that much of what he recounts is "apocryphal memory," the fruit of fantasy. Thus, in movingly lyrical prose, he describes his birth, his suckling, the magical garden outside his childhood apartment. It is difficult to reconcile this delicate sensitivity with the ugly, awkward, maladjusted man whose life consists of violent encounters with homosexual gigolos, solitary nights in impersonal third-class hotel rooms, and equally lonely days in a two-room publishing firm where he translates worthless pamphlets. There is no doubt that most of us would avoid contact with such a person were we to come upon him in real life; Morante, instead, insists on intimate and disturbing contact, for it seems that she wished us to see this tale of woe as exemplary. Emanuele, it is implied, is not, after all, marginal. He is the norm, an exaggerated but not unrecognizable version of any one of us. Whether he is the result primarily of psychological, political, or physical forces is not explicitly answered, however. All aspects of adult life are ruinous: this is a book of lamentation, not of hope. (pp. 650-52)

Rebecca West, "Elsa Morante," in Partisan Review, *Vol. LIII, No. 4, Fall, 1986, pp. 649-52.*

Andrew (Peter) Motion

1952-

English poet, critic, editor, and biographer.

Motion is considered one of the most talented poets to have emerged in England during the 1970s. His most accomplished poems are narratives related from the perspective of a reticent speaker who dwells upon such topics as love, loss, and isolation. Seeking to avoid the intense self-consciousness of confessional poetry, Motion employs an understated tone and a precise use of conventional poetic forms, similar to the styles of Edward Thomas and Philip Larkin. Many of Motion's poems take the form of reminiscences, either of historical incidents recounted by actual or fictional characters or of his personal experiences.

Motion's first collection of verse, *The Pleasure Steamers* (1978), was commended for displaying his assured tone and accomplished use of various poetic techniques. Included in this volume is the long poem ''Inland,'' in which Motion focuses upon the insecurity and uprootedness experienced by villagers who relocate during a flood. John Mole stated that this piece reflects Motion's ''own acute sense of isolation'' and that ''it is the tension between his sense of belonging to, and being refined out of, the world he describes which gives Mr. Motion's work its distinctive strength.'' This book also includes several poems about Motion's mother, a vibrant woman who was comatose for several years following an accident while horseback riding. Like much of his verse, these pieces are written from the perspective of a happy and secure individual whose existence is suddenly undermined by grave misfortune. This scenario also informs Motion's next work, *Independence* (1981). Public and private meanings of ''independence'' intersect in this book-length poem, as the narrator recounts his life in India, particularly his marriage and the death of his wife and unborn child in 1947, the year India became an independent nation. The poem is framed by an image of the narrator wiping ''a hole / in the misted silvery glass'' of a window, symbolizing his fading recollections.

Most of Motion's poems in *Secret Narratives* (1983) are short pieces ranging in subject matter from personal reminiscences to narratives about such historical figures as Anne Frank and Albert Schweitzer. The title of this volume reflects the sense of mystery and cryptic meaning conveyed by the narrators of the pieces, who tend to obscure or withhold vital information. *Dangerous Play: Poems, 1974-1984* (1984) contains selections from Motion's earlier books, new poems, and ''Skating,'' a prose work about his childhood. In addition to his verse, Motion has authored two critical studies, *The Poetry of Edward Thomas* (1980) and *Philip Larkin* (1982), and a biography, *The Lamberts: George, Constance, and Kit* (1986). Motion also edited *The Penguin Book of Contemporary British Poetry* with Blake Morrison.

(See also *Dictionary of Literary Biography,* Vol. 40.)

© Jerry Bauer

ANNE STEVENSON

Andrew Motion, among the most gifted of younger English poets, . . . has a relaxed way with language, although his smoothness derives, I suspect, from a patient belief in his powers. For a first collection, ***The Pleasure Steamers*** is remarkable for its continuity of tone and skilful control of emotion. At a first reading, one might wonder whether passion has not been too much repressed. These are meditative, self-examining poems which proceed cautiously from the present to the past, or from the past to the present through careful shifts of imagination. A second reading reveals depth of feeling the calculated language disguises. . . . It is so easy for Motion to write well that he rarely risks giving language its head. If the feeling of restless yearning that smoulders in these poems does not quite break into flame, this may be because the poet is afraid of letting his fire get out of control. Still, this is an impressive collection. (p. 63)

Anne Stevenson, ''Night-Time Tongue,'' in The Listener, *Vol. 100, No. 2568, July 13, 1978, pp. 62-3.*

JOHN MOLE

The speaker of the historical sequence **''Inland''**, which makes up the central section of Andrew Motion's first collection—

The Pleasure Steamers—and with which he won the Newdigate Prize in 1975, traces the events whereby he and the other members of a displaced seventeenth-century fenland village become "strangers / in our own land". In the new village to which they have been moved by commercial pressures beyond their control "we wake further into the deep hill / we disown" and when the speaker revisits his old house, a mood of desolation is evoked with telling precision. . . . Finally, the sense of exile is complete: "we are / without past now, waiting for lights / to come on in foreign towns." Most survive, some—like the village preacher Jesse Sease—go under. Only love, treated in the sequence with a brief but sensuous tenderness which matches Mr Motion's skill in realizing the particular physical qualities of the fen landscape ("fields must open to the water's shove"), sustains and adds warmth to a bleak story. . . .

"Inland" is a considerable achievement in itself, but it becomes increasingly interesting as one reads and rereads the poems grouped around it in the collection's first and third sections. It can be seen as an historical paradigm of Andrew Motion's own acute sense of isolation. He too seems to be a stranger in his own land, and poem after poem finds him becoming the ghost of himself. There are moments of uncanny detachment, set against the natural world from which Mr Motion is constantly and enigmatically slipping out. . . .

Heightening this awareness of being cast out of himself into the enduring landscapes he observes is an equally acute sense of collective human loneliness. A recurrent image throughout ***The Pleasure Steamers*** is that of distant lights: "lights of late travellers", "rows of streetlamps", "lamps outside / drown in the river like rain", "Lights from the empty train / fall in flakes in the Thames." . . . Each of these examples comes from a different poem and (along with the recurrence of words such as "distance" and "absence") their cumulative effect is one of an insistent sense of alienation even as the details of urban and rural landscapes are richly evoked. Although, at times, this method threatens to become predictable, it is the tension between his sense of belonging to, and being refined out of, the world he describes which gives Mr Motion's work its distinctive strength. It is the tension between (to take the title of one of the best poems) Inside and Out, and it certainly suggests the comparisons which have been made with the poetry of Edward Thomas. An attractive, melancholy restlessness animates his controlled stanzas, and when in the final poem, **"The Legacy"**, he contemplates his hand signing his furniture on to children or friends and then being replaced again "transcribing itself for ever / like shadows" the debt is unmistakable. It is almost as if Mr Motion had rewritten Thomas's beautiful "The Long Small Room", and to look at the two poems together provides a striking example of the way a talented new poet can—as it were—surprise with the familiar. ***The Pleasure Steamers*** is an impressive book.

John Mole, "The Relief of Solitude," in The Times Literary Supplement, *No. 3984, August 11, 1978, p. 906.*

DAVID MIDDLETON

[In ***The Pleasure Steamers,*** Andrew Motion] addresses the problem of how the mature mind can find and foster a civilized sensibility in a world in which Eliot's "historical sense" is becoming a thing of the past. ***The Pleasure Steamers*** is divided into three sections: Part One, a miscellany of poems that examine the difficult English experience of the postwar welfare state against a (possibly) more glorious past, the relation of man to nature in the post-romantic era, and the idea of "home" as the personal equivalent to cultural history; Part Two, a long series of poems entitled **"Inland,"** based on the dislocating effects of seventeenth-century enclosure of the commons; and, Part Three, a final group of poems centering on the death of a mother and thereby embodying the themes of the earlier two sections. (p. 217)

[The] dual theme of our modern isolation from the very history that largely determines us informs the volume's second section, **"Inland,"** a series of poems that seems to pinpoint, in the disruption of ancient village life by the enclosure of the commons, the end of the old medieval order and the beginning of that fabulous sequence of dislocations—political, theological, philosophical—that culminates in modernism. . . . **"Inland"** traces an unnamed "speaker," a preacher Jesse Sease, and other Fen Country villagers as they face the arrival of the king's men, who force them from their ancestral land so that modern economic methods can be instigated to facilitate the wool trade. Spokesman for the old order of Christendom, the preacher finally commits suicide. The unnamed speaker meditates on the paradoxical co-presence of consanguinity and a death-struggle between the farmers and the sea, whose tidal waves annually threaten to break the dikes and flood the low fenland acres. Displaced to a new village, the speaker reacts to the change from the old to the new in words that could describe life in any modern megalopolis: "a lull / opens between two worlds: we are / without past now, waiting for lights / to come on in foreign towns."

Part Three of Motion's book presents a contemporary equivalent to the enclosure movement described in **"Inland."** Here, a landed English family, apparently Motion's own, suffers loss. The poet recalls his childhood on a country estate (**"A Dying Race"**), an absent mother's unused clothes now stored away (**"In the Attic"**), and, in five moving poems (**"Anniversaries"**), the trips to the hospital to see the mother, made permanently unconscious by a fall from a horse. Much of what a modern poet feels about his ability to draw sustaining power from the tradition evoked by the words *home, inheritance, history* is brilliantly dramatized in the poet's witnessing of the mother's single, brief awakening, in four years, from unconsciousness:

> . . . and whose
> astonishing word was it
> that day when leaving
> your sunlit room I heard
>
> "Stay; stay," and watched
> your eyes flick open once,
> look, refuse to recognize
> my own, and turn away?

Finally, in **"The Legacy,"** the mother's death leads to meditation on the transience yet ongoingness of tradition, our inheritance in mind and in body, which is "transcribing itself for ever / like shadows which follow it now, / uncurling themselves in silence / on printed paper and skin."

The Pleasure Steamers is a good first book, especially for a poet of Motion's age. There are, naturally, some faults. A few of the poems seem to hover uncertainly between description or statement and metaphorical or symbolic presentation, and the apparent metaphors are not always worked out. The lament for poor old England in the postwar days [in the first section] is a bit stale. . . . There is plenty of life in Old England yet, and the problem of one's relation to history remains both more complex and more possibly solvable than Motion seems to imagine. Also, the diction of the poems is, one has to say, that grey articulateness that impedes some English poets and makes much of their work sound like prize poems composed by an Oxbridge committee of brilliant undergraduates. Up to a point, this public-school English eloquence raises their poets' poems above nine-tenths of the work of their less frenetically articulate American counterparts. Past that same point, however, that very idiosyncratic, ingrained eloquence of upper-class English speech often seems to inhibit a profound, simultaneously emotional and intellectual response as, say, in the greatest poems by Winters, Stevens, or Edgar Bowers. This English "inheritance" plagues Motion, even at his best. (pp. 218-20)

David Middleton, "Beyond the Mere Modern: New Foetry from Britain," in The Southern Review *(Louisiana State University), Vol. 17, No. 1, Winter, 1981, pp. 214-24.*

EDNA LONGLEY

Andrew Motion's ***Independence*** weaves a sequence of lyrics around a fiction which concerns the marriage and widowing of a young Englishman in the last days of the Raj. This ambitious scheme, claiming for poetry the kind of historical territory that the novel has taken up, projects into its own time and place the 'post-imperial *tristesse*' detected by Blake Morrison in Larkin's "At Grass". However, neither the irony nor the interpenetration of public and private worlds advances beyond a fairly surface level. An elegy may dispense with political analysis, but the Indian atmosphere is also thinly spread, tending towards present participles which keep us informed of the state of the light. The numerous short-hand constructions testify to Motion's difficulty in sustaining a syntactical, rhythmic and dramatic momentum. And for all the understated austerity that muffles the metre and hushes the voice, the plot itself remains distinctly mawkish. (p. 20)

Edna Longley, "Cooked and Raw," in New Statesman, *Vol. 103, No. 2661, March 19, 1982, pp. 19-20.*

JOHN MOLE

Andrew Motion's ***Independence*** is, for the most part, set in India at the time indicated by his title. It is a story narrated in episodic flash-backs somewhat reminiscent of a film by James Ivory or passages from a novel by Paul Scott. Unfolding a sequence of bitter-sweet events through haunting particulars and carefully arranged detail, it is rich in sentiment but—despite the shifting images of a backward look and the occasional overlay of soft-focus—it avoids the sentimental. The narrator, "a month home and awake / at three expecting light", recalls India as another country in which his wife and child both died, following a miscarriage. The memories press in on him as he gazes out of the window, re-encountering—in a poignantly realized isolation—"the lost company" of a vanished society and a period of personal happiness. He was married in the year of Independence . . . but his own independence has become a widower's exile—the painful, tender imperiousness of insistent recall on the one hand and an empty horizon on the other.

The poem begins and ends with the narrator smearing a hole in the "misted silvery glass" of his father-in-law's house somewhere on the English coast and looking outward, but the dominant image is that of the sea "heavily sliding, its craters split / and slammed shut to the moon". The remorseless continuum of *heavily,* the finality of *slammed shut,* and the romantic echo of the moon amount to an effective image of the presence of loss which is characteristic of Motion's skill in rendering emotion through scenic description.

A further dimension is added to ***Independence*** by the deployment of "sound effects": the voice-over of a letter, banal lyrics from an Inkspots record played again and again at a Christmas dance, the onomatopoeic *"chomp chomp"* of the Benares-Lahore train (ominous, with its barred windows, and "the packed / vanishing faces of refugees"), and careful modulated snatches of dialogue. This all contributes to a satisfying texture of verisimilitude. ***Independence*** is a work of vivid surfaces and considerable depth.

John Mole, "Hearts of Darkness," in The Times Literary Supplement, *No. 4122, April 2, 1982, p. 392.*

CLAUDE RAWSON

[Andrew Motion's ***Independence*** is] a dramatic monologue, tending, like some of his other poems, to the short story. A man remembers, in his father-in-law's house by the sea in England, his courtship and marriage in India, in the year of Independence. . . . The riots, the slogans, the free 'replacement maps' with Pakistan on them, Ghandi's death provide the historical setting for a tender study in nostalgia and bereavement.

The hero works in the carpet business and marries the boss's daughter in Independence week. The idyll of their courtship and life together until her death of a miscarriage are the central matters of reminiscence. Their first assignation occurs when she is recovering from appendicitis. He climbs over the wall to her, a nurse interrupts them, and he hides, dragging 'the heavy tallboy door shut behind me'. Eventually, the coupling is completed with post-surgical awkwardness, the stitched lady riding her lover in a rhythmic posture carefully adapted to minimise pain, while the removed appendix looks on from a jar on the windowsill. The bizarrerie is rendered with a quiet unfussy humour, not the genial blowsiness with which a more ordinary poet might have invested it. In the poem's prevailing atmosphere of tenderness and loss, it is remarkable to find such an episode executed without a discordant or unbalancing note, and perhaps even more remarkable that it should have been risked at all.

Andrew Motion is very strong at rendering the particularities of grief—the objects, for example, which survive a bereavement and bring home its poignancy. The gift was vividly present in **"Anne Frank Huis"**: the pathos of the girl's possessions, the pictures of her family mingling with cuttings of famous actors and 'fashions chosen by Princess Elizabeth', will seem extraordinarily accurately captured to anyone who has visited the house in Amsterdam, but also have a deep imaginative rightness which is again achieved in the strongest parts of ***Independence.*** But in the latter, such things are sometimes allowed to become automatic:

> *Can I help you sahib?*
> Then evenings drunk alone—
> the bedroom shutters drawn
> and my shadow reeling to

and fro across their slats
folding dresses into tea-chests,
scooping up the baby-things,
your belts, a lacy petticoat,
shoes, blouses from the cupboard.

Here perhaps the verse tends towards a slightly falsifying emotional telegraphese, a suggestion of experiences uniformly intensified. The verse-medium imposes in such places a heightening which is not always earned, and which blurs the individuality of some remembered scenes. One sometimes longs for an unfussy prose, which would give the true texture of ordinariness where that is due. But the lapses are rare, and the poem is a bold as well as a delicately orchestrated success. (p. 21)

Claude Rawson, "Kelpers," in London Review of Books, *Vol. 4, No. 11, June 17-30, 1982, pp. 20-1.*

TIM DOOLEY

As its title suggests, [***Secret Narratives***] continues and extends the interest in narrative revealed in Motion's long poem ***Independence*** (1981). **"The Great Man"** and **"The Interval"** (accounts, respectively, of a disillusioning visit to Schweitzer and of links between Nazism and German theatrical life in the 1930s) use comparatively conventional devices to tell fairly familiar stories. Other poems, such as **"Writing"**, **"Open Secrets"** and **"The Letter"** are more innovative—playing with the expectations of narrative structure, with tensions between author and first-person narrator and with notions of fiction and truth.

These interests, however, are only tangentially connected with the qualities which continue to make Motion's poetry of value. His particular strength lies neither in originality of observation nor in an individual approach to poetic form. Rather, he is remarkable for the precision of his technique—particularly in relating speech rhythms to the line of verse and registering vivid physical impressions. **"The Lines"**, which intersperses quotation from a history of Victorian England with evocations of personal loss, is a virtuoso piece; but **"Wooding"**, a poem of no special intellectual ambition, shows most clearly the strength of feeling Motion can wring from a minimum of technical effects and explains why it is no insult to his predecessors to see this poet as a natural heir to the traditions of Edward Thomas and Ivor Gurney. . . . **"The Lines"**, **"Wooding"**, and **"The House Through"** also underline how persistently the subject of mourning has enabled Motion to produce writing of the finest quality. It is unfortunate, therefore, that the public themes which have engaged him most actively—memories of imperial decline or military disaster—have drawn to themselves the tone of bitter-sweet regret developed in his poems of personal loss. An impression is given, whether intended or not, of nostalgia for a Britain great in more than name that ought to be very difficult to justify. A parallel difficulty emerges in the readiness with which Motion's historical imagination populates his poems with the trappings of patrician élites. Whether faced with an aristocratic world of stag hunts and complaisant servant girls or an entrenched bourgeois view over side plates to fields of ripening wheat, I cannot be the only reader who responds to Motion's poetry with a feeling that his England is not mine.

Tim Dooley, "Magnificence and Mourning," in The Times Literary Supplement, *No. 4194, August 19, 1983, p. 886.*

CLAUDE RAWSON

Andrew Motion's poems, even when not actually narrative, often tend towards narrative. The story element is often 'secret', its circumstantial background undisclosed, so that what comes through are hints of an incident, usually in a disturbing sense of that term, thrusting into view with an odd clarity of outline from an incomplete set of 'facts':

There was a van

drawn up by the rushes, and on the mud
a diver, easing his mask off,
calling 'I couldn't see anything'.
Neither could I.

The lines are from the title-poem of Motion's first book, ***The Pleasure Steamers.*** We don't know much more about van, diver or object of search. The thing comes at us obliquely, at once low-key and vaguely sensational, adding a note of menace to the speaker's nostalgic meditation. He knows more than we do, but what we don't know (or the fact that we don't) troubles our composure in a manner which seems to reflect his mood.

It doesn't really matter what 'happened': as Tom Paulin said of one of his own poems, 'the poem isn't really about the implied narrative'. The incident feeds the meditation rather than belonging to a chain of events. It's an objectified extension of something which was already in the emotional scenario, since the steamers recall war and drownings as well as 'safety, and home'. . . . Motion's poems have always been strong in emotional exactitudes captured through a perception of objects, and his way with narrative seems to be an extension of this. His more recent work has opened up a strip of territory in which stories about other people (true or invented) coexist and interact with the movements of his own inner life.

"Open Secrets", the first poem of ***Secret Narratives,*** is both an example and a declaration of this. It starts with two stanzas narrated in quotes. . . . (p. 58)

Then the poem comes out of quotes, and the poet tells us he's made it all up:

Just now, prolonging my journey home to you,
I killed
an hour where my road lay over a moor, and
made this up.

'I killed' is a cheeky effect which matches what went before, however. Hung on the end of a line, straight after a gruesome tale, it has an explosive force all the greater, momentarily, for being outside the narrated 'story' and thus seeming more immediate and 'real'. And then both violences are defused at once: all he killed was 'an hour' and the earlier story was a hoax. The remainder of the poem is about the process of making it up, and concludes:

He was never
myself, this boy, but I know if I tell you his story
you'll think we are one and the same: both of
us hiding
in fictions which say what we cannot admit to
ourselves.

It's a way of asserting some old perceptions, that fictions are truer than facts, that our inventions reveal more of ourselves than we dare. The subject seems to call for tentativeness, not this air of triumphant definition. But it's a celebration of the truth of lies which I think Yeats or Thomas Mann might have respected. What is 'secret' about the narratives are not (as in

"The Pleasure Steamers") facts that have been withheld, but the fact that they aren't facts. Both the sensationalism of the story, and the cheekiness of its denial, come over with a brio one would have called facile if the poem wasn't so obviously defying one to do so.

It's very different from those cautious exactitudes, those gentle exploratory probes into personal maps of bereavement or of lost or interrupted love which distinguished Motion's first book. These too had their finalities, but finalities of temporary understanding, momentary settlements of feeling delicately apprehended. One poem in ***Secret Narratives***, **"Wooding"**, seems to go back to the subject-matter of the sequence **"Anniversaries"**. The aching personal loss is the old one: 'we buried you, / still destitute of ways to show our grief'. Father and sons, stared at by old people 'from windows in the Home' as they bury the body, suddenly seem engaged in some adventure, half cloak-and-dagger, half schoolboy yarn. This is the new element: styles of violent story-telling are evoked, though in a somewhat muffled way, in what would once have been a simple elegiac meditation with no formal story in tow.

It's as if the act of inventing fictions, to 'say what we cannot admit to ourselves', has come to be seen as itself a violence, something which 'kills' what, for a hung moment, you don't know to be 'unreal'. It strays into that imaginative terrain which Wallace Stevens wrote about in "Poetry is a Destructive Force". 'It can kill a man'. Many of the stories in ***Secret Narratives*** evoke wars (the two World Wars, Vietnam, the Falklands) in some poignant intersection with the poet's own life, as for that matter does **"The Pleasure Steamers"**. ***Secret Narratives*** is a moving book, strangely combining delicacy and brio. (pp. 58-9)

Claude Rawson, "Telling Stories," in Poetry Review, *Vol. 73, No. 3, September, 1983, pp. 58-61.*

JOHN MOLE

Andrew Motion's ***Secret Narratives*** is a book of fluent, pleasantly readable if rather gratuitously baffling poems. They have a quiet levelness of tone despite the multiplicity of voices at play within their modest confines. Full of ambiguous, fugitive pronouns which hide inside each other, seeming by turns to evade their author and to establish a complicity with him, they keep raising the question of who exactly is writing whom or what. The idea behind many of them seems to be that snatches of conversation and anecdote, held in place by a loose narrative structure, should resonate and expand into something resembling a completeness of story. Motion is good at establishing mood if you stop worrying about what it all adds up to. In fact, what it all adds up to does appear to be mood. He's an old-fashioned impressionist *à la mode,* experimenting with the latest techniques of fiction, and he achieves some poignant atmospheres of loneliness, desolation and betrayal. The best poems in ***Secret Narratives*** speak with a single voice, as in **"The House Through"**—a poem of sweetness and delicacy with a *frisson* of the supernatural. It's reminiscent of A. E. Coppard's wonderful short story "Adam and Eve and Pinch Me", and points up the essential Englishness of Motion's work. . . . Motion also has a touching sympathy with the Englishman in exile. His portrait, in **"From the Imperial"**, of Edward Lear "lonely / and bigongulous, wishing / he were an egg" is appropriately eccentric without being in the least sentimental. He could trust to his sense of oddity much more than he does. Often he seems far too intent on making safe, acceptable poems. (pp. 65-6)

John Mole, "Expanding Elements," in Encounter, *Vol. LXI, No. 4, December, 1983, pp. 60-7.*

STEPHEN REGAN

[For success, the long narrative poem] demands a continual justification of stanza divisions, rhyme and rhythm, a prolonged emphasis on precision, and a relentless concern for the nuances of the individual word.

Andrew Motion's ***Independence*** has adopted the resources of the long narrative, reworking and refining them with a scrupulous care for the experience which the poem conveys. The events take place mainly in India, but are presented through the memory of the narrator after his return to England. The narrator's private struggle to accommodate the loss of his wife and child is paralleled by dramatic incidents in the movement towards Independence, creating a subtle interplay of personal and historical perspectives.

The narrative and dramatic strengths of Andrew Motion's work are evident in his first collection of poems ***The Pleasure Steamers*** (especially in the Newdigate Prize poem **"Inland"**). Since then, there has been a noticeable broadening of subject matter, a movement from the stagnation of post-war England to its colourful, but imminently fateful, colonial past, along with an increased flexibility in technique. Whereas **"Inland"** employs a definite rhyme scheme as part of its narrative framework, ***Independence*** allows for a greater conversational freedom and more delicate adjustments in feeling.

The setting of ***Independence*** provides the poem with a fresh vocabulary—'godown', 'punkah', 'cicadas'—words which are incorporated naturally and unobtrusively to lend the poem its air of authenticity. One of its most appealing aspects is the detailed observation of the country and its climate, its people and their customs. The narrator's impressions of the landscape are lively and vigorous; images are conceived with immediacy and surprise. The descriptions of the monsoon, for instance, convey a sense of astonishment and alarm. Natural objects are seen and heard with the intense vividness and awareness that one associates with first impressive experiences. . . . (pp. 89-90)

The poem opens and closes with the narrator looking out through his window over the English coast, waiting for daybreak. There is a gentle and sensitive creation of atmosphere; the setting with its 'wavering grey moonlight' allows the memory to recall the events of the past. The transition into the movement for independence in India is effected convincingly by a subliminal connection: the narrator's anticipation of dawn leads him to consider the dawn journey which he made to Kamaria in a period of political unrest. There is no disruption of rhythm or strained technique in this transition; the five-line stanza adopted in the second section of the poem permits an extension of the narrative voice, and quickly conveys the immediate impact of political unrest. A long unfolding prose line incorporates both the narrator's feelings of apprehension at the ferment of opposition to Britain in riots and slogans, and his more personal recollections of a love affair which coincided with those political events: 'the quick freckled blush I saw beginning / and deepening there like a burn.' By maintaining a flexible prose rhythm, the poem is able to capture the inflections of ordinary speech, usually in ruminating monologue, sometimes in a remembered exchange of voices.

The interplay of personal and historical events is given progression by a close observation of seasonal changes, midwinter becoming spring. The narrator remembers 'courting all that spring / to Independence', before his marriage and honeymoon in the crucial week of political activity. Occasionally, his personal recollections transcend his social pressures, adopting a lyrical strain and finding their focus in a series of sensuous images. . . . Variations in stanza form determine each section of the poem and allow for subtle notations of feeling, from the wistfulness of the exiled father in law, 'homesick for England', to the impassioned regret and pained conscience of the narrator for the death of his wife and child during his absence. The poem follows the narrator's intense self-questioning, his collapse into remorse and his sudden emotional release with the coming of the monsoon.

The 'steady hissing downpour' of rain mingles with a long fitful dream to create a sense of distraction from which the narrator emerges to witness the flood and the reality of his wife's death. The poem gains its unity by returning through the remembered images of the final morning in India to the twilight scene of the narrator's meditation, conceding, finally, to the disappointment that the future holds. . . . The narrative strength of ***Independence*** lies in its ability to combine a sensitive record of impressions with a refined and subtle technique. The merits of technical precision become evident as the narrative moves outwards to capture the stirring events of colonial history and inwards to the central emotional experience of the poem: the achievement of a more harrowing and personal independence. (pp. 90-2)

Stephen Regan, in a review of "Independence," in Critical Quarterly, *Vol. 26, No. 3, Autumn, 1984, pp. 89-92.*

DENIS DONOGHUE

Andrew Motion's way of making sense is to imagine something, then something else apparently quite different, and let the poem accommodate both imaginings with or without specifying the relation between them. A girl and her father, quarrelling; the girl and a boy, making love; the double vision, which the speaker offers his lover, a love-poem 'hiding in fictions'. A girl with a love-letter; then a pilot, crashing. . . . A man studies the butterflies he has caught: hundreds of miles away his wife, dying, remembers a bowl of apples. The poetry is in the gap between the two images, the third sense they make. . . . In a few poems, the third sense is specified—notably in **"Open Secrets"**. But mostly we are given only the two images, and allowed to make the sense upon our own authority. We are left free, too, if we want to assume, as with Stevens in "The River of Rivers in Connecticut", that the force of the river 'is not to be seen beneath the appearances / That tell of it'. Andrew Motion gives us the two appearances, but not, as a general thing, an official syntax to bind them.

Secret Narratives comprises 17 fairly short poems about houses, foreign places in wartime, codes, communications, letters. That everything exists as a sign is their predicate: hence the bearing of secrets, whispers, unanswered telephones, Anne Frank's house, Albert Schweitzer's music, Edward Lear as 'dream companion'. These are the kind of poems a good poet would write if his 'one idea' for the moment were that everything in the world wants to be a message. Rain in London wants to 'whisper'. A shaken duster waves 'goodbye'. . . . But suppose everything weren't a message or a sign? Then these poems would seem complacent in the possession of sentiments they haven't earned. Or too happy in the happiness of a language determined to embrace the world and charm every event to become an epiphany. In that mood, it is hard to take Motion's sentiments upon his system of valuation. The poem **"Wooding"**, for instance, tells of a family—the father and two sons—in the days after the mother's death, and ends:

> The whole short afternoon we spoke
> of anything except your death,
> and then, next day, beyond that
> blank enormous wall we buried you,
> still destitute of ways to show our grief.

'Show' is an impurity, and the whole poem more a show than it ought to be. If the boy is destitute, it is not for the reason the last line claims but, presumably, because he has that within him, his mother's loss, which passes show. Motion has ascribed to the boy his own zealotry of communication. (p. 22)

Denis Donoghue, "Making Sense," in London Review of Books, *Vol. 6, No. 18, October 4, 1984, pp. 22-3.*

ROBIN BELL

Andrew Motion and Craig Raine are two young masters of the visual image who are themselves highly visible on the poetry circuit. In their plump new collections, ***Dangerous Play*** and *Rich,* they quite literally pass from the slim volume stage of development to stand or fall among our established contemporary poets.

The question of establishment is central to their thinking. They are not rebels brandishing ideals for a new world, but men seeking a secure place in an old one. Both spend a great deal of time examining their backgrounds, and curiously both include in the middle of the poems a long prose piece about their respective childhoods. . . .

These two collections draw together poems from previous books along with much material already published in literary magazines. Those readers who keep up with the magazines will find little surprising in ***Dangerous Play*** and *Rich*. This fits in with the authors' preference for things which are well-tried and tested. Both are preoccupied with the grey area between fact and fiction and with appearances rather than essences. (p. 34)

What makes Andrew Motion and Craig Raine interesting is the way in which they look at the world. They move away from the Sixties' and Seventies' fashion for peering into oneself and externalising the present inner moment in earnest phrases. But, rather than abandon self-examination completely, they do it in different ways. . . . [Andrew Motion] adopts different *personae* to look at events. He pops up in the first person in a French resort before he was born and appears in a long poem, ***Independence,*** in the last days of Imperial India. He tries to look through the eyes of others: an older man, a soldier, a woman. This is not just playing the game of dressing-up in a new skin-deep personality and parading in front of the mirror to see how it looks. There is a more serious purpose, to do with getting away from the all-pervasive 'I' that sticks out like a large off-switch from the poetry of the past two decades. . . .

[In the opening poem of ***Dangerous Play,*** Motion] acknowledges that there is a poetry to be written which is not all about self but nevertheless reveals something about the condition of the individual. Neither he nor Craig Raine, however, seem comfortable about committing themselves to pure fiction. It is as if they were saying that it is all right once more to write about Young Lochinvar coming out of the west—but only if the poet writes from the viewpoint of Young Lochinvar.

Along with the need for a new perspective, both poets have a discipline and implicit desire for order that makes their style crisp and lucid. Both have a feeling for the rhythms of natural speech and an ear for precise language. . . .

Both poets have moved a long way from the straggly free verse of the Sixties and Seventies, but neither goes so far as to make consistent use of regular poetic forms. Technical ability is important to them, but their techniques are refinements of previous trends rather than the creation of a new style or the revitalisation of more classical forms.

In short, these are poems of transition. They show the way that poetry in Britain is going and they open up greater possibilities for their authors and for other writers. (p. 35)

Robin Bell, "Self-Examiners," in The Spectator, *Vol. 253, No. 8159, November 24, 1984, pp. 34-5.*

DICK DAVIS

[Tennyson] looms behind Andrew Motion's ***Dangerous Play.*** The women, especially, in Motion's poetry—uncomprehending, frustrated, caught up in impossible situations, unable to take hold of the reality of their lives—could have stepped straight from *The Idylls of the King;* the soft wash of sad emotion, reducing all incidents to a misty chiaroscuro, also seems Tennysonian.

Motion's verse is extremely fastidiously written, the pathos presented through understatement; almost all of his poems have a lonely, unfulfilled character at their centre, and he writes of such people with sympathy and insight, if a little monotonously. His book contains a passage of autobiographical prose; this is a fashionable procedure at the moment . . . but prose is not, I feel, Motion's medium; his reminiscenccs are painfully clichéd ('blissfully contented', 'a sense of identity', 'a profound sense of community') and give little evidence of the sensitivity to language evident in his best verse. (pp. 26-7)

Dick Davis, "Prosy Childhoods," in The Listener, *Vol. 113, No. 2890, January 3, 1985, pp. 26-7.*

MICHAEL HOFMANN

Dangerous Play: Poems 1974-1984 is Andrew Motion's fourth book of poetry, and his third in four years. . . . By current standards, it's a rather early "selected". Correspondingly, there is something a bit fussy or busy about the book, an anxiety to prove its right to exist. That said, though, ***Dangerous Play*** will undoubtedly, and quite rightly, win new readers for Motion. . . .

Predictably, and, I think, wrongly, the selection veers towards the latest work: seven new poems, and sixteen out of seventeen from last year's ***Secret Narratives*** listed in the acknowledgements—although **"The Interval"**, Motion's defector poem, has done a bunk. The other, "purposely" omitted, **"Resident at the Club"**, would not have been my own choice for blackballing: I found it spirited and winning, a bright fragment of Anglo-Indian matter which had made itself independent of Motion's long Anglo-Indian poem ***Independence,*** which of course is included. . . .

First and foremost [***Dangerous Play***] is the latest phase in Motion's ongoing poetic conversion, his move from lyric to narrative. I imagine he would see the handful of his early poems in this new book not so much as a representation of his younger self, but as poems that he'd been able to rescue *from* his younger self. ***Dangerous Play*** asks us, quite brazenly, to reconsider extant poems—even those of last year, fifteen out of seventeen of them—under a different aspect, and it is surprisingly successful. To put it broadly, the new emphasis is on brushes with death, direct or indirect, real or imagined: with illness, murder, bereavement, war and revolution. The book is arranged, not chronologically, but thematically, and all its seven sections (except, for the pacific fourth) can be seen under this newly imposed aspect. Almost everywhere, there is a hint or aftermath of public violence, directly, bizarrely, in what one might take to be the poems *in propria persona,* more boldly and luridly in imagined or reconstructed work.

As I say, Motion is surprisingly successful in his re-situating, his relocation of work written with another purpose in mind. When ***Secret Narratives*** first appeared, taking as my text the best poem in it, **"West 23rd"**, I would have stressed the comic way the human actors gesture and pine and perform, at once free and inhibited, grandiose and powerless. . . . I would have talked about the association of tenderness and foolishness in Motion's work, and the almost ignominious unfolding of lives against a background not only of their words and ambitions, but also of a history which is nebulously and intermittently evoked. In this new book, though, my attention is drawn instead to Joey the draft-dodger, the "fucked up" veteran of no wars, "some almost-forgotten instinct reminding him: bolt the door". Every poem (barring those in the fourth section) now has its Joey, and is in contact with violence. The piece that looks best in its new context is ***Independence,*** probably Motion's most effective work to date.

In view of this re-orientation, it is interesting to note how little Motion's style has changed from its lyrical beginnings. Long, strongly syntactical sentences (***Independence*** is an interesting exception, where the character, an engineer, and shattered, speaks in notes) are folded into trim stanza-shapes, with very little end-stopping and a great deal of run-on. The poetry, you might say, is in the subclauses. There is an almost total absence of poetic devices and effects. The vocabulary of poem after poem is simple and small, with its only unusual life in skittish, harmless and gawky adjectives, like "jiggy-jaggy", "jittery", "jangly"; or "sluttish", "sluggish" and "scrumpled". The occasional toughness of phrase in poems of the 1970s has been dropped, the "stern geographies of punishment / and love" of **"Leaving Belfast"**, the "obsolete pastoral" and "lost, inexhaustible century" of **"The Pleasure Steamers"**.

It is a self-effacing, almost featureless style, entirely in the service of whatever scene or feeling is to be put over. Phanopoiea is all: you are far more likely to remember a scene than a verse or a phrase. And this is what Motion is: not a descriptive writer, even, but a *metteur en scène,* a designer. His poems are as clear, as expected and as compelling as blueprints. Their vividness comes sometimes from a quite inspired observation—the borderline of attention and illusion or auto-suggestion is often Motion's path—but sometimes from considering the unconsidered and inconsiderable: "our heavy brown teapot" and "our simple village" are almost brilliantly unremarkable details in **"The Letter"**. This nearly inarticulate descriptive calm is combined with extraordinary friendliness towards the reader. Adverbs like "clearly" and "distinctly" flatter and deceive him; the prose memoir has beautiful touches (like the Union Jack in the water-rat's hole) masked by many professions of ordinariness; the appeal to "imagine" a scene is made no fewer than fourteen times in the book, not to mention a few more "think ofs"; and then there is Motion's favourite style of participial self-depiction as he goes about his narratorial roles:

> but here I am
> by the window, stooping,
> quickly smearing a hole
> in the misted silvery glass.

This device—borrowed maybe from jokes or photo-albums—is typical of how well Motion treats his reader. What his poetry offers is the tension between the easy pleasure of reading him, and the weight and drama associated with his subjects. I happen to think he has published this book a little precipitately: given a year or two more, and say half a dozen different poems, it would have been quite irresistible. Given his publishing history, this may happen.

Michael Hofmann, "Brushes with Death," in The Times Literary Supplement, *No. 4268, January 18, 1985, p. 54.*

PETER PORTER

[***Dangerous Play***] is an assembly with a keynote: Motion wishes us to take heed of the current idea of poetry as narrative. To this end, he has selected a handful of poems from his first collection, ***The Pleasure Steamers,*** his longish poem ***Independence,*** most of the contents of ***Secret Narratives*** (1983) and some new pieces, and has arranged them to read like an artistic apologia for a way of seeing and making.

On the whole he succeeds, though it should be stressed that storytelling in verse can seem stiff and laborious compared with its more relaxed prose equivalent. Many of Motion's poems are no more than vignettes and others are denied the life-blood of hard fact which could nourish their lyrical posturing. His is rather a bare poetry, romantic in shape yet strangely without rhetoric. A ghostly end-of-empire feeling pervades much of the verse.

However, reading through the book produces a cumulative sense of power, of a sensibility which finds reticence a way of owning up. And the versification, which at first seems so self-effacing as to hardly register, finally comes into its own. It is a worry that several of these secret narratives acknowledge their start in life in other men's journalism, as did Blake Morrison's recent "Dark Glasses." The latest cryptics please me most, especially **"The Gorilla Girl."**

Peter Porter, "The Stars Look Down," in The Observer, *January 27, 1985, p. 50.*

MICHAEL HULSE

The more limited a poet's stylistic basis, the more both his strengths and his weaknesses are emphasized. In Andrew Motion's work, the stylistic basis reads in many respects like a classic prescription for elegy: landscapes are usually seen at a distance, often veiled by mist; settings of twilight, dusk and evening, with their cognates of *shadow, dark/darkness* and *moon/moonlit/moonlight* occur throughout; images of silence and stillness abound; situations of absence and loss, with the related vocabulary of distance, travel/journeys, and strangers, are central; the most frequently-used verbs are *remember, imagine, discover, turn/return* and *survive;* and the single most often-used noun is that one word at the core of human experience, *home*. Many of Motin's poems indeed deal directly with death, often with violent death. The elegiac texture of his poetry is deepened by the gentle circumspection of his syntax and by his constant qualifications and modifications (*might have, seem, almost, perhaps, I should say, come to that* etc.), which place his writing in an English tradition of uninsistent decorum with roots in the Movement and, beyond the Movement, in the work of Hardy and Edward Thomas. Motion's single most essential addition to this received fabric is his repeated use of *sun* and *sunlight* and *sunlit* settings, but close analysis of the poems will readily show that this imagery by no means dispels the misty gloom of twilit elegy but in fact is an essential component in Motion's experience of loss.

In **"Anniversaries"**, which follows the first four years after a riding accident from which Andrew Motion's mother never recovered but lay unconscious until death, a poignant moment occurs in his mother's 'sunlit room'. . . . At three points in **"Anniversaries"**, sunlight is linked either to a cold winter landscape or to the lingering experience of loss; and it is with a jolt that we learn that not only these closing memories of his mother but also his very first offer Andrew Motion a compounding of sun, shadow and cold:

> I am peering through a fringe of white silk tassels. There is a sun, but it is low and cold. Occasionally a warm shadow blots it out, looming down to my face with a smell of what I will come to recognise as *Blue Grass*. The shadow is my mother, and she is pushing me in my pram on a frozen mill pond. . . .

The sun in Andrew Motion bestows neither joy nor warmth. Instead, with first and last memories of his mother behind it, and thus the experience of lost warmth and accommodation, and of grief and tragedy, the sun is usually an adjunct of bleak scenes of doubt, loss and death.

The tragedy that stopped his mother's life is in every way at the core of Andrew Motion's work. The proximity of sexual experience and death, so emphatically behind the emotive force of poems such as ***Independence*** and **"Bathing at Glymenopoulo"**, astonishingly announces itself in the prose memoir **"Skating"** when Motion opens the section dealing with his mother's accident with the statement, 'My mother and I never talked much about sex', and goes on to juxtapose his own adolescent quest for first sexual experience with the tragic arresting of life. Of course **"Bathing at Glymenopoulo"** also takes over the association of horses with death from the facts of Motion's mother's accident. Central also is the experience of separation or absence: **"Skating"** shows us that Andrew Motion was not present at the events that led to his mother's death, just as his protagonist in ***Independence*** is absent when his wife dies in premature childbirth. Absence from a loved one or correspondent is a frequent foundation of other poems (**"Letter to an exile"**, **"No news from the old country"**, **"West 23rd"**). This in turn is related to the indirect, refracted nature of experience in much of Motion's work. After all, after describing a memory of being pushed in a pram by his skating mother he goes on to add, 'But this is a photograph', and a similar reluctance to be committed to positive representation of experience is characteristic of Motion throughout. It is this that underlies his reliance on the verbs *remember* and *imagine,* with all that they imply of nondefinite relativity, and this too produces frequent 'as if . . .' constructions, and indeed fondness for certain kinds of imagery—not only the images of shadow and mist, but also (for example) images of reflections in water.

If there is a tendency for Motion to view sexual love, death, separation, and even landscape through the refractive medium of his experience of his mother's dying, that experience also gave him his obsessive need to think his way imaginatively into situations characterised equally by loss and survival. . . . **"The letter"**, **"Writing"**, **"Inside and out"**, **"A dying race"**, **"The house through"**, **"Dangerous Play"** and other poems seem all, in their distinct ways, to derive a profound ambiguity of effect precisely from their balance of loss and survival. We think of Andrew Motion's mother, who for ten years survived but was effectively lost to the world: Motion projects this moving ambivalence into the situations he writes of, and in a sense his final subject always remains one—his mother. In **"Anniversaries"** he describes her as 'your own survivor', and the phrase reminds us that elsewhere, where Motion appears to be writing about himself, he is in fact speaking of a conflated persona which is as much his mother as himself. In **"The pleasure steamers"** Motion writes of

> a lost, inexhaustible century
>
> where I may sometimes visit
> but never stay, although
> I discover at every return
> I could have outlived myself there.

The 'lost, inexhaustible century' is finally the distant and uncommunicating dying of the poet's mother; the returns are his imaginative and emotional attempts to come to terms with his exile from the accommodated world of childhood; and his 'there' is the home to which there is no going back. (pp. 71-3)

In ***The Pleasure Steamers*** (1978), Andrew Motion's first collection, the sense of a lost home is present throughout, from the opening **"Letter to an exile"** to **"The legacy"**, which closes the volume with thoughts of the 'shadows which follow' in the chain of linked lives within which the individual is accommodated. Not counting titles, the word 'home' is used six times in the collection. . . . The vocabulary of *mist, river* and *moon, travellers* and *home, darkness* and *silence,* is all central to Motion's poetry; but so too is the condition of sleep, so like that unconsciousness in which his mother existed for years. The ambiguity of emotion in a poem like **"Past midnight"** is intimately linked to Andrew Motion's conflation of mother and lover: through the lover he longs to find his way back to his lost mother, but the more he is actually reminded by her of his mother ('seeming to sleep') the more he is confounded by the impossibility of intimate contact (for a son does not love his mother as he loves his lover) and keeps his distance ('not touching'), and so fails to re-connect with the accommodation he wants to have again. Whatever the dramatic situation posited by **"Past midnight"**, whatever the 'real' identity of the poem's first person, it becomes essential, given what we know both of Andrew Motion's personal history and of his lexical preoccupations, to read this text as a psychogenetic transcript of the poet's quest to repossess his mother and the security she represented.

Independence (1981), though in other ways the poem is highly unsatisfactory, treats the concept of *home* without the self-indulgent emphasis and larmoyance which is present at times in the poems of ***The Pleasure Steamers,*** and thus marks a move toward greater maturity and command. The third word of the poem is 'home':

> A month home and awake
> at three expecting light.

Only later in the poem do we become aware of a particular component in the irony of this statement: for the narrator's 'home' has in fact been the Indian home he has shared with his wife, and it is only after her death that he again thinks of England as home. This is a small but moving insight which takes a proper and effective place in the poem.

In later narrative poems in ***Secret Narratives*** (1983) and ***Dangerous Play*** (1984), *home* is at times only a label ('the Home', 'a holiday home') or part of a familiar collocation ('fly the wounded home'); but two poems in particular invite us to scrutinise the word more closely. **"One life"** describes a woman who has left her butterfly-catching husband in Nigeria and now, in the 'silence' of a 'distant room' where she is together with a 'stranger, her friend', is haunted by the recollection of

> the delicate pottery bowl she left
> forgotten at home, still loaded with apples
> and pears she knows by their English names.

That place she has left became home through marriage and shared experience, and her new absence from it is poignant because her present state is one of essential loneliness and isolation; but beyond this poignancy we are left speculating whether a home is created by domesticity alone, by apples and pears in a bowl. Somewhat factitiously, Motion lends this speculation an added colonial irony by implying that imported Englishness cannot find a true home in a continent and culture where it is alien. In the poem **"Dangerous play"**—like **"The letter"**, ***Independence,*** **"Bathing at Glymenopoulo"** and the poems on Motion's mother a piece that owes its strength to direct confrontation of death—we are again offered a typical Motion version of *home*. . . . (pp. 74-6)

I have emphasized Andrew Motion as elegist, writing scenes of twilit distance and longing for what is lost, writing of death and homelessness; but he is received, on his own terms, as a narrative poet, and it is when we consider him as such that we see clearly the weaknesses as well as the strengths of his stylistic basis. Emphasis of a core diction of *home, remember, imagine, discover, shadow, dark/darkness, moon, sun,* and related words, with emphasis of twilit settings, situations of absence, and misty landscapes, and with emphasis too of ample syntactic units consisting of grammatically whole sentences flexibly enjambed across fluent verse paragraphs, all expressed in a gentle, tentative tone: this guarantees a remarkable integrity and thrust in Andrew Motion's elegiac mode, and he sensitively chooses verse forms which seem (but are not) metrically 'traditional'. From this integrity derives Andrew Motion's strength, and it is an elegiac strength. From the strategies he adopts in his choice of narrative modes, however, come striking weaknesses, and I think it is from these that the frequent note of self-parody derives.

There is nothing modern or post-modern in Motion's narrative mode. Its first rule, like the first rule of the well-made popular fiction, is to tell the reader *when* the events took place. These are the opening words or phrases of poems by Motion: 'Today . . .'; 'This summer . . .'; 'Past midnight now . . .'; 'Driving at dusk . . .'; 'There were floods, I remember, / our final spring in the place . . .'; 'Now . . .'; 'Midnight . . .'; 'A month home . . .'; . . . and 'That Easter night . . .'. When we add to this remarkable list the countless adverbials of time embedded in the subsequent texts of his poems, we see that Motion in fact approaches his poetry as a pulp writer of adventure fiction might approach the communication of essential data in his story. Not all the poems from which I have quoted opening words could be described as narrative poems, and not all the narrative poems have the same kind of content or purpose; so that this failure to differentiate registers comes to seem a major shortcoming in Motion's style. A related weakness, similar in that its function appears to be to hurl the reader into the story, is an opening such as that of **"The great man"**: 'It was straight out of Conrad but true.' The use of a pronoun strikingly lacking its referent is reminiscent of journalistic usage in the reportage of *Time* and *Newsweek;* though here, in fairness to Motion, we should add that in fact the narrator of **"The great man"** is himself a journalist, and thus this particular opening line may well be Andrew Motion's stylistic joke.

To push and propel his narratives on their way, Motion uses a mixture of elliptical constructions and filmic selection of scenic moments. Elliptical usages . . . [appear in] **"Inside and out"** and **"Dangerous Play"**, in the passages beginning (in each case) 'As if . . .', and may be seen again in [**"The Letter"**]. . . . Not only the elliptical syntax and the cinematically-caught momentary scenes (the vignette of her mother at the door, the abrupt shift of attention to take in the entirely new camera-shot of the German fighter), but also two dramatically demonstrative phrases, 'and there in the lane I am running' and 'But suddenly there it was', are wholly typical elements in Motion's narrative manner. Elsewhere in ***Secret Narratives*** we read 'and there was the man himself', 'there he was / gone', 'Then she was facing him', 'There we were: me running', 'Then he was dancing', and in ***Independence*** 'but here I am / by the window, stooping', 'Then I was home / and my servant ran to greet me / whispering', 'A sudden unthinking / surprised rush from your room', 'Then it was midnight, and over the wall / I dropped down', 'Then I was out', 'and we were away', 'Then you were screaming', . . . and so forth. In ***The Pleasure Steamers*** we can already find formulations like 'and here I am, walking' and 'And I am still there, / seeing your horse return'. Taken together with Motion's compulsive use of *-ing* forms, both gerundial and participial, this *but-suddenly* narrative mode becomes both tiresome and self-parodying. It extensively replaces in later work the injunction to *look* which at times lent an exclamatory, peremptory note to the first collection; in replacing it, it does not modify the imperative excitability. In Motion's narratives, there is often a breathlessness which would seem more in place in naive adventure fiction for adolescent readers; and, while to an extent Motion may indeed be deliberately adopting that genre's characteristics, his gain in doing so appears perplexingly slight. A less gasping narrative manner might often serve him better.

It is of course extremely significant that Andrew Motion works within a thoroughly familiar, indeed clichéd mode when writing narratives, for it is an essential part of those poems that they do not disturb the reader, but instead recall an Edwardian or Victorian procedure of agreed sequence and perspective. A similar familiarity is foregrounded in the poet's subject matter. The 'ghostly end-of-empire feeling' Peter Porter identified in Motion's writings [see excerpt above] is partly created by the familiar syntax and rhetoric, but equally by Motion's subject matter: in **"The pleasure steamers"**, ***Independence***, **"The letter"**, **"Resident at the club"**, **"On dry land"**, **"Bathing at Glymenopoulo"** and even (obliquely) **"Anne Frank Huis"**, the (specifically British) experience of two world wars is re-created, while other poems (**"The great man"**, **"One life"**, **"Dangerous play"**) share through their meetings of Europeans with Africa a colonial texture. References to military ranks, to derelict pill-boxes, to a hotel called the Majestic, even to steamers or to stag-hunting, help to consolidate a sense of a Britain which may be pre-1939 or may be pre-1914, but at all events belongs emphatically to a past which Motion is as unable to re-appropriate as that home he feels exiled from. Certainly, Motion is in this one of many spokesmen for a national sense of unaccommodation and loss; but what limits his value seriously is that . . . he makes no attempt to understand or evaluate the historical processes he describes, but is satisfied merely to present them, as any trader in nostalgia might. He also (like Philip Larkin, from whom he has clearly learnt a great deal) identifies Englishness by name: England, Bristol, Dartmoor, the Thames, the Cambridgeshire fenland, the North Sea, Essex, an Austin car, the Downs, London, Edward Lear, Princess Elizabeth, the World Service News, Darwin and Crusoe and Shakespeare, are all specified in poems, England repeatedly, as are non-English places (Gallipoli, India) which carry an especially high emotional charge in Britain. While none of this need be disturbing in itself, the absence of any critical commentary within the texture of the poetry suggests that the names are being deployed in a spirit of club-mentality response-programming, calling upon a collective sense of rallying and (if the word were not too suggestive of a different context) solidarity. Viewed like this, Andrew Motion's love affair with an elegiac longing for what is irretrievably lost in his own life can seem as politically suspect as his Thatcherite revival of the Empire; both his personal grief and his national nostalgia carry a political charge, since both are predicated upon scrutiny of the past rather than of the present. (pp. 77-80)

Much needs to be said about a number of Andrew Motion's poems, partly because the political and ethical implications of his writing are customarily lost sight of in debate of his narrative mode and the nature of fictionality. His fictionality, it seems to me, is intrinsically of very little interest, depending as it does on a small number of linguistic and rhetorical tricks which are neither novel nor used with much distinctive power. To discuss these tricks is to accept (or to risk accepting) the current orthodox view of textual invention as a kind of games-playing, predicated in relativity and thus finally lacking in answerability to the criteria of 'real' life. In fact Andrew Motion's poetry is based firmly in values; some of those values, I feel, need to be rejected (his affection for the imperial past, the death-wish implicit in his fixation with what is irretrievably gone), while others need to be accepted and welcomed (his openness to the plurality of experience, his emphasis on the central importance of a sense of belonging, accommodation, home). To urge a more responsible debate of Motion's poetry is only partly to imply that his writings always reward close scrutiny, for they do not; but he is widely read and widely considered to be at the heart of the new narrative poetry, and therefore the terms in which discussion are framed will matter. (pp. 80-1)

Michael Hulse, "'I Could Have Outlived Myself There': The Poetry of Andrew Motion," in Critical Quarterly, *Vol. 28, No. 3, Autumn, 1986, pp. 71-81.*

Percy Mtwa

19??-

South African dramatist and actor.

In his plays, Mtwa, a black South African, satirizes his country's racial policy of apartheid. His dramas generally feature short vignettes and combine such theatrical forms as comedy, tragedy, farce, vaudeville, political theater, and folk play. *Woza Albert!* (1981), a collaboration involving Mtwa, actor Mbongeni Ngema, and director Barney Simon, illustrates the conflicts and conditions associated with South African existence. A satirical fantasy in which Jesus Christ's second coming takes place in South Africa, *Woza Albert!* depicts the unsuccessful attempts of the Afrikaaner government to use the Savior for its own political purposes. Although Christ is sentenced to solitary confinement on Robben Island, a high-security prison for black political prisoners, he appears in a graveyard at the play's end to resurrect such black resistance leaders as Albert Luthuli and Stephen Biko. While some critics faulted *Woza Albert!* for repetition and predictability, many lauded the play's original approach. Jack Kroll commented: "Mtwa and Ngema provide an indispensable counterpoint to the work of white South Africans like Athol Fugard, Alan Paton and Nadine Gordimer, who bring the complications of their sensibilities to the vexed question of South Africa."

Mtwa's second play, *Bopha!* (1986), explores the predicament of black township police officers who antagonize and alienate fellow blacks by serving the white South African government. *Bopha!* depicts the relationship between two brothers: one is a career police sergeant, while the other enlists in the police force only because he is unable to secure other employment. After being reprimanded for arresting a white lawbreaker, the latter brother quits the force. The police sergeant resigns as well when his house is burned by angry blacks and his son is imprisoned for involvement with student activists. While some reviewers faulted *Bopha!* for lacking subtlety, most praised Mtwa's direct and powerful presentation of political realities. Jane Edwardes deemed *Bopha!* "agitprop theatre as it should be: sharp, satirical and stunning entertainment."

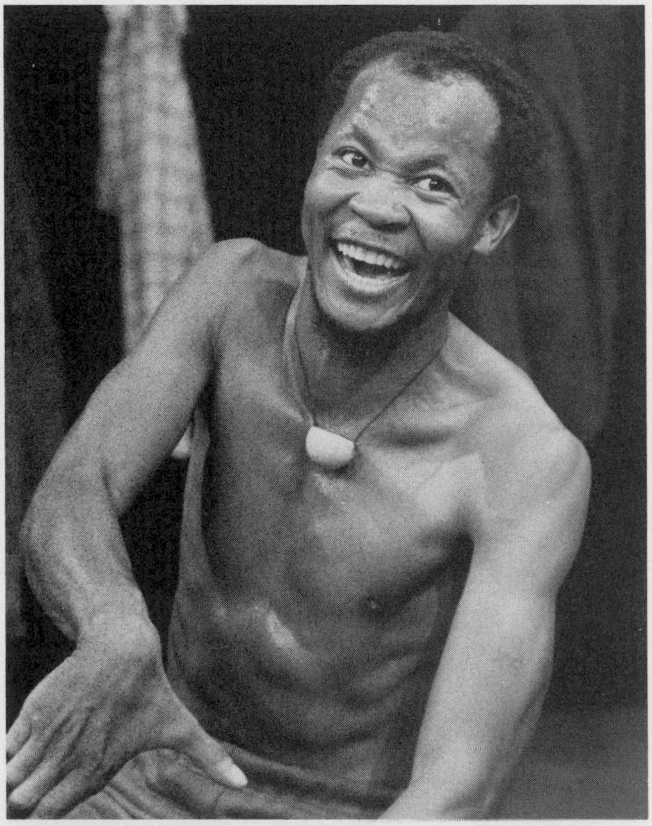

© Photograph by Chris Bennion

DOUGLAS WATT

The title of last night's two-man show . . . , ***Woza Albert!***, is a cry for a Zulu chieftain who defied the South African practice of apartheid to rise from the grave. And in the exultant finish to this 90-minute entertainment, a cemetery caretaker rouses a stranger sleeping by a tombstone, and together they call on all their black heroes to rise from their graves. But by that time our two winning and indefatigable players have just about worn us out.

This is a play only in the sense that its two young and exuberant black performers are continually at play as, in a series of mostly brief episodes, they illustrate various aspects of black life in South Africa, repeatedly calling upon or awaiting the arrival of their Deliverer, the Son of God, until that final outburst. It has neither the depth nor insight, and certainly not the power, of that earlier two-man black South African show, collaborated on and supervised by Athol Fugard, the twin bill of *Sizwe Bansi Is Dead* and *The Island*.

Instead, ***Woza Albert!*** is like a macabre vaudeville in which the two change roles by affixing bulbous rubber noses (for white characters) that hang from neck chains and donning one or another of the jackets on a pipe rack that, aside from a couple of crates, is the only "scenic" effect. . . .

They are hardly ever still as they limn the by-now familiar plight of Soweto blacks seeking employment in Johannesburg, try to account for lapses in their indispensable passbooks, beg for more of the slops they are dished out by their employers, deliver (as whites) official pronunciamentos, or kid around with each other. . . .

For what they do, they are excellent performers, skilled and astonishingly athletic. But what they do is both too little and too much: too much crowded into such a short space, and too litte attention given to individual subjects in their pell-mell race to imagined freedom.

Douglas Watt, " 'Woza Albert!': Macabre Vaudeville," in Daily News, *New York, February 24, 1984. Reprinted in* New York Theatre Critics' Reviews, *Vol. XXXXV, No. 3, 1984, p. 351.*

CLIVE BARNES

Can you be funny about South Africa? Is the racial segregation known there as Apartheid a fit subject for comic satire, even comic satire with a scalding hint of bitter tears?

Black South African actors Percy Mtwa and Mbongeni Ngema, and white South African director, Barney Simon, think so, and to prove their point they have devised a hilarious, corrosive, tragic, triumphant play about the survival of the human spirit called ***Woza Albert!*** . . .

[No] lover of the theater should miss [***Woza Albert!***]. It is basic theater—thought and emotion enclosed by an empty space and caught in a spotlight. . . .

There are between 20 and 30 sketches in the 90-minute intermissionless play. At first, it doesn't seem like a play. It is more like a revue—with bitter humor being directed at the so-called "black homelands," those tribal reservations South Africa puts aside for blacks.

But slowly—first almost as a side suggestion, a slight joke—the concept of Christ's return, he flies in on a South African Air jumbo jet, takes hold of the evening. The joke builds up . . . and explodes. There is a proud aftermath where hope is rallied and heroes recalled. The extraordinary evening is over. (p. 351)

[In ***Woza Albert!***, Mtwa and Ngema], and Simon their director, bring a whole world to vivid, vibrant life.

I could be their political opponent—the most boorish of Boars—and still admire them. They are wonderful.

And at the end—with their clarion call for political justice—as the new Christ raises like Lazarus, heroes of their cause, from the dead Albert Luthuli (leader of the African National Congress and Nobel Prize winner) flew a litany of martyrs and rebels, we rejoice in their courage.

Thus, the play's title—***Woza Albert!***. It means: Rise up Luthuli! But as Mtwa and Ngema raise our safe Liberal enthusiasm with their incantation, we must not forget what we have learned of Soweto, Albert Street, Robben Island and other placenames in the topography of man's inhumanity to man. See ***Woza Albert!*** You may see nothing quite like it again. (p. 352)

Clive Barnes, " 'Albert': Masterpiece Out of South Africa," in New York Post, *February 24, 1984. Reprinted in* New York Theatre Critics' Reviews, *Vol. XXXXV, No. 3, 1984, pp. 351-52.*

FRANK RICH

In ***Woza Albert!*** a new theater piece from South Africa, the gifted actors Percy Mtwa and Mbongeni Ngema play a wide variety of roles in a mosaic of roughly two dozen scenes. One of those scenes seems to summon up all the cruelty of apartheid.

The setting is outside the Pass Office on Albert Street, Johannesburg, where black laborers must wait endlessly for work permits and beg for jobs from potential white employers. Mr. Mtwa and Mr. Ngema play two such laborers. Facing us from the edge of the stage, they wave their passbooks and boast of their menial skills—all the while distorting their faces into wide, subservient smiles and stooping their bodies into postures of desperate supplication. And as they do so, the audience implicitly assumes the roles of the white men who are callously passing by. Pretty soon we feel the degradation of slavery—for both blacks and whites—as though it were a lash.

I wish I could say that the rest of ***Woza Albert!*** had as much bite. . . .

But much of ***Woza Albert!***—which was created by the actors in collaboration with Mr. Simon—seems predictable and mild. It lacks the blunt visceral impact of last season's similarly folkloric pageant of apartheid, *Poppie Nongena,* not to mention the impaling force of sophisticated works by such South African writers as Athol Fugard and Nadine Gordimer.

The show's intentions are satirical. ***Woza Albert!*** is a parable about what might happen if Jesus Christ were to descend on South Africa—by jumbo jet from Jerusalem. In many of the vignettes, we watch blacks tell a television interviewer what they expect from the Saviour, and those wishes are poignantly humble—from decent food to, most crushingly, real homes where men can at last live full time with their wives and children. The white government, meanwhile, at first tries to exploit Christ for its own nefarious purposes and then brands Him a Communist agitator. Eventually, He is locked up in solitary on Robben Island, along with the nation's political prisoners.

There is a great deal of repetition in the unfolding of this fable, and not nearly the quotient of humor the running time demands. One gets the feeling that a decent idea for a 20-minute sketch has been stretched to fill out an evening. ***Woza Albert!*** is at its impassioned best when it is dramatizing the harsh conditions of South Africa and the brave resilience of those who endure those conditions. The scenes of prison and deadening manual labor gnaw at us as the cute and more numerous comic sequences do not. . . .

It's in the final sequence that the meaning of the work's title becomes clear. The word "woza" means "rise up," and, at the end, Christ appears at a graveyard to resurrect dissident political heroes such as Albert Luthuli and Steven Biko. Watching Mr. Mtwa and Mr. Ngema dance in joy, we, too, are captured by this fantasy. But ***Woza Albert!*** makes South Africa's tragedy immediate only on those few occasions when it reminds us that the Saviour, as of yet, has failed to show up.

Frank Rich, "Two Actors in 'Woza Albert!': A Parable of Apartheid," in The New York Times, *February 24, 1984, p. C3.*

HOWARD KISSEL

[In ***Woza Albert!***], we see two innocent South African blacks, who suffer from economic and racial oppression, awaiting the return of Christ. He arrives by jumbo jet from Jerusalem and immediately falls athwart the white authorities, who treat him as brutally as they do the blacks. Only His knack for making comebacks—even when dead—enables Him to survive their assault.

The idea is certainly interesting but it probably could have been handled in a short, pointed sketch. Here it has been attenuated into a 90-minute play in which virtually every idea of interest is repeated and overdone to a point where it has almost no impact.

If one can learn anything from ***Woza Albert!*** it is the way theatricality can be used as a way to evade drama. ***Woza*** employs many techniques we associate with improvisation and "story theater." The actors make wonderful use of their voices to create the effect of trains, trucks, tools, musical instruments. It is an enormously demanding show for them physically—

they must mime much hard labor, much strenuous activity. But ultimately all that this exertion amounts to is an entertaining way to present platitudes. It appears imaginative—but how much more imaginative and meaningful (not to say moving) it might be had half this effort gone into writing a real play.

Another point must be made. Having the two actors imitate poor, naive blacks or, by having them don round clown noses, represent pompous whites, we see them as creatures of the theater—animated, fanciful, clowning. We can't really take them seriously. They're just too cute. If an apartheid apologist like John Vorster had wanted to show us "happy natives" to whom it is easy to condescend he couldn't have done a more effective job.

Mtwa and Ngema are clearly talented and skillful actors, but their craft is never really stretched or tested, because the material is meant merely to galvanize the already faithful. At the final preview I attended, a middle-aged white woman down the row from me stood and yelled bravo (which has become automatic—I saw the same response earlier this season at *Marilyn, A Musical Fable*). As if aware that something more was required to show how deeply she was moved, she shouted, "Thank you!"

For what? For teaching us something new about the way the world works? For any sort of unpredictable theatrical perceptions? No. Largely for reinforcing her—and our—complacency.

Howard Kissel, in a review of "Woza Albert!," in Women's Wear Daily, *February 24, 1984. Reprinted in* New York Theatre Critics' Reviews, *Vol. XXXXV, No. 3, 1984, p. 352.*

CATHARINE HUGHES

Anyone who attends the theater other than purely for entertainment is likely to be familiar with the plays of the white South African playwright Athol Fugard, among them *Master Harold . . . and the Boys, The Blood Knot* and *A Lesson From Aloes*. ***Woza Albert!*** is something entirely different, a distinctly black reaction, one that is far more visceral than intellectual, to some of the same concerns.

With humor, passion and sheer drive, two young black South African actors, Percy Mtwa and Mbongeni Ngema . . . , portray the harsh and humbling existence of the black man in South Africa. In the course of the 90 minutes in which they are on stage, the audience sees them depict what it means to rely on the passbooks that are essential to their existence and hears their scathing but funny reaction to the "black homelands" that the Government proposes as the solution to all the nation's racial problems. With the thread that ties all the diverse skits together, the play shows what the second coming of Christ, this time to the black of South Africa, might mean. . . .

Like much polemical theater, ***Woza Albert!*** suffers from its oversimplifications, but its cry of pain—and sometimes of expectation and joy—can be ignored no more than can be the more theoretically sophisticated pleas for freedom being voiced by [Janusz] Glowacki, [Vaclav] Havel and so many others who have found in theater a means to express both their anger and their hope. (p. 282)

Catharine Hughes, "Where Theatre Matters," in America, *Vol. 150, No. 14, April 14, 1984, pp. 281-2.*

ROGER DOWNEY

The Republic of South Africa is a split society, and its art reflects that schizophrenia: on the one hand, the polished, thoughtful prose of Nadine Gordimer and the poetic plays of Athol Fugard; on the other, the raucous popular music of the black slums of Johannesburg and Cape Town. . . .

[***Woza Albert!***] combines the divergent strands of South African culture, in one joyous, utterly sane, and overwhelmingly theatrical whole. The play has left audiences (and critics) gasping wherever it has been presented.

As impressive as the show itself is the story of its creation. Despite suspicion, misunderstanding, and an immense cultural gap, two ambitious, apolitical, black street entertainers got together with a politically radical, white, Jewish director trained in the avant-garde theater of Joseph Chaikin. Thus was one of the most exuberantly successful theater pieces of modern times created. . . .

Mtwa and Ngema give us a vivid, unsentimental portrait of life in the streets, markets, factories, and segregated townships of South Africa. Morena, or Christ, carries his message of peace and brotherhood to the people, only to be met with incomprehension on both sides of the racial barrier.

Roger Downey, "African Albert," in Horizon: A Magazine of the Arts, *Vol. XXVII, No. 5, June, 1984, p. 8.*

JANE EDWARDES

Bopha! (meaning 'Arrest!'), seen in Edinburgh last summer, is both a sympathetic explanation of why black South Africans become policemen thus enforcing a legal system which deprives their own kind of the most basic human rights and an exhortation to those same people to give up their jobs and to end the divisions within their families. The story may be simple but the technique is not. Using song, dance, gross caricature and comic scenarios, . . . three exciting actors know exactly how to make their point as they depict a black man, forced by financial circumstances to join the police, doggedly carrying out his duties until he is ordered to fire on a funeral procession attended by his own son. If the effect is rousing in Britain, it must be explosive in the townships. Not as imaginative or inventive as ***Woza Albert!***, this is nevertheless agitprop theatre as it should be: sharp, satirical and stunning entertainment.

Jane Edwardes, in a review of "Bopha!," in Time Out, *January 5, 1987. Reprinted in* London Theatre Record, *Vol. VII, No. 1, January 1-14, 1987, p. 21.*

MARTIN HOYLE

One of the more bewildering aspects of the South African agony, to outsiders at least, is the attitude of the black police. As [***Bopha!***] reveals, black brutality to black is a vital component of the present régime. Does becoming a policeman in the Republic automatically make a black man callous towards even his own? Or—a theory held in other continents besides Africa—does a police career attract a certain type in the first place? . . .

[***Bopha!*** is a] study of a black family's involvement with a police station where "we speak one language—bopha!" This means "arrest," resorted to for a multitude of crimes (a black is dragged from a whites only toilet, his trousers down) but applied selectively. As the sergeant earnestly reminds a newcomer, "The law say, never arrest a white man." . . .

We meet a black police sergeant, devoted to the force his father and grandfather served, and a comic disciplinarian in his domestic life. His student son is involved with activists, while his brother joins the police through expediency but resigns after humorously sabotaging the system (arresting a blubbering white man, for instance).

The sergeant, too, eventually resigns after his house is destroyed by petrol bombs. We are reminded of deaths in custody: cell suicides, falls from high windows during interrogation, "slipping in the shower"; of shanty homes wrecked and children shot in the back by frightened officers "doing the impossible for the ungrateful," as they put it.

As long as "there's security in the police force" it seems unlikely that black policemen will emulate the (literal) *volteface* at the Bastille and turn their guns on their masters. While [***Bopha!***] offers little insight into broader and deeper issues, it provides brisk, well-drilled playing in its episodic narrative. . . .

Martin Hoyle, in a review of "Bopha!," in Financial Times, *January 9, 1987. Reprinted in* London Theatre Record, *Vol. VII, No. 1, January 1-14, 1987, p. 22.*

MILTON SHULMAN

[***Bopha!***'s] one novel contribution is its partly accusatory and partly sympathetic look at the poor wretches who make up the black police force of the South African regime.

Like all policemen who have to support the State in a revolutionary or insurrectionist situation, the problem of divided loyalties is an added burden to the already onerous task of maintaining law and order.

But the strains must be almost intolerable in a racially segregated society where white officers expect loyalty from men they deride and ridicule, and where apartheid demands that black police live among the very people who consider them traitors.

What happens to the two policemen, who are brothers, in ***Bopha!,*** which means "arrest," is predictable. In their job, they are confronted with pathetic figures who have been charged with using white men's toilets, who have lost their pass cards, who complain that their family has not been told a son has committed suicide in prison, who have no place to sleep because their shack has been burnt down in a police operation.

Through a series of short scenes that shade from realism to symbolism, three actors . . . contrast the strict discipline needed for their well-drilled routines with the breakdown of their loyalties when one of their sons is accused of being a Communist and is flung into jail for not informing on his schoolmates. . . .

Since the play is an agitprop exercise with little regard for objectivity, it is impossible to assess from this distance whether this picture of universally stupid, brutal and crass white officers is anywhere near authenticity. It would have been a more effective work if only someone with a white skin had possessed a tiny flicker of humanity or compassion.

Milton Shulman, in a review of "Bopha!," in London Evening Standard, *January 9, 1987. Reprinted in* London Theatre Record, *Vol. VII, No. 1, January 1-14, 1987, p. 23.*

EDWARD PEARCE

Imagine three Africans in track suits singing a glee in Tswana then proceeding by the liquid and balletic means to send up the South African police drill in a style to throw Vincente Minnelli and you have the impressive opening to Percy Mtwa's own production of his play ***Bopha!***

The purple-faced friends of South Africa will doubtless object to the production of "agitprop" by the National Theatre. In fact what Mr Mtwa has written is a morality play, secular and irritatingly scatological at times, but lithe and cost-effective in its impact. The story could hardly be simpler. Take three blacks. One is an established, conservative policeman who loves the force, the second a sceptical homelands relative who, barred from work at anything else, joins the police. (One of the play's best lines: "There's only one way to beat influx control, join the South African police", fell upon wooden ears). The third black, Zwelakhe . . . , is a policeman's son and a radical of a mild, perhaps oversanitised sort.

The facts of South Africa, of everyday life in a township police station, then simply happen to them. (pp. 22-3)

First the whites are on top and the black policeman must humiliate himself, arresting a black for using a white toilet, then being officially reprimanded for also taking in a white who has urinated in public. Later comes the violence: "A woman was injured by a stray rubber bullet from a stray police force" and the balance of horror shifts. "There is smoke", says one character, "from burning people". Quite good at stop-you-dead one-liners is Mr Mtwa. For the burning necklaces saluted by the Mary Tudor of the townships, Winnie Mandela, have arrived. Finally they reach the door of the loyal black policeman, Njandini. . . . He gives up sucking on his pipe and demanding discipline and improbably joins with his own people and, as it were, throws in the sjambok. Even less probably he is instantly welcome. The message to an audience in Alexandra is not an artistic one. It is a play which any self respecting Minister of the Interior would ban if his writ ran to the Church Halls of the townships. . . .

As a piece of theatre it is crudely good, doing what it means to do, making them laugh, making them cry and making them scared in about equal proportions. Although verbally it is rougher than it is altogether ready. . . .

But this is theatre intended for township Africans on which a London audience eavesdrops. One senses Mr Mtwa's own unease at the horror of things on his own side. "Policemen killing people, people killing policemen", but the morality tale has *realpolitik* and Machiavelli in its weft—join the winning side.

For an 80-minute performance, as much sketch as play, it arouses disquiet, admiration and an uneasy feeling, in the case of somebody else's crisis, of being very close and real. (p. 23)

Edward Pearce, in a review of "Bopha!," in Daily Telegraph, *January 10, 1987. Reprinted in* London Theatre Record, *Vol. VII, No. 1, January 1-14, 1987, pp. 22-3.*

MICHAEL BILLINGTON

There is a natural liberal tendency to heap indiscriminate praise on all black productions coming out of South Africa. But we have seen enough now to start making distinctions. Percy Mtwa's ***Bopha!*** . . . is highly unusual in that it deploys the skill and energy of its three actors to pinpoint a tragic dilemma: that of the poor, jobless black who joins the South African police force to make a living and in so doing becomes a traitor to his own people.

Mtwa's play doesn't condemn: it attempts to explain. We see Naledi, born in the Johannesburg suburbs and lacking either income or passbook, enlisting in the police. For him it is a matter of survival: for his brother Njandini policing is an inherited family trade. And the different motivations of the siblings highlight the ludicrous double-standards the police have to enforce. Njandini plays by the rules in arresting a black for defecating in a white man's toilet; Naledi breaks them by arresting a white man for urinating in the street.

To complicate matters, Njandini's schoolboy son takes part in a peaceful funeral protest which ends in violence with the police shooting kids in the back. Njandini, in charge of the police contingent, sees his son imprisoned, his house burned down, and his whole faith in the law-enforcement ethic destroyed.

What is surprising is how much Mtwa manages to cram into 80 minutes. He not only gives us a domestic tragedy, he also delineates the impossible position of the black police. They are expected, as someone says, to be ministers, social workers, and Rambos, they are professionally obliged to buttress a detested system and they have to practise massive self-deception. Branded ''pigs'' by their own people, they kid themselves the initial letters stand for power, intelligence, and guts. This is possibly the most psychologically revealing point Mtwa makes: that to exist at all the black South African police have to cut off part of their consciousness and surrender to the commissioner's make-believe vaunt at the passing-out parade that they are the most envied force in the world.

TV documentaries have given us many of the facts: Mtwa's play and production impinge on our imagination.

Michael Billington, in a review of ''Bopha!,'' in The Guardian, *January 10, 1987. Reprinted in* London Theatre Record, *Vol. VII, No. 1, January 1-14, 1987, p. 22.*

R(asipuram) K(rishnaswami) Narayan

1906-

© Jerry Bauer

Indian novelist, short story writer, essayist, memoirist, travel writer, journalist, critic, and editor.

Widely considered India's foremost author writing in English, Narayan is noted for his creation of Malgudi, a fictitious village set in southern India which most critics consider a composite of his birthplace of Madras and his adult residence of Mysore. Writing in a spare, straightforward style derived from India's oral and literary traditions, Narayan uses wry, sympathetic humor to examine the universalized conflicts of Malgudi, usually focusing on ordinary characters who seek self-awareness through their struggles with ethical dilemmas. All of Narayan's characters, in accordance with principles of Hinduism, retain a calm, dignified acceptance of fate. Although critics often compare Narayan's creation of Malgudi to William Faulkner's fictional Yoknapatawpha County, most agree with Charles R. Larson's assessment: ''While Faulkner's vision remains essentially grotesque, Narayan's has been predominantly comic, reflecting with humor the struggle of the individual to find peace within the framework of public life.''

In his early fiction, Narayan makes use of personal experience to address conflicts between Indian and Western culture. His first novel, *Swami and Friends: A Novel of Malgudi* (1935), chronicles an extroverted schoolboy's rebellion against his missionary upbringing. Narayan's next work, *The Bachelor of Arts* (1937), depicts an idealistic college student who attacks the bourgeois order but eventually reconciles himself to an obedient, lawful existence. In *The English Teacher* (1945; published in the United States as *Grateful to Life and Death*), an educator who endures the premature death of his wife overcomes his grief through religion and philosophy. These novels, like Narayan's later works, were noted for his natural and unaffected language, his subtle humor, and his ability to transform a particular lifestyle into a universal human experience.

Narayan's novels written after 1945 blend humor and pathos in their portrayals of middle-class Indian characters who must reconcile Western ideals of financial and personal success with everyday reality. *Mr. Sampath* (1949; published in the United States as *The Printer of Malgudi*) chronicles a village printer's unsuccessful attempt to become a film producer. In *The Financial Expert* (1952), a man who makes his living obtaining loans for Malgudi's lower classes becomes wealthy by publishing a pornographic book but loses his money after provoking an influential businessman into discrediting him. *Waiting for the Mahatma* (1955), one of Narayan's few works to deal overtly with political themes, recounts the adventures of a man whose love for a young woman leads him to attempt to sabotage Mahatma Gandhi's peace movement.

The Guide (1958) is usually considered Narayan's most accomplished and popular novel. In this work, a former convict named Raju is mistaken for a holy man upon his arrival in Malgudi. Implored by the villagers to avert a famine, Raju is unable to convince them that he is a fraud. Deciding to embrace the role the townspeople have thrust upon him, Raju dies during a prolonged fast and is revered as a saint. In *The Sweet-Vendor* (1967; published in the United States as *The Vendor of Sweets*), a merchant abandons his profession and his family concerns for a life of tranquility and meditation. Ironic aspects of the clash between Indian and Western cultures are again examined in *The Painter of Signs* (1976), in which an Indian bachelor begins to question traditional mores after he falls in love with a female propagandizer for national birth control. Eve Auchincloss commented: ''[So] poised, so balanced a writer is Narayan, his sympathy and amusement so large, that even God's design for an overpopulated India seems defensible.''

In *A Tiger for Malgudi* (1983), Narayan makes use of Indian legends and folktales to suggest that beasts may be as capable of thought and feeling as human beings. Narrated by a tiger, this novel traces the animal's spiritual development in overcoming its potential for violence. According to Carlo Coppola, ''Narayan seems to be saying that not only is the universe basically one, but that animals too may attain spiritual growth . . . without assuming human form.'' Narayan's recent novel, *Talkative Man* (1986), addresses the tendency of Indians to overestimate Europeans. In this work, a journalist known as ''Talkative Man'' defends a mysterious stranger who arrives in Malgudi claiming to work for the United Nations but who is eventually revealed to be a con man.

Narayan's short stories, many written for the Madras newspaper *Hindu*, are praised for the same qualities that distinguish his novels. *Malgudi Days and Other Stories* (1941), *An Astrologer's Day and Other Stories* (1947), *Lawley Road and Other Stories* (1956), *Old and New* (1981), and *Under the Banyan Tree and Other Stories* (1985) are among his best-known collections. Narayan's travel books include two works on his native country, *Mysore* (1939) and *The Emerald Route* (1977), as well as *My Dateless Diary* (1960), an account of his travels in the United States. Narayan has also published *The Ramayana: A Shortened Modern Prose Version of the Indian Epic* (1972) and *The Mahabharata: A Shortened Modern Prose Version of the Indian Epic* (1978).

(See also *CLC*, Vols. 7, 28 and *Contemporary Authors*, Vols. 81-84.)

WILLIAM WALSH

Narayan's fifty years of writing fiction have left him with a faithful following, a distinguished reputation, and if not a great deal of critical attention—outside India, that is, where he has received pretty well every mark of that country's national distinction—at least the appreciation of novelists as different from one another as Somerset Maugham and E. M. Forster, each of whom has admired his low-toned but distinctive individuality, his unaffected literary *persona* and his professional dedication. (p. 163)

[An inner tranquility and unforced assurance] distinguish Narayan's fiction from so much Western fiction. This latter is a fiction which exists in a world of abstraction and technique and which derives its meanings and values from an unappeased appetite for change. (p. 164)

[Narayan is] a writer who is independent enough to abstain from fashionable abstractions in order to concentrate upon the particular, upon the exact stress, the precise tone, the exact feeling in the actual situation. Not that Narayan's stories are simply exercises in a specialism of the moment. They contain structures larger than this—lines of feeling, directions of attention, clusters of notions. But none of these is rarefied enough to be a generalisation of the contemporary kind. They are rather a thickening of the narrative line, a denser shading in the angle of a drawing, or chalky deposit in the joints of the characters. The thought in these stories is never at any great distance from the details. Instead of generalisations we have perceptions which are sharp, biting, immersed in the actual.

The effect on the reader is twofold. The world—or worlds—dealt with in the stories strikes him as enjoying an objective existence independent of the contribution of the author. There it is, existing with a certain solidity and authority. On the other hand, the attitude of the author is modest and unobstructive. It has the air of being dependent on, and responsive to, things outside himself. Actuality, one feels, is not being bullied or tricked into false positions. Nor is it being sucked up into some dominating and abstract symbolising system.

But, of course, there is a symbolic system, or rather universe, sustaining the fiction and attaching to its common particulars and events more profound, more richly orchestrated meanings derived from the history and experience of a whole race. At some points (the symbolic structure is never a matter of simple one-to-one correspondence) the symbolic pressure becomes if not explicit at least more insistent, as for example, in the sense of traditional holiness and divinity irradiating the dilapidated temple and embodied in the mysterious priest in ***The Financial Expert***. . . . But it is never necessary for the reader to have Narayan's complete familiarity with the Hindu myths and legends or his easy intimacy with *The Ramayana* and the *Mahabharata*. Such knowledge, at least if it were of the instinctive sort which Narayan claimed most of the millions in India had of the essential part of the epic, and its main figures, Rama and Sita, would only be of use to the reader if it were added to the essential qualification for the reader, a sensitive response to Narayan's original vision and independent sensibility. The truth is that the Hindu myths and religious parables, like D. H. Lawrence's Congregational hymns, are important not as theological scaffolding to the fiction but in being part of a whole economy of feeling itself sunk deep into the constitution of the novelist. These things are present and influential not as dogma or metaphysics but as part of a mode of perception and a habit of reaction. They flow in and out of the writer's thought and touch. The religious sense of Indian myth is part of Narayan's grip of reality, of his particular view of human life and his individual way of placing and ordering human feeling and experience. What one can say about Narayan without qualification is that he embodies the pure spirit of Hinduism. In Narayan Hinduism appears at the natural sub-stratum of a sensibility pre-occupied with individuality, with the specific, with particularisation. Not that he is concerned with a mere ticked collection of particulars. Each detail is seen and presented so as to imply an essential truth about its own nature, just as the aggregate of details is raised from a simple collection to an order or world or portrait. A detail in Narayan is not only close to the essential object but it contributes its part to a significant whole.

What this means is that Narayan's mind sees existence very much in the way of the ordinary man, except that in our case, our observation of a new fact or detail is relatively gross, relatively erratic. But what is blurred in us by inappropriate pre-conception or dimmed by reminiscence is in Narayan both natural and fresh, expected and surprising. Again, one must say that there is deeply in Narayan the profound Hindu conviction, or instinct for, the fundamental oneness of existence. But this sense operates in harmony with a quick feeling for the instantaneous present: an appreciation of the multiple and dispersed nature of existence. The tension between the one and the many, a sustaining theme of Hinduism, operates quietly and unpretentiously throughout Narayan's fiction. . . . [For] example, in ***The Financial Expert***, the one substance of money is both realised in and resisted by many guises, as coin, as a prey hunted by loan-forms, as a solid medium of exchange, a shadowy sophistication of capital movements, and even as a godhead to be worshipped. The general and specific create no friction in Narayan even in those places where philosophic Indian myths influence the text and the sub-text. This is because the metaphysical element creates no more than the faintest resonance under a meticulously accurate surface. . . . In Narayan Brahminical detachment never stands between the writer and a close and appreciative contact with his human subject. There is sadness in Narayan at a human capacity for deception and victimisation but never sourness, bitterness or disgust. The sadness comes from the most intimate experience at the centre of so many of his novels, namely the painful experience of dismantling the routine self (which the context, being Indian, seems less a private possession than something distilled by powerful and ancient conventions) and the reconstitution of another personality. The comedy arises from the sometimes bumbling, sometimes desperate, sometimes absurd exploration of different experiences in the search for a new, and it may be, an exquisitely inappropriate, role. The complex theme of Narayan's serious comedies, then, is the rebirth of self and the process and conditions of its pregnancy or education. Friction between the two parts of the composition is prevented by a subtle sense of acceptance, secreted both by the inclusive and tolerant attitude of the author, and an attitude of wry acceptance by the characters. These characters occupy a universe of which the substantial features are both the flux of being and the plurality of being. . . . To the author this is the nature of reality; to the characters living their day to day life, it is what they will, perhaps, with a moderate kind of happiness, finally accommodate themselves to.

Narayan's fastidious art, blending exact realism, poetic myth, sadness, perception and gaiety, is without precedent in literature in English and, as far as one can see, without following. It is kind but unsentimental, mocking but uncynical, profoundly Indian but distinctively individual. It fascinates by reason of the authenticity and attractiveness of its Indian setting, and engages because of the substantial human nature which it implies and embodies. It carries along with it at every point a kind of humour strange in English writing which mixes the melancholy and the amusing. Perhaps it is in this humour that there lies its deepest wisdom, which communicates a sense, crisp and unrebellious, of human limitation, and an appreciation, positively amiable but quite without illusion, of human achievement. (pp. 165-69)

William Walsh, in his R. K. Narayan: A Critical Appreciation, *The University of Chicago Press, 1982, 176 p.*

EDMUND FULLER

[Narayan's] mortal hand and eye have gentled lovingly the tiger's fearful symmetry in a charming novella, ***A Tiger for Malgudi.*** This fable takes us into the mind of Raja, a magnificent tiger, 11 feet from tip of nose to tip of tail. He is the narrator, except for a few third-person interludes. Don't question the logic of this; it is the given premise of the tale.

Raja, discovering how easy it is to seize stragglers from the sheep and cattle being driven into the villages for the night, becomes lazy and careless. A rash blunder leads to his capture by the people of Malgudi in spite of their fright and confusion. He is taken off their hands by an animal-taming circus proprietor. A movie maker wants to cast Raja as the adversary of a dim-brained human hulk named Jaggu, in a man-beast mini-epic. . . .

The project becomes a farcical fiasco. Raja, in spite of essential good will, can be innocently lethal. ". . . my species has an unfortunate reputation, and one's natural actions are misconstrued." Escaping, he wanders into the village school, throws it into panic and once again is cornered. An impasse.

Then appears a mysterious swami whom Raja recognizes at once as his master, and who chides the frightened villagers: "Never use the words *beast* or *brute*. They're ugly words coined by man in his arrogance. The human being thinks all other creatures are 'beasts.' Awful word!"

Raja, resentful of whips and prods, responds to the quiet psychic authority of the master and understands his words. They depart together for a mountain retreat, Raja unshackled, trotting along quietly, throwing panic into those who see him pass. There are funny, touching scenes on the mountain in which we learn something of the past of the master, whose gentle mysticism brings charm and a touch of practical reality to the close, as Raja ages. It is a lovely little book, at times a bit wordy and repetitious in some of its broader farce. Bear with it, for the closing section is most warming.

Edmund Fuller, "The Gentleness of a Beast and the Beastliness of Subversion," in The Wall Street Journal, *August 22, 1983, p. 14.*

ANITA DESAI

William Walsh [see excerpt above] has put forward the theory that the source of Narayan's deceptively gentle and elusive strength as a writer lies in his "rootedness" as contrasted to the "uprootedness" that is the theme of most Western fiction, the malady that is making it sicken and turn pale. Professor Walsh does not seem to be aware that in the 50 years that Narayan has been writing his tranquil fiction, his "rootedness" has become as unique in India as it is in the West, the traditional structure of rural existence that he celebrates having given way and collapsed irrevocably under the manifold pressures of an industrialized, urbanized and above all uncontrollable population. There are many of Narayan's readers who feel that his fiction does not reflect the chaos, the drift, the *angst* that characterizes a society in transition and that his "rootedness" is a relic of another, pastoral era now shaken and threatened beyond recovery. In criticizing him for what they see as a lack, they do not credit that it belongs not only to India's past but also to Narayan's. It could be on account of his constant peregrinations on two continents, as a reaction to physical flux, that when he takes up his pen he uses it as a compass to help his mind search out the stillness and stability of his memories of his earliest, "rooted" stage of existence. (p. 3)

[V. S. Naipaul] found a similarity between the world he had known as a child in the West Indies and Narayan's little town of Malgudi. "Disturbance, instability, development lay elsewhere; we, who had lost our wars and were removed from great events were at peace." . . . Naipaul understood the atmosphere, the pace, the rhythm of Malgudi perfectly because he had experienced it himself, on a different shore, yet he had rejected it and moved on, away; and when John Updike compared the work of the two authors, he found them at opposite poles of that once-colonial, now Third World—Naipaul harshly critical, castigating its laziness and delusion, and Narayan's attitude calmly fatalistic. Moreover, Naipaul used the Third World as a metaphor, an illustration for his philosophy of history, while Narayan shied away from anything abstract and theoretical, choosing to concern himself only with what is palpable and evident. . . . Updike examines Narayan's world closely as presented in the little stories that made up an earlier book, ***Malgudi Days,*** and . . . [finds] that poverty, cruelty and injustice are presented with "a touch of complacence and insubstantiality." Both underrate the dubious, skeptical tone that lies at the heart of [Narayan's] characteristic irony.

If one might accuse Narayan of failing to reflect recent political or social developments, one cannot accuse him of a lack of growth in his own world, Malgudi. The truth is that Narayan's voice as an author is in so low a key, the scale of his imagined world so small, that it can easily be overlooked. ***A Tiger for Malgudi*** is moreover a further stage in Narayan's own development as a novelist in that he does introduce "uprooted" characters to the scene. The circus ringmaster, Captain, not only travels constantly with the Grand Malgudi Circus and devises new ways of adding to its fame and coffers but also shows a constant change and fluctuation in his relationships with the animals he trains and with his wife, Rosie, the trapeze artiste. The Master who eventually tames the tiger is seen to have been an ordinary greedy businessman who goes through many stages of renunciation and penance to arrive at the state of *samadhi* in a cave in the forest where he fasts and meditates. The tiger undergoes the most radical change of all—from a vigorous beast of prey turned man-eater through sheer fury and frustration while in training to the gentle, ineffectual creature who has to be led to a zoo because he can no longer hunt and feed himself. But to Narayan these signs of outer development are only reflections of inner evolution: it is within that the true action always takes place, hence the superficial impression given of all change being too trivial to be of any note and of all his creatures being boringly, maddeningly "at peace." Updike summed up his theme as "Small lives seek their own solution within an insoluble mass" [see *CLC*, Vol. 28], which is surely heroism of a kind.

For all its philosophical basis, however, this novel is refreshing, like all Narayan's stories, precisely because it avoids abstractions and concentrates upon the concrete and particular. One is tempted to read the simple tale as a fable: the tiger representing the Seeker within the soul; the infant cub gamboling in the forest, the fiery youth snarling at the indignities and injustices of the circus, the aged creature finding tranquility at the feet of the Master and finally accepting the zoo as a kind of release from life, thus following the traditional cycle of Hindu life in India. It might sound like a rather precious device to transfer an ancient philosophical system onto a tiger, but Narayan can write of even outlandish topics like tigers and circuses and make them sound as familiar and commonplace as a cup of coffee and a newspaper.

As Naipaul says, he is "such a natural writer, so true to his experience and emotion" that no word ever rings false. When Captain is killed by a blow from the tiger's paw, his wife "stood looking at the body without a word or a tear; and when others tried to comfort her, said 'Leave me alone.' After that she went back to the circus tent, climbed to the top where the swings were clamped, took out one, took a full swing up and down, and when the swing touched the ceiling, let go her hold. . . ." There, only a very assured and very accomplished novelist could have brought that off, taking one's breath away at the smoothness and skill, so practiced as to be almost imperceptible. The language is simplicity itself, totally unaffected, the language of the ordinary man in the Indian streets, the man for whom the newspaper middles and the Sunday supplements are written, the "small lives" that "seek their own solution." (pp. 3, 9)

Anita Desai, "R. K. Narayan and the Grand Malgudi Circus," in Book World—The Washington Post, *September 4, 1983, pp. 3, 9.*

NOEL PERRIN

Beginning with ***Swami and Friends*** back in 1935, R. K. Narayan has now written a round dozen novels about Malgudi, his imaginary city in southern India. Because Mr. Narayan is probably the best of the Indian novelists who write in English and because Malgudi in all its god-soaked and humanity-drenched Indianness is so fully evoked, a lot of Americans derive their basic impression of Indian life from his work. That includes many who have never read a line of Mr. Narayan. His ideas now spread by osmosis as well as by direct contact, just as Mailer's or Hemingway's do in India.

A Tiger for Malgudi, the 12th in the series, is quite different from the others. The most obvious but not the most important difference is that it contains a talking animal. In fact, it's mostly narrated by one. Raja, the tiger, tells his own story: his early life in the jungle, his days with the Malgudi circus, his brief movie career, his final liberation from spiritual tigerhood by a holy man. The summary inevitably sounds comic, but the book itself isn't. Raja's enlightenment is meant seriously. . . .

What really distinguishes ***A Tiger for Malgudi*** from the other Malgudi novels is that Mr. Narayan is no longer much interested in the dailiness of life or the particularity of people. Or of tigers either. The book is god-soaked, all right, but it is distinctly not drenched with humanity. Most of the flavor of Malgudi is missing.

In the past, Mr. Narayan has had two main themes. He has written about the conflict for Indians between the enormous, overwhelming sense of duty they feel toward all blood relations and their frequent desire for a merely personal life. And he has written about the conflict between cool Western efficiency and warm Hindu inefficiency. . . .

[In his early works, neither] of Mr. Narayan's themes is explicit. Both are embedded in plots of wild complexity and in multitudes of vividly drawn characters and scenes.

In ***A Tiger for Malgudi,*** Mr. Narayan has pretty well left all that behind. . . .

Master excepted, [the characters] don't come to much. Some almost seem caricatures of what were already caricatures in Kipling's books about India. Alphonse is a more crudely sketched version of Buldeo, the blustering hunter in *The Jungle Book.* The Malgudi officials who appear are much like the pettifogging babu clerks Kipling loved to ridicule. The crowds of townspeople so easily terrified by Raja resemble Kipling's cowardly villagers. They will be disappointing to readers who have loved the richness of earlier Malgudi novels.

I think the truth is that Mr. Narayan is less interested in individuals, than in the oneness of all things and in broad symbols. The real subject of ***A Tiger for Malgudi*** is the principle of nonviolence, epitomized comically by the timid townspeople and seriously by Master. Raja himself is, of course, the epitome of violence. His two conversions to nonviolence—by force when he's with the circus, by spiritual teaching when he's with Master—represent right and wrong paths for India itself, I think.

In Brahman theory, there are four main stages of life: the student, the family man or woman, the ascetic and finally the withdrawn person, beyond the need not only for possessions but even for identity itself. This is a book about the fourth stage. It's difficult to portray in a novel, and Mr. Narayan has only partially succeeded.

Noel Perrin, "Conversions to Nonviolence," in The New York Times Book Review, *September 4, 1983, p. 4.*

CARLO COPPOLA

Essential to understanding any of R. K. Narayan's fiction are the Hindu notions of the unity of the universe and spiritual growth. *Brahman,* or roughly God, is the underlying cosmic force which sustains this universe, whose diversity emerges from an infinite number of *atmans,* individuated bits of *Brahman,* or roughly souls, caught up in an endless cycle of rebirths. The goal of all *atmans* is to achieve release from rebirths through spiritual growth and, eventually, to achieve union with *Brahman*. These concepts are probably nowhere more explicitly demonstrated in Narayan's literary output than in his twelfth and latest novel, ***A Tiger for Malgudi.***

This is the saga of the spiritual development of an *atman* captured in the form of a tiger named Raja from meat-eating hunter to placid, enlightened being. The novel exhibits many of the characteristics which are hallmarks of Narayan's fiction: simplicity of plot, gentle satire and irony that is intended both to make us slightly uncomfortable and to make us laugh. But there are a number of departures for the usual expectations one has regarding Narayan's fiction, the most obvious being that the narrator is a tiger, who is captured by a clever circus trainer. . . .

The novel possesses a number of complexities which belie its apparent simplicity. It is structured cyclically, starting and ending in the forest, away from ordinary people and the lure of action, egoism and involvement, which keep all beings enmeshed in the cycle of rebirths. In addition, the story is told as a flashback by a first-person narrator—the tiger—who, as a result of his own spiritual dimensions, has a deep, compassionate understanding and empathy not merely for the human but for the universal condition. . . . Narayan presents through the tiger a persona which is less than animal yet more than human. From this vantage point, the narrator is capable of astute observations about humankind, which provide the novel with much of its wit.

Most of Narayan's stories turn on the axis of spiritual progress, insight and self-understanding. This is the story of the development of Raja's base animal instincts into suprahuman enlightenment without the seemingly necessary intermediate step of taking on a human form. Narayan seems to be saying that not only is the universe basically one, but that animals too may attain spiritual growth and eventual release from the cycle of rebirths without assuming human form. To think that they must is merely one of man's more egotistical delusions.

In the final analysis, however, the novel falls short of Narayan's best achievements (viz., ***The Financial Expert, The Guide, The Man-Eater of Malgudi***) because the author fails to convince us of the final phase of Raja's quest. Indeed. Narayan spends some 154 pages getting Raja from the forest to the city and back to the forest again. The return to the forest and his "enlightenment" are presented in the last twenty pages of the novel. The detail, the dialogue, the tone and the narration itself seem scanty, off-center. There seems to be a rush to finish, with the result that at the end we are deprived of witnessing the process by which Raja attains his insight, a process which should be the central part of the work. In fact, it is not. Instead, this last section is excessively sober, perhaps even a bit pompous and, certainly, unconvincing. One almost pities Raja and wonders whether he might secretly yearn to be back in the hubbub of the circus world. Literarily speaking, the circus trainer is a much better developed character than the holy man, and common sense suggests that this should not be the case.

The inscription in the novel is to a friend who, Narayan states, "brought me back to the windmill again." This particular joust with the windmill has resulted in a story which, unlike earlier Narayan novels, fails to enchant us. Instead of pure-grained Narayan fare, we are left with a small loaf full of irritating bits of chaff and fluff.

Carlo Coppola, in a review of "A Tiger for Malgudi," in World Literature Today, *Vol. 58, No. 2, Spring, 1984, p. 325.*

FRANCES TALIAFERRO

Narayan wrote many of [the stories in ***Under the Banyan Tree***] some decades ago, when he was a contributor to *The Hindu* of Madras and "the driving force was the need to write two stories a month to survive." These slender pieces are quick glimpses of Malgudi characters—"human interest" stories, exotic in setting but not intention. A Malgudi householder may summon the snake charmer as casually as you or I would call the plumber, but there is no deliberate glamour in these journalistic snapshots of everyday Indian life.

For example, **"Like the Sun"** records the discomforts and eventual rewards of a man who vows to tell nothing but the truth all day. In **"At the Portal,"** the author observes a mother squirrel trying to teach her fearful baby to jump up into the squirrels' nest. The estranged husband and wife in **"The Shelter"** find themselves reunited under the same banyan tree during a heavy rain, but they squabble just as much as before they separated. (p. 7)

Of the 28 stories in ***Under the Banyan Tree,*** a good three fourths are slight sketches of this kind. Two colorful longer stories show Narayan at his best. The first, **"Nitya,"** is a wry tale of the generation gap. Nitya is a cynical youth of twenty, fond of filling his journal with worldly-wise observations on the human folly that surrounds him. Years ago, when he was two, he was very ill. His parents vowed that if Nitya survived, his head would be shaved clean and his hair would be offered to God. For various reasons, his parents forgot about the vow; now, they want to foreclose. The outraged Nitya blasphemously asks, "Where is God's hand in all this, if there is a God and if he is interested in my hair? . . . You have been carrying on negotiations with a commodity that did not belong to you." His parents prevail on him to travel to the shrine for the sacrifice, but numerous foolish complications allow Nitya to escape on a technicality.

"A Horse and Two Goats" is a classic of cross purposes. In Kritam, tiniest of all the 700,000 villages of India, old Muni and his wife eke out an abject existence. Once Muni was a prosperous shepherd with a flock of forty goats; now only two remain. One day he takes them to graze near the roadside statue of a horse. When a red-faced American tourist appears in his van, he cries "Marvellous!" and begins to negotiate with Muni to buy the statue. There follows a wonderfully ineffective "conversation" in which the foreigner speaks in English of suburban cocktail parties while Muni discourses in Tamil on the end of the world. At last the foreigner buys the horse from Muni, who does not own it. Neither man can believe his good fortune. In this delightful story, as in **"Nitya,"**Narayan presents the clash of generations and cultures, peasant and bourgeois, all in a humorous narrative that looks as easy as falling off a log. It isn't.

Narayan's art is one of condensation, and he renders his wisdom with affectionate simplicity. Western readers have much to learn from his amused acceptance of Fortune's lurches and from his tolerant interest in all created beings, from the squirrel to the swami. It seems, then, reprehensibly "western" to grow impatient with his sentimental ironies, but much of the present collection is not up to the writer's usual standard. It is likeable journalism, but it is second-rate Narayan. (pp. 7, 13)

Frances Taliaferro, "Main Street Malgudi," in Book World—The Washington Post, *July 28, 1985, pp. 7, 13.*

NEVILLE SHACK

Narayan's fictional world of folly and delusion offers scope for the finer points of story-telling, with everything in his ambit somehow shifting, not quite what it purports to be. Even the apparently fixed astrological course of fortune and its malign opposite can be played around with by the narrator for his own purposes—not least, that of surprise; human fallibility, being so strange, still manages to confound expectations. Narayan skilfully encompasses this capriciousness, draws out a sense of wonder and so suggests a poignancy beyond good-natured humour. . . .

Malgudi, an invented, embellished version of Mysore, the author's home city in southern India, has long framed his creations and lent them a strong sense of topography. . . . [***Under the Banyan Tree and Other Stories***] sees Narayan travelling in and out of the old environs at will, still maintaining a fine balance in his prose between a sense of place and universal homily. When, at the beginning of **"A Career"**, the seasoned narrator opens his store in Lawley Extension, the newly-built suburb, the salient details of his business routine are quickly and unobtrusively established. Narayan telescopes the scene yet never undermines its spatial dimensions or tangibility in the imagination. Ramu, a young confidence-trickster, cheats the shopkeeper, finally bankrupting him, only to abscond himself. The narrator and his family are reduced to beggary although, years later, they recover and become prosperous. The story's climax involves an affecting, masterfully restrained encounter between Ramu and his ex-employer. Narayan is too aware of the conflicting impulses in a person, in this case compassion and recrimination, to lapse into either glib sentimentality or the settling of old scores. He ranges in **"A Career"** from Malgudi to Madras to the southern hill country, from the rituals of daily commerce to one man's uneasy enlightenment: all this convincingly compressed into seven pages.

Narayan trips up a character in order to facilitate some vital process of discovery; the intention is benign rather than purely a comeuppance. **"Uncle's Letters"** sums up the author's position as a humane bystander, one whose world-weariness never turns into an excuse for grumpiness or misanthropy. The uncle in question writes letters to his nephew, marking the chief events in the latter's life from birth to the supposed serenity of old age. This epistolary form portrays the nephew as merely a recipient of his uncle's home-truths, but a clear picture emerges. . . .

Deception, self-deception and plain obtuseness take many whimsical turns in these stories. An archaeologist's assistant discovers a bogus Roman stone image. Some very credible charlatanism builds up around it, with lectures and monographs. The truth that finally transpires about the image's origins is rum in its own way, and effectively mocks so-called scholarly pretensions. An old servant might or might not have caught a cobra in his family's garden, but the uncertainty at the end of the incident makes the preceding fuss seem arch and ridiculous. On the subsistence level of village India there is a very curious meeting between an American tourist and a poor peasant [**"A Horse and Two Goats"**]; the encounter amounts to an absurd example of mutual autism, taking place with a flourish of banality, exasperating but quite moving at the same time, infused with humane drollery. . . .

Narayan tantalizingly exploits the ambiguity of a relatively petty situation; bewilderment here can be transformed into something almost lyrical rather than menacing or destructive. Defeat does not necessarily spell final humiliation. Sastri, the little man, an office clerk in **"All Avoidable Talk"**, comes across as both Chaplinesque and Thurberish, getting bruised in the big world and suffering at home. Sastri has reason to feel resigned, according to his horoscope, but poetic justice is on his side and he redeems his dignity with a small triumph.

By means of the "great consummate silence" chosen by the old village story-teller under the banyan tree, in the story which ends the book, Narayan seems modestly to advertise the limits of his craft as well as those of the practitioner. But questions linger. Is the story-teller's self-imposed vow a pointer to the ineffable Beyond or just a charming piece of obstinacy? Whatever it might be, it certainly gives a retrospective value to the business of peddling a narrative, something Narayan excels at.

Neville Shack, "A Vocation for Enchantment," in The Times Literary Supplement, *No. 4307, October 18, 1985, p. 1168.*

JACQUELINE AUSTIN

Like Faulkner's Yoknapatawpha County, R. K. Narayan's fictional South Indian town of Malgudi seems, at first sight, both small and sleepy. . . . Yet Malgudi compensates for its lack of physical grandeur in the quality and intimacy of its history.

Narayan notices every corner of his world and gives its tiniest moments worth. He shows the random visitor his town from the inside: the fall of a fruit from a drumstick tree is not just an insignificant act of gravity, of the season, but a complex of major yet unlabored exchanges. The human, the natural, and the artificial are one. Narayan's heroes, whether story-tellers, working folk, beggars, or saints, never force the reader to feel like a tourist. . . . Instead, Narayan's phenomena find their essence in a gentle, unpushy, seamless humanism. Because of the way details are seen and used, Malgudi's dust and noises, enmities and revelations simultaneously thrill and comfort, educate and entertain. . . .

Narayan has a knack with people. Annamalai, the gardener protagonist of a story in ***Under the Banyan Tree,*** grows evocative mysteries as well as exotic *poon chedi* (flowering plants), within a plot structured on small events and seemingly casual contacts. . . . Annamalai's 15 years of service in the narrator's garden hasn't led to intimacy (why should it?). The narrator's basement is as good a place as any to light a cooking fire; one lives by bizarre rules of conduct which are, it seems, dictated directly by Nature. In daily conversation, Annamalai talks to the wall, especially if he's defending himself from accusations. The narrator says, "No one is listening. Why do you address the wall?" Annamalai answers, "They are crouching behind it, not missing a word anyway." It is not that he's strange and paranoid, rather that his dignity and personality define their own terms. The narrator, a conventionally intelligent and perceptive man, is far more interested in Annamalai than Annamalai is in him.

This clash of character, of personal style, even of world view is a common theme in ***Banyan Tree***. . . .

In **"A Horse and Two Goats,"** Muni, the decrepit protagonist, is accosted by a red-faced foreign motorist as he sits in the shade of the town statue. Under the impression that he's selling the stupid foreigner his goats, Muni accepts a hundred rupees—an immense amount for him, but a pittance for the tourist; what he has really sold is the statue. The bargain, as off-kilter and misunderstood as it can be, symbolizes all human communication. The foreigner asks (from prejudice, or misguided sensitivity), "Have you any religious or spiritual scruples against English speech?" Muni does not understand a word he's saying.

The traveler continues on and on about his work on the 40th floor of the Empire State Building, and about a recent power failure. "All the way in the train I kept thinking, and the minute I reached home in Connecticut I told my wife, Ruth, 'We will visit India this winter, it's time to look at other civilizations . . .' " Neither Muni nor the foreigner can even see the other person before him, much less conduct a reasonable conversation, yet, as is typical in Narayan, everyone ends up with precisely what he deserves.

Nambi, the old storyteller who closes ***Banyan Tree,*** is one of the most touching examples of the tragedy, and comedy, inherent in attempts at human contact. After pleasuring his fellow villagers for decades with at least one 10-day-long story a month, Nambi's mind and tongue run dry. The Goddess, he feels, has withdrawn her inspiration. . . .

By the story's end, Nambi has made a decision. He goes "up and down the village street shouting, 'I have a most wonderful tale to tell tonight. Come one and all; don't miss it . . .' " The tale? Silence, now and for the rest of Nambi's days. . . .

It would be fair to call Narayan the Faulkner of South India if that label were not so ethnocentric, if the two writers were not so different in other ways, if Narayan were not so charmingly, gently funny. Faulkner had his moments. . . . But nobody would accuse Faulkner of being a sidesplitter. Narayan may share Faulkner's taste for the grotesque, but he keeps his readers smiling—his grotesqueries are more folklorish than nightmarish. . . . Malgudi's melodramas may share some motivating factors with those of Yoknapatawpha County, but the sensibility in charge is a far less tortured one.

Narayan's voice is musical, like Faulkner's, but it doesn't resound. He mixes a natural lilt and flow with a kind of reflexive prep-school stammer. . . . Narayan tends to stick to a simple diction, derived from oral tradition: his fanciest technique is to alternate chapters in first-person and third-person narration, doubling certain details and locutions to heighten the feeling of being absolutely present.

In the vast panorama of Narayan's Malgudi novels and stories, he has returned readers again and again to the same streets, the same sites. Through the eyes of different characters, he has created vastly different impressions. Mempi Hills, Sir Frederick Lawley, Albert Mission College, and the Untouchables' Village are at once multiple realities and sustained, singular ones. Nataraj the printer, Raman the painter of signs, even the dog that slinks time and again after the blind beggar, are all as different in their various incarnations (each of them appears in several stories) as they would be if their neighbors had written down the gossip, the wandering impressions, every time these characters walked by. This quality of intimate affect, combined with an engaging style, a pointed plot, a gently ironic delivery, and a thorough sense of location, has made Narayan's world a compelling one. Malgudi's strongest feature—sameness in multiplicity, pointedness in seeming diffusion—is also Narayan's greatest writerly virtue.

Jacqueline Austin, "Narayan's Hope," in The Village Voice, *Vol. XXX, No. 45, November 5, 1985, p. 55.*

GERALD MANGAN

Readers familiar with Malgudi, the fictional Indian town where R. K. Narayan's characters spend much of their time observing each other's lives, will probably recognize the eponymous narrator of his latest novel, [***Talkative Man***]. Talkative Man, who gave a droll account of himself in ***Lawley Road*** as an aspiring news-hound, has been set talking again, with another tale arising from his thirst for copy and his local fame. "I have earned this title", he begins, "because I cannot contain myself. My impulse to share an experience with others is irresistible . . .". ***Talkative Man,*** as a brief prelude gives us to understand, has been recounted by instalments to the owner of the Boardless Hotel, a "born listener". It is a short book, whose brevity has even drawn an apologetic postscript from Narayan ("I do not concern myself with quantity when writing . . ."), but it crowds a great deal into a simple framework.

"TM" has a pliable nature as well as a long nose, and it's this combination that embroils him in the odd affair of Dr Rann—a fair-haired stranger in a three-piece suit, who steps majestically off the Delhi train one day and instals himself, to the embarrassment of the overawed station-master, as a sitting tenant in the waiting-room. TM is drawn in when the mysterious visitor seeks him out in the Town Hall Library, casually mentions his vital role in a United Nations project, and enlists his help in seeking alternative accommodation. . . .

TM is also on the scent of a Story, in which a distinguished visitor honours a provincial backwater with his presence, and so on; and his fledgling career takes an encouraging step forward when it actually appears in print—a news item whose unwitting subject has had to be photographed by a comically elaborate subterfuge. Locked in with his paperwork, or lounging in pajamas in his host's favourite chair, Rann remains high-handedly evasive; but the unsought publicity throws a dramatic light on his past, when a dauntingly large woman turns up at the station, news-clipping in hand, to reclaim her long-lost husband.

TM's self-confessed garrulity is frequently contradicted by his dealings with other characters. When he decides to protect his guest from the vengeance of this termagant, TM shows a fine talent for keeping a secret; and in his own subsequent investigations of Rann, which expose him as a multiple bigamist with a fistful of passports, he acts with the discretion of a sleuth. . . . [TM's] eventual success in foiling the villain depends as much on silence as on cunning.

The novel's climax, in which Rann addresses a public meeting and inspires mass swooning with an apocalyptic vision of a globe-devouring tropical weed, is a small masterpiece of understated farce. TM's disenchantment with him makes for a satisfactory conclusion, but most of the comedy derives from his role as a bemused victim of his own innocence—which acts as a mirror, despite his affluence and education, to the wide-eyed curiosity in the peasant community around him. His initial deference to Rann as an "international figure" is plainly symptomatic of old forms of subservience, which still tends to overvalue all things European. Narayan satirizes his gullibility with an oblique and charmingly gentle touch, and is still able to remind us that "Malgudi climate has something in it that irons out outlandish habits".

Gerald Mangan, "Long-Nosed News-Hound," in The Times Literary Supplement, *No. 4357, October 3, 1986, p. 1113.*

ANITA DESAI

Narayan has written a postscript to his new novel [***Talkative Man***] which ought to have been a foreword, since it answers the exclamation practically every reader will make on seeing it: 'Such a short novel!' One hundred and nineteen pages of large print would hardly make a novella: it is only slightly more than a short story. Narayan is perfectly aware of this inevitable reaction from his devoted readers, who can never have enough of Malgudi. His reply is uncharacteristically forceful: 'Why *not* only 119 pages? I question. While a poet or dramatist rarely exceeds a hundred pages even in his most ambitious work, and is accepted without anyone commenting upon the length of his compositon, a writer of fiction is often subject to a quantitative evaluation.' Too true: we are conditioned by the size and weight of the classics . . . to take seriously only what has weight, although the weight of a book's worth ought surely not to be connected with its avoirdupois. . . .

It will be reassuring for [Narayan's] devotees to know that the little town of Malgudi still has treasures to be discovered and explored—eccentric and everyday characters, piquant and commonplace situations—and that Narayan is ready and waiting to record their tales. The question remains: can a novel that has 'no laboured detail and description of dress, deportment, facial features, furniture, food and drinks—passages I ruthlessly skip when reading a novel'—give the reader a sense of a whole world created, of characters of flesh and blood whose experiences take over one's imagination and convince one of their likelihood and importance? It is in Narayan's style that the secret lies, the style of which Graham Greene said: 'After the death of Evelyn Waugh, Narayan is the stylist I most admire.' Economy is, of course, its salient feature. . . . Narayan sees 'details' as an impediment to the smooth progress of the narrative: very kindly he removes them from the reader's way. How does he convey with any force what he wishes to say of his characters and their lives? By trimming each sentence so that its meaning stands out vividly, unobscured, unsoftened, making exactly the impact on the reader's mind that he wishes to make, no more and no other. . . .

Like all Narayan's characters, [the protagonist of ***Talkative Man***] has his unobtrusive eccentricities—sufficient to give him individuality, but not such as to make him grotesque or bizarre. He cannot hold his tongue, he must share every experience with everyone, particularly with his friend Varma who runs the Boardless Hotel and has an eccentricity of his own: he never throws away a calendar but keeps all those acquired in thirty years on his walls, 'sometimes four on nail, one behind another'. Varma is never too busy to pull out a chair for TM and listen to his latest tale.

The subject of the tale is an enigmatic Dr Rann, who arrives on one of the few trains that stop in Malgudi . . .

In sketching [Rann's] colourful past Narayan manages to pull the legs of a number of today's sacred cows. The puckish, understated, homespun humour is entirely his—although he might say it is Malgudi's, and by now the two are interchangeable. The resigned citizens of small-town India make these kinds of joke in order to live with the shortcomings of their lives. When Rann asks, "Shall I write to the Railway Board?' about the bugs that infest the waiting-room, TM replies: 'No use, the bugs being a part of the railway service—they are service bugs actually.'. . . Then there are the quick satiric sketches which recall the cartoons that appear daily on the front page of the *Times of India* and whose creator, R. K. Laxman, is Narayan's younger brother. . . . Laxman has borrowed the 'little man' from Malgudi—a bewildered, pained onlooker of the outrageous actions around him—for the corner or background of his political cartoons; Narayan's style has taken on both the sketchiness and the satiric edge of Laxman's cartoons. . . .

Narayan occasionally reveals an unexpected cynicism. . . . Generally, however, his satire is of the amused rather than the disgusted or the impassioned kind: the Deputy Minister who comes to introduce Rann's talk on Futurology to the Lotus Club in celebration of its silver jubilee is the man in charge of 'Town Planning, Cattle Welfare, Child Welfare, Family Planning, Co-operatives and Environment, Ecology and other portfolios too numerous even for him to remember'. (p. 23)

Many Indian readers, for whom reality is a much harsher affair than the sunlit state of Malgudi slumbering beside the sandy Sarayu, feel that the satire is so mild as to be no more than the nip of a non-malarial mosquito, and that present conditions call for much more ferocious attacks from India's writers, artists and film-makers. Narayan remains as inperturbable as Malgudi itself and has continued in the same amused, amusing strain since 1935. Fifty years of steady production, in a single vein and yet retaining the aroma and vigour of a tumbler of South Indian coffee, call for a look at those early novels that brought him to public attention. The very first, ***Swami and Friends,*** was scarcely more than a childhood idyll captured in a series of small, bright pictures remarkable on the Indian literary scene for their spontaneity and lack of pomposity. The first major novels were ***The Financial Expert*** and ***Waiting for the Mahatma,*** and it could be held that he has never surpassed them. They have an extra dimension which is suggested but never encompassed by his later novels. . . . [Narayan's] recent writing has been like a drying-out of his once ripe material: it is reduced in size; it still bears an aroma but a drier, sharper one—it is turning into a tobacco leaf or a pinch of snuff. There are still the familiar ingredients that one greets with delight: the railway platform as a symbol for the transitoriness of life and the ruined temple as a symbol for the solitude of the soul; the playful and enchanting child as the golden link to life; the moment of despair that is met with resignation and with common sense.

Readers in the West tend to take Malgudi as a metaphor, or as representative of India. It is unlikely that so modest a man as Narayan entertains such pretentions. The truth is that the India of Malgudi exists for a man like Narayan who is content to potter around its environs, registering its small, unimportant happenings and recording them plainly and honestly. It is the India of those who have managed to escape the holocausts that regularly embroil whole communities, and to exist on the fringes, grateful to survive without too much damage; the India that is capable of absorbing change and of transforming it into the perpetual. It is not the whole story, but, as Narayan warns us in his postscript, he has become the master of trimming and cutting, of excluding and making do with the barest essentials. No one who enjoys the tale of Malgudi will want exclusion to be carried any further at all. (p. 24)

Anita Desai, "Malgudi," in London Review of Books, *Vol. 8, No. 21, December 4, 1986, pp. 23-24.*

MICHIKO KAKUTANI

[In ***Talkative Man***], R. K. Narayan returns again to that fictional town in Southern India that he has memorialized so many times with such benevolence and precision. It's a small, populous world, Malgudi—located midway, in terms of comedy, between territories staked out by Dickens and Chekhov; and it's endowed with the sort of bustling timelessness you find in old-fashioned folk-art paintings. Though the tensions between tradition and change, old and new, East and West, often inform Mr. Narayan's works, it is the daily muddles of doing business and the mundane complexities of family life that form the core of his fiction.

A vendor of sweets, an illiterate gardener, a failed snake charmer, a meticulous painter of signs, a gullible moneylender and even a talking tiger—such are the heroes of Mr. Narayan's earlier stories and novels. This time, his narrator is a man blessed with his own storytelling gifts—an inveterate raconteur and sometime journalist known as TM or "Talkative Man." . . .

[The tale] that TM proceeds to relate bears a decided resemblance to an earlier Narayan story, namely ***The Man-Eater of Malgudi,*** in which an imperious womanizer and adventurer arrives in town and insinuates himself in the hapless narrator's life. In this case, the uninvited guest is one Dr. Rann, a mysterious traveler who wears expensive suits and claims to be working on a secret United Nations project. . . .

TM's feelings toward Rann vacillate between resentment and awe, anger and admiration, until he hits upon a scheme for using "the fat man" to advance his own fledging journalistic career: he will write a story about Rann and sell the article to a newspaper.

Although this article does little to boost TM's reputation as a writer, it does attract the attention of a strange woman, who suddenly turns up in Malgudi claiming that Rann is her long-lost husband. TM decides to try to protect his house guest from this threatening personage . . . and in doing so, he ends up listening to her life story. . . .

[As] the narrative of ***Talkative Man*** progresses, we realize that TM is not the only storyteller in this volume, but that Rann and his supposed wife are also in the process of inventing lives for themselves. Who is telling the truth here? Does Rann really work for the United Nations? Or is he using a phony identity as a cover for his own nefarious past? Did he really abandon this woman, as she claims? Or is he an innocent victim of her delusions? And what about the young girl on whom Rann is currently lavishing attention? Are his intentions the honorable ones of an old family friend? Or does he mean to make her one in a long line of seductions?

By raising such questions, Mr. Narayan clearly means to examine the very nature of the storytelling process, the subjectivity and self-interest involved in any attempt to articulate the past. Unfortunately, these issues never really engage the reader, so slight and glancing is this novel. Whereas Mr. Narayan's kindness and easygoing improvisations usually leave the reader with a pleasant sense of the ongoing rhythms of life—its muddled mixture of joy and sadness, grace and loss—those narrative qualities have dwindled, in this novel, into mere indifference.

On one hand, none of the characters in ***Talkative Man*** is very likable or sympathetic; each seems engaged in one kind of selfishness or another. On the other, none of them is delineated with sufficient satire or irony to jar the reader into laughter or recognition. In addition, the social matrix—of neighbors and colleagues, family and friends—that lends ballast to Mr. Narayan's earlier novels seems attenuated in this volume. Here, in fact, Malgudi is less a city or a town than a narrow street that we recognize only through its earlier incarnations.

Michiko Kakutani, "Telling Tall Tales," in The New York Times, *March 14, 1987, p. 14.*

BRUCE BAWER

[Narayan's] principal subjects are universal ones: dissension between husband and wife, parent and child, employer and employee; the difficulty that people have earning a living, finding a mate, and maintaining a home; the growth of boys into young men, and of young men into old. In Narayan's novels and stories, love blooms and dies; families are happy, then sad; businesses flourish and fail. And there is no lesson in any of it except that this is the way of all flesh—joy and sorrow will in their season come to each of us, no matter what we do, and the proportions that they happen to assume in a given life prove nothing. In "the rush of eternity" (Narayan's phrase), a single life is of no cosmic consequence—which means not that life should not be respected, but that to try to magnify oneself at the expense of other people is pointless. None of us are gods, in short, so we might as well recognize our common humanity and be decent to one another. Narayan affectionately mocks characters who cherish great ambitions or claim to have made earthshaking discoveries; he does the same for characters who take clubs, committees, statistics and other depersonalizing phenomena too seriously.

Universal as his themes are, Narayan's books are in many respects exotically Indian. "Without him," [Graham] Greene has written, "I could never have known what it is like to be Indian." Narayan's India is a place where ancient native traditions survive side-by-side with the trappings of contemporary Western culture. In modest, low-key, matter-of-fact prose, Narayan brings to life people who are as familiar with casting calls as with the caste system, who quote from the *Bhagavad-Gita* and Shelley with equal facility, who marry at the age of 9 and earn BAs at 20, and who invoke the name of a Hindu god one minute and that of Errol Flynn the next. . . .

The eponymous narrator and protagonist of ***Talkative Man*** has appeared over the years, in a variety of incarnations, in several of Narayan's short stories. . . . In ***Talkative Man*** he is an aspiring journalist—a rich, well-read bachelor who makes a career of submitting to newspapers human-interest articles that never get printed. The novel traces his involvement with Dr. Rann, a mysterious stranger (and dead ringer, TM tells us, for Adolphe Menjou) who appears in town one day claiming to be a native of Timbuctoo, visiting Malgudi on important United Nations business. . . .

At the center of the book is the contrast between the unpretentious, talkative, Malgudi-bound TM and the pompous, laconic, globetrotting Rann. The former is a good citizen of humble ambitions whose greatest pleasure, it seems, consists of watching other people live their lives; the latter, an exponent of the modern "scientific view," is essentially indifferent to others. . . .

Talkative Man is not a talky book—indeed, Narayan adds a postscript apologizing for its brevity. But there is nothing to apologize for. The story is not slight but economically told; every sentence serves to advance the narrative. And as important as the story is Narayan's masterly way with character and atmosphere. The book, like many of its predecessors, is rich in garrulous lecturers, insincere politicians, pretentious scholars, gossipy neighbors and the like. Charming and vivid touches abound. . . .

[***Talkative Man***] offers a distinctive and highly engaging glimpse into two things that R. K. Narayan knows intimately: human nature and South Indian life. For the reader who is interested in getting to know the world of Narayan, there could be no better place to start.

Bruce Bawer, "Magician of Malgudi," in Book World—The Washington Post, *April 5, 1987, p. 7.*

Flann O'Brien

1911-1966

(Pseudonym of Brian Ó Nualláin [also spelled O'Nolan and Nolan]; also wrote under pseudonyms of Myles na gCopaleen [also spelled na Copaleen and na gGopaleen], Brother Barnabas, and Count Blather) Irish novelist, journalist, short story writer, translator, and dramatist.

© *The Irish Times*

One of Ireland's most admired modern writers, O'Brien was virtually unknown outside his homeland until his first novel, *At Swim-Two-Birds* (1939), was republished in England in 1960. Deeply informed by Irish culture, history, and language, O'Brien's fiction often features such comic elements as parody, satire, exaggeration, and black humor while addressing serious concerns, including the relation of life to art and reality to fiction, the artificiality of literary convention, death and the afterlife, and the folly of pedantic knowledge. Characterized by a dexterity with language and regional Irish dialects, O'Brien's writing is also informed by his knowledge of science, philosophy, literature, and theology.

While attending University College, Dublin, in the late 1920s, O'Brien served as one of the most popular contributors to the university magazine, *Comhthrom Féinne*. In early 1935, he started work on his first novel, *At Swim-Two-Birds*. Structurally complicated, self-reflexive, and wildly humorous, *At Swim-Two-Birds* is narrated by an unnamed university student who lives under considerable duress with his uncle and spends most of his time either sleeping or engaging in "sparetime literary activities." These enterprises take the form of an unconventional book about Dermot Trellis, the owner of a public house, who, like the narrator, divides his time between sleeping and writing a novel. Through a scientific-literary process known as "aestho-autogamy," Trellis is able to create lifelike characters equipped with intellects and personalities. Trellis sexually assaults one of his female characters who, as a result of the rape, gives birth to a son. Incensed by what they consider inappropriate treatment by their author, the characters avenge themselves on Trellis by convincing his son, who has inherited his father's literary gifts, to construct a grotesque story involving the author. Trellis is eventually freed from his bondage when a servant accidentally burns the pages on which the characters exist, thereby banishing them to oblivion. The narrator ultimately passes his examinations and is reconciled with his uncle. *At Swim-Two-Birds* teems with satiric glimpses of Dublin life, burlesques of Celtic folk tales, exaggerated Irish regionalism and pedantry, and extraordinary recreations of Irish dialects, including lecture-hall jargon, legal patois, and Dublin pub banter. Often compared to James Joyce's *Ulysses* in part for sharing what Bernard Bergonzi called "the prevalent encyclopaedism . . . , the collage-like introduction of extraneous fragments of information . . . , [and] the tendency to present information in question-and-answer form," *At Swim-Two-Birds* is a caricature of the conventional, realistic novel and is primarily concerned with the creative process. Bergonzi concluded that O'Brien's novel "is one of the most brilliant works of modern English fiction."

As a result of an entertaining series of letters written to the editor of the *Irish Times* by O'Brien and other Irish writers under various pseudonyms, O'Brien was engaged to contribute a regular column to the *Times*. Entitled "Cruiskeen Lawn," the articles appeared several times a week from 1940 to 1966 under the pseudonym Myles na gCopaleen. In the column, O'Brien lampooned the absurdities of Irish life and often provided wry commentary on politics and government bureaucracy. Through his work as Myles na gCopaleen, O'Brien established a reputation in his homeland as a witty, intelligent, and insightful observer of Irish society.

As his relationship with the *Irish Times* progressed, O'Brien began writing his second novel, *The Third Policeman* (1967). Completed early in 1940, this book was refused by every publisher O'Brien approached and was not published until twenty-seven years later. *The Third Policeman* details the strange experiences of the narrator, a young Irishman and self-appointed scholar of the work of de Selby, an obscure, eccentric physicist and philosopher. The narrator conspires with a man named Divney to murder a wealthy farmer and steal his money in order to fund the publication of an index of de Selby's ideas. As the narrator attempts to retrieve the farmer's cash box, he becomes disoriented and is transformed into a dreamlike state. The narrator learns that the money box has been transported to a distant police barracks; in his quest for the box, he encounters a cast of bizarre characters in a land where the laws of the normal universe are suspended and where, in Anne

Clissmann's words, "reason is overthrown and a coherent type of unreason takes its place." After what appears to have been only a few days but has actually been twenty years, the narrator escapes from this nightmarish world and makes his way back to Divney, who dies of fright at the sight of him. The reader soon discovers that the cash box was a bomb planted by Divney; the narrator was killed while reaching for it, and the story has been an account of his journey through Hell. As the novel concludes, the narrator, joined by Divney, begins the same journey with no recollection of his previous experiences. Some critics regarded *The Third Policeman* as a parody of reality viewed through scientific and philosophical concepts. Anne Clissmann described the narrator as "the ordinary man who is faced with scientific ideas which he can grasp only in an incoherent fashion and which seem to deny the validity of the world around him." Other critics perceived *The Third Policeman* as a highly symbolic work in which O'Brien is primarily concerned, as in *At Swim-Two-Birds,* with the creative process. In lieu of such varyed interpretations, Kevin Sullivan observed that "*The Third Policeman* secures [O'Brien's] place . . . as the most original comic artist, after Joyce, to come out of Ireland in this century."

Between 1940 and 1960, O'Brien produced translations from poems in Irish, several short stories and plays, numerous newspaper articles, and a book in Gaelic, *An Béal Bocht* (1941; *The Poor Mouth: A Bad Story about the Hard Life*). While these works are generally considered inconsistent in quality, *The Poor Mouth* was hailed as a classic of Gaelic literature, and many admirers currently regard it as O'Brien's best book. Set in a fictional area of West Ireland in the days when the Gaels were ruled by the English and Gaelic was officially discouraged but unofficially defended and preserved, the book is a sendup of Gaelic literature and those who romanticize Ireland's past. Karl Miller observed that in *The Poor Mouth* O'Brien depicts West Ireland as a land overrun with "pigs, potatoes, rain, famine, Gael's guile, theft, and frenzied scarecrow Sweenies. To live 'in the old Gaelic manner' is to be 'wet and hungry by day and by night and unhealthy, having nothing in the future but rain, famine, and ill-luck.'" Characterized by O'Brien's use of sustained hyperbole, *The Poor Mouth* is more pointed in its satire than either of his earlier books.

O'Brien's second published novel in English, *The Hard Life: An Exegesis of Squalor* (1961), is set at the beginning of the twentieth century and presents a realistic account of the mental and physical degradation characteristic of the underside of life in Dublin. *The Hard Life* has been described as a parody of the repressive atmosphere James Joyce described in *Dubliners* and *A Portrait of the Artist as A Young Man,* and O'Brien himself called his work "a treatise on piss and vomit." The novel details the experiences of a young narrator and his immoral brother, beginning with the death of their mother and their deliverance into the household of Mr. Callopy. Callopy is involved in the construction of women's lavatories, and his work culminates in an audience with the pope. Another central character, Father Kurt Fahrt, is an incompetent theologian who often engages with Callopy in pedantic disputes over distorted views of the Irish Catholic Church and Irish history. Intended as a travesty of Jesuit priests, the character of Father Fahrt also serves to parody Joyce's preoccupation with Jesuits and continues the novel's theme of mental squalor. Anne Clissmann noted that "to a great extent the comedy of *The Hard Life* stems from its concentration on the basic functions of man set side by side with his intellectual pretensions."

O'Brien's last completed novel, *The Dalkey Archive* (1964), is in some ways a rewriting of *The Third Policeman,* as both works concern the effect of scientific and philosophic theories on humanity's perception of reality. The parody of Joyce and the use of pedantry as a comic mode are again central preoccupations, although in *The Dalkey Archive* O'Brien utilized these elements in a different manner than in his earlier books. The protagonist of this work, Mick Shaughnessy, simultaneously attempts to thwart De Selby, a scientist who plots to destroy the world with a time-altering invention, and to locate James Joyce, who appears in the novel as a bartender at a local Irish pub, attends mass daily, is embarrassed by his Parisian past, and denies authorship of all the works attributed to him except *Dubliners*. Set in the town of Dalkey, which resembles the Garden of Eden, the story passes freely between the material and immaterial worlds. Not intended to mock God or religion but, in O'Brien's words, "to roast the people who seriously do," *The Dalkey Archive* presents a humorous vision of a heaven in which unresolved mysteries abound and lend beauty to the universe. The novel has also been interpreted as a warning to those who, like De Selby, attempt to solve the mysteries of the universe by separating faith and intellect.

O'Brien's several posthumous collections include *The Best of Myles: A Selection from "Cruiskeen Lawn"* (1968), *The Hair of the Dogma: A Further Selection from "Cruiskeen Lawn"* (1977), and *Stories and Plays* (1973). *A Flann O'Brien Reader* (1978) contains excerpts from O'Brien's novels and selections from his newspaper columns, short fiction, and plays.

(See also *CLC,* Vols. 1, 4, 5, 7, 10; *Contemporary Authors,* Vols. 21-22, Vols. 25-28, rev. ed. [obituary]; and *Contemporary Authors Permanent Series,* Vol. 2.)

V. S. PRICHETT

This brilliant and wicked book [***At Swim-Two-Birds***] was first published in 1939, a bad year for originality and laughter. In spite of praise from James Joyce—who was parodied in it—and Mr Graham Greene, and from the best critics, it reached only a small public. Let us hope the prospects are brighter now, for Mr O'Brien's is one of the funniest 'novels' to come out of Ireland. To describe it is difficult. One could say that the author designed to reduce the total Irish literary tradition to farce and to make hay of the modern novel, but his irreverence is not journalistic. The book is not a skit. It is scholarly, vigorous and creative. The narrator is a slothful, verminous and drunken Dublin student who deceives his pious uncle and, while supposedly reading for his exams, is either fast asleep or working out a destructive theory of the novel. By now novelists merely copy one another. The only intellectually respectable thing to do is to pot, pillage, rearrange and summarise available literature and its techniques. But while he is writing a novel about a novelist called Trellis, the characters of Trellis's book—maimed by inadequate treatment—avenge themselves on their author by making up a grotesque yarn about him.

That is the ballast of the book; it hardly keeps on an even keel, but, at any rate, it rolls along comically half-capsized; in its course, it picks up a lot of Joyce, breaks into Celtic legend—Finn MacCool—Bardic exercises, Irish realism and Wild West yarning and fills up with the conceits, fantasies and enormities of talk in lecture halls, Law Courts and Dublin pubs. If Mr

O'Brien had waited ten years he could have taken Beckett on board and so reduced a whole tradition to laughter. But, as I say, Mr O'Brien is not out to kill a culture; by his vitality and impudence he adds to it. (p. 250)

Mr O'Brien's gifts are startling and heartless. He has the astounding Irish genius for describing the human animal, its shameless and dilapidated body, its touching and proliferating fancy, its terrible interest in useless conundrums. On top of this he has an extraordinary freedom of the English language, perhaps because he is a Gaelic scholar, perhaps because the Elizabethan tradition has survived in Ireland. His people are either seedy Dubliners or ludicrous giants, but their wits are alight; they live in language, in comic image, rather than in life. It looks as though his idea was to knock the regionalism out of Irish literature by magnifying it. . . .

The sloth of Mr O'Brien's sulky, superior narrator who, despite his beatnik behaviour, triumphs with cynical ease in his examinations at the end, is an enjoyable quality. I became tired of the joke only when Mr Trellis's characters started writing about him, simply because of the excess. This kind of fantasy is apt to be self-destructive. But I shall often return to Mr O'Brien's diverting brainstorm and shall often brood about one of his deluded characters who feared to sit down because he imagined his bottom was made of glass. (p. 251)

V. S. Pritchett, "Death of Finn," in New Statesman, *Vol. LX, No. 1536, August 20, 1960, pp. 250-51.*

KEVIN SULLIVAN

[***The Third Policeman***] is posthumous and may perhaps be said to be so in more ways than one. It was written in 1940 but not published until 1967, a year after the author's death. It is also a book about a man who is already dead, though the reader is not aware of this till the end, the dead man being the author of his own history—a sort of autothanatography. "When you are writing about the world of the dead," Flann O'Brien has said elsewhere, "none of the rules and laws (not even the law of gravity) holds good." This opens up all kinds of possibilities for grim fun which O'Brien exploits with dead-pan comic grace.

The form of the book is a circular *decensus Averni* and the idea behind it is set down briefly in a note of the author's which the publisher has sensibly included here as an appendix: "The beginning of the unfinished, the rediscovery of the familiar, the reexperience of the already suffered, the fresh forgetting of the unremembered. Hell goes round and round. In shape it is circular and by nature it is interminable, repetitive and very nearly unbearable."

The idea is not new; what is new is Flann O'Brien's ingenious embodiment of the idea in a series of weird and comical illustrations and in the singleness of their accumulative effect. Though summary is a thankless task, it will best serve to indicate both the simplicity and complexity of the comic genius here at work.

The anonymous narrator, a strange sort of Irish countryman, has conspired with a man named Divney to murder a rich old farmer and steal his cash box. After the murder, a savage and bloody affair, he goes to the farmer's house to fetch the box and as his fingers touch the lid the whole of his world is suddenly and utterly transmogrified. The dead farmer is alive again, the narrator's soul—"called Joe for convenience"—is present to him as a disembodied voice, and the cash box has been mysteriously transplanted to a police barracks located some distance away.

At the barracks the narrator is met by Sergeant Pluck, a man obsessed by bicycles, and Policeman MacCruiskeen, whose obsession it is to construct exquisite little boxes, one fitted within another Chinese-fashion, and the last so tiny and exquisitely made as to be entirely invisible. These two gentlemen, acting as guides and guardians to the narrator, introduce him to a place underground that looks like eternity, take readings and measurements on unknown instruments, and patiently explain to him the all-sufficient properties of a substance called omnium and the Law of the Interchange of Atomic Particles.

"Michael Gilhaney," says Sergeant Pluck, "is an example of a man that is nearly banjaxed from the principles of the Atomic Theory. Would it astonish you to hear that he is nearly half a bicycle?" but nothing really astonishes where all is astonishment, and the narrator, at one point condemned to be hanged, can still carry on with the policemen an amiable discussion of the technical difficulties to be encountered in gallows building and the unconscionable price of wood. All this fine talk—and there is no end to it—is conducted in what Anthony Burgess has called "Irish solecistic sesquipedalian raised to the ultimate power."

In the end the narrator returns to visit his accomplice, Divney, after what he thinks is an absence of only a few days. Actually it is twenty years later and Divney is quite literally scared to death at the sight of him. The justice of this is apparent in the knowledge now that it was Divney who had planted a bomb in the cash box that had blown the narrator to hell. Thereupon the two men set out across the same pleasant but breathless and static landscape through which the quest for that unholy grail had been begun. They encounter Sergeant Pluck. "Is it about a bicycle?" he asks. The wheel has come full circle. Behind Pluck is MacCruiskeen, and behind him the third policeman of the title. "Hell goes round and round." (pp. 181, 183)

A reader coming from ***At Swim-Two-Birds*** to ***The Third Policeman*** will be reminded again of Joyce, though it would be a mistake to exaggerate the influence. For there are other shades of influence lying over these pages, some vague, some wry, all right to the purpose and utterly transformed from the shape at their source, those of Swift and Berkeley, Sterne and Yeats, Kafka and Pirandello, and even of little Father Prout, alias Francis Sylvester Mahony, jogging along under the enveloping white shade of Dante Alighieri. But these are only shadows, the substance is all O'Brien. ***The Third Policeman*** secures his place, already indicated by ***At Swim-Two-Birds,*** as the most original comic artist, after Joyce, to come out of Ireland in this century. (p. 184)

Kevin Sullivan, "A Land of Lost Identities," in The Nation, *New York, Vol. 206, No. 6, February 5, 1968, pp. 181, 183-84.*

THE TIMES LITERARY SUPPLEMENT

It is good to have these fugitive pieces restrained within the covers of [***The Best of Myles: A Selection from "Cruiskeen Lawn"***]. Myles was a genial man, a wag, a humorist, himself a comic humour. Read one by one, his fragments were very funny, but there is a particular pleasure in the continuity of feeling and idiom provided by a book. The same themes turn up in diverse variations, the same absurdities, the characters resurrected for new trials and tribulations. In a book, it is possible to see the sources of the humour, the typical origins and patterns. The anecdotes, apocryphal conversations, curiosities of learning, tales of tubs, lists, names, satirical bites, these constitute a local history of Dublin in the age of de Valera. But they are not limited by locality. The reader who knows that NCR means the North Circular Road in Dublin has a slight advantage, but no more. Wisely, the editor has left the local names unglossed.

After a while it begins to emerge that Myles's several personalities were audible in the daily pieces. Suppose, to be specific, a man were to spend part of his day in a government office, another part in a pub, another in his own house, he would hear, in turn, the formal rhetoric of documentation, the informal bravado of the bar, and the pedantic euphuism of his own mind, last thing before bed. Myles's style includes all three, diversely apportioned. Much of his comedy is the result of setting these three idioms amiably at odds. The Civil Service idiom was represented all too powerfully, the new Ireland of Fanna Fail, the newly rich in high place. The pub talk was something else again, extravagant, subversive, eternal Opposition. The third Speaker was his own man, a scholar, a lover of dictionaries, a wordmonger, graduate of a time when Latin was compulsory.

Some of the best things in the book are essays in farcical discrimination, as if between a civil servant, a drinker, and a pedant. The discrimination of bores, for instance, is a brilliant section. . . .

But Myles was happiest in humour essentially verbal. His best anecdotes are traced back from the pun at the end. His famous characters Keats and Chapman live for the pun, spend their entire lives to make puns possible. . . . Then there is Myles's catechism of cliché, a dictionary of ideas received in Dublin. The moral of the story is given, reasonably, in Latin: "Vita sine litteris mors est"; the footnote reads; "Meaning, no doubt, that life without the guidance of books is a riddle, a closed book, a mors code".

"Mylestones," in The Times Literary Supplement, *No. 3473, September 19, 1968, p. 1046.*

BERNARD BENSTOCK

The appearance in 1967 of Flann O'Brien's fourth published novel, ***The Third Policeman,*** affords the reader an opportunity of testing his evaluations of the author's material in the three previous ones with the touchstone of a fourth, especially now that O'Nolan's death has cut off the source of Flann O'Brien books. There have been indications from Dublin circles that a new novel would be posthumously published (rumored title: *The Sago Saga*); ***The Third Policeman*** is obviously not that work, but a manuscript that has been lying dormant since 1940, from which the author had already extracted portions for use in ***The Dalkey Archive*** (the important bicycle theory, the name—but not the character of—De Selby, and the duplication of names and characteristics of at least one policeman). There is a possibility then that Brian O'Nolan never intended this new book to be published at all, and that the decision was made by others after his death.

It is important to realize that this new addition is not a work written by the author of ***The Dalkey Archive*** as much as it is a novel from the pen of the author of ***At Swim-Two-Birds.*** For those who had assumed that the significant falling-off of Flann O'Brien's talent had taken place because of twenty years of inactivity as a novelist, a retrenchment of thinking will be necessary. ***The Third Policeman*** proves in many respects to be a blood brother of the later ***Dalkey Archive,*** and only a distant cousin to the ***At Swim-Two-Birds*** that immediately preceded it. Whatever force reduced a major talent to a minor one was already in operation by 1940.

Nonetheless, it is apparent that Brian O'Nolan intended his second novel to be a more serious venture—in terms of moral commitment, that is—than his first: his letter to William Saroyan (dated 14 February 1940), affixed by the publishers at the end of the published version, describes the completed manuscript as involving a peregrination in hell, "the world of the dead—and the damned." . . . Surely the same sort of claim could not be made for ***At Swim-Two-Birds,*** where all immediate horrors and harrowings are intentionally fictitious (happening to individuals whose fictional identities are already established by the characters within the novel), and even they are allowed to awaken from their nightmares—or at least dissolve into a state of never-beens to whom nothing had actually happened. That first novel offers its readers a choice of three central characters, one supernatural, one legendary, and the last a fictional person existing in an unfinished manuscript by an author created by the narrator himself. It is only the fictional character then who has any real claim on reader sympathy, but even he is several steps removed from the kind of "reality" that is usually operative in a work of fiction. In contrast, ***The Third Policeman*** reverts to a traditional first-person narrator with whom the reader cannot but identify.

Did Brian O'Nolan consciously decide to sacrifice the multiple levels of a complex novel in which the characters are always at least once removed from the real for the existential vision of a single focus? If so, ***The Third Policeman*** deserves more serious attention than it has received in those kind reviews which hailed it as another *tour de force* of the Flann O'Brien wit.

For almost the entire length of the novel, while we assume that the anonymous protagonist is enduring three days of nightmare existence while alive, O'Brien is functioning within the confines described by Marlowe's Mephistopheles ("Why, this is hell, nor am I out of it"). With the surprising denouement, in which we learn that he has been dead for sixteen years, the emphasis shifts from the "nearly unbearable" temporary situation to the permanent recycling that gives hell its added dimension in eternal time. Yet the hell that O'Brien saw himself describing is hardly as horrible as he intended: the protagonist undergoes a fascinating series of adventures ranging from the terrifying to the blissfully delightful; half the time he finds himself under sentence of death, the other half in successful flight from execution; during the threatening portions he most often assumes that either escape or rescue is possible and even probable; and most soothing are those constant periods of pleasurable sleep in which he manages happily to escape (except for one rare nightmare) from his immediate predicament. The pleasures of sleep—along soft ditches, in comfortable beds, and even while sitting up blindfolded—recur frequently in ***The Third Policeman,*** an echo of O'Brien's familiar refrain: the escape from life and its adversities by taking up the horizontal. Both the nephew in ***At Swim-Two-Birds*** and Finbarr of ***The Hard Life*** are devoted to their beds. . . . By dint of the blissful periods of sleep that punctuate his sixteen years in hell, the hero of ***The Third Policeman*** escapes even those momentary tortures of the damned, and the novel is ironically Flann O'Brien's

Pilgrim's Progress and *Gulliver's Travels,* rather than his *Harrowing of Hell*—despite his own intentions.

Addiction to sleep and forgetfulness reinforces a corollary tendency in Flann O'Brien novels toward happy endings. The narrator of ***At Swim-Two-Birds*** is a chronic slugabed whose uncle is underwriting his education and expects more exertion for his money; yet the young scholar not only maintains his indolent habits, but actually succeeds in obtaining his university degree. Dermot Trellis, the beleaguered author that he created as the novelist-within-his-novel, is finally rescued from the torments of his own fictional characters when his maid carelessly burns the loose pages on which those characters had their existence. In ***The Dalkey Archive*** Mick Shaughnessy is out to foil the world-destructive scheme of a mad scientist, and manages to succeed in doing so, while winning the girl as well. And in ***The Hard Life*** both brothers, the fairly innocent Finbarr and the unscrupulous Manus, end up with their inheritances and are left to their own devices thereafter. Yet the O'Brien technique invariably rises above such self-imposed contrivances, and actual sentimentality is avoided by an extra fillip of imaginative wit. Amazed by his nephew's success at the University, the uncle comes forth with a laudatory speech and the traditional graduation watch; Dermot Trellis comes in out of the cold night dressed only in his nightshirt, to the amazement of the maid who is his unwitting rescuer. Finbarr's inheritance comes from the death of his uncle, who has been drinking Manus's concoction of gravid water, causing him to gain onerous weight, and resulting in his collapse through the old floorboards of a concert hall in Rome; while Finbarr himself reacts to the idea of marrying his cousin for the remainder of the inheritance by rushing off to vomit. And Mick's delight at the idea of marrying Mary is mitigated by the news of her pregnancy, a result of her probable affair with his friend Hackett.

The reversal in ***The Third Policeman*** (the protagonist arriving home in anticipation of fabulous wealth and power to learn that he has been dead for sixteen years) both conforms to the formula and reverses it. In the other three books the bittersweet ending eliminates all previous complications and poses newer, but lesser ones; here the conclusion eliminates the possibility that the adventures were only a dream and condemns the hero to repeating them over again. Yet it has the effect of comic relief: if death is the worst that the protagonist fears in his adventures through hell, then his punishment for murder is to endure the same hell in perpetuity. He may have forgotten what it was like, but the reader remembers—and it was rather endurable: there is stirabout and fresh warm milk for breakfast in hell. That the publisher finds it necessary to affix the author's comments indicates a discrepancy between O'Brien's intentions and his accomplishment. Flann O'Brien had hoped to conjure up the worst damnation possible and has instead (perhaps to his own relief) presented a rather tolerable Pandemonium.

In his own letter to Saroyan he describes his hero as "a heel" and what happens to him as "a sort of hell"; actually the hell is a mixed bag and the heel merely human. He is not much different from the bed-warmer of ***At Swim-Two-Birds*** or Finbarr or Mick Shaughnessy, O'Brien's usual *homme moyen sensuel.* Brian O'Nolan the letter-writer would have us believe that this man is being punished for his part in killing Mathers, but he has made it impossible for the reader to care really about the murder as such. His technique is to assault the reader with the shocking statement which opens the novel: "Not everybody knows how I killed old Phillip Mathers, smashing his jaw with my spade"; but thereafter the narrator presents himself with total ingenuousness as a pathetic orphan, a down-at-the-heels scholar, a naif in the process of being cheated by John Divney, and finally a weakling coaxed into collaborating in the murder of the senile miser in order to finance the publication of his scholarly work. Add to this his wooden leg, and it becomes impossible for the reader to condemn him as "a heel and a killer." Our murderer suffers fear and remorse immediately after the killing, but the remorse does not last very long; the novel then becomes his account of the journey to take possession of the black box that contains Mathers's money and to escape the police who are intent on hanging him. He is by turns terrified, astonished, exultant, becalmed; he discovers his conscience (named Joe), who speaks to him from inside him, but never chastises him for his misdeeds, except to remind him frequently that the gold watch he claims to have lost is only a subterfuge he uses with the police in order to find the black box. If this is the author's portrait of a villain, the novel is an artistic failure. But whatever O'Nolan's intention, he has created instead the sort of thing he does best: a comic novel based on a thin thread of a plot woven through a delightfully bizarre netherworld (or neverworld), but lacking the structural complexities that elevate ***At Swim-Two-Birds.*** Flann O'Brien's antihero is a homogenous creature equally recognizable in all four books: tempted often and often put-upon, vulnerable and corruptible, steering a middle course between most of the vices and most of the virtues, but definitely preferable to the cohort who is stronger, less scrupulous, more daring—the man of action. The protagonist here is an easy foil for the highly motivated John Divney, as Finbarr was for his older brother Manus, or as Mick feared he would become if allowed to fall under the sway of Hackett (a hint of this potent alter ego is seen in the success of Kelly in bringing the hero of ***At Swim-Two-Birds*** into the pubs). And an even stronger evil force than the Kelly-Divney-Manus-Hackett type is the Satanic manipulator: Dermot Trellis, the three policemen, and the De Selby of ***The Dalkey Archive.*** Compared to these two sets of dominant personalities, our wooden-legged killer is, like the trees along the Dodder, more sinned against than sinning.

It is not surprising that Flann O'Brien does not know his central character well enough to give him an accurate appraisal in his letter to Saroyan: he has never carried through with the novelist's obligation to establish an understandable relationship between himself and his protagonist. . . . If O'Brien is negligent in offering some necessary endorsements of the narrators of ***At Swim-Two-Birds*** and ***The Hard Life,*** he has certainly blundered badly with the narrator of ***The Third Policeman,*** especially if he intends that novel to have as definite a moral purpose as his letter suggests.

In attempting to determine the author's moral views in the other works, it is apparent that at best Flann O'Brien is safely teasing the Irish bourgeoisie, the "uncles" of ***At Swim-Two-Birds*** and ***The Hard Life,*** but with neither malice nor revolutionary intent. It is difficult to believe then that the naive bookworm-turned-homicide is to be condemned seriously by the man who condones the filling of Mr. Collopy with gravid water. Can the moralist who winks an eye at Manus's money-making schemes which cause a near-drowning in the Liffey and the dead uncle between collapsed floorboards be intent on exacting precise punishment from the murderer of old Mathers? Even with the attached addenda to ***The Third Policeman*** it is difficult to accept Flann O'Brien as a serious moralist, especially in a novel in which the usual Catholic material so prevalent in the other books is obviously missing. Not that the topography of O'Brien's hell is not fascinating: even without being designated as such it provides the most interesting material in the novel (along with the parody of academic scholarship found in the footnotes). A self-created ceiling map, whose cracks indicate the roads of the region, including one unseen on the earth surface that leads to Eternity; a landscape which takes on quietly mystic proportions when beheld by the narrator (O'Brien may have consigned him to hell, but he sees himself in paradise when he contemplates his natural surroundings); Eternity itself as a succession of identical rooms where time has stopped and where all wishes are fulfilled but nothing that has not been brought in may be taken out; and the private police barracks of Policeman Fox set inside a thick wall in old Mathers's house—these do service for Dante's nine circles. But the three policemen and the leader of the hoppy men add the best source for reader speculation in mapping out the cosmography of O'Brien's inferno. (pp. 69-75)

There is little profit, however, in speculating whether Flann O'Brien's vision of the afterlife has any orthodox or heterodox parallel with the Catholic world in which he lived (his kaleidoscopic focus never clarifies at any point to indicate a satiric target). Nor could speculation on his attitude toward his society be any more definite. Yet it is tempting to wonder whether hell is not a metaphor in ***The Third Policeman*** for the rural Ireland of his time, much as it is in Sean O'Casey's *Purple Dust, Cock-a-Doodle Dandy,* and *The Bishop's Bonfire*. Sergeant Pluck speaks darkly and menacingly about the County Council as some bureaucratic source for all the evils and shortcomings of the district. The three policemen operate both as devoted public officials and as individually anti-social aberrants. A Police Inspector appears from nowhere announcing a murder that took place two hours ago and demanding an arrested culprit to be already present: the Police Sergeant avails himself of the nearest person at hand and our hero stands condemned. A scaffold is built on the second day for an execution scheduled for the third, without any mention of a trial. Kafka could hardly have asked for a more nightmarish description of a sick society divided against itself. Yet in Flann O'Brien's comic world no direct accusation is ever made, but the reader is left with a definite suspicion that something somewhere is apparently rotten.

But Flann O'Brien is as difficult to catch in any definite trap as is a leprechaun—and for much the same reasons: his methods of approach are elliptical and perverse. In his editorial note to the issue of *Envoy* devoted to James Joyce, as Brian Nolan he posed the question, "What is the position of the artist in Ireland?", and to no one's surprise did nothing whatever to answer it. Instead he related the hilarious anecdote about "A Bash in the Tunnel," which equips him to summarize that "surely there you have the Irish artist? Sitting fully dressed, innerly locked in the toilet of a locked coach, where he has no right to be, resentfully drinking somebody else's whiskey, being whisked hither and thither by anonymous shunters, keeping fastidiously the while on the outer face of his door the simple word Engaged?" Joyce, he then decides, has the most Irish characteristic: "the transgressor's resentment with the nongressor." Flann O'Brien's transgressions are venial and apologetic, and the only sense in which he is *engagé* is that he is occupied, but not committed. (pp. 77-8)

Bernard Benstock, "Flann O'Brien in Hell: 'The Third Policeman'," in Bucknell Review, *Vol. XVII, No. 2, May, 1969, pp. 67-78.*

CATHARINE R. HUGHES

At Swim-Two-Birds, first published in the United States in 1951, is almost a state of mind—albeit one not to be indulged without proper discretion, lest it become a habit. It tells of a young college student who lives with his uncle ("Red-faced, bead-eyed, ball-bellied. Fleshy about the shoulders with long swinging arms giving ape-like effect to gait. Large moustache. Holder of Guinness clerkship the third class"), intermittently attends classes, more frequently attends pubs, and is involved in "spare-time literary activities." Another way of putting it: a book about a book about someone writing a book about characters who proceed to write a book about him; or words to that effect. All of which might seem a bit pretentious and labored, but never is. (p. 523)

What follows is a rich, cascading, often brilliant 300 pages of parody, satire and fantasy, which leaves little in Ireland altogether unscathed. From Irish prudery through Irish mythology and literature, the Irish clergy through the Irish way with a pint of porter or a whisky, and the sometimes resultant Irish way with a conversation, O'Brien indulges in his own particular brand of comic invention. The ear for dialogue, the establishment of atmosphere, the sheer vitality and mastery of the Irish gift for the telling of tales—the sort of thing that *New York Times* drama critic Clive Barnes had in mind when he noted, in another context, that "in comparison with the English, the Irish always sound as though they are talking in color"—are at times almost awe-inspiring. It is rather as if O'Brien had listened to his character Finn remark: "It is true that there has been ill-usage to the men of Erin from the book-poets of the world," had nodded his head and promptly set out to right all the wrongs but also to outdo all the wrongdoers.

From time to time, it seems impossible that ***At Swim-Two-Birds*** will ever manage to bring all its intertwining stories, all its seeming (and genuine) digressions, together. It is not merely that O'Brien's imagination is prodigious; so is his bizarre brand of scholarship, the latter occasionally indulged beyond the point of effectiveness. There are carefully denoted observations by the narrator: "description of my uncle" (promptly given), "quality of rasher in use in household" (likewise given), "nature of denial" ("inarticulate, of gesture"); extracts from assorted manuscripts, bursts of song and extended outpourings of poetry, "biographical reminiscences" and bits from the press. (p. 524)

From time to time, O'Brien steps in to present what is casually labeled a "synopsis, being a summary of what has gone before." By the time he reaches the first of them, Trellis has created not only the Pooka MacPhellimey and Furriskey, but Peggy, "a domestic servant," whom Furriskey is sent to "meet and betray," and Finn MacCool, "hired . . . to act as the girl's father and chastise her for her transgressions against the moral law," who instead endeavors to help her to indulge in them, and Paul Shanahan, "another man hired by Trellis for performing various small and unimportant parts in the story, also for running messages," and Sheila Lamont, created "in order to show how an evil man can debase the highest and the lowest in the same story," and her brother Antony, "so that there will be somebody to demand satisfaction off John Furriskey for betraying her—all this being provided for in the plot."

All this goes on for a bit, the characters acting out their own lives when not under Trellis' power, becoming enmeshed in Irish legend and myth. In time, there crops up Orlick Trellis, illegitimate offspring of Dermot, who following a "course of study" with the Pooka, takes up residence with Furriskey and is induced to begin a manuscript about Trellis *pater* as a "fitting punishment indeed for the usage he has given others." Thence to something carefully labeled "conclusion of the book, ultimate." Needless to say, it has been preceded by something equally carefully labeled "conclusion of the book, penultimate." And somehow, in the end, it all has become a whole, the manner and the means being known only to God and Brian O'Nolan.

There is a great deal of outrageous malarkey in ***At Swim-Two-Birds,*** a great deal of brilliant invention, and not a little genius. Since few writers have matched it, it is not surprising that O'Brien himself never did so either. Which is hardly to say that his three subsequent novels are lacking in their interests or their delights. In any event, reading O'Brien is rather like eating potato chips—once you begin you keep on going.

The Dalkey Archive is likely the most imaginative and inventive of the trio. Prefaced with O'Brien's dedication, "to my Guardian Angel, impressing upon him that I'm only fooling and warning him to see to it that there is no misunderstanding when I go home," it is certainly the most fun. There are, to name but a few of its elements: deliciously recorded meetings with St. Augustine, arranged with the aid of a substance known as D.M.T., with which its creator, De Selby, claims he is able "to stop the flow of time, or reverse it"; encounters by said creator—who also seems inclined to destroy the world—with John the Baptist, Jonah and Francis of Assisi; a police sergeant who has a vocabulary leaning toward such as "an indiscriminate exacerbation much to be inveighed against meticulously"; the discovery of a not in the least deceased James Joyce, who denies authorship of *Finnegans Wake* and *Ulysses,* admits only to ***Dubliners*** and "mostly pamphlets for the Catholic Truth Society of Ireland," "a man back from the grave, armed only with the plea that he had never gone there," and wants to join the Jesuits; people in danger of turning into bicycles (and bicycles in danger of turning into people) by virtue of "an exchange or infusion of bicycle atoms and human atoms," brought about by too close and extended proximity.

The Dalkey Archive also has a more or less central figure and catalyst in the form of one Mick Shaughnessy, who goes about the job of tracking down Joyce, thwarting De Selby (with the aid of the facilities of the Bank of Ireland), somewhat diffidently courting his girl friend, less diffidently courting the local pub (before in theory rejecting it entirely), and generally just managing to avoid and avert disaster. A very entertaining book, then, if not quite as impressive as ***At Swim-Two-Birds.***

The Hard Life bears the modest tongue-in-cheek dedication "I honorably present to Graham Greene, whose own forms of gloom I admire, this masterpiece," and the injunction "All the persons in this book are real and none is fictitious even in part." From the moment when Finbarr and Manus, otherwise known as "the brother," arrive at the home and hearth of their uncle Mr. Collopy, unpredicability abounds. Its main events include the development of Manus into something of an Irish Felix Krull, who sets about a brilliant career in mail fraud, first in Dublin, then in London, where he establishes "London University Academy," which, he informs Finbarr, aims "at the mass production of knowledge, human accomplishment and civilization." As he explains: "We plan the world of the future, a world of sophisticated and genial people, all well to do, impatient with snivelers, sneaks and politicians on the make." To that end, Manus is perfectly willing to deal with boxing, botany, fretwork, treatment of high blood pressure, acrobatics and wire-walking, care of the teeth, oil prospecting, a cure for cancer, Sausage Manufacture in the Home, and assorted other matters.

One of the other matters turns out to be Mr. Collopy, who, along with an obsession with a mysterious, not really identified, crusade (very likely for the establishment of ladies' comfort stations), also contracts rheumatism, for which Manus undertakes to prescribe his own treatment and patent medicine, Gravid Water, leading to unexpected consequences, including a bizarre audience at the Vatican.

The Third Policeman, although it is even more unusual, strikes me as the least successful of Flann O'Brien's novels. Part allegory, part mystery, part pure lunacy, it deals with the misadventures of a narrator who collaborates in the murder of "old Mathers" in order to acquire the funds necessary to pursue and publish his *De Selby Index,* a volume on the work of the physicist De Selby (whose fictitious works, and assorted commentaries on same, are quoted in extended, often very funny parodies of footnotes). Is Mathers dead? What are the real pursuits of the curious trio of policemen the narrator seeks out when he goes in quest of the black box he killed for? What of the army of one-legged men? And of those who, in an echo of ***The Dalkey Archive,*** are turning into bicycles? (Or, for that matter, those who are turning into horses?) Is the place where the policemen take the narrator *really* Eternity?

The Third Policeman is, in the end, almost a fantasized *Crime and Punishment,* perhaps what the narrator has in mind when he quotes his hero De Selby—"a journey is a hallucination." O'Nolan himself told William Saroyan that his anti-hero, who in reality has been dead during most of the book, walked "along the road to the hell place" and now must return to it again, that "this sort of thing goes on forever" as his punishment. Somehow, it does not entirely work. At least I do not *think* it does. But, of course, O'Brien being like not only potato chips, but like the Jameson's and porter his characters so dearly love, I shall probably go back to it again, indulging the idea that I may be wrong. (pp. 524-25)

Catharine R. Hughes, "Discovering Flann O'Brien," in America, *Vol. 120, No. 18, May 3, 1969, pp. 523-25.*

KARL MILLER

The Poor Mouth is a copious treatment of the subject of scarcity, and it reaches its climax, such as it is, in an imagined abundance, a magic windfall feast complete with fairy gold. History does not exist for the people of the tale. The present has swallowed the past, there has always been dearth, and the folk mind thinks hard about potatoes.

This wonderful book was published in 1941, two years after ***At Swim-Two-Birds,*** [O'Brien's] first major effort, and about a year before Patrick Kavanagh's long poem "The Great Hunger." "Patrick Power" has translated the third edition, which has emendations, and a set of satirical—or, in Dublin parlance, cod or codological—footnotes by the novelist. It is a better book, in my view, than either ***At Swim*** or ***The Third Policeman.*** All three books represent collections of episodes, but ***The Poor Mouth,*** copious but short, has more of a point, a pointed point. It has none of the desultoriness which the unending can produce, and which is produced in the other two works. It even has an ending. ***At Swim*** appears, significantly enough, to have been cut down to publishable size by another hand (so, of course, was *The Waste Land*). O'Brien prided himself on the "plot" of ***The Third Policeman,*** but this may have been codology. He also talked, in the same breath, of the narrator's being in hell, and of his being a heel and a killer. But the narrator is experienced by the reader as courteous, forlorn, and delightful, and he does not appear to experience the pains of the damned.

The narrator of ***The Poor Mouth*** is Bonaparte O'Coonassa, a pauper from the West of Ireland in the days when all Gaels were ruled by the English. Gaelic is officially discouraged, and it is also being defended and preserved. "Pauper" is a metonymy for any native of these parts, all of them being destitute or near it. O'Coonassa is a member of a caste of pauper distinguished for the rare quality of his poverty, and he picks his way, episode by episode, through the hunger, calamity, and vomiting oceanic downpours of the region, only to fetch up in jail for theft: but what is theft for the Anglo-Irish court which tries him is, for O'Coonassa, a lighting upon gold and streams of whisky. O'Coonassa is a kind of Candide, whose language parodies that used by Gaels who have told the story of their sufferings and scarcities.

A "poor mouth" is the native stratagem of pleading poverty, or grumbling, in order to gain advantage, but there is plenty of authentic poverty to plead. The poverty of the place is rendered by means of excess, exaggeration, the huge enlargement of specific features—by means of pleonasm and metonymy. The West of Ireland is pigs, potatoes, rain, famine, Gaels' guile, theft, and frenzied scarecrow Sweenies. To live "in the old Gaelic manner" is to be "wet and hungry by day and by night and unhealthy, having nothing in the future but rain, famine and ill-luck." Among these paupers arrive, each year, the Gaeligores from the East: middle-class men hungry for the old Gaelic manner, detaining paupers in awkward conversation, marveling at their poor mouths, savoring their high-grade destitution, and recording their precious, vulnerable folkways.

A foreword written in 1964, apparently by O'Brien, contains this: "As Standish Hayes O'Grady says 'the day is drawing to a close and the sweet wee maternal tongue has almost ebbed.'" Once the Irish had claimed their independence, the Gaeligores came into their own, and the sweet wee maternal tongue was made compulsory by a government which saw that it was taught in schools and which raised up bilingual street signs. Gaeligores can scarcely have approved of this novel, and it is odd that they did not try to ban it as an un-Irish activity. . . . [O'Brien's] book is decorated with Celtic conversational courtesies and mannered modes of address. It is delicately excessive and plethoric: you could say that it was written in a vein of sustained hyperbole. . . . The humor is often aimed, in contempt, at Gaeligoric falsity. The conduct of these men amounts to an unpropitious attempt to exploit people who have known how to deceive, but not how to defeat, previous exploiters. This, perhaps, is the main point. But there is another point too. O'Coonassa's dealings with his misfortunate mother and crafty grandfather, the Old-Grey-Fellow, and his departure for prison (on his way there, he meets and fails to recognize his father, jailed long before), come creeping out at you through the jokework and the artwork. They are very moving, though it is possible that O'Brien would not have wanted this said.

O'Brien is one of several Irish writers who are far from submissive to the moralistic attitudes of Anglo-Saxon criticism, who refuse to present, or elicit, a moving moral, and who will sometimes appear to be all stealth and obliquity, all averted eye and inverted comma: what might pass for an exercise of native cunning has a way, of course, of also being Modernism. For all his Irish or avant-garde avertedness, however, perhaps O'Brien would have been willing to grant that it need not be Gaeligoric to feel sorry for the Gaeligores' victims in ***The Poor Mouth,*** while laughing at their victimized airs and graces. (pp. 33-4)

Karl Miller, "Gael in Wonderland," in The New York Review of Books, *Vol. XXII, No. 7, May 1, 1975, pp. 31-4.*

MERVYN WALL

Flann O'Brien experienced a great deal of bad luck during his lifetime. Although writers of the status of James Joyce, Graham Greene and Dylan Thomas had expressed their admiration for him as a great comic genius while he was still in his twenties, his first book ***At Swim-Two-Birds*** did not sell sufficiently well for his publishers, worried by the shortage of paper and the general economic pressure on publishing brought about by the outbreak of the Second World War, to risk publishing his second novel ***The Third Policeman,*** a fact which embittered him greatly and turned him to the journalism without which he would have been altogether without an audience. . . .

During the past 10 years his reputation as a great satirist and as one of the outstanding humorists of our time has been growing with a steadiness which implies that it will be lasting. Stephen Jones . . . has now edited [***A Flann O'Brien Reader***], a compendium of extracts from the five novels, each extract sufficiently long to give a very good idea of the whole of each work, as well as being in themselves highly enjoyable; and to these he has added pieces from the shorter fiction and the plays, as well as examples of the author's journalistic work in his column "Cruiskeen Lawn" which he contributed to the conservative *Irish Times* for a period of 29 years. Each section is prefaced by a knowledgeable and understanding introduction, and there are examples of Flann O'Brien's lively correspondence with publishers and literary agents.

[The editor] has also contributed a pleasant and humorous General Introduction which gives an account of Flann O'Brien's life and presents a good picture of the personality which the public knew and whose journalistic outpourings they read avidly; and of the man, never rude or offensive in his daily contacts, but capable, when he got a pen in his hand, of using it like a whip. He sees his subject as a fierce scholar rebel, who was first a scholar, and only secondly a rebel. With great penetration and perception he sets out to display the unity of O'Brien's work as well as its diversity; and he is the first critic whose work I have read, to note O'Brien's sexual puritanism. (pp. 31-2)

For those unacquainted with O'Brien's work, the present volume will prove an excellent introduction, containing as it does not only lengthy extracts from all types of his writing, but in . . . [the] critical introductions to each section, a full study of the range of O'Brien's style and vision. (p. 33)

Mervyn Wall, in a review of "A Flann O'Brien Reader," in The New Republic, *Vol. 178, No. 7, February 18, 1978, pp. 31-3.*

RICHARD F. PETERSON

Though the time worlds of Flann O'Brien's Anglo-Irish novels are outrageously multidimensional, O'Brien's own attitude toward time and his use of time theories are relatively simple.

His basic approach, not surprising at all in a punster, is to take modern thought on time, no matter how abstract and complex, quite literally. The effect of such a strategy is to expose the incredible and laughable gap between our common perception of time and the non-human universes concocted by scientists and artists. He also throws a barb at our pretensions and ludicrous efforts to interpret and explain these theories to each other. (p. 30)

Flann O'Brien's time world is made up of characters who accept time theories as literal truths or encounter literal intrusions of "non-human truths" into their otherwise human world. Some of O'Brien's characters have no trouble at all accepting the incredible properties of either a microphysical or macroscopic universe. They live quite easily with the idea of relative or regressive time or a world of shifting molecules. Others, however, are caught between their belief in a predictable mechanical universe made up of time, space, and mass and their discovery of a nightmarish wonderland invented by science or art.

One of the most outrageous examples of an O'Brien character who accepts scientific thought as literal truth made his first appearance in print as the periphrastic Sergeant Fottrell, the archenemy of bicycles in ***The Dalkey Archive.*** Though he is often seen in the company of a bicycle, he refuses to get up on one because of what he mysteriously calls dangers inherent in the bicycle. During a chance meeting with Mick Shaughnessy, the Sergeant even admits that he deliberately steals bicycles or punctures their tires. When pressed to explain himself, the Sergeant calmly announces that "the Mollycule Theory is at work in the parish of Dalkey," and is doing "terrible destruction" to "half of the people." According to the Sergeant, the good people of Dalkey are in imminent danger of becoming bicycles.

Sergeant Fottrell's anti-bicycle crusade has been inspired by his practical application of quantum theory to the dynamic relationship between human beings and bicycles. He tells Mick that everything is made up of "small mollycules of itself and they are flying around in concentric circles and arcs and segments and innumerable various other routes too numerous to mention collectively, never standing still or resting but spinning away and darting hither and thither and back again, all the time on the go." All this whirling, however, cancels itself out within each object, thus our limited perception of a Newtonian universe of absolute solidity and determinable shape. Unfortunately, what we fail to see is that when two objects strike each other or are brought into contact frequently over a long period of time, there is an interchange of "mollycules." It follows for the quantum-minded Sergeant that people who have spent most of their time riding bicycles have mixed up their properties with those of their bicycles and that a surprising number of Irish citizens living in the country have become half-bicycles, while their bicycles, in the words of the Sergeant, "partake serenely of humanity." (pp. 31-2)

Sergeant Fottrell's mania for stealing bicycles or puncturing their tires to save mankind is an example of what happens to a character who takes a non-human truth or scientific theory too seriously. In ***The Dalkey Archive,*** however, modern scientific theory on the nature of time actually intrudes itself upon the physical world of the novel. The fantastic appearances of St. Augustine and James Joyce are actual, rather than imaginary or proposed, because time, as opposed to being absolute, true, and mathematical in its recording of passing events, emerges, according to O'Brien, "as a great flat motionless sea. Time does not pass; it is we who pass."

O'Brien believes that the responsibility for the concept of time as a vast, constant reality appearing to move and change only because of our limited understanding of its properties falls upon Einstein with his theory of relativity and J. W. Dunne with his serial universe. Both argued that our perception of time is dependent upon our position in the universe. Rather than accepting time as a mechanical movement, Einstein postulated that the time of an event is relative to the movement and position of the observer and that a single event observed by two people situated at different distances will appear to occur at different times. The implication of Einstein's theory is that events relegated to the past by our mechanical sense of time are actually still happening and that, theoretically, if a person generated enough speed to move faster than light waves, he could overtake an event and seemingly reverse time. Dunne argued that the idea of duration accepts time moving along a time length. If, however, the movement along the time length is everywhere at once, then indeed time is a motionless sea—it does not pass at all. The only way, then, we can observe the duration of an event is by moving to another observation or time level. This step backwards, however, begins a process or serial of regresses in which observer after observer withdraws from time to record its passage. Thus to measure time we move to another time level which, in turn, can be measured only by moving to a third level and on and on.

O'Brien's shortcut through light waves and endless regresses is De Selby's D.M.P. Another transfer from ***The Third Policeman,*** De Selby claims to have mastered time: "Time has been called an event, a repository, a continuum, an ingredient of the universe. I can suspend time, negative its apparent course." His reason for rejecting past explanations of time is his discovery that time is "a plenum, immobile, immutable, ineluctable, irrevocable, a condition of absolute stasis. Time does not pass. Change and movement may occur within time." De Selby simply does not need Einstein's relativity and Dunne's infinite regresses or any other intellectual or spatial construct of time because he has encountered and now can control what others have understood only in theory. He has no reason for spatializing time because he has experienced it as an unchanging, irresistible phenomenon. (pp. 33-4)

The immediate narrative effect of D.M.P. is to give Mick Shaughnessy the idea of saving the world from De Selby's mad plot, thereby setting in motion a bizarre sequence of events culminating in the unnecessary theft (De Selby changes his mind) of a circular four-gallon container of the deadly compound. As time's elixir, however, D.M.P. has far-reaching implications for the theme, unity, and general madness of ***The Dalkey Archive.*** It exposes as the basic flaw or blind spot in time theories, the pseudo-intellectualization of time. Once intellectual constructs about relative positions and infinite regresses are removed, true time appears as an undeniable, irresistible, and immutable reality. (p. 35)

The incredible resurrection of James Joyce in ***The Dalkey Archive*** has received a great deal of critical attention, most focusing on O'Brien's own obsession with Joyce. In terms of the timefoolery in the novel, however, Joyce's appearance offers yet another variation on O'Brien's parody of time speculators. While the words and deeds of Sergeant Fottrell and De Selby mock both microphysical and macroscopic time theories, Joyce's antics call into question the efforts of historians and biographers to rearrange and even deify the life and times of their subjects. The canonization or Ellmannization of Joyce by American scholars was always a sore spot for O'Brien, and in ***The Dalkey Archive,*** he clearly ridicules Joyceans as he has his sport with Joyce. (p. 36)

Whether it be Sergeant Fottrell and bicycles, De Selby and his D.M.P., or Joyce among the Jesuits, each character and his obsession expose the folly of modern efforts to define time. Rather than clarifying matters, these theories, at the very least, further muddle our understanding of time, and, at the very worst, lead to distortions of reality. On one level, because they are so abstract or so remote from human experience, they are perceptible, as Rampion says, only through non-human eyes. On another level, however, they can lead to potentially harmful efforts to manipulate reality by those who take the theories as literal truths. (p. 37)

At Swim-Two-Birds and ***The Third Policeman*** are not too different in conception from ***The Dalkey Archive,*** even though the techniques of the earlier novels are more elaborate and the humor more fantastic. Ironically, however, while the earlier novels are far more interesting for the critics, they are not as encompassing in their time themes as ***The Dalkey Archive.*** For all its mad dimensions, ***At Swim-Two-Birds*** is limited thematically to the world of art, particularly the tendency in some writers and readers to substitute literature for life, a grievous fault in literary critics (Joyceans are most susceptible) and literary-minded types like Walter Bidlake in *Point Counter Point*. Structurally, ***The Third Policeman*** parallels no less than Dante's *Inferno,* but it, too, is more limited than ***The Dalkey Archive*** because the dimensions of its hell are purely pseudoscientific.

Though O'Brien finished the manuscript of ***The Third Policeman*** by 1940, the book was not published until 1967, some three years after the publication of ***The Dalkey Archive.*** The failure to find a publisher for ***The Third Policeman*** for so many years eventually prompted O'Brien to use some of his material in his later novel, the most blatant example being Sergeant Fottrell's "Mollycule" theory, which appears as Sergeant Pluck's atomic theory in ***The Third Policeman.*** De Selby is also used in both novels, but for entirely different reasons. In ***The Dalkey Archive,*** De Selby is an actual character, a pneumatic chemist, who has mastered time with his D.M.P. and hopes to destroy the world with it. His mad scheme is a major part of a pattern of speculation and manipulation that shapes the novel. In ***The Third Policeman,*** de Selby (whose name is spelled with a lower case *d*) appears only through his theories and the writings of his commentators. As a parody of the pseudoscientific mind, he is a comic counter point to the hell prepared for the narrator, who has robbed and murdered old Mathers for the money to publish a complete edition of de Selby's work and has been murdered, in turn, by Divney, his partner in the crime. (pp. 39-40)

O'Brien's vision of hell is clearly Dantesque. Not only is it circular, but it imposes on the nameless narrator (one of his punishments is that he cannot remember his name) a punishment made up of literal transcriptions of de Selby's theories. Since de Selby is a parody of time theorists like Einstein and Dunne and the interpreters of their theories, this de Selbyish hell is a riot of minute particles, light waves, serial observers, and time loops. Our narrator, after murdering a man for de Selby's theories, faces an eternity of a recurring world literally created out of the half-truths, distortions, and absurdities that make up the best of de Selby's work. (pp. 40-1)

Omnium is the common element linking the parody of science in ***The Third Policeman*** and that in ***The Dalkey Archive,*** where De Selby's D.M.P. is the substance capable of interfering with time and reality. The major difference between the novels is the fate of the two main characters: Mick Shaughnessy comes to his senses, whereas the narrator of ***The Third Policeman*** has no exit, and at the end of the novel, is about to repeat his nightmarish experiences. O'Brien, using the *persona* of Joe, the narrator's newly discovered soul, wrote that hell eternally "goes round and round. In shape it is circular and by nature it is interminable, repetitive and very nearly unbearable." He could have added that hell is unbearable because its reality reflects our own distortions and misunderstandings of the truth.

As a symbol of the capacity of scientific theory to manipulate reality, omnium represents only one side of O'Brien's concern with notions that distort our perception of the true nature of things. In ***At Swim-Two-Birds,*** it is the artist's pen, rather than science, that plays havoc with reality. The equivalent of omnium in O'Brien's first novel is the theory of aestho-autogamy. As a literary phenomenon, it either eliminates conception and pregnancy or reduces "these processes to the same mysterious abstraction as that of the paternal factor in the commonplace case of unexplained maternity." In other words, aestho-autogamy gives the writer the power to create living characters *super spottum* or, like the holy spirit, to impregnate with the word a woman who will give birth some nine months later. What aestho-autogamy leads to in ***At Swim-Two-Birds*** is a series of outrageous literary events that completely subvert the normal order of time. We have characters being born instantly into adulthood and a writer so enamored with one of his female creations that he rapes her. We also have that same female character giving birth to the writer's son, who then seeks vengeance upon his father because his mother died in childbirth—an event not surprising considering her son was an adult at birth.

All this time and tomfoolery is part of O'Brien's parody of the notion shared by some artists and their most ardent critics, that art is life, or, even worse, that art, as a higher form of reality, has dominion over life. ***At Swim-Two-Birds*** has several levels of narration that give O'Brien free play in having fun with the idea that art is superior to life. On one level, the novel consists of several routine biographical reminiscences of a first-person narrator, a university student, who is writing a novel. The fun begins when the narrator creates a writer, Dermot Trellis, who is also writing a novel. The narrative becomes outrageous when characters created by Trellis (who steals material from William Tracy, a writer of Irish cowboy stories) become unhappy with their lot and collaborate on a novel chiefly written by Orlick Trellis, the son of Dermot, to revenge themselves upon their creator, who has been invented by the narrator of a book being written by Flann O'Brien.

The outcome of all this is a parody of several assumptions made about the art of fiction, particularly the books written by Joyce, and about the art of criticism, particularly Oscar Wilde's platonic dialogues, which portray the critic as the supreme artist. ***At Swim-Two-Birds*** mocks the novel as autobiography, epic, dream, and even revenge-book. It also pokes fun at the idea of the writer as the Artist-God who is his own father and his own son and at the belief in the power of the imagination to create a world unto itself. By the novel's end, poor Dermot Trellis, the epitome of the writer who lives entirely within the world of his imagination, has his powers entirely usurped by his characters. They put him through an ordeal and trial that rival those of Bloom and Joseph K. for sheer physical and mental humiliation. He is saved only by his servant, who puts an end to all this nonsense by accidentally burning several sheets of writing which had created Trellis's tormentors.

While all these preposterous literary events are taking place, practically every character in ***At Swim-Two-Birds*** steps forward to express himself as a literary critic. This leads to a variety of comments on plot and characterization, the novel as moral instruction, and art as an expression of the common folk. O'Brien also has some fun with the modern artist's tendency to plunder the literature of the past and with the critic's obsession with literary borrowings. The narrator offers an aesthetic based on the idea that the "entire corpus of existing literature should be regarded as a limbo from which discerning authors could draw their characters as required, creating only when they failed to find a suitable existing puppet. The modern novel should be largely a work of reference. Most authors spend their time saying what has been said before—usually said much better."

Two other aspects of the narrator's aesthetic clearly reveal what is behind O'Brien's literary games in ***At Swim-Two-Birds***. The narrator also says that if modern writers add a "wealth of reference" to their works it would eliminate the critic's job of offering tiresome explanations of character, theme, and structure and would effectively preclude the pseudo-critics or what the narrator calls "mountebanks, upstarts, thimbleriggers and persons of inferior education" from ever understanding modern literature. The surviving readers would then have the opportunity to read novels that are obvious shams, that make no pretensions to being more real than life, and that allow the reader to "regulate at will the degree of his credulity."

While the aesthetic is obviously a parody of the relationship between Joyce and his host of explicators, it also justifies the delightful insanity of ***At Swim-Two-Birds,*** a novel that explains itself and never really pretends to be anything more than it is. For O'Brien, the novel should be a bash in the tunnel, a chance to have a good time at someone else's expense, while discovering and experiencing what the Pooka calls "the seam between night and day, that is an aesthetic delight." ***At Swim-Two-Birds*** proves O'Brien's point that literature should not be taken too seriously, that it should be read for its potential fun and joy. His second novel, ***The Third Policeman,*** reflects the same view about scientific theory as it parodies the distortions of reality perpetuated in the name of science. What emerges in O'Brien's later novels, first through the squalor of ***The Hard Life*** and finally through the combined parody of art and science in ***The Dalkey Archive,*** is a warning against manipulators of reality, while at the same time the manipulation itself is a justification for art. Madness, for O'Brien, becomes a dangerous malady when it expresses itself as a political act (the manipulation of people) or a scientific one (the manipulation of reality). The former can cause delusions about a master race and lead to the mass murder of millions of people, while the latter justifies tampering with nature even for the sake of discovering a doomsday weapon.

Madness, however, is a blessing when it creates art, because it gives us an occasional bash in the tunnel, a chance to slip through a crack in time and make the sorrows and fears of life more bearable when we return. As violent as O'Brien could become on the subject of James Joyce, he also said that Joyce's great gift was his humor. The implication of this statement and the themes of O'Brien's fiction are that the world can afford a few more jokes like *Ulysses* and *Finnegans Wake,* but not another plan for a master race or the invention of the ultimate bomb. (pp. 42-5)

Richard F. Peterson, "Flann O'Brien's Timefoolery," in Irish Renaissance Annual III, *Vol. III, 1982, pp. 30-46.*

JOSÉ LANTERS

Both [***At Swim-Two-Birds*** and ***The Third Policeman***] are concerned with the relation between life and art, or more appropriately, between reality and fiction. ***At Swim*** is directly concerned with the concepts of writing and literature, and with the artificiality of literary conventions, and through these concepts it attempts to show that what is true for literature and writers is also true, in a wider sense, for life. ***The Third Policeman*** turns this approach around: instead of being concerned with the conventions of literature, it deals with the bewildering aspects of life (and death) in general. On another level, however, the conclusions reached with respect to life are shown to be equally valid for the limited world of the writer of fiction, for he attempts to depict life and reality in his work. The differences in approach are at the root of the apparent difference between the two novels, but a closer consideration of the themes of both novels reveals that, in spite of these differences, in the end they contain the same "message". (p. 267)

Briefly outlined, the structure of ***At Swim*** is as follows. The protagonist of the novel, a nameless university student, describes in biographical form his own life in the house of his uncle, as well as his "spare-time literary activities," that is, the novel he is writing about another novelist, Dermot Trellis, who is supposed to be writing a moralistic novel full of villains. The characters in Trellis's novel, however, disagree with the evil deeds they are forced to commit, and by drugging Trellis manage to lead their own virtuous lives. Trellis's son Orlick, born out of the union of Trellis and Sheila Lamont—one of Trellis's own characters—decides to avenge his mother's cruel treatment at the hands of Trellis by writing a novel about his father, in which he slowly tortures him to death.

The narrator in ***At Swim*** is a young man on the threshold of life. He is, moreover, a developing artist, and according to Ruth apRoberts, "the very type of the young hero of the *Bildungsroman*". Throughout the novel the narrator remains nameless; he has no parents that we hear of, and he lives with an equally nameless uncle. His self-conscious attitude betrays his search for a purpose in life, and his writing provides him with a means of searching for an identity. Orlick, another novelist, expresses the feeling that "wells up in the heart of every newcomer to this world that life is empty and hollow, disproportionately trivial compared with the trouble of entering it." Orlick, too, as a kind of second self to the narrator, looks for self-definition through his writing.

At Swim-Two-Birds is a novel about writing novels; it could hardly be about anything else. The student-narrator, in his adolescent *hubris,* appears to believe that he knows all there is to know about literature, and he is under the impression that he is quite an expert on the subject, which makes him approach it in a somewhat flippant and disrespectful manner. . . . This attitude leads him to put forward a "new" literary theory. The novel, he claims, as opposed to drama, "lacked the outward accidents of illusion, frequently inducing the reader to be outwitted in a shabby fashion and caused to experience a real concern for the fortunes of illusory characters." The result of this would be that "the novel, in the hands of an unscrupulous writer, could be despotic." In the narrator's opinion, a "satisfactory novel" should therefore be "a self-evident sham to which the reader could regulate at will the degree of his credulity.'' The author should ensure that the reader is aware that he is reading fiction.

The author, by breaking the conventions of literature, and thereby the illusion of reality in the novel, should expose his characters for what they really are: non-existent except on paper. It is this theory that induces the narrator to copy passages from existing works: characters should be interchangeable between books, and ''the modern novel should be largely a work of reference'' because ''most authors spend their time saying what has been said before—usually said much better.'' In Trellis's novel, characters are ''hired'' to perform a certain part in the novel. . . . By transposing the convention of drama (the actor) to his novel, the narrator effectively reduces the desired effect (creating a self-evident sham with illusory characters) to nil.

Taking his idea of the despotic novelist as his starting-point, the narrator then develops his theory with regard to his characters in such a way that it becomes paradoxical. Although his theory stresses their illusory existence, the characters should, according to this same theory, and in analogy with ''real'' actors, be given ''a private life, self-determination and a decent standard of living. This would make for self-respect, contentment and better service.'' The theory therefore returns to treating characters as ''real'' human beings, and this strange confusion of the real and the fictional is sustained throughout the novel. (pp. 268-70)

At Swim also pays attention to the conventions of time and logical order in the novel, and characteristically does so in physical terms:

> It was then that the Pooka MacPhellimey exercised the totality of his strange powers by causing with a twist of his hard hornthumb a stasis of the natural order and a surprising kinesis of many incalculable influences hitherto in suspense.

The Pooka's tricks are those of the writer as magician; he can conjure up the most fantastic and unnatural events. Under the influence of the Pooka's magic, ''a clock could be heard incessantly reciting the hours, a token that the free flight of time had also been interfered with.'' The conventions of the novel make such things possible, even if they defy the most basic laws of nature.

What makes ***At Swim*** special in its treatment of literary conventions is that it deals with the very ingredients of the novel as tangible objects. After the Pooka has worked his magic to torture Trellis, Orlick, the writer who is responsible for the story, has to pay a visit to the bathroom. Furriskey, Shanahan and Lamont, left behind with the unfinished novel, decide to give Trellis a little torture of their own. ''We'll put him back where we found him before the master comes back,'' they decide, and so they proceed (''never mind how it was done''), and the Pooka works his magic for them. The characters can be manipulated at will. A similar incident occurs when Shanahan ''inserted a brown tobacco finger in the texture of the story and in this manner caused a lacuna in the palimpsest.'' This again shows the folly of confusing paper characters with real people.

Flann O'Brien has no intention to depict an illusory reality; he wrote to Ethel Mannin about ***At Swim-Two-Birds*** that ''it is not a pale-faced sincere attempt to hold the mirror up'' and he declares that ''art has nothing to do with the 'delineation of creation' ''. The mirror in the possession of the narrator in ***At Swim*** is a special one:

> The mirror at which I shaved every second day was of the type supplied gratis by Messrs Watkins, Jameson and Pim and bore brief letterpress in reference to a proprietary brand of ale between the words of which I had acquired considerable skill in inserting the reflection of my countenance.

The mirror reflects the message of the novel: life, or reality, is seen through a muddle of words, and words spelling intoxication at that. The message is therefore that language intrudes upon, and to some extent distorts, our perception of reality, and that it makes it often more regular and comprehensible than it is. In this respect it should be remembered that the—unreliable—narrator is part of the same fiction, that the reader's perception of the novel takes place through him, and that the narrator's theory of fiction is written in the same intoxicating language.

At Swim-Two-Birds, for all its intricacy and structural tangles, is a unity all the same, and while its profusion of styles, levels and characters may seem immensely complex and intangible, it nevertheless forms the basis for this unity. The clue to this is given in the novel's epigraph from Euripides' *Hercules Furens* which, translated, reads: ''For all things go out and give way one to another.'' The most obvious instance of this is that one novel gives rise to another, and that one to yet another, so that the action of ***At Swim*** takes place at several levels. The effect thus created can be likened to a series of boxes of diminishing sizes, all fitting into one another. Policeman MacCruiskeen in ***The Third Policeman*** is in possession of just such a set of boxes, and the particular significance of these for that novel will be discussed hereafter.

The plot of ***The Third Policeman*** is more straightforward than that of ***At Swim,*** and its tone and atmosphere are very different too. The narrator whose name, even while he still remembers it, we are never told, murders old Philip Mathers with the help of his companion John Divney in order to obtain his cash-box. Divney hides the money, but after four years he allows his fellow-murderer to collect the black box from underneath the floor-boards of Mathers' house. When the narrator touches the box, however, he undergoes strange sensations, and the box disappears. After this, he undergoes a nightmarish sequence of events set in motion by two policemen, whose help he has sought for retrieving the box. Only at the end of the novel does it transpire that the narrator has been dead all the time, and that the box in Mathers' house was in fact a bomb planted there by Divney.

Throughout ***The Third Policeman*** the distinction is blurred between what is real and what is not, and between the existent and the non-existent. An example of this is Sergeant Pluck's inexorable logic:

> If you have no name you cannot own a watch and the watch that has been stolen does not exist and when it is found it will have to be restored to its rightful owner. If you have no name you possess nothing and you do not exist and even your trousers are not on you although they look as if they were from where I am sitting.

It is this same logic which causes the narrator's soul, Joe, to remark that "'*You are going to be hung for murdering a man you did not murder and now you will be shot for not finding a tiny thing that probably does not exist at all and which in any event you did not lose*'." A consistent application of this logic leads to the fundamental truth of the novel: "'*Anything can be said in this place and it will be true and will have to be believed*'."

This observation is an important one, for it introduces the preoccupation of this novel, too, with the relationship between reality and fiction. In his confrontation with Policeman MacCruiskeen, with the underground eternity full of impossible machinery, and with bicyclosis, the narrator has encountered phenomena that have no basis in reality as we know it; unknown dimensions, shapes and objects, non-existent colours or feelings and people who are really bicycles—such things contribute to a picture of a world that is beyond our comprehension. This means, effectively, that O'Brien points to a discrepancy between "reality" as it exists and "reality" as we experience it, or even as we create it, for instance in our imagination.

Reality and illusion are of course inherent to literature: the aim of the conventional novel is the depiction of an illusory reality. ***The Third Policeman*** obviously cannot be interpreted as being about a real world; the experiences of the narrator should rather be seen as a comment of a self-conscious writer on the aims and values of literature and writing itself. As ***At Swim-Two-Birds*** shows, O'Brien is very much concerned with the fictionality of fiction, and extremely conscious of the imaginary existence of fictional characters underneath the thin veneer of illusory reality. There is a distinct air of unnaturalness about all the characters in ***The Third Policeman.*** Mathers' eyes are described as "mechanical dummies animated by electricity or the like," and he appears to be hollow, pouring cups of tea into his mouth "as one would pour a bucket of milk into a churn at churning-time." MacCruiskeen is described as "'a comical man, . . . a walking emporium, you'd think he was on wires and worked with steam'." The Sergeant, too, appears to be hollow, for when he taps his forehead with his finger it produces a "booming hollow sound, slightly tinny, as if he had tapped an empty watering-can with his nail." All characters in the novel appear to be hollow, artificial puppets, incapable of functioning independently, but in ***The Third Policeman,*** unlike ***At Swim,*** there is no narrator to point out the obvious similarity between these puppets and fictional characters.

The narrator himself behaves very much as if he is being manipulated by an outside force. This force manifests itself as soon as he has set out from Mathers' house in search of the police-station; he finds that "I became surprised; surprising ideas were coming into my head from nowhere." From that moment on a large number of his own actions strike the narrator as inexplicable. . . . The mechanical behaviour of both the narrator and the other characters in the novel shows them up for what they really are: fictional characters in a novel manipulated like puppets by an author, who remains invisible behind the scenes, determining their actions.

Another strikingly unnatural feature in ***The Third Policeman*** is the landscape. Everything about it seems "almost too pleasant, too perfect, too finely made'." Just as the police-station looked as if it had been painted on cardboard, nature looks, in fact, as if it had been made by human hands, almost as if it were the scenery of a play. . . . (pp. 271-75)

The artificiality of nature posing as a "background" to the action is evinced in more than just its two-dimensional appearance; nature in ***The Third Policeman*** is purposeful and not, as in reality, haphazard and coincidental. . . . (p. 275)

The man-made setting is there, appropriately arranged by the author, and within it the two policemen Pluck and MacCruiskeen determine the narrator's future. Their method of never answering questions and turning everything to their own advantage makes them appear in perfect control of the situation, and of the narrator. The underground eternity, of which they keep on losing control, is the only source of problems in their otherwise untroubled existence. At the end of the novel it transpires that it is mad policeman Fox who has been controlling the lives of Pluck and MacCruiskeen by means of the black box, which turns out to contain four ounces of *omnium:* "'that is how I worked the fun with Pluck and MacCruiskeen, it would make you smile to think of it, they had to run and work like horses every time I shoved the readings up to danger point'." The narrator is astounded at the thought that Fox had been "calmly making ribbons of the natural order, inventing intricate and unheard of machinery to delude the other policemen, interfering drastically with time to make them think they had been leading their magical lives for years, bewildering and enchanting the whole countryside'."

The third policeman, who has disappeared but who at will quietly manipulates the course of time and action from behind the scenes, is surely a representative of the "omniscient author class", influencing the course of events without revealing his presence. Omnium, as its name suggests, provides man with the means of creating anything he wishes, just as the writer of fiction is able to create anything he wishes within his fiction. Omnium is the imagination: it makes the impossible possible. This theory also fits in with the mad scientist de Selby's idea that life is an illusion: if everything consists of omnium, and if omnium is the imagination, then it follows that existence is an illusion, and this leads neatly back to the illusory reality of the novel. Fox's imagination has got out of hand and is running away with him, since Pluck and MacCruiskeen cannot keep it in check; Fox's preoccupation with creation for its own sake is O'Brien's comment on certain experimental writers that he detested for their arrogance, for instance the Joyce of *Finnegans Wake*. (pp. 276-77)

All through the strange experiences in the country of the policemen, the narrator never gives up believing in his own mental resources, and in his ability to explain rationally and to overcome intelligently the strange phenomena he encounters. His shocking confrontation with the dead Mathers is soon dismissed by him as "a mistake"; confronted with MacCruiskeen's inventions the narrator is extremely puzzled, but admits that "I tried to make myself look like a wise person who was trying to comprehend something that called for all his wisdom." Finding himself eye to eye with such improbabilities as an invisible chest, the narrator whistles a happy tune "for the purpose of pretending that I was not disturbed." All the time, however puzzled or frightened he is by what happens to him, the narrator acts as if nothing unusual is taking place, and is determined "to pretend that everybody was an ordinary person like myself." His arrogant refusal to admit defeat and bewilderment leads him by a circular path to his downfall.

When the narrator hears that the black box he is looking for contains four ounces of omnium,

> formless speculations crowded in upon me, fantastic fears and hopes, inexpressible fancies, intoxicating foreshadowings of creations, changes, annihilations and god-like interferences. Sitting at home with my box of omnium I could do anything, see anything and know anything with no limit to my powers save that of my own imagination. Perhaps I could use it even to extend my imagination. I could destroy, alter and improve the universe at will.

In O'Brien's work this kind of intellectual arrogance is always associated with the "tyrannical" author, interfering god-like with his creation and arranging everything according to his will, to the extent of its becoming meaningless, from behind the scenes. (pp. 279-80)

Policeman MacCruiskeen's inventions also support this theory about art. MacCruiskeen looks intelligent and "if his face alone were in question he would look more like a poet than a policeman." Moreover, his boxes have "the satisfying quality of true art," but since they are only fit for containing boxes of identical appearance, his craft is an instance of *l'art pour l'art* in the extreme. The smallest boxes are invisible and " 'nobody can see me making them because my little tools are invisible into the same bargain'." In the same vein MacCruiskeen's diminutive piano can only be heard by its inventor, and he plays his own tunes on it " 'in order to extract private satisfaction from the sweetness of them'." To O'Brien such an attitude to art is decadent in the extreme; the artist is concerned only about his own satisfaction and the art is meaningless to anyone except the artist himself.

One of the rules of thumb that underlie Sergeant Pluck's apparent control of a chaotic situation is to ask questions, but never to answer them, and this piece of wisdom contains O'Brien's real criticism of MacCruiskeen's self-sufficient art. In ***At Swim-Two-Birds,*** Shanahan remarks: "the riddle of the universe I might solve if I had a mind to, . . . but I prefer the question to the answer." The Good Fairy, too, thinks that "answers do not matter so much as questions." In O'Brien's opinion, the main task of the writer is to question aspects of the world in which we live, thereby searching for new ways of describing experience, but always realising that "reality cannot be expressed or conveyed—only the illusion of it". The artist should write first and foremost for an audience, or else not write at all, for fiction for its own sake leads nowhere. O'Brien's belief that man never learns from experience and never attains self-knowledge leads him to the inevitable conclusion that it is a sign of foolishness and conceit in a writer to make bold statements about the world and to create the impression, through excess of imagination, that he understands more than he does. The conclusion must be that unreason prevails in the world, and that it is folly to pretend, in literature or otherwise, that this unreason does not exist. Instead, the writer of fiction should use his imagination to probe and query that irrational part of experience that cannot be grasped by reason. (pp. 280-81)

José Lanters, "Fiction within Fiction: The Role of the Author in Flann O'Brien's 'At Swim-Two-Birds' and 'The Third Policeman'," in Dutch Quarterly Review of Anglo-American Letters, *Vol. 13, No. 4, 1983, pp. 267-81.*

Julia O'Faolain

1932-

(Has also written as Julia Martines) English-born Irish novelist, short story writer, translator, and editor.

Photograph by Mark Gerson

Set in such diverse locales as Ireland, Italy, France, and the west coast of the United States, O'Faolain's fiction reflects her international background. The daughter of writers Sean O'Faolain and Eileen Gould, O'Faolain was born in London and has resided in the Irish countryside, Paris, Rome, and Los Angeles. With satirical wit and and dark humor, she explores cultural attitudes and themes related to sexuality, male-female relationships, Catholicism, and politics, particularly as these issues concern female characters attempting to establish their identities. Roger Garfitt stated: "To call Julia O'Faolain a satirist . . . is to do her work only partial justice: it suggests the incisiveness of her talent . . . but not the strength nor the subtlety of her concern. There is a power of mind behind her work, as well as an irreverently perceptive eye, that catches the intensity of human drives, without swallowing any of the trends in self-deception."

O'Faolain gained recognition with her first book, *We Might See Sights! and Other Stories* (1968). This volume contains stories set in Ireland and Italy that explore such topics as hypocritical cultural attitudes and young females discovering their sexuality. Many of the pieces in her second collection, *Man in the Cellar* (1974), examine power struggles between men and women. Critics were particularly impressed with the darkly comic title story, which depicts an Englishwoman who chains her Italian husband in a cellar while attempting to convince him of the inequalities in their marriage. *Daughters of Passion* (1982) collects stories that originally appeared in magazines and anthologies. The protagonists of these pieces include women whose identities are shaped by men and characters who adopt political views that suit their immediate purposes.

O'Faolain's first novel, *Godded and Codded* (1970), centers on an Irish graduate student who travels to Paris to free herself from the stifling atmosphere of her family life. Related with bawdy humor, the novel details her sexual adventures and satirizes various character types among expatriates in Paris. *Women in the Wall* (1975) is based upon the life of Radegunda, a Frankish saint. Set in sixth-century Gaul, the novel recreates Radegunda's founding of the Convent of the Holy Cross and explores spiritual motivation and the role of women in medieval society. While opinion varied as to whether O'Faolain had successfully developed her themes, most critics praised her evocation of Europe's Dark Ages.

Several critics consider *No Country for Young Men* (1980) O'Faolain's most accomplished novel. In this work, she addresses the issue of Irish nationalism to explicate the destructive, cyclical pattern of her country's history. While developing several subplots, including a murder mystery, O'Faolain examines oppression of women in Ireland and dubious values related to patriotism through three generations of a family involved in the "troubles." *The Obedient Wife* (1982), her next novel, is set in Los Angeles and centers on an unhappily married woman whose husband encourages her to see other men while he is away on business. O'Faolain explores conflicts between Catholic values and personal needs through the woman's romantic relationship with a priest. Critics were particularly impressed with O'Faolain's depiction of the detrimental effects of an unstable famiily life on the woman's thirteen-year old son. In *The Irish Signorina* (1984), O'Faolain evokes a Gothic atmosphere. Set in an Italian villa, this novel concerns a young Irish woman who visits a friend of her deceased mother and becomes involved with both the friend's grandson and her middle-aged son. O'Faolain develops a comparison between romanticism and rationalism and explores differing philosophies of life and love.

Under the name Julia Martines, O'Faolain has also published several translations of nonfiction works by Italian historical figures and edited the acclaimed essay collection *Not in God's Image: Women in History from the Greeks to the Victorians* (1973) with her husband, historian Lauro Martines.

(See also *CLC,* Vols. 6, 19; *Contemporary Authors,* Vols. 81-84; *Contemporary Authors New Revision Series,* Vol. 12; *Contemporary Authors Autobiography Series,* Vol. 2; and *Dictionary of Literary Biography,* Vol. 14.)

MICHAEL WILDING

Julia O'Faolain is not at all an 'experimental' writer. She is sensitively conscious of form—especially diction and syntax expressive of the adopted point of view—but in order the more accurately to achieve the psychological realism she aims for. And she succeeds delightfully [in ***We Might See Sights! and Other Stories***]. The personality of the 21-year-old Irish virgin (these are the defining aspects of personality the 21-year-old I.V. presses on our notice in her narration) is finely and wittily evoked in **"A Pot of Soothing Herbs"** (receptacle for Cuchulain's out-of-control weapon: the imagery is all beautifully apt) by her encounter with Dublin bohemia. It is a story that could easily have been mishandled—but the traps of both sophisticated detached hindsight, and of schoolgirl giggly naïvety, are avoided. The latter quality escapes from the content and cloys the form of **"Love in the Marble Foot":** the formal problems of presenting, with both wit and sympathy, sexually aware, Irish Catholic, sub-hysterical femininity are considerable. Yet success is total in **"Afternoon on Elba"**, where a sweaty purgatory is unleashed on the temporarily business-widowed young wife, pawed by and screamed at by horrid Italians, helpless witness of her 4-year-old son's revolting sex games with little girls, torn by post Freudian liberalism and inherited taboos. There are 13 stories in this first collection: they are all enjoyable, but the most successful, and the most original, are those about the Irish girl, at home and in Italy, where from experience and empathy a contrivance-free authenticity is deftly established. (pp. 116, 118)

Michael Wilding, in a review of "We Might See Sights! and Other Stories," in London Magazine, *n.s., Vol. 8, No. 6, September, 1968, pp. 116, 118.*

THE TIMES LITERARY SUPPLEMENT

Julia O'Faolain writes of youthful sexuality in a languorous style, as if the child's narcissism had crept into the adult's writing:

> Her controlled vibrancy enthralled me as did an aloof pity for our simplicity, and the prodigality with which, perhaps for her private amusement, she proposed considerations too fine for our grasp.

This story, **"First Conjugation"**, . . . appears in her collection, ***We Might See Sights!***—several of which are marred by a similar, rather dated pomposity. She is free with adjectives and over-ready with an abstract noun for physical circumstances: "she probed the intimacy of flesh sweating through his back". But the Irish stories are full of liveliness and, in those with an Italian setting, the ardent manner often seems appropriate.

"Cool and Macabre," in The Times Literary Supplement, *No. 3491, January 23, 1969, p. 77.*

DEREK MAHON

[***Godded and Codded***] follows the fortunes of Sally Tyndal, fresh from Ireland to write her thesis at the Sorbonne, as she falls in love with Mesli, an Algerian revolutionary, and drifts away from the pious respectability of her middle-class Dublin background. Several delightful characters stick close to her: Fintan McCann, an expatriate nonpainter out of early Beckett and Flann O'Brien; Letty O'Keefe, 'Mummy's spy', a game, boozy *vielle fille;* and Letty's lover, Raimondo, an aging Italian count in the best silent-movie tradition. One could wish that Mesli himself were less wooden. He is presented as pure physique ('a design superior to that found in France or the British Isles') and decked out with a few revolutionary principles. One can see what Miss O'Faolain is getting at, but he doesn't quite come off. This is a pity, for the book shows great potential. A few deft strokes and Fintan stands before us, 'like cutlery slack in a bag'. . . .

Miss O'Faolain avoids heartlessness. Letty's attempted seduction of Fintan, and prim old Patrick Conneally's of Sally when she goes home for Christmas, are genuinely touching. The book ends on a curiously indecisive note, as if in anticipation of a sequel. Let's hope she picks a better title next time. (p. 459)

Derek Mahon, "Sleek Desolation," in The Listener, *Vol. 84, No. 2166, October 1, 1970, pp. 457, 459.*

THE TIMES LITERARY SUPPLEMENT

In the tradition of her most famous literary compatriot, Miss O'Faolain's first novel [***Godded and Codded***] is a Portrait of the Artist as a Young Woman. And although its setting—Paris during the Algerian "troubles"—offers scenes as headily nostalgic, as sozzled and bohemian, as any Dublin experience, her subject too is inescapably Irish, that burden it seems impossible for even the youngest most intelligent writer to leave behind in the Celtic Crepuscule—sexual guilt, and bitter rage against the backward, hypocritical, absurd society that has engendered it. Sally arrives in Paris greedily imagining she's shaken off her cloistered upbringing. . . .

But the dark eyes and smooth body of Mesli, a militant Arab student, offer the most dangerous kind of dusty answer; intoxicating hours, days on end of picknicking among the rumpled sheets in Sally's poky Left Bank room, the bliss of ignoring raised eyebrows and any thought of her thesis—how short-lived Sally's contented emancipation turns out to be! For just as she begins to realize that Algerian brothers-in-war mean more to Mesli than any woman, she also finds she's pregnant. Even the grisly endurance of an amateur abortion does not, it seems, equip a girl with the self-confidence which will deal with fathers, or with the "aquatic beasts" of remorse which keep surfacing. Men, or rather a man, in the shape of a suave middle-aged Italian antique-dealer whom she easily and meanly pinches from dear old lonely Letty, still offer too tempting a buffer of security and cosseting.

As a wilder and more original counterpoint to Sally's guilty progress we meet Fintan McCann, the ramshackle wreck of a painter from the bogs who scrounges a lonely existence in the room above. He's a soul already lost—or maybe a Holy Innocent at heart—ready to pirate scandalous diaries to bibliophiles, hurl paint at the cultural establishment, torture himself with lust and remorse—yet also to hold the hands of others, such as Sally, who easily persuade him their plight's worse than his own, worth even the sharing of Mortal Sin. Maybe it's rather too easy to recognize Fintan—as indeed it's easy enough to spot models, both literary and actual, for the most of Miss O'Faolain's Parisian characters. She is a slyly accurate caricaturist of Left Bank scenes as well as people. What makes her novel marvellously readable, and suggests the best possible auguries for her literary future, is not its obvious and hackneyed material but the sharp, whimsical, often bookish intelligence of her style. She skates brilliantly through the confused images of Sally's mind: agonized with sensual excitement, flippant, vain, bravely comic and endlessly self-critical.

"Hot from the Cloisters," in The Times Literary Supplement, *No. 3579, October 2, 1970, p. 1125.*

J. G. FARRELL

There is . . . a lot to be recommended in Julia O'Faolain's first novel ***Godded and Codded*** which concerns the misadventures of that most vulnerable of creatures: the Irish girl abroad. This time the girl is middle-class and a graduate. Abroad is Paris and she is there on a scholarship looking without much conviction for a suitable thesis subject. What she finds instead is an Arab lover, an elderly Italian count as first-reserve lover, and an eccentric Irish painter who is too uncouth to make it but comes in handy to help with an abortion, as well as to provide a drunken lecture scene of *Ginger Man*-like proportions. Miss O'Faolain knows her Paris: the Moroccan house at the Cité Universitaire where her heroine is deflowered is certainly the best place for boy and girl students to bed down together at student prices undisturbed by sterile authority. However, the best part of the novel is that which describes the girl returning home to spend Christmas with her parents in Dublin. The mixture of complacency, chauvinism and insecurity with which the Irish greet those of their compatriots who have lived abroad is beautifully conveyed. 'Don't we seem a stick-in-the-mud lot to you here?' demands a seedy Irish suitor with whom she finds herself going to mass on Christmas morning. As a whole the novel tends to be somewhat uneven but it suffers from no shortage of talent or vitality.

J. G. Farrell, "Girls and Boys," in The Spectator, *Vol. 225, No. 7424, October 10, 1970, p. 407.*

MIKE POOLE

Julia O'Faolain's urbane novels have frequently hinted at the kind of vacuum created by rapid secularisation in societies like Ireland. In ***The Obedient Wife*** she elevates this concern into a major theme. Carla is an Italian living in California and contemplating having an affair after fifteen years of being cheated on by an obnoxiously *macho* husband. She becomes involved with a Catholic priest, who is in a kind of limbo between renouncing his vocation and beginning new life as an academic. Their tentative and fragile relationship is conducted in the shadow cast by the two institutions that have dominated their adulthood—Marriage and the Church—and eventually comes to grief because Carla, in particular, can find nothing in the rootless, hedonistic society of the West Coast that is ordered or ritualised enough to be worth breaking away for.

This thorough-going conservative scenario—in which the pull of family life Italian-style is made to triumph over mere 'emotion'—is re-inforced in a number of sub-plots. An adolescent son in love with a girl whose childhood has been blighted by a broken home; a divorcée best friend permanently preyed on by a philandering neighbour; and, just to further stress the shallowness of California, a series of rain-induced land-slips that threaten to undermine house foundations in the suburban Los Angeles setting. It's a sophisticated metaphorical structure for dealing with a crisis of direction that is undoubtedly real enough. And the courage involved in centring a contemporary narrative on such a thoroughly unfashionable heroine is not to be underestimated. Yet one cannot help but feel that this is a novel which, for all its sympathy with its main character, somehow manages to collude in her oppression.

Mike Poole, "Creating New Identities," in New Statesman, *Vol. 103, No. 2671, May 28, 1982, p. 25.*

JAMES CAMPBELL

One of Julia O'Faolain's concerns as a novelist is to show the effect which the actions of one generation are likely to have on the generation which follows, particularly in an unstable environment. In ***No Country For Young Men*** . . . where the action spanned the years between 1921 and 1979 in battle-scarred Ireland, one of the themes was the inexorability of the past; with great skill, Julia O'Faolain revealed the links between past and present which, though not always visible, are always there.

At first glance, ***The Obedient Wife*** is less ambitious. The action is restricted to a few weeks in a hot summer in Los Angeles (a 'high-paranoid low-trust society'), centring on the marital and maternal worries of Carla, a thirty-six year old Italian woman living separately—temporarily, she hopes—from her husband. Julia O'Faolain has created a more domesticated prose to contain the emotions and actions of her heroine, quite different from the wilfully overwritten, occasionally jagged sentences of ***No Country For Young Men,*** and the result, for this reader at least, is more satisfying.

The awareness of how separate generations affect one another is still there: Carla cares about her overbearing in-laws, but not half as much as she does about the effect which her unstable home is having on her fourteen-year-old son, Maurizio, an intelligent, sensitive, crazy mixed up kid, who cannot be sure if he is Italian or American.

Carla thirsts for a life which is basically simple, but her husband throws her into confusion by fleeing, on suspect motives, to Italy. . . . However, by way of a friend who thinks she's going through a spiritual crisis but really can't wait to get under the frock of the local priest, Carla herself becomes involved with the unworldly curate, first as friend, then as counsellor, and finally—inevitably—as lover. (p. 86)

The relationship between Carla and Leo, the priest, (and the subordinate involvement of Leo's initial admirer and her husband Terry, a superb creation, who presents a radio show devoted to dishing out moral philosophy as profound as the kitchen sink) is only the book's main narrative; there is also the effect which all this is having on Maurizio to take into account, and in some ways the novel is about him.

Being unsure of his national identity, Maurizio is the focus of numerous small cultural crises, and a constant worry to Carla. Looking around him for a set of values, he can choose between what he sees in the movies (that movies are an alternative life-form, rather than a diverting entertainment, is a recurring motif), what he picks up from the assorted no-goods who are the neighbours, and what he is likely to see his mother doing with the priest in the living room. Carla's dilemma—or one of them—is between her own 'freedom' and ensuring that the 'difficult phase' which her son informs her he's going through, is not the first stage of a ruined life.

Carla is a woman seeking stability in a world where everything—in both the private and the public realms—acts against it. Her simple values and ambitions are anything but reaffirmed by the world about her, and she sees her son's well-being in danger. Does she, then, make the right decision by returning to her rather thick husband at the end of the book? Is she condemning herself to a lifetime of mimicking trust? Her choice will not appeal to everyone, but at least it is her own: she has, as it were, come through the fire to arrive at it, and therefore it is more likely to reinforce her sense of herself than anything in the high-paranoid low-trust society.

This is a beautifully-written, witty, well-structured novel, and I was sorry to reach the end of it. It contains many vivid scenes which grow in the mind, refusing to die out for the reason that, with genuine artistry, all the leading characters have been provided with wholly convincing inner lives. (p. 87)

James Campbell, "Returning to the Fold," in London Magazine, *n.s., Vol. 22, No. 3, June, 1982, pp. 86-7.*

JOHN MELLORS

When Carla, married with a 13-year-old son, listens to Leo, the Roman Catholic priest who becomes her lover, she believes that 'under cover of irony, he told the truth'. That is how Julia O'Faolain tells her home-truths. ***The Obedient Wife*** is a masterpiece of unlaboured irony. Also, every character in the book, major or minor, man, woman or child, is an individual personality, totally real. For example, when the priest has made up his mind to abandon celibacy: 'He was ecstatic with materialism and saw it as sacramental. "A car," he said, "an old jalopy," and it became Ezekiel's chariot, gilded with humility.' Place is equally real: a 'slide area' suburb of Los Angeles.

Is Carla an obedient wife out of principle, or, as her macho husband thinks, only because her upbringing has conditioned her to be 'a victim'? Carla tastes the pleasures of illicit love but comes back in the end to her self-centred husband and bewildered son. She has concluded that caring, even if it includes quarrelling and fighting, is more important than sensitivity. ***The Obedient Wife*** both stimulates and satisfies. (p. 23)

John Mellors, "Left Luggage," in The Listener, *Vol. 107, No. 2763, June 3, 1982, pp. 22-3.*

PATRICIA CRAIG

As a symbol of Catholic tenacity, the mass rock—associated with Ireland in the penal days—has been exchanged for the rock mass, which signifies the church's eagerness to present itself as a thoroughly modern institution—ease of manner, showmanship and all. An appropriate setting for rock masses and other travesties of church rituals is California, where such popularizations flourish. [In ***The Obedient Wife***] Julia O'Faolain places her Italian heroine, Carla Verdi, in a Los Angeles suburb, and ropes in natural and unnatural forces—seismic tremors, mudslides, fires, domestic violence, animal killings and so on—to reinforce the sense of disintegration her novel postulates.

Narrative irony is at work from the start. Carla, recommending adultery to a friend in the grip of an infatuation with a Catholic priest, quickly finds herself involved in an amorous liaison with the same priest, who likes to be known as Leo. Carla, possessor of a useless law degree from a Florentine university, has been left in Los Angeles with her thirteen-year-old son, while her overbearing husband Marco engages in business pursuits in Italy (from which location he sends out a sequence of letters advising his wife to broaden her sexual experience while she has the chance). Carla's stability, while everything around her shakes, is the product of a secular code which encompasses order, solicitude and fastidiousness. Brought up on Boccaccio, she is apt to view clerical lapses from celibacy in a worldly and tolerant spirit somewhat at odds with the intense austerities of Northern Catholicism—even in its debased state. Not that Carla has any feeling for religion at all: the church's efforts to make itself palatable embarrass her, its excesses dismay her and its compromises worry her, once she forgoes the right to be disinterested. In her relations with Leo, she cannot quite separate the priest from the man, and it is only the latter she has any use for. Leo, by his choice of profession, has placed himself outside the range of ordinary affections; on his own terms, he is either damned from the start of any carnal affair, or "living by marked-down values: an unlikeable trait in a lover". Can it be that adulteration of church doctrines encourages adultery? To play fast and loose with selected precepts while professing a fundamental belief in the church's moral imperatives indicates, at any rate, a certain infirmity of purpose. . . .

There is plenty of scope for comedy in Julia O'Faolain's novel, but she has chosen not to present her material in a comic mode. (That she can be funny is evident from certain asides, such as the following, summing up a traditional pronouncement on female adultery: "Men were less likely to lose their heads and hearts and what they did with their other parts was consequently of less account.") Instead, she coolly assesses the circumstances and traits that have got her characters into their present predicament, and still more coolly allows their defects and misapprehensions to become apparent in the course of the narrative. Carla's instinct, for example, is less sound than she imagines; where her son is concerned, it hasn't been working properly at all.

The Obedient Wife is an exceptionally polished work; if its ending disappoints feminists, who require gestures of social rebelliousness from their fiction, just as Catholic readers used to require wholesomeness from theirs, it is none the less appropriate, in that it represents an assertion of the values its heroine has lived by.

Patricia Craig, "Playing Fast and Loose," in The Times Literary Supplement, *No. 4138, July 23, 1982, p. 807.*

HARRIETT GILBERT

Daughters of Passion brings together, in an original paperback, nine of Julia O'Faolain's intense, and intensely personal stories. **"Legend for a Painting"**, the first, is both atypical and paradigmatic—a fairy story, its narrative voice is unusually formal and detached; but its subject matter is one that recurs throughout the ensuing collection. The dependence of women on men for their very identity, and the ways in which they abuse themselves in order to acquire that male-defined Self, these are O'Faolain's themes. The lady in the **"Legend"** appears to be chained to a dragon. A knight thunders up to rescue her (ignoring her insistence that she's perfectly happy as she is) and, as soon as he has killed the dragon, realises that he's got it all wrong—that *it* was chained to *her*. The lady, however,

> Picked up a link (from the chain) that had become detached. 'I'll wear this,' she said bitterly, 'in token of my servitude. I'm your prisoner now.'

In the more realistic, 'serious' stories, a woman describes herself to her sister as 'valueless, being manless'; another cuts herself off from her roots to fulfil a (gay) man's fantasies; another bounces from 'ugliness' to 'prettiness' depending on the last man's judgment . . . For all the anger, bitter pain and sardonic humour of the writing, the cumulative effect on the reader is one of frustrated irritation.

Harriett Gilbert, "Lunacies," in New Statesman, *Vol. 104, No. 2695, November 12, 1982, p. 33.*

FRANCIS KING

The initial story and the title story can often, between them, be relied upon to convey a writer's dominant themes throughout a collection. This is certainly true of Julia O'Faolain's ***Daughters of Passion.***

The first of these nine stories, eight of which have already appeared in magazines or anthologies, **"Legend for a Painting",** takes as its starting point one of those works of art in which a knight is depicted as having just ridden up, lance at the ready, to rescue some immaculately gowned and coiffeured lady from the dragon to which she is chained. In this case, in reply to the knight's declaration 'I have come to set you free!', the lady, puzzled, replies: 'What do you mean by free?' Deciding that the lady's long bondage must have perverted her sense of values, the knight kills the beast. It then becomes clear that, so far from the lady having been the dragon's prisoner, he has been hers. . . .

In fact, this story, so uncharacteristically whimsical in tone, is the weakest in a strong collection; but its theme, of the idea of freedom from men exerting on women a tyranny as oppressive as their former subjection to them, is one which keeps recurring. Thus, when, in **"Mad Marga",** a self-regarding, homosexual art-historian rescues a plain, dim, female colleague of his from the dragon-dream of Kuche, Kinder, Kirche by lending her subversive literature, extolling collective over individual passion and dragging her off to demos, he merely makes her the prisoner of people far more sinister, exacting and destructive than any husband she might have acquired in her small hometown in Iowa. . . .

In the story actually called **"Daughters of Passion",** an Irish woman, Maggy, guilty of having killed a Special Branch officer with a bomb, lies on a prison bed on the twelfth day of the hunger strike which she has been persuaded—by a man of course!—to undertake in protest at not being given special status as a political prisoner. Maggy carried the bomb for someone else—just as, throughout this fine collection, people are metaphorically carrying bombs for others and so ensuring their own destruction—being the victim of her flat-mate Dizzy, a woman of Anglo-Irish Protestant stock, whose revolutionary commitment eventually turns out to be little more than a perilously childish game. Terrorism is a disease of which people like Dizzy are carriers and from which people like Maggy die. . . .

The general tone of these stories is one of sympathy with radical and even violent action but of suspicion of the motives of those who precipitate it. Miss O'Faolain has a lethal way with the kind of people who descend into the dark, malodorous basement of society while at the same time ensuring that there is a lift, door open, behind them, to waft them up and away to their penthouses if the atmosphere should grow too poisonous. Such a character is the American girl in **"Bought",** who takes up with a dirty, big-bellied artist in Paris, toys with the idea of making him famous, and then abandons him for a return to a wealthy protector back in the States. Such a character, too, is the liberal-minded woman in **"Will You Please Go Now",** who invites an Asian, met at a demonstration, back to her home for Christmas, becomes increasingly embarrassed by his behaviour, and eventually dismisses him.

These are stories remarkable for their intellectual and emotional toughness. Apart from a reference to Frankenstein as though he were the monster—do publishers no longer edit their books?—they are also written with a faultless combination of grace, concision and exactness.

Francis King, "Monsters," in The Spectator, *Vol. 250, No. 8060, January 1, 1983, p. 22.*

GILLIAN GREENWOOD

The family and the multifarious relationships therein seem to be the continuing preoccupation of [Julia O'Faolain], in her novels at any rate. The settings may be foreign, Ireland and Los Angeles in the last two [***No Country for Young Men*** and ***The Obedient Wife***], now Tuscany [in ***The Irish Signorina***]; but the dilemmas of difficult children, unfaithful husbands, and women with decisions to make remain constant. That is not to say that she is a predictable writer. Her work merely reflects the limited permutations of life and her great strength is the creation of little worlds in which a rather odd group of folk impinges on the nucleus.

Her collection of stories, ***Daughters of Passion,*** was a departure from this structure, though the stories were all based on the rituals of love, with varying degrees of success. Her new novel, ***The Irish Signorina,*** seems intended as a love story in the Gothic Romance vein, but we are back in the bosom of an aristocratic Italian family whose awareness of position and inheritance further complicates some rather predictable complexities.

The young Irish girl of the title arrives to stay with the Marchesa Cavalcanti whom she has never met before. Anne's mother had been 'companion' to the Marchesa's simple and now dead daughter many years before. As she arrives, a memorial wake is taking place for the dead daughter. A gloomy beginning. Within hours of her arrival at the villa (which makes do as a Gothic castle for the purpose of this analogy) Anne spies the Beast in the Tower (a terrorist on the run who is being protected by the Marchesa's grandson, Neri). There are also: a handsome, if a bit elderly hero, Neri's father, Guido; two parallel mysteries to be solved (one past, one present); and an impediment to the course of true love in the shape of the Marchesa, a woman of determination and the lynchpin of both the family and the narrative.

It seems at first that it was the plot's clichés which make this a disappointing book, but Julia O'Faolain has achieved an idiosyncratic mastery over old chestnuts in the past (the sexual fall of a priest, for example, in ***The Obedient Wife***). It is true that she does not unravel the mysteries—the terrorist plot, the identity of Anne's mother's lover—very subtly. I, who can rarely tell who's dunnit, had no trouble with these. There is a particularly clumsy device whereby Anne happens to go into a café and overhear a conversation of particular interest to her: 'Anne opened her guide book and pretended to be absorbed. They seemed unaware of her . . .'

But all this would not have mattered had the characters revealed themselves along the way. They seem to be in hiding. The rough outlines of personalities are sketched, some more strongly than others—the Marchesa almost comes off, though unfortunately she's dying and can rally only briefly—but their fleshing-out is sacrificed to the weak storyline. This is a great shame when one thinks what Miss O'Faolain might have made of them. Her horrible D. J. Terry Steele—'Mr. Golden Voice of the Southland'—and the dreadful transient Briggs family in ***The Obedient Wife*** are alarmingly substantial. There is a very promising Monsignor in ***The Irish Signorina*** whose comic possibilities boded well. But he *knows too much* and is wheeled off whenever he begins to blossom. The one exception to this is a character who has nothing to do with the plot at all, Count Bonnacorso, or 'Bobo'.

Bobo has been in love with the Marchesa for 40 years or so. He has never married since she refused him. His observations and reflections hold the book together and it is his devotion to the Marchesa which delineates her presence more sharply than that of the other characters. . . .

Bobo is present, too, at the central set-piece of the novel: a dinner-party at which the verbal seduction of Anne by Guido takes place during a dialogue on the nobility of love. This is a rich episode despite its shadowy participants. . . .

Despite the clever artifice of this section, the ultimate problem of the book remains: what is one to make of this central coupling? Guido, a suave politician in his late forties, is a philanderer and seemingly insincere. Anne is 22, supposedly mature for her years. Much more than that we simply do not know. Julia O'Faolain's previous heroines are far more distinctive. Perhaps Anne's youth caused the writer problems, though she is more successful with her portrayal of young Neri [and his affair with Anne]. . . .

Despite this infidelity, Anne and Guido's love is the focus of the book, and it is utterly unconvincing. The limitations which Miss O'Faolain has set herself also prevent, for the most part, her graceful prose from transcending the banal. She has bricked herself in and, despite the Tuscan sunshine, delivered an unripe fruit.

Gillian Greenwood, "Bricked In," in The Spectator, *Vol. 253, No. 8150, September 15, 1984, p. 33.*

LINDA TAYLOR

The Irish Signorina begins and ends with mourning. Between death and death, the lives of the characters are filled with ghosts. The Cavalcanti family is steeped in its own past: the name of the Marchesa's son, Guido, is a remembrance of the fourteenth-century poet, the friend of Dante whose canzone on the nature of love was studied as a philosophical treatise. Guido's son, a revolutionary, is called Neri, recalling the "Black" faction in Florence, opposed to the Bianchi, of whom the original Guido became leader. These hints of old debates and opinions, of battles and allegiances, are central (if obscurely so) to the way in which Julia O'Faolain's latest novel grapples with the nature of life. On the one hand there are compromises, lies, patchings up, dullness, deals and marriage; on the other, passion, terrorism, change, wildness and sex. Anne's own parents (both dead) took opposing sides: "her mother had an unsafe laugh and her husband, the bomb expert, had handled her with care". Too careful of the wife who craved passion but had married him for safety, the bomb expert died when a bomb he was defusing exploded in his hands. The mother, in fact, was a spent shell, her energy all wasted in a love affair with Guido which began twenty-five years before Anne's present visit to the villa.

The plot—Anne falls in love with Guido who turns out to be her real father while Neri involves her, marginally, in a terrorist conspiracy—provides the bones for the real stuff of the novel: the debate between romanticism and rationalism, in which the characters are more at war with themselves than, as they seem to be, with one another. . . .

Is it more passionate, the novel asks, to love spiritually, as in the old Count Bonnacorso's obsessive platonic feeling for Niccolosa, or lustfully, as in Anne and Neri's comforting night on the library floor? (Is passion, anyway, a part of love?) Or is it better to reject idealism and lust for the pragmatic alliance—money, property and safety as the basis for marriage? O'Faolain provides no answers—everyone in the novel is defeated, cheated by life (its mortal appetites and energies) or God (God is love, or is He?) or fervour (political factions are beset with infiltrators and cover-ups). Guido, the skilful lawyer, unhappily, pragmatically married, preaches that love is ennobling. Bonnacorso sees "all that spew Guido had tossed forth [as] nothing but a mating song"—to catch Anne. Anne, the rationalist, plans to throw caution to the wind; to disregard taboos of incest; to live, as all the Tuscans seem to live, by stealth and lies; to marry (?) Guido. . . .

O'Faolain's characters, cynical, depressed and oppressed, are unconvinced by their own philosophical arguments; the world she portrays is dark, convoluted, Machiavellian. As Guido says to his mother and Anne: "we three, laughing over our champagne. . .are in a long and pessimistic tradition. Ours is a sad laughter."

Linda Taylor, "Mating Song," in The Times Literary Supplement, *No. 4256, October 26, 1984, p. 1224.*

DAVID BURLEIGH

With one significant exception, Julia O'Faolain's settings are all more or less contemporary. And her work is most commonly occupied with a theme of personal love, or, more specifically, the physical expression of it, with male and female sexuality. Cultural, religious and political concerns are introduced where they intrude upon areas that are private and sexual, but it is the latter which seem to interest the author most. (p. 8)

In the title piece of the author's first published volume, ***We Might See Sights! and other stories*** (1968), the protagonist, a girl called Madge, goes with her friend Bernie to visit a cave. But first Madge has to end another relationship with a girl who, according to Madge's mother, is socially unsuitable. The rejected companion is described thus:

> Rosie had blonde, naturally curly hair, abundant as an aureole and alive with lice. She had a mouthful of bossy teeth and foamy laugh.

This is an extremely vivid picture, rhythmically stated, showing how Julia O'Faolain's strong sense of language is present right from the beginning.

Her friendships rearranged, Madge goes off with Bernie and the latter's mentally defective baby brother to explore the cave. Here they catch sight of a couple making love. The girls withdraw but the defective child doesn't understand. Afterwards, Madge beats him in a rage of adolescent jealousy and frustration. Unreasonable urges, we learn, are lurking inside us, ready to burst out and seek expression, if not in one form then in another. Instances of sexual denial reappear in the author's work.

In another story from the same collection, also the title story from a later selection of these and other tales, ***Melancholy Baby*** (1978), lonely, selfish Aunt Adie, married but childless and sexually unfulfilled, tries to dominate her orphaned niece Gwennie: 'Like the poised claw of a crane, her affective energies remained in suspense'. But these energies will not be refused and do fight their way out, with extremely unpleasant results for Gwennie. It is a recognizable and convincing, if not entirely new, way of looking at Ireland, about which the author writes with sardonic humour and, it often seems, a kind of smouldering anger.

The object of Julia O'Faolain's anger in her first novel, ***Godded and Codded*** (1970), about a young woman seeking sexual adventure in Paris, is middle class convention, with its supply of platitudinous prohibitions. Sally, the young woman, says of herself: 'I am like a leaky gas jet. I shall poison the air if my fumes are not lit'. She then proceeds to shuck off the restrictive attitudes of her Dublin parents. The novel is written in a jaunty style suitable for a romp, and some of it is quite funny. But none of the characters seem either very real or very sympathetic, though they are shrewdly observed and entertainingly presented.

What the novel does do, however, is establish the theme of a female finding her independence. This is continued and expanded in the title story of another collection, ***Man in the Cellar*** (1974). Indeed, with this second collection, the focus of the stories shifts noticeably from questions of exploration, to those of continuation, from the making to the maintenance of marriage. Engaging and thought-provoking, they give life to a wide selection of personae and situations.

Women in the Wall (1975), Julia O'Faolain's next book, is a stunning departure, both chronologically and in its imaginative scope, from all the previous work. It is set in sixth century Gaul, after the collapse of the Roman Empire, a time of tribal rivalries and random violence. 'Gaul', we are told, 'was like a painted chessboard whose inks have run. Borders were vague'. Partly historical reconstruction, partly invention, it is basically the story of a woman named Radegunda and the convent she founds when she leaves her husband, the King, to turn her back on the sensual world.

Giving up the world, however, for the 'reverse world' of Christianity, Radegunda is just as passionately physical in her search for spiritual union with God—she tortures and brands herself—as she was in bed with the King. A reason for atonement is suggested, as it is again when the illegitimate daughter of the convent's abbess, Ingunda, decides to become an anchoress and have herself closed up in a wall as a gesture of devotion. In the background there are political plots both inside and outside the convent. It is a very exciting story, the most compelling that the author has written, and a much livelier book than Helen Waddell's classic, *Peter Abelard* (1933), which deals with the Middle Ages at a later century.

Thematic consistency is maintained with Julia O'Faolain's other work through her examination in this novel of the consequences of the peculiar lives that celibates lead. A disapproval of celibacy was already implicit in the early stories, and here we find constant references to 'waste of life' and 'living death':

> These women, who called each other 'Mother' and 'Sister' were neither, were so many stoppered bottles. Emotion fermented in them. Their tenderness was turned on a distant, inconceivable infant: the babe of Bethlehem, an image just persuasive enough to set the milk of human affection moving in their body ducts. They longed for reality. Any reality.

They are, however, unable to see themselves in this way, and continue to mortify their flesh in endeavours to release the spirit. Despite O'Faolain's evident scepticism about religious practices, and a circumspectness in describing miraculous happenings, this is a very powerful book, wide and deep in its sympathies.

Vestigially medieval values, and unexpected and improbable acts of violence, persist down to the present in Ireland. Puritanism, too, though much undermined, still holds on in many quarters. It is not dead and gone, as John Montague, parodying Yeats's "September 1913", would have us believe. But it is certainly dying. The current availability of books that were earlier banned is proof of that. But the social and political changes that have taken place have not produced a country that is rich with hope and opportunity. Reflecting this, Julia O'Faolain's Irish novel, parodying the opening line of Yeats's "Sailing to Byzantium", is entitled ***No Country for Young Men*** (1980).

A complex and rich book, this novel is her most ambitious work so far. The main narrative describes an American filmmaker's attempts to extract secret information about the troubles of the 1920s from an elderly nun. The film is intended to raise funds to be sent to the North through an organisation called, wittily, Banned Aid. While the old nun struggles with her recalcitrant memory, the events of an earlier time are brought before us. The political past is thus cleverly, and comically, telescoped into the present, and we can watch both unfolding at the same time. Sidelights are cast along the way on other matters, such as American interference in Ireland.

The novel has a full gallery of characters, many encountered only briefly, but Julia O'Faolain always fixes them with a sharp eye. James Duffy, the ingenuous film-man, first encounters the Irish at a radio station in California:

> There was an Orangeman from Belfast in a pair of bright new cowboy boots, a local priest whose cufflinks were slightly bigger than quarters, and a fierce, butch-looking girl from Ireland who turned out to have a remarkable knack for scoring debating points and keeping physical control of the mike. She spoke with the fluency of a mimeographed flyer . . .

The dialogue which ensues from a purported discussion between the priest and the young woman is hilarious, interleaved as it is with another conversation that James is having. The whole book contains a series of such vignettes which come together to create a broad portrait of a time and place.

The other crucial strand of the narrative is James's affair with Grainne O'Malley, in whose home the old nun is staying because they are distant relatives. Both Grainne and James are married, which means that their affair must be kept secret, though it doesn't succeed in remaining so. The difference in their backgrounds profoundly affects their sexual liaison. And the liaison itself affects the lives of Grainne's husband and son, and James's wife, who receives detailed letters chronicling its course which we are allowed to read. Contingent events precipitate the situation into one of crisis, while the attachment of James and Grainne to each other deepens.

Once more the theme is revealed to be an examination of sexual relations. In this novel, and the one succeeding it, there is a preoccupation with marriage: its uncertainties, its durability in a permissive age, its interracial possibilities, its adjustment to the changing social position of women. And those who stay outside it, celibates and virgins, especially if they oppose it in any way, are given short shrift by the author. Thus the crusading Jane, who runs a home for Battered Wives in which Grainne spends some time, is made to appear foolish. And the two acts of violence which occur in the book are both perpetrated by individuals who have denied, or been denied, any sexual experience. (pp. 8-11)

Julia O'Faolain's next novel, ***The Obedient Wife*** (1982), is in a way complementary to the book it succeeds. It gives the other side of the story, that of the wife who must wait in America while her husband philanders in Europe, and the future of the marriage hangs in the air. The difference is that the couple in this case are not American but Italian, and also that, unlike James and his wife, they have a child, a boy. Son and mother bide their time in California, in an area of mud-slides, surrounded by people living lives quite different from their own, and threatened by all of this. Carla, the wife, has a dalliance with a priest which is handled with generosity. Cazz Dobrinski, a parasite and layabout who is one of their neighbours, is perhaps the most evil, and also the most memorable, character in the book. The American idiom is brilliantly caught. At the close of the novel, the family are reunited, and marriage survives, reassuringly but not very surprisingly.

One of Julia O'Faolain's particular talents as a writer is her ability to allow people to speak for themselves, in such a way that they often uncover or condemn themselves out of their own mouths. That we have the feeling that we are listening to the personae she adopts, and not to the author herself, is a measure of her skill as a novelist. Considering the range in the backgrounds of the people in her books, from politicians to gardeners, Irish, American and Italian, this represents quite a considerable achievement. It also means that she can sustain short stories in monologue form remarkably well.

In her third collection of short stories, ***Daughters of Passion*** (1982), we find examples of such monologues. The tales have varied settings, only two of the nine being concerned with Ireland. One of these is the story of the title, about three women, two of them Catholic orphans and the third a Catholic convert of Anglo-Irish stock, who have attended the same convent, then meet again in London and become involved with the IRA. The central character, Maggy, is in Brixton gaol on hunger strike as the story opens. She has planted a bomb and murdered a policeman, her reason for doing so not being entirely clear, though it appears to be another case of displaced passion. Julia O'Faolain makes splendid play out of the differences between the three women, whose fates are unexpectedly intertwined.

The other piece from this collection with an Irish setting is also a very fine one. **"And Why Should Not Old Men Be Mad?"** (another title from Yeats) deals with an elderly bishop in a mental hospital and an old lawyer friend who comes to visit him. Written with great humour, it concludes somewhat in the manner of Chekhov's "Ward Six". The other stories pursue and extend themes of marriage and sexual relations. The author's prose in these later stories shows greater suppleness and repose, as do her sympathies, but with no diminishing in the tough intelligence with which the characters are drawn.

Though she has always been vivid and evocative, inventing fresh images to elucidate her meaning and please her readers, some passages in Julia O'Faolain's earlier books are jerky and difficult to read. In later work there is much less reliance on the stream of consciousness technique for representing inner thoughts. Sentences become longer and more fluid, alliteration is less clamorous, and there is a welcome decline in the use of exclamation marks. At its best, her writing has a refreshing ribaldry and a literate wit that make it continuously enjoyable to read. The author's cosmopolitanism is, of course, rare in Irish writing.

Without doubt ***No Country for Young Men*** is Julia O'Faolain's most substantial book to date. It is her most wide-ranging and complex work of fiction, and one of her most pleasurable. . . . It takes an admirably cool and critical look at Ireland, though its mixture of realism and farce is not completely successful. Her most remarkable book is the earlier ***Women in the Wall,*** with its extraordinary imaginative reconstruction and gripping tale of an age which, though long ago, continues to resonate down into our own mad, knee-capping time. (pp. 13-14)

David Burleigh, "Dead and Gone: The Fiction of Jennifer Johnston and Julia O'Faolain," in Irish Writers and Society at Large, *edited by Masaru Sekine, Barnes and Noble Books, 1985, pp. 1-15.*

JULIA WHEDON

The premise of [***The Irish Signorina***] is an interesting one, yet in [O'Faolain's] hands the characters and the story are strangely operatic (one scene is actually played with a character hidden "comically" behind a couch). . . . Further to continue the comparison, the libretto seems to exist just to prop up the music—in this case, the writing—which is speculative, ruminative, descriptive and overly gorgeous, as if too much had been made of this writer's gift for nuance and detail.

Ms. O'Faolain is clearly a gifted and devout observer. She writes of "olive groves and towers awash in . . . spinach-water light," a house like a "conch sour with the smells and echoes of dead tides," "a skin of wrinkled damp" clinging to windowpanes, and so on. But the descriptions get away from her. At an intense narrative moment, when the reader needs a no-nonsense answer from a character, we are obliged to observe that his "head bobbed in the dimness like a parsnip in simmering broth."

Superfatted descriptions, together with a surfeit of quotations and mythological references, finally topple the task at hand. The destruction is complete when the characters are betrayed. Just when you think they are about to speak, out comes the writer's voice. The result is that they all seem to have an uncanny literary sensibility, an epigram for every occasion and the wisdom of the ages. It is not wise, perhaps, to bend credulity all out of shape just when you're bringing the story home. Readers are so trusting, so grateful for dignified prose. But when they've been promised a mystery, told that lives are at stake and love is on the boil, it's more prudent to depict irony than to discourse upon it, sword in hand, so to speak.

Julia Whedon, "Mummy's Erotic Daydreams," in The New York Times Book Review, *July 20, 1986, p. 23.*

Walker Percy

1916-

American novelist and essayist.

Best known for his first novel, *The Moviegoer* (1961), for which he won the National Book Award, Percy explores such conditions of modern life as alienation, malaise, and conformity. Drawing upon the religious and philosophical ideas of Sören Kierkegaard and Gabriel Marcel and imbued with his knowledge of semiotics, science, Southern history, and popular culture, Percy's works promote Christian and existentialist values as means for counteracting contemporary psychological and social ills. Percy's heroes are usually contemplative, affluent, middle-aged men who seek spiritual meaning, identity, and love. These protagonists reject scientific humanism in favor of traditional Christian ideals to overcome despair and to confront an increasingly valueless, chaotic, and swiftly changing world. A major concern in Percy's work is the relationship between language, identity, and reality. Although some critics fault Percy for creating one-dimensional characters, many laud his insightful probing of social, moral, and philosophical issues.

Percy studied pathology at Columbia University and received his medical degree in 1941. The following year, he contracted tuberculosis while performing an autopsy, requiring a two-year convalescence. During this time, Percy read the works of such existentialist authors as Albert Camus, Jean-Paul Sartre, and Fedor Dostoevski. His philosophical outlook was also shaped by his uncle, the poet and lawyer William Alexander Percy, who adopted the teenaged Percy after his father committed suicide and his mother died in an automobile accident. According to Percy, his uncle instilled in him "the Greek-Roman Stoic view" that informs much of his fiction. In 1947, Percy converted to Roman Catholicism; religion figures prominently in all of his work as a source of morality and reform. After having gained recognition for philosophical and semiotic essays published in scholarly journals, Percy turned to fiction, believing that art can serve as a vital means for social and moral improvement.

The Moviegoer established Percy as a singular presence in American letters. A novel of ideas resembling Sartre's *Nausea* and Camus's *The Stranger, The Moviegoer* is a study of "Binx" Bolling's quest to transcend the routines of suburbia. Binx escapes the dreariness of his world through films; he ironically maintains a sense of identity by behaving like various movie actors. In this novel, Percy suggests that art can mitigate alienation—a motif evident in all of his fiction. Percy's second book, *The Last Gentleman* (1966), is a picaresque novel depicting Will Barrett's struggle to discover his true self. After witnessing a priest comfort a dying child, Will is raised from his abstracted state and attains self-knowledge. In a sequel, *The Second Coming* (1980), Will intends to wait in a cave until he receives proof of the existence of God. He becomes convinced after he falls in love with Allison, an escapee from a mental asylum. Critics regarded Percy's viewpoint in this novel as uncharacteristically optimistic.

Love in the Ruins (1971), considered by many critics Percy's most light-hearted novel, is a futuristic satire that analyzes the malaise afflicting twentieth-century America. Sensing that the world is on the brink of apocalypse, Dr. Tom More, a lapsed Catholic, construes the cause of modern ennui as a spiritual schism between humanity's conscience and nature. He tries to remedy this condition with an electronic instrument known as More's Qualitative Quantitative Ontological Lapsometer, which measures "the perturbations of the soul." In this work, Percy mocks the use of technology to cure psychological ailments and implies that only love and religious faith can result in true happiness. In *The Thanatos Syndrome* (1987), which involves many of the same characters, themes, and settings as *Love in the Ruins,* Percy examines the moral and religious implications of social engineering. Written in the style of a conspiracy thriller, this novel cautions against the hazards of using science to treat emotional and spiritual disorders. *The Thanatos Syndrome* focuses on a group of doctors who add chemicals to a local water supply to reduce antisocial behavior and depression but who diminish the citizens' humanity in the process.

Percy's other works include *Lancelot* (1977), a novel related in the form of a dramatic monologue by a man driven insane by his wife's infidelity. The secular protagonist recalls crucial events in his life and debates the nature of evil with a religious man in a sanitarium. The hero's perceptions convey Percy's view that secular humanism and conservative Christianity are inadequate to contemporary lifestyles and spiritual needs. Although acknowledging overbearing irony in *Lancelot,* Robert

D. Daniel noted that "Percy ranks with Swift as that rare accomplished acrobat, the novelist who can balance interesting fiction with serious ideas." *The Message in the Bottle* (1975) consists of scholarly essays on linguistics, existentialism, and psychology. As in his novels, Percy probes the relationship between alienation and communication. In *Lost in the Cosmos* (1983), Percy parodies "how-to" manuals and various forms of popular culture with the intention of promoting understanding of the human predicament.

(See also *CLC,* Vols. 2, 3, 6, 8, 14, 18; *Contemporary Authors,* Vols. 1-4, rev. ed.; *Contemporary Authors New Revision Series,* Vols. 1, 23; *Dictionary of Literary Biography,* Vol. 2; and *Dictionary of Literary Biography Yearbook: 1980.*)

EDMUND FULLER

Dr. Percy began to write novels after becoming convinced, rightly, that through fiction he could convey his philosophy more effectively and to a far wider audience than through scholarly discourse.

The title of [his] new book at once reveals that he has found a fresh middle ground in non-fiction: ***Lost in the Cosmos: The Last Self-Help Book.*** Original and imaginative, at times dazzlingly so, it conveys a serious, occasionally somber message in a vein of high comedy. I love the book. It is not just to be read once through, but to be reread, savored and pondered.

In form it parodies with hawk-eyed keenness the whole genre of how-to-books, promising nothing, "considering how useless self-help books generally are," except that it just might "help you discover who you are not and even—an outside chance—who you are." He is faithful to the form, offering quizzes, multiple choices ("check one") and a series of "Thought Experiments.". . .

Different in tone is what he calls "an intermezzo of some 40 pages" that "can be skipped without fatal consequences." It "attempts an elementary semiotical grounding of the theory of self taken for granted in these pages." Semiotics (related to semantics) is an often abstruse study of signs and sign-language in human communication, a field of long-time interest to Dr. Percy. He offers a lucid, brief exposition of its principles, with diagrams (signs, but a medium to which I have high resistance). For all its concentratedness, it is done without losing the humor that pervades the book. Decline his slightly crafty invitation to skip those few pages.

The final, finest section of the book, in two parts, is "A Space Odyssey" with the subheading, "The Self Marooned in the Cosmos." In one part of this, with deceptive amiability, he devastates Carl Sagan's *Cosmos* (both book and TV series). . . .

His finale is a variation on a theme from what he calls, justly, "Walter M. Miller's extraordinary novel, *A Canticle for Leibowitz* (the name regrettably misspelled, which nobody caught). If one wishes to hear the direct voice of Dr. Percy in this book which leaves all conclusions to the reader, I think it speaks through the mask of Abbot Liebowitz (his spelling) among options offered for a surviving remnant of mankind in an imagined future. . . .

Lost in the Cosmos may infuriate some readers. It will cause others to shout with joy. To whichever camp we belong, it makes us squirm at times, in self-recognition, in his wittily parodied quizzes and his demand for choices. You don't ever have to take a pencil and check one, but you can't avoid thinking it over.

Edmund Fuller, "You and the Universe, in Properly Readable Form," in The Wall Street Journal, *May 31, 1983, p. 28.*

FRANCINE DU PLESSIX GRAY

If I've managed to decipher this problematic book [***Lost in the Cosmos***]—Walker Percy's second venture into nonfiction—its subject is summed up in the following words: "How you can survive in the Cosmos about which you know more and more while knowing less and less about yourself."

The waning of our self-knowledge and clear identity, the roots of this malaise in the decline of religious faith and the cult of technology, has been a central theme in most of Mr. Percy's work. His protagonists are well-bred Southern gentlemen who, although endowed with all the trappings of contemporary comfort, are haunted by the fear that they lead meaningless and inauthentic lives. They are all the more doomed because their gentility curbs them from that searing self-questioning which might jolt them into admitting their despair and exploring its roots. "The specific character of despair is that it is unaware of its despair"—so reads Kierkegaard's epigraph to Mr. Percy's novel ***The Moviegoer.***

However familiar this topic—contemporary man as stranger to himself—the best of Mr. Percy's novels have modulated it with an irony and compassion matched by few current authors. And the religious dimension he has added to the theme of self-estrangement makes him, to my mind, our greatest Catholic novelist alongside Flannery O'Connor. So it is my very infatuation with Mr. Percy's fictions that makes me so disappointed by his forays into nonfiction. His first collection of essays—***The Message in the Bottle*** (1975)—was a dense, ambitious book that centered on the importance of language in understanding the human predicament. It offered several ill-digested summaries of contemporary theories of semiotics, lashed out at fashionable behaviorist views that reduce man to an organism reacting solely to its environment and attempted to provide a respiritualized ethos (the only redeeming sections of the book) based on those Christian existentialists who have most deeply influenced Mr. Percy's work: Kierkegaard, Heidegger, Gabriel Marcel.

Lost in the Cosmos is more playful, less ambitious, less turgid than ***The Message in the Bottle.*** But I find it, alas, equally exasperating. Its oddball structure can best be described as pop-Socratic. Two-thirds of the volume consists of 20 long-winded questionnaires with multiple-choice answers, a parody of magazine quizzes and self-help books that plumbs different modes of despair allegedly suffered by contemporary Americans. . . .

Although I share Mr. Percy's Christian, existential and anti-technological convictions, I found his mishmash of satire and seriousness totally confusing. Furthermore, his diatribes against specific aspects of contemporary mores offended me by their priggishness. There is a hostility toward homosexuals in his pages that is particularly odious. And Mr. Percy's stand on women is hardly more palatable. "Are there not still religious folk, women who give their very lives to serve God and their fellowman, all for the love of God?" he asks. "Well some," he answers, "though for every Mother Teresa, there seem to be 1,800 nutty American nuns, female Clint Eastwoods who have it in for men and are out to get the pope."

Also offensive are the excesses of Mr. Percy's pop-Soc style, which inspires him to people his moral fables with a swarm of media personalities—Robert Redford, Al Pacino, Mickey Rooney, Tom Snyder, Phil Donahue. In such passages Mr. Percy's botched attempts at humor make him sound like a hippie clergyman trying to "level" with his audience—turning the author into someone akin to the swinging cleric he parodied so brilliantly in his novel ***The Second Coming.***

It takes Mr. Percy some 120 pages to get through the 20 questionnaires. The other segments of ***Lost in the Cosmos*** are less objectionable but equally tedious. They consist of two ineffectual attempts at "Space Odyssey" science fiction and a 40-page "intermezzo" that attempts to define "an elementary semiotical grounding of the theory of self." Its central insight, already elaborated ad nauseam in ***The Message in the Bottle,*** is that "of all the objects in the entire Cosmos which the sign-user can apprehend through the conjoining of signifier and signified (word uttered and thing beheld), there is one which forever escapes his comprehension—and that is the sign-user himself."

And so ***Lost in the Cosmos*** remains curiously schizophrenic. Percy the satirist tries to make us laugh at some of the excesses of American culture. Percy the twice-converted moralist (from science to art, from agnosticism to the Roman Catholic Church) tries to awaken us to the dangers of those excesses and to uncover the despair he suspects lurks in all of us. Both attempts fail. It would take a considerably broader and more inventive comic gift to satirize successfully such hackneyed subjects as the sexual revolution, the inanity of self-help manuals or the numbing effect of the electronic media. As for my attempt to play along with the author and answer his self-help quizzes, it thrust me into the worst form of despair I know—boredom. I fear that those who are as enamored as I am of Mr. Percy's fictions will feel like jilted lovers while trying to find their way in this particular cosmos.

Francine Du Plessix Gray, "A Pop-Socratic Survey of Despair," in The New York Times Book Review, *June 5, 1983, p. 9.*

GEOFFREY STOKES

Walker Percy is unhappy with us. He dislikes homosexuality, precocious children, pop psychology, and the *Phil Donahue Show*. He thinks that we—that is to say, more or less post-Christian, rationalistic, Western men and women of the 1980s—have blown it. Dazed by the breakdown of the great chain, befuddled by our frequent and erratic veerings between self-importance and self-abnegation, exhausted by sexual adventuring, we have lost our way, and Doctor Percy, that lovable old curmudgeon, has written a book to bring us to our senses. It is called ***Lost in the Cosmos,*** and it is a mess.

It is also something of a mystery, for the scope of the disaster cannot be explained merely by the tediousness of Percy's prescriptions. (For the record, he urges a return to preindustrial, maybe pre-Reformation, Judeo-Christian values.) His aren't the worst ideas ever propounded between hard covers by an author of literary merit (consider Pound, Wells, or Huxley), but they are hardly as *daring* as Percy pretends. Eccentric in these times, perhaps, but not page-one stuff. St. Augustine did it better; even across the cultural gap Percy laments, it remains clear that Augustine not only loved his fellow humans, but liked them.

Except for the fact that we seem to have overdrawn his reserves of charity, Percy is more inclined to the Pauline; yet Paul wasn't much of an ironist, and ***Lost in the Cosmos*** seethes with a sort of hamfisted bitterness. . . .

A prime difficulty with preaching to people one believes are beyond, even beneath, salvation is that the preacher has a tendency to get lazy. . . .

With Percy perhaps inadvertently having foreclosed the prospect of genuine dialogue, the book reduces itself to snippets of elephantine playfulness. These afford the reader moments of modest pleasure, but fatally undercut Percy's claims to seriousness. Which is too bad, for he is—or at least has been—a serious writer. From his early essays in *Thought* magazine through the peaks and valleys of his novelistic career (and though mine is a minority opinion, I thought ***Love in the Ruins*** was as fine a philosophic novel as any of its decade), he has always had something to say, and usually the craft and courage to say it clearly.

There are, indeed, three comparatively straightforward sections of ***Lost in the Cosmos*** that demonstrate how mistaken his choice of the cutesy-poo is. A long footnote deftly disposes of Carl Sagan, a dozen precise pages explore the reasons why writers drink, and a lengthy analysis uses the semiotic model to locate the roots of human loneliness within our language. An elegance of both language and thought in these particular pages provides the satisfaction one associates with neatly proven equations or pyramiding syllogisms. But, typical of ***Lost in the Cosmos,*** Percy prefaces the semiotic chapters with the note that "the following section, an intermezzo of some forty pages, can be skipped without fatal consequences." The, you should pardon the expression, subtext of that disclaimer is that we are too dumb, or too depraved by the incursions of television, or maybe just too stubborn to give Percy-in-serious-mode the benefit of attentive doubt.

Believing this, as he all too obviously does, he chooses to dispense cheap thrills. Given his contempt for us, the logic of Percy's choice is unassailable, but he is simply not the man for the job. After a while, one wearies of a juggler who keeps letting the crockery crash to the floor—especially when he's so smugly certain we won't notice.

Geoffrey Stokes, "Dr. Percy's Medicine Show," in The Village Voice, *Vol. XXVIII, No. 24, June 14, 1983, p. 39.*

JACK BEATTY

To put [Walker Percy's] message in a sentence, our alienation from each other, our estrangement from religious faith, and our semiological pathos as the creature that can name everything in the cosmos except itself, have us in a permanently awful fix. Despite [the subtitle of ***Lost in the Cosmos: The Last Self-Help Book***], this book won't help, though it does contain one form of comfort: intellectual delight. It crackles with thought, ideas, exotic information.

Most intellectuals in the Percy class have the same mentors—Marx, Freud, and the Frenchman of the month. That's why Harold Rosenberg called them "a herd of independent minds." Percy has this shifting trinity down pat, but he also is familiar with subjects rarely conned by our intellectual class. Science, for example, and medicine (he is an M.D.), theology and semiology . . . , Southern history and existentialism, plus an intimate knowledge of junk culture—TV, the movies, and the juicy divorce and infidelity sweepstakes. He lets all this mental stuff tumble out in this book, and the result is by turns a sharp sermon made up of highly imaginative examples, quizzes, and thought exercises, and a formless, how-do-I-stop-this-book ramble.

It's a good thing Percy is so witty; otherwise his parade of the profundities would put you off. Self-consciously deep, spiritual, concerned with damnation and redemption, he is, one feels, always searching for new metaphors for that old libel, Original Sin. (His account of the semiological situation of the self, unable to define or place itself in the world, is one of these.) I find it remarkable that such a rigid categorical notion, an idea with no shade in it at all, can enable so much thinking. The trouble is that the thinking is all along the same line. You keep hoping the author will board another train of thought. Instead, he tends irresistibly toward a single doctrinal destination. According the Percy, the self, by which he sometimes means the postreligious self but more often the thing itself, is fundamentally out of place in the cosmos. Nothing to be done but ride out the ennui. If, like me, you think people who say they have existential problems are avoiding calling their emotional conflicts by the right name, then Percy will strike you as barking, eloquently and with impressive originality, up the wrong tree.

After all, you can say anything you want about the human condition; but the test of truth in these matters is not how much reality you can conjure with your wand of words, but how much you can capture. For example, you can say this about the self: I feel empty because I am depressed, and I am depressed because I am afraid of my own aggression—I turn it against myself rather than use it on the world. Or, following Walker Percy, you can say this: I feel empty for a good reason—I am empty. So are you. We are all maws of negation. We are not only empty ourselves, we smear our emptiness all over the world, like an invisible but fatal stain, until the world and everything in it mirrors our condition. Those who take the first view of the empty self believe that psychotherapy can help them; they are willing to try pills, even self-help books, to get a little relief. They are not worried about saving their souls; they will settle for an afternoon without a repetition of their major problem. Those who take the second view come on sounding bleak but then tag on some such hopeful codicil as this: I feel empty only up to a point. Basically, I'm not empty. How could I be? I'm made in the image and likeness of God. Sure, I'm not doing so well now, but that's because I don't belong here. My place is with Him, and I'll reach it when I die if only I believe hard enough.

If you think that's deep, then Father Percy will speak to your hopes and fears. As for me, I liberally underlined his book, took many notes, cheered this clever touch, that inspired phrase, but finally tuned out. I got the messsage, and for all the color and celerity of Percy's mind, the message does not change. In this book, at any rate, he repeatedly posits the reality he would like to reveal. He conjures; he does not, to my mind, capture. (pp. 38-9)

Read ***Lost in the Cosmos*** for its parody of "The Phil Donahue Show," for its challenging chapter on the semiological dilemma of the self, and for its mordant discussion of why writers drink. Read it to find out why you can't look anyone in the eye, why Johnny Carson can't think of anything to say at a party, and why John Cheever was right when he said that "the main emotion of the adult North Eastern American who has had all the advantages of wealth, education, and culture is disappointment." Read it and be grateful that you're stuck in the saving muck of the quotidian, too immersed in the world to listen to the turbid music of your soul. Leave that to Walker Percy, our maestro of fear and trembling. (p. 39)

Jack Beatty, "Travels with My Angst," in The New Republic, *Vol. 189, No. 2, July 11, 1983, pp. 38-9.*

ROBERT ROYAL

The title of [***Lost in the Cosmos***] obliquely confronts Carl Sagan, suave popularizer of science and philosophical illiterate, who once intoned seriously on his television series *Cosmos* that if we admit the existence of God we then have to ask, "Where did God come from?" Percy, as the reader of his novels will know, is a Catholic who believes that religion is the resolution of our dilemmas. But he is not happy with most of the current religious banner carriers.

The institutional churches have largely been overtaken by the self-induced torpor. In the Catholic Church, the only group with any vigor seems to be pugnacious nuns: "female Clint Eastwoods who have it in for men and who are out to get the Pope." On the Protestant side, cutting across all the traditional denominations, the action seems focused on a born-again movement led eerily by TV preachers with blow-dry hairdos.

The current version of the struggle to reconcile science and faith thus becomes a put-up job. . . . (p. 1149)

Percy believes that a comprehensive scientific account of man would include a recognition of how human language puts a distance between human nature and the rest of nature. He has even elaborated a semiotic theory here and in his earlier work of nonfiction, ***The Message in the Bottle,*** to show how this traditional concept may be recast in modern form. In Percy's terms, the physical world is an intelligible cosmos, the world of plants and animals is an environment, but the world of human beings is a *world.* A world is not like the cosmos or an environment. In the cosmos, two galaxies may collide; in a world, two ideas can also conflict. In an environment, an organism seeks its physical necessitities and then rests; in a world, a human being can have all his "basic needs" met, yet be thoroughly dissatisfied. Only in a world can the Vietnam War, a Sunday doubleheader, someone's funeral, and the theory of evolution exist.

This rough outline of Percy's thesis may make ***Lost in the Cosmos*** seem stuffily intellectual and abstract. Instead of arguing in the dialectical manner used above, however, this book makes its point by a wicked parodying of current lunacies. Short scenarios or anecdotes are followed by questionnaires that are apparently meant to lead the reader to an overwhelming question. In the author's hands, this odd method of catechesis has much to recommend it.

Sound quirky? It is. Also: repetitive, desultory, obsessed, exasperating, brilliant, comic, passionate, illuminating, and finally compelling. The whole is brought off with that sly humor and intellectual verve that have made the author's novels exceptional in an age of eminently forgettable fiction.

If you are a fan of Percy's novels or appreciate satire turned with consummate skill against the idols of the age, do not miss this book. Have you been waiting for revenge on that harebrained crackpot, Phil Donahue? Don't miss the section called, "The Last Donahue Show." . . . Have you been wondering when our intellectual iconoclasts would get around to the real wackiness: the Esalen Institutes, the Leo Buscaglias, the apologists for gay promiscuity, the sex therapists and other gurus of lust under the guise of "loving and caring commitments"? Wonder no more.

Percy sees no easy escape from our condition. The road back to sanity is a long one and the hour is late. But he has identified some of the contemporary sources of our disease and given the traditional solutions a convincing freshness. (pp. 1149-50)

Robert Royal, "Invisible Man," in National Review, *New York, Vol. XXXV, No. 18, September 16, 1983, pp. 1149-50.*

EDMUND FULLER

The complicated plot [of ***The Thanatos Syndrome***] is spun skillfully. Dr. Percy would not claim it is original, although he gives it fresh twists aplenty. It is the familiar motif of an elite group, here a cabal of doctors, that has found and deployed a secret method of eliminating crime and all other forms of aggression, antisocial behavior and unhappiness. This involves tranquillizing an unsuspecting population and intervening, with "tender" intentions, in every medical situation that, again in the doctors' closed-council superior judgment, diminishes "quality" of life. The hero, flawed Dr. Thomas More, psychiatrist and lapsed Catholic, finds himself waging a struggle against odds to thwart this totalitarian scheme of doing good. Another element of suspense concerns sexual abuse of children, masked by the same means that are used for attaining the alleged improvement of society.

What truly matters in the book, giving it distinction and moral urgency, all comes after the nominal story has ended. Though the major themes are introduced earlier, the massive punch is packed into the final 47 pages of the book, which, except for its eloquent moral theology, would be just an old-fashioned summing-up of what happened to all the characters afterward. In fact, it is the true message in this bottle, and it is what makes ***The Thanatos Syndrome*** the most explicitly Catholic of Dr. Percy's novels.

In some quarters, this book has been called, carelessly, a sequel to his ***Love in the Ruins*** (1971), which has the subtitle "The Adventures of a Bad Catholic at a Time Near the End of the World." Significantly, the present book's jacket-copy contains no allusion to that earlier work. The two versions, as I prefer to call them, share some of the same characters—Dr. Tom More, his good friend Dr. Max Gottlieb, and Tom's wife, Ellen, but in the newer appearance all have undergone great changes. The earlier book even has a Father Smith, who sometimes occupies a fire tower and asserts, "Death is winning, life is losing." But there he is called "Rinaldo Smith." In the new novel he has become Simon Smith, and the more important fire tower is the explicit modern equivalent of the pillar atop which his baptismal patron, St. Simon the Stylite, dwelt in self-mortification. . . .

Each of the novels is projected a little ahead of present time. The chief science-fiction instrumentality in both is heavy sodium, but the device is employed utterly differently. There is no internal way in which either of these novels is sequential to the other. ***The Thanatos Syndrome*** is Walker Percy's second coming to the themes of ***Love in the Ruins,*** a new try that succeeds far more powerfully in its apocalyptic vision than does the earlier. Reading both reminds us that current events have a way of catching up with the most fantastic satirical scenes. It is hard for the imagination to keep ahead of madness. Also in the cryptic closing pages of ***The Thanatos Syndrome*** there are hints, obscure enough that you may make of them what you will, of a millenarian Second Coming.

Walker Percy is deservedly one of the most esteemed current American writers. This may become his most commercially successful novel. . . . Not wholly smooth as a novel but conceptually powerful, this book speaks with forthright courage about moral quandaries that are immemorial yet made freshly urgent by the rapid changes and new technologies of the world.

Edmund Fuller, "Death and Modern Morality," in The Wall Street Journal, *March 24, 1987, p. 34.*

DOUGLAS BAUER

From the publication of ***The Moviegoer,*** in 1961, through this, [Percy's] sixth, novel, ***The Thanatos Syndrome,*** we've encountered an interchangeable cast of protagonists composing one identity: a bemused, even somewhat addled man of middle age, standing (though prey to falling down) in the midst of a world gone enthusiastically haywire, scratching his head, nipping frequently from his bottle of bourbon, and desperately trying to make sense of it all. It's an affluent exurban world in the American South, hard by a country-club fairway, where there has recently begun an ill-motivated conspiracy, often some swindle in the name of human kindness, which the hero suspects, detects, and stops, with the help of a briskly affectionate Girl Friday who tells him when it's time to eat. Such is the recurrent narrative fabric of Percy's fiction, through which he weaves his constant fascinations and convictions—the resonant symbolism of language; the relative advantages of the cloistered and the participatory life; the persistent impulse of science to encroach on that which is properly left to mystery; and, within it all, the necessity for a resilient, dogmatic Catholicism in order to make the world one we *can* actively accept.

But if this suggests that his work seems redundant, the product of a regurgitant imagination, such is emphatically not the case. Within his single sturdy grid of theme and tale, Percy is reachlessly inventive and always freshly funny. (p. 86)

Consequently, ***The Thanatos Syndrome*** doesn't seem so much a discretely conceived novel, though it's certainly self-sufficient, as the latest installment in a body of work that Percy's narrow resolve has made serial. And in this instance the work is in fact a sequel—to his third novel, ***Love in the Ruins***—continuing the life of Dr. Tom More, patient/psychiatrist. At the close of ***Love in the Ruins*** More stood, clothed in sackcloth (John XXIV having revived public penance), over his grill cooking a Christmas turkey for his new wife. He had survived the near apocalypse of a world set in an unspecified and blatantly improbable future—after guerrilla bands of Bantus had driven frightened locals into hiding in the swamps, and the Roman Catholic Church had become hopelessly fragmented, its most prominent faction the new American Catholic Church, headquartered in Cicero, Illinois. Violent revolution had been avoided through a *coup de commerce,* the suddenly oil-lease-rich Bantus having simply bought up all the contested land. Still, though life had resumed a tenuous calm, More remained frustrated. He had invented a device that, when moved over the skull, recorded the degree to which a man's "self" had fallen away from itself, measuring "the perturbations of the soul." But that was as far as it could go—calibration without solution—and he vowed at novel's end to refine his invention, past diagnosis, to "cure the new plague . . . that rives soul from body."

Now we learn that though the world in the interim on its surface seemed to prosper, Tom More did not. His practice foundered, he again became a drunk, and, needing money, he sold pills wholesale to long-distance truckers, a felony that sent him to minimum-security prison. Having returned home, he finds the time in captivity to have been altogether salutary. He has emerged a calmly contemplative and newly curious shrink on parole. Whereas before he thought "the world was going mad and that it was up to me to diagnose the madness and treat it," now he asks, "What's a cure in this day and age? Maybe a cure is knowing there is no cure." Why, he wonders gratefully, does it take "two years of prison for a man to be able to sit still, listen, notice his children, watch the sunlight on the ceiling?"

Unfortunately, More finds himself alone in this regard, for all around him people seem bizarrely extroverted. While he admits that they no longer suffer "the ancient anxiety, guilt, obsessions, rage repressed, sex suppressed," he sees, too, that they've lost something he calls "the old ache of self."

All the people he meets now seem to share an odd disinterest, a flatness of affect. Further, their language has been cryptically reduced to infantile two-word sentences. And some of the women abruptly, unabashedly, come on to him, "presenting rearward," like primates in a cage. Still, More asks, unsettling as all this is, are they better or worse in their anxiety-free state?" "Happy is better than unhappy, right?" Maybe. Maybe not. But in either case, "What's going on?"

Well, all manner of wildly unlikely things, which are mainly the result of a plot by a small group of psychiatrist-bureaucrats concerned with halting the systematic erosion of Western culture. By diverting heavy-sodium waste from the local nuclear reactor into the water supply, they've been able to alter an entire population's social behavior. Steady doses of heavy sodium to the brains of the residents have so far reduced street crime by 85 percent, child abuse by 87, and teenage pregnancy by 85, and have all but eliminated prison violence and homosexuality. In other words, with a little harmless pharmacology these vigilantes of morality are accomplishing in Feliciana parish a kind of, yes, Utopia.

Which, of course, is what's *really* going on in this novel, so far as Percy is concerned—a realization that requires not nearly so much detective work as More has to do to get to the bottom of things. For Percy's clues are generously unsubtle: an imprisoned hero named Tom More; the litany "Happy is better than unhappy, right?" By applying central features of Sir Thomas's *Utopia*—the broadcast use of propaganda and diplomatic intrigue, a humanitarian penal code, the practice of euthanasia, much more—and satirically setting them down in that "most befouled" paradise of Feliciana, Percy has imagined the doomed and dire consequences of a concerted man-made effort to manipulate the world into something sublime.

To the persistent scholarly argument over whether Thomas More himself was sincere or satirical in writing *Utopia*, Percy answers, not surprisingly, that the whole impulse toward a secular perfecting, an ordering of one's life, is farcical. ("Maybe a cure is knowing there is no cure.") Ruefully he has watched us try to find happiness through fad religions and harmonious diet and group gropes, to employ more sophisticated science to find God or be Him. ("I aim to settle the question of God once and for all," Will Barrett says in ***The Second Coming***.)

What, then, would Percy have us do? Near the end of the novel, in conversation with More, Father Smith, the batty priest, speaks of a reported apparition of the Virgin Mary before some children. She apparently told them that the twentieth century has been uniquely monstrous, because "God agreed to let the Great Prince Satan have his way with men for a hundred years—this one hundred years. . . . And he has. How did he do it? . . . All he had to do was leave us alone. We did it. Faith gave way to reason, right? Superstition to science."

In other words, Percy would have us believe. But belief will hardly make our life perfect or even orderly; more essential, it makes the disorder endurable.

There is ample evidence of Percy's brilliance in ***The Thanatos Syndrome***—the droll Dixie anthropology, the pitch-perfect comic dialogue, the sheer intelligence alive everywhere on the page. But the book is seriously marred by the byzantine melodrama of its plot, which begins to seem like a movie made for the prime-time television Percy so frequently refers to. And the character of Lucy, More's companion and, fleetingly, lover, is a one-dimensional figure, especially in comparison with the marvelously memorable Allie of ***The Second Coming***. Considering the obligatory love interest and the incredible turns of narrative, it's as if Percy, having so explicitly clobbered us with his utopian conception and his abiding appeal to a literal faith, felt that he must also divert our attention, "content our normal expectations," to a corresponding degree. He need not. Walker Percy's vision is not only rigorously Catholic. It is splendidly, uproariously catholic, as well. (pp. 86, 88-9)

Douglas Bauer, "To Live and Die in Dixie," in The Atlantic Monthly, *Vol. 259, No. 4, April, 1987, pp. 86, 88-9.*

MICHIKO KAKUTANI

Mr. Percy, of course, has always been more of a philosophical novelist in the European tradition than a straightforward narrative storyteller; and this time [in ***The Thanatos Syndrome***] he uses [a] clumsy plot as an armature on which to hang his favorite theme—as he once put it, "the dislocation of man in the modern age." As in earlier novels and essays, behavioralist theory is contrasted with the author's own existential outlook, scientific positivism with a more old-fashioned brand of Christian humanism.

On one side, in ***The Thanatos Syndrome,*** there are the advocates of sodium-fortified water, who argue that drugs can suppress such nasty human symptoms as anxiety, depression, stress and insomnia and in doing so also reduce the crime rate and other social ills. Taking the opposing view is Tom, who doubtless speaks for the author when he points out the dangers of trying to use technology to solve emotional and spiritual problems and reiterates the important rewards (as well as painful costs) of remaining human.

In the past, Mr. Percy has dramatized such issues with enormous wit and intellectual passion, but this time his argument—not to mention history—bogs down in a succession of ill-connected and all too obvious scenes. We don't need to see the water-doping conspirators fall in with child molesters to realize the moral dangers of their position. Nor do we need to listen to analogies between their arguments and those used by Nazi eugenicists to grasp the terrible consequences of social engineering.

In fact, the main result of these heavy-handed illustrations is to make the reader overly aware of the novel's creaky plot machinery. So intent does Mr. Percy become in pushing his story along that he neglects to use his most distinctive talents. His lyrical way with language—so mesmerizing in some of his earlier novels—is barely in evidence here, and his gift for portraying the inner life of angst-ridden individuals like Binx Bolling (in ***The Moviegoer***) and Will Barrett (in ***The Last Gentleman*** and ***The Second Coming***) is similarly given little display.

No doubt Mr. Percy hoped, in writing ***The Thanatos Syndrome,*** to try something different; to look at today's soul-sickness in terms of society rather than the individual—something he achieved with a measure of success in ***Love in the Ruins.*** But while ***The Thanatos Syndrome*** contains a couple of satiric passages reminiscent of that volume—Mr. Percy is especially good at poking fun at the New South of country clubs and "plantation style" houses—the novel as a whole lacks the earlier book's fierceness of language and imagination. It stands, in the end, as one of the weakest efforts of one of our most talented and original authors.

Michiko Kakutani, in a review of "The Thanatos Syndrome," in The New York Times, *April 1, 1987, p. 28.*

GAIL GODWIN

Walker Percy has availed himself of the knowledge the prophet Jonah had to learn the hard way. "The novelist writes about the coming end in order to warn about present ills and so avert the end," Mr. Percy tells us in **"Notes for a Novel About the End of the World,"** one of his essays collected in ***The Message in the Bottle*** (1975). By "the end," he goes on to explain, he means "the passing of one age and the beginning of another." The novelist setting out to write a serious novel about the end, he maintains, "must reckon not merely like H. G. Wells with changes in the environment but also with changes in man's consciousness which might be quite as radical."

The changes in consciousness that engage Mr. Percy have to do with our abandonment of God and the concept of the soul for the new religions of science and sociology. And in his own two novelistic forays into the prophetic genre, he has poked some wicked fun at our self-important, jargon-filled secular age, while at the same time raising some thought-provoking questions about where we may be headed next.

Love in the Ruins, published in 1971, described the "last days" of 1983. Set in a future only nine years away, ***The Thanatos Syndrome*** is a perceptive mirror of Right Now and an entertaining assault on our society's besetting sins: the manipulative and reductionist practices of social science, the zeal and self-righteousness of ultra-conservatives, the splintering of the Government into clandestine groups, often working at cross purposes inside the same organization.

And though the novel's surface action spins along at a brisk thriller pace, laced with escapes and chase scenes and risky, ingenious detective work (including a burlesque episode in which an elusive ring of child abusers is exposed when their own methods are turned against them), the real plot, as with all this writer's fiction, chronicles the continuing battle between good and evil in a modern society where both words are out of fashion, if not downright suspect. (p. 1)

Walker Percy has the rare gift of being able to dramatize metaphysics. It is this gift that has won him his most devoted readers, eager to follow him through book after book, turning a kind eye when necessary on his lapses and foibles. In the recent novels, he often slips into a nuanceless, slapdash tempo, and the folksy, reiterative tone of his narrators can be tiresome in extensive doses. And after the memorable great-aunt in ***The Moviegoer,*** and the disquieting Cousin Kate, Mr. Percy's female characters have been disappointing. They exist as representative types, seen from the outside, prone to fickleness and fads or hellbent on marrying, or bedding, the hero. To give Mr. Percy credit, however, he is trying to work his way out of stereotypes in ***The Thanatos Syndrome.*** At least Cousin Lucy gets to be a doctor; but as soon as she has Dr. More safely tucked away in her guest room for an overnight stay, she turns into a succubus. I wish Mr. Percy would allow a future female character to worry about the big questions as much as he and his male protagonists do.

By choice as well as inclination, Mr. Percy is primarily a novelist of ideas, but he is a fine novelist of manners, too. He is uncommonly good at evoking the atmosphere and language of his region; he is dead on target when depicting the subtle, often devious locutions of Southern American talk. . . .

If Mr. Percy's theory about the novelist as prophet is right—that, like the canary coal miners used to take down into the mine shafts, his job is to test the air and thus help us avert the end—we ought to be able, by absorbing the scenarios he has provided us with in ***The Thanatos Syndrome,*** to outgrow our current sins and be well into new ones by the real 1996. By which time we will be ready for another diagnosis from a prophet-novelist—perhaps again by Mr. Percy himself. (p. 23)

Gail Godwin, "The Devil's Own Century," in The New York Times Book Review, *April 5, 1987, pp. 1, 22-3.*

SVEN BIRKERTS

[Percy] seems to be making the reincarnation of characters a feature of his literary practice. First he brought back Will Barrett, the youthful protagonist of ***The Last Gentleman,*** to play the middle-aged lead in ***The Second Coming;*** but that title was little more than a sly wink, since the passing of decades, as well as Percy's determined focus on the events of the present, dissolved any sense that a single Barrett was persisting in time. Now ***The Thanatos Syndrome*** picks up another Percy familiar. When we last saw Dr. Tom More, at the end of ***Love in the Ruins,*** he was settling in to spend his golden years with his lovely new wife, Ellen. (p. 31)

Percy is a novelist of ideas who just happens to have a knack for creating distinctive (if somewhat flat) characters and riveting (if somewhat improbable) plots. His interests and methods have changed considerably over the years. His first novel, ***The Moviegoer,*** was a Kierkegaardian meditation on the attainment of authentic selfhood. Its thrust was philosophical, not psychological; Binx Bolling's intriguing reflections all but buried the plot. Since then, however, Percy has become ever more venturesome about devising situations and complications that can embody contending concepts. He has decided that it is the reader, not the characters, who should do most of the thinking. And his scope has widened accordingly. The later novels turn from the malaise of individual consciousness to the larger infections of the social organism.

More's serenity at the close of ***Love in the Ruins*** was, it seems, an illusory triumph. At the beginning of [***The Thanatos Syndrome***], we learn that he has just returned from a two-year stint in a minimum-security prison for supplying amphetamines to truck drivers. Now under the probationary care of Drs. Max Gottlieb and Bob Comeaux, he resumes his private practice. Still, as indicated, something is amiss. His old patients are showing the most curious behavioral symptoms: an absence of former (indeed any) anxieties, verbal simplification, uncanny factual recall, and, among some of the females, a tendency to "present rearward." Nor is this monkey business confined to the consulting room. Ellen has quite suddenly—under the tutelage of doctor, educator, and bridge wizard John Van Dorn—revealed an almost superhuman ability to compute bridge combinations. She has also lost her former pudency; More finds her striking an inviting quadruped pose in the bedroom. (pp. 31-2)

More quickly teams up with his cousin Lucy, one of Percy's many can-do Southern women. As luck would have it, Lucy is both an epidemiologist and a crackerjack computer hacker. Together they map out the geographical distribution pattern of the cases. They discover in progress a high-level (and highly illegal) experiment in social control. A group of scientists, including Gottlieb, Comeaux, and Van Dorn, has been diverting sodium waste from the Grand Mer reactor into the regional water supply. . . .

The doctors are armed with some stunning statistics: the suppression of isolated cortical functions by sodium ions has brought about dramatic reductions in crime, homosexual activity, reports of AIDS. Street kids are volunteering for community service. The football team is unbeatable. When More eventually raises the tricky question of ethics, the doctors have a ready answer: they compare their project to the initially covert, and finally beneficial, fluoridation of water. What is involved here, however, is something more like a fluoridation of the psyche—a riskier venture. The doctors naturally want More on their side. They offer him a high-paying research post with perks. But More, old-style doctor that he is, cannot be persuaded. He mistrusts any kind of spiritual quick fix. Where there is no suffering, there can be no soul, no grace; God disappears. More, another of Percy's lapsed-Catholic narrators, never says this directly; but anyone who knows Percy's work can fill in the blanks.

Percy takes obvious pleasure in playing More's curmudgeonly skepticism off the slick cajolery of his colleagues. Over the years he has perfected his rendering of the subtle signals of Southern male bonhomie. The procedure is set, but it works. More refuses the moralistic pose; his opponents hoist themselves with their own petard. Here Comeaux has taken the doctor out for a drive and a "chat": . . .

> "Okay, one thing. Tell me honestly. Don't pull punches. Has anything you've heard in the last few minutes about the behavioral effects of the sodium additive struck you as undesirable?"
>
> "Not offhand, though it's hard to say. I'll have to think it over."
>
> "There you go!" Again the soft congratulatory fist on my knee. "That's the answer we're looking for. Be hard on us! Be our Dutch uncle!"
>
> "But what about the cases of gratuitous violence—Mickey LaFaye shooting all her horses—the rogue violence of that postal worker in St. Francisville who shot everybody in the post office?"
>
> Now he socks himself. "You've already put a finger on it!" he cries aloud. "That's why we need you."

The complexity of human exchange has always fascinated Percy (as his two essay collections, ***The Message in the Bottle*** and ***Lost in the Cosmos,*** demonstrate). He wishes to understand how two people can be speaking on one level while understanding each other on another. Once we catch on to More's strategically (and psychiatrically) neutral style, we realize that the whole novel turns on these semantically overdetermined interchanges. Their cumulative resonance grows by the chapter, turning what could be a conspiracy plot by Crichton or Cook into a statement of genuine minatory power. (p. 32)

Though ***The Thanatos Syndrome*** reads like a good thriller, it plays for bigger stakes. And in one respect it plays too hard. Perhaps out of fear that a one-track narrative might prevent his message from shining forth, Percy has outfitted the novel with a most perplexing subplot. Father Simon Smith (he made a cameo appearance in ***Love in the Ruins***) has shut himself up in a fire-watcher's tower and refuses to come down. Comeaux prevails upon More to exercise his therapeutic gifts. But the old priest . . . won't budge. He is suffering from some peculiar sickness of the soul. During More's first visit, he moves in and out of catatonia, ranting during his "lucid" moments about Jews and the evacuation of all meaning from our word-signs. "Tenderness," he says, fixing on his interlocutor, "leads to the gas chamber."

It turns out that as a young man Smith had traveled to Germany with his father, where they visited with a Dr. Jäger, an eminent psychiatrist, and his two sons. He formed a close friendship with Helmut, the younger son, who was about to join an SS officer school. At their parting, Helmut presented Smith with a dagger etched with the words *Blut und Ehre*. Grabbing More's arm now, the priest confesses: "If I had been German, not American, I would have joined him."

As we know very little of Father Smith, except for his dementia, it's hard to know what to make of this information. But the rest of his tale is perfectly clear. Returning to Germany in 1945 as a soldier with the Seventh Army, Smith participated in the liberation of the very hospital at which Dr. Jäger had worked. The doctor himself had fled, but one of the nurses showed him the *Kinderhaus,* where lethal experiments were carried out upon children. Jäger—musician, scholar, the same man who had expressed his outrage at the brownshirt thugs—had been the chief researcher. "I'm not sure I understand what you're trying to tell me—about your memory of—about Germany," says More. To this the priest replies: "What is there to understand?"

We are in the century of mass death, the Age of Thanatos. Percy wants to ensure that we make no mistake about the moral and historical connection: the logic of the sodium project is, slightly extended, the logic of the Nazi exterminators. *Any* action undertaken in the name of a principle or an abstraction is dangerous. The ethical conclusion is to treat all human beings with reference to their individuality, not their similarity. (pp. 32-3)

The Thanatos Syndrome manifests this calling with great vigor, even without the counternarrative. If Percy's intent was to intrude the Father Smith chapters as an irritant, as a way of forcing the reader to look past the seductive surface of his novel's plot, he has succeeded. But I can't help feeling that these more loaded episodes could have been worked in with greater elegance. ''Tenderness leads to the gas chamber'' certainly strikes one as, shall we say, a contradiction; but it does not shock, and it isn't placed in a way that would make it a ''lever of transcendence'' (the phrase is Simone Weil's).

This problem by no means hobbles the novel. Percy controls his main narrative with great sureness; it is suspenseful, it is provocative, it is witty. Nobody presently writing has so keen an eye for the surreal quality of our cultural topography. Percy is especially good at catching the way that media figures and media usages infiltrate every corner of daily life. Afternoon soaps, Dr. Ruth, Robin Leach, ''M*A*S*H'' reruns: little escapes Percy's whirring darts. And though his quips are never didactic, we can sense a more serious concern in the background. There's a hint, nothing more, that the happy vacuousness streaming from the screens of several hundred million televisions somehow makes his fantasy scenario less and less impossible.

The Thanatos Syndrome ends . . . well, happily. In the last chapter, More is back in his office, listening to what suddenly sounds like beautiful music: a patient's litany of anxiety and despair. It's a masterful final stroke. For only by this contrast do we register the true horror of the sodium cure: that the end of suffering and dread is for us, paradoxical creatures, the end of the path to awareness. Indeed, as we leave Tom More, old Kierkegaardian soul doctor, back in his element, we feel decidedly better about our own unmedicated condition. (p. 33)

Sven Birkerts, ''The Plot Sickens,'' in The New Republic, *Vol. 196, No. 15, April 13, 1987, pp. 31-3.*

TERRENCE RAFFERTY

The Thanatos Syndrome continues the adventures of Dr. Tom More, the ''bad Catholic'' of ***Love in the Ruins,*** as the world nears its end yet again. . . . Percy's project is bizarre enough to be rather fascinating. ***The Thanatos Syndrome***, with its mock-trashy, Ludlumish title, is a remake of ***Love in the Ruins,*** stripped (relatively speaking) for action: eschatology made simple. (p. 91)

Reading ***The Thanatos Syndrome*** is a little like tuning in, unawares, to the Christian Broadcasting Network, whose mixture of talk shows, Bible-thumping oratory, commercials for Jesus, and ''Man from U.N.C.L.E.'' reruns is so rivetingly weird. As in ***Love in the Ruins,*** Percy's Dr. More, a mildly unstable Louisiana psychiatrist, has to save the world from the destruction threatened by others' misuse of one of his scientific discoveries. In the earlier novel, it's a device called an Ontological Lapsometer, which measures an individual's sense of self; in ***Thanatos,*** it's a breakthrough in ''cortex pharmacology''—the discovery that large doses of heavy sodium tend to increase memory and reduce sexual inhibitions. . . . In both books, Dr. Tom, the author's stand-in, fights the good fight against the social engineers. For all his carefully planted human frailties—a weakness for drink, a hint of scientific arrogance, the occasional stirring of lust in his heart—he's a beacon of superego in the darkness of American culture. There are minor topical differences in emphasis between the two novels: ***Love in the Ruins,*** a product of the Nixon era, is more concerned with violence and political polarization, ***Thanatos*** more with sex (crimes and diseases). But basically they're as alike as an early and a late episode of a long-running series. The later one is just glibber, more streamlined, more cozily familiar—you don't have to pay as much attention to follow it. Percy must know he's repeating himself. Has he begun to believe that in literature, as in television, repetition is power?

The most generous explanation for what this very serious novelist is up to is that he's trying to get his message across in what he takes to be the authentic language of his times—the language of the tube. He doesn't use the pop idiom with much instinct or irony, though; it's something he seems to have fallen into awkwardly, like an author on a talk show who finds himself babbling about Vegas with the celebs. Of all the characters in Percy's recent books, the only one who is truly convincing, precisely observed, is Phil Donahue, as he appears in a brief parodic sketch called ''The Last Donahue Show'' in ***Lost in the Cosmos.*** And the reason that this short, funny routine is better than anything in ***The Thanatos Syndrome*** is, well, ontological. The real, largely unspoken subject of all Percy's novels at least from ***Love in the Ruins*** on, has been the impotent rage of the armchair viewer, who fumes and twitches as the horrible news flashes by—direr and more threatening, somehow, at second hand, because of the unassimilable density and speed of the presentation—and talks back, out loud, to the smug experts who presume to make sense of it all for him. The point of ''The Last Donahue Show,'' which ends with a ''Cosmic stranger'' (accompanied by John Calvin and a Confederate officer) bursting in on Phil's breezy psychosexual discussion group and announcing the approach of Armageddon, is debatable, but here the form that Percy's viewer-revenge fantasy takes is absolutely appropriate: Percy projects himself into the alien world of television, and his malicious satire has the same dizzying half-reality as its original. In Lapsometer terms, this bit of throwaway wit has a stronger sense of self, a greater congruence between the form of perception and the form of expression, than most of Percy's more ''literary'' work.

The real problem with ***The Thanatos Syndrome***—what makes Percy's message about the decline of American civilization so hard to accept—is a kind of formal bad faith. His imperfect Southern knight, Tom More, is less a vehicle for genuine social satire than a prime-time fantasy avenger, an Equalizer who embodies the combined virtues of Kierkegaard, Harry Stack Sullivan, and Robert E. Lee. If his creator showed any awareness that the need for such figures is itself an expression of impotence—a product of the living-room philosopher's frustration at his remoteness from the culture's catastrophes—he'd be a lot more persuasive. Everything seems to be in the wrong register. The human foibles satirized in ***The Thanatos Syndrome*** are barely recognizable, because they seem to come not out of the author's own experience but from his perception of significant experience *out there,* the data that have arrived from a distance, over the airwaves. His observations on, say, the dangers of female sexuality (one of the first symptoms of the ''syndrome'' Dr. More discovers is that his women patients ''present rearward'' to express interest in sex, like apes) and the spiritual emptiness of golfers and bridge players are recklessly imprecise, crusty with resentment. The benign do-gooder that Percy has invented to cure these imagined ills is something of a blind: if the world were truly as Percy describes it, only a wrathful god could make it right again. (pp. 91-2)

Binx Bolling, the narrator of ***The Moviegoer,*** has a theory—Kierkegaard's—about repetition: ''A repetition is the re-enactment of past experience toward the end of isolating the time segment which has lapsed in order that it, the lapsed time, can be savored of itself and without the usual adulteration of events that clog time like peanuts in brittle.'' And that's pretty much what ***The Thanatos Syndrome*** does. The time elapsed between ***Love in the Ruins*** and its reenactment certainly doesn't appear to have been adulterated by anything like an event: it's as pure as a blank screen, with even the traumatic self-revelation of ***Lancelot*** wiped out. It's not easy being a visionary satirist—the very attempt makes Percy worthy of our attention, and even respect—and it's just about impossible if you cling, as Percy does, to a philosophy that's fundamentally ahistorical. The apocalyptic imagination is innocent of the kinds of fine distinctions a cultural critic has to make. It's all marking time until the end, the fiery climax, the series finale, with events in the lapse-time between the original sin and the last judgment erasing themselves continually as we formulate and reformulate their meaning, until all that's left of them is a blinding-white constant significance—the last word. This is where the mystic and the talk-show crank meet: ***The Thanatos Syndrome***, like all Percy's novels, seems to be taking place in the greenroom of the apocalypse. (p. 92)

Terrence Rafferty, ''The Last Fiction Show,'' in The New Yorker, *Vol. LXIII, No. 17, June 15, 1987, pp. 91-4.*

ROBERT TOWERS

As a crazed but prophetic priest in ***The Thanatos Syndrome*** says of the Jews, Walker Percy as a writer is ''unsubsumable.'' Certainly he cannot be comfortably subsumed under any of the categories to which his fellow American writers are likely to be assigned. He seems to enjoy playing the part of the provincial loner who, snug in his corner of Louisiana, rides his hobby horses, railing cheerfully against the myriad evils of this disastrous century. If, in the eyes of some critic, he is ''our cool Dostoevsky,'' he might also be called, on the basis of his new novel, ''the adults' Kurt Vonnegut.'' As with all the novels that have followed his minor classic ***The Moviegoer***, ***The Thanatos Syndrome*** releases a cageful of themes, which dart off in all directions. Percy's pursuit of them is exhilarating. . . .

Much of ***The Thanatos Syndrome*** treats Percy's serious concerns in a manner more playful than impassioned. The search for the source of the heavy-sodium contaminant and the perils encountered along the way build up into a story strong and dramatic enough to moderate the novel's tendency to introduce one social theme after another. While many characters are too briskly sketched in to be memorable, they keep things moving, and the reader may ignore that they and their speech tend to be stereotypical and do not seem to have been felt in any deep way. Though conceived chiefly as people who stand for one attitude or another, they still contribute some degree of color and variety to Percy's panorama of the soon-to-be contemporary South.

But once the central mystery is solved, the novel spins out of control. Comedy broadens into fairly crude farce when the child abusers are forced to take their own medicine. As if not quite knowing what to do with the last third of his book, Percy allows his narrator simply to pack in more and more observations not only about the grand evils of our time but about the banalities as well, ranging from Disney World to born-again Christianity. Care about form (never a major preoccupation of Percy's), a concern to concentrate rather than to broadcast his effects, a degree of subtlety and surprise in the rendering of characters and their speech—these have all been sacrificed (in greater or lesser degree) in the author's headlong rush to fictionalize his diagnostic observations and his tragicomic vision of horrors to come. Percy's willingness to deal with big issues is no doubt salutary in a period of narrowly conceived novels, but ***The Thanatos Syndrome***, for all its energy and inventiveness, lacks the shapeliness and substance of achieved literary art. (p. 45)

Robert Towers, ''Danger Zones,'' in The New York Review of Books, *Vol. XXXIV, No. 11, June 25, 1987, pp. 45-6.*

Carl Rakosi

1903-

(Name legally changed to Callman Rawley) American poet and essayist.

Rakosi is identified primarily with the Objectivist movement, which attained prominence during the 1930s and included such poets as Louis Zukofsky, Charles Reznikoff, George Oppen, and William Carlos Williams. The Objectivists valued perception as one of the primary faculties of the poet and expanded upon the imagist concern with sight and sound by also emphasizing thought and feeling. Rakosi extends these preoccupations by employing complex linguistic associations and rich imagery, combining classical diction with American idioms, and frequently countering the observation of factual information with the bizarre, grotesque, and irrational. Rakosi attempts to accurately depict the relationship between objective reality and emotion by preserving both the integrity of the external world and the emotional presence of the poet.

Rakosi gained recognition when several of his poems appeared in *An "Objectivist" Anthology,* edited by Louis Zukofsky, in 1931. Rakosi's first book, *Selected Poems* (1941), gathers many of these pieces as well as revised versions of several previously published works. In these poems, Rakosi displays the influence of Wallace Stevens through his preoccupation with what he termed "the elegance of language, the imaginative associations of words." Although not completely disengaged from the political, social, and economic issues of the time, Rakosi deemphasized these themes in his early work.

Employed in New York as a social worker during the Depression, Rakosi was acutely aware of the economic hardship that confronted many people. In an attempt to actively improve these conditions, he became involved with the Marxist movement. Perceiving personal lyricism as an inappropriate instrument for change, Rakosi ceased writing poetry for more than twenty-five years and dedicated himself to social work. He resumed composing verse in 1965; his second book, *Amulet* (1967), includes revised versions of his early poems and many new works. Rakosi's poems written after 1965 emphasize his commitment to the evocation of an individual poetic persona.

Rakosi's subsequent volumes retain many of the themes and techniques introduced in *Amulet. Ere-Voice* (1971), like much of Rakosi's work, features colloquial language and natural speech rhythms accentuated by arresting imagery. In *Ex Cranium, Night* (1975), Rakosi alternates sections of verse and prose, prompting one critic to compare the volume to James Dickey's *Sorties.* In *Drôles de journal* (1981), a sequence of twenty pieces comprising reworkings of earlier poems and new verse, Rakosi examines such topics as aesthetics, academia, and the experiences of everyday life. *Spiritus, I* (1983) is a meditative volume containing descriptions of animals and epigrammatic reflections on a variety of subjects. Rakosi's best-regarded work appears in *Carl Rakosi: Collected Prose* (1983) and *The Collected Poems of Carl Rakosi* (1986).

(See also *Contemporary Authors,* Vols. 21-24, rev. ed.; *Contemporary Authors New Revision Series,* Vol. 12; and *Contemporary Authors Autobiography Series,* Vol. 5.)

NEW YORK HERALD TRIBUNE BOOKS

Carl Rakosi has been known to poetry readers chiefly through his association with the Objectivists, anthologized and defined by Louis Zukofsky some ten years ago. Of this group, William Carlos Williams has exemplified, in his work, the best utilization of the Objectivist aims; and among American poets it is Carlos Williams who has most influenced Mr. Rakosi. Like Mr. Williams, he uses the short, direct phrase, breaking the single object into clear, sharply reflected facets. But Mr. Rakosi's comment [in his ***Selected Poems***] is less spare, his images and associations richer, more varied and complex. He has drawn a good deal from the Surrealists (whom he satirizes), putting in apposition to factual observation the irrational or grotesque. And one finds the usual combination of formal, classical diction and racy American idiom. Wit, and no little ironic indignation, mark his comments on the American scene: the status quo of a city, the "nonpolitical" citizen, the portrait of an anti-Semite. There is honest analysis, too, of a poetic creed in **"Declaration."** Though he has published less than most of his contemporaries, and though what he has written will appeal only to a limited, discriminating audience, Carl Rakosi turns out the carefully disciplined and distinguished work of a mature poet.

"Objectivism," in New York Herald Tribune Books, *May 10, 1942, p. 30.*

PETER MONRO JACK

Carl Rakosi makes no pretense of social significance. His poems belong to a movement never properly defined, called Objectivism. It stems from Imagism and is brief, hard, clear and simple. The less said the better is a brief etc. way of expressing it. In 1928 Mr. Rakosi wrote for Ezra Pound's magazine, *Exile*, a long rambling poem called **"Extracts From a Private Life."** This he has reduced in his ***Selected Poems*** to four lines called **"News From the Old Country"** and which read:

> The eye of your second cousin
> An obscure cigarmaker from Smyrna
> Gluts on the dancing girls
> Like on oyster in the head of Bacchus.

It is a good process, since that was all that was interesting in the poem. The poetry is meticulous and somewhat elegant and is distinguished by a sense of strangeness, especially in the under-sea images of **"Lobster"** (written for W. C. Williams and probably influenced by Mr. Williams), which I think the best poem. It is factual, and it has a slight edge of that curious lore that makes Marianne Moore interesting reading. . . . It is a small poetry but, carefully considered, one sees that it has come from a mind that could be expansive but cares only for the ultimate aristocracy of the word.

Peter Monro Jack, in a review of "Selected Poems," in The New York Times Book Review, *May 17, 1942, p. 5.*

JIM HARRISON

After maintaining total silence for over 25 years, Carl Rakosi has begun writing poems again. ***Amulet*** is his second collection, containing many poems, though often in revised form, from his first book which appeared in 1941. Rakosi had been a well-thought-of member of the Objectivist Group (William Carlos Williams, Louis Zukofsky, Charles Reznikoff, George Oppen) when he dropped from sight in disgust with society and a dedication to his family and social work. He had a Marxist conviction that, in the wake of the Depression and World War II, his intensely individual lyricism was irrelevant and impossible to continue.

We should not necessarily regret this silence. There is a gnomic quality to Rakosi's work that would forbid profusion, and though he obviously lacks the range of Williams and Zukofsky, his short lyrics are consistently stronger. (This is not said at their expense, but in his praise.) It should also be noted that the positive effect of Rakosi's social concerns are direct and evident; there is a total concern for the "here and now," a sense too that poetry as an art can be but one of the sacraments replacing none of the others. It is a tremendously engaged poetry, humane, attentive to the ordinary until the ordinary ceases to be so, but scarcely ever committing the usual objectivist sin of mere attitude, that of expecting dumb, unequal objects to stand by themselves as poems. These poems are "made things" and throughout the book we sense the intelligence that directed the craft.

The faults in the lesser and generally earlier poems are obvious—a certain atrophied sense of range, an inability to let the poem seek its limits, the tendency to let his rhythms whisper a bit when they should remain harsh. But this is quibbling when we think of the poet returned virtually from the dead. There are at least a dozen poems here that should be consistently anthologized or given any other small portion of immortality that they so flatly deserve. . . .

There are a number of delights in Rakosi's work, not the least the use of words which often betray a purely esthetic intoxication, the celebration of the rite of language for its own sake. The vocabulary is not any more quirkish than that of Wallace Stevens—who was much maligned for his curiosity about language, as is Robert Duncan in our own day. Among bad poets there is a sort of "let's roll up our sleeves and get down to brass language" attitude. In Rakosi we find such words as chevron, egopedes, microskeptic, ariette, coryphee, cairngorm, Archimandrite, misinterem, fumous.

It is said that Rakosi began writing again at the urging of a young Englishman, Andrew Crozier. Crozier, it is evident, found his poet ready to begin again. . . . Rakosi begs our attention with these fine poems; he has not sought the art of landing without first being intimate with the art of flight. Rakosi is a maker, not a bearer, and should be read and saluted by those who care for the life of the poem.

Jim Harrison, "Gnomic Verse," in The New York Times Book Review, *January 28, 1968, p. 10.*

LAURENCE LIEBERMAN

Carl Rakosi's chief strength is the constant surgical purposefulness in the management of his line—each line is an incision, adroitly executed with care for tone and measure. Only rarely does a reader sense a lapse in the controlling hand behind the line. But the surprises of the line-to-line ingenuity are not enough to sustain the structure. In the best poems [contained in ***Amulet***], imagistic adventurousness—alluring to the ear and eye—saves the arbitrary framework, a verbal necessity inhering in the poem's music. . . . In most poems, however, the enticing sequence of images is interrupted by turn of wit, the voice skipping from imagism to clever fancifulness. Usually, the formal observation and wry extraneous remarks don't mix well, causing a disjunction in the poem's structure. A studied lightness—the insistent illogic of associations—is pursued programmatically as a technique; it becomes, finally, as predictable and unvivacious as ordinary discursive prose.

Ideas in Rakosi's poems are usually delivered obliquely, weaving, at odd angles, through a field of essentially "unconnected images". A few lines of personal discovery seem in deadly earnest, but they are quickly resorbed in the poem's prevailing timbre of whimsy and archness. All parts of the poem's content are reduced to inert components of an over-tenacious line movement. Due to this quality of reductiveness, a single aspect of style—the line-weave—dominates all other quantities in the poems. This disturbing mannerism often leaves me feeling as though I'm reading the same poem over and over as I move through the book, despite a resourceful variety of subjects. (pp. 340-42)

Laurence Lieberman, in a review of "Amulet," in Poetry, *Vol. CXII, No. 5, August, 1968, pp. 340-42.*

STANLEY COOPERMAN

Carl Rakosi's [***Amulet***], the work of one of the "objectivist" writers of the nineteen-forties, breaks a silence of more than two decades. Actually, we are in familiar country here: the metronome, after all, has tic-tocked the years away, and suddenly the objectivist mode seems almost quaintly orthodox. The short, broken line; the asides; the surface casualness of "real talk, small talk" (that is, of course, no "realer" than any other poetic talk, only more self-conscious about it), the play of wit and verbal surprise—it's all here.

Rakosi will, I believe, come as something of an unexpected pleasure to those readers who have been so bullied by academic theorists, and anti-academic academic theorists, that they approach objectivist poetry with the foolish solemnity of society matrons attending a light-show. Because the quality that one admires most about Rakosi is the ease and comfort and wit of his work: untheorized, we can actually enjoy the stuff. . . . I mean, how is it possible *not* to like a poet who dedicates his book to (among other things) "Izaak Walton's English / sounding like the small bell / of the knife-grinder"? What Rakosi has, delightfully, is an ability to translate emotion into objects, tastes, smells: and these, in turn, are completely familiar—except that the familiarity itself occurs in unexpected juxtapositions of sound and theme.

The result of Rakosi's *using* of the world immediately before him—tables, birds, "statues / with the noses / knocked off," lamp-shades, books—is that the reader is almost surprised to find himself moving from a homely, apparently naïve, sometimes even domestic landscape into a mind that is neither naïve nor domestic; and it is the casual leap into serious thought and back again, that keeps us balancing on the points of our mind, doing a verbal and intellectual jig to a fiddle that sometimes—and unexpectedly—becomes an orchestration. Quickness is needed: the ability to shift tones both on the linguistic and intellectual level. For Rakosi's work is at once irreverent and serious; highly intellectual and simplistic. Neither solemn nor sloppy readers will cope with his work easily—or rather, they will be irritated by his dancing finger, which comes to the same thing.

To be sure, the object sometimes is not enough; the bare play of a scene or thing makes no leap at all:

"Lamp"

with goddess,
  ivory-carved
Japanese lady,
  hands crossed
over breast, holding
  on her head
electric bulbs
  and batik
lamp shade

This, for me, is simply *flat:* the miracle of is-ness (even the is-ness of those electric bulbs) is not translated enough, so that—between the lamp and Rakosi's poem about the lamp—I would much prefer seeing the one than reading the other: that is, the poem becomes gratuitous; who needs it? But this is a risk of Rakosi's method: like all good ways of making poems, the risk is always there.

Oddly (or not so oddly) enough, it is when Rakosi tries to bolster his poems with *importances* that he is least interesting, and approaches the hedging of poetic bets. Because there is a kind of safety in posturing—any posturing, whether political or aesthetic: let a man be too afraid of becoming angry, Rakosi tells us, or shrill, and he will "spend too much time goosing"; let him cherish his High Calling of Poet too closely, too seriously, and he will fare no better. . . . (pp. 271-72)

As for Carl Rakosi: whether he repeats stories of Americana, or teases Wallace Stevens, or looks at a city, or joyful-mocks old movies (there is that too), or stands up with Shakespeare's Jew, we can say—along with Hayden Carruth—"Good news. Carl Rakosi is writing again!" (p. 272)

Stanley Cooperman, "The Experience of Having Poemed," in Prairie Schooner, *Vol. XLII, No. 3, Fall, 1968, pp. 266-72.*

W. G. REGIER

Carl Rakosi's [***Ere-Voice***], as its jacket indicates, is the latest contribution of a poet whose career began with the same years and theory of Oppen and Reznikoff. All three are brothers-in-ink if not blood of William Carlos Williams, and the similarities are unavoidably obvious. This fraternity has an aristocratic confidence mingled with rebellious energy, resolutely, assuredly offering its own special variety of poem. Despite the pre-eminence of Williams, his peers in perspective have attained high status themselves. Rakosi is no exception.

His poems, like most of those associated with Williams, possess the self-consciousness of a mind wringing itself out. There is the familiar non-distribution of lines, easier to watch than to read. There is the submerged imagery, moving like a squid beneath the surface; slippery, obscure, but there. Rakosi's book is acutely reminiscent of Theodore Roosevelt's letters to Bismarck: there is that kind of muscle and pride, that kind of narrow sensitivity, as if the words were half obvious and half code.

The section of sixteen poems subtitled **"Americana"** shows Rakosi in his most exemplary distillation. One of the sixteen, **"Atmosphere Anthrax,"** is most interesting in its title.

I would rather sing folk songs against injustice
and sound like ash cans in the early morning
or bark like a wolf
from the open doorway of a red-hot freight
than sit like Chopin on my exquisite ass.

Among a string of growling, forceful similes, Rakosi sticks in a tone of self-satire ("exquisite ass") rising to self-righteousness. This is the poem of a self-appointed prophet (we are in the habit of electing prophets these days), showing off his moral superiority. And superior to whom? Chopin? Could Rakosi ever be Chopin or sit like him, even if he wanted to? Doubtful. The comparison becomes poor sport.

It is finally this tone that ruins most of Rakosi's work. He is capable, and proves it, in such poems as **"In Thy Sleep / Little Sorrows Sit and Weep,"** and **"No One Talks About This,"** shirking his wilderness attitude for awhile to concentrate on the demands of the poems. But usually he is briared and brambled, and too proud of it, dominating excellent images with the absurd tone of an eighteenth-century missionary to the Iroquois. Or rather, a mountain man shooting missionaries.

Rakosi has as many faults as the California coastline. What a wonder that he can be just as attractive. When the passage is made through his wasteland, Rakosi rewards his readers with jewels. **"In a Warm Bath"** is a splendid example of what reverie can do when poured into recognizable phrases. Of his son, Rakosi writes:

The clarity I taught him
he has turned against me, and I am satisfied.
I say a man has integrity. For this he cares.
And I. Looks at me long and deep,
a straight beam unavoidable. And I to him.
I was made father for this.

Here there is substance supporting tone, and making it function gorgeously.

In a few rigidly controlled protests, **"1968"** and **"Simplicity,"** Rakosi produces undeniable rhythms, timed like the clenching and unclenching of fists. (pp. 85-6)

It is an acknowledged fact that good poets sometimes write bad poems, and idiots sometimes blunder into beauty. Rakosi is of the former: ***Ere-Voice*** is a bunch of bad poems gathered around a few rare blossoms. And those few make the whole worth picking. (p. 86)

W. G. Regier, "The Touring Word," in Prairie Schooner, *Vol. XLVI, No.1, Spring, 1972, pp. 85-6.*

CHOICE

[***Ex Cranium, Night***] is only Rakosi's fifth volume in 42 years, but unlike ***Ere-voice,*** this shows both Rakosi's verse and prose as mannered and affected. Starting out as Objectivist verse like Zukovsky's or Resnikoff's, Rakosi's is now almost indistinguishable from prose (indeed, it quotes prose statements). As if to confirm this shift in his work, Rakosi alternates sections of verse with longer sections of prose, mostly aphorisms, observations, and comments somewhat in the manner of James Dickey in *Sorties* but nowhere nearly so penetrating or insightful. The reader will find it difficult to be as interested in Rakosi's dreams as he himself is, for his reports of them, while not entirely pointless, seem irrelevant to anything much beyond the writer's own personal experience.

A review of "Ex Cranium, Night," in Choice, *Vol. 13, No. 1, March, 1976, p. 73.*

MICHAEL HULSE

Carl Rakosi is a survivor of that loose "Objectivist" group that was active in Pound's ambit in the 1920s and 30s; his name comes to mind with Zukofsky, Oppen, Williams and Reznikoff, and his strengths and weaknesses remain similar to theirs. ***Spiritus, I*** contains the mellowed, meditative work of advanced age, but the poems are still powered by a forceful motor. . . . The two-ply line favoured by Rakosi is a wiry, resourceful form that he uses with initiative, adapting it equally effectively to affectionate description of a goat and an epigrammatic reflection called **"Walkers passing each other in the park":**

Had I been eighty-five
he would have stopped
to compare notes,
but what was there
to talk about
with a man only sixty-five?

The dangers of such writing are that it can be too indulgent towards slight subject matter, and that it can result in pedestrian flatness if its rhythms are not always fully alert. Rakosi can provide examples of both failures, but he is nevertheless rewarding.

Michael Hulse, "Taking on the Alien," in The Times Literary Supplement, *No. 4254, October 12, 1984, p. 1169.*

MICHAEL HELLER

Within the larger framework of Objectivist possibilities, Carl Rakosi's work seems to explore the ground between intercommunication and divination, to, indeed, propose a poetics that, like a divining rod, sets itself between the human who wishes, who loves, and who fears and the object of his passions. For Rakosi's poetry shows forth the desire to possess, even as it reminds poet and reader of deep, unbridgeable gaps between wish and fulfillment. This poetry, then, is concerned not only with rendering the concreteness and feel of an actual world but also with accurately depicting the life of the emotions as they swarm between object and person; it is an attempt to articulate a kind of depth of field, to give substantiality to a phenomenologically constructed "reality" in which the perceived shapes of objects are dictated not only by their actuality but also by the mind that longs after them.

Rakosi's poetry exhibits an almost Blakean affinity for the contraries and oppositions of emotional life. In contrast to the far too typical contemporary poetry of the injured ego with its due bill of insults and hurts against society and the world, Rakosi presents an exploration of the poem as the agency of personal healing and redemption, as a kind of linguistic *modus vivendi* which interweaves the traces of subject and object, of passion and passion's claim. (pp. 36-7)

Rakosi's poetry continually speaks—or brings its energy to bear, however obliquely—in opposition to the prevailing egotism of much literature. Cast against the contemporary world, Rakosi's work suggests sanity in its most transcendent form (what I would call a form of sadness and regret) by imagining the possibility of a deep relation with the world and its orderings. (p. 37)

Rakosi's subject is the curious equation we make between life and emotions, curious because in Rakosi we sense a poet unconvinced of the equation's aptness. A close reading of his work shows that above all it embodies a deep resistance to the idea of mind (as postulated in much modern poetry) as something which desires to be possessed, to be victimized and pounced upon by the wave of its own self-centered feelings. Such a poetry as Rakosi's is obviously at odds with many of the hidden guilts and resentments of our time. Indeed, his work seems, by its very nature, to be an indirect exposé of the shabby rhetorics, the misused formal inventiveness of much contemporary poetry.

"The poet," Rakosi claims, "is more modest than the ancient philosopher: he doesn't claim that what he has thought out is the ultimate reality." As this statement implies, Rakosi's poetics involve a taking up of the Objectivist meaning of "objectification" within the context of self-irony and distance. Such irony is a version of Objectivist "sincerity" cast into a comic or investigative format. As such, we could say of Rakosi's poems that, rather than being 'emotional', they follow the path and texture of emotion, the curve of thought and impulse, as they mediate among images.

Reading Rakosi, one discovers that among the Objectivists his work embraces perhaps the widest range of emotions and feeling tones: in the poems there is awe, humor, anger, despair. And indeed, it can be said that his work is 'about' certain things, that subjects give rise to sentiments, to a range of responses. But this is to miss the character of its deeper effect, an effect that strikes one as something between contemplation and meditation. The poems do not really attempt to capture an essence; they seem rather to arrive out of a middle distance, a distance at once palpable and creative. They are the linguistic equivalent of the "patina" Rakosi mentions in an early poem, "more durable" even than the subject of the poet's perceptions.

Distance of this sort is less a matter of sentiment (or sentimentality) than of recognition. It has more to do with understanding the root or ground of contemporary alienation than with bemoaning it or with seeking alleviation from its effects. This understanding is intimately connected to the techniques of Rakosi's poetry, which is based, first of all, on that loss of "aura" to objects in the world as described by Walter Benjamin in his study of Baudelaire. In Benjamin, as objects and their representations in words acquire an increasingly pragmatic and utilitarian character, the sense of their human use, their luster of tradition and purposefulness, which he calls "aura," is destroyed. The rich and straightforward connections to the world and its objects fall away and are replaced by alienated and mechanized relationships. Rakosi's work is, in a sense, a response to this state of affairs. (pp. 38-9)

Rakosi's poetry is concerned with recovering the aura, the "patina" described above, and aims to become a vehicle for enabling reconnections between mind and world. But such reconnections involve a willingness on the part of the poet to dwell in that area where identity is fluctual, where things out there can no longer be defined by the pragmatic, alienated constructs dictated by modern consumerized and rationalized society. In **"Instructions to the Player,"** Rakosi likens this area, this distance between the hardened thing and the equally hardened notion of identity, to the musical interval, a space which must be entered with both courage and tact. (p. 39)

Of this "pause," one can only say that it is profoundly in between, that the poet is attempting to give imaginative life to the link between subject and object. The pause is sweet, infinite, i.e., saturated with possibilities even as the poet has rescued and formulated it out of chaos. Thus, the creative dynamics of such a poem lie in its ability not only to restore a link but to suggest an opening on an infinity of linkages. Such an opening is meant to cut through the rigidified and utilitarian constructs that characterize contemporary life.

Rakosi's importance lies not so much in this understanding as in his ability to mobilize a sense of loss and distance into a reflexive, non-aggressive poetics; the result is a poetry of regret without resentment, a poetry of healthy—I can think of no better word—self-knowledge and self-consciousness.

Of course, we are talking about poetry and not philosophy, and the issue of an outlook into poetry, the transcription of a private complexity into a public document, is a matter of craft.

In order to understand what Rakosi is doing, we have to consider briefly what the matter of poetic technique has become in the present. For the most part, craft and technique, under our tartarean modernity, have lost their old associations, have become ends in themselves, implicitly pointing towards attempts at mastery and control. The resulting manipulation of language is no longer concerned with outlook, but with a kind of inlook, with self-regard, with an attempt to create an object which can be sold off as an extension of personality. We see this most clearly in the inflated imagery, in the fantasticated surreality of the contemporary poem, in which the image has become a matter of seduction aimed at oneself. Everything from having paid one's dues to one's cleverness is subsumed as product. I mention this because it is necessary to see in precisely what way Rakosi departs from this contemporary ethos, why his use of imagery, in particular, is a kind of example for the poet writing today.

Form and imagery with Rakosi, as with the other Objectivists and with most twentieth-century modernist poets, are less the fixed elements of a technical repertoire than they are horizons for discovery. . . . [A prose passage in Rakosi's ***Ex Cranium, Night***] suggests, among other possibilities, the poet's desire to avoid any notion of form as imposition. Yet form there must be, for the formal properties of the poem, the very marks which distinguish the poem from other phenomena in the world, are the means by which it embodies conviction. Form, seen from this viewpoint, is not the mold into which content is poured but something captured or rescued by the desire to give materiality (or voice) to an occasion imbedded in the existential world. Thus, form, from this perspective, is the intersection of the desire and the occasion.

In Objectivist formulations, desire is unarmed and, in a sense, has no preconceived notions of the nature of the encounter; its only givens are appearances, emotions aroused, intellectual stimulations, that is, elements in the occasion. These, we could say, are dictated by the occasion.

In terms of the above, Rakosi's poetics can be said to be ways of entering these dictates, in particular, the dictates of seeing. Yet this entering is by no means an adopting of the Imagist's "literary" image with its overtones of strained metaphorization. Nor is Rakosi employing, strictly speaking, the Williams / Pound sense of imagery with its light flavor of encoding and reifying reality. Instead, Rakosi's poetics are techniques for reentering the dictation, for speaking, as it were, of the "existential world," which is, in the deepest sense, both given and not given; the poetics are primarily involved in the sense of recovery which I mentioned above. . . . [In the poem **"Shore Line,"** collected in ***Amulet***], the poet finds himself in significant relation with the "raw data," the scene come upon, and the poem is less concerned with rendering that data than with following the tracings of the "mystery" by which it is transformed into the "figure of will / and language," the "inevitable quartz" (read "rested totality") of the Objectivist poem.

It is because of this tracing, this linguistic interconnecting, that Rakosi strikes one as, above all, the poet of the lived world, the phenomenal world radiating out from us, the world under the double sign of self and otherness. And it is his sense of rootedness in that world, his tact with regard to the accuracy with which one can communicate what is not entirely given, the very humor of that situation, which constitutes the dynamics of his poems.

At Rakosi's command is the entire armament of modernist poetry: irony, complexity, a mordant hilarity, and a willingness to examine the folly of the self and that of the community. Yet underlying these is the hard classical commitment to the eye in its paradoxical function of orienting us towards otherness. In Rakosi, this function is raised to the level of morality, to a kind of open intentionality. (pp. 40-3)

Looked at from yet another point of view, Rakosi's craft is, in its own way, an act not only of discovery but also of permission. The clarity of line and the measured, sometimes hesitant cadences are means for admitting material into the structure of the poem. One sees this clearly in the earlier, less "existential" work, where there is a cluttering of objects, often a catalog of metonymies meant to re-create or hint at an entire structure of reality, of relations, by the most economical means. . . . Rakosi's admittance of these materials is an expression of unconditional curiosity, of an active desire to be with the things of the world, the wedding of vision and mind, which, for Rakosi, is a joy almost before all others.

In Rakosi's later work, in accordance with his existential poetics, the act of perception is transformed. It becomes the exacting rendition of the physical world as both the ground of our psychology and the possibility of a simultaneity of existential modes. . . . Here, between the seen and the seer, only contingency exists, exists as thought, as possibility, that is, as language. Rakosi is the poet of this contingency; the substantive quality of his work lies not in the things it renders but in this arrested quality, the shapely contour of interacting thought and emotion, thought and object. In this sense, we could say that the possibility of possession and identification is given up for the sake of communication, or that in terms of its readers, Rakosi's work enacts a kind of rescue. (pp. 44-6)

There is nothing more elusive to the critical mind than this kind of work. Perhaps it is that, finally, all questions of art, in a master's hands, become subsumed under the question or quality of their humaneness and, at the same time, involve a totality or bearing which does not easily lend itself to exegesis. This totality demands of us the giving up of preconceptions and biases. Rakosi's late work, certainly, is of such a character. To be a mediator between things, and thus to be able to give up for a moment all egocentric views, all flimsy and abstract humanism, is perhaps to be most human after all. Rakosi's work is among the most compassionate bodies of poetry, compassionate because so much seems to be transformed for the express purposes of communication and seems to have been given over to directness of statement and the recognition that another human is reading it. This is not to say that Rakosi has explained away or made sense of our condition, but that he has sought to witness both the self and the world, as it were, religiously. (pp. 46-7)

Michael Heller, "Carl Rakosi: Profoundly in Between," in his Conviction's Net of Branches: Essays on the Objectivist Poets and Poetry, *Southern Illinois University Press, 1985, pp. 36-47.*

MICHAEL HELLER

[***The Collected Poems of Carl Rakosi***], powerful, moving and delightful, recall to mind what Samuel Johnson praised as "easy writing," a poetry so limber and subtle that it seemed to be constructed of "naked elegance and simple purity." Mr. Rakosi, who has spent 55 years first as a social worker and then a psychotherapist, has had a distinguished career as a poet stemming from the 1920's and the poetic ferment surrounding the Imagists and Objectivists. He is very much in the line of other American "easy" poets such as Walt Whitman and William Carlos Williams. Like them, he is a maker of clear, supple lines that can create a poem as compact as a haiku or as discursive as an essay. What he has in common with his forebears is fluidity and capaciousness. His poetry, while always precise and assured, can soar on a scale of tonalities from the bite of Jewish slang to the higher, more philosophical reaches of poetry.

Mr. Rakosi's muse is the clear, physical eye, the "supreme governor." His *ars poetica* is sketched out in **"The Vow."** "Matter, / with this look / I wed thee," he says, "and become / thy very / attribute." Seeing and looking, the conscious acts of attention to the physical world, are for him essentially religious occasions. . . .

[A] major theme of Mr. Rakosi's poetry is the irreducible tension between a perceiving human and physical reality. The eye always portrays otherness to us; its encounter with form can have moral resonances which, for Mr. Rakosi, are constraining forces. In fact, where he parts company with the Whitmanian impulse is that, for him, perception is never appropriation; the song of "it" is not necessarily synonymous with the song of oneself. His most serious poems try to capture the knowledge of the shifty, duplicitous nature of what he calls "our deadly assignation" with the physical world. . . . [Yet], no matter what the theme of a particular poem, in Mr. Rakosi the comic is nearly always at hand; in his view it is an essential constituent of the poetic process.

In his most complex works, the comic has a deep instrumental function. In **"The Transmutation Into English,"** Aristotle, Paracelsus, the "Law of England" and "Giorgione's horse" are ironically deployed in a commentary on the meaning of "quintessence," the word, according to the poem, by which poets "will try to sneak into heaven." For Mr. Rakosi, the quintessential and the imagination are identical *and* ineffable; they can be approached only through irony—"in other words, in the fifth element / if all matter is composed of three elements / and the fourth is comedy."

In lighter moments, particularly in two lengthy sections of the book, the **"Americana"** series and ***Drôles de Journal,*** Mr. Rakosi can be—as few poets can—a downright funny social critic, a stand-up comedian or back-porch codger. Whether contemplating the mythos of American history or some bit of contemporary life, he tends, in the main, toward the deflationary. . . .

A poem, as Mr. Rakosi envisions it, is meant to give articulation to "the soundless order," as he puts it in one of his most intensely meditative poems, **"Yaddo"**—a weave of observation and self-reflection on the imagination and the ironies embedded in the themes of time and timelessness. Reality, and even sentience, is paradoxical, but this paradox, as in so much of his work, is itself the deepest source, and reward, of the poem. . . .

Michael Heller, "Heaven and the Modern World," in The New York Times Book Review, *March 8, 1987, p. 22.*

GEOFFREY O'BRIEN

It has taken far too long—Carl Rakosi is 83—but here at last are his ***Collected Poems,*** a monument so free from monumental posturings that its 490 pages could conceivably be read in a single delighted sitting. I can think of no contemporary poet who radiates such an aura of enjoyment—enjoyment of the senses, of the oddness of language, of the mind's capacity to make something out of nothing:

> If there is no connection between
> the wild
> hemp of Kashmir
> and the plectrum on a Persian lute,
> the mind
> will make one before the mallet comes down
> on the cymbalo.

So begins a poem characteristically entitled **"Discoveries, Trade Names, Genitals and Ancient Instruments."** Rakosi's unfettered range of association takes him readily from Finmarken to China to an eighth century Ireland where "the ram leaped / and the seal disported on small rocks / and birds and geese cackled in the glen / and Castlekirk was built in one night by a cock and a hen." Lost imagined worlds surface continually from the humblest objects; an avocado pit is "darkened and faded / like an old Roman mural / from the bath house / of Menander." Words are permitted to lead a life of their own, so that at his merriest, in **"The Glass of Madeira,"** Rakosi within a few lines juxtaposes "Eskimo" and "placebo" and "limbic" before calling in Prospero, Beethoven, and his wife, Leah, for an exuberant wind-up.

At the same time the poet reminds us that "although he is fanciful, / he loves / salt and iron, / and absolutes make him belch." His poems thrive on a tensile oscillation between the particularity of raw data and the whimsical unpredictability of the mind's music. Rakosi can write with scientific precision of "the jonquils whose air within / was irradiated topaz, / silent as in an ear, / the stems leaning lightly / against the glass, / trisecting its inner circle / in the water, / crossed like reverent hands"—and then, following a twist of thought, let the metaphor carry him off into a sudden manic digression: "(ah, the imagination! / Benedicite, / Enter monks. / Oops, sorry! / Trespassing / on Japanese space. / Exit Monks / and all their lore / from grace.)" Although often inclined to make the poem an elegantly self-enclosed artifact, he lacks the hermetic solemnity to take the exercise altogether seriously. Abrupt shifts of tone and perspective become a technique for reminding himself where he is; the music of the spheres is prone to unscheduled interruption by honks, growls, and rude squeaks.

Rakosi's flair for comic deflation reflects his distaste for more grandiose strains of modern poetry. Commenting on Pound's *Cantos* he once remarked: "All that pretense and double-dealing are nauseating to me. And irrelevant. People today are not heroic, and modern human nature is not epic. It's just human, and anything else is just playing games." Rakosi's humor is multiform, ranging from the simplest burlesque and one-liners to elaborate parody and satiric dissection. Even the crudest jokes have their place, since Rakosi wants above all to be true to his own experience of himself. There is a time for contemplating island universes or Aristotle's poetics or the ravages of war, and there is a time for contemplating Calvin Coolidge: "His lips were sealed / tighter / than an old man's / scrotum / backing up from / winter water." Rakosi strikes a balance of high and low, of pratfalls and philosophic flights, closer to certain Medieval and Renaissance writers than to most current practitioners.

He has arranged this book not chronologically but by theme, assembling all the pieces into a complex self-portrait. In so doing he elides the curious structure of his career: his "Objectivist" writing of the '20s and '30s, culminating in the 1941 ***Poems,*** was followed by a 20-year silence while he devoted himself to social work. His return to poetry in the early '60s generated an outpouring of writing more expansive and less calculatingly dazzling than in the earlier period. Between them, Rakosi and his friend George Oppen (movingly eulogized here in **"The Old Poet's Tale"**), whose career followed a similar course, testify to the rejuvenating effects of such prolonged sabbaticals. Rakosi's late phase is not so much a resumption as a rebirth. The "Ancient image" which he prays will "restore / my ancient relation / to words / in which I have set / my hope" seems to have answered him generously.

These ***Collected Poems*** have a companion volume, a ***Collected Prose,*** issued by the same publisher a few years back, which admirers of the poems are advised to pounce on. It reveals the same virtues of humor, concision, and frankness, and established Rakosi as a master of epigram: "When I sit down to write, I must not forget that one does not strike an attitude in front of a mountain." "The larger the crowd, the larger the rhetoric." "Not enough distinction is made between metaphors which transform a subject into poetry and those in which a poet escapes from his subject." Rakosi's day books are an indispensable adjunct to his work as a poet, a rich sample of the ground from which his clusters of particulars are culled. (pp. 50, 52)

Geoffrey O'Brien, "Enjoy!" in The Village Voice, *Vol. XXXII, No. 2, June 13, 1987, pp. 50, 52.*

Peter Reading

1946-

English poet.

Acknowledged as one of England's most innovative young poets, Reading uses both unorthodox and traditional verse forms to lament the barbaric tendencies of humanity and the transitory, anonymous nature of existence. Combining working-class colloquialisms with formal language, Reading infuses his verse with irony and caustic wit to develop his pessimistic outlook. Although some critics claim that Reading is more interested in shocking his readers than in enlightening them, many praise his provocative imagination and brash structural experiments.

Reading's first full-length collection of poems, *For the Municipality's Elderly* (1974), reflects the influence of W. H. Auden in its solemn diction, stately tone, and preponderance of alliteration. Throughout the volume, Reading displays a preoccupation with death and seasonal cycles, instilling in his poems an aura of gravity. In his next book, *The Prison Cell and Barrel Mystery* (1976), Reading focuses on complications arising from love relationships and offers brief dramatic monologues that reveal tangled emotions. This work introduces the pungent wit and acute irony that have become Reading's trademark. *Nothing for Anyone* (1977) concentrates on such recurring subjects as marriage and death and furthers Reading's experimentation with black humor. In *Fiction* (1979), Reading adopts the postmodernist fascination with authorial self-awareness to ironically examine the writer's liberty to manipulate invented lives. In *Tom o'Bedlam's Beauties* (1981), Reading explores insanity by detailing the personalities of inmates of a lunatic asylum. Through his use of such forms as the sonnet, the villanelle, and unrhymed hexameter, as well as his propensity for wordplay and parody, Reading exhibits compassion for society's outsiders. John Saunders noted: "Reading's combination of unbuttoned attitudes and strictly controlled versification accounts for the piquancy of his poetry."

With *Diplopic* (1983), Reading began to experiment with unusual structures. "Diplopic" is defined as "double vision"; Reading utilizes this meaning to organize his grotesque portraits of archaeologists, evangelists, circus performers, and violent teenagers. The events in each poem are told twice—once from the protagonist's perspective, and again in a detached, dispassionate tone. Michael O'Neill observed that this technique allows Reading to demonstrate "an acute sense of the distance between art and suffering," adding that he "at once confesses and exploits the artist's unhealthy interest in the callous and subhuman." In *5 x 5 x 5 x 5 x 5* (1983), Reading chronicles the mundane or fatal destinies of five characters. The volume is composed of five sections, each comprising five poems, with five stanzas per poem, five lines per stanza, and five syllables per line. In his next collection, *C* (1984), Reading confronts the fear of cancer through an examination of the realities of the disease. Reading's narrator, a cancer victim, plans his final hundred days in one hundred units, each consisting of one hundred words. The verse forms Reading employs in *C* are so grossly unsuited to the subject matter, asserted Mick Imlah, "that we relish all the more their impotence to explain, console, or cure."

Photograph by W. G. Reading. Courtesy of Peter Reading.

In *Ukulele Music* (1985), Reading delineates atrocities as reported by the media to convey the commonplace sordidness and desensitizing effects of modern life. *Stet* (1986) further develops themes posited in *Ukulele Music,* blending contemporary history and autobiography to form a collage of poetic voices and styles. Damian Grant deemed *Stet* "an updated downmarket *Waste Land* which assails us with the sights and sounds of a world gone terribly wrong." Reading's best-regarded work is collected in *Essential Reading* (1986).

(See also *Contemporary Authors,* Vol. 103 and *Dictionary of Literary Biography,* Vol. 40.)

ALASDAIR MACLEAN

Peter Reading loves nobody and is unloved and he does not think much of the past or the present or the future. He tells us so, interminably, in [***For the Municipality's Elderly***], a series of languid elegies for little bits of his life. Certainly he writes well and would write better still if he abandoned his literary-aesthetic pose. But to lay claim to such a huge melancholy and world-weariness at the age of only twenty-nine you need better credentials than commuter boredom and job-dissatisfaction. Mr Reading is a would-be Hamlet who has nothing more to offer by way of tragedy than fatness and scantness of breath.

Alasdair Maclean, "Matters of Concern," in The Times Literary Supplement, *No. 3820, May 23, 1975, p. 552.*

COLIN FALCK

Peter Reading's verse seems to be more or less premised on the impossibility of any kind of usefully durable imaginative comparisons, and his new book ***The Prison Cell & Barrel Mystery*** shows no more signs of slowing down into imagistic tentativeness or contemplative polishing than its predecessor (***For the Municipality's Elderly,*** less than two years previously) did. As refreshingly astringent in its pop poet's indifference to the received pieties, ***The Prison Cell & Barrel Mystery*** seems otherwise thinner and scrappier, perhaps because Reading had already come up with his main themes ('Will there be any tangible thing to remember us by? / I think not'; 'What they left is unimpressive / compared with their having been here and left it') and didn't find himself wanting to come up with them again.... If Reading seems school-of-Henri-and-McGough pushed to a higher level it's the higher level that makes the difference. One might wonder how long he can go on turning the stuff out at this rate, though; and one might also wonder—though there are some poignantly personal-sounding experiences behind these tales (as they mostly are) of failed marriages and relationships—whether when he's got his more urgent subjectivities out of his system he may not find himself abandoning verse altogether for some more satisfying dramatic medium.

Colin Falck, in a review of "The Prison Cell & Barrel Mystery," in The New Review, *Vol. III, No. 26, May, 1976, p. 59.*

D. M. THOMAS

Peter Reading's second collection, ***The Prison Cell and Barrel Mystery,*** comes as a Poetry Book Society recommendation. The opening poem, **"Early Stuff",** has a spring and zest, lyrical yet realistic, that promises excellence.... However, it turns out that this is deliberate parody, and the book settles into a drab, rhythm-less demotic. The dominant, indeed almost the only, theme of the book is a sad triangular situation in which a married man visits a past love, herself unhappily married. It is explored relentlessly but sentimentally, without ever probing the realities that lie underneath the surface wistfulness, and without distinction of style. "Young / We loved each other and were ignorant", wrote Yeats in "After Long Silence". Here, as a 1970s version of that reticent irony, we have "When we could have done something about it / our affection was inarticulate / —now, a dozen years late, all we *can* do is / write affectionate things to each other. . ."—which would serve in a letter to an agony column, but not in a collection of poems. There are moments where talent shows through, as in **"Widow"** and a few lively Shropshire dialect pieces in which lads and girls in Ludlow pine over unhappy triangles; but the book as a whole produces an embarrassed voyeurism rather than any sharing of pain or any transcending of pain through art.

D. M. Thomas, "The Adamic Silence," in The Times Literary Supplement, *No. 3880, July 23, 1976, p. 910.*

DESMOND GRAHAM

The Prison Cell and Barrel Mystery by Peter Reading is really a couple of splendid pamphlets grossly outclassing themselves in hardcovers . . . : excellent fun is here truly oversold. The tricksy title is warning. We are in the land where gloss means not interpretation but shine. The land where George MacBeth, the Welsh Arts Council and Dante give tone to Ray Conniff, Minovlar and Weetabix. It would be misleading to observe simply that this, Reading's second collection, has a recurrent motif of two people in love with each other, but at different times; that it is intrigued by the way we can be right and wrong in thinking of others; that it riddles, with the interactions of art and life, with the poet as appropriator of experience and his friends as appropriators of his art. It would also be misleading to suggest that it looks cliché straight in the eye and outstares it: misleading because such suggestions of seriousness would open the book to criteria which must damage it. As light verse, observant of how the trivial entraps us, aware of the difficulty of finding our realest feelings commonplace, clever at catching the reader out and giving him amusing entertainment, the knowledge that this is disposable art does not matter. Only the ponderousness of the moments where the poet turns to direct feeling make me qualify each item of praise. When . . . Reading aims for art rather than the artful, the banality of this poetry of feeling looks like the revenge of art upon the sensitivity of the achievements of such as Peter Dale. (pp. 78-9)

Desmond Graham, "Neatness and Truth," in Stand Magazine, *Vol. 18, No. 2, 1977, pp. 72-9.*

GAVIN EWART

Nothing for Anyone is Peter Reading's third book of verse and the best so far. We are surrounded by poetry that is well-intentioned but dull; Reading's book is an oasis of intellect and wit. Experimenting with styles and word-games, he achieves some very entertaining and interesting effects. These include a **"Hymn"** written in the style of Very Late Auden ("We're crusted enough to know / we can't immortalize this"), a disillusioned marital **"Sonnet"** and a sad and sinister one, **"Zygmunt"**. . . .

In his generally loose-textured verse he fills in the details of that ordinary life.... Parody is certainly one of his talents (letters by not-over-literate ladies concerning everyday events) and so is dialogue, of the kind that occurs in plays; both make **"The John O'Groats Theory"** funny as well as a pertinent comment on love and marriage. **"Placed By The Gideons"** does the same for Bible-worshipping Christianity. He is also master of a narrative and descriptive strain (**"Travelogue", "Dr. Cooper's Story", "10 x 10 x 10"**—the last being the invention of a new art form). A bitter wit marks almost all these poems. Of their kind—and there are not many poems of their kind now that George MacBeth has temporarily gone out of business as a poetic experimenter—they are quite remarkably good. John Fuller, Alan Brownjohn, and Edwin Morgan are writers who might be compared.

Gavin Ewart, "Accepting the Inevitable," in The Times Literary Supplement, *No. 3948, November 25, 1977, p. 1381.*

ALAN BROWNJOHN

Peter Reading's fourth book, ***Fiction,*** . . . is hardly more than a small batch of sardonic jokes and wheezes: a near-found poem about price increases for gravestones, several shots at easy targets (young freaks with their Tarot cards and joss-sticks, the local Thespians), a mock correspondence with an admirer who has invited him to give a reading. It's a give-away when the best poem is "found" in a discourse on "Mens Talents in Difcours Shadowed out by Muficall Inftruments" published in 1713; though I'm prepared to recant and say it's cleverer than most of Reading's latest if the joke is on the reader and he has actally *written* it. (p. 77)

Alan Brownjohn, "Cosmic, Comic, Casual, Careful," in Encounter, *Vol. LIII, No. 5, November, 1979, pp. 70-7.*

GREVEL LINDOP

From a modest beginning—the drably titled, Larkinesque volume ***For the Municipality's Elderly***—Peter Reading has steadily made his way into a territory explored by no one else in contemporary British poetry. A typical Reading poem greets us with a beguiling grin and welcomes us into situations so terrible that they pass into black comedy and out on the other side, while in the margins paradoxes and uncertainties multiply to infinity.

Tom o'Bedlam's Beauties, his fifth book (the title, we are told, is old Herefordshire for a kind of eating-apple), is a tangle of riddles, a maze with the dual enigma of madness and sanity—or madness/sanity, as Peter Reading, who has a nice way with the oblique stroke, might prefer to call it—at its centre. The characteristic flavour is conveyed by the epigraph—seemingly autobiographical, though one never knows—which sets up an engaging, irritating irony:

(I once considered nursing them
—even went for an interview
—magnanimous of me, eh?

and then puts a fast, paradoxical spin on it:

Backed out—like them, eschewing
the risky Real for Illusion.)

The poems which follow deal with mental oddity at every level from genial eccentricity to breakdown and suicide. An element of discipline is imposed on the gallimaufry by the technical proficiency of the verse, which ranges in form from sonnet and villanelle to unrhymed hexameter and Anglo-Saxon alliterative measure—the latter used for a riddle which offers a series of kennings for an item of apparel traditionally associated with the mental hospital.

As this detail perhaps implies, it is the grotesque that predominates in ***Tom o'Bedlam's Beauties.*** Probably the strangest exercise in this vein is **"Hardfhip Aboard American Sloop The Peggy, 1765",** a stark tale of maritime cannibalism told by a deranged survivor and further, arbitrarily, unbalanced by the simple typographical device of printing *f* for long *s,* so that as the narrative grows increasingly horrific, the intrusive absurdity of the spelling simultaneously undermines its seriousness. . . . The same quirk helps to derange **"Phrenfy",** an account of Swift's last days of mental twilight given by his housekeeper, Mrs Ridgeway. . . .

Other poems are more tranquil and communicate personal reminiscences with a deceptive simplicity. . . .

Peter Reading is adept at intensifying the sharp visual image by extreme plainness of diction. **"Bereft"** laconically describes an old man who was "The only one left who could use a scythe / in all Onibury" but was ignorant of how to use the electric cooker or even—"and this takes some believing", as Reading admits—the electric light: "when his wife died he sat in the dark, hungry". Shown how to telephone the doctor, he "held the phone in two paws like a sad dog / gnawing a bone, not knowing which end spoke". Here, the danger of sentimentality is averted by a concentration on the unwieldy, even sinister oddity of everyday objects.

More often, however, the poems are informed by a delight in elaborate game-playing. This not only shapes individual poems such as **"The Euphemisms",** whose rhyming quatrains are constructed entirely from seventy-nine different expressions for madness or folly, but leads to curious interconnections between poems, so that the book as a whole reads rather like a detective story with half the clues left out. . . .

Those who seek a general statement of Peter Reading's poetic aims can perhaps find it in **"65th",** a cheerful poem written for Gavin Ewart's birthday and concerned, it should be emphasized, with sanity and health. Reading takes Ewart as a heartening example, proof that "As well as bruising, / poems, and life, can also be amusing / and dignified and commonsensed and sexy / and much more fun and certainly more flexi- / ble than they seemed before." The poems in ***Tom o'Bedlam's Beauties*** are often painfully amusing; but their very pursuit of "fun" and "flexibility" threatens to diminish their humanity and lead them into the realm of the whimsical and self-admiring. It seems likely that a change of direction may now be needed to make further development possible. Reading's work has depended for much of its impact on teasing humour and an angular vision. The danger is that these qualities may become merely a cultivated eccentricity, the liberating disguises tightening to form a straitjacket.

Grevel Lindop, "Madness Stroke Sanity," in The Times Literary Supplement, *No. 4133, June 18, 1982, p. 662.*

ALAN JENKINS

The risks of opting for the resolutely anti-poetic are demonstrated by the few failures in Peter Reading's ***Tom o'Bedlam's Beauties.*** Reading clearly owes something to Ewart's example; behind him stands Auden again, and behind him one of Auden's masters, Skelton. So Reading can align himself with a strong team of English social commentators and satirists. His subject in this collection is, as its title indicates, the asylum: Bedlam, the loony-bin, the funny-farm and the inhabitants thereof. The first part of the book details the variety of ways in which people end up in a strait-jacket or padded cell; the second part . . . sketches in a few of the human documents—or at least the human voices, the messy reality of pain and breakdown—behind the findings of "Glibber and Crass" on "The therapeutic value of Poetry practised amongst the mentally disturbed." The personae of this tragi-comedy . . . range from the simple-minded, through the victims of "stress", to the suicidally depressed.

The point about all of them is not that they are mad, but that they have such good reason to be so. . . . Some of the same personae crop up in more than one poem; events in one piece will in another be seen from a different point of view. The book's unity derives not just from these linkages and cross-referrings, but also, perhaps most importantly, from the powerful if muted sense of compassion and anger which plays over all the *vignettes:* and this is the ground-note of Reading's laconic, flexible tone. One or two pieces are unsatisfactory because they tend to a clichéd neatness or over-simplification in the delineating of plot or character; for the most part the poems are persuasive and unsettling. (p. 60)

Alan Jenkins, "A Barbarous Eloquence," in Encounter, *Vol. LIX, No. 2, August, 1982, pp. 55-61.*

MICHAEL O'NEILL

Peter Reading's sardonic ***Diplopic*** has . . . an acute sense of the distance between art and suffering. It isn't, however, a distance his cleverly self-conscious poems do much to diminish. He at once confesses and exploits the artist's unhealthy interest in the callous and sub-human. He tries to sidestep, by making an exhibition of, the difficulty of feeling. With the exception of the moving **"P.S."**, this results in cheapness. Often the poems spring their stomach-turning effects chillingly and skilfully, like a well-told sick joke. . . . But the diplopic vision would seem, on the evidence of these poems, to lead down a blind alley. (p. 73)

Michael O'Neill, "Colliding Styles," in Poetry Review, *Vol. 73, No. 3, September, 1983, pp. 72-3.*

GAVIN EWART

[***Diplopic***] is not quite so tightly organized [as ***Tom o'Bedlam's Beauties***]—but it does have a small cast of characters who reappear. Diplopia is double vision, and Reading's belief that things can be both funny and sad is at the heart of this book. The nasty side of industrial society is under consideration in most of his poems, and some are capable of moving us to pity and terror. A few are, perhaps, too concerned to be nasty . . . , but mostly they are effective—**"Editorial"**, **"Dark Continent"**, **"Receipt"** (Evelyn Waugh-style cannibalism), **"The Big Cats"** (sex in terms of circus), **"Telecommunication"** (the demotic sonnet, Tony Harrison type) and many others. **"Epithalamium"** and **"Carte Postale"** are especially good. Wit, experiment with forms, and intelligent criticism of the unsophisticated, are desirable attributes. Ordinariness and the received idea are altogether absent.

Gavin Ewart, in a review of "Diplopic," in British Book News, *November, 1983, p. 706.*

JOHN MOLE

There's nothing safe about Peter Reading's work. He slaps on the detail with relish—great splashes of angry, viscous colour—and his poems are often as hilarious as they are painful. At one point, in [***Diplopic***], he quotes Graham Greene's remark "There is a splinter of ice in the heart of a writer" and adds, "I savour / the respective merits of one / kind of mayhem over another." He is obviously attracted to the desperate and awful but there's nothing gratuitous about the way he dramatises the droll horrors. . . . The more one laughs at Reading's brilliant scenarios, the more one recognises the real private and social horrors they represent, and in several cases one is pushed beyond laughter to sheer amazement and despair. **"At Home"**, an account of a brutal attack on an old lady, is an extraordinary poem: its last section is spoken, in persona, by one of the teenage thugs who invade her house, and his gross, semi-articulate itemising of the gang's various acts of cruelty is chillingly done. . . . My only reservations concern the inevitable element of performance in this, as in much of Reading's work, and the sense given that things are often so desperate that merely to reveal them becomes the full extent of possibility. Perhaps they are, and perhaps it does. Certainly Reading has no time for humanitarian cant, and lines like "Accentuate the dignified resilience / that humans, or some, are capable of still" are immediately undercut and deflated by irony. ***Diplopic*** is an entertaining, worrying book by a talented, idiosyncratic writer. If the double-vision is sometimes the *reader's,* after the battering administered, at least that reader is compelled to think about *why* he got hurt. (p. 66)

John Mole, "Expanding Elements," in Encounter, *Vol. LXI, No. 4, December, 1983, pp. 60-7.*

ALAN JENKINS

The letter C announces the subject-matter of Peter Reading's [***C***] (the big one, cancer) and its governing formal principle, the number 100. 'Incongruously I plan / 100 100-word units' announces the epigraph, and the amazing Reading proceeds to deliver them. They are all about dying, and about the need both to probe and hold off horror and dread by analytically precise notation of the facts. The facts are very nasty indeed; Reading balances an appalled descriptive clarity and directness in dealing with them against an almost manic sophistication in handling the gruesome ironies of helplessness.

For the most part 'rhythmic' prose (to call them prose-poems would be a travesty of everything Reading is trying to do), the 'units' summon a variety of voices (mock pastoral, hysterical, rigorously neutral) and a cast of characters. They are revolved before us in a series of linked episodes, the narrative threads crossing most strikingly in the 'single vertical column' of verse that represents the five floors of a hospital.

There are echoes, unexpected linkages, recapitulations; there is real and cod learning. One voice, a palaeontologist's, makes repeated attempts to establish the insignificance of human life, suffering and death in the vast perspectives of geological time; another's domestic and erotic memories counter him with an unbearable sense of impending loss. Both the former's insane passion for scholarly data and the latter's insouciant suicide fantasy sound a bit desperate by the closing stages, with their cancers well advanced and things getting *pretty* nasty. The book is outrageous, even pitiless. But it springs from outrage and pity, and is Reading's best by far.

Alan Jenkins, "Noises of Apocalypse," in The Observer, *December 23, 1984, p. 29.*

MICK IMLAH

Intimations of ***C***—Peter Reading's brilliant but ruthless new book of "poems" about cancer—are to be found in the pamphlet ***5x5x5x5x5,*** produced last year in collaboration with the Sunderland artist David Butler. In five sections, each of five poems, each of five stanzas, each of five lines, each of five syllables, we meet five dismal drunkards in the **"Railway Hotel"**, each of whom suffers some more or less terminal misadventure before the end. . . .

We look on these kinds of death and pain as the legitimate fictions of the light-verse black comedian; grotesque retribution on those who are only invented to deserve it, redeemable in joke resurrections. In ***5^4***, poet and surgeon alike have the power of life and death; in ***C***, by a bold intensification of its author's morbidity, poet and surgeon have no power at all. The difference in atmosphere is pointed by the presence in each book of a stock Reading figure; when the weak-hearted palaeontologist comforts himself in ***5⁴***, "What's 40 years / here or there on the / chronostratigraph?" he sounds drunk, but when the cancerous palaeontologist comforts himself in ***C***, with the same phrase, he sounds insane.

C is an even more demanding numerological structure. It pretends to be the work of a versifying cancer victim, charting his last 100 days in 100 units each of 100 words; and around this central figure Reading builds fossil layers of "poor frail dear frightened little vulnerable creatures" dying in isolation (the excellent acrostic "IN THE SAME VERTICAL COLUMN" follows five storeys of hospital suffering down to the stoker in the basement). The strange excitement of the book lies in the inappropriateness of the admirable design, and especially of the medium of verse, to such a very unliterary subject. Verse, indeed, is ***C***'s first casualty: "Verse is for healthy / arty-farties. The dying / and surgeons use prose" chimes an early haiku; and prose subsequently outweighs verse three to one. Where they survive, verse forms are gruesomely misapplied, so that we relish all the more their impotence to explain, console, or cure. There is a sixteen-liner on bedsores (from two angles); a limerick plus "cutely-adapted Adonic" for fatal haemorrhage; catelectic (truncated) tetrameters to lament cut-off breasts; a Japanese sonnet on a "stiff" in the chip shop; the thirteen-line sonnet, invented "for unlucky people" in general; and a limerick with "pretty Choriamb" to hymn the after-effects of a botched colostomy. In a different admission of verse's inadequacy, other pieces are hidden away in prose settings; as the stunned craftsman instructs himself, *"Run them together, set as justified prose, / the inadequately blank pentameters"*. Harder puns than these link the breakdown of verse and body. Can metre and punctuation contain the leakage of collapsed bowels? No—"pentameters, like colons, inadequate". Likewise, after the operation, "*ars*" is "*brevis*".

Still, we ought to detach Reading's *ars* from the arse of his persona. Its most apparently reductive flourishes are carefully placed and prepared for. The last words on verse, for example, are spoken by the tramp Tucker who, in various guises, and in contrived partnerships with the "pale horse" from Revelation, attends gloatingly on death throughout. . . .

So Reading, with a barrage of "Shit, blood, puke", etc, takes us as close to the facts of disease as any work of literature—including the medical dictionary which supplies some of his text—is likely to want to do. He has no interest in the distancing demeanour which more reverent poets might adopt to deal with dying subjects; the dying "hate" us (Reading's word) and want our life, not our verse. His solution—sick in its way, no doubt—is to join them, posing as "the Master of the 100 100-Word Units" who "*chronicles his death in the third Person*" in a game which is deadlier by far than the average earnestness. His daring even induces a certain dread for his health—a peculiar achievement for imaginative writing. . . . More than Reading's, though, our own health concerns us, and the book tweaks and probes at the general anxiety. One of its truest episodes is that of a victim, not of cancer, but of fear of it, who kills herself with twenty pills in Section Forty-four. There is the merest shadow of an ironic triumph in the fact that our nameless hero, who contemplates a bowery Virgilian suicide throughout, and collects the same twenty pills, is too weak by the close—too nearly dead—to do the job. And if the book's coda displaces poetical emphasis, nevertheless it borrows something of poetry's affirmative habit as it moves unexpectedly to its muted ten-thousandth word: "My wife patiently washes my faece-besmirched pyjamas, for *prosaic* love."

Mick Imlah, "Thanatoptic Designs," in The Times Literary Supplement, *No. 4266, January 4, 1985, p. 10.*

ROBERT GREACEN

At his best Peter Reading has shown himself to be clever, inventive, sophisticated, but in ***C*** he chooses to use material concerned with terminal disease, particularly focusing on the more disgusting physical aspects, and death. Some readers—and not only the squeamish—will find this distasteful. The book is divided into a hundred units, each of a hundred words. One must say 'unit' rather than 'poem' since Peter Reading's 'units' consist of conversations, medical reports, extracts from learned journals as well as statements made by patients in pain or desperately asking for help. He explores, clinically rather than sympathetically, the six emotional states (outlined, it seems, by one Kubler-Ross) of the terminally ill: denial, isolation, anger, bargaining, depression and acceptance. Reading certainly emphasizes the view that life shortly before death is nasty and brutish. It is to be regretted that he has not used his talent, and interest in medicine and nursing, more positively. The publishers claim that ***C*** entertains. They must be joking.

Robert Greacen, in a review of "C," in British Book News, *March, 1985, p. 181.*

JOHN LUCAS

Ukulele Music is about making music while the ship goes down. Reading's last volume, ***C***, concentrated on one man's death from cancer. The new volume is about the imminent death of the world. 'I didn't invent death,' Philip Larkin is supposed to have remarked, in answer to a question as to why so many of his poems dealt with the subject. ***Ukulele Music*** doesn't invent many of the horrors that Reading collects from newspapers, TV stories, radio reports. . . . (pp. 29-30)

The problem with this is not that it's too black but that it comes too easily. In the sense that Auden meant when he said that poetry makes nothing happen, elegiacs never *can* fix the horrors of the world. In another, a poet whose blend of satire and outrage looks back to—say—the tradition that produced Juvenal needs to convince us that he's doing more than playing self-reflexive games, or requiring our assent simply because he parades himself as the person ready to confront terrible realities from which more timid souls shrink. ***Ukulele Music*** seems to me badly compromised both by this posturing and by the invented charwoman whose semiliterate letters punctuate and are meant in some sense to counter the poem's catalogue of disasters. She is as sentimental and reductive a presence as Orwell's Proles, to whom she bears a close family resemblance. Reading is a clever, properly shocking writer (***Diplopic*** and ***C*** contain his best work), but he runs the risk of becoming holier-than-thou. (p. 30)

John Lucas, "Gruesomely Gooey," in New Statesman, *Vol. 110, No. 2843, September 20, 1985, pp. 29-30.*

CHARLES BOYLE

Peter Reading's poems in ***Ukulele Music*** are concerned with subjects that most British poetry is too well-mannered to do more than allude to in passing. . . . The comprehensive nastiness of the subject matter is tempered by wry, hard-edged comedy and the dramatic interplay of colloquial idioms, but the literary devices in no way disguise Reading's disgust, indignation and self-mocking awareness that his poems are no more than lyrics for the ukulele, chords strummed as the ship goes down.

The landscape of the title-sequence, which forms the first part of this book, comprises the streets and playgrounds of urban Britain now plus the writer's desk. The writer is upstaged by the Captain, a reclusive character whose memories are confused with bookish seafaring lore, and by Viv, the charlady who 'does' for them both, a stock sitcom character whose heart of gold redeems nothing at all but cannot be traduced. Both these characters are more directly implicated in the surrounding violence than they can realize. Survivor of shipwreck, storm and fire, the Captain's accomplishments in his fantastical yarns include the introduction of firearms to the natives, who proceed forthwith to shoot their prisoners ('We objected upon this last, / explained inhumanity / unto ye simple minds,'). . . . The writer himself, fiddling at his desk, passively recording the cycles of violence and stunted response . . . , claims no superiority, and in the book's second and overlapping sequence his doodlings are ruthlessly anatomized. . . . (pp. 79-80)

Courtroom statements and newspaper reports are mixed in with the Lyrical Fragments of the Reverend Wolly and replies to critics of the writer's recent work. The preferred forms of both Reading and Wolly are derived from Alcaeus and Alcman, an ironic gesture towards literary / classical decorum: the 'roam Kings' were hardly models of virtue, and in Nero they had the most famous ukulele player of all time. Over-the-top bad taste is what Reading is commonly accused of; an objection more to the point is that his avowed disgust with Grub Street and the 'media elbow deep in the offal bin', with lounge-bar 'beetrooty colonels' and 'reps and execs in Plastics and Packaging', betrays more than a trace of that reciprocal malice he righteously condemns. Not being cricket, however, is the essence of this book, and its rejection of any chat-show notion of 'balance' is, in the circumstances, entirely justifiable. (p. 80)

Charles Boyle, "Not Cricket," in London Magazine, *n.s. Vol. 25, No. 8, November, 1985, pp. 79-83.*

PETER PORTER

Stet seems an appropriate title, given Peter Reading's intention of reinstating the unswervably dreadful into that warp of received beauty known as poetry. It also serves notice that this new can of words is to be placed on Reading's shelf alongside ***C*** and ***Ukulele Music.*** Standard English here is discoloured by scientific circumlocution and jargon, and by various sorts cf nasty illiteracies. There is an *idée fixe*—'Muse! sing the Grotty (scant alternative).'

Human Nature keeps obliging Reading with its horrors, and he, in turn, keeps putting them in Alcaics for our proper disgust. Mixed in there somewhere is Reading's eye for natural beauty and his affection for the pleasures of eating and drinking.

Peter Porter, "English, Their English," in The Observer, *November 9, 1986, p. 28.*

JOSEPH BRISTOW

The punning title of [***Essential Reading***] . . . , representing the best of [Peter Reading's] work from all nine of his collections published since 1976, raises a number of questions about their 'essential' nature. For a start, these poems are ostensibly unserious, dealing with domestic trivia, marital dramas—as often as not with the sensational stuff of soap operas. But, at the same time, this is deeply disturbing work, telling, in playful tones and jaunty rhythms, a good many tales of gratuitous violence— of brutal vandalism, thuggery, sexual assault, and the popular appeal of these in urban (mostly working-class) life, particularly the news and gossip they generate. Reading reports on emotional and physical damage by means of a variety of verbal tricks—puns, slogans, acrostics, and this linguistic virtuosity successfully grabs the reader's attention with inventive visual layouts. This makes for demanding reading—'mordant' (to use one of Reading's words for defining himself and his work), wry, and both exhibitionist and self-effacing at once. Throughout, Reading refuses to be serious in so far as his writing brings together such a range of materials and ways of speaking that it is impossible to locate any certainty of tone. His work self-consciously asks the reader to consider who is speaking—Reading or one of his vibrant personae? The poet's voice keeps intruding but it is one so aware of its own presence that it begins to look factitious—indeed, 'Peter Reading' becomes one of his own protagonists. At times, the self-attentiveness of this work chases its own tale in a manner that, if formally neat, becomes tedious in its avowed tedium. . . .

[Reading's] frequently tight structures are in tension with the loose, fragmented bits of language that fill out his latest book, ***Stet.*** Stet is a printer's word that means 'leave the deleted word to stand as originally set'—and here Reading contemplates what might and might not be allowed to remain in a text that admits all kinds of overhead conversation and diary entry, plus pastiches of appalling competition poetry. Both books interrogate the status of 'art' more compellingly than most mainstream British poetry—and even if Reading's gestures are not always serious he certainly is, as he mockingly claims, Essential Reading: no one else is like him.

Joseph Bristow, in a review of "Essential Reading" and "Stet," in British Book News, *March, 1987, p. 151.*

DAMIAN GRANT

Poems like **"Opinions of the Press"** and the self-interrogating sections from ***Ukulele Music*** warn the reviewer of Peter Reading that he risks becoming entangled in his subject like a gladiator in a net. Even his editors . . . (not to mention the printer) must feel unnerved—which is excellent. This is poetry at its most unpredictable: we wouldn't be surprised to find a pop-up V-sign over the page. Alan Jenkins has made a good job of selecting from Reading's ten previous volumes for this ***Essential Reading***. . . .

[In this volume we] encounter the startling originality of Reading's formal devices. It could be argued that these wonderfully arbitrary structures (such as ***5x5x5x5x5*** or ***C***: 'Incongruously I plan / 100 100-word units') are necessary to cope with the disintegrating subject-matter. . . . It is as if a brain surgeon were to turn vivisectionist and perform a delicate operation on a patient—such as himself—still writhing on the table. One can only urge anyone who has not yet discovered Reading to begin here: satisfaction—and stupefaction—guaranteed. . . .

Reading's new volume, ***Stet,*** presents all his virtues in a concentrated form. It is a remarkable work, an updated downmarket *Waste Land* which assails us with the sights and sounds of a world gone terribly wrong. . . . The self-deprecating 'Poet Pete's' unavailing protest is allowed to stand; the printing metaphor is justified with an appalling pun:

> [Re-draft the sick obsessional chuntering,
> strike out the old gratuitous cruelties . . .
> (re-draft be buggered, leave as printed,
> Hail!, uncorrectable Age of Floored Proofs).]

There are echoes here of the great Augustan satires, rank with printers' ink: the Gutenberg *Dunciad,* and the author-ejecting "Tale of a Tub". The volume's 40 leaves are unpaginated: the very structure of The Book is under attack. What we have is 79 (unnumbered) poems, fragments and one-liners, linked together in a pared-down plot of novelistic scope and complexity. I dare say it's the first book of poems that could be filmed. The outer plot is contemporary history, from the Coronation to the present reign of 'Great Britain's / Satrapess gloatingly self-applauding'. The hinge is autobiography, anchored in the unswinging and unsung Fifties or Reading's childhood. . . .

Tony Harrison is once again brought to mind by Reading's world of classrooms, comics, cinemas and working-class interiors: these two poets of the classical demotic have a lot in common. There is a remarkable 'secular ecstasy' recorded in the Headmaster's study, alerting us to Reading's lyrical voice—a voice deriving from Hopkins, Frost and Edward Thomas. This voice is exercised in the fine, fraught elegy for a friend, killed in a car accident, with whom he shared an early passion for birdwatching. Orwell maintained that fishing was the opposite of war; Peter Reading seems to offer birdwatching as the antithesis of atrocity.

This ecstatic voice is interrupted here by the caustic, cryptic countermining of the other, lurking in square brackets, who regards lyrical poetry as 'Hippocrene hogwash' and elegy as 'arrogant therapy / piffle, claptrap':

> [Who do you think you are whining to? No
> reader { wants / shares } your bereavement,
> and it's pathetic and mad to address yourself to
> the dead.]

The anti-poet has most of the say. He provides typical Reading horror stories. . . . But it is the dialogic principle that provides the true Reading taste: where the 'especial, pseudo-rural, scene' (from Hopkins) contends with the 'holed Nuform, empty Long Life, laid-flat oats' (from Eliot); where the early migrants and melodious warblers are drowned out by the shattering Harriers and hedge-hopping Tornadoes. These discordant voices are jostled by a gang of others to create a true Bakhtinian polyphony. There is a gloriously illiterate pub politician who fears that 'this bleeding / nuclear warflair' will soon have us all 'dead as a yo-yo mate', and meanwhile leave 'Prodestants, Catherlic, Jews, Isleramics' to 'blow bloody buggery out of each other'; a demented scientist of Swiftian extraction interested only in the laws of 'reasonless causal physics' at the extreme fringes of the universe; a grief-crazed widow who writes to the 'Miss Prudence' of a provincial newspaper, and 'Miss Prudence' himself, a disreputable literary editor who supplements his income by submitting vapid verses under different aliases to win the £10-per-week poetry prize. There is also the resource of the lady's album of 1826, which provides two one-liners, 'unexplained' but expressive: the pentameter 'This waiting bravely to be badly hurt', and the alexandrine, 'Something ridiculous and sad will happen soon.' The note of fearful prognostication makes these natural epigraphs to the volume. (p. 23)

Damian Grant, "An Englishman, an Irishman and a Scotsman," in London Review of Books, *Vol. 9, No. 9, May 7, 1987, pp. 22-3.*

Philip (Milton) Roth

1933-

American novelist, short story writer, essayist, and critic.

© Thomas Victor 1987

A prominent and controversial figure in contemporary American letters, Roth draws heavily upon his Jewish upbringing and his life as a successful author to explore his predominant thematic concerns—the search for self-identity, conflicts between traditional and contemporary moral values, and the relationship between fiction and reality. The scatological content of some of Roth's works and his satiric portraits of Jewish life have inspired a considerable amount of critical debate. While some critics view his work as anti-Semitic, perverse, and self-indulgent, others extol Roth's skill at rendering Jewish-American dialect, his exuberant inventiveness, and his outrageous sense of humor. John N. McDaniel remarked: "No other living writer has so rigorously and actively attempted to describe the destructive element of experience in American life—the absurdities and banalities that impinge upon self-realization."

Roth received the National Book Award for his first book, *Goodbye, Columbus, and Five Short Stories* (1959), which focuses upon the individual's search for identity. In the acclaimed novella, *Goodbye, Columbus,* which was adapted for film, Roth examines conflicting emotions and the struggle to accommodate an unfamiliar lifestyle as Neil Klugman, a poor young Jewish man, falls in love with a wealthy Jewish suburbanite. By contrasting the cultural backgrounds of these two young people, Roth satirizes American materialistic values. In *Letting Go* (1962), his first novel, Roth explores the anxieties and moral dilemmas experienced by a young Jew facing manhood. *When She Was Good* (1967) offers a humorless portrait of an imperious gentile housewife.

Alexander Portnoy, the protagonist of *Portnoy's Complaint* (1969), is Roth's most flamboyant depiction of an individual searching for identity. Written in a first-person narrative style, the book chronicles Portnoy's profane, contemptuous, guilt-ridden apologia to his psychiatrist in which he decries his Jewish upbringing. *Portnoy's Complaint* was a tremendous commercial success and vaulted Roth into widespread public and critical scrutiny. While some reviewers objected to the book's sexual explicitness and what they considered Roth's degrading treatment of Jewish life, others praised its ribald humor and reacted sympathetically to the hero's machinations to free himself from the restrictions of his cultural background. James Gindin commented that the the novel "is playfully and painfully moving, but also a work that is certainly catholic in appeal—and, perhaps more important, a deliciously funny book, absurd and exuberant, wild and uproarious." Roth followed *Portnoy's Complaint* with three satirical novels that are generally regarded as inferior efforts: *Our Gang* (1971) is a political satire of President Nixon and his administration; *The Breast* (1972) is a Kafkaesque fantasy about a professor who is transformed into a six-foot mammary gland; and *The Great American Novel* (1973) lampoons the myths surrounding baseball and American culture.

Much of Roth's later work investigates the relationship of fiction to reality. In *My Life as a Man* (1974), Roth depicts novelist Peter Tarnopol, who is writing about a novelist named Nathan Zuckerman. The character of Zuckerman reappears in several of Roth's later novels which satirize artistic success in America. In the first of these works, *The Ghost Writer* (1978), Zuckerman is a young author who gains notoriety and sparks intense critical debate with his salacious novel *Carnovsky,* much as Roth did with *Portnoy's Complaint*. *The Ghost Writer* also recounts Zuckerman's association with mentor E. I. Lonoff, an older, established novelist. Roth uses this scenario to pose questions concerning literature's relationship to life and the pressures of being a literary celebrity. Two subsequent volumes, *Zuckerman Unbound* (1981) and *The Anatomy Lesson* (1983), trace Zuckerman as he experiences the joys and disadvantages of fame and then succumbs to the terrors of writer's block. In these books, Roth examines such topics as the difficulties of familial and male-female relationships and the conflicts between traditional and contemporary moral values. In *The Prague Orgy* (1985), Zuckerman travels to Czechoslovakia in an attempt to secure the unpublished manuscripts of a deceased Yiddish writer. While continuing to develop themes and conflicts characteristic of the Zuckerman books, Roth compares the roles of literature and writers in the free world with those in the Eastern European communist states. The first four Zuckerman books were collected in *Zuckerman Bound: A Trilogy and an Epilogue* (1985).

Roth's recent work, *The Counterlife* (1986), which won the National Book Critics Circle Award, is widely considered the best of his Zuckerman books as well as his most ambitious effort. In this novel, Zuckerman travels to Israel, where his brother has joined a militant terrorist group, and then to England, where he attacks English anti-Semitism. While employing a self-reflexive narrative structure, a characteristic of several of his later books, Roth introduces abrupt shifts in plot development and the lives of his characters to offer various perspectives on such subjects as death, literature, and what it means to be Jewish. According to William H. Gass, *The Counterlife* "constitutes a fulfillment of tendencies, a successful integration of themes, and the final working through of obsessions that have previously troubled if not marred [Roth's] work. I hope it felt, as Mr. Roth wrote it, like a triumph, because that is certainly how it reads to me."

(See also *CLC,* Vols. 1, 2, 3, 4, 6, 9, 15, 22, 31; *Contemporary Authors,* Vols. 1-4, rev. ed.; *Contemporary Authors New Revision Series,* Vols. 1, 22; *Dictionary of Literary Biography,* Vols. 2, 28; and *Dictionary of Literary Biography Yearbook: 1982.*)

MICHIKO KAKUTANI

In bringing together in [***Zuckerman Bound: A Trilogy and Epilogue***] his last three novels (***The Ghost Writer, Zuckerman Unbound*** and ***The Anatomy Lesson***) and a new comic novella, titled ***The Prague Orgy,*** Philip Roth has presumably completed the saga of his fictional hero, Nathan Zuckerman. It is the story of how an earnest young student of literature grows up, writes a scandalous best seller and experiences the debilitating effects of fame. And it is also a story about the unforeseen consequences of art, the strange, predatory relationship that exists between literature and life, and an American writer's anomalous sense of vocation.

It's hard to say whether the parts of this volume add up to something more than their sum. In the first place, reading the Zuckerman fictions together, one is more acutely aware of fluctuations in Mr. Roth's style—the limber, Jamesian prose and delicate ironies of ***The Ghost Writer*** stand in marked contrast to the more staccato rhythms of ***Zuckerman Unbound*** and the frenzied, almost incoherent mannerisms of ***The Anatomy Lesson.*** The self-reflexive nature of the three novels also feels more pronounced when they are read all at once: just as Mr. Roth is constantly teasing us to draw parallels between his own career and that of his hero, so too does Nathan continually comment upon the relationship between his life and *his* fiction—complaining about people who misread his stories as gossip, even as he's taking notes on their lives for his next book. As a result, ***Zuckerman Bound*** becomes a kind of Möbius strip that is forever turning back on itself: charges of solipsism are anticipated and countered even before they can be leveled. . . .

Mr. Roth's orchestration of his hero's dilemmas is clever and sometimes very funny, but his narrative—filled with little but Nathan's attempts at self-explanation—feels increasingly constricted, increasingly whiny and narcissistic. Indeed, Nathan's self-consciousness so permeates the second two novels that the reader begins to share his feeling of being trapped inside his skin. The other characters in ***Zuckerman Unbound*** are really little more than two-dimensional stage props, used to give Nathan someone to argue with. And in ***The Anatomy Lesson,*** they've grown even more attenuated. They feel less like distinct individuals than antiphonal voices inside Nathan's head—voices charged with articulating his own conflicts or playing the role of devil's advocate. By the end of ***The Anatomy Lesson,*** the reader cannot help but feel that Nathan—like his hero Carnovsky—is another obsessive onanist.

In contrasting Nathan's dilemma with that of writers in Eastern Europe, ***The Prague Orgy*** puts his self-conscious concerns in perspective and also casts them in a ludicrously comic light. Where the celebrated American writer receives money and fame for writing a sensational novel, the East European writer receives a jail sentence. Where the American writer gets thrown to the critics, the East European writer gets arrested by the police. And where the American writer suffers paranoia over importunate fans, the East European writer suffers real anxiety over informers and bugged rooms.

The irony of all this, Mr. Roth implies, is that the freedom enjoyed by writers in the West also reduces them to celebrities—their work is not taken with the moral seriousness conferred upon the work of their comrades in Eastern Europe. But if Nathan seems to envy the sense of purpose and history enjoyed by his friends in Prague, he also realizes that he cannot make their stories his, that "one's story isn't a skin to be shed—it's inescapable, one's body and blood."

Nathan will no doubt go on writing about himself—and he will no doubt go on complaining about his inability to write about anything else. As for Mr. Roth, he demonstrates, in this story, that he is a writer of far greater subtlety and inventiveness than his fictional hero. ***The Prague Orgy*** is free of the shrillness and self-pity that mar earlier sections of this volume, and it also possesses a new range and density of ambition. Roth fans can only hope that instead of merely marking the end of the Zuckerman saga, it marks another beginning.

Michiko Kakutani, in a review of "Zuckerman Bound: A Trilogy and Epilogue," in The New York Times, *May 15, 1985, p. C21.*

HAROLD BLOOM

Philip Roth's ***Zuckerman Bound*** binds together ***The Ghost Writer, Zuckerman Unbound*** and ***The Anatomy Lesson,*** adding to them as epilogue a wild short novel, ***The Prague Orgy,*** which is at once the bleakest and the funniest writing Roth has done. The totality is certainly the novelist's finest achievement to date, eclipsing even his best single fictions, the exuberantly notorious ***Portnoy's Complaint*** and the undervalued and ferocious ***My Life as a Man. Zuckerman Bound*** is a classic apologia, an aggressive defense of Roth's moral stance as an author. Its cosmos derives candidly from the Freudian interpretation of ambivalence as being primal, and the Kafkan evasion of interpretation as being unbearable. (p. 1)

Zuckerman Bound merits something reasonably close to the highest level of esthetic praise for tragi-comedy, partly because as a formal totality it becomes much more than the sum of its parts. Those parts are surprisingly diverse: ***The Ghost Writer*** is a Jamesian parable of fictional influence, economical and shapely, beautifully modulated, while ***Zuckerman Unbound*** is more characteristically Rothian, being freer in form and more joyously expressionistic in its diction. ***The Anatomy Lesson*** is a farce bordering on fantasy, closer in mode and spirit to Nathanael West than is anything else by Roth. With ***The Prague Orgy,*** Roth has transcended himself, or perhaps shown himself and others that, being just past 50, he has scarcely begun to display his powers. I have read nothing else in recent American fiction that rivals Thomas Pynchon in *The Crying of Lot 49* and episodes like the story of Bryon the light bulb in the same author's *Gravity's Rainbow*. ***The Prague Orgy*** is of that disturbing eminence: obscenely outrageous and yet brilliantly reflective of a paranoid reality that has become universal.

But the Rothian difference from Nathanael West and Thomas Pynchon also should be emphasized. Roth paradoxically is still engaged in moral prophecy; he continues to be outraged by the outrageous—in societies, others and himself. There is in him nothing of West's gnostic preference for the posture of the satanic editor, Shrike, in *Miss Lonelyhearts*, or of Mr. Pynchon's cabalistic doctrine of sado-anarchism. Roth's negative exuberance is not in the service of a negative theology, but intimates instead a nostalgia for the morality once engendered by the Jewish normative tradition.

This is the harsh irony, obsessively exploited throughout ***Zuckerman Bound***, of the attack made upon Zuckerman's *Carnovsky* (Roth's ***Portnoy's Complaint***) by the literary critic Milton Appel (Irving Howe). Zuckerman has received a mortal wound from Appel, and Roth endeavors to commemorate the wound and the wounder, in the spirit of James Joyce permanently impaling the Irish poet, physician and general roustabout, Oliver St. John Gogarty, as the immortally egregious Malachi (Buck) Mulligan of *Ulysses*. . . . Roth, characteristically scrupulous, presents Appel as dignified, serious and sincere, and Zuckerman as dangerously lunatic in this matter, but since the results are endlessly hilarious, the revenge is sharp nevertheless.

Zuckerman Unbound makes clear, at least to me, that Roth indeed is a Jewish writer in a sense that Saul Bellow and Bernard Malamud are not, and do not care to be. Bellow and Malamud, in their fiction, strive to be North American Jewish only as Tolstoy was Russian, or Faulkner was American Southern. Roth seems prophetic in the biblical tradition. His absolute concern never ceases to be the pain of the relations between children and parents, and between husband and wife, and in him this pain invariably results from the incommensurability between a rigorously moral normative tradition whose expectations rarely can be satisfied, and the reality of the way we live now. Zuckerman's insane resentment of the moralizing Milton Appel, and of even fiercer feminist critics, is a deliberate self-parody of Roth's more-than-ironic reaction to how badly he has been read. Against both Appel and the swarms of maenads, Roth defends Zuckerman (and so himself) as a kind of Talmudic Orpheus, by defining any man as "clay with aspirations."

What wins over the reader is that both defense and definition are conveyed by the highest humor now being written. ***The Anatomy Lesson*** and ***The Prague Orgy***, in particular, provoke a cleansing and continuous laughter, sometimes so intense that in itself it becomes astonishingly painful. One of the many esthetic gains of binding together the entire Zuckerman ordeal (it cannot be called a saga) is to let the reader experience the gradual acceleration of wit from the gentle Chekhovian wistfulness of ***The Ghost Writer*** on to the Gogolian sense of the ridiculous in ***Zuckerman Unbound*** and then to the boisterous Westian farce of ***The Anatomy Lesson***, only to end in the merciless Kafkan irrealism of ***The Prague Orgy***. . . .

When last we saw the afflicted Zuckerman, at the close of ***The Anatomy Lesson***, he had progressed (or regressed) from painfully lying back on his play-mat, Roget's Thesaurus propped beneath his head and four women serving his many needs, to wandering the corridors of a university hospital, a patient playing at being an intern. A few years later, a physically recovered Zuckerman is in Prague, as visiting literary lion, encountering so paranoid a social reality that New York seems by contrast the Forest of Arden. Zuckerman, "the American authority on Jewish demons," quests for the unpublished Yiddish stories of the elder Sisovsky, perhaps murdered by the Nazis. The exiled younger Sisovsky's abandoned wife, Olga, guards the manuscripts in Prague. In a deliberate parody of Henry James's *Aspern Papers*, Zuckerman needs somehow to seduce the alcoholic and insatiable Olga into releasing stories supposedly worthy of Sholom Aleichem or Isaac Babel, written in "the Yiddish of Flaubert."

Being Zuckerman, he seduces no one, and secures the Yiddish manuscripts anyway, only to have them confiscated by the Czechoslovak Minister of Culture and his thugs, who proceed to expel "Zuckerman the Zionist agent" back to "the little world around the corner" in New York City. In a final scene subtler, sadder and funnier than all previous Roth, the frustrated Zuckerman endures the moralizing of the Minister of Culture, who attacks America for having forgotten that "masterpiece" by Betty MacDonald, *The Egg and I*. Associating himself with K., Kafka's hero in *The Castle*, Zuckerman is furious at his expulsion, and utters a lament for the more overt paranoia he must abandon:

> Here where there's no nonsense about purity and goodness, where the division is not that easy to discern between the heroic and the perverse, where every sort of repression foments a parody of freedom and the suffering of their historical misfortune engenders in its imaginative victims these clownish forms of human despair.

That farewell-to-Prague has as its undersong: here where Zuckerman is not an anomaly, but indeed a model of decorum and restraint compared to anyone else who is at all interesting. Perhaps there is another undertone: a farewell-to-Zuckerman on Roth's part. The author of ***Zuckerman Bound*** at last may have exorcised the afterglow of ***Portnoy's Complaint***. (p. 42)

Harold Bloom, "His Long Ordeal by Laughter," in The New York Times Book Review, *May 19, 1985, pp. 1, 42.*

BRUCE ALLEN

To his three previously published novels about the career of (Roth-like) novelist Nathan Zuckerman. . . , Roth now adds an 84-page "Epilogue" entitled ***The Prague Orgy***. And here is the completed work, in an imposing omnibus volume [***Zuckerman Bound: A Trilogy and an Epilogue***]. This new story finds Zuckerman uneasy over his own literary success vis-à-vis the oppressions visited on writers living in societies less hospitable to art: He meets a displaced Czech writer, Sisovsky, in America, and agrees to go to Prague on an "espionage mission," in the service of literature and also as a kind of penance. . . .

The novella is static and talky; its characters never stop lecturing one another. There are, sporadically, splendid one-liners, and gritty characterizations. But the spark isn't there; the story doesn't *take off* the way Roth's best writing does. Furthermore, its bitter conclusion, leaving Zuckerman "bound" to his realization that he's only "a shallow, sentimental American Jew who thinks there is virtue in suffering,'' feels like a holding action. I don't believe Roth has said all he means to say by way of this self-tormenting alter ego—and I expect to see the Zuckerman story keep on expanding.

Bruce Allen, '' 'Zuckerman Bound' Stays on Ground,'' in The Christian Science Monitor, *August 5, 1985, p. 26.*

CLIVE SINCLAIR

[***The Prague Orgy*** closes the Zuckerman] circle by concluding a few months before ***The Ghost Writer***—the first in the Zuckerman sequence—was composed, if I have read the internal evidence correctly.

The Ghost Writer begins with a mixture of precision and vagueness that characterizes the ghost story (which is what it is, in part): ''It was the last daylight hour of a December afternoon more than twenty years ago. . .'. Darkness and December, words to make you catch your breath, as any reader of *The Turn of the Screw* will know. It is some pages later that we learn, in passing, that the year is 1956. However, by 1976, when ***The Prague Orgy*** commences (very precisely on January 11) Zuckerman has become firmly rooted in history and its concomitant moral concerns; primarily his own and those of his family, but also those of the Jews of America and Czechoslovakia. Since ***The Ghost Writer*** takes place in December 1956 and was composed, as we have seen, more than twenty years later, it is clear that Zuckerman must have written it some months after his return from Prague (only ***The Ghost Writer*** and ***The Prague Orgy*** are narrated in the first person, in a voice that introduces a Jamesian concern for precision and plot to a Kafkaesque sense of self), presumably in early 1977. The epilogue thereby becomes a prologue. In a way Zuckerman has fulfilled his own prophesy, made in ***The Anatomy Lesson,*** and disappeared up his own asshole. But, if so, it turns out to be a triumphant exit, as we shall see.

The Ghost Writer describes Zuckerman's pilgrimage to his literary father-figure, Emmanuel Isidore Lonoff, but by 1976 that position is his. It is to him that Prague émigré Zdenek Sisovsky comes with the words, ''Your novel . . . is absolutely one of the five or six books of my life'', the novel in question being the infamous *Carnovsky,* which changed Zuckerman's life as ***Portnoy's Complaint*** changed Roth's. Art draws on life and then, as if dissatisfied with that minor role, seeks to influence the subsequent lives of the artist and his subjects in completely unexpected ways, so that real people are forced to act out sequels to fictions. Zuckerman's brother Henry is consequently able to blame Nathan and his scandalous book for the death of their father, the same father whom poor, guilty Zuckerman wanted to replace with Lonoff anyway. Thus he is a soft touch for honey-tongued Sisovsky, who tells the sad story of his own father's death at the hands of the Nazis, a death that may yet be redeemed if only Zuckerman would go to Prague and rescue his father's manuscripts, now in the hands of Sisovsky's ex-wife. . . .

Sisovsky, aged thirty, is accompanied by forty-year-old Eva Kalinova, formerly Czechoslovakia's greatest Chekhovian actress, *formerly* because of an even greater predilection for Jews. The fact that she once played Anne Frank on the stage is given as evidence of this unhealthy philosemitism by the Vice-Minister of Culture. . . .

What gives Sisovsky and Kalinova most credibility in Zuckerman's eyes is the mere fact that Prague was once their home. Prague is a revelatory city; a city in which the human struggle for freedom against repression, long waged by Zuckerman, is played out not in the head or on the psychoanalyst's couch but in cafés, streets and prisons. It is a place where all the demons that plague Zuckerman's conscience are alive and kicking. It is a metropolis where the consequences of art are neither psychological nor ambiguous but crystal-clear; break the rules and you don't get a ticking off in *Commentary,* it's the pokey for you. As a result the intelligentsia, unable to put pen to paper, act out what Zuckerman has only imagined; the Prague Orgy, life without the moral salvation of the written word. Compared to them Zuckerman is indeed a regular Henry James.

Roth has been to Prague before, of course. In 1977 he sent David Kepesh there in search of Kafka, the visit being wonderfully described in ***The Professor of Desire.*** Well, Kepesh found Kafka's tomb and that of his barber and also, most memorably (although, alas, only in a dream), Kafka's whore. All this ancient trollop can remember is that Kafka didn't beat her and that, like all the other good Jewish boys, he was fastidiously clean. In the interests of literature she is prepared to let Kepesh see her pudenda, since she is convinced of his seriousness of purpose. Kepesh looks but declines to touch. Even for Kafka the Professor cannot summon up the necessary desire. Zuckerman, in his turn, rejects a similar offer from Olga (the ex-Mrs Sisovsky), guardian of the manuscripts, who also habitually displays herself (*pace The Aspern papers*). It is the old exchange; life for art, a not so heroic sacrifice. Yet Zuckerman, like Kepesh, declines—with less reason, for Olga is still voluptuous. She is also sharp. Any man may see her secret flesh, but she in turn can see through every man. She knows better than Zuckerman why he wants Sisovsky's father's stories. . . . Worse, she sees through Sisovsky. Did Zuckerman really believe that he was concerned about his father's memory? Oh no, says Olga, he wants to publish the stories under his own name and claim the credit for himself. Even worse, the tale of Sisovsky senior's demise is a falsehood. According to Olga he sat out the war in hiding and was killed, not by the Nazis, but by a bus. In the end, however, it all becomes irrelevant. The stories, retrieved from Olga by Zuckerman, are taken into custody minutes thereafter by the Minister of Culture's police.

There is no redemption for the Sisovskys, father and son; no lives are changed by publication in America. Sisovsky senior, finding no Brod, will receive none of Kafka's posthumous fame. Yet again Zuckerman has failed, both as father and son. In ***The Professor of Desire*** Roth quoted from Kafka's ''Letter to His Father'': ''My writing is all about you'', Kafka wrote, ''. . . yet it did take its course in the direction determined by me.'' Following on from that the whole of ***Zuckerman Bound*** (as the trilogy is known in America) can be seen as a search for ''patriarchal validation'' to counterbalance familial and critical vituperation. Not that Zuckerman could have expected anything but the latter in Prague. Indeed, even as the Minister of Culture is expelling him personally he cannot resist mythologizing his own father, the salt of the earth—''yet another fabricated father manufactured to serve the purposes of a storytelling son'', notes Zuckerman.

Has he learned at last that no patriarchal validation is possible for a post-Freudian son? Fathers—even Kafka's father—are filial constructions. To be sure, the guilt they engender is real enough, but it is essentially self-inflicted. In the final analysis the stories are just as important as the lives, perhaps more so, for it is in such stories that our most acute moral dilemmas are most finely articulated. Even as he is kicked out of Prague—presumed guilty (cf Kafka's K)—and returned in humiliation to his "little world around the corner", Zuckerman can still manage this valediction:

> No, one's story isn't a skin to be shed—it's inescapable, one's body and blood. You go on pumping it out till you die, the story veined with the themes of your life, the ever-recurring story that's at once your invention and the invention of you.

Zuckerman lives, and blessed be his creator.

Clive Sinclair, "The Son in the Father," in The Times Literary Supplement, *No. 4307, October 18, 1985, p. 1167.*

CHRISTOPHER LEHMANN-HAUPT

Near the end of Philip Roth's experimental new novel, ***The Counterlife,*** there occurs a scene that this reader particularly wished he could have felt more directly. In it, the writer Nathan Zuckerman and his English wife, Maria, have just returned home from celebrating her 28th birthday at a London restaurant. During dinner, Nathan is the target of an anti-Semitic outburst from a woman at a neighboring table. Earlier in the evening, at a reception at the end of a Christmas carol service at a church in the West End, Maria's older sister, Sarah, attacks Nathan's Jewishness. She warns him not to "stand in the way of a christening" after Maria gives birth to their child. Now, at the end of a nerve-racking day, Nathan begins to press Maria for her real feelings about his Jewishness.

We would like very much to feel the full impact of this scene. The tension is terrific. The dialogue is passionately articulate. The characters are brilliantly defined. The stakes are nothing less than the future of the marriage. Yet we simply cannot believe the scene. Or, more exactly, Mr. Roth does not permit us to suspend our disbelief completely. We cannot help recalling that, according to Maria's earlier testimony in the book, the entire chapter in which the scene occurs is a wild distortion of what has actually happened between her and Nathan. . . .

We can't rid ourselves of the awareness that Nathan Zuckerman is no more than a figment of Mr. Roth's imagination and that anything can happen to him at his creator's whim, including his death from quintuple-bypass surgery, which indeed (or rather in fantasy) occurs some 90 pages earlier. In short, we can't give in to the scene between Nathan and Maria because too many things are going on in the background that undermine its credibility.

There is of course a purpose to this subversion of the novel's surface reality. Apparently not yet recovered from the shock of having his earlier novels, especially ***Portnoy's Complaint,*** taken literally by the American reading public, Mr. Roth is determined to prove in as many ways as possible that autobiographical fiction, no matter how seemingly personal, is not the same thing as confession.

So, Mr. Roth makes it absolutely impossible for the reader to identify Nathan Zuckerman with his creator. Contradictory things keep happening to Nathan in ***The Counterlife.*** Halfway through the book, he dies and yet witnesses his funeral service, where a eulogy is delivered that explains, among other things, why his fiction can't be taken literally. On a flight from Tel Aviv to London, he is drawn into a hijacking plot hatched by one of his fans; a few dozen pages later, he takes the same flight uneventfully, suggesting that, in the earlier version, he is merely the fantasy of his fan.

Made impotent by his heart medication, he decides to submit to bypass surgery so he can marry Maria and conceive a child. (By doing this, he reverses the role of his younger brother, Henry, who has undergone the same surgery so he can go on having a mistress.). . .

So the writer Nathan Zuckerman is not to be equated with the novelist Philip Roth. And ***The Counterlife*** is not to be read as a record of Mr. Roth's life, but rather as an "ever-enlarging storage plant for" Zuckerman's "narrative factory, where there is no clear demarcation dividing actual happenings eventually consigned to the imagination from imaginings that are treated as having actually occurred—memory as entwined with fantasy as it is in the brain."

It's as if the novelist were saying, since I can make you believe in anything, the ultimate challenge is to make you believe in nothing. So we learn to count on nothing. Yet the novel pays a price for sabotaging its own reality. We become so aware of the narrative's duplicity that all that is left to us is the burden of the author's self-consciousness as an artist and a Jew. . . .

By the time we have finished ***The Counterlife,*** we have begun to wonder if Mr. Roth has anything to write about except his fear of being misjudged as an artist. Like Pirandello's mad King Henry IV, he becomes the king of a court of illusions. We respect the tricky epistemology. And go hungering for something more substantial.

Christopher Lehmann-Haupt, in a review of "The Counterlife," in The New York Times, *December 29, 1986, p. C19.*

WILLIAM H. GASS

There have been thousands of different drawings of the world, many maps made of reality. Each puts the gods, the good, the false and the true in a different place. They cannot each be correct—there are too many counterclaims—yet society after society has sailed to greatness (not simply to the doom they also doomed themselves to) following these false charts, these fictions that have been projected upon the planet. And the planet, like the great screen of a drive-in movie, accepts them all, lighted by the illusions of passion, for as long as the passions last. If so, then our lives are made of fictions, beliefs we construct and then dwell in like a beach house in Malibu. When we change our life—one of the central themes of Philip Roth's magnificent new novel [***The Counterlife***], a remarkable change of direction itself—we recreate "a counterlife that is one's own anti-myth," as Mr. Roth's protagonist, Nathan Zuckerman, surmises. (p. 1)

In novel after novel, Mr. Roth has asked what Jews want with somewhat the same irritated bewilderment we associate with Freud's question: "What do women want?" In ***The Counterlife,*** the query has become more riddling, more radical and, despite the antic flipflops of the plot, more serious yet no less witty for all that: can a Jew, if he wishes—if he wants—change into a Jew? And in what direction should he go to do that? And why should the quiet course of a comfortable life be shattered by such questions, which were always there to be put, but were answered by not being asked? And is not the anti-Semitism of a Jew the refusal of a Jew to be one?

These are a few of the questions Philip Roth's latest novel considers, turning them round like meat on a spit. With respect to his own past as an author, there are many questions—the hedges, qualifications, objections entertained by critics—to which it gives a resounding answer. ***The Counterlife,*** it seems to me, constitutes a fulfillment of tendencies, a successful integration of themes, and the final working through of obsessions that have previously troubled if not marred his work. I hope it felt, as Mr. Roth wrote it, like a triumph, because that is certainly how it reads to me.

The style is a triumph too. It is no longer a style at war with itself, as Mr. Roth's sometimes used to be, its cleverness undercutting its own emotions, its satire thinning a subject already sliced. Its combativeness is no longer pointed at the reader, the critic, the family or some other ancient adversary. The world of the ***The Counterlife*** is made of intelligent, argumentative, witty, observant words. They are words woven now, after the practice of many years, into a rich, muscular, culturally complex style that even in purely narrative moments seems to come not from the end of a pen but through the flow of the voice. . . . (pp. 1, 24)

The book comes to us wrapped in more than its dust jacket. It continues and seems to conclude a series of affairs, ambitions and other anxieties taken from the life of Nathan Zuckerman. . . .

However, Mr. Roth would now have us believe that Nathan Zuckerman is the invention of Peter Tarnopol, the professor and novelist of ***My Life as a Man.*** Tarnopol endeavors to come to some understanding of himself by composing a series of fictions that are then topped off by the real thing, Tarnopol's autobiography (which we should no more believe is true of Tarnopol than ***My Life as a Man*** is true of Mr. Roth). And this conjunction of fact with fancy presumably allows us to estimate the alterations imagination makes to any fictionalized biography. In a Roth novel, it is not unusual for characters to cross from one text to another as though they were crossing a street. . . .

Nathan Zuckerman is the author of a notoriously dirty book, an alleged libel of the Jews, *Carnovsky,* which has made him both rich and reviled, just as ***Portnoy's Complaint*** made Philip Roth well known, well off and the target of slings. So if we follow this tangle from head to tail, we shall discover that Mr. Roth has created a character, Peter Tarnopol, who has in turn invented Nathan Zuckerman, who has, for his part, written the same book Mr. Roth has (since *Carnovsky* equals ***Portnoy***). This ring of real and fictive authors puts us at least a touch back, if not smack back at the beginning. It is consequently not stretching the facts but admitting them to say that ***The Counterlife*** is both thematically and structurally connected to the general body of Philip Roth's work. (p. 24)

So the Zuckerman chronicles continue. Nothing is changed. Every old quarrel has a home in this text. There are references, naturally, to previous books. We are still teased by details taken from the author's life and we are encouraged to search for more, while at the same time the fundamental connection is denied. Sexual expression, phallic power, oral fixation: each is present. Family oppression and familial duties: these too. But above all, there is the presence of the question of what it means to be a Jew. Nevertheless, everything has changed after all. These themes no longer possess our author. He has become their master.

The book begins with the brother's death. Henry, the dentist, has heart trouble. The medicine he is taking for it makes him impotent. Unable to sport with his hygienist any longer, Henry grows desperate and undergoes a bypass operation that will remove him from his medicine, restore his manhood and incidentally repair his heart. His wife chooses to believe it is for her he has run this risk. But soon Mr. Roth will skillfully split the narrative. Henry will unaccountably recover from his death at the hands of the text, and with his revived heart will hasten abruptly away to Israel to take up righteousness and seek the faith. . . .

We learn that Nathan Zuckerman, Henry's nemesis, has refused to speak at his brother's funeral. For reasons, of course. Well, wait. Henry will get his opportunity to refuse to speak at Nathan's. These are counterlives but suspiciously parallel tales: woman against woman, marriage against marriage, both or neither brother surviving the knife, as the novel continues its surprises. For Nathan's story could be said to commence with his death, too, at a later date in the text, though from similar causes and resembling motives. Nathan has the same punning problem—a troubled heart—with its emasculating consequences, which means he cannot marry the sweet young object of his present affections and beget the child he finally thinks he wants. So he too will seek a remedy beneath the surgeon's knife and receive his quietus for it. . . .

We follow Nathan as he follows Henry to Israel. There he receives doses of rhetoric from every mouth sufficient to cure complacency by killing it. Hope is killed as well. . . . The arguments concern Jews, are about Jewishness, about power, and are wholly political. The political and the moral are artfully confused. So this is not a novel about ideas only, but about beliefs—those beliefs that, like bombs, we daily drop on one another. The speakers' rhetoric is their rifle. And the characters establish their character by means of their speech, through the defense, the advocacy, the oppressiveness of their opinions.

This speech does not turn back upon itself as Stanley Elkin's often does, nor are its rhythms so obviously Yiddish as Bernard Malamud's sometimes were, nor is it quite as continuously civilized as Saul Bellow's. It has an insistently forward push toward the next thought, the next feeling, a future desire; it does not normally dawdle in description, or stop for meditative poesy, or paralyze its movement with refinements and indecisions. In this it is urban, male (no matter the sex of the speaker), quick, artful yet blunt, overbearing, mean, street smart but worldly wise. In each case, it seems superb for its purposes and complete.

Every belief is buttressed, not with reasons, but with the crimes of opponents. The gentiles have done thus and so; the Arabs, also, have done thus and so; therefore we, the Jews, should do thus, and thus, and thus and so. . . . And every Jew, except for the secular, corrupt, pluralistic and skeptically minded Nathan, believes it essential that every Jew believe the same as every other Jew, achieve the solidarity of the Wailing Wall. The speeches which give air to these opinions are intensely interesting, passionately convincing and perfectly phrased. Although each view is by its fevered nature a partial one, such is Mr. Roth's skill that the accumulation of these partials makes for an impressive whole. . . .

Each often painful encounter with . . . Jewish love and Jewish hate has cleansed Nathan Zuckerman, who has sought the solution to his nature through book after book, of one more trapping of his type, until he finally sees himself as "a Jew without Jews, without Judaism, without Zionism, without Jewishness, without a temple or an army or even a pistol, a Jew clearly without a home, just the object itself, like a glass or an apple.'' Except for the phallic scar, the venereal voodoo he desires to have performed upon his son—a futile mark of difference, it would seem to me, since circumcision is now more fashionable among the gentiles than pierced ears.

A little past its middle, in a brilliant post-modern maneuver, the book becomes posthumous, and begins reading itself both front and rear, before and after, like a swing. With Nathan dead of Henry's heart, Henry seizes and censors the manuscript of his brother's latest book. It is a draft of ***The Counterlife.*** Our surprise at these developments, and a number of others, is honestly accounted for by the structure of the book and brilliantly brought off each time. . . .

When a woman becomes a character, not a lover or a wife; when this character expresses her desire to leave the work the way she might a husband; when *goy* and *galuth* quarrel over, of all things, circumcision; when we remember, as good readers ought, what St. Paul said it took to make a Christian: a faith in Jesus as the Saviour that (not to hold back the knife) was the equivalent in spirit to the circumcision of the heart; and when a man (a character) who is already dead when we read the words that render his forthcoming life is heatedly arguing with his wife about one more operation, insisting that the paper tale we've been passing through in their company is ''as close to life as you, and I, and our child can ever hope to come''; and when we know, or think we know, that Zuckerman, now only ashes, wrote his own maybe-marriage with its male offspring and the boy's disputed penis into being the way he wrote his own funeral eulogy; when we realize that Zuckerman himself is Tarnopol's creation, and that Tarnopol lives only in another book by Mr. Roth, and that Mr. Roth, too, in the guise of Portnoy, Zuckerman and others, is in this same work as well, thrashing around; then we may be willing to agree that all of them have changed their nature right in front of us, passing, as it were, behind the page like a cloud; but such is the rightness of the form, the richness of the theme and the eloquence in the execution of this splendid novel that we can assent to the conventions, to the fiction, to the disclaimers and the harmless piles of paper it after all comes to, and still feel the words, still be moved and still care. (p. 25)

William H. Gass, ''Deciding to Do the Impossible,'' in The New York Times Book Review, *January 4, 1987, pp. 1, 24-5.*

J. HOBERMAN

Zuckerman has now preoccupied Roth for the better part of a decade, and although he resembles his creator in many respects, he originated as a doubly imaginary character—making his debut in ***My Life as a Man*** as the fictional alter ego of Roth's ostensive alter ego Peter Tarnopol. . . .

The Prague Orgy seemed Zuckerman's farewell performance—until ***The Counterlife,*** set two years later, in 1978. As befits the convoluted Zuckerman saga, this textual Möbius strip flips from first to third person and back, oscillating between two parallel worlds while entwining all manner of letters, manuscripts, and notebook entries around one basic plot. Afflicted with a sick heart and rendered impotent by his medication, a middle-aged man—alternately Nathan and his brother Henry, a New Jersey dentist—submits to high-risk bypass surgery. Henry dies and, abandoning his family, goes to Israel, where he joins a militant Zionist group on the West Bank; Nathan dies and, having married a young Englishwoman named Maria, moves to London, where he's lacerated for his trouble by the local anti-Semites.

Hilarious it's not. ***The Counterlife*** is at once self-consciously literary and grossly obsessed with sex and death and Jews. The opening movement, devoted to the demise of Henry, is comically devious and characteristically wicked. Moving on to Nathan, the novel grows increasingly straightforward, even sentimental, plunging to its nadir with a stratospheric Punch-and-Judy show that features a third-rate version of Alvin Pepler, before regrouping—Henry revenging himself upon the dead Nathan's manuscript and another character walking out on the novel—for a bravura coda.

Although no more devoid of pleasure than it is innocent of virtuosity, ***The Counterlife*** suffers from a case of the would-be magisterial. (Indeed, the *New York Times Book Review*'s front-page rave [see excerpt above by William H. Gass] reads like an engraved invitation to the Postmodernist Club. But really, what could be more postmodern than ***Portnoy's Complaint***?) Scarcely the manic Zuck of ***The Anatomy Lesson,*** Roth's hero—and much of his narrative voice—is flat, depressed, and almost stuffy. It's Zuckerman under glass. The problem with the novel is that although Roth's dogged invention can be read as a non-stop attempt to wriggle off the hook, Zuckerman's consciousness remains always the same. Neither Roth's pyrotechnics nor the gaseous *Times* review conceals ***The Counterlife***'s oppressive overfamiliarity. The mouth, dentist Henry tells his hygienist, is ''the primary organ of experience.'' In ***The Counterlife,*** however, it's more like the mouthpiece.

To a degree, Zuckerman is a trap Roth has set for his critics—''all those astute book reviewers who are sure that I am the only novelist in the history of literature who has never made anything up.'' Still, Roth is not Balzac, and whether he's called Nathan Zuckerman or Peter Tarnopol, Neil Klugman or David Kepesh, Portnoy or Carnovsky, there is a recognizable species of *homo rothicus.* The pampered scion of an uneducated petit bourgeois Jewish family, born in the mid-1930s (usually in New Jersey), *homo rothicus* is a serious writer or an academic, successful (if not world famous), obsessed with his family and his own Jewishness, typically (and tormentedly) involved with a shiksa. (The undeveloped psyche of the female *homo rothicus* has the effect of making the male of the species seem all the more self-preoccupied.)

It has been suggested that, in rejecting intimacy and shirking fatherhood, *homo rothicus* suffers a terminal case of arrested psychosexual development. Should analysts of this persuasion crack ***The Counterlife,*** they'll find the patient has made some progress, even to the point of conceiving a child with his fourth shiksa wife. (The crisis will come with the prospect of circumcision or christening.) But like the novel's kiss-and-*Tel Quel* structure, this maturity is more problem than solution. (p. 51)

The Counterlife is set in late 1978, at the time of the Camp David accords—the very moment when Israel bent over backwards to appear reasonable to the goyim. (Never mentioned, the treaty with Egypt might be considered a structuring absence.) Actually, insofar as ***The Counterlife*** is a novel of ideas, its ''Judea'' section seems a response to Saul Bellow's more pious *To Jerusalem and Back.* Perhaps Roth was thinking of Bellow's unruffled, affably imperial tour cum defense of Israel when, in a neat reversal, he has the Sabra leftist Shuki assure visiting Nathan that "we [Israelis] are the excitable, ghettoized, jittery little Jews of the Diaspora, and you [Americans] are the Jews with all the confidence and cultivation that comes of feeling at home where you are." ("Only to an Israeli," Zuckerman replies, "could an American-Jewish intellectual look like a charming Frenchman.")

Or perhaps, in writing ***The Counterlife,*** Roth was defending, not Israel, but himself. One need only remember the (anti) climax of ***Portnoy's Complaint,*** in which, under the most humiliating of circumstances, the randiest *homo rothicus* twice failed to get an erection, suggesting that his sexual identity was bound up inextricably in his sense of himself as a Diaspora Jew. Something similar is happening here. Israel is as overwhelming as the nuclear family. Mordecai Lippman, the Gush Emunim-style, Meir Kahane-like fanatic, is not simply the negation of the *galut* mentality. Zuckerman regards him as the embodiment of potency.

Among other things, ***The Counterlife*** seems written to contest "the bold claims of militant Zionism that they have the patent on Jewish self-transformation, if not on boldness itself." (In a letter to Henry, Nathan explains Zionism in literary terms as "the construction of a counterlife that is one's own anti-myth.") According to Zuckerman, Jews not only reinvented themselves in America but in American novels as well. In the battle between Zionism and literature, one is never in doubt where *homo rothicus* stands. On Rosh Hashanah, Neil Klugman goes not to synagogue but to the library.

While religious faith never complicates Bellow's Nobel *oblige,* Roth permits Zuckerman to define himself in opposition to it. The holiest relic in Judaism appears in Bellow's text only as the yellowed image on a pre-Hitler German postcard, but there's nothing insubstantial about Zuckerman's experience of the Wailing Wall:

> Standing singly at the Wall, some rapidly swaying and rhythmically bobbing as they recited their prayers, others motionless but for the lightning flutter of their mouths, were seventeen of the world's twelve million Jews communing with the King of the Universe. To me it looked as though they were communing solely with the stones in whose crevices pigeons were roosting some twenty feet above their heads. I thought (as I am predisposed to think), 'If there is a God who plays a role in our world, I will eat every hat in this town'—nonetheless, I couldn't help but be gripped by the sight of this rock-worship, exemplifying as it did to me the most awesomely retarded aspect of the human mind. Rock is just about right, I thought: what on earth could be less responsive? . . .

Homo rothicus actually treasures the sense of Jewish absurdity and Jewish superfluity, which is more a legacy of Central European "enlightenment" than East European captivity. (No wonder that Zuckerman is half at home in Prague or that Roth, like [Woody Allen], is a culture hero in Budapest.) "I object to people clinging to an identity just for the sake of it," Maria finally cries, comparing the irate Zuckerman to Lippman. "You disguise yourself as rational and moderate when *you* are the wild nut." In her world that is. Out in Christendom (as he calls England), Zuckerman is taken aback by the hostility he encounters (or, in the meta-novel, orchestrates): "Usually it was the Semites and not the anti-Semites who assaulted me for being the Jew I was," he muses after some ancient crone spots him in an exclusive London restaurant and proceeds to go wild.

As a Christian in Christendom and the daughter of a family that for 300 years raised sheep in Gloucestershire, Maria has no problem with her identity. And while she fumes over the "bloody fuss" Jews make over being Jewish, the eyes of Mordecai Lippman's contented wife shine

> with love for a life free of Jewish cringing, deference, diplomacy, apprehension, alienation, self-pity, self-satire, self-mistrust, depression, clowning, bitterness, nervousness, inwardness, hypercriticalness, hypertouchiness, social anxiety, social assimilation—a way of life absolved, in short, of all the Jewish 'abnormalities,' those peculiarities of self-division whose traces remained imprinted in just about every engaging Jew I knew.

The Counterlife attempts a "mature" solution by globalizing these "abnormalities" on the level of form, but *homo rothicus* remains terminally unresolved. In a final tantrum of ambivalence, ***The Counterlife*** ends with Zuckerman's fantasy of a new critical Jew, a cubist Jew, a formalist Jew: "A Jew without Jews, without Judaism, without Zionism, without Jewishness, without a temple or an army or even a pistol, a Jew clearly without a home, just the object itself, like a glass or an apple." An apple! That's how history began. Like all Jews, Zuckerman is defined by history—by the internalized presence of tribal ancestors, by desire to inscribe that history upon the penis of his hypothetical son and, perhaps, even by the impossible longing to transcend the happenstance of birth. (There are no born-again Jews; it's a contradiction in terms.)

Even at his second best, Roth reminds us that, in this age of the neo *frum,* Jewish history can neither be represented by a static model nor appropriated by a single group. "Jews are to history what Eskimos are to snow," Zuckerman maintains. The man without an igloo, *homo rothicus* has always wanted us to admire his frostbite. (p. 52)

J. Hoberman, "Up against the Wailing Wall," in The Village Voice, *Vol. XXXII, No. 4, January 27, 1987, pp. 51-2.*

MARTIN AMIS

Philip Roth's [***The Counterlife***] is so formidably good, and so perversely surprising, that it prompts a question: How did he get here? How did he wind up with *this*? Over the space of ten books and almost twenty years Roth has endured an odd kind of impatience from his public, an impatience resembling pique or obscurely hurt feelings. The reason for this seems to me quite straightforward. Roth is a comic genius, and there is never an embarrassment of comic geniuses—there are never enough to go around. In 1969 he published ***Portnoy's Complaint.*** It was his fourth work of fiction; the dutiful tyro stuff was out of the way; he had found his voice. We sat back, asking for more. And he gave us less.

What *did* he give us? First a trio of formal satires, if you please: ***Our Gang, The Breast,*** and ***The Great American Novel.*** These were comic in shape but, contrary to our wishes, only glancingly comic in execution. Looking on with expressions of strained indulgence, we allowed Roth this holiday, and calmly waited for the comic genius to resume his obligations. Next came ***My***

Life as a Man and ***The Professor of Desire,*** two novels that, it was widely felt, were not funny enough. And where did Roth get off, not being funny enough? No, ***My Life*** and ***The Prof.*** erred on the side of bookishness, introspection, and anguish. We wanted the old get up and go. For our pains we were zapped by the Zuckerman quartet, perhaps the most cramped and stubborn exercise in self-examination known to modern letters. As its title suggests, ***The Counterlife*** marks a parting of the ways, which, though, lead in unexpected directions. Zuckerman is still there; Zuckerman is still in prison (newly reinforced, with extra guards). Zuckerman is still in solitary. But Roth is back on the streets.

There aren't supposed to be degrees or intensities of uniqueness, and yet Roth is somehow inordinately *sui generis*. He is bloody-mindedly himself, himself, himself. The trouble with Zuckerman, the trouble with the self as a literary idea, is that *there is no subject*. Ironically, it is Zuckerman whom we thank for this elusive truth, at the end of ***The Counterlife,*** one thousand pages having gone by since the experiment began. Hence the desperate thinness, the unbearable lightness of much of the earlier Zuckerman work. How it yearned for escape into the concrete, how it sobbed and pleaded for substance. One felt that Roth couldn't possibly go further—that, indeed, there was nowhere further to go. But on he went, with typical and (it now seems) heroic intransigence. Like a dying star, Roth hovered on the point of catastrophic collapse. With ***The Counterlife,*** however, the supernova has arrived, and it almost hurts the eye.

The agent, the catalyst, is unquestionably Israel. Here is a subject, all right, and it may even be that Roth has spent half his life readying himself to take it on. He went there before, carrying Portnoy's passport, and the place defeated him: the Israel section was the only major weakness of ***Portnoy's Complaint,*** and that is a measure of how far we have come. Set against ***The Counterlife,*** the earlier book looks regressive and dead-ended, for all its savage splendors. . . .

The Israel chapters [in ***The Counterlife***], "Judea" and "Aloft" (aboard an El Al jet), are choric songs for vying voices, successions of dramatic monologues coolly marshaled by the man with the golden ear. (p. 89)

Zuckerman seems to steer his way through the cacophony with impeccable skepticism. . . . In a brush with a wailer at the Wailing Wall, Zuckerman confesses that all four of his wives have been shiksas. "Why, mister?" "That's the sort of Jew I am, Mac." He is contentedly assimilated, contentedly "decadent." When, in Judea, Zuckerman is informed that "what Hitler couldn't achieve with Auschwitz, American Jews are doing to themselves in the bedroom," he shrugs and keeps his counsel, fondly anticipating his return to London, to his pregnant Maria, his new intermarriage, his new life in "Christendom." But it doesn't work out; it never does in Roth's world. A radical epiphany, an uncovenanted conversion, is at hand. On Dizengoff Street, Zuckerman has told Shuki [a Tel Aviv journalist] that circumcision, like every other biblical injunction, "was probably irrelevant to my 'I'." Practically the next day his entire existence is hinging on that one question, circumcision, the mark of the Jewish reality, "this old, old stuff."

To engineer such an about-turn it is additionally necessary for Zuckerman to apprehend anti-Semitism in England, "deep, insidious Establishment anti-Semitism," and to apprehend it, moreover, in the space of a single evening. Writing in my capacity as an Englishman, I am both ashamed and surprised to say that Roth pulls it off—he makes this murky thing happen on the page. (p. 90)

There is a good deal else going on in ***The Counterlife.*** It is, for instance, a rare addition to the corpus of successful—one could almost say readable—post-modernist fiction. Here Roth is audacious, grimly playful, almost Parisian (but Paris of the exile—Milan Kundera, say). He takes a dilemma and runs it past two different lives, that of Zuckerman and that of his "uninteresting" brother, Henry. How brothers "know each other, in my experience, is as a kind of deformation of themselves"; by crosshatching their realities, Roth can undertake his characteristic search for "the real wisdom of the predicament." The predicament has to do with impotence and its opposite, death and its opposite, with the longing to escape inherited identities, and with the helpless addiction to a supposed authenticity, the hamming up of a self that barely exists outside the perceptions of others. . . .

The book unites in the theme of Israel, but loosely, not too schematically, not too *teachably,* above all. One of the things that can't be thematically squared, it seems to me, is Roth's entirely personal bedevilment by the abuses of autobiographical fiction. For what must be historical reasons, modern fiction is unprecedentedly close to the authors' peculiar realities: the idea of the freely gamboling fancy doesn't appear to cut much mustard anymore. Roth has never looked at these questions historically or indeed artistically—only morally, only personally. How does this fit in with Israel? In its tendency to exploit and gobble up half-formed lives? Well, here I think we are stretching it; and there is no need or inclination to stretch it elsewhere. One equation feels particularly satisfying: that between Israel and Philip Roth. In *Ulysses* Joyce calls Judea "the grey sunken cunt of the world." I wouldn't like to say what Roth does to the place, or with what mixture of emotions; but the union is explosive. Like Israel, he exhausts you, he unsettles you, he galvanizes your responses. In this book (wonderfully sharp, worryingly tense) he is an electrifier. (p. 91)

Martin Amis, "Found in Jerusalem," in The Atlantic Monthly, *Vol. 259, No. 2, February, 1987, pp. 89-91.*

ROBERT ALTER

It is surprising that a novel this compelling should have emerged as a sequel from the shambles of Philip Roth's Zuckerman trilogy. Neither riding an obsession nor paying off scores against critics and editors is a very happy substitute for fictional invention; ***Zuckerman Bound*** ends up being the work of a mature talent determined, through sheer spite against the world, to reduce itself to embarrassing puerility. ***The Counterlife*** still exhibits certain vestiges of Roth's gnawing preoccupation with the hostility his fiction has provoked in the Jewish public—a concern that, 28 years after the publication of ***Goodbye, Columbus,*** is bound to be much more interesting to the author than to most of his readers. By and large, however, the new novel manages to put behind it Roth's fixation on reception, and instead to focus suggestively on the ambiguous transactions between fiction and life.

Although Roth has often written about writers and their quandaries, this is his first "self-reflexive" novel—that is, a novel that pointedly exposes its own condition as fictional artifice, and by so doing leads us to ponder the insoluble conundrums of fiction's relation to reality, fiction's claim to be a kind of reality. . . .

In effect ***The Counterlife*** has four different plots, two alternative destinies for each of the Zuckerman brothers, so that each lives a life both counter to the other and counter to himself. These alternatives correspond to the different parts, or five long chapters, of the novel, with the exception of the third part, which continues the fictional hypothesis of the previous chapter. The common denominators in this multiplication of fictional alternatives are the problematic Jewishness and the threatened sexuality of the protagonists. . . .

By the time we get to the fourth of the novel's five parts, we begin to wonder who exactly is inventing either of the Zuckermans, or the multiple selves of Zuckerman. For Nathan Zuckerman turns out to be the inventor of almost everything, but not quite everything, that seems to be "reality" in the book. The live, contentious Zuckerman of the concluding section, which is a supposedly posthumous piece of first-person writing, is finally more real than the Zuckerman who gives up the ghost in the preceding section. If both the novelist's brother and his wife (his fourth) eventually complain rather bitterly that he has reduced them to "just one of a series of fictive propositions," that he is "utterly unable to involve himself in anything not entirely of his own making," Zuckerman, who has the last word, responds by affirming the validity of the novelist's need to invent the world. (p. 36)

This could be, the novel suggests, a questionable way of living, peculiar to the haunted theatricality of the novelistic imagination. But perhaps the world that others assume or construct is no more real. . . .

What is remarkable is that in being Roth's first self-reflexive novel, it is also his first Jewish novel. Jewish types abound, of course, in his previous fiction. . . . But the middle-class, second-generation American Jews of northern New Jersey, with their characteristic family constellation, their attitudes and tics, are in these books the familiar social materials of an American realist. . . .

The Counterlife, on the other hand, is a Jewish novel in a more substantive sense. It uses the fictional medium to wrestle with the intractable question of Jewish identity (hence the appositeness of the theme of self-making). And this involves an imaginative confrontation within the fictional frame of clashing Jewish ideologies. . . . Roth's resourcefulness in representing conflicting options, personal and political, for persistent or residual Jewish identity, is remarkable. It makes his new novel one of the best American examples—alongside Cynthia Ozick's novella *Envy, or Yiddish in America*—of the Jewish fiction of ideas.

This concentration of ideas is so intense that it leads Roth into the one entirely implausible episode of the novel. A tough Israeli security agent, in the midst of brutally apprehending a deranged would-be skyjacker who has drawn the hapless Zuckerman into his wake, delivers to Zuckerman a long harangue on Jewish history, on Jewish power and powerlessness, on the anti-Semitism of T. S. Eliot. It is a moment when the internal argument of the novel is pursued at the cost of verisimilitude. The bizarre introduction of T. S. Eliot by a knife-wielding counterterrorist points forward to the concluding section, "Christendom," in which Zuckerman's Jewish juices will begin to bubble in a series of unexpected encounters with British genteel anti-Semitism; and the equally improbable detail that the knife in question is a circumcision scalpel prepares for the very end of the novel, when Zuckerman proposes his own symbolic reinterpretation of circumcision.

Elsewhere in the book, Roth is more successful in giving the clash of ideas a plausible human place and habitation. The most remarkable piece of writing in this regard occurs in the long second section, "Judea," in which Henry, the assimilated, affluent suburbanite, reacts to a postoperative depression by a precipitous return to the Jewish fold, a return that carries him all the way to a Gush Emunim settlement on the West Bank, where he changes his name to Hanoch and becomes the follower of a zealot rabbi. One measure of the difference between this novel and Roth's earlier work is the acuteness with which the Israeli scene, though represented only by a few fragments, is observed—in contrast to the Israel of ***Portnoy's Complaint,*** which is alternately a mirror for Portnoy's sexual neuroses and a tissue of stereotypes inherited from the New Jersey Jewish summer camps of the 1940s. Anyone who knows the country well should recognize . . . that Roth has got things just right. . . . (p. 37)

It is hard to say precisely what happens in ***The Counterlife*** because it contains four different, mutually contradictory fictional hypotheses about two lives. Similarly, it is hard to say what is concluded ideologically because ideas and outlooks remain, as they should, in restless circulation. But the Zuckerman of the final section does resolve to resist all visions of a harmonious accommodation with reality—all "pastoral" prospects, as he calls them, whether in assimilation or in a Zionist normalization of Jewish existence. This resistance is itself a minimal Jewish credo.

Zuckerman chooses as its symbol the rite of circumcision. For him it confirms our banishment from the comforts of the womb, seals in the flesh the moral necessity to live in strife, bearing the scars inflicted by society and history. The concluding image of the novel is of Zuckerman's erect penis. This may sound Portnoyan, but it is not. What is stressed is not just resurgent virility, but the condition of circumcision, with all that it symbolically portends. In an odd but instructive conjunction, this conclusion might be read as a gloss on three lines from "Jews in the Land of Israel," one of Yehuda Amichai's most striking poems, lines that in turn gloss a phrase from Genesis 32:25, "when they were in pain": "The circumcision does it to us, / as in the Bible, in the story of Shechem and the sons of Jacob, / when we are in pain all our lives." (p. 38)

Robert Alter, "Déjà Jew," in The New Republic, *Vol. 196, No. 5, February 2, 1987, pp. 36-8.*

JOSH RUBINS

Philip Roth dedicates [***The Counterlife***] "To my father at eighty-five," and those who have been keeping up with Roth's recent fiction will probably suspect that—on this very first page of text—something more than a heartwarming personal note is being sounded. After all, the centerpiece of ***Zuckerman Unbound*** (1981) was the deathbed curse of Zuckerman senior: a devastating retort to his son's "artistic license" and "writer's freedom." In case the reader (unlike some of Roth's critics) is not inclined toward biographical research, Roth is now telling us that *his* father isn't dead at all, that the real son is perhaps not so painfully estranged from the real father, that "Zuckerman" (whatever his usefulness as an alter ego may be) does not necessarily equal "Roth." And so begins a cautionary lecture series—How *Not* To Read Philip Roth—that will form, both implicitly and very explicitly indeed, one layer of this elaborate, impassioned, fitfully commanding new novel.

The role of instructor isn't a new one for Roth, of course. In one manner or another (essays, interviews, stories), he has been trying to clarify the nature of autobiographical fiction ever since such seeming self-portraits as Neil Klugman and Alexander Portnoy began drawing shocked responses from critics, rabbis, and (apparently) relatives. With ***My Life as a Man*** (1974), an entire novel was on one level turned into a lecture-demonstration, an explanatory exercise. The book's first section consists of two very different stories about writer Nathan Zuckerman (his first appearance in the Roth *oeuvre*), "drawn from the writings of" fictional novelist Peter Tarnopol. These "Useful Fictions," as they're labeled, are in some fundamental respects autobiographical—for Philip Roth the novelist and, as we soon learn from the Tarnopol memoir that follows the Zuckerman tales ("My True Story"), for his fictional counterpart Peter Tarnopol. . . .

The point? Roth spells it out, repeatedly, pedagogically, in ***The Counterlife:*** "Contrary to the general belief, it is the *distance* between the writer's life and his novel that is the most intriguing aspect of his imagination." In fact, to an even greater extent than ***My Life as a Man,*** this new novel is itself—on its most superficial, pyrotechnical level—an impressive show-and-tell performance, reminding all slow learners once again that the novelist is not a slave to his "real-life" materials, that verisimilitude is achieved through craft, not confession. (p. 40)

[When] read as part of an ongoing dialogue between Roth and his readers (particularly some critics), ***The Counterlife*** scores a series of quick triumphs, it ultimately may be more undone than enhanced by that very element of interplay between writer and audience. The insistent repetition of the art-is-not-life message—in literal, hectoring (if frequently eloquent) terms—is likely to alienate or distract most readers through the novel's weaker second half, certainly those readers who recall similar harangues from ***My Life as a Man*** and the Zuckerman trilogy. In his argumentative excess, even perhaps in his stubborn proffering of yet another Zuckerman novel (when the trilogy's conclusion was greeted with considerable relief), Roth emerges here, more transparently than ever before, as a writer fiercely preoccupied—despite his apparent aloofness—with his critics. . . . It's difficult not to be reminded of the Nathan Zuckerman of "Courting Disaster" in ***My Life as a Man,*** who sees in himself a pattern of Bartleby-like defiance—passive, irrational, sometimes self-destructive; or the Nathan Zuckerman of "Salad Days," who revels in his role of "enemy of the world" and in his inability to "get along better with people."

Such chronic, all-purpose defiance is usually, as Nathan Zuckerman himself acknowledges, the flip side of, or a reaction against, the "dreamy, needy, and helpless child" in desperate search of approval and acceptance. And while a defiant author's presence can be felt (sometimes to an oppressive degree) through ***The Counterlife,*** the escalating proliferation of narrative gimmicks suggests the simultaneous presence of another overcompensating force: the author as showman, up-to-date and eager to please. At the novel's midpoint, after Roth has made arresting, distinctive use of "metafictional" devices, the self-conscious, book-within-a-book artifice becomes denser, cleverer, more generic. There are brain-teaser games with stolen manuscripts, shuffled time frames, characters who rebel against their author. Reminiscent of the contortions of such postmodernist watershed volumes as John Barth's stupefying *Letters* and Gilbert Sorrentino's infectious *Mulligan Stew,* these maneuvers seem designed—with undeniable energy and intricacy—to grab the attention of critics (academic, trendy) who've had limited interest in Roth's plainer, deceptively straightforward narratives. But, like the other excesses that arise in part from Roth's apparent compulsion to battle or seduce his readers in text or subtext, the metafictional overkill in ***The Counterlife*** may help to obscure the novel's sporadic brilliance.

The book's opening sequence, for instance, succeeds in investing one of metafiction's central clichés—the heightened awareness that what we're reading is a made-up story—with the sort of emotional power that's rarely found in postmodernism's brittle precincts. Henry Zuckerman, contemplating his medico-psychosexual crisis and nostalgically recalling his childhood, feels a dislocation, as if watching or reading two stories simultaneously. . . . When Nathan then takes over the narration and attends Henry's funeral, listening to a fundamentally distorted eulogy from the widow ("a subtle and persuasive writer of domestic fiction"), that sense of life as a *life story*—impossible to rewrite, except in the imagination—deepens. The word "story" reverberates effectively through the novel's first half: the sudden changes in the narrative seem not just received devices, not just aggressive display, but desperate maneuvers in the face of mortality. And storytelling—as a way of reclaiming the past, defying death, escaping pain—develops as an independent theme, but one that usually intensifies the basic human material in the early chapters: grieving, loss, family, fatherhood. . . .

"The kind of stories that people turn life into, the kind of lives that people turn stories into. . . ." Roth clearly intends for his book-length gamesmanship to remain grounded in this tough-minded yet warmblooded recognition; but the later convolutions eventually overwhelm the novel, retroactively blurring the singular impact of the book's first one hundred pages. Similarly, the theme announced in the title—the attempted escape from ourselves into some "counterlife" offered by new roles, places, romances, allegiances—is a promising one that's only erratically sustained. At first elegantly paralleled by the quick-change escapes of the narrative itself, the broad counterlife theme is soon lost in the postmodernist thicket. It's also undermined by the fact that one specific manifestation of the theme—Jewishness as an identity to escape into, or escape from—becomes ungainly, throwing the novel (a precarious study in crosspurposes to begin with) off balance.

The Counterlife, in fact, often seems to be at least two books roughly cobbled into one—not because of the contradictory story lines, but because of a lack of selectivity and shape. Jewishness—almost always a controversial issue in Roth's work, yet rarely the frankly primary one—this time virtually demands a book of its own, one without the larger patterns, without the slippery distractions of metafiction (even if there's something inarguably Talmudic about the either/or, back-and-forth quality of the narrative). (p. 41)

The Counterlife is a frustrating book, and an especially disappointing one for admirers of ***The Ghost Writer.*** In that much shorter novel, Roth turned comparably ambitious material—entangled themes (most of the *same* entangled themes, in fact), farce and fantasy along with moody realism—into something both involving and richly ambiguous: an unlikely triumph of restraint, of implicit connections, from a writer whose stock in trade is the energy of uninhibited full disclosure.

But if structural miscalculations and floundering impulses make ***The Counterlife*** a much less absorbing novel than it might have been, its feverish imaginings are proof that the main quest of Roth's career thus far—the exploration of the self through a fictional alter ego—continues to yield powerful, disturbing material. . . . And if Roth and Zuckerman can sometimes be exasperating company as they pursue the idea of autobiographical fiction to its furthest limits, the partnership is often unnerving and grimly fascinating—and even, oddly, gallant. (p. 42)

Josh Rubins, "The Wandering Jew," in The New York Review of Books, *Vol. XXXIV, No. 5, March 26, 1987, pp. 40-2.*

Georges (Jacques Christian) Simenon

1903-

(Has also written under pseudonyms of Bobette, Christian Brulls, Germain d'Antibes, Jacques Dersonnes, Georges d'Isly, Luc Dorsan, Jean Dorsange, Jean Dossage, Jean du Perry, Georges Martin Georges, Gom Gut, Kim, Plick et Plock, Georges Sim, Gaston Vialis, and G. Violis) Belgian-born French novelist, short story writer, autobiographer, essayist, and nonfiction writer.

With over five hundred titles to his credit and translations of his work into more than forty languages, Simenon is quite possibly the world's most widely published living writer. He is probably best known for his series of detective novels featuring French police inspector Jules Maigret. Through this protagonist, Simenon introduced to detective fiction the exploration of character as the central means for solving a crime. Simenon is also highly respected for his non-Maigret novels, most of which revolve around protagonists who are driven to commit crimes by psychological crises. Central to all of Simenon's work is his view of the inevitability of destiny, which renders his characters helpless to stop themselves from taking part in criminal actions. Some of the topics explored in Simenon's novels are guilt, flight, solitude and alienation, xenophobia, and difficulties in communication. His works are marked by terse prose, a detached narrative style, credible plots and characters, and perceptive psychological insights. Simenon is often praised for his evocation of place. According to Lis Harris, "the relish with which [Simenon] describes the atmosphere of the little worlds he writes about distinguishes him most from his European contemporaries, and will make him remembered . . . long after writers of far greater ambition have been forgotten."

Simenon's Maigret novels, or "Maigrets," depart from most crime and mystery stories in their reliance on intuition, as opposed to deductive reasoning, for their solutions. Maigret attempts to fully understand the victim and suspect by immersing himself in their lifestyles and by examining the psychological reasons that provoked the crime. An element of immeasurable importance in Maigret's investigations is his extraordinary patience, which sometimes allows him to spend weeks observing the milieu of a crime. The Maigret novels are set mainly in Paris, but some of the stories also take place in other cities in France, Holland, England, Mexico, Tahiti, and the United States. Critics praise Simenon for his innovation in the detective genre, his narrative skill, and his insights, as well as for his fully realized depiction of Maigret, a quiet, unexcitable, stolid man whose compassion and profound insight help him solve his cases without relying upon such traditional tools as fingerprints and laboratory reports. Maigret's deep compassion and sensitivity are reflected in the sorrow and pity he often feels after catching a criminal. Simenon gained instant popularity with the publication of his first Maigret novel, *Pietr-le-Letton* (1931; *The Strange Case of Peter the Lett,* republished as *Maigret and the Enigmatic Lett*). Other well-regarded Maigret novels include *La tete d'un homme* (1931; *A Battle of Nerves*), *L'affaire Saint Fiacre* (1932; *The Saint-Fiacre Affair*), *Mon ami Maigret* (1949; *My Friend Maigret*, republished as *The Methods of Maigret*), *Maigret et la vieille dame* (1949; *Maigret and the Old Lady*), *Maigret en mueble* (1951; *Maigret Takes a Room*), *Maigret chez le ministre* (1954; *Maigret and the Calame Report*), and *Maigret et les braves gens* (1962; *Maigret and the Black Sheep*). Numerous films and a television series have been based on the Maigret character and novels.

Although Simenon's serious novels retain many elements of his Maigret works, they also differ in several significant ways. Both types of novels center upon an illegal act; unlike the Maigrets, however, Simenon's serious works are concerned less with the solution of the crime than with the emotional states of his protagonists. Often described through the guise of a narrator who is directly involved in the story, these novels usually center on characters who are driven to commit a felony. Simenon builds tension by focusing on events leading up to the deed; while leaving little doubt that a crime will be committed, Simenon's protagonists often strike when least expected. Among the most highly regarded of these novels are *Lettre à mon juge* (1947; *Act of Passion), La neige était sale* (1948; *The Snow Was Black*), *Le grand Bob* (1954; *Big Bob*), *Le train* (1961; *The Train*), *Les anneaux de Bicêtre* (1963; *The Bells of Bicêtre*), and *Le petit saint* (1965; *The Little Saint*). Critics generally consider Simenon's psychological novels more complex and ambitious but less entertaining than his Maigret works.

Simenon wrote approximately two hundred pulp novels under numerous pseudonyms at the beginning of his career. These works encompass various genres, including the adventure story, the crime novel, and the romance, and have not been translated into English. In addition to his fiction, Simenon has also published many nonfiction works. *Long cours dur les rivieres et cannaux* (1952), *La femme en France* (1960), and *Le Paris de Simenon* (1969; *Simenon's Paris*) are illustrated topological books. *Je me souviens* (1945), *Pedigree* (1948), *Quand j'étais vieux* (1971; *When I Was Old*), and *Lettre à ma mère* (1974; *Letter to My Mother*) are among his numerous autobiographical works, while *Des traces de pas* (1975), *Les petits hommes* (1976), and *Tant que je suis vivant* (1978) are diaries.

(See also *CLC*, Vols. 1, 2, 3, 8, 18 and *Contemporary Authors*, Vols. 85-88.)

In this volume commentary on Georges Simenon will focus on his works featuring detective Jules Maigret.

ISAAC ANDERSON

The young Frenchman who writes under the name of Georges Simenon and who is introduced to the American public by the simultaneous publication of [***The Crime of Inspector Maigret*** and ***The Death of Monsieur Gallet***] is only 28 years old and has already written 280 detective stories. He turns them out at the rate of four a month, and he has been known to write a book in four days. What is more to the point, they are, if one may judge from these two samples, well-constructed stories with unusual plots. In ***The Crime of Inspector Maigret,*** the inspector, having completed another case upon which he has been working, sees a man acting in a suspicious manner and decides to follow him. Technically, he becomes guilty of the crime of driving a man to suicide, but the net result of his investigations is the uncovering of a most bizarre crime committed many years earlier. In ***The Death of Monsieur Gallet,*** Inspector Maigret again finds that the death he has been assigned to investigate is the concluding episode of a drama of the past. Inspector Maigret's outstanding characteristics are infinite patience, dogged perseverance and a disinclination to be satisfied with anything less than a complete and logical solution of the problem upon which he happens to be engaged.

Isaac Anderson, in a review of "The Crime of Inspector Maigret" and "The Death of Monsieur Gallet," in The New York Times Book Review, *September 4, 1932, p. 14.*

ISAAC ANDERSON

[In ***The Crossroad Murders,*** a] black monocle which conceals a glass eye is the distinguishing feature of the man who is first suspected of the murder at the crossroad of the Three Widows, but the severest grilling of which Inspector Maigret and his colleagues of the Judiciary Police are capable fails to break the man down or make him alter his story in the slightest degree. Further investigation at the scene of the crime puts Maigret in possession of various bits of information which, when fitted together, provide the solution of a puzzle whose component parts appear at first glance to be utterly incongruous. Compared with the general run of detective novels, this one is relatively short, but the reader need not feel that he has been cheated, [because] Georges Simenon has the happy faculty of being able to pack large gobs of mystery and excitement into a small number of pages.

Isaac Anderson, in a review of "The Crossroad Murders," in The New York Times Book Review, *February 5, 1933, p. 16.*

ISAAC ANDERSON

[***The Shadow in the Courtyard*** and ***The Crime at Lock 14***] are two detective stories for the price of one. To be sure, each of them is somewhat shorter than the average novel printed in this country, but there never has been any reason to believe that the merit of a story is directly proportional to its length. Inspector Maigret, who, if we remember correctly, has appeared in all of the Simenon books printed in this country, is the central figure in both stories. Maigret is a patient and untiring investigator. There is little of the spectacular in his methods, nor does he depend upon inspiration for his results. He examines everybody and everything even remotely connected with the matter in hand, and eventually he finds that certain pieces of the information that he has gathered match up to form an intelligible pattern.

Of the two stories presented here, ***The Crime at Lock 14*** seems to us to be the better, although that may be merely because the setting is so out of the ordinary. The body of a fashionably dressed woman is found under the straw in a stable near a canal lock, about the last place in the world where one would expect to find a woman of her type. Even when the body is identified as the French wife of an Englishman whose yacht is passing through the canal, there is still no reasonable explanation of her presence there—none, that is, until Maigret finds one that is a surprise to every one concerned. [***The Shadow in the Courtyard***] is but little, if at all, inferior, although its solution is, perhaps, less of a surprise.

Although Georges Simenon is said to turn out his detective yarns at a rate of speed that even the late Edgar Wallace might have envied, his novels show no signs of too hasty construction. They are, indeed, about the best French detective stories appearing in English at the present time. (pp. 11, 21)

Isaac Anderson, in a review of "The Shadow in the Courtyard" and "The Crime at Lock 14," in The New York Times Book Review, *March 4, 1934, pp. 11, 21.*

RALPH PARTRIDGE

There are two cases in ***Maigret Travels South,*** each only half as long as its English counterpart would have been. Inspector Maigret is one of those psychological detectives who get all their results by studying character. What a temptation to indulge in superfluous characterisation for the misleading of readers! But M. Simenon never allows his characters to take liberties; they can present themselves distinctly, but must not expand their chests to our annoyance. Maigret himself is a reel of sensitised celluloid exposed to a criminal atmosphere; every phenomenon of light and shade is recorded impartially and the detective claims no advantage over the reader in interpretation. All you have to do is to get the right snapshots in focus in order to see the villain staring you in the face. Yet it is not quite so easy as it looks, or M. Simenon would have failed as an artist. The complete passivity of the recording machine is most deceptive. An English reader is always on the lookout for trick photography, and there is none; not a shadow of emphasis intrudes. Possibly with more experience of Maigret's technique the solutions will come easier, for we shall know exactly what we expect to see, i.e. the one character not only physically but *morally* capable of the crime in question. If ***Maigret Travels South*** is a fair sample, M. Simenon is going to make a great many English friends. He may not be the equal of our Mrs. Christie, but he trounces the tedious prolixity of our second-class writers. He may even, by his example, introduce into our detection a new era of brevity and sincerity. But one might as well hope that the Expeditionary Force will come back liking French cooking! (p. 184)

Ralph Partridge, "Detection in France," in The New Statesman & Nation, *Vol. XIX, No. 468, February 10, 1940, pp. 184, 186.*

B. E. BETTINGER

Monsieur Georges Sim is a young Frenchman of Dutch-Breton stock who looks like Maurice Chevalier and produces like Henry Ford. At the age of twenty-nine he had, under sixteen pseudonyms (Simenon is the one used for the Maigret series), around 150 novels to his credit. He then decided to go in for bigger and better models. Among these are the Maigret stories, the first of which were published in this country in 1932-4 . . .—three volumes, each containing two mysteries. The present project . . . will follow the same plan—two stories to a volume, released at intervals of a few months—and will eventually cover twenty-five more of the yarns.

Of the two in [***The Patience of Maigret***], the first, ***A Battle of Nerves,*** has a Dostoevskyan touch. A condemned convict escapes, on the eve of execution, with the collusion of his conscience-plagued captor Maigret. The nerves of the real murderer play chess with those of the detective and lose. The second, ***A Face for a Clue,*** is concerned with a crime wave in a provincial town. M. Maigret is no exotic attraction like Charlie Chan; he is one of us, patient and plodding. To make an average dub a personage takes penetration and craftsmanship.

It's a business, this Sim fiction. . . . But it's not a luxury trade, for in France the Maigret stories are available in cheap editions at six francs. You don't expect Rolls quality from a Flivver plant, but each new model has enough variations to attract buyers; it can take you to new places and persons and situations. And M. Sim's characters and plots have a roundness and wit unusual in the genre. (pp. 319-20)

B. E. Bettinger, in a review of "The Patience of Maigret," in The New Republic, *Vol. 102, No. 10, March 4, 1940, pp. 319-20.*

RALPH PARTRIDGE

When M. Simenon's Maigret novels were first introduced in an English translation a few months ago, it was not merely a question of recognising a distinguished foreign Professor of Detection and welcoming him to a seat at High Table that faced a reviewer. M. Simenon is a luminary of the first magnitude but he cannot be placed in the old firmament; his course cannot be plotted alongside that of Mrs. Christie; his spectrum reveals lines that do not correspond to any known detective substance. There are two more Maigret stories in ***Maigret Abroad.*** The first, ***A Crime in Holland,*** is presented in M. Simenon's best detective manner that we understand and appreciate. The scene is Delfzijl, a small Dutch town opposite Emden; a teacher in a Dutch training-ship has been shot while a French professor on a lecture tour is staying in his house. The characters are all lined up for our inspection, the visiting professor, the wife, the sister-in-law, the neighbours; one of them must be capable of the crime—which? The emphasis with Simenon is always on the psychological problem. Murders are committed, not because people have the physical ability or opportunity to kill each other, but because somebody has been able to work himself or herself up to killing point. The role of Maigret, and of the reader, is to size up the characters until one fits; but, with the pieces so well cut, one must have a jig-saw eye to manage it at the first attempt.

The second story in ***Maigret Abroad*** runs on different lines and shows that Simenon is heading for an eventual destination far removed from detection. The scene is Liège, where a rich Greek is murdered; the characters are no longer presented gratis by the author but begin to present themselves; and not till halfway through does Maigret figure in person. One gains the impression that the Maigret mechanism of evolving character is being discarded for more direct introspection. The result is not detection, but a crime novel; and even crimes will soon become superfluous, for the author's evident intention is to delineate, with as deft a touch as Proust's, the inflexible threads of destiny on which are strung all the vagaries and ambiguities of the human soul. Maigret is doomed to extinction, but European literature will profit by his demise. (p. 680)

Ralph Partridge, "The Progress of Simenon," in The New Statesman & Nation, *Vol. XIX, No. 483, May 25, 1940, pp. 678, 680.*

THE TIMES LITERARY SUPPLEMENT

Whether M. Simenon's work should be classed as crime fiction starts a hopeless argument. Maigret is a detective and he is engaged on baffling murder mysteries. This will satisfy the specialized public that reads in order to be puzzled. On the other hand it may scare the public that has no wish to be puzzled. As long as Maigret keeps his author under the heading of "Detective Stories" many people may not know how high M. Simenon ranks among writers of stories undivided by class.

Another difficulty is that the Maigret cases are too long to be tales and too short to be novels. There are a pair of them under this title of ***Maigret Keeps a Rendez-vous.*** The first, a quiet, almost casual, inquiry into the last voyage of a skipper in a fishing fleet, reveals M. Simenon's mastery in the drawing of scenes and characters. Crime is not to him a species of fiction. He begins, as a rule, by distinguishing in a vaguely ominous atmosphere the stray scents that form an aftermath. Then, working backwards, he discerns the first signs of the ominous at an earlier date when the thought of the murder first clouded a man's brain. A trawler, back in port while townspeople are taking their summer holiday, is inspected by Maigret for traces of the skipper's death when he was about to step ashore. There is a hint of something sinister in the queer behaviour of the man who has been arrested; the secret he keeps begins to trouble everybody. Before Maigret has finished, the reader almost has the feel of a fishing voyage in his bones. The second story, though less gripping, also evokes the past of the people and the place Maigret examines.

"Detective Stories," in The Times Literary Supplement, *No. 2028, December 14, 1940, p. 632.*

JOHN PEALE BISHOP

In the old days in Paris there was a friend of mine who could not sleep without reading for an hour or so. Often at night he would come back alone to his apartment to find there nothing he had not already read and would go out again in search of a book, whose print could be put between him and the day's disquiet, any book, to distract his mind so that he could sleep. Now the only places in Paris where books could be bought at a late hour were the railroad stations. One night, in the dimly lit stall of the Gare Saint-Lazare, on the shelf of *romans policiers* in their lurid covers, he came on a book by Georges Simenon. He went off with ***Monsieur Gallet, Décedé*** and the next night found ***Le Pendu de Saint-Pholien;*** a month later there was a third, for it was at intervals of one month that the volumes devoted to the adventures of Maigret appeared. It was at this point that he passed the books on to me, with the enthusiastic announcement that there had been nothing so original in detective fiction since Sherlock Holmes was carried to the immortals in a hansom cab.

I must say that it took more than one volume to overcome my distrust. I am no great reader of detective tales, but even I knew that in France they belong to the lower depths of literature. Nothing lower was allowed to be sold in the railroad stations. And yet, Simenon's originality was at once obvious to me, and it was not long before I discovered that he was a serious writer, serious in a way that Conan Doyle could never have dreamed of being.

To be sure, his detective is not startlingly original. Simenon, when he made him, might have gone round to the Quai des Orfèvres and taken the first member of the Police Judiciaire he happened to run into as model. Outwardly, there is nothing much to distinguish Maigret from any professional detective under the Third Republic. He smokes a pipe and drinks a fair amount of beer. He lives, appropriately enough, in the République quarter with an Alsatian wife, who, as one might expect of a good housewife from that region, makes excellent *quiches*. Maigret is trustworthy. He is a heavy-set man; but more important is the impression he gives—to use words which Simenon applies not to him, but to another character—"of a sort of stability, both phsyical and moral, that is positively staggering." His nerves are sensitive as they must be, but sound; he is sure of his skill, and only rarely is his self-assurance exaggerated. About all that Simenon has done to turn a professional detective into Maigret is to make him into a decent man. He is a capable paid servant of the Third Republic. But there are times when he seems much more than that, when, with his comprehending pity and his patience in applying power, Maigret comes close to being what was best, what was most human, in the Third Republic.

Simenon's originality consists in this, that, in the thirty volumes which he has written about the adventures of Maigret, he has created a form of detective fiction into which real characters can enter. For if his detective is convincing, his criminals are credible. They are the same small people who used to be reported in the *faits divers* of the Paris newspapers, as having run foul of the police. They are those provincials whose crimes were ignored in Paris save by the police. In Simenon's novels they are simply brought closer and made comprehensible. Their crimes, most of them, arise out of the sordidness of living and are only remotely provoked by passion. They may have come about—and this is the most frequent situation—through the necessity to shore up some small threatened position, some meager and dismal security, too hardly won to be let go for a scruple. In ***The Flemish Shop,*** which is one of the two stories [included in ***Maigret to the Rescue***], murder is committed to prevent the son of the house from compromising his future by marriage to a factory girl, whom he loves just enough to have got her with child. In ***The "Guinguette" by the Seine,*** the other story, crime occurs as the result of an escapade which, as it turned out, was not the escape it promised to be from the inexorable dullness of existence on a thousand francs a month. Simenon's are almost always middle-class crimes.

French literature has always been more conscious of its own conventions than any other literature. The story goes that Georges Simenon began by writing four straight novels and, only when he was convinced that these were failures, turned to the detective novel. But having done so, he is nothing if not scrupulous in observing its conventions. He does not, as so many British and American writers of detective stories do when they get a little above themselves, mix his *genres*. As long as Simenon holds to Maigret, he continues to write *romans policiers,* and now that he has dropped his policeman, he still holds to that most valuable literary convention of the detective story—that is, the story itself, which, simply because they considered it to be a literary convention, was discarded by most serious French writers of fiction after Maupassant. (p. 345)

Simenon begins by reminding us, both in his gifts and his limitations, of Maupassant. When he tells a story, it is done with a conscious skill and at the same time it seems to have been prompted by some inner compulsion, as though to tell stories were a necessary activity of his being. His characters have until recently been created like those of Maupassant from outside; but they belong not to a France which had just known the Franco-Prussian War, but to a France between two wars, between a defeat of the Germans and a defeat by the Germans. And the air they breathe is alive with an immense disquietude, which increases as Simenon goes on, until in the latest of his novels to reach this country, ***Malempin,*** which was printed just ten days before the Germans invaded his country, the atmosphere is heavy with helplessness and tense with dread. It is a simple little story, but as sinister in its implications as anything ever written by Julian Green. War is not mentioned, and I cannot remember much mention of politics in Simenon. Yet the position of the people in his novels is, in a small way, the position of France in the world. They are trying, as France was between Versailles and Munich, to maintain a situation beyond their means. To outward appearance they are sound, but as I reread Simenon it seems to me that it is not altogether because the detective story demands such devices that the outward show of his characters is so deceiving. (pp. 345-46)

John Peale Bishop, "Georges Simenon," in The New Republic, *Vol. 104, No. 10, March 10, 1941, pp. 345-46.*

JOHN FAIRFIELD

Of the two new Maigret stories [included in ***Maigret Sits It Out***] it is difficult to speak. [Simenon] has almost dropped the police side of the Inspector's work, and the first story [***The Lock at Charenton***] in particular is a sustained cry of doubt about the law and the working of justice. The Man of Instinct kills, an aged bargee appears in the garments of Primitive Law to claim the blood-price, and Maigret as the agent of Roman-Mosaic Law appears to lift the scales of justice in trembling hands and to protect and destroy his quarry. It is a harrowing exhibition of the post-Freudian dilemma and the paralysis of the will that comes of examining the roots of action too deeply. The doubt and agony of the first story is underlined by the second [***Maigret Returns***], in which Maigret runs down a murderer after his retirement with the aid of an unregistered prostitute and various ratting members of a white-slave-cum-dope gang. Here everyone is outside the law. Maigret has no legal status, and the hares and hounds circle among each other and swap identity now and again. The regular police work against an innocent man, a member of their own organisation, the criminal is a police-informer and head of a gang simultaneously. There is no mercy, and justice is served by kicking holes in the law and acting with greater ruthlessness than the criminals. It is a little disturbing in its intensity, as if one found a man afraid to go out for fear of slipping between the molecules of the road-surface into the bowels of the earth. Simenon seems to be in the depressing circumstances of a Manichean who yet does not believe that man is capable of turning towards the light, much less of fighting his way back to it. But the connexion of Manicheanism and detective stories is scarcely germane to the matter of making out library-lists. (p. 640)

John Fairfield, "Murder Everywhere," in The Spectator, *Vol. 166, No. 5894, June 13, 1941, pp. 638, 640.*

JOHN FAIRFIELD

[***Maigret and M. Labbé***] is made up of a very good Maigret story [***The Man from Everywhere***] yoked to an extremely bad story [***Death of a Harbour Master***] about a retired master criminal whose patent absurdity drags the affair into the Sexton Blake class. Maigret's little problem is set in one of those misty northern ports of which his creator is so fond and his technique of solution by attrition is the same as ever; he has also apparently regained his official status and the retirement of ***Maigret Sits It Out*** has lapsed without leaving a trace behind. Attractive as the people and the scenery are, however, the story ends with a group of resounding improbabilities unusual in Simenon and of a somewhat disturbing character. Maigret has in the past suffered from considerable doubt about the laws he has had to enforce, but he has not hitherto kicked them about for sentimental reasons. Any reader of ***Death of a Harbour Master*** who has had any little difficulty in France and has come into contact with the law and the police will find the conclusion of the book an affair of farce. The murderer has committed suicide and to clear his good name Maigret delivers himself of the following remark:

> I wonder now . . . ? We might say that the crime was the work of some foreign sailor with a grudge against the Captain. And that he's gone back to his own country. I'll think it over.

It is unlike Maigret to suggest putting up such fluff for the *Juge d'Instruction* to blow upon, and it is very unlike a member of the *Sûreté* to use the phrase "Good Fellows All" when referring to a crowd of extremely obstructive witnesses whose reticence has been responsible for a very great deal of trouble. Maigret is becoming a cosy sentimental figure. (p. 338)

John Fairfield, "Six Crimes," in The Spectator, *Vol. 167, No. 5910, October 3, 1941, pp. 338, 340.*

CHARLES J. ROLO

[*The essay excerpted below was originally published in the magazine* New World Writing *in 1952.*]

In addition to pleasing [millions of readers], Simenon has been highly praised by exacting judges—not merely as a superior confectioner of mysteries but as a literary artist. André Gide has described him as "the most novelistic novelist in French literature today"; and a leading British critic, Raymond Mortimer, says: "I suspect Simenon to be among the most gifted novelists now alive."

Simenon has said that thanks to mass communications—the press and radio, photography, the movies, and now television—the reader's horizon has been so enormously enlarged that elaborate documentation no longer has any place in the novel; the novelist should be able to suggest a setting, evoke an atmosphere, in a few swift strokes. The time has therefore come, Simenon believes, to try to write what he calls *"le roman pur"*—the quintessential novel—which should do for our time what was done by the tragedies of ancient Greece. Starting at the moment of decisive crisis, it should pose the problem of man's destiny; should give an accounting of a man's life. Simenon was attracted to the murder mystery because it offers a convenient way of doing just this in terms of the murderer, the detective serving as an explanatory prop akin to the Chorus in Greek tragedy.

In working his way toward the *roman pur* via detective fiction, Simenon brought a crucial innovation to the whodunit. He made it an exploration of personality—a quest whose goal is not so much punishment of the crime as understanding of the criminal; a mystery whose solution unravels not so much a tangled skein of events as a tangled skein of motives. In Simenon's hands, the whodunit is essentially a whydunit.

Though the detective story leaves no room for portraiture-in-depth, Simenon's sharply sketched characters are living, three-dimensional individuals. His décor, achieved with masterly economy, is marvelously authentic. His plots seldom contain anything far-fetched.

It is impossible to categorize the world of Maigret because it is the real world—Paris, the provincial towns of France, the Riviera—and the crimes in it are committed by ordinary people deranged by jealousy, or ambition, or greed, or to cover up some scandal which threatens them with ruin. Maigret himself, in his habits and appearance, is a typical French *bourgeois,* married to a *bonne bourgeoise* who tries, vainly, to make him cut down his incessant pipe-smoking, and who knows better than any chef how to prepare her husband's favorite dishes—creamed cod and *créme au citron*. Always clad in a black suit and a derby, Maigret is a quiet, unexcitable man, who detests hurry; a stolid, peaceable figure who might be a schoolmaster or a country doctor.

Maigret has little interest in fingerprints, footprints, alibis, how the murderer entered and how he got away, in most of the data which are the foundation of the conventional whodunit. Sometimes he doesn't even give the corpse itself more than a casual glance. In one sense, Maigret is the least realistic of Simenon's characters; he will hardly pass, under rigorous scrutiny, as an Inspector of the Paris Police Judiciare—he simply doesn't know his job. He is very real, however, as a man, a man of deep humanity, with a profound insight into people.

Maigret's compass is not the logic of events but the logic of passions. The clues he follows are looks, words, gestures. He works through his feelings, his intuition, his knowledge of men. He tries, and the reader tries with him, to grope his way toward the psychological crisis which provoked the murder. The disclosure of the truth, with its revelation of the dire pressures that shape human conduct, usually brings a measure of sympathy for the criminal, a kind of absolution. The leitmotif of Simenon's work is: "It is a difficult job to be a man." (pp. 172-73)

The answers in Simenon's books always penetrate to the deepest recesses of the unconscious and they are never glib or patly presented. Simenon is too much of "a natural"—a born storyteller and a magnificent creator of character—to write clinical case histories. A comment he made on the work of another writer admirably conveys the flavor of his own work: "There is no psychologizing, and yet every personage has a private life which is his own and his alone. There is no sound and fury, no striving for the picturesque, but always the people having the universe glued to their skin."

Like the psychoanalyst, Simenon does not condemn. Nothing shocks him, for he believes that between the cruelest murder and the most decent citizen there lies but the turn of a screw in the psyche. The catharsis his climaxes provide lies in the revelation that human beings are not evil but merely human. (p. 174)

Charles J. Rolo, "Simenon and Spillane: The Metaphysics of Murder for the Millions," in Mass Culture: The Popular Arts in America, *edited by Bernard Rosenberg and David Manning White, The Free Press, 1957, pp. 165-75.*

ANTHONY BOUCHER

Any list of the world's greatest fictional detectives must perforce include Georges Simenon's patient, shrewd, stolid yet sensitive Commissaire Jules Maigret (who is regularly demoted in English to inspector, a lowly rank in the French police force). I doubt if anyone knows how many Maigret stories exist. . . .

Only a handful of these stories have been vouchsafed to Americans. . . . [Since the early 1940s] Maigret has been as absent from publishers' lists as he has been present in all serious critical discussion of the *roman policier*.

Now at last the Crime Club has undertaken to reintroduce Maigret to American readers with ***No Vacation for Maigret,*** and one hopes that reader response will insure a regular flow of novels to catch up with past neglect. This one presents Maigret in an unofficial role—bored with a vacation on which his wife gets appendicitis, curious about an oddity in the hospital—and so gradually uncovering a series of murders and preventing several more. As I've often observed in reviewing Simenon's more ambitious "straight" novels, these criminal episodes are at least their equal in texture and sensitivity; this one is masterly in its economic evocation of a seaside town, a provincial society, a nursing order—and as always superb in the interplay between Maigret and the murderer, with one of the finest of Simenon's individually subtle climactic scenes *à deux*.

Anthony Boucher, in a review of "No Vacation for Maigret," in The New York Times Book Review, *October 11, 1953, p. 34.*

ANTHONY BOUCHER

Georges Simenon usually presents a portrait of a murderer comparable to the reports of fact-crime; but in ***Maigret au 'Picratt's,'*** translated as ***Inspector Maigret and the Strangled Stripper,*** he keeps the killer entirely offstage until the dénouement. You're unlikely to find any other source of disappointment in this atmospheric study of Montmartre, with its well-characterized victims, its adroitly handled sub-plot of a young policeman tragically in love, and its minutely observed picture of a dive as memorable as any since Simenon's ***Liberty Bar.***

Anthony Boucher, in a review of "Inspector Maigret and the Strangled Stripper," in The New York Times Book Review, *July 11, 1954, p. 10.*

ANTHONY BOUCHER

In ***Inspector Maigret and the Killers,*** Georges Simenon imports American crime to Paris, where gangsters from St. Louis ride roughshod over French law. The book starts off amusingly with the woes of Lognon, the policeman with delusions of inferiority and persecution, but winds up as a lesser entry in the Maigret canon, chiefly because the inspector has little to do with action or solution.

Anthony Boucher, in a review of "Inspector Maigret and the Killers," in The New York Times Book Review, *November 28, 1954, p. 42.*

RALPH PARTRIDGE

Maigret, the leading exponent of the long, deep look, is faced with unpromising material when an unknown girl is found with her head bashed in on a pavement in Montmartre. As there is no one else to look at, Maigret concentrates his gaze on the girl, unravels her past, and deduces the only possible reason for killing her. ***Maigret and the Young Girl*** is not vintage Simenon but a palatable *vin ordinaire;* only readers must be warned that there is no more than a tumblerful, which will not slake their thirst for detection for more than a couple of hours at most. (pp. 194-95)

Ralph Partridge, "Detection and Crime," in The New Statesman & Nation, *Vol. L, No. 1275, August 13, 1955, pp. 194-95.*

ANTHONY BOUCHER

The detectives of fiction's Scotland Yard have had some peculiar assignments, but few odder than that of Inspector Pyke, who, in the latest Simenon novel, is sent to France to study ***The Methods of Maigret.***

Now the methods of Maigret, as all students know, resemble the activities of the dog in the night-time in being non-existent; but the worthy Pyke has no cause to regret a job that takes him to the island of Porquerolles. There in the south of France, where the Parisian is as much a foreigner as the Englishman, the two detectives observe a curious assortment of types, relish some fine meridional eating and drinking, enjoy the beachcombing lassitude of the Mediterranean and finally capture a murderer by dint of that patience which is the only observable method of Maigret. Richly evocative in its depiction of a place and a way of life, quietly humorous in its interplay of two police systems, the short novel is reminiscent of some of the best early-Maigret episodes of the Nineteen Thirties.

Anthony Boucher, in a review of "The Methods of Maigret," in The New York Times Book Review, *January 27, 1957, p. 35.*

JAMES SANDOE

By one chance and another Maigret and Mme. Maigret are vacationing in Paris in August when the murder of the doctor's wife occurs. So that it becomes ambitious Inspector Janvier's case and ***None of Maigret's Business,*** Georges Simenon lets him view it as a reader of daily newspapers striving to put aside his professional temptation to interfere.

Maigret has been with us a good many years and is soundly wound in our affections. His cases are never stated or remembered in primary colors and a good many of them have been gray. This one is done charmingly in pastels and is one of the more delightful.

James Sandoe, in a review of "None of Maigret's Business," in New York Herald Tribune Book Review, *May 11, 1958, p. 36.*

JAMES SANDOE

Maigret at Christmas, Maigret remembering his country boyhood, Maigret considering the quandary of "Stan the Killer" and the curious death of the Old Lady of Bayeaux are among the five rich, long ***Short Cases of Inspector Maigret*** . . . and comprising our first assembly of Simenon's shorter tales. Within his handsome economy Simenon finds space for a puzzle and for a wonderfully keen evocation of milieu. It is an admirable and memorable assembly, gathered from the pages of *Ellery Queen's Mystery Magazine,* that persisting storehouse of most of the best in mystery, crime and detection.

James Sandoe, in a review of "The Short Cases of Inspector Maigret," in New York Herald Tribune Book Review, *July 19, 1959, p. 11.*

THE TIMES LITERARY SUPPLEMENT

Paris, like London, is a city of villages. "Some people's universe", says M. Simenon in ***Maigret Takes a Room,*** "consists only of a few streets." When one of his assistants is shot while watching outside a boarding-house, Chief Inspector Maigret takes up temporary residence there and straightway finds himself in a village-within-a-city. He learns the habits of each of his fellow-lodgers, observes the comings and goings of the houses opposite, takes his meals in the little café down the street.

What started as a simple search for a young gunman soon turns into quite another case. Maigret, solid, pipe-smoking, infinitely compassionate, plods on until at last he makes an arrest which saddens rather than satisfies him. This is Simenon at his best, moving with the confidence of an old professional across familiar ground; the writing tight-packed, the plot exactly controlled, the Parisian atmosphere created with a few deft strokes.

"Dons at Play," in The Times Literary Supplement, *No. 3065, November 25, 1960, p. 762.*

JAY JACOBS

Originally, Simenon appears to have been about as trashy a novelist as any ever enjoyed by a serving-maid from the provinces. And this is what I considered him awhile back. In his early years, he banged out as many as eighty pages a night under a variety of pseudonyms (ranging from Georges Sim to Gom Gut) and a flood of books that included such provocative titles as ***Captain S.O.S., Le Sang des Gitanes, Le Gorille Roi, Hélas, Je T'aime!,*** and ***Les Pirates du Texas.*** But his youthful indiscretions and a good many later potboilers notwithstanding, Simenon is essentially a fine novelist. He has been taken with the utmost seriousness by a number of literary mandarins in Europe—notably by Gide, whose copies of Simenon's books were so heavily annotated that they were, in Simenon's words, "almost more Gide than Simenon." (p. 38)

The exigencies of Simenon's early working schedule were of incalculable value in developing an almost telegraphic brevity, a narrative pace of extreme rapidity, and a clean, stripped-down style. He published his first book—written in ten days—at seventeen, and for some time afterwards was under contract to write a novel a month, plus a short story each week. Working at that rate, though sacrificing none of the perquisites of the young man about town, he had no time for nonessential description, convoluted syntax, or ornamental turns of phrase.

From the start, Simenon regarded his hackwork as a lucrative apprenticeship. The ultimate aim was always the serious novel, and around the end of the 1920's he worked tentatively in that direction. Inspector Maigret made his first appearances in 1931 (***Maigret Stonewalled*** and ***Maigret and the Hundred Gibbets*** . . .); and while his debut was auspicious mostly in retrospect, one casual assertion—"I shall know the murderer when I know the victim well"—marked what was to become a revolutionary departure from the prevailing concepts of detective fiction. The devious plot, the bizarre twist, the fortuitous clue were to have little place in the Maigret books. . . . Instead, while his colleagues busy themselves to little purpose with fingerprints, ballistics, and chemical analyses, Maigret bibs the local *blanc,* gossips with concierges and *garçons du café,* observes the state of the weather, or languidly looks on at a game of *belote.* His "clues" are a gradually developing awareness of the pressures, exerted by a particular ambience, that drive an ordinary human being like himself to an extraordinary act.

The early Maigret books were conceived as a bridge between the cheap popular romances, written *"pour gagner ma vie,"* and the serious efforts for which he did not yet consider himself ready. In ***Maigret's Memoirs,*** an ingenious apologia written some twenty years after the first Maigret volumes, the roles of author and protagonist ostensibly are reversed, and the detective "recalls" an exchange in which the young Simenon is described as thinking this time not of a popular series but of what he calls . . . "what do you call it, Monsieu Sim?" "Semi-literature," Simenon answers.

The Maigret books were an immediate popular success in Europe and Britain. Moreover, they are so novelistic in their treatment and so far removed, both in degree and kind, from the mindless jigsaw-puzzle escapism of most whodunits that they have attracted a devoted and highly literate group of readers to whom the "detective story" ordinarily is anathema. In the best of the Maigrets, ***A Battle of Nerves,*** for example, the offender is not simply motivated, but driven, as relentlessly as a Raskolnikov, and what ensues is not a chase so much as a dialogue held on common ground.

In a discussion of his more serious efforts . . . Simenon remarks: ". . . I try to make each one of those characters heavy, like a statue, and to be the brother of everybody in the world." And while he denies the possibility of achieving "the weight that a stroke of Cézanne's gave to an apple" in the Maigret novels, weight—or presence, if you will—*is* there. And, given the limitations of the form, Maigret himself is something very like a brother to everyone in the world, including his adversaries. (pp. 38-9)

In most of the Maigret books, the conventional good-guy-bad-guy alignment is replaced by a colloquy that often ends not with triumph and defeat but with mutual relief, leaving Maigret somewhat wistful and the transgressor in a state of near-exaltation. The judicial processes to follow can only be anticlimactic. . . .

In one of his rare prefaces (to ***No Vacation for Maigret***), Simenon wrote in 1953: "When, twenty-four years ago . . . I created Inspector Maigret, I certainly did not foresee that he would one day acquire, so to speak, a life of his own that would even, at times, overshadow mine." In spite of the affection the author goes on to profess for his character (an affection somewhat grudgingly returned in the ***Memoirs***), a curious sort of rivalry, almost like that between a ventriloquist and his puppet, is evident in their relationship. In the [discussion of his works quoted above], for example, Simenon dismisses the Maigret novels from serious consideration, saying: "Maigret can't go inside a character. He will see, explain, and understand; but he does not give the character the weight the character should have in another of my novels." . . .

Maigret's much-misunderstood "methods," however, are nothing but a novelist's attempt to give "weight" to the character he is describing. Essentially, Maigret is no policeman at all, but the author-reader of his own novels, who must flesh out his characters before he can possibly apprehend them. . . .

The methods of Maigret, in other words, are the methods of Conrad (whose influence on the "serious" novels is apparent): "My task is . . . to make you hear, to make you feel—it is, before all, to make you *see*." (p. 39)

Jay Jacobs, "Simenon's Mosaic," in The Reporter, *Vol. 32, No. 1, January 14, 1965, pp. 38-40.*

RICHARD MAYNE

[There's] surely a fascination about this somnambulistic Ancient Mariner from the narrows between novels and detective stories, fixing us time after time with his riveting stare. His secret, I suspect, is the intensity of his own imagination: it doesn't extend to complexity or even, in some cases, credibility of plot. Often, there's no more real mystery than in a newspaper crime story; and yet we read on, absorbed. ***Maigret Loses His Temper*** is a good routine Maigret with some evocative scenes of hot summer Paris and a weekend fishing pub; ***The Blue Room*** is the story of what might be called, aping a current French news item, *'les amants diaboliques'*. (p. 367)

Richard Mayne, "Top Ten," in New Statesman, *Vol. LXIX, No. 1773, March 5, 1965, pp. 366-67.*

ANTHONY BOUCHER

The first case of Jules Amédée François Maigret appears as one of five entries in Simenon's ***Maigret Cinq***. This is far from a first-published case (although now first published in this country): it is Simenon in 1948 going back to describe the first solo investigation of the 26-year-old Maigret in 1913—a complicated affair among coffee tycoons in which the young policeman learned, bitterly, that truth can weigh less, in the scales of the blind goddess, than the status of the individuals involved. It's a lovely story, beautifully evocative of Paris before World War I and full of nice touches on Maigret as a young man (and Mme. Maigret as a bride).

This grand omnibus also contains the first appearance of ***Maigret and the Old Lady,*** a Grade-A Maigret set in Etretat, richly evocative (the word one keeps using for Simenon) of a Norman seacoast town, with a fine subtle relationship between the detective and the titular old lady (whose sleeping-potion has been poisoned). The other entries have been seen here before under other titles: ***Maigret and the Young Girl*** (***Inspector Maigret and the Dead Girl,*** 1955), ***Maigret Takes a Room*** (***Maigret Rents a Room,*** 1961), and ***Maigret's Little Joke*** (***None of Maigret's Business,*** 1958). All the repeated stories are worth rereading, especially the last, one of the delights of the Maigret canon.

Anthony Boucher, in a review of "Maigret Cinq," in The New York Times Book Review, *June 20, 1965, p. 25.*

ALLEN J. HUBIN

Georges Simenon's Chief Inspector Maigret belongs to the Paris of today as surely as Holmes did to gaslit London. In ***Maigret's Pickpocket,*** he suffers the indignity of having his wallet lifted by an amateur. This brings him into contact with François Ricain, an aspiring but vastly unsuccessful writer, who came home to find his wife shot to death. Maigret pursues her killer in his characteristic fashion. He worries the case like a dog with a favorite bone; he roams among the people involved like an amiable but purposeful agent of vengeance; he asks endless and seemingly irrelevant questions as he peers behind well-established facades. In the end, a clever murderer almost trips him up. It's good, quietly entertaining Simenon.

Allen J. Hubin, in a review of "Maigret's Pickpocket," in The New York Times Book Review, *August 18, 1968, p. 20.*

JAMES FENTON

[***Maigret and the Minister***] takes the inspector much against his will into the world of high politics and big business. A government minister is being framed by a colleague and the newspapers are determined to bring the crisis and scandal to a peak. With the scantiest knowledge of the workings of politics and very little evidence to go on, Maigret not only has to pit his wits against the big men but also has to put up with his detectives being preceded everywhere by men from Security. We are granted no triumphant conclusion, but the scope of the case makes for exceptionally good and exciting reading.

James Fenton, "Simple & Classic," in New Statesman, *Vol. 78, No. 2014, October 17, 1969, p. 542.*

THE NEW YORKER

[In ***Maigret and the Calame Report***], Superintendent Maigret, of the Paris police, goes dangerously far out on a limb in an attempt to save the good name of a Cabinet Minister who is about to be destroyed by a vindictive power maniac in the Chamber of Deputies. The Minister is a man of integrity and simplicity, and Maigret searches out his persecutor with an implacable determination that has in it not one trace of the pity or the reluctant, half-irritable sympathy he usually gives to those who break the law. This subtle story, vibrating with tension from its sinister beginning to its positive and satisfactory ending, shows Simenon writing at his best. It is a very, very good book.

A review of "Maigret and the Calame Report," in The New Yorker, *Vol. XLV, No. 48, January 17, 1970, p. 84.*

A. L. ROSENZWEIG

Georges Simenon has taken another look at the past through the eyes of stolid old Maigret. It is called ***Maigret's Boyhood Friend,*** and that sort of title, you had better believe, sells only to the faithful. Maigret's friend has come to report the murder of his mistress; or, more accurately, the mistress of four men. The deceased was one of those interesting women (now almost extinct) who lived virtuously in sin. The friend is a shabby fraud living on the edge of things, as well as a compulsive liar who embarrasses Maigret by his presence. Simenon seems more than ever a historian of disappearing times. The boyhood friend is a useful vehicle to explore the solid dead days of provincial France. The plot, as always, is rather simple, and ancillary to the revelations of time and place which remain, in Simenon's hands, subtle and pervasive.

A. L. Rosenzweig, in a review of "Maigret's Boyhood Friend," in Book World—The Washington Post, *September 27, 1970, p. 2.*

NEWGATE CALLENDAR

A wealthy wine merchant is shot down [in ***Maigret and the Wine Merchant***]. His wife takes the news with complete unsurprise and a shrug of the shoulders. His business associates discuss him as some sort of artifact, coolly, unemotionally. His mistresses neither liked nor disliked him. Eventually the murderer comes into Maigret's sight. No heroics, no great intellectual feats of deduction, very little action—and yet a story of human beings, with a sad, ineffectual murderer. A typical Simenon job, in short, this story about a bourgeois murder in a bourgeois Paris, solved by a bourgeois policeman with a running nose and infinite sympathy for his fellow man.

Newgate Callendar, in a review of "Maigret and the Wine Merchant," in The New York Times Book Review, *August 8, 1971, p. 23.*

***THE CRITIC,* CHICAGO**

The Common Market prosperity has caught up with Superintendent Maigret [in ***Maigret and the Killer***]. He owns a car, though he is afraid to drive it and even the redoubtable Mme. Maigret is quite tense at the wheel. He is a TV addict, enjoying particularly Gary Cooper Westerns. He even has a weekend home at Meung-sur-Loire where he fishes (skillfully) and plays cards with the locals (unskillfully). Despite the fact that he is sixty-three he recently received a new lease on life professionally when the retirement age was changed from 65 to 68.

But while Maigret is doing well in his golden years he is still the same man he always was. Janvier, Lucas, and Lapointe are still with him. He still has the same office on the Quai des Orfevres. . . . He still deals with events that occur on streets like the Rue Popincourt, the Quai de Bethune, the Rue St. Louis-en-Isle, and the Place de la Bastille. And of course he still lives with Mme. Maigret on the Boulevard Richard-Lenoir.

The story in this latest Maigret? It is completely unimportant: Maigret persuades a mentally deranged killer to give himself up, mostly by listening to him on the telephone. You read one Maigret, you've read them all. But that doesn't mean that we won't eagerly await the appearance of the next one—and hope that Mme. Maigret doesn't pile the two of them up on one of their weekly pilgrimages to Meung-sur-Loire.

A review of "Maigret and the Killer," in The Critic, *Chicago, Vol. 30, No. 3, January-February, 1972, p. 90.*

JOHN R. COYNE, JR.

No one ever worries about suspense in a Simenon novel. There isn't any, and [***Maigret Sets a Trap***] is no exception. The plot is standard Jack the Ripper. A loon prowls Montmartre, slicing up the young ladies he meets. Maigret does some of his simple-minded psychologizing, sets up a simple-minded trap, and then proceeds to lull us to sleep by displaying for us the incredibly mundane little components of his simple little mind.

For one of the very few times in my life, I find myself in total agreement with Jacques Barzun and Wendell Taylor, who say of Maigret in their comprehensive *Catalogue of Crime*. . . . "[What readers of Maigret] enjoy is his boredom, fatigue, wet feet and hunger—all skilfully interwoven with his shrewd speculations as he looks across the road from behind the curtain in a tavern—ideal fiction for a born member of a Watch and Ward society."

If you want suspense, read [Robert] O'Brien and [Michael] Crichton. If you want a sure cure for insomnia, try Simenon. (p. 701)

John R. Coyne, Jr., "Suspense and Insomnia," in National Review, *New York, Vol. XXIV, No. 24, June 23, 1972, pp. 700-01.*

MAURICE RICHARDSON

The Flea [of ***Maigret and the Flea***] is the nickname of a well-known Montmartre character—a ponce of course—who tips Maigret off about the shooting of a restaurant proprietor who is also a planner of large-scale robberies. His young wife and two gangster brothers, one of them her lover, are all heavily suspect from the start. A bit slapdash and timeless as to background but brisk and readable enough.

Maurice Richardson, in a review of "Maigret and the Flea," in The Observer, *October 1, 1972, p. 40.*

MAURICE RICHARDSON

Recent Maigrets, as compared with the pre-war classics such as ***Liberty Bar*** and ***A Battle of Nerves,*** have been rather stereotyped with their settings not seeming to belong to any specified period. ***Maigret and Monsieur Charles*** is a case in point. Yet it has plenty of the familiar compulsion. The victim, a successful solicitor with a double life in which he is addicted to nightclub hostesses, is fished out of the Seine, shot. His wife is a hopeless alcoholic who was once one of his pickups, and has retained a connection with the underworld. She manages to be just enigmatic enough to keep Maigret and the reader panting along in her wake.

Maurice Richardson, "Valedictory Simenon," in The Observer, *June 3, 1973, p. 37.*

NEWGATE CALLENDAR

Georges Simenon, it was recently announced, has stopped writing. One of the most prolific authors in history, he has reached the age of 70 and is calling it quits. Maigret addicts need not despair for a while: any number of Maigrets are awaiting translation. The most recent to be published in America is ***Maigret and the Bum***. . . .

[In this novel, a] bum is fished out of the Seine, barely alive. He turns out to be an ex-doctor, an intellectual. Revived in the hospital, he won't talk. Maigret, fascinated by the contrast between the victim's past and present, plods here and there, asking questions. Little by little, things come out. All this is prime Simenon—quiet, slow-moving, yet filled with constant tension. The ending, too, is prime Simenon. It leaves a lot unsaid. (pp. 78-9)

Newgate Callendar, in a review of "Maigret and the Bum," in The New York Times Book Review, *November 4, 1973, pp. 78-9.*

MAURICE RICHARDSON

Ambitious embittered Lognon disappears for two days and two American-Italian gangsters search his flat [in ***Maigret and the Gangsters.***] When he reappears with a story of a disappearing corpse Maigret handles him with benevolent tact before concentrating on rounding up the gangsters to the tune of dire muttered threats from pimps and pushers. Written in 1952 soon after Simenon settled in America, and rather far from his par.

Maurice Richardson, in a review of "Maigret and the Gangsters," in The Observer, *September 22, 1974, p. 29.*

NEWGATE CALLENDAR

Maigret is always with us. In Georges Simenon's ***Maigret and the Millionaires,*** originally written in 1958, the famous French detective moves in a world of high society and big money, but he is uncomfortable; this is not his normal milieu. On his agenda is a multi-millionaire murdered in the great hotel George V. There is a flighty countess, and Maigret has to chase her from Paris to Monte Carlo to Lausanne. This is not one of the better Maigret books; it is a bit perfunctory and the solution is, for Simenon, altogether stagy. One can understand this; it is impossible for any writer to turn out as much as Simenon does and have every book a winner. Yet his standard is so high that even a slight lapse seems magnified.

Newgate Callendar, in a review of "Maigret and the Millionaires," in The New York Times Book Review, *November 24, 1974, p. 39.*

THE NEW YORKER

In noting a disappointing Simenon a few weeks ago, we predicted that a better one was probably making its way toward us. This delightful and deeply nostalgic Maigret [***Maigret and the Loner***], set chiefly in Montmartre, keeps the Chief Superintendent staring gloomily into his beer foam until the last possible moment as he attempts to find out who murdered an elegantly barbered old tramp in a building near Les Halles. With the help of the usual satisfyingly seedy hoteliers, sweaty detectives, cynical workingmen, and vindictive servants, he discovers that the man left his wife and daughter for another woman twenty years ago, then disappeared. But there he gets stuck, and he has to try to reconstruct the dead man's life. This enables Simenon, of course (one feels it is half the reason for the book), to recapture the France that the French have taken away from him: the country of intimate neighborhoods, open-platform buses, long, hearty lunches, and, above all, Les Halles when, as Simenon says with an almost audible sigh, it "had not yet been transferred." (pp. 139-40)

A review of "Maigret and the Loner," in The New Yorker, *Vol. LI, No. 7, April 7, 1975, pp. 139-40.*

ANATOLE BROYARD

Some of the better new writers in [the crime and detective] genre make Georges Simenon's mysteries seem rather unadventurous—and the more I read them the more I begin to suspect that they actually are. I don't mean adventurous in the sense of derring-do, but of breaking away from the old formulas, developing three-dimensional characters, writing an occasional sentence that may in itself be risky, muscling in on the topical, being guilty of a few mischievous literary misdemeanors himself.

In his way, Mr. Simenon is as pure, formal or classical as Racine—only I'm afraid one may need grandeur to carry off that kind of classicism. A few years ago, I described the author of ***Maigret and the Man on the Bench*** as the Zola or Balzac of suspense, but it seems to me now that his books would have to teem with more life, provide a denser ambiance, come closer to the *zeitgeist* for him to qualify as a naturalist of the *roman policier*.

There is such a sameness in his novels: the weather; Maigret's immediate obsession with the case; Madame Maigret's monosyllabic tact; the office at the Quai des Orfèvres with its winter cold or summer heat; Maigret's pipes and emergency bottle of brandy; the sandwiches and beer sent up from the neighboring brasserie; the dull, patient, methodical investigations of Maigret's men, against which his own intuitions figure like the featured instrument in a concerto; the Gallic inevitability of the crime under the given circumstances; the bitter woman in the case; the doubtful justness of justice . . . I could go on.

In Mr. Simenon's works, some readers mistake a predictable formula for psychological inevitability. I would say, rather, that books like ***Maigret and the Man on the Bench*** represent a primitive form of behaviorism. Corner a rat and he will fight. A worm, under certain conditions, will turn.

On the positive side, Paris is the perfect place to take a vacation from a world too much with us. "Gallic" crimes are preferable to the rapes and muggings whose rising statistics we read in the paper. Predictability, in our discontinuous lives, can come to seem like a virtue. Besides, Mr. Simenon is in unusually good form for most of this book. Young Lapointe even gets to spend a night, in line of duty, with a lively and attractive prostitute. This is vintage Simenon, published in 1953 and just now translated into English.

The only real flaw in [***Maigret and the Man on the Bench***], within the limits just described, is the author's disconcerting trick of ringing in a last-minute stranger for the most dramatic crime of all. This leaves the book looking like a hastily packed valise with a loose shirttail still sticking out.

Anatole Broyard, "Classical vs. Romantic Crime," in The New York Times Book Review, *August 4, 1975, p. 17.*

PUBLISHERS WEEKLY

[In ***Maigret in Exile***], Maigret, in disfavor with his superiors, has been transferred to a sleepy provincial town. He is restless, bored—until a body turns up in the bedroom of one of l'Aiguillon's most distinguished citizens, Judge Forelacroix. So begins this satisfying Simenon mystery, an early Maigret. . . . Written in Simenon's spare style which adroitly captures nuances of character and telling details of scenes and events, it focuses attention on Maigret's seemingly random cerebrations, his instinctive compulsion to seek in his suspects the one characteristic that will illumine the true motive for the crime. In this case, he finds himself dealing with a bizarre family situation that spills over into the community. One meets a vivid cast of idiosyncratic personalities, and enjoys Maigret's logical deductions, as the identity of the murderer is carefully shielded until the end.

A review of "Maigret in Exile," in Publishers Weekly, *Vol. 214, No. 20, November 13, 1978, p. 54.*

JEAN M. WHITE

In ***Maigret's Rival,*** the stolid, pipe-smoking Parisian police inspector finds himself in an uncomfortable, unfamiliar setting.

As a personal favor to an examining magistrate, Maigret goes to a small French village to help the magistrate's brother-in-law. Etienne Naud, a well-to-do farmer, has complained that he is being slandered by village gossip. A young man has been found dead on the train tracks near his land, and people are saying that the victim was the secret lover of his daughter and that his death may not have been an accident or suicide.

Maigret finds himself without the help of his trusted aides and without official standing to question and investigate. The villagers, and even the family that he has come to help, obviously don't want him to meddle in their affairs. Still worse, Maigret has to deal with Cavre, nicknamed Cadaver, a dismissed colleague who has become a private investigator. But Inspector Maigret plods his way to the truth, with Simenon, the master storyteller, marvelously catching the atmosphere of an inbred French village. This is vintage (1944) Maigret.

Jean M. White, in a review of "Maigret's Rival," in Book World—The Washington Post, *May 18, 1980, p. 6.*

MARK TODD

Maigret and the Coroner, first published in French in 1949, has Maigret a member of the audience at a public inquest in a small town near the Mexican border. A night of drink and casual sexual encounter ends with the death in a lonely part of the desert of a girl who has been travelling around for a lark in a car with a group of young airmen; she has been run over by a train. The solution is not intricate, but the leading up to it is masterly, the characters of the barely post-adolescent airmen and the murdered girl's brother gradually being revealed, with Maigret taking mostly a bystander's role. The mixture of wildness and innocence in the airmen, casually brought together from backgrounds all over the US, and the parochial atmosphere of the town in the middle of vast open space are unerringly caught. (p. 974)

Mark Todd, "Private Eyes," in New Statesman, *Vol. 99, No. 2571, June 27, 1980, pp. 974-75.*

JEAN M. WHITE

Away from the streets of Paris and the French countryside, Inspector Maigret is an unhappy and forlorn figure. He never should have come to the United States for ***Maigret at the Coroner's.*** Without his friends at the Sureté, the chidings of Madame Maigret, the glasses of brandy, and his heavy overcoat, Maigret is a strangely inept, puzzled, and, worst of all, uninteresting character.

This 1952 novel by Georges Simenon, recently translated, finds Maigret, in Tucson, Arizona, on an exchange program to observe American police methods. While he is there, a girl is messily murdered during a drink-and-sex orgy with a group of American soldiers. Maigret doesn't understand the working of the American judicial system or U.S. drinking habits. In the end, he arrives at the same solution as the county sheriff. May Maigret never leave France again.

Jean M. White, in a review of "Maigret at the Coroner's," in Book World—The Washington Post, *January 18, 1981, p. 6.*

PAUL STUEWE

Simenon's Maigret novels are cosier and more formulaic [than his "straight" novels], but here too reality keeps breaking in upon the famous suprintendent of the Paris police. In ***Maigret on the Defensive*** a young woman charges him with sexual harassment, and before Maigret clears himself he has been brushed by the same web of circumstantial evidence and equivocal testimony that has entangled the innocent in several of his previous cases. It's one of the most satisfying of a generally excellent series of police procedurals, and if you ever feel that you're being culturally manipulated into reading *Auto-Da-Fé* or some other overnight sensation, take two Maigrets with a glass of white wine and go straight to bed. (p. 30)

Paul Stuewe, "In Translation," in Books in Canada, *Vol. 11, No. 5, May, 1982, pp. 29-30.*

THE NEW YORKER

[In ***Maigret Has Doubts***], Maigret is dining with his old friend Dr. Pardon, and the Doctor tells him of his worries about a dying patient with a wife and five children. Maigret, in turn, recalls a worrisome case of his own, in which the younger husband of a rich woman is accused of murdering her in order to marry his secretary. The case has many confusing elements; Maigret is convinced neither of the man's guilt nor of his innocence. There is an equivocal dénouement. This is Maigret at his moody, broody, reflective best.

A review of "Maigret Has Doubts," in The New Yorker, *Vol. LVIII, No. 19, June 28, 1982, p. 120.*

THE NEW YORKER

[In ***Maigret and the Nahour Case***], Maigret becomes involved in *l'affaire Nahour* some hours before it is recognized as a case, by way of a midnight telephone call from his friend Dr. Pardon. Pardon has just treated a well-dressed young woman for a gunshot wound in the back. She was brought to his office by a similarly well-dressed young man, who explained he found her wounded in the street. When Dr. Pardon leaves them for a moment, they flee. A few hours later, Maigret is informed in an official way that a rich Lebanese named Felix Nahour has been found shot to death in his house in the Fourteenth Arrondissement, and his wife has disappeared. This is one of M. Simenon's later novels, dating from 1967, and this is its first appearance in this country. It ranks—in atmosphere, in tricks and twists of plot, in the quality of Maigret's insights—among his very best.

A review of "Maigret and the Nahour Case," in The New Yorker, *Vol. LVIII, No. 48, January 17, 1983, p. 114.*

RICHARD COBB

Part of the charm of Simenon's books is that they satisfy an enormous range of readers in quite different ways. Enthusiasts for detective stories will settle on Maigret when he comes to terms with a problem and ends up, as much by intuition (*au pifomètre,* to use Simenon's own words to me) as by systematic elimination, by finding a solution. Furthermore, each reader will construct his own Maigret. I have always seen him as very large and burly, wearing a rather battered bowler, a hard white collar, the front stud showing above the carelessly knotted tie, black boots, a black overcoat with velvet collar: a man with a red face, dark eyes, shaggy eyebrows and greying curly hair. Others will picture him in mac and trilby. My own 40-year-long appreciation of Simenon comes above all from what I regard as his unique sense of place, of ambience, his slow, apparently haphazard exploration of topography, his ability to look at the backs of houses, as seen from canals or railway cuttings—his perspectives are always unusual—his genius in giving, in a few brief brushstrokes, the feeling of a town, a village, a landscape, the smell of the wind, of the sea, a moving sky. (pp. 8-9)

I suppose everyone has his own favourite Simenon topography. I feel he is at his best, his surest, in his native Belgium, Northern France, canal-country, the coast of the Charentes, Lower Normandy (Port-en-Bessin, for instance), and, of course, Paris, *all* of Paris, in its immense variety, smallness, in its once-identifiable quarters and villages, in the colour of its walls. But he can manage *Alphaville* equally well.

Although Simenon himself fell in love with Porquerolles, I don't think that he writes as well about the Midi, about the Mediterranean, as he does about, let us say, Moulins, Nevers, Meung-sur-Loire, Vichy or, for that matter, Alsace. There is something stagey about his Midi, the south as seen and appreciated by a northerner. My own view is that he does not get London right, that he is rather out of his depth with England and the English. I enjoy the seedy, steamy exoticism of his accounts of the Canal Zone, West Africa and Tahiti—the stories of white men going native and taking to drink; I enjoy his gleeful descriptions of the sordid, mean-minded tensions of long journeys by sea; and I have no doubt that, once again, he has got the atmosphere just right.

He never sits in judgment on people, he tries to understand them, and to make them understandable to us. I find him compassionate, as well as intuitive and imaginative. He would describe himself as a collector of souls; and I think he is; but they are not disembodied souls, nor do they languish in some dramatic Hell. Hell is where they are, like the couple each of whom has his or her own key to the two separate larders.

Simenon will be 80 this month. His achievement has been stupendous. Having found his form at about 26, he has been writing steadily for over 50 years: 400 books, 200 of them novels, of which, perhaps, a score or more first-rate. ***Au bout du rouleau, Lettre à mon juge, La maison du canal, Le train, L'aîné des Fercheaux, La tante, Le déménagement, Les anneaux de Bicêtre*** would come at the top of my list. I prefer the straight novels to the Maigrets. But this is a matter of taste. (p. 9)

Richard Cobb, "Simenon at 80," in The Listener, *Vol. 109, No. 2799, February 17, 1983, pp. 8-10.*

ALAN BRIEN

[Simenon], three of whose novellas from the Thirties have been re-issued as ***Maigret at the Crossroads,*** now seems to me to have faded to a thin bundle of tricks. His device of confusing the reader by making his people subject to sudden fits of depression or manic verbosity at random now looks more like desperation than imagination, and his habit of stringing out . . . all conversations . . . followed by three different translators . . . by bursts of dots . . . as if they all spat when they talked . . . grows wearisome . . . Even in this trio, the same character-plot occurs twice, and it is disillusioning to find the supposed expert at police methods falling back on the faked shadow on the blind for an alibi, or the pistol fired by a spring-timer to make suicide seem like murder. Just how far Simenon, even at his peak, relied on double-bluff can be gauged from the ease with which titles are swapped—what in 1934 was ***The Triumph of Inspector Maigret*** is in 1983 called ***Maigret Mystified.*** (p. 27)

Alan Brien, "Committed," in New Statesman, *Vol. 106, No. 2744, October 21, 1983, pp. 26-7.*

PIERRE WEISZ

Maigret stumbled into [the world of crime fiction] almost by accident and established himself in the span of a few novels. From Dupin to Nero Wolfe, from Sherlock Holmes to Father Brown, the detective is expected to be, by tradition, a 'character' in the common, non-literary sense of the word. Dupin is an exotic Frenchman, Philo Vance an aristocratic aesthete, Holmes a freakish genius with a cocaine habit, Nero Wolfe an elephantine refugee from Montenegro. Most important of all, our fictional detective is usually an amateur. If murder is to be enjoyed, it should be a hobby, not a matter of routine. Maigret upsets the apple-cart. Although not the first policeman in crime fiction, he is the first true professional to meddle with the Art of Murder. Maigret smells cop. He fills his 'plebeian frame' with blood, flesh and bones. His physical presence is imposed upon the reader as it is upon witnesses, bereaved relatives, bartenders and prostitutes: 'He had a way quite his own to stand where he was.' Whether he stays still or walks—the two main 'activities' of police work—Maigret's great asset is *being there:* '[he was] cast in one piece against which everything seemed destined to break, whether he was moving forward or just standing, set on his two legs slightly apart.' This snapshot from ***Pietr-le-Letton,*** which marks Maigret's first appearance in 1931, was to be polished throughout some sixty novels. Maigret's clothes, tastes, habits are so ordinary that they would pass unnoticed if Simenon did not pointedly mention them again and again, thus making *le Commissaire* a striking antithesis to the great aesthetes of detective fiction. Maigret wears a bulky overcoat, a hat; he washes down his sandwiches with cheap beer; he drinks Calvados or *gros rouge* in little neighbourhood cafés; spurning Holmes' Latakia, he fills his pipe with *gris,* the coarsest grade of French tobacco. He is a common man. Larger than most.

Simenon is playing another game but he still makes use of the old material. Crime fiction never was entirely abstract or preposterous and it did keep tabs on the real world, evolving with the times, adapting its themes and techniques to a changing environment. Conan Doyle understood the importance of material clues and the place of science in police work. Professor Locard, the French criminologist, saluted Sherlock Holmes as a forerunner of modern investigative techniques. A *Commissaire de la Police Judiciaire* could hardly ignore the realities of police work. What Simenon destroys, however, is the nineteenth-century sense of wonder which equates Holmes to a magician because he can trace a mudstain or identify a footprint. Maigret uses the resources of *l'Institut Médico-Légal* as a good cop should; he even has a special relationship with Moers, the lab technician at Quai des Orfèvres. In ***Maigret and his Corpse,*** he follows examplary police routine by determining the occupation of the victim from his hands, his feet, his clothes. He then proceeds to find out where he lived and where he was a short time before his death. A shirt, a pair of shoes, a stain of varnish on his trousers will play their parts. Such deductions will not, however, be presented as strokes of genius: Maigret simply has to justify his procedure before his superiors. In an almost perfect parallel to the Holmes-Watson situation, Maigret patiently explains facts and conclusions to a certain Juge Coméliau who does not view crime as a hobby. The reader finds his satisfaction; he does see bits of the puzzle falling into place, but he remains in a Paris that is not a tourist's playground or a high place of culture or a faraway dreamland. In Maigret's Paris most people are at work or eating, or sleeping; if they make love, body secretions and odours are present. Maigret's great idiosyncrasy is that he can feel other people live at their own rhythms, he can experience the exhaustion of their tired bodies, taste their food, hear their heart beats. The purely technical part of his work is no concession to the genre, it is part of the physical environment which conditions the problem.

The ideal triangle is still there: a victim, a murderer, a detective, but each element is treated in a new way. The victim usually comes first, which, after all, is only natural since its very existence is the source of the problem. Most authors treat it rather casually, reserving strange and striking characteristics for the criminal whose discovery has to be a dramatic climax. Simenon reverses the process. Maigret's first task or, rather, first labour is to *know* the victim. The corpse has to talk. Sometimes it talks before being killed, sometimes after, but the information released is always essential. ***Mr Gallet, Deceased,*** one of Simenon's first efforts, sets the pattern in exemplary fashion: the whole book is an investigation of the mysterious Mr Gallet, a very quiet, modest person who will prove to be an extraordinary combination of misery and guile, of guilt and innocence. Maigret will uncover dark secrets about most of the characters; he will upset their peaceful lives, ruin their little schemes and, in the end, wrap up the case by showing that murderer and victim are one and the same, that Mr Gallet died a double death as he lived a double life. Most writers would not get away with it: changing murder into suicide is one of the cardinal sins of crime fiction, and *aficionados* will not forgive where archbishops might. Strangely enough, the revelation does not frustrate the reader from his pleasure. The book does contain its share of problematic hardware in the form of a self-shooting device, but it is essentially devoted to searching the soul of a man, not his pockets. The answer is not so much the solution of a riddle as the resolution of a human paradox: the deep complexity of a nondescript individual. Maigret's approach does not entirely break with tradition; he still proceeds from the known to the unknown as does every other sleuth, but the object of his inquiry is highly original: he invades a domain that had always been the *chasse-gardée* of the novel, from Balzac to Dostoievski.

Establishing the facts is still a must. Maigret is the equal of his fictional peers but he treats very casually what used to be the bread and butter of crime fiction. Smaller versions of himself, Inspectors Lucas, Torrence or Janvier, deal with the material aspects of the investigation as they are supposed to in books as well as in life. Maigret's contribution is of a subtle order. If he decides to do leg-work, it is because he chooses to do so—one of the few liberties that Simenon takes with verisimilitude. Everybody can *understand,* but Maigret must *feel* in order to *know*. This is the poetic part of Simenon's creation. Maigret attunes his senses to the world. He takes in everything—the weather, the wet cobblestones, the smell of *fricandeau à l'oseille* and even the memory of the smell of *fricandeau à l'oseille,* and he gives the reader an uncanny sense of being there, whether the place is a train station in Belgium or a court-house in Arizona. 'It was full tide and a south-west storm made the little boats knock against one another in the harbour'—we are at a fisherman's village in Brittany. 'The houses glared white in the lowering light of late afternoon'—Loire Valley. 'The way the weather was going, it would rain all day, a cold and monotonous rain, with a low sky and the lights on in all the offices, with wet tracks on the floor'—Quai des Orfèvres in the Fall. Through a miracle of a sort, the perceptions of all kinds that Maigret soaks in seem to say something to readers in all parts of the world. The French text gives a sense of inevitability and still its many translations seem to be just as effective. 'Better put on your heavy coat,' says Mme Maigret, and a Japanese or Israeli reader prepares to face a Paris winter day.

Whether it is dialogue or description, a Simenon text seems deceptively simple. It says just what it means in the most economical way. There are very few adjectives and they all belong to everyday usage; verbs are all to be found in a pocket-dictionary; nouns stand for ordinary objects, well-known concepts or common feelings. Both Simenon and Maigret believe in essentials. 'Balzac is the novelist of the clothed man, I am the novelist of the naked man,' Simenon said in a radio interview. This does not keep him from being specific, taking us with each novel on a trip to a certain neighbourhood of Paris, a particular corner of provincial France, a city, a country, each with a flavour entirely its own. So much so that Simenon was long dubbed as a novelist of 'atmosphere', until the diversity of his characters and situations and the wealth of his invention made it obvious that he was not limited to local colour.

Although there undoubtedly is a Simenon manner that pervades all his novels, it can hardly be reduced to some ingredients of time, place and weather, or to the presence of the hulking commissaire solving crimes through the ingestion of vast quantities of food and beverages. It is rather characterised by the way Simenon uses his material, by the delicate balance he maintains between the various elements. He is very close to tradition and miles away at the same time. (pp. 175-79)

Maigret is not guided by a particular method or theory but rather by a deep-rooted feeling that all men are mirrored in each and every man. He will be able to solve his case only if he can apprehend the victim, the criminal, and their mutual relationship from the inside. This has little to do with the idea, sometimes expressed by other fictional sleuths like Hercule Poirot, that the victim brought about his own fate. Simenon's murders are not the sanction of imprudent behaviour or light-headed rashness; they generally occur at the end of a causal chain, but that chain is so long that it is hardly possible to speak of cause and effect. A subtle interplay between chance and determinism, between freedom and fate results in a death, and there is no way to pin down any of these entities as the 'cause': two human beings crossed paths and a murder 'happened'; it cannot be ascribed to accidental circumstances, but individual responsibility seems inadequate to explain it. No spur of activity of the 'little grey cells' will deliver the guilty party.

This is why, aside from the investigation proper, Maigret usually goes into a sort of crisis of identification with both the victim and the killer. He immerses himself in the environment and opens up the gates of perception. The more important side of his work does not take place on the intellectual level. To questions about the case in hand, he usually answers with 'I never have ideas' or 'I do not believe anything'. Although he follows an intuitive path, he certainly does not solve his case through intuition: such a reversal of the rules of the genre would not be too effective and would leave the reader dissatisfied. In Simenon, the intuitive element does not replace logic, it is part of it; it puts Maigret on the right track without muddying up the issue. If the old comparison of the bloodhound applies to one sleuth, it is to Maigret. A complicated bloodhound, though, a human bloodhound whose perceptions go further than the sense of smell. Maigret knows that everything is both simpler and more complex than it looks. The simpler aspects are the causal chain that leads up to a murder, the more complex ones lie in the motivations. Maigret shifts the centre of gravity of crime fiction from the *who* and *how* to the *why*.

Local colour is thus not a device but an essential component of Simenon's novels. All authors of crime fiction situate every misdeed or murder in a world of its own; with Simenon, it is just as important to investigate that world as it is to solve the puzzle. This shift of focus changes all the rules. Simenon does not even have to start with a murder: the intimation of murder is enough. He does not have to wait till the last chapter to unmask the criminal: 'Whodunit?' is not the question. So we sometimes see Maigret looking for the victim even before the crime has been committed. We know that a crime is pending; we know that, contrary to thriller tradition, Maigret will be unable to prevent that crime, but we relish another kind of suspense based on character rather than events. In ***Maigret et son mort,*** for instance, if Maigret can learn enough about the future victim who calls him at intervals on the telephone, we know that he will be able to capture the killer. In ***Maigret et le client du samedi,*** we have the same pattern and quite another novel: the motivations, the setting, the characters are entirely different, but the main clue still is in the victim. At other times, the killer himself talks to Maigret for the better part of the book. Another kind of challenge: will Maigret find the words that will bring him to surrender? Usually, Maigret adopts a quietly amoral attitude: he is no judge; he is the perfect listener, gently encouraging the other fellow to go on talking and eventually to stumble on the only solution, which is to give himself up. Quite often, Maigret and the killer come face to face at Maigret's home. They talk and drink and a sort of complicity is established. Two members of the human race have to recognise their bonds in order for peace to be restored.

We could look at Maigret's cases from three main viewpoints: those where the investigation is confined to a well-defined environment; those where it has to go beyond those limits; those where it has to reach into the past in order to unearth a deeply buried secret. In the closed-field variety, the approach is, so to speak, horizontal. Maigret spreads his inspectors as well as his mental tentacles throughout a certain *milieu* and, having sifted clues and weighed characters, comes up with a solution that will satisfy both logic and psychology. The interest is focused on the individual in his 'natural' environment: the intimacy of the family in ***Maigret se trompe,*** the network of interferences between personal and professional relations in ***Maigret et le marchand de vin,*** the chance association of some soldiers on a binge in ***Maigret chez le Coroner.*** Maigret performs his task in a very static way: he mainly stands or sits around. The open-field variety, on the contrary, shows a sort of quest. The criminal is lost in the crowd and Maigret has to ferret him out. He walks. The investigation spreads to a broader group or area. This is the occasion for us to discover the hidden realities of a supposedly familiar world. Such is ***Maigret et son mort,*** where the commissaire takes us through the Marais quarter of Paris, with its refugees from central Europe. The third category shows Maigret travelling in time: a 'vertical' approach. The present does not seem to hold the answers to his questions; he has to go into the past, just as he would go to another part of town or take a trip to another country in order to get the evidence. Material clues play an essential part here. Some discrepancy will put Maigret on the trail, he will start digging into the past of the victim, he will discover past associations, the memory of friends that would be better forgotten, of a sin that never led to atonement; a motive will finally emerge, a mask will crack. We could see ***Maigret in New York*** and many others in this light.

Needless to say, Simenon did not write novels in order for us to classify them. Most of the time, there is no definite border between novels of various moods. The restricted group, the small town, the emergence of the past; if one element is dominant, all are generally present at the same time. It is difficult to treat Simenon in a systematic way. Just as Maigret will not confine himself to a 'method', Simenon will not let himself be pinned down under a critic's magnifying glass. We have to open up, to take in what we are given. Perhaps one fruitful approach would be to extend Maigret's special relationship with his murderers and victims to include the author and the reader. Is there, in this respect, something peculiar to the work of Simenon that makes it different from the rest of crime fiction? The detective novel has always given a special place to the reader by inviting him to match wits with the sleuth. Most stories reach a point where it is theoretically possible to solve the case and, although authors play with a stacked deck, the reader usually lets himself be drawn into the game. This trait is unique in the field of art in so far as it challenges the public to participate in the creation itself. Perhaps this is the reason why so many addicts of fiction feel the itch to write a detective novel. Simenon does not elicit exactly the same responses. There is a body, a crime, a puzzle, and we do want an answer, but we rarely try to second-guess Maigret. The game he plays is so close to life that it has no fixed rules; the puzzle he is putting together is so complicated that it can be arranged into different pictures. We are quite content to put our trust into the good commissaire and let him assume the burden. Burden of proof it is not, but burden of guilt. Every Simenon novel shows that the line is thin between criminal and victim, so much so that Maigret sometimes does not bother to deliver a killer to justice. Crime and punishment are identified to each other, a lesson that we also received from other quarters. It is not too much to say that there is an affinity between Simenon and Dostoievski. A Simenon novel differs from 'serious literature' in only one way: it accepts the conventions of a genre by replacing analysis with formal investigation. We might say that Simenon has created a new genre which combines two apparently irreconcilable approaches to literature.

The Maigret-Simenon relationship falls in with the tradition of the mainstream novel rather than that of crime fiction, which is not surprising since Simenon concentrates on character rather than oddities. Maigret's personal habits, his love for little cafés, his closeness to people of all callings and descriptions, his taste for the simpler pleasures of life are direct transpositions of Simenon's own tastes and idiosyncrasies. Maigret's investigations, his travels, his encounters always run parallel to Simenon's own experiences. Although sequences might be different, Maigret's biography would very much read like the author's. Maigret, however, is no duplicate of Simenon. His 'job', in the first place, is different. A writer (or a man in the street) can take his time analysing characters; a detective has to conclude his inquiry. The natural limits of the genre impose a certain one-sidedness on Maigret, a quantitative rather than a qualitative difference. There are, however, differences of another order.

There is an aloofness about Maigret which is certainly not shared by Simenon. He keeps the world at a distance. He understands all passions and vices but seems immune to them. If not entirely innocent, his pleasures are none the less severely limited to those that will not shock bourgeois morality. Mme Maigret is a provider of good food and tender care, but a mistress she is not. Maigret, 'who always regretted not having a child', goes to the conjugal bed only to get a restful sleep. He, who penetrates the most carefully hidden secrets in the sexual life of others, will not ever yield to the temptation of the flesh. The closest hint that he is not totally indifferent to sex is a touch of jealousy he feels when a prostitute falls in love with a criminal from whom Maigret expected her to worm out information. Apparently a curious return to the old values of crime fiction, which forbade the hero to engage in such lowly matters as sex and love. The reasons, however, are quite different. Crime fiction used to sacrifice the human element to the intellectual pleasure of solving riddles. A Simenon novel, based on opposite principles, generally has its share of sex and love, often described in starkly naturalistic style, but they exist for the reader's sake, not the Commissaire's, whose function it is to bring order to the world. The priest is not supposed to dally with the parishioner he is confessing; the analyst is not supposed to join the patient on the couch.

Simenon has been reproached by some bilious critics with rehashing his material and churning out his novels like so many hot cakes. To the sympathetic reader the astounding abundance of his production does not seem repetitive. It is true that the general trend of his novels is predictable, but it reminds one of five-finger exercises composed by a master. Is it coincidence if Simenon is a great admirer of Bach? Old Johann-Sebastian did not lose his genius while composing for Anna-Magdalena. In the post-war period of the Maigret saga, Simenon collects vignettes. The virtuoso is using his well-honed technique for his own pleasure and ours. There is no artificiality in these *pièces de circonstance*. Simenon always keeps to what he knows, emotions, anecdotes, countries, people. In mature life, he discovers humour, which certainly does not diminish him. (pp. 179-84)

Throughout his long career, Georges Simenon has shown rare unity of inspiration. He has succeeded in the paradoxical endeavour to bring together two genres that were apparently impossible to reconcile. We can understand Agatha Christie, who once refused to comment on his talent: their approaches to literature are so different that they hardly belong to the same trade. Crime fiction changed a lot since Commissaire Maigret made his first appearance in the 1930s. Writers like Raymond Chandler and Dashiell Hammett have also brought a valuable contribution, bringing it closer to the great current of realism which started in the nineteenth century. In Simenon's own words, it has introduced 'a new way to look at man'. (p. 184)

Pierre Weisz, "Simenon and 'Le Commissaire'," in Art in Crime Writing: Essays on Detective Fiction, *edited by Bernard Benstock, St. Martin's Press, 1983, pp. 174-88.*

CONNIE FLETCHER

Maigret's Revolver . . . leads Simenon's hero from the discovery that an agitated young man has carried off his .45 revolver to the knowledge that the youth has dangerous plans in which the gun plays a key role. Alain Lagrange may be involved in a political murder, in which the body of a government official is found in a trunk in the Gare du Nord. Lagrange is certainly involved in a murder plot (though whether as instigator, accomplice, or victim is unclear) that carries Maigret from Paris to London. Here, Simenon devotes himself almost exclusively to the workings of the intricate plot, rather than (as in so many other Maigrets) to the inner workings of the detective himself.

Connie Fletcher, in a review of "Maigret's Revolver," in The Booklist, *Vol. 81, No. 3, October 1, 1984, p. 193.*

MARY F. PERKINS

[In ***Maigret Afraid***], Chief Inspector Maigret is asked by his friend Julien Chabot, the Examining Magistrate, to help solve a series of three unrelated murders. Thinking that these murders could only have been perpetrated by a madman, Maigret tries to remain uninvolved, but his detective instinct persuades him to examine the evidence at hand. Lurking in the background are the upholders of local justice threatening in a silent way the guilty as well as the innocent. Truly a mystery must!

Mary F. Perkins, in a review of "Maigret Afraid," in Kliatt Young Adult Paperback Book Guide, *Vol. XIX, No. 1, January, 1985, p. 14.*

KIRKUS REVIEWS

[In ***Maigret Bides His Time***], Manuel Palmari, one of the detective's older criminal acquaintances (he's long been suspected of directing a series of jewel thefts from his wheelchair), has been murdered. But Maigret doesn't have enough evidence to arrest Palmari's young mistress Aline for the crime—so he plays a kind of waiting-game with her while he uncovers her ownership of much property that once belonged to Palmari. Meanwhile, he also discovers that Aline has a married lover, Fernand Barillard, who occupies an adjacent apartment. Then *that* connection leads to the poignant link between Barillard's wife and elderly Jef Claes, a deaf-and-dumb man who lives in an attic room in the same building. And Maigret continues to pressure all the suspects while he puts these pieces together, ending with a watertight case . . . but not in time to prevent another murder. Fast, neat, absorbing.

A review of "Maigret Bides His Time," in Kirkus Reviews, *Vol. LIII, No. 6, March 15, 1985, p. 254.*

THE NEW YORKER

We have [in ***Maigret's Memoirs***] an interesting convolution: an autobiographical memoir in which Jules Maigret tells us how he and Simenon became acquainted and how his recollection of certain unusual cases became the vast Simenon-Maigret oeuvre. Maigret seems to be pretty much the same person we have known in the novels, but his tone is frequently that of mild annoyance. Maigret feels that only too often Simenon has distorted the facts of a case, or the nature of police procedure, or some aspect of him. "I have felt a certain embarrassment," he notes, "on seeing attributed to me in his books certain smiles, certain attitudes I have never assumed." And "How many times, after the publication of one of Simenon's books, have my colleagues looked at me mockingly as I went into my office!"

A review of "Maigret's Memoirs," in The New Yorker, *Vol. LXI, No. 44, December 23, 1985, p. 92.*

PUBLISHERS WEEKLY

[***Maigret's War of Nerves***] remains as intensely absorbing as when it first appeared in 1939. Here again is Inspector Maigret, guided by humane feelings behind his stolid facade, putting himself at grave risk to arrange the escape of a condemned man from prison. Judged guilty and awaiting execution for the killing of a rich American woman, Mrs. Henderson, and her maid, Joseph Heurtin is innocent, as Maigret suspects. Unaware that the police have deliberately let him escape, Heurtin dodges about the streets, leading the inspector and his detectives to cafes where they observe their quarry's interest in Henderson's free-spending heir and the women with him, as well as Heurtin's concentration on a penniless, eccentric student. The results of Maigret's scheme are utterly unexpected. Without one unnecessary word, Simenon brings all the characters to life and keeps the reader engrossed right up to the shattering denouement. (pp. 63-4)

A review of "Maigret's War of Nerves," in Publishers Weekly, *Vol. 229, No. 4, January 24, 1986, pp. 63-4.*

Tristan Tzara

1896-1963

(Pseudonym of Samuel Rosenfeld) Rumanian-born French poet, dramatist, essayist, and critic.

© Lutfi Özkök

Tzara is remembered as a proponent and theoretician for Dadaism, an intellectual movement of the World War I era whose adherents espoused intentional irrationality and urged individuals to repudiate traditional artistic, historical, and religious values. In response to the alienation and absurdity of World War I and the staid, unimaginative art forms predominant in Europe during that era, Tzara and other European artists sought to establish a new style in which random associations would serve to evoke a vitality free from the restraints of logic and grammar. Tzara articulated the aesthetic theories of Dadaism in his seminal collection of essays, *Sept manifestes dada* (1924; *Seven Dada Manifestos*). This volume, in which Tzara advocates ''absolute faith in every god that is the immediate product of spontaneity,'' represents a chaotic assault on reason and convention. Although his work often defies standard classification and is regarded by most contemporary English-speaking scholars as little more than a literary curiosity, Tzara is esteemed in France for his large and diverse body of poetry, which is unified by his critique of and search for a universal language and cosmic wisdom.

Tzara's first published poetry appeared in a literary review in 1912. Many of these poems, written in Rumanian and influenced by French symbolist writers, appear in *Les premiers poèmes* (1965; *Primele poèmes: First Poems*). Tzara immigrated to Switzerland from Rumania in 1916. Together with Jean Arp, Hugo Ball, and others, Tzara founded Dadaism and staged Dadaist performances at the Cabaret Voltaire in Zurich. Tzara left Switzerland in 1919 and settled in Paris, where he engaged in Dadaist experiments with such literary figures as André Breton and Louis Aragon. Serious philosophical differences caused a split between Tzara and Breton in 1921; soon after, Breton founded Surrealism, and by 1922 the Dada movement had dissolved. Tzara's early Dadaist verse, written between 1916 and 1924, utilizes agglomerations of obscure images, nonsense syllables, outrageous juxtapositions, ellipses, and inscrutable maxims to perplex readers and to illustrate the limitations of language. Volumes such as *Vingt-cinq poèmes* (1918) and *De nos oiseaux* (1923) display the propositions outlined in Tzara's manifestos and critical essays, often blending criticism and poetry to create hybrid literary forms.

From 1929 to 1934, Tzara participated in the activities of the Surrealist group in Paris. In this environment, he created a more sustained and coherent poetry that places less emphasis on the ridiculous than his Dadaist verse. Tzara's works published during this period include *L'homme approximatif* (1931; *Approximate Man and Other Writings*), an epic poem that is widely considered a landmark of twentieth-century French literature. This work portrays an unfulfilled wayfarer's search for a universal knowledge and language. Roger Cardinal asserted: ''[In] this apocalyptic explosion of language, Tzara finally approaches the primal seat of creativity, the point where the naked word reveals the naked truth about the world.'' This and Tzara's later Surrealist volumes—*L'arbre des voyageurs* (1930), *Où boivent les loups* (1932) *L'antitête* (1933), and *Grains et issues* (1935)—reveal his obsession with language, his vision of humanity's destiny of tedium and alienation, and his concern with the struggle to achieve completeness and enlightenment.

In 1934, Tzara left the Surrealists to join France's communist party. As his commitment to left-wing politics increased, his poetry included greater political content and stressed revolutionary and humanistic values while maintaining his lifelong interest in free imagery and linguistic experiments. *Midis gagnés* (1939) focuses on Tzara's impressions of Spain during the country's Civil War, while *La fuite* (1947) depicts the frantic German evacuation of Nazi-occupied France during World War II. The prose poems *Sans coup férir* (1949) and *À haute flamme* (1955) also address political topics related to the Second World War. Critics generally regard such later works as *Terre sur terre* (1946), *Parler seul* (1950), and *Le fruit permis* (1956) as less vigorous and inventive but more controlled than his earlier poetry.

Tzara's dramas have received less critical attention than his manifestos and poetry. Written during his Dadaist phase, Tzara's best-known plays, *La coeur à gaz* (1920; *The Gas Heart*) and *Mouchoir de nuages* (1925), rely on absurdity and wordplay, parodying such literary forms as classical Greek and Shakespearean theater and French symbolist poetry. In *Essai sur la situation de la poésie* (1931), a collection of critical essays, Tzara celebrates poetry as a liberating force from conventional modes of expression.

(See also *Contemporary Authors,* Vols. 89-92 [obituary].)

MARY ANN CAWS

At first reading, Tzara's early Dada poetry, such as ***Vingt-cinq poèmes*** (1918) and ***De nos oiseaux*** (1923), seems to consist of unusual images gratuitously linked to each other in an order invisible to the logical mind and in complete accord with Dada principles of rapidity and vitality. There is no immediately apparent structure exterior to the images which would hold them together in a definite form and thus mute the impact of their collision; the type of linking which becomes apparent on a second reading is only thematic and therefore totally flexible. It is usually thought that Dada poetry is a sort of random catalogue, that the words pulled out of a hat according to the famous method advocated by Tzara are in no way joined to each other, that his statements about the poem formed by the random words and its necessary resemblance to the man making the poem are only another Dada joke. Yet one of the primary elements of the Dada joke, like its parallel, the surrealist game, is its seriousness; its particular type of humor lies precisely there. Tzara always claims for Dada creations an essential interior ordering, a "constellation" of necessary clarity below the obvious surface. Of course we are meant to look at the surface as at a spectacle, and Dada poetry is full of references to vision: "Look at me"; "see." According to Tzara, the inner order is only apparent to the intuition; whether the thematic links that can be perceived are signs of the subsurface order or accidental manifestations of the continuity of certain Dada attitudes, we cannot know—but the links are incontrovertibly there.

In brief, if the early Dada poems are examined, these main themes, all of which are exact parallels to the themes of the Dada manifestos and critical essays, are to be found: vivid color, motion, a certain direction or grouping, definite geometrical figures, and light or its variants. . . . The images or themes might, of course, be differently characterized, but in any case, they are all related to the spectacle Dada is supposed to be, and to its motion and invisible purity of order. But these thematic links never fall into any fixed (non-Dada) or predictable form or succession, nor could they ever be said to soften the literally *spectacular* shock of the images against each other: they are, rather, *intensifiers* for those images.

In the later ***L'Arbre des voyageurs*** (1930) there is an equally rich profusion of brilliant imagery, which is only partly absurd. The fact that the American with "pointed leaves" holding a "marriage in her beak" in one poem and the ear feeding on the sound of a "muscled waterfall" in another have certain possible supports in reality . . . in no way subtracts from the power of the images or from the spontaneity of the poetic imagination: they are witnesses to its correspondence with the world outside it. The same statement could be made about much surrealist imagery.

On another level, it is also clear that surrealist word play is prefigured by Dada word play, as they are reflections of the aesthetic theories of the movements and intended to expand the range of possible significations of vocabulary and to intensify the poetic effect by doubling it in sense and in sound. Some of the puns and more obvious tricks of sound Tzara uses in his poetry, both early and late, are decidedly trivial. . . . But at their best the word experiments can result in passages of singular beauty, where each sentence leads to the next in an unbroken lyricism. (pp. 97-9)

Frequently the chief difference between Dada and surrealism (or between the theoretical writing of their most prominent exponents, Tzara and Breton), seems to be only a difference of tone or of style, since the themes they deal with are so similar. . . . At other times, even their styles are similar, especially in the more "poetic" writings. After the initial period of Dada and before the period of his political commitment, Tzara lays as heavy a stress on the romantic themes of solitude and ennui as Breton. . . . [In ***Le Désespéranto*** (from ***L'antitête***)], Tzara declares the same enthusiasm for the notion of *ennui* as Breton: "Tedium, before it reaches death, when I abandon myself to it completely, is my most delightful waking state." Here the violent energy and the sense of action are less prized than the acute intensity of consciousness to be found in the endless waiting which Tzara describes as full of charm.

As for the many other points of similarity between Breton and Tzara already mentioned, they are not by any means confined to Tzara's early Dada period. In 1932 Tzara asserts that his activity and his interests are those of the surrealists, and they remain so until 1934. The prose parts of his ***Abrégé de la nuit*** (1934) are very close in tone and content to Breton's *Vases communicants,* especially in the description of the salutary deforming action of the dream on the world of everyday thought ("night in the fermentation of its profound possibilities"). (pp. 100-02)

From this point on, Tzara lays a decided stress on the definitions of poetry or art itself. In his essay on Max Ernst and his "reversible images" (1934) he speaks not just of the dream but of all forms of poetry as an ideal means of deformation, always leading to new types of knowledge. In ***Grains et issues*** (1935), poetry becomes the supreme method for bringing about the required "transparency of things and beings." It is at the same time the act of knowledge and the way of knowing. Like the dream, it exalts thought and goes beyond it. In fact, thought and poetry seem to have somewhat the same relationship as that indicated by "communicating vessels," since Tzara calls for the absorption of one in the other as the goal of a necessary and significant revolution. He treats his own images as though they were thoughts, joining in this way the realm of poetry and the realm of knowledge. There is no possible separation in Tzara's essays between the idea and the image—so that, for instance, the mirages perceived by the mind when it is paralyzed by the strength of the sun actually themselves augment the understanding and the vitality of the man who sees them. . . . (pp. 102-03)

[Tzara's] will to unite elements, ordinarily considered separate (like the image and the idea, poetry and thought) extends to other realms also. Like Breton and the other poets connected with surrealism, one of the ideas to which he refers with the greatest frequency in all the periods of his life is that of the *union* of all things, however contrary in appearance. He calls poetry a way of living, a "condition of existence." Attacking, in ***Le surréalisme et l'après-guerre*** (1947), his former friends the surrealists from whom he had separated for permitting what he considers a divorce between their action and their theories, he insists on a *unicité* of action, which he describes as "action confused with dream,'' or, in his presentation of Rimbaud (1948), as a state of activity ''where the terms of absence and presence are both unthinkable separately and where dream and action are linked in one unique projection.'' As an ex-surrealist, he sees the surrealists overcome with despair at the duality of man and the world and he calls for a humanistic hope in the power of man to rearrange his world by his creative will, to make the ''immense transparency'' of his work mirror that of his life in all its purity and integrity. (pp. 103-04)

A description Tzara once gave of modern poetry (**"Gestes, ponctuation, et langage poétique"** in *Europe,* January 1953) is the best clue we have to his own poetry. There he speaks of the ''*poetic fields* which are electrically charged by certain conduit images with the help of meanings recalled, of assonances and auditive echoes.'' The reader who is troubled by the profusion of assonance, alliteration, repetition of key words and key sounds, and various other sorts of word play must realize that these poetic devices furnish the verbal echoes Tzara has always used to reinforce his images in the memory. By means of these images the poet sets up a ''current of induction'' which flows in the way he determines. Tzara's insistence on transparency and on the family of images with which it is associated is a deliberate ''charging'' of his poetry to make possible the eventual creation of a *poetic reality,* that is, a reality as convincing in the realm of poetry as the objects surrounding us are in theirs. And in this interior reality, we have only his images for landmarks. (pp. 104-05)

The extremely diverse and unequally brilliant images of Tzara's masterpiece ***L'Homme approximatif*** (1931) are themselves appropriate to the theme of approximation. Taken together they form a full-scale portrait of multiple-natured and imperfect man as he wanders aimlessly about in the ''à peu près'' (the almosts) of destiny, with labyrinths hanging on the shadow of his steps and others weighing heavily on his back, without direction outside and in (''lost inside myself lost''). Even the space of his existence is rented; the only continuity he possesses is the series of worries he puts on in the morning like underclothes. Inconstant in his relationships with others, he is no more constant with himself, changing into ''another self at every turning.'' . . . Always conscious of the ''deadly punctuations'' which mark his flesh, he feels his horizons limited to the border of a watch face and his prospects gambled away in a universal lottery, feels insignificant and shrunken into himself. . . . Mocked by space and time, impoverished and confused, this man who is all of us (''approximate man like me like you reader and like the others'') often betrays his incomplete nature by his inconclusive style, where one line of verse breaks off unfinished and the next line begins a totally different idea. . . . In a similar manner, the frequent repetitions of lines, and of words (. . . ''consolation . . . consolation'') may be considered repeated attempts at, or approximations of, completeness.

Insofar as he is not even completely man, but ''un peu animal un peu fleur un peu métal un peu homme,'' approximate man belongs not only to the human realm but to the world beyond man which is as incomplete as he is; in fact, the whole sweep of the poem is determined by the constant mixture of human and natural elements. An important series of images represents a serious state of imperfection: like man, the night and the moon are described as shriveled, and, like him, the mirror and the drinking glasses are broken. . . . But the desolation of the outside world may be only a human interpretation, since the mind often serves as an intensifier of catastrophe. At other times natural objects are the only consolation for the sadness and impoverishment that haunt man's dwellings, and it is their ''inexpressible plénitude'' that compensates for human shortcomings and human wants. Unable to rely on his own constancy, man can count at least on the unfailing cycle of nature. . . . Here he learns to renew his vision and expand it.

Far less flexible than man's vision, and far more important to the poet Tzara, is his language. From the sound of the bells and of the chains, felt more than heard at the beginning of [***L' Homme approximatif***] (''this language which lashes us'') to the stammering sounds of hell at the end, the theme of nonhuman expression runs through the poem, and it is always counterbalanced by the theme of the human word. . . . Language alone provokes the drunkenness which can deliver us from what Tzara calls the ''lazy habit'' of living. Our faith in the word has even retarded our adventures into other spheres: ''word that I wait for . . . / around the hive of your chance sweetness / we are so many bees whose flight your promises have checked.'' And yet this faith is often disappointed. The language approximate man has chosen, perhaps the only one he could have chosen, is a language befitting his imperfect nature, full of words that are ''rotten unhealthy moth-eaten.'' It is both static and nonvisionary. . . . (pp. 107-10)

As an absolute opposition to the imperfect character of human life and language (including, of course, the language in which the poem is written), ***L'Homme approximatif*** offers a theme of distant perfection and ''brightness forever immeasurable,'' of luminous forgetfulness and an eternal warmth of sun raining down upon the earth. . . . [There] is a lengthy passage, comprising at least three of the nineteen sections of the poem, in which the outstanding images are linked by the color white—so that ''la blancheur invincible immaculée'' joins tufts of souls, swans gargling sprays of water, birds, glaciers, clouds, the white finger of the stone thinker, a woman's body, fog, and the frequent recurrences of the more general statement: ''outside all is white'' or its variations. The unforgettably simple affirmations of the natural and human realm find a celestial and sterile counterpart in the often reiterated ''up there all is stone.'' The ''rigid clarity'' of the absolute has none of the approximate character of man, and the changing spectacle of nature and of man's own desperate attempts at courage seem tarnished by its light. . . . (p. 111)

The only possible link seen at first between celestial perfection and earthly incompleteness is an exterior one. The wolf lost or bogged down in the confusion of the forest bears the same relation to ordinary sheep as does Tzara's hero of language to ordinary unheroic man; in these years Tzara frequently compares the poet to the wolf, in his revolt against his circumstances, for his ''state of turbulence.'' Lycanthropy, he says, is an ''affective mode'' of the poets' consciousness. . . . When, in the final section of the poem, the slow furnace identified with man's spirit and his hope rises to a litany of fire, and when there is a new and decided stress on the notions of height, strength, violent gestures, and infinite presumption, all modest approximate language and all principles of human logic are rejected (or redeemed) simultaneously: ''harmony—let this word be banished from the feverish world that I visit.'' With them disappear the timid distinctions of limited earthly vision, as the tones of hell are heard among the ''dizzying salvoes of stars.'' And finally the extended accumulation of seemingly disparate images receives an absolute retrospective unity as the epic tone of the poem prevails over the pathetic human theme of approximation.

Infinite in "the holy variety" of his species, as magnificent as he is miserable, man is now able to move toward completeness without physical motion. The universal refrain, "and others and so many others," which returns throughout the poem and particularly in the next to last section gives way to the heroic vow concluding the long journey which is the poem: . . .

> (and rugged in my clothing of schist
> I have pledged my waiting to the oxidized desert of torment
> to the unshakeable advent of its flame).

In the most difficult way possible, the poet here takes upon himself the will to immobile perfection and the necessary torment of purification. His attitude of waiting and his garments of rock are a human echo of the permanence and the static completeness of the preceding refrain: "all is stone." The certain flame he accepts at the end is the response to and the double of the nocturnal peace he implores near the beginning: . . .

> (peace on the outside of this world inverted in the mold of unanimous approximations
> and on so many others and on so many others).

But the universe which was the subject of the former outward vision of the poet is now absorbed into his interior landscape. Pilgrimage and waiting, torment and repose, flame and stone, Tzara and his reader, language and absence of language, imperfect attempts and absolute commitment—all the elements of the journey meet in the space and time of the poet's own mind. And since it is only an outward witness to the interior realization, and is formed of the imperfect matter of human language, the poem itself is finally no more than an approximation of the inward journey "beyond surfaces and reality."

Où boivent les loups (1931) mixes images of suffering and darkness, of a black thirst and a night for blind men, of shadows, dead men, and dying laughter, of velvet griefs and nights flowing under the tears on the cheeks of summer, with brighter images of the depth of the sun and its "peaceful imprint the radiance of its surging word." But most of the images of hope here are predictions rather than certainties, where the main actions are expressed as problematic and where all the forms are future in implication. . . . More serious than the inevitability of future oppositions is the grim warning expressed earlier in the poem that even words will come to an end, a warning justified as the poet is finally imprisoned by silence. Loneliness waits for him not only on the crystal mountains and in the glass corridors, where the encounter would be heroic, as it is in the flaming desert of ***L'Homme approximatif,*** but at the end of bronze streets, where the vertical dimension and the transparent purity are utterly lacking. The hero does not struggle against the silence waiting to enslave him, and there is not even an aura of elevation or mystery to his fate, for the silence is spun by "the bastard and quavering fingers of an old woman." The words of sun and the language of youth are more seriously threatened by a complete cessation of interior power than by the natural fall of outside darkness. Silence is perhaps more perfect than nonsilence, just as it is less human: this is of course the problem suggested by ***L'Homme approximatif,*** the man who makes successive attempts at human language and then commits himself to a perfection beyond the space of language and silence. But the stylistic technique of repetition continues in the poetry of Tzara himself as in that of his fellow Dada-surrealist poets: the linkings of images by a theme, the refrains, and the litanic form can all be considered recurring *approximations* or steps toward a perfect language, the accumulated efforts of the surrealist poet toward a perfect poetry in a formal journey parallel to the metaphysical one.

In the volumes ***La Main passe, Mutations radieuses, Midis gagnés,*** and ***Entretemps*** of the years 1935 to 1940, when Tzara's poetry begins to take on a strong political orientation, the same themes continue and are amplified, acquiring a "realistic correlation" and a more *apparent* structure. There is the familiar insistence on fullness, vitality, and luminosity. . . . In these poems, however, Tzara begins to stress the necessity of the interweaving of hope and despair, no longer in a formal conception or in a mere poetic balance, but as the basis of life itself as man can best perceive it. The darkness and the light seem at first to exist side by side: "l'aveugle dort la flamme règne" (the blind man sleeps the flame rules). But in reality, one is *within* the other, as in the game of *l'un dans l'autre* already discussed: "Sale vie mélangée à la mort" (dirty life mixed into death). This theme is responsible for many of the most memorable of Tzara's poems and images, such as "midi éclaté dans l'obscurité de sa force" (noon exploded in the darkness of its strength). . . . (pp. 111-17)

[In his poetry], Tzara refuses the concept of stability and unchangeable order; the most superficial study of his manuscripts shows that he often experiments with the location of a line or a group of lines, and that this is especially true for what might be called the key lines, those which include the most often repeated images, such as that of fire, or which form part of a litanic series. Many "necessary" lines may come into the head at once, but their position can be rearranged without destroying any *a priori* fabric of the poem. Furthermore, some of the parts of ***L'Homme approximatif*** originate in simple sets of bizarre words, listed by association (geological, botanical, etc.) which Tzara then combines in various groups which are to be shifted about as the poem grows. A particular and preconceived *form* would scarcely be appropriate to a poem on approximate man and his language.

The emphasis on motion in all the Dada manifestos and in the Dada poetry is striking; in a poem of 1917, even "the crystal dissolves in motion." But Tzara shows a permanent concern for all manifestations of movement. In ***Le Désespéranto*** he maintains that the will to action is more interesting than the act accomplished, and that desire is far more important than the attainment (compare Breton's "abandon the prey for the shadow"). He insists here also that the stable appearance of things, if overturned, would show an intense verbal activity as the starting point of all matter: "Under each stone, there is a nest of words and it is from their rapid spinning that the world's substance is formed." . . . Tzara never ceases to be a Dadaist in spirit, insofar as Dada represents a state of ceaseless and unformalized activity: "The poem forces or digs a crater, is silent, murders or shrieks along the accelerated degrees of speed." The poet's task, as Tzara envisions it, is to "*break* the winter of things," to "*shake* the laugh from the appletree," or to "*seize* the flux of wings at the moment of transparency." All of these expressions reveal his concern that poetry should be *active*—not a passive perception of the world but an involvement in its seasons and changes of mood and rhythm. He calls this "la fidélité de vivre" and opposes it to the stupid gaping of the man who only watches as the procession of other lives goes by. (pp. 119-20)

Of all the values Tzara finds necessary to good poetry, simplicity seems always to be the most important for him, together with the qualities of entirety, immediacy, and necessity he sees as its primary components. (p. 122)

[The] distinguishing mark of Tzara's poetry which remains constant from the time of Dada is the sharp condensation in one or a few lines of the sort of image which perfectly illustrates the *merveilleux* of Dada-surrealist poetry, fusing transparency and all its allied qualities of luminosity, intensity, elevation, and immediacy into a perfect whole. In the 1961 poem **"Juste présent,"** the poet sees, with the clarity of a child's vision . . . and with the full range of human experience: . . .

> (the flock of mists dispersed
> the incandescence of time
> and the lofty smile of man everywhere
> at the stroke of noon).

Here in these lines is concentrated, in the single and simple image of the "lofty smile," all the force of the most powerful Dada and surrealist inspiration. (p. 128)

The necessary complement to Tzara's simplicity is the emphasis he places on the notion of *plénitude* ("fullness" or "completeness"). . . . Tzara's faithfulness to the principle of simplicity never entails a passive agreement in the narrow sense, for he is equally faithful to the spirit of his ***L'Homme approximatif:*** "Harmony—let this word be banished from the feverish world I visit." The concept of *plénitude,* then, is not only compatible with the extreme variance of light and dark images constant in Tzara—it is in just this dramatic play of differences visible to the poet that the concept acquires its greatest scope and intensity.

As early as 1931, the theme of *plénitude* can be plainly identified in Tzara's poetry and essays among all the other lesser but related themes. Tzara describes ***L'Homme approximatif*** aware of his own possibilities as . . .

> (man bearing in his fruit morning's burning and
> propitious blossoming).

The burning and the brilliance of the morning sun are of course closely allied to all the images of clarity and intensity which provide the major focus for Tzara's early poetry, whereas the image of ripening fruit and the adjective "propice" announce the atmosphere of his later poems. All the themes of presence and of the bounty and wisdom of the natural world are already indicated here by phrases such as "objects are still there a consolation alongside feelings" and "the slow consciousness of plants and of things." (pp. 129-30)

The poems of ***Terre sur terre*** could all be placed under the heading of the rhetorical question posed in one of them: "What is this space that radiates in me?" Here the contrasts of light and dark images are less important than the force of the whole to which they contribute. (p. 131)

[In ***Terre sur terre,*** the] poem is no longer a spectacle but a witness to what the poet himself has seen and comprehended, as mystery ("à la merveilleuse à la flamme future") and as the ordinary course of nature. The smallest elements of man's daily life (bread, wine, salt) are elevated with those of the natural world (wind, rain, fruits) in a splendid pagan communion of the future (birth, the future flame). Once more the emotional texture of the poem depends on a contrast of elements: blindness and vision, rain and sun, man and child, radiance and shadow, song and silence—and these uncomplicated, undramatic, and obvious elements form a poem of great depth and epic vision. (p. 132)

The long poem of 1953, ***La Face intérieure,*** gives what is perhaps the best and most complete summation of all Tzara's favorite images of earth—of its seasons and its fruits, of the dualities of presence and absence, pain and hope, misery and grandeur, the word and the cessation of the word. More than any other of his poems it is a poem of *plénitude;*. . . . The clarity and the assurance of totality so highly prized by Tzara throughout all the periods of his poetic and critical evolution is finally perceived in its simple presence within the concrete world of natural objects, whose inner surface and depth (***La Face intérieure***) is identical with their exterior and universal reality. From one point of view, nothing could be further from the obvious anti-natural violence of Dada. But that point of view is perhaps not the one closest to the more profound spirit of Dada as Tzara expresses it. (pp. 133-35)

Mary Ann Caws, "Tristan Tzara," in her The Poetry of Dada and Surrealism: Aragon, Breton, Tzara, Eluard & Desnos, *Princeton University Press, 1970, pp. 95-135.*

AILEEN ROBBINS

[***Mouchoir de nuages,*** or ***Handkerchief of Clouds***], is an eclectic piece, offering a great variety of literary and theatrical styles; the poetic-romantic-comic tone of the play is quite unlike any of Tzara's other dramatic works. It is the only one of his plays that has a conventional dramatic form: The easily discernible romantic plot, based on a love-triangle, is a slight parody of Huysmans' novel, *Là-bas*. Though there are occasional bursts of poetry and non-sequiturs, the language is straightforward, with most of the syntax intact.

Its sources range from classical Greek theatre, to Shakespeare, to French Symbolist poets, to popular novels and films of the early '20's. The play consists of fifteen very short acts, each followed by an even shorter Commentary, reminiscent of a Greek chorus. Though the protagonists pursue their activities with dead seriousness, the Commentary on their action is mock-heroic and even farcical, serving to undercut the deadpan quality. Tzara thus presents a romantic melodrama which is, at the same time, a parody of itself.

Tzara also parodies the Shakespearean tradition. He lifts portions of three scenes from *Hamlet* and puts them together to make Act XII of ***Handkerchief of Clouds.*** The analogy between this play's hero, the Poet, and Hamlet, is possible, but ridiculous. The choice of *Hamlet* is quite deliberate, however, since it serves a deeper purpose: to parody the obsession with the figure of Hamlet that was endemic to European novelists and poets of the late 19th Century. It was one of the central myths of the Symbolist poets and figured in the work of Mallarmé, who regarded Hamlet not as a man struggling to resolve an Oedipal dilemma but as a morbid dreamer who spent long hours staring at a skull, obsessed and tempted by death. This was the inspiration for Mallarmé's long prose-poem, *Igitur,* as well as a host of other creations, including Villiers de l'Isle-Adam's *Axël*. The contrast of the Symbolists' use of the myth with Tzara's is obvious.

Twisted literary allusions to Symbolist poetry are scattered throughout the play. In Act X, for example, the Poet describes how he killed an enormous creature that he found stalking through a foreign land. The "creature" turns out to be a huge flower. This is an echo of an image from one of Mallarmé's most hermetic poems, "Prose pour Des Esseintes," in which he speaks of hyperbolic flowers ("Toute fleur s'etalait plus large''). In Mallarmé's poems, as well as those of Baudelaire (see his *Les Fleurs du Mal*), a flower was often a symbol for a poem. Tzara's image, though superficially absurd, therefore exists on multiple levels; the Poet who shoots the flower is symbolically murdering poetry, or at least traditional Romantic poetry, a task that appealed to Tzara. On one level, this play is a discussion of the art, and the proposed non-art, of poetry.

Apart from these literary parodies, the play can be appreciated in terms of its innovative staging. The fact that the actors and the stage crew were visible at all times to the audience, as well as the arbitrary division of the play into separate (and sometimes unrelated) Acts and Commentaries, creates a type of Brechtian alienation. The Commentators themselves discuss the problem of illusion and reality, in theatre and life, which is further complicated by the fact that the actors use their real names. This contrasting of realities was a theme that Pirandello was also developing in the 1920's.

Another interesting technique that Tzara uses is the ''flashback.'' Tzara was aware of the discoveries in avant-garde film at the time and this play is one of the earlier examples of the influence of cinema on the theatre. Every time a scene takes place in the past, a tulle curtain is lowered (eg., Act VII). This condensation of space and time—the jumping over distance and mixture of past and present—may be a convention for us today, but it was unusual in 1924. (pp. 110-11)

Aileen Robbins, ''Tristan Tzara's 'Handkerchief of Clouds','' in The Drama Review, *Vol. 16, No. 4, December, 1972, pp. 110-11.*

MARY ANN CAWS

All his life, Tzara wrote prolifically: poetry, plays, essays on art and literature, and even an abortive autobiographical novel. In these writings he remained a poet, in the sense given to that word by the Dadaists and the surrealists, irrespective of political and personal tendencies or of considerations of subject and genre. Despite the changes in affiliation and the obvious alterations of tone from his sentimental and slightly ironic Rumanian poetry, through the disconnected or catalog style of his earliest French poetry to his later epic style, a number of themes recur: the alternations of sun and shadow, of motion and fixity, of imperfection or approximation and completeness or fullness *(plénitude)*. All reveal the dialectic of opposites and resolution familiar to surrealist theory and characteristic of all the poets connected with this group. Tzara's preferred images of the crystal and the flame, the intoxication and melancholy of night, and in particular, the deliberate dizziness provoked by the contrast between them are characteristic of both surrealism and Dada. (pp. 17-18)

Tzara's situation in French literature is unique: he is the only poet who has left us a vast body of significant material from both the Dada and the surrealist epochs. The former movement, revolting against bourgeois commonplaces and polite ''art,'' created a public nuisance with its manifestly ridiculous, brilliantly and definitely illogical statements. All the Dada manifestations were eulogies of the spontaneous negative gesture which was to be the opposite of art, of the violent language which was to be the executioner of existing poetry. Defining Dada in the essay **''Picasso and Poetry,''** Tzara called it: ''the abolition of all art for the benefit of a sort of poetic function, spontaneous expression of individuality.'' In conformity with these principles, Tzara recommended the following recipe for poetry: words clipped from a newspaper article, drawn from a hat in which they have been shaken, and then pasted together in that order. In his own early poems, nouns, adjectives, and verbs are simply juxtaposed in a collage or catalog. Ironically, these poems have a strong and positive appeal for the modern reader, bourgeois or not. Tzara's essays on poetry and art, furthermore, go far beyond other Dada statements to reach a personal style and series of coherent principles, in which present-day readers can on occasion see an extraordinary beauty and brilliance. His frequent protestations about his deliberate incoherence are partly genuine and partly mocking.

Of the Dadaists Tzara expressed most convincingly the essential Dada revolution against the sentimentality of previous literary movements. Since Dada is not literary, it cannot be judged by literary standards. Tzara applies to Dada poetry, for instance, the primary criterion of rapidity: the poem must push, shove, scream, and murder all in its path as it rushes along at faster and faster tempos. Tzara's other criterion for the possible evaluation of Dada ''products'' is their capability for self-transformation as they gather the procession of changing moments into the ultimate *instant*. It is for this instant that the strongest positive adjectives are reserved: crystal-clear, vital, multicolored, vibrant, radiant, joyous. This accent on the mobile present in its unique reality presumes a theory of underlying structure convincing only for the partisans of Dada. For the Dada poem is rigorously constructed but with an effortless instantaneity whose effect is only visible *a posteriori*. The poet ''structures'' his work around an inaudible rhythmical arrangement which Tzara describes as the light sent out from interior groupings of radiant constellations of order. Each element in the poem is independent, has its proper place and its own distinct nature (singularity). Each image is a singular entity, a constructor of fervor and density, a brazenly violent involvement with life, intensity at its highest peak but it is always a part of the intuitive order. Dada reveals its most positive qualities precisely in its enthusiastic contradictions: these alone provide its character and its certainty. For Tzara, Dada is the poetry of TODAY, of a vital abundance, explosion, and purity, so obscure that its blinding light radiates everywhere. (pp. 18-19)

It was during his surrealist period that Tzara wrote his poetic masterpiece, ***Approximate Man (L'Homme approximatif)***, and the great prose poems of ***The Antihead (L'Antitête)*** and ***Seeds and Bran (Grains et issues)***. In these mature works the themes of the intermingling of night and day, of dream and reality predominate—themes which, together with the meditation on language, form the basis of Tzara's surrealist theories and expression. When closely examined, however, these works exhibit the best aspects of Dada and of the surrealist inspiration. (pp. 19-20)

[In making the transition from Dadaism to Surrealism, Tzara's style ranges] from the deliberately disconnected to the sustained and lyric; from the fragmentary to the visionary and the epic; from the tormented or the nostalgic to the serene; from the simple to the complex. The accent falls constantly on two recurring elements, however, on action or the spectacle of action and on the attempt to find a language which will translate it.

Tzara's Rumanian poems, written from 1911 to 1915 [and collected in ***Les premiers poèmes***], are postsymbolist in imagery and sentimental in tone. Of particular interest are the alternations from light to dark imagery and the ironic asides, both of which continue and are intensified in the later poetry, which also occasionally exhibits the accompanying accent of romantic melancholy especially in the period from 1925 to 1935.

The great works of the Dada years, that we can date from 1916 to 1924 approximately, the works for which Tzara is best known, are structurally simple but brilliantly colored cinematic panoramas of motion and antirational violence. The elements of action are juxtaposed without any apparent grammatical or semantic links. This lack of cohesion is partly due to the awkwardness of Tzara's French at this time (although there is some controversy even about that), but, more importantly, it represents a stylistic choice. This technique produces the instantaneous effect of vivid discontinuity. Even on the surface, however, there are indications of an interior order which Tzara describes as the genuine orientation of the poetic vision and of an underlying rhythm that he views as characteristic of the apparently frenetic transcription. (pp. 20-1)

By the time of ***Travelers' Tree (L'Arbre des voyageurs)***, published in 1930, Tzara's concern for language is of an equal interest with that of the examination of the poet's own feeling and the display of the violence done to logic by his poetry. The leitmotif of voyage prefigured in the sea journey of ***Cloud Handkerchief (Mouchoir de nuages)*** and in the allusions to roads and paths in ***Heartway Guide (Indicateur des chemins de coeur)*** and ***Circuit by the Moon and Color (Circuit par la lune et par la couleur)*** is transformed into the epic interior pilgrimage of ***Approximate Man.*** Here the theme is interwoven with a reflection on the progress, the power, and the severe limits of language. During this period, Tzara's most intensive linguistic experimentation and poetic development can be described as a lyric journey in itself, as the early unevenness and catalog of spectacle give way to a poetry of range and continuity. Gradually, the bizarre and the bright join with the deeply pathetic and the majestic in a total impression of cosmic inspiration.

In the period from 1931 to 1938, a more sustained lyricism emerges from the linguistic and visionary force of the preceding years, as the image of ***Noontimes Gained (Midis gagnés)*** leads finally to an emphasis on clarity, combined with the profound impulses of night and the dream world. The bizarre is given less weight. The manuscript changes, for example, are frequently a simple substitution of one term, perhaps more euphonious, for another of the same tone, in contrast to the preceding period, where the changes were overwhelmingly toward the more startling or the more grandiose. Tzara now demonstrates a personal involvement in the concerns of the surrealists with whom he is once more, although temporarily, associated. The concept of *ennui,* dear to Breton, dominates a good part of ***The Despairing (Le Désespéranto)*** in ***The Antihead.*** The experimental use of the dream as a transforming and scientific process, an idea advocated by the group of *Inquisitions* which attracted Gaston Bachelard and others of equal eminence, is responsible for the title **"Radiant Mutations" ("Les Mutations radieuses")** and for much of ***Seeds and Bran.***

After 1938, Tzara enters a period of increasing political commitment. In his work, he places an even stronger emphasis on fullness, illumination, and height, as in ***At Full Flame (A haute flamme)***, on the possible generosity of the earth, ***Permitted Fruit (Le Fruit permis), Earth upon Earth (Terre sur terre)***, together with man's necessary acceptance of the ways of nature, **"Acceptance of Spring"** (**"Acceptation du printemps"**"), and on the possible efficacity of human action in the world. Tzara's late poems, centered rather weakly on repeated unspecified images of clarity, fullness, immobility, and vague movement and on simple verbs of vision and motion do not have the poetic strength of his earlier work. . . . His taste and his own tendencies inclined toward the powerful rather than the subtle, direct primitive force rather than the indirect sensitivity, the massive and the epic rather than the understated and the brief. His conception in the earlier ***Approximate Man*** of the dubious and slow-moving approximation of a hero who follows on the overtly negative steps of the earlier ***Antiphilosopher*** is presented not as an incoherent and modest lament but as a great and deliberately prolonged poetic journey. This is the focal point for a great pilgrimage of language, of which all the other writings are only stages along the way. (pp. 21-2)

Probably the clearest insight into Tzara's poetic personality is afforded by his incomplete autobiographical novel ***Place Your Bets*** (***Faites vos jeux***). . . . As the title indicates, the novel is concerned with a game played, in this case, by the poet against himself. The more tragic elements of his nature win out over the others as he balances the concepts of risk, error, and failure against pride in individual assertion: "I play my life on the tornado of every present moment." The romantic "snobbism of melancholy" and the consciousness of a heart constantly bankrupt prevent the poet from acquiring the "taint of mediocrity," as he says. At times, Tzara describes himself ideally as an adventurer with sweeping gestures; but here he calls his actions nearsighted and terms the experiments he makes with language as much of a failure as the sentimental ones he makes in life. He views himself as only a "word merchant, changing ideas and elements of life into images and crystallized sentences and vice versa." (p. 23)

Tzara's spirit of negativity is also reflected in a wide range of poems, beginning with the first melancholy neo-symbolist effusions. Tzara speaks of undergoing a severe psychological crisis around 1916 and then of trying to efface the sentimental from his poems. For this purpose, he incorporates into the poems sounds, scraps of pseudo-language, and phrases resembling African dialects. . . . However, the negative intensity continues with images of burning, breaking, imprisoning, cutting, and other modes of suffering in the ***Twenty-Five Poems (Vingt-cinq poèmes)*** and in all the later works. This melancholy vision was never absent from Tzara's writing. (pp. 23-4)

[Poetry] is for Tzara the transcendence of language from its tragic incompetence and necessary artifice into the purest demonstration of mental freedom. Tzara describes poetry in ***Place Your Bets*** as an instrument of life opened at a certain angle under the light, a property like dampness of color. "Poetry starts where the specificity of painting or verse leaves off." In advocating the "predominance of the human over the aesthetic," Dada "made a poetry a way of life more than the accessory manifestation of intelligence and of will. For art was one of the forces, common to all men, of this poetic activity, whose deep roots mingle with the primitive structure of affective life." (Essay on **"Primitive Art"**)

At the same time that poetry provides the means of living beyond individual self-consciousness and the impotence of language, it also becomes the means of heightening self-consciousness. A strong sense of self and of one's own reactions forms the basis for the extreme sensitivity to the tragic and to the poetic. Tzara speaks in 1917 of his "nerves zigzagged in a cosmic harmonica." Indeed, Tzara's consistent emphasis on self-awareness in his poetry prevents the reader from an unselfconscious absorption in the work. In ***Mr. Aa the Antiphilosopher,*** the first part of ***The Antihead,*** the themes of language and self-consciousness merge. . . . The half-amused, half-serious consciousness of the Dada writing gesture in all its personal and linguistic excessiveness never leaves Tzara: "By being drunk on ourselves." It is the determining element in his numerous and extensive corrections of his own texts.

Of course the approximate nature of language would prevent it from an idle and *fixed* perfection, contrary to the Dada ideals of vertigo and violence. A Dada manifesto of 1918 calls on the poet to jab a trident into the lazy flesh of all who are non-Dada. Tzara repeatedly proclaims his desire to write brutally, to incise with a stiletto the placid appearance of a world too sure of its own logic and the language based on it. In ***Seeds and Bran,*** he describes at length the "vital instinct corrosive and intense," inclining him toward terror, manias, and deliberate depreciation. Poetry offers the best means to "sabotage the realization of the exterior world and its unacceptable manifestations." (pp. 24-5)

There are instances throughout the pre-1936 manuscripts, particularly in Tzara's middle period (1925-1932), of his deliberate effort to *create* a language of shock and of the unexpected. The spontaneous astonishment of Dada is replaced by a more carefully structured epic which has as a basis not its own gyrations, but the no less dramatic plight of man told in an accumulation of images, refrains, fugal rhythms, narrative, litany of plaints, and majestic descant. The many modifications of set phrases and obvious images or clichés, from concrete presentations to abstract ones, from a simple thematic modulation (as in the first stages of ***Approximate Man***) to the infinitely complex series of elaborations and modifications of the final masterpiece seem perplexing at first glance. The poetic progression from the "newspaper poems" to the epic, where Tzara works and reworks his poetry into an odd combination of the sentimental and the bizarre, is astounding. Nevertheless, within the complexity of the epic's imagery certain clusters can be distinguished: images associated with the sky or the seasons, with death and dream, and with water. As in other surrealist writings, they create an atmosphere of the fluid state, the liberated consciousness called poetry. Even the deliberately rough surface of the poetry, the often irritating imagery and overloaded texture, and the seemingly non-sequential nature of the lines serve as signals. They point to the inadequacy of language, to Tzara's doubts concerning the role of poetry. Moreover, they place the reader in a position exterior to the epic from which he can judge its brilliant but uneven character, the extraordinary power and the tragic failure of the poetic word. This strength and this weakness can only be seen approximately, as if there were another more absolute text behind the visible one, which the Dadaist would call "the groupings of an interior order."

In the puzzling and diverse nature of ***Approximate Man*** can be seen the poet's struggle between his desire to recapture the bizarre imagery of his former poetry, on one hand, and, on the other, his spontaneously lyric effusions, emphasized by repetition. Thus a whole series of remarkable extensions of verbally induced images is interrupted by a sort of tragic chorus, repeated from time to time at key points. Appearing at the conclusion of a part, the reiterated phrase casts an emotional aura over all the disjointed brilliance before it. These lyric patterns serve as guides to the rest; in contrast to the other passages in the notebooks, manuscripts, typed pages, and printer's proofs, where Tzara patiently complicates the imagery, these passages are almost never touched. Only their position is changed, as Tzara makes of them the changing centers of his mobile poem on motion:

consolation . . . consolation . . . consolation

morning/ morning/ morning sealed in crystal

above nocturnal peace nocturnal peace/ and
so many others and so many others
peace on the outside of this world reversed
in the mold of unanimous approximations/
and on so many others and on so many others

I have pledged my waiting . . . I have pledged my waiting

These refrains express a certain universality, patience, and peace. They are the obvious threads leading to the final hope, as incomplete man in all the humility and uncertainty of his vocabulary is led by a shepherd of absolute language toward a final ordeal of fire and waiting, the agents of his possible transformation. They are not only the visible centers of lyric continuity and the sustained focus of the mutual involvement of poet and reader, but also the stages of an invisible progression toward unity and completeness in language and in vision.

Even as early as ***The Second Celestial Adventure of Mr. Antipyrine,*** the concept of *centers* forms the focus of an eight-line incantation. Tzara himself refers to the roundness of his "semi-language"; and a passage from ***The Antihead*** reads as a description of the rapid, wheel-like motion of the ideal gyratory language as it revolves about the specific center of its desire. . . . Corresponding to this roundness is the fundamental notion of centers, or kernels. . . . Tzara refers constantly to images of centers, as if language continued to be the *circus* it had been during the Dada epoch. . . . The refrains themselves in ***Approximate Man*** are the centers of the rest: in many cases, they appear before the rest of the work and are never altered.

Like ***Approximate Man,*** the prose poems of the latter part of ***The Antihead*** (the first parts of which date from the same period as the ***Twenty-Five Poems*** and ***Seeds and Bran***) are based on continuous thematic structures and repetitions of corresponding verbal rearrangements. Through their lengthy accumulations of details and their eloquent invocations of night, boredom, and dream, there is built up a linguistic and dramatic momentum of unmistakable force. They are structurally as impressive as ***Approximate Man.*** (pp. 25-8)

Mary Ann Caws, in an introduction to Approximate Man and Other Writings *by Tristan Tzara, translated by Mary Ann Caws, Wayne State University Press, 1973, pp. 15-35.*

JACQUES BERSANI

[The title ***Oeuvres complètes, Volume I: 1912-1924***] is too classic with its chilly whiff of the grave and academe. Its cover is sagely, too sagely, Art Nouveau, in dark brown and blue on white. And inside this misleading package there are 746 of the craziest and most serious, the gayest and most violent, the most amazing, most explosive pages possible. Here is Tzara as he's never been read before: everything at once, everything at least up to 1924.

Thanks are due to Henri Behar, the editor of these ***Oeuvres completes*** . . . , for having managed to group, date and classify texts dispersed at random in magazines and anthologies, not to mention desk drawers and file folders. But even greater thanks are due for his having managed, through a discreet use of notes, to show the singlemindedness and consistency of Tzara's concerns: "His approach, however violent, is totally unified in its overriding determination to construct a poetic edifice." . . .

Perhaps it's time to see ***Vingt-cinq poemes, Cinema calendrier du coeur abstrait, De nos signaux,*** all those admirable texts. Here reprinted at last, for what they are: the undeniable saboteurs of both traditional and modern poetic tradition, but also, and chiefly, the revelation, through that same destruction, of poetry's true path. We must get rid of the legends and the cliches: "**Amer Aile Soir**" and "**Soleil Nuit**" weren't pulled out of a hat, and if their own meaning isn't obvious, it's certainly obvious that they're anything but nonsense.

As in the "poemes negres" which Tzara, far from inventing, enthusiastically translated after an extremely pallid debut in the wake of Maeterlinck and Laforgue, here are words restored to their primeval force, replenished with the "quantity of life" they carry and transmit to us. In a plentitude of sound, of rhythmic intensity, poetry becomes, or becomes once again, a system of physics; language becomes a cosmos whose laws are no longer logic and good taste but attraction and repulsion.

So thick a volume weighs so light in the hand because it obeys the rule laid down by Tzara himself in his famous 1918 manifesto: "Every page must explode, whether in deep and heavy seriousness; in vortex, vertigo, novelty, eternity; in cutting jest; in zealous ideals; or in the way it's printed."

Tzara lives: the [***Oeuvres complètes***] prove it.

Jacques Bersani, "Tzara Lives!," in Manchester Guardian Weekly, *December 28, 1975, p. 12.*

ROGER CARDINAL

All views of the world are relative, nothing is sacred, [Tzara] proclaims [in ***Seven Dada Manifestos and Lampisteries***], and in the same dismissive breath announces the advent of chaos and his intention "to destroy the drawers of the brain, and those of social organization; to sow demoralization everywhere. . .".

The reader of the first English versions of the Dada manifestos can only guess what it must have been like to experience them at first hand at those legendary evenings arranged by Tzara in Zurich and Paris. The author wrote them to be read aloud and did so, we are told, to the accompaniment of sobs, screams and whistles, gestures, and dance-steps, in a combination of expressive modes calculated to intensify their immediate impact on the audience.

Reading the bare words on the page some sixty years after the event, one can none the less catch Tzara's distinctive tone. His is an incisively witty voice, practised in ironies and tricks of speech, that slickly delivers sardonic jokes and shrill denunciations directed at a host of targets—the voice of a wizard in words, a hysteric chatterbox, who, defying all logic and propriety, somehow manages to communicate and even to entrance. Tzara loves to baffle his listener with a barrage of obscure aphorisms and paradoxes and to court his disgust by announcing "I consider myself very likeable".

As a result it is hard for us to see that Tzara is in fact more deeply serious than the tomfoolery and provocation seemed to allow. Yet Dada was for him, not simply a means to raise a riot . . . , but above all a crusade to establish a new approach to art and thereby to existence.

For, far from desiring the global annihilation of art, Dada was a tonic prelude to the exploration of fresh perspectives. Attend to what Tzara is actually saying in these manifestos, as distinct from his persona, and you will hear the entirely earnest voice of a man who badly wants art to recover from the drastic surgery it is undergoing.

In denouncing the imperialism of the cultural establishment, in rejecting Cubism and Futurism as fashionable luxuries, in voicing the outrageous call to abolish all logic, all hierarchies, all good manners, all systems, Tzara is ultimately hoping to break through the crust of received ideas that separates the artist from his public, and to convey an urgent intuition of the authentic sensibility that might emerge from anarchy.

If for example Tzara announces "Dada is working with all its might towards the universal installation of the idiot" he will scandalize those who see in this an ignoble attack on intellect; whereas a few attentive spirits may realize that he is in fact positing the ideal of an intelligence uncontaminated by established culture. Dada aims at a new simplicity, allied to individual spontaneity and to the notion that life itself is something blissfully absurd, irreducible to an objective logic, yet not sheer vacancy, but the ground of authentic freedom.

The texts of ***Lampisteries*** date from the same period, and provide firm support for the view that Tzara genuinely hoped for reconstruction after the Dada state of emergency. In these reviews and theoretical notes, he comes across as anything but a nihilist.

The crucial text is the 1922 **"Lecture on Dada",** Tzara's public farewell to the experiment. Though it echoes the old manner in an opening quip about refusing to grant an explanation about Dada to the audience which has paid to hear just that, the lecture does in fact offer a clear definition of the Dada spirit. Its metaphysical basis, Tzara indicates, is a sense of indifference, "an even, calm state of mind, in which everything is equal and unimportant"—which seems close on the one hand to the Pataphysics of Jarry, and on the other to Taoism. (Did not Tzara once remark that Chuang Tzu, the Taoist sage, was the first Dadaist?) Of course, such calm did not prevent Dada from also being explosive and destructive, but, as Tzara argues, this is because all contraries are equivalent anyway, or as he says elsewhere, "everything is the same as everything that is not the same".

In the context of an almost pious acceptance of contradiction and nothingness, Tzara insists on holding on to two strands which sustain the positive creative value implicit in Dada: spontaneity and subjectivism. The one determines the other, for "everything that comes from us freely without any intervention from speculative ideas, represents us" that is, the value of art is that it finally outweighs the meaninglessness of existence, not by erecting fake values such as Beauty and Truth, but by transmitting the "intensity of a personality, transposed directly and clearly".

The sober lesson of Tzara's lecture on Dada is thus the same as the one visible through the effervescent ravings of the manifestoes. What we engage with here is the mystery of a living subjectivity. As much as key documents in the public chronology of the avant-garde, we may therefore see these Dada texts as occasions for Tzara to test himself, to explore his fund of spontaneity as a prelude to mature creation.

Roger Cardinal, "States of Emergency," in The Times Literary Supplement, *No. 3955, January 13, 1978, p. 27.*

ROGER CARDINAL

[The] first two bulky volumes of Tzara's prolific life-work [***Oeuvres complètes, Volume I: 1912-1924*** and ***Oeuvres complètes, Volume II: 1925-1933***] take us from the poems of his adolescence in Bucharest, through the classic texts of Zürich and Paris Dadaism, and on into his Surrealist period in the late 1920s and early 1930s. Tzara himself refused to accept that his different "periods" were discontinuous, and kept a careful archive of his own. From this and from Henri Béhar's painstaking editorial researches, we now have the material from which the overall shape of Tzara's achievement as a counter-cultural writer can be elicited. . . .

From the outset, Tzara's outrageous onslaughts on syntax and linguistic coherence are accompanied by a reassuring sense that even as it succumbed to his aggressive manipulations, the French language remained attractive. It is fascinating to observe how the writer's style develops in these volumes: lyrical beauty seems to be fostered by the very ravages that the Dada experiments dictated.

Tzara's literary terrorism took the form of experimental writing based on an astounding variety of techniques. The texts include spontaneous or automatic poems (more or less consistent with the principles of composition defined by Breton in the Surrealist Manifesto), sound poems using nonsense syllables, and poems adapted from Negro and Maori folk-songs. Tzara experimented in "fold-in" techniques à la William Burroughs whereby, boasting that he was a "self-kleptomaniac", he would rejuvenate old texts of his own by cutting them up and shuffling the bits. He would delightedly appropriate any manuscript or printing errors, and introduce meaningless coinages ("tzaca tzac tzacatzac"), abstruse scientific terms, newspaper headlines, publicity slogans, anagrams, puns ("mississicri") and frenzied repetitions (as witness the page from the 1918 ***Manifeste Dada*** on which the single word *hurle* appears in a block eleven rows wide by twenty-five lines deep). Together with their typographical inconsistencies and their general submission to the principle of syntactic and semantic illogicality, the resulting texts are almost impossible to read in any coherent way. They are manifestations of disorder and absurdity, and defy all normal logic.

There is a wild and nihilistic glitter about the Dada poems of ***Vingt-cinq poèmes*** (1918) and ***De nos oiseaux*** (1923), for instance. Tonal shifts occur from line to line, thrusting the reader through staccato transitions—calm, querulous, sly, disdainful. The vocabulary is in constant flux; all sense of sequence or form is absent. To read is to speed through an alien country where landmarks flash past too fast for recognition. There is no centre and no shape to these poems; their message is purely one of aggressive self-manifestation: "Danse crie casse". They are spectacular provocations which deliberately obstruct the intelligence in search of meaning and implicitly challenge the reader—"Dare you take this to be Literature?" . . .

Tzara's ideal text would seem to be one in which words emerge in a naked state, not as carriers of meaning proper but as manifestations of a kind of pure electrical energy. And each word is as highly charged as the next. . . . Each word comes out of the blue, so to speak, lacking a context and yet bristling with its own urgent singularity. The author himself is nowhere to be seen, so that what he offers is a random texture, an anonymous surface from which no intention or meaning can be read. However, no writer would want to keep up such an illegible mode for ever, and Tzara's savage zest generates occasional passages of accessible lyricism. The reader battling his way through the blizzard of unintelligibility is rewarded by abrupt transitions into zones of radiant meaning. Random islets of unexpected beauty float up, images which glow with the strange and moving colours of a dream. . . .

There is a sense, then, in which this most formless and anarchic of poetry eventually coheres and reveals some sort of purpose and shape. The climax of **"Maison Flake"** (1919) expresses a vision which it is not hard to read as being consciously constructive rather than terroristic. . . . Here the poetic meaning emerges clearly enough in the form of an apologia for the poem itself. Sounding much like Apollinaire in "La Jolie Rousse", Tzara describes his aim of uncovering poetic images which will suggest to his reader that a deeper harmony underlies the surface discontinuities of reality and language.

The more one reads Tzara, the more one becomes attuned to the notion of the creative stance as sketched in the 1919 **"Note sur la Poésie".** There Tzara sees poetry as a juggling with disparates whereby the juggler stands at the central point of serene communion with his innermost being: "Eye, water, equilibrium, sun, kilometre, and everything that I can imagine as belonging together and which represents a potential human asset: sensibility". The continuity which underlies the torrential generation of texts is that of the sensibility at their centre. Tzara may insist on remaining impersonal, on setting value only on work produced by one who remains "demanding and cruel, pure and honest", that is: committed to no intentional meaning. Yet the immediacy and sheer verve of his writing is such as to convey a lively sense of his involvement: the author's euphoric pleasure in his own text transmits a kind of presence after all. We witness "l'intensité d'une personnalité transposée directement" as, like a watermark on soiled paper, the temper of thc propelling consciousness shimmers beneath the flux of words. And here one can find confirmation of a paradox that has haunted French poetry since Rimbaud and Mallarmé: that the more a writer strives to extinguish his individuality, the more idiosyncratic and personal his style becomes.

Tzara evidently saw himself as fitting more and more into the French poetic tradition as he developed. The love poems of ***Indicateur des chemins du coeur*** (1928) and ***L'Arbre des voyageurs*** (1930) contain elegiac echoes of Lamartine and Apollinaire, while the major poetic performance of ***L'Homme approximatif*** (composed during 1925-30) is a deliberate attempt on Tzara's part to stake a claim to a place in French literary history as a poet confident enough to sustain a long poem, on a par with Apollinaire ("Zone"), Saint-John Perse (*Vents*) and Eluard (*Poésie ininterrompue*).

While, in this ninety-page poem, Tzara remains very much the literary "savage", he demonstrably draws upon all sorts of sophisticated effects, many of them entirely traditional. Most noticeably, the verbal flux now falls into rhythmic clusters, long lines reminiscent of the epic *laisses* of a Perse, and is punctuated by recurring words or leitmotif phrases that communicate an overall sense of an insistent, structured argument.

[***L'Homme approximatif***] is centred on the consciousness of the "approximate man." . . . This is Tzara's persona, a timid yet hopeful pilgrim who battles for meaning in a universe of absurdity. . . . No longer absent from the verbal struggle, the poet reveals his frailty in the face of the "inexpressible plenitude" of his surroundings. Words seem hostile, and he can only succumb to their terrifying meaninglessness as they flash through consciousness: ''words streaking / leaving the merest trace majestic trace behind their meaning scarcely meaningful.'' . . .

Like Perse or (as Jean Cassou suggested) Walt Whitman, Tzara had in mind in [***L'Homme approximatif***] to build up a catalogue of allusions that would support a poetic vision of elemental depth and encyclopedic completeness. Animals, minerals, cities, jungles—all are evoked in a polymorphous discourse voiced by a subject who, at first bewildered, grows in confidence, being gradually borne upon the tide of words to achieve a position of confidence and all-surveying dominance. Henri Béhar comments that the poet ''transforms himself into mineral, vegetable, bird, insect: he is himself *natura naturata*''.

That is, in this apocalyptic explosion of language, the poet finally approaches the primal seat of creativity, the point where the naked word reveals the naked truth about the world. . . . A language which at last takes root and generates profound meaning, this is Tzara's ultimate aim.

At the same time, however, his tone has a certain shrillness which makes his grand theme less overwhelming than does, say, the more majestic rhetoric of Perse. Prolonged reading of the poem has left this reader unsatisfied that it succeeds in approximating a visionary grasp on cosmic realities. Much of ***L'Homme approximatif*** is too wordy, the modulation from chaos to confidence too sleekly *verbal*. ''La parole seule suffit pour voir'', claims Tzara, in echo of a prime Surrealist tenet; but this text is often too mannered and wilful to create the full visionary effect.

One turns therefore to the last section in these two volumes, ***L'Antitête,*** which groups texts written across the Dada and Surrealist years (1919-32). The most impressive are a set of automatic prose pieces under the heading ***Le Désespéranto,*** a title which ties in the two strands of Tzara's poetic effort: a desire to achieve the condition of a universal language, an ''esperanto'' which will touch on all aspects of human feeling and thought; and the acknowledgment that true intensity of expression can only be found in circumstances of stress and desperation—the courting of self-extinction is a corollary of verbal authenticity.

These are indeed texts of moving authority and incisiveness, which suggests that it was in prose that Tzara was best able to sustain his characteristic ''attack''. In the closing piece, **''Les Consciences atténuantes'',** the adventure into language comes across most powerfully, truly convincing the reader that ''beneath each stone, there is a nest of words and it is from their rapid spinning that the substance of the world is formed''. It is in such texts, stripped of self-conscious flourishes and rhetorical supports, that Tzara comes closest to that ''stenography of feeling'' which he came to see as his poetic goal, and thus demonstrates the remarkable way in which his uncompromising poetics of non-intentionality finally communicates ''l'aignë intensité de la conscience'', the naked energy of his singular consciousness.

Roger Cardinal, ''Adventuring into Language,'' in The Times Literary Supplement, *No. 3993, October 13, 1978, p. 1156.*

RUTH L. CALDWELL

As we consider [Tristan Tzara's] work between 1918, date of his first published volume of poetry, and 1961, date of his last published volume, we see that while his style undergoes radical changes, there are no breaks in his conception of the unity of nature, which becomes a dominant theme in his work and a justification for his variety of techniques.

Three common elements of ''nature,'' as perceived by and set against ''man,'' are the sky, the sea and the earth. Taking these elements in all their allusive possibilities, we can see how in his first published work, ***Vingt-cinq poèmes,*** Tzara makes these elements clash, in unexpected and sometimes violent ways. The first poem of the volume, **''Le géant blanc lépreux du paysage,''** has a number of unsettling signs: . . .

> (salt groups in a constellation of birds on the cotton
> wool tumor
> in his lungs starfish and bugs balance
> microbes crystallize into palm trees of muscles swings
> hello without cigarette tzantzantza ganga
> bouzdouc zdouc nfounfa mbaah mbaah nfounfa
> macrocystis perifera kiss the boats surgeon of the boats
> humid clean scar)

From the beginning of the poem, strange syllables, coming from Tzara's interest in African poetry, jump to our eyes. The lack of punctuation and capitalization aggravate the irregularity of the lines. Within the first three lines, the three nature images are already present, all within the context of the sick body: the image of ''a constellation of birds on the cotton wool tumor'' brings the sky into the sickness. In the second line, the sea enters, with the presence of starfish in the lungs. Finally, in the third line, we find the ''palm trees of muscles,'' where the plant image suggests the earth. The confrontation between the human being and the world seen in this first poem appears again and again in Tzara's work.

Sometimes the confrontation emphasizes sickness, where the world outside seems to invade the inside, signified by various organs of the body. The transformations going on in the body or beyond it also give strange images, whether one chooses to call them Dada or surrealist. Finally, there is a confrontation between the reader and these images: . . .

> (. . . . here the reader starts to shout
> the reader wants to die perhaps or dance and
> starts to shout
> he is thin stupid dirty he doesn't understand my verses
> he shouts
> he is one-eyed)

To the kind of reader insulted toward the end of the poem the universe presented appears distorted or offensive, which is not the least of the effects desired by the Dada poet.

Indeed, aside from the unusual imagery of nature, the vocabulary of nature is another possible source of reader irritation. Alongside meaningless sounds or African-inspired syllables we find the word *macrocystis perifera,* a brown alga. In other texts we find words like *lithophanie* (a process which obtains opaque shadows or translucid reflections in porcelain, glass and the like), *aniline* (an amino acid used in fabricating synthetic colors), and *gymnotes,* eel-like fresh water fishes of South America. It is ironic that the scientific words, scattered throughout the texts in this volume, although part of our dictionaries, prevent our easy access to reading, because they are not part of our everyday language. Thus scientific words—precisely the things used by human beings to clarify their world—are used here to distort it.

However, we might also see the emergence of coherent themes, linked to the nature images. In this text, allusions to the sky or that which is above or beyond, such as "the family of sounds," "the origin," or "beyond the starboard," suggest a distant goal, a desire for unity. The search for such unity is often linked to marine imagery, represented in . . . [some] poems by a descent into the sea (which could also signify the subconscious). . . . On the other hand, earth imagery suggests growth and transformation, although of an unusual kind. Usually, in [***Vingt-cinq poèmes***], earth references such as rocks, trees and the seasons, are juxtaposed in unexpected ways, as in the "palm trees of muscles" of [**"Le géant blanc lépreux du paysage"**]. In the poem entitled **"printemps,"** the habitual images associated with springtime are not present. Everything goes on in obscurity and the lack of freshness. The sowing of seeds is more nearly a preparation of a witches' brew. Thus, in this first volume, we see the goal of new visions, represented by the sky, and the search for and even the process of transformations, represented by earth images. But the emphasis is on searching, as seen in the marine images.

In the 1920's Tzara's writing changes. The disappearance of techniques like mere sounds and meaningless syllables, or simultaneism and juxtaposition, seems to suggest a growing concern for meaning. Even so, the language is not necessarily simplified and the lines often conserve an effect of an avalanche of images. We can consider as representative of these years Tzara's masterpiece, ***L'homme approximatif,*** composed between 1925 and 1931. This work might be thought of as Tzara's *De Rerum Natura;* it is his key poetical work, in which he sets forth the ideas which have occupied him for years. This long epic poem, which depicts a search for a knowledge and a language that would incorporate all things in the universe, develops the three main natural elements previously identified.

In general, we find a closer association of these images, with metaphor becoming metamorphosis: . . .

> (even beneath birch bark life loses itself in bloody hypotheses
> where peaks peck at stars and foxes sneeze insular echoes
> but from what depths loom these flakes of damned souls
> that intoxicate the ponds with their warm idleness)

The opening lines of the sixth part of the poem set up a transformational universe, where life is presented as "hypotheses" and where the interior ("beneath birch bark") has a movement of its own ("loses itself"), capable of change. The lines that follow show the possible linking of the interior with the exterior, which we remember was an impossibility in the texts of ***Vingt-cinq poèmes.*** Outward movement is suggested by elements of the earth reaching the sky or the air (line 2) and things beneath the earth touching the surface of water (last two lines). Here there is a mixture of plants, animals, human qualities, and the sky. (pp. 18-21)

Elsewhere in [***L'homme approximatif***], Tzara evokes "correspondences" and "immense and eternal coincidences." In a free imagery that mixes animals, vegetables and minerals, bushes have fins, a poplar tree can fly, mountains have throats, children change into grasshoppers, plants climb in the veins of man, and in the pores of the skin one finds a garden and the "complete fauna" of suffering. Man is evoked in one line as "man somewhat animal somewhat flower somewhat metal somewhat man." Here we see that while Tzara's writing may show the influence of surrealism, it also puts a special stamp on certain techniques associated with surrealism. Thus the possessive formation (such as "the earth's lip" or "the climbing plants of your veins"), an image which juxtaposes nouns not usually associated together and of which the surrealists were so fond, is not a momentary ornament of surprise, but a constant factor in the universe of transformations that is continuously proclaimed in Tzara's works.

Another development of the earth, water and sky images concerns the search for a cosmic language, which is the main theme of this poem. Here we see perhaps the old conflict between Nominalism and Realism, with Tzara seeming to take a Realist's stand, attacking the convention of words which have become "rotten" because they no longer apply to things, but rather to their own grammatical system. Tzara seems to want to bring words closer to the things they represent. After attacking man's language, the speaker of [***L'homme approximatif***] presents a language that participates in all the elements. There exist "multiple languages," the sky has tongues or languages (Tzara exploits the double meaning of the French word), there are "flying words," and "shooting words," rain is described as "writing without respite," and there is an "unspeakable theory of vocabularies and thoraces," an "alphabet of your necklace of teeth," a "grammar of eyes," and mollusks have hieroglyphics. Tzara in fact changes a line in his manuscript from "the sky's agricultural instruments" to "the sky's languages." The speaker must find the cosmic language so he might decipher the "unreadable sun."

A dominant element seems to emerge at the end of the poem. This last section begins with an apocalyptic rupture: mountains have whooping cough, the sky is a new ground that is broken, the rain is rapid, and "essences" are drowned. The only element that seems to remain untouched is man, although in his rock-like closure, he awaits expectantly his own rupture, and at four separate times we see a powerful refrain: . . .

> (and rugged in my clothing of schist
> I have pledged my waiting to the oxidized desert of torment
> to the robust advent of its flame)

In the end of the poem, before the final repetition of this refrain, the speaker compares man to a "slow furnace" and implores fire to come, rejecting harmony. Although ascendance is always possible, with the image of fire (which is linked to the earth, but moves upward), the "approximate man" of the poem seems to remain linked to the earth. He feels the "despair of granite" and speaks of the "sparse vegetation" of his being. His search settles into a determined and continual struggle. These earth images are important to Tzara's later works, which reflect his political involvement.

Critics generally agree that Tzara's poetry becomes clearer after 1935. This change has been associated with a political orientation in Tzara's writing, which appeared as early as the ***Essai sur la situation de la poésie,*** published in 1931, and in the footnotes to a volume of poetic prose, published in 1935 and entitled ***Grains et Issues,*** where we see, indeed, the earth-linked image of grains. Doubtless, such activities as going to the front during the Spanish Civil War and writing in clandestine magazines in the south of France during the Resistance encouraged a realism that we find in many texts, especially some long poems (***Sans coup férir,*** and ***A haute flamme***) which are organized around a political significance.

This realism is also reflected in the development of the earth images. Generally, the sense of struggle becomes calmer, more determined and more coherent. Travel imagery is less often associated with flight and searching and more often indicative of the determined march or advancement. The opposition between seasons and light and darkness tends towards a balanced, interdependent relationship. (pp. 21-2)

In these later works there is also a greater emphasis on plenitude and on the concreteness of the earth: in rocks, fruits, and trees. We can see examples of this development in the titles: ***Le Signe de Vie*** (1946), ***Terre sur terre*** (1946), ***Le Fruit permis*** (1956), ***Frère Bois*** (1958). This latter small volume is probably the most radically simple of all of Tzara's works. These texts all evoke concrete aspects of nature (woods, stones, hills, the sun, sky and fruits) and they give a sense of the close presence of nature, where the forest is a "brother," and the stone a "sister." There is warmth in the personalization of the sun and sensuality in the attributes of a date. There is also in these texts a sense of surprise and mystery, as the sun is associated with Botticelli, an artist known for his fine lines and colors, and a date and a smile are sources of wonder to the speaker in the last text. It is as if Tzara had finally made his peace with the things that people his world.

What we have seen in this poetic itinerary is how one idea, the unity and totality of nature, can have many forms, from a Dada outburst to a text with the lightness of a song. Different images of nature as sky, sea, and earth (associated with distant goals, searching or transformation, and finally, a determined struggle) are emphasized at different times within a context of totality. Of course, the idea itself of the totality of nature is scarcely original. Tzara was, however, bucking a serious linguistic trend in the twentieth century in his refusal to accept words as mere signs, or as he says contemptuously in one poem: "postage stamps on things." Ecologists of today can perhaps sympathize with the almost Franciscan statements of ***Frère Bois.*** Tzara in fact is arguing for a cosmic language, in which humans and nature are no longer alienated from each other. In Tzara's life and work much commitment and many varied poems grew out of the idea that nature, in its total workings, is a symbol and ally for process, both political and poetical. (pp. 22-3)

Ruth L. Caldwell, "From Chemical Explosion to Simple Fruits: Nature in the Poetry of Tristan Tzara," in Perspectives on Contemporary Literature, *Vol. 5, 1979, pp. 18-23.*

Constance (Henriette) Urdang

1922-

American poet, novelist, and editor.

In much of her work, Urdang responds to women's issues from various historical periods and geographical locations. In her experimental novel *Natural History* (1969), Urdang combines newspaper clippings, journal entries, and nonlinear narration to examine, in Jay Neugeboren's words, "time, birth, generation, old age, love, death." Urdang's recent novella, *Lucha* (1986), centers on the Mexican heritage and stoical resignation of the title character while depicting the repression of women. Urdang's poetry collections *Charades and Celebrations* (1965), *The Picnic in the Cemetery* (1975), *The Lone Woman and Others* (1981), and *Only the World* (1983) are respected for her austere handling of such themes as alienation, death, sexuality, and feminism.

(See also *Contemporary Authors,* Vols. 21-24, rev. ed. and *Contemporary Authors New Revision Series,* Vol. 9.)

Photograph by Ida Robbins. Courtesy of Constance Urdang.

CHOICE

In her first book [***Charades and Celebrations,*** Urdang] demonstrates decided talent and a sensibility and style that have not quite shaken down into something distinctively her own. At times she is fragmentary and imagistic. At other times, her verse reads like the early Auden reborn, as in **"The Madman."** Often she tries too hard to be cute, and occasionally, especially in her satire, she labors the obvious with more heaviness than wit. . . . Certain of the poems have a direct and touching emotional impact; a particularly moving one is **"Lines for My Grandmother's Grave."** . . . Uneven and still awkwardly derivative in spots, this first collection of verse reveals a versatile and interesting talent, still in process of formation.

A review of "Charades and Celebrations," in Choice, *Vol. 2, No. 10, December, 1965, p. 686.*

JAY NEUGEBOREN

Natural History, by Constance Urdang, is a novel in search of a novel—in format, a St. Louis housewife's notes, mingled with scrapbook items: clippings, excerpts from letters, quotations, descriptions of old photos. Despite this anti-fiction pattern, and despite the fact that the narrator is endlessly concerned with her own and with all writing, ***Natural History*** itself seems quite old-fashioned.

The narrator (who remains nameless), involves us in her own life (past, present, future), in the life of her family, in a trip she takes to New York (where she was born) and in the lives of three woman friends. . . . Like the narrator's own life and thoughts, however, the actuality of what happens to these friends is always in question; the difference between what they *are* and the parts they play in this novel-in-search-of-a-novel. Eventually their reality—their childbearing, their love affairs, their very words—become suspect. . . .

In spite of the book's fragmented surface, in spite of its disclaimers ("Not a novel . . ."), it becomes, due to its sure and singular voice, a coherent, evocative and real object in its own right. Rapid juxtapositions of materials (e.g., a quotation from Lenny Bruce followed by a loving rumination on the narrator's grandmother), news stories about marijuana, booby-trapped Vietnamese dolls, birth control, the Kama Sutra, lengthy excerpts from testimony in an "obscene book case" (to which the narrator's husband has been called as witness)—none of these seem jarring, out of place. The novel's concerns remain fundamental, traditional: time, birth, generation, old age, love, death. It is unified as much by these concerns as by its quiet tone, by the voice which itself imposes a sense of these things.

Natural History is best when it is lodged in the physical. Miss Urdang (who has published a book of poetry) has a sharp eye for detail, and the hard, lyric gifts to project it. Her speculations on abstract matters are less convincing. The surface of the book remains, alas, less interesting than the intelligence that created it.

Even the capsule stories, brief histories and lovely character sketches are here, it often seems, for purposes of argument—as if to prove that the author *could* have written a conventional novel had she wished to. Moreover, the thinness, the very brevity of the book seems to reinforce its languid, dispassionate tone, to make it seem insufficient, empty.

If, as one reading might suggest, this is somehow the point; if the author's intention is to *not* involve us in a world, in "media" which "effect a homogenization of the most bizarre aspects of contemporary experience, thereby divesting all experience of any particular significance," then ***Natural History*** still lacks—despite its gifts of observation, its fine intelligence—the freshness and substance to compel our attention. One finishes it hungry for more of its too-infrequent magic. . . . (pp. 30-1)

Jay Neugeboren, "A St. Louis Housewife Broods on Life and Love," in The New York Times Book Review, *July 20, 1969, pp. 30-1.*

THE VIRGINIA QUARTERLY REVIEW

[***Natural History***] is a novel which should, but probably won't, be widely read. It's a difficult, mature novel, a "novel of ideas"—as Miss Urdang herself admits, immediately disinfecting the phrase by noting that, as usual in such cases, the ideas are not necessarily the author's but rather the "political, philosophical, moral ideas 'going around.'" Miss Urdang is a poet, and ***Natural History*** is written with a precision and economy of language altogether unexpected in a novel. She has also constructed ***Natural History*** as a poem, with its "emotional impact to implode, as in a poem, rather than empathy, antipathy, etc., as in a novel." Her strategy fails—the disparate elements, scenes, quotations never quite merge to produce the desired implosion—but her novel is probably more interesting, and illuminating, as a failure than it could have been a success. . . . The narrative is an honest, moving, and intelligent questioning of what a woman's rôle is, and can be, in our society. ***Natural History,*** without becoming self-indulgent and without the glib confidences of confessional literature, has the fascination of a brilliant journal and, despite Miss Urdang's disclaimers, the emotional resonance that distinguishes the art of the novel. (pp. cxxviii-cxxix)

A review of "Natural History," in The Virginia Quarterly Review, *Vol. 45, No. 4, Autumn, 1969, pp. cxxviii-cxxix.*

RICHARD HOWARD

Ten years ago, Constance Urdang published her first book of poems, ***Charades & Celebrations.*** And then she published her first novel, ***Natural History.*** [In ***The Picnic in the Cemetery,*** the] charades have been discarded, and the celebrations are riddled with a kind of somatic resignation which reminds us that doom means no more than judgment, the verdict of our flesh upon itself, natural history. . . . She has made herself a poet of stoical transformations, of becomings and ongoings, in the tumultuous, often convulsive course whereof there are no constants in experience: nothing stays the same. It is why so often this poetry, so often this spellbinding, refuses to take the *given* for itself. What is the use of being a little boy, Gertrude Stein used to ask, if you are going to grow up to be a man? It is not a use, Constance Urdang answers—speaking as the mother of daughters and a son, as the daughter of dead parents, as a *member* who knows that dismembering is far more likely, more to be looked for than remembering—it is a tragedy. And her poems are the purging of pity and terror, the drama of having a body which keeps us from our only felicity, forgetting.

The speech here is from the center, it is therefore gnomic and ready for the shortest distance—no need to take the long way around when the remarked helplessness is at hand, within reach: put out a hand and the opaque realities are there, to be touched, to be scarred, to be hugged close to the self. And in that repository, to be altered: brought to birth. The rhythms of parturition and the vehemence of the childbed: blood, pain, and travail are everywhere offered here, without much confidence in the taking. It is still a celebration, the new Constance Urdang poem—the picnic in the cemetery is a feast aware of the dead underground, in the sandwiches, on the mind. . . .

In the Villa Giulia, in Rome, is the principal museum of Etruscan art, and in the center of that museum is the sarcophagus of a married couple, from Cerveteri, carved or modeled in the second half of the sixth century B.C. The pair are reclining together on a couch, with the upper part of the bodies raised, and are turned toward the spectator; there is no precedence, no preference, in fact, in the handling of the man, the woman—they are together in their death, he rests his right arm on her shoulder, his left hand touches her elbow, and their bodies melt together at the loins. As you look at them, the four hands extend toward you in a bouquet of gestures, unspecified but significant. The faunlike faces (as D. H. Lawrence saw them) have a tiny smile which does not even draw the flesh over the bones—it is the smile not of pleasure but of acceptance, of acknowledgment. These know they have died, for they know that only what has been alive can die. Their frank sexuality and their freedom to accept mortality make them unique in all Western art—unique because there is no placing or grading, no refusing and no choosing.

Such an object is the analogy I want for a Constance Urdang poem—for any group of her poems. Though of course she writes most deliberately as a woman, a wife, a daughter, a mother, a maiden, a whore, a crone (the nurse, the sibyl, and the hag are favorite inflections), she is astonishing among the women poets I know for her egalitarianism, for her coupled measurements of what it must be to be fully human. What bothers her into poetry is not resentment but response, not competition but compassion, not replacement but replenishment. For she is supremely aware of the metamorphoses—even in the cemetery, even in the nursery, in the nursery most of all. Death is not something that comes from outside and takes life away; death in her poems is there, a presence within, which affords life its careful meaning, its meaningful care. And the poem will be accountable to these immense perceptions

> by the glass, wherein all images are clear
> by the needle, that pricks and lets no one rest
> by fire, that burns and is not consumed
> by song
> by praise
> by silence

A lot of winnowing, a lot of paring, a lot of *undoing* has gone into these charms and hexes. Their patience is exemplary, for it has accommodated the eager hopes of what will not be stilled, as well as the pressure of what will be only still. They do not make grand gestures, though they have the presence of a certain grandeur in them: the grandeur to hold still and watch, to sit by the fire and wait. Laboring, waiting, noticing—these are the actions which afford, sometimes, a cosmic insight, as in the poem **"Nightfall,"** and sometimes a comic one (though the joke is always on her, on the properly named Constance), as in **"MidAmerica."** They are poems of wisdom which has shucked off knowledge, which has shucked off information—there will not be many facts here, and there will not be many fables. There will be the sediment, the precipitate, the residue of facts and fables, and we call it wisdom, a word whose root has something to do with our word *guide* and with that word for appearances *guise* or *wise,* as when we say a thing is done in a certain wise. Hence the cool *sagesse* of a poem like **"The Fruit,"** which appears to come out of the ritual practice of proscribed lineages, but which is no more (no more!) than the long, loving look at the guise of things, and the guidance such a look yields up. It is the look I have seen on the Etruscan funerary figures, and the likeness, too, of this poem, which will do—if the reader goes no further than this note—as a liminary specimen of this remarkable artist, this wise woman who, like a man, is never disgusted. . . . The authority of ["**The Fruit**"] speaks for itself—indeed that is for whom it must speak. The beauty and the justice of it is that there is a "whom," that there is a person *paying,* as the French say, for the wisdom achieved, won from nothing less than the whole range of the life lived, the suffering known, the joy divined. (pp. vii-xi)

Richard Howard, "A Note on Constance Urdang," in The Picnic in the Cemetery: Poems *by Constance Urdang, George Braziller, 1975, pp. vii-xi.*

WILLIAM LOGAN

"Outside the circle around the campfire / beyond where the lamplight reaches" is where Constance Urdang's imagination travels, and where her fears lurk [in ***The Picnic in the Cemetery***]. This poetry, not of things but of presences, suggests habitation in emptiness, or by emptiness: "No footsteps in the house / no shouting in the house / no love in the house". The world outside the world of the protective campfire repels the seeker, but lures her on. "No! I don't want to see it", she says, even as she sees it, and describes it with the loving care that tells us that at fear's root lies desire. That fear and that desire are transformation, "an old grandpa turned into a tree". The ability to alter is the presence within things. (p. 223)

"'If only there were some adventure other than death'", someone writes on a window. Circled by the idea of endings ("Nothing was real enough / it was all a sham / only his own death / could live up to his expectation"), these poems concentrate on death to the exclusion of everything else (which, of course, it is), until death is no longer an intruder, but a guest, then a friend. One senses the writer caressing the notion. From repetition the word, like a lover's name, loses power and becomes mere sound. Suddenly one wonders what "deth" signifies, as one wonders what might be denoted by her other exhausted nouns: "blud", "bōnz", "stärz", "emp·tē·nes".

The repetitions suggest ceremony, litany, the incantation of language against fear. The lines are kept short, since nothing matters except the getting said, the getting out: "let there be no more owners / and no more ownership / no more plats lots liens mortgages / let there be no property". And no properties. Punctuation is often scrapped, so the poems run on—they are fairly unstoppable. Such poems suppose a world of urgency, where silence threatens, where everything must be said before it can be unsaid, undone. At their best, the poems toss overboard the extraneous cargo to keep the ship above water. At worst, they hurl the dreck in all directions: "They believe in Juicy Fruit Gum. / They believe in Hollywood. / They believe in the Fourth of July. / They believe in Dick Tracy." They throw away until the only images left must be recycled: "lips drawn back / from toothless gums", "lips drawn back, grinning, from black gums".

This nakedness is both beautiful and horrible:

> Blind, naked as a new-born
> rat under my new dress
>
> despair keeps me pale
> I sewed my own shroud

But the unclothed may lack the mysterious power of the clothed. The naked emperor looks merely foolish, though we may not have the courage to tell him so. The topless waitress is soon just another waitress, no more remarkable than the soup. Even deprived of their clothing, the poems are intensely, even aggressively, private. They make few concessions to communication. The landscapes are all interiors, even when trees, grass, and animals are elaborately carted in and arranged. This imagination has collapsed under the weight of its obsessions, until nothing, certainly not light or matter, can emerge. We learn not what is beyond the campfire, only what the mind believes is there.

None of the poems in this, Urdang's second volume of poetry, is completely successful. The means are finally too limited, the concerns too private to transmute the matter, to turn metamorphosis into metaphysics. There are many fine lines, especially those mapping out the terrain of sexuality, but measured against the poems of Adrienne Rich, which chart similar regions, though not so morbidly, Urdang's work seems imitative, less complex, and less moving. (pp. 224-25)

William Logan, "Language against Fear," in Poetry, *Vol. CXXX, No. 4, July, 1977, pp. 221-29.*

JAMES FINN COTTER

In [***The Lone Woman and Others***] Constance Urdang encounters the outer worlds of one's country, other people, and one's own body. From within, she reaches out to the limits of her dreams and fantasies. In **"Portrait,"** for example, she pictures herself as a trespasser in her own house, "my own alter ego." She is a stranger to her dog, to a rude woman in a grocery store, to her childhood. She sums up her dilemma in **"Missouri"** when she ironically observes: "Even inside, I'm an outsider." **"The Brother Poems"** offers sharp detail and focus, recalling Thanksgiving dinners at home, a secret clubhouse, a dead friend, and her brother today, hiding "Inside this fat uncle." She waits for him now to jump out and declare "it was only a joke, / He didn't really mean it." Of course, the brother mirrors everyone, including the poet. As **"The Lone Woman of San Nicolas Island"**, she lives like an anchorite and wild woman, "no longer daughter, sister, mother." A strong feminist viewpoint underlies two series of prose poems, **"Artificial Illuminations"** and **"Reinventing America"**; both employ surrealistic comments on real events, private and public. The four poems on **"Family Life"** also juxtapose the ordinary and the imaginary, aligning real memories of relatives with gothic fiction. A clear eye for comedy keeps their purpose in perspective. Urdang can write matter-of-factly about the most intimate thoughts. . . . [In *The Lone Woman,* a] sense of alienation spreads outward; it drives people into the suburban grasslands, a flight well sketched in **"In the Suburbs"** and **"Safe Places." "The Foreigner,"** a poem about a nervous tourist trying conversation in a café, captures the plight of the displaced; **"Baked Potatoes"** reminds us that even back home we can be absent: ''As if back there it is all going on without me.'' Perhaps **''The Kites''** most graphically telescopes the experience of being-outside when the kites, the children holding them, and the observers ''inside / windows,'' all fly aloft with astronauts, satellites, and stars. (pp. 281-82)

James Finn Cotter, in a review of ''The Lone Woman and Others,'' in The Hudson Review, *Vol. XXXIV, No. 2, Summer, 1981, pp. 281-82.*

RICHARD JACKSON

For Constance Urdang, the Other is more internalized and so the language of the poems is more introspective, taut. ''Somewhere inside me lives / the lone woman of San Nicolas Island'' (the title is the second line) she says in the opening lines of ***The Lone Woman and Others.*** Indeed, the aim of the book is to discover the ''Trespasser in my own house, / My own alter ego'' (**''Portrait''**), ''the woman in the / woman'' (**''Being a Woman''**). Each of the selves, the *Others* of the title, has a history, a separate time structure, a memory from which the speaker is detached. The problem is, then, that the self seems lost, ''rootless'' as she says in **''Missouri.''** The pasts of these Others cannot be experienced: ''In fact, if anything, what they had wished for had receded even further into the distance; curiously, it seemed to have traveled from the future into the past without ever passing through the present, which was where they lived'' (**''Artificial Illuminations''**). The solution for Urdang is to find a precise, detailed and photographic language that will not view the past as ''mazy, obscure, / Cowering in corners,'' but rather as the grandchildren of Missouri pioneers do when they ''Tidy away the past / Until the polished surfaces (of old photos) / Reflect not apparitions, pinched / Parched, craving, unsatisfied, / But only their own faces'' (**''Reflections on History In Missouri''**).

One way, then, of creating these ''polished surfaces,'' the past made present, is to see the self not as a ''lone'' and ''isolate'' being, but as the reflection of Others. A couple of poems, for example, strive to interpenetrate the self (or selves) with the histories of external Others. In **''Somebody's Life''** the speaker sees other lives as ''the landscape seen through a train window'' and in ''windows of tenements . . . crowded with somebody's life,'' only to realize that someone out there ''will remember / The rumble and clatter of the lighted train . . . / That used to punctuate his nights.'' In **''Adventures''** an old man is selling photographs of a revolutionary hero and the poem goes on to describe the old man's life as a lost alternative history for the hero's early death. In each case, the doublings or mirrorings mutually internalize the histories of self and Other. As a result of such doublings, the self, even if the speaker finds herself, as in **''Deja Vu,''** situated ''At the crossroads where Indians believed / The soul might go astray,'' may catch ''sight of myself in a mirror / Silent, monochrome / Moving through depthless space,'' and . . . resituate herself ''on the margins of the world'' she paradoxically gathers within her. The ''margins,'' become the taut surfaces of the language in her poems. As the book progresses, in fact, the lone woman allies herself not only with all her possible selves, but with all the possible Others that define her culture; ''moving through'' the photographic surfaces of her language, she and America, by the end, ''have become one another'' (**''American Suite''**). (pp. 93-4)

Richard Jackson, ''No Language but the Language of the Heart,'' in Prairie Schooner, *Vol. 56, No. 1, Spring, 1982, pp. 91-9.*

JAMES FINN COTTER

Traveling is the theme of Constance Urdang's fourth collection of poetry [***Only the World***]. Victorian ladies setting out for far places, immigrants moving steadily westward—''not *toward* / But *away from,* not into the future, / But away from the past''—and travelers returning home to find things changed—''another way of discovering'' that they are what has altered. Here again is the same stranger encountered as if for the first time, the familiar newly seen from another viewpoint. Absence may not make the heart grow fonder, but it does sharpen the mind. . . . A century ago women tasted their ''civilizing mission'' by turning their backs on domesticity to show that ''a woman could travel as easily as a man.'' Other themes, like childhood and nature, appear in this volume, but women and travel occupy the central spot. The tone is personal, but not autobiographical; the style is pre-set and the form fairly fixed, but the poems do not become repetitious. While there remains an underlying note of life's estrangements, a warmth of observation and concern kindles the poet's vision; the trees, birds, and children's cries are ''carried away on the wind: / They are only the world. / It is enough.'' The final poem, **''The World Is Full of Poets,''** celebrates poets near and far, under trees, on subways or streetcars.

James Finn Cotter, in a review of ''Only the World,'' in The Hudson Review, *Vol. XXXVI, No. 4, Winter, 1983-84, p. 714.*

LORRIE GOLDENSOHN

The first section of ***Only the World*** introduces a brace of Victorian heroines, cheerily radiant, and largely two-dimensional, and then, in contrast to these unrelenting ladies, a bunch of unnamed, disgruntled first person wanderers who see the world in more dispirited terms. Declares one Victorian lady, in the brightness of her confidence: '''I see no wonder / In this shrubbery, equal to seeing myself in it.''' Yet Urdang's more timid traveler hesitates to affirm trip benefits as the better personal backdrop, and sees his travel, like a magnet, pulling ''not *toward* / But *away from,* not into the future, / But away from the past.'' If to move towards the seductions of the future means to eradicate the past, we may awake to loss: ''aware / Of the empty place, and what might have belonged there.'' . . . Urdang projects spatial gain as temporal loss.

Although the poet describes distant or imaginary landscapes seen in a variety of exotic and prosaic neighborhoods, and writes about different gardens with different edibles and weathers, acreage is not coverage. Urdang turns resolutely towards the more familiar and inward home ground, to more interiors, and . . . defines her task as the recognition of Presence in the known and ordinary. She favors occasional portraits, tiny flashes of family narrative, or domestic life remembered or shrunk by fantasy into miniature; she rarely does close-up, daylight present-tense seeing. Her epigraph takes this sentence from Martin Buber: ''There is no world of appearances, there is only the world.'' The fuller poems, however, seem to subvert this premise, and draw from the troubling world of appearances Urdang's richer and more animated speculations. . . . In **''After Illness in Childhood,''** she asks, ''Does Mother dream she is fleeing, or flying, to a lover?'' From **''Interpretations,''** her interlocutor wants to know if those are ''screams coming from behind the police station'' or ''simple drunken raillery''? The poems appear to doubt that these questions can be answered; perhaps in the world there are only appearances. It may be rather awful to contemplate—who likes to worry?—but the more apprehensive interpreter of these ambiguous sights and sounds is livelier and more engrossing than the quietist in Urdang's title piece in tribute to Buber, **"Only the World,"** who inclines to accept the world's more painful contradictions. Urdang is more persuasive when she worries.

If there is a weakness in this collection, it is the drift to charm. Too many of the poems rely on fancifulness, or static pictures with remote-focus group scenes, or *idées reçues*. They quit; they lie down on the job; too many poems leave us very quickly. (pp. 41-2)

Lorrie Goldensohn, "Flight Home," in Poetry, *Vol. CXLIV, No. 1, April, 1984, pp. 40-7.*

PUBLISHERS WEEKLY

Lucha is the Spanish word for "struggle," as well as the nickname of one of the protagonists, who escapes an impoverished life on a barren *ranchecito* through marriage to a prosperous factory owner. . . . Lucha concludes that, as much as the outside world changes, a passive, fatalistic Mexico, whose poor women have too many babies and whose citizens dump garbage in the streets, remains the same. More akin to journalism than literature, this disappointing novella by the poet and author of ***Natural History*** mixes dispassionate observations with dogmatic conclusions. Narrative supersedes dialogue while expository passages are given as much weight as dramatic ones, and the reader may accurately determine that all are equally unimportant.

A review of "Lucha," in Publishers Weekly, *Vol. 230, No. 9, August 29, 1986, p. 393.*

SUSAN WOOD

Luz Filomena, the protagonist of [***Lucha***] by the poet Constance Urdang, is fond of saying "*La vida es lucha*" ("Life is a struggle"). In fact, since childhood she herself has been called Lucha because, her sister Julia says, she was always "a great one for struggling against the world." However, in this spare, often elegant tale of three generations of women in a small Mexican town, Lucha seems to have lost much of the grit and determination that took her from poverty to middle-class comfort and into the complacent, conventional life of the wife of a prosperous rug manufacturer. She spends her days running her household, going to the movies on Fridays, sitting in the public garden on Sundays, happily ignoring the absences and affairs of her husband, who is called only Señor Tio. . . . Years pass very quickly in these 94 pages and suddenly Lucha is spending most of her time in the United States as a representative of her husband's expanding business. A family tragedy reminds her of the persistence of struggle, the constancy of suffering on "this bleak, rejecting earth." Ms. Urdang obviously knows Mexico and she writes about the country and its people with feeling and understanding. But Lucha herself is traced only in the barest outlines; so much time and so many characters are covered in so few pages that one feels something is curiously missing.

Susan Wood, in a review of "Lucha," in The New York Times Book Review, *January 11, 1987, p. 18.*

Janwillem van de Wetering

1931-

Dutch novelist, nonfiction writer, short story writer, and author of children's books.

Photograph by Douglas Bruce.

Van de Wetering is a popular and critically respected author of detective novels and nonfiction books that reflect his interest in Zen Buddhism. In his detective works, van de Wetering engages his readers with colorful characterizations, vivid evocations of social milieus, particularly those of Amsterdam, and a blending of philosophical speculation, mysticism, and police procedure. His best-known works feature detectives Henk Grijpstra and Rinus de Gier and their superior, a police commissioner known as the Commissaris. Van de Wetering subordinates plot and action to focus on the attitudes, troubles, and desires of his investigators and the people they encounter.

Van de Wetering's first books to receive critical attention, *De Lege spiegel* (1971; *The Empty Mirror: Experiences in a Japanese Zen Monastery*) and *A Glimpse of Nothingness: Experiences in an American Zen Community* (1975), document his initiation into the rites and beliefs of Zen Buddhism. The first book details van de Wetering's experiences in a monastery, where he spent more than a year as a novice monk adhering to a strict program of meditation. In the second work, van de Wetering observes the workings of an American Zen community that was founded by a monastic pupil whom he had met in Japan.

Van de Wetering's knowledge of Zen and his experiences as a reserve on the Amsterdam police force inform his detective fiction. These novels feature striking descriptions of the beauty and squalor of Amsterdam and explore the enigmas and ambiguities of crime and human life. Critics frequently call these works "Zen mysteries," as van de Wetering attempts to blend Zen concepts of nothingness and the totality of existence with dream sequences, surrealistic images, and realistic details of police routine. John Leonard commented: "Mr. van de Wetering is less a mystery writer than he is a mystagogue. His odd-angled novels more and more resemble the sort of thing Simenon might have done if Albert Camus and Kōbō Abé had sublet his skull."

As van de Wetering's detectives undertake unsolved murder cases, they also encounter other criminal and unconventional activities. These include drug dealing in *Outsider in Amsterdam* (1975), prostitution in *Tumbleweed* (1976), counterculture lifestyles in *The Corpse on the Dike* (1976), and the black market in *Death of a Hawker* (1977). The latter book, in which the detectives are caught in a riot over the razing of a decaying neighborhood, reflects van de Wetering's penchant for examining social issues. The influence of Zen is particularly apparent in the mysteries, illusions, and philosophizing of *The Mind Murders* (1981), a novel which prompted Jeffrey Burke to state: "That van de Wetering uses the genre to explore life's bright and bland tenuities (Zen cousins of Joyce's epiphanies) is as remarkable as his skill in subtly carrying forward at the same time a concrete and intriguing plot."

Van de Wetering's other detective novels include two books set outside Amsterdam, *The Japanese Corpse* (1977) and *The Maine Massacre* (1979); *The Butterfly Hunter,* which focuses on an amoral protagonist's adventures as a murderer, a spy, and an actor; *Streetbird* (1983), which is set in the black community of Amsterdam; and *Hard Rain* (1986), in which a successful businessman and longtime rival of the Commissaris is exposed as a thief, a murderer, and a drug peddler. Van de Wetering has also written *Inspector Saito's Small Satori* (1985), a collection of short stories featuring a young Japanese detective who solves crimes through his application of Zen principles.

(See also *Contemporary Authors,* Vols. 49-52 and *Contemporary Authors New Revision Series,* Vol. 4.)

JOHN SKOW

This small and admirable memoir [***The Empty Mirror: Experiences in a Japanese Zen Monastery***] records the experiences of a young Dutch student who spent a year and a half as a novice monk in a Japanese Zen Buddhist monastery. As might be expected, the author shows a deep respect for the teachings of Zen. What makes his account extraordinary, however, is that the book contains none of the convert's irritating certitude, and no suggestion that the reader rush to follow the author's example.

Janwillem van de Wetering sailed for Japan by freighter in the summer of 1958. He was 27, and a misfit in the bustling Dutch society. He had read a few books on Buddhism, and, he writes, he wanted to find a door he could knock on: "a real door, made of wood, with a live man behind it who would say something I could hear." Japan, he knew, had living masters who would accept disciples. . . .

The monastery that Van de Wetering found was in the holy city of Kyoto. He appeared there without introduction and was accepted without surprise. . . . The strain of monastery routine was much more severe than he was prepared for. . . . Meditation suggests tranquillity not torture, but sitting motionless for even a few minutes in an approximation of the lotus position left the author's stiff Western legs cramped and shaking. The younger Japanese monks did not have a much better time of it. The holiest and most arduous week of the year—Rohatsu—came in December. The period of sleep was reduced to two hours, from midnight to 2 a.m. The monks meditated for 15 hours a day. Anyone who seemed inattentive was beaten with a long piece of board. Van de Wetering lasted out the ordeal, surprising himself and his superiors, but his account of it might be that of a survivor of some calamitous polar expedition.

The author visited the Zen master each day. During the first of these encounters he received his *koan,* or Zen riddle. A postulant's first *koan* usually is one of formidable difficulty, and solving it may take years. On each day of each of these years, the master asks in a sharp and businesslike manner for the answer. The learning monk may attempt some reply or say nothing. When the master decides that no progress will be made on that day, he rings a small bell, and the interview is over.

The sessions proved humbling. "You are asleep," the Zen master would say, "you are snoring." Then later, "If ever you succeed in waking up a bit, be careful that it doesn't go to your head.". . .

His eventual decision to leave the monastery and return to Europe and a life in business came during a period of discouragement. He seemed to be getting nowhere. He went to say goodbye to his master, who accepted his departure as simply as he had accepted his arrival. The master raised his spirits, reassuring him that "by leaving here nothing is broken. Your training continues. . . . You are now a little awake, so awake that you can never fall asleep again."

With those words this honest and absorbing account ends. . . . There is, in fact, not a word about his life from 1959 to the present in ***The Empty Mirror.*** It would have been interesting to learn whether he did indeed stay awake, but the silence seems right. A book about Zen should end with a question.

John Skow, "Waking Up in Kyoto," in Time, *New York, Vol. CIII, No. 6, February 11, 1974, p. 80.*

ANNIE GOTTLIEB

"And that was why I had come, to visit an old Japanese gentleman who ridiculed everything I said or could say, and to sit still for fifteen hours a day on a mat, for seven days on end, while the monks whacked me on the back with a four-foot-long lath made of strong wood." So writes Janwillem van de Wetering, a wandering Dutchman, in [***The Empty Mirror***] a memoir of his wits'-end state of mind just before Rohatsu, the most strenuous week of meditation in the Japanese Zen monastery where he had lived and trained for over a year. He dreaded the "week of weeks" because, even on an ordinary day, his stiff thigh muscles made sitting in the half-lotus-position an agony, because he couldn't help falling asleep and toppling over during meditation, and because the morning interview with the master fiercely demanding an answer to his *koan*—the paradoxical knot every Zen student is given to untie—left his mind a paralyzed blank.

Janwillem made it through Rohatsu, but he left the monastery soon after and today is co-director of a textile company in Amsterdam. This slender, wry memoir of his Zen experiences gives an unusually objective account of the big frustrations and modest revelations of mystical training in another culture. . . .

[Seekers'] responses tend to fall into one of two categories: reverence or skepticism. Of the two, perhaps the skeptics like van de Wetering (or Carlos Castaneda in his far more "major," melodramatic and revelatory books) tell us more about what "actually" happens in such a mystical training system as seen through Western eyes. . . .

Whatever "enlightenment" is—and it is very clearly not an intellectual attainment—it frankly eludes Janwillem. Like a good impatient Westerner, he can't just practice quietly and wait for it. What's more, his ego is wounded by his inability to achieve even an instant of it, and he's wryly aware of a good bit of this. . . .

In van de Wetering's book a heavy black line divides those who have solved *koans* and thus tasted *satori* from those who toil away outside. (Or so it seems to the latter.) For just this reason, his portrayal of the strenuous monastery routine and of the young Japanese monks' often comical attempts to evade it (many of them have been committed to the discipline by their fathers) is more vivid and human than a "reverent" account of the same goings-on.

At the same time, he is deeply impressed by the master, whose "little room trembled with power"; by the head monk, a serene and cryptic presence who is said to have come to the monastery as a spoiled neurotic boy; and by Peter, an American pianist, one of those few Westerners who have persisted long enough to begin to penetrate or be penetrated by the mystery. They seem to him to be "beings of a higher order, who wore their bodies as actors wear masks and costumes." They must know the answer to the painful question that has brought him to Zen: What is the meaning, the purpose of life?

When Janwillem leaves the monastery in frustration, the master tells him gently, "By leaving here nothing is broken. Your training continues. The world is a school where the sleeping are woken up." The *koan* is compared to a time bomb that goes on ticking by itself, to explode, perhaps years later, in *satori*. Whether it ever did so explode for Janwillem van de Wetering, he never tells us, any more than he tells us much else about his life before or after the monastery. He presents himself here simply as a kind of Western Everyman, on whose cranky sensibility the delicate ironies, hard knocks and ultimate mystery of Zen record themselves with a low-key clarity.

Annie Gottlieb, "A Wandering Dutchman Finds His Koan but Not Satori," in The New York Times Book Review, *March 3, 1974, p. 2.*

PAUL KAGAN

In [***A Glimpse of Nothingness: Experiences in an American Zen Community***] we learn that Zen Buddhism is a skeptic's way. It is a way full of doubt, pathos and ordinary cares and woes. Underlying the negations of the Zen master, the pain of sitting still for long periods and the annoyance of fellow students is a burning question. Put into extra-logical form by a master, the question . . . calls for an awareness of action in everyday life and an ever-deepening and more centered practice of meditation in order to respond with the right final manifestation—perhaps even without words. But it is a true answer recognized by both master and disciple.

It is this answer that Janwillem van de Wetering sought—and has chronicled in his book about his experiences in an American Zen community. After the time he spent in a Japanese Zen monastery (which he described in ***The Empty Mirror: Experiences in a Japanese Zen Monastery***), a sense of searching unfulfillment led him to the United States, where a fellow student, an American, had assumed the mantle of the now dead Japanese master. With candid accounts of his continuing disillusioning experiences, and with help from the American master, van de Wetering, a Dutchman, attempts the personal style of literary *vérité* that is so effective in the works of Carlos Castaneda. Van de Wetering tries to evoke a living *koan* from an account of his own short, but intense, Zen experience. . . .

There is an intimate picture here of the relation of master to disciple. The master, pink-faced and American though he may be, who even smokes cigarettes when he is nervous, requires of van de Wetering not spoken "correct" answers, but the attainment of a certain level of understanding that may or may not manifest in word and thoughts or in conventionally recognizable "spiritual" comportment. This is a personal picture of that state: the humanness of this path extends to a description of great Zen sages who were alcoholics; the two-natured personality of Zen masters who enjoy sex and cowboy movies, knowing that the development of real morality grows out of the unrelenting attempt to become more conscious of the inexorable mechanical forces that govern all of us, master and student alike.

Van de Wetering shows a healthy skepticism of his own Zen tradition. He questions authority, sometimes with just cause and points out the historic inevitability of the forces that institutionalize a religion. . . .

A Glimpse of Nothingness makes two major contributions in a sociological context. The author describes the routine (along with his own personal reactions) in a New England Zen community, and he describes the work, finances and delegation of tasks in such a tradition-based yet very American community. . . .

The "nothingness" which the author glimpses is actually an experience of momentary freedom from the habitual forms of thought, reaction and behavior that imprison us in a false sense of who we are and where we are going. . . .

This is a book that deserves serious attention, in spite (and partly because) of a slightly résumé quality of reporting ordinary subjective impressions. While this quality is often no more than humorous, it often gives those impressions a richness that makes a metaphor for the whole Zen experience. It makes the book eminently readable, easy to relate to on several different levels, and a fascinating and encouraging tale of human communal endeavor.

Paul Kagan, in a review of "A Glimpse of Nothingness," in The New York Times Book Review, *June 29, 1975, p. 21.*

DOUGLAS AUCHINCLOSS

Janwillem van de Wetering has finally solved his *koan.*

It wasn't easy. He spent a year and a half working on it in Japan—a tall, pink-faced Hollander, surrounded by short, shaven-headed Zen monks and suffering from culture shock, language barrier, 3:30 a.m. reveilles and agonizing leg pains from thousands of hours of cross-legged *zazen*. His first book, ***The Empty Mirror,*** . . . described the ordeal in Van de Wetering's own wry, crisp English. . . . [***A Glimpse of Nothingness***] picked up the story of the dogged Dutchman's search for enlightenment 10 years later. But ***Glimpse*** is not simply a subjective sequel on the author's spiritual development but an absorbing story of Zen American style. It is also more artfully constructed, with careful characterizations and revealing incidents. For Van de Wetering, Zen student and Amsterdam businessman, has become a full-fledged writer. His newest book, ***Outsider in Amsterdam,*** is a detective novel.

In Japan, Van de Wetering made no apparent progress with his *koan*—an intentionally illogical question (example: "What is the sound of one hand clapping?"), assigned pupils in the Rinzai sect of Zen Buddhism to help break the domination of the intellectual mind. And when he decided to leave, his old master was kindly and encouraging. . . . Doing his nine-to-five as a family man in Amsterdam, he kept a statue of the Buddha on his office desk and the unsolved *koan* smoldered in his mind.

One day, a familiar voice sounded on the telephone. An American he calls Peter, who had spent many years working with the same master and had helped him over several rough spots in Japan, was in Holland for a week. It turned out that the old man had died and that Peter was his spiritual successor—a Zen master in his own right with his own monastery on a farm in the northeastern United States. Van de Wetering asked Peter's permission to become his disciple and visit his American *zendo*. . . .

Janwillem's visit coincided with Rohatsu—a week of intensive meditation (10 hours a day) leading up to December 8, the day on which the Buddha had attained enlightenment 2,500 years ago. Janwillem, trudging through the snow, slipping on the ice, slept fully clothed beneath a pile of horse blankets in a waterless cabin with a stove that gave more smoke than heat.

In Rinzai Zen the master gives an interview each day to each of his disciples to check on progress with their *koans* and offer helpful advice, sharp reproof or electric silence, as the case may be. It was at one of these *sanzen* sessions with Peter (whose face had "the round innocence of Charlie Brown") that Janwillem achieved his breakthrough. His description of the event is rich with Zen-like ambiguity: "You say nothing. The master asks nothing. Who or what you are is paper-thin. The veil is torn. The master smiles. The silence continues and then he gives you the next *koan*. You have a new question and you are in another world. For a very short moment."

This is *satori?* After leaving the master's room with tears in his eyes, Janwillem wondered what, if anything, had happened. Solving one's first *koan* was supposed, as he understood it, to be accompanied by enlightenment, but he had to admit that everything felt just about the same. . . .

Van de Wetering's *koans* and aching legs go on, but they will result in no more books on Buddhism, he says. ***Outsider in Amsterdam*** derives from quite another kind of discipline—the Amsterdam police force, on which Van de Wetering serves as a part-time sergeant. To carry the story (and presumably a series of sequels) he has invented a two-man team of detectives: Adjutant Grijpstra—middle-aged, unhappily married, muddling, philosophical—and Sergeant de Gier—hip and humorous, with a bachelor apartment and a nutty Siamese cat. The outsider in question is a mysterious Papuan, and the action is a smoothly paced, pleasantly ungritty amalgam of murder and drug dealing in international Amsterdam.

Douglas Auchincloss, "One Hand Clapping," in Book World—The Washington Post, *September 7, 1975, p. 3.*

T. J. BINYON

[In ***Outsider in Amsterdam***] detectives Grijpstra and de Gier of the Amsterdam police are called in to investigate an apparent suicide: the owner of a commune, which might be the front for a drugs racket, has been found hanging from the ceiling of his room. . . . Janwillem van de Wetering concentrates more on police work than personality, and his detectives are not as bumptious as [Nicolas Freeling's Dutch detective Piet Van der Valk]. This is a solid, well-constructed and well-written first novel with a more serious intent than most of its genre.

T. J. Binyon, in a review of "Outsider in Amsterdam," in The Times Literary Supplement, *No. 3872, May 28, 1976, p. 656.*

ANATOLE BROYARD

I'm tired of the detective as catalyst, he who moves without being moved. . . . While it is not true of all American suspense novels, it seems to me that, in too many of them, the detective is laconic and detached, an outsider who brings no mystery of his own to the mystery to be solved, no personal intimacy to the intimacy of murder. . . .

In ***Tumbleweed,*** Janwillem van de Wetering offers us not one, but *three* detectives who are all recognizable people incapable of putting aside their personalities simply because someone has been killed. It is not they who have been murdered: Their lives go on, under protest, perhaps, but nevertheless. In his office at police headquarters in Amsterdam, Adjutant-Detective Grijpstra has a set of drums that was left over from a case and somehow never removed. When he wishes to discharge a feeling of frustration, or to punctuate the logic of his remarks, he takes up the sticks and indulges in an autodidact's expression. Detective-Sergeant de Gier, his assistant, adapts himself to the situation by accompanying his superior on the flute. . . .

While she is a high-priced whore, the woman who is murdered is not denied a personality either—when the knife enters her back, she is sewing and listening to the phonograph.

The Commissioner is even better. When he hears of the murder, he says to himself, "We cannot allow a man to throw a knife into the living back of a fellow citizen," as if to remind himself of the commonsensical basis of the law. To the scene of every crime, the Commissioner also brings "the secret of life which he had never solved." When he learns that the murdered woman had come from, and still visited, the island of Curaçao, the Commissioner looks up the place in one of his books. "A land of grasshoppers and prophets," he reads and finds this riddle irresistible. It is clearly his duty to go to Curaçao, where the warm, dry weather stills the ache of rheumatism in his legs, where he hits the numbers, buys his wife a batik dress, and meets a sorcerer who teaches him the power of silence. In this last scene, Mr. van de Wetering draws effectively on his first, nonfiction book, ***The Empty Mirror: Experiences in a Japanese Zen Monastery.***

In ***Tumbleweed,*** the woman is killed for an extremely contemporary reason—she liked to make powerful men feel powerless. She is a kind of guerrilla arm of the feminist movement and her "sorcery," disguised by such bric-a-brac as Mandrake roots and deadly nightshade, is the silent or "witchlike" power of an attractive woman to alienate a man from what he regards as his true self.

One of the most curious characters in ***Tumbleweed*** is Holman, a fat, unromantic fellow who wears a red velvet waistcoat. While he was in the habit of visiting the victim, we are never able to discover the slightest clue as to the nature of their relationship. Both of the obvious answers seem improbable. Mr. van de Wetering is telling us, in his sly way, that not all human actions are accountable. Also, that he is inventive enough to be able to waste a character. . . .

In other words, everything about the author's characters is more real than the murder one of them commits, and this has the effect of surrounding the murder with suspicion and incredulity, which is as it should be. As the Commissioner might say: We cannot have people merely taking murder for granted.

Anatole Broyard, "Case of the Orange Undershirt," in The New York Times, *June 9, 1976, p. 37.*

JEAN M. WHITE

In Van de Wetering's ***The Corpse on the Dike,*** third in the Amsterdam-based series, Detectives Grijpstra and De Gier and the wise old *commissaris* have to deal with life's mysteries as well as the mysterious death of a young, well-to-do dropout from society. The first suspect is an abrasive lesbian, and the commissaris finds it hard to explain why he likes her and doesn't think she is the killer. "We laughed together," he says simply. And then there's the Cat, who has brought pride to the dike residents and inspired a community urban renewal project with filched materials. Van de Wetering has a villain (a cunning Arab businessman), a breathless car chase, and a plot puzzler. You can get these elsewhere, but not such memorable characters. . . .

Jean M. White, in a review of "The Corpse on the Dike," in Book World—The Washington Post, *September 26, 1976, p. H2.*

NEWGATE CALLENDAR

[***The Corpse on the Dike***] has an Amsterdam locale and three main characters—two cops and an old, tired, wise police official. The action is anything but strenuous. There is the murder of a young man who apparently has no enemies. A lesbian neighbor is booked on suspicion. Interesting characters come into the picture. There is some gnomic speech: "No, sir, I believe in cleverness, not in violence. Violence flies in a small circle and burns its own wings." To which the old police officer says, "So does cleverness, perhaps." There is a good deal of quiet humor and a nice, relaxed feeling. ***The Corpse on the Dike*** is hard to resist.

Newgate Callendar, in a review of "The Corpse on the Dike," in The New York Times Book Review, *November 7, 1976, p. 54.*

T. J. BINYON

After ***Outsider in Amsterdam,*** Janwillem van de Wetering's outstandingly good first novel, [***Tumbleweed***] comes as rather a disappointment. The murder . . . is one of those annoying crimes which solves itself without any detection; there is a lot of irrelevant material, and detectives Grijpstra and de Gier are in danger of becoming as nauseatingly cosy a pair as television's Starsky and Hutch. A pleasant read, though, with an interesting, if pointless, side trip to Curaçao.

T. J. Binyon, in a review of "Tumbleweed," in The Times Literary Supplement, *No. 3902, December 24, 1976, p. 1601.*

ANATOLE BROYARD

As ***Death of a Hawker*** opens, there is rioting in Amsterdam because part of the old quarter of the town is about to be razed to make way for a subway entrance. Various conservationists of tradition have gone crazy with indignation and are throwing bricks at the police. Don't be too hard on them, the commissaris urges. "Crazy people are special people. They carry the country's genius, its urge to create, to find new ways." While they're driving through the streets, the commissaris asks his chauffeur to stop and back up: he wants to have another look at a heron that is holding a goldfish in its beak. . . .

These are some of the reasons I liked Janwillem van de Wetering's fourth suspense novel, ***Death of a Hawker.*** There are more: There is a former police constable who is now a believable transvestite, justly proud of a bell pull he has made in half cross-stitch. There is a moment when the dead man's sister asks Sergeant de Gier whether she can come home with him for the night and the handsome sergeant is so taken aback that he can only scratch his bottom, which makes her laugh and ask, "Are you nervous?" When they are in his apartment, the sergeant searches his conscience in these unpretentious terms: "She can't feel like it now . . . her brother died today." He also considers the fact that he will be duty-bound to report her whereabouts and all his colleagues will know about them.

Adjutant Grijpstra wonders whether he himself, "flatfooted sleuth, bogey-man of the underworld, restless wanderer of canals, alleyways, cul-de-sacs, would like to be happy," as a young father he sees sitting on a balcony is happy. It is interesting to watch the adjutant eat snails for the first time. When the commissaris warns that his wife will not welcome his garlicky kiss, Grijpstra answers, "I never kiss my wife.". . .

Death of a Hawker even includes a parrot who imitates its master vomiting after a night of drinking. A scene in a wildlife sanctuary in which a police car runs over hundreds of migrating toads supplies most of the violence without which suspense novels cannot do. When a bulldozer is used as a weapon in an attempt to flatten the commissaris against a wall, it only succeeds in pulling down flowering vines over the driver.

I enjoy Mr. van de Wetering's murder mysteries partly because the policemen in them are even richer in antic impulses than the criminals. . . . The author has another appealing peculiarity: He describes Amsterdam as a very pleasant place to live, while so many mystery writers work up all their worst rhetoric to make all cities seem insupportable.

I have only two complaints—relatively small ones—about ***Death of a Hawker.*** Someone must have been telling the author that if he wanted to sell his books, they would have to be sexier. I disagree. If his women characters get any sexier, they are going to lose all their charm. I believe, too, that Mr. van de Wetering has been advised to think of more outré ways of killing his victims, so that in the present book the device is so farfetched as to resemble the labored inventions of your run-of-the-mill mystery writer. If I were advising him, I would tell Mr. van de Wetering to stick to his half cross-stitched bell pulls and women weeping over Surrealism.

Anatole Broyard, "A Tear for Surrealism," in The New York Times, *February 24, 1977, p. 33.*

MARTHA DUFFY

Agatha Christie said that if she had ever imagined, as a young woman, that she would spend 50 years writing thrillers, she would never have made Hercule Poirot and Jane Marple so old. Perhaps, but several of the elderly detectives prove to be the hardiest. The latest ancient to carry a series on his frail back is an Amsterdam police commissioner, or *commissaris.* He wears waistcoats and a watch chain; he has rheumatism, unfailing gaiety and humor, but no name. ***The Japanese Corpse*** is the fifth mystery he has appeared in, and he gives every promise of providing an annuity for his creator. . . .

[Van de Wetering's] new book draws on his knowledge of Japan. In outline the plot is very conventional. The *commissaris* and his two assistants, Adjutant Grijpstra and Sergeant De Gier, are required to search out and destroy a Japanese connection that supplies drugs and stolen art to Amsterdam. The villains are the *yakusa,* Japan's Mafia, who of course have their own extralegal culture with its warriors, taboos, codes and pretty girls.

The author obviously knows the methods of his florid villains very well—but seems to have only a casual interest in them. He nudges the story along every so often, but the entire climax is accomplished in exactly one paragraph. The rest of the time he browses amiably among his policemen. At one point the *commissaris* quotes a Chinese philosopher: "Hurry is a fundamental error." It is not one Van de Wetering is guilty of.

Fortunately the author has a genuine gift for characterization. . . .

Van de Wetering's trio [of detectives] are quirky, but compassionate, peaceable men. Even his *yakusa* are complex people who are neither James Bond cartoons nor clinical studies in sadism. This series will probably flourish not because of ingenious plots but because the characters are good enough to carry a conventional novel.

In their offhand approach to this rather rigid form, the *commissaris* books most closely resemble the mysteries of Nicolas Freeling. But Van de Wetering's inspiration was the late Robert van Gulik, a mystery writer and Oriental scholar who was once the Dutch Ambassador to Japan. He appears briefly in ***The Japanese Corpse***—as a helpful ambassador.

Martha Duffy, "Zen Cops," in Time, *New York, Vol. CX, No. 10, September 5, 1977, p. 67.*

NEWGATE CALLENDAR

Janwillem van de Wetering's procedurals about the Amsterdam Police Department have been attracting an American following. The latest in this series is ***The Blond Baboon.*** The same characters are present—Detectives de Gier, Grijpstra and Cardozo, and above all the Commissaris, the old cop, that frail, all-wise father figure. They are looking into the death of a woman who may have been murdered. Of course she was murdered, and of course the Commissaris (the highest rank of Amsterdam's municipal police) breaks the case.

This is one of the better books in the series, but basically the writing is calculated and artificial. Mr. van de Wetering is so nervously determined to make his characters come to life that he adds all kinds of unnecessary corroborative detail. None of that makes his people any more interesting, mostly because the author has a conventional mind and a stiff writing style. (pp. 38-9)

Newgate Callendar, in a review of "The Blond Baboon," in The New York Times Book Review, *April 16, 1978, pp. 38-9.*

JEAN M. WHITE

Fate is the result of previous actions, Buddhist thought tells us. If this is so, then we have fate as well as Janwillem van de Wetering to thank for those marvellously ambiguous Zen mysteries written under the guise of Amsterdam police procedurals. Those are the ones with the non-dynamic duo of detectives Grijpstra and de Gier and the Commissaris, their Buddha-figure boss—an odd trio of quirky policemen who puzzle more over the mysteries of everyday life than the murders to be solved. They always are asking why as well as whodunit. . . .

In his work, as a writer using the device of the police procedural, van de Wetering goes deeper than the surface of chase and pursuit of the criminal. The Commissaris and Detectives de Gier and Grijpstra must deal with the ambiguities of human nature and life as they dig into a victim's past and personality, seek the murderer and his motives, and try to sort out their own lives and thoughts.

There is Grijpstra, miserably married to a woman grown out of the girl that he married into a "blob of semi-solid fats" sitting before the TV and pushing him out of his home. . . . He bangs away at his frustration on a set of drums dumped in his office and sometimes remembers the dreams of his youth when he planned to become a jazz musician.

Sometimes de Gier, who fancies denim suits with a dash of kerchief at the neck, joins Grijpstra on the flute that he carries in his pocket. De Gier, a loner, has his apartment, his balcony plants of geraniums and alyssum, and Oliver, the Siamese cat who loves chopped heart and is jealous of de Gier's bedmates. As a restorative of spirit, he puts the cat on his lap, switches off the lights, opens the balcony door, lights a cigar, and listens to jazz records for hours. (p. 34)

And then there is the frail Commissaris (never given a name but addressed only by his commissioned rank), who strokes the painful rheumatism in his left leg and keeps a pet turtle in a wooden box under his garden's rhododendron bushes.

He is a police officer who pauses to listen to the evening song of a thrush on the way to interview a suspect. He treats a lesbian with courtly respect and honestly praises the embroidered bellpull of an ex-cop transvestite. . . .

More often than not, it is the criminals who turn out to be the most interesting characters in mystery novels. But it is the three policemen, originals as human beings, who take over van de Wetering's novels, although his villains and victims also have their fascination. We are more concerned about Grijpstra's escape from his miserable, drab life than we are about the identity of the murderer of the fake religious fanatic in ***Outsider in Amsterdam.*** And we worry more about de Gier's sorrow over the loss of his cat and mistress than we do about the culprit in ***The Japanese Corpse.***

It is not that van de Wetering is writing a Zen philosopher's treatise to the neglect of plot or action. He has ingenious plot puzzles. . . .

But it is mood, character, and atmosphere that dominate van de Wetering's Zen mysteries. We remember Louis, the hostile young man who makes sculpture of wire, string and beads to show a body moved only by outside forces, rather than the details of the murder plot in ***Death of a Hawker.*** The scene of van de Wetering's novels is Amsterdam today, a civilized, gracious city of old gable houses, bridges, and lovely canals beset with riots over subway construction, drug traffic, and bureaucratic bungling. But unlike [Maj Sjöwall and Per Wahlöö], who used the police procedural as a vehicle for criticism of the Swedish welfare state, van de Wetering is more interested in personal documentary than social commentary.

Van de Wetering, like Ross Macdonald, often finds the clues to crime buried in the past of human relationships. Maria van Buren, the sex witch who dies on her lavishly-furnished houseboat in ***Tumbleweed,*** experiments with the magical plants and brews of her native Curaçao. It is her bastard half-brother, grown into a religious fanatic, who becomes the instrument of her death under the manipulations of a clever murderer. . . .

Over glasses of jenever in a topless bar or a Chinese restaurant, Grijpstra, de Gier, and the Commissaris sigh, marvel and brood over such ironies of life and the ways of human nature. (p. 35)

Jean M. White, "Murder by Zen," in The New Republic, *Vol. 179, No. 4, July 22, 1978, pp. 34-5.*

MARTHA DUFFY

[In ***The Maine Massacre***] Janwillem van de Wetering writes about Amsterdam policemen and the statutes and terrors that govern their lives, but this casual author makes Sjöwal-Wahlöö look like Ellery Queen. Van de Wetering's novels meander along, with asides on the foibles of human nature and gracefully written filaments of Eastern philosophy. The plot is announced early in the narrative and dispatched at the end as quickly as a victim. . . . The new book is set [in Maine], in a coastal town called Jameson, just below the Canadian border. The author's usual characters are on hand: the old *commissaris,* who has arrived in the U. S. to help his sister settle her affairs after her husband's sudden death, and his young sergeant, Rinus de Gier. The *commissaris'* brother-in-law is only one of several people who have lived on a peninsula called Cape Orca and who died or disappeared, leaving the land a cursed place. The motive for all this is not very deep. The story would not be tenable if the local sheriff were not a very new man in the territory and his helpers foreign. As the old man notes, the townspeople are not mystified at all: "They know the country, the undercurrents." In ***The Maine Massacre,*** the plot is the undercurrents.

The principal character is the snow. It isolates the town and stills all action. The escapes and chases that fill an ordinary story are stalled in Jameson. A marksman in snowshoes is the only prowling menace. In the *commissaris'* whining sister Suzanne, van de Wetering finds a way to spoof his native country and contrast it to Maine. The old lady lives surrounded by tacky reproductions of Dutch scenes and execrable examples of porcelain. Her brother briefly thinks that she may have killed her husband but concludes that he is overinfluenced by the fact that her meals constitute the foulest kind of home cooking.

Since van de Wetering lives in Maine permanently, he could have set his story during a summer tourist season or the fiery glories of autumn. Instead he takes the harder route: bare, muted landscapes filled with ravens, seals and deer. He is aware of the violence in the town and casual cruelty of the hunters. But the book's strongest writing is about the satisfactions of surviving a hard winter: wooden stoves, good drink, a safe journey home made in a blizzard. These are worth more than a tricky plot. Van de Wetering is an amateur who is good enough to get away with it. (p. 101)

Martha Duffy, "Chiller," in Time, *New York, Vol. CXIII, No. 7, February 12, 1979, pp. 99, 101.*

JULIAN SYMONS

Janwillem van de Wetering's first crime story, ***Outsider in Amsterdam,*** appeared only four years ago, but in the United States his work is already the subject of a cult (British reactions have been less enthusiastic). This following is based at least as much upon the author's quizzical attitude toward his characters and his occasionally starry-eyed philosophizing about the virtues of being a loner as it is upon plot and characterization. . . .

The series depends largely on [three Dutch detectives] and their relationships: the physically feeble but supremely intelligent and cunning commissaris; the shrewdly practical Grijpstra; the enthusiastic and passionate de Gier. These last two are very close. They joke constantly with each other: about police inefficiency ("If the civilians knew how silly their police are they would commit more crimes"); about their salaries being less than that of garbage collectors ("There are no garbage collectors anymore, there are only sanitation engineers"). . . . All this is done with charm and freshness, and so is the blend of awe and protective affection with which the two view the commissaris. . . .

Now comes ***The Maine Massacre.*** The commissaris has a telephone call from his sister Suzanne in Maine to say that her husband has died in an accident. He flies out to help her clear up the estate. But he has been ill, and Grijpstra and de Gier feel that the old man needs an eye kept on him. By an ingenious fiddle about police exchange visits, de Gier flies out to wintry Maine.

It soon appears that not only was Suzanne's husband murdered, but five other people have died in mysterious circumstances. There is some fun with the innocent Dutch sliding and falling about in the snow; a youthful gang of near-anarchists appears; a hermit living in a house on a 10-acre island reached by letting down a drawbridge over a ravine favors them with some cracker-barrel philosophy about the virtues of self-contained living and some hints about the crimes; de Gier gets out of an awkward spot by playing his flute; a lovely lubricous lady falls into bed with the handsome sergeant; there is a brief session in Boston's red-light Combat Zone; and, after confrontations and a bit of violence, the commissaris traps the principal villain with the assistance of a concealed microphone.

All this sounds, and is, fairly conventional. Mr. van de Wetering's books rely on the three principal figures, and on the relaxed geniality of the author, who has been both an Amsterdam policeman and a Buddhist monk. The settings add something, and the books with an Amsterdam background are notably more convincing than those in which the Dutch team are playing away from home. But there are limits to the variations one can play on characters who are defined chiefly by a limp or by playing the flute. If one puts the commissaris, Grijpstra and de Gier up against Maigret, Nicolas Freeling's Van der Valk or Sjöwall and Wahlöö's Martin Beck, the three Dutchmen are seen to be something less than original creations.

Sometimes de Gier sounds like Philip Marlowe or Lew Archer, and the exchanges between de Gier and Grijpstra are uncomfortably reminiscent of Ed McBain. Occasionally the generally deft touches of quirkiness are overemphasized. . . .

It may seem hard to make comparisons between the three Dutchmen and Maigret or Van der Valk, but Mr. van de Wetering's more passionate enthusiasts invite them. The fact that they are overstating the case in calling him a superlative mystery writer, however, shouldn't obscure recognition that these are stories of much more than average merit in their field. They are written with an alertness and a genuine feeling for amusing dialogue that keep them constantly lively. Janwillem van de Wetering is a considerable asset to the criminal-entertainment industry.

Julian Symons, "Dutch Fuzz," in The New York Times Book Review, *February 18, 1979, p. 15.*

JOHN LEONARD

[In ***The Mind Murders*** we are back] with Janwillem van de Wetering in the underworld of Amsterdam as seen through Buddhist goggles. Our policemen, once again, are Grijpstra and de Gier. Of course, de Gier will tell Grijpstra: "There is nothing more glorious than zero, adjutant. You can multiply it at will, you can divide it at will, and it will always be the same. We can lose ourself in nothing and go as far as we like; we'll never hit the end of it."

And yet both de Gier and Grijpstra "move in empty space." The streets they patrol are full of "gaping holes," into which automobiles and human bodies disappear. Their suspects move in "a horrifying circle.". . .

What is outside the circle, the glorious zero? Various characters speak: "To know that you have nothing can be encouraging." And, "Without obstructions one can see far.". . . Finally: "I've never accepted the chaos. Perhaps I should."

A policeman is not permitted to accept chaos. Grijpstra, de Gier and the commissaris are trying in ***The Mind Murders*** to make sense of a missing wife and her equally missing household furniture, a dead drug dealer and haunted saloon, a masked motorcyclist, the world of publishing and the riddle of life. There are also references to "the Bardo of Tibetan migrants" and "the Great Clearing." Meanwhile, de Gier has given up cigarettes, and the people he meets have names like Fortune, Titania, Carate, Ketchup and the Other Son of God.

As usual, Amsterdam is perfectly evoked. There are drums and flutes and geese and fish and too many dogs, not to mention parapsychology and psychosomatic disorder. Inside a circle, someone wears a paper hat. The commissaris explains to the murderer: ''There is the law. I don't mean the law in our books, that's no more than a projection. The true law is in all of us, in our center, in the core of our being, where we are all connected and where the illusion of identity no longer obscures our insight.''

Mr. van de Wetering is less a mystery writer than he is a mystagogue. His odd-angled novels more and more resemble the sort of thing Simenon might have done if Albert Camus or Kobo Abe had sublet his skull. They make a sinister music as they seek the true law. They are quite wonderful, and ***The Mind Murders,*** perhaps more self-indulgent than the rest, is nevertheless one of his best.

John Leonard, in a review of ''The Mind Murders,'' in The New York Times, *April 17, 1981, p. C23.*

JULIAN SYMONS

Janwillem van de Wetering, his publisher says, ''works, lives and meditates in Maine,'' and his last story, ***The Maine Massacre,*** was set there, but his Dutch detectives are still most at home in Amsterdam. And it is a pleasure to find them back on native ground in ***The Mind-Murders,*** which begins with two roughish policemen throwing a customer from the Beelema cafe into the Emperorscanal to cool him off. It is only recently that European crime writers have begun to use cities with something of the sensibility Georges Simenon showed for Paris. Maj Sjöwall and Per Wahlöö treat Stockholm brilliantly, Nicolas Freeling and Mr. van de Wetering's books seem most authentic when set in Amsterdam, but Rome, Berlin, Copenhagen offer possibilities so far untapped by native crime writers.

The investigation in Mr. van de Wetering's novel is conducted as usual by his three police musketeers. . . . They are characters now firmly fixed in readers' affections, and they offer the pleasures of the customary. The relationship between these three, the in-jokes and easy chat, the quirkiness and gentle philosophizing, are among the chief pleasures in reading Mr. van de Wetering. The theorizing, however, is not always gentle. ''People are no good, Jurriaans,'' Grijpstra says at one point to another sergeant. ''If you haven't found out by now, you should leave the police.''

The story embedded in the philosophizing tends to confirm another remark made by Grijpstra, that everybody is abnormal in Amsterdam. When the wife of Frits Fortune (the man who was tossed into the canal) disappears, his apartment is stripped so thoroughly that even the toilet paper is taken, along with the cast-iron bars that were drilled into the wall by Fortune to support his bookshelves. Grijpstra suspects that Fortune has killed his wife—but where is the body? Too much of the first half of the story is conducted through dialogues in which other people are inclined to be as philosophical as the detectives. ''I disagree with her motivation.'' Fortune says about his wife. ''All she wanted was wealth, happiness, some short-range goal like that. She's a silly woman really.'' (p. 12)

The solution of the puzzle, about which no more should be said than that it makes the title meaningful, is in keeping with the characters' wayward astuteness. The criminal goes free, but in the end suffers according to the true law, which, the commissaris tells him, is ''in the core of our being, where we are all connected and where the illusion of identity no longer obscures our insight.'' They are great talkers, these Dutch policemen. (p. 34)

Julian Symons, ''Dutch Policemen and Florida Lowlife,'' in The New York Times Book Review, *May 3, 1981, pp. 12, 34-5.*

JEFFREY BURKE

[A] detective series worth discovering is that of Janwillem van de Wetering, whose Grijpstra and de Gier have been curiously covering a beat in Amsterdam for several books before ***The Mind Murders.*** In the author's biographical note, these books are said to reflect ''his training in a Buddhist monastery in Kyoto.'' That helps explain the apparent non sequiturs, the startling digressions, the crime that isn't quite a crime yet takes up half the book, the murder with no corpse and the corpse with no murder, and passages like this:

> ''That'll be four meatrolls,'' Grijpstra said worriedly, ''two for him and two for me, that makes four. Not two, not one for him and one for me, but two each, that's four, but only with two rolls, one for him and one for me. Can you remember that?''

That van de Wetering uses the genre to explore life's bright and bland tenuities (Zen cousins of Joyce's epiphanies) is as remarkable as his skill in subtly carrying forward at the same time a concrete and intriguing plot. Readers shopping for enlightenment might do better to look elsewhere: here the play's the thing. (p. 74)

Jeffrey Burke, ''Mysteries for the Misbegotten: The Literary Corpse,'' in Harper's, *Vol. 263, No. 1574, July, 1981, pp. 72, 74.*

PUBLISHERS WEEKLY

Eddy Sachs [in ***The Butterfly Hunter***] is a handsome blond Dutchman. He's been a model for the Nazis as a perfect Aryan, a spy-commando for the Allies, a movie star, a Western spy in East Berlin, a tour guide, a drug dealer, always with his choice of women and, from his childhood, a killer. . . . This novel follows Eddy from the 1930s to the present, when he's planning to retrieve a fortune in buried Nazi gold with the aid of his young (amoral, if not actually crazy) mistress and her husband. The scenes move through Europe to South and Central America, where Eddy and his partners end up in the middle of the Nicaraguan revolt. The characters are sharply drawn, there is much humor and action, and the reader keeps turning the pages. . . . [Van de Wetering] is best known for mysteries heavily laced with philosophizing. Here he shows, until the almost slow-motion climax and final twist, how to keep a slam-bang story going about a totally amoral and loveless character.

A review of ''The Butterfly Hunter,'' in Publishers Weekly, *Vol. 222, No. 9, August 27, 1982, p. 347.*

MELANIE AXEL-LUTE

From the time [Eddy Sachs, the protagonist of ***The Butterfly Hunter***], goaded his hated brother into a fatal accident, he's been able to get what he wants—as a spy, an officer in occupied Germany, a movie actor, a drug runner. Occasionally he kills someone. . . . This riveting dissection of an amoral personality deals on a brutal level with sex, cruelty, and greed, and finally with morality. Bleak and devastating.

Melanie Axel-Lute, in a review of "The Butterfly Hunter," in Library Journal, *Vol. 107, No. 17, October 1, 1982, p. 1898.*

ANATOLE BROYARD

The action and the violence in ***Streetbird*** are precisely where they should be: in Janwillem van de Wetering's invention. His Amsterdam policemen are almost reckless in the indulgence of their personalities. Their method of crime detection is to free associate ad libitum until the necessary clues arise out of a welter of improvisation.

Mr. van de Wetering's triad of heroes represent the three ages of man. Sergeant de Gier is irrepressible youth; Adjutant Grijpstra is heavy, middle-aged, philosophical and still hanging on to the possibility of happiness by his fingernails. The Commissaris, or chief, is elderly and afflicted with rheumatism, which resembles what a French author calls ontalgia, a pain of being.

Cardozo, another policeman, is like a beginning poet, his head full of far-fetchedness. Jurriaans, the sergeant in the red-light district of Amsterdam, owns a monumental irony. The streets are full of suspects, he points out, but "how many remain once we have applied discernment to our thoughtful structure?"

The crime in ***Streetbird*** is a particularly interesting one, for it involves an investigation of the still coherent ethnicity of the black community in Amsterdam. Luko Obrian, the black prince of the red-light quarter, had announced to the police when he originally arrived from Surinam that he would "disconcert" them. And he did. He ran the quarter with a majestic unyieldingness until his body was riddled with a machine pistol fired from a burned-out sex shop. The symbolism is sly, and Luko's death is his final disconcertment. Everyone had believed that he was untouchable.

As he lies dead in an alley, a vulture flies over him and perches on a television antenna. But there are no vultures in Amsterdam, one of the policemen protests. Known as Streetbird, the vulture is the pet of Uncle Wisi, an ancient black medicine man. Wisi's relationship to Luko is a skein of anthropological complexities. Originally a prodigal son, Luko disobeyed Wisi, and it was the old man's curse that undermined his habitual alertness and rendered him vulnerable.

Mr. van de Wetering has a pleasant fondness for motherly fallen women, and there is one in ***Streetbird*** called Nellie, who is both Grijpstra's mistress and the Commissaris's nurse. . . .

There's a fine incidental character, a philosophical playboy with a nostalgie de la boue, who says when his identity papers are stolen, "The liberty which the undefinable offers frightens me." When there is a riot in Amsterdam, tanks have to be called out, and one of them crushes a Pekingese dog. Grijpstra, who is sentimental enough to have tried to save a rat from a hungry tomcat, is so taken by the incongruity of a tank mashing a Pekingese that he gets carried away and calls the image "horrifying, of course, but almost subtly beautiful."

When Grijpstra asks Uncle Wisi whether he is good or bad, Wisi replies that he is neither, adding, "It took some doing to be done with definitions, or to soar out of them." Much of the action of ***Streetbird*** revolves around the idea of "the honor of the station," and it is refreshing to hear of policemen who think in these terms. In fact, everything about Mr. van de Wetering's 11th novel is refreshing.

Anatole Broyard, in a review of "Streetbird," in The New York Times, *May 26, 1983, p. C23.*

FRANCIS H. CURTIS

[***Streetbird***] lacks a compelling or convincing plot. The story seems to have been created as a vehicle for crude language and episodes, some of which are clung to tenaciously as though the book depended on them for any coherence, continuity, reader attention or reason for existence. I presume a murder mystery involving pimps, prostitutes and the rest of a city's lower life is bound to involve some bawdy and ribald scenes. In this case, however, the scenes seem to be the focus around which mystery is concocted.

A mystery should be a challenge and be fun to read. This book was neither.

Francis H. Curtis, in a review of "Streetbird," in Best Sellers, *Vol. 43, No. 5, August, 1983, p. 172.*

JOHN C. CARR

Van de Wetering spent a number of years on the Amsterdam police force doing his national service, so he knows the people, the cops, and the city. But his police procedurals are rather unique in that each policeman has dreams and visions that are as important to him, ultimately, as the "real" world through which he moves. Grijpstra dreams of a world of sensual memories and fantasies, de Gier sees visions that are symbolic and indirectly solve the mysteries he's working on, and the old Commissaris has thoughts that soar above ethics and even above religion into the emptiness that van de Wetering himself found in the Zen monasteries he lived in.

Tumbleweed has an overtly religious theme. Maria van Buren, a lady of the evening, or certainly an inhabitant of the more elegant precincts of the demimonde, is found dead on her houseboat and her collection of plants and potions suggest she's a witch. De Gier is the first to put a name to it and the rest of the novel is devoted to finding her murderer, who it turns out is another witch. This novel sets the pattern that van de Wetering usually adheres to: the justice in these finely rendered, vivid novels is usually poetic rather than statutory.

The Japanese Corpse is probably his best novel before the current crop and has to do, again, with the smuggling of drugs into Holland, this time from Japan by the *yakusa,* a society of gangsters that has functioned (indeed, flourished) in Japan since the end of their middle ages. The book, aside from its suspense and mystery and chilling bits of murder and mayhem, is a meditation on Zen and on Japan.

One of the latest novels is ***The Maine Massacre,*** set in the mythical town of Jameson, Maine. Van de Wetering lives in fact near Ellsworth, Maine, way up the coast, almost on the edge of the cliffs of Maine, in a wooden house he built himself. The flavor of rural Maine is captured perfectly in this book, which features the unraveling of the mystery of Cape Orca by de Gier and the Commissaris (who has come over to help liquidate the estate of his brother-in-law, who died in an "accident" outside his home on the Cape). Grijpstra never gets to go on these jaunts; perhaps he is the presiding genius of the Amsterdam police and cannot travel. Regardless of the setting, however, those who have never read van de Wetering are in for a treat. (pp. 291-92)

John C. Carr, "Janwillem Van de Wetering," in his The Craft of Crime: Conversations with Crime Writers, *Houghton Mifflin Company, 1983, pp. 289-321.*

JEAN M. WHITE

Janwillem van de Wetering, the author of the distinctive series of Amsterdam police procedurals with Dutch detectives Grijpstra and De Gier, each an original, introduces a new sleuth in ***Inspector Saito's Small Satori***. . . .

[Readers] get 11 short stories loosely linked together. In each, young Inspector Matsuo Saito applies Zen Logic to detection and waits for *satori*, outbursts of sudden enlightenment, to solve cases. . . .

Saito, who irritates his superiors on the Kyoto Municipal Police force with his aristocratic, slightly arrogant manner, also uses his trusty 13th-century manual, *Parallel Cases Under the Pear Tree*, for guidance as he searches for parallel situations in contemporary life. . . .

It is difficult to warm to Saito until the last two cases, in which he recognizes his own arrogance and thinks about leaving the police force. Within the constraints of short stories, he emerges as only a half-formed character. We must wait to see whether Van de Wetering will have a *satori* about his new character.

Jean M. White, "The Zen of Detection," in Book World—The Washington Post, *May 19, 1985, p. 8.*

NJEGOS M. PETROVIC

While living in Japan [Van de Wetering] discovered in the Zen monastery a thirteenth century manual listing 144 criminal cases solved by Chinese magistrates, inspired by buddhist wisdom, and more specifically, Zen logic. The discovery inspired Van de Wetering to create a new hero, Inspector Saito of the Kyoto Police Department. This charming and witty detective [who appears in the stories in ***Inspector Saito's Small Satori***] has a touch of Charlie Chan's oriental wisdom, a bit of the famous French Inspector Clouseau's perfection, and Hercule Poirot's seventh sense of deduction. The action is fast, thrilling and usually further complicated by oriental mystery. Crime is, however, always crime, and solving it is always challenging and exciting. Each section of the book is to be read as a separate little story. The only common link among all of them is, of course, Inspector Saito, who never fails to surprise us.

Njegos M. Petrovic, in a review of "Inspector Saito's Small Satori," in Best Sellers, *Vol. 45, No. 5, August, 1985, p. 176.*

JOHN MICHIELSEN

In ***Death of a Hawker***, Van de Wetering's two detectives with the homicide squad of the Amsterdam municipal police force, De Gier and Grijpstra, are on their way to investigate a murder in the inner city when they are held up by a demonstration in the Newmarket area. A mob is trying to prevent wreckers from demolishing houses so the city can build a subway station. As Grijpstra smokes a cigar while he waits for the violence to subside so he and his colleague can proceed to the scene of the crime, he ponders on the reasons for the demonstration:

> Why? Grijpstra thought, but he knew the answer. This wasn't just a protest against the building of an underground station. There had always been violence in the city. Amsterdam, by its tolerance for unconventional behavior, attracts crazy people. Holland is a conventional country; crazy people have to go somewhere. They go to the capital, where the lovely canals, thousands and thousands of gable houses, hundreds of bridges of every shape and form, lines of old trees, clusters of offbeat bars and cafes, dozens of small cinemas and theatres encourage and protect the odd. Crazy people are special people. They carry the country's genius, its urge to create, to find new ways. The State smiles and is proud of its crazy people. But the State does not approve of anarchism. It limits the odd.

This passage illustrates two important features of Van de Wetering's work, namely the combination of crazy and eccentric people with whom his detectives come into contact in the course of their work and the description of lovely canals, gable houses, bridges, and trees that make his Amsterdam so vibrant. As someone who worked for the Amsterdam police force and who loves the city, the author is especially skillful at evoking the latter's atmosphere—not just the gabled houses, canals, bridges, and trees the tourist admires, but also the ugliness, violence, and rubbish contained in these houses and canals. The juxtaposition of the ugliness and the beauty of the city, and the acceptance of both as essential to its life is what makes his portrayal of Amsterdam work. In his acceptance of the totality of life the author is, of course, influenced by his studies of Buddhism and the time he spent in a monastery. The physical appearance of the city mirrors what he considers to be human life which is, on the whole, positive.

Like their creator, Van de Wetering's three main detectives are aware of the ugliness of the city as a reflection of the human condition, but they find solace in its beauty at the same time. . . . They do not find Amsterdam alienating as Alistair Maclean depicts it in *Puppet on a Chain*, for example. At the beginning of ***The Mind Murders*** there is a fight going on at the Keizersgracht and the Brouwersgracht while De Gier studies a row of gabled houses displaying their seventeenth-century splendor through the branches of the majestic elms lining both canals. De Gier takes the time to remark: "A lovely spot, Grijpstra. This, I believe, is one of the better locations of the inner city, we are surrounded by decorative and beautiful architecture." At this moment, however, Grijpstra is more concerned with getting a drink than admiring the architectural beauty. Against their will, the detectives do get involved in the disturbance caused by a drunk in the canal. The motley crowd assembled to witness the scene, among others a fat man dressed in leather, a male model in his nighties, and a screaming young female, admires De Gier's physique after he strips and jumps into the canal to rescue the man. While De Gier swims to the man with a soggy newspaper brushing past his mouth, seaweed around his wrists, and a condom around his toe, Grijpstra admires the view: "a perfect square bordered by bridge, quaysides and a tumbled elm tree—the arena where the law fought its formidable opponent." (pp. 39-41)

Not only the fine old houses in the inner city admired by tourists are described, but other areas such as the Lamsburger Dike, which is a street with humble wooden houses inhabited by petty criminals and unemployed people in a poor section of Amsterdam North. This street is the setting for ***The Corpse on the Dike,*** and in the same novel there is a description of Bickers Eiland, a forgotten section of the city which has a maze of narrow streets and dock-sides, lined with tall sixteenth century warehouses. The commissaris often goes there for a walk and he usually ends up in a pub, the last of its kind where the landlord, who is described as a living skeleton, still pours a shot of Geneva from a stone bottle for his few guests. (pp. 42-3)

If we turn from the description of the streetscapes to the various aspects of life that can be considered characteristic of Amsterdam, we find that these are also evocative. There are traffic jams, of course, usually when our detectives are on their way to investigate a crime. (p. 43)

On other occasions the detectives are delayed by riots organized by squatters occupying empty houses that the police attempt to break up. This happens again and again in ***Death of a Hawker,*** and the riots are glossed over as part of life in Amsterdam. Elsewhere, however, the riots are treated with irony and are the cause for social commentary. . . .

Drug dealing and prostitution are important problems in Amsterdam and these are also mentioned by Van de Wetering. In ***The Corpse on the Dike*** there is an excellent description of the Dam Square on a hot summer night. (p. 44)

Prostitution, which has always been part of life in Amsterdam, is also discussed at length in the novels. ***Streetbird***'s plot centers around the murder of the pimp Luku Obrian, who compelled a beautiful popular prostitute to perform fellatio on him on a bridge in full daylight in front of many tourists strolling through the red-light district in the city. In other novels Van de Wetering treats this aspect of life in Holland's capital with the same tolerance with which the Dutch accept it; if there is no crime involved, the police ignore it. In ***The Mind Murders,*** for example, it is mentioned that the police have had apple pies delivered to them because they have not interfered with the operation of the brothel across the street in the last five years. "Madame baked the pie with her own puffy hands. . . . She sent her two prize whores to carry the basket; the handle was decorated with a plastic rose." Grijpstra's mistress, Nellie, is a former prostitute who in ***Streetbird*** has been able to buy a small hotel in the inner city where the commissaris lodges when he investigates Obrian's murder. In ***The Corpse on the Dike*** there is a lengthy description of an evening spent by De Gier and the commissaris in the course of an investigation at an expensive, discreetly managed brothel. In not one of these cases does Van de Wetering condemn prostitution as such. When drugs or extortion are involved, however, the police do interfere. (p. 46)

And finally, the characters that appear in Van de Wetering's novels reflect the various socio-economic and ethnic groups that make up the diversity of the population of the city. At the lowest end of the scale there are, of course, the drug addicts, pimps, and prostitutes mentioned. There are also the petty thieves and people on welfare who live on the Lamsburger Dike in ***The Corpse on the Dike.*** Hawkers play an important role in ***Death of a Hawker,*** where the colorful scenes of Dutch markets are described, and black market dealers, who constitute an important element of Dutch society, appear in most of the novels. On the other hand, the reader also catches glimpses of the lives of powerful Dutch industrialists, like Maria van Buren's lover, Drachtsma, and the patrician gentry, still living in the houses that their forefathers built, such as Frits Fortune's aunt and uncle in ***The Mind Murders.*** There are also such colorful characters as a retired transvestite policeman who is a friend of the commissaris and lives alone on his houseboat with his cat, various Turks, Chinese aliens, and blacks from the former Dutch colonies.

In summary, Van de Wetering's portrayal of Amsterdam and its inhabitants works for two reasons. The author is skillful at evoking both the beauty and richness of the life in the city that is admired by those who visit it and live in it, and miserable lives of some of the inhabitants with whom the police come into contact. The acceptance of both of these aspects and the juxtaposition of the ugliness and the crimes committed within these surroundings is one important factor in his novels. Such a scene as the one described earlier where Grijpstra admires the splendor of the houses reflected in the canal while De Gier swims through the rubbish which collects in these same canals is typical. In spite of its size and cosmopolitan population Amsterdam strikes one as a friendly town that is not alienating. The other aspect that makes Van de Wetering's works delightful to read is his humorous approach to all facets of life in Amsterdam and his ability to put what could be tragic situations into a positive context. (pp. 46-7)

John Michielsen, "Van de Wetering's Amsterdam," in Clues: A Journal of Detection, *Vol. 7, No. 1, Spring-Summer, 1986, pp. 39-48.*

ART SEIDENBAUM

Plenty of bodies fall in the course of ***Hard Rain,*** and the climate—drugs, prostitution, official corruption, computer manipulation—is about what you'd expect this literary season. . . . Yet a couple of attending virtues make Janwillem van de Wetering's new novel more than a routine case of venality and violence. One is a world-weary humor, the sort of exchanges heard among the hirelings of police stations, political campaigns and hospitals. The other is an exploration of a good guy's ethic and a bad guy's ethos.

Jan and Willem—not so oddly both sides of the author's first name—grew up together, competed for the same teacher's admiration and, later, the same girl's affection. They even grew up to look like each other in their mutual middle ages. Jan became a policeman, rising to the rank of *commissaris,* the equivalent of a deputy chief. Willem became a banker, power broker, head of a philanthropic foundation and one of the most prominent men in modern Netherlands. He was less well known as a thief, child-murderer and owner of a lavish brothel-casino for the lowest creatures of the Low Countries.

The first killing begins during a downpour, murder muffled in a thunderclap. The resolution follows a downpour, setting up another parallel. In between storms come some engaging explanations of how law enforcers operate and behave, almost putting the book in a category called "police procedurals.". . .

Philosophy dominates procedure here. Younger police officers discuss the morality of the way they break laws in order to enforce them. They argue about the burdens of owning anything and the temptations of selling out to the enemy. Selling out is the most active verb in the novel; high officials are more likely to be in the pay of the bad guys than of the government they serve. The bad guys at the top, the ones who do the buying and bribing, have already purchased trappings of respectability. Principles die as quickly as sniper victims.

Jan, the *commissaris,* remains uncorrupted; he must battle headquarters even while having his final fight with Willem. . . .

Hero Jan and villain Willem have a couple of reunions along the way. Willem wants to know whether they are "starting up our old argument about negativity again? The infinite enters the finite, and ultimately there's nothing there and in nothingness everything exists? Wasn't that David Hume?"

Jan accuses Willem of repressing his "true nature," then suggests, "You're not really a devil, Willem, you're a good man hiding behind a demonic mask."

By the end of the bloodletting, the *commissaris* cannot be so charitable. Willem lies dying—of natural causes—in a hospital bed, all the while plotting to murder Jan by remote means and even enjoying the prospect of hell. Jan, not so hale himself, admits, "Hell could be exciting. Heaven will be dull." The pure of heart, especially, understand the limits allowed. But the good guy, of course, must go to heaven. Good thrillers, like Western movies and morality plays, require victories of faith; ***Hard Rain*** is an engaging victory of form within formula.

Art Seidenbaum, in a review of "Hard Rain," in Los Angeles Times Book Review, *December 7, 1986, p. 3.*

PAUL STUEWE

[***Hard Rain***] is on much more solid ground than its immediate predecessors, which tended to emphasize Zen-influenced, metaphysical speculations at the expense of narrative interest. Here the dynamic Dutch duo [of de Gier and Grijpstra] becomes involved in a most down-to-earth affair of murder, drug dealing, and police corruption. There's lots of action to complement van de Wetering's compelling portraits of de Gier and Grijpstra, which lifts ***Hard Rain*** well above the standard police procedural. . . . Fortunately they're also adept at tracking down criminals and dishing them out their just deserts. ***Hard Rain*** is one of the few truly sophisticated thrillers available to readers in search of literate entertainment.

Paul Stuewe, "A Lively Deal . . . Tubeside Companion . . . Stellar Stella," in Quill and Quire, *Vol. 53, No. 1, January, 1987, p. 33.*

Keith (Spencer) Waterhouse

1929-

English novelist, dramatist, journalist, scriptwriter, essayist, and critic.

Photograph by Gered Mankowitz. Courtesy of Keith Waterhouse.

Waterhouse is best known for his satiric novels that examine contemporary British society. He often focuses upon the misfortunes of irreverent and immature antiheroes who frequently rely on their imagination to escape their plight. These protagonists, as well as the sardonic tone of his novels, have led some critics to associate Waterhouse with the ''Angry Young Men,'' a group of English writers, including Kingsley Amis, John Braine, and John Osborne, who bitterly condemned the social and political values of post-World War II Britain during the late 1950s. Although some critics have admonished Waterhouse for the formulaic quality of his fiction, he is generally praised for his humorously precise depictions of working-class life and his ability to faithfully render English dialects.

Waterhouse first won critical plaudits with the publication of *Billy Liar* (1959). This novel, which is generally considered Waterhouse's most successful work, recounts the misadventures of teenage pathological liar Billy Fisher. Like James Thurber's Walter Mitty, with whom Waterhouse's protagonist has been compared, Billy eschews the tedium of his working-class existence by daydreaming of heroic escapades in fantastic worlds. John Updike commented that in this novel Waterhouse ''gives us adolescence full-bodied in its raucous ferocity.'' Waterhouse later wrote a sequel, *Billy Liar on the Moon* (1975), in which he details the mishaps of an older but still childlike Billy Fisher. Waterhouse's other early novels include *Jubb* (1963), a darkly humorous, introspective portrait of a psychopath, and *The Bucket Shop* (1968), which chronicles the business and personal failures of an antique dealer who longs for a superior existence. Although reviews of *The Bucket Shop* were mixed, A. DeVitis contended that the novel ''demonstrates again the author's wit and moral detachment, a detachment . . . reminiscent in many ways of the early [Evelyn] Waugh.''

Many of Waterhouse's novels of the late 1970s and 1980s demonstrate his proficiency with satire and parody. In *Office Life* (1978), Waterhouse lampoons modern corporations while focusing upon office clerk Clement Gryce's efforts to discover his company's objectives within its bureaucratic complexities. *Maggie Muggins; or, Spring in Earl's Court* (1981) is a portrait of an alternately amusing and pathetic London vagrant, and *In the Mood* (1983) concerns the lustful desires of three adolescent boys. Waterhouse based his next two novels, *Mrs. Pooter's Diary* (1983) and *The Collected Letters of a Nobody* (1986), on *The Diary of a Nobody,* a nineteenth-century satire by George and Weedon Grossmith. Critics extolled Waterhouse's ability to faithfully reproduce the style and tone of the earlier work. In his review of *The Collected Letters of a Nobody,* Nicolas Wollaston remarked: ''Waterhouse has done for [letters] what the Grossmiths did for the diary, keeping the same cunning balance between affection and ridicule, conjuring another vaudeville of comic fiction.''

In addition to his novels, Waterhouse has collaborated on several plays with Willis Hall that are lauded for their witty dialogue and vivid characterizations. Waterhouse and Hall's first play, an adaptation of *Billy Liar* produced in 1960, met with financial and critical success. Their next work, *Celebration: The Wedding and the Funeral* (1961), is an insightful examination of two disparate family gatherings. In the musical revue *England, Our England* (1962), Waterhouse and Hall satirize the perplexities of their country's working-class citizens. *The Sponge Room and Squat Betty* (1962) consists of two one-act comedies that evidence Waterhouse and Hall's talent for writing sexual farce. In the first play, a married man and his mistress futilely search for a secret place to consummate their affair; in the second, a woman's extramarital activities expose suicidal tendencies in her husband and herself. Roger Gellert observed that ''these hilarious plays are not to be judged by their documentary likelihood, but by the charm of their fantasy and their underlying emotional truth.'' *Say Who You Are* (1965) is another farce involving a woman's revenge for her husband's infidelity, and *Whoops-a-Daisy* (1968) details the comical interaction between a reticent family and their boisterous new neighbors. *Children's Days* (1969) centers on the puerile behavior of adults chaperoning a children's party.

Waterhouse is also a popular journalist whose work has appeared in such publications as *Punch* and the *Daily Mirror*. Collections of his sketches and columns include *The Passing of the Third-Floor Buck* (1974), *Mondays, Thursdays* (1976), and *Rhubarb, Rhubarb, and Other Noises* (1979).

(See also *Contemporary Authors,* Vols. 5-8, rev. ed. and *Dictionary of Literary Biography,* Vols. 13, 15.)

THE TIMES LITERARY SUPPLEMENT

[In ***Billy Liar,*** we] are in familiar fictional territory, England A.D. 1959. Billy Fisher, the now traditionally unheroic hero of this kind of novel, is a hapless welfare-state Yorkshire chap. By profession he is an undertakers' assistant. What he wants to be is a script-writer for a comedian, whom some would call light, on television. There are lots of catch-phrases, instead of a dressing-gown he wears an old raincoat—with a packet of Weights in the pocket—he has a "Gran"—and in addition to face-twitching, noise-making, scientific yawning, &c., he indulges in two kinds of "thinking," the first being chiefly concerned with a fantasy world called Ambrosia, where his day-dream ideal self is carried to surrealistic lengths, and the second with his bedraggled scoured Mum and loud-mouthed Dad in the front parlour. Billy also has two fiancées and one wedding ring and a third girl he loves; or, in other words, he has problems. Yet, all in all, this is a brilliantly funny book, rich in absurdities and beautifully edged writing.

"Joking Apart," in The Times Literary Supplement, *No. 3001, September 4, 1959, p. 505.*

JOHN COLEMAN

[***Billy Liar***], Keith Waterhouse's second novel, set in that humorist's playground, the grim North, is calculated to bring a rush of names to the head—Amis, Osborne, even Peter de Vries—but it shows, for all the reminiscences, as something more than a Yorkshire posy of other men's flowers. The narrator, Billy Fisher, is an original: a young undertaker's clerk given to gag-writing and a gamut of private and public fantasies. . . . The book swiftly sees him through one claustrophobic Saturday when all manner of retributions fall from the air; from a cliché-ridden breakfast *en famille,* through a botched idyll in a cemetery, down to his nasty Gran's death in the evening. The assault on one's sense of humour is conducted from several angles. There is the hideously convincing fake-dialect ('Ah'm just about thraiped,' 'It's neither muckling nor mickling') that Billy finds himself using on Councillor Duxbury in an aberrant moment; the de Vries-like Ambrosia, all nobility and left-handed salutes, where he takes refuge when things get too hot; the panic Amis incidents (doing a funny turn before bored drinkers; flushing torn calendars down a reluctant lavatory); and, setting it off, the spare needling accuracy of his seedy small-town backcloth. Mr. Waterhouse, in fact, has written such a funny book that it seems almost ungracious to accuse him of having tried to write a serious one as well. But there are conventions in comedy as in anything else: Wooster with cancer is unthinkable; and Mr. Waterhouse undoes much of his good work before the end. His Billy keeps trying to see the decent, 'human' side of his victims, there is that death, and you are left, as he trudges home, with the uneasy sensation of having been slipped an unwarranted draught of morality. (p. 342)

John Coleman, "Comic Turn," in The Spectator, *Vol. 203, No. 6846, September 11, 1959, pp. 342-43.*

MAURICE RICHARDSON

Bleuler would have classed Mr Waterhouse's comic hero [in ***Billy Liar***] as a case of *Pseudologia fantastica*. The label covers a variety of types from swindlers and con-men to daydreamers and schizoids. They are very strange people, these pathological liars. You might expect the symptom to be part of some insidious degeneration of the character, but this is not always so. I know three cases of intermittent *Pseudologia fantastica* all of whom are neat, dapper, competent persons who lead tidy, successful lives. The most capable of them, also the most reliable and scrupulous, is the one who tells the biggest lies.

It seems that the condition can exist in isolation, like a tic or a perversion. If I had not known this I might have thought Billy Liar, the Yorkshire small-town undertaker's clerk whose misadventures, occupational and amorous, during 24 hectic hours, as his lies catch up with him, was not quite dotty enough to be consistent. In spite of some rather artificial-seeming intellectual's properties, such as his Guilt Chest—the trunk in which he keeps his passion pills for his girls, and the hundreds of calendars which he is supposed to have sent off for his firm—he just passes the test for an original character, though occurring in his improbable environment you need to think of him as a rare mutation. The affinity with Kingsley Amis's Jim, which several reviewers have stressed is, I think, only superficial, due to their similar predicaments and attitudes of self-mockery, all part of the same farcical genre. Mr Waterhouse has a remarkable gift for projecting himself under the skin of the modern adolescent. Billy's daydreams, with their amalgam of telly-formed consciousness and literary ideas and juke-box sex, and his dialogue, with its scriptwriter's wisecracks and puns, are contemporary right up to the minute. The small-town and family background is richly detailed. The writing is nice and tight. A lot of it is really funny. The characters of Billy's three girls with whom he gets into such dreadful troubles, the Witch, Liz, and Rita, are strikingly differentiated. Under the harsh surface of farce, there is a good deal of human sympathy.

Maurice Richardson, in a review of "Billy Liar," in New Statesman, *Vol. LVIII, No. 1487, September 12, 1959, p. 328.*

JOHN UPDIKE

This pungent, shapely and instructive novel [***Billy Liar***] begins, and for the first half continues, comically. Billy Fisher, an ambitious and mendacious teenager in the Yorkshire town of Stradhoughton, describes his progress through one critical Saturday. As he tells it, his family is a pack of harping drudges, his employers (undertakers) are a pair of futile fools, and his town is a dismal muddle of moldering churchyards and modernist record shops, of despairing institutions and desperate Americanisms.

Along these drab streets Billy trundles a complicated apparatus of fantasy worlds: Ambrosia, an imaginary nation of which he is President and, repeatedly, savior: a companion nether world of "daymares," where diseases like ingrowing hair and Fisher's Yawn beset him; a vaguely envisioned London, where he hopes to go and live as a gag-writer. . . .

The friction of all these revolving spheres strikes a wonderful number of comic sparks. And it all seems true. The author gives us adolescence full-bodied, in its raucous ferocity. . . .

In the second half of the book the demands of that wearisome old fellow Plot, or perhaps the inherent seriousness of the material itself, press hard upon the humor. Apparently Billy must, if he cannot unravel, at least confront the tangle he has made. His bad checks roll in. His ebullience weakens, and with it the mainspring of the comedy. Mr. Waterhouse rushes new, more somber resources to the fore. He creates several harrowing and touching scenes. But he is handicapped, I think, by the determinedly comic tone of the beginning. (p. 4)

It comes down to the doubtful compatibility, over the length of the book, of comedy and realism. Even novels as funny as Joyce Cary's *Herself Surprised* and Henry Green's *Nothing* do not strike us as purposely comic, but, rather, accidently so, like reality itself. The publicized Anger of England's younger writers may seem to lead easily into satire and hence into the also publicized Renascence of the Comic Novel. But, in Mr. Waterhouse's case, there is much more at stake than a view, indignant or amused, of the contemporary scene; and, while I would not really want this excellent book (except for a phrase about "the eyes that laughed aloud") any different, I hope that the author in his future work does not confine himself to a genre possibly too small for his experiences and his feelings about them. (p. 22)

John Updike, "Nightmares and Daymares," in The New York Times Book Review, *January 3, 1960, pp. 4, 22.*

MARTIN PRICE

What gives Mr. Waterhouse's book [***Billy Liar***] its distinction is that his angry man is so much younger than usual; he is, in fact, an adolescent boy, restive in the progressive funeral establishment of Shadrack and Duxbury, dreaming of writing scripts for a London television comedian. Billy lives much of his life in wonderfully callow daydreams or nightmares. He sends the armies of Ambrosia to victory; he is indulged by an unutterably worldly mother; he broods about polio, gingivitis, and ingrown hair. His actual nagging mother and blustering father, and his savage old gran, are hardly more real than the creatures he invents, and he constantly recreates his family in a series of obsessive lies. . . . Billy's fears are as genuine as his bravado, and Mr. Waterhouse is enormously inventive in creating the elaborate and protective world of fantasy into which he retreats.

But it is all too comfortable. For Billy at every point recalls those older and more bitterly farcical heroes of John Osborne, Kingsley Amis, Alan Sillitoe. The feeling for music-hall style, the risk of living out impromptu lies, the grotesque humiliation at the hands of employers—all of these have an urgency in other works which is largely dissipated here. At first it seems all too revealingly apt to give these gestures to an adolescent boy, and Billy's collapse back into Stradhoughton at the close has its pathos, but the collapse is something more painful and threatening in the others. The cultivation of fantasy, of irresponsibility, of destructiveness by maturer men has a weight of implication that Mr. Waterhouse's more innocent hero can hardly suggest. Billy is amusingly outrageous, but he is not very tellingly outraged. (pp. 443-44)

Martin Price, "Deeps and Shallows: Some Recent Fiction," in The Yale Review, *Vol. XLIX, No. 3, March, 1960, pp. 443-51.*

JEREMY BROOKS

[***Billy Liar***] is a study of a compulsive liar, a youth—again of the north country, but more Amis than Delaney—who lives in a fantasy world, which he acts out at home and at work: getting engaged to three girls at once, telling lies about his background, his friends, his prospects. Living his lies, he is the slave of them, and finally the prisoner of his own inventions. . . . Like *Hancock's Half-Hour,* the play is funny, exact, and often penetrating—as an extended music-hall sketch it is marvellous entertainment. . . . The second act curtain commits the authors, however funny their material, to making some serious statement about their subject; yet Billy is allowed to dwindle into nothing more than a sad-eyed funny man. Our hopes come crashing to the ground. (p. 378)

Jeremy Brooks, "Chunks of Life," in New Statesman, *Vol. LX, No. 1540, September 17, 1960, pp. 377-78)*

***THE TIMES,* LONDON**

It is some 20 years since Mr. Willis Hall and Mr. Keith Waterhouse began to collaborate as writers, and one might have taken [***Celebration***] for an early work of theirs, if the programme did not say that it has been written quite recently. Perhaps, now that they are established singly and jointly, they have imagined themselves back in the West Riding of their youth and tried to write about it exactly as they once saw it, adding nothing to the picture that experience of life has taught them since.

For this picture of two gatherings of the same two families, one before a wedding, the other immediately after a funeral six months later, is not at all a remarkable one. Its merit is consistency. There is an equal amount, a very small amount, of over emphasis in the drawing of every character, so that all of them move on one level plane of comedy.

It is as though they wore high heeled shoes and accordingly to us, but not to one another, have a slightly odd and absurd look. But apart from this they appear not only to each other but also to us to be their normal everyday selves. This is an achievement of a kind but it is not in any way exciting. While the moderation and up to a point the skill in the composition of the picture are engaging qualities, one cannot think that the exercise was worth these two writers' while.

"Family Gatherings," in The Times, *London, February 21, 1961, p. 15.*

DENIS DONOGHUE

Questions of choice, action, and dialogue are proposed . . . in ***Billy Liar,*** a play by Keith Waterhouse and Willis Hall based on Waterhouse's novel. The shadow of English domestic farce may be discerned in the wings, and most of the characters are to be found any evening in the green room of the B.B.C. Light Programme. The play becomes interesting only when we see Billy Fisher dreaming dreams rarely entertained in English domestic farce and never condoned by the Light Programme. Billy is Walter Mitty set down in a post-war-and-probably-pre-WAR Welfare State called England; the game is rougher than Thurber's. . . . Billy is a boy-man for whom life has been inadequate, fitful where he wanted focus; so he supplies form and focus in daydreams, ideal but not abstract, trying to devise a reality for himself since he is unable to find one in life. . . . I wish I could say that in Billy's dreams begin Billy's responsibilities, but here is the major defect of the play. Toward the end of the third act Billy and Liz talk about going to London and getting married and having children. They arrange to meet at the station at eleven. Billy has a row with Mum and Dad, packs his bag, sets off—and slinks back. The play ends with Billy unpacking. Going to London with Liz stands for all the positive acts which a Billy Fisher might perform; he is not asked to be a saint or to replace Walter Winchell or to find the Abominable Snowman. But he can't go to London; at least he doesn't. Why not? He doesn't say, because he doesn't know. Presumably he could dream just as engrossingly in London as in Stradhoughton, so the answer is not that he can't break out of the closed circuit of an invented reality. London is not a dream; Liz, who knows about these matters, vouches for its existence. The only answer is the play's modish 'you can't win.' (pp. 95-6)

Denis Donoghue, "London Letter: Moral West End," in The Hudson Review, *Vol. XIV, No. 1, Spring, 1961, pp. 93-103.*

THE TIMES, LONDON

If inexperience in the theatre is not the inevitable liability we once took it to be, it is not either the automatic advantage we now, in our passion for the "fresh" and the "unspoilt", tend to suppose it. Not that in this new revue [***England, Our England***] by Mr. Willis Hall and Mr. Keith Waterhouse absolute theatrical inexperience is at issue. . . . But they do not know revue, and revue, like it or not, is a form with its own very special requirements.

Novelty, of course, has its attractions. In this show, for instance, how new, and how true, are the trials of the loving relatives trying to get their favoured design of headstone past the prejudices of the local vicars; the sad case of the young housewife on a new estate who wants to make her home different when all the rules force her to keep it exactly the same; the problems of the mail-order shoplifter dazzled by the glittering prizes of the seven-day free trial offer. . . .

But—and there is a but—new ideas, however good, are not enough by themselves to make a good revue. Here and there this show has numbers which come off perfectly: "**Home Town**" is a favourable example. . . . But there are too many sketches which just drag on without either hitting their target or pointedly failing to hit it.

"Bright, Polished Ideas but Not a Revue," in The Times, *London, May 8, 1962, p. 15.*

ROGER GELLERT

The activities of that dual chameleon Waterhouse 'n' Hall continue to proliferate in the London theatre. ***All Things Bright and Beautiful*** was a straightforward piece of Northern anecdotage, but their new double-bill . . . makes a surprisingly successful thrust into John Mortimer country. . . . The first play, ***The Sponge Room*** (its action unfolds in this particular backwater of the BM), tackles from a more poetic angle the matter of Mortimer's disappointing and frenetic one-acter *Lunch Hour:* an unmarried couple's search for a love-nest. Colin . . . has a wife of his own, is convinced she is having him shadowed, but keeps sad, furtive trysts with Hilary . . . in London museums and art galleries. Frustrated, they hunt contacts who might lend rooms, think of advertising in windows, speculate on distant bliss: until a *deus ex machina* intervenes in the person of Leslie, a helpful museum attendant . . . who offers them the use of his bed-sitter if, in exchange, they will smuggle out a few coveted stuffed birds for him. . . .

The scene of the second play, ***Squat Betty,*** is a Cumberland mountain hostel (Betty is the local peak) where marital drama is brewing between the warden Stanley . . . and his wife Elizabeth. . . . He suspects her of misconduct with another warden over the hill, but her real paramour, Jonathan Pearce . . . turns up as a young mountaineering ad-man from London. When Stanley learns the truth he tries, for the umpteenth time, to kill himself: the hostel by now is a perfect machine for dying in, with a rope dangling from the ceiling and pills rattling in every drawer. When Elizabeth learns that Jonathan has in fact come to break off the affair, she too starts munching pills and trying the noose for size. These hilarious plays are not to be judged by their documentary likelihood, but by the charm of their fantasy and their underlying emotional truth. The suicidal farce is less beautifully constructed than the spongy idyll, but as pure theatre it has some sublime moments.

Roger Gellert, "Love and Sponges," in New Statesman, *Vol. LXIV, No. 1659, December 28, 1962, p. 936.*

BAMBER GASCOIGNE

[***The Sponge Room***] is a poor specimen in an overworked fashion—the fashion this time being for the quaintly trivial, as established by the lesser plays of John Mortimer. In such plays pathetic little characters are nudged into reciting strings of suburban place-names or lists of Formica-type details of interior decoration. The authors are aiming at a poetry of the commonplace, but the result is only whimsical-literary. Two drooping would-be lovers meet in the Sponge Room of the Natural History Museum. They pretend to be searching eagerly for a room somewhere with a bed, but during the play this pretence is shattered—they could have found one long ago, the difficulties are all trumped up. This revelation has no noticeable effect on them. Within moments they are back at the old pretence. This is typical of such plays. The pathos is laid on and laid bare just for us, without any real relevance to the characters concerned. But if it means so little to them, it is certainly going to mean no more to us.

Bamber Gascoigne, "The Child and the Man," in The Spectator, *Vol. 209, No. 7018, December 28, 1962, p. 991.*

J. C. TREWIN

[In ***All Things Bright and Beautiful***] Keith Waterhouse and Willis Hall present to us what the programme describes as "a combined living room and kitchen and the communal yard outside." At curtain-rise, when I observed the dustbin and the outside lavatory, my spirits drooped. Though there was not a great deal in the night to lift them, the play could have been much worse. A half-hearted phrase, but all I can muster. Maybe the trouble is that Mr. Hall and Mr. Waterhouse have not bothered about a narrative; though they can create character and establish a scene, there is no real development.

The piece is about a crude, scrounging slum family that may or may not reach a Council housing estate. The latest piece of scrounging is the removal of a church lectern—a wooden eagle that has to be concealed somewhere when the hunt is up. Surprisingly little comes of this. Throughout the night I watched and listened hopefully, observing a glint of truth here, a moment of comedy there, but looking in vain for real progress or genuine wit. The liveliest personage never appears: the demon-child of the family who is heard singing (off) and who is talked about so much that we feel we know him and his crimes to the last article. It is a pity that he never gets to us. . . . But though the piece is not less than competent, it does not offer much of a night. It gives the impression that the dramatists, hoping for the best but without inspiration, settled down resolutely to write, the paper blank before them.

J. C. Trewin, "All and Nothing," in The Illustrated London News, *Vol. 241, No. 6439, December 29, 1962, p. 1060.*

THE TIMES LITERARY SUPPLEMENT

[***Jubb***] seems intended to shock. Those who chuckled over Billy Liar's wholesome tangles with sex and respectability are warned from the very first lines that ***Jubb*** is concerned with a very different sort of anti-hero: "Man found dead in plastic wardrobe. That's the way you'll finish up if you're not careful, I tell myself."

Cyril Jubb, thus opening the sad, startling and uncomfortably perspicacious confession of his downfall in a society of hypocrites and hyenas, is a keen member of the community centre in Chapel Langtry New Town. . . . Jubb recognizes that he is an anomaly in Chapel Langtry—one of the ugly, dirty, lonely, longing Herberts who cannot compete with the bronzed and confident "lions" of the human race. . . .

Jubb's idea of starting a Camera Club for the Youth Group rips open the façade of decency in Chapel Langtry, letting out all the savage herd instincts which reject this unhealthy Jonah in its midst. Poor Jubb does not stand a chance. A coloured lady in arrears accuses him of assault when he offers to make up the books out of his own pocket; his wife cannot stand the nasty demands to dress up and excite him any longer, so she runs off with a Bible-bashing man next door; no one turns up to his little party; a visitor from Ghana writes rude articles about the Peeping Toms in public office. Even *Follow Your Thoughts (1961)* Ltd. does not want his help distributing leaflets—a back-door pornographic bookshop provides them with ample funds—and the True Nationals do not consider Jubb's admiration for Mussolini an adequate qualification for membership. . . .

Squalid and pathetic Jubb may be, but Mr. Waterhouse has somehow managed to make him a gloriously comic character. He is so absurdly inept at being a lecher and a pervert, so meticulously and pompously correct and careful in analysing his problems and recounting his humiliating experiences—rather as a police constable reads out his statement concerning some unspeakably shocking investigation. And the laugh, of course, is not on the Jubbs plotting sadly to derive some kind of satisfaction in their blighted and lonely lives, but on the successful Jeremiahs who proclaim their "normality" so lustily. Mr. Waterhouse's criticism of our society is no less angry for being very funny, and he has achieved the remarkable feat of writing in the character of a man not only psychopathic, but also a repulsive bore, who nevertheless emerges as profoundly sane and even, in his own odd way, quite jolly.

"Heading for a Fall," in The Times Literary Supplement, *No. 3213, September 27, 1963, p. 730.*

EDITH OLIVER

Keith Waterhouse, who wrote the novel ***Billy Liar*** and collaborated on the play and the movie that were made from it, is a very funny writer, but this would be hard to tell from ***Squat Betty*** and ***The Sponge Room,*** a couple of one-act plays he wrote with Willis Hall, which have already been done in London, and which opened last week at the East End. Although both have comic lines, original, quirky nonsense, and amusing characters (three apiece), neither is nearly as funny in performance as it ought to be. Perhaps the plays just didn't travel well, but I doubt it. It is more likely that two of the three actors who appear in them—and possibly the director, too—never hit the right note. (p. 122)

On opening night, ***Squat Betty,*** which is the more obvious and farcical of the two, went better than ***The Sponge Room,*** but I think ***The Sponge Room*** is a better and more revealing play, for all its nuttiness. (p. 124)

Edith Oliver, "Vive la Compagnie," in The New Yorker, *Vol. XL, No. 3, March 7, 1964, pp. 120, 122, 124.*

THE TIMES, LONDON

The farce revival is one of the healthiest recent developments in the West End, but—with the possible exception of Henry Livings—no writer has yet made any serious attempt to revitalize the form for modern audiences.

Peter Shaffer's *Black Comedy* succeeded by means of combining a structural innovation with an ostentatiously stereotyped set of characters. Keith Waterhouse and Willis Hall's new play [***Say Who You Are***] pursues the opposite, and far less rewarding course of coating a traditional structure with contemporary decoration. A three-sided phone-box is the only technical novelty they have to offer: otherwise modernity consists of equipping their puppets with lines about French films and travel agencies.

The play is a bedroom variant on the *Box and Cox* situation. To repay her husband's infidelity without "losing her honour" (this phrase is spoken in all seriousness) a wife lets off her flat to a friend as a Friday night love-nest. The friend, who wants sex without marriage, assumes the wife's identity as an alibi against involvement. In the first act this situation is unfolded to the audience; in the second, the characters (all in some state of ignorance) discover it for themselves, and the evening grows increasingly strident with slamming doors, tumblers of whisky flung in the face, and symbolic acts of castration with wild women amputating the sleeves from their men's suits.

Comedy of this kind makes its effect when it provides a safety valve for acts of violence we wish to, but dare not, commit. The weakness here is that the violence seems quite arbitrary.

Disabled though it is, the plan is the work of a pair of deft professionals, and there is some pleasure in the economy of their technique—as much in the conversational echo effects as in the use of properties.

"A Friday Night Love-Nest Farce," in The Times, *London, October 15, 1965, p. 18.*

WALTER KERR

Help Stamp Out Marriage [produced in Great Britain as ***Say Who You Are***], which overexerted itself by opening . . . last night, is a British-born sex comedy in which the four principal funmakers are willing to do absolutely anything to avoid engaging in sex. Let the night be available, the room ready, the feathery green peignoirs afloat in the breeze and off they go—dashing down stairwells, whooshing up elevator shafts, hot-footing it nattily to the bright orange public phone booth that waits to welcome them at the corner. They are all, I would say, on the wrong track. . . .

What we have here, really, is a nice-naughty little relic of all the *Up in Mabel's Room* leftovers from an earlier, more innocent time of our lives, a time in which we didn't much mind how frayed the jokes were provided the breathless, spinning, double-talking and double-taking comedians did—or did not—bump into one another with split-second timing. The . . . [director] has seen to it that the timing is always right, but somehow he can't quite keep us from—heaven help us—hearing the jokes.

Walter Kerr, "Comedy from Britain Opens at Booth," in The New York Times, *September 30, 1966, p. 50.*

GILLIAN TINDALL

[In ***The Bucket Shop***] Keith Waterhouse's hero is obsessed by a vain hope that his life may appear more interesting to others than it does to himself. This contemporary man is hounded not by guilt but by humiliation: 'one of his preoccupations was a nagging consciousness that he had nothing to think about.' Lest such a fundamental theme should suggest that the book must be heavy-going, I hasten to say that the tale is almost too light, and compulsively readable. The Contemporary Man sells, incompetently, junk that is hopefully considered amusing. He has a boring wife (whom he calls 'Poodle' in the hope of making her more of a character) and a conventional small daughter whom he cannot induce to clamour for his whimsy stories. . . . [Husband and wife] take lovers, tragi-farce ensues. Readers may feel only laughing patronage toward characters so bogged-down in calculations about their status, but the hunger for identity is real.

Gillian Tindall, "Bright Brute," in New Statesman, *Vol. 76, No. 1960, October 4, 1968, p. 435.*

IRVING WARDLE

The playwriting partnership of Keith Waterhouse and Willis Hall has yielded a number of comedies that assail middle-class subjects with working-class derision. It sounds, and sometimes it is, a good formula. But in the case of their new piece, ***Whoops-a-Daisy,*** it seems that a cheap and nasty method is being used to demolish a cheap and nasty target. . . .

The object of scorn is the provincial suburban environment. . . . Here live the Wormalds, a trio of lugubrious stay-at-homes. . . .

Life changes for them with the arrival of new neighbors—a raw extrovert pair who invade the living room to make shocking phone calls and belabor their stuffy hosts into letting their hair down—rather more than hair in the daughter's case. This leads up to a last act reversal in which the Wormalds regain their joie de vivre, passing on their mean-spirited apathy to the newcomers.

Something no doubt is being said about the poison of suburban life; but nothing earlier in the play predicts it. . . .

Much of the action consists of party scenes and gags, both well within the range of the authors. . . . But the general impression is one of glib contempt: You are left wishing that a play that criticizes the clichés of modern living were less prone to the same faults itself.

Irving Wardle, "'Whoops-a-Daisy,' Play on Suburbia, Is Given in London," in The New York Times, *December 13, 1968, p. 61.*

JOHN BOWEN

The dramatic critic of *The London Times* writing recently of the new Waterhouse and Hall play described it as being from their "factory." Well, it is true that Keith Waterhouse and Willis Hall are a prolific pair. . . . [And] perhaps it is true that their writing has become a manufacturing process in which fairly similar jokes and characteristics and incidents are fitted together to make a salable object.

Worse, I suspect that the process itself may have become teleological. A novel, after all, is not a *very* salable object, and since [***Everything Must Go,*** published in England as ***The Bucket Shop***] is only Keith Waterhouse's fourth novel (and is not written in collaboration) one might expect to find it more individual, more important to its creator. Not so. In spite of some good jokes and neat writing, I found ***Everything Must Go*** easy to put down.

William, its hero, is an antique dealer who knows nothing about antiques, so he runs what is effectively a tat-shop. He lives in the unfashionable part of Fulham with a whining daughter, who is becoming a petty thief, and a wife whom he has nicknamed "Poodle" in the hope that she will behave whimsically, but she won't. He has a neurotic mistress with whom, owing to his own timidity, he has come to sexual grips only three and a half times in an entire year. During the course of the action he breaks with this mistress, and acquires a new one, who cons him out of the money for an abortion twice in six months, and finally commits suicide. (p. 4)

Perhaps deadness is a stylistic device, since William himself is clearly dead in most important senses. Dead to what are called "the finer feelings": the feelings he has are of guilt and fear. Dead to desire, except the desire for esteem. Dead selfish. Dead stupid. If so, it is a device that misfires, because the surface of this novel is a comic surface, and comedy demands at least the appearance of life. . . .

Everything Must Go is "expertly made" in the sense that it has been made by an expert. But it is not well made, because it does not seem to have been made for use. Mr. Waterhouse obviously doesn't care what happens to William, as long as the pieces fit together, and there is no reason why anyone else should care. (p. 34)

John Bowen, in a review of "Everything Must Go," in The New York Times Book Review, *January 26, 1969, pp. 4, 34.*

HENRY RAYNOR

As Keith Waterhouse and Willis Hall worked out exactly what happened to the adults during a children's party they kept two serious ideas tucked firmly away at the back of their minds. The first is about the responsibility of bringing up children: the second is about the disastrous effect children may have on a marriage. Each of these themes produces a long speech—long, that is, in the context of [***Children's Day***'s] snappy chatter—in which it is treated with impassioned seriousness. The authors place these pills so neatly in the middle of the jam that they actually contribute to the hilarity.

For the rest, unspeakable things are done by the children off stage; their activities chill the blood and keep all their seniors in frenzied action. . . . A wild proliferation of incidents prevents Emma and Robin, who are responsible for the party, and Polly and Peter, who are there to help, from discussing their complex matrimonial problems. . . .

For the rest the comic invention of Mr. Waterhouse and Mr. Hall does not flag. We might not be tempted to anthologize their jokes in any collection of The Year's Wittiest Repartee, but they still make us laugh while working out elaborate comic schemes and coincidences, and they make sure that the players enjoy themselves as well.

Henry Raynor, "A Party for Children," in The Times, *London, September 4, 1969, p. 7.*

THE TIMES LITERARY SUPPLEMENT

The title [of this book, ***The Passing of the Third-Floor Buck***], suggests S.J. Perelman and so at first does the style—the solemn dedication to fantasy, the drive and timing as well as the economy of gesture. But these satirical jabs (collected from *Punch*) never go really wild; they have a reach and versatility rare in the casual journalism of our day. Above all, ***The Passing of the Third-Floor Buck*** shows Keith Waterhouse to be a brilliant parodist. He observes life with some care before sending it up. . . .

Mr. Waterhouse is particularly good with jargon and idioms of all kinds—the elevated leader, sociological fieldwork study, court or company report, swift investigation-in-depth, resonant rural note. He is not afraid of traditional modes such as the humour of simple inversion. . . . [In] his best pieces, like the hilarious correspondence between Dickens and the Brontës, he distances just about every professional droll in the business. He steals notes like a starling and can even imitate the cosy disquiet of old *Strand* magazines. . . .

Now and again he rises to high satirical stature, most notably in the punchy copy he has written for the Virgins for Industry campaign, obviously booked for full national distribution. "I would like to join Virgins for Industry", it ends. "How do I set about becoming a virgin?"

"High-Rise Humour," in The Times Literary Supplement, *No. 3790, October 25, 1974, p. 1205.*

PETER ACKROYD

Keith Waterhouse has picked Billy Liar up again, dusted him off and set him back on his feet somewhere in his mid-thirties. I know that professional comics are always complaining about the shortage of jokes, but it should be a matter of deep concern for us all that the old jokes are not necessarily the best ones. ***Billy Liar On The Moon*** is not nearly as funny as ***Billy Liar,*** and I have a sinking feeling that it is not even meant to be. There is another old truth which Keith Waterhouse may well have taken to heart. It goes something to the effect that, for writers, the door closes at twenty; they are condemned to the mines of adolescence. This new novel again plumbs the depths of pubescent insecurity with Billy, now the Peter Pan of a high-rise, struggling to cause some fission within his nuclear family, trying very hard to belong nowhere and to nobody. He plays at being adult, continually imitating the mannerisms of his peers in a hopeless struggle to keep abreast of events and, when alone, weaving fantasies to keep himself company.

The plot of the book has a lot to do with Billy's torrid affair with Helen, a woman of today and wife of a pet-food manufacturer; it almost destroys his appalling marriage to Jeanette (but bad marriages always last) and makes the life and times of his local Council office, where he is on something like Rung Three of the ladder, even harder than they should be. Like all good comedy, and good farce, tragedy, melodrama and masque for that matter, one lie leads to further and greater lies until Billy Liar becomes three or four characters looking for a human being, woefully inadequate though that person may be. Keith Waterhouse is a sharp observer of all these things, and he is very adept with the cliches of everyday life: the lugubrious routines, the tacky interiors and what he calls "Council clerk patois." And as long as Waterhouse stays the observer, he writes very well and very amusingly. But this is not enough for him, since he also insists upon giving Billy Liar an interior life: he wants to be "free," he says, he wants to "relieve the monotony." Since this is the theme of the whole book, it is a little flat-footed to say it out loud; there are no circumstances in which Billy's soul-searching could be funnier than his behaviour, and the suburban blues are such a familiar refrain nowadays that Waterhouse devalues his comedy by giving voice to them. (pp. 540-41)

Peter Ackroyd, "Fantasies," in The Spectator, *Vol. 235, No. 7687, October 25, 1975, pp. 540-41.*

NEIL HEPBURN

Keith Waterhouse has waited a long time to write the sequel to ***Billy Liar,*** and it is uncharitable to suspect that that might be because of the stamina of the first book as film, TV series and so on. [***Billy Liar on the Moon***] was worth waiting for. Billy, grown older but not up, is now in local government, feeding official lies to questioners about the moonscape of redeveloped Shepford, keeping a mistress, avoiding contact with his empty-headed, clinging and baby-lusting wife, holding off the rat-faces and rat-bags as best he can by fantasy, virtuoso lying and fiddling expenses.

It is not just fun, of course. There is a serious point, rammed home lightly by Billy's escapades and last, mad shambles in the festive market square of ratty Shepford: that it is possible to live entirely separate from the 'real' world and survive. Indeed, Mr. Waterhouse's precise laceration of the squalid reality being born out of decently slummy, comfortably inconvenient, old provincial towns makes the fantasy-life dangerously attractive. He has a marvellous ear for spoken provincial English, a splendid, venomous way with the manifestations of greed, socially mobile snobbery and predatory fiddling to be found in taken-over town halls, and real pain and hatred to fuel this appallingly funny indictment of 'progress'.

Neil Hepburn, "England in Hollywood," in The Listener, *Vol. 94, No. 2431, November 6, 1975, p. 622.*

MARGARET DRABBLE

Keith Waterhouse's ***Billy Liar on the Moon,*** which continues the story begun in ***Billy Liar,*** is not funny . . . , although, alas, it tries hard to be so. Billy, now in his thirties, has a job, a wife and a mistress who drinks vodka martinis. By the end of the book we are supposed to believe that he has at last faced reality and decided to grow up and become a man and a father—but the narration is so tired, the jokes so forced, the world so dreary, that one does not believe a word of it. It is also, surprisingly, rather offensively patronizing in tone. Northern suburbs and local councillors may be dull, but they are not like this. [***Billy Liar on the Moon*** is a] most unmemorable sequel to a deservedly popular book.

Margaret Drabble, in a review of "Billy Liar on the Moon," in The New York Times Book Review, *February 8, 1976, p. 3.*

ANTHONY THWAITE

Keith Waterhouse's ***Office Life*** may look like facetious frivolity. So it is, up to a point, and Mr Waterhouse should ration his running gags a bit; Kingsley Amis has already patented the transliteration of laughter-sounds as individual leitmotifs, and the Waterhouse repertoire of *coh*!, *tuh*!, *sha*!, *haaark*!, *tchair*!, *keeesh*! etc. runs to tedium, as does his tenacious orthographic tactic when dealing with cockneys or men with marbles in their mouths.

But ***Office Life*** is better than its mannerisms: the good-humoured caricature of big corporation inanities gradually becomes twitchily sub-Kafka as Clement Gryce, a cheerful clerk, stumbles on the sinister puzzle of what British Albion actually *does*. Mr Waterhouse may have something to say about the work-ethic, under all that larkiness.

Anthony Thwaite, "The New Elizabethans," in The Observer, *November 5, 1978, p. 30.*

CHARLES NICHOLL

[***Office Life***] is a witty etching of the grossly featureless face of corporate bureaucracy. Clement Gryce, archetypal timid clerk, joins the Stationery Supplies department of the British Albion company. He becomes uneasy about its sinisterly seamless operations: the telephones never ring, the paperwork is minimal and repetitive, the whole carbon-copy and luncheon-voucher ritual begins to seem like a front. But for what? What, exactly, is British Albion? As a kind of Kafkaesque thriller, or as an allegory on bloodsucking bureaucracy, this is an amusing book. Its questions are worth asking. What Londoners persist in calling 'the City' is now more like a glass and concrete mountain-range. To what end and for whose benefit?

Charles Nicholl, "Wain and Waterhouse," in Books and Bookmen, *Vol. 24, No. 4, January, 1979, p. 56.*

CAROL RUMENS

Despite a richly varied cast of "office types", the major character of Keith Waterhouse's previous novel, ***Office Life,*** often seemed to be British Albion itself, that incestuous, sprawling Civil Service of a bumph factory. Unfortunately there were times when Waterhouse's brilliant satirical sparkle became damped down by his obligation to lead the reader through rigmaroles of explanation as complex and meticulous as those no doubt contained in the missing "guidelines for staff" leaflet. Now, in his new novel, ***Maggie Muggins,*** it is good to find the author once again basing his narrative on the complexities of personal, as opposed to bureaucratic, character, with a result that is both funny and humane.

The action takes place in a single Mugginsday, during which we follow Maggie on an odyssey of previous addresses, most of them bedsits of varying degrees of inner-London grottiness. Originally a Doncaster lass (she was Margaret Moon in those days), Maggie is as rooted in London's sub-culture as Leopold Bloom was in Dublin's, even though she says that she would rather have branches than put down roots. Her passion for privacy leads her into deviousness (there's an echo of the Billy Liar mentality in her anxious slitherings between "fact" and "fiction", though her fundamental sense of reality is far more pervasive and harsh than that of the adolescent fantasist), and she rarely gives her right address to the various "authorities"—social workers, the clap clinic, TV rental firms, etc—who shadow her life. . . .

There is an almost Dickensian zestfulness in the writer's descriptions of working-class London—the tube stations, the peeling flat-shares of Earls' Court (a terrain briefly charted in an earlier novel, ***Jubb***), the bleak council blocks and fug-filled pubs. By putting Maggie's age at around thirty, Waterhouse can even allow himself a fleeting touch of Lyons-Tea-Shop nostalgia. But otherwise his places and people are firmly of the tawdry, cut-back present, with a teeming, vandalized, seam-bursting London, its flats chopped into rooms and its rooms into smaller rooms by landlords handy with the chipboard, its social services departments exiled in outcrops of "Portakabins".

Waterhouse's narrative style is at its raciest best here: in the third-person, it also makes use of the rich medley of Northern and Cockney slang which is Maggie's own. This abrasive slang guards Waterhouse against the mawkishness he might otherwise have risked by introducing a number of tragedies into Maggie's career. . . .

As in ***Jubb,*** that rather more blackly-comic masterpiece, Waterhouse seems to be at his best when writing about those on the fringes of society, finely drawing out the pathos and dignity, as well as, in Jubb's case, the anguished lunacy of their condition. Maggie, too, is light years away from the comic stereotyping that occasionally afflicts Waterhouse's minor figures. With her anarchic, bawdy wit, her haunted fecklessness and her deeply English mixture of self-denigration and stubborn self-esteem, she is a fascinating recruit to Waterhouse's cast of memorable individuals: again he has created a character who is more than merely "a character".

Carol Rumens, "Down the Tube," in The Times Literary Supplement, *No. 4078, May 29, 1981, p. 596.*

ALAN HOLLINGHURST

In Keith Waterhouse's succession of funny and original novels since ***Billy Liar*** in 1960 he has compacted two kinds of comedy: a relentlessly observant ridicule of the world, and a private systematisation of things carried out by the characters to protect themselves from their uncharitable and ridiculous circumstances. . . . In ***Maggie Muggins*** this inward and outward bifocal view, with its capacity for pathos as well as resilience, is presented in a new way.

Maggie Moon is a victim of life, constantly moving from bedsit to bedsit, leaving a trail of old addresses and failed lives behind her. She is now making the final arrangements to have her illegitimate child adopted, on the same day that her one true friend, gay Sean, throws himself under a train at Fulham Broadway. But Maggie, when not so 'legless' as to remember nothing, is observant, and Waterhouse conspires with her in the task of anatomising the meanness and oddness of modern London. . . . Few novelists have noticed so much of the cityscape or reported it with such unfailing accuracy as Waterhouse, but for him sanity is preserved by the mordant humour and satirical toughness of his vision.

Maggie's further means of keeping sane is the Dickensian fashion in which her imagination transmogrifies the London streets: the entrance to Earl's Court Station is humanised by a habit of fantasy, and in which the crowds of people are tamed by her categorisation of them. . . . Waterhouse makes Maggie's act more pathetic by giving her a faded slang to speak—'bijou surprisette' &c—which is not intended to be funny and which in its monotony realistically shows the extent to which she is trapped in her anonymous jargon just as she is in the anonymous city. The excellently tight circular construction of the novel further consolidates the impression of a life which avoids the tyranny of despair only by the fertility and anarchy of the sense of humour.

Alan Hollinghurst, "Ways of Escape," in New Statesman, *Vol. 101, No. 2621, June 12, 1981, p. 18.*

J. K. L. WALKER

Forsaking the splendours and miseries of contemporary London which made ***Maggie Muggins,*** his last novel, such a rich if somewhat indigestible night out, Waterhouse has retreated north and backwards in time for his new comedy. ***In the Mood*** is set in the period immediately prior to the Festival of Britain of 1951; that time of nationalized jollification, and is concerned with the amorous escapades of three young Yorkshire clerks, newly extruded from Grippenshaw College of Commerce. From the vantage point of the present day, the narrator, Raymond Watmough, looks back thirty years in the opening pages of the novel on that different country to which "youth was our visa . . . Although we were only visitors, yet it had no other inhabitants while we were there, or none that we recognised." Ray, and the other members of the triumvirate, Douglas Beckett and Terry Liversedge, set out on their careers in, respectively a travel agency, a bank and a building society, guided less by ambition than by lust, the "single smiling glance" that shapes their lives.

The ever-changing chorus line leads the three of them a pretty dance through the urban glades of the Youth Guild Social, the Kismet Café, the Clock Ballroom, and above all the back rows of the cinemas—the Gaumont Coliseum, the Gainsborough, the Paramount or, if they are down to their last shilling, the Gem Picture Palace. Here (or, if dry, in the less public areas of the public park) they inch forward on their adventurous journeys into the unknown terrain of girls' bodies. . . .

Waterhouse evokes this vanished world with great skill. Although the story is simple, it commands acceptance by the densely plotted shifts of allegiance—the narrator alone has gone through five girls by the end of the novel—and by the careful and authentic build-up of detail that brings time and place vividly to life. Grippenshaw thirty years ago emerges as a more agreeable place than London today, and no doubt Waterhouse will be reproached for romanticizing the recent past. ***In the Mood,*** however, is not a simple trip down nostalgia lane but a warm, delicately observed and realistic comedy about adolescent emotions which is set in this particular period because, as the author has confessed, he doesn't know how seventeen-year-olds feel today. One wonders how far any such reader of this novel would identify with Raymond's preoccupation with "making a steady territorial advance down the front of Janet Gill's dress."

J. K. L. Walker, "Territorial Advances," in The Times Literary Supplement, *No. 4180, May 13, 1983, p. 481.*

JOHN MELLORS

Keith Waterhouse is a master of light prose, and ***In the Mood*** shows him in top form. Raymond, his narrator, 'pushing 50', recalls that sex-struck year when he left the Grippenshaw College of Commerce without a thought in his head 'that did not directly or obliquely touch on acts of lust'. . . .

Waterhouse's evocation of times past is as vivid as a sudden smell—'a heady potpourri of privet, creosoted chestnut palings, woodsmoke, fog or plum blossom according to season' in a Yorkshire suburb between town and moors. One of the funniest scenes in a very funny book is Ray's attempt in the recreation ground to get to 'first base' with Janet. After his fingers have discovered 'a small, soft protuberance that seemed to be hardening to the touch', Ray is triumphant, until Janet asks him what he finds so fascinating about the mole under her armpit. One of the virtues of ***In the Mood*** is that we laugh with as well as at Ray and Terry and Duggerlugs. Waterhouse takes his characters seriously even when he is being funny about them; a girl's nipple can loom like Everest to a teenage boy.

John Mellors, "Light Lust," in The Listener, *Vol. 109, No. 2815, June 30, 1983, p. 28.*

GEOFFREY ELBORN

It has been suggested that *Punch* never makes you laugh, only smile, but Keith Waterhouse in [***Fanny Peculiar,*** a] selection of pieces, which originally appeared in that magazine, is not only fanny peculiar but fanny ha-ha.

Nothing dates so much as humour, but Waterhouse has cleverly guarded against his wit ever being regarded as 'period' or 'quaint' in the future by his skilful variety of styles. He is at his best as a parodist and several sacred institutions such as *Hansard,* Dickens' *Christmas Carol* and *Crossroads* are quietly but forcefully sent up by his pen. They will easily survive the Waterhouse treatment, for the parodies are never malicious or nasty, but poke fun rather than stab.

The success of parodies depends on an almost instant recognition of the original, and Waterhouse never selects from the obscure or academic, that would make us struggle to recall. If he had, the point of his humour would be lost. Instead, *Marx Twain* and other schoolday favourites seem doubly delightful here, because certain familiarity with Tom Sawyer and his chums, allows direct access to the message of the parody. For despite the laughter evoked from each paragraph, Waterhouse is not just raising the chuckles for nothing. His skilful rerendering of *William the Red* with apologies to Richmal Crompton, is hilarious, but also points a finger at the National Front and the extreme left. In the best of the short pieces, the **"Prince of Wails,"** Waterhouse ingeniously thumbs his nose at the press for concentrating so much fuss and attention on a baby who has after all, done nothing. Prince William is his subject of several pages of biography, and with Waterhouse's fertile imagination, one feels certain he could write a thesis on a discarded burnt match, and still make the readers feel they want more.

Geoffrey Elborn, in a review of "In the Mood" and "Fanny Peculiar," in Books and Bookmen, *No. 334, July, 1983, p. 37.*

SIMON HOGGART

[Keith Waterhouse's ***Mrs Pooter's Diary***] is a cunning idea which quite a few people must wish they had thought of first. Carrie Pooter's diary is exactly contemporaneous with her husband's *Diary of a Nobody,* which, having discovered its hiding place, she reads every day. Naturally she has her own versions of the great events in her husband's work: the Mansion House reception, Lupin's engagement, but she also describes scores of new incidents and fresh characters, including the Pooters' dreadful neighbours and Mrs Shrike, a comic invention of which the Grossmiths would have been proud.

Waterhouse manages to give the existing characters new dimensions too: we learn much about Annie Fuller (now Mrs James) of Sutton, and we see with greater clarity than Pooter himself what appalling parasites Gowing and Cummings are.

But the book is most revealing on the Pooters themselves. She clearly adores him, but in a much more critical way than his own work implies. Pooter keeps his dignity through both books because in spite of his silliness and his limp self-congratulation he is a good man, whose main concern is to do the right thing, socially or morally. Yet he would be deeply shocked to see how well his wife understood him and baffled that she loved him in spite of it. . . .

What Waterhouse has managed is to re-create the whole Pooter world, as if in a three-dimensional model, and then show it to us from a quite different perspective. Like the Grossmiths, he has managed to tread lightly between scoffing and sentimentality. Most readers like the Pooters, and I suspect that quite a few of us admire them and even envy them; Waterhouse has left that affection intact.

Simon Hoggart, "The Lady of 'The Laurels'," in The Observer, *October 2, 1983, p. 30.*

BRYN CALESS

One of the most amusing satires on late-Victorian domestic manners and social propriety was *The Diary of a Nobody* by George and Weedon Grossmith, published in 1892 after appearing serially in *Punch*. Almost one hundred years later, we have presented to us the distaff side of Charles Pooter's life, written by his wife Carrie in secret session. If you know (and love) the original diary, you will find a great deal to relish in Keith Waterhouse's affectionate and accurate pastiche [***Mrs. Pooter's Diary***]. However, the book can be enjoyed entirely on its own merits. . . .

Waterhouse is already well known as a humorous writer . . . , but with this new book he surpasses himself. Not only has he done his research thoroughly, created a character whose gentle whimsy is delightful to know, and offered a 'footnote' to the original diary, he has created a work which stands both alone and in close harmony with its precursor. I recommend it without reservation—it is a *tour de force* and easily the funniest thing published so far this year.

Bryn Caless, in a review of "Mrs. Pooter's Diary," in British Book News, *December, 1983, p. 778.*

JOHN MELLORS

[An] excess of cleverness sinks ***Thinks,*** Edgar Samuel Bapty is given to 'vicious thoughts'—about yobs, about inoffensive ticket collectors, about people who are not even there, let alone doing him any harm. Bapty is the author's safety valve, letting off steam from the hot Waterhouse, ventilating pet hates, prejudices and obsessions. Sometimes Bapty emits only a quick 'thought-flash', like 'British Piss-piddling Rail'. Sometimes he goes in for elaborately staged daydreams, sexual fantasies with one of his three ex-wives or with a Soho model.

Keith Waterhouse invents complicated rules for the reader's access to Bapty's thoughts, laying down no-go areas, as it were, such as actual spoken conversations as opposed to remembered or imagined speech. Enforced audience participation in the theatre is bad enough. One did not expect to see it extended to novel-reading. The final indignity is when the reader, cast as Bapty's conscience, soul, *alter ego,* avenging angel or whatever, is held responsible for Bapty's death. This 'swining bloody-minded pig-faced snot-gobbling' reviewer refuses to be conned into pleading guilty.

John Mellors, "Conmen," in The Listener, *Vol. 112, No. 2874, September 6, 1984, p. 26.*

BRYN CALESS

Keith Waterhouse gets better and better. In ***Thinks*** he has surpassed himself, and has written an original, entertaining and thoughtful novel. Edgar Samuel Bapty is a perfectly ordinary man, who is 'as sane as anyone on the 08.33 from Portsea to Victoria' except that he is overweight, his blood pressure is up and he thinks 'vicious thoughts'. The reader is invited to 'play a game', involving entry into Bapty's thoughts. All readers of fiction play a game something like it because all novels, to some degree, invite us into the characters' minds. This time the difference is that Bapty 'exists in the flesh'; he does not know what we are doing as we eavesdrop on his thoughts. We cannot hear what he says, nor follow him wherever he goes. All we can be privy to are his internal monologues, his wrestling with ideas and his unspoken diatribes. (p. 619)

So we go with Bapty through his day, learning as we listen. . . . The novel ends with a surprising twist. All along, the reader has been reminded by Waterhouse that the eavesdropping has been a privilege. It is anarchic, funny and chaotic in its absurdity. Bapty's death on the final page is unexpected and reminds us, chillingly, what we have always known in the real world: that we cannot enter other minds, and that fiction really is a lie. (pp. 619-20)

Bryn Caless, in a review of "Thinks," in British Book News, *October, 1984, pp. 619-20.*

NICHOLAS WOLLASTON

At a time when everybody who was anybody was publishing their memoirs, somebody who was a Nobody brought out his immortal Diary. But the Grossmith brothers responsible for its appearance in 1892 failed to exhaust the complete Pooter archive. It lay, we are told, for almost a century in a tin trunk behind the water cistern in the loft of the Pooter residence, till

Keith Waterhouse reopened it in 1983 and discreetly, hilariously, edited ***Mrs Pooter's Diary.*** Now he has dug out Mr Pooter's letters [***The Collected Letters of a Nobody***].

Charles Pooter, a stockbroker's clerk, lived with his wife in a rented terrace house, 'The Laurels,' backing on to the railway in Holloway, north London. Even by the standards of those Victorian times, when the penny post ensured a reply by the day after tomorrow, he was a prolific letter-writer and took such pains that he would make 29 drafts for a four-line acceptance of an invitation to the Mansion House Ball. Preservation of his correspondence was guaranteed by the purchase, for 25 shillings, of a secondhand Ee-zee-kopi patent copying device on the Jellygraph principle. . . .

[Pooter] writes to a gardening magazine for advice on growing vegetables that do well near a steam railway; to his MP about the hurdy-gurdy menace in the streets; to a firm of wholesale fancy stationery, in disgust at the price of their Valentines. He is forever taking his business elsewhere, replying to petty humiliations with blistering sarcasm, keeping his end up, boasting of his connections, squabbling with his neighbours and composing deadly snubs. . . .

The marvel is that we still like him. But with his jokes and puns and misunderstandings that aren't quite accidental, he elbows his way through suburban gentility . . . , making more than the most of his very thin social life. To Pooter nothing is as nice or nasty as it seems, and to his readers everything is funny.

When the Ee-zee-kopi company folded he could no longer buy the special ink for it, and the letters end in outrage. Keith Waterhouse has done for them what the Grossmiths did for the diary, keeping the same cunning balance between affection and ridicule, conjuring another vaudeville of comic fiction. Mr Pooter lives.

Nicholas Wollaston, ''Letters from 'The Laurels','' *in* The Observer, *April 13, 1986, p. 24.*

CRAIG BROWN

So often the posthumously published letters of an author reveal improprieties damaging to a reputation. Happily, Mr Pooter's letters [***The Collected Letters of a Nobody***], lovingly edited by Mr Waterhouse, further convince the reader of his basic rectitude.

Many of these letters are alluded to in the Diary, particularly those of a ''satiric'' bent. The sense of humour hinted at in the Diary is paraded gloriously in the letters: puns (particularly those inspired by surnames) abound, and are awarded greater emphasis by generous deployment of the exclamation mark. Sometimes, inevitably, the sense of humour misfires. Having made a jest to Mr Spellman (''Forgive me if I have mis-*spelled* your name (!)'') on the surname of a Mr Steam, Pooter is obliged in a subsequent letter to withdraw the pun (''I was not to know that he was in mourning for his sister''). As Mr Waterhouse observes in his exquisitely judged commentary, ''while appreciative of his own flair for sustained irony, he often failed to recognize the quality in others'', and certainly Mr Pooter is quick to take offence at affronts to his dignity; but Mr Waterhouse wisely understands that it is for Pooter's frailties as much as for his aspirations that he has come to be held in such affection.

The collection is subtitled *Including Mr Pooter's advice to his son*. It must be admitted that much of the poignancy of the book lies in the fact that the larger amount of this advice goes unheeded. Lupin Pooter seems to have little regard for the Victorian values of thrift, delicacy, industry, promptitude or sobriety; against his father's wishes, he is a willing herald for a new age of ostentatious jollity, blunt talk and informality. As his father tries unsuccessfully to pull him back from the brink of debauchery . . . the young Pooter loafs uncaringly onwards.

Craig Brown, ''Propriety Undimmed,'' in The Times Literary Supplement, *No. 4333, April 18, 1986, p. 417.*

Appendix

The following is a listing of all sources used in Volume 47 of *Contemporary Literary Criticism*. Included in this list are all copyright and reprint rights and acknowledgments for those essays for which permission was obtained. Every effort has been made to trace copyright, but if omissions have been made, please let us know.

THE EXCERPTS IN CLC, VOLUME 47, WERE REPRINTED FROM THE FOLLOWING PERIODICALS:

Agenda, v. 16, Spring, 1978./ v. 4, Autumn, 1966 for "Experience into Music: The Poetry of Basil Bunting" by Charles Tomlinson; v. 4, Autumn, 1966 for "The Aesthetic of Basil Bunting" by Kenneth Cox. Both reprinted by permission of the respective authors.

America, v. 150, April 14, 1984 for "Where Theatre Matters" by Catharine Hughes. © 1984. All rights reserved. Reprinted with permission of the Literary Estate of Catharine Hughes./ v. 152, May 4, 1985 for a review of "Collected Stories" by Robert Phillips. © 1985. All rights reserved. Reprinted with permission of the author./ v. 120, May 3, 1969. © 1969. All rights reserved. Reprinted with permission of America Press, Inc., 106 West 56th Street, New York, NY 10019.

The American Book Review, v. 1, December-January, 1978-1979; v. 3, November-December, 1980; v. 3, March-April, 1981; v. 4, January-February, 1982; v. 6, November-December, 1983; v. 8, November-December, 1985; v. 8, September-October, 1986. © 1979, 1980, 1981, 1982, 1983, 1985, 1986 by *The American Book Review*. All reprinted by permission of the publisher.

Analog Science Fiction/Science Fact, v. CIII, July, 1983 for a review of "Hart's Hope" by Tom Easton. © 1983 by Davis Publications, Inc. Reprinted by permission of the author.

Anglo-Welsh Review, 1982. Reprinted by permission of the publisher.

The Atlantic Monthly, v. 111, April, 1913./ v. 259, February, 1987 for "Found in Jerusalem" by Martin Amis. Copyright 1987 by The Atlantic Monthly Company, Boston, MA. Reprinted by permission of A. D. Peters & Co. Ltd./ v. 259, April, 1987 for "To Live and Die in Dixie" by Douglas Bauer. Copyright 1987 by The Atlantic Monthly Company, Boston, MA. Reprinted by permission of the author.

Best Sellers, v. 43, August, 1983; v. 45, August, 1985. Copyright © Helen Dwight Reid Educational Foundation. Both reprinted by permission of the publisher.

Book Week—New York Herald Tribune, October 23, 1966. © 1966, *The Washington Post*. Reprinted by permission of the publisher.

Book World—The Washington Post, September 27, 1970. © 1970 Postrib Corp. Reprinted by permission of *The Washington Post.*/ March 9, 1975; September 7, 1975; September 26, 1976; May 15, 1977; May 18, 1980; August 24, 1980; January 18, 1981; January 25, 1981; September 13, 1981; April 3, 1983; September 4, 1983; May 13, 1984; November 11, 1984; November 18, 1984; April 7, 1985; May 19, 1985; July 28, 1985; February 23, 1986; June 8, 1986; June 15, 1986; January 18, 1987; March 22, 1987; April 5, 1987; May 24, 1987. © 1975, 1976, 1977, 1980, 1981, 1983, 1984, 1985, 1986, 1987, *The Washington Post*. All reprinted by permission of the publisher.

Booklist, v. 80, September 15, 1982. Copyright © 1982 by the American Library Association. Reprinted by permission of the publisher.

The Booklist, v. 81, October 1, 1984. Copyright © 1984 by the American Library Association. Reprinted by permission of the publisher.

The Bookman, v. XLVI, December, 1917.

Books and Bookmen, n. 371, September, 1986 for "Oddities" by Sylvia Clayton. © copyright the author 1986./ v. 16, September, 1971 for a review of "National Winner" by Roger Baker; v. 24, January, 1979 for "Wain and Waterhouse" by Charles Nicholl; n. 334, July, 1983 for a review of "In the Mood" and "Fanny Peculiar" by Geoffrey Elborn. © copyright the respective authors 1971, 1979, 1983. All reprinted by permission of the respective authors./ n. 336, September, 1983 for a review of "Magic" by Miranda Seymour; n. 357, July, 1985 for "Perfect Happiness" by Miranda Seymour. © copyright the author 1983, 1985. Both reprinted by permission of David Higham Associates Limited.

Books in Canada, v. 11, May, 1982 for "In Translation" by Paul Stuewe; v. 13, May, 1984 for "Lost in the Maze" by Brian L. Flack; v. 13, June-July, 1984 for "Mud and Metaphor" by George Galt; v. 14, November, 1985 for a review of "Craft Slices" by Karl Jirgens; v. 16, June-July, 1987 for "As for Me and My Horse" by Kenneth McGoogan. All reprinted by permission of the respective authors.

Boston Review, v. XII, April, 1987 for a review of "In the Country of Last Things" by Daniel Max. Copyright © 1987 by the Boston Critic, Inc. Reprinted by permission of the author.

boundary 2, v. V, Fall, 1976. Copyright © *boundary 2*, 1976. Reprinted by permission of the publisher.

Brick: A Journal of Reviews, n. 28, Fall, 1986. Reprinted by permission of the publisher.

British Book News, November, 1983; December, 1983; October, 1984; March, 1985; June, 1985; March, 1987. © *British Book News*, 1983, 1984, 1985, 1987. All courtesy of *British Book News*.

Bucknell Review, v. XVII, May, 1969. Reprinted by permission of the publisher.

The Canadian Forum, v. XLVII, May, 1967; v. LXII, October, 1982; v. LXIII, February, 1984. All reprinted by permission of the publisher.

Canadian Literature, n. 4, Autumn, 1969 for "Virtue Is Not Enough" by Ralph Gustafson; n. 64, Spring, 1975 for "Insistent Fluidity" by Donald Stephens; n. 89, Summer, 1981 for "Fast-Forward Man" by Janet Giltrow; n. 98, Autumn, 1983 for "The Scratch, Not the Itch" by John Orange; n. 112, Spring, 1987 for "For People" by Noah Zacharin. All reprinted by permission of the respective authors.

Canadian Review of Comparative Literature, Winter, 1981. *Canadian Review of Comparative Literature*, © Canadian Comparative Literature Association. Reprinted by permission of the publisher.

Canto: Review of the Arts, v. 3, 1979 for "Three Poets" by J. D. McClatchy. Copyright © 1975 by Canto, Inc. All rights reserved. Reprinted by permission of the author.

Carolina Quarterly, v. XXXV, Fall, 1982. © copyright 1982 *Carolina Quarterly*. Reprinted by permission of the publisher.

Chicago Review, v. 29, Summer, 1977; v. 32, Autumn, 1980. Copyright © 1977, 1980 by *Chicago Review*. Both reprinted by permission of the publisher.

Chicago Tribune, April 24, 1960 for "Spy Novel Caricature" by Richard B. Harwell; January 25, 1987 for "Spies in Chicago" by Jack Hurst. © copyrighted 1960, 1987, Chicago Tribune Company. All rights reserved. Both reprinted by permission of the respective authors.

Choice, v. 2, December, 1965; v. 12, June, 1975; v. 13, March, 1976. Copyright © 1965, 1975, 1976 by American Library Association. All reprinted by permission of the publisher.

The Christian Science Monitor, August 5, 1985 for "'Zuckerman Bound' Stays on Ground" by Bruce Allen. © 1985 the author. All rights reserved. Reprinted by permission of the author./ November 24, 1980; November 12, 1986; December 22, 1986; February 11, 1987. © 1980, 1986, 1987 The Christian Science Publishing Society. All rights reserved. All reprinted by permission from *The Christian Science Monitor*.

Clues: A Journal of Detection, v. 6, Spring-Summer, 1985; v. 7, Spring-Summer, 1986. Copyright 1985, 1986 by Pat Browne. Both reprinted by permission of the publisher.

Commentary, v. 64, August, 1977 for "History into Art" by John Romano; v. 76, August, 1983 for "Aharon Appelfeld, Survivor" by Ruth R. Wisse. Copyright © 1977, 1983 by American Jewish Committee. All rights reserved. Both reprinted by permission of the publisher and the respective authors.

Comparative Literature Studies, v. XVII, September, 1980. Copyright © 1980 by The Pennsylvania State University Press, University Park, PA. Reprinted by permission of the publisher.

Contemporary Literature, v. 19, Winter, 1978; v. 21, Winter, 1980. © 1978, 1980 by the Board of Regents of the University of Wisconsin System. Both reprinted by permission of The University of Wisconsin Press.

Contemporary Poetry: A Journal of Criticism, v. III, Winter, 1978. Reprinted by permission of the publisher.

The Critic, Chicago, v. 30, January-February, 1972. © *The Critic* 1972. Reprinted with the permission of the Thomas More Association, Chicago, IL.

Critical Quarterly, v. 26, Autumn, 1984; v. 28, Autumn, 1986. © Manchester University Press 1984, 1986. Both reprinted by permission of Manchester University Press.

Critique: Studies in Modern Fiction, v. XXIV, Summer, 1983. Copyright © 1983, Helen Dwight Reid Educational Foundation. Reprinted with permission of the Helen Dwight Reid Educational Foundation, published by Heldref Publications, 4000 Albemarle Street N.W., Washington, DC 20016.

Daily News, February 24, 1984. © 1984 New York News Inc. Reprinted with permission.

Daily Telegraph, January 10, 1987. Reprinted by permission of the publisher.

The Drama Review, v. 16, December, 1972. Copyright © 1972, *The Drama Review.* Reprinted by permission of MIT Press.

Dutch Quarterly Review of Anglo-American Letters, v. 13, 1983. Reprinted by permission of the publisher.

Encounter, v. LIII, November, 1979; v. LVIII & LIX, June & July, 1982; v. LIX, August, 1982; v. LXI, December, 1983. © 1979, 1982, 1983 by Encounter Ltd. All reprinted by permission of the publisher.

English Journal, v. XV, January, 1926.

Essays on Canadian Writing, n. 12, Fall, 1978. © Essays on Canadian Writing Ltd. Reprinted by permission of the publisher.

Exquisite Corpse, v. 2, May-July, 1984. Reprinted by permission of the publisher.

Fantasy Review, v. 9, February, 1986 for "Three Magic Realists" by Jessica Amanda Salmonson. Copyright © 1986 by the author. Reprinted by permission of the author.

fiction international, n. 2-3, 1974; n. 16:1, 1985. Copyright © 1974, 1985 by the Editors. Both reprinted by permission of the publisher.

The Fiddlehead, n. 92, Winter, 1972 for a review of "Touch: Selected Poems, 1960-1970" by John L. Nugent; n. 116, Winter, 1978 for "Clever, Curious, Sometimes Composed George" by Michael Brian Oliver. Copyright by the respective authors./ n. 121, Spring, 1979 for a review of "Concentric Circles," "A Short Sad Book" and "Protective Footwear" by Gwendolyn Davies; n. 131, January, 1982 for a review of "Burning Water" by Anthony S. Brennan. Copyright by the respective authors. Both reprinted by permission of the respective authors.

Financial Times, January 9, 1987. Reprinted by permission of the publisher.

Forum for Modern Language Studies, v. XIII, January, 1977 for "Basil Bunting's Linguistic Poetics" by Karl Muller. Copyright © 1977 by *Forum for Modern Language Studies* and the author. Reprinted by permission of the publisher.

French Forum, v. 6, September, 1981. Copyright 1981 by French Forum, Inc. Reprinted by permission of the publisher.

The Guardian, August 24, 1974; January 10, 1987. © Guardian and Manchester Evening News Ltd., 1974, 1987. Both reprinted by permission of Los Angeles Times—Washington Post News Service.

Harper's, v. 263, July, 1981. Copyright © 1981 by *Harper's Magazine.* All rights reserved. Reprinted by special permission.

Horizon: A Magazine of the Arts, v. XXVII, June, 1984 for "African Albert" by Roger Downey. © June, 1984 by Horizon Publishers, Inc. Reprinted by permission of the publisher and the author.

The Hudson Review, v. XIV, Spring, 1961; v. XXXIV, Summer, 1981; v. XXXVI, Winter, 1983-84; v. XXXVII, Autumn, 1984. Copyright © 1961, 1981, 1984 by The Hudson Review, Inc. All reprinted by permission of the publisher.

The Illustrated London News, v. 241, December 29, 1962. © 1962 The Illustrated London News & Sketch Ltd. Reprinted by permission of the publisher.

Irish Renaissance Annual III, v. III, 1982. © 1982 by Associated Presses, Inc. Reprinted by permission of the publisher.

The Journal of American History, v. LI, December, 1964; v. LIII, March, 1967. Copyright Organization of American Historians, 1964, 1967. Both reprinted by permission of the publisher.

Journal of American Studies, v. 14, December, 1980 for ''Stirring Things Up: Dashiell Hammett's Continental Op'' by John S. Whitley. © Cambridge University Press 1980. Reprinted with the permission of Cambridge University Press and the author.

Kirkus Reviews, v. XLVII, December 1, 1980; v. LIII, March 15, 1985. Copyright © 1980, 1985 The Kirkus Service, Inc. All rights reserved. Both reprinted by permission of the publisher.

Kliatt Young Adult Paperback Book Guide, v. XIX, January, 1985. Copyright © by Kliatt Paperback Book Guide. Reprinted by permission of the publisher.

Library Journal, v. 107, October 1, 1982 for a review of ''The Butterfly Hunter'' by Melanie Axel-Lute; v. 110, November 1, 1985 for a review of ''Robeson Street'' by Rochelle Ratner. Copyright © 1982, 1985 by Reed Publishing, USA, Division of Reed Holdings, Inc. Both reprinted from *Library Journal,* published by R. R. Bowker, Co., Division of Reed Publishing, USA, by permission of the publisher and the respective authors.

The Listener, v. LXXIX, February 29, 1968; v. 109, February 17, 1983. © British Broadcasting Corp. 1968, 1983./ v. 88, November 2, 1972 for ''Aristocrat'' by J. G. Farrell. © British Broadcasting Corp. 1972. Reprinted by permission of the Literary Estate of J. G. Farrell./ v. LXIX, January 31, 1963 for a review of ''The Gift'' by Laurence Lerner; v. LXXI, April 23, 1964 for a review of ''The Somnambulists'' by Elizabeth Jennings; v. LXXIX, February 15, 1968 for ''Only Project'' by John Hemmings; v. 84, October 1, 1970 for ''Sleek Desolation'' by Derek Mahon; v. 93, March 6, 1975 for ''Out of Eden'' by Sara Maitland; v. 94, November 6, 1975 for ''England in Hollywood'' by Neil Hepburn; v. 100, July 13, 1978 for ''Night-Time Tongue'' by Anne Stevenson; v. 100, November 2, 1978 for ''The Nice and the Nasty'' by Peter Kemp; v. 103, April 10, 1980 for ''Dreadful Things'' by John Mellors; v. 104, July 31, 1980 for ''Norse Winds'' by John Mellors; v. 107, June 3, 1982 for ''Left Luggage'' by John Mellors; v. 109, June 30, 1983 for ''Light Lust'' by John Mellors; v. 112, September 6, 1984 for ''Conmen'' by John Mellors; v. 113, January 3, 1985 for ''Prosy Childhoods'' by Dick Davis; v. 115, February 20, 1986 for ''Atoms Not Actors'' by Vernon Bogdanor; v. 116, November 13, 1986 for ''Man Overboard'' by John Archer. © British Broadcasting Corp. 1963, 1964, 1968, 1970, 1975, 1978, 1980, 1982, 1983, 1984, 1985, 1986. All reprinted by permission of the respective authors.

The Living Age, v. CCLXXVIII, July 19, 1913.

London Evening Standard, January 9, 1987 for a review of ''Bopha!'' by Milton Shulman. Reprinted by permission of the author.

London Magazine, v. 2, February, 1955./ n.s. v. 8, September, 1968; n.s. v. 22, June, 1982; n.s. v. 23, November, 1983; n.s. v. 25, November, 1985. © *London Magazine* 1955, 1968, 1982, 1983, 1985. All reprinted by permission of the publisher.

London Review of Books, v. 4, June 17-30, 1982 for ''Kelpers'' by Claude Rawson; v. 6, October 4, 1984 for ''Making Sense'' by Denis Donoghue; v. 8, December 4, 1986 for ''Malgudi'' by Anita Desai; v. 9, February 19, 1987 for ''Darkest Peru'' by John Sturrock; v. 9, April 23, 1987 for ''Charmed Lives'' by Patrick Parrinder; v. 9, May 7, 1987 for ''An Englishman, an Irishman and a Scotsman'' by Damian Grant. All appear here by permission of the *London Review of Books* and the respective authors.

Los Angeles Times Book Review, March 6, 1983; April 3, 1983; May 27, 1984; July 8, 1984; July 22, 1984; September 23, 1984; December 16, 1984; January 6, 1985; February 9, 1986; April 27, 1986; November 23, 1986; December 7, 1986; June 17, 1987. Copyright, 1983, 1984, 1985, 1986, 1987, *Los Angeles Times.* All reprinted by permission of the publisher.

The Magazine of Fantasy and Science Fiction, v. 58, January, 1980 for a review of ''Hot Sleep'' by Michael Bishop. © 1980 by Mercury Press Inc. Reprinted by permission of *The Magazine of Fantasy and Science Fiction* and the author.

Manchester Guardian Weekly, May 20, 1965; December 28, 1975. Copyright © 1965, 1975 by Guardian Publications Ltd. Both reprinted by permission of Los Angeles Times—Washington Post News Service.

Modern Fiction Studies, v. XVI, Spring, 1970. Copyright © 1970 by Purdue Research Foundation, West Lafayette, IN 47907. All rights reserved. Reprinted with permission.

The Modern Language Journal, v. L, November, 1966. © 1966 *The Modern Language Journal.* Reprinted by permission of The University of Wisconsin Press.

Mosaic: A Journal for the Comparative Study of Literature and Ideas, v. VIII, Spring, 1975. Copyright © *MOSAIC,* 1975. Acknowledgement of previous publication is herewith made.

The Nation, New York, v. 205, September 11, 1967; v. 206, February 5, 1968; v. 207, September 23, 1968; v. 209, December 8, 1969; v. 212, February 15, 1971; v. 236, February 5, 1983; v. 239, October 13, 1984; v. 243, November 1, 1986. Copyright 1967, 1968, 1969, 1971, 1983, 1984, 1986 *The Nation* magazine, The Nation Company, Inc. All reprinted by permission of the publisher./ v. 173, October 27, 1951; v. 183, September 8, 1956. Copyright 1951, renewed 1979; copyright 1956, renewed 1984 *The Nation* magazine, The Nation Company, Inc. Both reprinted by permission of the publisher.

The National Observer, October 7, 1968; February 26, 1977. © Dow Jones & Company, Inc. 1968, 1977. All rights reserved. Both reprinted by permission of *The National Observer*.

National Review, New York, v. XIX, October 31, 1967; v. XXIV, June 23, 1972; v. XXXV, September 16, 1983; v. XXXVI, May 18, 1984. © 1967, 1972, 1983, 1984 by National Review, Inc., 150 East 35th Street, New York, NY 10016. All reprinted with permission of the publisher.

The New Leader, v. LII, November 24, 1969; v. LVIII, May 12, 1975; v. LXIX, February 10, 1986; v. LXX, February 9-23, 1987. © 1969, 1975, 1986, 1987 by The American Labor Conference on International Affairs, Inc. All reprinted by permission of the publisher.

The New Republic, v. 102, March 4, 1940; v. 104, March 10, 1941./ v. 178, February 18, 1978; v. 178, May 6, 1978; v. 179, July 22, 1978; v. 189, July 11, 1983; v. 192, February 4, 1985; v. 195, December 29, 1986; v. 196, February 2, 1987; v. 196, April 13, 1987. © 1978, 1983, 1985, 1987 The New Republic, Inc. All reprinted by permission of *The New Republic*.

The New Review, v. III, May, 1976. © TNR Publications, Ltd., London. Reprinted by permission of the publisher.

New Statesman, v. LVIII, September 12, 1959; v. LX, August 20, 1960; v. LX, September 17, 1960; v. LXIV, December 28, 1962; v. LXIX, March 5, 1965; v. 76, October 4, 1968; v. 78, September 5, 1969; v. 78, October 17, 1969; v. 79, June 12, 1970; v. 81, February 5, 1971; v. 82, July 16, 1971; v. 82, July 23, 1971; v. 82, October 1, 1971; v. 88, August 9, 1974; v. 94, July 29, 1977; v. 94, September 20, 1977; v. 99, June 27, 1980; v. 101, March 6, 1981; v. 101, June 12, 1981; v. 103, March 19, 1982; v. 103, May 28, 1982; v. 104, November 12, 1982; v. 106, October 21, 1983; v. 109, May 3, 1985; v. 110, September 20, 1985; v. 112, November 14, 1986; v. 113, May 22, 1987. © 1959, 1960, 1962, 1965, 1968, 1969, 1970, 1971, 1974, 1977, 1980, 1981, 1982, 1983, 1985, 1986, 1987 The Statesman & Nation Publishing Co. Ltd. All reprinted by permission of the publisher.

The New Statesman & Nation, v. XIX, February 10, 1940; v. XIX, May 25, 1940; v. L, August 13, 1955.

New World Writing, v. 1, 1952 for ''Simenon and Spillane: The Metaphysics of Murder for the Millions'' by Charles J. Rolo. Copyright, 1952, renewed 1980, by The New American Library. Reprinted by permission of the Literary Estate of Charles J. Rolo.

New York Magazine, v. 17, September 3, 1984; v. 20, January 5, 1987; v. 20, February 23, 1987. Copyright © 1984, 1987 by News America Publishing, Inc. All reprinted with the permission of *New York* Magazine.

New York Herald Tribune Book Review, April 13, 1958; May 11, 1958./ June 1, 1958; July 19, 1959. © 1958, 1959 I.H.T. Corporation. All reprinted by permission of the publisher.

New York Herald Tribune Books, May 10, 1942./ January 10, 1926. Copyright 1926 I.H.T. Corporation. Renewed 1953 by New York Herald Tribune, Inc. Reprinted by permission of the publisher.

New York Herald Tribune Weekly Book Review, November 18, 1945.

New York Post, November 21, 1980; February 24, 1984; December 23, 1985; December 19, 1986. © 1980, 1984, 1985, 1986, News America Publishing, Incorporated. All reprinted from the *New York Post* by permission.

The New York Review of Books, v. XXII, May 1, 1975; v. XXX, June 16, 1983; v. XXXIV, March 26, 1987; v. XXXIV, June 25, 1987. Copyright © 1975, 1983, 1987 Nyrev, Inc. All reprinted with permission from *The New York Review of Books*.

The New York Times, August 12, 1956; May 25, 1958; September 30, 1966; December 13, 1968; March 8, 1969; June 9, 1976; February 24, 1977; November 21, 1980; April 17, 1981; May 26, 1983; February 24, 1984; March 15, 1984; April 3, 1984; September 1, 1984; May 15, 1985; December 23, 1985; April 26, 1986; October 24, 1986; December 28, 1986; December 29, 1986; January 4, 1987; February 9, 1987; March 14, 1987; April 1, 1987; June 1, 1987. Copyright © 1956, 1958, 1966, 1968, 1969, 1976, 1977, 1980, 1981, 1983, 1984, 1985, 1986, 1987 by The New York Times Company. All reprinted by permission of the publisher.

The New York Times Book Review, September 4, 1932; February 5, 1933; March 4, 1934; May 17, 1942; November 18, 1945; October 7, 1951; October 11, 1953; July 11, 1954; November 28, 1954; December 5, 1954. Copyright 1932, 1933, 1934, 1942, 1945, 1951, 1953, 1954 by The New York Times Company. All reprinted by permission of the publisher./ January 27, 1957; April 20, 1958; January 3, 1960; May 31, 1964; June 20, 1965; September 11, 1966; April 2, 1967; November 26, 1967; January 28, 1968; August 18, 1968; September 8, 1968; January 26, 1969; July 20, 1969; December 14, 1969; May 30, 1971; August 8, 1971; October 1, 1972; November 4, 1973; March 3, 1974; November 24, 1974; June 29, 1975; August 4, 1975; February 8, 1976; May 9, 1976; November 7, 1976; April 16, 1978; February 18, 1979; February 3, 1980; May 3, 1981; September 20, 1981; November 7, 1982; February 27, 1983; May 15, 1983; June 5, 1983; September 4, 1983; March 18, 1984; April 1, 1984; May 20, 1984; June 3, 1984; June 10, 1984; September 9, 1984; November 18, 1984; January 13, 1985; March 24, 1985; April 7, 1985; May 19, 1985; November 3, 1985; November 24, 1985; April 27, 1986; June 1, 1986; June 29, 1986; July 20, 1986; August 31, 1986; November 30, 1986; January 4, 1987; January 11, 1987; February 1, 1987; March 8, 1987; April 5, 1987; April 12, 1987; May 17, 1987; June 21, 1987. Copyright © 1957, 1958, 1960, 1964, 1965, 1966, 1967, 1968, 1969, 1971, 1972, 1973, 1974, 1975, 1976, 1978, 1979, 1980, 1981, 1982, 1983, 1984, 1985, 1986, 1987 by The New York Times Company. All reprinted by permission of the publisher.

The New Yorker, v. LXI, May 20, 1985 for "Living Death" by John Updike; v. LXIII, June 15, 1987 for "The Last Fiction Show" by Terrence Rafferty. © 1985, 1987 by the respective authors. Both reprinted by permission of the publisher./ v. XL, March 7, 1964; v. XLV, January 17, 1970; v. LI, April 7, 1975; v. LVIII, June 28, 1982; v. LVIII, January 17, 1983; v. LXI, December 23, 1985. © 1964, 1970, 1975, 1982, 1983, 1985 by The New Yorker Magazine, Inc. All reprinted by permission of the publisher.

Newsweek, v. LXXII, September 9, 1968; v. LXXXIX, May 2, 1977; v. CI, March 28, 1983. Copyright 1968, 1977, 1983, by Newsweek, Inc. All rights reserved. All reprinted by permission of the publisher.

The North American Review, v. 271, March, 1986. Copyright © 1986 by the University of Northern Iowa. Reprinted by permission from *The North American Review*.

The Observer, January 21, 1968; October 1, 1972; June 3, 1973; September 22, 1974; November 5, 1978; October 2, 1983; November 13, 1983; December 23, 1984; January 27, 1985; March 31, 1985; January 26, 1986; April 13, 1986; November 9, 1986. All reprinted by permission of The Observer Limited.

The Ontario Review, Fall-Winter, 1976-77. Copyright © 1976 by The Ontario Review, Inc. Reprinted by permission of the publisher.

Parnassus: Poetry in Review, v. 8, Fall-Winter, 1979; v. 8, 1980; v. 13, Spring-Summer, 1986. Copyright © 1979, 1980, 1986 Poetry in Review Foundation. All reprinted by permission of the publisher.

Partisan Review, v. LIII, Fall, 1986 for "Elsa Morante" by Rebecca West. Copyright © 1986 by *Partisan Review*. Reprinted by permission of A. D. Peters & Co. Ltd.

Perspectives on Contemporary Literature, v. 5, 1979. Copyright © 1979 by The University Press of Kentucky. Reprinted by permission of the publisher.

Plays & Players, n. 369, June, 1984. © 1984 Brevet Limited. Reprinted with permission of the publisher.

Poetry, v. I, February, 1913; v. XXXVIII, June, 1931./ v. CIX, November, 1966 for "New Lines" by Thomas Clark; v. CX, June, 1967 for a review of "The Spoils" by Richard Howard; v. CXII, August, 1968 for a review of "Amulet" by Laurence Lieberman; v. CXV, March, 1970 for "Sensibilities" by William Heyen; v. CXXX, July, 1977 for "Language against Fear" by William Logan; v. CXXXVII, March, 1981 for "The Strength of James Dickey" by Dave Smith; v. CXLIV, April, 1984 for "Flight Home" by Lorrie Goldensohn; v. CXLV, February, 1985 for "Weaving and Unweaving" by J. D. McClatchy. © 1966, 1967, 1968, 1970, 1977, 1981, 1984, 1985 by the Modern Poetry Association. All reprinted by permission of the Editor of *Poetry* and the respective authors./ v. CXVIII, August, 1971 for "A Range of Six" by Frank MacShane. © 1971 by the Modern Poetry Association. Reprinted by permission of the Editor of *Poetry* and The Aaron M. Priest Literary Agency, Inc./ v. LXXVIII, September, 1951 for "A Resurrected Poet: The Chisel" by Hugh Kenner; v. LXXVIII, September, 1951 for "Bunting: Formal Aspects" by Thomas Cole. Copyright 1951, renewed 1979, by the Modern Poetry Association. Both reprinted by permission of the Editor of *Poetry* and the respective authors.

Poetry Review, v. 73, September, 1983 for "Telling Stories" by Claude Rawson; v. 73, September, 1983 for "Colliding Styles" by Michael O'Neill. Copyright © The Poetry Society 1983. Both reprinted by permission of the respective authors.

Prairie Schooner, v. XLII, Fall, 1968; v. XLVI, Spring, 1972; v. 56, Spring, 1982. © 1968, 1972, 1982 by University of Nebraska Press. All reprinted from *Prairie Schooner* by permission of the University of Nebraska Press.

Publishers Weekly, v. 197, May 4, 1970; v. 202, July 17, 1972; v. 209, March 22, 1976; v. 214, November 13, 1978; v. 214, December 4, 1978; v. 215, March 26, 1979; v. 219, January 2, 1981; v. 222, August 27, 1982; v. 224, November 25, 1983. Copyright © 1969, 1972, 1976, 1978, 1979, 1981, 1982, 1983 by Xerox Corporation. All reprinted from *Publishers Weekly*, published by R. R. Bowker Company, a Xerox company, by permission./ v. 229, January 24, 1986; v. 230, August 29, 1986. Copyright 1986 by Reed Publishing USA. Both reprinted from *Publishers Weekly*, published by the Bowker Magazine Group of Cahners Publishing Co., a division of Reed Publishing USA.

Queen's Quarterly, v. 90, Autumn, 1983 for "Céline: Art and Politics" by George Grant; v. 93, Summer, 1986 for a review of "Craft Slices," "Seventy-One Poems for People," and "Feeling the Worlds: New Poems" by David Leahy; v. 94, Spring, 1987 for "Louis-Ferdinand Céline Observed and Translated" by Stephen Day. Copyright © 1983, 1986, 1987 by the respective authors. All reprinted by permission of the respective authors.

Quill and Quire, v. 53, January, 1987 for "A Lively Deal ... Tubeside Companion ... Stellar Stella" by Paul Stuewe; v. 53, May, 1987 for "Bowering's Western: Woolly Post-Modernist Chic" by Paul Roberts. Both reprinted by permission of *Quill and Quire* and the respective authors.

The Reporter, v. 32, January 14, 1965 for "Simenon's Mosaic" by Jay Jacobs. © 1965 by The Reporter Magazine Company. All rights reserved. Reprinted by permission of the author.

San Francisco Review of Books, v. XI, Fall, 1986. Copyright © by the *San Francisco Review of Books* 1986. Reprinted by permission of the publisher.

Saturday Night, v. 82, May, 1967 for a review of "Mirror on the Floor" by Phyllis Grosskurth; v. 86, November, 1971 for "Two Bowerings Embrace Past, Present, Future" by Eldon Garnet. Copyright © 1967, 1971 by *Saturday Night*. Both reprinted by permission of the respective authors.

Saturday Review, v. LIII, October 10, 1970. © 1970 *Saturday Review* magazine. Reprinted by permission of the publisher.

The Saturday Review, New York, v. XXXVI, May 30, 1953.

The Saturday Review of Literature, v. XXXIV, October 20, 1951.

Science Fiction & Fantasy Book Review, v. I, April, 1979; v. I, December, 1979. Copyright © 1979 by The Borgo Press. Both reprinted by permission of the publisher.

Science Fiction and Fantasy Book Review, n. 15, June, 1983. Copyright © 1983 by Science Fiction Research Association. Reprinted by permission of the publisher.

The Sewanee Review, v. LXXVIII, Autumn, 1970. © 1970 by The University of the South. Reprinted by permission of the editor of *The Sewanee Review*.

The Small Press Review, v. 16, February, 1984. © 1984 by Dustbooks. Reprinted by permission of the publisher.

The Southern Review, Louisiana State University, v. 17, Winter, 1981 for "Beyond the Merely Modern: New Poetry from Britain" by David Middleton; v. 17, Spring, 1981 for "The Growth of James Dickey" by Richard Tillinghast. Copyright, 1981, by the respective authors. Both reprinted by permission of the respective authors.

The Spectator, v. 166, June 13, 1941; v. 167, October 3, 1941./ v. 257, September 6, 1986 for "Surreal Oxford Junketings" by Anita Brookner. © 1986 by *The Spectator*. Reprinted by permission of the author./ v. 203, September 11, 1959; v. 209, December 28, 1962; v. 225, October 10, 1970; v. 235, October 25, 1975; v. 239, August 13, 1977; v. 244, April 5, 1980; v. 250, January 1, 1983; v. 251, September 17, 1983; v. 253, September 15, 1984; v. 253, November 24, 1984. © 1959, 1962, 1970, 1975, 1977, 1980, 1983, 1984 by *The Spectator*. All reprinted by permission of Special Features.

Stand Magazine, v. 18, 1977 for "Neatness and Truth" by Desmond Graham. Copyright © by the author. Reprinted by permission of the publisher.

The Sunday Times, London, April, 1964; March 14, 1982. © Times Newspapers Limited 1964, 1982. Both reproduced from *The Sunday Times*, London by permission.

Theatre Journal, v. 35, December, 1983. © 1983, University and College Theatre Association of the American Theatre Association. Reprinted by permission of the publisher.

Time, New York, v. CIII, February 11, 1974; v. CX, September 5, 1977; v. CXIII, February 12, 1979. Copyright 1974, 1977, 1979 Time Inc. All rights reserved. All reprinted by permission from *Time*.

Time & Tide, v. 43, September 13-20, 1962.

Time Out, January 5, 1987. Reprinted by permission of the publisher.

The Times, London, February 21, 1961; May 8, 1962; October 15, 1965; September 4, 1969. © Times Newspapers Limited 1961, 1962, 1965, 1969. All reproduced from *The Times*, London by permission.

The Times Literary Supplement, n. 2028, December 14, 1940; n. 2412, April 24, 1948; n. 2747, September 24, 1954./ n. 2985, May 15, 1959; n. 3001, September 4, 1959; n. 3065, November 25, 1960; n. 3160, September 21, 1962; n. 3177, January 18, 1963; n. 3213, September 27, 1963; n. 3300, May 27, 1965; n. 3349, May 5, 1966; n. 3404, May 25, 1967; n. 3431, November 30, 1967; n. 3444, February 29, 1968; n. 3457, May 30, 1968; n. 3473, September 19, 1968; n. 3491, January 23, 1969; n. 3494, February 13, 1969; n. 3523, September 4, 1969; n. 3563, June 11, 1970; n. 3579, October 2, 1970; n. 3621, July 23, 1971; n. 3687, November 3, 1972; n. 3787, October 4, 1974; n. 3790, October 25, 1974; n. 3809, March 7, 1975; n. 3820, May 23, 1975; n. 3872, May 28, 1976; n. 3880, July 23, 1976; n. 3902, December 24, 1976; n. 3948, November 25, 1977; n. 3955, January 13, 1978; n. 3978, June 30, 1978; n. 3984, August 11, 1978; n. 3989, September 15, 1978; n. 3993, October 13, 1978; n. 4021, April 18, 1980; n. 4036, August 1, 1980; n. 4067, March 13, 1981; n. 4078, May 29, 1981; n. 4120, March 19, 1982; n. 4122, April 2, 1982; n. 4133, June 18, 1982; n. 4138, July 23, 1982; n. 4157, December 3, 1982; n. 4180, May 13, 1983; n. 4194, August 19, 1983; n. 4205, November 4, 1983; n. 4218, February 3, 1984; n. 4245, August 10, 1984; n. 4254, October 12, 1984; n. 4256, October 26, 1984; n. 4266, January 4, 1985; n. 4268, January 18, 1985; n. 4282, April 26, 1985; n. 4307, October 18, 1985; n. 4333, April 18, 1986; n. 4340, June 6, 1986; n. 4355, September 19, 1986; n. 4357, October 3, 1986; n. 4365, November 28, 1986; n. 4378, February 27, 1987. © Times Newspapers Ltd. (London) 1959, 1960, 1962, 1963, 1965, 1966, 1967, 1968, 1969, 1970, 1971, 1972, 1974, 1975, 1976, 1977, 1978, 1980, 1981, 1982, 1983, 1984, 1985, 1986, 1987. All reproduced from *The Times Literary Supplement* by permission.

University of Toronto Quarterly, v. XXXIV, July, 1965. Reprinted by permission of University of Toronto Press.

USA Today, February 9, 1987. Copyright 1987, *USA Today*. Excerpted with permission of the publisher.

The Village Voice, v. XXIV, August 13, 1979 for "Unwanted Guests" by James Wolcott; v. XXV, February 4, 1980 for "A Poet for the Bleachers" by Seymour Krim; v. XXVI, November 4-10, 1981 for a review of "Take this Man" and "Rounds" by Susan Lydon; v. XXVIII, June 14, 1983 for "Dr. Percy's Medicine Show" by Geoffrey Stokes; v. XXIX, June 5, 1984 for "End of the Holocaust Myth" by Vivian Gornick; v. XXIX, June 19, 1984 for "Feudal Gesture or Capitalist Plot?: Arthur Miller Takes on China" by Paul Berman; v. XXX, November 5, 1985 for "Narayan's Hope" by Jacqueline Austin; v. XXXI, January 21, 1986 for "Solid as a Rock: Country Poems, Made to Last" by Geoffrey O'Brien; v. XXXI, July 22, 1986 for "And Then What Happened?" by Geoffrey O'Brien; v. XXXII, January 27, 1987 for "Up against the Wailing Wall" by J. Hoberman; v. XXXII, February 17, 1987 for "Treadmiller" by Gordon Rogoff; v. XXXII, May 5, 1987 for "More Is More: Joseph McElroy's New-Age Epic" by Albert Mobilio; v. XXXII, June 13, 1987 for "Enjoy!" by Geoffrey O'Brien. Copyright © News Group Publications, Inc., 1979, 1980, 1981, 1983, 1984, 1985, 1986, 1987. All reprinted by permission of *The Village Voice* and the respective authors.

The Virginia Quarterly Review, v. 45, Autumn, 1969. Copyright, 1969, by *The Virginia Quarterly Review,* The University of Virginia. Reprinted by permission of the publisher.

VLS, n. 34, April, 1985 for a review of "Weir & Pouce" by Albert Mobilio. Copyright © 1985 News Group Publications, Inc. Reprinted by permission of *The Village Voice* and the author.

The Wall Street Journal, May 31, 1983; August 22, 1983; March 24, 1987. © Dow Jones & Company, Inc. 1983, 1987. All rights reserved. All reprinted by permission of *The Wall Street Journal*.

Western Humanities Review, v. XXIII, Autumn, 1969; v. XXXIV, Spring, 1980. Copyright, 1969, 1980, University of Utah. Both reprinted by permission of the publisher.

The University of Windsor Review, v. XI, Spring-Summer, 1976 for a review of "Flycatcher & Other Stories" by Louis K. MacKendrick. Reprinted by permission of the publisher and the author.

Women's Wear Daily, November 21, 1980; February 24, 1984. Copyright 1980, 1984, Fairchild Publications. Both reprinted by permission of the publisher.

World Literature Today, v. 51, Winter, 1977; v. 52, Winter, 1978; v. 52, Autumn, 1978; v. 56, Spring, 1982; v. 57, Summer, 1983; v. 57, Autumn, 1983; v. 58, Spring, 1984; v. 58, Autumn, 1984; v. 59, Winter, 1985; v. 60, Spring, 1986; v. 60, Autumn, 1986. Copyright 1977, 1978, 1982, 1983, 1984, 1985, 1986 by the University of Oklahoma Press. All reprinted by permission of the publisher.

The Yale Review, v. XLIX, March, 1960; v. 71, Winter, 1982; v. 72, Spring, 1983. Copyright 1960, 1982, 1983, by Yale University. All reprinted by permission of the editors.

THE EXCERPTS IN CLC, VOLUME 47, WERE REPRINTED FROM THE FOLLOWING BOOKS:

Aiken, Conrad. From *Scepticisms: Notes on Contemporary Poetry*. Alfred A. Knopf, 1919.

Allen, Mary. From *Animals in American Literature*. University of Illinois Press, 1983. © 1983 by the Board of Trustees of the University of Illinois. Reprinted by permission of the publisher and the author.

Bhatia, Santosh K. From *Arthur Miller: Social Drama as Tragedy*. Arnold-Heinemann, 1985. © Santosh K. Bhatia, 1985. Reprinted by permission of the publisher.

Burleigh, David. From ''Dead and Gone: The Fiction of Jennifer Johnston and Julia O'Faolain,'' in *Irish Writers and Society at Large*. Edited by Masaru Sekine. Colin Smythe, 1985. Copyright © 1985 by David Burleigh. All rights reserved. Reprinted by permission of the publisher.

Caesar, Michael. From ''Elsa Morante,'' in *Writers & Society in Contemporary Italy: A Collection of Essays*. Edited by Michael Caesar and Peter Hainsworth. St. Martin's Press, 1984. © Michael Caesar and Peter Hainsworth 1984. Reprinted by permission of St. Martin's Press, Inc.

Callander, Margaret. From ''Pierre Jean Jouve: The Idea of Poetry,'' in *Order and Adventure in Post-Romantic French Poetry: Essays Presented to C. A. Hackett*. E. M. Beaumont, J. M. Cocking, J. Cruickshank, eds. Basil Blackwell, 1973. © Basil Blackwell, 1973. All rights reserved. Reprinted by permission of the publisher.

Callander, Margaret. From *The Poetry of Pierre Jean Jouve*. Manchester University Press, 1965. © 1965 Margaret Callander. Reprinted by permission of the publisher.

Carr, John C. From *The Craft of Crime: Conversations with Crime Writers*. Houghton Mifflin, 1983. Copyright © 1983 by John C. Carr. All rights reserved. Reprinted by permission of Houghton Mifflin Company.

Caws, Mary Ann. From an introduction to *Approximate Man and Other Writings*. By Tristan Tzara, translated by Mary Ann Caws. Wayne State University Press, 1973. Reprinted by permission of the Wayne State University Press and Mary Ann Caws.

Caws, Mary Ann. From *The Poetry of Dada and Surrealism: Aragon, Breton, Tzara, Eluard & Desnos*. Princeton University Press, 1970. Copyright © 1970 by Princeton University Press. All rights reserved. Reprinted with permission of the publisher.

Daiches, David. From *Poetry and the Modern World: A Study of Poetry in England between 1900 and 1939*. The University of Chicago Press, 1940.

Fenton, James. From an introduction to *The Original Michael Frayn: Satirical Essays*. By Michael Frayn, edited by James Fenton. The Salamander Press, 1983. Introduction © James Fenton 1983. All rights reserved. Reprinted by permission of Sterling Lord Literistic, Inc.

Heller, Michael. From *Conviction's Net of Branches: Essays on the Objectivist Poets and Poetry*. Southern Illinois University Press, 1985. Copyright © 1985 by the Board of Trustees, Southern Illinois University. All rights reserved. Reprinted by permission of the publisher.

Howard, Richard. From ''A Note on Constance Urdang,'' in *The Picnic in the Cemetery: Poems*. By Constance Urdang. Braziller, 1975. Copyright © 1975 by Constance Urdang. All rights reserved. Reprinted by permission of George Braziller, Inc., Publishers.

Kauffmann, Stanley. From *Theater Criticisms*. Performing Arts Journal Publications, 1983. © 1983 copyright by Stanley Kauffmann. All rights reserved. Reprinted by permission of the publisher.

Knapp, Bettina. From *Andrée Chedid*. Rodopi, 1984. © Editions Rodopi B.V., 1984. Reprinted by permission of the publisher.

McCaffery, Larry. From ''Form, Formula, and Fantasy: Generative Structures in Contemporary Fiction,'' in *Bridges to Fantasy*. George E. Slusser, Eric S. Rabkin, Robert Scholes, eds. Southern Illinois University Press, 1982. Copyright © 1982 by Southern Illinois University Press. All rights reserved. Reprinted by permission of the publisher.

Naremore, James. From ''Dashiell Hammett and the Poetics of Hard-Boiled Detection,'' in *Art in Crime Writing: Essays on Detective Fiction*. Edited by Bernard Benstock. St. Martin's Press, 1983. © Bernard Benstock 1983. All rights reserved. Reprinted by permission of St. Martin's Press, Inc.

Ortega, Julio. From *Poetics of Change: The New Spanish-American Narrative*. Translated by Galen D. Greaser, in collaboration with the author. University of Texas Press, 1984. Copyright © 1984 by the University of Texas Press. All rights reserved. Reprinted by permission of the publisher and the author.

Pearce, Richard. From *The Novel in Motion: An Approach to Modern Fiction*. Ohio State University Press, 1983. Copyright © 1983 by the Ohio State University Press. All rights reserved. Reprinted by permission of the publisher.

Sorrentino, Gilbert. From *Something Said*. North Point Press, 1984. Copyright © 1984 by Gilbert Sorrentino. Reprinted by permission of the publisher.

Spark, Muriel. From *John Masefield*. Peter Nevill, 1953. Copyright 1953, renewed 1981, by Muriel Spark. Reproduced by permission of the Hamlyn Publishing Group Limited.

Symons, Julian. From ''Dashiell Hammett: A Writer and His Time,'' in *Crime Writers: Reflections on Crime Fiction*. By Reginald Hill and others, edited by H. R. F. Keating. British Broadcasting Corporation, 1978. Reprinted by permission of Julian Symons.

Walsh, William. From *R. K. Narayan: A Critical Appreciation*. University of Chicago Press, 1982. © 1982 by William Walsh. All rights reserved. Reprinted by permission of The University of Chicago Press.

Weisz, Pierre. From ''Simenon and 'Le commissaire',''' in *Art in Crime Writing: Essays on Detective Fiction*. Edited by Bernard Benstock. St. Martin's Press, 1983. © Bernard Benstock 1983. All rights reserved. Reprinted by permission of St. Martin's Press, Inc.

Williams, Ioan. From *Emyr Humphreys*. University of Wales Press on behalf of the Welsh Arts Council, 1980. Reprinted by permission of the publisher.

□ Contemporary Literary Criticism Indexes

Literary Criticism Series
Cumulative Author Index
Cumulative Nationality Index
Title Index, Volume 47

This Index Includes References to Entries in These Gale Series

Contemporary Literary Criticism

Presents excerpts of criticism on the works of novelists, poets, dramatists, short story writers, scriptwriters, and other creative writers who are now living or who have died since 1960. Cumulative indexes to authors and nationalities and an index to titles discussed are included in each volume. Volumes 1-47 are in print.

Twentieth-Century Literary Criticism

Contains critical excerpts by the most significant commentators on poets, novelists, short story writers, dramatists, and philosophers who died between 1900 and 1960. Cumulative indexes to authors, nationalities, and titles discussed are included in each new volume. Volumes 1-27 are in print.

Nineteenth-Century Literature Criticism

Offers significant passages from criticism on authors who died between 1800 and 1899. Cumulative indexes to authors, nationalities, and titles discussed are included in each new volume. Volumes 1-17 are in print.

Literature Criticism from 1400 to 1800

Compiles significant passages from the most noteworthy criticism on authors of the fifteenth through eighteenth centuries. Cumulative indexes to authors, nationalities, and titles discussed are included in each new volume. Volumes 1-7 are in print.

Children's Literature Review

Includes excerpts from reviews, criticism, and commentary on works of authors and author/illustrators who create books for children. Cumulative indexes to authors, nationalities, and titles discussed are included in each new volume. Volumes 1-14 are in print.

Contemporary Authors Series

Encompasses five related series. *Contemporary Authors* provides biographical and bibliographical information on more than 89,000 writers of fiction, nonfiction, poetry, journalism, drama, motion pictures, and other fields. Each new volume contains sketches on authors not previously covered in the series. Volumes 1-121 are in print. *Contemporary Authors New Revision Series* provides completely updated information on active authors covered in previously published volumes of *CA*. Only entries requiring significant change are revised for *CA New Revision Series.* Volumes 1-22 are in print. *Contemporary Authors Permanent Series* consists of updated listings for deceased and inactive authors removed from original volumes 9-36 when these volumes were revised. Volumes 1-2 are in print. *Contemporary Authors Autobiography Series* presents specially commissioned autobiographies by leading contemporary writers. Volumes 1-6 are in print. *Contemporary Authors Bibliographical Series* contains primary and secondary bibliographies as well as analytical bibliographical essays by authorities on major modern authors. Volumes 1-2 are in print.

Dictionary of Literary Biography

Encompasses three related series. *Dictionary of Literary Biography* furnishes illustrated overviews of authors' lives and works and places them in the larger perspective of literary history. Volumes 1-64 are in print. *Dictionary of Literary Biography Documentary Series* illuminates the careers of major figures through a selection of literary documents, including letters, notebook and diary entries, interviews, book reviews, and photographs. Volumes 1-4 are in print. *Dictionary of Literary Biography Yearbook* summarizes the past year's literary activity with articles on genres, major prizes, conferences, and other timely subjects and includes udpated and new entries on individual authors. Yearbooks for 1980-1986 are in print. A cumulative index to authors and articles is included in each new volume.

Concise Dictionary of American Literary Biography

A six-volume series that collects revised and updated sketches on major American authors that were originally presented in *Dictionary of Literary Biography.* Volume 1 is in print.

Something about the Author Series

Encompasses two related series. *Something about the Author* contains heavily illustrated biographical sketches on juvenile and young adult authors and illustrators from all eras. Volumes 1-49 are in print. *Something about the Author Autobiography Series* presents specially commissioned autobiographies by prominent authors and illustrators of books for children and young adults. Volumes 1-4 are in print.

Authors in the News

Reprints news stories and feature articles from American newspapers and magazines covering writers and other members of the communications media. A cumulative index to authors and a list of surveyed periodicals are included in each volume. Volumes 1-2, both published in 1976, are in print.

Yesterday's Authors of Books for Children

Contains heavily illustrated entries on children's writers who died before 1961. Two volumes only. Volumes 1-2 are in print.

Literary Criticism Series Cumulative Author Index

This index lists all author entries in the Gale Literary Criticism Series and includes cross-references to other Gale sources. For the convenience of the reader, references to the *Yearbook* in the *Contemporary Literary Criticism* series include the page number (in parentheses) after the volume number. References in the index are identified as follows:

AITN: *Authors in the News,* Volumes 1-2
CAAS: *Contemporary Authors Autobiography Series,* Volumes 1-6
CA: *Contemporary Authors* (original series), Volumes 1-121
CABS: *Contemporary Authors Bibliographical Series,* Volumes 1-2
CANR: *Contemporary Authors New Revision Series,* Volumes 1-22
CAP: *Contemporary Authors Permanent Series,* Volumes 1-2
CA-R: *Contemporary Authors* (revised editions), Volumes 1-44
CDALB: *Concise Dictionary of American Literary Biography*
CLC: *Contemporary Literary Criticism,* Volumes 1-47
CLR: *Children's Literature Review,* Volumes 1-14
CMLC: *Classical and Medieval Literature Criticism,* Volume 1
DLB: *Dictionary of Literary Biography,* Volumes 1-64
DLB-DS: *Dictionary of Literary Biography Documentary Series,* Volumes 1-4
DLB-Y: *Dictionary of Literary Biography Yearbook,* Volumes 1980-1986
LC: *Literature Criticism from 1400 to 1800,* Volumes 1-7
NCLC: *Nineteenth-Century Literature Criticism,* Volumes 1-17
SAAS: *Something about the Author Autobiography Series,* Volumes 1-4
SATA: *Something about the Author,* Volumes 1-49
SSC: *Short Story Criticism,* Volume 1
TCLC: *Twentieth-Century Literary Criticism,* Volumes 1-27
YABC: *Yesterday's Authors of Books for Children,* Volumes 1-2

Author Index

Author Index

Author Index

Author Index

Author Index

Author Index

Author Index

Author Index

Author Index

Author Index

CLC Cumulative Nationality Index

Nationality Index

Nationality Index

CLC-47 Title Index